Three Translations of The Koran (Al-Qur'an) side by side

Tranlated By

Abdullah Yusuf Ali
Marmaduke Pickthall
Mohammad Habib Shaki

Cover Photograph: mmechtley

© 2011 Benediction Classics, Oxford.

Contents

Chapter 1: 1
AL-FATIHA (THE OPENING)
Total Verses: 7 Revealed At: MAKKA

Chapter 2: 1
AL-BAQARA (THE COW)
Total Verses: 286 Revealed At: MADINA

Chapter 3: 43
AL-E-IMRAN (THE FAMILY OF 'IMRAN, THE HOUSE OF 'IMRAN)
Total Verses: 200 Revealed At: MADINA

Chapter 4: 67
AN-NISA (WOMEN)
Total Verses: 176 Revealed At: MADINA

Chapter 5: 92
AL-MAEDA (THE TABLE, THE TABLE SPREAD)
Total Verses: 120 Revealed At: MADINA

Chapter 6: 111
AL-ANAAM (CATTLE, LIVESTOCK)
Total Verses: 165 Revealed At: MAKKA

Chapter 7: 132
AL-ARAF (THE HEIGHTS)
Total Verses: 206 Revealed At: MAKKA

Chapter 8: 155
AL-ANFAL (SPOILS OF WAR, BOOTY)
Total Verses: 75 Revealed At: MADINA

Chapter 9: 163
AL-TAWBA (REPENTANCE, DISPENSATION)
Total Verses: 129 Revealed At: MADINA

Chapter 10: 181
YUNUS (JONAH)
Total Verses: 109 Revealed At: MAKKA

Chapter 11: 193
HUD (HUD)
Total Verses: 123 Revealed At: MAKKA

Chapter 12: 206
YUSUF (JOSEPH)
Total Verses: 111 Revealed At: MAKKA

Chapter 13: 219
AL-RAD (THE THUNDER)
Total Verses: 43 Revealed At: MAKKA

Chapter 14: 225
IBRAHIM (ABRAHAM)
Total Verses: 52 Revealed At: MAKKA

Chapter 15: 231
AL-HIJR (AL-HIJR, STONELAND, ROCK CITY)
Total Verses: 99 Revealed At: MAKKA

Chapter 16: 236
AN-NAHL (THE BEE)
Total Verses: 128 Revealed At: MAKKA

Chapter 17: 249
AL-ISRA (ISRA', THE NIGHT JOURNEY, CHILDREN OF ISRAEL)
Total Verses: 111 Revealed At: MAKKA

Chapter 18: 260
AL-KAHF (THE CAVE)
Total Verses: 110 Revealed At: MAKKA

Chapter 19: ....272 MARYAM (MARY) Total Verses: 98 Revealed At: MAKKA	Chapter 28: ....347 AL-QASAS (THE STORY, STORIES) Total Verses: 88 Revealed At: MAKKA
Chapter 20: ....279 TA-HA (TA-HA) Total Verses: 135 Revealed At: MAKKA	Chapter 29: ....357 AL-ANKABOOT (THE SPIDER) Total Verses: 69 Revealed At: MAKKA
Chapter 21: ....289 AL-ANBIYA (THE PROPHETS) Total Verses: 112 Revealed At: MAKKA	Chapter 30: ....364 AL-ROOM (THE ROMANS, THE BYZANTINES) Total Verses: 60 Revealed At: MAKKA
Chapter 22: ....297 AL-HAJJ (THE PILGRIMAGE) Total Verses: 78 Revealed At: MADINA	Chapter 31: ....370 LUQMAN (LUQMAN) Total Verses: 34 Revealed At: MAKKA
Chapter 23: ....306 AL-MUMENOON (THE BELIEVERS) Total Verses: 118 Revealed At: MAKKA	Chapter 32: ....374 AS-SAJDA (THE PROSTRATION, WORSHIP, ADORATION) Total Verses: 30 Revealed At: MAKKA
Chapter 24: ....314 AL-NOOR (THE LIGHT) Total Verses: 64 Revealed At: MADINA	Chapter 33: ....377 AL-AHZAB (THE CLANS, THE COALITION, THE COMBINED FORCES) Total Verses: 73 Revealed At: MADINA
Chapter 25: ....322 AL-FURQAN (THE CRITERION, THE STANDARD) Total Verses: 77 Revealed At: MAKKA	Chapter 34: ....386 SABA (SABA, SHEBA) Total Verses: 54 Revealed At: MAKKA
Chapter 26: ....329 AL-SHUARA (THE POETS) Total Verses: 227 Revealed At: MAKKA	Chapter 35: ....392 FATIR (THE ANGELS, ORIGINATOR) Total Verses: 45 Revealed At: MAKKA
Chapter 27: ....339 AL-NAML (THE ANT, THE ANTS) Total Verses: 93 Revealed At: MAKKA	Chapter 36: ....397 YA-SEEN (YA-SEEN) Total Verses: 83 Revealed At: MAKKA
O Moses! Lo! it is I, Allah, the Mighty, the Wise.	

Chapter 37: 403
AS-SAAFFAT (THOSE WHO SET THE RANKS, DRAWN UP IN RANKS)
Total Verses: 182 Revealed At: MAKKA

Chapter 38: 411
SAD (THE LETTER SAD)
Total Verses: 88 Revealed At: MAKKA

Chapter 39: 417
AZ-ZUMAR (THE TROOPS, THRONGS)
Total Verses: 75 Revealed At: MAKKA

Chapter 40: 425
AL-GHAFIR (THE FORGIVER (GOD))
Total Verses: 85 Revealed At: MAKKA

Chapter 41: 434
FUSSILAT (EXPLAINED IN DETAIL)
Total Verses: 54 Revealed At: MAKKA

Chapter 42: 440
ASH-SHURA (COUNCIL, CONSULTATION)
Total Verses: 53 Revealed At: MAKKA

Chapter 43: 446
AZ-ZUKHRUF (ORNAMENTS OF GOLD, LUXURY)
Total Verses: 89 Revealed At: MAKKA

Chapter 44: 452
AD-DUKHAN (SMOKE)
Total Verses: 59 Revealed At: MAKKA

Chapter 45: 455
AL-JATHIYA (CROUCHING)
Total Verses: 37 Revealed At: MAKKA

Chapter 46: 459
AL-AHQAF (THE WIND-CURVED SANDHILLS, THE DUNES)
Total Verses: 35 Revealed At: MAKKA

Chapter 47: 463
MUHAMMAD (MUHAMMAD)
Total Verses: 38 Revealed At: MADINA

Chapter 48: 468
AL-FATH (VICTORY, CONQUEST)
Total Verses: 29 Revealed At: MADINA

Chapter 49: 472
AL-HUJRAAT (THE PRIVATE APARTMENTS, THE INNER APARTMENTS)
Total Verses: 18 Revealed At: MADINA

Chapter 50: 475
QAF (THE LETTER QAF)
Total Verses: 45 Revealed At: MAKKA

Chapter 51: 478
ADH-DHARIYAT (THE WINNOWING WINDS)
Total Verses: 60 Revealed At: MAKKA

Chapter 52: 481
AT-TUR (THE MOUNT)
Total Verses: 49 Revealed At: MAKKA

Chapter 53: 484
AN-NAJM (THE STAR)
Total Verses: 62 Revealed At: MAKKA

Chapter 54: 487
AL-QAMAR (THE MOON)
Total Verses: 55 Revealed At: MAKKA

Chapter 55: ....490 AR-RAHMAN (THE BENEFICENT, THE MERCY GIVING) Total Verses: 78 Revealed At: MAKKA	**Chapter 63:** ....514 AL-MUNAFIQOON (THE HYPOCRITES) Total Verses: 11 Revealed At: MADINA
Chapter 56: ....493 AL-WAQIA (THE EVENT, THE INEVITABLE) Total Verses: 96 Revealed At: MAKKA	**Chapter 64:** ....516 AT-TAGHABUN (MUTUAL DISILLUSION, HAGGLING) Total Verses: 18 Revealed At: MAKKA
Chapter 57: ....497 AL-HADID (THE IRON) Total Verses: 29 Revealed At: MADINA	**Chapter 65:** ....518 AT-TALAQ (DIVORCE) Total Verses: 12 Revealed At: MADINA
Chapter 58: ....502 AL-MUJADILA (SHE THAT DISPUTETH, THE PLEADING WOMAN) Total Verses: 22 Revealed At: MADINA	**Chapter 66:** ....520 AT-TAHRIM (BANNING, PROHIBITION) Total Verses: 12 Revealed At: MADINA
Chapter 59: ....505 AL-HASHR (EXILE, BANISHMENT) Total Verses: 24 Revealed At: MADINA	**Chapter 67:** ....522 AL-MULK (THE SOVEREIGNTY, CONTROL) Total Verses: 30 Revealed At: MAKKA
Chapter 60: ....509 AL-MUMTAHINA (SHE THAT IS TO BE EXAMINED, EXAMINING HER) Total Verses: 13 Revealed At: MADINA	**Chapter 68:** ....524 AL-QALAM (THE PEN) Total Verses: 52 Revealed At: MAKKA
Chapter 61: ....511 AS-SAFF (THE RANKS, BATTLE ARRAY) Total Verses: 14 Revealed At: MADINA	**Chapter 69:** ....527 AL-HAAQQA (THE REALITY) Total Verses: 52 Revealed At: MAKKA
Chapter 62: ....513 AL-JUMUA (THE CONGREGATION, FRIDAY) Total Verses: 11 Revealed At: MADINA	**Chapter 70:** ....530 AL-MAARIJ (THE ASCENDING STAIRWAYS) Total Verses: 44 Revealed At: MAKKA
	Chapter 71: ....532 NOOH (NOOH) Total Verses: 28 Revealed At: MAKKA
	Chapter 72: ....534 AL-JINN (THE JINN) Total Verses: 28 Revealed At: MAKKA

Chapter 73: 536
   AL-MUZZAMMIL (THE ENSHROUDED ONE, BUNDLED UP)
   Total Verses: 20 Revealed At: MAKKA

Chapter 74: 538
   AL-MUDDATHTHIR (THE CLOAKED ONE, THE MAN WEARING A CLOAK)
   Total Verses: 56 Revealed At: MAKKA

Chapter 75: 541
   AL-QIYAMA (THE RISING OF THE DEAD, RESURRECTION)
   Total Verses: 40 Revealed At: MAKKA

Chapter 76: 543
   AL-INSAN (MAN)
   Total Verses: 31 Revealed At: MAKKA

Chapter 77: 545
   AL-MURSALAT (THE EMISSARIES, WINDS SENT FORTH)
   Total Verses: 50 Revealed At: MAKKA

Chapter 78: 547
   AN-NABA (THE TIDINGS, THE ANNOUNCEMENT)
   Total Verses: 40 Revealed At: MAKKA

Chapter 79: 549
   AN-NAZIAT (THOSE WHO DRAG FORTH, SOUL-SNATCHERS)
   Total Verses: 46 Revealed At: MAKKA

Chapter 80: 551
   ABASA (HE FROWNED)
   Total Verses: 42 Revealed At: MAKKA

Chapter 81: 553
   AT-TAKWIR (THE OVERTHROWING)
   Total Verses: 29 Revealed At: MAKKA

Chapter 82: 554
   AL-INFITAR (THE CLEAVING, BURSTING APART)
   Total Verses: 19 Revealed At: MAKKA

Chapter 83: 555
   AL-MUTAFFIFIN (DEFRAUDING, THE CHEATS, CHEATING)
   Total Verses: 36 Revealed At: MAKKA

Chapter 84: 557
   AL-INSHIQAQ (THE SUNDERING, SPLITTING OPEN)
   Total Verses: 25 Revealed At: MAKKA

Chapter 85: 558
   AL-BUROOJ (THE MANSIONS OF THE STARS, CONSTELLATIONS)
   Total Verses: 22 Revealed At: MAKKA

Chapter 86: 559
   AT-TARIQ (THE MORNING STAR, THE NIGHTCOMER)
   Total Verses: 17 Revealed At: MAKKA

Chapter 87: 560
   AL-ALA (THE MOST HIGH, GLORY TO YOUR LORD IN THE HIGHEST)
   Total Verses: 19 Revealed At: MAKKA

Chapter 88: 561
   AL-GHASHIYA (THE OVERWHELMING, THE PALL)
   Total Verses: 26 Revealed At: MAKKA

Chapter 89: 562
AL-FAJR (THE DAWN, DAYBREAK)
Total Verses: 30 Revealed At: MAKKA

Chapter 90: 563
AL-BALAD (THE CITY, THIS COUNTRYSIDE)
Total Verses: 20 Revealed At: MAKKA

Chapter 91: 564
ASH-SHAMS (THE SUN)
Total Verses: 15 Revealed At: MAKKA

Chapter 92: 565
AL-LAIL (THE NIGHT)
Total Verses: 21 Revealed At: MAKKA

Chapter 93: 566
AD-DHUHA (THE MORNING HOURS, MORNING BRIGHT)
Total Verses: 11 Revealed At: MAKKA

Chapter 94: 567
AL-INSHIRAH (SOLACE, CONSOLATION, RELIEF)
Total Verses: 8 Revealed At: MAKKA

Chapter 95: 567
AT-TIN (THE FIG, THE FIGTREE)
Total Verses: 8 Revealed At: MAKKA

Chapter 96: 568
AL-ALAQ (THE CLOT, READ)
Total Verses: 19 Revealed At: MAKKA

Chapter 97: 569
AL-QADR (POWER, FATE)
Total Verses: 5 Revealed At: MAKKA

Chapter 98: 569
AL-BAYYINA (THE CLEAR PROOF, EVIDENCE)
Total Verses: 8 Revealed At: MADINA

Chapter 99: 570
AL-ZALZALA (THE EARTHQUAKE)
Total Verses: 8 Revealed At: MAKKA

Chapter 100: 570
AL-ADIYAT (THE COURSER, THE CHARGERS)
Total Verses: 11 Revealed At: MAKKA

Chapter 101: 571
AL-QARIA (THE CALAMITY, THE STUNNING BLOW, THE DISASTER)
Total Verses: 11 Revealed At: MAKKA

Chapter 102: 572
AT-TAKATHUR (RIVALRY IN WORLD INCREASE, COMPETITION)
Total Verses: 8 Revealed At: MAKKA

Chapter 103: 572
AL-ASR (THE DECLINING DAY, EVENTIDE, THE EPOCH)
Total Verses: 3 Revealed At: MAKKA

Chapter 104: 573
AL-HUMAZA (THE TRADUCER, THE GOSSIPMONGER)
Total Verses: 9 Revealed At: MAKKA

Chapter 105: 573
AL-FIL (THE ELEPHANT)
Total Verses: 5 Revealed At: MAKKA

Chapter 106: 574
QURAISH (WINTER, QURAYSH)
Total Verses: 4 Revealed At: MAKKA

Chapter 107: 574
AL-MAUN (SMALL KINDNESSES, ALMSGIVING, HAVE YOU SEEN)
Total Verses: 7 Revealed At: MAKKA

Chapter 108: 575
AL-KAUTHER (ABUNDANCE, PLENTY)
Total Verses: 3 Revealed At: MAKKA

Chapter 109: 575
AL-KAFIROON (THE DISBELIEVERS, ATHEISTS)
Total Verses: 6 Revealed At: MAKKA

Chapter 110: 575
AN-NASR (SUCCOUR, DIVINE SUPPORT)
Total Verses: 3 Revealed At: MADINA

Chapter 111: 576
AL-MASADD (PALM FIBRE, THE FLAME)
Total Verses: 5 Revealed At: MAKKA

Chapter 112: 576
AL-IKHLAS (SINCERITY)
Total Verses: 4 Revealed At: MAKKA

Chapter 113: 577
AL-FALAQ (THE DAYBREAK, DAWN)
Total Verses: 5 Revealed At: MAKKA

Chapter 114: 577
AN-NAS (MANKIND)
Total Verses: 6 Revealed At: MAKKA

In the following pages the text is shown in 3 columns, these are the translations of Abdullah Yusuf Ali, Marmaduke Pickthall and Mohammad Habib Shaki respectively.

Chapter 1:

AL-FATIHA (THE OPENING)

Total Verses: 7 Revealed At: MAKKA

1	001	In the name of Allah, the Most Beneficent, the Most Merciful.	In the name of Allah, the Beneficent, the Merciful.	In the name of Allah, the Beneficent, the Merciful.
1	002	Praise be to Allah, the Cherisher and Sustainer of the worlds;	Praise be to Allah, Lord of the Worlds,	All praise is due to Allah, the Lord of the Worlds.
1	003	Most Gracious, Most Merciful;	The Beneficent, the Merciful.	The Beneficent, the Merciful.
1	004	Master of the Day of Judgment.	Master of the Day of Judgment,	Master of the Day of Judgment.
1	005	Thee do we worship, and Thine aid we seek.	Thee (alone) we worship; Thee (alone) we ask for help.	Thee do we serve and Thee do we beseech for help.
1	006	Show us the straight way,	Show us the straight path,	Keep us on the right path.
1	007	The way of those on whom Thou hast bestowed Thy Grace, those whose (portion) is not wrath, and who go not astray.	The path of those whom Thou hast favoured; Not the (path) of those who earn Thine anger nor of those who go astray.	The path of those upon whom Thou hast bestowed favors. Not (the path) of those upon whom Thy wrath is brought down, nor of those who go astray.

Chapter 2:

AL-BAQARA (THE COW)

Total Verses: 286 Revealed At: MADINA

In the name of Allah, the Most Beneficent, the Most Merciful.

2	001	A.L.M.	Alif. Lam. Mim.	Alif Lam Mim.
2	002	This is the Book; in it is guidance sure, without doubt, to those who fear Allah;	This is the Scripture whereof there is no doubt, a guidance unto those who ward off (evil).	This Book, there is no doubt in it, is a guide to those who guard (against evil).
2	003	Who believe in the Unseen, are steadfast in prayer, and spend out of what We have provided for them;	Who believe in the Unseen, and establish worship, and spend of that We have bestowed upon them;	Those who believe in the unseen and keep up prayer and spend out of what We have given them.
2	004	And who believe in the Revelation sent to thee, and sent before thy time, and (in their hearts) have the assurance of the Hereafter.	And who believe in that which is revealed unto thee (Muhammad) and that which was revealed before thee, and are certain of the Hereafter.	And who believe in that which has been revealed to you and that which was revealed before you and they are sure of the hereafter.
2	005	They are on (true) guidance, from their Lord, and it is these who will prosper.	These depend on guidance from their Lord. These are the successful.	These are on a right course from their Lord and these it is that shall be successful.
2	006	As to those who reject Faith, it is the same to them whether thou warn them or do not warn them; they will not believe.	As for the Disbelievers, Whether thou warn them or thou warn them not it is all one for them; they believe not.	Surely those who disbelieve, it being alike to them whether you warn them, or do not warn them, will not believe.

2 007	Allah hath set a seal on their hearts and on their hearing, and on their eyes is a veil; great is the penalty they (incur).	Allah hath sealed their hearing and their hearts, and on their eyes there is a covering. Theirs will be an awful doom.	Allah has set a seal upon their hearts and upon their hearing and there is a covering over their eyes, and there is a great punishment for them.
2 008	Of the people there are some who say: "We believe in Allah and the Last Day;" but they do not (really) believe.	And of mankind are some who say: We believe in Allah and the Last Day, when they believe not.	And there are some people who say: We believe in Allah and the last day; and they are not at all believers.
2 009	Fain would they deceive Allah and those who believe, but they only deceive themselves, and realise (it) not!	They think to beguile Allah and those who believe, and they beguile none save themselves; but they perceive not.	They desire to deceive Allah and those who believe, and they deceive only themselves and they do not perceive.
2 010	In their hearts is a disease; and Allah has increased their disease: And grievous is the penalty they (incur), because they are false (to themselves).	In their hearts is a disease, and Allah increaseth their disease. A painful doom is theirs because they lie.	There is a disease in their hearts, so Allah added to their disease and they shall have a painful chastisement because they lied.
2 011	When it is said to them: "Make not mischief on the earth," they say: Why, we only Want to make peace!	And when it is said unto them: Make not mischief in the earth, they say: We are peacemakers only.	And when it is said to them, Do not make mischief in the land, they say: We are but peace-makers.
2 012	Of a surety, they are the ones who make mischief, but they realise (it) not.	Are not they indeed the mischief-makers? But they perceive not.	Now surely they themselves are the mischief makers, but they do not perceive.
2 013	When it is said to them: "Believe as the others believe:" They say: Shall we believe as the fools believe? Nay, of a surety they are the fools, but they do not know.	And when it is said unto them: believe as the people believe, they say: shall we believe as the foolish believe? are not they indeed the foolish? But they know not.	And when it is said to them: Believe as the people believe they say: Shall we believe as the fools believe? Now surely they themselves are the fools, but they do not know.
2 014	When they meet those who believe, they say: "We believe;" but when they are alone with their evil ones, they say: "We are really with you: We (were) only jesting."	And when they fall in with those who believe, they say: We believe; but when they go apart to their devils they declare: Lo! we are with you; verily we did but mock.	And when they meet those who believe, they say: We believe; and when they are alone with their Shaitans, they say: Surely we are with you, we were only mocking.
2 015	Allah will throw back their mockery on them, and give them rope in their trespasses; so they will wander like blind ones (To and fro).	Allah (Himself) doth mock them, leaving them to wander blindly on in their contumacy.	Allah shall pay them back their mockery, and He leaves them alone in their inordinacy, blindly wandering on.
2 016	These are they who have bartered Guidance for error: But their traffic is profitless, and they have lost true direction,	These are they who purchase error at the price of guidance, so their commerce doth not prosper, neither are they guided.	These are they who buy error for the right direction, so their bargain shall bring no gain, nor are they the followers of the right direction.
2 017	Their similitude is that of a man who kindled a fire; when it lighted all around him, Allah took away their light and left them in utter darkness. So they could not see.	Their likeness is as the likeness of one who kindleth fire, and when it sheddeth its light around him Allah taketh away their light and leaveth them in darkness, where they cannot see,	Their parable is like the parable of one who kindled a fire but when it had illumined all around him, Allah took away their light, and left them in utter darkness--they do not see.
2 018	Deaf, dumb, and blind, they will not return (to the path).	Deaf, dumb and blind; and they return not.	Deaf, dumb (and) blind, so they will not turn back.

2 019	Or (another similitude) is that of a rain-laden cloud from the sky: In it are zones of darkness, and thunder and lightning: They press their fingers in their ears to keep out the stunning thunder-clap, the while they are in terror of death. But Allah is ever round the rejecters of Faith!	Or like a rainstorm from the sky, wherein is darkness, thunder and the flash of lightning. They thrust their fingers in their ears by reason of the thunder-claps, for fear of death, Allah encompasseth the disbelievers (in His guidance, His omniscience and His omnipotence).	Or like abundant rain from the cloud in which is utter darkness and thunder and lightning; they put their fingers into their ears because of the thunder peal, for fear of death, and Allah encompasses the unbelievers.
2 020	The lightning all but snatches away their sight; every time the light (Helps) them, they walk therein, and when the darkness grows on them, they stand still. And if Allah willed, He could take away their faculty of hearing and seeing; for Allah hath power over all things.	The lightning almost snatcheth away their sight from them. As often as it flasheth forth for them they walk therein, and when it darkeneth against them they stand still. If Allah willed, He could destroy their hearing and their sight. Lo! Allah is able to do all things.	The lightning almost takes away their sight; whenever it shines on them they walk in it, and when it becomes dark to them they stand still; and if Allah had pleased He would certainly have taken away their hearing and their sight; surely Allah has power over all things.
2 021	O ye people! Adore your Guardian-Lord, who created you and those who came before you, that ye may have the chance to learn righteousness;	O mankind! worship your Lord, Who hath created you and those before you, so that ye may ward off (evil).	O men! serve your Lord Who created you and those before you so that you may guard (against evil).
2 022	Who has made the earth your couch, and the heavens your canopy; and sent down rain from the heavens; and brought forth therewith Fruits for your sustenance; then set not up rivals unto Allah when ye know (the truth).	Who hath appointed the earth a resting-place for you, and the sky a canopy; and causeth water to pour down from the sky, thereby producing fruits as food for you. And do not set up rivals to Allah when ye know (better).	Who made the earth a resting place for you and the heaven a canopy and (Who) sends down rain from the cloud then brings forth with it subsistence for you of the fruits; therefore do not set up rivals to Allah while you know.
2 023	And if ye are in doubt as to what We have revealed from time to time to Our servant, then produce a Sura like thereunto; and call your witnesses or helpers (If there are any) besides Allah, if your (doubts) are true.	And if ye are in doubt concerning that which We reveal unto Our slave (Muhammad), then produce a surah of the like thereof, and call your witness beside Allah if ye are truthful.	And if you are in doubt as to that which We have revealed to Our servant, then produce a Chapter like it and call on your witnesses besides Allah if you are truthful.
2 024	But if ye cannot- and of a surety ye cannot- then fear the Fire whose fuel is men and stones,- which is prepared for those who reject Faith.	And if ye do it not- and ye can never do it - then guard yourselves against the Fire prepared for disbelievers, whose fuel is of men and stones.	But if you do (it) not and never shall you do (it), then be on your guard against the fire of which men and stones are the fuel; it is prepared for the unbelievers.
2 025	But give glad tidings to those who believe and work righteousness, that their portion is Gardens, beneath which rivers flow. Every time they are fed with fruits therefrom, they say: "Why, this is what we were fed with before," for they are given things in similitude; and they have therein companions pure (and holy); and they abide therein (for ever).	And give glad tidings (O Muhammad) unto those who believe and do good works; that theirs are Gardens underneath which rivers flow; as often as they are regaled with food of the fruit thereof, they say: this is what was given us aforetime; and it is given to them in resemblance. There for them are pure companions; there forever they abide.	And convey good news to those who believe and do good deeds, that they shall have gardens in which rivers flow; whenever they shall be given a portion of the fruit thereof, they shall say: This is what was given to us before; and they shall be given the like of it, and they shall have pure mates in them, and in them, they shall abide.

2 026	Allah disdains not to use the similitude of things, lowest as well as highest. Those who believe know that it is truth from their Lord; but those who reject Faith say: "What means Allah by this similitude?" By it He causes many to stray, and many He leads into the right path; but He causes not to stray, except those who forsake (the path),-	Lo! Allah disdaineth not to coin the similitude even of a gnat. Those who believe know that it is the truth from their Lord; but those who disbelieve say: What doth Allah wish (to teach) by such a similitude? He misleadeth many thereby, and He guideth many thereby; and He misleadeth thereby only miscreants;	Surely Allah is not ashamed to set forth any parable-- (that of) a gnat or any thing above that; then as for those who believe, they know that it is the truth from their Lord, and as for those who disbelieve, they say: What is it that Allah means by this parable: He causes many to err by it and many He leads aright by it! but He does not cause to err by it (any) except the transgressors,
2 027	Those who break Allah's Covenant after it is ratified, and who sunder what Allah has ordered to be joined, and do mischief on earth: These cause loss (only) to themselves.	Those who break the covenant of Allah after ratifying it, and sever that which Allah ordered to be joined, and (who) make mischief in the earth: Those are they who are the losers.	Who break the covenant of Allah after its confirmation and cut asunder what Allah has ordered to be joined, and make mischief in the land; these it is that are the losers.
2 028	How can ye reject the faith in Allah?- seeing that ye were without life, and He gave you life; then will He cause you to die, and will again bring you to life; and again to Him will ye return.	How disbelieve ye in Allah when ye were dead and He gave life to you! Then He will give you death, then life again, and then unto Him ye will return.	How do you deny Allah and you were dead and He gave you life? Again He will cause you to die and again bring you to life, then you shall be brought back to Him.
2 029	It is He Who hath created for you all things that are on earth; Moreover His design comprehended the heavens, for He gave order and perfection to the seven firmaments; and of all things He hath perfect knowledge.	He it is Who created for you all that is in the earth. Then turned He to the heaven, and fashioned it as seven heavens. And He is knower of all things.	He it is Who created for you all that is in the earth, and He directed Himself to the heaven, so He made them complete seven heavens, and He knows all things.
2 030	Behold, thy Lord said to the angels: "I will create a vicegerent on earth." They said: "Wilt Thou place therein one who will make mischief therein and shed blood?- whilst we do celebrate Thy praises and glorify Thy holy (name)?" He said: "I know what ye know not."	And when thy Lord said unto the angels: Lo! I am about to place a viceroy in the earth, they said: Wilt thou place therein one who will do harm therein and will shed blood, while we, we hymn Thy praise and sanctify Thee? He said: Surely I know that which ye know not.	And when your Lord said to the angels, I am going to place in the earth a khalif, they said: What! wilt Thou place in it such as shall make mischief in it and shed blood, and we celebrate Thy praise and extol Thy holiness? He said: Surely I know what you do not know.
2 031	And He taught Adam the names of all things; then He placed them before the angels, and said: "Tell me the names of these if ye are right."	And He taught Adam all the names, then showed them to the angels, saying: Inform Me of the names of these, if ye are truthful.	And He taught Adam all the names, then presented them to the angels; then He said: Tell me the names of those if you are right.
2 032	They said: "Glory to Thee, of knowledge We have none, save what Thou Hast taught us: In truth it is Thou Who art perfect in knowledge and wisdom."	They said: Be glorified! We have no knowledge saving that which Thou hast taught us. Lo! Thou, only Thou, art the Knower, the Wise.	They said: Glory be to Thee! we have no knowledge but that which Thou hast taught us; surely Thou art the Knowing, the Wise.
2 033	He said: "O Adam! Tell them their names." When he had told them, Allah said: "Did I not tell you that I know the secrets of heaven and earth, and I know what ye reveal and what ye conceal?"	He said: O Adam! Inform them of their names, and when he had informed them of their names, He said: Did I not tell you that I know the secret of the heavens and the earth? And I know that which ye disclose and which ye hide.	He said: O Adam! inform them of their names. Then when he had informed them of their names, He said: Did I not say to you that I surely know what is ghaib in the heavens and the earth and (that) I know what you manifest and what you hide?

2 034	And behold, We said to the angels: "Bow down to Adam" and they bowed down. Not so Iblis: he refused and was haughty: He was of those who reject Faith.	And when We said unto the angels: Prostrate yourselves before Adam, they fell prostrate, all save Iblis. He demurred through pride, and so became a disbeliever.	And when We said to the angels: Make obeisance to Adam they did obeisance, but Iblis (did it not). He refused and he was proud, and he was one of the unbelievers.
2 035	We said: "O Adam! dwell thou and thy wife in the Garden; and eat of the bountiful things therein as (where and when) ye will; but approach not this tree, or ye run into harm and transgression."	And We said: O Adam! Dwell thou and thy wife in the Garden, and eat ye freely (of the fruits) thereof where ye will; but come not nigh this tree lest ye become wrong-doers.	And We said: O Adam! Dwell you and your wife in the garden and eat from it a plenteous (food) wherever you wish and do not approach this tree, for then you will be of the unjust.
2 036	Then did Satan make them slip from the (garden), and get them out of the state (of felicity) in which they had been. We said: "Get ye down, all (ye people), with enmity between yourselves. On earth will be your dwelling-place and your means of livelihood- for a time."	But Satan caused them to deflect therefrom and expelled them from the (happy) state in which they were; and We said: Fall down, one of you a foe unto the other! There shall be for you on earth a habitation and provision for a time.	But the Shaitan made them both fall from it, and caused them to depart from that (state) in which they were; and We said: Get forth, some of you being the enemies of others, and there is for you in the earth an abode and a provision for a time.
2 037	Then learnt Adam from his Lord words of inspiration, and his Lord Turned towards him; for He is Oft-Returning, Most Merciful.	Then Adam received from his Lord words (of revelation), and He relented toward him. Lo! He is the relenting, the Merciful.	Then Adam received (some) words from his Lord, so He turned to him mercifully; surely He is Oft-returning (to mercy), the Merciful.
2 038	We said: "Get ye down all from here; and if, as is sure, there comes to you Guidance from me," whosoever follows My guidance, on them shall be no fear, nor shall they grieve.	We said: Go down, all of you, from hence; but verily there cometh unto you from Me a guidance; and whoso followeth My guidance, there shall no fear come upon them neither shall they grieve.	We said: Go forth from this (state) all; so surely there will come to you a guidance from Me, then whoever follows My guidance, no fear shall come upon them, nor shall they grieve.
2 039	"But those who reject Faith and belie Our Signs, they shall be companions of the Fire; they shall abide therein."	But they who disbelieve, and deny Our revelations, such are rightful Peoples of the Fire. They will abide therein.	And (as to) those who disbelieve in and reject My communications, they are the inmates of the fire, in it they shall abide.
2 040	O Children of Israel! call to mind the (special) favour which I bestowed upon you, and fulfil your covenant with Me as I fulfil My Covenant with you, and fear none but Me.	O Children of Israel! Remember My favour wherewith I favoured you, and fulfil your (part of the) covenant, I shall fulfil My (part of the) covenant, and fear Me.	O children of Israel! call to mind My favor which I bestowed on you and be faithful to (your) covenant with Me, I will fulfill (My) covenant with you; and of Me, Me alone, should you be afraid.
2 041	And believe in what I reveal, confirming the revelation which is with you, and be not the first to reject Faith therein, nor sell My Signs for a small price; and fear Me, and Me alone.	And believe in that which I reveal, confirming that which ye possess already (of the Scripture), and be not first to disbelieve therein, and part not with My revelations for a trifling price, and keep your duty unto Me.	And believe in what I have revealed, verifying that which is with you, and be not the first to deny it, neither take a mean price in exchange for My communications; and Me, Me alone should you fear.
2 042	And cover not Truth with falsehood, nor conceal the Truth when ye know (what it is).	Confound not truth with falsehood, nor knowingly conceal the truth.	And do not mix up the truth with the falsehood, nor hide the truth while you know (it).
2 043	And be steadfast in prayer; practise regular charity; and bow down your heads with those who bow down (in worship).	Establish worship, pay the poor-due, and bow your heads with those who bow (in worship).	And keep up prayer and pay the poor-rate and bow down with those who bow down.
2 044	Do ye enjoin right conduct on the people, and forget (To practise it) yourselves, and yet ye study the Scripture? Will ye not understand?	Enjoin ye righteousness upon mankind while ye yourselves forget (to practise it)? And ye are readers of the Scripture! Have ye then no sense?	What! do you enjoin men to be good and neglect your own souls while you read the Book; have you then no sense?

2 045	Nay, seek (Allah's) help with patient perseverance and prayer: It is indeed hard, except to those who bring a lowly spirit,-	Seek help in patience and prayer; and truly it is hard save for the humble-minded,		And seek assistance through patience and prayer, and most surely it is a hard thing except for the humble ones,
2 046	Who bear in mind the certainty that they are to meet their Lord, and that they are to return to Him.	Who know that they will have to meet their Lord, and that unto Him they are returning.		Who know that they shall meet their Lord and that they shall return to Him.
2 047	Children of Israel! call to mind the (special) favour which I bestowed upon you, and that I preferred you to all other (for My Message).	O Children of Israel! Remember My favour wherewith I favoured you and how I preferred you to (all) creatures.		O children of Israel! call to mind My favor which I bestowed on you and that I made you excel the nations.
2 048	Then guard yourselves against a day when one soul shall not avail another nor shall intercession be accepted for her, nor shall compensation be taken from her, nor shall anyone be helped (from outside).	And guard yourselves against a day when no soul will in aught avail another, nor will intercession be accepted from it, nor will compensation be received from it, nor will they be helped.		And be on your guard against a day when one soul shall not avail another in the least, neither shall intercession on its behalf be accepted, nor shall any compensation be taken from it, nor shall they be helped.
2 049	And remember, We delivered you from the people of Pharaoh: They set you hard tasks and punishments, slaughtered your sons and let your women-folk live; therein was a tremendous trial from your Lord.	And (remember) when We did deliver you from Pharaoh's folk, who were afflicting you with dreadful torment, slaying your sons and sparing your women: that was a tremendous trial from your Lord.		And when We delivered you from Firon's people, who subjected you to severe torment, killing your sons and sparing your women, and in this there was a great trial from your Lord.
2 050	And remember We divided the sea for you and saved you and drowned Pharaoh's people within your very sight.	And when We brought you through the sea and rescued you, and drowned the folk of Pharaoh in your sight.		And when We parted the sea for you, so We saved you and drowned the followers of Firon and you watched by.
2 051	And remember We appointed forty nights for Moses, and in his absence ye took the calf (for worship), and ye did grievous wrong.	And when We did appoint for Moses forty nights (of solitude), and then ye chose the calf, when he had gone from you, and were wrong-doers.		And when We appointed a time of forty nights with Musa, then you took the calf (for a god) after him and you were unjust.
2 052	Even then We did forgive you; there was a chance for you to be grateful.	Then, even after that, We pardoned you in order that ye might give thanks.		Then We pardoned you after that so that you might give thanks.
2 053	And remember We gave Moses the Scripture and the Criterion (Between right and wrong): There was a chance for you to be guided aright.	And when We gave unto Moses the Scripture and the criterion (of right and wrong), that ye might be led aright.		And when We gave Musa the Book and the distinction that you might walk aright.
2 054	And remember Moses said to his people: "O my people! Ye have indeed wronged yourselves by your worship of the calf: So turn (in repentance) to your Maker, and slay yourselves (the wrong-doers); that will be better for you in the sight of your Maker." Then He turned towards you (in forgiveness): For He is Oft-Returning, Most Merciful.	And when Moses said unto his people: O my people! Ye have wronged yourselves by your choosing of the calf (for worship) so turn in penitence to your Creator, and kill (the guilty) yourselves. That will be best for you with your Creator and He will relent toward you. Lo! He is the Relenting, the Merciful.		And when Musa said to his people: O my people! you have surely been unjust to yourselves by taking the calf (for a god), therefore turn to your Creator (penitently), so kill your people, that is best for you with your Creator: so He turned to you (mercifully), for surely He is the Oft-returning (to mercy), the Merciful.
2 055	And remember ye said: "O Moses! We shall never believe in thee until we see Allah manifestly," but ye were dazed with thunder and lighting even as ye looked on.	And when ye said: O Moses! We will not believe in thee till we see Allah plainly; and even while ye gazed the lightning seized you.		And when you said: O Musa! we will not believe in you until we see Allah manifestly, so the punishment overtook you while you looked on.

2 056	Then We raised you up after your death: Ye had the chance to be grateful.	Then We revived you after your extinction, that ye might give thanks.		Then We raised you up after your death that you may give thanks.
2 057	And We gave you the shade of clouds and sent down to you Manna and quails, saying: "Eat of the good things We have provided for you:" (But they rebelled); to us they did no harm, but they harmed their own souls.	And We caused the white cloud to overshadow you and sent down on you the manna and the quails, (saying): Eat of the good things wherewith We have provided you-they wronged Us not, but they did wrong themselves.		And We made the clouds to give shade over you and We sent to you manna and quails: Eat of the good things that We have given you; and they did not do Us any harm, but they made their own souls suffer the loss.
2 058	And remember We said: "Enter this town, and eat of the plenty therein as ye wish; but enter the gate with humility, in posture and in words, and We shall forgive you your faults and increase (the portion of) those who do good."	And when We said: Go into this township and eat freely of that which is therein, and enter the gate prostrate, and say: "Repentance." We will forgive you your sins and will increase (reward) for the right-doers.		And when We said: Enter this city, then eat from it a plenteous (food) wherever you wish, and enter the gate making obeisance, and say, forgiveness. We will forgive you your wrongs and give more to those who do good (to others).
2 059	But the transgressors changed the word from that which had been given them; so We sent on the transgressors a plague from heaven, for that they infringed (Our command) repeatedly.	But those who did wrong changed the word which had been told them for another saying, and We sent down upon the evil-doers wrath from heaven for their evil-doing.		But those who were unjust changed it for a saying other than that which had been spoken to them, so We sent upon those who were unjust a pestilence from heaven, because they transgressed.
2 060	And remember Moses prayed for water for his people; We said: Strike the rock with thy staff. Then gushed forth therefrom twelve springs. Each group knew its own place for water. So eat and drink of the sustenance provided by Allah, and do no evil nor mischief on the (face of the) earth.	And when Moses asked for water for his people, We said: Smite with thy staff the rock. And there gushed out therefrom twelve springs (so that) each tribe knew their drinking-place. Eat and drink of that which Allah hath provided, and do not act corruptly, making mischief in the earth.		And when Musa prayed for drink for his people, We said: Strike the rock with your staff So there gushed from it twelve springs; each tribe knew its drinking place: Eat and drink of the provisions of Allah and do not act corruptly in the land, making mischief.
2 061	And remember ye said: "O Moses! we cannot endure one kind of food (always); so beseech thy Lord for us to produce for us of what the earth groweth,- its pot-herbs, and cucumbers, its garlic, lentils, and onions." He said: "Will ye exchange the better for the worse? Go ye down to any town, and ye shall find what ye want!" They were covered with humiliation and misery; they drew on themselves the wrath of Allah. This because they went on rejecting the Signs of Allah and slaying His Messengers without just cause. This because they rebelled and went on transgressing.	And when ye said: O Moses! We are weary of one kind of food; so call upon thy Lord for us that He bring forth for us of that which the earth groweth - of its herbs and its cucumbers and its corn and its lentils and its onions. He said: Would ye exchange that which is higher for that which is lower? Go down to settled country, thus ye shall get that which ye demand. And humiliation and wretchedness were stamped upon them and they were visited with wrath from Allah. That was because they disbelieved in Allah's revelations and slew the prophets wrongfully. That was for their disobedience and transgression.		And when you said: O Musa! we cannot bear with one food, therefore pray Lord on our behalf to bring forth for us out of what the earth grows, of its herbs and its cucumbers and its garlic and its lentils and its onions. He said: Will you exchange that which is better for that which is worse? Enter a city, so you will have what you ask for. And abasement and humiliation were brought down upon them, and they became deserving of Allah's wrath; this was so because they disbelieved in the communications of Allah and killed the prophets unjustly; this was so because they disobeyed and exceeded the limits.

2 062	Those who believe (in the Qur'an), and those who follow the Jewish (scriptures), and the Christians and the Sabians,- any who believe in Allah and the Last Day, and work righteousness, shall have their reward with their Lord; on them shall be no fear, nor shall they grieve.	Lo! Those who believe (in that which is revealed unto thee, Muhammad), and those who are Jews, and Christians, and Sabaeans - whoever believeth in Allah and the Last Day and doeth right - surely their reward is with their Lord, and there shall no fear come upon them neither shall they grieve.	Surely those who believe, and those who are Jews, and the Christians, and the Sabians, whoever believes in Allah and the Last day and does good, they shall have their reward from their Lord, and there is no fear for them, nor shall they grieve.
2 063	And remember We took your covenant and We raised above you (The towering height) of Mount (Sinai) (Saying): "Hold firmly to what We have given you and bring (ever) to remembrance what is therein: Perchance ye may fear Allah."	And (remember, O Children of Israel) when We made a covenant with you and caused the mount to tower above you, (saying): Hold fast that which We have given you, and remember that which is therein, that ye may ward off (evil).	And when We took a promise from you and lifted the mountain over you: Take hold of the law (Tavrat) We have given you with firmness and bear in mind what is in it, so that you may guard (against evil).
2 064	But ye turned back thereafter: Had it not been for the Grace and Mercy of Allah to you, ye had surely been among the lost.	Then, even after that, ye turned away, and if it had not been for the grace of Allah and His mercy ye had been among the losers.	Then you turned back after that; so were it not for the grace of Allah and His mercy on you, you would certainly have been among the losers.
2 065	And well ye knew those amongst you who transgressed in the matter of the Sabbath: We said to them: "Be ye apes, despised and rejected."	And ye know of those of you who broke the Sabbath, how We said unto them: Be ye apes, despised and hated!	And certainly you have known those among you who exceeded the limits of the Sabbath, so We said to them: Be (as) apes, despised and hated.
2 066	So We made it an example to their own time and to their posterity, and a lesson to those who fear Allah.	And We made it an example to their own and to succeeding generations, and an admonition to the Allah-fearing.	So We made them an example to those who witnessed it and those who came after it, and an admonition to those who guard (against evil).
2 067	And remember Moses said to his people: "Allah commands that ye sacrifice a heifer." They said: "Makest thou a laughing-stock of us?" He said: "Allah save me from being an ignorant (fool)!"	And when Moses said unto his people: Lo! Allah commandeth you that ye sacrifice a cow, they said: Dost thou make game of us? He answered: Allah forbid that I should be among the foolish!	And when Musa said to his people: Surely Allah commands you that you should sacrifice a cow; they said: Do you ridicule us? He said: I seek the protection of Allah from being one of the ignorant.
2 068	They said: "Beseech on our behalf Thy Lord to make plain to us what (heifer) it is!" He said; "He says: The heifer should be neither too old nor too young, but of middling age. Now do what ye are commanded!"	They said: Pray for us unto thy Lord that He make clear to us what (cow) she is. (Moses) answered: Lo! He saith, Verily she is a cow neither with calf nor immature; (she is) between the two conditions; so do that which ye are commanded.	They said: Call on your Lord for our sake to make it plain to us what she is. Musa said: He says, Surely she is a cow neither advanced in age nor too young, of middle age between that (and this); do therefore what you are commanded.
2 069	They said: "Beseech on our behalf Thy Lord to make plain to us Her colour." He said: "He says: A fawn-coloured heifer, pure and rich in tone, the admiration of beholders!"	They said: Pray for us unto thy Lord that He make clear to us of what colour she is. (Moses) answered: Lo! He saith: Verily she is a yellow cow. Bright is her colour, gladdening beholders.	They said: Call on your Lord for our sake to make it plain to us what her color is. Musa said: He says, Surely she is a yellow cow; her color is intensely yellow, giving delight to the beholders.
2 070	They said: "Beseech on our behalf Thy Lord to make plain to us what she is: To us are all heifers alike: We wish indeed for guidance, if Allah wills."	They said: Pray for us unto thy Lord that He make clear to us what (cow) she is. Lo! cows are much alike to us; and Lo! if Allah wills, we may be led aright.	They said: Call on your Lord for our sake to make it plain to us what she is, for surely to us the cows are all alike, and if Allah please we shall surely be guided aright.

2 071	He said: "He says: A heifer not trained to till the soil or water the fields; sound and without blemish." They said: "Now hast thou brought the truth." Then they offered her in sacrifice, but not with good-will.	(Moses) answered: Lo! He saith: Verily she is a cow unyoked; she plougheth not the soil nor watereth the tilth; whole and without mark. They said: Now thou bringest the truth. So they sacrificed her, though almost they did not.	Musa said: He says, Surely she is a cow not made submissive that she should plough the land, nor does she irrigate the tilth; sound, without a blemish in her. They said: Now you have brought the truth; so they sacrificed her, though they had not the mind to do (it).
2 072	Remember ye slew a man and fell into a dispute among yourselves as to the crime: But Allah was to bring forth what ye did hide.	And (remember) when ye slew a man and disagreed concerning it and Allah brought forth that which ye were hiding.	And when you killed a man, then you disagreed with respect to that, and Allah was to bring forth that which you were going to hide.
2 073	So We said: "Strike the (body) with a piece of the (heifer)." Thus Allah bringeth the dead to life and showeth you His Signs: Perchance ye may understand.	And We said: Smite him with some of it. Thus Allah bringeth the dead to life and showeth you His portents so that ye may understand.	So We said: Strike the (dead body) with part of the (Sacrificed cow), thus Allah brings the dead to life, and He shows you His signs so that you may understand.
2 074	Thenceforth were your hearts hardened: They became like a rock and even worse in hardness. For among rocks there are some from which rivers gush forth; others there are which when split asunder send forth water; and others which sink for fear of Allah. And Allah is not unmindful of what ye do.	Then, even after that, your hearts were hardened and became as rocks, or worse than rocks, for hardness. For indeed there are rocks from out which rivers gush, and indeed there are rocks which split asunder so that water floweth from them. And indeed there are rocks which fall down for the fear of Allah. Allah is not unaware of what ye do.	Then your hearts hardened after that, so that they were like rocks, rather worse in hardness; and surely there are some rocks from which streams burst forth, and surely there are some of them which split asunder so water issues out of them, and surely there are some of them which fall down for fear of Allah, and Allah is not at all heedless of what you do.
2 075	Can ye (O ye men of Faith) entertain the hope that they will believe in you?- Seeing that a party of them heard the Word of Allah, and perverted it knowingly after they understood it.	Have ye any hope that they will be true to you when a party of them used to listen to the word of Allah, then used to change it, after they had understood it, knowingly?	Do you then hope that they would believe in you, and a party from among them indeed used to hear the Word of Allah, then altered it after they had understood it, and they know (this).
2 076	Behold! when they meet the men of Faith, they say: "We believe": But when they meet each other in private, they say: "Shall you tell them what Allah hath revealed to you, that they may engage you in argument about it before your Lord?"- Do ye not understand (their aim)?	And when they fall in with those who believe, they say: We believe. But when they go apart one with another they say: Prate ye to them of that which Allah hath disclosed to you that they may contend with you before your Lord concerning it? Have ye then no sense?	And when they meet those who believe they say: We believe, and when they are alone one with another they say: Do you talk to them of what Allah has disclosed to you that they may contend with you by this before your Lord? Do you not then understand?
2 077	Know they not that Allah knoweth what they conceal and what they reveal?	Are they then unaware that Allah knoweth that which they keep hidden and that which they proclaim?	Do they not know that Allah knows what they keep secret and what they make known?
2 078	And there are among them illiterates, who know not the Book, but (see therein their own) desires, and they do nothing but conjecture.	Among them are unlettered folk who know the Scripture not except from hearsay. They but guess.	And there are among them illiterates who know not the Book but only lies, and they do but conjecture.
2 079	Then woe to those who write the Book with their own hands, and then say: "This is from Allah," to traffic with it for miserable price!- Woe to them for what their hands do write, and for the gain they make thereby.	Therefore woe be unto those who write the Scripture with their hands and then say, "This is from Allah," that they may purchase a small gain therewith. Woe unto them for that their hands have written, and woe unto them for that they earn thereby.	Woe, then, to those who write the book with their hands and then say: This is from Allah, so that they may take for it a small price; therefore woe to them for what their hands have written and woe to them for what they earn.

2 080	And they say: "The Fire shall not touch us but for a few numbered days:" Say: "Have ye taken a promise from Allah, for He never breaks His promise? or is it that ye say of Allah what ye do not know?"	And they say: The Fire (of punishment) will not touch us save for a certain number of days. Say: Have ye received a covenant from Allah - truly Allah will not break His covenant - or tell ye concerning Allah that which ye know not?	And they say: Fire shall not touch us but for a few days. Say: Have you received a promise from Allah, then Allah will not fail to perform His promise, or do you speak against Allah what you do not know?
2 081	Nay, those who seek gain in evil, and are girt round by their sins,- they are companions of the Fire: Therein shall they abide (For ever).	Nay, but whosoever hath done evil and his sin surroundeth him; such are rightful owners of the Fire; they will abide therein.	Yea, whoever earns evil and his sins beset him on every side, these are the inmates of the fire; in it they shall abide.
2 082	But those who have faith and work righteousness, they are companions of the Garden: Therein shall they abide (For ever).	And those who believe and do good works: such are rightful owners of the Garden. They will abide therein.	And (as for) those who believe and do good deeds, these are the dwellers of the garden; in it they shall abide.
2 083	And remember We took a covenant from the Children of Israel (to this effect): Worship none but Allah; treat with kindness your parents and kindred, and orphans and those in need; speak fair to the people; be steadfast in prayer; and practise regular charity. Then did ye turn back, except a few among you, and ye backslide (even now).	And (remember) when We made a covenant with the Children of Israel, (saying): Worship none save Allah (only), and be good to parents and to kindred and to orphans and the needy, and speak kindly to mankind; and establish worship and pay the poor-due. Then, after that, ye slid back, save a few of you, being averse.	And when We made a covenant with the children of Israel: You shall not serve any but Allah and (you shall do) good to (your) parents, and to the near of kin and to the orphans and the needy, and you shall speak to men good words and keep up prayer and pay the poor-rate. Then you turned back except a few of you and (now too) you turn aside.
2 084	And remember We took your covenant (to this effect): Shed no blood amongst you, nor turn out your own people from your homes: and this ye solemnly ratified, and to this ye can bear witness.	And when We made with you a covenant (saying): Shed not the blood of your people nor turn (a party of) your people out of your dwellings. Then ye ratified (Our covenant) and ye were witnesses (thereto).	And when We made a covenant with you: You shall not shed your blood and you shall not turn your people out of your cities; then you gave a promise while you witnessed.
2 085	After this it is ye, the same people, who slay among yourselves, and banish a party of you from their homes; assist (Their enemies) against them, in guilt and rancour; and if they come to you as captives, ye ransom them, though it was not lawful for you to banish them. Then is it only a part of the Book that ye believe in, and do ye reject the rest? but what is the reward for those among you who behave like this but disgrace in this life?- and on the Day of Judgment they shall be consigned to the most grievous penalty. For Allah is not unmindful of what ye do.	Yet ye it is who slay each other and drive out a party of your people from their homes, supporting one another against them by sin and transgression? - and if they came to you as captives ye would ransom them, whereas their expulsion was itself unlawful for you - Believe ye in part of the Scripture and disbelieve ye in part thereof? And what is the reward of those who do so save ignominy in the life of the world, and on the Day of Resurrection they will be consigned to the most grievous doom. For Allah is not unaware of what ye do.	Yet you it is who slay your people and turn a party from among you out of their homes, backing each other up against them unlawfully and exceeding the limits; and if they should come to you, as captives you would ransom them-- while their very turning out was unlawful for you. Do you then believe in a part of the Book and disbelieve in the other? What then is the reward of such among you as do this but disgrace in the life of this world, and on the day of resurrection they shall be sent back to the most grievous chastisement, and Allah is not at all heedless of what you do.
2 086	These are the people who buy the life of this world at the price of the Hereafter: their penalty shall not be lightened nor shall they be helped.	Such are those who buy the life of the world at the price of the Hereafter. Their punishment will not be lightened, neither will they have support.	These are they who buy the life of this world for the hereafter, so their chastisement shall not be lightened nor shall they be helped.

2 087	We gave Moses the Book and followed him up with a succession of messengers; We gave Jesus the son of Mary Clear (Signs) and strengthened him with the holy spirit. Is it that whenever there comes to you a messenger with what ye yourselves desire not, ye are puffed up with pride?- Some ye called impostors, and others ye slay!	And verily We gave unto Moses the Scripture and We caused a train of messengers to follow after him, and We gave unto Jesus, son of Mary, clear proofs (of Allah's sovereignty), and We supported him with the Holy spirit. Is it ever so, that, when there cometh unto you a messenger (from Allah) with that which ye yourselves desire not, ye grow arrogant, and some ye disbelieve and some ye slay?	And most certainly We gave Musa the Book and We sent messengers after him one after another; and We gave Isa, the son of Marium, clear arguments and strengthened him with the holy spirit, What! whenever then a messenger came to you with that which your souls did not desire, you were insolent so you called some liars and some you slew.
2 088	They say, "Our hearts are the wrappings (which preserve Allah's Word: we need no more)." Nay, Allah's curse is on them for their blasphemy: Little is it they believe.	And they say: Our hearts are hardened. Nay, but Allah hath cursed them for their unbelief. Little is that which they believe.	And they say: Our hearts are covered. Nay, Allah has cursed them on account of their unbelief; so little it is that they believe.
2 089	And when there comes to them a Book from Allah, confirming what is with them,- although from of old they had prayed for victory against those without Faith,- when there comes to them that which they (should) have recognised, they refuse to believe in it but the curse of Allah is on those without Faith.	And when there cometh unto them a scripture from Allah, confirming that in their possession - though before that they were asking for a signal triumph over those who disbelieved - and when there cometh unto them that which they know (to be the truth) they disbelieve therein. The curse of Allah is on disbelievers.	And when there came to them a Book from Allah verifying that which they have, and aforetime they used to pray for victory against those who disbelieve, but when there came to them (Prophet) that which they did not recognize, they disbelieved in him; so Allah's curse is on the unbelievers.
2 090	Miserable is the price for which they have sold their souls, in that they deny (the revelation) which Allah has sent down, in insolent envy that Allah of His Grace should send it to any of His servants He pleases: Thus have they drawn on themselves Wrath upon Wrath. And humiliating is the punishment of those who reject Faith.	Evil is that for which they sell their souls: that they should disbelieve in that which Allah hath revealed, grudging that Allah should reveal of His bounty unto whom He will of His slaves. They have incurred anger upon anger. For disbelievers is a shameful doom.	Evil is that for which they have sold their souls-- that they should deny what Allah has revealed, out of envy that Allah should send down of His grace on whomsoever of His servants He pleases; so they have made themselves deserving of wrath upon wrath, and there is a disgraceful punishment for the unbelievers.
2 091	When it is said to them: "Believe in what Allah Hath sent down," they say, "We believe in what was sent down to us": yet they reject all besides, even if it be Truth confirming what is with them. Say: "Why then have ye slain the prophets of Allah in times gone by, if ye did indeed believe?"	And when it is said unto them: Believe in that which Allah hath revealed, they say: We believe in that which was revealed unto us. And they disbelieve in that which cometh after it, though it is the truth confirming that which they possess. Say (unto them, O Muhammad): Why then slew ye the prophets of Allah aforetime, if ye are (indeed) believers?	And when it is said to them, Believe in what Allah has revealed, they say: We believe in that which was revealed to us; and they deny what is besides that, while it is the truth verifying that which they have. Say: Why then did you kill Allah's Prophets before if you were indeed believers?
2 092	There came to you Moses with clear (Signs); yet ye worshipped the calf (Even) after that, and ye did behave wrongfully.	And Moses came unto you with clear proofs (of Allah's Sovereignty), yet, while he was away, ye chose the calf (for worship) and ye were wrong-doers.	And most certainly Musa came to you with clear arguments, then you took the calf (for a god) in his absence and you were unjust.

2 093	And remember We took your covenant and We raised above you (the towering height) of Mount (Sinai): (Saying): "Hold firmly to what We have given you, and hearken (to the Law)": They said: "We hear, and we disobey": And they had to drink into their hearts (of the taint) of the calf because of their Faithlessness. Say: "Vile indeed are the behests of your Faith if ye have any faith!"	And when We made with you a covenant and caused the Mount to tower above you, (saying): Hold fast by that which We have given you, and hear (Our Word), they said: We hear and we rebel. And (worship of) the calf was made to sink into their hearts because of their rejection (of the covenant). Say (unto them): Evil is that which your belief enjoineth on you, if ye are believers.	And when We made a covenant with you and raised the mountain over you: Take hold of what We have given you with firmness and be obedient. They said: We hear and disobey. And they were made to imbibe (the love of) the calf into their hearts on account of their unbelief Say: Evil is that which your belief bids you if you are believers.
2 094	Say: "If the last Home, with Allah, be for you specially, and not for anyone else, then seek ye for death, if ye are sincere."	Say (unto them): If the abode of the Hereafter in the providence of Allah is indeed for you alone and not for others of mankind (as ye pretend), then long for death (for ye must long for death) if ye are truthful.	Say: If the future abode with Allah is specially for you to the exclusion of the people, then invoke death if you are truthful.
2 095	But they will never seek for death, on account of the (sins) which their hands have sent on before them. And Allah is well-acquainted with the wrong-doers.	But they will never long for it, because of that which their own hands have sent before them. Allah is aware of evil-doers.	And they will never invoke it on account of what their hands have sent before, and Allah knows the unjust.
2 096	Thou wilt indeed find them, of all people, most greedy of life,-even more than the idolaters: Each one of them wishes He could be given a life of a thousand years: But the grant of such life will not save him from (due) punishment. For Allah sees well all that they do.	And thou wilt find them greediest of mankind for life and (greedier) than the idolaters. (Each) one of them would like to be allowed to live a thousand years. And to live (a thousand years) would be no means remove him from the doom. Allah is Seer of what they do.	And you will most certainly find them the greediest of men for life (greedier) than even those who are polytheists; every one of them loves that he should be granted a life of a thousand years, and his being granted a long life will in no way remove him further off from the chastisement, and Allah sees what they do.
2 097	Say: Whoever is an enemy to Gabriel-for he brings down the (revelation) to thy heart by Allah's will, a confirmation of what went before, and guidance and glad tidings for those who believe,-	Say (O Muhammad, to mankind): Who is an enemy to Gabriel! For he it is who hath revealed (this Scripture) to thy heart by Allah's leave, confirming that which was (revealed) before it, and a guidance and glad tidings to believers;	Say: Whoever is the enemy of Jibreel-- for surely he revealed it to your heart by Allah's command, verifying that which is before it and guidance and good news for the believers.
2 098	Whoever is an enemy to Allah and His angels and messengers, to Gabriel and Michael,- Lo! Allah is an enemy to those who reject Faith.	Who is an enemy to Allah, and His angels and His messengers, and Gabriel and Michael! Then, lo! Allah (Himself) is an enemy to the disbelievers.	Whoever is the enemy of Allah and His angels and His messengers and Jibreel and Meekaeel, so surely Allah is the enemy of the unbelievers.
2 099	We have sent down to thee Manifest Signs (ayat); and none reject them but those who are perverse.	Verily We have revealed unto thee clear tokens, and only miscreants will disbelieve in them.	And certainly We have revealed to you clear communications and none disbelieve in them except the transgressors.
2 100	Is it not (the case) that every time they make a covenant, some party among them throw it aside?- Nay, most of them are faithless.	Is it ever so that when they make a covenant a party of them set it aside? The truth is, most of them believe not.	What! whenever they make a covenant, a party of them cast it aside? Nay, most of them do not believe.

2 101	And when there came to them a messenger from Allah, confirming what was with them, a party of the people of the Book threw away the Book of Allah behind their backs, as if (it had been something) they did not know!	And when there cometh unto them a messenger from Allah, confirming that which they possess, a party of those who have received the Scripture fling the Scripture of Allah behind their backs as if they knew not,	And when there came to them a Messenger from Allah verifying that which they have, a party of those who were given the Book threw the Book of Allah behind their backs as if they knew nothing.
2 102	They followed what the evil ones gave out (falsely) against the power of Solomon: the blasphemers Were, not Solomon, but the evil ones, teaching men Magic, and such things as came down at Babylon to the angels Harut and Marut. But neither of these taught anyone (Such things) without saying: "We are only for trial; so do not blaspheme." They learned from them the means to sow discord between man and wife. But they could not thus harm anyone except by Allah's permission. And they learned what harmed them, not what profited them. And they knew that the buyers of (magic) would have no share in the happiness of the Hereafter. And vile was the price for which they did sell their souls, if they but knew!	And follow that which the devils falsely related against the kingdom of Solomon. Solomon disbelieved not; but the devils disbelieved, teaching mankind magic and that which was revealed to the two angels in Babel, Harut and Marut. Nor did they (the two angels) teach it to anyone till they had said: We are only a temptation, therefore disbelieve not (in the guidance of Allah). And from these two (angles) people learn that by which they cause division between man and wife; but they injure thereby no-one save by Allah's leave. And they learn that which harmeth them and profiteth them not. And surely they do know that he who trafficketh therein will have no (happy) portion in the Hereafter; and surely evil is the price for which they sell their souls, if they but knew.	And they followed what the Shaitans chanted of sorcery in the reign of Sulaiman, and Sulaiman was not an unbeliever, but the Shaitans disbelieved, they taught men sorcery and that was sent down to the two angels at Babel, Harut and Marut, yet these two taught no man until they had said, "Surely we are only a trial, therefore do not be a disbeliever." Even then men learned from these two, magic by which they might cause a separation between a man and his wife; and they cannot hurt with it any one except with Allah's permission, and they learned what harmed them and did not profit them, and certainly they know that he who bought it should have no share of good in the hereafter and evil was the price for which they sold their souls, had they but known this.
2 103	If they had kept their Faith and guarded themselves from evil, far better had been the reward from their Lord, if they but knew!	And if they had believed and kept from evil, a recompense from Allah would be better, if they only knew.	And if they had believed and guarded themselves (against evil), reward from Allah would certainly have been better; had they but known (this).
2 104	O ye of Faith! Say not (to the Messenger) words of ambiguous import, but words of respect; and hearken (to him): To those without Faith is a grievous punishment.	O ye who believe, say not (unto the Prophet): "Listen to us" but say Look upon us, and be ye listeners. For disbelievers is a painful doom.	O you who believe! do not say Raina and say Unzurna and listen, and for the unbelievers there is a painful chastisement.
2 105	It is never the wish of those without Faith among the People of the Book, nor of the Pagans, that anything good should come down to you from your Lord. But Allah will choose for His special Mercy whom He will - for Allah is Lord of grace abounding.	Neither those who disbelieve among the people of the Scripture nor the idolaters love that there should be sent down unto you any good thing from your Lord. But Allah chooseth for His mercy whom He will, and Allah is of Infinite Bounty.	Those who disbelieve from among the followers of the Book do not like, nor do the polytheists, that the good should be sent down to you from your Lord, and Allah chooses especially whom He pleases for His mercy, and Allah is the Lord of mighty grace.
2 106	None of Our revelations do We abrogate or cause to be forgotten, but We substitute something better or similar: Knowest thou not that Allah Hath power over all things?	Nothing of our revelation (even a single verse) do we abrogate or cause be forgotten, but we bring (in place) one better or the like thereof. Knowest thou not that Allah is Able to do all things?	Whatever communications We abrogate or cause to be forgotten, We bring one better than it or like it. Do you not know that Allah has power over all things?
2 107	Knowest thou not that to Allah belongeth the dominion of the heavens and the earth? And besides Him ye have neither patron nor helper.	Knowest thou not that it is Allah unto Whom belongeth the Sovereignty of the heavens and the earth; and ye have not, beside Allah, any guardian or helper?	Do you not know that Allah's is the kingdom of the heavens and the earth, and that besides Allah you have no guardian or helper?

2 108	Would ye question your Messenger as Moses was questioned of old? but whoever changeth from Faith to Unbelief, Hath strayed without doubt from the even way.	Or would ye question your messenger as Moses was questioned aforetime? He who chooseth disbelief instead of faith, verily he hath gone astray from a plain road.	Rather you wish to put questions to your Messenger, as Musa was questioned before; and whoever adopts unbelief instead of faith, he indeed has lost the right direction of the way.
2 109	Quite a number of the People of the Book wish they could Turn you (people) back to infidelity after ye have believed, from selfish envy, after the Truth hath become Manifest unto them: But forgive and overlook, Till Allah accomplish His purpose; for Allah Hath power over all things.	Many of the people of the Scripture long to make you disbelievers after your belief, through envy on their own account, after the truth hath become manifest unto them. Forgive and be indulgent (toward them) until Allah give command. Lo! Allah is Able to do all things.	Many of the followers of the Book wish that they could turn you back into unbelievers after your faith, out of envy from themselves, (even) after the truth has become manifest to them; but pardon and forgive, so that Allah should bring about His command; surely Allah has power over all things.
2 110	And be steadfast in prayer and regular in charity: And whatever good ye send forth for your souls before you, ye shall find it with Allah: for Allah sees Well all that ye do.	Establish worship, and pay the poor-due; and whatever of good ye send before (you) for your souls, ye will find it with Allah. Lo! Allah is Seer of what ye do.	And keep up prayer and pay the poor-rate and whatever good you send before for yourselves, you shall find it with Allah; surely Allah sees what you do.
2 111	And they say: "None shall enter Paradise unless he be a Jew or a Christian." Those are their (vain) desires. Say: "Produce your proof if ye are truthful."	And they say: None entereth paradise unless he be a Jew or a Christian. These are their own desires. Say: Bring your proof (of what ye state) if ye are truthful.	And they say: None shall enter the garden (or paradise) except he who is a Jew or a Christian. These are their vain desires. Say: Bring your proof if you are truthful.
2 112	Nay,- whoever submits His whole self to Allah and is a doer of good,- He will get his reward with his Lord; on such shall be no fear, nor shall they grieve.	Nay, but whosoever surrendereth his purpose to Allah while doing good, his reward is with his Lord; and there shall no fear come upon them neither shall they grieve.	Yes! whoever submits himself entirely to Allah and he is the doer of good (to others) he has his reward from his Lord, and there is no fear for him nor shall he grieve.
2 113	The Jews say: "The Christians have naught (to stand) upon"; and the Christians say: "The Jews have naught (To stand) upon." Yet they (Profess to) study the (same) Book. Like unto their word is what those say who know not; but Allah will judge between them in their quarrel on the Day of Judgment.	And the Jews say the Christians follow nothing (true), and the Christians say the Jews follow nothing (true); yet both are readers of the Scripture. Even thus speak those who know not. Allah will judge between them on the Day of Resurrection concerning that wherein they differ.	And the Jews say: The Christians do not follow anything (good) and the Christians say: The Jews do not follow anything (good) while they recite the (same) Book. Even thus say those who have no knowledge, like to what they say; so Allah shall judge between them on the day of resurrection in what they differ.
2 114	And who is more unjust than he who forbids that in places for the worship of Allah, Allah's name should be celebrated? - whose zeal is (in fact) to ruin them? It was not fitting that such should themselves enter them except in fear. For them there is nothing but disgrace in this world, and in the world to come, an exceeding torment.	And who doth greater wrong than he who forbiddeth the approach to the sanctuaries of Allah lest His name should be mentioned therein, and striveth for their ruin. As for such, it was never meant that they should enter them except in fear. Theirs in the world is ignominy and theirs in the Hereafter is an awful doom.	And who is more unjust than he who prevents (men) from the masjids of Allah, that His name should be remembered in them, and strives to ruin them? (As for) these, it was not proper for them that they should have entered them except in fear; they shall meet with disgrace in this world, and they shall have great chastisement in the hereafter.
2 115	To Allah belong the east and the West: Whithersoever ye turn, there is the presence of Allah. For Allah is All-Pervading, All-Knowing.	Unto Allah belong the East and the West, and whithersoever ye turn, there is Allah's Countenance. Lo! Allah is All-Embracing, All-Knowing.	And Allah's is the East and the West, therefore, whither you turn, thither is Allah's purpose; surely Allah is Amplegiving, Knowing.
2 116	They say: "Allah hath begotten a son": Glory be to Him.-Nay, to Him belongs all that is in the heavens and on earth: everything renders worship to Him.	And they say: Allah hath taken unto Himself a son. Be He glorified! Nay, but whatsoever is in the heavens and the earth is His. All are subservient unto Him.	And they say: Allah has taken to himself a son. Glory be to Him; rather, whatever is in the heavens and the earth is His; all are obedient to Him.

2 117	To Him is due the primal origin of the heavens and the earth: When He decreeth a matter, He saith to it: "Be," and it is.	The Originator of the heavens and the earth! When He decreeth a thing, He saith unto it only: Be! and it is.	Wonderful Originator of the heavens and the earth, and when He decrees an affair, He only says to it, Be, so there it is.
2 118	Say those without knowledge: "Why speaketh not Allah unto us? or why cometh not unto us a Sign?" So said the people before them words of similar import. Their hearts are alike. We have indeed made clear the Signs unto any people who hold firmly to Faith (in their hearts).	And those who have no knowledge say: Why doth not Allah speak unto us, or some sign come unto us? Even thus, as they now speak, spake those (who were) before them. Their hearts are all alike. We have made clear the revelations for people who are sure.	And those who have no knowledge say: Why does not Allah speak to us or a sign come to us? Even thus said those before them, the like of what they say; their hearts are all alike. Indeed We have made the communications clear for a people who are sure.
2 119	Verily We have sent thee in truth as a bearer of glad tidings and a warner: But of thee no question shall be asked of the Companions of the Blazing Fire.	Lo! We have sent thee (O Muhammad) with the truth, a bringer of glad tidings and a warner. And thou wilt not be asked about the owners of hell-fire.	Surely We have sent you with the truth as a bearer of good news and as a warner, and you shall not be called upon to answer for the companions of the flaming fire.
2 120	Never will the Jews or the Christians be satisfied with thee unless thou follow their form of religion. Say: "The Guidance of Allah,-that is the (only) Guidance." Wert thou to follow their desires after the knowledge which hath reached thee, then wouldst thou find neither Protector nor helper against Allah.	And the Jews will not be pleased with thee, nor will the Christians, till thou follow their creed. Say: Lo! the guidance of Allah (Himself) is Guidance. And if thou shouldst follow their desires after the knowledge which hath come unto thee, then wouldst thou have from Allah no protecting guardian nor helper.	And the Jews will not be pleased with you, nor the Christians until you follow their religion. Say: Surely Allah's guidance, that is the (true) guidance. And if you follow their desires after the knowledge that has come to you, you shall have no guardian from Allah, nor any helper.
2 121	Those to whom We have sent the Book study it as it should be studied: They are the ones that believe therein: Those who reject faith therein,- the loss is their own.	Those unto whom We have given the Scripture, who read it with the right reading, those believe in it. And whoso disbelieveth in it, those are they who are the losers.	Those to whom We have given the Book read it as it ought to be read. These believe in it; and whoever disbelieves in it, these it is that are the losers.
2 122	O Children of Israel! call to mind the special favour which I bestowed upon you, and that I preferred you to all others (for My Message).	O Children of Israel! Remember My favour wherewith I favoured you and how I preferred you to (all) creatures.	O children of Israel, call to mind My favor which I bestowed on you and that I made you excel the nations.
2 123	Then guard yourselves against a-Day when one soul shall not avail another, nor shall compensation be accepted from her nor shall intercession profit her nor shall anyone be helped (from outside).	And guard (yourselves) against a day when no soul will in aught avail another, nor will compensation be accepted from it, nor will intercession be of use to it; nor will they be helped.	And be on your guard against a day when no soul shall avail another in the least neither shall any compensation be accepted from it, nor shall intercession profit it, nor shall they be helped.
2 124	And remember that Abraham was tried by his Lord with certain commands, which he fulfilled: He said: "I will make thee an Imam to the Nations." He pleaded: "And also (Imams) from my offspring!" He answered: But My Promise is not within the reach of evil-doers.	And (remember) when his Lord tried Abraham with (His) commands, and he fulfilled them, He said: Lo! I have appointed thee a leader for mankind. (Abraham) said: And of my offspring (will there be leaders)? He said: My covenant includeth not wrong-doers.	And when his Lord tried Ibrahim with certain words, he fulfilled them. He said: Surely I will make you an Imam of men. Ibrahim said: And of my offspring? My covenant does not include the unjust, said He.

2 125	Remember We made the House a place of assembly for men and a place of safety; and take ye the station of Abraham as a place of prayer; and We covenanted with Abraham and Isma'il, that they should sanctify My House for those who compass it round, or use it as a retreat, or bow, or prostrate themselves (therein in prayer).	And when We made the House (at Makka) a resort for mankind and sanctuary, (saying): Take as your place of worship the place where Abraham stood (to pray). And We imposed a duty upon Abraham and Ishmael, (saying): Purify My house for those who go around and those who meditate therein and those who bow down and prostrate themselves (in worship).	And when We made the House a pilgrimage for men and a (place of) security, and: Appoint for yourselves a place of prayer on the standing-place of Ibrahim. And We enjoined Ibrahim and Ismail saying: Purify My House for those who visit (it) and those who abide (in it) for devotion and those who bow down (and) those who prostrate themselves.	
2 126	And remember Abraham said: "My Lord, make this a City of Peace, and feed its people with fruits,-such of them as believe in Allah and the Last Day." He said: "(Yea), and such as reject Faith,-for a while will I grant them their pleasure, but will soon drive them to the torment of Fire,- an evil destination (indeed)!"	And when Abraham prayed: My Lord! Make this a region of security and bestow upon its people fruits, such of them as believe in Allah and the Last Day, He answered: As for him who disbelieveth, I shall leave him in contentment for a while, then I shall compel him to the doom of Fire - a hapless journey's end!	And when Ibrahim said: My Lord, make it a secure town and provide its people with fruits, such of them as believe in Allah and the last day. He said: And whoever disbelieves, I will grant him enjoyment for a short while, then I will drive him to the chastisement of the fire; and it is an evil destination.	
2 127	And remember Abraham and Isma'il raised the foundations of the House (With this prayer): "Our Lord! Accept (this service) from us: For Thou art the All-Hearing, the All-Knowing."	And when Abraham and Ishmael were raising the foundations of the House, (Abraham prayed): Our Lord! Accept from us (this duty). Lo! Thou, only Thou, art the Hearer, the Knower.	And when Ibrahim and Ismail raised the foundations of the House: Our Lord! accept from us; surely Thou art the Hearing, the Knowing:	
2 128	"Our Lord! make of us Muslims, bowing to Thy (Will), and of our progeny a people Muslim, bowing to Thy (will); and show us our place for the celebration of (due) rites; and turn unto us (in Mercy); for Thou art the Oft-Returning, Most Merciful."	Our Lord! And make us submissive unto Thee and of our seed a nation submissive unto Thee, and show us our ways of worship, and relent toward us. Lo! Thou, only Thou, art the Relenting, the Merciful.	Our Lord! and make us both submissive to Thee and (raise) from our offspring a nation submitting to Thee, and show us our ways of devotion and turn to us (mercifully), surely Thou art the Oft-returning (to mercy), the Merciful.	
2 129	"Our Lord! send amongst them a Messenger of their own, who shall rehearse Thy Signs to them and instruct them in scripture and wisdom, and sanctify them: For Thou art the Exalted in Might, the Wise."	Our Lord! And raise up in their midst a messenger from among them who shall recite unto them Thy revelations, and shall instruct them in the Scripture and in wisdom and shall make them grow. Lo! Thou, only Thou, art the Mighty, Wise.	Our Lord! and raise up in them a Messenger from among them who shall recite to them Thy communications and teach them the Book and the wisdom, and purify them; surely Thou art the Mighty, the Wise.	
2 130	And who turns away from the religion of Abraham but such as debase their souls with folly? Him We chose and rendered pure in this world: And he will be in the Hereafter in the ranks of the Righteous.	And who forsaketh the religion of Abraham save him who befooleth himself? Verily We chose him in the world, and lo! in the Hereafter he is among the righteous.	And who forsakes the religion of Ibrahim but he who makes himself a fool, and most certainly We chose him in this world, and in the hereafter he is most surely among the righteous.	
2 131	Behold! his Lord said to him: "Bow (thy will to Me):" He said: "I bow (my will) to the Lord and Cherisher of the Universe."	When his Lord said unto him: Surrender! he said: I have surrendered to the Lord of the Worlds.	When his Lord said to him, Be a Muslim, he said: I submit myself to the Lord of the worlds.	
2 132	And this was the legacy that Abraham left to his sons, and so did Jacob; "Oh my sons! Allah hath chosen the Faith for you; then die not except in the Faith of Islam."	The same did Abraham enjoin upon his sons, and also Jacob, (saying): O my sons! Lo! Allah hath chosen for you the (true) religion; therefore die not save as men who have surrendered (unto Him).	And the same did Ibrahim enjoin on his sons and (so did) Yaqoub. O my sons! surely Allah has chosen for you (this) faith, therefore die not unless you are Muslims.	

2 133	Were ye witnesses when death appeared before Jacob? Behold, he said to his sons: "What will ye worship after me?" They said: "We shall worship Thy god and the god of thy fathers, of Abraham, Isma'il and Isaac,- the one (True) Allah: To Him we bow (in Islam)."	Or were ye present when death came to Jacob, when he said unto his sons: What will ye worship after me? They said: We shall worship thy god, the god of thy fathers, Abraham and Ishmael and Isaac, One Allah, and unto Him we have surrendered.	Nay! were you witnesses when death visited Yaqoub, when he said to his sons: What will you serve after me? They said: We will serve your God and the God of your fathers, Ibrahim and Ismail and Ishaq, one Allah only, and to Him do we submit.
2 134	That was a people that hath passed away. They shall reap the fruit of what they did, and ye of what ye do! Of their merits there is no question in your case!	Those are a people who have passed away. Theirs is that which they earned, and yours is that which ye earn. And ye will not be asked of what they used to do.	This is a people that have passed away; they shall have what they earned and you shall have what you earn, and you shall not be called upon to answer for what they did.
2 135	They say: "Become Jews or Christians if ye would be guided (To salvation)." Say thou: "Nay! (I would rather) the Religion of Abraham the True, and he joined not gods with Allah."	And they say: Be Jews or Christians, then ye will be rightly guided. Say (unto them, O Muhammad): Nay, but (we follow) the religion of Abraham, the upright, and he was not one of the idolaters.	And they say: Be Jews or Christians, you will be on the right course. Say: Nay! (we follow) the religion of Ibrahim, the Hanif, and he was not one of the polytheists.
2 136	Say ye: "We believe in Allah, and the revelation given to us, and to Abraham, Isma'il, Isaac, Jacob, and the Tribes, and that given to Moses and Jesus, and that given to (all) prophets from their Lord: We make no difference between one and another of them: And we bow to Allah (in Islam)."	Say (O Muslims): We believe in Allah and that which is revealed unto us and that which was revealed unto Abraham, and Ishmael, and Isaac, and Jacob, and the tribes, and that which Moses and Jesus received, and that which the prophets received from their Lord. We make no distinction between any of them, and unto Him we have surrendered.	Say: We believe in Allah and (in) that which had been revealed to us, and (in) that which was revealed to Ibrahim and Ismail and Ishaq and Yaqoub and the tribes, and (in) that which was given to Musa and Isa, and (in) that which was given to the prophets from their Lord, we do not make any distinction between any of them, and to Him do we submit.
2 137	So if they believe as ye believe, they are indeed on the right path; but if they turn back, it is they who are in schism; but Allah will suffice thee as against them, and He is the All-Hearing, the All-Knowing.	And if they believe in the like of that which ye believe, then are they rightly guided. But if they turn away, then are they in schism, and Allah will suffice thee (for defence) against them. He is the Hearer, the Knower.	If then they believe as you believe in Him, they are indeed on the right course, and if they turn back, then they are only in great opposition, so Allah will suffice you against them, and He is the Hearing, the Knowing.
2 138	(Our religion is) the Baptism of Allah: And who can baptize better than Allah? And it is He Whom we worship.	(We take our) colour from Allah, and who is better than Allah at colouring. We are His worshippers.	(Receive) the baptism of Allah, and who is better than Allah in baptising? and Him do we serve.
2 139	Say: Will ye dispute with us about Allah, seeing that He is our Lord and your Lord; that we are responsible for our doings and ye for yours; and that We are sincere (in our faith) in Him?	Say (unto the People of the Scripture): Dispute ye with us concerning Allah when He is our Lord and your Lord? Ours are our works and yours your works. We look to Him alone.	Say: Do you dispute with us about Allah, and He is our Lord and your Lord, and we shall have our deeds and you shall have your deeds, and we are sincere to Him.
2 140	Or do ye say that Abraham, Isma'il Isaac, Jacob and the Tribes were Jews or Christians? Say: Do ye know better than Allah? Ah! who is more unjust than those who conceal the testimony they have from Allah? but Allah is not unmindful of what ye do!	Or say ye that Abraham, and Ishmael, and Isaac, and Jacob, and the tribes were Jews or Christians? Say: Do ye know best, or doth Allah? And who is more unjust than he who hideth a testimony which he hath received from Allah? Allah is not unaware of what ye do.	Nay! do you say that Ibrahim and Ismail and Yaqoub and the tribes were Jews or Christians? Say: Are you better knowing or Allah? And who is more unjust than he who conceals a testimony that he has from Allah? And Allah is not at all heedless of what you do.

2 141	That was a people that hath passed away. They shall reap the fruit of what they did, and ye of what ye do! Of their merits there is no question in your case:	Those are a people who have passed away; theirs is that which they earned and yours that which ye earn. And ye will not be asked of what they used to do.	This is a people that have passed away; they shall have what they earned and you shall have what you earn, and you shall not be called upon to answer for what they did.
2 142	The fools among the people will say: "What hath turned them from the Qibla to which they were used?" Say: To Allah belong both east and West: He guideth whom He will to a Way that is straight.	The foolish of the people will say: What hath turned them from the qiblah which they formerly observed? Say: Unto Allah belong the East and the West. He guideth whom He will unto a straight path.	The fools among the people will say: What has turned them from their qiblah which they had? Say: The East and the West belong only to Allah; He guides whom He likes to the right path.
2 143	Thus, have We made of you an Ummat justly balanced, that ye might be witnesses over the nations, and the Messenger a witness over yourselves; and We appointed the Qibla to which thou wast used, only to test those who followed the Messenger from those who would turn on their heels (From the Faith). Indeed it was (A change) momentous, except to those guided by Allah. And never would Allah Make your faith of no effect. For Allah is to all people most surely full of kindness, Most Merciful.	Thus We have appointed you a middle nation, that ye may be witnesses against mankind, and that the messenger may be a witness against you. And We appointed the qiblah which ye formerly observed only that We might know him who followeth the messenger, from him who turneth on his heels. In truth it was a hard (test) save for those whom Allah guided. But it was not Allah's purpose that your faith should be in vain, for Allah is Full of Pity, Merciful toward mankind.	And thus We have made you a medium (just) nation that you may be the bearers of witness to the people and (that) the Messenger may be a bearer of witness to you; and We did not make that which you would have to be the qiblah but that We might distinguish him who follows the Messenger from him who turns back upon his heels, and this was surely hard except for those whom Allah has guided aright; and Allah was not going to make your faith to be fruitless; most surely Allah is Affectionate, Merciful to the people.
2 144	We see the turning of thy face (for guidance) to the heavens: now Shall We turn thee to a Qibla that shall please thee. Turn then Thy face in the direction of the sacred Mosque: Wherever ye are, turn your faces in that direction. The people of the Book know well that that is the truth from their Lord. Nor is Allah unmindful of what they do.	We have seen the turning of thy face to heaven (for guidance, O Muhammad). And now verily We shall make thee turn (in prayer) toward a qiblah which is dear to thee. So turn thy face toward the Inviolable Place of Worship, and ye (O Muslims), wheresoever ye may be, turn your faces (when ye pray) toward it. Lo! Those who have received the Scripture know that (this revelation) is the Truth from their Lord. And Allah is not unaware of what they do.	Indeed We see the turning of your face to heaven, so We shall surely turn you to a qiblah which you shall like; turn then your face towards the Sacred Mosque, and wherever you are, turn your face towards it, and those who have been given the Book most surely know that it is the truth from their Lord; and Allah is not at all heedless of what they do.
2 145	Even if thou wert to bring to the people of the Book all the Signs (together), they would not follow Thy Qibla; nor art thou going to follow their Qibla; nor indeed will they follow each other's Qibla. If thou after the knowledge hath reached thee, Wert to follow their (vain) desires,-then wert thou Indeed (clearly) in the wrong.	And even if thou broughtest unto those who have received the Scripture all kinds of portents, they would not follow thy qiblah, nor canst thou be a follower of their qiblah; nor are some of them followers of the qiblah of others. And if thou shouldst follow their desires after the knowledge which hath come unto thee, then surely wert thou of the evil-doers.	And even if you bring to those who have been given the Book every sign they would not follow your qiblah, nor can you be a follower of their qiblah, neither are they the followers of each other's qiblah, and if you follow their desires after the knowledge that has come to you, then you shall most surely be among the unjust.
2 146	The people of the Book know this as they know their own sons; but some of them conceal the truth which they themselves know.	Those unto whom We gave the Scripture recognise (this revelation) as they recognise their sons. But lo! a party of them knowingly conceal the truth.	Those whom We have given the Book recognize him as they recognize their sons, and a party of them most surely conceal the truth while they know (it).

2 147	The Truth is from thy Lord; so be not at all in doubt.	It is the Truth from thy Lord (O Muhammad), so be not thou of those who waver.	The truth is from your Lord, therefore you should not be of the doubters.
2 148	To each is a goal to which Allah turns him; then strive together (as in a race) Towards all that is good. Wheresoever ye are, Allah will bring you Together. For Allah Hath power over all things.	And each one hath a goal toward which he turneth; so vie with one another in good works. Wheresoever ye may be, Allah will bring you all together. Lo! Allah is Able to do all things.	And every one has a direction to which he should turn, therefore hasten to (do) good works; wherever you are, Allah will bring you all together; surely Allah has power over all things.
2 149	From whencesoever Thou startest forth, turn Thy face in the direction of the sacred Mosque; that is indeed the truth from the Lord. And Allah is not unmindful of what ye do.	And whencesoever thou comest forth (for prayer, O Muhammad) turn thy face toward the Inviolable Place of Worship. Lo! it is the Truth from thy Lord. Allah is not unaware of what ye do.	And from whatsoever place you come forth, turn your face towards the Sacred Mosque; and surely it is the very truth from your Lord, and Allah is not at all heedless of what you do.
2 150	So from whencesoever Thou startest forth, turn Thy face in the direction of the sacred Mosque; and wheresoever ye are, Turn your face thither: that there be no ground of dispute against you among the people, except those of them that are bent on wickedness; so fear them not, but fear Me; and that I may complete My favours on you, and ye May (consent to) be guided;	Whencesoever thou comest forth turn thy face toward the Inviolable Place of Worship; and wheresoever ye may be (O Muslims) turn your faces toward it (when ye pray) so that men may have no argument against you, save such of them as do injustice - Fear them not, but fear Me! - and so that I may complete My grace upon you, and that ye may be guided.	And from whatsoever place you come forth, turn your faces towards the Sacred Mosque; and wherever you are turn your faces towards it, so that people shall have no accusation against you, except such of them as are unjust; so do not fear them, and fear Me, that I may complete My favor on you and that you may walk on the right course.
2 151	A similar (favour have ye already received) in that We have sent among you a Messenger of your own, rehearsing to you Our Signs, and sanctifying you, and instructing you in Scripture and Wisdom, and in new knowledge.	Even as We have sent unto you a messenger from among you, who reciteth unto you Our revelations and causeth you to grow, and teacheth you the Scripture and wisdom, and teacheth you that which ye knew not.	Even as We have sent among you a Messenger from among you who recites to you Our communications and purifies you and teaches you the Book and the wisdom and teaches you that which you did not know.
2 152	Then do ye remember Me; I will remember you. Be grateful to Me, and reject not Faith.	Therefore remember Me, I will remember you. Give thanks to Me, and reject not Me.	Therefore remember Me, I will remember you, and be thankful to Me, and do not be ungrateful to Me.
2 153	O ye who believe! seek help with patient perseverance and prayer; for Allah is with those who patiently persevere.	O ye who believe! Seek help in steadfastness and prayer. Lo! Allah is with the steadfast.	O you who believe! seek assistance through patience and prayer; surely Allah is with the patient.
2 154	And say not of those who are slain in the way of Allah: "They are dead." Nay, they are living, though ye perceive (it) not.	And call not those who are slain in the way of Allah "dead." Nay, they are living, only ye perceive not.	And do not speak of those who are slain in Allah's way as dead; nay, (they are) alive, but you do not perceive.
2 155	Be sure we shall test you with something of fear and hunger, some loss in goods or lives or the fruits (of your toil), but give glad tidings to those who patiently persevere,	And surely We shall try you with something of fear and hunger, and loss of wealth and lives and crops; but give glad tidings to the steadfast,	And We will most certainly try you with somewhat of fear and hunger and loss of property and lives and fruits; and give good news to the patient,
2 156	Who say, when afflicted with calamity: "To Allah We belong, and to Him is our return":-	Who say, when a misfortune striketh them: Lo! we are Allah's and lo! unto Him we are returning.	Who, when a misfortune befalls them, say: Surely we are Allah's and to Him we shall surely return.
2 157	They are those on whom (Descend) blessings from Allah, and Mercy, and they are the ones that receive guidance.	Such are they on whom are blessings from their Lord, and mercy. Such are the rightly guided.	Those are they on whom are blessings and mercy from their Lord, and those are the followers of the right course.

2 158	Behold! Safa and Marwa are among the Symbols of Allah. So if those who visit the House in the Season or at other times, should compass them round, it is no sin in them. And if any one obeyeth his own impulse to good,- be sure that Allah is He Who recogniseth and knoweth.	Lo! (the mountains) As-Safa and Al-Marwah are among the indications of Allah. It is therefore no sin for him who is on pilgrimage to the House (of Allah) or visiteth it, to go around them (as the pagan custom is). And he who doeth good of his own accord, (for him) lo! Allah is Responsive, Aware.	Surely the Safa and the Marwa are among the signs appointed by Allah; so whoever makes a pilgrimage to the House or pays a visit (to it), there is no blame on him if he goes round them both; and whoever does good spontaneously, then surely Allah is Grateful, Knowing.
2 159	Those who conceal the clear (Signs) We have sent down, and the Guidance, after We have made it clear for the people in the Book,- on them shall be Allah's curse, and the curse of those entitled to curse,-	Lo! Those who hide the proofs and the guidance which We revealed, after We had made it clear to mankind in the Scripture: such are accursed of Allah and accursed of those who have the power to curse.	Surely those who conceal the clear proofs and the guidance that We revealed after We made it clear in the Book for men, these it is whom Allah shall curse, and those who curse shall curse them (too).
2 160	Except those who repent and make amends and openly declare (the Truth): To them I turn; for I am Oft-Returning, Most Merciful.	Except those who repent and amend and make manifest (the truth). These it is toward whom I relent. I am the Relenting, the Merciful.	Except those who repent and amend and make manifest (the truth), these it is to whom I turn (mercifully); and I am the Oft-returning (to mercy), the Merciful.
2 161	Those who reject Faith, and die rejecting,- on them is Allah's curse, and the curse of angels, and of all mankind;	Lo! Those who disbelieve, and die while they are disbelievers; on them is the curse of Allah and of angels and of men combined.	Surely those who disbelieve and die while they are disbelievers, these it is on whom is the curse of Allah and the angels and men all;
2 162	They will abide therein: Their penalty will not be lightened, nor will respite be their (lot).	They ever dwell therein. The doom will not be lightened for them, neither will they be reprieved.	Abiding in it; their chastisement shall not be lightened nor shall they be given respite.
2 163	And your Allah is One Allah: There is no god but He, Most Gracious, Most Merciful.	Your Allah is One Allah; there is no God save Him, the Beneficent, the Merciful.	And your Allah is one Allah! there is no god but He; He is the Beneficent, the Merciful.
2 164	Behold! in the creation of the heavens and the earth; in the alternation of the night and the day; in the sailing of the ships through the ocean for the profit of mankind; in the rain which Allah Sends down from the skies, and the life which He gives therewith to an earth that is dead; in the beasts of all kinds that He scatters through the earth; in the change of the winds, and the clouds which they Trail like their slaves between the sky and the earth;- (Here) indeed are Signs for a people that are wise.	Lo! In the creation of the heavens and the earth, and the difference of night and day, and the ships which run upon the sea with that which is of use to men, and the water which Allah sendeth down from the sky, thereby reviving the earth after its death, and dispersing all kinds of beasts therein, and (in) the ordinance of the winds, and the clouds obedient between heaven and earth: are signs (of Allah's Sovereignty) for people who have sense.	Most surely in the creation of the heavens and the earth and the alternation of the night and the day, and the ships that run in the sea with that which profits men, and the water that Allah sends down from the cloud, then gives life with it to the earth after its death and spreads in it all (kinds of) animals, and the changing of the winds and the clouds made subservient between the heaven and the earth, there are signs for a people who understand.
2 165	Yet there are men who take (for worship) others besides Allah, as equal (with Allah): They love them as they should love Allah. But those of Faith are overflowing in their love for Allah. If only the unrighteous could see, behold, they would see the penalty: that to Allah belongs all power, and Allah will strongly enforce the penalty.	Yet of mankind are some who take unto themselves (objects of worship which they set as) rivals to Allah, loving them with a love like (that which is the due) of Allah (only) - those who believe are stauncher in their love for Allah - Oh, that those who do evil had but known, (on the day) when they behold the doom, that power belongeth wholly to Allah, and that Allah is severe in punishment!	And there are some among men who take for themselves objects of worship besides Allah, whom they love as they love Allah, and those who believe are stronger in love for Allah and O, that those who are unjust had seen, when they see the chastisement, that the power is wholly Allah's and that Allah is severe in requiting (evil).

2 166	Then would those who are followed clear themselves of those who follow (them): They would see the penalty, and all relations between them would be cut off.	(On the day) when those who were followed disown those who followed (them), and they behold the doom, and all their aims collapse with them.	When those who were followed shall renounce those who followed (them), and they see the chastisement and their ties are cut asunder.
2 167	And those who followed would say: "If only We had one more chance, We would clear ourselves of them, as they have cleared themselves of us." Thus will Allah show them (The fruits of) their deeds as (nothing but) regrets. Nor will there be a way for them out of the Fire.	And those who were but followers will say: If a return were possible for us, we would disown them even as they have disowned us. Thus will Allah show them their own deeds as anguish for them, and they will not emerge from the Fire.	And those who followed shall say: Had there been for us a return, then we would renounce them as they have renounced us. Thus will Allah show them their deeds to be intense regret to them, and they shall not come forth from the fire.
2 168	O ye people! Eat of what is on earth, Lawful and good; and do not follow the footsteps of the evil one, for he is to you an avowed enemy.	O mankind! Eat of that which is lawful and wholesome in the earth, and follow not the footsteps of the devil. Lo! he is an open enemy for you.	O men! eat the lawful and good things out of what is in the earth, and do not follow the footsteps of the Shaitan; surely he is your open enemy.
2 169	For he commands you what is evil and shameful, and that ye should say of Allah that of which ye have no knowledge.	He enjoineth upon you only the evil and the foul, and that ye should tell concerning Allah that which ye know not.	He only enjoins you evil and indecency, and that you may speak against Allah what you do not know.
2 170	When it is said to them: "Follow what Allah hath revealed:" They say: Nay! we shall follow the ways of our fathers. What! even though their fathers Were void of wisdom and guidance?	And when it is said unto them: Follow that which Allah hath revealed, they say: We follow that wherein we found our fathers. What! Even though their fathers were wholly unintelligent and had no guidance?	And when it is said to them, Follow what Allah has revealed, they say: Nay! we follow what we found our fathers upon. What! and though their fathers had no sense at all, nor did they follow the right way.
2 171	The parable of those who reject Faith is as if one were to shout Like a goat-herd, to things that listen to nothing but calls and cries: Deaf, dumb, and blind, they are void of wisdom.	The likeness of those who disbelieve (in relation to the messenger) is as the likeness of one who calleth unto that which heareth naught except a shout and cry. Deaf, dumb, blind, therefore they have no sense.	And the parable of those who disbelieve is as the parable of one who calls out to that which hears no more than a call and a cry; deaf, dumb (and) blind, so they do not understand.
2 172	O ye who believe! Eat of the good things that We have provided for you, and be grateful to Allah, if it is Him ye worship.	O ye who believe! Eat of the good things wherewith We have provided you, and render thanks to Allah if it is (indeed) He Whom ye worship.	O you who believe! eat of the good things that We have provided you with, and give thanks to Allah if Him it is that you serve.
2 173	He hath only forbidden you dead meat, and blood, and the flesh of swine, and that on which any other name hath been invoked besides that of Allah. But if one is forced by necessity, without wilful disobedience, nor transgressing due limits,- then is he guiltless. For Allah is Oft-Forgiving Most Merciful.	He hath forbidden you only carrion, and blood, and swineflesh, and that which hath been immolated to (the name of) any other than Allah. But he who is driven by necessity, neither craving nor transgressing, it is no sin for him. Lo! Allah is Forgiving, Merciful.	He has only forbidden you what dies of itself, and blood, and flesh of swine, and that over which any other (name) than (that of) Allah has been invoked; but whoever is driven to necessity, not desiring, nor exceeding the limit, no sin shall be upon him; surely Allah is Forgiving, Merciful.
2 174	Those who conceal Allah's revelations in the Book, and purchase for them a miserable profit,- they swallow into themselves naught but Fire; Allah will not address them on the Day of Resurrection. Nor purify them: Grievous will be their penalty.	Lo! those who hide aught of the Scripture which Allah hath revealed and purchase a small gain therewith, they eat into their bellies nothing else than fire. Allah will not speak to them on the Day of Resurrection, nor will He make them grow. Theirs will be a painful doom.	Surely those who conceal any part of the Book that Allah has revealed and take for it a small price, they eat nothing but fire into their bellies, and Allah will not speak to them on the day of resurrection, nor will He purify them, and they shall have a painful chastisement.

2 175	They are the ones who buy Error in place of Guidance and Torment in place of Forgiveness. Ah! what boldness (They show) for the Fire!	Those are they who purchase error at the price of guidance, and torment at the price of pardon. How constant are they in their strife to reach the Fire!	These are they who buy error for the right direction and chastisement for forgiveness; how bold they are to encounter fire.
2 176	(Their doom is) because Allah sent down the Book in truth but those who seek causes of dispute in the Book are in a schism Far (from the purpose).	That is because Allah hath revealed the Scripture with the truth. Lo! those who find (a cause of) disagreement in the Scripture are in open schism.	This is because Allah has revealed the Book with the truth; and surely those who go against the Book are in a great opposition.
2 177	It is not righteousness that ye turn your faces Towards east or West; but it is righteousness- to believe in Allah and the Last Day, and the Angels, and the Book, and the Messengers; to spend of your substance, out of love for Him, for your kin, for orphans, for the needy, for the wayfarer, for those who ask, and for the ransom of slaves; to be steadfast in prayer, and practice regular charity; to fulfil the contracts which ye have made; and to be firm and patient, in pain (or suffering) and adversity, and throughout all periods of panic. Such are the people of truth, the Allah-fearing.	It is not righteousness that ye turn your faces to the East and the West; but righteous is he who believeth in Allah and the Last Day and the angels and the Scripture and the prophets; and giveth wealth, for love of Him, to kinsfolk and to orphans and the needy and the wayfarer and to those who ask, and to set slaves free; and observeth proper worship and payeth the poor-due. And those who keep their treaty when they make one, and the patient in tribulation and adversity and time of stress. Such are they who are sincere. Such are the Allah-fearing.	It is not righteousness that you turn your faces towards the East and the West, but righteousness is this that one should believe in Allah and the last day and the angels and the Book and the prophets, and give away wealth out of love for Him to the near of kin and the orphans and the needy and the wayfarer and the beggars and for (the emancipation of) the captives, and keep up prayer and pay the poor-rate; and the performers of their promise when they make a promise, and the patient in distress and affliction and in time of conflicts-- these are they who are true (to themselves) and these are they who guard (against evil).
2 178	O ye who believe! the law of equality is prescribed to you in cases of murder: the free for the free, the slave for the slave, the woman for the woman. But if any remission is made by the brother of the slain, then grant any reasonable demand, and compensate him with handsome gratitude, this is a concession and a Mercy from your Lord. After this whoever exceeds the limits shall be in grave penalty.	O ye who believe! Retaliation is prescribed for you in the matter of the murdered; the freeman for the freeman, and the slave for the slave, and the female for the female. And for him who is forgiven somewhat by his (injured) brother, prosecution according to usage and payment unto him in kindness. This is an alleviation and a mercy from your Lord. He who transgresseth after this will have a painful doom.	O you who believe! retaliation is prescribed for you in the matter of the slain, the free for the free, and the slave for the slave, and the female for the female, but if any remission is made to any one by his (aggrieved) brother, then prosecution (for the bloodwit) should be made according to usage, and payment should be made to him in a good manner; this is an alleviation from your Lord and a mercy; so whoever exceeds the limit after this he shall have a painful chastisement.
2 179	In the Law of Equality there is (saving of) Life to you, O ye men of understanding; that ye may restrain yourselves.	And there is life for you in retaliation, O men of understanding, that ye may ward off (evil).	And there is life for you in (the law of) retaliation, O men of understanding, that you may guard yourselves.
2 180	It is prescribed, when death approaches any of you, if he leave any goods that he make a bequest to parents and next of kin, according to reasonable usage; this is due from the Allah-fearing.	It is prescribed for you, when death approacheth one of you, if he leave wealth, that he bequeath unto parents and near relatives in kindness. (This is) a duty for all those who ward off (evil).	Bequest is prescribed for you when death approaches one of you, if he leaves behind wealth for parents and near relatives, according to usage, a duty (incumbent) upon those who guard (against evil).
2 181	If anyone changes the bequest after hearing it, the guilt shall be on those who make the change. For Allah hears and knows all things.	And whoso changeth (the will) after he hath heard it - the sin thereof is only upon those who change it. Lo! Allah is Hearer, Knower.	Whoever then alters it after he has heard it, the sin of it then is only upon those who alter it; surely Allah is Hearing, Knowing.

2 182	But if anyone fears partiality or wrong-doing on the part of the testator, and makes peace between (The parties concerned), there is no wrong in him: For Allah is Oft-Forgiving, Most Merciful.	But he who feareth from a testator some unjust or sinful clause, and maketh peace between the parties, (it shall be) no sin for him. Lo! Allah is Forgiving, Merciful.	But he who fears an inclination to a wrong course or an act of disobedience on the part of the testator, and effects an agreement between the parties, there is no blame on him. Surely Allah is Forgiving, Merciful.
2 183	O ye who believe! Fasting is prescribed to you as it was prescribed to those before you, that ye may (learn) self-restraint,-	O ye who believe! Fasting is prescribed for you, even as it was prescribed for those before you, that ye may ward off (evil);	O you who believe! fasting is prescribed for you, as it was prescribed for those before you, so that you may guard (against evil).
2 184	(Fasting) for a fixed number of days; but if any of you is ill, or on a journey, the prescribed number (Should be made up) from days later. For those who can do it (With hardship), is a ransom, the feeding of one that is indigent. But he that will give more, of his own free will,- it is better for him. And it is better for you that ye fast, if ye only knew.	(Fast) a certain number of days; and (for) him who is sick among you, or on a journey, (the same) number of other days; and for those who can afford it there is a ransom: the feeding of a man in need - but whoso doeth good of his own accord, it is better for him: and that ye fast is better for you if ye did but know -	For a certain number of days; but whoever among you is sick or on a journey, then (he shall fast) a (like) number of other days; and those who are not able to do it may effect a redemption by feeding a poor man; so whoever does good spontaneously it is better for him; and that you fast is better for you if you know.
2 185	Ramadhan is the (month) in which was sent down the Qur'an, as a guide to mankind, also clear (Signs) for guidance and judgment (Between right and wrong). So every one of you who is present (at his home) during that month should spend it in fasting, but if any one is ill, or on a journey, the prescribed period (Should be made up) by days later. Allah intends every facility for you; He does not want to put to difficulties. (He wants you) to complete the prescribed period, and to glorify Him in that He has guided you; and perchance ye shall be grateful.	The month of Ramadan in which was revealed the Qur'an, a guidance for mankind, and clear proofs of the guidance, and the Criterion (of right and wrong). And whosoever of you is present, let him fast the month, and whosoever of you is sick or on a journey, (let him fast the same) number of other days. Allah desireth for you ease; He desireth not hardship for you; and (He desireth) that ye should complete the period, and that ye should magnify Allah for having guided you, and that peradventure ye may be thankful.	The month of Ramazan is that in which the Quran was revealed, a guidance to men and clear proofs of the guidance and the distinction; therefore whoever of you is present in the month, he shall fast therein, and whoever is sick or upon a journey, then (he shall fast) a (like) number of other days; Allah desires ease for you, and He does not desire for you difficulty, and (He desires) that you should complete the number and that you should exalt the greatness of Allah for His having guided you and that you may give thanks.
2 186	When My servants ask thee concerning Me, I am indeed close (to them): I listen to the prayer of every supplicant when he calleth on Me: Let them also, with a will, Listen to My call, and believe in Me: That they may walk in the right way.	And when My servants question thee concerning Me, then surely I am nigh. I answer the prayer of the suppliant when he crieth unto Me. So let them hear My call and let them trust in Me, in order that they may be led aright.	And when My servants ask you concerning Me, then surely I am very near; I answer the prayer of the suppliant when he calls on Me, so they should answer My call and believe in Me that they may walk in the right way.

2 187	Permitted to you, on the night of the fasts, is the approach to your wives. They are your garments and ye are their garments. Allah knoweth what ye used to do secretly among yourselves; but He turned to you and forgave you; so now associate with them, and seek what Allah Hath ordained for you, and eat and drink, until the white thread of dawn appear to you distinct from its black thread; then complete your fast Till the night appears; but do not associate with your wives while ye are in retreat in the mosques. Those are Limits (set by) Allah: Approach not nigh thereto. Thus doth Allah make clear His Signs to men: that they may learn self-restraint.	It is made lawful for you to go in unto your wives on the night of the fast. They are raiment for you and ye are raiment for them. Allah is Aware that ye were deceiving yourselves in this respect and He hath turned in mercy toward you and relieved you. So hold intercourse with them and seek that which Allah hath ordained for you, and eat and drink until the white thread becometh distinct to you from the black thread of the dawn. Then strictly observe the fast till nightfall and touch them not, but be at your devotions in the mosques. These are the limits imposed by Allah, so approach them not. Thus Allah expoundeth His revelation to mankind that they may ward off (evil).	It is made lawful to you to go into your wives on the night of the fast; they are an apparel for you and you are an apparel for them; Allah knew that you acted unfaithfully to yourselves, so He has turned to you (mercifully) and removed from you (this burden); so now be in contact with them and seek what Allah has ordained for you, and eat and drink until the whiteness of the day becomes distinct from the blackness of the night at dawn, then complete the fast till night, and have not contact with them while you keep to the mosques; these are the limits of Allah, so do not go near them. Thus does Allah make clear His communications for men that they may guard (against evil).
2 188	And do not eat up your property among yourselves for vanities, nor use it as bait for the judges, with intent that ye may eat up wrongfully and knowingly a little of (other) people's property.	And eat not up your property among yourselves in vanity, nor seek by it to gain the hearing of the judges that ye may knowingly devour a portion of the property of others wrongfully.	And do not swallow up your property among yourselves by false means, neither seek to gain access thereby to the judges, so that you may swallow up a part of the property of men wrongfully while you know.
2 189	They ask thee concerning the New Moons. Say: They are but signs to mark fixed periods of time in (the affairs of) men, and for Pilgrimage. It is no virtue if ye enter your houses from the back: It is virtue if ye fear Allah. Enter houses through the proper doors: And fear Allah: That ye may prosper.	They ask thee, (O Muhammad), of new moons, say: They are fixed seasons for mankind and for the pilgrimage. It is not righteousness that ye go to houses by the backs thereof (as do the idolaters at certain seasons), but the righteous man is he who wardeth off (evil). So go to houses by the gates thereof, and observe your duty to Allah, that ye may be successful.	They ask you concerning the new moon. Say: They are times appointed for (the benefit of) men, and (for) the pilgrimage; and it is not righteousness that you should enter the houses at their backs, but righteousness is this that one should guard (against evil); and go into the houses by their doors and be careful (of your duty) to Allah, that you may be successful.
2 190	Fight in the cause of Allah those who fight you, but do not transgress limits; for Allah loveth not transgressors.	Fight in the way of Allah against those who fight against you, but begin not hostilities. Lo! Allah loveth not aggressors.	And fight in the way of Allah with those who fight with you, and do not exceed the limits, surely Allah does not love those who exceed the limits.
2 191	And slay them wherever ye catch them, and turn them out from where they have Turned you out; for tumult and oppression are worse than slaughter; but fight them not at the Sacred Mosque, unless they (first) fight you there; but if they fight you, slay them. Such is the reward of those who suppress faith.	And slay them wherever ye find them, and drive them out of the places whence they drove you out, for persecution is worse than slaughter. And fight not with them at the Inviolable Place of Worship until they first attack you there, but if they attack you (there) then slay them. Such is the reward of disbelievers.	And kill them wherever you find them, and drive them out from whence they drove you out, and persecution is severer than slaughter, and do not fight with them at the Sacred Mosque until they fight with you in it, but if they do fight you, then slay them; such is the recompense of the unbelievers.
2 192	But if they cease, Allah is Oft-Forgiving, Most Merciful.	But if they desist, then lo! Allah is Forgiving, Merciful.	But if they desist, then surely Allah is Forgiving, Merciful.

2 193	And fight them on until there is no more Tumult or oppression, and there prevail justice and faith in Allah; but if they cease, Let there be no hostility except to those who practise oppression.	And fight them until persecution is no more, and religion is for Allah. But if they desist, then let there be no hostility except against wrong-doers.	And fight with them until there is no persecution, and religion should be only for Allah, but if they desist, then there should be no hostility except against the oppressors.	
2 194	The prohibited month for the prohibited month,- and so for all things prohibited,- there is the law of equality. If then any one transgresses the prohibition against you, Transgress ye likewise against him. But fear Allah, and know that Allah is with those who restrain themselves.	The forbidden month for the forbidden month, and forbidden things in retaliation. And one who attacketh you, attack him in like manner as he attacked you. Observe your duty to Allah, and know that Allah is with those who ward off (evil).	The Sacred month for the sacred month and all sacred things are (under the law of) retaliation; whoever then acts aggressively against you, inflict injury on him according to the injury he has inflicted on you and be careful (of your duty) to Allah and know that Allah is with those who guard (against evil).	
2 195	And spend of your substance in the cause of Allah, and make not your own hands contribute to (your) destruction; but do good; for Allah loveth those who do good.	Spend your wealth for the cause of Allah, and be not cast by your own hands to ruin; and do good. Lo! Allah loveth the beneficent.	And spend in the way of Allah and cast not yourselves to perdition with your own hands, and do good (to others); surely Allah loves the doers of good.	
2 196	And complete the Hajj or 'umra in the service of Allah. But if ye are prevented (From completing it), send an offering for sacrifice, such as ye may find, and do not shave your heads until the offering reaches the place of sacrifice. And if any of you is ill, or has an ailment in his scalp, (Necessitating shaving), (He should) in compensation either fast, or feed the poor, or offer sacrifice; and when ye are in peaceful conditions (again), if any one wishes to continue the 'umra on to the hajj, He must make an offering, such as he can afford, but if he cannot afford it, He should fast three days during the hajj and seven days on his return, Making ten days in all. This is for those whose household is not in (the precincts of) the Sacred Mosque. And fear Allah, and know that Allah Is strict in punishment.	Perform the pilgrimage and the visit (to Makka) for Allah. And if ye are prevented, then send such gifts as can be obtained with ease, and shave not your heads until the gifts have reached their destination. And whoever among you is sick or hath an ailment of the head must pay a ransom of fasting or almsgiving or offering. And if ye are in safety, then whosoever contenteth himself with the visit for the pilgrimage (shall give) such gifts as can be had with ease. And whosoever cannot find (such gifts), then a fast of three days while on the pilgrimage, and of seven when ye have returned; that is, ten in all. That is for him whoso folk are not present at the Inviolable Place of Worship. Observe your duty to Allah, and know that Allah is severe in punishment.	And accomplish the pilgrimage and the visit for Allah, but if, you are prevented, (send) whatever offering is easy to obtain, and do not shave your heads until the offering reaches its destination; but whoever among you is sick or has an ailment of the head, he (should effect) a compensation by fasting or alms or sacrificing, then when you are secure, whoever profits by combining the visit with the pilgrimage (should take) what offering is easy to obtain; but he who cannot find (any offering) should fast for three days during the pilgrimage and for seven days when you return; these (make) ten (days) complete; this is for him whose family is not present in the Sacred Mosque, and be careful (of your duty) to Allah, and know that Allah is severe in requiting (evil).	
2 197	For Hajj are the months well known. If any one undertakes that duty therein, Let there be no obscenity, nor wickedness, nor wrangling in the Hajj. And whatever good ye do, (be sure) Allah knoweth it. And take a provision (With you) for the journey, but the best of provisions is right conduct. So fear Me, O ye that are wise.	The pilgrimage is (in) the well-known months, and whoever is minded to perform the pilgrimage therein (let him remember that) there is (to be) no lewdness nor abuse nor angry conversation on the pilgrimage. And whatsoever good ye do Allah knoweth it. So make provision for yourselves (hereafter); for the best provision is to ward off evil. Therefore keep your duty unto Me, O men of understanding.	The pilgrimage is (performed in) the well-known months; so whoever determines the performance of the pilgrimage therein, there shall be no intercourse nor fornication nor quarrelling amongst one another; and whatever good you do, Allah knows it; and make provision, for surely the provision is the guarding of oneself, and be careful (of your duty) to Me, O men of understanding.	

2 198	It is no crime in you if ye seek of the bounty of your Lord (during pilgrimage). Then when ye pour down from (Mount) Arafat, celebrate the praises of Allah at the Sacred Monument, and celebrate His praises as He has directed you, even though, before this, ye went astray.	It is no sin for you that ye seek the bounty of your Lord (by trading). But, when ye press on in the multitude from 'Arafat, remember Allah by the sacred monument. Remember Him as He hath guided you, although before ye were of those astray.		There is no blame on you in seeking bounty from your Lord, so when you hasten on from "Arafat", then remember Allah near the Holy Monument, and remember Him as He has guided you, though before that you were certainly of the erring ones.
2 199	Then pass on at a quick pace from the place whence it is usual for the multitude so to do, and ask for Allah's forgiveness. For Allah is Oft-Forgiving, Most Merciful.	Then hasten onward from the place whence the multitude hasteneth onward, and ask forgiveness of Allah. Lo! Allah is Forgiving, Merciful.		Then hasten on from the Place from which the people hasten on and ask the forgiveness of Allah; surely Allah is Forgiving, Merciful.
2 200	So when ye have accomplished your holy rites, celebrate the praises of Allah, as ye used to celebrate the praises of your fathers,- yea, with far more Heart and soul. There are men who say: "Our Lord! Give us (Thy bounties) in this world!" but they will have no portion in the Hereafter.	And when ye have completed your devotions, then remember Allah as ye remember your fathers or with a more lively remembrance. But of mankind is he who saith: "Our Lord! Give unto us in the world," and he hath no portion in the Hereafter.		So when you have performed your devotions, then laud Allah as you lauded your fathers, rather a greater lauding. But there are some people who say, Our Lord! give us in the world, and they shall have no resting place.
2 201	And there are men who say: "Our Lord! Give us good in this world and good in the Hereafter, and defend us from the torment of the Fire!"	And of them (also) is he who saith: "Our Lord! Give unto us in the world that which is good and in the Hereafter that which is good, and guard us from the doom of Fire."		And there are some among them who say: Our Lord! grant us good in this world and good in the hereafter, and save us from the chastisement of the fire.
2 202	To these will be allotted what they have earned; and Allah is quick in account.	For them there is in store a goodly portion out of that which they have earned. Allah is swift at reckoning.		They shall have (their) portion of what they have earned, and Allah is swift in reckoning.
2 203	Celebrate the praises of Allah during the Appointed Days. But if any one hastens to leave in two days, there is no blame on him, and if any one stays on, there is no blame on him, if his aim is to do right. Then fear Allah, and know that ye will surely be gathered unto Him.	Remember Allah through the appointed days. Then whoso hasteneth (his departure) by two days, it is no sin for him, and whoso delayeth, it is no sin for him; that is for him who wardeth off (evil). Be careful of your duty to Allah, and know that unto Him ye will be gathered.		And laud Allah during the numbered days; then whoever hastens off in two days, there is no blame on him, and whoever remains behind, there is no blame on him, (this is) for him who guards (against evil), and be careful (of your duty) to Allah, and know that you shall be gathered together to Him.
2 204	There is the type of man whose speech about this world's life May dazzle thee, and he calls Allah to witness about what is in his heart; yet is he the most contentious of enemies.	And of mankind there is he whoso conversation on the life of this world pleaseth thee (Muhammad), and he calleth Allah to witness as to that which is in his heart; yet he is the most rigid of opponents.		And among men is he whose speech about the life of this world causes you to wonder, and he calls on Allah to witness as to what is in his heart, yet he is the most violent of adversaries.
2 205	When he turns his back, His aim everywhere is to spread mischief through the earth and destroy crops and cattle. But Allah loveth not mischief.	And when he turneth away (from thee) his effort in the land is to make mischief therein and to destroy the crops and the cattle; and Allah loveth not mischief.		And when he turns back, he runs along in the land that he may cause mischief in it and destroy the tilth and the stock, and Allah does not love mischief-making.
2 206	When it is said to him, "Fear Allah", He is led by arrogance to (more) crime. Enough for him is Hell;-An evil bed indeed (To lie on)!	And when it is said unto him: Be careful of thy duty to Allah, pride taketh him to sin. Hell will settle his account, an evil resting-place.		And when it is said to him, guard against (the punishment of) Allah; pride carries him off to sin, therefore hell is sufficient for him; and certainly it is an evil resting place.

2	207	And there is the type of man who gives his life to earn the pleasure of Allah: And Allah is full of kindness to (His) devotees.	And of mankind is he who would sell himself, seeking the pleasure of Allah; and Allah hath compassion on (His) bondmen.	And among men is he who sells himself to seek the pleasure of Allah; and Allah is Affectionate to the servants.
2	208	O ye who believe! Enter into Islam whole-heartedly; and follow not the footsteps of the evil one; for he is to you an avowed enemy.	O ye who believe! Come, all of you, into submission (unto Him); and follow not the footsteps of the devil. Lo! he is an open enemy for you.	O you who believe! enter into submission one and all and do not follow the footsteps of Shaitan; surely he is your open enemy.
2	209	If ye backslide after the clear (Signs) have come to you, then know that Allah is Exalted in Power, Wise.	And if ye slide back after the clear proofs have come unto you, then know that Allah is Mighty, Wise.	But if you slip after clear arguments have come to you, then know that Allah is Mighty, Wise.
2	210	Will they wait until Allah comes to them in canopies of clouds, with angels (in His train) and the question is (thus) settled? but to Allah do all questions go back (for decision).	Wait they for naught else than that Allah should come unto them in the shadows of the clouds with the angels? Then the case would be already judged. All cases go back to Allah (for judgment).	They do not wait aught but that Allah should come to them in the shadows of the clouds along with the angels, and the matter has (already) been decided; and (all) matters are returned to Allah.
2	211	Ask the Children of Israel how many clear (Signs) We have sent them. But if any one, after Allah's favour has come to him, substitutes (something else), Allah is strict in punishment.	Ask of the Children of Israel how many a clear revelation We gave them! He who altereth the grace of Allah after it hath come unto him (for him), lo! Allah is severe in punishment.	Ask the Israelites how many a clear sign have We given them; and whoever changes the favor of Allah after it has come to him, then surely Allah is severe in requiting (evil).
2	212	The life of this world is alluring to those who reject faith, and they scoff at those who believe. But the righteous will be above them on the Day of Resurrection; for Allah bestows His abundance without measure on whom He will.	Beautified is the life of the world for those who disbelieve; they make a jest of the believers. But those who keep their duty to Allah will be above them on the Day of Resurrection. Allah giveth without stint to whom He will.	The life of this world is made to seem fair to those who disbelieve, and they mock those who believe, and those who guard (against evil) shall be above them on the day of resurrection; and Allah gives means of subsistence to whom he pleases without measure.
2	213	Mankind was one single nation, and Allah sent Messengers with glad tidings and warnings; and with them He sent the Book in truth, to judge between people in matters wherein they differed; but the People of the Book, after the clear Signs came to them, did not differ among themselves, except through selfish contumacy. Allah by His Grace Guided the believers to the Truth, concerning that wherein they differed. For Allah guided whom He will to a path that is straight.	Mankind were one community, and Allah sent (unto them) prophets as bearers of good tidings and as warners, and revealed therewith the Scripture with the truth that it might judge between mankind concerning that wherein they differed. And only those unto whom (the Scripture) was given differed concerning it, after clear proofs had come unto them, through hatred one of another. And Allah by His Will guided those who believe unto the truth of that concerning which they differed. Allah guideth whom He will unto a straight path.	(All) people are a single nation; so Allah raised prophets as bearers of good news and as warners, and He revealed with them the Book with truth, that it might judge between people in that in which they differed; and none but the very people who were given it differed about it after clear arguments had come to them, revolting among themselves; so Allah has guided by His will those who believe to the truth about which they differed and Allah guides whom He pleases to the right path.

2 214	Or do ye think that ye shall enter the Garden (of bliss) without such (trials) as came to those who passed away before you? they encountered suffering and adversity, and were so shaken in spirit that even the Messenger and those of faith who were with him cried: "When (will come) the help of Allah?" Ah! Verily, the help of Allah is (always) near!	Or think ye that ye will enter paradise while yet there hath not come unto you the like of (that which came to) those who passed away before you? Affliction and adversity befell them, they were shaken as with earthquake, till the messenger (of Allah) and those who believed along with him said: When cometh Allah's help? Now surely Allah's help is nigh.	Or do you think that you would enter the garden while yet the state of those who have passed away before you has not come upon you; distress and affliction befell them and they were shaken violently, so that the Messenger and those who believed with him said: When will the help of Allah come? Now surely the help of Allah is nigh!
2 215	They ask thee what they should spend (In charity). Say: Whatever ye spend that is good, is for parents and kindred and orphans and those in want and for wayfarers. And whatever ye do that is good,- Allah knoweth it well.	They ask thee, (O Muhammad), what they shall spend. Say: that which ye spend for good (must go) to parents and near kindred and orphans and the needy and the wayfarer. And whatsoever good ye do, lo! Allah is Aware of it.	They ask you as to what they should spend. Say: Whatever wealth you spend, it is for the parents and the near of kin and the orphans and the needy and the wayfarer, and whatever good you do, Allah surely knows it.
2 216	Fighting is prescribed for you, and ye dislike it. But it is possible that ye dislike a thing which is good for you, and that ye love a thing which is bad for you. But Allah knoweth, and ye know not.	Warfare is ordained for you, though it is hateful unto you; but it may happen that ye hate a thing which is good for you, and it may happen that ye love a thing which is bad for you. Allah knoweth, ye know not.	Fighting is enjoined on you, and it is an object of dislike to you; and it may be that you dislike a thing while it is good for you, and it may be that you love a thing while it is evil for you, and Allah knows, while you do not know.
2 217	They ask thee concerning fighting in the Prohibited Month. Say: Fighting therein is a grave (offence); but graver is it in the sight of Allah to prevent access to the path of Allah, to deny Him, to prevent access to the Sacred Mosque, and drive out its members." Tumult and oppression are worse than slaughter. Nor will they cease fighting you until they turn you back from your faith if they can. And if any of you turn back from their faith and die in unbelief, their works will bear no fruit in this life and in the Hereafter; they will be companions of the Fire and will abide therein.	They question thee (O Muhammad) with regard to warfare in the sacred month. Say: Warfare therein is a great (transgression), but to turn (men) from the way of Allah, and to disbelieve in Him and in the Inviolable Place of Worship, and to expel His people thence, is a greater sin with Allah; for persecution is worse than killing. And they will not cease from fighting against you till they have made you renegades from your religion, if they can. And whoso becometh a renegade and dieth in his disbelief: such are they whose works have fallen both in the world and the Hereafter. Such are rightful owners of the Fire: they will abide therein.	They ask you concerning the sacred month about fighting in it. Say: Fighting in it is a grave matter, and hindering (men) from Allah's way and denying Him, and (hindering men from) the Sacred Mosque and turning its people out of it, are still graver with Allah, and persecution is graver than slaughter; and they will not cease fighting with you until they turn you back from your religion, if they can; and whoever of you turns back from his religion, then he dies while an unbeliever-- these it is whose works shall go for nothing in this world and the hereafter, and they are the inmates of the fire; therein they shall abide.
2 218	Those who believed and those who suffered exile and fought (and strove and struggled) in the path of Allah,- they have the hope of the Mercy of Allah: And Allah is Oft-Forgiving, Most Merciful.	Lo! those who believe, and those who emigrate (to escape the persecution) and strive in the way of Allah, these have hope of Allah's mercy. Allah is Forgiving, Merciful.	Surely those who believed and those who fled (their home) and strove hard in the way of Allah these hope for the mercy of Allah and Allah is Forgiving, Merciful.

2 219	They ask thee concerning wine and gambling. Say: "In them is great sin, and some profit, for men; but the sin is greater than the profit." They ask thee how much they are to spend; Say: "What is beyond your needs." Thus doth Allah Make clear to you His Signs: In order that ye may consider-	They question thee about strong drink and games of chance. Say: In both is great sin, and (some) utility for men; but the sin of them is greater than their usefulness. And they ask thee what they ought to spend. Say: that which is superfluous. Thus Allah maketh plain to you (His) revelations, that haply ye may reflect.	They ask you about intoxicants and games of chance. Say: In both of them there is a great sin and means of profit for men, and their sin is greater than their profit. And they ask you as to what they should spend. Say: What you can spare. Thus does Allah make clear to you the communications, that you may ponder,
2 220	(Their bearings) on this life and the Hereafter. They ask thee concerning orphans. Say: "The best thing to do is what is for their good; if ye mix their affairs with yours, they are your brethren; but Allah knows the man who means mischief from the man who means good. And if Allah had wished, He could have put you into difficulties: He is indeed Exalted in Power, Wise."	Upon the world and the Hereafter. And they question thee concerning orphans. Say: To improve their lot is best. And if ye mingle your affairs with theirs, then (they are) your brothers. Allah knoweth him who spoileth from him who improveth. Had Allah willed He could have overburdened you. Allah is Mighty, Wise.	On this world and the hereafter. And they ask you concerning the orphans Say: To set right for them (their affairs) is good, and if you become co-partners with them, they are your brethren; and Allah knows the mischief-maker and the pace-maker, and if Allah had pleased, He would certainly have caused you to fall into a difficulty; surely Allah is Mighty, Wise.
2 221	Do not marry unbelieving women (idolaters), until they believe: A slave woman who believes is better than an unbelieving woman, even though she allures you. Nor marry (your girls) to unbelievers until they believe: A man slave who believes is better than an unbeliever, even though he allures you. Unbelievers do (but) beckon you to the Fire. But Allah beckons by His Grace to the Garden (of bliss) and forgiveness, and makes His Signs clear to mankind: That they may celebrate His praise.	Wed not idolatresses till they believe; for lo! a believing bondwoman is better than an idolatress though she please you; and give not your daughters in marriage to idolaters till they believe, for lo! a believing slave is better than an idolater though he please you. These invite unto the Fire, and Allah inviteth unto the Garden, and unto forgiveness by His grace, and expoundeth His revelations to mankind that haply they may remember.	And do not marry the idolatresses until they believe, and certainly a believing maid is better than an idolatress woman, even though she should please you; and do not give (believing women) in marriage to idolaters until they believe, and certainly a believing servant is better than an idolater, even though he should please you; these invite to the fire, and Allah invites to the garden and to forgiveness by His will, and makes clear His communications to men, that they may be mindful.
2 222	They ask thee concerning women's courses. Say: They are a hurt and a pollution: So keep away from women in their courses, and do not approach them until they are clean. But when they have purified themselves, ye may approach them in any manner, time, or place ordained for you by Allah. For Allah loves those who turn to Him constantly and He loves those who keep themselves pure and clean.	They question thee (O Muhammad) concerning menstruation. Say: It is an illness, so let women alone at such times and go not in unto them till they are cleansed. And when they have purified themselves, then go in unto them as Allah hath enjoined upon you. Truly Allah loveth those who turn unto Him, and loveth those who have a care for cleanness.	And they ask you about menstruation. Say: It is a discomfort; therefore keep aloof from the women during the menstrual discharge and do not go near them until they have become clean; then when they have cleansed themselves, go in to them as Allah has commanded you; surely Allah loves those who turn much (to Him), and He loves those who purify themselves.
2 223	Your wives are as a tilth unto you; so approach your tilth when or how ye will; but do some good act for your souls beforehand; and fear Allah. And know that ye are to meet Him (in the Hereafter), and give (these) good tidings to those who believe.	Your women are a tilth for you (to cultivate) so go to your tilth as ye will, and send (good deeds) before you for your souls, and fear Allah, and know that ye will (one day) meet Him. Give glad tidings to believers, (O Muhammad).	Your wives are a tilth for you, so go into your tilth when you like, and do good beforehand for yourselves, and be careful (of your duty) to Allah, and know that you will meet Him, and give good news to the believers.

2	224	And make not Allah's (name) an excuse in your oaths against doing good, or acting rightly, or making peace between persons; for Allah is One Who heareth and knoweth all things.	And make not Allah, by your oaths, a hindrance to your being righteous and observing your duty unto Him and making peace among mankind. Allah is Hearer, Knower.	And make not Allah because of your swearing (by Him) an obstacle to your doing good and guarding (against evil) and making peace between men, and Allah is Hearing, Knowing.
2	225	Allah will not call you to account for thoughtlessness in your oaths, but for the intention in your hearts; and He is Oft-Forgiving, Most Forbearing.	Allah will not take you to task for that which is unintentional in your oaths. But He will take you to task for that which your hearts have garnered. Allah is Forgiving, Clement.	Allah does not call you to account for what is vain in your oaths, but He will call you to account for what your hearts have earned, and Allah is Forgiving, Forbearing.
2	226	For those who take an oath for abstention from their wives, a waiting for four months is ordained; if then they return, Allah is Oft-Forgiving, Most Merciful.	Those who forswear their wives must wait four months; then, if they change their mind, lo! Allah is Forgiving, Merciful.	Those who swear that they will not go in to their wives should wait four months; so if they go back, then Allah is surely Forgiving, Merciful.
2	227	But if their intention is firm for divorce, Allah heareth and knoweth all things.	And if they decide upon divorce (let them remember that) Allah is Hearer, Knower.	And if they have resolved on a divorce, then Allah is surely Hearing, Knowing.
2	228	Divorced women shall wait concerning themselves for three monthly periods. Nor is it lawful for them to hide what Allah Hath created in their wombs, if they have faith in Allah and the Last Day. And their husbands have the better right to take them back in that period, if they wish for reconciliation. And women shall have rights similar to the rights against them, according to what is equitable; but men have a degree (of advantage) over them. And Allah is Exalted in Power, Wise.	Women who are divorced shall wait, keeping themselves apart, three (monthly) courses. And it is not lawful for them that they should conceal that which Allah hath created in their wombs if they are believers in Allah and the Last Day. And their husbands would do better to take them back in that case if they desire a reconciliation. And they (women) have rights similar to those (of men) over them in kindness, and men are a degree above them. Allah is Mighty, Wise.	And the divorced women should keep themselves in waiting for three courses; and it is not lawful for them that they should conceal what Allah has created in their wombs, if they believe in Allah and the last day; and their husbands have a better right to take them back in the meanwhile if they wish for reconciliation; and they have rights similar to those against them in a just manner, and the men are a degree above them, and Allah is Mighty, Wise.
2	229	A divorce is only permissible twice: after that, the parties should either hold Together on equitable terms, or separate with kindness. It is not lawful for you, (Men), to take back any of your gifts (from your wives), except when both parties fear that they would be unable to keep the limits ordained by Allah. If ye (judges) do indeed fear that they would be unable to keep the limits ordained by Allah, there is no blame on either of them if she give something for her freedom. These are the limits ordained by Allah; so do not transgress them if any do transgress the limits ordained by Allah, such persons wrong (Themselves as well as others).	Divorce must be pronounced twice and then (a woman) must be retained in honour or released in kindness. And it is not lawful for you that ye take from women aught of that which ye have given them; except (in the case) when both fear that they may not be able to keep within the limits (imposed by) Allah. And if ye fear that they may not be able to keep the limits of Allah, in that case it is no sin for either of them if the woman ransom herself. These are the limits (imposed by) Allah. Transgress them not. For whoso transgresseth Allah's limits: such are wrong-doers.	Divorce may be (pronounced) twice, then keep (them) in good fellowship or let (them) go with kindness; and it is not lawful for you to take any part of what you have given them, unless both fear that they cannot keep within the limits of Allah; then if you fear that they cannot keep within the limits of Allah, there is no blame on them for what she gives up to become free thereby. These are the limits of Allah, so do not exceed them and whoever exceeds the limits of Allah these it is that are the unjust.

2 230	So if a husband divorces his wife (irrevocably), He cannot, after that, re-marry her until after she has married another husband and He has divorced her. In that case there is no blame on either of them if they re-unite, provided they feel that they can keep the limits ordained by Allah. Such are the limits ordained by Allah, which He makes plain to those who understand.	And if he hath divorced her (the third time), then she is not lawful unto him thereafter until she hath wedded another husband. Then if he (the other husband) divorce her it is no sin for both of them that they come together again if they consider that they are able to observe the limits of Allah. These are the limits of Allah. He manifesteth them for people who have knowledge.	So if he divorces her she shall not be lawful to him afterwards until she marries another husband; then if he divorces her there is no blame on them both if they return to each other (by marriage), if they think that they can keep within the limits of Allah, and these are the limits of Allah which He makes clear for a people who know.
2 231	When ye divorce women, and they fulfil the term of their ('Iddat), either take them back on equitable terms or set them free on equitable terms; but do not take them back to injure them, (or) to take undue advantage; if any one does that; He wrongs his own soul. Do not treat Allah's Signs as a jest, but solemnly rehearse Allah's favours on you, and the fact that He sent down to you the Book and Wisdom, for your instruction. And fear Allah, and know that Allah is well acquainted with all things.	When ye have divorced women, and they have reached their term, then retain them in kindness or release them in kindness. Retain them not to their hurt so that ye transgress (the limits). He who doeth that hath wronged his soul. Make not the revelations of Allah a laughing-stock (by your behaviour), but remember Allah's grace upon you and that which He hath revealed unto you of the Scripture and of wisdom, whereby He doth exhort you. Observe your duty to Allah and know that Allah is Aware of all things.	And when you divorce women and they reach their prescribed time, then either retain them in good fellowship or set them free with liberality, and do not retain them for injury, so that you exceed the limits, and whoever does this, he indeed is unjust to his own soul; and do not take Allah's communications for a mockery, and remember the favor of Allah upon you, and that which He has revealed to you of the Book and the Wisdom, admonishing you thereby; and be careful (of your duty to) Allah, and know that Allah is the Knower of all things.
2 232	When ye divorce women, and they fulfil the term of their ('Iddat), do not prevent them from marrying their (former) husbands, if they mutually agree on equitable terms. This instruction is for all amongst you, who believe in Allah and the Last Day. That is (the course Making for) most virtue and purity amongst you and Allah knows, and ye know not.	And when ye have divorced women and they reach their term, place not difficulties in the way of their marrying their husbands if it is agreed between them in kindness. This is an admonition for him among you who believeth in Allah and the Last Day. That is more virtuous for you, and cleaner. Allah knoweth; ye know not.	And when you have divorced women and they have ended-- their term (of waiting), then do not prevent them from marrying their husbands when they agree among themselves in a lawful manner; with this is admonished he among you who believes in Allah and the last day, this is more profitable and purer for you; and Allah knows while you do not know.

2 233	The mothers shall give suck to their offspring for two whole years, if the father desires to complete the term. But he shall bear the cost of their food and clothing on equitable terms. No soul shall have a burden laid on it greater than it can bear. No mother shall be Treated unfairly on account of her child. Nor father on account of his child, an heir shall be chargeable in the same way. If they both decide on weaning, by mutual consent, and after due consultation, there is no blame on them. If ye decide on a foster-mother for your offspring, there is no blame on you, provided ye pay (the mother) what ye offered, on equitable terms. But fear Allah and know that Allah sees well what ye do.	Mothers shall suckle their children for two whole years; (that is) for those who wish to complete the suckling. The duty of feeding and clothing nursing mothers in a seemly manner is upon the father of the child. No-one should be charged beyond his capacity. A mother should not be made to suffer because of her child, nor should he to whom the child is born (be made to suffer) because of his child. And on the (father's) heir is incumbent the like of that (which was incumbent on the father). If they desire to wean the child by mutual consent and (after) consultation, it is no sin for them; and if ye wish to give your children out to nurse, it is no sin for you, provide that ye pay what is due from you in kindness. Observe your duty to Allah, and know that Allah is Seer of what ye do.	And the mothers should suckle their children for two whole years for him who desires to make complete the time of suckling; and their maintenance and their clothing must be-- borne by the father according to usage; no soul shall have imposed upon it a duty but to the extent of its capacity; neither shall a mother be made to suffer harm on account of her child, nor a father on account of his child, and a similar duty (devolves) on the (father's) heir, but if both desire weaning by mutual consent and counsel, there is no blame on them, and if you wish to engage a wet-nurse for your children, there is no blame on you so long as you pay what you promised for according to usage; and be careful of (your duty to) Allah and know that Allah sees what you do.
2 234	If any of you die and leave widows behind, they shall wait concerning themselves four months and ten days: When they have fulfilled their term, there is no blame on you if they dispose of themselves in a just and reasonable manner. And Allah is well acquainted with what ye do.	Such of you as die and leave behind them wives, they (the wives) shall wait, keeping themselves apart, four months and ten days. And when they reach the term (prescribed for them) then there is no sin for you in aught that they may do with themselves in decency. Allah is informed of what ye do.	And (as for) those of you who die and leave wives behind, they should keep themselves in waiting for four months and ten days; then when they have fully attained their term, there is no blame on you for what they do for themselves in a lawful manner; and Allah is aware of what you do.
2 235	There is no blame on you if ye make an offer of betrothal or hold it in your hearts. Allah knows that ye cherish them in your hearts: But do not make a secret contract with them except in terms honourable, nor resolve on the tie of marriage till the term prescribed is fulfilled. And know that Allah Knoweth what is in your hearts, and take heed of Him; and know that Allah is Oft-Forgiving, Most Forbearing.	There is no sin for you in that which ye proclaim or hide in your minds concerning your troth with women. Allah knoweth that ye will remember them. But plight not your troth with women except by uttering a recognised form of words. And do not consummate the marriage until (the term) prescribed is run. Know that Allah knoweth what is in your minds, so beware of Him; and know that Allah is Forgiving, Clement.	And there is no blame on you respecting that which you speak indirectly in the asking of (such) women in marriage or keep (the proposal) concealed within your minds; Allah knows that you will mention them, but do not give them a promise in secret unless you speak in a lawful manner, and do not confirm the marriage tie until the writing is fulfilled, and know that Allah knows what is in your minds, therefore beware of Him, and know that Allah is Forgiving, Forbearing.
2 236	There is no blame on you if ye divorce women before consummation or the fixation of their dower; but bestow on them (A suitable gift), the wealthy according to his means, and the poor according to his means;- A gift of a reasonable amount is due from those who wish to do the right thing.	It is no sin for you if ye divorce women while yet ye have not touched them, nor appointed unto them a portion. Provide for them, the rich according to his means, and the straitened according to his means, a fair provision. (This is) a bounden duty for those who do good.	There is no blame on you if you divorce women when you have not touched them or appointed for them a portion, and make provision for them, the wealthy according to his means and the straitened in circumstances according to his means, a provision according to usage; (this is) a duty on the doers of good (to others).

2 237	And if ye divorce them before consummation, but after the fixation of a dower for them, then the half of the dower (Is due to them), unless they remit it or (the man's half) is remitted by him in whose hands is the marriage tie; and the remission (of the man's half) is the nearest to righteousness. And do not forget Liberality between yourselves. For Allah sees well all that ye do.	If ye divorce them before ye have touched them and ye have appointed unto them a portion, then (pay the) half of that which ye appointed, unless they (the women) agree to forgo it, or he agreeth to forgo it in whose hand is the marriage tie. To forgo is nearer to piety. And forget not kindness among yourselves. Allah is Seer of what ye do.	And if you divorce them before you have touched them and you have appointed for them a portion, then (pay to them) half of what you have appointed, unless they relinquish or he should relinquish in whose hand is the marriage tie; and it is nearer to righteousness that you should relinquish; and do not neglect the giving of free gifts between you; surely Allah sees what you do.
2 238	Guard strictly your (habit of) prayers, especially the Middle Prayer; and stand before Allah in a devout (frame of mind).	Be guardians of your prayers, and of the midmost prayer, and stand up with devotion to Allah.	Attend constantly to prayers and to the middle prayer and stand up truly obedient to Allah.
2 239	If ye fear (an enemy), pray on foot, or riding, (as may be most convenient), but when ye are in security, celebrate Allah's praises in the manner He has taught you, which ye knew not (before).	And if ye go in fear, then (pray) standing or on horseback. And when ye are again in safety, remember Allah, as He hath taught you that which (heretofore) ye knew not.	But if you are in danger, then (say your prayers) on foot or on horseback; and when you are secure, then remember Allah, as. He has taught you what you did not know.
2 240	Those of you who die and leave widows should bequeath for their widows a year's maintenance and residence; but if they leave (The residence), there is no blame on you for what they do with themselves, provided it is reasonable. And Allah is Exalted in Power, Wise.	(In the case of) those of you who are about to die and leave behind them wives, they should bequeath unto their wives a provision for the year without turning them out, but if they go out (of their own accord) there is no sin for you in that which they do of themselves within their rights. Allah is Mighty, Wise.	And those of you who die and leave wives behind, (make) a bequest in favor of their wives of maintenance for a year without turning (them) out, then if they themselves go away, there is no blame on you for what they do of lawful deeds by themselves, and Allah is Mighty, Wise.
2 241	For divorced women Maintenance (should be provided) on a reasonable (scale). This is a duty on the righteous.	For divorced women a provision in kindness: a duty for those who ward off (evil).	And for the divorced women (too) provision (must be made) according to usage; (this is) a duty on those who guard (against evil).
2 242	Thus doth Allah Make clear His Signs to you: In order that ye may understand.	Thus Allah expoundeth unto you His revelations so that ye may understand.	Allah thus makes clear to you His communications that you may understand.
2 243	Didst thou not Turn by vision to those who abandoned their homes, though they were thousands (In number), for fear of death? Allah said to them: "Die": Then He restored them to life. For Allah is full of bounty to mankind, but most of them are ungrateful.	Bethink thee (O Muhammad) of those of old, who went forth from their habitations in their thousands, fearing death, and Allah said unto them: Die; and then He brought them back to life. Lo! Allah is a Lord of Kindness to mankind, but most of mankind give not thanks.	Have you not considered those who went forth from their homes, for fear of death, and they were thousands, then Allah said to them, Die; again He gave them life; most surely Allah is Gracious to people, but most people are not grateful.
2 244	Then fight in the cause of Allah, and know that Allah Heareth and knoweth all things.	Fight in the way of Allah, and know that Allah is Hearer, Knower.	And fight in the way of Allah, and know that Allah is Hearing, Knowing.
2 245	Who is he that will loan to Allah a beautiful loan, which Allah will double unto his credit and multiply many times? It is Allah that giveth (you) Want or plenty, and to Him shall be your return.	Who is it that will lend unto Allah a goodly loan, so that He may give it increase manifold? Allah straiteneth and enlargeth. Unto Him ye will return.	Who is it that will offer of Allah a goodly gift, so He will multiply it to him manifold, and Allah straitens and amplifies, and you shall be returned to Him.

2 246	Hast thou not Turned thy vision to the Chiefs of the Children of Israel after (the time of) Moses? they said to a prophet (That was) among them: "Appoint for us a king, that we May fight in the cause of Allah." He said: "Is it not possible, if ye were commanded to fight, that that ye will not fight?" They said: "How could we refuse to fight in the cause of Allah, seeing that we were turned out of our homes and our families?" but when they were commanded to fight, they turned back, except a small band among them. But Allah Has full knowledge of those who do wrong.	Bethink thee of the leaders of the Children of Israel after Moses, how they said unto a prophet whom they had: Set up for us a king and we will fight in Allah's way. He said: Would ye then refrain from fighting if fighting were prescribed for you? They said: Why should we not fight in Allah's way when we have been driven from our dwellings with our children? Yet, when fighting was prescribed for them, they turned away, all save a few of them. Allah is aware of evil-doers.	Have you not considered the chiefs of the children of Israel after Musa, when they said to a prophet of theirs: Raise up for us a king, (that) we may fight in the way of Allah. He said: May it not be that you would not fight if fighting is ordained for you? They said: And what reason have we that we should not fight in the way of Allah, and we have indeed been compelled to abandon our homes and our children. But when fighting was ordained for them, they turned back, except a few of them, and Allah knows the unjust.
2 247	Their Prophet said to them: "Allah hath appointed Talut as king over you." They said: "How can he exercise authority over us when we are better fitted than he to exercise authority, and he is not even gifted, with wealth in abundance?" He said: "Allah hath Chosen him above you, and hath gifted him abundantly with knowledge and bodily prowess: Allah Granteth His authority to whom He pleaseth. Allah careth for all, and He knoweth all things."	Their Prophet said unto them: Lo! Allah hath raised up Saul to be a king for you. They said: How can he have kingdom over us when we are more deserving of the kingdom than he is, since he hath not been given wealth enough? He said: Lo! Allah hath chosen him above you, and hath increased him abundantly in wisdom and stature. Allah bestoweth His Sovereignty on whom He will. Allah is All-Embracing, All-Knowing.	And their prophet said to them: Surely Allah has raised Talut to be a king over you. They said: How can he hold kingship over us while we have a greater right to kingship than he, and he has not been granted an abundance of wealth? He said: Surely Allah has chosen him in preference to you, and He has increased him abundantly in knowledge and physique, and Allah grants His kingdom to whom He pleases, and Allah is Amplegiving, Knowing.
2 248	And (further) their Prophet said to them: "A Sign of his authority is that there shall come to you the Ark of the covenant, with (an assurance) therein of security from your Lord, and the relics left by the family of Moses and the family of Aaron, carried by angels. In this is a symbol for you if ye indeed have faith."	And their Prophet said unto them: Lo! the token of his kingdom is that there shall come unto you the ark wherein is peace of reassurance from your Lord, and a remnant of that which the house of Moses and the house of Aaron left behind, the angels bearing it. Lo! herein shall be a token for you if (in truth) ye are believers.	And the prophet said to them: Surely the sign of His kingdom is, that there shall come to you the chest in which there is tranquillity from your Lord and residue of the relics of what the children of Musa and the children of Haroun have left, the angels bearing it; most surely there is a sign in this for those who believe.
2 249	When Talut set forth with the armies, he said: "Allah will test you at the stream: if any drinks of its water, He goes not with my army: Only those who taste not of it go with me: A mere sip out of the hand is excused." but they all drank of it, except a few. When they crossed the river,- He and the faithful ones with him,- they said: "This day We cannot cope with Goliath and his forces." but those who were convinced that they must meet Allah, said: "How oft, by Allah's will, Hath a small force vanquished a big one? Allah is with those who steadfastly persevere."	And when Saul set out with the army, he said: Lo! Allah will try you by (the ordeal of) a river. Whosoever therefore drinketh thereof he is not of me, and whosoever tasteth it not he is of me, save him who taketh (thereof) in the hollow of his hand. But they drank thereof, all save a few of them. And after he had crossed (the river), he and those who believed with him, they said: We have no power this day against Goliath and his hosts. But those who knew that they would meet Allah exclaimed: How many a little company hath overcome a mighty host by Allah's leave! Allah is with the steadfast.	So when Talut departed with the forces, he said: Surely Allah will try you with a river; whoever then drinks from it, he is not of me, and whoever does not taste of it, he is surely of me, except he who takes with his hand as much of it as fills the hand; but with the exception of a few of them they drank from it. So when he had crossed it, he and those who believed with him, they said: We have today no power against Jalut and his forces. Those who were sure that they would meet their Lord said: How often has a small party vanquished a numerous host by Allah's permission, and Allah is with the patient.

2 250	When they advanced to meet Goliath and his forces, they prayed: Our Lord! Pour out constancy on us and make our steps firm: Help us against those that reject faith."	And when they went into the field against Goliath and his hosts they said: Our Lord! Bestow on us endurance, make our foothold sure, and give us help against the disbelieving folk.	And when they went out against Jalut and his forces they said: Our Lord, pour down upon us patience, and make our steps firm and assist us against the unbelieving people.
2 251	By Allah's will they routed them; and David slew Goliath; and Allah gave him power and wisdom and taught him whatever (else) He willed. And did not Allah Check one set of people by means of another, the earth would indeed be full of mischief: But Allah is full of bounty to all the worlds.	So they routed them by Allah's leave and David slew Goliath; and Allah gave him the kingdom and wisdom, and taught him of that which He willeth. And if Allah had not repelled some men by others the earth would have been corrupted. But Allah is a Lord of Kindness to (His) creatures.	So they put them to flight by Allah's permission. And Dawood slew Jalut, and Allah gave him kingdom and wisdom, and taught him of what He pleased. And were it not for Allah's repelling some men with others, the earth would certainly be in a state of disorder; but Allah is Gracious to the creatures.
2 252	These are the Signs of Allah: we rehearse them to thee in truth: verily Thou art one of the messengers.	These are the portents of Allah which We recite unto thee (Muhammad) with truth, and lo! thou art of the number of (Our) messengers;	These are the communications of Allah: We recite them to you with truth; and most surely you are (one) of the messengers.
2 253	Those messengers We endowed with gifts, some above others: To one of them Allah spoke; others He raised to degrees (of honour); to Jesus the son of Mary We gave clear (Signs), and strengthened him with the holy spirit. If Allah had so willed, succeeding generations would not have fought among each other, after clear (Signs) had come to them, but they (chose) to wrangle, some believing and others rejecting. If Allah had so willed, they would not have fought each other; but Allah Fulfilleth His plan.	Of those messengers, some of whom We have caused to excel others, and of whom there are some unto whom Allah spake, while some of them He exalted (above others) in degree; and We gave Jesus, son of Mary, clear proofs (of Allah's Sovereignty) and We supported him with the holy Spirit. And if Allah had so wiled it, those who followed after them would not have fought one with another after the clear proofs had come unto them. But they differed, some of them believing and some disbelieving. And if Allah had so willed it, they would not have fought one with another; but Allah doeth what He will.	We have made some of these messengers to excel the others among them are they to whom Allah spoke, and some of them He exalted by (many degrees of) rank; and We gave clear miracles to Isa son of Marium, and strengthened him with the holy spirit. And if Allah had pleased, those after them would not have fought one with another after clear arguments had come to them, but they disagreed; so there were some of them who believed and others who denied; and if Allah had pleased they would not have fought one with another, but Allah brings about what He intends.
2 254	O ye who believe! Spend out of (the bounties) We have provided for you, before the Day comes when no bargaining (Will avail), nor friendship nor intercession. Those who reject Faith they are the wrong-doers.	O ye who believe! Spend of that wherewith We have provided you ere a day come when there will be no trafficking, nor friendship, nor intercession. The disbelievers, they are the wrong-doers.	O you who believe! spend out of what We have given you before the day comes in which there is no bargaining, neither any friendship nor intercession, and the unbelievers-- they are the unjust.

2 255	Allah! There is no god but He,-the Living, the Self-subsisting, Eternal. No slumber can seize Him nor sleep. His are all things in the heavens and on earth. Who is there can intercede in His presence except as He permitteth? He knoweth what (appeareth to His creatures as) before or after or behind them. Nor shall they compass aught of His knowledge except as He willeth. His Throne doth extend over the heavens and the earth, and He feeleth no fatigue in guarding and preserving them for He is the Most High, the Supreme (in glory).		Allah! There is no deity save Him, the Alive, the Eternal. Neither slumber nor sleep overtaketh Him. Unto Him belongeth whatsoever is in the heavens and whatsoever is in the earth. Who is he that intercedeth with Him save by His leave? He knoweth that which is in front of them and that which is behind them, while they encompass nothing of His knowledge save what He will. His throne includeth the heavens and the earth, and He is never weary of preserving them. He is the Sublime, the Tremendous.	Allah is He besides Whom there is no god, the Everliving, the Self-subsisting by Whom all subsist; slumber does not overtake Him nor sleep; whatever is in the heavens and whatever is in the earth is His; who is he that can intercede with Him but by His permission? He knows what is before them and what is behind them, and they cannot comprehend anything out of His knowledge except what He pleases, His knowledge extends over the heavens and the earth, and the preservation of them both tires Him not, and He is the Most High, the Great.
2 256	Let there be no compulsion in religion: Truth stands out clear from Error: whoever rejects evil and believes in Allah hath grasped the most trustworthy hand-hold, that never breaks. And Allah heareth and knoweth all things.		There is no compulsion in religion. The right direction is henceforth distinct from error. And he who rejecteth false deities and believeth in Allah hath grasped a firm hand-hold which will never break. Allah is Hearer, Knower.	There is no compulsion in religion; truly the right way has become clearly distinct from error; therefore, whoever disbelieves in the Shaitan and believes in Allah he indeed has laid hold on the firmest handle, which shall not break off, and Allah is Hearing, Knowing.
2 257	Allah is the Protector of those who have faith: from the depths of darkness He will lead them forth into light. Of those who reject faith the patrons are the evil ones: from light they will lead them forth into the depths of darkness. They will be companions of the fire, to dwell therein (For ever).		Allah is the Protecting Guardian of those who believe. He bringeth them out of darkness into light. As for those who disbelieve, their patrons are false deities. They bring them out of light into darkness. Such are rightful owners of the Fire. They will abide therein.	Allah is the guardian of those who believe. He brings them out of the darkness into the light; and (as to) those who disbelieve, their guardians are Shaitans who take them out of the light into the darkness; they are the inmates of the fire, in it they shall abide.
2 258	Hast thou not Turned thy vision to one who disputed with Abraham About his Lord, because Allah had granted him power? Abraham said: "My Lord is He Who giveth life and death." He said: "I give life and death". Said Abraham: "But it is Allah that causeth the sun to rise from the east: Do thou then cause him to rise from the West." Thus was he confounded who (in arrogance) rejected faith. Nor doth Allah Give guidance to a people unjust.		Bethink thee of him who had an argument with Abraham about his Lord, because Allah had given him the kingdom; how, when Abraham said: My Lord is He Who giveth life and causeth death, he answered: I give life and cause death. Abraham said: Lo! Allah causeth the sun to rise in the East, so do thou cause it to come up from the West. Thus was the disbeliever abashed. And Allah guideth not wrongdoing folk.	Have you not considered him (Namrud) who disputed with Ibrahim about his Lord, because Allah had given him the kingdom? When Ibrahim said: My Lord is He who gives life and causes to die, he said: I give life and cause death. Ibrahim said: So surely Allah causes the sun to rise from the east, then make it rise from the west; thus he who disbelieved was confounded; and Allah does not guide aright the unjust people.

2 259	Or (take) the similitude of one who passed by a hamlet, all in ruins to its roofs. He said: "Oh! how shall Allah bring it (ever) to life, after (this) its death?" but Allah caused him to die for a hundred years, then raised him up (again). He said: "How long didst thou tarry (thus)?" He said: "(Perhaps) a day or part of a day." He said: "Nay, thou hast tarried thus a hundred years; but look at thy food and thy drink; they show no signs of age; and look at thy donkey: And that We may make of thee a sign unto the people, Look further at the bones, how We bring them together and clothe them with flesh." When this was shown clearly to him, he said: "I know that Allah hath power over all things."	Or (bethink thee of) the like of him who, passing by a township which had fallen into utter ruin, exclaimed: How shall Allah give this township life after its death? And Allah made him die a hundred years, then brought him back to life. He said: How long hast thou tarried? (The man) said: I have tarried a day or part of a day. (He) said: Nay, but thou hast tarried for a hundred years. Just look at thy food and drink which have not rotted! Look at thine ass! And, that We may make thee a token unto mankind, look at the bones, how We adjust them and then cover them with flesh! And when (the matter) became clear unto him, he said: I know now that Allah is Able to do all things.	Or the like of him (Uzair) who passed by a town, and it had fallen down upon its roofs; he said: When will Allah give it life after its death? So Allah caused him to die for a hundred years, then raised him to life. He said: How long have you tarried? He said: I have tarried a day, or a part of a day. Said He: Nay! you have tarried a hundred years; then look at your food and drink-- years have not passed over it; and look at your ass; and that We may make you a sign to men, and look at the bones, how We set them together, then clothed them with flesh; so when it became clear to him, he said: I know that Allah has power over all things.
2 260	When Abraham said: "Show me, Lord, how You will raise the dead," He replied: "Have you no faith?" He said "Yes, but just to reassure my heart." Allah said, "Take four birds, draw them to you, and cut their bodies to pieces. Scatter them over the mountain-tops, then call them back. They will come swiftly to you. Know that Allah is Mighty, Wise."	And when Abraham said (unto his Lord): My Lord! Show me how Thou givest life to the dead, He said: Dost thou not believe? Abraham said: Yea, but (I ask) in order that my heart may be at ease. (His Lord) said: Take four of the birds and cause them to incline unto thee, then place a part of them on each hill, then call them, they will come to thee in haste, and know that Allah is Mighty, Wise.	And when Ibrahim said: My Lord! show me how Thou givest life to the dead, He said: What! and do you not believe? He said: Yes, but that my heart may be at ease. He said: Then take four of the birds, then train them to follow you, then place on every mountain a part of them, then call them, they will come to you flying; and know that Allah is Mighty, Wise.
2 261	The parable of those who spend their substance in the way of Allah is that of a grain of corn: it groweth seven ears, and each ear Hath a hundred grains. Allah giveth manifold increase to whom He pleaseth: And Allah careth for all and He knoweth all things.	The likeness of those who spend their wealth in Allah's way is as the likeness of a grain which groweth seven ears, in every ear a hundred grains. Allah giveth increase manifold to whom He will. Allah is All-Embracing, All-Knowing.	The parable of those who spend their property in the way of Allah is as the parable of a grain growing seven ears (with) a hundred grains in every ear; and Allah multiplies for whom He pleases; and Allah is Ample-giving, Knowing.
2 262	Those who spend their substance in the cause of Allah, and follow not up their gifts with reminders of their generosity or with injury,-for them their reward is with their Lord: on them shall be no fear, nor shall they grieve.	Those who spend their wealth for the cause of Allah and afterward make not reproach and injury to follow that which they have spent; their reward is with their Lord, and there shall no fear come upon them, neither shall they grieve.	(As for) those who spend their property in the way of Allah, then do not follow up what they have spent with reproach or injury, they shall have their reward from their Lord, and they shall have no fear nor shall they grieve.
2 263	Kind words and the covering of faults are better than charity followed by injury. Allah is free of all wants, and He is Most-Forbearing.	A kind word with forgiveness is better than almsgiving followed by injury. Allah is Absolute, Clement.	Kind speech and forgiveness is better than charity followed by injury; and Allah is Self-sufficient, Forbearing.

2 264	O ye who believe! cancel not your charity by reminders of your generosity or by injury,- like those who spend their substance to be seen of men, but believe neither in Allah nor in the Last Day. They are in parable like a hard, barren rock, on which is a little soil: on it falls heavy rain, which leaves it (Just) a bare stone. They will be able to do nothing with aught they have earned. And Allah guideth not those who reject faith.	O ye who believe! Render not vain your almsgiving by reproach and injury, like him who spendeth his wealth only to be seen of men and believeth not in Allah and the Last Day. His likeness is as the likeness of a rock whereon is dust of earth; a rainstorm smiteth it, leaving it smooth and bare. They have no control of aught of that which they have gained. Allah guideth not the disbelieving folk.	O you who believe! do not make your charity worthless by reproach and injury, like him who spends his property to be seen of men and does not believe in Allah and the last day; so his parable is as the parable of a smooth rock with earth upon it, then a heavy rain falls upon it, so it leaves it bare; they shall not be able to gain anything of what they have earned, and Allah does not guide the unbelieving people.	
2 265	And the likeness of those who spend their substance, seeking to please Allah and to strengthen their souls, is as a garden, high and fertile: heavy rain falls on it but makes it yield a double increase of harvest, and if it receives not Heavy rain, light moisture sufficeth it. Allah seeth well whatever ye do.	And the likeness of those who spend their wealth in search of Allah's pleasure, and for the strengthening of their souls, is as the likeness of a garden on a height. The rainstorm smiteth it and it bringeth forth its fruit twofold. And if the rainstorm smite it not, then the shower. Allah is Seer of what ye do.	And the parable of those who spend their property to seek the pleasure of Allah and for the certainty 'of their souls is as the parable of a garden on an elevated ground, upon which heavy rain falls so it brings forth its fruit twofold but if heavy rain does not fall upon it, then light rain (is sufficient); and Allah sees what you do.	
2 266	Does any of you wish that he should have a garden with date-palms and vines and streams flowing underneath, and all kinds of fruit, while he is stricken with old age, and his children are not strong (enough to look after themselves)- that it should be caught in a whirlwind, with fire therein, and be burnt up? Thus doth Allah make clear to you (His) Signs; that ye may consider.	Would any of you like to have a garden of palm-trees and vines, with rivers flowing underneath it, with all kinds of fruit for him therein; and old age hath stricken him and he hath feeble offspring; and a fiery whirlwind striketh it and it is (all) consumed by fire. Thus Allah maketh plain His revelations unto you, in order that ye may give thought.	Does one of you like that he should have a garden of palms and vines with streams flowing beneath it; he has in it all kinds of fruits; and old age has overtaken him and he has weak offspring, when, (lo!) a whirlwind with fire in it smites it so it becomes blasted; thus Allah makes the communications clear to you, that you may reflect.	
2 267	O ye who believe! Give of the good things which ye have (honourably) earned, and of the fruits of the earth which We have produced for you, and do not even aim at getting anything which is bad, in order that out of it ye may give away something, when ye yourselves would not receive it except with closed eyes. And know that Allah is Free of all wants, and worthy of all praise.	O ye who believe! Spend of the good things which ye have earned, and of that which We bring forth from the earth for you, and seek not the bad (with intent) to spend thereof (in charity) when ye would not take it for yourselves save with disdain; and know that Allah is Absolute, Owner of Praise.	O you who believe! spend (benevolently) of the good things that you earn and or what We have brought forth for you out of the earth, and do not aim at what is bad that you may spend (in alms) of it, while you would not take it yourselves unless you have its price lowered, and know that Allah is Self-sufficient, Praiseworthy.	
2 268	The Evil one threatens you with poverty and bids you to conduct unseemly. Allah promiseth you His forgiveness and bounties. And Allah careth for all and He knoweth all things.	The devil promiseth you destitution and enjoineth on you lewdness. But Allah promiseth you forgiveness from Himself with bounty. Allah is All-Embracing, All-Knowing.	Shaitan threatens you with poverty and enjoins you to be niggardly, and Allah promises you forgiveness from Himself and abundance; and Allah is Ample-giving, Knowing.	
2 269	He granteth wisdom to whom He pleaseth; and he to whom wisdom is granted receiveth indeed a benefit overflowing; but none will grasp the Message but men of understanding.	He giveth wisdom unto whom He will, and he unto whom wisdom is given, he truly hath received abundant good. But none remember except men of understanding.	He grants wisdom to whom He pleases, and whoever is granted wisdom, he indeed is given a great good and none but men of understanding mind.	

2 270	And whatever ye spend in charity or devotion, be sure Allah knows it all. But the wrong-doers have no helpers.	Whatever alms ye spend or vow ye vow, lo! Allah knoweth it. Wrong-doers have no helpers.	And whatever alms you give or (whatever) vow you vow, surely Allah knows it; and the unjust shall have no helpers.
2 271	If ye disclose (acts of) charity, even so it is well, but if ye conceal them, and make them reach those (really) in need, that is best for you: It will remove from you some of your (stains of) evil. And Allah is well acquainted with what ye do.	If ye publish your almsgiving, it is well, but if ye hide it and give it to the poor, it will be better for you, and will atone for some of your ill-deeds. Allah is Informed of what ye do.	If you give alms openly, it is well, and if you hide it and give it to the poor, it is better for you; and this will do away with some of your evil deeds; and Allah is aware of what you do.
2 272	It is not required of thee (O Messenger), to set them on the right path, but Allah sets on the right path whom He pleaseth. Whatever of good ye give benefits your own souls, and ye shall only do so seeking the "Face" of Allah. Whatever good ye give, shall be rendered back to you, and ye shall not Be dealt with unjustly.	The guiding of them is not thy duty (O Muhammad), but Allah guideth whom He will. And whatsoever good thing ye spend, it is for yourselves, when ye spend not save in search of Allah's Countenance; and whatsoever good thing ye spend, it will be repaid to you in full, and ye will not be wronged.	To make them walk in the right way is not incumbent on you, but Allah guides aright whom He pleases; and whatever good thing you spend, it is to your own good; and you do not spend but to seek Allah's pleasure; and whatever good things you spend shall be paid back to you in full, and you shall not be wronged.
2 273	(Charity is) for those in need, who, in Allah's cause are restricted (from travel), and cannot move about in the land, seeking (For trade or work): the ignorant man thinks, because of their modesty, that they are free from want. Thou shalt know them by their (Unfailing) mark: They beg not importunately from all the sundry. And whatever of good ye give, be assured Allah knoweth it well.	(Alms are) for the poor who are straitened for the cause of Allah, who cannot travel in the land (for trade). The unthinking man accounteth them wealthy because of their restraint. Thou shalt know them by their mark: They do not beg of men with importunity. And whatsoever good thing ye spend, lo! Allah knoweth it.	(Alms are) for the poor who are confined in the way of Allah-- they cannot go about in the land; the ignorant man thinks them to be rich on account of (their) abstaining (from begging); you can recognise them by their mark; they do not beg from men importunately; and whatever good thing you spend, surely Allah knows it.
2 274	Those who (in charity) spend of their goods by night and by day, in secret and in public, have their reward with their Lord: on them shall be no fear, nor shall they grieve.	Those who spend their wealth by night and day, by stealth and openly, verily their reward is with their Lord, and their shall no fear come upon them neither shall they grieve.	(As for) those who spend their property by night and by day, secretly and openly, they shall have their reward from their Lord and they shall have no fear, nor shall they grieve.
2 275	Those who devour usury will not stand except as stand one whom the Evil one by his touch Hath driven to madness. That is because they say: Trade is like usury, but Allah hath permitted trade and forbidden usury. Those who after receiving direction from their Lord, desist, shall be pardoned for the past; their case is for Allah (to judge); but those who repeat (The offence) are companions of the Fire: They will abide therein (for ever).	Those who swallow usury cannot rise up save as he ariseth whom the devil hath prostrated by (his) touch. That is because they say: Trade is just like usury; whereas Allah permitteth trading and forbiddeth usury. He unto whom an admonition from his Lord cometh, and (he) refraineth (in obedience thereto), he shall keep (the profits of) that which is past, and his affair (henceforth) is with Allah. As for him who returneth (to usury) - Such are rightful owners of the Fire. They will abide therein.	Those who swallow down usury cannot arise except as one whom Shaitan has prostrated by (his) touch does rise. That is because they say, trading is only like usury; and Allah has allowed trading and forbidden usury. To whomsoever then the admonition has come from his Lord, then he desists, he shall have what has already passed, and his affair is in the hands of Allah; and whoever returns (to it)-- these arc the inmates of the fire; they shall abide in it.
2 276	Allah will deprive usury of all blessing, but will give increase for deeds of charity: For He loveth not creatures ungrateful and wicked.	Allah hath blighted usury and made almsgiving fruitful. Allah loveth not the impious and guilty.	Allah does not bless usury, and He causes charitable deeds to prosper, and Allah does not love any ungrateful sinner.

2 277	Those who believe, and do deeds of righteousness, and establish regular prayers and regular charity, will have their reward with their Lord: on them shall be no fear, nor shall they grieve.	Lo! those who believe and do good works and establish worship and pay the poor-due, their reward is with their Lord and there shall no fear come upon them neither shall they grieve.	Surely they who believe and do good deeds and keep up prayer and pay the poor-rate they shall have their reward from their Lord, and they shall have no fear, nor shall they grieve.
2 278	O ye who believe! Fear Allah, and give up what remains of your demand for usury, if ye are indeed believers.	O ye who believe! Observe your duty to Allah, and give up what remaineth (due to you) from usury, if ye are (in truth) believers.	O you who believe! Be careful of (your duty to) Allah and relinquish what remains (due) from usury, if you are believers.
2 279	If ye do it not, Take notice of war from Allah and His Messenger: But if ye turn back, ye shall have your capital sums: Deal not unjustly, and ye shall not be dealt with unjustly.	And if ye do not, then be warned of war (against you) from Allah and His messenger. And if ye repent, then ye have your principal (without interest). Wrong not, and ye shall not be wronged.	But If you do (it) not, then be apprised of war from Allah and His Messenger; and if you repent, then you shall have your capital; neither shall you make (the debtor) suffer loss, nor shall you be made to suffer loss.
2 280	If the debtor is in a difficulty, grant him time Till it is easy for him to repay. But if ye remit it by way of charity, that is best for you if ye only knew.	And if the debtor is in straitened circumstances, then (let there be) postponement to (the time of) ease; and that ye remit the debt as almsgiving would be better for you if ye did but know.	And if (the debtor) is in straitness, then let there be postponement until (he is in) ease; and that you remit (it) as alms is better for you, if you knew.
2 281	And fear the Day when ye shall be brought back to Allah. Then shall every soul be paid what it earned, and none shall be dealt with unjustly.	And guard yourselves against a day in which ye will be brought back to Allah. Then every soul will be paid in full that which it hath earned, and they will not be wronged.	And guard yourselves against a day in which you shall be returned to Allah; then every soul shall be paid back in full what it has earned, and they shall not be dealt with unjustly.

2 282 O ye who believe! When ye deal with each other, in transactions involving future obligations in a fixed period of time, reduce them to writing Let a scribe write down faithfully as between the parties: let not the scribe refuse to write: as Allah has taught him, so let him write. Let him who incurs the liability dictate, but let him fear His Lord Allah, and not diminish aught of what he owes. If they party liable is mentally deficient, or weak, or unable Himself to dictate, Let his guardian dictate faithfully, and get two witnesses, out of your own men, and if there are not two men, then a man and two women, such as ye choose, for witnesses, so that if one of them errs, the other can remind her. The witnesses should not refuse when they are called on (For evidence). Disdain not to reduce to writing (your contract) for a future period, whether it be small or big: it is juster in the sight of Allah, More suitable as evidence, and more convenient to prevent doubts among yourselves but if it be a transaction which ye carry out on the spot among yourselves, there is no blame on you if ye reduce it not to writing. But take witness whenever ye make a commercial contract; and let neither scribe nor witness suffer harm. If ye do (such harm), it would be wickedness in you. So fear Allah; For it is Good that teaches you. And Allah is well acquainted with all things. If ye are on a journey, and cannot find a scribe, a pledge with possession (may serve the purpose). And if one of you deposits a thing on trust with another, let the trustee (faithfully) discharge his trust, and let him Fear his Lord conceal not evidence; for whoever conceals it, - his heart is tainted with sin. And Allah knoweth all that ye do.

O ye who believe! When ye contract a debt for a fixed term, record it in writing. Let a scribe record it in writing between you in (terms of) equity. No scribe should refuse to write as Allah hath taught him, so let him write, and let him who incurreth the debt dictate, and let him observe his duty to Allah his Lord, and diminish naught thereof. But if he who oweth the debt is of low understanding, or weak, or unable himself to dictate, then let the guardian of his interests dictate in (terms of) equity. And call to witness, from among your men, two witnesses. And if two men be not (at hand) then a man and two women, of such as ye approve as witnesses, so that if the one erreth (through forgetfulness) the other will remember. And the witnesses must not refuse when they are summoned. Be not averse to writing down (the contract) whether it be small or great, with (record of) the term thereof. That is more equitable in the sight of Allah and more sure for testimony, and the best way of avoiding doubt between you; save only in the case when it is actual merchandise which ye transfer among yourselves from hand to hand. In that case it is no sin for you if ye write it not. And have witnesses when ye sell one to another, and let no harm be done to scribe or witness. If ye do (harm to them) lo! it is a sin in you. Observe your duty to Allah. Allah is teaching you. And Allah is knower of all things.

O you who believe! when you deal with each other in contracting a debt for a fixed time, then write it down; and let a scribe write it down between you with fairness; and the scribe should not refuse to write as Allah has taught him, so he should write; and let him who owes the debt dictate, and he should be careful of (his duty to) Allah, his Lord, and not diminish anything from it; but if he who owes the debt is unsound in understanding, or weak, or (if) he is not able to dictate himself, let his guardian dictate with fairness; and call in to witness from among your men two witnesses; but if there are not two men, then one man and two women from among those whom you choose to be witnesses, so that if one of the two errs, the second of the two may remind the other; and the witnesses should not refuse when they are summoned; and be not averse to writing it (whether it is) small or large, with the time of its falling due; this is more equitable in the sight of Allah and assures greater accuracy in testimony, and the nearest (way) that you may not entertain doubts (afterwards), except when it is ready merchandise which you give and take among yourselves from hand to hand, then there is no blame on you in not writing it down; and have witnesses when you barter with one another, and let no harm be done to the scribe or to the witness; and if you do (it) then surely it will be a transgression in you, and be careful of (your duty) to Allah, Allah teaches you, and Allah knows all things.

2 283	If ye are on a journey, and cannot find a scribe, a pledge with possession (may serve the purpose). And if one of you deposits a thing on trust with another, Let the trustee (Faithfully) discharge His trust, and let him fear his Lord. Conceal not evidence; for whoever conceals it,- His heart is tainted with sin. And Allah Knoweth all that ye do.	If ye be on a journey and cannot find a scribe, then a pledge in hand (shall suffice). And if one of you entrusteth to another let him who is trusted deliver up that which is entrusted to him (according to the pact between them) and let him observe his duty to Allah his Lord. Hide not testimony. He who hideth it, verily his heart is sinful. Allah is Aware of what ye do.	And if you are upon a journey and you do not find a scribe, then (there may be) a security taken into possession; but if one of you trusts another, then he who is trusted should deliver his trust, and let him be careful (of his duty to) Allah, his Lord; and do not conceal testimony, and whoever conceals it, his heart is surely sinful; and Allah knows what you do.
2 284	To Allah belongeth all that is in the heavens and on earth. Whether ye show what is in your minds or conceal it, Allah Calleth you to account for it. He forgiveth whom He pleaseth, and punisheth whom He pleaseth, for Allah hath power over all things.	Unto Allah (belongeth) whatsoever is in the heavens and whatsoever is in the earth; and whether ye make known what is in your minds or hide it, Allah will bring you to account for it. He will forgive whom He will and He will punish whom He will. Allah is Able to do all things.	Whatever is in the heavens and whatever is in the earth is Allah's; and whether you manifest what is in your minds or hide it, Allah will call you to account according to it; then He will forgive whom He pleases and chastise whom He pleases, and Allah has power over all things.
2 285	The Messenger believeth in what hath been revealed to him from his Lord, as do the men of faith. Each one (of them) believeth in Allah, His angels, His books, and His messengers. "We make no distinction (they say) between one and another of His messengers." And they say: We hear, and we obey: (We seek) Thy forgiveness, our Lord, and to Thee is the end of all journeys."	The messenger believeth in that which hath been revealed unto him from his Lord and (so do) believers. Each one believeth in Allah and His angels and His scriptures and His messengers - We make no distinction between any of His messengers - and they say: We hear, and we obey. (Grant us) Thy forgiveness, our Lord. Unto Thee is the journeying.	The messenger believes in what has been revealed to him from his Lord, and (so do) the believers; they all believe in Allah and His angels and His books and His messengers; We make no difference between any of His messengers; and they say: We hear and obey, our Lord! Thy forgiveness (do we crave), and to Thee is the eventual course.
2 286	On no soul doth Allah Place a burden greater than it can bear. It gets every good that it earns, and it suffers every ill that it earns. (Pray:) "Our Lord! Condemn us not if we forget or fall into error; our Lord! Lay not on us a burden Like that which Thou didst lay on those before us; Our Lord! Lay not on us a burden greater than we have strength to bear. Blot out our sins, and grant us forgiveness. Have mercy on us. Thou art our Protector; Help us against those who stand against faith."	Allah tasketh not a soul beyond its scope. For it (is only) that which it hath earned, and against it (only) that which it hath deserved. Our Lord! Condemn us not if we forget, or miss the mark! Our Lord! Lay not on us such a burden as thou didst lay on those before us! Our Lord! Impose not on us that which we have not the strength to bear! Pardon us, absolve us and have mercy on us, Thou, our Protector, and give us victory over the disbelieving folk.	Allah does not impose upon any soul a duty but to the extent of its ability; for it is (the benefit of) what it has earned and upon it (the evil of) what it has wrought: Our Lord! do not punish us if we forget or make a mistake; Our Lord! do not lay on us a burden as Thou didst lay on those before us, Our Lord do not impose upon us that which we have not the strength to bear; and pardon us and grant us protection and have mercy on us, Thou art our Patron, so help us against the unbelieving people.

Chapter 3:

AL-E-IMRAN (THE FAMILY OF 'IMRAN, THE HOUSE OF 'IMRAN)

Total Verses: 200 Revealed At: MADINA

In the name of Allah, the Most Beneficent, the Most Merciful.

3 001	A. L. M.	Alim. Lam. Mim.	Alif Lam Mim.
3 002	Allah! There is no god but He,-the Living, the Self-Subsisting, Eternal.	Allah! There is no God save Him, the Alive, the Eternal.	Allah, (there is) no god but He, the Everliving, the Self-subsisting by Whom all things subsist.
3 003	It is He Who sent down to thee (step by step), in truth, the Book, confirming what went before it; and He sent down the Law (of Moses) and the Gospel (of Jesus) before this, as a guide to mankind, and He sent down the criterion (of judgment between right and wrong).	He hath revealed unto thee (Muhammad) the Scripture with truth, confirming that which was (revealed) before it, even as He revealed the Torah and the Gospel.	He has revealed to you the Book with truth, verifying that which is before it, and He revealed the Tavrat and the Injeel aforetime, a guidance for the people, and He sent the Furqan.
3 004	Then those who reject Faith in the Signs of Allah will suffer the severest penalty, and Allah is Exalted in Might, Lord of Retribution.	Aforetime, for a guidance to mankind; and hath revealed the Criterion (of right and wrong). Lo! those who disbelieve the revelations of Allah, theirs will be a heavy doom. Allah is Mighty, Able to Requite (the wrong).	Surely they who disbelieve in the communications of Allah they shall have a severe chastisement; and Allah is Mighty, the Lord of retribution.
3 005	From Allah, verily nothing is hidden on earth or in the heavens.	Lo! nothing in the earth or in the heavens is hidden from Allah.	Allah-- surely nothing is hidden from Him in the earth or in the heaven.
3 006	He it is Who shapes you in the wombs as He pleases. There is no god but He, the Exalted in Might, the Wise.	He it is Who fashioneth you in the wombs as pleaseth Him. There is no Allah save Him, the Almighty, the Wise.	He it is Who shapes you in the wombs as He likes; there is no god but He, the Mighty, the Wise.
3 007	He it is Who has sent down to thee the Book: In it are verses basic or fundamental (of established meaning); they are the foundation of the Book: others are allegorical. But those in whose hearts is perversity follow the part thereof that is allegorical, seeking discord, and searching for its hidden meanings, but no one knows its hidden meanings except Allah. And those who are firmly grounded in knowledge say: "We believe in the Book; the whole of it is from our Lord:" and none will grasp the Message except men of understanding.	He it is Who hath revealed unto thee (Muhammad) the Scripture wherein are clear revelations - they are the substance of the Book - and others (which are) allegorical. But those in whose hearts is doubt pursue, forsooth, that which is allegorical seeking (to cause) dissension by seeking to explain it. None knoweth its explanation save Allah. And those who are of sound instruction say: We believe therein; the whole is from our Lord; but only men of understanding really heed.	He it is Who has revealed the Book to you; some of its verses are decisive, they are the basis of the Book, and others are allegorical; then as for those in whose hearts there is perversity they follow the part of it which is allegorical, seeking to mislead and seeking to give it (their own) interpretation, but none knows its interpretation except Allah, and those who are firmly rooted in knowledge say: We believe in it, it is all from our Lord; and none do mind except those having understanding.

3 008	"Our Lord!" (they say), "Let not our hearts deviate now after Thou hast guided us, but grant us mercy from Thine own Presence; for Thou art the Grantor of bounties without measure."	Our Lord! Cause not our hearts to stray after Thou hast guided us, and bestow upon us mercy from Thy Presence. Lo! Thou, only Thou, art the Bestower.	Our Lord! make not our hearts to deviate after Thou hast guided us aright, and grant us from Thee mercy; surely Thou art the most liberal Giver.
3 009	"Our Lord! Thou art He that will gather mankind Together against a day about which there is no doubt; for Allah never fails in His promise."	Our Lord! Lo! it is Thou Who gatherest mankind together to a Day of which there is no doubt. Lo! Allah faileth not to keep the tryst.	Our Lord! surely Thou art the Gatherer of men on a day about which there is no doubt; surely Allah will not fail (His) promise.
3 010	Those who reject Faith,- neither their possessions nor their (numerous) progeny will avail them aught against Allah: They are themselves but fuel for the Fire.	(On that Day) neither the riches nor the progeny of those who disbelieve will aught avail them with Allah. They will be fuel for Fire.	(As for) those who disbelieve, surely neither their wealth nor their children shall avail them in the least against Allah, and these it is who are the fuel of the fire.
3 011	(Their plight will be) no better than that of the people of Pharaoh, and their predecessors: They denied our Signs, and Allah called them to account for their sins. For Allah is strict in punishment.	Like Pharaoh's folk and those who were before them, they disbelieved Our revelations and so Allah seized them for their sins. And Allah is severe in punishment.	Like the striving of the people of Firon and those before them; they rejected Our communications, so Allah destroyed them on account of their faults; and Allah is severe in requiting (evil).
3 012	Say to those who reject Faith: "Soon will ye be vanquished and gathered together to Hell,-an evil bed indeed (to lie on)!"	Say (O Muhammad) unto those who disbelieve: Ye shall be overcome and gathered unto Hell, an evil resting-place.	Say to those who disbelieve: You shall be vanquished, and driven together to hell; and evil is the resting-place.
3 013	"There has already been for you a Sign in the two armies that met (in combat): One was fighting in the cause of Allah, the other resisting Allah; these saw with their own eyes Twice their number. But Allah doth support with His aid whom He pleaseth. In this is a warning for such as have eyes to see."	There was a token for you in two hosts which met: one army fighting in the way of Allah, and another disbelieving, whom they saw as twice their number, clearly, with their very eyes. Thus Allah strengtheneth with His succour whom He will. Lo! herein verily is a lesson for those who have eyes.	Indeed there was a sign for you in the two hosts (which) met together in encounter; one party fighting in the way of Allah and the other unbelieving, whom they saw twice as many as themselves with the sight of the eye and Allah strengthens with His aid whom He pleases; most surely there is a lesson in this for those who have sight.
3 014	Fair in the eyes of men is the love of things they covet: Women and sons; Heaped-up hoards of gold and silver; horses branded (for blood and excellence); and (wealth of) cattle and well-tilled land. Such are the possessions of this world's life; but in nearness to Allah is the best of the goals (To return to).	Beautified for mankind is love of the joys (that come) from women and offspring; and stored-up heaps of gold and silver, and horses branded (with their mark), and cattle and land. That is comfort of the life of the world. Allah! With Him is a more excellent abode.	The love of desires, of women and sons and hoarded treasures of gold and silver and well bred horses and cattle and tilth, is made to seem fair to men; this is the provision of the life of this world; and Allah is He with Whom is the good goal (of life).
3 015	Say: Shall I give you glad tidings of things Far better than those? For the righteous are Gardens in nearness to their Lord, with rivers flowing beneath; therein is their eternal home; with companions pure (and holy); and the good pleasure of Allah. For in Allah's sight are (all) His servants,-	Say: Shall I inform you of something better than that? For those who keep from evil, with their Lord, are Gardens underneath which rivers flow wherein they will abide, and pure companions, and contentment from Allah. Allah is Seer of His bondmen,	Say: Shall I tell you what is better than these? For those who guard (against evil) are gardens with their Lord, beneath which rivers flow, to abide in them, and pure mates and Allah's pleasure; and Allah sees the servants.
3 016	(Namely), those who say: "Our Lord! we have indeed believed: forgive us, then, our sins, and save us from the agony of the Fire;"-	Those who say: Our Lord! Lo! we believe. So forgive us our sins and guard us from the punishment of Fire;	Those who say: Our Lord! surely we believe, therefore forgive us our faults and save us from the chastisement of the fire.

3 017	Those who show patience, Firmness and self-control; who are true (in word and deed); who worship devoutly; who spend (in the way of Allah); and who pray for forgiveness in the early hours of the morning.	The steadfast, and the truthful, and the obedient, those who spend (and hoard not), those who pray for pardon in the watches of the night.	The patient, and the truthful, and the obedient, and those who spend (benevolently) and those who ask forgiveness in the morning times.
3 018	There is no god but He: That is the witness of Allah, His angels, and those endued with knowledge, standing firm on justice. There is no god but He, the Exalted in Power, the Wise.	Allah (Himself) is Witness that there is no God save Him. And the angels and the men of learning (too are witness). Maintaining His creation in justice, there is no God save Him the Almighty, the Wise.	Allah bears witness that there is no god but He, and (so do) the angels and those possessed of knowledge, maintaining His creation with justice; there is no god but He, the Mighty, the Wise.
3 019	The Religion before Allah is Islam (submission to His Will): Nor did the People of the Book dissent therefrom except through envy of each other, after knowledge had come to them. But if any deny the Signs of Allah, Allah is swift in calling to account.	Lo! religion with Allah (is) the Surrender (to His Will and Guidance). Those who (formerly) received the Scripture differed only after knowledge came unto them, through transgression among themselves. Whoso disbelieveth the revelations of Allah (will find that) lo! Allah is swift at reckoning.	Surely the (true) religion with Allah is Islam, and those to whom the Book had been given did not show opposition but after knowledge had come to them, out of envy among themselves; and whoever disbelieves in the communications of Allah then surely Allah is quick in reckoning.
3 020	So if they dispute with thee, say: "I have submitted My whole self to Allah and so have those who follow me." And say to the People of the Book and to those who are unlearned: "Do ye (also) submit yourselves?" If they do, they are in right guidance, but if they turn back, Thy duty is to convey the Message; and in Allah's sight are (all) His servants.	And if they argue with thee, (O Muhammad), say: I have surrendered my purpose to Allah and (so have) those who follow me. And say unto those who have received the Scripture and those who read not: Have ye (too) surrendered? If they surrender, then truly they are rightly guided, and if they turn away, then it is thy duty only to convey the message (unto them). Allah is Seer of (His) bondmen.	But if they dispute with you, say: I have submitted myself entirely to Allah and (so) every one who follows me; and say to those who have been given the Book and the unlearned people: Do you submit yourselves? So if they submit then indeed they follow the right way; and if they turn back, then upon you is only the delivery of the message and Allah sees the servants.
3 021	As to those who deny the Signs of Allah and in defiance of right, slay the prophets, and slay those who teach just dealing with mankind, announce to them a grievous penalty.	Lo! those who disbelieve the revelations of Allah, and slay the prophets wrongfully, and slay those of mankind who enjoin equity: promise them a painful doom.	Surely (as for) those who disbelieve in the communications of Allah and slay the prophets unjustly and slay those among men who enjoin justice, announce to them a painful chastisement.
3 022	They are those whose works will bear no fruit in this world and in the Hereafter nor will they have anyone to help.	Those are they whose works have failed in the world and the Hereafter; and they have no helpers.	Those are they whose works shall become null in this world as well as the hereafter, and they shall have no helpers.
3 023	Hast thou not turned Thy vision to those who have been given a portion of the Book? They are invited to the Book of Allah, to settle their dispute, but a party of them Turn back and decline (The arbitration).	Hast thou not seen how those who have received a portion of the Scripture invoke the Scripture of Allah (in their disputes) that it may judge between them; then a faction of them turn away, being opposed (to it)?	Have you not considered those (Jews) who are given a portion of the Book? They are invited to the Book of Allah that it might decide between them, then a part of them turn back and they withdraw.
3 024	This because they say: "The Fire shall not touch us but for a few numbered days": For their forgeries deceive them as to their own religion.	That is because they say: The Fire will not touch us save for a certain number of days. That which they used to invent hath deceived them regarding their religion.	This is because they say: The fire shall not touch us but for a few days; and what they have forged deceives them in the matter of their religion.

3 025	But how (will they fare) when we gather them together against a day about which there is no doubt, and each soul will be paid out just what it has earned, without (favour or) injustice?	How (will it be with them) when We have brought them all together to a Day of which there is no doubt, when every soul will be paid in full what it hath earned, and they will not be wronged.	Then how will it be when We shall gather them together on a day about which there is no doubt, and every soul shall be fully paid what it has earned, and they shall not be dealt with unjustly?
3 026	Say: "O Allah! Lord of Power (And Rule), Thou givest power to whom Thou pleasest, and Thou strippest off power from whom Thou pleasest: Thou enduest with honour whom Thou pleasest, and Thou bringest low whom Thou pleasest: In Thy hand is all good. Verily, over all things Thou hast power."	Say: O Allah! Owner of Sovereignty! Thou givest sovereignty unto whom Thou wilt, and Thou withdrawest sovereignty from whom Thou wilt. Thou exaltest whom Thou wilt, and Thou abasest whom Thou wilt. In Thy hand is the good. Lo! Thou art Able to do all things.	Say: O Allah, Master of the Kingdom! Thou givest the kingdom to whomsoever Thou pleasest and takest away the kingdom from whomsoever Thou pleasest, and Thou exaltest whom Thou pleasest and abasest whom Thou pleasest in Thine hand is the good; surety, Thou hast power over all things.
3 027	"Thou causest the night to gain on the day, and thou causest the day to gain on the night; Thou bringest the Living out of the dead, and Thou bringest the dead out of the Living; and Thou givest sustenance to whom Thou pleasest, without measure."	Thou causest the night to pass into the day, and Thou causest the day to pass into the night. And Thou bringest forth the living from the dead, and Thou bringest forth the dead from the living. And Thou givest sustenance to whom Thou choosest, without stint.	Thou makest the night to pass into the day and Thou makest the day to pass into the night, and Thou bringest forth the living from the dead and Thou bringest forth the dead from the living, and Thou givest sustenance to whom Thou pleasest without measure.
3 028	Let not the believers Take for friends or helpers Unbelievers rather than believers: if any do that, in nothing will there be help from Allah: except by way of precaution, that ye may Guard yourselves from them. But Allah cautions you (To remember) Himself; for the final goal is to Allah.	Let not the believers take disbelievers for their friends in preference to believers. Whoso doeth that hath no connection with Allah unless (it be) that ye but guard yourselves against them, taking (as it were) security. Allah biddeth you beware (only) of Himself. Unto Allah is the journeying.	Let not the believers take the unbelievers for friends rather than believers; and whoever does this, he shall have nothing of (the guardianship of) Allah, but you should guard yourselves against them, guarding carefully; and Allah makes you cautious of (retribution from) Himself; and to Allah is the eventual coming.
3 029	Say: "Whether ye hide what is in your hearts or reveal it, Allah knows it all: He knows what is in the heavens, and what is on earth. And Allah has power over all things."	Say, (O Muhammad): Whether ye hide that which is in your breasts or reveal it, Allah knoweth it. He knoweth that which is in the heavens and that which is in the earth, and Allah is Able to do all things.	Say: Whether you hide what is in your hearts or manifest it, Allah knows it, and He knows whatever is in the heavens and whatever is in the earth, and Allah has power over all things.
3 030	"On the Day when every soul will be confronted with all the good it has done, and all the evil it has done, it will wish there were a great distance between it and its evil. But Allah cautions you (To remember) Himself. And Allah is full of kindness to those that serve Him."	On the Day when every soul will find itself confronted with all that it hath done of good and all that it hath done of evil (every soul) will long that there might be a mighty space of distance between it and that (evil). Allah biddeth you beware of Him. And Allah is Full of Pity for (His) bondmen.	On the day that every soul shall find present what it has done of good and what it has done of evil, it shall wish that between it and that (evil) there were a long duration of time; and Allah makes you to be cautious of (retribution from) Himself; and Allah is Compassionate to the servants.
3 031	Say: "If ye do love Allah, Follow me: Allah will love you and forgive you your sins: For Allah is Oft-Forgiving, Most Merciful."	Say, (O Muhammad, to mankind): If ye love Allah, follow me; Allah will love you and forgive you your sins. Allah is Forgiving, Merciful.	Say: If you love Allah, then follow me, Allah will love you and forgive you your faults, and Allah is Forgiving, Merciful.
3 032	Say: "Obey Allah and His Messenger": But if they turn back, Allah loveth not those who reject Faith.	Say: Obey Allah and the messenger. But if they turn away, lo! Allah loveth not the disbelievers (in His guidance).	Say: Obey Allah and the Messenger; but if they turn back, then surely Allah does not love the unbelievers.

3 033	Allah did choose Adam and Noah, the family of Abraham, and the family of 'Imran above all people,-	Lo! Allah preferred Adam and Noah and the Family of Abraham and the Family of 'Imran above (all His) creatures.		Surely Allah chose Adam and Nuh and the descendants of Ibrahim and the descendants of Imran above the nations.
3 034	Offspring, one of the other: And Allah heareth and knoweth all things.	They were descendants one of another. Allah is Hearer, Knower.		Offspring one of the other; and Allah is Hearing, Knowing.
3 035	Behold! a woman of 'Imran said: "O my Lord! I do dedicate unto Thee what is in my womb for Thy special service: So accept this of me: For Thou hearest and knowest all things."	(Remember) when the wife of 'Imran said: My Lord! I have vowed unto Thee that which is in my belly as a consecrated (offering). Accept it from me. Lo! Thou, only Thou, art the Hearer, the Knower!		When a woman of Imran said: My Lord! surely I vow to Thee what is in my womb, to be devoted (to Thy service); accept therefore from me, surely Thou art the Hearing, the Knowing.
3 036	When she was delivered, she said: "O my Lord! Behold! I am delivered of a female child!"- and Allah knew best what she brought forth- And no wise is the male Like the female. I have named her Mary, and I commend her and her offspring to Thy protection from the Evil One, the Rejected."	And when she was delivered she said: My Lord! Lo! I am delivered of a female - Allah knew best of what she was delivered - the male is not as the female; and lo! I have named her Mary, and lo! I crave Thy protection for her and for her offspring from Satan the outcast.		So when she brought forth, she said: My Lord! Surely I have brought it forth a female-- and Allah knew best what she brought forth-- and the male is not like the female, and I have named it Marium, and I commend her and her offspring into Thy protection from the accursed Shaitan.
3 037	Right graciously did her Lord accept her: He made her grow in purity and beauty: To the care of Zakariya was she assigned. Every time that he entered (Her) chamber to see her, He found her supplied with sustenance. He said: "O Mary! Whence (comes) this to you?" She said: From Allah: for Allah Provides sustenance to whom He pleases without measure."	And her Lord accepted her with full acceptance and vouchsafed to her a goodly growth; and made Zachariah her guardian. Whenever Zachariah went into the sanctuary where she was, he found that she had food. He said: O Mary! Whence cometh unto thee this (food)? She answered: It is from Allah. Allah giveth without stint to whom He will.		So her Lord accepted her with a good acceptance and made her grow up a good growing, and gave her into the charge of Zakariya; whenever Zakariya entered the sanctuary to (see) her, he found with her food. He said: O Marium! whence comes this to you? She said: It is from Allah. Surely Allah gives to whom He pleases without measure.
3 038	There did Zakariya pray to his Lord, saying: "O my Lord! Grant unto me from Thee a progeny that is pure: for Thou art He that heareth prayer!"	Then Zachariah prayed unto his Lord and said: My Lord! Bestow upon me of Thy bounty goodly offspring. Lo! Thou art the Hearer of Prayer.		There did Zakariya pray to his Lord; he said: My Lord! grant me from Thee good offspring; surely Thou art the Hearer of prayer.
3 039	While he was standing in prayer in the chamber, the angels called unto him: "Allah doth give thee glad tidings of Yahya, witnessing the truth of a Word from Allah, and (be besides) noble, chaste, and a prophet,- of the (goodly) company of the righteous."	And the angels called to him as he stood praying in the sanctuary: Allah giveth thee glad tidings of (a son whose name is) John, (who cometh) to confirm a word from Allah lordly, chaste, a prophet of the righteous.		Then the angels called to him as he stood praying in the sanctuary: That Allah gives you the good news of Yahya verifying a Word from Allah, and honorable and chaste and a prophet from among the good ones.
3 040	He said: "O my Lord! How shall I have son, seeing I am very old, and my wife is barren?" "Thus," was the answer, "Doth Allah accomplish what He willeth."	He said: My Lord! How can I have a son when age hath overtaken me already and my wife is barren? (The angel) answered: So (it will be). Allah doeth what He will.		He said: My Lord! when shall there be a son (born) to me, and old age has already come upon me, and my wife is barren? He said: even thus does Allah what He pleases.
3 041	He said: "O my Lord! Give me a Sign!" "Thy Sign," was the answer, Shall be that thou shalt speak to no man for three days but with signals. Then celebrate the praises of thy Lord again and again, and glorify Him in the evening and in the morning."	He said: My Lord! Appoint a token for me. (The angel) said: The token unto thee (shall be) that thou shalt not speak unto mankind three days except by signs. Remember thy Lord much, and praise (Him) in the early hours of night and morning.		He said: My Lord! appoint a sign for me. Said He: Your sign is that you should not speak to men for three days except by signs; and remember your Lord much and glorify Him in the evening and the morning.

3 042	Behold! the angels said: "O Mary! Allah hath chosen thee and purified thee- chosen thee above the women of all nations."	And when the angels said: O Mary! Lo! Allah hath chosen thee and made thee pure, and hath preferred thee above (all) the women of creation.	And when the angels said: O Marium! surely Allah has chosen you and purified you and chosen you above the women of the world.
3 043	"O Mary! worship Thy Lord devoutly: Prostrate thyself, and bow down (in prayer) with those who bow down."	O Mary! Be obedient to thy Lord, prostrate thyself and bow with those who bow (in worship).	O Marium! keep to obedience to your Lord and humble yourself, and bow down with those who bow.
3 044	This is part of the tidings of the things unseen, which We reveal unto thee (O Messenger!) by inspiration: Thou wast not with them when they cast lots with arrows, as to which of them should be charged with the care of Mary: Nor wast thou with them when they disputed (the point).	This is of the tidings of things hidden. We reveal it unto thee (Muhammad). Thou wast not present with them when they threw their pens (to know) which of them should be the guardian of Mary, nor wast thou present with them when they quarrelled (thereupon).	This is of the announcements relating to the unseen which We reveal to you; and you were not with them when they cast their pens (to decide) which of them should have Marium in his charge, and you were not with them when they contended one with another.
3 045	Behold! the angels said: "O Mary! Allah giveth thee glad tidings of a Word from Him: his name will be Christ Jesus, the son of Mary, held in honour in this world and the Hereafter and of (the company of) those nearest to Allah;"	(And remember) when the angels said: O Mary! Lo! Allah giveth thee glad tidings of a word from him, whose name is the Messiah, Jesus, son of Mary, illustrious in the world and the Hereafter, and one of those brought near (unto Allah).	When the angels said: O Marium, surely Allah gives you good news with a Word from Him (of one) whose name is the '. Messiah, Isa son of Marium, worthy of regard in this world and the hereafter and of those who are made near (to Allah).
3 046	"He shall speak to the people in childhood and in maturity. And he shall be (of the company) of the righteous."	He will speak unto mankind in his cradle and in his manhood, and he is of the righteous.	And he shall speak to the people when in the cradle and when of old age, and (he shall be) one of the good ones.
3 047	She said: "O my Lord! How shall I have a son when no man hath touched me?" He said: "Even so: Allah createth what He willeth: When He hath decreed a plan, He but saith to it, 'Be,' and it is!"	She said: My Lord! How can I have a child when no mortal hath touched me? He said: So (it will be). Allah createth what He will. If He decreeth a thing, He saith unto it only: Be! and it is.	She said: My Lord! when shall there be a son (born) to I me, and man has not touched me? He said: Even so, Allah creates what He pleases; when He has decreed a matter, He only says to it, Be, and it is.
3 048	"And Allah will teach him the Book and Wisdom, the Law and the Gospel,"	And He will teach him the Scripture and wisdom, and the Torah and the Gospel,	And He will teach him the Book and the wisdom and the Tavrat and the Injeel.
3 049	"And (appoint him) a messenger to the Children of Israel, (with this message): 'I have come to you, with a Sign from your Lord, in that I make for you out of clay, as it were, the figure of a bird, and breathe into it, and it becomes a bird by Allah's leave: And I heal those born blind, and the lepers, and I quicken the dead, by Allah's leave; and I declare to you what ye eat, and what ye store in your houses. Surely therein is a Sign for you if ye did believe;"	And will make him a messenger unto the Children of Israel, (saying): Lo! I come unto you with a sign from your Lord. Lo! I fashion for you out of clay the likeness of a bird, and I breathe into it and it is a bird, by Allah's leave. I heal him who was born blind, and the leper, and I raise the dead, by Allah's leave. And I announce unto you what ye eat and what ye store up in your houses. Lo! herein verily is a portent for you, if ye are to be believers.	And (make him) a messenger to the children of Israel: That I have come to you with a sign from your Lord, that I determine for you out of dust like the form of a bird, then I breathe into it and it becomes a bird with Allah's permission and I heal the blind and the leprous, and bring the dead to life with Allah's permission and I inform you of what you should eat and what you should store in your houses; most surely there is a sign in this for you, if you are believers.

3 050	"'(I have come to you), to attest the Law which was before me. And to make lawful to you part of what was (Before) forbidden to you; I have come to you with a Sign from your Lord. So fear Allah, and obey me.'"	And (I come) confirming that which was before me of the Torah, and to make lawful some of that which was forbidden unto you. I come unto you with a sign from your Lord, so keep your duty to Allah and obey me.	And a verifier of that which is before me of the Taurat and that I may allow you part of that which has been forbidden to you, and I have come to you with a sign from your Lord therefore be careful of (your duty to) Allah and obey me.
3 051	"'It is Allah Who is my Lord and your Lord; then worship Him. This is a Way that is straight.'"	Lo! Allah is my Lord and your Lord, so worship Him. That is a straight path.	Surely Allah is my Lord and your Lord, therefore serve Him; this is the right path.
3 052	When Jesus found Unbelief on their part He said: "Who will be My helpers to (the work of) Allah?" Said the disciples: "We are Allah's helpers: We believe in Allah, and do thou bear witness that we are Muslims."	But when Jesus became conscious of their disbelief, he cried: Who will be my helpers in the cause of Allah? The disciples said: We will be Allah's helpers. We believe in Allah, and bear thou witness that we have surrendered (unto Him).	But when Isa perceived unbelief on their part, he said Who will be my helpers in Allah's way? The disciples said: We are helpers (in the way) of Allah: We believe in Allah and bear witness that we are submitting ones.
3 053	"Our Lord! we believe in what Thou hast revealed, and we follow the Messenger; then write us down among those who bear witness."	Our Lord! We believe in that which Thou hast revealed and we follow him whom Thou hast sent. Enroll us among those who witness (to the truth).	Our Lord! we believe in what Thou hast revealed and we follow the messenger, so write us down with those who bear witness.
3 054	And (the unbelievers) plotted and planned, and Allah too planned, and the best of planners is Allah.	And they (the disbelievers) schemed, and Allah schemed (against them): and Allah is the best of schemers.	And they planned and Allah (also) planned, and Allah is the best of planners.
3 055	Behold! Allah said: "O Jesus! I will take thee and raise thee to Myself and clear thee (of the falsehoods) of those who blaspheme; I will make those who follow thee superior to those who reject faith, to the Day of Resurrection: Then shall ye all return unto me, and I will judge between you of the matters wherein ye dispute."	(And remember) when Allah said: O Jesus! Lo! I am gathering thee and causing thee to ascend unto Me, and am cleansing thee of those who disbelieve and am setting those who follow thee above those who disbelieve until the Day of Resurrection. Then unto Me ye will (all) return, and I shall judge between you as to that wherein ye used to differ.	And when Allah said: O Isa, I am going to terminate the period of your stay (on earth) and cause you to ascend unto Me and purify you of those who disbelieve and make those who follow you above those who disbelieve to the day of resurrection; then to Me shall be your return, so I will decide between you concerning that in which you differed.
3 056	"As to those who reject faith, I will punish them with terrible agony in this world and in the Hereafter, nor will they have anyone to help."	As for those who disbelieve I shall chastise them with a heavy chastisement in the world and the Hereafter; and they will have no helpers.	Then as to those who disbelieve, I will chastise them with severe chastisement in this world and the hereafter, and they shall have no helpers.
3 057	"As to those who believe and work righteousness, Allah will pay them (in full) their reward; but Allah loveth not those who do wrong."	And as for those who believe and do good works, He will pay them their wages in full. Allah loveth not wrong-doers.	And as to those who believe and do good deeds, He will pay them fully their rewards; and Allah does not love the unjust.
3 058	"This is what we rehearse unto thee of the Signs and the Message of Wisdom."	This (which) We recite unto thee is a revelation and a wise reminder.	This We recite to you of the communications and the wise reminder.
3 059	The similitude of Jesus before Allah is as that of Adam; He created him from dust, then said to him: "Be". And he was.	Lo! the likeness of Jesus with Allah is as the likeness of Adam. He created him of dust, then He said unto him: Be! and he is.	Surely the likeness of Isa is with Allah as the likeness of Adam; He created him from dust, then said to him, Be, and he was.
3 060	The Truth (comes) from Allah alone; so be not of those who doubt.	(This is) the truth from thy Lord (O Muhammad), so be not thou of those who waver.	(This is) the truth from your Lord, so be not of the disputers.

3 061	If any one disputes in this matter with thee, now after (full) knowledge Hath come to thee, say: "Come! let us gather together,- our sons and your sons, our women and your women, ourselves and yourselves: Then let us earnestly pray, and invoke the curse of Allah on those who lie!"	And whoso disputeth with thee concerning him, after the knowledge which hath come unto thee, say (unto him): Come! We will summon our sons and your sons, and our women and your women, and ourselves and yourselves, then we will pray humbly (to our Lord) and (solemnly) invoke the curse of Allah upon those who lie.	But whoever disputes with you in this matter after what has come to you of knowledge, then say: Come let us call our sons and your sons and our women and your women and our near people and your near people, then let us be earnest in prayer, and pray for the curse of Allah on the liars.
3 062	This is the true account: There is no god except Allah; and Allah - He is indeed the Exalted in Power, the Wise.	Lo! This verily is the true narrative. There is no God save Allah, and lo! Allah, He verily is, is the Mighty, the Wise.	Most surely this is the true explanation, and there is no god but Allah; and most surely Allah-- He is the Mighty, the Wise.
3 063	But if they turn back, Allah hath full knowledge of those who do mischief.	And if they turn away, then lo! Allah is Aware of (who are) the corrupters.	But if they turn back, then surely Allah knows the mischief-makers.
3 064	Say: "O People of the Book! come to common terms as between us and you: That we worship none but Allah; that we associate no partners with him; that we erect not, from among ourselves, Lords and patrons other than Allah." If then they turn back, say ye: "Bear witness that we (at least) are Muslims (bowing to Allah's Will)."	Say: O People of the Scripture! Come to an agreement between us and you: that we shall worship none but Allah, and that we shall ascribe no partner unto Him, and that none of us shall take others for lords beside Allah. And if they turn away, then say: Bear witness that we are they who have surrendered (unto Him).	Say: O followers of the Book! come to an equitable proposition between us and you that we shall not serve any but Allah and (that) we shall not associate aught with Him, and (that) some of us shall not take others for lords besides Allah; but if they turn back, then say: Bear witness that we are Muslims.
3 065	Ye People of the Book! Why dispute ye about Abraham, when the Law and the Gospel Were not revealed Till after him? Have ye no understanding?	O People of the Scripture! Why will ye argue about Abraham, when the Torah and the Gospel were not revealed till after him? Have ye then no sense?	O followers of the Book! why do you dispute about Ibrahim, when the Taurat and the Injeel were not revealed till after him; do you not then understand?
3 066	Ah! Ye are those who fell to disputing (Even) in matters of which ye had some knowledge! but why dispute ye in matters of which ye have no knowledge? It is Allah Who knows, and ye who know not!	Lo! ye are those who argue about that whereof ye have some knowledge: Why then argue ye concerning that whereof ye have no knowledge? Allah knoweth. Ye know not.	Behold! you are they who disputed about that of which you had knowledge; why then do you dispute about that of which you have no knowledge? And Allah knows while you do not know.
3 067	Abraham was not a Jew nor yet a Christian; but he was true in Faith, and bowed his will to Allah's (Which is Islam), and he joined not gods with Allah.	Abraham was not a Jew, nor yet a Christian; but he was an upright man who had surrendered (to Allah), and he was not of the idolaters.	Ibrahim was not a Jew nor a Christian but he was (an) upright (man), a Muslim, and he was not one of the polytheists.
3 068	Without doubt, among men, the nearest of kin to Abraham, are those who follow him, as are also this Prophet and those who believe: And Allah is the Protector of those who have faith.	Lo! those of mankind who have the best claim to Abraham are those who followed him, and this Prophet and those who believe (with him); and Allah is the Protecting Guardian of the believers.	Most surely the nearest of people to Ibrahim are those who followed him and this Prophet and those who believe and Allah is the guardian of the believers.
3 069	It is the wish of a section of the People of the Book to lead you astray. But they shall lead astray (Not you), but themselves, and they do not perceive!	A party of the People of the Scripture long to make you go astray; and they make none to go astray except themselves, but they perceive not.	A party of the followers of the Book desire that they should lead you astray, and they lead not astray but themselves, and they do not perceive.
3 070	Ye People of the Book! Why reject ye the Signs of Allah, of which ye are (Yourselves) witnesses?	O People of the Scripture! Why disbelieve ye in the revelations of Allah, when ye (yourselves) bear witness (to their truth)?	O followers of the Book! Why do you disbelieve in the communications of Allah while you witness (them)?

3 071	Ye People of the Book! Why do ye clothe Truth with falsehood, and conceal the Truth, while ye have knowledge?	O People of the Scripture! Why confound ye truth with falsehood and knowingly conceal the truth?	O followers of the Book! Why do you confound the truth with the falsehood and hide the truth while you know?
3 072	A section of the People of the Book say: "Believe in the morning what is revealed to the believers, but reject it at the end of the day; perchance they may (themselves) Turn back;"	And a party of the People of the Scripture say: Believe in that which hath been revealed unto those who believe at the opening of the day, and disbelieve at the end thereof, in order that they may return;	And a party of the followers of the Book say: Avow belief in that which has been revealed to those who believe, in the first part of the day, and disbelieve at the end of it, perhaps they go back on their religion.
3 073	"And believe no one unless he follows your religion." Say: "True guidance is the Guidance of Allah: (Fear ye) Lest a revelation be sent to someone (else) Like unto that which was sent unto you? or that those (Receiving such revelation) should engage you in argument before your Lord?" Say: "All bounties are in the hand of Allah: He granteth them to whom He pleaseth: And Allah careth for all, and He knoweth all things."	And believe not save in one who followeth your religion - Say (O Muhammad): Lo! the guidance is Allah's Guidance - that anyone is given the like of that which was given unto you or that they may argue with you in the presence of their Lord. Say (O Muhammad): Lo! the bounty is in Allah's hand. He bestoweth it on whom He will. Allah is All-Embracing, All-Knowing.	And do not believe but in him who follows your religion. Say: Surely the (true) guidance is the guidance of Allah-- that one may be given (by Him) the like of what you were given; or they would contend with you by an argument before your Lord. Say: Surely grace is in the hand of Allah, He gives it to whom He pleases; and Allah is Ample-giving, Knowing.
3 074	For His Mercy He specially chooseth whom He pleaseth; for Allah is the Lord of bounties unbounded.	He selecteth for His mercy whom He will. Allah is of Infinite Bounty.	He specially chooses for His mercy whom He pleases; and Allah is the Lord of mighty grace.
3 075	Among the People of the Book are some who, if entrusted with a hoard of gold, will (readily) pay it back; others, who, if entrusted with a single silver coin, will not repay it unless thou constantly stoodest demanding, because, they say, "there is no call on us (to keep faith) with these ignorant (Pagans)." but they tell a lie against Allah, and (well) they know it.	Among the People of the Scripture there is he who, if thou trust him with a weight of treasure, will return it to thee. And among them there is he who, if thou trust him with a piece of gold, will not return it to thee unless thou keep standing over him. That is because they say: We have no duty to the Gentiles. They speak a lie concerning Allah knowingly.	And among the followers of the Book there are some such that if you entrust one (of them) with a heap of wealth, he shall pay it back to you; and among them there are some such that if you entrust one (of them) with a dinar he shall not pay it back to you except so long as you remain firm in demanding it; this is because they say: There is not upon us in the matter of the unlearned people any way (to reproach); and they tell a lie against Allah while they know.
3 076	Nay.- Those that keep their plighted faith and act aright,-verily Allah loves those who act aright.	Nay, but (the chosen of Allah is) he who fulfilleth his pledge and wardeth off (evil); for lo! Allah loveth those who ward off (evil).	Yea, whoever fulfills his promise and guards (against evil)-- then surely Allah loves those who guard (against evil).
3 077	As for those who sell the faith they owe to Allah and their own plighted word for a small price, they shall have no portion in the Hereafter: Nor will Allah (Deign to) speak to them or look at them on the Day of Judgment, nor will He cleans them (of sin): They shall have a grievous penalty.	Lo! those who purchase a small gain at the cost of Allah's covenant and their oaths, they have no portion in the Hereafter. Allah will neither speak to them nor look upon them on the Day of Resurrection, nor will He make them grow. Theirs will be a painful doom.	(As for) those who take a small price for the covenant of Allah and their own oaths-- surely they shall have no portion in the hereafter, and Allah will not speak to them, nor will He look upon them on the day of resurrection nor will He purify them, and they shall have a painful chastisement.

3 078	There is among them a section who distort the Book with their tongues: (As they read) you would think it is a part of the Book, but it is no part of the Book; and they say, "That is from Allah," but it is not from Allah: It is they who tell a lie against Allah, and (well) they know it!	And lo! there is a party of them who distort the Scripture with their tongues, that ye may think that what they say is from the Scripture, when it is not from the Scripture. And they say: It is from Allah, when it is not from Allah; and they speak a lie concerning Allah knowingly.	Most surely there is a party amongst those who distort the Book with their tongue that you may consider it to be (a part) of the Book, and they say, It is from Allah, while it is not from Allah, and they tell a lie against Allah whilst they know.	
3 079	It is not (possible) that a man, to whom is given the Book, and Wisdom, and the prophetic office, should say to people: "Be ye my worshippers rather than Allah's": on the contrary (He would say) "Be ye worshippers of Him Who is truly the Cherisher of all: For ye have taught the Book and ye have studied it earnestly."	It is not (possible) for any human being unto whom Allah had given the Scripture and wisdom and the prophethood that he should afterwards have said unto mankind: Be slaves of me instead of Allah; but (what he said was): Be ye faithful servants of the Lord by virtue of your constant teaching of the Scripture and of your constant study thereof.	It is not meet for a mortal that Allah should give him the Book and the wisdom and prophethood, then he should say to men: Be my servants rather than Allah's; but rather (he would say): Be worshippers of the Lord because of your teaching the Book and your reading (it yourselves).	
3 080	Nor would he instruct you to take angels and prophets for Lords and patrons. What! would he bid you to unbelief after ye have bowed your will (To Allah in Islam)?	And he commanded you not that ye should take the angels and the prophets for lords. Would he command you to disbelieve after ye had surrendered (to Allah)?	And neither would he enjoin you that you should take the angels and the prophets for lords; what! would he enjoin you with unbelief after you are Muslims?	
3 081	Behold! Allah took the covenant of the prophets, saying: "I give you a Book and Wisdom; then comes to you a messenger, confirming what is with you; do ye believe in him and render him help." Allah said: "Do ye agree, and take this my Covenant as binding on you?" They said: "We agree." He said: "Then bear witness, and I am with you among the witnesses."	When Allah made (His) covenant with the prophets, (He said): Behold that which I have given you of the Scripture and knowledge. And afterward there will come unto you a messenger, confirming that which ye possess. Ye shall believe in him and ye shall help him. He said: Do ye agree, and will ye take up My burden (which I lay upon you) in this (matter)? They answered: We agree. He said: Then bear ye witness. I will be a witness with you.	And when Allah made a covenant through the prophets: Certainly what I have given you of Book and wisdom-- then a messenger comes to you verifying that which is with you, you must believe in him, and you must aid him. He said: Do you affirm and accept My compact in this (matter)? They said: We do affirm. He said: Then bear witness, and I (too) am of the bearers of witness with you.	
3 082	If any turn back after this, they are perverted transgressors.	Then whosoever after this shall turn away: they will be miscreants.	Whoever therefore turns back after this, these it is that are the transgressors.	
3 083	Do they seek for other than the Religion of Allah?-while all creatures in the heavens and on earth have, willing or unwilling, bowed to His Will (Accepted Islam), and to Him shall they all be brought back.	Seek they other than the religion of Allah, when unto Him submitteth whosoever is in the heavens and the earth, willingly or unwillingly, and unto Him they will be returned.	Is it then other than Allah's religion that they seek (to follow), and to Him submits whoever is in the heavens and the earth, willingly or unwillingly, and to Him shall they be returned.	
3 084	Say: "We believe in Allah, and in what has been revealed to us and what was revealed to Abraham, Isma'il, Isaac, Jacob, and the Tribes, and in (the Books) given to Moses, Jesus, and the prophets, from their Lord: We make no distinction between one and another among them, and to Allah do we bow our will (in Islam)."	Say (O Muhammad): We believe in Allah and that which is revealed unto us and that which was revealed unto Abraham and Ishmael and Isaac and Jacob and the tribes, and that which was vouchsafed unto Moses and Jesus and the prophets from their Lord. We make no distinction between any of them, and unto Him we have surrendered.	Say: We believe in Allah and what has been revealed to us, and what was revealed to Ibrahim and Ismail and Ishaq and Yaqoub and the tribes, and what was given to Musa and Isa and to the prophets from their Lord; we do not make any distinction between any of them, and to Him do we submit.	

3 085	If anyone desires a religion other than Islam (submission to Allah), never will it be accepted of him; and in the Hereafter He will be in the ranks of those who have lost (all spiritual good).	And whoso seeketh as religion other than the Surrender (to Allah) it will not be accepted from him, and he will be a loser in the Hereafter.	And whoever desires a religion other than Islam, it shall not be accepted from him, and in the hereafter he shall be one of the losers.
3 086	How shall Allah Guide those who reject Faith after they accepted it and bore witness that the Messenger was true and that Clear Signs had come unto them? but Allah guides not a people unjust.	How shall Allah guide a people who disbelieved after their belief and (after) they bore witness that the messenger is true and after clear proofs (of Allah's Sovereignty) had come unto them. And Allah guideth not wrongdoing folk.	How shall Allah guide a people who disbelieved after their believing and (after) they had borne witness that the Messenger was true and clear arguments had come to them; and Allah does not guide the unjust people.
3 087	Of such the reward is that on them (rests) the curse of Allah, of His angels, and of all mankind;-	As for such, their guerdon is that on them rests the curse of Allah and of angels and of men combined.	(As for) these, their reward is that upon them is the curse of Allah and the angels and of men, all together.
3 088	In that will they dwell; nor will their penalty be lightened, nor respite be (their lot);-	They will abide therein. Their doom will not be lightened, neither will they be reprieved;	Abiding in it; their chastisement shall not be lightened nor shall they be respited.
3 089	Except for those that repent (Even) after that, and make amends; for verily Allah is Oft-Forgiving, Most Merciful.	Save those who afterward repent and do right. Lo! Allah is Forgiving, Merciful.	Except those who repent after that and amend, then surely Allah is Forgiving, Merciful.
3 090	But those who reject Faith after they accepted it, and then go on adding to their defiance of Faith,- never will their repentance be accepted; for they are those who have (of set purpose) gone astray.	Lo! those who disbelieve after their (profession of) belief, and afterward grow violent in disbelief: their repentance will not be accepted. And such are those who are astray.	Surely, those who disbelieve after their believing, then increase in unbelief, their repentance shall not be accepted, and these are they that go astray.
3 091	As to those who reject Faith, and die rejecting,- never would be accepted from any such as much gold as the earth contains, though they should offer it for ransom. For such is (in store) a penalty grievous, and they will find no helpers.	Lo! those who disbelieve, and die in disbelief, the (whole) earth full of gold would not be accepted from such an one if it were offered as a ransom (for his soul). Theirs will be a painful doom and they will have no helpers.	Surely, those who disbelieve and die while they are unbelievers, the earth full of gold shall not be accepted from one of them, though he should offer to ransom himself with it, these it is who shall have a painful chastisement, and they shall have no helpers.
3 092	By no means shall ye attain righteousness unless ye give (freely) of that which ye love; and whatever ye give, of a truth Allah knoweth it well.	Ye will not attain unto piety until ye spend of that which ye love. And whatsoever ye spend, Allah is Aware thereof.	By no means shall you attain to righteousness until you spend (benevolently) out of what you love; and whatever thing you spend, Allah surely knows it.
3 093	All food was lawful to the Children of Israel, except what Israel Made unlawful for itself, before the Law (of Moses) was revealed. Say: Bring ye the Law and study it, if ye be men of truth.	All food was lawful unto the Children of Israel, save that which Israel forbade himself, (in days) before the Torah was revealed. Say: Produce the Torah and read it (unto us) if ye are truthful.	All food was lawful to the children of Israel except that which Israel had forbidden to himself, before the Taurat was revealed. Say: Bring then the Taurat and read it, if you are truthful.
3 094	If any, after this, invent a lie and attribute it to Allah, they are indeed unjust wrong-doers.	And whoever shall invent a falsehood after that concerning Allah, such will be wrong-doers.	Then whoever fabricates a lie against Allah after this, these it is that are the unjust.
3 095	Say: "Allah speaketh the Truth: follow the religion of Abraham, the sane in faith; he was not of the Pagans."	Say: Allah speaketh truth. So follow the religion of Abraham, the upright. He was not of the idolaters.	Say: Allah has spoken the truth, therefore follow the religion of Ibrahim, the upright one; and he was not one of the polytheists.

3 096	The first House (of worship) appointed for men was that at Bakka: Full of blessing and of guidance for all kinds of beings:	Lo! the first Sanctuary appointed for mankind was that at Becca, a blessed place, a guidance to the peoples;	Most surely the first house appointed for men is the one at Bekka, blessed and a guidance for the nations.
3 097	In it are Signs Manifest; (for example), the Station of Abraham; whoever enters it attains security; Pilgrimage thereto is a duty men owe to Allah,- those who can afford the journey; but if any deny faith, Allah stands not in need of any of His creatures.	Wherein are plain memorials (of Allah's guidance); the place where Abraham stood up to pray; and whosoever entereth it is safe. And pilgrimage to the House is a duty unto Allah for mankind, for him who can find a way thither. As for him who disbelieveth, (let him know that) lo! Allah is Independent of (all) creatures.	In it are clear signs, the standing place of Ibrahim, and whoever enters it shall be secure, and pilgrimage to the House is incumbent upon men for the sake of Allah, (upon) every one who is able to undertake the journey to it, and whoever disbelieves, then surely Allah is Self-sufficient, above any need of the worlds.
3 098	Say: "O People of the Book! Why reject ye the Signs of Allah, when Allah is Himself witness to all ye do?"	Say: O People of the Scripture! Why disbelieve ye in the revelations of Allah, when Allah (Himself) is Witness of what ye do?	Say: O followers of the Book! why do you disbelieve in the communications of Allah? And Allah is a witness of what you do.
3 099	Say: "O ye People of the Book! Why obstruct ye those who believe, from the path of Allah, Seeking to make it crooked, while ye were yourselves witnesses (to Allah's Covenant)? but Allah is not unmindful of all that ye do."	Say: O People of the Scripture! Why drive ye back believers from the way of Allah, seeking to make it crooked, when ye are witnesses (to Allah's guidance)? Allah is not unaware of what ye do.	Say: O followers of the Book! why do you hinder him who believes from the way of Allah? You seek (to make) it crooked, while you are witness, and Allah is not heedless of what you do.
3 100	O ye who believe! If ye listen to a faction among the People of the Book, they would (indeed) render you apostates after ye have believed!	O ye who believe! If ye obey a party of those who have received the Scripture they will make you disbelievers after your belief.	O you who believe! if you obey a party from among those who have been given the Book, they will turn you back as unbelievers after you have believed.
3 101	And how would ye deny Faith while unto you are rehearsed the Signs of Allah, and among you Lives the Messenger? Whoever holds firmly to Allah will be shown a way that is straight.	How can ye disbelieve, when it is ye unto whom Allah's revelations are recited, and His messenger is in your midst? He who holdeth fast to Allah, he indeed is guided unto a right path.	But how can you disbelieve while it is you to whom the communications of Allah are recited, and among you is His Messenger? And whoever holds fast to Allah, he indeed is guided to the right path.
3 102	O ye who believe! Fear Allah as He should be feared, and die not except in a state of Islam.	O ye who believe! Observe your duty to Allah with right observance, and die not save as those who have surrendered (unto Him)	O you who believe! be careful of (your duty to) Allah with the care which is due to Him, and do not die unless you are Muslims.
3 103	And hold fast, all together, by the rope which Allah (stretches out for you), and be not divided among yourselves; and remember with gratitude Allah's favour on you; for ye were enemies and He joined your hearts in love, so that by His Grace, ye became brethren; and ye were on the brink of the pit of Fire, and He saved you from it. Thus doth Allah make His Signs clear to you: That ye may be guided.	And hold fast, all of you together, to the cable of Allah, and do not separate. And remember Allah's favour unto you: How ye were enemies and He made friendship between your hearts so that ye became as brothers by His grace; and (how) ye were upon the brink of an abyss of fire, and He did save you from it. Thus Allah maketh clear His revelations unto you, that haply ye may be guided,	And hold fast by the covenant of Allah all together and be not disunited, and remember the favor of Allah on you when you were enemies, then He united your hearts so by His favor you became brethren; and you were on the brink of a pit of fire, then He saved you from it, thus does Allah make clear to you His communications that you may follow the right way.
3 104	Let there arise out of you a band of people inviting to all that is good, enjoining what is right, and forbidding what is wrong: They are the ones to attain felicity.	And there may spring from you a nation who invite to goodness, and enjoin right conduct and forbid indecency. Such are they who are successful.	And from among you there should be a party who invite to good and enjoin what is right and forbid the wrong, and these it is that shall be successful.

3 105	Be not like those who are divided amongst themselves and fall into disputations after receiving Clear Signs: For them is a dreadful penalty,-	And be ye not as those who separated and disputed after the clear proofs had come unto them. For such there is an awful doom,	And be not like those who became divided and disagreed after clear arguments had come to them, and these it is that shall have a grievous chastisement.
3 106	On the Day when some faces will be (lit up with) white, and some faces will be (in the gloom of) black: To those whose faces will be black, (will be said): "Did ye reject Faith after accepting it? Taste then the penalty for rejecting Faith."	On the Day when (some) faces will be whitened and (some) faces will be blackened; and as for those whose faces have been blackened, it will be said unto them: Disbelieved ye after your (profession of) belief? Then taste the punishment for that ye disbelieved.	On the day when (some) faces shall turn white and (some) faces shall turn black; then as to those whose faces turn black: Did you disbelieve after your believing? Taste therefore the chastisement because you disbelieved.
3 107	But those whose faces will be (lit with) white,- they will be in (the light of) Allah's mercy: therein to dwell (for ever).	And as for those whose faces have been whitened, in the mercy of Allah they dwell for ever.	And as to those whose faces turn white, they shall be in Allah's mercy; in it they shall-abide.
3 108	These are the Signs of Allah: We rehearse them to thee in Truth: And Allah means no injustice to any of His creatures.	These are revelations of Allah. We recite them unto thee in truth. Allah willeth no injustice to (His) creatures.	These are the communications of Allah which We recite to you with truth, and Allah does not desire any injustice to the creatures.
3 109	To Allah belongs all that is in the heavens and on earth: To Him do all questions go back (for decision).	Unto Allah belongeth whatsoever is in the heavens and whatsoever is in the earth; and unto Allah all things are returned.	And whatever is in the heavens and whatever is in the earth is Allah's; and to Allah all things return.
3 110	Ye are the best of peoples, evolved for mankind, enjoining what is right, forbidding what is wrong, and believing in Allah. If only the People of the Book had faith, it were best for them: among them are some who have faith, but most of them are perverted transgressors.	Ye are the best community that hath been raised up for mankind. Ye enjoin right conduct and forbid indecency; and ye believe in Allah. And if the People of the Scripture had believed it had been better for them. Some of them are believers; but most of them are evil-livers.	You are the best of the nations raised up for (the benefit of) men; you enjoin what is right and forbid the wrong and believe in Allah; and if the followers of the Book had believed it would have been better for them; of them (some) are believers and most of them are transgressors.
3 111	They will do you no harm, barring a trifling annoyance; if they come out to fight you, they will show you their backs, and no help shall they get.	They will not harm you save a trifling hurt, and if they fight against you they will turn and flee. And afterward they will not be helped.	They shall by no means harm you but with a slight evil; and if they fight with you they shall turn (their) backs to you, then shall they not be helped.
3 112	Shame is pitched over them (Like a tent) wherever they are found, except when under a covenant (of protection) from Allah and from men; they draw on themselves wrath from Allah, and pitched over them is (the tent of) destitution. This because they rejected the Signs of Allah, and slew the prophets in defiance of right; this because they rebelled and transgressed beyond bounds.	Ignominy shall be their portion wheresoever they are found save (where they grasp) a rope from Allah and a rope from men. They have incurred anger from their Lord, and wretchedness is laid upon them. That is because they used to disbelieve the revelations of Allah, and slew the prophets wrongfully. That is because they were rebellious and used to transgress.	Abasement is made to cleave to them wherever they are found, except under a covenant with Allah and a covenant with men, and they have become deserving of wrath from Allah, and humiliation is made to cleave to them; this is because they disbelieved in the communications of Allah and slew the prophets unjustly; this is because they disobeyed and exceeded the limits.
3 113	Not all of them are alike: Of the People of the Book are a portion that stand (For the right): They rehearse the Signs of Allah all night long, and they prostrate themselves in adoration.	They are not all alike. Of the People of the Scripture there is a staunch community who recite the revelations of Allah in the night season, falling prostrate (before Him).	They are not all alike; of the followers of the Book there is an upright party; they recite Allah's communications in the nighttime and they adore (Him).

3 114	They believe in Allah and the Last Day; they enjoin what is right, and forbid what is wrong; and they hasten (in emulation) in (all) good works: They are in the ranks of the righteous.	They believe in Allah and the Last Day, and enjoin right conduct and forbid indecency, and vie one with another in good works. These are of the righteous.	They believe in Allah and the last day, and they enjoin what is right and forbid the wrong and they strive with one another in hastening to good deeds, and those are among the good.
3 115	Of the good that they do, nothing will be rejected of them; for Allah knoweth well those that do right.	And whatever good they do, they will not be denied the meed thereof. Allah is Aware of those who ward off (evil).	And whatever good they do, they shall not be denied it, and Allah knows those who guard (against evil).
3 116	Those who reject Faith, neither their possessions nor their (numerous) progeny will avail them aught against Allah: They will be companions of the Fire,-dwelling therein (for ever).	Lo! the riches and the progeny of those who disbelieve will not avail them aught against Allah; and such are rightful owners of the Fire. They will abide therein.	(As for) those who disbelieve, surely neither their wealth nor their children shall avail them in the least against Allah; and these are the inmates of the fire; therein they shall abide.
3 117	What they spend in the life of this (material) world May be likened to a wind which brings a nipping frost: It strikes and destroys the harvest of men who have wronged their own souls: it is not Allah that hath wronged them, but they wrong themselves.	The likeness of that which they spend in this life of the world is as the likeness of a biting, icy wind which smiteth the harvest of a people who have wronged themselves, and devastateth it. Allah wronged them not, but they do wrong themselves.	The likeness of what they spend in the life of this world is as the likeness of wind in which is intense cold (that) smites the seed produce of a people who haw done injustice to their souls and destroys it; and Allah is not unjust to them, but they are unjust to themselves.
3 118	O ye who believe! Take not into your intimacy those outside your ranks: They will not fail to corrupt you. They only desire your ruin: Rank hatred has already appeared from their mouths: What their hearts conceal is far worse. We have made plain to you the Signs, if ye have wisdom.	O ye who believe! Take not for intimates others than your own folk, who would spare no pains to ruin you; they love to hamper you. Hatred is revealed by (the utterance of) their mouths, but that which their breasts hide is greater. We have made plain for you the revelations if ye will understand.	O you who believe! do not take for intimate friends from among others than your own people; they do not fall short of inflicting loss upon you; they love what distresses you; vehement hatred has already appeared from out of their mouths, and what their breasts conceal is greater still; indeed, We have made the communications clear to you, if you will understand.
3 119	Ah! ye are those who love them, but they love you not,- though ye believe in the whole of the Book. When they meet you, they say, "We believe": But when they are alone, they bite off the very tips of their fingers at you in their rage. Say: "Perish in you rage; Allah knoweth well all the secrets of the heart."	Lo! ye are those who love them though they love you not, and ye believe in all the Scripture. When they fall in with you they say: We believe; but when they go apart they bite their finger-tips at you, for rage. Say: Perish in your rage! Lo! Allah is Aware of what is hidden in (your) breasts.	Lo! you are they who will love them while they do not love you, and you believe in the Book (in) the whole of it; and when they meet you they say: We believe, and when they are alone, they bite the ends of their fingers in rage against you. Say: Die in your rage; surely Allah knows what is in the breasts.
3 120	If aught that is good befalls you, it grieves them; but if some misfortune overtakes you, they rejoice at it. But if ye are constant and do right, not the least harm will their cunning do to you; for Allah Compasseth round about all that they do.	If a lucky chance befall you, it is evil unto them, and if disaster strike you they rejoice thereat. But if ye persevere and keep from evil their guile will never harm you. Lo! Allah is Surrounding what they do.	If good befalls you, it grieves them, and if an evil afflicts you, they rejoice at it; and if you are patient and guard yourselves, their scheme will not injure you in any way; surely Allah comprehends what they do.
3 121	Remember that morning Thou didst leave Thy household (early) to post the faithful at their stations for battle: And Allah heareth and knoweth all things:	And when thou settedst forth at daybreak from thy housefolk to assign to the believers their positions for the battle, Allah was Hearer, Knower.	And when you did go forth early in the morning from your family to lodge the believers in encampments for war and Allah is Hearing, Knowing.

3	122	Remember two of your parties Meditated cowardice; but Allah was their protector, and in Allah should the faithful (Ever) put their trust.	When two parties of you almost fell away, and Allah was their Protecting Friend. In Allah let believers put their trust.	When two parties from among you had determined that they should show cowardice, and Allah was the guardian of them both, and in Allah should the believers trust.
3	123	Allah had helped you at Badr, when ye were a contemptible little force; then fear Allah; thus may ye show your gratitude.	Allah had already given you the victory at Badr, when ye were contemptible. So observe your duty to Allah in order that ye may be thankful.	And Allah did certainly assist you at Badr when you were weak; be careful of (your duty to) Allah then, that you may give thanks.
3	124	Remember thou saidst to the Faithful: Is it not enough for you that Allah should help you with three thousand angels (Specially) sent down?	When thou didst say unto the believers: Is it not sufficient for you that your Lord should support you with three thousand angels sent down (to your help)?	When you said to the believers: Does it not suffice you that your Lord should assist you with three thousand of the angels sent down?
3	125	"Yea, - if ye remain firm, and act aright, even if the enemy should rush here on you in hot haste, your Lord would help you with five thousand angels Making a terrific onslaught."	Nay, but if ye persevere, and keep from evil, and (the enemy) attack you suddenly, your Lord will help you with five thousand angels sweeping on.	Yea! if you remain patient and are on your guard, and they come upon you in a headlong manner, your Lord will assist you with five thousand of the havoc-making angels.
3	126	Allah made it but a message of hope for you, and an assurance to your hearts: (in any case) there is no help except from Allah. The Exalted, the Wise:	Allah ordained this only as a message of good cheer for you, and that thereby your hearts might be at rest - Victory cometh only from Allah, the Mighty, the Wise -	And Allah did not make it but as good news for you, and that your hearts might be at ease thereby, and victory is only from Allah, the Mighty, the Wise.
3	127	That He might cut off a fringe of the Unbelievers or expose them to infamy, and they should then be turned back, frustrated of their purpose.	That He may cut off a part of those who disbelieve, or overwhelm them so that they retire, frustrated.	That He may cut off a portion from among those who disbelieve, or abase them so that they should return disappointed of attaining what they desired.
3	128	Not for thee, (but for Allah), is the decision: Whether He turn in mercy to them, or punish them; for they are indeed wrong-doers.	It is no concern at all of thee (Muhammad) whether He relent toward them or punish them; for they are evil-doers.	You have no concern in the affair whether He turns to them (mercifully) or chastises them, for surely they are unjust.
3	129	To Allah belongeth all that is in the heavens and on earth. He forgiveth whom He pleaseth and punisheth whom He pleaseth; but Allah is Oft-Forgiving, Most Merciful.	Unto Allah belongeth whatsoever is in the heavens and whatsoever is in the earth. He forgiveth whom He will, and punisheth whom He will. Allah is Forgiving, Merciful.	And whatever is in the heavens and whatever is in the earth is Allah's; He forgives whom He pleases and chastises whom He pleases; and Allah is Forgiving, Merciful.
3	130	O ye who believe! Devour not usury, doubled and multiplied; but fear Allah; that ye may (really) prosper.	O ye who believe! Devour not usury, doubling and quadrupling (the sum lent). Observe your duty to Allah, that ye may be successful.	O you who believe! do not devour usury, making it double and redouble, and be careful of (your duty to) Allah, that you may be successful.
3	131	Fear the Fire, which is repaired for those who reject Faith:	And ward off (from yourselves) the Fire prepared for disbelievers.	And guard yourselves against the fire which has been prepared for the unbelievers.
3	132	And obey Allah and the Messenger; that ye may obtain mercy.	And obey Allah and the messenger, that ye may find mercy.	And obey Allah and the Messenger, that you may be shown mercy.
3	133	Be quick in the race for forgiveness from your Lord, and for a Garden whose width is that (of the whole) of the heavens and of the earth, prepared for the righteous,-	And vie one with another for forgiveness from your Lord, and for a paradise as wide as are the heavens and the earth, prepared for those who ward off (evil);	And hasten to forgiveness from your Lord; and a Garden, the extensiveness of which is (as) the heavens and the earth, it is prepared for those who guard (against evil).

3 134	Those who spend (freely), whether in prosperity, or in adversity; who restrain anger, and pardon (all) men;- for Allah loves those who do good;-	Those who spend (of that which Allah hath given them) in ease and in adversity, those who control their wrath and are forgiving toward mankind; Allah loveth the good;	Those who spend (benevolently) in ease as well as in straitness, and those who restrain (their) anger and pardon men; and Allah loves the doers of good (to others).
3 135	And those who, having done something to be ashamed of, or wronged their own souls, earnestly bring Allah to mind, and ask for forgiveness for their sins, and who can forgive sins except Allah?- and are never obstinate in persisting knowingly in (the wrong) they have done.	And those who, when they do an evil thing or wrong themselves, remember Allah and implore forgiveness for their sins - Who forgiveth sins save Allah only? - and will not knowingly repeat (the wrong) they did.	And those who when they commit an indecency or do injustice to their souls remember Allah and ask forgiveness for their faults-- and who forgives the faults but Allah, and (who) do not knowingly persist in what they have done.
3 136	For such the reward is forgiveness from their Lord, and Gardens with rivers flowing underneath,- an eternal dwelling: How excellent a recompense for those who work (and strive)!	The reward of such will be forgiveness from their Lord, and Gardens underneath which rivers flow, wherein they will abide for ever - a bountiful reward for workers!	(As for) these-- their reward is forgiveness from their Lord, and gardens beneath which rivers flow, to abide in them, and excellent is the reward of the laborers.
3 137	Many were the Ways of Life that have passed away before you: travel through the earth, and see what was the end of those who rejected Truth.	Systems have passed away before you. Do but travel in the land and see the nature of the consequence for those who did deny (the messengers).	Indeed there have been examples before you; therefore travel in the earth and see what was the end of the rejecters.
3 138	Here is a plain statement to men, a guidance and instruction to those who fear Allah!	This is a declaration for mankind, a guidance and an admonition unto those who ward off (evil)	This is a clear statement for men, and a guidance and an admonition to those who guard (against evil).
3 139	So lose not heart, nor fall into despair: For ye must gain mastery if ye are true in Faith.	Faint not nor grieve, for ye will overcome them if ye are (indeed) believers.	And be not infirm, and be not grieving, and you shall have the upper hand if you are believers.
3 140	If a wound hath touched you, be sure a similar wound hath touched the others. Such days (of varying fortunes) We give to men and men by turns: that Allah may know those that believe, and that He may take to Himself from your ranks Martyr-witnesses (to Truth). And Allah loveth not those that do wrong.	If ye have received a blow, the (disbelieving) people have received a blow the like thereof. These are (only) the vicissitudes which We cause to follow one another for mankind, to the end that Allah may know those who believe and may choose witnesses from among you; and Allah loveth not wrong-doers.	If a wound has afflicted you (at Ohud), a wound like it has also afflicted the (unbelieving) people; and We bring these days to men by turns, and that Allah may know those who believe and take witnesses from among you; and Allah does not love the unjust.
3 141	Allah's object also is to purge those that are true in Faith and to deprive of blessing Those that resist Faith.	And that Allah may prove those who believe, and may blight the disbelievers.	And that He may purge those who believe and deprive the unbelievers of blessings.
3 142	Did ye think that ye would enter Heaven without Allah testing those of you who fought hard (In His Cause) and remained steadfast?	Or deemed ye that ye would enter paradise while yet Allah knoweth not those of you who really strive, nor knoweth those (of you) who are steadfast?	Do you think that you will enter the garden while Allah has not yet known those who strive hard from among you, and (He has not) known the patient.
3 143	Ye did indeed wish for death before ye met him: Now ye have seen him with your own eyes, (And ye flinch!)	And verily ye used to wish for death before ye met it (in the field). Now ye have seen it with your eyes!	And certainly you desired death before you met it, so indeed you have seen it and you look (at it)

3 144	Muhammad is no more than a messenger: many Were the messenger that passed away before him. If he died or were slain, will ye then Turn back on your heels? If any did turn back on his heels, not the least harm will he do to Allah; but Allah (on the other hand) will swiftly reward those who (serve Him) with gratitude.	Muhammad is but a messenger, messengers (the like of whom) have passed away before him. Will it be that, when he dieth or is slain, ye will turn back on your heels? He who turneth back on his heels doth no hurt to Allah, and Allah will reward the thankful.	And Muhammad is no more than a messenger; the messengers have already passed away before him; if then he dies or is killed will you turn back upon your heels? And whoever turns back upon his heels, he will by no means do harm to Allah in the least and Allah will reward the grateful.
3 145	Nor can a soul die except by Allah's leave, the term being fixed as by writing. If any do desire a reward in this life, We shall give it to him; and if any do desire a reward in the Hereafter, We shall give it to him. And swiftly shall We reward those that (serve us with) gratitude.	No soul can ever die except by Allah's leave and at a term appointed. Whoso desireth the reward of the world, We bestow on him thereof; and whoso desireth the reward of the Hereafter, We bestow on him thereof. We shall reward the thankful.	And a soul will not die but with the permission of Allah the term is fixed; and whoever desires the reward of this world, I shall give him of it, and whoever desires the reward of the hereafter I shall give him of it, and I will reward the grateful.
3 146	How many of the prophets fought (in Allah's way), and with them (fought) Large bands of godly men? but they never lost heart if they met with disaster in Allah's way, nor did they weaken (in will) nor give in. And Allah Loves those who are firm and steadfast.	And with how many a prophet have there been a number of devoted men who fought (beside him). They quailed not for aught that befell them in the way of Allah, nor did they weaken, nor were they brought low. Allah loveth the steadfast.	And how many a prophet has fought with whom were many worshippers of the Lord; so they did not become weak-hearted on account of what befell them in Allah's way, nor did they weaken, nor did they abase themselves; and Allah loves the patient.
3 147	All that they said was: "Our Lord! Forgive us our sins and anything We may have done that transgressed our duty: Establish our feet firmly, and help us against those that resist Faith."	Their cry was only that they said: Our Lord! forgive us for our sins and wasted efforts, make our foothold sure, and give us victory over the disbelieving folk.	And their saying was no other than that they said: Our Lord! forgive us our faults and our extravagance in our affair and make firm our feet and help us against the unbelieving people.
3 148	And Allah gave them a reward in this world, and the excellent reward of the Hereafter. For Allah Loveth those who do good.	So Allah gave them the reward of the world and the good reward of the Hereafter. Allah loveth those whose deeds are good.	So Allah gave them the reward of this world and better reward of the hereafter and Allah loves those who do good (to others).
3 149	O ye who believe! If ye obey the Unbelievers, they will drive you back on your heels, and ye will turn back (from Faith) to your own loss.	O ye who believe! if ye obey those who disbelieve, they will make you turn back on your heels, and ye turn back as losers.	O you who believe! if you obey those who disbelieve they will turn you back upon your heels, so you will turn back losers.
3 150	Nay, Allah is your protector, and He is the best of helpers.	But Allah is your Protector, and He is the Best of Helpers.	Nay! Allah is your Patron and He is the best of the helpers.
3 151	Soon shall We cast terror into the hearts of the Unbelievers, for that they joined companions with Allah, for which He had sent no authority: their abode will be the Fire: And evil is the home of the wrong-doers!	We shall cast terror into the hearts of those who disbelieve because they ascribe unto Allah partners, for which no warrant hath been revealed. Their habitation is the Fire, and hapless the abode of the wrong-doers.	We will cast terror into the hearts of those who disbelieve, because they set up with Allah that for which He has sent down no authority, and their abode is the fire, and evil is the abode of the unjust.

3 152	Allah did indeed fulfil His promise to you when ye with His permission Were about to annihilate your enemy,-until ye flinched and fell to disputing about the order, and disobeyed it after He brought you in sight (of the booty) which ye covet. Among you are some that hanker after this world and some that desire the Hereafter. Then did He divert you from your foes in order to test you but He forgave you: For Allah is full of grace to those who believe.	Allah verily made good His promise unto you when ye routed them by His leave, until (the moment) when your courage failed you, and ye disagreed about the order and ye disobeyed, after He had shown you that for which ye long. Some of you desired the world, and some of you desired the Hereafter. Therefore He made you flee from them, that He might try you. Yet now He hath forgiven you. Allah is a Lord of Kindness to believers.	And certainly Allah made good to you His promise when you slew them by His permission, until when you became weak-hearted and disputed about the affair and disobeyed after He had shown you that which you loved; of you were some who desired this world and of you were some who desired the hereafter; then He turned you away from them that He might try you; and He has certainly pardoned you, and Allah is Gracious to the believers.
3 153	Behold! ye were climbing up the high ground, without even casting a side glance at any one, and the Messenger in your rear was calling you back. There did Allah give you one distress after another by way of requital, to teach you not to grieve for (the booty) that had escaped you and for (the ill) that had befallen you. For Allah is well aware of all that ye do.	When ye climbed (the hill) and paid no heed to anyone, while the messenger, in your rear, was calling you (to fight). Therefor He rewarded you grief for (his) grief, that (He might teach) you not to sorrow either for that which ye missed or for that which befell you. Allah is Informed of what ye do.	When you ran off precipitately and did not wait for any one, and the Messenger was calling you from your rear, so He gave you another sorrow instead of (your) sorrow, so that you might not grieve at what had escaped you, nor (at) what befell you; and Allah is aware of what you do.
3 154	After (the excitement) of the distress, He sent down calm on a band of you overcome with slumber, while another band was stirred to anxiety by their own feelings, Moved by wrong suspicions of Allah-suspicions due to ignorance. They said: "What affair is this of ours?" Say thou: Indeed, this affair is wholly Allah's. They hide in their minds what they dare not reveal to thee. They say (to themselves): "If we had had anything to do with this affair, We should not have been in the slaughter here." Say: "Even if you had remained in your homes, those for whom death was decreed would certainly have gone forth to the place of their death"; but (all this was) that Allah might test what is in your breasts and purge what is in your hearts. For Allah knoweth well the secrets of your hearts.	Then, after grief, He sent down security for you. As slumber did it overcome a party of you, while (the other) party, who were anxious on their own account, thought wrongly of Allah, the thought of ignorance. They said: Have we any part in the cause? Say (O Muhammad): The cause belongeth wholly to Allah. They hide within themselves (a thought) which they reveal not unto thee, saying: Had we had any part in the cause we should not have been slain here. Say: Even though ye had been in your houses, those appointed to be slain would have gone forth to the places where they were to lie. (All this hath been) in order that Allah might try what is in your breasts and prove what is in your hearts. Allah is Aware of what is hidden in the breasts (of men).	Then after sorrow He sent down security upon you, a calm coming upon a party of you, and (there was) another party whom their own souls had rendered anxious; they entertained about Allah thoughts of ignorance quite unjustly, saying: We have no hand in the affair. Say: Surely the affair is wholly (in the hands) of Allah. They conceal within their souls what they would not reveal to you. They say: Had we any hand in the affair, we would not have been slain here. Say: Had you remained in your houses, those for whom slaughter was ordained would certainly have gone forth to the places where they would be slain, and that Allah might test what was in your breasts and that He might purge what was in your hearts; and Allah knows what is in the breasts.
3 155	Those of you who turned back on the day the two hosts Met,-it was Satan who caused them to fail, because of some (evil) they had done. But Allah Has blotted out (their fault): For Allah is Oft-Forgiving, Most Forbearing.	Lo! those of you who turned back on the day when the two hosts met, Satan alone it was who caused them to backslide, because of some of that which they have earned. Now Allah hath forgiven them. Lo! Allah is Forgiving, Clement.	(As for) those of you who turned back on the day when the two armies met, only the Shaitan sought to cause them to make a slip on account of some deeds they had done, and certainly Allah has pardoned them; surely Allah is Forgiving, Forbearing.

3 156	O ye who believe! Be not like the Unbelievers, who say of their brethren, when they are travelling through the Earth or engaged in fighting: "If they had stayed with us, they would not have died, or been slain." This that Allah may make it a cause of sighs and regrets in their hearts. It is Allah that gives Life and Death, and Allah sees well all that ye do.	O ye who believe! Be not as those who disbelieved and said of their brethren who went abroad in the land or were fighting in the field: If they had been (here) with us they would not have died or been killed: that Allah may make it anguish in their hearts. Allah giveth life and causeth death; and Allah is Seer of what ye do.	O you who believe! be not like those who disbelieve and say of their brethren when they travel in the earth or engage in fighting: Had they been with us, they would not have died and they would not have been slain; so Allah makes this to be an intense regret in their hearts; and Allah gives life and causes death and Allah sees what you do.
3 157	And if ye are slain, or die, in the way of Allah, forgiveness and mercy from Allah are far better than all they could amass.	And what though ye be slain in Allah's way or die therein? Surely pardon from Allah and mercy are better than all that they amass.	And if you are slain in the way of Allah or you die, certainly forgiveness from Allah and mercy is better than what they amass.
3 158	And if ye die, or are slain, Lo! it is unto Allah that ye are brought together.	What though ye be slain or die, when unto Allah ye are gathered?	And if indeed you die or you are slain, certainly to Allah shall you be gathered together.
3 159	It is part of the Mercy of Allah that thou dost deal gently with them Wert thou severe or harsh-hearted, they would have broken away from about thee: so pass over (Their faults), and ask for (Allah's) forgiveness for them; and consult them in affairs (of moment). Then, when thou hast Taken a decision put thy trust in Allah. For Allah loves those who put their trust (in Him).	It was by the mercy of Allah that thou wast lenient with them (O Muhammad), for if thou hadst been stern and fierce of heart they would have dispersed from round about thee. So pardon them and ask forgiveness for them and consult with them upon the conduct of affairs. And when thou art resolved, then put thy trust in Allah. Lo! Allah loveth those who put their trust (in Him).	Thus it is due to mercy from Allah that you deal with them gently, and had you been rough, hard hearted, they would certainly have dispersed from around you; pardon them therefore and ask pardon for them, and take counsel with them in the affair; so when you have decided, then place your trust in Allah; surely Allah loves those who trust.
3 160	If Allah helps you, none can overcome you: If He forsakes you, who is there, after that, that can help you? in Allah, then, let believers put their trust.	If Allah is your helper none can overcome you, and if He withdraw His help from you, who is there who can help you after Him? In Allah let believers put their trust.	If Allah assists you, then there is none that can overcome you, and if He forsakes you, who is there then that can assist you after Him? And on Allah should the believers rely.
3 161	No prophet could (ever) be false to his trust. If any person is so false, He shall, on the Day of Judgment, restore what he misappropriated; then shall every soul receive its due,- whatever it earned,- and none shall be dealt with unjustly.	It is not for any prophet to embezzle. Whoso embezzleth will bring what he embezzled with him on the Day of Resurrection. Then every soul will be paid in full what it hath earned; and they will not be wronged.	And it is not attributable to a prophet that he should act unfaithfully; and he who acts unfaithfully shall bring that in respect of which he has acted unfaithfully on the day of resurrection; then shall every soul be paid back fully what it has earned, and they shall not be dealt with unjustly.
3 162	Is the man who follows the good pleasure of Allah Like the man who draws on himself the wrath of Allah, and whose abode is in Hell?- A woeful refuge!	Is one who followeth the pleasure of Allah as one who hath earned condemnation from Allah, whose habitation is the Fire, a hapless journey's end?	Is then he who follows the pleasure of Allah like him who has made himself deserving of displeasure from Allah, and his abode is hell; and it is an evil destination.
3 163	They are in varying gardens in the sight of Allah, and Allah sees well all that they do.	There are degrees (of grace and reprobation) with Allah, and Allah is Seer of what they do.	There are (varying) grades with Allah, and Allah sees what they do.

3 164	Allah did confer a great favour on the believers when He sent among them a messenger from among themselves, rehearsing unto them the Signs of Allah, sanctifying them, and instructing them in Scripture and Wisdom, while, before that, they had been in manifest error.	Allah verily hath shown grace to the believers by sending unto them a messenger of their own who reciteth unto them His revelations, and causeth them to grow, and teacheth them the Scripture and wisdom; although before (he came to them) they were in flagrant error.	Certainly Allah conferred a benefit upon the believers when He raised among them a Messenger from among themselves, reciting to them His communications and purifying them, and teaching them the Book and the wisdom, although before that they were surely in manifest error.
3 165	What! When a single disaster smites you, although ye smote (your enemies) with one twice as great, do ye say?- "Whence is this?" Say (to them): "It is from yourselves: For Allah hath power over all things."	And was it so, when a disaster smote you, though ye had smitten (them with a disaster) twice (as great), that ye said: How is this? Say (unto them, O Muhammad): It is from yourselves. Lo! Allah is Able to do all things.	What! when a misfortune befell you, and you had certainly afflicted (the unbelievers) with twice as much, you began to say: Whence is this? Say: It is from yourselves; surely Allah has power over all things.
3 166	What ye suffered on the day the two armies Met, was with the leave of Allah, in order that He might test the believers,-	That which befell you, on the day when the two armies met, was by permission of Allah; that He might know the true believers;	And what befell you on the day when the two armies met (at Ohud) was with Allah's knowledge, and that He might know the believers.
3 167	And the Hypocrites also. These were told: "Come, fight in the way of Allah, or (at least) drive (The foe from your city)." They said: "Had we known how to fight, we should certainly have followed you." They were that day nearer to Unbelief than to Faith, saying with their lips what was not in their hearts but Allah hath full knowledge of all they conceal.	And that He might know the hypocrites, unto whom it was said: Come, fight in the way of Allah, or defend yourselves. They answered: If we knew aught of fighting we would follow you. On that day they were nearer disbelief than faith. They utter with their mouths a thing which is not in their hearts. Allah is Best Aware of what they hide.	And that He might know the hypocrites; and it was said to them: Come, fight in Allah's way, or defend yourselves. They said: If we knew fighting, we would certainly have followed you. They were on that day much nearer to unbelief than to belief. They say with their mouths what is not in their hearts, and Allah best knows what they conceal.
3 168	(They are) the ones that say, (of their brethren slain), while they themselves sit (at ease): "If only they had listened to us they would not have been slain." Say: "Avert death from your own selves, if ye speak the truth."	Those who, while they sat at home, said of their brethren (who were fighting for the cause of Allah): If they had been guided by us they would not have been slain. Say (unto them, O Muhammad): Then avert death from yourselves if ye are truthful.	Those who said of their brethren whilst they (themselves) held back: Had they obeyed us, they would not have been killed. Say: Then avert death from yourselves if you speak the truth.
3 169	Think not of those who are slain in Allah's way as dead. Nay, they live, finding their sustenance in the presence of their Lord;	Think not of those, who are slain in the way of Allah, as dead. Nay, they are living. With their Lord they have provision.	And reckon not those who are killed in Allah's way as dead; nay, they are alive (and) are provided sustenance from their Lord;
3 170	They rejoice in the bounty provided by Allah: And with regard to those left behind, who have not yet joined them (in their bliss), the (Martyrs) glory in the fact that on them is no fear, nor have they (cause to) grieve.	Jubilant (are they) because of that which Allah hath bestowed upon them of His bounty, rejoicing for the sake of those who have not joined them but are left behind: That there shall no fear come upon them neither shall they grieve.	Rejoicing in what Allah has given them out of His grace and they rejoice for the sake of those who, (being left) behind them, have not yet joined them, that they shall have no fear, nor shall they grieve.
3 171	They glory in the Grace and the bounty from Allah, and in the fact that Allah suffereth not the reward of the Faithful to be lost (in the least).	They rejoice because of favour from Allah and kindness, and that Allah wasteth not the wage of the believers.	They rejoice on account of favor from Allah and (His) grace, and that Allah will not waste the reward of the believers.

3 172	Of those who answered the call of Allah and the Messenger, even after being wounded, those who do right and refrain from wrong have a great reward;-	As for those who heard the call of Allah and His messenger after the harm befell them (in the fight); for such of them as do right and ward off (evil), there is great reward.	(As for) those who responded (at Ohud) to the call of Allah and the Messenger after the wound had befallen them, those among them who do good (to others) and guard (against evil) shall have a great reward.
3 173	Men said to them: "A great army is gathering against you": And frightened them: But it (only) increased their Faith: They said: "For us Allah sufficeth, and He is the best disposer of affairs."	Those unto whom men said: Lo! the people have gathered against you, therefor fear them. (The threat of danger) but increased the faith of them and they cried: Allah is Sufficient for us! Most Excellent is He in Whom we trust!	Those to whom the people said: Surely men have gathered against you, therefore fear them, but this increased their faith, and they said: Allah is sufficient for us and most excellent is the Protector.
3 174	And they returned with Grace and bounty from Allah: no harm ever touched them: For they followed the good pleasure of Allah: And Allah is the Lord of bounties unbounded.	So they returned with grace and favour from Allah, and no harm touched them. They followed the good pleasure of Allah, and Allah is of Infinite Bounty.	So they returned with favor from Allah and (His) grace, no evil touched them and they followed the pleasure of Allah; and Allah is the Lord of mighty grace.
3 175	It is only the Evil One that suggests to you the fear of his votaries: Be ye not afraid of them, but fear Me, if ye have Faith.	It is only the devil who would make (men) fear his partisans. Fear them not; fear Me, if ye are true believers.	It is only the Shaitan that causes you to fear from his friends, but do not fear them, and fear Me if you are believers.
3 176	Let not those grieve thee who rush headlong into Unbelief: Not the least harm will they do to Allah: Allah's plan is that He will give them no portion in the Hereafter, but a severe punishment.	Let not their conduct grieve thee, who run easily to disbelief, for lo! they injure Allah not at all. It is Allah's Will to assign them no portion in the Hereafter, and theirs will be an awful doom.	And let not those grieve you who fall into unbelief hastily; surely they can do no harm to Allah at all; Allah intends that He should not give them any portion in the hereafter, and they shall have a grievous chastisement.
3 177	Those who purchase Unbelief at the price of faith,- not the least harm will they do to Allah, but they will have a grievous punishment.	Those who purchase disbelief at the price of faith harm Allah not at all, but theirs will be a painful doom.	Surely those who have bought unbelief at the price of faith shall do no harm at all to Allah, and they shall have a painful chastisement.
3 178	Let not the Unbelievers think that our respite to them is good for themselves: We grant them respite that they may grow in their iniquity: But they will have a shameful punishment.	And let not those who disbelieve imagine that the rein We give them bodeth good unto their souls. We only give them rein that they may grow in sinfulness. And theirs will be a shameful doom.	And let not those who disbelieve think that Our granting them respite is better for their souls; We grant them respite only that they may add to their sins; and they shall have a disgraceful chastisement.
3 179	Allah will not leave the believers in the state in which ye are now, until He separates what is evil from what is good nor will He disclose to you the secrets of the Unseen. But He chooses of His Messengers (For the purpose) whom He pleases. So believe in Allah. And His messengers: And if ye believe and do right, ye have a reward without measure.	It is not (the purpose) of Allah to leave you in your present state till He shall separate the wicked from the good. And it is not (the purpose of) Allah to let you know the Unseen. But Allah chooseth of His messengers whom He will, (to receive knowledge thereof). So believe in Allah and His messengers. If ye believe and ward off (evil), yours will be a vast reward.	On no account will Allah leave the believers in the condition which you are in until He separates the evil from the good; nor is Allah going to make you acquainted with the unseen, but Allah chooses of His messengers whom He pleases; therefore believe in Allah and His messengers; and if you believe and guard (against evil), then you shall have a great reward.

3 180	And let not those who covetously withhold of the gifts which Allah Hath given them of His Grace, think that it is good for them: Nay, it will be the worse for them: soon shall the things which they covetously withheld be tied to their necks Like a twisted collar, on the Day of Judgment. To Allah belongs the heritage of the heavens and the earth; and Allah is well-acquainted with all that ye do.	And let not those who hoard up that which Allah hath bestowed upon them of His bounty think that it is better for them. Nay, it is worse for them. That which they hoard will be their collar on the Day of Resurrection. Allah's is the heritage of the heavens and the earth, and Allah is Informed of what ye do.	And let not those deem, who are niggardly in giving away that which Allah has granted them out of His grace, that it is good for them; nay, it is worse for them; they shall have that whereof they were niggardly made to cleave to their necks on the resurrection day; and Allah's is the heritage of the heavens and the earth; and Allah is aware of what you do.
3 181	Allah hath heard the taunt of those who say: "Truly, Allah is indigent and we are rich!"- We shall certainly record their word and (their act) of slaying the prophets in defiance of right, and We shall say: "Taste ye the penalty of the Scorching Fire!"	Verily Allah heard the saying of those who said, (when asked for contributions to the war): "Allah, forsooth, is poor, and we are rich!" We shall record their saying with their slaying of the prophets wrongfully and We shall say: Taste ye the punishment of burning!	Allah has certainly heard the saying of those who said: Surely Allah is poor and we are rich. I will record what they say, and their killing the prophets unjustly, and I will say: Taste the chastisement of burning.
3 182	"This is because of the (unrighteous deeds) which your hands sent on before ye: For Allah never harms those who serve Him."	This is on account of that which your own hands have sent before (you to the judgment). Allah is no oppressor of (His) bondmen.	This is for what your own hands have sent before and because Allah is not in the least unjust to the servants.
3 183	They (also) said: "Allah took our promise not to believe in an messenger unless He showed us a sacrifice consumed by Fire (From heaven)." Say: "There came to you messengers before me, with clear Signs and even with what ye ask for: why then did ye slay them, if ye speak the truth?"	(The same are) those who say: Lo! Allah hath charged us that we believe not in any messenger until he bring us an offering which fire (from heaven) shall devour. Say (unto them, O Muhammad): Messengers came unto you before me with miracles, and with that (very miracle) which ye describe. Why then did ye slay them? (Answer that) if ye are truthful!	(Those are they) who said: Surely Allah has enjoined us that we should not believe in any messenger until he brings us an offering which the fire consumes. Say: Indeed, there came to you messengers before me with clear arguments and with that which you demand; why then did you kill them if you are truthful?
3 184	Then if they reject thee, so were rejected messengers before thee, who came with Clear Signs, Books of dark prophecies, and the Book of Enlightenment.	And if they deny thee, even so did they deny messengers who were before thee, who came with miracles and with the Psalms and with the Scripture giving light.	But if they reject you, so indeed were rejected before you messengers who came with clear arguments and scriptures and the illuminating book.
3 185	Every soul shall have a taste of death: And only on the Day of Judgment shall you be paid your full recompense. Only he who is saved far from the Fire and admitted to the Garden will have attained the object (of Life): For the life of this world is but goods and chattels of deception.	Every soul will taste of death. And ye will be paid on the Day of Resurrection only that which ye have fairly earned. Whoso is removed from the Fire and is made to enter paradise, he indeed is triumphant. The life of this world is but comfort of illusion.	Every soul shall taste of death, and you shall only be paid fully your reward on the resurrection day; then whoever is removed far away from the fire and is made to enter the garden he indeed has attained the object; and the life of this world is nothing but a provision of vanities.
3 186	Ye shall certainly be tried and tested in your possessions and in your personal selves; and ye shall certainly Hear much that will grieve you, from those who received the Book before you and from those who worship many gods. But if ye persevere patiently, and guard against evil,-then that will be a determining factor in all affairs.	Assuredly ye will be tried in your property and in your persons, and ye will hear much wrong from those who were given the Scripture before you, and from the idolaters. But if ye persevere and ward off (evil), then that is of the steadfast heart of things.	You shall certainly be tried respecting your wealth and your souls, and you shall certainly hear from those who have been given the Book before you and from those who are polytheists much annoying talk; and if you are patient and guard (against evil), surely this is one of the affairs (which should be) determined upon.

3 187	And remember Allah took a covenant from the People of the Book, to make it known and clear to mankind, and not to hide it; but they threw it away behind their backs, and purchased with it some miserable gain! And vile was the bargain they made!	And (remember) when Allah laid a charge on those who had received the Scripture (He said): Ye are to expound it to mankind and not to hide it. But they flung it behind their backs and bought thereby a little gain. Verily evil is that which they have gained thereby.	And when Allah made a covenant with those who were given the Book: You shall certainly make it known to men and you shall not hide it; but they cast it behind their backs and took a small price for it; so evil is that which they buy.
3 188	Think not that those who exult in what they have brought about, and love to be praised for what they have not done,- think escape the penalty. For them is a penalty Grievous indeed.	Think not that those who exult in what they have given, and love to be praised for what they have not done - Think not, they are in safety from the doom. A painful doom is theirs.	Do not think those who rejoice for what they have done and love that they should be praised for what they have not done-- so do by no means think them to be safe from the chastisement, and they shall have a painful chastisement.
3 189	To Allah belongeth the dominion of the heavens and the earth; and Allah hath power over all things.	Unto Allah belongeth the Sovereignty of the heavens and the earth. Allah is Able to do all things.	And Allah's is the kingdom of the heavens and the earth, and Allah has power over all things.
3 190	Behold! in the creation of the heavens and the earth, and the alternation of night and day,- there are indeed Signs for men of understanding,-	Lo! In the creation of the heavens and the earth and (in) the difference of night and day are tokens (of His Sovereignty) for men of understanding,	Most surely in the creation of the heavens and the earth and the alternation of the night and the day there are signs for men who understand.
3 191	Men who celebrate the praises of Allah, standing, sitting, and lying down on their sides, and contemplate the (wonders of) creation in the heavens and the earth, (With the thought): "Our Lord! not for naught Hast Thou created (all) this! Glory to Thee! Give us salvation from the penalty of the Fire."	Such as remember Allah, standing, sitting, and reclining, and consider the creation of the heavens and the earth, (and say): Our Lord! Thou createdst not this in vain. Glory be to Thee! Preserve us from the doom of Fire.	Those who remember Allah standing and sitting and lying on their sides and reflect on the creation of the heavens and the earth: Our Lord! Thou hast not created this in vain! Glory be to Thee; save us then from the chastisement of the fire:
3 192	"Our Lord! any whom Thou dost admit to the Fire, Truly Thou coverest with shame, and never will wrong-doers Find any helpers!"	Our Lord! Whom Thou causest to enter the Fire: him indeed Thou hast confounded. For evil-doers there will be no helpers.	Our Lord! surely whomsoever Thou makest enter the fire, him Thou hast indeed brought to disgrace, and there shall be no helpers for the unjust:
3 193	"Our Lord! we have heard the call of one calling (Us) to Faith, 'Believe ye in the Lord,' and we have believed. Our Lord! Forgive us our sins, blot out from us our iniquities, and take to Thyself our souls in the company of the righteous."	Our Lord! Lo! we have heard a crier calling unto Faith: "Believe ye in your Lord!" So we believed. Our Lord! Therefor forgive us our sins, and remit from us our evil deeds, and make us die the death of the righteous.	Our Lord! surely we have heard a preacher calling to the faith, saying: Believe in your Lord, so we did believe; Our Lord! forgive us therefore our faults, and cover our evil deeds and make us die with the righteous.
3 194	"Our Lord! Grant us what Thou didst promise unto us through Thine messengers, and save us from shame on the Day of Judgment: For Thou never breakest Thy promise."	Our Lord! And give us that which Thou hast promised to us by Thy messengers. Confound us not upon the Day of Resurrection. Lo! Thou breakest not the tryst.	Our Lord! and grant us what Thou hast promised us by Thy messengers; and disgrace us not on the day of resurrection; surely Thou dost not fail to perform the promise.

3 195	And their Lord hath accepted of them, and answered them: "Never will I suffer to be lost the work of any of you, be he male or female: Ye are members, one of another: Those who have left their homes, or been driven out therefrom, or suffered harm in My Cause, or fought or been slain,- verily, I will blot out from them their iniquities, and admit them into Gardens with rivers flowing beneath;- A reward from the presence of Allah, and from His presence is the best of rewards."	And their Lord hath heard them (and He saith): Lo! I suffer not the work of any worker, male or female, to be lost. Ye proceed one from another. So those who fled and were driven forth from their homes and suffered damage for My cause, and fought and were slain, verily I shall remit their evil deeds from them and verily I shall bring them into Gardens underneath which rivers flow - A reward from Allah. And with Allah is the fairest of rewards.	So their Lord accepted their prayer: That I will not waste the work of a worker among you, whether male or female, the one of you being from the other; they, therefore, who fled and were turned out of their homes and persecuted in My way and who fought and were slain, I will most certainly cover their evil deeds, and I will most certainly make them enter gardens beneath which rivers flow; a reward from Allah, and with Allah is yet better reward.
3 196	Let not the strutting about of the Unbelievers through the land deceive thee:	Let not the vicissitude (of the success) of those who disbelieve, in the land, deceive thee (O Muhammad).	Let it not deceive you that those who disbelieve go to and fro in the cities fearlessly.
3 197	Little is it for enjoyment: Their ultimate abode is Hell: what an evil bed (To lie on)!	It is but a brief comfort. And afterward their habitation will be hell, an ill abode.	A brief enjoyment! then their abode is hell, and evil is the resting-place.
3 198	On the other hand, for those who fear their Lord, are Gardens, with rivers flowing beneath; therein are they to dwell (for ever),- a gift from the presence of Allah; and that which is in the presence of Allah is the best (bliss) for the righteous.	But those who keep their duty to their Lord, for them are Gardens underneath which rivers flow, wherein they will be safe for ever. A gift of welcome from their Lord. That which Allah hath in store is better for the righteous.	But as to those who are careful of (their duty to) their Lord, they shall have gardens beneath which rivers flow, abiding in them; an entertainment from their Lord, and that which is with Allah is best for the righteous.
3 199	And there are, certainly, among the People of the Book, those who believe in Allah, in the revelation to you, and in the revelation to them, bowing in humility to Allah: They will not sell the Signs of Allah for a miserable gain! For them is a reward with their Lord, and Allah is swift in account.	And lo! of the People of the Scripture there are some who believe in Allah and that which is revealed unto you and that which was revealed unto them, humbling themselves before Allah. They purchase not a trifling gain at the price of the revelations of Allah. Verily their reward is with their Lord. Lo! Allah is swift to take account.	And most surely of the followers of the Book there are those who believe in Allah and (in) that which has been revealed to you and (in) that which has been revealed to them, being lowly before Allah; they do not take a small price for the communications of Allah; these it is that have their reward with their Lord; surely Allah is quick in reckoning.
3 200	O ye who believe! Persevere in patience and constancy; vie in such perseverance; strengthen each other; and fear Allah; that ye may prosper.	O ye who believe! Endure, outdo all others in endurance, be ready, and observe your duty to Allah, in order that ye may succeed.	O you who believe! be patient and excel in patience and remain steadfast, and be careful of (your duty to) Allah, that you may be successful.

Chapter 4:

AN-NISA (WOMEN)

Total Verses: 176 Revealed At: MADINA

In the name of Allah, the Most Beneficent, the Most Merciful.

4 001	O mankind! reverence your Guardian-Lord, who created you from a single person, created, of like nature, His mate, and from them twain scattered (like seeds) countless men and women;- reverence Allah, through whom ye demand your mutual (rights), and (reverence) the wombs (That bore you): for Allah ever watches over you.	O mankind! Be careful of your duty to your Lord Who created you from a single soul and from it created its mate and from them twain hath spread abroad a multitude of men and women. Be careful of your duty toward Allah in Whom ye claim (your rights) of one another, and toward the wombs (that bare you). Lo! Allah hath been a watcher over you.	O people! be careful of (your duty to) your Lord, Who created you from a single being and created its mate of the same (kind) and spread from these two, many men and women; and be careful of (your duty to) Allah, by Whom you demand one of another (your rights), and (to) the ties of relationship; surely Allah ever watches over you.
4 002	To orphans restore their property (When they reach their age), nor substitute (your) worthless things for (their) good ones; and devour not their substance (by mixing it up) with your won. For this is indeed a great sin.	Give unto orphans their wealth. Exchange not the good for the bad (in your management thereof) nor absorb their wealth into your own wealth. Lo! that would be a great sin.	And give to the orphans their property, and do not substitute worthless (things) for (their) good (ones), and do not devour their property (as an addition) to your own property; this is surely a great crime.
4 003	If ye fear that ye shall not be able to deal justly with the orphans, Marry women of your choice, Two or three or four; but if ye fear that ye shall not be able to deal justly (with them), then only one, or (a captive) that your right hands possess, that will be more suitable, to prevent you from doing injustice.	And if ye fear that ye will not deal fairly by the orphans, marry of the women, who seem good to you, two or three or four; and if ye fear that ye cannot do justice (to so many) then one (only) or (the captives) that your right hands possess. Thus it is more likely that ye will not do injustice.	And if you fear that you cannot act equitably towards orphans, then marry such women as seem good to you, two and three and four; but if you fear that you will not do justice (between them), then (marry) only one or what your right hands possess; this is more proper, that you may not deviate from the right course.
4 004	And give the women (on marriage) their dower as a free gift; but if they, of their own good pleasure, remit any part of it to you, Take it and enjoy it with right good cheer.	And give unto the women (whom ye marry) free gift of their marriage portions; but if they of their own accord remit unto you a part thereof, then ye are welcome to absorb it (in your wealth).	And give women their dowries as a free gift, but if they of themselves be pleased to give up to you a portion of it, then eat it with enjoyment and with wholesome result.
4 005	To those weak of understanding Make not over your property, which Allah hath made a means of support for you, but feed and clothe them therewith, and speak to them words of kindness and justice.	Give not unto the foolish (what is in) your (keeping of their) wealth, which Allah hath given you to maintain; but feed and clothe them from it, and speak kindly unto them.	And do not give away your property which Allah has made for you a (means of) support to the weak of understanding, and maintain them out of (the profits of) it, and clothe them and speak to them words of honest advice.

4 006	Make trial of orphans until they reach the age of marriage; if then ye find sound judgment in them, release their property to them; but consume it not wastefully, nor in haste against their growing up. If the guardian is well-off, Let him claim no remuneration, but if he is poor, let him have for himself what is just and reasonable. When ye release their property to them, take witnesses in their presence: But all-sufficient is Allah in taking account.	Prove orphans till they reach the marriageable age; then, if ye find them of sound judgment, deliver over unto them their fortune; and devour it not by squandering and in haste lest they should grow up Whoso (of the guardians) is rich, let him abstain generously (from taking of the property of orphans); and whoso is poor let him take thereof in reason (for his guardianship). And when ye deliver up their fortune unto orphans, have (the transaction) witnessed in their presence. Allah sufficeth as a Reckoner.	And test the orphans until they attain puberty; then if you find in them maturity of intellect, make over to them their property, and do not consume it extravagantly and hastily, lest they attain to full age; and whoever is rich, let him abstain altogether, and whoever is poor, let him eat reasonably; then when you make over to them their property, call witnesses in their presence; and Allah is enough as a Reckoner.	
4 007	From what is left by parents and those nearest related there is a share for men and a share for women, whether the property be small or large,-a determinate share.	Unto the men (of a family) belongeth a share of that which parents and near kindred leave, and unto the women a share of that which parents and near kindred leave, whether it be little or much - a legal share.	Men shall have a portion of what the parents and the near relatives leave, and women shall have a portion of what the parents and the near relatives leave, whether there is little or much of it; a stated portion.	
4 008	But if at the time of division other relatives, or orphans or poor, are present, feed them out of the (property), and speak to them words of kindness and justice.	And when kinsfolk and orphans and the needy are present at the division (of the heritage), bestow on them therefrom and speak kindly unto them.	And when there are present at the division the relatives and the orphans and the needy, give them (something) out of it and speak to them kind words.	
4 009	Let those (disposing of an estate) have the same fear in their minds as they would have for their own if they had left a helpless family behind: Let them fear Allah, and speak words of appropriate (comfort).	And let those fear (in their behaviour toward orphans) who if they left behind them weak offspring would be afraid for them. So let them mind their duty to Allah, and speak justly.	And let those fear who, should they leave behind them weakly offspring, would fear on their account, so let them be careful of (their duty to) Allah, and let them speak right words.	
4 010	Those who unjustly eat up the property of orphans, eat up a Fire into their own bodies: They will soon be enduring a Blazing Fire!	Lo! Those who devour the wealth of orphans wrongfully, they do but swallow fire into their bellies, and they will be exposed to burning flame.	(As for) those who swallow the property of the orphans unjustly, surely they only swallow fire into their bellies and they shall enter burning fire.	

4 011	Allah (thus) directs you as regards your Children's (Inheritance): to the male, a portion equal to that of two females: if only daughters, two or more, their share is two-thirds of the inheritance; if only one, her share is a half. For parents, a sixth share of the inheritance to each, if the deceased left children; if no children, and the parents are the (only) heirs, the mother has a third; if the deceased Left brothers (or sisters) the mother has a sixth. (The distribution in all cases is) after the payment of legacies and debts. Ye know not whether your parents or your children are nearest to you in benefit. These are settled portions ordained by Allah; and Allah is All-Knowing, All-Wise.	Allah chargeth you concerning (the provision for) your children: to the male the equivalent of the portion of two females, and if there be women more than two, then theirs is two-thirds of the inheritance, and if there be one (only) then the half. And to each of his parents a sixth of the inheritance, if he have a son; and if he have no son and his parents are his heirs, then to his mother appertaineth the third; and if he have brethren, then to his mother appertaineth the sixth, after any legacy he may have bequeathed, or debt (hath been paid). Your parents and your children: Ye know not which of them is nearer unto you in usefulness. It is an injunction from Allah. Lo! Allah is Knower, Wise.	Allah enjoins you concerning your children: The male shall have the equal of the portion of two females; then if they are more than two females, they shall have two-thirds of what the deceased has left, and if there is one, she shall have the half; and as for his parents, each of them shall have the sixth of what he has left if he has a child, but if he has no child and (only) his two parents inherit him, then his mother shall have the third; but if he has brothers, then his mother shall have the sixth after (the payment of) a bequest he may have bequeathed or a debt; your parents and your children, you know not which of them is the nearer to you in usefulness; this is an ordinance from Allah: Surely Allah is Knowing, Wise.
4 012	In what your wives leave, your share is a half, if they leave no child; but if they leave a child, ye get a fourth; after payment of legacies and debts. In what ye leave, their share is a fourth, if ye leave no child; but if ye leave a child, they get an eighth; after payment of legacies and debts. If the man or woman whose inheritance is in question, has left neither ascendants nor descendants, but has left a brother or a sister, each one of the two gets a sixth; but if more than two, they share in a third; after payment of legacies and debts; so that no loss is caused (to any one). Thus is it ordained by Allah; and Allah is All-Knowing, Most Forbearing.	And unto you belongeth a half of that which your wives leave, if they have no child; but if they have a child then unto you the fourth of that which they leave, after any legacy they may have bequeathed, or debt (they may have contracted, hath been paid). And unto them belongeth the fourth of that which ye leave if ye have no child, but if ye have a child then the eighth of that which ye leave, after any legacy ye may have bequeathed, or debt (ye may have contracted, hath been paid). And if a man or a woman have a distant heir (having left neither parent nor child), and he (or she) have a brother or a sister (only on the mother's side) then to each of them twain (the brother and the sister) the sixth, and if they be more than two, then they shall be sharers in the third, after any legacy that may have been bequeathed or debt (contracted) not injuring (the heirs by willing away more than a third of the heritage) hath been paid. A commandment from Allah. Allah is Knower, Indulgent.	And you shall have half of what your wives leave if they have no child, but if they have a child, then you shall have a fourth of what they leave after (payment of) any bequest they may have bequeathed or a debt; and they shall have the fourth of what you leave if you have no child, but if you have a child then they shall have the eighth of what you leave after (payment of) a bequest you may have bequeathed or a debt; and if a man or a woman leaves property to be inherited by neither parents nor offspring, and he (or she) has a brother or a sister, then each of them two shall have the sixth, but if they are more than that, they shall be sharers in the third after (payment of) any bequest that may have been bequeathed or a debt that does not harm (others); this is an ordinance from Allah: and Allah is Knowing, Forbearing.
4 013	Those are limits set by Allah: those who obey Allah and His Messenger will be admitted to Gardens with rivers flowing beneath, to abide therein (for ever) and that will be the supreme achievement.	These are the limits (imposed by) Allah. Whoso obeyeth Allah and His messenger, He will make him enter Gardens underneath which rivers flow, where such will dwell for ever. That will be the great success.	These are Allah's limits, and whoever obeys Allah and His Messenger, He will cause him to enter gardens beneath which rivers flow, to abide in them; and this is the great achievement.

4 014	But those who disobey Allah and His Messenger and transgress His limits will be admitted to a Fire, to abide therein: And they shall have a humiliating punishment.	And whoso disobeyeth Allah and His messenger and transgresseth His limits, He will make him enter Fire, where he will dwell for ever; his will be a shameful doom.	And whoever disobeys Allah and His Messenger and goes beyond His limits, He will cause him to enter fire to abide in it, and he shall have an abasing chastisement.
4 015	If any of your women are guilty of lewdness, Take the evidence of four (Reliable) witnesses from amongst you against them; and if they testify, confine them to houses until death do claim them, or Allah ordain for them some (other) way.	As for those of your women who are guilty of lewdness, call to witness four of you against them. And if they testify (to the truth of the allegation) then confine them to the houses until death take them or (until) Allah appoint for them a way (through new legislation).	And as for those who are guilty of an indecency from among your women, call to witnesses against them four (witnesses) from among you; then if they bear witness confine them to the houses until death takes them away or Allah opens some way for them.
4 016	If two men among you are guilty of lewdness, punish them both. If they repent and amend, Leave them alone; for Allah is Oft-Returning, Most Merciful.	And as for the two of you who are guilty thereof, punish them both. And if they repent and improve, then let them be. Lo! Allah is ever relenting, Merciful.	And as for the two who are guilty of indecency from among you, give them both a punishment; then if they repent and amend, turn aside from them; surely Allah is Oft-returning (to mercy), the Merciful.
4 017	Allah accept the repentance of those who do evil in ignorance and repent soon afterwards; to them will Allah turn in mercy: For Allah is full of knowledge and wisdom.	Forgiveness is only incumbent on Allah toward those who do evil in ignorance (and) then turn quickly (in repentance) to Allah. These are they toward whom Allah relenteth. Allah is ever Knower, Wise.	Repentance with Allah is only for those who do evil in ignorance, then turn (to Allah) soon, so these it is to whom Allah turns (mercifully), and Allah is ever Knowing, Wise.
4 018	Of no effect is the repentance of those who continue to do evil, until death faces one of them, and he says, "Now have I repented indeed;" nor of those who die rejecting Faith: for them have We prepared a punishment most grievous.	The forgiveness is not for those who do ill-deeds until, when death attendeth upon one of them, he saith: Lo! I repent now; nor yet for those who die while they are disbelievers. For such We have prepared a painful doom.	And repentance is not for those who go on doing evil deeds, until when death comes to one of them, he says: Surely now I repent; nor (for) those who die while they are unbelievers. These are they for whom We have prepared a painful chastisement.
4 019	O ye who believe! Ye are forbidden to inherit women against their will. Nor should ye treat them with harshness, that ye may Take away part of the dower ye have given them,-except where they have been guilty of open lewdness; on the contrary live with them on a footing of kindness and equity. If ye take a dislike to them it may be that ye dislike a thing, and Allah brings about through it a great deal of good.	O ye who believe! It is not lawful for you forcibly to inherit the women (of your deceased kinsmen), nor (that) ye should put constraint upon them that ye may take away a part of that which ye have given them, unless they be guilty of flagrant lewdness. But consort with them in kindness, for if ye hate them it may happen that ye hate a thing wherein Allah hath placed much good.	O you who believe! it is not lawful for you that you should take women as heritage against (their) will, and do not straiten them in order that you may take part of what you have given them, unless they are guilty of manifest indecency, and treat them kindly; then if you hate them, it may be that you dislike a thing while Allah has placed abundant good in it.
4 020	But if ye decide to take one wife in place of another, even if ye had given the latter a whole treasure for dower, Take not the least bit of it back: Would ye take it by slander and manifest wrong?	And if ye wish to exchange one wife for another and ye have given unto one of them a sum of money (however great), take nothing from it. Would ye take it by the way of calumny and open wrong?	And if you wish to have (one) wife in place of another and you have given one of them a heap of gold, then take not from it anything; would you take it by slandering (her) and (doing her) manifest wrong?
4 021	And how could ye take it when ye have gone in unto each other, and they have Taken from you a solemn covenant?	How can ye take it (back) after one of you hath gone in unto the other, and they have taken a strong pledge from you?	And how can you take it when one of you has already gone in to the other and they have made with you a firm covenant?

4 022	And marry not women whom your fathers married,- except what is past: It was shameful and odious,- an abominable custom indeed.	And marry not those women whom your fathers married, except what hath already happened (of that nature) in the past. Lo! it was ever lewdness and abomination, and an evil way.	And marry not woman whom your fathers married, except what has already passed; this surely is indecent and hateful, and it is an evil way.
4 023	Prohibited to you (For marriage) are:- Your mothers, daughters, sisters; father's sisters, Mother's sisters; brother's daughters, sister's daughters; foster-mothers (Who gave you suck), foster-sisters; your wives' mothers; your step-daughters under your guardianship, born of your wives to whom ye have gone in,- no prohibition if ye have not gone in;- (Those who have been) wives of your sons proceeding from your loins; and two sisters in wedlock at one and the same time, except for what is past; for Allah is Oft-Forgiving, Most Merciful;-	Forbidden unto you are your mothers, and your daughters, and your sisters, and your father's sisters, and your mother's sisters, and your brother's daughters and your sister's daughters, and your foster-mothers, and your foster-sisters, and your mothers-in-law, and your step-daughters who are under your protection (born) of your women unto whom ye have gone in - but if ye have not gone in unto them, then it is no sin for you (to marry their daughters) - and the wives of your sons who (spring) from your own loins. And (it is forbidden unto you) that ye should have two sisters together, except what hath already happened (of that nature) in the past. Lo! Allah is ever Forgiving, Merciful.	Forbidden to you are your mothers and your daughters and your sisters and your paternal aunts and your maternal aunts and brothers' daughters and sisters' daughters and your mothers that have suckled you and your foster-sisters and mothers of your wives and your step-daughters who are in your guardianship, (born) of your wives to whom you have gone in, but if you have not gone in to them, there is no blame on you (in marrying them), and the wives of your sons who are of your own loins and that you should have two sisters together, except what has already passed; surely Allah is Forgiving, Merciful.
4 024	Also (prohibited are) women already married, except those whom your right hands possess: Thus hath Allah ordained (Prohibitions) against you: Except for these, all others are lawful, provided ye seek (them in marriage) with gifts from your property,- desiring chastity, not lust, seeing that ye derive benefit from them, give them their dowers (at least) as prescribed; but if, after a dower is prescribed, agree Mutually (to vary it), there is no blame on you, and Allah is All-Knowing, All-Wise.	And all married women (are forbidden unto you) save those (captives) whom your right hands possess. It is a decree of Allah for you. Lawful unto you are all beyond those mentioned, so that ye seek them with your wealth in honest wedlock, not debauchery. And those of whom ye seek content (by marrying them), give unto them their portions as a duty. And there is no sin for you in what ye do by mutual agreement after the duty (hath been done). Lo! Allah is ever Knower, Wise.	And all married women except those whom your right hands possess (this is) Allah's ordinance to you, and lawful for you are (all women) besides those, provided that you seek (them) with your property, taking (them) in marriage not committing fornication. Then as to those whom you profit by, give them their dowries as appointed; and there is no blame on you about what you mutually agree after what is appointed; surely Allah is Knowing, Wise.

4 025	If any of you have not the means wherewith to wed free believing women, they may wed believing girls from among those whom your right hands possess: And Allah hath full knowledge about your faith. Ye are one from another: Wed them with the leave of their owners, and give them their dowers, according to what is reasonable: They should be chaste, not lustful, nor taking paramours: when they are taken in wedlock, if they fall into shame, their punishment is half that for free women. This (permission) is for those among you who fear sin; but it is better for you that ye practise self-restraint. And Allah is Oft-Forgiving, Most Merciful.	And whoso is not able to afford to marry free, believing women, let them marry from the believing maids whom your right hands possess. Allah knoweth best (concerning) your faith. Ye (proceed) one from another; so wed them by permission of their folk, and give unto them their portions in kindness, they being honest, not debauched nor of loose conduct. And if when they are honourably married they commit lewdness they shall incur the half of the punishment (prescribed) for free women (in that case). This is for him among you who feareth to commit sin. But to have patience would be better for you. Allah is Forgiving, Merciful.	And whoever among you has not within his power ampleness of means to marry free believing women, then (he may marry) of those whom your right hands possess from among your believing maidens; and Allah knows best your faith: you are (sprung) the one from the other; so marry them with the permission of their masters, and give them their dowries justly, they being chaste, not fornicating, nor receiving paramours; and when they are taken in marriage, then if they are guilty of indecency, they shall suffer half the punishment which is (inflicted) upon free women. This is for him among you who fears falling into evil; and that you abstain is better for you, and Allah is Forgiving, Merciful.	
4 026	Allah doth wish to make clear to you and to show you the ordinances of those before you; and (He doth wish to) turn to you (In Mercy): And Allah is All-Knowing, All-Wise.	Allah would explain to you and guide you by the examples of those who were before you, and would turn to you in mercy. Allah is Knower, Wise.	Allah desires to explain to you, and to guide you into the ways of those before you, and to turn to you (mercifully), and Allah is Knowing, Wise.	
4 027	Allah doth wish to Turn to you, but the wish of those who follow their lusts is that ye should turn away (from Him),- far, far away.	And Allah would turn to you in mercy; but those who follow vain desires would have you go tremendously astray.	And Allah desires that He should turn to you (mercifully), and those who follow (their) lusts desire that you should deviate (with) a great deviation.	
4 028	Allah doth wish to lighten your (difficulties): For man was created Weak (in flesh).	Allah would make the burden light for you, for man was created weak.	Allah desires that He should make light your burdens, and man is created weak.	
4 029	O ye who believe! Eat not up your property among yourselves in vanities: But let there be amongst you Traffic and trade by mutual good-will: Nor kill (or destroy) yourselves: for verily Allah hath been to you Most Merciful!	O ye who believe! Squander not your wealth among yourselves in vanity, except it be a trade by mutual consent, and kill not one another. Lo! Allah is ever Merciful unto you.	O you who believe! do not devour your property among yourselves falsely, except that it be trading by your mutual consent; and do not kill your people; surely Allah is Merciful to you.	
4 030	If any do that in rancour and injustice,- soon shall We cast them into the Fire: And easy it is for Allah.	Whoso doeth that through aggression and injustice, we shall cast him into Fire, and that is ever easy for Allah.	And whoever does this aggressively and unjustly, We will soon cast him into fire; and this is easy to Allah.	
4 031	If ye (but) eschew the most heinous of the things which ye are forbidden to do, We shall expel out of you all the evil in you, and admit you to a gate of great honour.	If ye avoid the great (things) which ye are forbidden, We will remit from you your evil deeds and make you enter at a noble gate.	If you shun the great sins which you are forbidden, We will do away with your small sins and cause you to enter an honorable place of entering.	

4 032	And in no wise covet those things in which Allah Hath bestowed His gifts More freely on some of you than on others: To men is allotted what they earn, and to women what they earn: But ask Allah of His bounty. For Allah hath full knowledge of all things.	And covet not the thing in which Allah hath made some of you excel others. Unto men a fortune from that which they have earned, and unto women a fortune from that which they have earned. (Envy not one another) but ask Allah of His bounty. Lo! Allah is ever Knower of all things.	And do not covet that by which Allah has made some of you excel others; men shall have the benefit of what they earn and women shall have the benefit of what they earn; and ask Allah of His grace; surely Allah knows all things.	
4 033	To (benefit) every one, We have appointed shares and heirs to property left by parents and relatives. To those, also, to whom your right hand was pledged, give their due portion. For truly Allah is witness to all things.	And unto each We have appointed heirs of that which parents and near kindred leave; and as for those with whom your right hands have made a covenant, give them their due. Lo! Allah is ever Witness over all things.	And to every one We have appointed heirs of what parents and near relatives leave; and as to those with whom your rights hands have ratified agreements, give them their portion; surely Allah is a witness over all things.	
4 034	Men are the protectors and maintainers of women, because Allah has given the one more (strength) than the other, and because they support them from their means. Therefore the righteous women are devoutly obedient, and guard in (the husband's) absence what Allah would have them guard. As to those women on whose part ye fear disloyalty and ill-conduct, admonish them (first), (Next), refuse to share their beds, (And last) beat them (lightly); but if they return to obedience, seek not against them Means (of annoyance): For Allah is Most High, great (above you all).	Men are in charge of women, because Allah hath made the one of them to excel the other, and because they spend of their property (for the support of women). So good women are the obedient, guarding in secret that which Allah hath guarded. As for those from whom ye fear rebellion, admonish them and banish them to beds apart, and scourge them. Then if they obey you, seek not a way against them. Lo! Allah is ever High, Exalted, Great.	Men are the maintainers of women because Allah has made some of them to excel others and because they spend out of their property; the good women are therefore obedient, guarding the unseen as Allah has guarded; and (as to) those on whose part you fear desertion, admonish them, and leave them alone in the sleeping-places and beat them; then if they obey you, do not seek a way against them; surely Allah is High, Great.	
4 035	If ye fear a breach between them twain, appoint (two) arbiters, one from his family, and the other from hers; if they wish for peace, Allah will cause their reconciliation: For Allah hath full knowledge, and is acquainted with all things.	And if ye fear a breach between them twain (the man and wife), appoint an arbiter from his folk and an arbiter from her folk. If they desire amendment Allah will make them of one mind. Lo! Allah is ever Knower, Aware.	And if you fear a breach between the two, then appoint judge from his people and a judge from her people; if they both desire agreement, Allah will effect harmony between them, surely Allah is Knowing, Aware.	
4 036	Serve Allah, and join not any partners with Him; and do good- to parents, kinsfolk, orphans, those in need, neighbours who are near, neighbours who are strangers, the companion by your side, the wayfarer (ye meet), and what your right hands possess: For Allah loveth not the arrogant, the vainglorious;-	And serve Allah. Ascribe no thing as partner unto Him. (Show) kindness unto parents, and unto near kindred, and orphans, and the needy, and unto the neighbour who is of kin (unto you) and the neighbour who is not of kin, and the fellow-traveller and the wayfarer and (the slaves) whom your right hands possess. Lo! Allah loveth not such as are proud and boastful,	And serve Allah and do not associate any thing with Him and be good to the parents and to the near of kin and the orphans and the needy and the neighbor of (your) kin and the alien neighbor, and the companion in a journey and the wayfarer and those whom your right hands possess; surely Allah does not love him who is proud, boastful;	
4 037	(Nor) those who are niggardly or enjoin niggardliness on others, or hide the bounties which Allah hath bestowed on them; for We have prepared, for those who resist Faith, a punishment that steeps them in contempt;-	Who hoard their wealth and enjoin avarice on others, and hide that which Allah hath bestowed upon them of His bounty. For disbelievers We prepare a shameful doom;	Those who are niggardly and bid people to be niggardly and hide what Allah has given them out of His grace; and We have prepared for the unbelievers a disgraceful chastisement.	

4 038	Not those who spend of their substance, to be seen of men, but have no faith in Allah and the Last Day: If any take the Evil One for their intimate, what a dreadful intimate he is!	And (also) those who spend their wealth in order to be seen of men, and believe not in Allah nor the Last Day. Whoso taketh Satan for a comrade, a bad comrade hath he.	And those who spend their property (in alms) to be seen of the people and do not believe in Allah nor in the last day; and as for him whose associate is the Shaitan, an evil associate is he!
4 039	And what burden Were it on them if they had faith in Allah and in the Last Day, and they spent out of what Allah hath given them for sustenance? For Allah hath full knowledge of them.	What have they (to fear) if they believe in Allah and the Last Day and spend (aright) of that which Allah hath bestowed upon them, when Allah is ever Aware of them (and all they do)?	And what (harm) would it have done them if they had believed in Allah and the last day and spent (benevolently) of what Allah had given them? And Allah knows them.
4 040	Allah is never unjust in the least degree: If there is any good (done), He doubleth it, and giveth from His own presence a great reward.	Lo! Allah wrongeth not even of the weight of an ant; and if there is a good deed, He will double it and will give (the doer) from His presence an immense reward.	Surely Allah does not do injustice to the weight of an atom, and if it is a good deed He multiplies it and gives from Himself a great reward.
4 041	How then if We brought from each people a witness, and We brought thee as a witness against these people!	But how (will it be with them) when We bring of every people a witness, and We bring thee (O Muhammad) a witness against these?	How will it be, then, when We bring from every people a witness and bring you as a witness against these?
4 042	On that day those who reject Faith and disobey the messenger will wish that the earth Were made one with them: But never will they hide a single fact from Allah!	On that day those who disbelieved and disobeyed the messenger will wish that they were level with the ground, and they can hide no fact from Allah.	On that day will those who disbelieve and disobey the Messenger desire that the earth were levelled with them, and they shall not hide any word from Allah.
4 043	O ye who believe! Approach not prayers with a mind befogged, until ye can understand all that ye say,- nor in a state of ceremonial impurity (Except when travelling on the road), until after washing your whole body. If ye are ill, or on a journey, or one of you cometh from offices of nature, or ye have been in contact with women, and ye find no water, then take for yourselves clean sand or earth, and rub therewith your faces and hands. For Allah doth blot out sins and forgive again and again.	O ye who believe! Draw not near unto prayer when ye are drunken, till ye know that which ye utter, nor when ye are polluted, save when journeying upon the road, till ye have bathed. And if ye be ill, or on a journey, or one of you cometh from the closet, or ye have touched women, and ye find not water, then go to high clean soil and rub your faces and your hands (therewith). Lo! Allah is Benign, Forgiving.	O you who believe! do not go near prayer when you are Intoxicated until you know (well) what you say, nor when you are under an obligation to perform a bath-- unless (you are) travelling on the road-- until you have washed yourselves; and if you are sick, or on a journey, or one of you come from the privy or you have touched the women, and you cannot find water, betake yourselves to pure earth, then wipe your faces and your hands; surely Allah is Pardoning, Forgiving.
4 044	Hast thou not turned Thy vision to those who were given a portion of the Book? they traffic in error, and wish that ye should lose the right path.	Seest thou not those unto whom a portion of the Scripture hath been given, how they purchase error, and seek to make you (Muslims) err from the right way?	Have you not considered those to whom a portion of the Book has been given? They buy error and desire that you should go astray from the way.
4 045	But Allah hath full knowledge of your enemies: Allah is enough for a protector, and Allah is enough for a Helper.	Allah knoweth best (who are) your enemies. Allah is sufficient as a Guardian, and Allah is sufficient as a Supporter.	And Allah best knows your enemies; and Allah suffices as a Guardian, and Allah suffices as a Helper.

4 046	Of the Jews there are those who displace words from their (right) places, and say: "We hear and we disobey"; and "Hear what is not Heard"; and "Ra'ina"; with a twist of their tongues and a slander to Faith. If only they had said: "We hear and we obey"; and "Do hear"; and "Do look at us"; it would have been better for them, and more proper; but Allah hath cursed them for their Unbelief; and but few of them will believe.	Some of those who are Jews change words from their context and say: We hear and disobey; hear thou as one who heareth not and "Listen to us!" distorting with their tongues and slandering religion. If they had said: "We hear and we obey: hear thou, and look at us" it had been better for them, and more upright. But Allah hath cursed them for their disbelief, so they believe not, save a few.	Of those who are Jews (there are those who) alter words from their places and say: We have heard and we disobey and: Hear, may you not be made to hear! and: Raina, distorting (the word) with their tongues and taunting about religion; and if they had said (instead): We have heard and we obey, and hearken, and unzurna it would have been better for them and more upright; but Allah has cursed them on account of their unbelief, so they do not believe but a little.
4 047	O ye People of the Book! believe in what We have (now) revealed, confirming what was (already) with you, before We change the face and fame of some (of you) beyond all recognition, and turn them hindwards, or curse them as We cursed the Sabbath-breakers, for the decision of Allah must be carried out.	O ye unto whom the Scripture hath been given! Believe in what We have revealed confirming that which ye possess, before We destroy countenances so as to confound them, or curse them as We cursed the Sabbath-breakers (of old time). The commandment of Allah is always executed.	O you who have been given the Book! believe that which We have revealed, verifying what you have, before We alter faces then turn them on their backs, or curse them as We cursed the violaters of the Sabbath, and the command of Allah shall be executed.
4 048	Allah forgiveth not that partners should be set up with Him; but He forgiveth anything else, to whom He pleaseth; to set up partners with Allah is to devise a sin most heinous indeed.	Lo! Allah forgiveth not that a partner should be ascribed unto Him. He forgiveth (all) save that to whom He will. Whoso ascribeth partners to Allah, he hath indeed invented a tremendous sin.	Surely Allah does not forgive that anything should be associated with Him, and forgives what is besides that to whomsoever He pleases; and whoever associates anything with Allah, he devises indeed a great sin.
4 049	Hast thou not turned Thy vision to those who claim sanctity for themselves? Nay-but Allah Doth sanctify whom He pleaseth. But never will they fail to receive justice in the least little thing.	Hast thou not seen those who praise themselves for purity? Nay, Allah purifieth whom He will, and they will not be wronged even the hair upon a date-stone.	Have you not considered those who attribute purity to themselves? Nay, Allah purifies whom He pleases; and they shall not be wronged the husk of a date stone.
4 050	Behold! how they invent a lie against Allah! but that by itself is a manifest sin!	See, how they invent lies about Allah! That of itself is flagrant sin.	See how they forge the lie against Allah, and this is sufficient as a manifest sin.
4 051	Hast thou not turned Thy vision to those who were given a portion of the Book? they believe in sorcery and Evil, and say to the Unbelievers that they are better guided in the (right) way Than the believers!	Hast thou not seen those unto whom a portion of the Scripture hath been given, how they believe in idols and false deities, and how they say of those (idolaters) who disbelieve: "These are more rightly guided than those who believe"?	Have you not seen those to whom a portion of the Book has been given? They believe in idols and false deities and say of those who disbelieve: These are better guided in the path than those who believe.
4 052	They are (men) whom Allah hath cursed: And those whom Allah Hath cursed, thou wilt find, have no one to help.	Those are they whom Allah hath cursed, and he whom Allah hath cursed, thou (O Muhammad) wilt find for him no helper.	Those are they whom Allah has cursed, and whomever Allah curses you shall not find any helper for him.
4 053	Have they a share in dominion or power? Behold, they give not a farthing to their fellow-men?	Or have they even a share in the Sovereignty? Then in that case, they would not give mankind even the speck on a date-stone.	Or have they a share in the kingdom? But then they would not give to people even the speck in the date stone.

4 054	Or do they envy mankind for what Allah hath given them of his bounty? but We had already given the people of Abraham the Book and Wisdom, and conferred upon them a great kingdom.	Or are they jealous of mankind because of that which Allah of His bounty hath bestowed upon them? For We bestowed upon the house of Abraham (of old) the Scripture and wisdom, and We bestowed on them a mighty kingdom.	Or do they envy the people for what Allah has given them of His grace? But indeed We have given to Ibrahim's children the Book and the wisdom, and We have given them a grand kingdom.
4 055	Some of them believed, and some of them averted their faces from him: And enough is Hell for a burning fire.	And of them were (some) who believed therein and of them were (some) who turned away from it. Hell is sufficient for (their) burning.	So of them is he who believes in him, and of them is he who turns away from him, and hell is sufficient to burn.
4 056	Those who reject our Signs, We shall soon cast into the Fire: as often as their skins are roasted through, We shall change them for fresh skins, that they may taste the penalty: for Allah is Exalted in Power, Wise.	Lo! Those who disbelieve Our revelations, We shall expose them to the Fire. As often as their skins are consumed We shall exchange them for fresh skins that they may taste the torment. Lo! Allah is ever Mighty, Wise.	(As for) those who disbelieve in Our communications, We shall make them enter fire; so oft as their skins are thoroughly burned, We will change them for other skins, that they may taste the chastisement; surely Allah is Mighty, Wise.
4 057	But those who believe and do deeds of righteousness, We shall soon admit to Gardens, with rivers flowing beneath,- their eternal home: Therein shall they have companions pure and holy: We shall admit them to shades, cool and ever deepening.	And as for those who believe and do good works, We shall make them enter Gardens underneath which rivers flow - to dwell therein for ever; there for them are pure companions - and We shall make them enter plenteous shade.	And (as for) those who believe and do good deeds, We will make them enter gardens beneath which rivers flow, to abide in them for ever; they shall have therein pure mates, and We shall make them enter a dense shade.
4 058	Allah doth command you to render back your Trusts to those to whom they are due; And when ye judge between man and man, that ye judge with justice: Verily how excellent is the teaching which He giveth you! For Allah is He Who heareth and seeth all things.	Lo! Allah commandeth you that ye restore deposits to their owners, and, if ye judge between mankind, that ye judge justly. Lo! comely is this which Allah admonisheth you. Lo! Allah is ever Hearer, Seer.	Surely Allah commands you to make over trusts to their owners and that when you judge between people you judge with justice; surely Allah admonishes you with what is excellent; surely Allah is Seeing, Hearing.
4 059	O ye who believe! Obey Allah, and obey the Messenger, and those charged with authority among you. If ye differ in anything among yourselves, refer it to Allah and His Messenger, if ye do believe in Allah and the Last Day: That is best, and most suitable for final determination.	O ye who believe! Obey Allah, and obey the messenger and those of you who are in authority; and if ye have a dispute concerning any matter, refer it to Allah and the messenger if ye are (in truth) believers in Allah and the Last Day. That is better and more seemly in the end.	O you who believe! obey Allah and obey the Messenger and those in authority from among you; then if you quarrel about anything, refer it to Allah and the Messenger, if you believe in Allah and the last day; this is better and very good in the end.
4 060	Hast thou not turned Thy vision to those who declare that they believe in the revelations that have come to thee and to those before thee? Their (real) wish is to resort together for judgment (in their disputes) to the Evil One, though they were ordered to reject him. But Satan's wish is to lead them astray far away (from the right).	Hast thou not seen those who pretend that they believe in that which is revealed unto thee and that which was revealed before thee, how they would go for judgment (in their disputes) to false deities when they have been ordered to abjure them? Satan would mislead them far astray.	Have you not seen those who assert that they believe in what has been revealed to you and what was revealed before you? They desire to summon one another to the judgment of the Shaitan, though they were commanded to deny him, and the Shaitan desires to lead them astray into a remote error.
4 061	When it is said to them: "Come to what Allah hath revealed, and to the Messenger": Thou seest the Hypocrites avert their faces from thee in disgust.	And when it is said unto them: Come unto that which Allah hath revealed and unto the messenger, thou seest the hypocrites turn from thee with aversion.	And when it is said to them: Come to what Allah has revealed and to the Messenger, you will see the hypocrites turning away from you with (utter) aversion.

4 062	How then, when they are seized by misfortune, because of the deeds which they hands have sent forth? Then they come to thee, swearing by Allah: "We meant no more than good-will and conciliation!"	How would it be if a misfortune smote them because of that which their own hands have sent before (them)? Then would they come unto thee, swearing by Allah that they were seeking naught but harmony and kindness.	But how will it be when misfortune befalls them on account of what their hands have sent before? Then they will come to you swearing by Allah: We did not desire (anything) but good and concord.
4 063	Those men,-Allah knows what is in their hearts; so keep clear of them, but admonish them, and speak to them a word to reach their very souls.	Those are they, the secrets of whose hearts Allah knoweth. So oppose them and admonish them, and address them in plain terms about their souls.	These are they of whom Allah knows what is in their hearts; therefore turn aside from them and admonish them, and speak to them effectual words concerning themselves.
4 064	We sent not a messenger, but to be obeyed, in accordance with the will of Allah. If they had only, when they were unjust to themselves, come unto thee and asked Allah's forgiveness, and the Messenger had asked forgiveness for them, they would have found Allah indeed Oft-Returning, Most Merciful.	We sent no messenger save that he should be obeyed by Allah's leave. And if, when they had wronged themselves, they had but come unto thee and asked forgiveness of Allah, and asked forgiveness of the messenger, they would have found Allah Forgiving, Merciful.	And We did not send any messenger but that he should be obeyed by Allah's permission; and had they, when they were unjust to themselves, come to you and asked forgiveness of Allah and the Messenger had (also) asked forgiveness for them, they would have found Allah Oft-returning (to mercy), Merciful.
4 065	But no, by the Lord, they can have no (real) Faith, until they make thee judge in all disputes between them, and find in their souls no resistance against Thy decisions, but accept them with the fullest conviction.	But nay, by thy Lord, they will not believe (in truth) until they make thee judge of what is in dispute between them and find within themselves no dislike of that which thou decidest, and submit with full submission.	But no! by your Lord! they do not believe (in reality) until they make you a judge of that which has become a matter of disagreement among them, and then do not find any straitness in their hearts as to what you have decided and submit with entire submission.
4 066	If We had ordered them to sacrifice their lives or to leave their homes, very few of them would have done it: But if they had done what they were (actually) told, it would have been best for them, and would have gone farthest to strengthen their (faith);	And if We had decreed for them: Lay down your lives or go forth from your dwellings, but few of them would have done it; though if they did what they are exhorted to do it would be better for them, and more strengthening;	And if We had prescribed for them: Lay down your lives or go forth from your homes, they would not have done it except a few of them; and if they had done what they were admonished, it would have certainly been better for them and best in strengthening (them);
4 067	And We should then have given them from our presence a great reward;	And then We should bestow upon them from Our presence an immense reward,	And then We would certainly have given them from Ourselves a great reward.
4 068	And We should have shown them the Straight Way.	And should guide them unto a straight path.	And We would certainly have guided them in the right path.
4 069	All who obey Allah and the messenger are in the company of those on whom is the Grace of Allah,- of the prophets (who teach), the sincere (lovers of Truth), the witnesses (who testify), and the Righteous (who do good): Ah! what a beautiful fellowship!	Whoso obeyeth Allah and the messenger, they are with those unto whom Allah hath shown favour, of the prophets and the saints and the martyrs and the righteous. The best of company are they!	And whoever obeys Allah and the Messenger, these are with those upon whom Allah has bestowed favors from among the prophets and the truthful and the martyrs and the good, and a goodly company are they!
4 070	Such is the bounty from Allah: And sufficient is it that Allah knoweth all.	That is bounty from Allah, and Allah sufficeth as Knower.	This is grace from Allah, and sufficient is Allah as the Knower.
4 071	O ye who believe! Take your precautions, and either go forth in parties or go forth all together.	O ye who believe! Take your precautions, then advance the proven ones, or advance all together.	O you who believe! take your precaution, then go forth in detachments or go forth in a body.

4 072	There are certainly among you men who would tarry behind: If a misfortune befalls you, they say: "Allah did favour us in that we were not present among them."	Lo! among you there is he who loitereth; and if disaster overtook you, he would say: Allah hath been gracious unto me since I was not present with them.	And surely among you is he who would certainly hang back! If then a misfortune befalls you he says: Surely Allah conferred a benefit on me that I was not present with them.
4 073	But if good fortune comes to you from Allah, they would be sure to say - as if there had never been Ties of affection between you and them Oh! I wish I had been with them; a fine thing should I then have made of it!"	And if a bounty from Allah befell you, he would surely cry, as if there had been no love between you and him: Oh, would that I had been with them, then should I have achieved a great success!	And if grace from Allah come to you, he would certainly cry out, as if there had not been any friendship between you and him: Would that I had been with them, then I should have attained a mighty good fortune.
4 074	Let those fight in the cause of Allah Who sell the life of this world for the hereafter. To him who fighteth in the cause of Allah,- whether he is slain or gets victory - Soon shall We give him a reward of great (value).	Let those fight in the way of Allah who sell the life of this world for the other. Whoso fighteth in the way of Allah, be he slain or be he victorious, on him We shall bestow a vast reward.	Therefore let those fight in the way of Allah, who sell this world's life for the hereafter; and whoever fights in the way of Allah, then be he slain or be he victorious, We shall grant him a mighty reward.
4 075	And why should ye not fight in the cause of Allah and of those who, being weak, are ill-treated (and oppressed)?- Men, women, and children, whose cry is: "Our Lord! Rescue us from this town, whose people are oppressors; and raise for us from thee one who will protect; and raise for us from thee one who will help!"	How should ye not fight for the cause of Allah and of the feeble among men and of the women and the children who are crying: Our Lord! Bring us forth from out this town of which the people are oppressors! Oh, give us from thy presence some protecting friend! Oh, give us from Thy presence some defender!	And what reason have you that you should not fight in the way of Allah and of the weak among the men and the women and the children, (of) those who say: Our Lord! cause us to go forth from this town, whose people are oppressors, and give us from Thee a guardian and give us from Thee a helper.
4 076	Those who believe fight in the cause of Allah, and those who reject Faith Fight in the cause of Evil: So fight ye against the friends of Satan: feeble indeed is the cunning of Satan.	Those who believe do battle for the cause of Allah; and those who disbelieve do battle for the cause of idols. So fight the minions of the devil. Lo! the devil's strategy is ever weak.	Those who believe fight in the way of Allah, and those who disbelieve fight in the way of the Shaitan. Fight therefore against the friends of the Shaitan; surely the strategy of the Shaitan is weak.
4 077	Hast thou not turned Thy vision to those who were told to hold back their hands (from fight) but establish regular prayers and spend in regular charity? When (at length) the order for fighting was issued to them, behold! a section of them feared men as - or even more than - they should have feared Allah: They said: "Our Lord! Why hast Thou ordered us to fight? Wouldst Thou not Grant us respite to our (natural) term, near (enough)?" Say: "Short is the enjoyment of this world: the Hereafter is the best for those who do right: Never will ye be dealt with unjustly in the very least!"	Hast thou not seen those unto whom it was said: Withhold your hands, establish worship and pay the poor due, but when fighting was prescribed for them behold! a party of them fear mankind even as their fear of Allah or with greater fear, and say: Our Lord! Why hast Thou ordained fighting for us? If only Thou wouldst give us respite yet a while! Say (unto them, O Muhammad): The comfort of this world is scant; the Hereafter will be better for him who wardeth off (evil); and ye will not be wronged the down upon a date-stone.	Have you not seen those to whom it was said: Withhold your hands, and keep up prayer and pay the poor-rate; but when fighting is prescribed for them, lo! a party of them fear men as they ought to have feared Allah, or (even) with a greater fear, and say: Our Lord! why hast Thou ordained fighting for us? Wherefore didst Thou not grant us a delay to a near end? Say: The provision of this world is short, and the hereafter is better for him who guards (against evil); and you shall not be wronged the husk of a date stone.

4 078	"Wherever ye are, death will find you out, even if ye are in towers built up strong and high!" If some good befalls them, they say, "This is from Allah"; but if evil, they say, "This is from thee" (O Prophet). Say: "All things are from Allah." But what hath come to these people, that they fail to understand a single fact?	Wheresoever ye may be, death will overtake you, even though ye were in lofty towers. Yet if a happy thing befalleth them they say: This is from Allah; and if an evil thing befalleth them they say: This is of thy doing (O Muhammad). Say (unto them): All is from Allah. What is amiss with these people that they come not nigh to understand a happening?	Wherever you are, death will overtake you, though you are in lofty towers, and if a benefit comes to them, they say: This is from Allah; and if a misfortune befalls them, they say: This is from you. Say: All is from Allah, but what is the matter with these people that they do not make approach to understanding what is told (them)?
4 079	Whatever good, (O man!) happens to thee, is from Allah; but whatever evil happens to thee, is from thy (own) soul. And We have sent thee as a messenger to (instruct) mankind. And enough is Allah for a witness.	Whatever of good befalleth thee (O man) it is from Allah, and whatever of ill befalleth thee it is from thyself. We have sent thee (Muhammad) as a messenger unto mankind and Allah is sufficient as Witness.	Whatever benefit comes to you (O man!), it is from Allah, and whatever misfortune befalls you, it is from yourself, and We have sent you (O Prophet!), to mankind as a messenger; and Allah is sufficient as a witness.
4 080	He who obeys the Messenger, obeys Allah: But if any turn away, We have not sent thee to watch over their (evil deeds).	Whoso obeyeth the messenger hath obeyed Allah, and whoso turneth away: We have not sent thee as a warder over them.	Whoever obeys the Messenger, he indeed obeys Allah, and whoever turns back, so We have not sent you as a keeper over them.
4 081	They have "Obedience" on their lips; but when they leave thee, a section of them Meditate all night on things very different from what thou tellest them. But Allah records their nightly (plots): So keep clear of them, and put thy trust in Allah, and enough is Allah as a disposer of affairs.	And they say: (It is) obedience; but when they have gone forth from thee a party of them spend the night in planning other than what thou sayest. Allah recordeth what they plan by night. So oppose them and put thy trust in Allah. Allah is sufficient as Trustee.	And they say: Obedience. But when they go out from your presence, a party of them decide by night upon doing otherwise than what you say; and Allah writes down what they decide by night, therefore turn aside from them and trust in Allah, and Allah is sufficient as a protector.
4 082	Do they not consider the Qur'an (with care)? Had it been from other Than Allah, they would surely have found therein Much discrepancy.	Will they not then ponder on the Qur'an? If it had been from other than Allah they would have found therein much incongruity.	Do they not then meditate on the Quran? And if it were from any other than Allah, they would have found in it many a discrepancy.
4 083	When there comes to them some matter touching (Public) safety or fear, they divulge it. If they had only referred it to the Messenger, or to those charged with authority among them, the proper investigators would have Tested it from them (direct). Were it not for the Grace and Mercy of Allah unto you, all but a few of you would have fallen into the clutches of Satan.	And if any tidings, whether of safety or fear, come unto them, they noise it abroad, whereas if they had referred it to the messenger and to such of them as are in authority, those among them who are able to think out the matter would have known it. If it had not been for the grace of Allah upon you and His mercy ye would have followed Satan, save a few (of you).	And when there comes to them news of security or fear they spread it abroad; and if they had referred it to the Messenger and to those in authority among them, those among them who can search out the knowledge of it would have known it, and were it not for the grace of Allah upon you and His mercy, you would have certainly followed the Shaitan save a few.
4 084	Then fight in Allah's cause - Thou art held responsible only for thyself - and rouse the believers. It may be that Allah will restrain the fury of the Unbelievers; for Allah is the strongest in might and in punishment.	So fight (O Muhammad) in the way of Allah Thou art not taxed (with the responsibility for anyone) except thyself - and urge on the believers. Peradventure Allah will restrain the might of those who disbelieve. Allah is stronger in might and stronger in inflicting punishment.	Fight then in Allah's way; this is not imposed on you except In relation to yourself, and rouse the believers to ardor maybe Allah will restrain the fighting of those who disbelieve and Allah is strongest in prowess and strongest to give an exemplary punishment.

4 085	Whoever recommends and helps a good cause becomes a partner therein: And whoever recommends and helps an evil cause, shares in its burden: And Allah hath power over all things.	Whoso interveneth in a good cause will have the reward thereof, and whoso interveneth in an evil cause will bear the consequence thereof. Allah overseeth all things.	Whoever joins himself (to another) in a good cause shall have a share of it, and whoever joins himself (to another) in an evil cause shall have the responsibility of it, and Allah controls all things.
4 086	When a (courteous) greeting is offered you, meet it with a greeting still more courteous, or (at least) of equal courtesy. Allah takes careful account of all things.	When ye are greeted with a greeting, greet ye with a better than it or return it. Lo! Allah taketh count of all things.	And when you are greeted with a greeting, greet with a better (greeting) than it or return it; surely Allah takes account of all things.
4 087	Allah! There is no god but He: of a surety He will gather you together against the Day of Judgment, about which there is no doubt. And whose word can be truer than Allah's?	Allah! There is no God save Him. He gathereth you all unto a Day of Resurrection whereof there is no doubt. Who is more true in statement than Allah?	Allah, there is no god but He-- He will most certainly gather you together on the resurrection day, there is no doubt in it; and who is more true in word than Allah?
4 088	Why should ye be divided into two parties about the Hypocrites? Allah hath upset them for their (evil) deeds. Would ye guide those whom Allah hath thrown out of the Way? For those whom Allah hath thrown out of the Way, never shalt thou find the Way.	What aileth you that ye are become two parties regarding the hypocrites, when Allah cast them back (to disbelief) because of what they earned? Seek ye to guide him whom Allah hath sent astray? He whom Allah sendeth astray, for him thou (O Muhammad) canst not find a road.	What is the matter with you, then, that you have become two parties about the hypocrites, while Allah has made them return (to unbelief) for what they have earned? Do you wish to guide him whom Allah has caused to err? And whomsoever Allah causes to err, you shall by no means find a way for him.
4 089	They but wish that ye should reject Faith, as they do, and thus be on the same footing (as they): But take not friends from their ranks until they flee in the way of Allah (From what is forbidden). But if they turn renegades, seize them and slay them wherever ye find them; and (in any case) take no friends or helpers from their ranks;-	They long that ye should disbelieve even as they disbelieve, that ye may be upon a level (with them). So choose not friends from them till they forsake their homes in the way of Allah; if they turn back (to enmity) then take them and kill them wherever ye find them, and choose no friend nor helper from among them,	They desire that you should disbelieve as they have disbelieved, so that you might be (all) alike; therefore take not from among them friends until they fly (their homes) in Allah's way; but if they turn back, then seize them and kill them wherever you find them, and take not from among them a friend or a helper.
4 090	Except those who join a group between whom and you there is a treaty (of peace), or those who approach you with hearts restraining them from fighting you as well as fighting their own people. If Allah had pleased, He could have given them power over you, and they would have fought you: Therefore if they withdraw from you but fight you not, and (instead) send you (Guarantees of) peace, then Allah Hath opened no way for you (to war against them).	Except those who seek refuge with a people between whom and you there is a covenant, or (those who) come unto you because their hearts forbid them to make war on you or make war on their own folk. Had Allah willed He could have given them power over you so that assuredly they would have fought you. So, if they hold aloof from you and wage not war against you and offer you peace, Allah alloweth you no way against them.	Except those who reach a people between whom and you there is an alliance, or who come to you, their hearts shrinking from fighting you or fighting their own people; and if Allah had pleased, He would have given them power over you, so that they should have certainly fought you; therefore if they withdraw from you and do not fight you and offer you peace, then Allah has not given you a way against them.

4 091	Others you will find that wish to gain your confidence as well as that of their people: Every time they are sent back to temptation, they succumb thereto: if they withdraw not from you nor give you (guarantees) of peace besides restraining their hands, seize them and slay them wherever ye get them: In their case We have provided you with a clear argument against them.	Ye will find others who desire that they should have security from you, and security from their own folk. So often as they are returned to hostility they are plunged therein. If they keep not aloof from you nor offer you peace nor hold their hands, then take them and kill them wherever ye find them. Against such We have given you clear warrant.	You will find others who desire that they should be safe from you and secure from their own people; as often as they are sent back to the mischief they get thrown into it headlong; therefore if they do not withdraw from you, and (do not) offer you peace and restrain their hands, then seize them and kill them wherever you find them; and against these We have given you a clear authority.
4 092	Never should a believer kill a believer; but (If it so happens) by mistake, (Compensation is due): If one (so) kills a believer, it is ordained that he should free a believing slave, and pay compensation to the deceased's family, unless they remit it freely. If the deceased belonged to a people at war with you, and he was a believer, the freeing of a believing slave (Is enough). If he belonged to a people with whom ye have treaty of Mutual alliance, compensation should be paid to his family, and a believing slave be freed. For those who find this beyond their means, (is prescribed) a fast for two months running: by way of repentance to Allah: for Allah hath all knowledge and all wisdom.	It is not for a believer to kill a believer unless (it be) by mistake. He who hath killed a believer by mistake must set free a believing slave, and pay the blood-money to the family of the slain, unless they remit it as a charity. If he (the victim) be of a people hostile unto you, and he is a believer, then (the penance is) to set free a believing slave. And if he cometh of a folk between whom and you there is a covenant, then the blood-money must be paid unto his folk and (also) a believing slave must be set free. And whoso hath not the wherewithal must fast two consecutive months. A penance from Allah. Allah is Knower, Wise.	And it does not behoove a believer to kill a believer except by mistake, and whoever kills a believer by mistake, he should free a believing slave, and blood-money should be paid to his people unless they remit it as alms; but if he be from a tribe hostile to you and he is a believer, the freeing of a believing slave (suffices), and if he is from a tribe between whom and you there is a convenant, the blood-money should be paid to his people along with the freeing of a believing slave; but he who cannot find (a slave) should fast for two months successively: a penance from Allah, and Allah is Knowing, Wise.
4 093	If a man kills a believer intentionally, his recompense is Hell, to abide therein (For ever): And the wrath and the curse of Allah are upon him, and a dreadful penalty is prepared for him.	Whoso slayeth a believer of set purpose, his reward is hell for ever. Allah is wroth against him and He hath cursed him and prepared for him an awful doom.	And whoever kills a believer intentionally, his punishment is hell; he shall abide in it, and Allah will send His wrath on him and curse him and prepare for him a painful chastisement.
4 094	O ye who believe! When ye go abroad in the cause of Allah, investigate carefully, and say not to any one who offers you a salutation: "Thou art none of a believer!" Coveting the perishable goods of this life: with Allah are profits and spoils abundant. Even thus were ye yourselves before, till Allah conferred on you His favours: Therefore carefully investigate. For Allah is well aware of all that ye do.	O ye who believe! When ye go forth (to fight) in the way of Allah, be careful to discriminate, and say not unto one who offereth you peace: Thou art not a believer, seeking the chance profits of this life (so that ye may despoil him). With Allah are plenteous spoils. Even thus (as he now is) were ye before; but Allah hath since then been gracious unto you. Therefore take care to discriminate. Allah is ever Informed of what ye do.	O you who believe! when you go to war in Allah's way, make investigation, and do not say to any one who offers you peace: You are not a believer. Do you seek goods of this world's life! But with Allah there are abundant gains; you too were such before, then Allah conferred a benefit on you; therefore make investigation; surely Allah is aware of what you do.

4 095	Not equal are those believers who sit (at home) and receive no hurt, and those who strive and fight in the cause of Allah with their goods and their persons. Allah hath granted a grade higher to those who strive and fight with their goods and persons than to those who sit (at home). Unto all (in Faith) Hath Allah promised good: But those who strive and fight Hath He distinguished above those who sit (at home) by a special reward,-	Those of the believers who sit still, other than those who have a (disabling) hurt, are not on an equality with those who strive in the way of Allah with their wealth and lives. Allah hath conferred on those who strive with their wealth and lives a rank above the sedentary. Unto each Allah hath promised good, but He hath bestowed on those who strive a great reward above the sedentary;	The holders back from among the believers, not having any injury, and those who strive hard in Allah's way with their property and their persons are not equal; Allah has made the strivers with their property and their persons to excel the holders back a (high) degree, and to each (class) Allah has promised good; and Allah shall grant to the strivers above the holders back a mighty reward:
4 096	Ranks specially bestowed by Him, and Forgiveness and Mercy. For Allah is Oft-Forgiving, Most Merciful.	Degrees of rank from Him, and forgiveness and mercy. Allah is ever Forgiving, Merciful.	(High) degrees from Him and protection and mercy, and Allah is Forgiving, Merciful.
4 097	When angels take the souls of those who die in sin against their souls, they say: "In what (plight) Were ye?" They reply: "Weak and oppressed Were we in the earth." They say: "Was not the earth of Allah spacious enough for you to move yourselves away (From evil)?" Such men will find their abode in Hell,- What an evil refuge! -	Lo! as for those whom the angels take (in death) while they wrong themselves, (the angels) will ask: In what were ye engaged? They will say: We were oppressed in the land. (The angels) will say: Was not Allah's earth spacious that ye could have migrated therein? As for such, their habitation will be hell, an evil journey's end;	Surely (as for) those whom the angels cause to die while they are unjust to their souls, they shall say: In what state were you? They shall say: We were weak in the earth. They shall say: Was not Allah's earth spacious, so that you should have migrated therein? So these it is whose abode is hell, and it is an evil resort;
4 098	Except those who are (really) weak and oppressed - men, women, and children - who have no means in their power, nor (a guide-post) to their way.	Except the feeble among men, and the women, and the children, who are unable to devise a plan and are not shown a way.	Except the weak from among the men and the children who have not in their power the means nor can they find a way (to escape);
4 099	For these, there is hope that Allah will forgive: For Allah doth blot out (sins) and forgive again and again.	As for such, it may be that Allah will pardon them. Allah is ever Clement, Forgiving.	So these, it may be, Allah will pardon them, and Allah is Pardoning, Forgiving.
4 100	He who forsakes his home in the cause of Allah, finds in the earth Many a refuge, wide and spacious: Should he die as a refugee from home for Allah and His Messenger, His reward becomes due and sure with Allah: And Allah is Oft-Forgiving, Most Merciful.	Whoso migrateth for the cause of Allah will find much refuge and abundance in the earth, and whoso forsaketh his home, a fugitive unto Allah and His messenger, and death overtaketh him, his reward is then incumbent on Allah. Allah is ever Forgiving, Merciful.	And whoever flies in Allah's way, he will find in the earth many a place of refuge and abundant resources, and whoever goes forth from his house flying to Allah and His Messenger, and then death overtakes him, his reward is indeed with Allah and Allah is Forgiving, Merciful.
4 101	When ye travel through the earth, there is no blame on you if ye shorten your prayers, for fear the Unbelievers May attack you: For the Unbelievers are unto you open enemies.	And when ye go forth in the land, it is no sin for you to curtail (your) worship if ye fear that those who disbelieve may attack you. In truth the disbelievers are an open enemy to you.	And when you journey in the earth, there is no blame on you if you shorten the prayer, if you fear that those who disbelieve will cause you distress, surely the unbelievers are your open enemy.

4 102	When thou (O Messenger) art with them, and standest to lead them in prayer, Let one party of them stand up (in prayer) with thee, taking their arms with them: When they finish their prostrations, let them take their position in the rear. And let the other party come up which hath not yet prayed - and let them pray with thee, taking all precaution, and bearing arms: the Unbelievers wish, if ye were negligent of your arms and your baggage, to assault you in a single rush. But there is no blame on you if ye put away your arms because of the inconvenience of rain or because ye are ill; but take (every) precaution for yourselves. For the Unbelievers Allah hath prepared a humiliating punishment.	And when thou (O Muhammad) art among them and arrangest (their) worship for them, let only a party of them stand with thee (to worship) and let them take their arms. Then when they have performed their prostrations let them fall to the rear and let another party come that hath not worshipped and let them worship with thee, and let them take their precaution and their arms. Those who disbelieve long for you to neglect your arms and your baggage that they may attack you once for all. It is no sin for you to lay aside your arms, if rain impedeth you or ye are sick. But take your precaution. Lo! Allah prepareth for the disbelievers shameful punishment.	And when you are among them and keep up the prayer for them, let a party of them stand up with you, and let them take their arms; then when they have prostrated themselves let them go to your rear, and let another party who have not prayed come forward and pray with you, and let them take their precautions and their arms; (for) those who disbelieve desire that you may be careless of your arms and your luggage, so that they may then turn upon you with a sudden united attack, and there is no blame on you, if you are annoyed with rain or if you are sick, that you lay down your arms, and take your precautions; surely Allah has prepared a disgraceful chastisement for the unbelievers.
4 103	When ye pass (Congregational) prayers, celebrate Allah's praises, standing, sitting down, or lying down on your sides; but when ye are free from danger, set up Regular Prayers: For such prayers are enjoined on believers at stated times.	When ye have performed the act of worship, remember Allah, standing, sitting and reclining. And when ye are in safety, observe proper worship. Worship at fixed times hath been enjoined on the believers.	Then when you have finished the prayer, remember Allah standing and sitting and reclining; but when you are secure (from danger) keep up prayer; surely prayer is a timed ordinance for the believers.
4 104	And slacken not in following up the enemy: If ye are suffering hardships, they are suffering similar hardships; but ye have Hope from Allah, while they have none. And Allah is full of knowledge and wisdom.	Relent not in pursuit of the enemy. If ye are suffering, lo! they suffer even as ye suffer and ye hope from Allah that for which they cannot hope. Allah is ever Knower, Wise.	And be not weak hearted in pursuit of the enemy; if you suffer pain, then surely they (too) suffer pain as you suffer pain, and you hope from Allah what they do not hope; and Allah is Knowing, Wise.
4 105	We have sent down to thee the Book in truth, that thou mightest judge between men, as guided by Allah: so be not (used) as an advocate by those who betray their trust;	Lo! We reveal unto thee the Scripture with the truth, that thou mayst judge between mankind by that which Allah showeth thee. And be not thou a pleader for the treacherous;	Surely We have revealed the Book to you with the truth that you may judge between people by means of that which Allah has taught you; and be not an advocate on behalf of the treacherous.
4 106	But seek the forgiveness of Allah; for Allah is Oft-Forgiving, Most Merciful.	And seek forgiveness of Allah. Lo! Allah is ever Forgiving, Merciful.	And ask forgiveness of Allah; surely Allah is Forgiving, Merciful.
4 107	Contend not on behalf of such as betray their own souls; for Allah loveth not one given to perfidy and crime:	And plead not on behalf of (people) who deceive themselves. Lo! Allah loveth not one who is treacherous and sinful.	And do not plead on behalf of those who act unfaithfully to their souls; surely Allah does not love him who is treacherous, sinful;
4 108	They may hide (Their crimes) from men, but they cannot hide (Them) from Allah, seeing that He is in their midst when they plot by night, in words that He cannot approve: And Allah Doth compass round all that they do.	They seek to hide from men and seek not to hide from Allah. He is with them when by night they hold discourse displeasing unto Him. Allah ever surroundeth what they do.	They hide themselves from men and do not hide themselves from Allah, and He is with them when they meditate by night words which please Him not, and Allah encompasses what they do.

4 109	Ah! These are the sort of men on whose behalf ye may contend in this world; but who will contend with Allah on their behalf on the Day of Judgment, or who will carry their affairs through?	Ho! ye are they who pleaded for them in the life of the world. But who will plead with Allah for them on the Day of Resurrection, or who will then be their defender?	Behold! you are they who (may) plead for them in this world's life, but who will plead for them with Allah on the resurrection day, or who shall be their protector?
4 110	If any one does evil or wrongs his own soul but afterwards seeks Allah's forgiveness, he will find Allah Oft-Forgiving, Most Merciful.	Yet whoso doeth evil or wrongeth his own soul, then seeketh pardon of Allah, will find Allah Forgiving, Merciful.	And whoever does evil or acts unjustly to his soul, then asks forgiveness of Allah, he shall find Allah Forgiving, Merciful.
4 111	And if any one earns sin, he earns it against His own soul: for Allah is full of knowledge and wisdom.	Whoso committeth sin committeth it only against himself. Allah is ever Knower, Wise.	And whoever commits a sin, he only commits it against his own soul; and Allah is Knowing, Wise.
4 112	But if any one earns a fault or a sin and throws it on to one that is innocent, He carries (on himself) (Both) a falsehood and a flagrant sin.	And whoso committeth a delinquency or crime, then throweth (the blame) thereof upon the innocent, hath burdened himself with falsehood and a flagrant crime.	And whoever commits a fault or a sin, then accuses of it one innocent, he indeed takes upon himself the burden of a calumny and a manifest sin.
4 113	But for the Grace of Allah to thee and his Mercy, a party of them would certainly have plotted to lead thee astray. But (in fact) they will only Lead their own souls astray, and to thee they can do no harm in the least. For Allah hath sent down to thee the Book and wisdom and taught thee what thou Knewest not (before): And great is the Grace of Allah unto thee.	But for the grace of Allah upon thee (Muhammad), and His mercy, a party of them had resolved to mislead thee, but they will mislead only themselves and they will hurt thee not at all. Allah revealeth unto thee the Scripture and wisdom, and teacheth thee that which thou knewest not. The grace of Allah toward thee hath been infinite.	And were it not for Allah's grace upon you and His mercy a party of them had certainly designed to bring you to perdition and they do not bring (aught) to perdition but their own souls, and they shall not harm you in any way, and Allah has revealed to you the Book and the wisdom, and He has taught you what you did not know, and Allah's grace on you is very great.
4 114	In most of their secret talks there is no good: But if one exhorts to a deed of charity or justice or conciliation between men, (Secrecy is permissible): To him who does this, seeking the good pleasure of Allah, We shall soon give a reward of the highest (value).	There is no good in much of their secret conferences save (in) him who enjoineth almsgiving and kindness and peace-making among the people. Whoso doeth that, seeking the good pleasure of Allah, We shall bestow on him a vast reward.	There is no good in most of their secret counsels except (in his) who enjoins charity or goodness or reconciliation between people; and whoever does this seeking Allah's pleasure, We will give him a mighty reward.
4 115	If anyone contends with the Messenger even after guidance has been plainly conveyed to him, and follows a path other than that becoming to men of Faith, We shall leave him in the path he has chosen, and land him in Hell,- what an evil refuge!	And whoso opposeth the messenger after the guidance (of Allah) hath been manifested unto him, and followeth other than the believer's way, We appoint for him that unto which he himself hath turned, and expose him unto hell - a hapless journey's end!	And whoever acts hostilely to the Messenger after that guidance has become manifest to him, and follows other than the way of the believers, We will turn him to that to which he has (himself) turned and make him enter hell; and it is an evil resort.
4 116	Allah forgiveth not (The sin of) joining other gods with Him; but He forgiveth whom He pleaseth other sins than this: one who joins other gods with Allah, Hath strayed far, far away (from the right).	Lo! Allah pardoneth not that partners should be ascribed unto Him. He pardoneth all save that to whom He will. Whoso ascribeth partners unto Allah hath wandered far astray.	Surely Allah does not forgive that anything should be associated with Him, and He forgives what is besides this to whom He pleases; and whoever associates anything with Allah, he indeed strays off into a remote error.
4 117	(The Pagans), leaving Him, call but upon female deities: They call but upon Satan the persistent rebel!	They invoke in His stead only females; they pray to none else than Satan, a rebel.	They do not call besides Him on anything but idols, and they do not call on anything but a rebellious Shaitan.
4 118	Allah did curse him, but he said: "I will take of Thy servants a portion Marked off;"	Whom Allah cursed, and he said: Surely I will take of Thy bondmen an appointed portion,	Allah has cursed him; and he said: Most certainly I will take of Thy servants an appointed portion:

4	119	"I will mislead them, and I will create in them false desires; I will order them to slit the ears of cattle, and to deface the (fair) nature created by Allah." Whoever, forsaking Allah, takes Satan for a friend, hath of a surety suffered a loss that is manifest.	And surely I will lead them astray, and surely I will arouse desires in them, and surely I will command them and they will cut the cattle' ears, and surely I will command them and they will change Allah's creation. Whoso chooseth Satan for a patron instead of Allah is verily a loser and his loss is manifest.	And most certainly I will lead them astray and excite in them vain desires, and bid them so that they shall slit the ears of the cattle, and most certainly I will bid them so that they shall alter Allah's creation; and whoever takes the Shaitan for a guardian rather than Allah he indeed shall suffer a manifest loss.
4	120	Satan makes them promises, and creates in them false desires; but Satan's promises are nothing but deception.	He promiseth them and stirreth up desires in them, and Satan promiseth them only to beguile.	He gives them promises and excites vain desires in them; and the Shaitan does not promise them but to deceive.
4	121	They (his dupes) will have their dwelling in Hell, and from it they will find no way of escape.	For such, their habitation will be hell, and they will find no refuge therefrom.	These are they whose abode is hell, and they shall not find any refuge from it.
4	122	But those who believe and do deeds of righteousness,- we shall soon admit them to gardens, with rivers flowing beneath,-to dwell therein for ever. Allah's promise is the truth, and whose word can be truer than Allah's?	But as for those who believe and do good works We shall bring them into Gardens underneath which rivers flow, wherein they will abide for ever. It is a promise from Allah in truth; and who can be more truthful than Allah in utterance?	And (as for) those who believe and do good, We will make them enter into gardens beneath which rivers flow, to abide therein for ever; (it is) a promise of Allah, true (indeed), and who is truer of word than Allah?
4	123	Not your desires, nor those of the People of the Book (can prevail): whoever works evil, will be requited accordingly. Nor will he find, besides Allah, any protector or helper.	It will not be in accordance with your desires, nor the desires of the People of the Scripture. He who doeth wrong will have the recompense thereof, and will not find against Allah any protecting friend or helper.	(This) shall not be in accordance with your vain desires nor in accordance with the vain desires of the followers of the Book; whoever does evil, he shall be requited with it, and besides Allah he will find for himself neither a guardian nor a helper.
4	124	If any do deeds of righteousness,- be they male or female - and have faith, they will enter Heaven, and not the least injustice will be done to them.	And whoso doeth good works, whether of male or female, and he (or she) is a believer, such will enter paradise and they will not be wronged the dint in a date-stone.	And whoever does good deeds whether male or female and he (or she) is a believer-- these shall enter the garden, and they shall not be dealt with a jot unjustly.
4	125	Who can be better in religion than one who submits his whole self to Allah, does good, and follows the way of Abraham the true in Faith? For Allah did take Abraham for a friend.	Who is better in religion than he who surrendereth his purpose to Allah while doing good (to men) and followeth the tradition of Abraham, the upright? Allah (Himself) chose Abraham for friend.	And who has a better religion than he who submits himself entirely to Allah? And he is the doer of good (to others) and follows the faith of Ibrahim, the upright one, and Allah took Ibrahim as a friend.
4	126	But to Allah belong all things in the heavens and on earth: And He it is that Encompasseth all things.	Unto Allah belongeth whatsoever is in the heavens and whatsoever is in the earth. Allah ever surroundeth all things.	And whatever is in the heavens and whatever is in the earth is Allah's; and Allah encompasses all things.

4 127	They ask thy instruction concerning the women say: Allah doth instruct you about them: And (remember) what hath been rehearsed unto you in the Book, concerning the orphans of women to whom ye give not the portions prescribed, and yet whom ye desire to marry, as also concerning the children who are weak and oppressed: that ye stand firm for justice to orphans. There is not a good deed which ye do, but Allah is well-acquainted therewith.	They consult thee concerning women. Say: Allah giveth you decree concerning them, and the Scripture which hath been recited unto you (giveth decree), concerning female orphans and those unto whom ye give not that which is ordained for them though ye desire to marry them, and (concerning) the weak among children, and that ye should deal justly with orphans. Whatever good ye do, lo! Allah is ever Aware of it.	And they ask you a decision about women. Say: Allah makes known to you His decision concerning them, and that which is recited to you in the Book concerning female orphans whom you do not give what is appointed for them while you desire to marry them, and concerning the weak among children, and that you should deal towards orphans with equity, and whatever good you do, Allah surely knows it.
4 128	If a wife fears cruelty or desertion on her husband's part, there is no blame on them if they arrange an amicable settlement between themselves; and such settlement is best; even though men's souls are swayed by greed. But if ye do good and practise self-restraint, Allah is well-acquainted with all that ye do.	If a woman feareth ill treatment from her husband, or desertion, it is no sin for them twain if they make terms of peace between themselves. Peace is better. But greed hath been made present in the minds (of men). If ye do good and keep from evil, lo! Allah is ever Informed of what ye do.	And if a woman fears ill usage or desertion on the part of her husband, there is no blame on them, if they effect a reconciliation between them, and reconciliation is better, and avarice has been made to be present in the (people's) minds; and if you do good (to others) and guard (against evil), then surely Allah is aware of what you do.
4 129	Ye are never able to be fair and just as between women, even if it is your ardent desire: But turn not away (from a woman) altogether, so as to leave her (as it were) hanging (in the air). If ye come to a friendly understanding, and practise self-restraint, Allah is Oft-Forgiving, Most Merciful.	Ye will not be able to deal equally between (your) wives, however much ye wish (to do so). But turn not altogether away (from one), leaving her as in suspense. If ye do good and keep from evil, lo! Allah is ever Forgiving, Merciful.	And you have it not in your power to do justice between wives, even though you may wish (it), but be not disinclined (from one) with total disinclination, so that you leave her as it were in suspense; and if you effect a reconciliation and guard (against evil), then surely Allah is Forgiving, Merciful.
4 130	But if they disagree (and must part), Allah will provide abundance for all from His all-reaching bounty: for Allah is He that careth for all and is Wise.	But if they separate, Allah will compensate each out of His abundance. Allah is ever All-Embracing, All-Knowing.	And if they separate, Allah will render them both free from want out of His ampleness, and Allah is Ample-giving, Wise.
4 131	To Allah belong all things in the heavens and on earth. Verily we have directed the People of the Book before you, and you (O Muslims) to fear Allah. But if ye deny Him, lo! unto Allah belong all things in the heavens and on earth, and Allah is free of all wants, worthy of all praise.	Unto Allah belongeth whatsoever is in the heavens and whatsoever is in the earth. And We charged those who received the Scripture before you, and (We charge) you, that ye keep your duty toward Allah. And if ye disbelieve, lo! unto Allah belongeth whatsoever is in the heavens and whatsoever is in the earth, and Allah is ever Absolute, Owner of Praise.	And whatever is in the heavens and whatever is in the earth is Allah's and certainly We enjoined those who were given the Book before you and (We enjoin) you too that you should be careful of (your duty to) Allah; and if you disbelieve, then surely whatever is in the heavens and whatever is in the earth is Allah's and Allah is Self-sufficient, Praise-worthy.
4 132	Yea, unto Allah belong all things in the heavens and on earth, and enough is Allah to carry through all affairs.	Unto Allah belongeth whatsoever is in the heavens and whatsoever is in the earth. And Allah is sufficient as Defender.	And whatever is in the heavens and whatever is in the earth is Allah's, and Allah is sufficient as a Protector.
4 133	If it were His will, He could destroy you, O mankind, and create another race; for He hath power this to do.	If He will, He can remove you, O people, and produce others (in your stead). Allah is Able to do that.	If He please, He can make you pass away, O people! and bring others; and Allah has the power to do this.

4	134	If any one desires a reward in this life, in Allah's (gift) is the reward (both) of this life and of the hereafter: for Allah is He that heareth and seeth (all things).	Whoso desireth the reward of the world, (let him know that) with Allah is the reward of the world and the Hereafter. Allah is ever Hearer, Seer.	Whoever desires the reward of this world, then with Allah is the reward of this world and the hereafter; and Allah is Hearing, Seeing.
4	135	O ye who believe! stand out firmly for justice, as witnesses to Allah, even as against yourselves, or your parents, or your kin, and whether it be (against) rich or poor: for Allah can best protect both. Follow not the lusts (of your hearts), lest ye swerve, and if ye distort (justice) or decline to do justice, verily Allah is well-acquainted with all that ye do.	O ye who believe! Be ye staunch in justice, witnesses for Allah, even though it be against yourselves or (your) parents or (your) kindred, whether (the case be of) a rich man or a poor man, for Allah is nearer unto both (them ye are). So follow not passion lest ye lapse (from truth) and if ye lapse or fall away, then lo! Allah is ever Informed of what ye do.	O you who believe! be maintainers of justice, bearers of witness of Allah's sake, though it may be against your own selves or (your) parents or near relatives; if he be rich or poor, Allah is nearer to them both in compassion; therefore do not follow (your) low desires, lest you deviate; and if you swerve or turn aside, then surely Allah is aware of what you do.
4	136	O ye who believe! Believe in Allah and His Messenger, and the scripture which He hath sent to His Messenger and the scripture which He sent to those before (him). Any who denieth Allah, His angels, His Books, His Messengers, and the Day of Judgment, hath gone far, far astray.	O ye who believe! Believe in Allah and His messenger and the Scripture which He hath revealed unto His messenger, and the Scripture which He revealed aforetime. Whoso disbelieveth in Allah and His angels and His scriptures and His messengers and the Last Day, he verily hath wandered far astray.	O you who believe! believe in Allah and His Messenger and the Book which He has revealed to His Messenger and the Book which He revealed before; and whoever disbelieves in Allah and His angels and His messengers and the last day, he indeed strays off into a remote error.
4	137	Those who believe, then reject faith, then believe (again) and (again) reject faith, and go on increasing in unbelief,- Allah will not forgive them nor guide them nor guide them on the way.	Lo! those who believe, then disbelieve and then (again) believe, then disbelieve, and then increase in disbelief, Allah will never pardon them, nor will He guide them unto a way.	Surely (as for) those who believe then disbelieve, again believe and again disbelieve, then increase in disbelief, Allah will not forgive them nor guide them in the (right) path.
4	138	To the Hypocrites give the glad tidings that there is for them (but) a grievous penalty;-	Bear unto the hypocrites the tidings that for them there is a painful doom;	Announce to the hypocrites that they shall have a painful chastisement:
4	139	Yea, to those who take for friends unbelievers rather than believers: is it honour they seek among them? Nay,- all honour is with Allah.	Those who chose disbelievers for their friends instead of believers! Do they look for power at their hands? Lo! all power appertaineth to Allah.	Those who take the unbelievers for guardians rather than believers. Do they seek honor from them? Then surely all honor is for Allah.
4	140	Already has He sent you Word in the Book, that when ye hear the signs of Allah held in defiance and ridicule, ye are not to sit with them unless they turn to a different theme: if ye did, ye would be like them. For Allah will collect the hypocrites and those who defy faith - all in Hell:-	He hath already revealed unto you in the Scripture that, when ye hear the revelations of Allah rejected and derided, (ye) sit not with them (who disbelieve and mock) until they engage in some other conversation. Lo! in that case (if ye stayed) ye would be like unto them. Lo! Allah will gather hypocrites and disbelievers, all together, into hell;	And indeed He has revealed to you in the Book that when you hear Allah's communications disbelieved in and mocked at do not sit with them until they enter into some other discourse; surely then you would be like them; surely Allah will gather together the hypocrites and the unbelievers all in hell.

4 141	(These are) the ones who wait and watch about you: if ye do gain a victory from Allah, they say: "Were we not with you?"- but if the unbelievers gain a success, they say (to them): "Did we not gain an advantage over you, and did we not guard you from the believers?" but Allah will judge betwixt you on the Day of Judgment. And never will Allah grant to the unbelievers a way (to triumphs) over the believers.	Those who wait upon occasion in regard to you and, if a victory cometh unto you from Allah, say: Are we not with you? and if the disbelievers meet with a success say: Had we not the mastery of you, and did we not protect you from the believers? - Allah will judge between you at the Day of Resurrection, and Allah will not give the disbelievers any way (of success) against the believers.	Those who wait for (some misfortune to befall) you; then if you have a victory from Allah they say: Were we not with you? And if there is a chance for the unbelievers, they say: Did we not acquire the mastery over you and defend you from the believers? So Allah shall Judge between you on the day of resurrection, and Allah will by no means give the unbelievers a way against the believers.
4 142	The Hypocrites - they think they are over-reaching Allah, but He will over-reach them: When they stand up to prayer, they stand without earnestness, to be seen of men, but little do they hold Allah in remembrance;	Lo! the hypocrites seek to beguile Allah, but it is He Who beguileth them. When they stand up to worship they perform it languidly and to be seen of men, and are mindful of Allah but little;	Surely the hypocrites strive to deceive Allah, and He shall requite their deceit to them, and when they stand up to prayer they stand up sluggishly; they do it only to be seen of men and do not remember Allah save a little.
4 143	(They are) distracted in mind even in the midst of it,- being (sincerely) for neither one group nor for another whom Allah leaves straying,- never wilt thou find for him the way.	Swaying between this (and that), (belonging) neither to these nor to those. He whom Allah causeth to go astray, thou (O Muhammad) wilt not find a way for him:	Wavering between that (and this), (belonging) neither to these nor to those; and whomsoever Allah causes to err, you shall not find a way for him.
4 144	O ye who believe! Take not for friends unbelievers rather than believers: Do ye wish to offer Allah an open proof against yourselves?	O ye who believe! Choose not disbelievers for (your) friends in place of believers. Would ye give Allah a clear warrant against you?	O you who believe! do not take the unbelievers for friends rather than the believers; do you desire that you should give to Allah a manifest proof against yourselves?
4 145	The Hypocrites will be in the lowest depths of the Fire: no helper wilt thou find for them;-	Lo! the hypocrites (will be) in the lowest deep of the Fire, and thou wilt find no helper for them;	Surely the hypocrites are in the lowest stage of the fire and you shall not find a helper for them.
4 146	Except for those who repent, mend (their lives) hold fast to Allah, and purify their religion as in Allah's sight: if so they will be (numbered) with the believers. And soon will Allah grant to the believers a reward of immense value.	Save those who repent and amend and hold fast to Allah and make their religion pure for Allah (only). Those are with the believers. And Allah will bestow on the believers an immense reward.	Except those who repent and amend and hold fast to Allah and are sincere in their religion to Allah, these are with the believers, and Allah will grant the believers a mighty reward.
4 147	What can Allah gain by your punishment, if ye are grateful and ye believe? Nay, it is Allah that recogniseth (all good), and knoweth all things.	What concern hath Allah for your punishment if ye are thankful (for His mercies) and believe (in Him)? Allah was ever Responsive, Aware.	Why should Allah chastise you if you are grateful and believe? And Allah is the Multiplier of rewards, Knowing.
4 148	Allah loveth not that evil should be noised abroad in public speech, except where injustice hath been done; for Allah is He who heareth and knoweth all things.	Allah loveth not the utterance of harsh speech save by one who hath been wronged. Allah is ever Hearer, Knower.	Allah does not love the public utterance of hurtful speech unless (it be) by one to whom injustice has been done; and Allah is Hearing, Knowing.
4 149	Whether ye publish a good deed or conceal it or cover evil with pardon, verily Allah doth blot out (sins) and hath power (in the judgment of values).	If ye do good openly or keep it secret, or forgive evil, lo! Allah is ever Forgiving, Powerful.	If you do good openly or do it in secret or pardon an evil then surely Allah is Pardoning, Powerful.

4 150	Those who deny Allah and His messengers, and (those who) wish to separate Allah from His messengers, saying: "We believe in some but reject others": And (those who) wish to take a course midway,-	Lo! those who disbelieve in Allah and His messengers, and seek to make distinction between Allah and His messengers, and say: We believe in some and disbelieve in others, and seek to choose a way in between;		Surely those who disbelieve in Allah and His messengers and (those who) desire to make a distinction between Allah and His messengers and say: We believe in some and disbelieve in others, and desire to take a course between (this and) that.
4 151	They are in truth (equally) unbelievers; and we have prepared for unbelievers a humiliating punishment.	Such are disbelievers in truth; and for disbelievers We prepare a shameful doom.		These it is that are truly unbelievers, and We have prepared for the unbelievers a disgraceful chastisement.
4 152	To those who believe in Allah and His messengers and make no distinction between any of the messengers, we shall soon give their (due) rewards: for Allah is Oft-Forgiving, Most Merciful.	But those who believe in Allah and His messengers and make no distinction between any of them, unto them Allah will give their wages; and Allah was ever Forgiving, Merciful.		And those who believe in Allah and His messengers and do not make a distinction between any of them-- Allah will grant them their rewards; and Allah is Forgiving, Merciful.
4 153	The people of the Book ask thee to cause a book to descend to them from heaven: Indeed they asked Moses for an even greater (miracle), for they said: "Show us Allah in public," but they were dazed for their presumption, with thunder and lightning. Yet they worshipped the calf even after clear signs had come to them; even so we forgave them; and gave Moses manifest proofs of authority.	The people of the Scripture ask of thee that thou shouldst cause an (actual) Book to descend upon them from heaven. They asked a greater thing of Moses aforetime, for they said: Show us Allah plainly. The storm of lightning seized them for their wickedness. Then (even after that) they chose the calf (for worship) after clear proofs (of Allah's Sovereignty) had come unto them. And We forgave them that! And We bestowed on Moses evident authority.		The followers of the Book ask you to bring down to them a book from heaven; so indeed they demanded of Musa a greater thing than that, for they said: Show us Allah manifestly; so the lightning overtook them on account of their injustice. Then they took the calf (for a god), after clear signs had come to them, but We pardoned this; and We gave to Musa clear authority.
4 154	And for their covenant we raised over them (the towering height) of Mount (Sinai); and (on another occasion) we said: "Enter the gate with humility"; and (once again) we commanded them: "Transgress not in the matter of the Sabbath." And we took from them a solemn covenant.	And We caused the Mount to tower above them at (the taking of) their covenant: and We bade them: Enter the gate, prostrate! and We bode them: Transgress not the Sabbath! and We took from them a firm covenant.		And We lifted the mountain (Sainai) over them at (the taking of the covenant) and We said to them: Enter the door making obeisance; and We said to them: Do not exceed the limits of the Sabbath, and We made with them a firm covenant.
4 155	(They have incurred divine displeasure): In that they broke their covenant; that they rejected the signs of Allah; that they slew the Messengers in defiance of right; that they said, "Our hearts are the wrappings (which preserve Allah's Word; We need no more)";- Nay, Allah hath set the seal on their hearts for their blasphemy, and little is it they believe;-	Then because of their breaking of their covenant, and their disbelieving in the revelations of Allah, and their slaying of the prophets wrongfully, and their saying: Our hearts are hardened - Nay, but Allah set a seal upon them for their disbelief, so that they believe not save a few -		Therefore, for their breaking their covenant and their disbelief in the communications of Allah and their killing the prophets wrongfully and their saying: Our hearts are covered; nay! Allah set a seal upon them owing to their unbelief, so they shall not believe except a few.
4 156	That they rejected Faith; that they uttered against Mary a grave false charge;	And because of their disbelief and of their speaking against Mary a tremendous calumny;		And for their unbelief and for their having uttered against Marium a grievous calumny.

4 157	That they said (in boast), "We killed Christ Jesus the son of Mary, the Messenger of Allah";- but they killed him not, nor crucified him, but so it was made to appear to them, and those who differ therein are full of doubts, with no (certain) knowledge, but only conjecture to follow, for of a surety they killed him not:-	And because of their saying: We slew the Messiah, Jesus son of Mary, Allah's messenger - they slew him not nor crucified him, but it appeared so unto them; and lo! those who disagree concerning it are in doubt thereof; they have no knowledge thereof save pursuit of a conjecture; they slew him not for certain.	And their saying: Surely we have killed the Messiah, Isa son of Marium, the messenger of Allah; and they did not kill him nor did they crucify him, but it appeared to them so (like Isa) and most surely those who differ therein are only in a doubt about it; they have no knowledge respecting it, but only follow a conjecture, and they killed him not for sure.
4 158	Nay, Allah raised him up unto Himself; and Allah is Exalted in Power, Wise;-	But Allah took him up unto Himself. Allah was ever Mighty, Wise.	Nay! Allah took him up to Himself; and Allah is Mighty, Wise.
4 159	And there is none of the People of the Book but must believe in him before his death; and on the Day of Judgment he will be a witness against them;-	There is not one of the People of the Scripture but will believe in him before his death, and on the Day of Resurrection he will be a witness against them -	And there is not one of the followers of the Book but most certainly believes in this before his death, and on the day of resurrection he (Isa) shall be a witness against them.
4 160	For the iniquity of the Jews We made unlawful for them certain (foods) good and wholesome which had been lawful for them;- in that they hindered many from Allah's Way;-	Because of the wrongdoing of the Jews We forbade them good things which were (before) made lawful unto them, and because of their much hindering from Allah's way,	Wherefore for the iniquity of those who are Jews did We disallow to them the good things which had been made lawful for them and for their hindering many (people) from Allah's way.
4 161	That they took usury, though they were forbidden; and that they devoured men's substance wrongfully;- we have prepared for those among them who reject faith a grievous punishment.	And of their taking usury when they were forbidden it, and of their devouring people's wealth by false pretences, We have prepared for those of them who disbelieve a painful doom.	And their taking usury though indeed they were forbidden it and their devouring the property of people falsely, and We have prepared for the unbelievers from among them a painful chastisement.
4 162	But those among them who are well-grounded in knowledge, and the believers, believe in what hath been revealed to thee and what was revealed before thee: And (especially) those who establish regular prayer and practise regular charity and believe in Allah and in the Last Day: To them shall We soon give a great reward.	But those of them who are firm in knowledge and the believers believe in that which is revealed unto thee, and that which was revealed before thee, especially the diligent in prayer and those who pay the poor-due, the believers in Allah and the Last Day. Upon these We shall bestow immense reward.	But the firm in knowledge among them and the believers believe in what has been revealed to you and what was revealed before you, and those who keep up prayers and those who give the poor-rate and the believers in Allah and the last day, these it is whom We will give a mighty reward.
4 163	We have sent thee inspiration, as We sent it to Noah and the Messengers after him: we sent inspiration to Abraham, Isma'il, Isaac, Jacob and the Tribes, to Jesus, Job, Jonah, Aaron, and Solomon, and to David We gave the Psalms.	Lo! We inspire thee as We inspired Noah and the prophets after him, as We inspired Abraham and Ishmael and Isaac and Jacob and the tribes, and Jesus and Job and Jonah and Aaron and Solomon, and as We imparted unto David the Psalms;	Surely We have revealed to you as We revealed to Nuh, and the prophets after him, and We revealed to Ibrahim and Ismail and Ishaq and Yaqoub and the tribes, and Isa and Ayub and Yunus and Haroun and Sulaiman and We gave to Dawood Psalms.
4 164	Of some messengers We have already told thee the story; of others We have not;- and to Moses Allah spoke direct;-	And messengers We have mentioned unto thee before and messengers We have not mentioned unto thee; and Allah spake directly unto Moses;	And (We sent) messengers We have mentioned to you before and messengers we have not mentioned to you; and to Musa, Allah addressed His Word, speaking (to him):

4 165	Messengers who gave good news as well as warning, that mankind, after (the coming) of the messengers, should have no plea against Allah: For Allah is Exalted in Power, Wise.	Messengers of good cheer and of warning, in order that mankind might have no argument against Allah after the messengers. Allah was ever Mighty, Wise.	(We sent) messengers as the givers of good news and as warners, so that people should not have a plea against Allah after the (coming of) messengers; and Allah is Mighty, Wise.
4 166	But Allah beareth witness that what He hath sent unto thee He hath sent from His (own) knowledge, and the angels bear witness: But enough is Allah for a witness.	But Allah (Himself) testifieth concerning that which He hath revealeth unto thee; in His knowledge hath He revealed it; and the angels also testify. And Allah is sufficient Witness.	But Allah bears witness by what He has revealed to you that He has revealed it with His knowledge, and the angels bear witness (also); and Allah is sufficient as a witness.
4 167	Those who reject Faith and keep off (men) from the way of Allah, have verily strayed far, far away from the Path.	Lo! those who disbelieve and hinder (others) from the way of Allah, they verily have wandered far astray.	Surely (as for) those who disbelieve and hinder (men) from Allah's way, they indeed have strayed off into a remote error.
4 168	Those who reject Faith and do wrong,- Allah will not forgive them nor guide them to any way-	Lo! those who disbelieve and deal in wrong, Allah will never forgive them, neither will He guide them unto a road,	Surely (as for) those who disbelieve and act unjustly Allah will not forgive them nor guide them to a path,
4 169	Except the way of Hell, to dwell therein for ever. And this to Allah is easy.	Except the road of hell, wherein they will abide for ever. And that is ever easy for Allah.	Except the path of hell, to abide in it for ever, and this is easy to Allah.
4 170	O Mankind! The Messenger hath come to you in truth from Allah: believe in him: It is best for you. But if ye reject Faith, to Allah belong all things in the heavens and on earth: And Allah is All-Knowing, All-Wise.	O mankind! The messenger hath come unto you with the Truth from your Lord. Therefor believe; (it is) better for you. But if ye disbelieve, still, lo! unto Allah belongeth whatsoever is in the heavens and the earth. Allah is ever Knower, Wise.	O people! surely the Messenger has come to you with the truth from your Lord, therefore believe, (it shall be) good for you and If you disbelieve, then surely whatever is in the heavens and the earth is Allah's; and Allah is Knowing, Wise.
4 171	O People of the Book! Commit no excesses in your religion: Nor say of Allah aught but the truth. Christ Jesus the son of Mary was (no more than) a messenger of Allah, and His Word, which He bestowed on Mary, and a spirit proceeding from Him: so believe in Allah and His messengers. Say not "Trinity": desist: it will be better for you: for Allah is one Allah: Glory be to Him: (far Exalted is He) above having a son. To Him belong all things in the heavens and on earth. And enough is Allah as a Disposer of affairs.	O People of the Scripture! Do not exaggerate in your religion nor utter aught concerning Allah save the truth. The Messiah, Jesus son of Mary, was only a messenger of Allah, and His word which He conveyed unto Mary, and a spirit from Him. So believe in Allah and His messengers, and say not "Three" - Cease! (it is) better for you! - Allah is only One Allah. Far is it removed from His Transcendent Majesty that He should have a son. His is all that is in the heavens and all that is in the earth. And Allah is sufficient as Defender.	O followers of the Book! do not exceed the limits in your religion, and do not speak (lies) against Allah, but (speak) the truth; the Messiah, Isa son of Marium is only a messenger of Allah and His Word which He communicated to Marium and a spirit from Him; believe therefore in Allah and His messengers, and say not, Three. Desist, it is better for you; Allah is only one Allah; far be It from His glory that He should have a son, whatever is in the heavens and whatever is in the earth is His, and Allah is sufficient for a Protector.
4 172	Christ disdaineth nor to serve and worship Allah, nor do the angels, those nearest (to Allah): those who disdain His worship and are arrogant,-He will gather them all together unto Himself to (answer).	The Messiah will never scorn to be a slave unto Allah, nor will the favoured angels. Whoso scorneth His service and is proud, all such will He assemble unto Him;	The Messiah does by no means disdain that he should be a servant of Allah, nor do the angels who are near to Him, and whoever disdains His service and is proud, He will gather them all together to Himself.

4 173	But to those who believe and do deeds of righteousness, He will give their (due) rewards,- and more, out of His bounty: But those who are disdainful and arrogant, He will punish with a grievous penalty; Nor will they find, besides Allah, any to protect or help them.	Then, as for those who believed and did good works, unto them will He pay their wages in full, adding unto them of His bounty; and as for those who were scornful and proud, them will He punish with a painful doom. And they will not find for them, against Allah, any protecting friend or helper.	Then as for those who believe and do good, He will pay them fully their rewards and give them more out of His grace; and as for those who disdain and are proud, He will chastise them with a painful chastisement. And they shall not find for themselves besides Allah a guardian or a helper.
4 174	O mankind! verily there hath come to you a convincing proof from your Lord: For We have sent unto you a light (that is) manifest.	O mankind! Now hath a proof from your Lord come unto you, and We have sent down unto you a clear light;	O people! surely there has come to you manifest proof from your Lord and We have sent to you clear light.
4 175	Then those who believe in Allah, and hold fast to Him,- soon will He admit them to mercy and grace from Himself, and guide them to Himself by a straight way.	As for those who believe in Allah, and hold fast unto Him, them He will cause to enter into His mercy and grace, and will guide them unto Him by a straight road.	Then as for those who believe in Allah and hold fast by Him, He will cause them to enter into His mercy and grace and guide them to Himself on a right path.
4 176	They ask thee for a legal decision. Say: Allah directs (thus) about those who leave no descendants or ascendants as heirs. If it is a man that dies, leaving a sister but no child, she shall have half the inheritance: If (such a deceased was) a woman, who left no child, Her brother takes her inheritance: If there are two sisters, they shall have two-thirds of the inheritance (between them): if there are brothers and sisters, (they share), the male having twice the share of the female. Thus doth Allah make clear to you (His law), lest ye err. And Allah hath knowledge of all things.	They ask thee for a pronouncement. Say: Allah hath pronounced for you concerning distant kindred. If a man die childless and he have a sister, hers is half the heritage, and he would have inherited from her had she died childless. And if there be two sisters, then theirs are two-thirds of the heritage, and if they be brethren, men and women, unto the male is the equivalent of the share of two females. Allah expoundeth unto you, so that ye err not. Allah is Knower of all things.	They ask you for a decision of the law. Say: Allah gives you a decision concerning the person who has neither parents nor offspring; if a man dies (and) he has no son and he has a sister, she shall have half of what he leaves, and he shall be her heir she has no son; but if there be two (sisters), they shall have two-thirds of what he leaves; and if there are brethren, men and women, then the male shall have the like of the portion of two females; Allah makes clear to you, lest you err; and Allah knows all things.

Chapter 5:

AL-MAEDA (THE TABLE, THE TABLE SPREAD)

Total Verses: 120 Revealed At: MADINA

In the name of Allah, the Most Beneficent, the Most Merciful.

5 001	O ye who believe! fulfil (all) obligations. Lawful unto you (for food) are all four-footed animals, with the exceptions named: But animals of the chase are forbidden while ye are in the sacred precincts or in pilgrim garb: for Allah doth command according to His will and plan.	O ye who believe! Fulfil your indentures. The beast of cattle is made lawful unto you (for food) except that which is announced unto you (herein), game being unlawful when ye are on the pilgrimage. Lo! Allah ordaineth that which pleaseth Him.	O you who believe! fulfill the obligations. The cattle quadrupeds are allowed to you except that which is recited to you, not violating the prohibition against game when you are entering upon the performance of the pilgrimage; surely Allah orders what He desires.

5 002	O ye who believe! Violate not the sanctity of the symbols of Allah, nor of the sacred month, nor of the animals brought for sacrifice, nor the garlands that mark out such animals, nor the people resorting to the sacred house, seeking of the bounty and good pleasure of their Lord. But when ye are clear of the sacred precincts and of pilgrim garb, ye may hunt and let not the hatred of some people in (once) shutting you out of the Sacred Mosque lead you to transgression (and hostility on your part). Help ye one another in righteousness and piety, but help ye not one another in sin and rancour: fear Allah: for Allah is strict in punishment.	O ye who believe! Profane not Allah's monuments nor the Sacred Month nor the offerings nor the garlands, nor those repairing to the Sacred House, seeking the grace and pleasure of their Lord. But when ye have left the sacred territory, then go hunting (if ye will). And let not your hatred of a folk who (once) stopped your going to the inviolable place of worship seduce you to transgress; but help ye one another unto righteousness and pious duty. Help not one another unto sin and transgression, but keep your duty to Allah. Lo! Allah is severe in punishment.	O you who believe! do not violate the signs appointed by Allah nor the sacred month, nor (interfere with) the offerings, nor the sacrificial animals with garlands, nor those going to the sacred house seeking the grace and pleasure of their Lord; and when you are free from the obligations of the pilgrimage, then hunt, and let not hatred of a people-- because they hindered you from the Sacred Masjid-- incite you to exceed the limits, and help one another in goodness and piety, and do not help one another in sin and aggression; and be careful of (your duty to) Allah; surely Allah is severe in requiting (evil).	
5 003	Forbidden to you (for food) are: dead meat, blood, the flesh of swine, and that on which hath been invoked the name of other than Allah; that which hath been killed by strangling, or by a violent blow, or by a headlong fall, or by being gored to death; that which hath been (partly) eaten by a wild animal; unless ye are able to slaughter it (in due form); that which is sacrificed on stone (altars); (forbidden) also is the division (of meat) by raffling with arrows: that is impiety. This day have those who reject faith given up all hope of your religion: yet fear them not but fear Me. This day have I perfected your religion for you, completed My favour upon you, and have chosen for you Islam as your religion. But if any is forced by hunger, with no inclination to transgression, Allah is indeed Oft-Forgiving, Most Merciful.	Forbidden unto you (for food) are carrion and blood and swineflesh, and that which hath been dedicated unto any other than Allah, and the strangled, and the dead through beating, and the dead through falling from a height, and that which hath been killed by (the goring of) horns, and the devoured of wild beasts, saving that which ye make lawful (by the death-stroke), and that which hath been immolated unto idols. And (forbidden is it) that ye swear by the divining arrows. This is an abomination. This day are those who disbelieve in despair of (ever harming) your religion; so fear them not, fear Me! This day have I perfected your religion for you and completed My favour unto you, and have chosen for you as religion al-Islam. Whoso is forced by hunger, not by will, to sin: (for him) lo! Allah is Forgiving, Merciful.	Forbidden to you is that which dies of itself, and blood, and flesh of swine, and that on which any other name than that of Allah has been invoked, and the strangled (animal) and that beaten to death, and that killed by a fall and that killed by being smitten with the horn, and that which wild beasts have eaten, except what you slaughter, and what is sacrificed on stones set up (for idols) and that you divide by the arrows; that is a transgression. This day have those who disbelieve despaired of your religion, so fear them not, and fear Me. This day have I perfected for you your religion and completed My favor on you and chosen for you Islam as a religion; but whoever is compelled by hunger, not inclining willfully to sin, then surely Allah is Forgiving, Merciful.	
5 004	They ask thee what is lawful to them (as food). Say: lawful unto you are (all) things good and pure: and what ye have taught your trained hunting animals (to catch) in the manner directed to you by Allah: eat what they catch for you, but pronounce the name of Allah over it: and fear Allah; for Allah is swift in taking account.	They ask thee (O Muhammad) what is made lawful for them. Say: (all) good things are made lawful for you. And those beasts and birds of prey which ye have trained as hounds are trained, ye teach them that which Allah taught you; so eat of that which they catch for you and mention Allah's name upon it, and observe your duty to Allah. Lo! Allah is swift to take account.	They ask you as to what is allowed to them. Say: The good things are allowed to you, and what you have taught the beasts and birds of prey, training them to hunt-- you teach them of what Allah has taught you-- so eat of that which they catch for you and mention the name of Allah over it; and be careful of (your duty to) Allah; surely Allah is swift in reckoning.	

5 005	This day are (all) things good and pure made lawful unto you. The food of the People of the Book is lawful unto you and yours is lawful unto them. (Lawful unto you in marriage) are (not only) chaste women who are believers, but chaste women among the People of the Book, revealed before your time,- when ye give them their due dowers, and desire chastity, not lewdness, nor secret intrigues if any one rejects faith, fruitless is his work, and in the Hereafter he will be in the ranks of those who have lost (all spiritual good).	This day are (all) good things made lawful for you. The food of those who have received the Scripture is lawful for you, and your food is lawful for them. And so are the virtuous women of the believers and the virtuous women of those who received the Scripture before you (lawful for you) when ye give them their marriage portions and live with them in honour, not in fornication, nor taking them as secret concubines. Whoso denieth the faith, his work is vain and he will be among the losers in the Hereafter.	This day (all) the good things are allowed to you; and the food of those who have been given the Book is lawful for you and your food is lawful for them; and the chaste from among the believing women and the chaste from among those who have been given the Book before you (are lawful for you); when you have given them their dowries, taking (them) in marriage, not fornicating nor taking them for paramours in secret; and whoever denies faith, his work indeed is of no account, and in the hereafter he shall be one of the losers.	
5 006	O ye who believe! when ye prepare for prayer, wash your faces, and your hands (and arms) to the elbows; Rub your heads (with water); and (wash) your feet to the ankles. If ye are in a state of ceremonial impurity, bathe your whole body. But if ye are ill, or on a journey, or one of you cometh from offices of nature, or ye have been in contact with women, and ye find no water, then take for yourselves clean sand or earth, and rub therewith your faces and hands, Allah doth not wish to place you in a difficulty, but to make you clean, and to complete his favour to you, that ye may be grateful.	O ye who believe! When ye rise up for prayer, wash you faces, and your hands up to the elbows, and lightly rub your heads and (wash) your feet up to the ankles. And if ye are unclean, purify yourselves. And if ye are sick or on a journey, or one of you cometh from the closet, or ye have had contact with women, and ye find not water, then go to clean, high ground and rub your faces and your hands with some of it. Allah would not place a burden on you, but He would purify you and would perfect His grace upon you, that ye may give thanks.	O you who believe! when you rise up to prayer, wash your faces and your hands as far as the elbows, and wipe your heads and your feet to the ankles; and if you are under an obligation to perform a total ablution, then wash (yourselves) and if you are sick or on a journey, or one of you come from the privy, or you have touched the women, and you cannot find water, betake yourselves to pure earth and wipe your faces and your hands therewith, Allah does not desire to put on you any difficulty, but He wishes to purify you and that He may complete His favor on you, so that you may be grateful.	
5 007	And call in remembrance the favour of Allah unto you, and His covenant, which He ratified with you, when ye said: "We hear and we obey": And fear Allah, for Allah knoweth well the secrets of your hearts.	Remember Allah's grace upon you and His covenant by which He bound you when ye said: We hear and we obey; And keep your duty to Allah. Lo! He knoweth what is in the breasts (of men).	And remember the favor of Allah on you and His covenant with which He bound you firmly, when you said: We have heard and we obey, and be careful of (your duty to) Allah, surely Allah knows what is in the breasts.	
5 008	O ye who believe! stand out firmly for Allah, as witnesses to fair dealing, and let not the hatred of others to you make you swerve to wrong and depart from justice. Be just: that is next to piety: and fear Allah. For Allah is well-acquainted with all that ye do.	O ye who believe! Be steadfast witnesses for Allah in equity, and let not hatred of any people seduce you that ye deal not justly. Deal justly, that is nearer to your duty. Observe your duty to Allah. Lo! Allah is Informed of what ye do.	O you who believe! Be upright for Allah, bearers of witness with justice, and let not hatred of a people incite you not to act equitably; act equitably, that is nearer to piety, and he careful of (your duty to) Allah; surely Allah is Aware of what you do.	
5 009	To those who believe and do deeds of righteousness hath Allah promised forgiveness and a great reward.	Allah hath promised those who believe and do good works: Theirs will be forgiveness and immense reward.	Allah has promised to those who believe and do good deeds (that) they shall have forgiveness and a mighty reward.	
5 010	Those who reject faith and deny our signs will be companions of Hell-fire.	And they who disbelieve and deny Our revelations, such are rightful owners of hell.	And (as for) those who disbelieve and reject our communications, these are the companions of the name.	

5 011	O ye who believe! Call in remembrance the favour of Allah unto you when certain men formed the design to stretch out their hands against you, but (Allah) held back their hands from you: so fear Allah. And on Allah let believers put (all) their trust.	O ye who believe! Remember Allah's favour unto you, how a people were minded to stretch out their hands against you but He withheld their hands from you; and keep your duty to Allah. In Allah let believers put their trust.	O you who believe! remember Allah's favor on you when a people had determined to stretch forth their hands towards you, but He withheld their hands from you, and be careful of (your duty to) Allah; and on Allah let the believers rely.
5 012	Allah did aforetime take a covenant from the Children of Israel, and we appointed twelve captains among them. And Allah said: "I am with you: if ye (but) establish regular prayers, practise regular charity, believe in my messengers, honour and assist them, and loan to Allah a beautiful loan, verily I will wipe out from you your evils, and admit you to gardens with rivers flowing beneath; but if any of you, after this, resisteth faith, he hath truly wandered from the path or rectitude."	Allah made a covenant of old with the Children of Israel and We raised among them twelve chieftains, and Allah said: Lo! I am with you. If ye establish worship and pay the poor-due, and believe in My messengers and support them, and lend unto Allah a kindly loan, surely I shall remit your sins, and surely I shall bring you into Gardens underneath which rivers flow. Whoso among you disbelieveth after this will go astray from a plain road.	And certainly Allah made a covenant with the children of Israel, and We raised up among them twelve chieftains; and Allah said: Surely I am with you; if you keep up prayer and pay the poor-rate and believe in My messengers and assist them and offer to Allah a goodly gift, I will most certainly cover your evil deeds, and I will most certainly cause you to enter into gardens beneath which rivers flow, but whoever disbelieves from among you after that, he indeed shall lose the right way.
5 013	But because of their breach of their covenant, We cursed them, and made their hearts grow hard; they change the words from their (right) places and forget a good part of the message that was sent them, nor wilt thou cease to find them- barring a few - ever bent on (new) deceits: but forgive them, and overlook (their misdeeds): for Allah loveth those who are kind.	And because of their breaking their covenant, We have cursed them and made hard their hearts. They change words from their context and forget a part of that whereof they were admonished. Thou wilt not cease to discover treachery from all save a few of them. But bear with them and pardon them. Lo! Allah loveth the kindly.	But on account of their breaking their covenant We cursed them and made their hearts hard; they altered the words from their places and they neglected a portion of what they were reminded of; and you shall always discover treachery in them excepting a few of them; so pardon them and turn away; surely Allah loves those who do good (to others).
5 014	From those, too, who call themselves Christians, We did take a covenant, but they forgot a good part of the message that was sent them: so we estranged them, with enmity and hatred between the one and the other, to the Day of Judgment. And soon will Allah show them what it is they have done.	And with those who say: "Lo! we are Christians," We made a covenant, but they forgot a part of that whereof they were admonished. Therefor We have stirred up enmity and hatred among them till the Day of Resurrection, when Allah will inform them of their handiwork.	And with those who say, We are Christians, We made a covenant, but they neglected a portion of what they were reminded of, therefore We excited among them enmity and hatred to the day of resurrection; and Allah will inform them of what they did.
5 015	O people of the Book! There hath come to you our Messenger, revealing to you much that ye used to hide in the Book, and passing over much (that is now unnecessary): There hath come to you from Allah a (new) light and a perspicuous Book, -	O People of the Scripture! Now hath Our messenger come unto you, expounding unto you much of that which ye used to hide in the Scripture, and forgiving much. Now hath come unto you light from Allah and plain Scripture.	O followers of the Book! indeed Our Messenger has come to you making clear to you much of what you concealed of the Book and passing over much; indeed, there has come to you light and a clear Book from Allah;
5 016	Wherewith Allah guideth all who seek His good pleasure to ways of peace and safety, and leadeth them out of darkness, by His will, unto the light,- guideth them to a path that is straight.	Whereby Allah guideth him who seeketh His good pleasure unto paths of peace. He bringeth them out of darkness unto light by His decree, and guideth them unto a straight path.	With it Allah guides him who will follow His pleasure into the ways of safety and brings them out of utter darkness into light by His will and guides them to the right path.

5 017	In blasphemy indeed are those that say that Allah is Christ the son of Mary. Say: "Who then hath the least power against Allah, if His will were to destroy Christ the son of Mary, his mother, and all every-one that is on the earth? For to Allah belongeth the dominion of the heavens and the earth, and all that is between. He createth what He pleaseth. For Allah hath power over all things."	They indeed have disbelieved who say: Lo! Allah is the Messiah, son of Mary. Say: Who then can do aught against Allah, if He had willed to destroy the Messiah son of Mary, and his mother and everyone on earth? Allah's is the Sovereignty of the heavens and the earth and all that is between them. He createth what He will. And Allah is Able to do all things.	Certainly they disbelieve who say: Surely, Allah-- He is the Messiah, son of Marium. Say: Who then could control anything as against Allah when He wished to destroy the Messiah son of Marium and his mother and all those on the earth? And Allah's is the kingdom of the heavens and the earth and what is between them; He creates what He pleases; and Allah has power over all things,
5 018	(Both) the Jews and the Christians say: "We are sons of Allah, and his beloved." Say: "Why then doth He punish you for your sins? Nay, ye are but men,- of the men he hath created: He forgiveth whom He pleaseth, and He punisheth whom He pleaseth: and to Allah belongeth the dominion of the heavens and the earth, and all that is between: and unto Him is the final goal (of all)"	The Jews and Christians say: We are sons of Allah and His loved ones. Say: Why then doth He chastise you for your sins? Nay, ye are but mortals of His creating. He forgiveth whom He will, and chastiseth whom He will. Allah's is the Sovereignty of the heavens and the earth and all that is between them, and unto Him is the journeying.	And the Jews and the Christians say: We are the sons of Allah and His beloved ones. Say: Why does He then chastise you for your faults? Nay, you are mortals from among those whom He has created, He forgives whom He pleases and chastises whom He pleases; and Allah's is the kingdom of the heavens and the earth and what is between them, and to Him is the eventual coming.
5 019	O People of the Book! Now hath come unto you, making (things) clear unto you, Our Messenger, after the break in (the series of) our messengers, lest ye should say: "There came unto us no bringer of glad tidings and no warner (from evil)": But now hath come unto you a bringer of glad tidings and a warner (from evil). And Allah hath power over all things.	O People of the Scripture! Now hath Our messenger come unto you to make things plain unto you after an interval (of cessation) of the messengers, lest ye should say: There came not unto us a messenger of cheer nor any warner. Now hath a messenger of cheer and a warner come unto you. Allah is Able to do all things.	O followers of the Book! indeed Our Messenger has come to you explaining to you after a cessation of the (mission of the) messengers, lest you say: There came not to us a giver of good news or a warner, so indeed there has come to you a giver of good news and a warner; and Allah has power over all things.
5 020	Remember Moses said to his people: "O my people! Call in remembrance the favour of Allah unto you, when He produced prophets among you, made you kings, and gave you what He had not given to any other among the peoples."	And (remember) when Moses said unto his people: O my people! Remember Allah's favour unto you, how He placed among you prophets, and He made you kings, and gave you that (which) He gave not to any (other) of (His) creatures.	And when Musa said to his people: O my people! remember the favor of Allah upon you when He raised prophets among you and made you kings and gave you what He had not given to any other among the nations.
5 021	"O my people! Enter the holy land which Allah hath assigned unto you, and turn not back ignominiously, for then will ye be overthrown, to your own ruin."	O my people! Go into the holy land which Allah hath ordained for you. Turn not in flight, for surely ye turn back as losers:	O my people! enter the holy land which Allah has prescribed for you and turn not on your backs for then you will turn back losers.
5 022	They said: "O Moses! In this land are a people of exceeding strength: Never shall we enter it until they leave it: if (once) they leave, then shall we enter."	They said: O Moses! Lo! a giant people (dwell) therein and lo! we go not in till they go forth from thence. When they go forth from thence, then we will enter (not till then).	They said: O Musa! surely there is a strong race in it, and we will on no account enter it until they go out from it, so if they go out from it, then surely we will enter.

5 023	(But) among (their) Allah-fearing men were two on whom Allah had bestowed His grace: They said: "Assault them at the (proper) Gate: when once ye are in, victory will be yours; But on Allah put your trust if ye have faith."	Then out spake two of those who feared (their Lord, men) unto whom Allah had been gracious: Enter in upon them by the gate, for if ye enter by it, lo! ye will be victorious. So put your trust (in Allah) if ye are indeed believers.	Two men of those who feared, upon both of whom Allah had bestowed a favor, said: Enter upon them by the gate, for when you have entered it you shall surely be victorious, and on Allah should you rely if you are believers.
5 024	They said: "O Moses! while they remain there, never shall we be able to enter, to the end of time. Go thou, and thy Lord, and fight ye two, while we sit here (and watch)."	They said: O Moses! We will never enter (the land) while they are in it. So go thou and thy Lord and fight! We will sit here.	They said: O Musa! we shall never enter it so long as they are in it; go therefore you and your Lord, then fight you both surely we will here sit down.
5 025	He said: "O my Lord! I have power only over myself and my brother: so separate us from this rebellious people!"	He said: My Lord! I have control of none but myself and my brother, so distinguish between us and the wrong-doing folk.	He said: My Lord! Surely I have no control (upon any) but my own self and my brother; therefore make a separation between us and the nation of transgressors.
5 026	Allah said: "Therefore will the land be out of their reach for forty years: In distraction will they wander through the land: But sorrow thou not over these rebellious people."	(Their Lord) said: For this the land will surely be forbidden them for forty years that they will wander in the earth, bewildered. So grieve not over the wrongdoing folk.	He said: So it shall surely be forbidden to them for forty years, they shall wander about in the land, therefore do not grieve for the nation of transgressors.
5 027	Recite to them the truth of the story of the two sons of Adam. Behold! they each presented a sacrifice (to Allah): It was accepted from one, but not from the other. Said the latter: "Be sure I will slay thee." "Surely," said the former, "Allah doth accept of the sacrifice of those who are righteous."	But recite unto them with truth the tale of the two sons of Adam, how they offered each a sacrifice, and it was accepted from the one of them and it was not accepted from the other. (The one) said: I will surely kill thee. (The other) answered: Allah accepteth only from those who ward off (evil).	And relate to them the story of the two sons of Adam with truth when they both offered an offering, but it was accepted from one of them and was not accepted from the other. He said: I will most certainly slay you. (The other) said: Allah only accepts from those who guard (against evil).
5 028	"If thou dost stretch thy hand against me, to slay me, it is not for me to stretch my hand against thee to slay thee: for I do fear Allah, the cherisher of the worlds."	Even if thou stretch out thy hand against me to kill me, I shall not stretch out my hand against thee to kill thee, lo! I fear Allah, the Lord of the Worlds.	If you will stretch forth your hand towards me to slay me, I am not one to stretch forth my hand towards you to slay you surely I fear Allah, the Lord of the worlds:
5 029	"For me, I intend to let thee draw on thyself my sin as well as thine, for thou wilt be among the companions of the fire, and that is the reward of those who do wrong."	Lo! I would rather thou shouldst bear the punishment of the sin against me and thine own sin and become one of the owners of the fire. That is the reward of evildoers.	Surely I wish that you should bear the sin committed against me and your own sin, and so you would be of the inmates of the fire, and this is the recompense of the unjust.
5 030	The (selfish) soul of the other led him to the murder of his brother: he murdered him, and became (himself) one of the lost ones.	But (the other's) mind imposed on him the killing of his brother, so he slew him and became one of the losers.	Then his mind facilitated to him the slaying of his brother so he slew him; then he became one of the losers.
5 031	Then Allah sent a raven, who scratched the ground, to show him how to hide the shame of his brother. "Woe is me!" said he; "Was I not even able to be as this raven, and to hide the shame of my brother?" then he became full of regrets-	Then Allah sent a raven scratching up the ground, to show him how to hide his brother's naked corpse. He said: Woe unto me! Am I not able to be as this raven and so hide my brother's naked corpse? And he became repentant.	Then Allah sent a crow digging up the earth so that he might show him how he should cover the dead body of his brother. He said: Woe me! do I lack the strength that I should be like this crow and cover the dead body of my brother? So he became of those who regret.

5 032	On that account: We ordained for the Children of Israel that if any one slew a person - unless it be for murder or for spreading mischief in the land - it would be as if he slew the whole people: and if any one saved a life, it would be as if he saved the life of the whole people. Then although there came to them Our messengers with clear signs, yet, even after that, many of them continued to commit excesses in the land.	For that cause We decreed for the Children of Israel that whosoever killeth a human being for other than manslaughter or corruption in the earth, it shall be as if he had killed all mankind, and whoso saveth the life of one, it shall be as if he had saved the life of all mankind. Our messengers came unto them of old with clear proofs (of Allah's Sovereignty), but afterwards lo! many of them became prodigals in the earth.	For this reason did We prescribe to the children of Israel that whoever slays a soul, unless it be for manslaughter or for mischief in the land, it is as though he slew all men; and whoever keeps it alive, it is as though he kept alive all men; and certainly Our messengers came to them with clear arguments, but even after that many of them certainly act extravagantly in the land.	
5 033	The punishment of those who wage war against Allah and His Messenger, and strive with might and main for mischief through the land is: execution, or crucifixion, or the cutting off of hands and feet from opposite sides, or exile from the land: that is their disgrace in this world, and a heavy punishment is theirs in the Hereafter;	The only reward of those who make war upon Allah and His messenger and strive after corruption in the land will be that they will be killed or crucified, or have their hands and feet on alternate sides cut off, or will be expelled out of the land. Such will be their degradation in the world, and in the Hereafter theirs will be an awful doom;	The punishment of those who wage war against Allah and His messenger and strive to make mischief in the land is only this, that they should be murdered or crucified or their hands and their feet should be cut off on opposite sides or they should be imprisoned; this shall be as a disgrace for them in this world, and in the hereafter they shall have a grievous chastisement,	
5 034	Except for those who repent before they fall into your power: in that case, know that Allah is Oft-Forgiving, Most Merciful.	Save those who repent before ye overpower them. For know that Allah is Forgiving, Merciful.	Except those who repent before you have them in your power; so know that Allah is Forgiving, Merciful.	
5 035	O ye who believe! Do your duty to Allah, seek the means of approach unto Him, and strive with might and main in his cause: that ye may prosper.	O ye who believe! Be mindful of your duty to Allah, and seek the way of approach unto Him, and strive in His way in order that ye may succeed.	O you who believe! be careful of (your duty to) Allah and seek means of nearness to Him and strive hard in His way that you may be successful.	
5 036	As to those who reject Faith,- if they had everything on earth, and twice repeated, to give as ransom for the penalty of the Day of Judgment, it would never be accepted of them, theirs would be a grievous penalty.	As for those who disbelieve, lo! if all that is in the earth were theirs, and as much again therewith, to ransom them from the doom on the Day of Resurrection, it would not be accepted from them. Theirs will be a painful doom.	Surely (as for) those who disbelieve, even if they had what is in the earth, all of it, and the like of it with it, that they might ransom themselves with it from the punishment of the day of resurrection, it shall not be accepted from them, and they shall have a painful punishment.	
5 037	Their wish will be to get out of the Fire, but never will they get out therefrom: their penalty will be one that endures.	They will wish to come forth from the Fire, but they will not come forth from it. Theirs will be a lasting doom.	They would desire to go forth from the fire, and they shall not go forth from it, and they shall have a lasting punishment.	
5 038	As to the thief, Male or female, cut off his or her hands: a punishment by way of example, from Allah, for their crime: and Allah is Exalted in power.	As for the thief, both male and female, cut off their hands. It is the reward of their own deeds, an exemplary punishment from Allah. Allah is Mighty, Wise.	And (as for) the man who steals and the woman who steals, cut off their hands as a punishment for what they have earned, an exemplary punishment from Allah; and Allah is Mighty, Wise.	
5 039	But if the thief repents after his crime, and amends his conduct, Allah turneth to him in forgiveness; for Allah is Oft-Forgiving, Most Merciful.	But whoso repenteth after his wrongdoing and amendeth, lo! Allah will relent toward him. Lo! Allah is Forgiving, Merciful.	But whoever repents after his iniquity and reforms (himself), then surely Allah will turn to him (mercifully); surely Allah is Forgiving, Merciful.	

5 040	Knowest thou not that to Allah (alone) belongeth the dominion of the heavens and the earth? He punisheth whom He pleaseth, and He forgiveth whom He pleaseth: and Allah hath power over all things.	Knowest thou not that unto Allah belongeth the Sovereignty of the heavens and the earth? He punisheth whom He will, and forgiveth whom He will. Allah is Able to do all things.	Do you not know that Allah-- His is the kingdom of the heavens and the earth; He chastises whom He pleases; and forgives whom He pleases and Allah has power over all things.
5 041	O Messenger! let not those grieve thee, who race each other into unbelief: (whether it be) among those who say "We believe" with their lips but whose hearts have no faith; or it be among the Jews,- men who will listen to any lie,- will listen even to others who have never so much as come to thee. They change the words from their (right) times and places: they say, "If ye are given this, take it, but if not, beware!" If any one's trial is intended by Allah, thou hast no authority in the least for him against Allah. For such - it is not Allah's will to purify their hearts. For them there is disgrace in this world, and in the Hereafter a heavy punishment.	O Messenger! Let not them grieve thee who vie one with another in the race to disbelief, of such as say with their mouths: "We believe," but their hearts believe not, and of the Jews: listeners for the sake of falsehood, listeners on behalf of other folk who come not unto thee, changing words from their context and saying: If this be given unto you, receive it, but if this be not given unto you, then beware! He whom Allah doometh unto sin, thou (by thine efforts) wilt avail him naught against Allah. Those are they for whom the Will of Allah is that He cleanse not their hearts. Theirs in the world will be ignominy, and in the Hereafter an awful doom;	O Messenger! let not those grieve you who strive together in hastening to unbelief from among those who say with their mouths: We believe, and their hearts do not believe, and from among those who are Jews; they are listeners for the sake of a lie, listeners for another people who have not come to you; they alter the words from their places, saying: If you are given this, take it, and if you are not given this, be cautious; and as for him whose temptation Allah desires, you cannot control anything for him with Allah. Those are they for whom Allah does not desire that He should purify their hearts; they shall have disgrace in this world, and they shall have a grievous chastisement in the hereafter.
5 042	(They are fond of) listening to falsehood, of devouring anything forbidden. If they do come to thee, either judge between them, or decline to interfere. If thou decline, they cannot hurt thee in the least. If thou judge, judge in equity between them. For Allah loveth those who judge in equity.	Listeners for the sake of falsehood! Greedy for illicit gain! If then they have recourse unto thee (Muhammad) judge between them or disclaim jurisdiction. If thou disclaimest jurisdiction, then they cannot harm thee at all. But if thou judgest, judge between them with equity. Lo! Allah loveth the equitable.	(They are) listeners of a lie, devourers of what is forbidden; therefore if they come to you, judge between them or turn aside from them, and if you turn aside from them, they shall not harm you in any way; and if you judge, judge between them with equity; surely Allah loves those who judge equitably.
5 043	But why do they come to thee for decision, when they have (their own) law before them?- therein is the (plain) command of Allah; yet even after that, they would turn away. For they are not (really) People of Faith.	How come they unto thee for judgment when they have the Torah, wherein Allah hath delivered judgment (for them)? Yet even after that they turn away. Such (folk) are not believers.	And how do they make you a judge and they have the Taurat wherein is Allah's judgment? Yet they turn back after that, and these are not the believers.
5 044	It was We who revealed the law (to Moses): therein was guidance and light. By its standard have been judged the Jews, by the prophets who bowed (as in Islam) to Allah's will, by the rabbis and the doctors of law: for to them was entrusted the protection of Allah's book, and they were witnesses thereto: therefore fear not men, but fear me, and sell not my signs for a miserable price. If any do fail to judge by (the light of) what Allah hath revealed, they are (no better than) Unbelievers.	Lo! We did reveal the Torah, wherein is guidance and a light, by which the prophets who surrendered (unto Allah) judged the Jews, and the rabbis and the priests (judged) by such of Allah's Scripture as they were bidden to observe, and thereunto were they witnesses. So fear not mankind, but fear Me. And My revelations for a little gain. Whoso judgeth not by that which Allah hath revealed: such are disbelievers.	Surely We revealed the Taurat in which was guidance and light; with it the prophets who submitted themselves (to Allah) judged (matters) for those who were Jews, and the masters of Divine knowledge and the doctors, because they were required to guard (part) of the Book of Allah, and they were witnesses thereof; therefore fear not the people and fear Me, and do not take a small price for My communications; and whoever did not judge by what Allah revealed, those are they that are the unbelievers.

5 045	We ordained therein for them: "Life for life, eye for eye, nose or nose, ear for ear, tooth for tooth, and wounds equal for equal." But if any one remits the retaliation by way of charity, it is an act of atonement for himself. And if any fail to judge by (the light of) what Allah hath revealed, they are (No better than) wrong-doers.	And We prescribed for them therein: The life for the life, and the eye for the eye, and the nose for the nose, and the ear for the ear, and the tooth for the tooth, and for wounds retaliation. But whoso forgoeth it (in the way of charity) it shall be expiation for him. Whoso judgeth not by that which Allah hath revealed: such are wrong-doers.	And We prescribed to them in it that life is for life, and eye for eye, and nose for nose, and ear for ear, and tooth for tooth, and (that there is) reprisal in wounds; but he who foregoes it, it shall be an expiation for him; and whoever did not judge by what Allah revealed, those are they that are the unjust.
5 046	And in their footsteps We sent Jesus the son of Mary, confirming the Law that had come before him: We sent him the Gospel: therein was guidance and light, and confirmation of the Law that had come before him: a guidance and an admonition to those who fear Allah.	And We caused Jesus, son of Mary, to follow in their footsteps, confirming that which was (revealed) before him in the Torah, and We bestowed on him the Gospel wherein is guidance and a light, confirming that which was (revealed) before it in the Torah - a guidance and an admonition unto those who ward off (evil).	And We sent after them in their footsteps Isa, son of Marium, verifying what was before him of the Taurat and We gave him the Injeel in which was guidance and light, and verifying what was before it of Taurat and a guidance and an admonition for those who guard (against evil).
5 047	Let the people of the Gospel judge by what Allah hath revealed therein. If any do fail to judge by (the light of) what Allah hath revealed, they are (no better than) those who rebel.	Let the People of the Gospel judge by that which Allah hath revealed therein. Whoso judgeth not by that which Allah hath revealed: such are evil-livers.	And the followers of the Injeel should have judged by what Allah revealed in it; and whoever did not judge by what Allah revealed, those are they that are the transgressors.
5 048	To thee We sent the Scripture in truth, confirming the scripture that came before it, and guarding it in safety: so judge between them by what Allah hath revealed, and follow not their vain desires, diverging from the Truth that hath come to thee. To each among you have we prescribed a law and an open way. If Allah had so willed, He would have made you a single people, but (His plan is) to test you in what He hath given you: so strive as in a race in all virtues. The goal of you all is to Allah; it is He that will show you the truth of the matters in which ye dispute;	And unto thee have We revealed the Scripture with the truth, confirming whatever Scripture was before it, and a watcher over it. So judge between them by that which Allah hath revealed, and follow not their desires away from the truth which hath come unto thee. For each We have appointed a divine law and a traced-out way. Had Allah willed He could have made you one community. But that He may try you by that which He hath given you (He hath made you as ye are). So vie one with another in good works. Unto Allah ye will all return, and He will then inform you of that wherein ye differ.	And We have revealed to you the Book with the truth, verifying what is before it of the Book and a guardian over it, therefore judge between them by what Allah has revealed, and do not follow their low desires (to turn away) from the truth that has come to you; for every one of you did We appoint a law and a way, and if Allah had pleased He would have made you (all) a single people, but that He might try you in what He gave you, therefore strive with one another to hasten to virtuous deeds; to Allah is your return, of all (of you), so He will let you know that in which you differed;
5 049	And this (He commands): Judge thou between them by what Allah hath revealed, and follow not their vain desires, but beware of them lest they beguile thee from any of that (teaching) which Allah hath sent down to thee. And if they turn away, be assured that for some of their crime it is Allah's purpose to punish them. And truly most men are rebellious.	So judge between them by that which Allah hath revealed, and follow not their desires, but beware of them lest they seduce thee from some part of that which Allah hath revealed unto thee. And if they turn away, then know that Allah's Will is to smite them for some sin of theirs. Lo! many of mankind are evil-livers.	And that you should judge between them by what Allah has revealed, and do not follow their low desires, and be cautious of them, lest they seduce you from part of what Allah has revealed to you; but if they turn back, then know that Allah desires to afflict them on account of some of their faults; and most surely many of the people are transgressors.

5 050	Do they then seek after a judgment of (the days of) ignorance? But who, for a people whose faith is assured, can give better judgment than Allah?	Is it a judgment of the time of (pagan) ignorance that they are seeking? Who is better than Allah for judgment to a people who have certainty (in their belief)?	Is it then the judgment of (the times of) ignorance that they desire? And who is better than Allah to judge for a people who are sure?
5 051	O ye who believe! take not the Jews and the Christians for your friends and protectors: They are but friends and protectors to each other. And he amongst you that turns to them (for friendship) is of them. Verily Allah guideth not a people unjust.	O ye who believe! Take not the Jews and the Christians for friends. They are friends one to another. He among you who taketh them for friends is (one) of them. Lo! Allah guideth not wrongdoing folk.	O you who believe! do not take the Jews and the Christians for friends; they are friends of each other; and whoever amongst you takes them for a friend, then surely he is one of them; surely Allah does not guide the unjust people.
5 052	Those in whose hearts is a disease - thou seest how eagerly they run about amongst them, saying: "We do fear lest a change of fortune bring us disaster." Ah! perhaps Allah will give (thee) victory, or a decision according to His will. Then will they repent of the thoughts which they secretly harboured in their hearts.	And thou seest those in whose heart is a disease race toward them, saying: We fear lest a change of fortune befall us. And it may happen that Allah will vouchsafe (unto thee) the victory, or a commandment from His presence. Then will they repent them of their secret thoughts.	But you will see those in whose hearts is a disease hastening towards them, saying: We fear lest a calamity should befall us; but it may be that Allah will bring the victory or a punishment from Himself, so that they shall be regretting on account of what they hid in their souls.
5 053	And those who believe will say: "Are these the men who swore their strongest oaths by Allah, that they were with you?" All that they do will be in vain, and they will fall into (nothing but) ruin.	Then will the believers say (unto the people of the Scripture): are these they who swore by Allah their most binding oaths that they were surely with you? Their works have failed, and they have become the losers.	And those who believe will say: Are these they who swore by Allah with the most forcible of their oaths that they were most surely with you? Their deeds shall go for nothing, so they shall become losers.
5 054	O ye who believe! if any from among you turn back from his Faith, soon will Allah produce a people whom He will love as they will love Him,- lowly with the believers, mighty against the rejecters, fighting in the way of Allah, and never afraid of the reproaches of such as find fault. That is the grace of Allah, which He will bestow on whom He pleaseth. And Allah encompasseth all, and He knoweth all things.	O ye who believe! Whoso of you becometh a renegade from his religion, (know that in his stead) Allah will bring a people whom He loveth and who love Him, humble toward believers, stern toward disbelievers, striving in the way of Allah, and fearing not the blame of any blamer. Such is the grace of Allah which He giveth unto whom He will. Allah is All-Embracing, All-Knowing.	O you who believe! whoever from among you turns back from his religion, then Allah will bring a people, He shall love them and they shall love Him, lowly before the believers, mighty against the unbelievers, they shall strive hard in Allah's way and shall not fear the censure of any censurer; this is Allah's Face, He gives it to whom He pleases, and Allah is Ample-giving, Knowing.
5 055	Your (real) friends are (no less than) Allah, His Messenger, and the (fellowship of) believers,- those who establish regular prayers and regular charity, and they bow down humbly (in worship).	Your guardian can be only Allah; and His messenger and those who believe, who establish worship and pay the poordue, and bow down (in prayer).	Only Allah is your Vali and His Messenger and those who believe, those who keep up prayers and pay the poor-rate while they bow.
5 056	As to those who turn (for friendship) to Allah, His Messenger, and the (fellowship of) believers,- it is the fellowship of Allah that must certainly triumph.	And whoso taketh Allah and His messenger and those who believe for guardian (will know that), lo! the party of Allah, they are the victorious.	And whoever takes Allah and His messenger and those who believe for a guardian, then surely the party of Allah are they that shall be triumphant.

5 057	O ye who believe! take not for friends and protectors those who take your religion for a mockery or sport,- whether among those who received the Scripture before you, or among those who reject Faith; but fear ye Allah, if ye have faith (indeed).	O Ye who believe! Choose not for guardians such of those who received the Scripture before you, and of the disbelievers, as make a jest and sport of your religion. But keep your duty to Allah if ye are true believers.	O you who believe! do not take for guardians those who take your religion for a mockery and a joke, from among those who were given the Book before you and the unbelievers; and be careful of (your duty to) Allah if you are believers.
5 058	When ye proclaim your call to prayer they take it (but) as mockery and sport; that is because they are a people without understanding.	And when ye call to prayer they take it for a jest and sport. That is because they are a folk who understand not.	And when you call to prayer they make it a mockery and a joke; this is because they are a people who do not understand.
5 059	Say: "O people of the Book! Do ye disapprove of us for no other reason than that we believe in Allah, and the revelation that hath come to us and that which came before (us), and (perhaps) that most of you are rebellious and disobedient?"	Say: O People of the Scripture! Do ye blame us for aught else than that we believe in Allah and that which is revealed unto us and that which was revealed aforetime, and because most of you are evil-livers?	Say: O followers of the Book! do you find fault with us (for aught) except that we believe in Allah and in what has been revealed to us and what was revealed before, and that most of you are transgressors?
5 060	Say: "Shall I point out to you something much worse than this, (as judged) by the treatment it received from Allah? those who incurred the curse of Allah and His wrath, those of whom some He transformed into apes and swine, those who worshipped evil;- these are (many times) worse in rank, and far more astray from the even path!"	Shall I tell thee of a worse (case) than theirs for retribution with Allah? (Worse is the case of him) whom Allah hath cursed, him on whom His wrath hath fallen and of whose sort Allah hath turned some to apes and swine, and who serveth idols. Such are in worse plight and further astray from the plain road.	Say: Shall I inform you of (him who is) worse than this in retribution from Allah? (Worse is he) whom Allah has cursed and brought His wrath upon, and of whom He made apes and swine, and he who served the Shaitan; these are worse in place and more erring from the straight path.
5 061	When they come to thee, they say: "We believe": but in fact they enter with a mind against Faith, and they go out with the same but Allah knoweth fully all that they hide.	When they come unto you (Muslims), they say: We believe; but they came in unbelief and they went out in the same; and Allah knoweth best what they were hiding.	And when they come to you, they say: We believe; and indeed they come in with unbelief and indeed they go forth with it; and Allah knows best what they concealed.
5 062	Many of them dost thou see, racing each other in sin and rancour, and their eating of things forbidden. Evil indeed are the things that they do.	And thou seest many of them vying one with another in sin and transgression and their devouring of illicit gain. Verily evil is what they do.	And you will see many of them striving with one another to hasten in sin and exceeding the limits, and their eating of what is unlawfully acquired; certainly evil is that which they do.
5 063	Why do not the rabbis and the doctors of Law forbid them from their (habit of) uttering sinful words and eating things forbidden? Evil indeed are their works.	Why do not the rabbis and the priests forbid their evil-speaking and their devouring of illicit gain? Verily evil is their handiwork.	Why do not the learned men and the doctors of law prohibit them from their speaking of what is sinful and their eating of what is unlawfully acquired? Certainly evil is that which they work.

5 064	The Jews say: "Allah's hand is tied up." Be their hands tied up and be they accursed for the (blasphemy) they utter. Nay, both His hands are widely outstretched: He giveth and spendeth (of His bounty) as He pleaseth. But the revelation that cometh to thee from Allah increaseth in most of them their obstinate rebellion and blasphemy. Amongst them we have placed enmity and hatred till the Day of Judgment. Every time they kindle the fire of war, Allah doth extinguish it; but they (ever) strive to do mischief on earth. And Allah loveth not those who do mischief.	The Jews say: Allah's hand is fettered. Their hands are fettered and they are accursed for saying so. Nay, but both His hands are spread out wide in bounty. He bestoweth as He will. That which hath been revealed unto thee from thy Lord is certain to increase the contumacy and disbelief of many of them, and We have cast among them enmity and hatred till the Day of Resurrection. As often as they light a fire for war, Allah extinguisheth it. Their effort is for corruption in the land, and Allah loveth not corrupters.	And the Jews say: The hand of Allah is tied up! Their hands shall be shackled and they shall be cursed for what they say. Nay, both His hands are spread out, He expends as He pleases; and what has been revealed to you from your Lord will certainly make many of them increase in inordinacy and unbelief; and We have put enmity and hatred among them till the day of resurrection; whenever they kindle a fire for war Allah puts it out, and they strive to make mischief in the land; and Allah does not love the mischief-makers.
5 065	If only the People of the Book had believed and been righteous, We should indeed have blotted out their iniquities and admitted them to gardens of bliss.	If only the People of the Scripture would believe and ward off (evil), surely We should remit their sins from them and surely We should bring them into Gardens of Delight.	And if the followers of the Book had believed and guarded (against evil) We would certainly have covered their evil deeds and We would certainly have made them enter gardens of bliss,
5 066	If only they had stood fast by the Law, the Gospel, and all the revelation that was sent to them from their Lord, they would have enjoyed happiness from every side. There is from among them a party on the right course: but many of them follow a course that is evil.	If they had observed the Torah and the Gospel and that which was revealed unto them from their Lord, they would surely have been nourished from above them and from beneath their feet. Among them there are people who are moderate, but many of them are of evil conduct.	And if they had kept up the Taurat and the Injeel and that which was revealed to them from their Lord, they would certainly have eaten from above them and from beneath their feet there is a party of them keeping to the moderate course, and (as for) most of them, evil is that which they do.
5 067	O Messenger! proclaim the (message) which hath been sent to thee from thy Lord. If thou didst not, thou wouldst not have fulfilled and proclaimed His mission. And Allah will defend thee from men (who mean mischief). For Allah guideth not those who reject Faith.	O Messenger! Make known that which hath been revealed unto thee from thy Lord, for if thou do it not, thou wilt not have conveyed His message. Allah will protect thee from mankind. Lo! Allah guideth not the disbelieving folk.	O Messenger! deliver what bas been revealed to you from your Lord; and if you do it not, then you have not delivered His message, and Allah will protect you from the people; surely Allah will not guide the unbelieving people.
5 068	Say: "O People of the Book! ye have no ground to stand upon unless ye stand fast by the Law, the Gospel, and all the revelation that has come to you from your Lord." It is the revelation that cometh to thee from thy Lord, that increaseth in most of them their obstinate rebellion and blasphemy. But sorrow thou not over (these) people without Faith.	Say O People of the Scripture! Ye have naught (of guidance) till ye observe the Torah and the Gospel and that which was revealed unto you from your Lord. That which is revealed unto thee (Muhammad) from thy Lord is certain to increase the contumacy and disbelief of many of them. But grieve not for the disbelieving folk.	Say: O followers of the Book! you follow no good till you keep up the Taurat and the Injeel and that which is revealed to you from your Lord; and surely that which has been revealed to you from your Lord shall make many of them increase in inordinacy and unbelief; grieve not therefore for the unbelieving people.
5 069	Those who believe (in the Qur'an), those who follow the Jewish (scriptures), and the Sabians and the Christians,- any who believe in Allah and the Last Day, and work righteousness,- on them shall be no fear, nor shall they grieve.	Lo! those who believe, and those who are Jews, and Sabaeans, and Christians - Whosoever believeth in Allah and the Last Day and doeth right - there shall no fear come upon them neither shall they grieve.	Surely those who believe and those who are Jews and the Sabians and the Christians whoever believes in Allah and the last day and does good-- they shall have no fear nor shall they grieve.

5 070	We took the covenant of the Children of Israel and sent them messengers, every time, there came to them a messenger with what they themselves desired not - some (of these) they called impostors, and some they (go so far as to) slay.	We made a covenant of old with the Children of Israel and We sent unto them messengers. As often as a messenger came unto them with that which their souls desired not (they became rebellious). Some (of them) they denied and some they slew.	Certainly We made a covenant with the children of Israel and We sent to them messengers; whenever there came to them a messenger with what that their souls did not desire, some (of them) did they call liars and some they slew.
5 071	They thought there would be no trial (or punishment); so they became blind and deaf; yet Allah (in mercy) turned to them; yet again many of them became blind and deaf. But Allah sees well all that they do.	They thought no harm would come of it, so they were wilfully blind and deaf. And afterward Allah turned (in mercy) toward them. Now (even after that) are many of them wilfully blind and deaf. Allah is Seer of what they do.	And they thought that there would be no affliction, so they became blind and deaf, then Allah turned to them mercifully, but many of them became blind and deaf; and Allah is well seeing what they do.
5 072	They do blaspheme who say: "Allah is Christ the son of Mary." But said Christ: "O Children of Israel! worship Allah, my Lord and your Lord." Whoever joins other gods with Allah,- Allah will forbid him the garden, and the Fire will be his abode. There will for the wrong-doers be no one to help.	They surely disbelieve who say: Lo! Allah is the Messiah, son of Mary. The Messiah (himself) said: O Children of Israel, worship Allah, my Lord and your Lord. Lo! whoso ascribeth partners unto Allah, for him Allah hath forbidden paradise. His abode is the Fire. For evil-doers there will be no helpers.	Certainly they disbelieve who say: Surely Allah, He is the Messiah, son of Marium; and the Messiah said: O Children of Israel! serve Allah, my Lord and your Lord. Surely whoever associates (others) with Allah, then Allah has forbidden to him the garden, and his abode is the fire; and there shall be no helpers for the unjust.
5 073	They do blaspheme who say: Allah is one of three in a Trinity: for there is no god except One Allah. If they desist not from their word (of blasphemy), verily a grievous penalty will befall the blasphemers among them.	They surely disbelieve who say: Lo! Allah is the third of three; when there is no God save the One Allah. If they desist not from so saying a painful doom will fall on those of them who disbelieve.	Certainly they disbelieve who say: Surely Allah is the third (person) of the three; and there is no god but the one Allah, and if they desist not from what they say, a painful chastisement shall befall those among them who disbelieve.
5 074	Why turn they not to Allah, and seek His forgiveness? For Allah is Oft-Forgiving, Most Merciful.	Will they not rather turn unto Allah and seek forgiveness of Him? For Allah is Forgiving, Merciful.	Will they not then turn to Allah and ask His forgiveness? And Allah is Forgiving, Merciful.
5 075	Christ the son of Mary was no more than a messenger; many were the messengers that passed away before him. His mother was a woman of truth. They had both to eat their (daily) food. See how Allah doth make His signs clear to them; yet see in what ways they are deluded away from the truth!	The Messiah, son of Mary, was no other than a messenger, messengers (the like of whom) had passed away before him. And his mother was a saintly woman. And they both used to eat (earthly) food. See how We make the revelations clear for them, and see how they are turned away!	The Messiah, son of Marium is but a messenger; messengers before him have indeed passed away; and his mother was a truthful woman; they both used to eat food. See how We make the communications clear to them, then behold, how they are turned away.
5 076	Say: "Will ye worship, besides Allah, something which hath no power either to harm or benefit you? But Allah,- He it is that heareth and knoweth all things."	Say: Serve ye in place of Allah that which possesseth for you neither hurt nor use? Allah it is Who is the Hearer, the Knower.	Say: Do you serve besides Allah that which does not control for you any harm, or any profit? And Allah-- He is the Hearing, the Knowing.
5 077	Say: "O people of the Book! exceed not in your religion the bounds (of what is proper), trespassing beyond the truth, nor follow the vain desires of people who went wrong in times gone by,- who misled many, and strayed (themselves) from the even way."	Say: O People of the Scripture! Stress not in your religion other than the truth, and follow not the vain desires of folk who erred of old and led many astray, and erred from a plain road.	Say: O followers of the Book! be not unduly immoderate in your religion, and do not follow the low desires of people who went astray before and led many astray and went astray from the right path.

5 078	Curses were pronounced on those among the Children of Israel who rejected Faith, by the tongue of David and of Jesus the son of Mary: because they disobeyed and persisted in excesses.	Those of the Children of Israel who went astray were cursed by the tongue of David, and of Jesus, son of Mary. That was because they rebelled and used to transgress.	Those who disbelieved from among the children of Israel were cursed by the tongue of Dawood and Isa, son of Marium; this was because they disobeyed and used to exceed the limit.
5 079	Nor did they (usually) forbid one another the iniquities which they committed: evil indeed were the deeds which they did.	They restrained not one another from the wickedness they did. Verily evil was that they used to do!	They used not to forbid each other the hateful things (which) they did; certainly evil was that which they did.
5 080	Thou seest many of them turning in friendship to the Unbelievers. Evil indeed are (the works) which their souls have sent forward before them (with the result), that Allah's wrath is on them, and in torment will they abide.	Thou seest many of them making friends with those who disbelieve. Surely ill for them is that which they themselves send on before them: that Allah will be wroth with them and in the doom they will abide.	You will see many of them befriending those who disbelieve; certainly evil is that which their souls have sent before for them, that Allah became displeased with them and in chastisement shall they abide.
5 081	If only they had believed in Allah, in the Prophet, and in what hath been revealed to him, never would they have taken them for friends and protectors, but most of them are rebellious wrong-doers.	If they believed in Allah and the Prophet and that which is revealed unto him, they would not choose them for their friends. But many of them are of evil conduct.	And had they believed in Allah and the prophet and what was revealed to him, they would not have taken them for friends but! most of them are transgressors.
5 082	Strongest among men in enmity to the believers wilt thou find the Jews and Pagans; and nearest among them in love to the believers wilt thou find those who say, "We are Christians": because amongst these are men devoted to learning and men who have renounced the world, and they are not arrogant.	Thou wilt find the most vehement of mankind in hostility to those who believe (to be) the Jews and the idolaters. And thou wilt find the nearest of them in affection to those who believe (to be) those who say: Lo! We are Christians. That is because there are among them priests and monks, and because they are not proud.	Certainly you will find the most violent of people in enmity for those who believe (to be) the Jews and those who are polytheists, and you will certainly find the nearest in friendship to those who believe (to be) those who say: We are Christians; this is because there are priests and monks among them and because they do not behave proudly.
5 083	And when they listen to the revelation received by the Messenger, thou wilt see their eyes overflowing with tears, for they recognise the truth: they pray: "Our Lord! we believe; write us down among the witnesses."	When they listen to that which hath been revealed unto the messengers, thou seest their eyes overflow with tears because of their recognition of the Truth. They say: Our Lord, we believe. Inscribe us as among the witnesses.	And when they hear what has been revealed to the messenger you will see their eyes overflowing with tears on account of the truth that they recognize; they say: Our Lord! we believe, so write us down with the witnesses (of truth).
5 084	"What cause can we have not to believe in Allah and the truth which has come to us, seeing that we long for our Lord to admit us to the company of the righteous?"	How should we not believe in Allah and that which hath come unto us of the Truth. And (how should we not) hope that our Lord will bring us in along with righteous folk?	And what (reason) have we that we should not believe in Allah and in the truth that has come to us, while we earnestly desire that our Lord should cause us to enter with the good people?
5 085	And for this their prayer hath Allah rewarded them with gardens, with rivers flowing underneath,- their eternal home. Such is the recompense of those who do good.	Allah hath rewarded them for that their saying - Gardens underneath which rivers flow, wherein they will abide for ever. That is the reward of the good.	Therefore Allah rewarded them on account of what they said, with gardens in which rivers flow to abide in them; and this is the reward of those who do good (to others).
5 086	But those who reject Faith and belie our Signs,- they shall be companions of Hell-fire.	But those who disbelieve and deny Our revelations, they are owners of hell-fire.	And (as for) those who disbelieve and reject Our communications, these are the companions of the flame.

5 087	O ye who believe! make not unlawful the good things which Allah hath made lawful for you, but commit no excess: for Allah loveth not those given to excess.	O ye who believe! Forbid not the good things which Allah hath made lawful for you, and transgress not, Lo! Allah loveth not transgressors.	O you who believe! do not forbid (yourselves) the good things which Allah has made lawful for you and do not exceed the limits; surely Allah does not love those who exceed the limits.
5 088	Eat of the things which Allah hath provided for you, lawful and good; but fear Allah, in Whom ye believe.	Eat of that which Allah hath bestowed on you as food lawful and good, and keep your duty to Allah in Whom ye are believers.	And eat of the lawful and good (things) that Allah has given you, and be careful of (your duty to) Allah, in Whom you believe.
5 089	Allah will not call you to account for what is futile in your oaths, but He will call you to account for your deliberate oaths: for expiation, feed ten indigent persons, on a scale of the average for the food of your families; or clothe them; or give a slave his freedom. If that is beyond your means, fast for three days. That is the expiation for the oaths ye have sworn. But keep to your oaths. Thus doth Allah make clear to you His signs, that ye may be grateful.	Allah will not take you to task for that which is unintentional in your oaths, but He will take you to task for the oaths which ye swear in earnest. The expiation thereof is the feeding of ten of the needy with the average of that wherewith ye feed your own folk, or the clothing of them, or the liberation of a slave, and for him who findeth not (the wherewithal to do so) then a three days' fast. This is the expiation of your oaths when ye have sworn; and keep your oaths. Thus Allah expoundeth unto you His revelations in order that ye may give thanks.	Allah does not call you to account for what is vain in your oaths, but He calls you to account for the making of deliberate oaths; so its expiation is the feeding of ten poor men out of the middling (food) you feed your families with, or their clothing, or the freeing of a neck; but whosoever cannot find (means) then fasting for three days; this is the expiation of your oaths when you swear; and guard your oaths. Thus does Allah make clear to you His communications, that you may be Fateful.
5 090	O ye who believe! Intoxicants and gambling, (dedication of) stones, and (divination by) arrows, are an abomination,- of Satan's handwork: eschew such (abomination), that ye may prosper.	O ye who believe! Strong drink and games of chance and idols and divining arrows are only an infamy of Satan's handiwork. Leave it aside in order that ye may succeed.	O you who believe! intoxicants and games of chance and (sacrificing to) stones set up and (dividing by) arrows are only an uncleanness, the Shaitan's work; shun it therefore that you may be successful.
5 091	Satan's plan is (but) to excite enmity and hatred between you, with intoxicants and gambling, and hinder you from the remembrance of Allah, and from prayer: will ye not then abstain?	Satan seeketh only to cast among you enmity and hatred by means of strong drink and games of chance, and to turn you from remembrance of Allah and from (His) worship. Will ye then have done?	The Shaitan only desires to cause enmity and hatred to spring in your midst by means of intoxicants and games of chance, and to keep you off from the remembrance of Allah and from prayer. Will you then desist?
5 092	Obey Allah, and obey the Messenger, and beware (of evil): if ye do turn back, know ye that it is Our Messenger's duty to proclaim (the message) in the clearest manner.	Obey Allah and obey the messenger, and beware! But if ye turn away, then know that the duty of Our messenger is only plain conveyance (of the message).	And obey Allah and obey the messenger and be cautious; but if you turn back, then know that only a clear deliverance of the message is (incumbent) on Our messenger.
5 093	On those who believe and do deeds of righteousness there is no blame for what they ate (in the past), when they guard themselves from evil, and believe, and do deeds of righteousness,- (or) again, guard themselves from evil and believe,- (or) again, guard themselves from evil and do good. For Allah loveth those who do good.	There shall be no sin (imputed) unto those who believe and do good works for what they may have eaten (in the past). So be mindful of your duty (to Allah), and believe, and do good works; and again: be mindful of your duty, and believe; and once again: be mindful of your duty, and do right. Allah loveth the good.	On those who believe and do good there is no blame for what they eat, when they are careful (of their duty) and believe and do good deeds, then they are careful (of their duty) and believe, then they are careful (of their duty) and do good (to others), and Allah loves those who do good (to others).

5 094	O ye who believe! Allah doth but make a trial of you in a little matter of game well within reach of your hands and your lances, that He may test who feareth him unseen: any who transgress thereafter, will have a grievous penalty.	O ye who believe! Allah will surely try you somewhat (in the matter) of the game which ye take with your hands and your spears, that Allah may know him who feareth Him in secret. Whoso transgresseth after this, for him there is a painful doom.	O you who believe! Allah will certainly try you in respect of some game which your hands and your lances can reach, that Allah might know who fears Him in secret; but whoever exceeds the limit after this, he shall have a painful punishment.
5 095	O ye who believe! Kill not game while in the sacred precincts or in pilgrim garb. If any of you doth so intentionally, the compensation is an offering, brought to the Ka'ba, of a domestic animal equivalent to the one he killed, as adjudged by two just men among you; or by way of atonement, the feeding of the indigent; or its equivalent in fasts: that he may taste of the penalty of his deed. Allah forgives what is past: for repetition Allah will exact from him the penalty. For Allah is Exalted, and Lord of Retribution.	O ye who believe! Kill no wild game while ye are on the pilgrimage. Whoso of you killeth it of set purpose he shall pay its forfeit in the equivalent of that which he hath killed, of domestic animals, the judge to be two men among you known for justice, (the forfeit) to be brought as an offering to the Ka'bah; or, for expiation, he shall feed poor persons, or the equivalent thereof in fasting, that he may taste the evil consequences of his deed. Allah forgiveth whatever (of this kind) may have happened in the past, but whoso relapseth, Allah will take retribution from him. Allah is Mighty, Able to Requite (the wrong).	O you who believe! do not kill game while you are on pilgrimage, and whoever among you shall kill it intentionally, the compensation (of it) is the like of what he killed, from the cattle, as two just persons among you shall judge, as an offering to be brought to the Kaaba or the expiation (of it) is the feeding of the poor or the equivalent of it in fasting, that he may taste the unwholesome result of his deed; Allah has pardoned what is gone by; and whoever returns (to it), Allah will inflict retribution on him; and Allah is Mighty, Lord of Retribution.
5 096	Lawful to you is the pursuit of water-game and its use for food,- for the benefit of yourselves and those who travel; but forbidden is the pursuit of land-game;- as long as ye are in the sacred precincts or in pilgrim garb. And fear Allah, to Whom ye shall be gathered back.	To hunt and to eat the fish of the sea is made lawful for you, a provision for you and for seafarers; but to hunt on land is forbidden you so long as ye are on the pilgrimage. Be mindful of your duty to Allah, unto Whom ye will be gathered.	Lawful to you is the game of the sea and its food, a provision for you and for the travellers, and the game of the land is forbidden to you so long as you are on pilgrimage, and be careful of (your duty to) Allah, to Whom you shall be gathered.
5 097	Allah made the Ka'ba, the Sacred House, an asylum of security for men, as also the Sacred Months, the animals for offerings, and the garlands that mark them: That ye may know that Allah hath knowledge of what is in the heavens and on earth and that Allah is well acquainted with all things.	Allah hath appointed the Ka'bah, the Sacred House, a standard for mankind, and the Sacred Month and the offerings and the garlands. That is so that ye may know that Allah knoweth whatsoever is in the heavens and whatsoever is in the earth, and that Allah is Knower of all things.	Allah has made the Kaaba, the sacred house, a maintenance for the people, and the sacred month and the offerings and the sacrificial animals with garlands; this is that you may know that Allah knows whatever is in the heavens and whatever is in the earth, and that Allah is the Knower of all things.
5 098	Know ye that Allah is strict in punishment and that Allah is Oft-Forgiving, Most Merciful.	Know that Allah is severe in punishment, but that Allah (also) is Forgiving, Merciful.	Know that Allah is severe in requiting (evil) and that Allah is Forgiving, Merciful.
5 099	The Messenger's duty is but to proclaim (the message). But Allah knoweth all that ye reveal and ye conceal.	The duty of the messenger is only to convey (the message). Allah knoweth what ye proclaim and what ye hide.	Nothing is (incumbent) on the Messenger but to deliver (the message), and Allah knows what you do openly and what you hide.
5 100	Say: "Not equal are things that are bad and things that are good, even though the abundance of the bad may dazzle thee; so fear Allah, O ye that understand; that (so) ye may prosper."	Say: The evil and the good are not alike even though the plenty of the evil attract thee. So be mindful of your duty to Allah, O men of understanding, that ye may succeed.	Say: The bad and the good are not equal, though the abundance of the bad may please you; so be careful of (your duty to) Allah, O men of understanding, that you may be successful.

5 101	O ye who believe! Ask not questions about things which, if made plain to you, may cause you trouble. But if ye ask about things when the Qur'an is being revealed, they will be made plain to you, Allah will forgive those: for Allah is Oft-Forgiving, Most Forbearing.	O ye who believe! Ask not of things which, if they were made unto you, would trouble you; but if ye ask of them when the Qur'an is being revealed, they will be made known unto you. Allah pardoneth this, for Allah is Forgiving, Clement.	O you who believe! do not put questions about things which if declared to you may trouble you, and if you question about them when the Quran is being revealed, they shall be declared to you; Allah pardons this, and Allah is Forgiving, Forbearing.
5 102	Some people before you did ask such questions, and on that account lost their faith.	A folk before you asked (for such disclosures) and then disbelieved therein.	A people before you indeed asked such questions, and then became disbelievers on account of them.
5 103	It was not Allah who instituted (superstitions like those of) a slit-ear she-camel, or a she-camel let loose for free pasture, or idol sacrifices for twin-births in animals, or stallion-camels freed from work: It is blasphemers who invent a lie against Allah; but most of them lack wisdom.	Allah hath not appointed anything in the nature of a Bahirah or a Sa'ibah or a Wasilah or a Hami, but those who disbelieve invent a lie against Allah. Most of them have no sense.	Allah has not ordained (the making of) a bahirah or a saibah or a wasilah or a hami but those who disbelieve fabricate a lie against Allah, and most of them do not understand.
5 104	When it is said to them: "Come to what Allah hath revealed; come to the Messenger": They say: "Enough for us are the ways we found our fathers following." what! even though their fathers were void of knowledge and guidance?	And when it is said unto them: Come unto that which Allah hath revealed and unto the messenger, they say: Enough for us is that wherein we found our fathers. What! Even though their fathers had no knowledge whatsoever, and no guidance?	And when it is said to them, Come to what Allah has revealed and to the Messenger, they say: That on which we found our fathers is sufficient for us. What! even though their fathers knew nothing and did not follow the right way.
5 105	O ye who believe! Guard your own souls: If ye follow (right) guidance, no hurt can come to you from those who stray. To goal of you all is to Allah: it is He that will show you the truth of all that ye do.	O ye who believe! Ye have charge of your own souls. He who erreth cannot injure you if ye are rightly guided. Unto Allah ye will all return; and then He will inform you of what ye used to do.	O you who believe! take care of your souls; he who errs cannot hurt you when you are on the right way; to Allah is your return, of all (of you), so He will inform you of what you did.
5 106	O ye who believe! When death approaches any of you, (take) witnesses among yourselves when making bequests,- two just men of your own (brotherhood) or others from outside if ye are journeying through the earth, and the chance of death befalls you (thus). If ye doubt (their truth), detain them both after prayer, and let them both swear by Allah: "We wish not in this for any worldly gain, even though the (beneficiary) be our near relation: we shall hide not the evidence before Allah: if we do, then behold! the sin be upon us!"	O ye who believe! Let there be witnesses between you when death draweth nigh unto one of you, at the time of bequest - two witnesses, just men from among you, or two others from another tribe, in case ye are campaigning in the land and the calamity of death befall you. Ye shall empanel them both after the prayer, and, if ye doubt, they shall be made to swear by Allah (saying): We will not take a bribe, even though it were (on behalf of) a near kinsman nor will we hide the testimony of Allah, for then indeed we should be of the sinful.	O you who believe! call to witness between you when death draws nigh to one of you, at the time of making the will, two just persons from among you, or two others from among others than you, if you are travelling in the land and the calamity of death befalls you; the two (witnesses) you should detain after the prayer; then if you doubt (them), they shall both swear by Allah, (saying): We will not take for it a price, though there be a relative, and we will not hide the testimony of Allah for then certainly we should be among the sinners.

5	107	But if it gets known that these two were guilty of the sin (of perjury), let two others stand forth in their places,- nearest in kin from among those who claim a lawful right: let them swear by Allah: "We affirm that our witness is truer than that of those two, and that we have not trespassed (beyond the truth): if we did, behold! the wrong be upon us!"	But then, if it is afterwards ascertained that both of them merit (the suspicion of) sin, let two others take their place of those nearly concerned, and let them swear by Allah, (saying): Verily our testimony is truer than their testimony and we have not transgressed (the bounds of duty), for them indeed we should be of the evil-doers.	Then if it becomes known that they both have been guilty of a sin, two others shall stand up in their place from among those who have a claim against them, the two nearest in kin; so they two should swear by Allah: Certainly our testimony is truer than the testimony of those two, and we have not exceeded the limit, for then most surely we should be of the unjust.
5	108	That is most suitable: that they may give the evidence in its true nature and shape, or else they would fear that other oaths would be taken after their oaths. But fear Allah, and listen (to His counsel): for Allah guideth not a rebellious people:	Thus it is more likely that they will bear true witness or fear that after their oaths the oaths (of others) will be taken. So be mindful of your duty (to Allah) and hearken. Allah guideth not the froward folk.	This is more proper in order that they should give testimony truly or fear that other oaths be given after their oaths; and be careful of (your duty to) Allah, and hear; and Allah does not guide the transgressing people.
5	109	One day will Allah gather the messengers together, and ask: "What was the response ye received (from men to your teaching)?" They will say: We have no knowledge: it is Thou Who knowest in full all that is hidden."	In the day when Allah gathereth together the messengers, and saith: What was your response (from mankind)? they say: We have no knowledge. Lo! Thou, only Thou art the Knower of Things Hidden,	On the day when Allah will assemble the messengers, then say: What answer were you given? They shall say: We have no knowledge, surely Thou art the great Knower of the unseen things.
5	110	Then will Allah say: "O Jesus the son of Mary! Recount My favour to thee and to thy mother. Behold! I strengthened thee with the holy spirit, so that thou didst speak to the people in childhood and in maturity. Behold! I taught thee the Book and Wisdom, the Law and the Gospel and behold! thou makest out of clay, as it were, the figure of a bird, by My leave, and thou breathest into it and it becometh a bird by My leave, and thou healest those born blind, and the lepers, by My leave. And behold! thou bringest forth the dead by My leave. And behold! I did restrain the Children of Israel from (violence to) thee when thou didst show them the clear Signs, and the unbelievers among them said: 'This is nothing but evident magic.'"	When Allah saith: O Jesus, son of Mary! Remember My favour unto thee and unto thy mother; how I strengthened thee with the holy Spirit, so that thou spakest unto mankind in the cradle as in maturity; and how I taught thee the Scripture and Wisdom and the Torah and the Gospel; and how thou didst shape of clay as it were the likeness of a bird by My permission, and didst blow upon it and it was a bird by My permission, and thou didst heal him who was born blind and the leper by My permission; and how thou didst raise the dead by My permission; and how I restrained the Children of Israel from (harming) thee when thou camest unto them with clear proofs, and those of them who disbelieved exclaimed: This is naught else than mere magic;	When Allah will say: O Isa son of Marium! Remember My favor on you and on your mother, when I strengthened you I with the holy Spirit, you spoke to the people in the cradle and I when of old age, and when I taught you the Book and the wisdom and the Taurat and the Injeel; and when you determined out of clay a thing like the form of a bird by My permission, then you breathed into it and it became a bird by My permission, and you healed the blind and the leprous by My permission; and when you brought forth the dead by My permission; and when I withheld the children of Israel from you when you came to them with clear arguments, but those who disbelieved among them said: This is nothing but clear enchantment.
5	111	"And behold! I inspired the disciples to have faith in Me and Mine Messenger: they said, 'We have faith, and do thou bear witness that we bow to Allah as Muslims'".	And when I inspired the disciples, (saying): Believe in Me and in My messenger, they said: We believe. Bear witness that we have surrendered (unto Thee) "we are muslims".	And when I revealed to the disciples, saying, Believe in Me and My messenger, they said: We believe and bear witness that we submit (ourselves).

5 112	Behold! the disciples, said: "O Jesus the son of Mary! can thy Lord send down to us a table set (with viands) from heaven?" Said Jesus: Fear Allah, if ye have faith.	When the disciples said: O Jesus, son of Mary! Is thy Lord able to send down for us a table spread with food from heaven? He said: Observe your duty to Allah, if ye are true believers.	When the disciples said: O Isa son of Marium! will your Lord consent to send down to us food from heaven? He said: Be careful of (your duty to) Allah if you are believers.
5 113	They said: "We only wish to eat thereof and satisfy our hearts, and to know that thou hast indeed told us the truth; and that we ourselves may be witnesses to the miracle."	(They said:) We wish to eat thereof, that we may satisfy our hearts and know that thou hast spoken truth to us, and that thereof we may be witnesses.	They said: We desire that we should eat of it and that our hearts should be at rest, and that we may know that you have indeed spoken the truth to us and that we may be of the witnesses to it.
5 114	Said Jesus the son of Mary: "O Allah our Lord! Send us from heaven a table set (with viands), that there may be for us - for the first and the last of us - a solemn festival and a sign from thee; and provide for our sustenance, for thou art the best Sustainer (of our needs)."	Jesus, son of Mary, said: O Allah, Lord of us! Send down for us a table spread with food from heaven, that it may be a feast for us, for the first of us and for the last of us, and a sign from Thee. Give us sustenance, for Thou art the Best of Sustainers.	Isa the son of Marium said: O Allah, our Lord! send down to us food from heaven which should be to us an ever-recurring happiness, to the first of us and to the last of us, and a sign from Thee, and grant us means of subsistence, and Thou art the best of the Providers.
5 115	Allah said: "I will send it down unto you: But if any of you after that resisteth faith, I will punish him with a penalty such as I have not inflicted on any one among all the peoples."	Allah said: Lo! I send it down for you. And whoso disbelieveth of you afterward, him surely will I punish with a punishment wherewith I have not punished any of (My) creatures.	Allah said: Surely I will send it down to you, but whoever shall disbelieve afterwards from among you, surely I will chastise him with a chastisement with which I will not chastise, anyone among the nations.
5 116	And behold! Allah will say: "O Jesus the son of Mary! Didst thou say unto men, worship me and my mother as gods in derogation of Allah'?" He will say: "Glory to Thee! never could I say what I had no right (to say). Had I said such a thing, thou wouldst indeed have known it. Thou knowest what is in my heart, Thou I know not what is in Thine. For Thou knowest in full all that is hidden."	And when Allah saith: O Jesus, son of Mary! Didst thou say unto mankind: Take me and my mother for two gods beside Allah? he saith: Be glorified! It was not mine to utter that to which I had no right. If I used to say it, then Thou knewest it. Thou knowest what is in my mind, and I know not what is in Thy Mind. Lo! Thou, only Thou, art the Knower of Things Hidden?	And when Allah will say: O Isa son of Marium! did you say to men, Take me and my mother for two gods besides Allah he will say: Glory be to Thee, it did not befit me that I should say what I had no right to (say); if I had said it, Thou wouldst indeed have known it; Thou knowest what is in my mind, and I do not know what is in Thy mind, surely Thou art the great Knower of the unseen things.
5 117	"Never said I to them aught except what Thou didst command me to say, to wit, 'worship Allah, my Lord and your Lord'; and I was a witness over them whilst I dwelt amongst them; when Thou didst take me up Thou wast the Watcher over them, and Thou art a witness to all things."	I spake unto them only that which Thou commandedst me, (saying): Worship Allah, my Lord and your Lord. I was a witness of them while I dwelt among them, and when Thou tookest me Thou wast the Watcher over them. Thou art Witness over all things.	I did not say to them aught save what Thou didst enjoin me with: That serve Allah, my Lord and your Lord, and I was a witness of them so long as I was among them, but when Thou didst cause me to die, Thou wert the watcher over them, and Thou art witness of all things.
5 118	"If Thou dost punish them, they are Thy servant: If Thou dost forgive them, Thou art the Exalted in power, the Wise."	If Thou punish them, lo! they are Thy slaves, and if Thou forgive them (lo! they are Thy slaves). Lo! Thou, only Thou, art the Mighty, the Wise.	If Thou shouldst chastise them, then surely they are Thy servants; and if Thou shouldst forgive them, then surely Thou art the Mighty, the Wise.

5 119	Allah will say: "This is a day on which the truthful will profit from their truth: theirs are gardens, with rivers flowing beneath,- their eternal Home: Allah well-pleased with them, and they with Allah: That is the great salvation, (the fulfilment of all desires)."	Allah saith: This is a day in which their truthfulness profiteth the truthful, for theirs are Gardens underneath which rivers flow, wherein they are secure for ever, Allah taking pleasure in them and they in Him. That is the great triumph.	Allah will say: This is the day when their truth shall benefit the truthful ones; they shall have gardens beneath which rivers flow to abide in them for ever: Allah is well pleased with them and they are well pleased with Allah; this is the mighty achievement.	
5 120	To Allah doth belong the dominion of the heavens and the earth, and all that is therein, and it is He Who hath power over all things.	Unto Allah belongeth the Sovereignty of the heavens and the earth and whatsoever is therein, and He is Able to do all things.	Allah's is the kingdom of the heavens and the earth and what is in them; and He has power over all things.	

Chapter 6:

AL-ANAAM (CATTLE, LIVESTOCK)

Total Verses: 165 Revealed At: MAKKA

In the name of Allah, the Most Beneficent, the Most Merciful.

6 001	Praise be Allah, Who created the heavens and the earth, and made the darkness and the light. Yet those who reject Faith hold (others) as equal, with their Guardian-Lord.	Praise be to Allah, Who hath created the heavens and the earth, and hath appointed darkness and light. Yet those who disbelieve ascribe rivals unto their Lord.	All praise is due to Allah, Who created the heavens and the earth and made the darkness and the light; yet those who disbelieve set up equals with their Lord.	
6 002	He it is created you from clay, and then decreed a stated term (for you). And there is in His presence another determined term; yet ye doubt within yourselves!	He it is Who hath created you from clay, and hath decreed a term for you. A term is fixed with Him. Yet still ye doubt!	He it is Who created you from clay, then He decreed a term; and there is a term named with Him; still you doubt.	
6 003	And He is Allah in the heavens and on earth. He knoweth what ye hide, and what ye reveal, and He knoweth the (recompense) which ye earn (by your deeds).	He is Allah in the heavens and in the earth. He knoweth both your secret and your utterance, and He knoweth what ye earn.	And He is Allah in the heavens and in the earth; He knows your secret (thoughts) and your open (words), and He knows what you earn.	
6 004	But never did a single one of the signs of their Lord reach them, but they turned away therefrom.	Never came there unto them a revelation of the revelations of Allah but they did turn away from it.	And there does not come to them any communication of the communications of their Lord but they turn aside from it.	
6 005	And now they reject the truth when it reaches them: but soon shall they learn the reality of what they used to mock at.	And they denied the truth when it came unto them. But there will come unto them the tidings of that which they used to deride.	So they have indeed rejected the truth when it came to them; therefore the truth of what they mocked at will shine upon them.	
6 006	See they not how many of those before them We did destroy?- generations We had established on the earth, in strength such as We have not given to you - for whom We poured out rain from the skies in abundance, and gave (fertile) streams flowing beneath their (feet): yet for their sins We destroyed them, and raised in their wake fresh generations (to succeed them).	See they not how many a generation We destroyed before them, whom We had established in the earth more firmly than We have established you, and We shed on them abundant showers from the sky, and made the rivers flow beneath them. Yet we destroyed them for their sins, and created after them another generation.	Do they not consider how many a generation We have destroyed before them, whom We had established in the earth as We have not established you, and We sent the clouds pouring rain on them in abundance, and We made the rivers to flow beneath them, then We destroyed them on account of their faults and raised up after them another generation.	

6 007	If We had sent unto thee a written (message) on parchment, so that they could touch it with their hands, the Unbelievers would have been sure to say: "This is nothing but obvious magic!"	Had we sent down unto thee (Muhammad) (actual) writing upon parchment, so that they could feel it with their hands, those who disbelieve would have said: This is naught else than mere magic.	And if We had sent to you a writing on a paper, then they had touched it with their hands, certainly those who disbelieve would have said: This is nothing but clear enchantment.
6 008	They say: "Why is not an angel sent down to him?" If we did send down an angel, the matter would be settled at once, and no respite would be granted them.	They say: Why hath not an angel been sent down unto him? If We sent down an angel, then the matter would be judged; no further time would be allowed them (for reflection).	And they say: Why has not an angel been sent down to him? And had We sent down an angel, the matter would have certainly been decided and then they would not have been respited.
6 009	If We had made it an angel, We should have sent him as a man, and We should certainly have caused them confusion in a matter which they have already covered with confusion.	Had we appointed him (Our messenger) an angel, We assuredly had made him (as) a man (that he might speak to men); and (thus) obscured for them (the truth) they (now) obscure.	And if We had made him angel, We would certainly have made him a man, and We would certainly have made confused to them what they make confused.
6 010	Mocked were (many) messengers before thee; but their scoffers were hemmed in by the thing that they mocked.	Messengers (of Allah) have been derided before thee, but that whereat they scoffed surrounded such of them as did deride.	And certainly messengers before you were mocked at, but that which they mocked at encompassed the scoffers among them.
6 011	Say: "Travel through the earth and see what was the end of those who rejected Truth."	Say (unto the disbelievers): Travel in the land, and see the nature of the consequence for the rejecters!	Say: Travel in the land, then see what was the end of the rejecters.
6 012	Say: "To whom belongeth all that is in the heavens and on earth?" Say: "To Allah. He hath inscribed for Himself (the rule of) Mercy. That He will gather you together for the Day of Judgment, there is no doubt whatever. It is they who have lost their own souls, that will not believe."	Say: Unto whom belongeth whatsoever is in the heavens and the earth? Say: Unto Allah. He hath prescribed for Himself mercy, that He may bring you all together to the Day of Resurrection whereof there is no doubt. Those who ruin their souls will not believe.	Say: To whom belongs what is in the heavens and the earth? Say: To Allah; He has ordained mercy on Himself; most certainly He will gather you on the resurrection day-- there is no doubt about it. (As for) those who have lost their souls, they will not believe.
6 013	"To him belongeth all that dwelleth (or lurketh) in the night and the day. For he is the one who heareth and knoweth all things."	Unto Him belongeth whatsoever resteth in the night and the day. He is the Hearer, the Knower.	And to Him belongs whatever dwells in the night and the day; and He is the Hearing, the Knowing.
6 014	Say: "Shall I take for my protector any other than Allah, the Maker of the heavens and the earth? And He it is that feedeth but is not fed." Say: "Nay! but I am commanded to be the first of those who bow to Allah (in Islam), and be not thou of the company of those who join gods with Allah."	Say: Shall I choose for a protecting friend other than Allah, the Originator of the heavens and the earth, Who feedeth and is never fed? Say: I am ordered to be the first to surrender (unto Him). And be not thou (O Muhammad) of the idolaters.	Say: Shall I take a guardian besides Allah, the Originator of the heavens and the earth, and He feeds (others) and is not (Himself) fed. Say: I am commanded to be the first who submits himself, and you should not be of the polytheists.
6 015	Say: "I would, if I disobeyed my Lord, indeed have fear of the penalty of a Mighty Day."	Say: I fear, if I rebel against my Lord, the retribution of an Awful Day.	Say: Surely I fear, if I disobey my Lord, the chastisement of a grievous day.
6 016	"On that day, if the penalty is averted from any, it is due to Allah's mercy; And that would be (Salvation), the obvious fulfilment of all desire."	He from whom (such retribution) is averted on that day, (Allah) hath in truth had mercy on him. That will be the signal triumph.	He from whom it is averted on that day, Allah indeed has shown mercy to him; and this is a manifest achievement.

6 017	"If Allah touch thee with affliction, none can remove it but He; if He touch thee with happiness, He hath power over all things."	If Allah touch thee with affliction, there is none that can relieve therefrom save Him, and if He touch thee with good fortune (there is none that can impair it); for He is Able to do all things.	And if Allah touch you with affliction, there is none to take it off but He; and if He visit you with good, then He has power over all things.
6 018	"He is the irresistible, (watching) from above over His worshippers; and He is the Wise, acquainted with all things."	He is the Omnipotent over His slaves, and He is the Wise, the Knower.	And He is the Supreme, above His servants; and He is the Wise, the Aware.
6 019	Say: "What thing is most weighty in evidence?" Say: "Allah is witness between me and you; This Qur'an hath been revealed to me by inspiration, that I may warn you and all whom it reaches. Can ye possibly bear witness that besides Allah there is another Allah?" Say: Nay! I cannot bear witness! Say: "But in truth He is the one Allah, and I truly am innocent of (your blasphemy of) joining others with Him."	Say (O Muhammad): What thing is of most weight in testimony? Say: Allah is Witness between me and you. And this Qur'an hath been inspired in me, that I may warn therewith you and whomsoever it may reach. Do ye in sooth bear witness that there are gods beside Allah? Say: I bear no such witness. Say: He is only One Allah. Lo! I am innocent of that which ye associate (with Him).	Say: What thing is the weightiest in testimony? Say: Allah is witness between you and me; and this Quran has been revealed to me that with it I may warn you and whomsoever it reaches. Do you really bear witness that there are other gods with Allah? Say: I do not bear witness. Say: He is only one Allah, and surely I am clear of that which you set up (with Him).
6 020	Those to whom We have given the Book know this as they know their own sons. Those who have lost their own souls refuse therefore to believe.	Those unto whom We gave the Scripture recognise (this revelation) as they recognise their sons. Those who ruin their own souls will not believe.	Those whom We have given the Book recognize him as they recognize their sons; (as for) those who have lost their souls, they will not believe.
6 021	Who doth more wrong than he who inventeth a lie against Allah or rejecteth His signs? But verily the wrong-doers never shall prosper.	Who doth greater wrong than he who inventeth a lie against Allah or denieth His revelations? Lo! the wrongdoers will not be successful.	And who is more unjust than he who forges a lie against Allah or (he who) gives the lie to His communications; surely the unjust will not be successful.
6 022	One day shall We gather them all together: We shall say to those who ascribed partners (to Us): "Where are the partners whom ye (invented and) talked about?"	And on the day We gather them together We shall say unto those who ascribed partners (unto Allah): Where are (now) those partners of your make-believe?	And on the day when We shall gather them all together, then shall We say to those who associated others (with Allah): Where are your associates whom you asserted?
6 023	There will then be (left) no subterfuge for them but to say: "By Allah our Lord, we were not those who joined gods with Allah."	Then will they have no contention save that they will say: By Allah, our Lord, we never were idolaters.	Then their excuse would be nothing but that they would say: By Allah, our Lord, we were not polytheists.
6 024	Behold! how they lie against their own souls! But the (lie) which they invented will leave them in the lurch.	See how they lie against themselves, and (how) the thing which they devised hath failed them!	See how they lie against their own souls, and that which they forged has passed away from them.
6 025	Of them there are some who (pretend to) listen to thee; but We have thrown veils on their hearts, So they understand it not, and deafness in their ears; if they saw every one of the signs, not they will believe in them; in so much that when they come to thee, they (but) dispute with thee; the Unbelievers say: "These are nothing but tales of the ancients."	Of them are some who listen unto thee, but We have placed upon their hearts veils, lest they should understand, and in their ears a deafness. If they saw every token they would not believe therein; to the point that, when they come unto thee to argue with thee, the disbelievers say: This is naught else than fables of the men of old.	And of them is he who hearkens to you, and We have cast veils over their hearts lest they understand it and a heaviness into their ears; and even if they see every sign they will not believe in it; so much so that when they come to you they only dispute with you; those who disbelieve say: This is naught but the stories of the ancients.

6 026	Others they keep away from it, and themselves they keep away; but they only destroy their own souls, and they perceive it not.	And they forbid (men) from it and avoid it, and they ruin none save themselves, though they perceive not.	And they prohibit (others) from it and go far away from it, and they only bring destruction upon their own souls while they do not perceive.
6 027	If thou couldst but see when they are confronted with the Fire! They will say: "Would that we were but sent back! Then would we not reject the signs of our Lord, but would be amongst those who believe!"	If thou couldst see when they are set before the Fire and say: Oh, would that we might return! Then would we not deny the revelations of our Lord but we would be of the believers!	And could you see when they are made to stand before the fire, then they shall say: Would that we were sent back, and we would not reject the communications of our Lord and we would be of the believers.
6 028	Yea, in their own (eyes) will become manifest what before they concealed. But if they were returned, they would certainly relapse to the things they were forbidden, for they are indeed liars.	Nay, but that hath become clear unto them which before they used to hide. And if they were sent back they would return unto that which they are forbidden. Lo! they are liars.	Nay, what they concealed before shall become manifest to them; and if they were sent back, they would certainly go back to that which they are forbidden, and most surely they are liars.
6 029	And they (sometimes) say: "There is nothing except our life on this earth, and never shall we be raised up again."	And they say: There is naught save our life of the world, and we shall not be raised (again).	And they say: There is nothing but our life of this world, and we shall not be raised.
6 030	If thou couldst but see when they are confronted with their Lord! He will say: "Is not this the truth?" They will say: "Yea, by our Lord!" He will say: "Taste ye then the penalty, because ye rejected Faith."	If thou couldst see when they are set before their Lord! He will say: Is not this real? They will say: Yea, verily, by our Lord! He will say: Taste now the retribution for that ye used to disbelieve.	And could you see when they are made to stand before their Lord. He will say: Is not this the truth? They will say: Yea! by our Lord. He will say: Taste then the chastisement because you disbelieved.
6 031	Lost indeed are they who treat it as a falsehood that they must meet Allah,- until on a sudden the hour is on them, and they say: "Ah! woe unto us that we took no thought of it"; for they bear their burdens on their backs, and evil indeed are the burdens that they bear?	They indeed are losers who deny their meeting with Allah until, when the Hour cometh on them suddenly, they cry: Alas for us, that we neglected it! They bear upon their backs their burdens. Ah, evil is that which they bear!	They are losers indeed who reject the meeting of Allah; until when the hour comes upon them all of a sudden they shall say: O our grief for our neglecting it! and they shall bear their burdens on their backs; now surely evil is that which they bear.
6 032	What is the life of this world but play and amusement? But best is the home in the hereafter, for those who are righteous. Will ye not then understand?	Naught is the life of the world save a pastime and a spot. Better far is the abode of the Hereafter for those who keep their duty (to Allah). Have ye then no sense?	And this world's life is naught but a play and an idle sport and certainly the abode of the hereafter is better for those who guard (against evil); do you not then understand?
6 033	We know indeed the grief which their words do cause thee: It is not thee they reject: it is the signs of Allah, which the wicked contemn.	We know well how their talk grieveth thee, though in truth they deny not thee (Muhammad) but evil-doers flout the revelations of Allah.	We know indeed that what they say certainly grieves you, but surely they do not call you a liar; but the unjust deny the communications of Allah.
6 034	Rejected were the messengers before thee: with patience and constancy they bore their rejection and their wrongs, until Our aid did reach them: there is none that can alter the words (and decrees) of Allah. Already hast thou received some account of those messengers.	Messengers indeed have been denied before thee, and they were patient under the denial and the persecution till Our succour reached them. There is none to alter the decisions of Allah. Already there hath reached thee (somewhat) of the tidings of the messengers (We sent before).	And certainly messengers before you were rejected, but they were patient on being rejected and persecuted until Our help came to them; and there is none to change the words of Allah, and certainly there has come to you some information about the messengers.

6 035	If their spurning is hard on thy mind, yet if thou wert able to seek a tunnel in the ground or a ladder to the skies and bring them a sign,- (what good?). If it were Allah's will, He could gather them together unto true guidance: so be not thou amongst those who are swayed by ignorance (and impatience)!	And if their aversion is grievous unto thee, then, if thou canst, seek a way down into the earth or a ladder unto the sky that thou mayst bring unto them a portent (to convince them all)! - If Allah willed, He could have brought them all together to the guidance - So be not thou among the foolish ones.	And if their turning away is hard on you, then if you can seek an opening (to go down) into the earth or a ladder (to ascend up) to heaven so that you should bring them a sign and if Allah had pleased He would certainly have gathered them all on guidance, therefore be not of the ignorant.
6 036	Those who listen (in truth), be sure, will accept: as to the dead, Allah will raise them up; then will they be turned unto Him.	Only those can accept who hear. As for the dead, Allah will raise them up; then unto Him they will be returned.	Only those accept who listen; and (as to) the dead, Allah will raise them, then to Him they shall be returned.
6 037	They say: "Why is not a sign sent down to him from his Lord?" Say: Allah hath certainly power to send down a sign: but most of them understand not."	They say: Why hath no portent been sent down upon him from his Lord? Say: Lo! Allah is Able to send down a portent. But most of them know not.	And they say: Why has not a sign been sent down to him from his Lord? Say: Surely Allah is able to send down a sign, but most of them do not know.
6 038	There is not an animal (that lives) on the earth, nor a being that flies on its wings, but (forms part of) communities like you. Nothing have we omitted from the Book, and they (all) shall be gathered to their Lord in the end.	There is not an animal in the earth, nor a flying creature flying on two wings, but they are peoples like unto you. We have neglected nothing in the Book (of Our decrees). Then unto their Lord they will be gathered.	And there is no animal that walks upon the earth nor a bird that flies with its two wings but (they are) genera like yourselves; We have not neglected anything in the Book, then to their Lord shall they be gathered.
6 039	Those who reject our signs are deaf and dumb,- in the midst of darkness profound: whom Allah willeth, He leaveth to wander: whom He willeth, He placeth on the way that is straight.	Those who deny Our revelations are deaf and dumb in darkness. Whom Allah will sendeth astray, and whom He will He placeth on a straight path.	And they who reject Our communications are deaf and dumb, in utter darkness; whom Allah pleases He causes to err and whom He pleases He puts on the right way.
6 040	Say: "Think ye to yourselves, if there come upon you the wrath of Allah, or the Hour (that ye dread), would ye then call upon other than Allah?- (reply) if ye are truthful!"	Say: Can ye see yourselves, if the punishment of Allah come upon you or the Hour come upon you, (calling upon other than Allah)? Do ye then call (for help) to any other than Allah? (Answer that) if ye are truthful.	Say: Tell me if the chastisement of Allah should overtake you or the hour should come upon you, will you call (on others) besides Allah, if you are truthful?
6 041	"Nay,- On Him would ye call, and if it be His will, He would remove (the distress) which occasioned your call upon Him, and ye would forget (the false gods) which ye join with Him!"	Nay, but unto Him ye call, and He removeth that because of which ye call unto Him, if He will, and ye forget whatever partners ye ascribed unto Him.	Nay, Him you call upon, so He clears away that for which you pray if He pleases and you forget what you set up (with Him).
6 042	Before thee We sent (messengers) to many nations, and We afflicted the nations with suffering and adversity, that they might learn humility.	We have sent already unto peoples that were before thee, and We visited them with tribulation and adversity, in order that they might grow humble.	And certainly We sent (messengers) to nations before you then We seized them with distress and affliction in order that they might humble themselves.
6 043	When the suffering reached them from us, why then did they not learn humility? On the contrary their hearts became hardened, and Satan made their (sinful) acts seem alluring to them.	If only, when Our disaster came on them, they had been humble! But their hearts were hardened and the devil made all that they used to do seem fair unto them!	Yet why did they not, when Our punishment came to them, humble themselves? But their hearts hardened and the Shaitan made what they did fair-seeming to them.

6 044	But when they forgot the warning they had received, We opened to them the gates of all (good) things, until, in the midst of their enjoyment of Our gifts, on a sudden, We called them to account, when lo! they were plunged in despair!	Then, when they forgot that whereof they had been reminded, We opened unto them the gates of all things till, even as they were rejoicing in that which they were given, We seized them unawares, and lo! they were dumbfounded.	But when they neglected that with which they had been admonished, We opened for them the doors of all things, until when they rejoiced in what they were given We seized them suddenly; then lo! they were in utter despair.
6 045	Of the wrong-doers the last remnant was cut off. Praise be to Allah, the Cherisher of the worlds.	So of the people who did wrong the last remnant was cut off. Praise be to Allah, Lord of the Worlds!	So the roots of the people who were unjust were cut off; and all praise is due to Allah, the Lord of the worlds.
6 046	Say: "Think ye, if Allah took away your hearing and your sight, and sealed up your hearts, who - a god other than Allah - could restore them to you?" See how We explain the signs by various (symbols); yet they turn aside.	Say: Have ye imagined, if Allah should take away your hearing and your sight and seal your hearts, who is the God who could restore it to you save Allah? See how We display the revelations unto them! Yet still they turn away.	Say: Have you considered that if Allah takes away your hearing and your sight and sets a seal on your hearts, who is the god besides Allah that can bring it to you? See how We repeat the communications, yet they turn away.
6 047	Say: "Think ye, if the punishment of Allah comes to you, whether suddenly or openly, will any be destroyed except those who do wrong?"	Say: Can ye see yourselves, if the punishment of Allah come upon you unawares or openly? Would any perish save wrongdoing folk?	Say: Have you considered if the chastisement of Allah should overtake you suddenly or openly, will any be destroyed but the unjust people?
6 048	We send the messengers only to give good news and to warn: so those who believe and mend (their lives),- upon them shall be no fear, nor shall they grieve.	We send not the messengers save as bearers of good news and warners. Whoso believeth and doeth right, there shall no fear come upon them neither shall they grieve.	And We send not messengers but as announcers of good news and givers of warning, then whoever believes and acts aright, they shall have no fear, nor shall they grieve.
6 049	But those who reject our signs,- them shall punishment touch, for that they ceased not from transgressing.	But as for those who deny Our revelations, torment will afflict them for that they used to disobey.	And (as for) those who reject Our communications, chastisement shall afflict them because they transgressed.
6 050	Say: "I tell you not that with me are the treasures of Allah, nor do I know what is hidden, nor do I tell you I am an angel. I but follow what is revealed to me." Say: "can the blind be held equal to the seeing?" Will ye then consider not?	Say (O Muhammad, to the disbelievers): I say not unto you (that) I possess the treasures of Allah, nor that I have knowledge of the Unseen; and I say not unto you: Lo! I am an angel. I follow only that which is inspired in me. Say: Are the blind man and the seer equal? Will ye not then take thought?	Say: I do not say to you, I have with me the treasures of Allah, nor do I know the unseen, nor do I say to you that I am an angel; I do not follow aught save that which is revealed to me. Say: Are the blind and the seeing one alike? Do you not then reflect?
6 051	Give this warning to those in whose (hearts) is the fear that they will be brought (to judgment) before their Lord: except for Him they will have no protector nor intercessor: that they may guard (against evil).	Warn hereby those who fear (because they know) that they will be gathered unto their Lord, for whom there is no protecting ally nor intercessor beside Him, that they may ward off (evil).	And warn with it those who fear that they shall be gathered to their Lord-- there is no guardian for them, nor any intercessor besides Him-- that they may guard (against evil).
6 052	Send not away those who call on their Lord morning and evening, seeking His face. In naught art thou accountable for them, and in naught are they accountable for thee, that thou shouldst turn them away, and thus be (one) of the unjust.	Repel not those who call upon their Lord at morn and evening, seeking His Countenance. Thou art not accountable for them in aught, nor are they accountable for thee in aught, that thou shouldst repel them and be of the wrong-doers.	And do not drive away those who call upon their Lord in the morning and the evening, they desire only His favor; neither are you answerable for any reckoning of theirs, nor are they answerable for any reckoning of yours, so that you should drive them away and thus be of the unjust.

6 053	Thus did We try some of them by comparison with others, that they should say: "Is it these then that Allah hath favoured from amongst us?" Doth not Allah know best those who are grateful?	And even so do We try some of them by others, that they say: Are these they whom Allah favoureth among us? Is not Allah best Aware of the thanksgivers?	And thus do We try some of them by others so that they say: Are these they upon whom Allah has conferred benefit from among us? Does not Allah best know the grateful?
6 054	When those come to thee who believe in Our signs, Say: "Peace be on you: Your Lord had inscribed for Himself (the rule of) mercy: verily, if any of you did evil in ignorance, and thereafter repented, and amend (his conduct), lo! He is Oft-Forgiving, Most Merciful."	And when those who believe in Our revelations come unto thee, say: Peace be unto you! Your Lord hath prescribed for Himself mercy, that whoso of you doeth evil through ignorance and repenteth afterward thereof and doeth right, (for him) lo! He is Forgiving, Merciful.	And when those who believe in Our communications come to you, say: Peace be on you, your Lord has ordained mercy on Himself, (so) that if any one of you does evil in ignorance, then turns after that and acts aright, then He is Forgiving, Merciful.
6 055	Thus do We explain the signs in detail: that the way of the sinners may be shown up.	Thus do We expound the revelations that the way of the unrighteous may be manifest.	And thus do We make distinct the communications and so that the way of the guilty may become clear.
6 056	Say: "I am forbidden to worship those - others than Allah - whom ye call upon." Say: "I will not follow your vain desires: If I did, I would stray from the path, and be not of the company of those who receive guidance."	Say: I am forbidden to worship those on whom ye call instead of Allah. Say: I will not follow your desires, for then should I go astray and I should not be of the rightly guided.	Say: I am forbidden to serve those whom you call upon besides Allah. Say: I do not follow your low desires, for then indeed I should have gone astray and I should not be of those who go aright.
6 057	Say: "For me, I (work) on a clear sign from my Lord, but ye reject Him. What ye would see hastened, is not in my power. The command rests with none but Allah: He declares the truth, and He is the best of judges."	Say: I am (relying) on clear proof from my Lord, while ye deny Him. I have not that for which ye are impatient. The decision is for Allah only. He telleth the truth and He is the Best of Deciders.	Say: Surely I have manifest proof from my Lord and you call it a lie; I have not with me that which you would hasten; the judgment is only Allah's; He relates the truth and He is the best of deciders.
6 058	Say: "If what ye would see hastened were in my power, the matter would be settled at once between you and me. But Allah knoweth best those who do wrong."	Say: If I had that for which ye are impatient, then would the case (ere this) have been decided between me and you. Allah is Best Aware of the wrong-doers.	Say: If that which you desire to hasten were with me, the matter would have certainly been decided between you and me; and Allah best knows the unjust.
6 059	With Him are the keys of the unseen, the treasures that none knoweth but He. He knoweth whatever there is on the earth and in the sea. Not a leaf doth fall but with His knowledge: there is not a grain in the darkness (or depths) of the earth, nor anything fresh or dry (green or withered), but is (inscribed) in a record clear (to those who can read).	And with Him are the keys of the Invisible. None but He knoweth them. And He knoweth what is in the land and the sea. Not a leaf falleth but He knoweth it, not a grain amid the darkness of the earth, naught of wet or dry but (it is noted) in a clear record.	And with Him are the keys of the unseen treasures-- none knows them but He; and He knows what is in the land and the sea, and there falls not a leaf but He knows it, nor a grain in the darkness of the earth, nor anything green nor dry but (it is all) in a clear book.
6 060	It is He who doth take your souls by night, and hath knowledge of all that ye have done by day: by day doth He raise you up again; that a term appointed be fulfilled; In the end unto Him will be your return; then will He show you the truth of all that ye did.	He it is Who gathereth you at night and knoweth that which ye commit by day. Then He raiseth you again to life therein, that the term appointed (for you) may be accomplished. And afterward unto Him is your return. Then He will proclaim unto you what ye used to do.	And He it is Who takes your souls at night (in sleep), and He knows what you acquire in the day, then He raises you up therein that an appointed term may be fulfilled; then to Him is your return, then He will inform you of what you were doing.

6 061	He is the irresistible, (watching) from above over His worshippers, and He sets guardians over you. At length, when death approaches one of you, Our angels take his soul, and they never fail in their duty.	He is the Omnipotent over His slaves. He sendeth guardians over you until, when death cometh unto one of you, Our messengers receive him, and they neglect not.	And He is the Supreme, above His servants, and He sends keepers over you; until when death comes to one of you, Our messengers cause him to die, and they are not remiss.
6 062	Then are men returned unto Allah, their protector, the (only) reality: Is not His the command? and He is the swiftest in taking account.	Then are they restored unto Allah, their Lord, the Just. Surely His is the judgment. And He is the most swift of reckoners.	Then are they sent back to Allah, their Master, the True one; now surely His is the judgment and He is swiftest in taking account.
6 063	Say: "Who is it that delivereth you from the dark recesses of land and sea, when ye call upon Him in humility and silent terror: 'If He only delivers us from these (dangers), (we vow) we shall truly show our gratitude'?"	Say: Who delivereth you from the darkness of the land and the sea? Ye call upon Him humbly and in secret, (saying): If we are delivered from this (fear) we truly will be of the thankful.	Say: Who is it that delivers you from the dangers of the land and the sea (when) you call upon Him (openly) humiliating yourselves, and in secret: If He delivers us from this, we should certainly be of the grateful ones.
6 064	Say "It is Allah that delivereth you from these and all (other) distresses: and yet ye worship false gods!"	Say: Allah delivereth you from this and from all affliction. Yet ye attribute partners unto Him.	Say: Allah delivers you from them and from every distress, but again you set up others (with Him).
6 065	Say: "He hath power to send calamities on you, from above and below, or to cover you with confusion in party strife, giving you a taste of mutual vengeance - each from the other." See how We explain the signs by various (symbols); that they may understand.	Say: He is able to send punishment upon you from above you or from beneath your feet, or to bewilder you with dissension and make you taste the tyranny one of another. See how We display the revelations so that they may understand.	Say: He has the power that He should send on you a chastisement from above you or from beneath your feet, or that He should throw you into confusion, (making you) of different parties; and make some of you taste the fighting of others. See how We repeat the communications that they may understand.
6 066	But thy people reject this, though it is the truth. Say: "Not mine is the responsibility for arranging your affairs;"	Thy people (O Muhammad) have denied it, though it is the Truth. Say: I am not put in charge of you.	And your people call it a lie and it is the very truth. Say: I am not placed in charge of you.
6 067	"For every message is a limit of time, and soon shall ye know it."	For every announcement there is a term, and ye will come to know.	For every prophecy is a term, and you will come to know (it).
6 068	When thou seest men engaged in vain discourse about Our signs, turn away from them unless they turn to a different theme. If Satan ever makes thee forget, then after recollection, sit not thou in the company of those who do wrong.	And when thou seest those who meddle with Our revelations, withdraw from them until they meddle with another topic. And if the devil cause thee to forget, sit not, after the remembrance, with the congregation of wrong-doers.	And when you see those who enter into false discourses about Our communications, withdraw from them until they enter into some other discourse, and if the Shaitan causes you to forget, then do not sit after recollection with the unjust people.
6 069	On their account no responsibility falls on the righteous, but (their duty) is to remind them, that they may (learn to) fear Allah.	Those who ward off (evil) are not accountable for them in aught, but the Reminder (must be given them) that haply they (too) may ward off (evil).	And nought of the reckoning of their (deeds) shall be against those who guard (against evil), but (theirs) is only to remind, haply they may guard.

6 070	Leave alone those who take their religion to be mere play and amusement, and are deceived by the life of this world. But proclaim (to them) this (truth): that every soul delivers itself to ruin by its own acts: it will find for itself no protector or intercessor except Allah: if it offered every ransom, (or reparation), none will be accepted: such is (the end of) those who deliver themselves to ruin by their own acts: they will have for drink (only) boiling water, and for punishment, one most grievous: for they persisted in rejecting Allah.		And forsake those who take their religion for a pastime and a jest, and whom the life of the world beguileth. Remind (mankind) hereby lest a soul be destroyed by what it earneth. It hath beside Allah no protecting ally nor intercessor, and though it offer every compensation it will not be accepted from it. Those are they who perish by their own deserts. For them is drink of boiling water and a painful doom, because they disbelieved.	And leave those who have taken their religion for a play and an idle sport, and whom this world's life has deceived, and remind (them) thereby lest a soul should be given up to destruction for what it has earned; it shall not have besides Allah any guardian nor an intercessor, and if it should seek to give every compensation, it shall not be accepted from it; these are they who shall be given up to destruction for what they earned; they shall have a drink of boiling water and a painful chastisement because they disbelieved.
6 071	Say: "Shall we indeed call on others besides Allah,- things that can do us neither good nor harm,- and turn on our heels after receiving guidance from Allah? - like one whom the evil ones have made into a fool, wandering bewildered through the earth, his friends calling, come to us', (vainly) guiding him to the path." Say: "Allah's guidance is the (only) guidance, and we have been directed to submit ourselves to the Lord of the worlds;-"		Say: Shall we cry, instead of unto Allah, unto that which neither profiteth us nor hurteth us, and shall we turn back after Allah hath guided us, like one bewildered whom the devils have infatuated in the earth, who hath companions who invite him to the guidance (saying): Come unto us? Say: Lo! the guidance of Allah is Guidance, and we are ordered to surrender to the Lord of the Worlds,	Say: Shall we call on that besides Allah, which does not benefit us nor harm us, and shall we be returned back on our heels after Allah has guided us, like him whom the Shaitans have made to fall down perplexed in the earth? He has companions who call him to the right way, (saying): Come to us. Say: Surely the guidance of Allah, that is the (true) guidance, and we are commanded that we should submit to the Lord of the worlds.
6 072	"To establish regular prayers and to fear Allah: for it is to Him that we shall be gathered together."		And to establish worship and be dutiful to Him, and He it is unto Whom ye will be gathered.	And that you should keep up prayer and be careful of (your duty to) Him; and He it is to Whom you shall be gathered.
6 073	It is He who created the heavens and the earth in true (proportions): the day He saith, "Be," behold! it is. His word is the truth. His will be the dominion the day the trumpet will be blown. He knoweth the unseen as well as that which is open. For He is the Wise, well acquainted (with all things).		He it is Who created the heavens and the earth in truth. In the day when He saith: Be! it is. His Word is the Truth, and His will be the Sovereignty on the day when the trumpet is blown. Knower of the Invisible and the Visible, He is the Wise, the Aware.	And He it is Who has created the heavens and the earth with truth, and on the day He says: Be, it is. His word is the truth, and His is the kingdom on the day when the trumpet shall be blown; the Knower of the unseen and the seen; and He is the Wise, the Aware.
6 074	Lo! Abraham said to his father Azar: "Takest thou idols for gods? For I see thee and thy people in manifest error."		(Remember) when Abraham said unto his father Azar: Takest thou idols for gods? Lo! I see thee and thy folk in error manifest.	And when Ibrahim said to his sire, Azar: Do you take idols for gods? Surely I see you and your people in manifest error.
6 075	So also did We show Abraham the power and the laws of the heavens and the earth, that he might (with understanding) have certitude.		Thus did We show Abraham the kingdom of the heavens and the earth that he might be of those possessing certainty:	And thus did We show Ibrahim the kingdom of the heavens and the earth and that he might be of those who are sure.
6 076	When the night covered him over, He saw a star: He said: "This is my Lord." But when it set, He said: "I love not those that set."		When the night grew dark upon him he beheld a star. He said: This is my Lord. But when it set, he said: I love not things that set.	So when the night over-shadowed him, he saw a star; said he: Is this my Lord? So when it set, he said: I do not love the setting ones.

6 077	When he saw the moon rising in splendour, he said: "This is my Lord." But when the moon set, He said: "unless my Lord guide me, I shall surely be among those who go astray."	And when he saw the moon uprising, he exclaimed: This is my Lord. But when it set, he said: Unless my Lord guide me, I surely shall become one of the folk who are astray.	Then when he saw the moon rising, he said: Is this my Lord? So when it set, he said: If my Lord had not guided me I should certainly be of the erring people.
6 078	When he saw the sun rising in splendour, he said: "This is my Lord; this is the greatest (of all)." But when the sun set, he said: "O my people! I am indeed free from your (guilt) of giving partners to Allah."	And when he saw the sun uprising, he cried: This is my Lord! This is greater! And when it set he exclaimed: O my people! Lo! I am free from all that ye associate (with Him).	Then when he saw the sun rising, he said: Is this my Lord? Is this the greatest? So when it set, he said: O my people! surely I am clear of what you set up (with Allah).
6 079	"For me, I have set my face, firmly and truly, towards Him Who created the heavens and the earth, and never shall I give partners to Allah."	Lo! I have turned my face toward Him Who created the heavens and the earth, as one by nature upright, and I am not of the idolaters.	Surely I have turned myself, being upright, wholly to Him Who originated the heavens and the earth, and I am not of the polytheists.
6 080	His people disputed with him. He said: "(Come) ye to dispute with me, about Allah, when He (Himself) hath guided me? I fear not (the beings) ye associate with Allah: Unless my Lord willeth, (nothing can happen). My Lord comprehendeth in His knowledge all things. Will ye not (yourselves) be admonished?"	His people argued with him. He said: Dispute ye with me concerning Allah when He hath guided me? I fear not at all that which ye set up beside Him unless my Lord willeth aught. My Lord includeth all things in His knowledge. Will ye not then remember?	And his people disputed with him. He said: Do you dispute with me respecting Allah? And He has guided me indeed; and I do not fear in any way those that you set up with Him, unless my Lord pleases; my Lord comprehends all things in His knowledge; will you not then mind?
6 081	"How should I fear (the beings) ye associate with Allah, when ye fear not to give partners to Allah without any warrant having been given to you? Which of (us) two parties hath more right to security? (tell me) if ye know."	How should I fear that which ye set up beside Him, when ye fear not to set up beside Allah that for which He hath revealed unto you no warrant? Which of the two factions hath more right to safety? (Answer me that) if ye have knowledge.	And how should I fear what you have set up (with Him), while you do not fear that you have set up with Allah that for which He has not sent down to you any authority; which then of the two parties is surer of security, if you know?
6 082	"It is those who believe and confuse not their beliefs with wrong - that are (truly) in security, for they are on (right) guidance."	Those who believe and obscure not their belief by wrongdoing, theirs is safety; and they are rightly guided.	Those who believe and do not mix up their faith with iniquity, those are they who shall have the security and they are those who go aright.
6 083	That was the reasoning about Us, which We gave to Abraham (to use) against his people: We raise whom We will, degree after degree: for thy Lord is full of wisdom and knowledge.	That is Our argument. We gave it unto Abraham against his folk. We raise unto degrees of wisdom whom We will. Lo! thy Lord is Wise, Aware.	And this was Our argument which we gave to Ibrahim against his people; We exalt in dignity whom We please; surely your Lord is Wise, Knowing.
6 084	We gave him Isaac and Jacob: all (three) guided: and before him, We guided Noah, and among his progeny, David, Solomon, Job, Joseph, Moses, and Aaron: thus do We reward those who do good:	And We bestowed upon him Isaac and Jacob; each of them We guided; and Noah did We guide aforetime; and of his seed (We guided) David and Solomon and Job and Joseph and Moses and Aaron. Thus do We reward the good.	And We gave to him Ishaq and Yaqoub; each did We guide, and Nuh did We guide before, and of his descendants, Dawood and Sulaiman and Ayub and Yusuf and Haroun; and thus do We reward those who do good (to others).
6 085	And Zakariya and John, and Jesus and Elias: all in the ranks of the righteous:	And Zachariah and John and Jesus and Elias. Each one (of them) was of the righteous.	And Zakariya and Yahya and Isa and Ilyas; every one was of the good;
6 086	And Isma'il and Elisha, and Jonas, and Lot: and to all We gave favour above the nations:	And Ishmael and Elisha and Jonah and Lot. Each one (of them) did We prefer above (Our) creatures,	And Ismail and Al-Yasha and Yunus and Lut; and every one We made to excel (in) the worlds:

6 087	(To them) and to their fathers, and progeny and brethren: We chose them, and we guided them to a straight way.	With some of their forefathers and their offspring and their brethren; and We chose them and guided them unto a straight path.	And from among their fathers and their descendants and their brethren, and We chose them and guided them into the right way.
6 088	This is the guidance of Allah: He giveth that guidance to whom He pleaseth, of His worshippers. If they were to join other gods with Him, all that they did would be vain for them.	Such is the guidance of Allah wherewith He guideth whom He will of His bondmen. But if they had set up (for worship) aught beside Him, (all) that they did would have been vain.	This is Allah's guidance, He guides thereby whom He pleases of His servants; and if they had set up others (with Him), certainly what they did would have become ineffectual for them.
6 089	These were the men to whom We gave the Book, and authority, and prophethood: if these (their descendants) reject them, Behold! We shall entrust their charge to a new people who reject them not.	Those are they unto whom We gave the Scripture and command and prophethood. But if these disbelieve therein, then indeed We shall entrust it to a people who will not be disbelievers therein.	These are they to whom We gave the book and the wisdom and the prophecy; therefore if these disbelieve in it We have already entrusted with it a people who are not disbelievers in it.
6 090	Those were the (prophets) who received Allah's guidance: Copy the guidance they received; Say: "No reward for this do I ask of you: This is no less than a message for the nations."	Those are they whom Allah guideth, so follow their guidance. Say (O Muhammad, unto mankind): I ask of you no fee for it. Lo! it is naught but a Reminder to (His) creatures.	These are they whom Allah guided, therefore follow their guidance. Say: I do not ask you for any reward for it; it is nothing but a reminder to the nations.
6 091	No just estimate of Allah do they make when they say: "Nothing doth Allah send down to man (by way of revelation)" Say: "Who then sent down the Book which Moses brought?- a light and guidance to man: But ye make it into (separate) sheets for show, while ye conceal much (of its contents): therein were ye taught that which ye knew not- neither ye nor your fathers." Say: "Allah (sent it down)": Then leave them to plunge in vain discourse and trifling.	And they measure not the power of Allah its true measure when they say: Allah hath naught revealed unto a human being. Say (unto the Jews who speak thus): Who revealed the Book which Moses brought, a light and guidance for mankind, which ye have put on parchments which ye show, but ye hide much (thereof), and (by which) ye were taught that which ye knew not yourselves nor (did) your fathers (know it)? Say: Allah. Then leave them to their play of cavilling.	And they do not assign to Allah the attributes due to Him when they say: Allah has not revealed anything to a mortal. Say: Who revealed the Book which Musa brought, a light and a guidance to men, which you make into scattered writings which you show while you conceal much? And you were taught what you did not know, (neither) you nor your fathers. Say: Allah then leave them sporting in their vain discourses.
6 092	And this is a Book which We have sent down, bringing blessings, and confirming (the revelations) which came before it: that thou mayest warn the mother of cities and all around her. Those who believe in the Hereafter believe in this (Book), and they are constant in guarding their prayers.	And this is a blessed Scripture which We have revealed, confirming that which (was revealed) before it, that thou mayst warn the Mother of Villages and those around her. Those who believe in the Hereafter believe herein, and they are careful of their worship.	And this is a Book We have revealed, blessed, verifying that which is before it, and that you may warn the metropolis and those around her; and those who believe in the hereafter believe in it, and they attend to their prayers constantly.

6 093	Who can be more wicked than one who inventeth a lie against Allah, or saith, "I have received inspiration," when he hath received none, or (again) who saith, "I can reveal the like of what Allah hath revealed"? If thou couldst but see how the wicked (do fare) in the flood of confusion at death! - the angels stretch forth their hands, (saying), "Yield up your souls: this day shall ye receive your reward,- a penalty of shame, for that ye used to tell lies against Allah, and scornfully to reject of His signs!"	Who is guilty of more wrong than he who forgeth a lie against Allah, or saith: I am inspired, when he is not inspired in aught; and who saith: I will reveal the like of that which Allah hath revealed? If thou couldst see, when the wrong-doers reach the pangs of death and the angels stretch their hands out (saying): Deliver up your souls. This day ye are awarded doom of degradation for that ye spake concerning Allah other than the truth, and used to scorn His portents.	And who is more unjust than he who forges a lie against Allah, or says: It has been revealed to me; while nothing has been revealed to him, and he who says: I can reveal the like of what Allah has revealed? and if you had seen when the unjust shall be in the agonies of death and the angels shall spread forth their hands: Give up your souls; today shall you be recompensed with an ignominious chastisement because you spoke against Allah other than the truth and (because) you showed pride against His communications.
6 094	"And behold! ye come to us bare and alone as We created you for the first time: ye have left behind you all (the favours) which We bestowed on you: We see not with you your intercessors whom ye thought to be partners in your affairs: so now all relations between you have been cut off, and your (pet) fancies have left you in the lurch!"	Now have ye come unto Us solitary as We did create you at the first, and ye have left behind you all that We bestowed upon you, and We behold not with you those your intercessors, of whom ye claimed that they possessed a share in you. Now is the bond between you severed, and that which ye presumed hath failed you.	And certainly you have come to Us alone as We created you at first, and you have left behind your backs the things which We gave you, and We do not see with you your intercessors about whom you asserted that they were (Allah's) associates in respect to you; certainly the ties between you are now cut off and what you asserted is gone from you.
6 095	It is Allah Who causeth the seed-grain and the date-stone to split and sprout. He causeth the living to issue from the dead, and He is the one to cause the dead to issue from the living. That is Allah: then how are ye deluded away from the truth?	Lo! Allah (it is) Who splitteth the grain of corn and the date-stone (for sprouting). He bringeth forth the living from the dead, and is the bringer-forth of the dead from the living. Such is Allah. How then are ye perverted?	Surely Allah causes the grain and the stone to germinate; He brings forth the living from the dead and He is the bringer forth of the dead from the living; that is Allah! how are you then turned away.
6 096	He it is that cleaveth the day-break (from the dark): He makes the night for rest and tranquillity, and the sun and moon for the reckoning (of time): Such is the judgment and ordering of (Him), the Exalted in Power, the Omniscient.	He is the Cleaver of the Daybreak, and He hath appointed the night for stillness, and the sun and the moon for reckoning. That is the measuring of the Mighty, the Wise.	He causes the dawn to break; and He has made the night for rest, and the sun and the moon for reckoning; this is an arrangement of the Mighty, the Knowing.
6 097	It is He Who maketh the stars (as beacons) for you, that ye may guide yourselves, with their help, through the dark spaces of land and sea: We detail Our signs for people who know.	And He it is Who hath set for you the stars that ye may guide your course by them amid the darkness of the land and the sea. We have detailed Our revelations for a people who have knowledge.	And He it is Who has made the stars for you that you might follow the right way thereby in the darkness of the land and the sea; truly We have made plain the communications for a people who know.
6 098	It is He Who hath produced you from a single person: here is a place of sojourn and a place of departure: We detail Our signs for people who understand.	And He it is Who hath produced you from a single being, and (hath given you) a habitation and a repository. We have detailed Our revelations for a people who have understanding.	And He it is Who has brought you into being from a single soul, then there is (for you) a resting-place and a depository; indeed We have made plain the communications for a people who understand.

6 099	It is He Who sendeth down rain from the skies: with it We produce vegetation of all kinds: from some We produce green (crops), out of which We produce grain, heaped up (at harvest); out of the date-palm and its sheaths (or spathes) (come) clusters of dates hanging low and near: and (then there are) gardens of grapes, and olives, and pomegranates, each similar (in kind) yet different (in variety): when they begin to bear fruit, feast your eyes with the fruit and the ripeness thereof. Behold! in these things there are signs for people who believe.	He it is Who sendeth down water from the sky, and therewith We bring forth buds of every kind; We bring forth the green blade from which We bring forth the thick-clustered grain; and from the date-palm, from the pollen thereof, spring pendant bunches; and (We bring forth) gardens of grapes, and the olive and the pomegranate, alike and unlike. Look upon the fruit thereof, when they bear fruit, and upon its ripening. Lo! herein verily are portents for a people who believe.	And He it is Who sends down water from the cloud, then We bring forth with it buds of all (plants), then We bring forth from it green (foliage) from which We produce grain piled up (in the ear); and of the palm-tree, of the sheaths of it, come forth clusters (of dates) within reach, and gardens of grapes and olives and pomegranates, alike and unlike; behold the fruit of it when it yields the fruit and the ripening of it; most surely there are signs in this for a people who believe.
6 100	Yet they make the jinns equals with Allah, though Allah did create the jinns; and they falsely, having no knowledge, attribute to Him sons and daughters. Praise and glory be to Him! (for He is) above what they attribute to Him!	Yet they ascribe as partners unto Him the jinn, although He did create them, and impute falsely, without knowledge, sons and daughters unto Him. Glorified be He and High Exalted above (all) that they ascribe (unto Him).	And they make the jinn associates with Allah, while He created them, and they falsely attribute to Him sons and daughters without knowledge; glory be to Him, and highly exalted is He above what they ascribe (to Him).
6 101	To Him is due the primal origin of the heavens and the earth: How can He have a son when He hath no consort? He created all things, and He hath full knowledge of all things.	The Originator of the heavens and the earth! How can He have a child, when there is for Him no consort, when He created all things and is Aware of all things?	Wonderful Originator of the heavens and the earth! How could He have a son when He has no consort, and He (Himself) created everything, and He is the Knower of all things.
6 102	That is Allah, your Lord! there is no god but He, the Creator of all things: then worship ye Him: and He hath power to dispose of all affairs.	Such is Allah, your Lord. There is no God save Him, the Creator of all things, so worship Him. And He taketh care of all things.	That is Allah, your Lord, there is no god but He; the Creator of all things, therefore serve Him, and He has charge of all things.
6 103	No vision can grasp Him, but His grasp is over all vision: He is above all comprehension, yet is acquainted with all things.	Vision comprehendeth Him not, but He comprehendeth (all) vision. He is the Subtle, the Aware.	Vision comprehends Him not, and He comprehends (all) vision; and He is the Knower of subtleties, the Aware.
6 104	"Now have come to you, from your Lord, proofs (to open your eyes): if any will see, it will be for (the good of) his own soul; if any will be blind, it will be to his own (harm): I am not (here) to watch over your doings."	Proofs have come unto you from your Lord, so whoso seeth, it is for his own good, and whoso is blind is blind to his own hurt. And I am not a keeper over you.	Indeed there have come to you clear proofs from your Lord; whoever will therefore see, it is for his own soul and whoever will be blind, it shall be against himself and I am not a keeper over you.
6 105	Thus do we explain the signs by various (symbols): that they may say, Thou hast taught (us) diligently, and that We may make the matter clear to those who know.	Thus do We display Our revelations that they may say (unto thee, Muhammad): "Thou hast studied," and that We may make (it) clear for people who have knowledge.	And thus do We repeat the communications and that they may say: You have read; and that We may make it clear to a people who know.
6 106	Follow what thou art taught by inspiration from thy Lord: there is no god but He: and turn aside from those who join gods with Allah.	Follow that which is inspired in thee from thy Lord; there is no Allah save Him; and turn away from the idolaters.	Follow what is revealed to you from your Lord; there is no god but He; and withdraw from the polytheists.

6 107	If it had been Allah's plan, they would not have taken false gods: but We made thee not one to watch over their doings, nor art thou set over them to dispose of their affairs.	Had Allah willed, they had not been idolatrous. We have not set thee as a keeper over them, nor art thou responsible for them.	And if Allah had pleased, they would not have set up others (with Him) and We have not appointed you a keeper over them, and you are not placed in charge of them.
6 108	Revile not ye those whom they call upon besides Allah, lest they out of spite revile Allah in their ignorance. Thus have We made alluring to each people its own doings. In the end will they return to their Lord, and We shall then tell them the truth of all that they did.	Revile not those unto whom they pray beside Allah lest they wrongfully revile Allah through ignorance. Thus unto every nation have We made their deed seem fair. Then unto their Lord is their return, and He will tell them what they used to do.	And do not abuse those whom they call upon besides Allah, lest exceeding the limits they should abuse Allah out of ignorance. Thus have We made fair seeming to every people their deeds; then to their Lord shall be their return, so He will inform them of what they did.
6 109	They swear their strongest oaths by Allah, that if a (special) sign came to them, by it they would believe. Say: "Certainly (all) signs are in the power of Allah: but what will make you (Muslims) realise that (even) if (special) signs came, they will not believe."?	And they swear a solemn oath by Allah that if there come unto them a portent they will believe therein. Say; Portents are with Allah and (so is) that which telleth you that if such came unto them they would not believe.	And they swear by Allah with the strongest of their oaths, that if a sign came to them they would most certainly believe in it. Say: Signs are only with Allah; and what should make you know that when it comes they will not believe?
6 110	We (too) shall turn to (confusion) their hearts and their eyes, even as they refused to believe in this in the first instance: We shall leave them in their trespasses, to wander in distraction.	We confound their hearts and their eyes. As they believed not therein at the first, We let them wander blindly on in their contumacy.	And We will turn their hearts and their sights, even as they did not believe in it the first time, and We will leave them in their inordinacy, blindly wandering on.
6 111	Even if We did send unto them angels, and the dead did speak unto them, and We gathered together all things before their very eyes, they are not the ones to believe, unless it is in Allah's plan. But most of them ignore (the truth).	And though We should send down the angels unto them, and the dead should speak unto them, and We should gather against them all things in array, they would not believe unless Allah so willed. Howbeit, most of them are ignorant.	And even if We had sent down to them the angels and the dead had spoken to them and We had brought together all things before them, they would not believe unless Allah pleases, but most of them are ignorant.
6 112	Likewise did We make for every Messenger an enemy,- evil ones among men and jinns, inspiring each other with flowery discourses by way of deception. If thy Lord had so planned, they would not have done it: so leave them and their inventions alone.	Thus have We appointed unto every prophet an adversary - devils of humankind and jinn who inspire in one another plausible discourse through guile. If thy Lord willed, they would not do so; so leave them alone with their devising;	And thus did We make for every prophet an enemy, the Shaitans from among men and jinn, some of them suggesting to others varnished falsehood to deceive (them), and had your Lord pleased they would not have done it, therefore leave them and that which they forge.
6 113	To such (deceit) let the hearts of those incline, who have no faith in the hereafter: let them delight in it, and let them earn from it what they may.	That the hearts of those who believe not in the Hereafter may incline thereto, and that they may take pleasure therein, and that they may earn what they are earning.	And that the hearts of those who do not believe in the hereafter may incline to it and that they may be well pleased with it and that they may earn what they are going to earn (of evil).
6 114	Say: "Shall I seek for judge other than Allah? - when He it is Who hath sent unto you the Book, explained in detail." They know full well, to whom We have given the Book, that it hath been sent down from thy Lord in truth. Never be then of those who doubt.	Shall I seek other than Allah for judge, when He it is Who hath revealed unto you (this) Scripture, fully explained? Those unto whom We gave the Scripture (aforetime) know that it is revealed from thy Lord in truth. So be not thou (O Muhammad) of the waverers.	Shall I then seek a judge other than Allah? And He it is Who has revealed to you the Book (which is) made plain; and those whom We have given the Book know that it is revealed by your Lord with truth, therefore you should not be of the disputers.

6 115	The word of thy Lord doth find its fulfilment in truth and in justice: None can change His words: for He is the one who heareth and knoweth all.	Perfected is the Word of thy Lord in truth and justice. There is naught that can change His words. He is the Hearer, the Knower.	And the word of your Lord has been accomplished truly and justly; there is none who can change His words, and He is the Hearing, the Knowing.
6 116	Wert thou to follow the common run of those on earth, they will lead thee away from the way of Allah. They follow nothing but conjecture: they do nothing but lie.	If thou obeyedst most of those on earth they would mislead thee far from Allah's way. They follow naught but an opinion, and they do but guess.	And if you obey most of those in the earth, they will lead you astray from Allah's way; they follow but conjecture and they only lie.
6 117	Thy Lord knoweth best who strayeth from His way: He knoweth best who they are that receive His guidance.	Lo! thy Lord, He knoweth best who erreth from His way; and He knoweth best (who are) the rightly guided.	Surely your Lord-- He best knows who goes astray from His way, and He best knows those who follow the right course.
6 118	So eat of (meats) on which Allah's name hath been pronounced, if ye have faith in His signs.	Eat of that over which the name of Allah hath been mentioned, if ye are believers in His revelations.	Therefore eat of that on which Allah's name has been mentioned if you are believers in His communications.
6 119	Why should ye not eat of (meats) on which Allah's name hath been pronounced, when He hath explained to you in detail what is forbidden to you - except under compulsion of necessity? But many do mislead (men) by their appetites unchecked by knowledge. Thy Lord knoweth best those who transgress.	How should ye not eat of that over which the name of Allah hath been mentioned, when He hath explained unto you that which is forbidden unto you unless ye are compelled thereto. But lo! many are led astray by their own lusts through ignorance. Lo! thy Lord, He is Best Aware of the transgressors.	And what reason have you that you should not eat of that on which Allah's name has been mentioned, and He has already made plain to you what He has forbidden to you-- excepting what you are compelled to; and most surely many would lead (people) astray by their low desires out of ignorance; surely your Lord-- He best knows those who exceed the limits.
6 120	Eschew all sin, open or secret: those who earn sin will get due recompense for their "earnings."	Forsake the outwardness of sin and the inwardness thereof. Lo! those who garner sin will be awarded that which they have earned.	And abandon open and secret sin; surely they who earn sin shall be recompensed with what they earned.
6 121	Eat not of (meats) on which Allah's name hath not been pronounced: That would be impiety. But the evil ones ever inspire their friends to contend with you if ye were to obey them, ye would indeed be Pagans.	And eat not of that whereon Allah's name hath not been mentioned, for lo! it is abomination. Lo! the devils do inspire their minions to dispute with you. But if ye obey them, ye will be in truth idolaters.	And do not eat of that on which Allah's name has not been mentioned, and that is most surely a transgression; and most surely the Shaitans suggest to their friends that they should contend with you; and if you obey them, you shall most surely be polytheists.
6 122	Can he who was dead, to whom We gave life, and a light whereby he can walk amongst men, be like him who is in the depths of darkness, from which he can never come out? Thus to those without faith their own deeds seem pleasing.	Is he who was dead and We have raised him unto life, and set for him a light wherein he walketh among men, as him whose similitude is in utter darkness whence he cannot emerge? Thus is their conduct made fairseeming for the disbelievers.	Is he who was dead then We raised him to life and made for him a light by which he walks among the people, like him whose likeness is that of one in utter darkness whence he cannot come forth? Thus what they did was made fair seeming to the unbelievers.
6 123	Thus have We placed leaders in every town, its wicked men, to plot (and burrow) therein: but they only plot against their own souls, and they perceive it not.	And thus have We made in every city great ones of its wicked ones, that they should plot therein. They do but plot against themselves, though they perceive not.	And thus have We made in every town the great ones to be its guilty ones, that they may plan therein; and they do not plan but against their own souls, and they do not perceive.

6 124	When there comes to them a sign (from Allah), They say: "We shall not believe until we receive one (exactly) like those received by Allah's messengers." Allah knoweth best where (and how) to carry out His mission. Soon will the wicked be overtaken by humiliation before Allah, and a severe punishment, for all their plots.	And when a token cometh unto them, they say: We will not believe till we are given that which Allah's messengers are given. Allah knoweth best with whom to place His message. Humiliation from Allah and heavy punishment will smite the guilty for their scheming.	And when a communication comes to them they say: We will not believe till we are given the like of what Allah's messengers are given. Allah best knows where He places His message. There shall befall those who are guilty humiliation from Allah and severe chastisement because of what they planned.
6 125	Those whom Allah (in His plan) willeth to guide,- He openeth their breast to Islam; those whom He willeth to leave straying,- He maketh their breast close and constricted, as if they had to climb up to the skies: thus doth Allah (heap) the penalty on those who refuse to believe.	And whomsoever it is Allah's will to guide, He expandeth his bosom unto the Surrender, and whomsoever it is His Will to send astray, He maketh his bosom close and narrow as if he were engaged in sheer ascent. Thus Allah layeth ignominy upon those who believe not.	Therefore (for) whomsoever Allah intends that He would guide him aright, He expands his breast for Islam, and (for) whomsoever He intends that He should cause him to err, He makes his breast strait and narrow as though he were ascending upwards; thus does Allah lay uncleanness on those who do not believe.
6 126	This is the way of thy Lord, leading straight: We have detailed the signs for those who receive admonition.	This is the path of thy Lord, a straight path. We have detailed Our revelations for a people who take heed.	And this is the path of your Lord, (a) right (path); indeed We have made the communications clear for a people who mind.
6 127	For them will be a home of peace in the presence of their Lord: He will be their friend, because they practised (righteousness).	For them is the abode of peace with their Lord. He will be their Protecting Friend because of what they used to do.	They shall have the abode of peace with their Lord, and He is their guardian because of what they did.
6 128	One day will He gather them all together, (and say): "O ye assembly of jinns! Much (toll) did ye take of men." Their friends amongst men will say: "Our Lord! we made profit from each other: but (alas!) we reached our term - which thou didst appoint for us." He will say: "The Fire be your dwelling-place: you will dwell therein for ever, except as Allah willeth." for thy Lord is full of wisdom and knowledge.	In the day when He will gather them together (He will say): O ye assembly of the jinn! Many of humankind did ye seduce. And their adherents among humankind will say: Our Lord! We enjoyed one another, but now we have arrived at the appointed term which Thou appointedst for us. He will say: Fire is your home. Abide therein for ever, save him whom Allah willeth (to deliver). Lo! thy Lord is Wise, Aware.	And on the day when He shall gather them all together: O assembly of jinn! you took away a great part of mankind. And their friends from among the men shall say: Our Lord! some of us profited by others and we have reached our appointed term which Thou didst appoint for us. He shall say: The fire is your abode, to abide in it, except as Allah is pleased; surely your Lord is Wise, Knowing.
6 129	Thus do we make the wrong-doers turn to each other, because of what they earn.	Thus We let some of the wrong-doers have power over others because of what they are wont to earn.	And thus do We make some of the iniquitous to befriend others on account of what they earned.
6 130	"O ye assembly of jinns and men! came there not unto you messengers from amongst you, setting forth unto you My signs, and warning you of the meeting of this Day of yours?" They will say: "We bear witness against ourselves." It was the life of this world that deceived them. So against themselves will they bear witness that they rejected Faith.	O ye assembly of the jinn and humankind! Came there not unto you messengers of your own who recounted unto you My tokens and warned you of the meeting of this your Day? They will say: We testify against ourselves. And the life of the world beguiled them. And they testify against themselves that they were disbelievers.	O assembly of jinn and men! did there not come to you messengers from among you, relating to you My communications and warning you of the meeting of this day of yours? They shall say: We bear witness against ourselves; and this world's life deceived them, and they shall bear witness against their own souls that they were unbelievers.

6 131	(The messengers were sent) thus, for thy Lord would not destroy for their wrong-doing men's habitations whilst their occupants were unwarned.	This is because thy Lord destroyeth not the townships arbitrarily while their people are unconscious (of the wrong they do).	This is because your Lord would not destroy towns unjustly while their people were negligent.
6 132	To all are degrees (or ranks) according to their deeds: for thy Lord is not unmindful of anything that they do.	For all there will be ranks from what they did. Thy Lord is not unaware of what they do.	And all have degrees according to what they do; and your Lord is not heedless of what they do.
6 133	Thy Lord is self-sufficient, full of Mercy: if it were His will, He could destroy you, and in your place appoint whom He will as your successors, even as He raised you up from the posterity of other people.	Thy Lord is the Absolute, the Lord of Mercy. If He will, He can remove you and can cause what He will to follow after you, even as He raised you from the seed of other folk.	And your Lord is the Self-sufficient one, the Lord of mercy; if He pleases, He may take you off, and make whom He pleases successors after you, even as He raised you up from the seed of another people.
6 134	All that hath been promised unto you will come to pass: nor can ye frustrate it (in the least bit).	Lo! that which ye are promised will surely come to pass, and ye cannot escape.	Surely what you are threatened with must come to pass and you cannot escape (it).
6 135	Say: "O my people! Do whatever ye can: I will do (my part): soon will ye know who it is whose end will be (best) in the Hereafter: certain it is that the wrong-doers will not prosper."	Say (O Muhammad): O my people! Work according to your power. Lo! I too am working. Thus ye will come to know for which of us will be the happy sequel. Lo! the wrong-doers will not be successful.	Say: O my people! act according to your ability; I too am acting; so you will soon come to know, for whom (of us) will be the (good) end of the abode; surely the unjust shall not be successful.
6 136	Out of what Allah hath produced in abundance in tilth and in cattle, they assigned Him a share: they say, according to their fancies: This is for Allah, and this - for our "partners"! but the share of their "partners" reacheth not Allah, whilst the share of Allah reacheth their "partners"! evil (and unjust) is their assignment!	They assign unto Allah, of the crops and cattle which He created, a portion, and they say: "This is Allah's" - in their make-believe - "and this is for (His) partners in regard to us." Thus that which (they assign) unto His partners in them reacheth not Allah and that which (they assign) unto Allah goeth to their (so-called) partners. Evil is their ordinance.	And they set apart a portion for Allah out of what He has created of tilth and cattle, and say: This is for Allah-- so they assert-- and this for our associates; then what is for their associates, it reaches not to Allah, and whatever is (set apart) for Allah, it reaches to their associates; evil is that which they judge.
6 137	Even so, in the eyes of most of the pagans, their "partners" made alluring the slaughter of their children, in order to lead them to their own destruction, and cause confusion in their religion. If Allah had willed, they would not have done so: But leave alone them and their inventions.	Thus have their (so-called) partners (of Allah) made the killing of their children to seem fair unto many of the idolaters, that they may ruin them and make their faith obscure for them. Had Allah willed (it otherwise), they had not done so. So leave them alone with their devices.	And thus their associates have made fair seeming to most of the polytheists the killing of their children, that they may cause them to perish and obscure for them their religion; and if Allah had pleased, they would not have done it, therefore leave them and that which they forge.
6 138	And they say that such and such cattle and crops are taboo, and none should eat of them except those whom - so they say - We wish; further, there are cattle forbidden to yoke or burden, and cattle on which, (at slaughter), the name of Allah is not pronounced; - inventions against Allah's name: soon will He requite them for their inventions.	And they say: Such cattle and crops are forbidden. No-one is to eat of them save whom we will - in their make-believe - cattle whose backs are forbidden, cattle over which they mention not the name of Allah. (All that is) a lie against Him. He will repay them for that which they invent.	And they say: These are cattle and tilth prohibited, none shall eat them except such as We please-- so they assert-- and cattle whose backs are forbidden, and cattle on which they would not mention Allah's name-- forging a lie against Him; He shall requite them for what they forged.

6 139	They say: "What is in the wombs of such and such cattle is specially reserved (for food) for our men, and forbidden to our women; but if it is still-born, then all have share therein." For their (false) attribution (of superstitions to Allah), He will soon punish them: for He is full of wisdom and knowledge.	And they say: That which is in the bellies of such cattle is reserved for our males and is forbidden to our wives; but if it be born dead, then they (all) may be partakers thereof. He will reward them for their attribution (of such ordinances unto Him). Lo, He is Wise, Aware.	And they say: What is in the wombs of these cattle is specially for our males, and forbidden to our wives, and if it be stillborn, then they are all partners in it; He will reward them for their attributing (falsehood to Allah); surely He is Wise, Knowing.
6 140	Lost are those who slay their children, from folly, without knowledge, and forbid food which Allah hath provided for them, inventing (lies) against Allah. They have indeed gone astray and heeded no guidance.	They are losers who besottedly have slain their children without knowledge, and have forbidden that which Allah bestowed upon them, inventing a lie against Allah. They indeed have gone astray and are not guided.	They are lost indeed who kill their children foolishly without knowledge, and forbid what Allah has given to them forging a lie against Allah; they have indeed gone astray, and they are not the followers of the right course.
6 141	It is He Who produceth gardens, with trellises and without, and dates, and tilth with produce of all kinds, and olives and pomegranates, similar (in kind) and different (in variety): eat of their fruit in their season, but render the dues that are proper on the day that the harvest is gathered. But waste not by excess: for Allah loveth not the wasters.	He it is Who produceth gardens trellised and untrellised, and the date-palm, and crops of divers flavour, and the olive and the pomegranate, like and unlike. Eat ye of the fruit thereof when it fruiteth, and pay the due thereof upon the harvest day, and be not prodigal. Lo! Allah loveth not the prodigals.	And He it is Who produces gardens (of vine), trellised and untrellised, and palms and seed-produce of which the fruits are of various sorts, and olives and pomegranates, like and unlike; eat of its fruit when it bears fruit, and pay the due of it on the day of its reaping, and do not act extravagantly; surely He does not love the extravagant.
6 142	Of the cattle are some for burden and some for meat: eat what Allah hath provided for you, and follow not the footsteps of Satan: for he is to you and avowed enemy.	And of the cattle (He produceth) some for burdens, some for food. Eat of that which Allah hath bestowed upon you, and follow not the footsteps of the devil, for lo! he is an open foe to you.	And of cattle (He created) beasts of burden and those which are fit for slaughter only; eat of what Allah has given you and do not follow the footsteps of the Shaitan; surely he is your open enemy.
6 143	(Take) eight (head of cattle) in (four) pairs: of sheep a pair, and of goats a pair; say, hath He forbidden the two males, or the two females, or (the young) which the wombs of the two females enclose? Tell me with knowledge if ye are truthful:	Eight pairs: Of the sheep twain, and of the goats twain. Say: Hath He forbidden the two males or the two females, or that which the wombs of the two females contain? Expound to me (the case) with knowledge, if ye are truthful.	Eight in pairs-- two of sheep and two of goats. Say: Has He forbidden the two males or the two females or that which the wombs of the two females contain? Inform me with knowledge if you are truthful.
6 144	Of camels a pair, and oxen a pair; say, hath He forbidden the two males, or the two females, or (the young) which the wombs of the two females enclose? - Were ye present when Allah ordered you such a thing? But who doth more wrong than one who invents a lie against Allah, to lead astray men without knowledge? For Allah guideth not people who do wrong.	And of the camels twain and of the oxen twain. Say: Hath He forbidden the two males or the two females, or that which the wombs of the two females contain; or were ye by to witness when Allah commanded you (all) this? Then who doth greater wrong than he who deviseth a lie concerning Allah, that he may lead mankind astray without knowledge. Lo! Allah guideth not wrongdoing folk.	And two of camels and two of cows. Say: Has He forbidden the two males or the two females or that which the wombs of the two females contain? Or were you witnesses when Allah enjoined you this? Who, then, is more unjust than he who forges a lie against Allah that he should lead astray men without knowledge? Surely Allah does not guide the unjust people.

6 145	Say: "I find not in the message received by me by inspiration any (meat) forbidden to be eaten by one who wishes to eat it, unless it be dead meat, or blood poured forth, or the flesh of swine,- for it is an abomination - or, what is impious, (meat) on which a name has been invoked, other than Allah's". But (even so), if a person is forced by necessity, without wilful disobedience, nor transgressing due limits,- thy Lord is Oft-Forgiving, Most Merciful.	Say: I find not in that which is revealed unto me aught prohibited to an eater that he eat thereof, except it be carrion, or blood poured forth, or swineflesh - for that verily is foul - or the abomination which was immolated to the name of other than Allah. But whoso is compelled (thereto), neither craving nor transgressing, (for him) lo! thy Lord is Forgiving, Merciful.	Say: I do not find in that which has been revealed to me anything forbidden for an eater to eat of except that it be what has died of itself, or blood poured forth, or flesh of swine-- for that surely is unclean-- or that which is a transgression, other than (the name of) Allah having been invoked on it; but whoever is driven to necessity, not desiring nor exceeding the limit, then surely your Lord is Forgiving, Merciful.
6 146	For those who followed the Jewish Law, We forbade every (animal) with undivided hoof, and We forbade them that fat of the ox and the sheep, except what adheres to their backs or their entrails, or is mixed up with a bone: this in recompense for their wilful disobedience: for We are true (in Our ordinances).	Unto those who are Jews We forbade every animal with claws. And of the oxen and the sheep forbade We unto them the fat thereof save that upon the backs or the entrails, or that which is mixed with the bone. That we awarded them for their rebellion. And lo! we verily are truthful.	And to those who were Jews We made unlawful every animal having claws, and of oxen and sheep We made unlawful to them the fat of both, except such as was on their backs or the entrails or what was mixed with bones: this was a punishment We gave them on account of their rebellion, and We are surely Truthful.
6 147	If they accuse thee of falsehood, say: "Your Lord is full of mercy all-embracing; but from people in guilt never will His wrath be turned back."	So if they give the lie to thee (Muhammad), say: Your Lord is a Lord of all-embracing Mercy, and His wrath will never be withdrawn from guilty folk.	But if they give you the lie, then say: Your Lord is the Lord of All-encompassing mercy; and His punishment cannot be averted from the guilty people.
6 148	Those who give partners (to Allah) will say: "If Allah had wished, we should not have given partners to Him nor would our fathers; nor should we have had any taboos." So did their ancestors argue falsely, until they tasted of Our wrath. Say: "Have ye any (certain) knowledge? If so, produce it before us. Ye follow nothing but conjecture: ye do nothing but lie."	They who are idolaters will say: Had Allah willed, we had not ascribed (unto Him) partners neither had our fathers, nor had we forbidden aught. Thus did those who were before them give the lie (to Allah's messengers) till they tasted of the fear of Us. Say: Have ye any knowledge that ye can adduce for Us? Lo! ye follow naught but an opinion, Lo! ye do but guess.	Those who are polytheists will say: If Allah had pleased we would not have associated (aught with Him) nor our fathers, nor would we have forbidden (to ourselves) anything; even so did those before them reject until they tasted Our punishment. Say: Have you any knowledge with you so you should bring it forth to us? You only follow a conjecture and you only tell lies.
6 149	Say: "With Allah is the argument that reaches home: if it had been His will, He could indeed have guided you all."	Say - For Allah's is the final argument - Had He willed He could indeed have guided all of you.	Say: Then Allah's is the conclusive argument; so if He please, He would certainly guide you all.
6 150	Say: "Bring forward your witnesses to prove that Allah did forbid so and so." If they bring such witnesses, be not thou amongst them: Nor follow thou the vain desires of such as treat our signs as falsehoods, and such as believe not in the Hereafter: for they hold others as equal with their Guardian-Lord.	Say: Come, bring your witnesses who can bear witness that Allah forbade (all) this. And if they bear witness, do not thou bear witness with them. Follow thou not the whims of those who deny Our revelations, those who believe not in the Hereafter and deem (others) equal with their Lord.	Say: Bring your witnesses who should bear witness that Allah has forbidden this, then if they bear witness, do not bear witness with them; and follow not the low desires of those who reject Our communications and of those who do not believe in the hereafter, and they make (others) equal to their Lord.

6 151	Say: "Come, I will rehearse what Allah hath (really) prohibited you from": Join not anything as equal with Him; be good to your parents; kill not your children on a plea of want;- We provide sustenance for you and for them;- come not nigh to shameful deeds. Whether open or secret; take not life, which Allah hath made sacred, except by way of justice and law: thus doth He command you, that ye may learn wisdom.	Say: Come, I will recite unto you that which your Lord hath made a sacred duty for you: That ye ascribe no thing as partner unto Him and that ye do good to parents, and that ye slay not your children because of penury - We provide for you and for them - and that ye draw not nigh to lewd things whether open or concealed. And that ye slay not the life which Allah hath made sacred, save in the course of justice. This He hath command you, in order that ye may discern.	Say: Come I will recite what your Lord has forbidden to you-- (remember) that you do not associate anything with Him and show kindness to your parents, and do not slay your children for (fear of) poverty-- We provide for you and for them-- and do not draw nigh to indecencies, those of them which are apparent and those which are concealed, and do not kill the soul which Allah has forbidden except for the requirements of justice; this He has enjoined you with that you may understand.
6 152	And come not nigh to the orphan's property, except to improve it, until he attain the age of full strength; give measure and weight with (full) justice;- no burden do We place on any soul, but that which it can bear;- whenever ye speak, speak justly, even if a near relative is concerned; and fulfil the covenant of Allah: thus doth He command you, that ye may remember.	And approach not the wealth of the orphan save with that which is better, till he reach maturity. Give full measure and full weight, in justice. We task not any soul beyond its scope. And if ye give your word, do justice thereunto, even though it be (against) a kinsman; and fulfil the covenant of Allah. This He commandeth you that haply ye may remember.	And do not approach the property of the orphan except in the best manner until he attains his maturity, and give full measure and weight with justice-- We do not impose on any soul a duty except to the extent of its ability; and when you speak, then be just though it be (against) a relative, and fulfill Allah's covenant; this He has enjoined you with that you may be mindful;
6 153	Verily, this is My way, leading straight: follow it: follow not (other) paths: they will scatter you about from His (great) path: thus doth He command you, that ye may be righteous.	And (He commandeth you, saying): This is My straight path, so follow it. Follow not other ways, lest ye be parted from His way. This hath He ordained for you, that ye may ward off (evil).	And (know) that this is My path, the right one therefore follow it, and follow not (other) ways, for they will lead you away from His way; this He has enjoined you with that you may guard (against evil).
6 154	Moreover, We gave Moses the Book, completing (Our favour) to those who would do right, and explaining all things in detail,- and a guide and a mercy, that they might believe in the meeting with their Lord.	Again, We gave the Scripture unto Moses, complete for him who would do good, an explanation of all things, a guidance and a mercy, that they might believe in the meeting with their Lord.	Again, We gave the Book to Musa to complete (Our blessings) on him who would do good (to others), and making plain all things and a guidance and a mercy, so that they should believe in the meeting of their Lord.
6 155	And this is a Book which We have revealed as a blessing: so follow it and be righteous, that ye may receive mercy:	And this is a blessed Scripture which We have revealed. So follow it and ward off (evil), that ye may find mercy.	And this is a Book We have revealed, blessed; therefore follow it and guard (against evil) that mercy may be shown to you.
6 156	Lest ye should say: "The Book was sent down to two Peoples before us, and for our part, we remained unacquainted with all that they learned by assiduous study:"	Lest ye should say: The Scripture was revealed only to two sects before us, and we in sooth were unaware of what they read;	Lest you say that the Book was only revealed to two parties before us and We were truly unaware of what they read.

6 157	Or lest ye should say: "If the Book had only been sent down to us, we should have followed its guidance better than they." Now then hath come unto you a clear (sign) from your Lord,- and a guide and a mercy: then who could do more wrong than one who rejecteth Allah's signs, and turneth away therefrom? In good time shall We requite those who turn away from Our signs, with a dreadful penalty, for their turning away.	Or lest ye should say: If the Scripture had been revealed unto us, we surely had been better guided than are they. Now hath there come unto you a clear proof from your Lord, a guidance and mercy; and who doeth greater wrong than he who denieth the revelations of Allah, and turneth away from them? We award unto those who turn away from Our revelations an evil doom because of their aversion.	Or lest you should say: If the Book had been revealed to us, we would certainly have been better guided than they, so indeed there has come to you clear proof from your Lord, and guidance and mercy. Who then is more unjust than he who rejects Allah's communications and turns away from them? We will reward those who turn away from Our communications with an evil chastisement because they turned away.
6 158	Are they waiting to see if the angels come to them, or thy Lord (Himself), or certain of the signs of thy Lord! the day that certain of the signs of thy Lord do come, no good will it do to a soul to believe in them then if it believed not before nor earned righteousness through its faith. Say: "Wait ye: we too are waiting."	Wait they, indeed, for nothing less than that the angels should come unto them, or thy Lord should come, or there should come one of the portents from thy Lord? In the day when one of the portents from thy Lord cometh, its belief availeth naught a soul which theretofore believed not, nor in its belief earned good (by works). Say: Wait ye! Lo! We (too) are waiting.	They do not wait aught but that the angels should come to them, or that your Lord should come, or that some of the signs of your Lord should come. On the day when some of the signs of your Lord shall come, its faith shall not profit a soul which did not believe before, or earn good through its faith. Say: Wait; we too are waiting.
6 159	As for those who divide their religion and break up into sects, thou hast no part in them in the least: their affair is with Allah: He will in the end tell them the truth of all that they did.	Lo! As for those who sunder their religion and become schismatics, no concern at all hast thou with them. Their case will go to Allah, Who then will tell them what they used to do.	Surely they who divided their religion into parts and became sects, you have no concern with them; their affair is only with Allah, then He will inform them of what they did.
6 160	He that doeth good shall have ten times as much to his credit: He that doeth evil shall only be recompensed according to his evil: no wrong shall be done unto (any of) them.	Whoso bringeth a good deed will receive tenfold the like thereof, while whoso bringeth an ill-deed will be awarded but the like thereof; and they will not be wronged.	Whoever brings a good deed, he shall have ten like it, and whoever brings an evil deed, he shall be recompensed only with the like of it, and they shall not be dealt with unjustly.
6 161	Say: "Verily, my Lord hath guided me to a way that is straight,- a religion of right,- the path (trod) by Abraham the true in Faith, and he (certainly) joined not gods with Allah."	Say: Lo! As for me, my Lord hath guided me unto a straight path, a right religion, the community of Abraham, the upright, who was no idolater.	Say: Surely, (as for) me, my Lord has guided me to the right path; (to) a most right religion, the faith of Ibrahim the upright one, and he was not of the polytheists.
6 162	Say: "Truly, my prayer and my service of sacrifice, my life and my death, are (all) for Allah, the Cherisher of the Worlds:"	Say: Lo! my worship and my sacrifice and my living and my dying are for Allah, Lord of the Worlds.	Say. Surely my prayer and my sacrifice and my life and my death are (all) for Allah, the Lord of the worlds;
6 163	No partner hath He: this am I commanded, and I am the first of those who bow to His will.	He hath no partner. This am I commanded, and I am first of those who surrender (unto Him).	No associate has He; and this am I commanded, and I am the first of those who submit.

6 164	Say: "Shall I seek for (my) Cherisher other than Allah, when He is the Cherisher of all things (that exist)? Every soul draws the meed of its acts on none but itself: no bearer of burdens can bear of burdens can bear the burden of another. Your goal in the end is towards Allah: He will tell you the truth of the things wherein ye disputed."	Say: Shall I seek another than Allah for Lord, when He is Lord of all things? Each soul earneth only on its own account, nor doth any laden bear another's load. Then unto your Lord is your return and He will tell you that wherein ye differed.	Say: What! shall I seek a Lord other than Allah? And He is the Lord of all things; and no soul earns (evil) but against itself, and no bearer of burden shall bear the burden of another; then to your Lord is your return, so He will inform you of that in which you differed.
6 165	It is He Who hath made you (His) agents, inheritors of the earth: He hath raised you in ranks, some above others: that He may try you in the gifts He hath given you: for thy Lord is quick in punishment: yet He is indeed Oft-Forgiving, Most Merciful.	He it is Who hath placed you as viceroys of the earth and hath exalted some of you in rank above others, that He may try you by (the test of) that which He hath given you. Lo! Thy Lord is swift in prosecution, and Lo! He verily is Forgiving, Merciful.	And He it is Who has made you successors in the land and raised some of you above others by (various) grades, that He might try you by what He has given you; surely your Lord is quick to requite (evil), and He is most surely the Forgiving, the Merciful.

Chapter 7:

AL-ARAF (THE HEIGHTS)

Total Verses: 206 Revealed At: MAKKA

In the name of Allah, the Most Beneficent, the Most Merciful.

7 001	Alif, Lam, Mim, Sad.	Alif. Lam. Mim. Sad.	Alif Lam Mim Suad.
7 002	A Book revealed unto thee,- So let thy heart be oppressed no more by any difficulty on that account,- that with it thou mightest warn (the erring) and teach the Believers.	(It is) a Scripture that is revealed unto thee (Muhammad) - so let there be no heaviness in thy heart therefrom - that thou mayst warn thereby, and (it is) a Reminder unto believers.	A Book revealed to you-- so let there be no straitness in your breast on account of it-- that you may warn thereby, and a reminder close to the believers.
7 003	Follow (O men!) the revelation given unto you from your Lord, and follow not, as friends or protectors, other than Him. Little it is ye remember of admonition.	(Saying): Follow that which is sent down unto you from your Lord, and follow no protecting friends beside Him. Little do ye recollect!	Follow what has been revealed to you from your Lord and do not follow guardians besides Him, how little you mind.
7 004	How many towns have We destroyed (for their sins)? Our punishment took them on a sudden by night or while they slept for their afternoon rest.	How many a township have We destroyed! As a raid by night, or while they slept at noon, Our terror came unto them.	And how many a town that We destroyed, so Our punishment came to it by night or while they slept at midday.
7 005	When (thus) Our punishment took them, no cry did they utter but this: Indeed we did wrong.	No plea had they, when Our terror came unto them, save that they said: Lo! We were wrong-doers.	Yet their cry, when Our punishment came to them, was nothing but that they said: Surely we were unjust.
7 006	Then shall we question those to whom Our message was sent and those by whom We sent it.	Then verily We shall question those unto whom (Our message) hath been sent, and verily We shall question the messengers.	Most certainly then We will question those to whom (the messengers) were sent, and most certainly We will also question the messengers;

7 007	And verily, We shall recount their whole story with knowledge, for We were never absent (at any time or place).	Then verily We shall narrate unto them (the event) with knowledge, for We were not absent (when it came to pass).	Then most certainly We will relate to them with knowledge, and We were not absent.
7 008	The balance that day will be true (to nicety): those whose scale (of good) will be heavy, will prosper:	The weighing on that day is the true (weighing). As for those whose scale is heavy, they are the successful.	And the measuring out on that day will be just; then as for him whose measure (of good deeds) is heavy, those are they who shall be successful;
7 009	Those whose scale will be light, will be their souls in perdition, for that they wrongfully treated Our signs.	And as for those whose scale is light: those are they who lose their souls because they used to wrong Our revelations.	And as for him whose measure (of good deeds) is light those are they who have made their souls suffer loss because they disbelieved in Our communications.
7 010	It is We Who have placed you with authority on earth, and provided you therein with means for the fulfilment of your life: small are the thanks that ye give!	And We have given you (mankind) power in the earth, and appointed for you therein livelihoods. Little give ye thanks!	And certainly We have established you in the earth and made in it means of livelihood for you; little it is that you give thanks.
7 011	It is We Who created you and gave you shape; then We bade the angels prostrate to Adam, and they prostrate; not so Iblis; He refused to be of those who prostrate.	And We created you, then fashioned you, then told the angels: Fall ye prostrate before Adam! And they fell prostrate, all save Iblis, who was not of those who make prostration.	And certainly We created you, then We fashioned you, then We said to the angels: Prostrate to Adam. So they did prostrate except Iblis; he was not of those who prostrated.
7 012	(Allah) said: "What prevented thee from prostrating when I commanded thee?" He said: "I am better than he: Thou didst create me from fire, and him from clay."	He said: What hindered thee that thou didst not fall prostrate when I bade thee? (Iblis) said: I am better than him. Thou createdst me of fire while him Thou didst create of mud.	He said: What hindered you so that you did not prostrate when I commanded you? He said: I am better than he: Thou hast created me of fire, while him Thou didst create of dust.
7 013	(Allah) said: "Get thee down from this: it is not for thee to be arrogant here: get out, for thou art of the meanest (of creatures)."	He said: Then go down hence! It is not for thee to show pride here, so go forth! Lo! thou art of those degraded.	He said: Then get forth from this (state), for it does not befit you to behave proudly therein. Go forth, therefore, surely you are of the abject ones.
7 014	He said: "Give me respite till the day they are raised up."	He said: Reprieve me till the day when they are raised (from the dead).	He said: Respite me until the day when they are raised up.
7 015	(Allah) said: "Be thou among those who have respite."	He said: Lo! thou art of those reprieved.	He said: Surely you are of the respited ones.
7 016	He said: "Because thou hast thrown me out of the way, lo! I will lie in wait for them on thy straight way:"	He said: Now, because Thou hast sent me astray, verily I shall lurk in ambush for them on Thy Right Path.	He said: As Thou hast caused me to remain disappointed I will certainly lie in wait for them in Thy straight path.
7 017	"Then will I assault them from before them and behind them, from their right and their left: Nor wilt thou find, in most of them, gratitude (for thy mercies)."	Then I shall come upon them from before them and from behind them and from their right hands and from their left hands, and Thou wilt not find most of them beholden (unto Thee).	Then I will certainly come to them from before them and from behind them, and from their right-hand side and from their left-hand side; and Thou shalt not find most of them thankful.
7 018	(Allah) said: "Get out from this, disgraced and expelled. If any of them follow thee,- Hell will I fill with you all."	He said: Go forth from hence, degraded, banished. As for such of them as follow thee, surely I will fill hell with all of you.	He said: Get out of this (state), despised, driven away; whoever of them will follow you, I will certainly fill hell with you all.

7 019	"O Adam! dwell thou and thy wife in the Garden, and enjoy (its good things) as ye wish: but approach not this tree, or ye run into harm and transgression."	And (unto man): O Adam! Dwell thou and thy wife in the Garden and eat from whence ye will, but come not nigh this tree lest ye become wrong-doers.	And (We said): O Adam! Dwell you and your wife in the garden; so eat from where you desire, but do not go near this tree, for then you will be of the unjust.
7 020	Then began Satan to whisper suggestions to them, bringing openly before their minds all their shame that was hidden from them (before): he said: "Your Lord only forbade you this tree, lest ye should become angels or such beings as live for ever."	Then Satan whispered to them that he might manifest unto them that which was hidden from them of their shame, and he said: Your Lord forbade you from this tree only lest ye should become angels or become of the immortals.	But the Shaitan made an evil suggestion to them that he might make manifest to them what had been hidden from them of their evil inclinations, and he said: Your Lord has not forbidden you this tree except that you may not both become two angels or that you may (not) become of the immortals.
7 021	And he swore to them both, that he was their sincere adviser.	And he swore unto them (saying): Lo! I am a sincere adviser unto you.	And he swore to them both: Most surely I am a sincere adviser to you.
7 022	So by deceit he brought about their fall: when they tasted of the tree, their shame became manifest to them, and they began to sew together the leaves of the garden over their bodies. And their Lord called unto them: "Did I not forbid you that tree, and tell you that Satan was an avowed enemy unto you?"	Thus did he lead them on with guile. And when they tasted of the tree their shame was manifest to them and they began to hide (by heaping) on themselves some of the leaves of the Garden. And their Lord called them, (saying): Did I not forbid you from that tree and tell you: Lo! Satan is an open enemy to you?	Then he caused them to fall by deceit; so when they tasted of the tree, their evil inclinations became manifest to them, and they both began to cover themselves with the leaves of the garden; and their Lord called out to them: Did I not forbid you both from that tree and say to you that the Shaitan is your open enemy?
7 023	They said: "Our Lord! We have wronged our own souls: If thou forgive us not and bestow not upon us Thy Mercy, we shall certainly be lost."	They said: Our Lord! We have wronged ourselves. If thou forgive us not and have not mercy on us, surely we are of the lost!	They said: Our Lord! We have been unjust to ourselves, and if Thou forgive us not, and have (not) mercy on us, we shall certainly be of the losers.
7 024	(Allah) said: "Get ye down. With enmity between yourselves. On earth will be your dwelling-place and your means of livelihood,- for a time."	He said: Go down (from hence), one of you a foe unto the other. There will be for you on earth a habitation and provision for a while.	He said: Get forth, some of you, the enemies of others, and there is for you in the earth an abode and a provision for a time.
7 025	He said: "Therein shall ye live, and therein shall ye die; but from it shall ye be taken out (at last)."	He said: There shall ye live, and there shall ye die, and thence shall ye be brought forth.	He (also) said: Therein shall you live, and therein shall you die, and from it shall you be raised.
7 026	O ye Children of Adam! We have bestowed raiment upon you to cover your shame, as well as to be an adornment to you. But the raiment of righteousness,- that is the best. Such are among the Signs of Allah, that they may receive admonition!	O Children of Adam! We have revealed unto you raiment to conceal your shame, and splendid vesture, but the raiment of restraint from evil, that is best. This is of the revelations of Allah, that they may remember.	O children of Adam! We have indeed sent down to you clothing to cover your shame, and (clothing) for beauty and clothing that guards (against evil), that is the best. This is of the communications of Allah that they may be mindful.
7 027	O ye Children of Adam! Let not Satan seduce you, in the same manner as He got your parents out of the Garden, stripping them of their raiment, to expose their shame: for he and his tribe watch you from a position where ye cannot see them: We made the evil ones friends (only) to those without faith.	O Children of Adam! Let not Satan seduce you as he caused your (first) parents to go forth from the Garden and tore off from them their robe (of innocence) that he might manifest their shame to them. Lo! he seeth you, he and his tribe, from whence ye see him not. Lo! We have made the devils protecting friends for those who believe not.	O children of Adam! let not the Shaitan cause you to fall into affliction as he expelled your parents from the garden, pulling off from them both their clothing that he might show them their evil inclinations, he surely sees you, he as well as his host, from whence you cannot see them; surely We have made the Shaitans to be the guardians of those who do not believe.

7 028	When they do aught that is shameful, they say: "We found our fathers doing so"; and "Allah commanded us thus": Say: "Nay, Allah never commands what is shameful: do ye say of Allah what ye know not?"	And when they do some lewdness they say: We found our fathers doing it and Allah hath enjoined it on us. Say: Allah, verily, enjoineth not lewdness. Tell ye concerning Allah that which ye know not?	And when they commit an indecency they say: We found our fathers doing this, and Allah has enjoined it on us. Say: Surely Allah does not enjoin indecency; do you say against Allah what you do not know?
7 029	Say: "My Lord hath commanded justice; and that ye set your whole selves (to Him) at every time and place of prayer, and call upon Him, making your devotion sincere as in His sight: such as He created you in the beginning, so shall ye return."	Say: My Lord enjoineth justice. And set your faces upright (toward Him) at every place of worship and call upon Him, making religion pure for Him (only). As He brought you into being, so return ye (unto Him).	Say: My Lord has enjoined justice, and set upright your faces at every time of prayer and call on Him, being sincere to Him in obedience; as He brought you forth in the beginning, so shall you also return.
7 030	Some He hath guided: Others have (by their choice) deserved the loss of their way; in that they took the evil ones, in preference to Allah, for their friends and protectors, and think that they receive guidance.	A party hath He led aright, while error hath just hold over (another) party, for lo! they choose the devils for protecting supporters instead of Allah and deem that they are rightly guided.	A part has He guided aright and (as for another) part, error is justly their due, surely they took the Shaitans for guardians beside Allah, and they think that they are followers of the right way.
7 031	O Children of Adam! wear your beautiful apparel at every time and place of prayer: eat and drink: But waste not by excess, for Allah loveth not the wasters.	O Children of Adam! Look to your adornment at every place of worship, and eat and drink, but be not prodigal. Lo! He loveth not the prodigals.	O children of Adam! attend to your embellishments at every time of prayer, and eat and drink and be not extravagant; surely He does not love the extravagant.
7 032	Say: Who hath forbidden the beautiful (gifts) of Allah, which He hath produced for His servants, and the things, clean and pure, (which He hath provided) for sustenance? Say: They are, in the life of this world, for those who believe, (and) purely for them on the Day of Judgment. Thus do We explain the signs in detail for those who understand.	Say: Who hath forbidden the adornment of Allah which He hath brought forth for His bondmen, and the good things of His providing? Say: Such, on the Day of Resurrection, will be only for those who believed during the life of the world. Thus do we detail Our revelations for people who have knowledge.	Say: Who has prohibited the embellishment of Allah which He has brought forth for His servants and the good provisions? Say: These are for the believers in the life of this world, purely (theirs) on the resurrection day; thus do We make the communications clear for a people who know.
7 033	Say: the things that my Lord hath indeed forbidden are: shameful deeds, whether open or secret; sins and trespasses against truth or reason; assigning of partners to Allah, for which He hath given no authority; and saying things about Allah of which ye have no knowledge.	Say: My Lord forbiddeth only indecencies, such of them as are apparent and such as are within, and sin and wrongful oppression, and that ye associate with Allah that for which no warrant hath been revealed, and that ye tell concerning Allah that which ye know not.	Say: My Lord has only prohibited indecencies, those of them that are apparent as well as those that are concealed, and sin and rebellion without justice, and that you associate with Allah that for which He has not sent down any authority, and that you say against Allah what you do not know.
7 034	To every people is a term appointed: when their term is reached, not an hour can they cause delay, nor (an hour) can they advance (it in anticipation).	And every nation hath its term, and when its term cometh, they cannot put it off an hour nor yet advance (it).	And for every nation there is a doom, so when their doom is come they shall not remain behind the least while, nor shall they go before.
7 035	O ye Children of Adam! whenever there come to you messengers from amongst you, rehearsing My signs unto you,- those who are righteous and mend (their lives),- on them shall be no fear nor shall they grieve.	O Children of Adam! When messengers of your own come unto you who narrate unto you My revelations, then whosoever refraineth from evil and amendeth - there shall no fear come upon them neither shall they grieve.	O children of Adam! if there come to you messengers from among you relating to you My communications, then whoever shall guard (against evil) and act aright-- they shall have no fear nor shall they grieve.

7 036	But those who reject Our signs and treat them with arrogance,- they are companions of the Fire, to dwell therein (for ever).	But they who deny Our revelations and scorn them - each are rightful owners of the Fire; they will abide therein.	And (as for) those who reject Our communications and turn away from them haughtily-- these are the inmates of the fire they shall abide in it.
7 037	Who is more unjust than one who invents a lie against Allah or rejects His Signs? For such, their portion appointed must reach them from the Book (of decrees): until, when our messengers (of death) arrive and take their souls, they say: "Where are the things that ye used to invoke besides Allah?" They will reply, "They have left us in the lurch," And they will bear witness against themselves, that they had rejected Allah.	Who doeth greater wrong than he who inventeth a lie concerning Allah or denieth Our tokens. (For such) their appointed portion of the Book (of destiny) reacheth them till, when Our messengers come to gather them, they say: Where (now) is that to which ye cried beside Allah? They say: They have departed from us. And they testify against themselves that they were disbelievers.	Who is then more unjust than he who forges a lie against Allah or rejects His communications? (As for) those, their portion of the Book shall reach them, until when Our messengers come to them causing them to die, they shall say: Where is that which you used to call upon besides Allah? They would say: They are gone away from us; and they shall bear witness against themselves that they were unbelievers.
7 038	He will say: "Enter ye in the company of the peoples who passed away before you - men and jinns, - into the Fire." Every time a new people enters, it curses its sister-people (that went before), until they follow each other, all into the Fire. Saith the last about the first: Our Lord! it is these that misled us: so give them a double penalty in the Fire." He will say: "Doubled for all": but this ye do not understand.	He saith: Enter into the Fire among nations of the jinn and humankind who passed away before you. Every time a nation entereth, it curseth its sister (nation) till, when they have all been made to follow one another thither, the last of them saith unto the first of them: Our Lord! These led us astray, so give them double torment of the Fire. He saith: For each one there is double (torment), but ye know not.	He will say: Enter into fire among the nations that have passed away before you from among jinn and men; whenever a nation shall enter, it shall curse its sister, until when they have all come up with one another into it; the last of them shall say with regard to the foremost of them: Our Lord! these led us astray therefore give them a double chastisement of the fire. He will say: Every one shall have double but you do not know.
7 039	Then the first will say to the last: "See then! No advantage have ye over us; so taste ye of the penalty for all that ye did!"	And the first of them saith unto the last of them: Ye were no whit better than us, so taste the doom for what ye used to earn.	And the foremost of them will say to the last of them: So you have no preference over us; therefore taste the chastisement for what you earned.
7 040	To those who reject Our signs and treat them with arrogance, no opening will there be of the gates of heaven, nor will they enter the garden, until the camel can pass through the eye of the needle: Such is Our reward for those in sin.	Lo! they who deny Our revelations and scorn them, for them the gates of heaven will nor be opened not will they enter the Garden until the camel goeth through the needle's eye. Thus do We requite the guilty.	Surely (as for) those who reject Our communications and turn away from them haughtily, the doors of heaven shall not be opened for them, nor shall they enter the garden until the camel pass through the eye of the needle; and thus do We reward the guilty.
7 041	For them there is Hell, as a couch (below) and folds and folds of covering above: such is Our requital of those who do wrong.	Theirs will be a bed of hell, and over them coverings (of hell). Thus do We requite wrong-doers.	They shall have a bed of hell-fire and from above them coverings (of it); and thus do We reward the unjust.
7 042	But those who believe and work righteousness,- no burden do We place on any soul, but that which it can bear,- they will be Companions of the Garden, therein to dwell (for ever).	But (as for) those who believe and do good works - We tax not any soul beyond its scope - Such are rightful owners of the Garden. They abide therein.	And (as for) those who believe and do good We do not impose on any soul a duty except to the extent of its ability-- they are the dwellers of the garden; in it they shall abide.

7 043	And We shall remove from their hearts any lurking sense of injury;- beneath them will be rivers flowing;- and they shall say: "Praise be to Allah, who hath guided us to this (felicity): never could we have found guidance, had it not been for the guidance of Allah: indeed it was the truth, that the messengers of our Lord brought unto us." And they shall hear the cry: "Behold! the garden before you! Ye have been made its inheritors, for your deeds (of righteousness)."	And We remove whatever rancour may be in their hearts. Rivers flow beneath them. And they say: The praise to Allah, Who hath guided us to this. We could not truly have been led aright if Allah had not guided us. Verily the messengers of our Lord did bring the Truth. And it is cried unto them: This is the Garden. Ye inherit it for what ye used to do.	And We will remove whatever of ill-feeling is in their breasts; the rivers shall flow beneath them and they shall say: All praise is due to Allah Who guided us to this, and we would not have found the way had it not been that Allah had guided us; certainly the messengers of our Lord brought the truth; and it shall be cried out to them that this is the garden of which you are made heirs for what you did.
7 044	The Companions of the Garden will call out to the Companions of the Fire: "We have indeed found the promises of our Lord to us true: Have you also found Your Lord's promises true?" They shall say, "Yes"; but a crier shall proclaim between them: "The curse of Allah is on the wrong-doers;-"	And the dwellers of the Garden cry unto the dwellers of the Fire: We have found that which our Lord promised us (to be) the Truth. Have ye (too) found that which your Lord promised the Truth? They say: Yea, verily. And a crier in between them crieth: The curse of Allah is on evil-doers,	And the dwellers of the garden will call out to the inmates of the fire: Surely we have found what our Lord promised us to be true; have you too found what your Lord promised to be true? They will say: Yes. Then a crier will cry out among them that the curse of Allah is on the unjust.
7 045	"Those who would hinder (men) from the path of Allah and would seek in it something crooked: they were those who denied the Hereafter."	Who debar (men) from the path of Allah and would have it crooked, and who are disbelievers in the Last Day.	Who hinder (people) from Allah's way and seek to make it crooked, and they are disbelievers in the hereafter.
7 046	Between them shall be a veil, and on the heights will be men who would know every one by his marks: they will call out to the Companions of the Garden, "peace on you": they will not have entered, but they will have an assurance (thereof).	Between them is a veil. And on the Heights are men who know them all by their marks. And they call unto the dwellers of the Garden: Peace be unto you! They enter it not although they hope (to enter).	And between the two there shall be a veil, and on the most elevated places there shall be men who know all by their marks, and they shall call out to the dwellers of the garden: Peace be on you; they shall not have yet entered it, though they hope.
7 047	When their eyes shall be turned towards the Companions of the Fire, they will say: "Our Lord! send us not to the company of the wrong-doers."	And when their eyes are turned toward the dwellers of the Fire, they say: Our Lord! Place us not with the wrong-doing folk.	And when their eyes shall be turned towards the inmates of the fire, they shall say: Our Lord! place us not with the unjust people.
7 048	The men on the heights will call to certain men whom they will know from their marks, saying: "Of what profit to you were your hoards and your arrogant ways?"	And the dwellers on the Heights call unto men whom they know by their marks, (saying): What did your multitude and that in which ye took your pride avail you?	And the dwellers of the most elevated places shall call out to men whom they will recognize by their marks saying: Of no avail were to you your amassings and your behaving haughtily:
7 049	"Behold! are these not the men whom you swore that Allah with His Mercy would never bless? Enter ye the Garden: no fear shall be on you, nor shall ye grieve."	Are these they of whom ye swore that Allah would not show them mercy? (Unto them it hath been said): Enter the Garden. No fear shall come upon you nor is it ye who will grieve.	Are these they about whom you swore that Allah will not bestow mercy on them? Enter the garden; you shall have no fear, nor shall you grieve.

7 050	The Companions of the Fire will call to the Companions of the Garden: Pour down to us water or anything that Allah doth provide for your sustenance." They will say: "Both these things hath Allah forbidden to those who rejected Him."	And the dwellers of the Fire cry out unto the dwellers of the Garden: Pour on us some water or some wherewith Allah hath provided you. They say: Lo! Allah hath forbidden both to disbelievers (in His guidance),	And the inmates of the fire shall call out to the dwellers of the garden, saying: Pour on us some water or of that which Allah has given you. They shall say: Surely Allah has prohibited them both to the unbelievers.
7 051	"Such as took their religion to be mere amusement and play, and were deceived by the life of the world." That day shall We forget them as they forgot the meeting of this day of theirs, and as they were wont to reject Our signs.	Who took their religion for a sport and pastime, and whom the life of the world beguiled. So this day We have forgotten them even as they forgot the meeting of this their Day and as they used to deny Our tokens.	Who take their religion for an idle sport and a play and this life's world deceives them; so today We forsake them, as they neglected the meeting of this day of theirs and as they denied Our communications.
7 052	For We had certainly sent unto them a Book, based on knowledge, which We explained in detail,- a guide and a mercy to all who believe.	Verily We have brought them a Scripture which We expounded with knowledge, a guidance and a mercy for a people who believe.	And certainly We have brought them a Book which We have made clear with knowledge, a guidance and a mercy for a people who believe.
7 053	Do they just wait for the final fulfilment of the event? On the day the event is finally fulfilled, those who disregarded it before will say: "The messengers of our Lord did indeed bring true (tidings). Have we no intercessors now to intercede on our behalf? Or could we be sent back? then should we behave differently from our behaviour in the past." In fact they will have lost their souls, and the things they invented will leave them in the lurch.	Await they aught save the fulfilment thereof? On the day when the fulfilment thereof cometh, those who were before forgetful thereof will say: The messengers of our Lord did bring the Truth! Have we any intercessors, that they may intercede for us? Or can we be returned (to life on earth), that we may act otherwise than we used to act? They have lost their souls, and that which they devised hath failed them.	Do they wait for aught but its final sequel? On the day when its final sequel comes about, those who neglected it before will say: Indeed the messengers of our Lord brought the truth; are there for us then any intercessors so that they should intercede on our behalf? Or could we be sent back so that we should do (deeds) other than those which we did? Indeed they have lost their souls and that which they forged has gone away from them.
7 054	Your Guardian-Lord is Allah, Who created the heavens and the earth in six days, and is firmly established on the throne (of authority): He draweth the night as a veil o'er the day, each seeking the other in rapid succession: He created the sun, the moon, and the stars, (all) governed by laws under His command. Is it not His to create and to govern? Blessed be Allah, the Cherisher and Sustainer of the worlds!	Lo! your Lord is Allah Who created the heavens and the earth in six Days, then mounted He the Throne. He covereth the night with the day, which is in haste to follow it, and hath made the sun and the moon and the stars subservient by His command. His verily is all creation and commandment. Blessed be Allah, the Lord of the Worlds!	Surely your Lord is Allah, Who created the heavens and the earth in six periods of time, and He is firm in power; He throws the veil of night over the day, which it pursues incessantly; and (He created) the sun and the moon and the stars, made subservient by His command; surely His is the creation and the command; blessed is Allah, the Lord of the worlds.
7 055	Call on your Lord with humility and in private: for Allah loveth not those who trespass beyond bounds.	(O mankind!) Call upon your Lord humbly and in secret. Lo! He loveth not aggressors.	Call on your Lord humbly and secretly; surely He does not love those who exceed the limits.
7 056	Do no mischief on the earth, after it hath been set in order, but call on Him with fear and longing (in your hearts): for the Mercy of Allah is (always) near to those who do good.	Work not confusion in the earth after the fair ordering (thereof). and call on Him in fear and hope. Lo! the mercy of Allah is nigh unto the good.	And do not make mischief in the earth after its reformation, and call on Him fearing and hoping; surely the mercy of Allah is nigh to those who do good (to others).

7 057	It is He Who sendeth the winds like heralds of glad tidings, going before His mercy: when they have carried the heavy-laden clouds, We drive them to a land that is dead, make rain to descend thereon, and produce every kind of harvest therewith: thus shall We raise up the dead: perchance ye may remember.	And He it is Who sendeth the winds as tidings heralding His mercy, till, when they bear a cloud heavy (with rain), We lead it to a dead land, and then cause water to descend thereon and thereby bring forth fruits of every kind. Thus bring We forth the dead. Haply ye may remember.	And He it is Who sends forth the winds bearing good news before His mercy, until, when they bring up a laden cloud, We drive it to a dead land, then We send down water on it, then bring forth with it of fruits of all kinds; thus shall We bring forth the dead that you may be mindful.
7 058	From the land that is clean and good, by the will of its Cherisher, springs up produce, (rich) after its kind: but from the land that is bad, springs up nothing but that which is niggardly: thus do we explain the signs by various (symbols) to those who are grateful.	As for the good land, its vegetation cometh forth by permission of its Lord; while as for that which is bad, only the useless cometh forth (from it). Thus do We recount the tokens for people who give thanks.	And as for the good land, its vegetation springs forth (abundantly) by the permission of its Lord, and (as for) that which is inferior (its herbage) comes forth but scantily; thus do We repeat the communications for a people who give thanks.
7 059	We sent Noah to his people. He said: "O my people! worship Allah! ye have no other god but Him. I fear for you the punishment of a dreadful day!"	We sent Noah (of old) unto his people, and he said: O my people! Serve Allah. Ye have no other Allah save Him. Lo! I fear for you the retribution of an Awful Day.	Certainly We sent Nuh to his people, so he said: O my people! serve Allah, you have no god other than Him; surely I fear for you the chastisement of a grievous day.
7 060	The leaders of his people said: "Ah! we see thee evidently wandering (in mind)."	The chieftains of his people said: Lo! we see thee surely in plain error.	The chiefs of his people said: Most surely we see you in clear error.
7 061	He said: "O my people! No wandering is there in my (mind): on the contrary I am a messenger from the Lord and Cherisher of the worlds!"	He said: O my people! There is no error in me, but I am a messenger from the Lord of the Worlds.	He said: O my people! there is no error in me, but I am a messenger from the Lord of the worlds.
7 062	"I but fulfil towards you the duties of my Lord's mission: Sincere is my advice to you, and I know from Allah something that ye know not."	I convey unto you the messages of my Lord and give good counsel unto you, and know from Allah that which ye know not.	I deliver to you the messages of my Lord, and I offer you good advice and I know from Allah what you do not know.
7 063	"Do ye wonder that there hath come to you a message from your Lord, through a man of your own people, to warn you,- so that ye may fear Allah and haply receive His Mercy?"	Marvel ye that there should come unto you a Reminder from your Lord by means of a man among you, that he may warn you, and that ye may keep from evil, and that haply ye may find mercy.	What! do you wonder that a reminder has come to you from your Lord through a man from among you, that he might warn you and that you might guard (against evil) and so that mercy may be shown to you?
7 064	But they rejected him, and We delivered him, and those with him, in the Ark: but We overwhelmed in the flood those who rejected Our signs. They were indeed a blind people!	But they denied him, so We saved him and those with him in the ship, and We drowned those who denied Our tokens. Lo! they were blind folk.	But they called him a liar, so We delivered him and those with him in the ark, and We drowned those who rejected Our communications; surely they were a blind people.
7 065	To the 'Ad people, (We sent) Hud, one of their (own) brethren: He said: "O my people! worship Allah! ye have no other god but Him will ye not fear (Allah)?"	And unto (the tribe of) A'ad (We sent) their brother, Hud. He said: O my people! Serve Allah. Ye have no other Allah save Him. Will ye not ward off (evil)?	And to Ad (We sent) their brother Hud. He said: O my people! serve Allah, you have no god other than Him; will you not then guard (against evil)?
7 066	The leaders of the Unbelievers among his people said: "Ah! we see thou art an imbecile!" and "We think thou art a liar!"	The chieftains of his people, who were disbelieving, said: Lo! we surely see thee in foolishness, and lo! we deem thee of the liars.	The chiefs of those who disbelieved from among his people said: Most surely we see you in folly, and most surely we think you to be of the liars.

7 067	He said: "O my people! I am no imbecile, but (I am) a messenger from the Lord and Cherisher of the Worlds!"	He said: O my people! There is no foolishness in me, but I am a messenger from the Lord of the Worlds.	He said: O my people! there is no folly in me, but I am a messenger of the Lord of the worlds.
7 068	"I but fulfil towards you the duties of my Lord's mission: I am to you a sincere and trustworthy adviser."	I convey unto you the messages of my Lord and am for you a true adviser.	I deliver to you the messages of my Lord and I am a faithful adviser to you:
7 069	"Do ye wonder that there hath come to you a message from your Lord through a man of your own people, to warn you? call in remembrance that He made you inheritors after the people of Noah, and gave you a stature tall among the nations. Call in remembrance the benefits (ye have received) from Allah: that so ye may prosper."	Marvel ye that there should come unto you a Reminder from your Lord by means of a man among you, that he may warn you? Remember how He made you viceroys after Noah's folk, and gave you growth of stature. Remember (all) the bounties of your Lord, that haply ye may be successful.	What! do you wonder that a reminder has come to you from your Lord through a man from among you that he might warn you? And remember when He made you successors after Nuh's people and increased you in excellence in respect of make; therefore remember the benefits of Allah, that you may be successful.
7 070	They said: "Comest thou to us, that we may worship Allah alone, and give up the cult of our fathers? bring us what thou threatenest us with, if so be that thou tellest the truth!"	They said: Hast come unto us that we should serve Allah alone, and forsake what our fathers worshipped? Then bring upon us that wherewith thou threatenest us if thou art of the truthful!	They said: Have you come to us that we may serve Allah alone and give up what our fathers used to serve? Then bring to us what you threaten us with, if you are of the truthful ones.
7 071	He said: "Punishment and wrath have already come upon you from your Lord: dispute ye with me over names which ye have devised - ye and your fathers,- without authority from Allah? then wait: I am amongst you, also waiting."	He said: Terror and wrath from your Lord have already fallen on you. Would ye wrangle with me over names which ye have named, ye and your fathers, for which no warrant from Allah hath been revealed? Then await (the consequence), lo! I (also) am of those awaiting (it).	He said: Indeed uncleanness and wrath from your Lord have lighted upon you; what! do you dispute with me about names which you and your fathers have given? Allah has not sent any authority for them; wait then, I too with you will be of those who wait.
7 072	We saved him and those who adhered to him. By Our mercy, and We cut off the roots of those who rejected Our signs and did not believe.	And We saved him and those with him by a mercy from Us, and We cut the root of those who denied Our revelations and were not believers.	So We delivered him and those with him by mercy from Us, and We cut off the last of those who rejected Our communications and were not believers.
7 073	To the Thamud people (We sent) Salih, one of their own brethren: He said: "O my people! worship Allah: ye have no other god but Him. Now hath come unto you a clear (Sign) from your Lord! This she-camel of Allah is a Sign unto you: So leave her to graze in Allah's earth, and let her come to no harm, or ye shall be seized with a grievous punishment."	And to (the tribe of) Thamud (We sent) their brother Salih. He said: O my people! Serve Allah. Ye have no other Allah save Him. A wonder from your Lord hath come unto you. Lo! this is the camel of Allah, a token unto you; so let her feed in Allah's earth, and touch her not with hurt lest painful torment seize you.	And to Samood (We sent) their brother Salih. He said: O my people! serve Allah, you have no god other than Him; clear proof indeed has come to you from your Lord; this is (as) Allah's she-camel for you-- a sign, therefore leave her alone to pasture on Allah's earth, and do not touch her with any harm, otherwise painful chastisement will overtake you.
7 074	"And remember how He made you inheritors after the 'Ad people and gave you habitations in the land: ye build for yourselves palaces and castles in (open) plains, and carve out homes in the mountains; so bring to remembrance the benefits (ye have received) from Allah, and refrain from evil and mischief on the earth."	And remember how He made you viceroys after A'ad and gave you station in the earth. Ye choose castles in the plains and hew the mountains into dwellings. So remember (all) the bounties of Allah and do not evil, making mischief in the earth.	And remember when He made you successors after Ad and settled you in the land-- you make mansions on its plains and hew out houses in the mountains-- remember therefore Allah's benefits and do not act corruptly in the land, making mischief.

7 075	The leaders of the arrogant party among his people said to those who were reckoned powerless - those among them who believed: "know ye indeed that Salih is a messenger from his Lord?" They said: "We do indeed believe in the revelation which hath been sent through him."	The chieftains of his people, who were scornful, said unto those whom they despised, unto such of them as believed: Know ye that Salih is one sent from his Lord? They said: Lo! In that wherewith he hath been sent we are believers.	The chief of those who behaved proudly among his people said to those who were considered weak, to those who believed from among them: Do you know that Salih is sent by his Lord? They said: Surely we are believers in what he has been sent with.
7 076	The Arrogant party said: "For our part, we reject what ye believe in."	Those who were scornful said: Lo! in that which ye believe we are disbelievers.	Those who were haughty said: Surely we are deniers of what you believe in.
7 077	Then they ham-strung the she-camel, and insolently defied the order of their Lord, saying: "O Salih! bring about thy threats, if thou art a messenger (of Allah)!"	So they hamstrung the she-camel, and they flouted the commandment of their Lord, and they said: O Salih! Bring upon us that thou threatenest if thou art indeed of those sent (from Allah).	So they slew the she-camel and revolted against their Lord's commandment, and they said: O Salih! bring us what you threatened us with, if you are one of the messengers.
7 078	So the earthquake took them unawares, and they lay prostrate in their homes in the morning!	So the earthquake seized them, and morning found them prostrate in their dwelling-place.	Then the earthquake overtook them, so they became motionless bodies in their abode.
7 079	So Salih left them, saying: "O my people! I did indeed convey to you the message for which I was sent by my Lord: I gave you good counsel, but ye love not good counsellors!"	And (Salih) turned from them and said: O my people! I delivered my Lord's message unto you and gave you good advice, but ye love not good advisers.	Then he turned away from them and said: O my people I did certainly deliver to you the message of my Lord, and I gave you good advice, but you do not love those who give good advice.
7 080	We also (sent) Lut: He said to his people: "Do ye commit lewdness such as no people in creation (ever) committed before you?"	And Lot! (Remember) when he said unto his folk: Will ye commit abomination such as no creature ever did before you?	And (We sent) Lut when he said to his people: What! do you commit an indecency which any one in the world has not done before you?
7 081	"For ye practise your lusts on men in preference to women: ye are indeed a people transgressing beyond bounds."	Lo! ye come with lust unto men instead of women. Nay, but ye are wanton folk.	Most surely you come to males in lust besides females; nay you are an extravagant people.
7 082	And his people gave no answer but this: they said, "Drive them out of your city: these are indeed men who want to be clean and pure!"	And the answer of his people was only that they said (one to another): Turn them out of your township. They are folk, forsooth, who keep pure.	And the answer of his people was no other than that they said: Turn them out of your town, surely they are a people who seek to purify (themselves).
7 083	But we saved him and his family, except his wife: she was of those who legged behind.	And We rescued him and his household, save his wife, who was of those who stayed behind.	So We delivered him and his followers, except his wife; she was of those who remained behind.
7 084	And we rained down on them a shower (of brimstone): Then see what was the end of those who indulged in sin and crime!	And We rained a rain upon them. See now the nature of the consequence of evil-doers!	And We rained upon them a rain; consider then what was the end of the guilty.
7 085	To the Madyan people We sent Shu'aib, one of their own brethren: he said: "O my people! worship Allah; Ye have no other god but Him. Now hath come unto you a clear (Sign) from your Lord! Give just measure and weight, nor withhold from the people the things that are their due; and do no mischief on the earth after it has been set in order: that will be best for you, if ye have Faith."	And unto Midian (We sent) their brother, Shu'eyb. He said: O my people! Serve Allah. Ye have no other Allah save Him. Lo! a clear proof hath come unto you from your Lord; so give full measure and full weight and wrong not mankind in their goods, and work not confusion in the earth after the fair ordering thereof. That will be better for you, if ye are believers.	And to Madyan (We sent) their brother Shu'aib. He said: O my people! serve Allah, you have no god other than Him; clear proof indeed has come to you from your Lord, therefore give full measure and weight and do not diminish to men their things, and do not make mischief in the land after its reform; this is better for you if you are believers:

7 086	"And squat not on every road, breathing threats, hindering from the path of Allah those who believe in Him, and seeking in it something crooked; But remember how ye were little, and He gave you increase. And hold in your mind's eye what was the end of those who did mischief."	Lurk not on every road to threaten (wayfarers), and to turn away from Allah's path him who believeth in Him, and to seek to make it crooked. And remember, when ye were but few, how He did multiply you. And see the nature of the consequence for the corrupters!	And do not lie in wait in every path, threatening and turning away from Allah's way him who believes in Him and seeking to make it crooked; and remember when you were few then He multiplied you, and consider what was the end of the mischief-makers.
7 087	"And if there is a party among you who believes in the message with which I have been sent, and a party which does not believe, hold yourselves in patience until Allah doth decide between us: for He is the best to decide."	And if there is a party of you which believeth in that wherewith I have been sent, and there is a party which believeth not, then have patience until Allah judge between us. He is the Best of all who deal in judgment.	And if there is a party of you who believe in that with which am sent, and another party who do not believe, then wait patiently until Allah judges between us; and He is the best of the Judges.
7 088	The leaders, the arrogant party among his people, said: "O Shu'aib! we shall certainly drive thee out of our city - (thee) and those who believe with thee; or else ye (thou and they) shall have to return to our ways and religion." He said: "What! even though we do detest (them)?"	The chieftains of his people, who were scornful, said: Surely we will drive thee out, O Shu'eyb, and those who believe with thee, from our township, unless ye return to our religion. He said: Even though we hate it?	The chiefs, those who were proud from among his people said: We will most certainly turn you out, O Shu'aib, and (also) those who believe with you, from our town, or you shall come back to our faith. He said: What! though we dislike (it)?
7 089	"We should indeed invent a lie against Allah, if we returned to your ways after Allah hath rescued us therefrom; nor could we by any manner of means return thereto unless it be as in the will and plan of Allah, Our Lord. Our Lord can reach out to the utmost recesses of things by His knowledge. In Allah is our trust. Our Lord! decide Thou between us and our people in truth, for Thou art the best to decide."	We should have invented a lie against Allah if we returned to your religion after Allah hath rescued us from it. It is not for us to return to it unless Allah our Lord should (so) will. Our Lord comprehendeth all things in knowledge. In Allah do we put our trust. Our Lord! Decide with truth between us and our folk, for Thou art the best of those who make decision.	Indeed we shall have forged a lie against Allah If we go back to your religion after Allah has delivered us from it, and it befits us not that we should go back to it, except if Allah our Lord please: Our Lord comprehends all things in His knowledge; in Allah do we trust: Our Lord! decide between us and our people with truth; and Thou art the best of deciders.
7 090	The leaders, the unbelievers among his people, said: "If ye follow Shu'aib, be sure then ye are ruined!"	But the chieftains of his people, who were disbelieving, said: If ye follow Shu'eyb, then truly ye shall be the losers.	And the chiefs of those who disbelieved from among his people said: If you follow Shu'aib, you shall then most surely be losers.
7 091	But the earthquake took them unawares, and they lay prostrate in their homes before the morning!	So the earthquake seized them and morning found them prostrate in their dwelling-place.	Then the earthquake overtook them, so they became motionless bodies in their abode.
7 092	The men who reject Shu'aib became as if they had never been in the homes where they had flourished: the men who rejected Shu'aib - it was they who were ruined!	Those who denied Shu'eyb became as though they had not dwelt there. Those who denied Shu'eyb, they were the losers.	Those who called Shu'aib a liar were as though they had never dwelt therein; those who called Shu'aib a liar, they were the losers.
7 093	So Shu'aib left them, saying: "O my people! I did indeed convey to you the messages for which I was sent by my Lord: I gave you good counsel, but how shall I lament over a people who refuse to believe!"	So he turned from them and said: O my people! I delivered my Lord's messages unto you and gave you good advice; then how can I sorrow for a people that rejected (truth)?	So he turned away from them and said: O my people! certainly I delivered to you the messages of my Lord and I gave you good advice; how shall I then be sorry for an unbelieving people?

7 094	Whenever We sent a prophet to a town, We took up its people in suffering and adversity, in order that they might learn humility.	And We sent no prophet unto any township but We did afflict its folk with tribulation and adversity that haply they might grow humble.	And We did not send a prophet in a town but We overtook its people with distress and affliction in order that they might humble themselves.
7 095	Then We changed their suffering into prosperity, until they grew and multiplied, and began to say: "Our fathers (too) were touched by suffering and affluence" ... Behold! We called them to account of a sudden, while they realised not (their peril).	Then changed We the evil plight for good till they grew affluent and said: Tribulation and distress did touch our fathers. Then We seized them unawares, when they perceived not.	Then We gave them good in the place of evil until they became many and said: Distress and happiness did indeed befall our fathers. Then We took them by surprise while they did not perceive.
7 096	If the people of the towns had but believed and feared Allah, We should indeed have opened out to them (All kinds of) blessings from heaven and earth; but they rejected (the truth), and We brought them to book for their misdeeds.	And if the people of the townships had believed and kept from evil, surely We should have opened for them blessings from the sky and from the earth. But (unto every messenger) they gave the lie, and so We seized them on account of what they used to earn.	And if the people of the towns had believed and guarded (against evil) We would certainly have opened up for them blessings from the heaven and the earth, but they rejected, so We overtook them for what they had earned.
7 097	Did the people of the towns feel secure against the coming of Our wrath by night while they were asleep?	Are the people of the townships then secure from the coming of Our wrath upon them as a night-raid while they sleep?	What! do the people of the towns then feel secure from Our punishment coming to them by night while they sleep?
7 098	Or else did they feel secure against its coming in broad daylight while they played about (care-free)?	Or are the people of the townships then secure from the coming of Our wrath upon them in the daytime while they play?	What! do the people of the towns feel secure from Our punishment coming to them in the morning while they play?
7 099	Did they then feel secure against the plan of Allah?- but no one can feel secure from the Plan of Allah, except those (doomed) to ruin!	Are they then secure from Allah's scheme? None deemeth himself secure from Allah's scheme save folk that perish.	What! do they then feel secure from Allah's plan? But none feels secure from Allah's plan except the people who shall perish.
7 100	To those who inherit the earth in succession to its (previous) possessors, is it not a guiding, (lesson) that, if We so willed, We could punish them (too) for their sins, and seal up their hearts so that they could not hear?	Is it not an indication to those who inherit the land after its people (who thus reaped the consequence of evil-doing) that, if We will, We can smite them for their sins and print upon their hearts so that they hear not?	Is it not clear to those who inherit the earth after its (former) residents that if We please We would afflict them on account of their faults and set a seal on their hearts so they would not hear.
7 101	Such were the towns whose story We (thus) relate unto thee: There came indeed to them their messengers with clear (signs): But they would not believe what they had rejected before. Thus doth Allah seal up the hearts of those who reject faith.	Such were the townships. We relate some tidings of them unto thee (Muhammad). Their messengers verily came unto them with clear proofs (of Allah's Sovereignty), but they could not believe because they had before denied. Thus doth Allah print upon the hearts of disbelievers (that they hear not).	These towns-- We relate to you some of their stories, and certainly their messengers came to them with clear arguments, but they would not believe in what they rejected at first; thus does Allah set a seal over the hearts of the unbelievers.
7 102	Most of them We found not men (true) to their covenant: but most of them We found rebellious and disobedient.	We found no (loyalty to any) covenant in most of them. Nay, most of them We found wrong-doers.	And We did not find in most of them any (faithfulness to) covenant, and We found most of them to be certainly transgressors.
7 103	Then after them We sent Moses with Our signs to Pharaoh and his chiefs, but they wrongfully rejected them: So see what was the end of those who made mischief.	Then, after them, We sent Moses with our tokens unto Pharaoh and his chiefs, but they repelled them. Now, see the nature of the consequence for the corrupters!	Then we raised after them Musa with Our communications to Firon and his chiefs, but they disbelieved in them; consider then what was the end of the mischief makers.

7 104	Moses said: "O Pharaoh! I am a messenger from the Lord of the worlds,-"	Moses said: O Pharaoh! Lo! I am a messenger from the Lord of the Worlds,	And Musa said: O Firon! surely I am a messenger from the Lord of the worlds:
7 105	"One for whom it is right to say nothing but truth about Allah. Now have I come unto you (people), from your Lord, with a clear (Sign): So let the Children of Israel depart along with me."	Approved upon condition that I speak concerning Allah nothing but the truth. I come unto you (lords of Egypt) with a clear proof from your Lord. So let the Children of Israel go with me.	(I am) worthy of not saying anything about Allah except the truth: I have come to you indeed with clear proof from your Lord, therefore send with me the children of Israel.
7 106	(Pharaoh) said: "If indeed thou hast come with a Sign, show it forth, if thou tellest the truth."	(Pharaoh) said: If thou comest with a token, then produce it, if thou art of those who speak the truth.	He said: If you have come with a sign, then bring it, if you are of the truthful ones.
7 107	Then (Moses) threw his rod, and behold! it was a serpent, plain (for all to see)!	Then he flung down his staff and lo! it was a serpent manifest;	So he threw his rod, then lo! it was a clear serpent.
7 108	And he drew out his hand, and behold! it was white to all beholders!	And he drew forth his hand (from his bosom), and lo! it was white for the beholders.	And he drew forth his hand, and lo! it was white to the beholders.
7 109	Said the Chiefs of the people of Pharaoh: "This is indeed a sorcerer well-versed."	The chiefs of Pharaoh's people said: Lo! this is some knowing wizard,	The chiefs of Firon's people said: most surely this is an enchanter possessed of knowledge:
7 110	"His plan is to get you out of your land: then what is it ye counsel?"	Who would expel you from your land. Now what do ye advise?	He intends to turn you out of your land. What counsel do you then give?
7 111	They said: "Keep him and his brother in suspense (for a while); and send to the cities men to collect-"	They said (unto Pharaoh): Put him off (a while) - him and his brother - and send into the cities summoners,	They said: Put him off and his brother, and send collectors into the cities:
7 112	"And bring up to thee all (our) sorcerers well-versed."	To bring each knowing wizard unto thee.	That they may bring to you every enchanter possessed of knowledge.
7 113	So there came the sorcerers to Pharaoh: They said, "of course we shall have a (suitable) reward if we win!"	And the wizards came to Pharaoh, saying: Surely there will be a reward for us if we are victors.	And the enchanters came to Firon (and) said: We must surely have a reward if we are the prevailing ones.
7 114	He said: "Yea, (and more),- for ye shall in that case be (raised to posts) nearest (to my person)."	He answered: Yes, and surely ye shall be of those brought near (to me).	He said: Yes, and you shall certainly be of those who are near (to me).
7 115	They said: "O Moses! wilt thou throw (first), or shall we have the (first) throw?"	They said: O Moses! Either throw (first) or let us be the first throwers?	They said: O Musa! will you cast, or shall we be the first to cast?
7 116	Said Moses: "Throw ye (first)." So when they threw, they bewitched the eyes of the people, and struck terror into them: for they showed a great (feat of) magic.	He said: Throw! And when they threw they cast a spell upon the people's eyes, and overawed them, and produced a mighty spell.	He said: Cast. So when they cast, they deceived the people's eyes and frightened them, and they produced a mighty enchantment.
7 117	We put it into Moses's mind by inspiration: "Throw (now) thy rod": and behold! it swallows up straight away all the falsehoods which they fake!	And We inspired Moses (saying): Throw thy staff! And lo! it swallowed up their lying show.	And We revealed to Musa, saying: Cast your rod; then lo! it devoured the lies they told.
7 118	Thus truth was confirmed, and all that they did was made of no effect.	Thus was the Truth vindicated and that which they were doing was made vain.	So the truth was established, and what they did became null.
7 119	So the (great ones) were vanquished there and then, and were made to look small.	Thus were they there defeated and brought low.	Thus they were vanquished there, and they went back abased.
7 120	But the sorcerers fell down prostrate in adoration.	And the wizards fell down prostrate,	And the enchanters were thrown down, prostrating (themselves).

7 121	Saying: "We believe in the Lord of the Worlds,-"	Crying: We believe in the Lord of the Worlds,		They said: We believe in the Lord of the worlds,
7 122	"The Lord of Moses and Aaron."	The Lord of Moses and Aaron.		The Lord of Musa and Haroun.
7 123	Said Pharaoh: "Believe ye in Him before I give you permission? Surely this is a trick which ye have planned in the city to drive out its people: but soon shall ye know (the consequences)."	Pharaoh said: Ye believe in Him before I give you leave! Lo! this is the plot that ye have plotted in the city that ye may drive its people hence. But ye shall come to know!		Firon said: Do you believe in Him before I have given you permission? Surely this is a plot which you have secretly devised in this city, that you may turn out of it its people, but you shall know:
7 124	"Be sure I will cut off your hands and your feet on apposite sides, and I will cause you all to die on the cross."	Surely I shall have your hands and feet cut off upon alternate sides. Then I shall crucify you every one.		I will certainly cut off your hands and your feet on opposite sides, then will I crucify you all together.
7 125	They said: "For us, We are but sent back unto our Lord:"	They said: Lo! We are about to return unto our Lord!		They said: Surely to our Lord shall we go back:
7 126	"But thou dost wreak thy vengeance on us simply because we believed in the Signs of our Lord when they reached us! Our Lord! pour out on us patience and constancy, and take our souls unto thee as Muslims (who bow to thy will)!"	Thou takest vengeance on us only forasmuch as we believed the tokens of our Lord when they came unto us. Our Lord! Vouchsafe unto us steadfastness and make us die as men who have surrendered (unto Thee).		And you do not take revenge on us except because we have believed in the communications of our Lord when they came to us! Our Lord: Pour out upon us patience and cause us to die in submission.
7 127	Said the chiefs of Pharaoh's people: "Wilt thou leave Moses and his people, to spread mischief in the land, and to abandon thee and thy gods?" He said: "Their male children will we slay; (only) their females will we save alive; and we have over them (power) irresistible."	The chiefs of Pharaoh's people said: (O King), wilt thou suffer Moses and his people to make mischief in the land, and flout thee and thy gods? He said: We will slay their sons and spare their women, for lo! we are in power over them.		And the chiefs of Firon's people said: Do you leave Musa and his people to make mischief in the land and to forsake you and your gods? He said: We will slay their sons and spare their women, and surely we are masters over them.
7 128	Said Moses to his people: "Pray for help from Allah, and (wait) in patience and constancy: for the earth is Allah's, to give as a heritage to such of His servants as He pleaseth; and the end is (best) for the righteous."	And Moses said unto his people: Seek help in Allah and endure. Lo! the earth is Allah's. He giveth it for an inheritance to whom He will. And lo! the sequel is for those who keep their duty (unto Him).		Musa said to his people: Ask help from Allah and be patient; surely the land is Allah's; He causes such of His servants to inherit it as He pleases, and the end is for those who guard (against evil).
7 129	They said: "We have had (nothing but) trouble, both before and after thou camest to us." He said: "It may be that your Lord will destroy your enemy and make you inheritors in the earth; that so He may try you by your deeds."	They said: We suffered hurt before thou camest unto us, and since thou hast come unto us. He said: It may be that your Lord is going to destroy your adversary and make you viceroys in the earth, that He may see how ye behave.		They said: We have been persecuted before you came to us and since you have come to us. He said: It may be that your Lord will destroy your enemy and make you rulers in the land, then He will see how you act.
7 130	We punished the people of Pharaoh with years (of droughts) and shortness of crops; that they might receive admonition.	And we straitened Pharaoh's folk with famine and dearth of fruits, that peradventure they might heed.		And certainly We overtook Firon's people with droughts and diminution of fruits that they may be mindful.
7 131	But when good (times) came, they said, "This is due to us;" When gripped by calamity, they ascribed it to evil omens connected with Moses and those with him! Behold! in truth the omens of evil are theirs in Allah's sight, but most of them do not understand!	But whenever good befell them, they said: This is ours; and whenever evil smote them they ascribed it to the evil auspices of Moses and those with him. Surely their evil auspice was only with Allah. But most of them knew not.		But when good befell them they said: This is due to us; and when evil afflicted them, they attributed it to the ill-luck of Musa and those with him; surely their evil fortune is only from Allah but most of them do not know.

7	132	They said (to Moses): "Whatever be the Signs thou bringest, to work therewith thy sorcery on us, we shall never believe in thee."	And they said: Whatever portent thou bringest wherewith to bewitch us, we shall not put faith in thee.	And they said: Whatever sign you may bring to us to charm us with it-- we will not believe in you.
7	133	So We sent (plagues) on them: Wholesale death, Locusts, Lice, Frogs, And Blood: Signs openly self-explained: but they were steeped in arrogance,- a people given to sin.	So We sent against them the flood and the locusts and the vermin and the frogs and the blood - a succession of clear signs. But they were arrogant and became a guilty folk.	Therefore We sent upon them widespread death, and the locusts and the lice and the frog and the blood, clear signs; but they behaved haughtily and they were a guilty people.
7	134	Every time the penalty fell on them, they said: "O Moses! on your behalf call on thy Lord in virtue of his promise to thee: If thou wilt remove the penalty from us, we shall truly believe in thee, and we shall send away the Children of Israel with thee."	And when the terror fell on them they cried: O Moses! Pray for us unto thy Lord, because He hath a covenant with thee. If thou removest the terror from us we verily will trust thee and will let the Children of Israel go with thee.	And when the plague fell upon them, they said: O Musa! pray for us to your Lord as He has promised with you, if you remove the plague from us, we will certainly believe in you and we will certainly send away with you the children of Israel.
7	135	But every time We removed the penalty from them according to a fixed term which they had to fulfil,- Behold! they broke their word!	But when We did remove from them the terror for a term which they must reach, behold! they broke their covenant.	But when We removed the plague from them till a term which they should attain lo! they broke (the promise).
7	136	So We exacted retribution from them: We drowned them in the sea, because they rejected Our Signs and failed to take warning from them.	Therefore We took retribution from them; therefore We drowned them in the sea: because they denied Our revelations and were heedless of them.	Therefore We inflicted retribution on them and drowned them in the sea because they rejected Our signs and were heedless of them.
7	137	And We made a people, considered weak (and of no account), inheritors of lands in both east and west, - lands whereon We sent down Our blessings. The fair promise of thy Lord was fulfilled for the Children of Israel, because they had patience and constancy, and We levelled to the ground the great works and fine buildings which Pharaoh and his people erected (with such pride).	And We caused the folk who were despised to inherit the eastern parts of the land and the western parts thereof which We had blessed. And the fair word of thy Lord was fulfilled for the Children of Israel because of their endurance; and We annihilated (all) that Pharaoh and his folk had done and that they had contrived.	And We made the people who were deemed weak to inherit the eastern lands and the western ones which We had blessed; and the good word of your Lord was fulfilled in the children of Israel because they bore up (sufferings) patiently; and We utterly destroyed what Firon and his people had wrought and what they built.
7	138	We took the Children of Israel (with safety) across the sea. They came upon a people devoted entirely to some idols they had. They said: O Moses! fashion for us a god like unto the gods they have. He said: Surely ye are a people without knowledge.	And We brought the Children of Israel across the sea, and they came unto a people who were given up to idols which they had. They said: O Moses! Make for us a god even as they have gods. He said: Lo! ye are a folk who know not.	And We made the children of Israel to pass the sea; then they came upon a people who kept to the worship of their idols They said: O Musa! make for us a god as they have (their) gods He said: Surely you are a people acting ignorantly:
7	139	"As to these folk,- the cult they are in is (but) a fragment of a ruin, and vain is the (worship) which they practise."	Lo! as for these, their way will be destroyed and all that they are doing is in vain.	(As to) these, surely that about which they are shall be brought to naught and that which they do is vain.
7	140	He said: "Shall I seek for you a god other than the (true) Allah, when it is Allah Who hath endowed you with gifts above the nations?"	He said: Shall I seek for you a god other than Allah when He hath favoured you above (all) creatures?	He said: What! shall I seek for you a god other than Allah while He has made you excel (all) created things?

7 141	And remember We rescued you from Pharaoh's people, who afflicted you with the worst of penalties, who slew your male children and saved alive your females: in that was a momentous trial from your Lord.	And (remember) when We did deliver you from Pharaoh's folk who were afflicting you with dreadful torment, slaughtering your sons and sparing your women. That was a tremendous trial from your Lord.	And when We delivered you from Firon's people who subjected you to severe torment, killing your sons and sparing your women, and in this there was a great trial from your Lord.
7 142	We appointed for Moses thirty nights, and completed (the period) with ten (more): thus was completed the term (of communion) with his Lord, forty nights. And Moses had charged his brother Aaron (before he went up): "Act for me amongst my people: Do right, and follow not the way of those who do mischief."	And when We did appoint for Moses thirty nights (of solitude), and added to them ten, and he completed the whole time appointed by his Lord of forty nights; and Moses said unto his brother, Aaron: Take my place among the people. Do right, and follow not the way of mischief-makers.	And We appointed with Musa a time of thirty nights and completed them with ten (more), so the appointed time of his Lord was complete forty nights, and Musa said to his brother Haroun: Take my place among my people, and act well and do not follow the way of the mischief-makers.
7 143	When Moses came to the place appointed by Us, and his Lord addressed him, He said: "O my Lord! show (Thyself) to me, that I may look upon thee." Allah said: "By no means canst thou see Me (direct); But look upon the mount; if it abide in its place, then shalt thou see Me." When his Lord manifested His glory on the Mount, He made it as dust. And Moses fell down in a swoon. When he recovered his senses he said: Glory be to Thee! to Thee I turn in repentance, and I am the first to believe."	And when Moses came to Our appointed tryst and his Lord had spoken unto him, he said: My Lord! Show me (Thy Self), that I may gaze upon Thee. He said: Thou wilt not see Me, but gaze upon the mountain! If it stand still in its place, then thou wilt see Me. And when his Lord revealed (His) glory to the mountain He sent it crashing down. And Moses fell down senseless. And when he woke he said: Glory unto Thee! I turn unto Thee repentant, and I am the first of (true) believers.	And when Musa came at Our appointed time and his Lord spoke to him, he said: My Lord! show me (Thyself), so that I may look upon Thee. He said: You cannot (bear to) see Me but look at the mountain, if it remains firm in its place, then will you see Me; but when his Lord manifested His glory to the mountain He made it crumble and Musa fell down in a swoon; then when he recovered, he said: Glory be to Thee, I turn to Thee, and I am the first of the believers.
7 144	(Allah) said: "O Moses! I have chosen thee above (other) men, by the mission I (have given thee) and the words I (have spoken to thee): take then the (revelation) which I give thee, and be of those who give thanks."	He said: O Moses! I have preferred thee above mankind by My messages and by My speaking (unto thee). So hold that which I have given thee, and be among the thankful.	He said: O Musa! surely I have chosen you above the people with My messages and with My words, therefore take hold of what I give to you and be of the grateful ones.
7 145	And We ordained laws for him in the tablets in all matters, both commanding and explaining all things, (and said): "Take and hold these with firmness, and enjoin thy people to hold fast by the best in the precepts: soon shall I show you the homes of the wicked,- (How they lie desolate)."	And We wrote for him, upon the tablets, the lesson to be drawn from all things and the explanation of all things, then (bade him): Hold it fast; and command thy people (saying): Take the better (course made clear) therein. I shall show thee the abode of evil-livers.	And We ordained for him in the tablets admonition of every kind and clear explanation of all things; so take hold of them with firmness and enjoin your people to take hold of what is best thereof; I will show you the abode of the transgressors.
7 146	Those who behave arrogantly on the earth in defiance of right - them will I turn away from My signs: Even if they see all the signs, they will not believe in them; and if they see the way of right conduct, they will not adopt it as the way; but if they see the way of error, that is the way they will adopt. For they have rejected our signs, and failed to take warning from them.	I shall turn away from My revelations those who magnify themselves wrongfully in the earth, and if they see each token believe it not, and if they see the way of righteousness choose it nor for (their) way, and if they see the way of error choose if for (their) way. That is because they deny Our revelations and are used to disregard them.	I will turn away from My communications those who are unjustly proud in the earth; and if they see every sign they will not believe in It; and if they see the way of rectitude they do not take It for a way, and if they see the way of error, they take it for a way; this is because they rejected Our communications and were heedless of them.

7 147	Those who reject Our signs and the meeting in the Hereafter,- vain are their deeds: Can they expect to be rewarded except as they have wrought?	Those who deny Our revelations and the meeting of the Hereafter, their works are fruitless. Are they requited aught save what they used to do?	And (as to) those who reject Our communications and the meeting of the hereafter, their deeds are null. Shall they be rewarded except for what they have done?
7 148	The people of Moses made, in his absence, out of their ornaments, the image of calf, (for worship): it seemed to low: did they not see that it could neither speak to them, nor show them the way? They took it for worship and they did wrong.	And the folk of Moses, after (he left them), chose a calf (for worship), (made) out of their ornaments, of saffron hue, which gave a lowing sound. Saw they not that it spake not unto them nor guided them to any way? They chose it, and became wrong-doers.	And Musa's people made of their ornaments a calf after him, a (mere) body, which gave a mooing sound. What! could they not see that it did not speak to them nor guide them in the way? They took it (for worship) and they were unjust.
7 149	When they repented, and saw that they had erred, they said: "If our Lord have not mercy upon us and forgive us, we shall indeed be of those who perish."	And when they feared the consequences thereof and saw that they had gone astray, they said: Unless our Lord have mercy on us and forgive us, we verily are of the lost.	And when they repented and saw that they had gone astray, they said: If our Lord show not mercy to us and forgive us we shall certainly be of the losers.
7 150	When Moses came back to his people, angry and grieved, he said: Evil it is that ye have done in my place in my absence: did ye make haste to bring on the judgment of your Lord?" He put down the tablets, seized his brother by (the hair of) his head, and dragged him to him. Aaron said: "Son of my mother! the people did indeed reckon me as naught, and went near to slaying me! Make not the enemies rejoice over my misfortune, nor count thou me amongst the people of sin."	And when Moses returned unto his people, angry and grieved, he said: Evil is that (course) which ye took after I had left you. Would ye hasten on the judgment of your Lord? And he cast down the tablets, and he seized his brother by the head, dragging him toward him. He said: Son of my mother! Lo! the folk did judge me weak and almost killed me. Oh, make not mine enemies to triumph over me and place me not among the evil-doers.	And when Musa returned to his people, wrathful (and) in violent grief, he said: Evil is it that you have done after me; did you turn away from the bidding of your Lord? And he threw down the tablets and seized his brother by the head, dragging him towards him. He said: Son of my mother! surely the people reckoned me weak and had well-nigh slain me, therefore make not the enemies to rejoice over me and count me not among the unjust people.
7 151	Moses prayed: "O my Lord! forgive me and my brother! admit us to Thy mercy! for Thou art the Most Merciful of those who show mercy!"	He said: My Lord! Have mercy on me and on my brother; bring us into Thy mercy, Thou the Most Merciful of all who show mercy.	He said: My Lord! forgive me and my brother and cause us to enter into Thy mercy, and Thou art the most Merciful of the merciful ones.
7 152	Those who took the calf (for worship) will indeed be overwhelmed with wrath from their Lord, and with shame in this life: thus do We recompense those who invent (falsehoods).	Lo! Those who chose the calf (for worship), terror from their Lord and humiliation will come upon them in the life of the world. Thus do We requite those who invent a lie.	(As for) those who took the calf (for a god), surely wrath from their Lord and disgrace in this world's life shall overtake them, and thus do We recompense the devisers of lies.
7 153	But those who do wrong but repent thereafter and (truly) believe,- verily thy Lord is thereafter Oft-Forgiving, Most Merciful.	But those who do ill-deeds and afterward repent and believe - lo! for them, afterward, Allah is Forgiving, Merciful.	And (as to) those who do evil deeds, then repent after that and believe, your Lord after that is most surely Forgiving, Merciful.
7 154	When the anger of Moses was appeased, he took up the tablets: in the writing thereon was guidance and Mercy for such as fear their Lord.	Then, when the anger of Moses abated, he took up the tablets, and in their inscription there was guidance and mercy for all those who fear their Lord.	And when Musa's anger calmed down he took up the tablets, and in the writing thereof was guidance and mercy for those who fear for the sake of their Lord.

7 155	And Moses chose seventy of his people for Our place of meeting: when they were seized with violent quaking, he prayed: "O my Lord! if it had been Thy will Thou couldst have destroyed, long before, both them and me: wouldst Thou destroy us for the deeds of the foolish ones among us? this is no more than Thy trial: by it Thou causest whom Thou wilt to stray, and Thou leadest whom Thou wilt into the right path. Thou art our Protector: so forgive us and give us Thy mercy; for Thou art the best of those who forgive."	And Moses chose of his people seventy men for Our appointed tryst and, when the trembling came on them, he said: My Lord! If Thou hadst willed Thou hadst destroyed them long before, and me with them. Wilt thou destroy us for that which the ignorant among us did? It is but Thy trial (of us). Thou sendest whom Thou wilt astray and guidest whom Thou wilt: Thou art our Protecting Friend, therefore forgive us and have mercy on us, Thou, the Best of all who show forgiveness.	And Musa chose out of his people seventy men for Our appointment; so when the earthquake overtook them, he said: My Lord! if Thou hadst pleased, Thou hadst destroyed them before and myself (too); wilt Thou destroy us for what the fools among us have done? It is naught but Thy trial, Thou makest err with it whom Thou pleasest and guidest whom Thou pleasest: Thou art our Guardian, therefore forgive us and have mercy on us, and Thou art the best of the forgivers.
7 156	"And ordain for us that which is good, in this life and in the Hereafter: for we have turned unto Thee." He said: "With My punishment I visit whom I will; but My mercy extendeth to all things. That (mercy) I shall ordain for those who do right, and practise regular charity, and those who believe in Our signs;-"	And ordain for us in this world that which is good, and in the Hereafter (that which is good), Lo! We have turned unto Thee. He said: I smite with My punishment whom I will, and My mercy embraceth all things, therefore I shall ordain it for those who ward off (evil) and pay the poor-due, and those who believe Our revelations;	And ordain for us good in this world's life and in the hereafter, for surely we turn to Thee. He said: (As for) My chastisement, I will afflict with it whom I please, and My mercy encompasses all things; so I will ordain it (specially) for those who guard (against evil) and pay the poor-rate, and those who believe in Our communications.
7 157	"Those who follow the messenger, the unlettered Prophet, whom they find mentioned in their own (scriptures),- in the law and the Gospel;- for he commands them what is just and forbids them what is evil; he allows them as lawful what is good (and pure) and prohibits them from what is bad (and impure); He releases them from their heavy burdens and from the yokes that are upon them. So it is those who believe in him, honour him, help him, and follow the light which is sent down with him,- it is they who will prosper."	Those who follow the messenger, the Prophet who can neither read nor write, whom they will find described in the Torah and the Gospel (which are) with them. He will enjoin on them that which is right and forbid them that which is wrong. He will make lawful for them all good things and prohibit for them only the foul; and he will relieve them of their burden and the fetters that they used to wear. Then those who believe in him, and honour him, and help him, and follow the light which is sent down with him: they are the successful.	Those who follow the Messenger-Prophet, the Ummi, whom they find written down with them in the Taurat and the Injeel (who) enjoins them good and forbids them evil, and makes lawful to them the good things and makes unlawful to them impure things, and removes from them their burden and the shackles which were upon them; so (as for) those who believe in him and honor him and help him, and follow the light which has been sent down with him, these it is that are the successful.
7 158	Say: "O men! I am sent unto you all, as the Messenger of Allah, to Whom belongeth the dominion of the heavens and the earth: there is no god but He: it is He That giveth both life and death. So believe in Allah and His Messenger, the Unlettered Prophet, who believeth in Allah and His words: follow him that (so) ye may be guided."	Say (O Muhammad): O mankind! Lo! I am the messenger of Allah to you all - (the messenger of) Him unto Whom belongeth the Sovereignty of the heavens and the earth. There is no God save Him. He quickeneth and He giveth death. So believe in Allah and His messenger, the Prophet who can neither read nor write, who believeth in Allah and in His Words, and follow him that haply ye may be led aright.	Say: O people! surely I am the Messenger of Allah to you all, of Him Whose is the kingdom of the heavens and the earth there is no god but He; He brings to life and causes to die therefore believe in Allah and His messenger, the Ummi Prophet who believes in Allah and His words, and follow him so that you may walk in the right way.
7 159	Of the people of Moses there is a section who guide and do justice in the light of truth.	And of Moses' folk there is a community who lead with truth and establish justice therewith.	And of Musa's people was a party who guided (people) with the truth, and thereby did they do justice.

7 160	We divided them into twelve tribes or nations. We directed Moses by inspiration, when his (thirsty) people asked him for water: "Strike the rock with thy staff": out of it there gushed forth twelve springs: Each group knew its own place for water. We gave them the shade of clouds, and sent down to them manna and quails, (saying): "Eat of the good things We have provided for you": (but they rebelled); to Us they did no harm, but they harmed their own souls.	We divided them into twelve tribes, nations; and We inspired Moses, when his people asked him for water, saying: Smite with thy staff the rock! And there gushed forth therefrom twelve springs, so that each tribe knew their drinking-place. And we caused the white cloud to overshadow them and sent down for them the manna and the quails (saying): Eat of the good things wherewith we have provided you. They wronged Us not, but they were wont to wrong themselves.	And We divided them into twelve tribes, as nations; and We revealed to Musa when his people asked him for water: Strike the rock with your staff, so outflowed from it twelve springs; each tribe knew its drinking place; and We made the clouds to give shade over them and We sent to them manna and quails: Eat of the good things We have given you. And they did not do Us any harm, but they did injustice to their own souls.
7 161	And remember it was said to them: "Dwell in this town and eat therein as ye wish, but say the word of humility and enter the gate in a posture of humility: We shall forgive you your faults; We shall increase (the portion of) those who do good."	And when it was said unto them: Dwell in this township and eat therefrom whence ye will, and say "Repentance," and enter the gate prostrate; We shall forgive you your sins; We shall increase (reward) for the right-doers.	And when it was said to them: Reside in this town and eat from it wherever you wish, and say, Put down from us our heavy burdens: and enter the gate making obeisance, We will forgive you your wrongs: We will give more to those who do good (to others).
7 162	But the transgressors among them changed the word from that which had been given them so we sent on them a plague from heaven. For that they repeatedly transgressed.	But those of them who did wrong changed the word which had been told them for another saying, and We sent down upon them wrath from heaven for their wrongdoing.	But those who were unjust among them changed it for a saying other than that which had been spoken to them; so We sent upon them a pestilence from heaven because they were unjust.
7 163	Ask them concerning the town standing close by the sea. Behold! they transgressed in the matter of the Sabbath. For on the day of their Sabbath their fish did come to them, openly holding up their heads, but on the day they had no Sabbath, they came not: thus did We make a trial of them, for they were given to transgression.	Ask them (O Muhammad) of the township that was by the sea, how they did break the Sabbath, how their big fish came unto them visibly upon their Sabbath day and on a day when they did not keep Sabbath came they not unto them. Thus did We try them for that they were evil-livers.	And ask them about the town which stood by the sea; when they exceeded the limits of the Sabbath, when their fish came to them on the day of their Sabbath, appearing on the surface of the water, and on the day on which they did not keep the Sabbath they did not come to them; thus did We try them because they transgressed.
7 164	When some of them said: "Why do ye preach to a people whom Allah will destroy or visit with a terrible punishment?"- said the preachers: "To discharge our duty to your Lord, and perchance they may fear Him."	And when a community among them said: Why preach ye to a folk whom Allah is about to destroy or punish with an awful doom, they said: In order to be free from guilt before your Lord, and that haply they may ward off (evil).	And when a party of them said: Why do you admonish a with a severe chastisement? They said: To be free from blame before your Lord, and that haply they may guard (against evil).
7 165	When they disregarded the warnings that had been given them, We rescued those who forbade Evil; but We visited the wrong-doers with a grievous punishment because they were given to transgression.	And when they forgot that whereof they had been reminded, We rescued those who forbade wrong, and visited those who did wrong with dreadful punishment because they were evil-livers.	So when they neglected what they had been reminded of, We delivered those who forbade evil and We overtook those who were unjust with an evil chastisement because they transgressed.
7 166	When in their insolence they transgressed (all) prohibitions, We said to them: "Be ye apes, despised and rejected."	So when they took pride in that which they had been forbidden, We said unto them: Be ye apes despised and loathed!	Therefore when they revoltingly persisted in what they had been forbidden, We said to them: Be (as) apes, despised and hated.

7	167	Behold! thy Lord did declare that He would send against them, to the Day of Judgment, those who would afflict them with grievous penalty. Thy Lord is quick in retribution, but He is also Oft-Forgiving, Most Merciful.	And (remember) when thy Lord proclaimed that He would raise against them till the Day of Resurrection those who would lay on them a cruel torment. Lo! verily thy Lord is swift in prosecution and lo! verily He is Forgiving, Merciful.	And when your Lord announced that He would certainly send against them to the day of resurrection those who would subject them to severe torment; most surely your Lord is quick to requite (evil) and most surely He is Forgiving, Merciful.
7	168	We broke them up into sections on this earth. There are among them some that are the righteous, and some that are the opposite. We have tried them with both prosperity and adversity: In order that they might turn (to us).	And We have sundered them in the earth as (separate) nations. Some of them are righteous, and some far from that. And We have tried them with good things and evil things that haply they might return.	And We cut them up on the earth into parties, (some) of them being righteous and (others) of them falling short of that, and We tried them with blessings and misfortunes that they might turn.
7	169	After them succeeded an (evil) generation: They inherited the Book, but they chose (for themselves) the vanities of this world, saying (for excuse): "(Everything) will be forgiven us." (Even so), if similar vanities came their way, they would (again) seize them. Was not the covenant of the Book taken from them, that they would not ascribe to Allah anything but the truth? and they study what is in the Book. But best for the righteous is the home in the Hereafter. Will ye not understand?	And a generation hath succeeded them who inherited the scriptures. They grasp the goods of this low life (as the price of evil-doing) and say: It will be forgiven us. And if there came to them (again) the offer of the like, they would accept it (and would sin again). Hath not the covenant of the Scripture been taken on their behalf that they should not speak aught concerning Allah save the truth? And they have studied that which is therein. And the abode of the Hereafter is better, for those who ward off (evil). Have ye then no sense?	Then there came after them an evil posterity who inherited the Book, taking only the frail good of this low life and saying: It will be forgiven us. And if the like good came to them, they would take it (too). Was not a promise taken from them in the Book that they would not speak anything about Allah but the truth, and they have read what is in it; and the abode of the hereafter is better for those who guard (against evil). Do you not then understand?
7	170	As to those who hold fast by the Book and establish regular prayer,- never shall We suffer the reward of the righteous to perish.	And as for those who make (men) keep the Scripture, and establish worship - lo! We squander not the wages of reformers.	And (as for) those who hold fast by the Book and keep up prayer, surely We do not waste the reward of the right doers.
7	171	When We shook the Mount over them, as if it had been a canopy, and they thought it was going to fall on them (We said): "Hold firmly to what We have given you, and bring (ever) to remembrance what is therein; perchance ye may fear Allah."	And when We shook the Mount above them as it were a covering, and they supposed that it was going to fall upon them (and We said): Hold fast that which We have given you, and remember that which is therein, that ye may ward off (evil).	And when We shook the mountain over them as if it were a covering overhead, and they thought that it was going to fall down upon them: Take hold of what We have given you with firmness, and be mindful of what is in it, so that you may guard (against evil).
7	172	When thy Lord drew forth from the Children of Adam - from their loins - their descendants, and made them testify concerning themselves, (saying): "Am I not your Lord (who cherishes and sustains you)?"- They said: "Yea! We do testify!" (This), lest ye should say on the Day of Judgment: "Of this we were never mindful":	And (remember) when thy Lord brought forth from the Children of Adam, from their reins, their seed, and made them testify of themselves, (saying): Am I not your Lord? They said: Yea, verily. We testify. (That was) lest ye should say at the Day of Resurrection: Lo! of this we were unaware;	And when your Lord brought forth from the children of Adam, from their backs, their descendants, and made them bear witness against their own souls: Am I not your Lord? They said: Yes! we bear witness. Lest you should say on the day of resurrection: Surely we were heedless of this.
7	173	Or lest ye should say: "Our fathers before us may have taken false gods, but we are (their) descendants after them: wilt Thou then destroy us because of the deeds of men who were futile?"	Or lest ye should say: (It is) only (that) our fathers ascribed partners to Allah of old and we were (their) seed after them. Wilt Thou destroy us on account of that which those who follow falsehood did?	Or you should say: Only our fathers associated others (with Allah) before, and we were an offspring after them: Wilt Thou then destroy us for what the vain doers did?

7 174	Thus do We explain the signs in detail; and perchance they may turn (unto Us).	Thus we detail the revelations, that haply they may return.	And thus do We make clear the communications, and that haply they might return.
7 175	Relate to them the story of the man to whom We sent Our signs, but he passed them by: so Satan followed him up, and he went astray.	Recite unto them the tale of him to whom We gave Our revelations, but he sloughed them off, so Satan overtook him and he became of those who lead astray.	And recite to them the narrative of him to whom We give Our communications, but he withdraws himself from them, so the Shaitan overtakes him, so he is of those who go astray.
7 176	If it had been Our will, We should have elevated him with Our signs; but he inclined to the earth, and followed his own vain desires. His similitude is that of a dog: if you attack him, he lolls out his tongue, or if you leave him alone, he (still) lolls out his tongue. That is the similitude of those who reject Our signs; So relate the story; perchance they may reflect.	And had We willed We could have raised him by their means, but he clung to the earth and followed his own lust. Therefor his likeness is as the likeness of a dog: if thou attackest him he panteth with his tongue out, and if thou leavest him he panteth with his tongue out. Such is the likeness of the people who deny Our revelations. Narrate unto them the history (of the men of old), that haply they may take thought.	And if We had pleased, We would certainly have exalted him thereby; but he clung to the earth and followed his low desire, so his parable is as the parable of the dog; if you attack him he lolls out his tongue; and if you leave him alone he lolls out his tongue; this is the parable of the people who reject Our communications; therefore relate the narrative that they may reflect.
7 177	Evil as an example are people who reject Our signs and wrong their own souls.	Evil as an example are the folk who denied Our revelations, and were wont to wrong themselves.	Evil is the likeness of the people who reject Our communications and are unjust to their own souls.
7 178	Whom Allah doth guide,- he is on the right path: whom He rejects from His guidance,- such are the persons who perish.	He whom Allah leadeth, he indeed is led aright, while he whom Allah sendeth astray - they indeed are losers.	Whomsoever Allah guides, he is the one who follows the right way; and whomsoever He causes to err, these are the losers.
7 179	Many are the jinns and men we have made for Hell: They have hearts wherewith they understand not, eyes wherewith they see not, and ears wherewith they hear not. They are like cattle,- nay more misguided: for they are heedless (of warning).	Already have We urged unto hell many of the jinn and humankind, having hearts wherewith they understand not, and having eyes wherewith they see not, and having ears wherewith they hear not. These are as the cattle - nay, but they are worse! These are the neglectful.	And certainly We have created for hell many of the jinn and the men; they have hearts with which they do not understand, and they have eyes with which they do not see, and they have ears with which they do not hear; they are as cattle, nay, they are in worse errors; these are the heedless ones.
7 180	The most beautiful names belong to Allah: so call on him by them; but shun such men as use profanity in his names: for what they do, they will soon be requited.	Allah's are the fairest names. Invoke Him by them. And leave the company of those who blaspheme His names. They will be requited what they do.	And Allah's are the best names, therefore call on Him thereby, and leave alone those who violate the sanctity of His names; they shall be recompensed for what they did.
7 181	Of those We have created are people who direct (others) with truth. And dispense justice therewith.	And of those whom We created there is a nation who guide with the Truth and establish justice therewith.	And of those whom We have created are a people who guide with the truth and thereby they do justice.
7 182	Those who reject Our signs, We shall gradually visit with punishment, in ways they perceive not;	And those who deny Our revelations - step by step We lead them on from whence they know not.	And (as to) those who reject Our communications, We draw them near (to destruction) by degrees from whence they know not.
7 183	Respite will I grant unto them: for My scheme is strong (and unfailing).	I give them rein (for) lo! My scheme is strong.	And I grant them respite; surely My scheme is effective.
7 184	Do they not reflect? Their companion is not seized with madness: he is but a perspicuous warner.	Have they not bethought them (that) there is no madness in their comrade? He is but a plain warner.	Do they not reflect that their companion has not unsoundness in mind; he is only a plain warner.

7 185	Do they see nothing in the government of the heavens and the earth and all that Allah hath created? (Do they not see) that it may well be that their term is nigh drawing to an end? In what message after this will they then believe?	Have they not considered the dominion of the heavens and the earth, and what things Allah hath created, and that it may be that their own term draweth nigh? In what fact after this will they believe?	Do they not consider the kingdom of the heavens and the earth and whatever things Allah has created, and that may be their doom shall have drawn nigh; what announcement would they then believe in after this?
7 186	To such as Allah rejects from His guidance, there can be no guide: He will leave them in their trespasses, wandering in distraction.	Those whom Allah sendeth astray, there is no guide for them. He leaveth them to wander blindly on in their contumacy.	Whomsoever Allah causes to err, there is no guide for him; and He leaves them alone in their inordinacy, blindly wandering on.
7 187	They ask thee about the (final) Hour - when will be its appointed time? Say: "The knowledge thereof is with my Lord (alone): None but He can reveal as to when it will occur. Heavy were its burden through the heavens and the earth. Only, all of a sudden will it come to you." They ask thee as if thou Wert eager in search thereof: Say: "The knowledge thereof is with Allah (alone), but most men know not."	They ask thee of the (destined) Hour, when will it come to port. Say: Knowledge thereof is with my Lord only. He alone will manifest it at its proper time. It is heavy in the heavens and the earth. It cometh not to you save unawares. They question thee as if thou couldst be well informed thereof. Say: Knowledge thereof is with Allah only, but most of mankind know not.	They ask you about the hour, when will be its taking place? Say: The knowledge of it is only with my Lord; none but He shall manifest it at its time; it will be momentous in the heavens and the earth; it will not come on you but of a sudden. They ask you as if you were solicitous about it. Say: Its knowledge is only with Allah, but most people do not know.
7 188	Say: "I have no power over any good or harm to myself except as Allah willeth. If I had knowledge of the unseen, I should have multiplied all good, and no evil should have touched me: I am but a warner, and a bringer of glad tidings to those who have faith."	Say: For myself I have no power to benefit, nor power to hurt, save that which Allah willeth. Had I knowledge of the Unseen, I should have abundance of wealth, and adversity would not touch me. I am but a warner, and a bearer of good tidings unto folk who believe.	Say: I do not control any benefit or harm for my own soul except as Allah please; and had I known the unseen I would have had much of good and no evil would have touched me; I am nothing but a warner and the giver of good news to a people who believe.
7 189	It is He Who created you from a single person, and made his mate of like nature, in order that he might dwell with her (in love). When they are united, she bears a light burden and carries it about (unnoticed). When she grows heavy, they both pray to Allah their Lord, (saying): "If Thou givest us a goodly child, we vow we shall (ever) be grateful."	He it is Who did create you from a single soul, and therefrom did make his mate that he might take rest in her. And when he covered her she bore a light burden, and she passed (unnoticed) with it, but when it became heavy they cried unto Allah, their Lord, saying: If thou givest unto us aright we shall be of the thankful.	He it is Who created you from a single being, and of the same (kind) did He make his mate, that he might incline to her; so when he covers her she bears a light burden, then moves about with it; but when it grows heavy, they both call upon Allah, their Lord: If Thou givest us a good one, we shall certainly be of the grateful ones.
7 190	But when He giveth them a goodly child, they ascribe to others a share in the gift they have received: but Allah is Exalted high above the partners they ascribe to Him.	But when He gave unto them aright, they ascribed unto Him partners in respect of that which He had given them. High is He Exalted above all that they associate (with Him).	But when He gives them a good one, they set up with Him associates in what He has given them; but high is Allah above what they associate (with Him).
7 191	Do they indeed ascribe to Him as partners things that can create nothing, but are themselves created?	Attribute they as partners to Allah those who created naught, but are themselves created,	What! they associate (with Him) that which does not create any thing, while they are themselves created!
7 192	No aid can they give them, nor can they aid themselves!	And cannot give them help, nor can they help themselves?	And they have no power to give them help, nor can they help themselves.

7	193	If ye call them to guidance, they will not obey: For you it is the same whether ye call them or ye hold your peace!	And if ye call them to the Guidance, they follow you not. Whether ye call them or are silent is all one for you.	And if you invite them to guidance, they will not follow you; it is the same to you whether you invite them or you are silent.
7	194	Verily those whom ye call upon besides Allah are servants like unto you: Call upon them, and let them listen to your prayer, if ye are (indeed) truthful!	Lo! those on whom ye call beside Allah are slaves like unto you. Call on them now, and let them answer you, if ye are truthful!	Surely those whom you call on besides Allah are in a state of subjugation like yourselves; therefore call on them, then let them answer you if you are truthful.
7	195	Have they feet to walk with? Or hands to lay hold with? Or eyes to see with? Or ears to hear with? Say: "Call your 'god-partners', scheme (your worst) against me, and give me no respite!"	Have they feet wherewith they walk, or have they hands wherewith they hold, or have they eyes wherewith they see, or have they ears wherewith they hear? Say: Call upon your (so-called) partners (of Allah), and then contrive against me, spare me not!	Have they feet with which they walk, or have they hands with which they hold, or have they eyes with which they see, or have they ears with which they hear? Say: Call your associates, then make a struggle (to prevail) against me and give me no respite.
7	196	"For my Protector is Allah, Who revealed the Book (from time to time), and He will choose and befriend the righteous."	Lo! my Protecting Friend is Allah Who revealeth the Scripture. He befriendeth the righteous.	Surely my guardian is Allah, Who revealed the Book, and He befriends the good.
7	197	"But those ye call upon besides Him, are unable to help you, and indeed to help themselves."	They on whom ye call beside Him have no power to help you, nor can they help themselves.	And those whom you call upon besides Him are not able to help you, nor can they help themselves.
7	198	If thou callest them to guidance, they hear not. Thou wilt see them looking at thee, but they see not.	And if ye (Muslims) call them to the guidance they hear not; and thou (Muhammad) seest them looking toward thee, but they see not.	And if you invite them to guidance, they do not hear; and you see them looking towards you, yet they do not see.
7	199	Hold to forgiveness; command what is right; But turn away from the ignorant.	Keep to forgiveness (O Muhammad), and enjoin kindness, and turn away from the ignorant.	Take to forgiveness and enjoin good and turn aside from the ignorant.
7	200	If a suggestion from Satan assail thy (mind), seek refuge with Allah; for He heareth and knoweth (all things).	And if a slander from the devil wound thee, then seek refuge in Allah. Lo! He is Hearer, Knower.	And if a false imputation from the Shaitan afflict you, seek refuge in Allah; surely He is Hearing, Knowing.
7	201	Those who fear Allah, when a thought of evil from Satan assaults them, bring Allah to remembrance, when lo! they see (aright)!	Lo! those who ward off (evil), when a glamour from the devil troubleth them, they do but remember (Allah's Guidance) and behold them seers!	Surely those who guard (against evil), when a visitation from the Shaitan afflicts them they become mindful, then lo! they see.
7	202	But their brethren (the evil ones) plunge them deeper into error, and never relax (their efforts).	Their brethren plunge them further into error and cease not.	And their brethren increase them in error, then they cease not.
7	203	If thou bring them not a revelation, they say: "Why hast thou not got it together?" Say: "I but follow what is revealed to me from my Lord: this is (nothing but) lights from your Lord, and Guidance, and mercy, for any who have faith."	And when thou bringest not a verse for them they say: Why hast thou not chosen it? Say: I follow only that which is inspired in me from my Lord. This (Qur'an) is insight from your Lord, and a guidance and a mercy for a people that believe.	And when you bring them not a revelation they say: Why do you not forge it? Say: I only follow what is revealed to me from my Lord; these are clear proofs from your Lord and a guidance and a mercy for a people who believe.
7	204	When the Qur'an is read, listen to it with attention, and hold your peace: that ye may receive Mercy.	And when the Qur'an is recited, give ear to it and pay heed, that ye may obtain mercy.	And when the Quran is recited, then listen to it and remain silent, that mercy may be shown to you.

7 205	And do thou (O reader!) Bring thy Lord to remembrance in thy (very) soul, with humility and in reverence, without loudness in words, in the mornings and evenings; and be not thou of those who are unheedful.	And do thou (O Muhammad) remember thy Lord within thyself humbly and with awe, below thy breath, at morn and evening. And be not thou of the neglectful.	And remember your Lord within yourself humbly and fearing and in a voice not loud in the morning and the evening and be not of the heedless ones.
7 206	Those who are near to thy Lord, disdain not to do Him worship: They celebrate His praises, and prostrate before Him.	Lo! those who are with thy Lord are not too proud to do Him service, but they praise Him and prostrate before Him.	Surely those who are with your Lord are not too proud to serve Him, and they declare His glory and prostrate in humility before Him.

Chapter 8:

AL-ANFAL (SPOILS OF WAR, BOOTY)

Total Verses: 75 Revealed At: MADINA

In the name of Allah, the Most Beneficent, the Most Merciful.

8 001	They ask thee concerning (things taken as) spoils of war. Say: (such) spoils are at the disposal of Allah and the Messenger: So fear Allah, and keep straight the relations between yourselves: Obey Allah and His Messenger, if ye do believe."	They ask thee (O Muhammad) of the spoils of war. Say: The spoils of war belong to Allah and the messenger, so keep your duty to Allah, and adjust the matter of your difference, and obey Allah and His messenger, if ye are (true) believers.	They ask you about the windfalls. Say: The windfalls are for Allah and the Messenger. So be careful of (your duty to) Allah and set aright matters of your difference, and obey Allah and His Messenger if you are believers.
8 002	For, Believers are those who, when Allah is mentioned, feel a tremor in their hearts, and when they hear His signs rehearsed, find their faith strengthened, and put (all) their trust in their Lord;	They only are the (true) believers whose hearts feel fear when Allah is mentioned, and when His revelations are recited unto them they increase their faith, and who trust in their Lord;	Those only are believers whose hearts become full of fear when Allah is mentioned, and when His communications are recited to them they increase them in faith, and in their Lord do they trust.
8 003	Who establish regular prayers and spend (freely) out of the gifts We have given them for sustenance:	Who establish worship and spend of that We have bestowed on them.	Those who keep up prayer and spend (benevolently) out of what We have given them.
8 004	Such in truth are the believers: they have grades of dignity with their Lord, and forgiveness, and generous sustenance:	Those are they who are in truth believers. For them are grades (of honour) with their Lord, and pardon, and a bountiful provision.	These are the believers in truth; they shall have from their Lord exalted grades and forgiveness and an honorable sustenance.
8 005	Just as thy Lord ordered thee out of thy house in truth, even though a party among the Believers disliked it,	Even as thy Lord caused thee (Muhammad) to go forth from thy home with the Truth, and lo! a party of the believers were averse (to it).	Even as your Lord caused you to go forth from your house with the truth, though a party of the believers were surely averse;
8 006	Disputing with thee concerning the truth after it was made manifest, as if they were being driven to death and they (actually) saw it.	Disputing with thee of the Truth after it had been made manifest, as if they were being driven to death visible.	They disputed with you about the truth after it had become clear, (and they went forth) as if they were being driven to death while they saw (it).

8 007	Behold! Allah promised you one of the two (enemy) parties, that it should be yours: Ye wished that the one unarmed should be yours, but Allah willed to justify the Truth according to His words and to cut off the roots of the Unbelievers;-	And when Allah promised you one of the two bands (of the enemy) that it should be yours, and ye longed that other than the armed one might be yours. And Allah willed that He should cause the Truth to triumph by His words, and cut the root of the disbelievers;	And when Allah promised you one of the two parties that it shall be yours and you loved that the one not armed should be yours and Allah desired to manifest the truth of what was true by His words and to cut off the root of the unbelievers.	
8 008	That He might justify Truth and prove Falsehood false, distasteful though it be to those in guilt.	That He might cause the Truth to triumph and bring vanity to naught, however much the guilty might oppose;	That He may manifest the truth of what was true and show the falsehood of what was false, though the guilty disliked.	
8 009	Remember ye implored the assistance of your Lord, and He answered you: "I will assist you with a thousand of the angels, ranks on ranks."	When ye sought help of your Lord and He answered you (saying): I will help you with a thousand of the angels, rank on rank.	When you sought aid from your Lord, so He answered you: I will assist you with a thousand of the angels following one another.	
8 010	Allah made it but a message of hope, and an assurance to your hearts: (in any case) there is no help except from Allah: and Allah is Exalted in Power, Wise.	Allah appointed it only as good tidings, and that your hearts thereby might be at rest. Victory cometh only by the help of Allah. Lo! Allah is Mighty, Wise.	And Allah only gave it as a good news and that your hearts might be at ease thereby; and victory is only from Allah; surely Allah is Mighty, Wise.	
8 011	Remember He covered you with a sort of drowsiness, to give you calm as from Himself, and he caused rain to descend on you from heaven, to clean you therewith, to remove from you the stain of Satan, to strengthen your hearts, and to plant your feet firmly therewith.	When He made the slumber fall upon you as a reassurance from him and sent down water from the sky upon you, that thereby He might purify you, and remove from you the fear of Satan, and make strong your hearts and firm (your) feet thereby.	When He caused calm to fall on you as a security from Him and sent down upon you water from the cloud that He might thereby purify you, and take away from you the uncleanness of the Shaitan, and that He might fortify your hearts and steady (your) footsteps thereby.	
8 012	Remember thy Lord inspired the angels (with the message): "I am with you: give firmness to the Believers: I will instil terror into the hearts of the Unbelievers: smite ye above their necks and smite all their finger-tips off them."	When thy Lord inspired the angels, (saying): I am with you. So make those who believe stand firm. I will throw fear into the hearts of those who disbelieve. Then smite the necks and smite of them each finger.	When your Lord revealed to the angels: I am with you, therefore make firm those who believe. I will cast terror into the hearts of those who disbelieve. Therefore strike off their heads and strike off every fingertip of them.	
8 013	This because they contended against Allah and His Messenger: If any contend against Allah and His Messenger, Allah is strict in punishment.	That is because they opposed Allah and His messenger. Whoso opposeth Allah and His messenger, (for him) lo! Allah is severe in punishment.	This is because they acted adversely to Allah and His Messenger; and whoever acts adversely to Allah and His Messenger-- then surely Allah is severe in requiting (evil).	
8 014	Thus (will it be said): "Taste ye then of the (punishment): for those who resist Allah, is the penalty of the Fire."	That (is the award), so taste it, and (know) that for disbelievers is the torment of the Fire.	This-- taste it, and (know) that for the unbelievers is the chastisement of fire.	
8 015	O ye who believe! when ye meet the Unbelievers in hostile array, never turn your backs to them.	O ye who believe! When ye meet those who disbelieve in battle, turn not your backs to them.	O you who believe! when you meet those who disbelieve marching for war, then turn not your backs to them.	
8 016	If any do turn his back to them on such a day - unless it be in a stratagem of war, or to retreat to a troop (of his own)- he draws on himself the wrath of Allah, and his abode is Hell,- an evil refuge (indeed)!	Whoso on that day turneth his back to them, unless maneuvering for battle or intent to join a company, he truly hath incurred wrath from Allah, and his habitation will be hell, a hapless journey's end.	And whoever shall turn his back to them on that day-- unless he turn aside for the sake of fighting or withdraws to a company-- then he, indeed, becomes deserving of Allah's wrath, and his abode is hell; and an evil destination shall it be.	

8 017	It is not ye who slew them; it was Allah: when thou threwest (a handful of dust), it was not thy act, but Allah'S: in order that He might test the Believers by a gracious trial from Himself: for Allah is He Who heareth and knoweth (all things).	Ye (Muslims) slew them not, but Allah slew them. And thou (Muhammad) threwest not when thou didst throw, but Allah threw, that He might test the believers by a fair test from Him. Lo! Allah is Hearer, Knower.	So you did not slay them, but it was Allah Who slew them, and you did not smite when you smote (the enemy), but it was Allah Who smote, and that He might confer upon the believers a good gift from Himself; surely Allah is Hearing, Knowing.
8 018	That, and also because Allah is He Who makes feeble the plans and stratagem of the Unbelievers.	That (is the case); and (know) that Allah (it is) Who maketh weak the plan of disbelievers.	This, and that Allah is the weakener of the struggle of the unbelievers.
8 019	(O Unbelievers!) if ye prayed for victory and judgment, now hath the judgment come to you: if ye desist (from wrong), it will be best for you: if ye return (to the attack), so shall We. Not the least good will your forces be to you even if they were multiplied: for verily Allah is with those who believe!	(O Qureysh!) If ye sought a judgment, now hath the judgment come unto you. And if ye cease (from persecuting the believers) it will be better for you, but if ye return (to the attack) We also shall return. And your host will avail you naught, however numerous it be, and (know) that Allah is with the believers (in His Guidance).	If you demanded a judgment, the judgment has then indeed come to you; and if you desist, it will be better for you; and if you turn back (to fight), We (too) shall turn back, and your forces shall avail you nothing, though they may be many, and (know) that Allah is with the believers.
8 020	O ye who believe! Obey Allah and His Messenger, and turn not away from him when ye hear (him speak).	O ye who believe! Obey Allah and His messenger, and turn not away from him when ye hear (him speak).	O you who believe! obey Allah and His Messenger and do not turn back from Him while you hear.
8 021	Nor be like those who say, "We hear," but listen not:	Be not as those who say, we hear, and they hear not.	And be not like those who said, We hear, and they did not obey.
8 022	For the worst of beasts in the sight of Allah are the deaf and the dumb,- those who understand not.	Lo! the worst of beasts in Allah's sight are the deaf, the dumb, who have no sense.	Surely the vilest of animals, in Allah's sight, are the deaf, the dumb, who do not understand.
8 023	If Allah had found in them any good. He would indeed have made them listen: (As it is), if He had made them listen, they would but have turned back and declined (Faith).	Had Allah known of any good in them He would have made them hear, but had He made them hear they would have turned away, averse.	And if Allah had known any good in them He would have made them hear, and if He makes them hear they would turn back while they withdraw.
8 024	O ye who believe! give your response to Allah and His Messenger, when He calleth you to that which will give you life; and know that Allah cometh in between a man and his heart, and that it is He to Whom ye shall (all) be gathered.	O ye who believe! Obey Allah, and the messenger when He calleth you to that which quickeneth you, and know that Allah cometh in between the man and his own heart, and that He it is unto Whom ye will be gathered.	O you who believe! answer (the call of) Allah and His Messenger when he calls you to that which gives you life; and know that Allah intervenes between man and his heart, and that to Him you shall be gathered.
8 025	And fear tumult or oppression, which affecteth not in particular (only) those of you who do wrong: and know that Allah is strict in punishment.	And guard yourselves against a chastisement which cannot fall exclusively on those of you who are wrong-doers, and know that Allah is severe in punishment.	And fear an affliction which may not smite those of you in particular who are unjust; and know that Allah is severe in requiting (evil).
8 026	Call to mind when ye were a small (band), despised through the land, and afraid that men might despoil and kidnap you; But He provided a safe asylum for you, strengthened you with His aid, and gave you Good things for sustenance: that ye might be grateful.	And remember, when ye were few and reckoned feeble in the land, and were in fear lest men should extirpate you, how He gave you refuge, and strengthened you with His help, and made provision of good things for you, that haply ye might be thankful.	And remember when you were few, deemed weak in the land, fearing lest people might carry you off by force, but He sheltered you and strengthened you with His aid and gave you of the good things that you may give thanks.

8 027	O ye that believe! betray not the trust of Allah and the Messenger, nor misappropriate knowingly things entrusted to you.	O ye who believe! Betray not Allah and His messenger, nor knowingly betray your trusts.		O you who believe! be not unfaithful to Allah and the Messenger, nor be unfaithful to your trusts while you know.
8 028	And know ye that your possessions and your progeny are but a trial; and that it is Allah with Whom lies your highest reward.	And know that your possessions and your children are a test, and that with Allah is immense reward.		And know that your property and your children are a temptation, and that Allah is He with Whom there is a mighty reward.
8 029	O ye who believe! if ye fear Allah, He will grant you a criterion (to judge between right and wrong), remove from you (all) evil (that may afflict) you, and forgive you: for Allah is the Lord of grace unbounded.	O ye who believe! If ye keep your duty to Allah, He will give you discrimination (between right and wrong) and will rid you of your evil thoughts and deeds, and will forgive you. Allah is of Infinite Bounty.		O you who believe! If you are careful of (your duty to) Allah, He will grant you a distinction and do away with your evils and forgive you; and Allah is the Lord of mighty grace.
8 030	Remember how the Unbelievers plotted against thee, to keep thee in bonds, or slay thee, or get thee out (of thy home). They plot and plan, and Allah too plans; but the best of planners is Allah.	And when those who disbelieve plot against thee (O Muhammad) to wound thee fatally, or to kill thee or to drive thee forth; they plot, but Allah (also) plotteth; and Allah is the best of plotters.		And when those who disbelieved devised plans against you that they might confine you or slay you or drive you away; and they devised plans and Allah too had arranged a plan; and Allah is the best of planners.
8 031	When Our Signs are rehearsed to them, they say: "We have heard this (before): if we wished, we could say (words) like these: these are nothing but tales of the ancients."	And when Our revelations are recited unto them they say: We have heard. If we wish we can speak the like of this. Lo! this is naught but fables of the men of old.		And when Our communications are recited to them, they say: We have heard indeed; if we pleased we could say the like of it; this is nothing but the stories of the ancients.
8 032	Remember how they said: "O Allah if this is indeed the Truth from Thee, rain down on us a shower of stones form the sky, or send us a grievous penalty."	And when they said: O Allah! If this be indeed the truth from Thee, then rain down stones on us or bring on us some painful doom!		And when they said: O Allah! if this is the truth from Thee, then rain upon us stones from heaven or inflict on us a painful punishment.
8 033	But Allah was not going to send them a penalty whilst thou wast amongst them; nor was He going to send it whilst they could ask for pardon.	But Allah would not punish them while thou wast with them, nor will He punish them while they seek forgiveness.		But Allah was not going to chastise them while you were among them, nor is Allah going to chastise them while yet they ask for forgiveness.
8 034	But what plea have they that Allah should not punish them, when they keep out (men) from the sacred Mosque - and they are not its guardians? No men can be its guardians except the righteous; but most of them do not understand.	What (plea) have they that Allah should not punish them, when they debar (His servants) from the Inviolable Place of Worship, though they are not its fitting guardians. Its fitting guardians are those only who keep their duty to Allah. But most of them know not.		And what (excuse) have they that Allah should not chastise them while they hinder (men) from the Sacred Mosque and they are not (fit to be) guardians of it; its guardians are only those who guard (against evil), but most of them do not know.
8 035	Their prayer at the House (of Allah) is nothing but whistling and clapping of hands: (Its only answer can be), "Taste ye the penalty because ye blasphemed."	And their worship at the (holy) House is naught but whistling and hand-clapping. Therefore (it is said unto them): Taste of the doom because ye disbelieve.		And their prayer before the House is nothing but whistling and clapping of hands; taste then the chastisement, for you disbelieved.
8 036	The Unbelievers spend their wealth to hinder (man) from the path of Allah, and so will they continue to spend; but in the end they will have (only) regrets and sighs; at length they will be overcome: and the Unbelievers will be gathered together to Hell;-	Lo! those who disbelieve spend their wealth in order that they may debar (men) from the way of Allah. They will spend it, then it will become an anguish for them, then they will be conquered. And those who disbelieve will be gathered unto hell,		Surely those who disbelieve spend their wealth to hinder (people) from the way of Allah; so they shall spend it, then it shall be to them an intense regret, then they shall be overcome; and those who disbelieve shall be driven together to hell.

8 037	In order that Allah may separate the impure from the pure, put the impure, one on another, heap them together, and cast them into Hell. They will be the ones to have lost.	That Allah may separate the wicked from the good, The wicked will He place piece upon piece, and heap them all together, and consign them unto hell. Such verily are the losers.	That Allah might separate the impure from the good, and put the impure, some of it upon the other, and pile it up together, then cast it into hell; these it is that are the losers.
8 038	Say to the Unbelievers, if (now) they desist (from Unbelief), their past would be forgiven them; but if they persist, the punishment of those before them is already (a matter of warning for them).	Tell those who disbelieve that if they cease (from persecution of believers) that which is past will be forgiven them; but if they return (thereto) then the example of the men of old hath already gone (before them, for a warning).	Say to those who disbelieve, if they desist, that which is past shall be forgiven to them; and if they return, then what happened to the ancients has already passed.
8 039	And fight them on until there is no more tumult or oppression, and there prevail justice and faith in Allah altogether and everywhere; but if they cease, verily Allah doth see all that they do.	And fight them until persecution is no more, and religion is all for Allah. But if they cease, then lo! Allah is Seer of what they do.	And fight with them until there is no more persecution and religion should be only for Allah; but if they desist, then surely Allah sees what they do.
8 040	If they refuse, be sure that Allah is your Protector - the best to protect and the best to help.	And if they turn away, then know that Allah is your Befriender - a Transcendent Patron, a Transcendent Helper!	And if they turn back, then know that Allah is your Patron; most excellent is the Patron and most excellent the Helper.
8 041	And know that out of all the booty that ye may acquire (in war), a fifth share is assigned to Allah,- and to the Messenger, and to near relatives, orphans, the needy, and the wayfarer,- if ye do believe in Allah and in the revelation We sent down to Our servant on the Day of Testing,- the Day of the meeting of the two forces. For Allah hath power over all things.	And know that whatever ye take as spoils of war, lo! a fifth thereof is for Allah, and for the messenger and for the kinsman (who hath need) and orphans and the needy and the wayfarer, if ye believe in Allah and that which We revealed unto Our slave on the Day of Discrimination, the day when the two armies met. And Allah is Able to do all things.	And know that whatever thing you gain, a fifth of it is for Allah and for the Messenger and for the near of kin and the orphans and the needy and the wayfarer, if you believe in Allah and in that which We revealed to Our servant, on the day of distinction, the day on which the two parties met; and Allah has power over all things.
8 042	Remember ye were on the hither side of the valley, and they on the farther side, and the caravan on lower ground than ye. Even if ye had made a mutual appointment to meet, ye would certainly have failed in the appointment: But (thus ye met), that Allah might accomplish a matter already enacted; that those who died might die after a clear Sign (had been given), and those who lived might live after a Clear Sign (had been given). And verily Allah is He Who heareth and knoweth (all things).	When ye were on the near bank (of the valley) and they were on the yonder bank, and the caravan was below you (on the coast plain). And had ye trysted to meet one another ye surely would have failed to keep the tryst, but (it happened, as it did, without the forethought of either of you) that Allah might conclude a thing that must be done; that he who perished (on that day) might perish by a clear proof (of His Sovereignty) and he who survived might survive by a clear proof (of His Sovereignty). Lo! Allah in truth is Hearer, Knower.	When you were on the nearer side (of the valley) and they were on the farthest side, while the caravan was in a lower place than you; and if you had mutually made an appointment, you would certainly have broken away from the appointment, but-- in order that Allah might bring about a matter which was to be done, that he who would perish might perish by clear proof, and he who would live might live by clear proof; and most surely Allah is Hearing, Knowing;
8 043	Remember in thy dream Allah showed them to thee as few: if He had shown them to thee as many, ye would surely have been discouraged, and ye would surely have disputed in (your) decision; but Allah saved (you): for He knoweth well the (secrets) of (all) hearts.	When Allah showed them unto thee (O Muhammad) in thy dream as few in number, and if He had shown them to thee as many, ye (Muslims) would have faltered and would have quarreled over the affair. But Allah saved (you). Lo! He knoweth what is in the breasts (of men).	When Allah showed them to you in your dream as few; and if He had shown them to you as many you would certainly have become weak-hearted and you would have disputed about the matter, but Allah saved (you); surely He is the Knower of what is in the breasts.

8 044	And remember when ye met, He showed them to you as few in your eyes, and He made you appear as contemptible in their eyes: that Allah might accomplish a matter already enacted. For to Allah do all questions go back (for decision).	And when He made you (Muslims), when ye met (them), see them with your eyes as few, and lessened you in their eyes, (it was) that Allah might conclude a thing that must be done. Unto Allah all things are brought back.	And when He showed them to you, when you met, as few in your eyes and He made you to appear little in their eyes, in order that Allah might bring about a matter which was to be done, and to Allah are all affairs returned.
8 045	O ye who believe! When ye meet a force, be firm, and call Allah in remembrance much (and often); that ye may prosper:	O ye who believe! When ye meet an army, hold firm and think of Allah much, that ye may be successful.	O you who believe! when you meet a party, then be firm, and remember Allah much, that you may be successful.
8 046	And obey Allah and His Messenger; and fall into no disputes, lest ye lose heart and your power depart; and be patient and persevering: For Allah is with those who patiently persevere:	And obey Allah and His messenger, and dispute not one with another lest ye falter and your strength depart from you; but be steadfast! Lo! Allah is with the steadfast.	And obey Allah and His Messenger and do not quarrel for then you will be weak in hearts and your power will depart, and be patient; surely Allah is with the patient.
8 047	And be not like those who started from their homes insolently and to be seen of men, and to hinder (men) from the path of Allah: For Allah compasseth round about all that they do.	Be not as those who came forth from their dwellings boastfully and to be seen of men, and debar (men) from the way of Allah, while Allah is surrounding all they do.	And be not like those who came forth from their homes in great exultation and to be seen of men, and (who) turn away from the way of Allah, and Allah comprehends what they do.
8 048	Remember Satan made their (sinful) acts seem alluring to them, and said: "No one among men can overcome you this day, while I am near to you": But when the two forces came in sight of each other, he turned on his heels, and said: "Lo! I am clear of you; lo! I see what ye see not; Lo! I fear Allah: for Allah is strict in punishment."	And when Satan made their deeds seem fair to them and said: No one of mankind can conquer you this day, for I am your protector. But when the armies came in sight of one another, he took flight, saying: Lo! I am guiltless of you. Lo! I see that which ye see not. Lo! I fear Allah. And Allah is severe in punishment.	And when the Shaitan made their works fair seeming to them, and said: No one can overcome you this day, and surely I am your protector: but when the two parties came in sight of each other he turned upon his heels, and said: Surely I am clear of you, surely I see what you do not see, surely I fear Allah; and Allah is severe in requiting (evil).
8 049	Lo! the hypocrites say, and those in whose hearts is a disease: These people,- their religion has misled them. But if any trust in Allah, behold! Allah is Exalted in might, Wise.	When the hypocrites and those in whose hearts is a disease said: Their religion hath deluded these. Whoso putteth his trust in Allah (will find that) lo! Allah is Mighty, Wise.	When the hypocrites and those in whose hearts was disease said: Their religion has deceived them; and whoever trusts in Allah, then surely Allah is Mighty, Wise.
8 050	If thou couldst see, when the angels take the souls of the Unbelievers (at death), (How) they smite their faces and their backs, (saying): "Taste the penalty of the blazing Fire-"	If thou couldst see how the angels receive those who disbelieve, smiting faces and their backs and (saying): Taste the punishment of burning!	And had you seen when the angels will cause to die those who disbelieve, smiting their faces and their backs, and (saying): Taste the punishment of burning.
8 051	"Because of (the deeds) which your (own) hands sent forth; for Allah is never unjust to His servants:"	This is for that which your own hands have sent before (to the Judgment), and (know) that Allah is not a tyrant to His slaves.	This is for what your own hands have sent on before, and because Allah is not in the least unjust to the servants;
8 052	"(Deeds) after the manner of the people of Pharaoh and of those before them: They rejected the Signs of Allah, and Allah punished them for their crimes: for Allah is Strong, and Strict in punishment:"	(Their way is) as the way of Pharaoh's folk and those before them; they disbelieved the revelations of Allah, and Allah took them in their sins. Lo! Allah is Strong, severe in punishment.	In the manner of the people of Firon and those before them; they disbelieved in Allah's communications, therefore Allah destroyed them on account of their faults; surely Allah is strong, severe in requiting (evil).

8 053	"Because Allah will never change the grace which He hath bestowed on a people until they change what is in their (own) souls: and verily Allah is He Who heareth and knoweth (all things)."	That is because Allah never changeth the grace He hath bestowed on any people until they first change that which is in their hearts, and (that is) because Allah is Hearer, Knower.	This is because Allah has never changed a favor which He has conferred upon a people until they change their own condition; and because Allah is Hearing, Knowing;
8 054	"(Deeds) after the manner of the people of Pharaoh and those before them": They treated as false the Signs of their Lord: so We destroyed them for their crimes, and We drowned the people of Pharaoh: for they were all oppressors and wrong-doers.	(Their way is) as the way of Pharaoh's folk and those before them; they denied the revelations of their Lord, so We destroyed them in their sins. And We drowned the folk of Pharaoh. All were evil-doers.	In the manner of the people of Firon and those before them; they rejected the communications of their Lord, therefore We destroyed them on account of their faults and We drowned Firon's people, and they were all unjust.
8 055	For the worst of beasts in the sight of Allah are those who reject Him: They will not believe.	Lo! the worst of beasts in Allah's sight are the ungrateful who will not believe.	Surely the vilest of animals in Allah's sight are those who disbelieve, then they would not believe.
8 056	They are those with whom thou didst make a covenant, but they break their covenant every time, and they have not the fear (of Allah).	Those of them with whom thou madest a treaty, and then at every opportunity they break their treaty, and they keep not duty (to Allah).	Those with whom you make an agreement, then they break their agreement every time and they do not guard (against punishment).
8 057	If ye gain the mastery over them in war, disperse, with them, those who follow them, that they may remember.	If thou comest on them in the war, deal with them so as to strike fear in those who are behind them, that haply they may remember.	Therefore if you overtake them in fighting, then scatter by (making an example of) them those who are in their rear, that they may be mindful.
8 058	If thou fearest treachery from any group, throw back (their covenant) to them, (so as to be) on equal terms: for Allah loveth not the treacherous.	And if thou fearest treachery from any folk, then throw back to them (their treaty) fairly. Lo! Allah loveth not the treacherous.	And if you fear treachery on the part of a people, then throw back to them on terms of equality; surely Allah does not love the treacherous.
8 059	Let not the unbelievers think that they can get the better (of the godly): they will never frustrate (them).	And let not those who disbelieve suppose that they can outstrip (Allah's Purpose). Lo! they cannot escape.	And let not those who disbelieve think that they shall come in first; surely they will not escape.
8 060	Against them make ready your strength to the utmost of your power, including steeds of war, to strike terror into (the hearts of) the enemies, of Allah and your enemies, and others besides, whom ye may not know, but whom Allah doth know. Whatever ye shall spend in the cause of Allah, shall be repaid unto you, and ye shall not be treated unjustly.	Make ready for them all thou canst of (armed) force and of horses tethered, that thereby ye may dismay the enemy of Allah and your enemy, and others beside them whom ye know not. Allah knoweth them. Whatsoever ye spend in the way of Allah it will be repaid to you in full, and ye will not be wronged.	And prepare against them what force you can and horses tied at the frontier, to frighten thereby the enemy of Allah and your enemy and others besides them, whom you do not know (but) Allah knows them; and whatever thing you will spend in Allah's way, it will be paid back to you fully and you shall not be dealt with unjustly.
8 061	But if the enemy incline towards peace, do thou (also) incline towards peace, and trust in Allah: for He is One that heareth and knoweth (all things).	And if they incline to peace, incline thou also to it, and trust in Allah. Lo! He, even He, is the Hearer, the Knower.	And if they incline to peace, then incline to it and trust in Allah; surely He is the Hearing, the Knowing.
8 062	Should they intend to deceive thee,- verily Allah sufficeth thee: He it is That hath strengthened thee with His aid and with (the company of) the Believers;	And if they would deceive thee, then lo! Allah is Sufficient for thee. He it is Who supporteth thee with His help and with the believers,	And if they intend to deceive you-- then surely Allah is sufficient for you; He it is Who strengthened you with His help and with the believers,

8 063	And (moreover) He hath put affection between their hearts: not if thou hadst spent all that is in the earth, couldst thou have produced that affection, but Allah hath done it: for He is Exalted in might, Wise.	And (as for the believers) hath attuned their hearts. If thou hadst spent all that is in the earth thou couldst not have attuned their hearts, but Allah hath attuned them. Lo! He is Mighty, Wise.	And united their hearts; had you spent all that is in the earth, you could not have united their hearts, but Allah united them; surely He is Mighty, Wise.
8 064	O Prophet! sufficient unto thee is Allah,- (unto thee) and unto those who follow thee among the Believers.	O Prophet! Allah is Sufficient for thee and those who follow thee of the believers.	O Prophet! Allah is sufficient for you and (for) such of the believers as follow you.
8 065	O Prophet! rouse the Believers to the fight. If there are twenty amongst you, patient and persevering, they will vanquish two hundred: if a hundred, they will vanquish a thousand of the Unbelievers: for these are a people without understanding.	O Prophet! Exhort the believers to fight. If there be of you twenty steadfast they shall overcome two hundred, and if there be of you a hundred (steadfast) they shall overcome a thousand of those who disbelieve, because they (the disbelievers) are a folk without intelligence.	O Prophet! urge the believers to war; if there are twenty patient ones of you they shall overcome two hundred, and if there are a hundred of you they shall overcome a thousand of those who disbelieve, because they are a people who do not understand.
8 066	For the present, Allah hath lightened your (task), for He knoweth that there is a weak spot in you: But (even so), if there are a hundred of you, patient and persevering, they will vanquish two hundred, and if a thousand, they will vanquish two thousand, with the leave of Allah: for Allah is with those who patiently persevere.	Now hath Allah lightened your burden, for He knoweth that there is weakness in you. So if there be of you a steadfast hundred they shall overcome two hundred, and if there be of you a thousand (steadfast) they shall overcome two thousand by permission of Allah. Allah is with the steadfast.	For the present Allah has made light your burden, and He knows that there is weakness in you; so if there are a hundred patient ones of you they shall overcome two hundred, and if there are a thousand they shall overcome two thousand by Allah's permission, and Allah is with the patient.
8 067	It is not fitting for a prophet that he should have prisoners of war until he hath thoroughly subdued the land. Ye look for the temporal goods of this world; but Allah looketh to the Hereafter: And Allah is Exalted in might, Wise.	It is not for any prophet to have captives until he hath made slaughter in the land. Ye desire the lure of this world and Allah desireth (for you) the Hereafter, and Allah is Mighty, Wise.	It is not fit for a prophet that he should take captives unless he has fought and triumphed in the land; you desire the frail goods of this world, while Allah desires (for you) the hereafter; and Allah is Mighty, Wise.
8 068	Had it not been for a previous ordainment from Allah, a severe penalty would have reached you for the (ransom) that ye took.	Had it not been for an ordinance of Allah which had gone before, an awful doom had come upon you on account of what ye took.	Were it not for an ordinance from Allah that had already gone forth, surely there would have befallen you a great chastisement for what you had taken to.
8 069	But (now) enjoy what ye took in war, lawful and good: but fear Allah: for Allah is Oft-Forgiving, Most Merciful.	Now enjoy what ye have won, as lawful and good, and keep your duty to Allah. Lo! Allah is Forgiving, Merciful.	Eat then of the lawful and good (things) which you have acquired in war, and be careful of (your duty to) Allah; surely Allah is Forgiving, Merciful.
8 070	O Prophet! say to those who are captives in your hands: "If Allah findeth any good in your hearts, He will give you something better than what has been taken from you, and He will forgive you: for Allah is Oft-Forgiving, Most Merciful."	O Prophet! Say unto those captives who are in your hands: If Allah knoweth any good in your hearts He will give you better than that which hath been taken from you, and will forgive you. Lo! Allah is Forgiving, Merciful.	O Prophet! say to those of the captives who are in your hands: If Allah knows anything good in your hearts, He will give to you better than that which has been taken away from you and will forgive you, and Allah is Forgiving, Merciful.

8 071	But if they have treacherous designs against thee, (O Messenger!), they have already been in treason against Allah, and so hath He given (thee) power over them. And Allah so He Who hath (full) knowledge and wisdom.	And if they would betray thee, they betrayed Allah before, and He gave (thee) power over them. Allah is Knower, Wise.	And if they intend to act unfaithfully towards you, so indeed they acted unfaithfully towards Allah before, but He gave (you) mastery over them; and Allah is Knowing, Wise.
8 072	Those who believed, and adopted exile, and fought for the Faith, with their property and their persons, in the cause of Allah, as well as those who gave (them) asylum and aid,- these are (all) friends and protectors, one of another. As to those who believed but came not into exile, ye owe no duty of protection to them until they come into exile; but if they seek your aid in religion, it is your duty to help them, except against a people with whom ye have a treaty of mutual alliance. And (remember) Allah seeth all that ye do.	Lo! those who believed and left their homes and strove with their wealth and their lives for the cause of Allah, and those who took them in and helped them: these are protecting friends one of another. And those who believed but did not leave their homes, ye have no duty to protect them till they leave their homes; but if they seek help from you in the matter of religion then it is your duty to help (them) except against a folk between whom and you there is a treaty. Allah is Seer of what ye do.	Surely those who believed and fled (their homes) and struggled hard in Allah's way with their property and their souls, and those who gave shelter and helped-- these are guardians of each other; and (as for) those who believed and did not fly, not yours is their guardianship until they fly; and if they seek aid from you in the matter of religion, aid is incumbent on you except against a people between whom and you there is a treaty, and Allah sees what you do.
8 073	The Unbelievers are protectors, one of another: Unless ye do this, (protect each other), there would be tumult and oppression on earth, and great mischief.	And those who disbelieve are protectors one of another - If ye do not so, there will be confusion in the land, and great corruption.	And (as for) those who disbelieve, some of them are the guardians of others; if you will not do it, there will be in the land persecution and great mischief.
8 074	Those who believe, and adopt exile, and fight for the Faith, in the cause of Allah as well as those who give (them) asylum and aid,- these are (all) in very truth the Believers: for them is the forgiveness of sins and a provision most generous.	Those who believed and left their homes and strove for the cause of Allah, and those who took them in and helped them - these are the believers in truth. For them is pardon, and bountiful provision.	And (as for) those who believed and fled and struggled hard in Allah's way, and those who gave shelter and helped, these are the believers truly; they shall have forgiveness and honorable provision.
8 075	And those who accept Faith subsequently, and adopt exile, and fight for the Faith in your company,- they are of you. But kindred by blood have prior rights against each other in the Book of Allah. Verily Allah is well-acquainted with all things.	And those who afterwards believed and left their homes and strove along with you, they are of you; and those who are akin are nearer one to another in the ordinance of Allah. Lo! Allah is Knower of all things.	And (as for) those who believed afterwards and fled and struggled hard along with you, they are of you; and the possessors of relationships are nearer to each other in the ordinance of Allah; surely Allah knows all things.

Chapter 9:

AL-TAWBA (REPENTANCE, DISPENSATION)

Total Verses: 129 Revealed At: MADINA

9 001	A (declaration) of immunity from Allah and His Messenger, to those of the Pagans with whom ye have contracted mutual alliances:-	Freedom from obligation (is proclaimed) from Allah and His messenger toward those of the idolaters with whom ye made a treaty.	(This is a declaration of) immunity by Allah and His Messenger towards those of the idolaters with whom you made an agreement.

9 002	Go ye, then, for four months, backwards and forwards, (as ye will), throughout the land, but know ye that ye cannot frustrate Allah (by your falsehood) but that Allah will cover with shame those who reject Him.	Travel freely in the land four months, and know that ye cannot escape Allah and that Allah will confound the disbelievers (in His Guidance).	So go about in the land for four months and know that you cannot weaken Allah and that Allah will bring disgrace to the unbelievers.
9 003	And an announcement from Allah and His Messenger, to the people (assembled) on the day of the Great Pilgrimage,- that Allah and His Messenger dissolve (treaty) obligations with the Pagans. If then, ye repent, it were best for you; but if ye turn away, know ye that ye cannot frustrate Allah. And proclaim a grievous penalty to those who reject Faith.	And a proclamation from Allah and His messenger to all men on the day of the Greater Pilgrimage that Allah is free from obligation to the idolaters, and (so is) His messenger. So, if ye repent, it will be better for you; but if ye are averse, then know that ye cannot escape Allah. Give tidings (O Muhammad) of a painful doom to those who disbelieve,	And an announcement from Allah and His Messenger to the people on the day of the greater pilgrimage that Allah and His Messenger are free from liability to the idolaters; therefore if you repent, it will be better for you, and if you turn back, then know that you will not weaken Allah; and announce painful punishment to those who disbelieve.
9 004	(But the treaties are) not dissolved with those Pagans with whom ye have entered into alliance and who have not subsequently failed you in aught, nor aided any one against you. So fulfil your engagements with them to the end of their term: for Allah loveth the righteous.	Excepting those of the idolaters with whom ye (Muslims) have a treaty, and who have since abated nothing of your right nor have supported anyone against you. (As for these), fulfil their treaty to them till their term. Lo! Allah loveth those who keep their duty (unto Him).	Except those of the idolaters with whom you made an agreement, then they have not failed you in anything and have not backed up any one against you, so fulfill their agreement to the end of their term; surely Allah loves those who are careful (of their duty).
9 005	But when the forbidden months are past, then fight and slay the Pagans wherever ye find them, an seize them, beleaguer them, and lie in wait for them in every stratagem (of war); but if they repent, and establish regular prayers and practise regular charity, then open the way for them: for Allah is Oft-Forgiving, Most Merciful.	Then, when the sacred months have passed, slay the idolaters wherever ye find them, and take them (captive), and besiege them, and prepare for them each ambush. But if they repent and establish worship and pay the poor-due, then leave their way free. Lo! Allah is Forgiving, Merciful.	So when the sacred months have passed away, then slay the idolaters wherever you find them, and take them captives and besiege them and lie in wait for them in every ambush, then if they repent and keep up prayer and pay the poor-rate, leave their way free to them; surely Allah is Forgiving, Merciful.
9 006	If one amongst the Pagans ask thee for asylum, grant it to him, so that he may hear the word of Allah; and then escort him to where he can be secure. That is because they are men without knowledge.	And if anyone of the idolaters seeketh thy protection (O Muhammad), then protect him so that he may hear the Word of Allah, and afterward convey him to his place of safety. That is because they are a folk who know not.	And if one of the idolaters seek protection from you, grant him protection till he hears the word of Allah, then make him attain his place of safety; this is because they are a people who do not know.
9 007	How can there be a league, before Allah and His Messenger, with the Pagans, except those with whom ye made a treaty near the sacred Mosque? As long as these stand true to you, stand ye true to them: for Allah doth love the righteous.	How can there be a treaty with Allah and with His messenger for the idolaters save those with whom ye made a treaty at the Inviolable Place of Worship? So long as they are true to you, be true to them. Lo! Allah loveth those who keep their duty.	How can there be an agreement for the idolaters with Allah and with His Messenger; except those with whom you made an agreement at the Sacred Mosque? So as long as they are true to you, be true to them; surely Allah loves those who are careful (of their duty).

9 008	How (can there be such a league), seeing that if they get an advantage over you, they respect not in you the ties either of kinship or of covenant? With (fair words from) their mouths they entice you, but their hearts are averse from you; and most of them are rebellious and wicked.	How (can there be any treaty for the others) when, if they have the upper hand of you, they regard not pact nor honour in respect of you? They satisfy you with their mouths the while their hearts refuse. And most of them are wrongdoers.	How (can it be)! while if they prevail against you, they would not pay regard in your case to ties of relationship, nor those of covenant; they please you with their mouths while their hearts do not consent; and most of them are transgressors.
9 009	The Signs of Allah have they sold for a miserable price, and (many) have they hindered from His way: evil indeed are the deeds they have done.	They have purchased with the revelations of Allah a little gain, so they debar (men) from His way. Lo! evil is that which they are wont to do.	They have taken a small price for the communications of Allah, so they turn away from His way; surely evil is it that they do.
9 010	In a Believer they respect not the ties either of kinship or of covenant! It is they who have transgressed all bounds.	And they observe toward a believer neither pact nor honour. These are they who are transgressors.	They do not pay regard to ties of relationship nor those of covenant in the case of a believer; and these are they who go beyond the limits.
9 011	But (even so), if they repent, establish regular prayers, and practise regular charity,- they are your brethren in Faith: (thus) do We explain the Signs in detail, for those who understand.	But if they repent and establish worship and pay the poor-due, then are they your brethren in religion. We detail Our revelations for a people who have knowledge.	But if they repent and keep up prayer and pay the poor-rate, they are your brethren in faith; and We make the communications clear for a people who know.
9 012	But if they violate their oaths after their covenant, and taunt you for your Faith,- fight ye the chiefs of Unfaith: for their oaths are nothing to them: that thus they may be restrained.	And if they break their pledges after their treaty (hath been made with you) and assail your religion, then fight the heads of disbelief - Lo! they have no binding oaths - in order that they may desist.	And if they break their oaths after their agreement and (openly) revile your religion, then fight the leaders of unbelief-- surely their oaths are nothing-- so that they may desist.
9 013	Will ye not fight people who violated their oaths, plotted to expel the Messenger, and took the aggressive by being the first (to assault) you? Do ye fear them? Nay, it is Allah Whom ye should more justly fear, if ye believe!	Will ye not fight a folk who broke their solemn pledges, and purposed to drive out the messenger and did attack you first? What! Fear ye them? Now Allah hath more right that ye should fear Him, if ye are believers.	What! will you not fight a people who broke their oaths and aimed at the expulsion of the Messenger, and they attacked you first; do you fear them? But Allah is most deserving that you should fear Him, if you are believers.
9 014	Fight them, and Allah will punish them by your hands, cover them with shame, help you (to victory) over them, heal the breasts of Believers,	Fight them! Allah will chastise them at your hands, and He will lay them low and give you victory over them, and He will heal the breasts of folk who are believers.	Fight them, Allah will punish them by your hands and bring them to disgrace, and assist you against them and heal the hearts of a believing people.
9 015	And still the indignation of their hearts. For Allah will turn (in mercy) to whom He will; and Allah is All-Knowing, All-Wise.	And He will remove the anger of their hearts. Allah relenteth toward whom He will. Allah is Knower, Wise.	And remove the rage of their hearts; and Allah turns (mercifully) to whom He pleases, and Allah is Knowing, Wise.
9 016	Or think ye that ye shall be abandoned, as though Allah did not know those among you who strive with might and main, and take none for friends and protectors except Allah, His Messenger, and the (community of) Believers? But Allah is well-acquainted with (all) that ye do.	Or deemed ye that ye would be left (in peace) when Allah yet knoweth not those of you who strive, choosing for familiar none save Allah and His messenger and the believers? Allah is Informed of what ye do.	What! do you think that you will be left alone while Allah has not yet known those of you who have struggled hard and have not taken any one as an adherent besides Allah and His Messenger and the believers; and Allah is aware of what you do.

9 017	It is not for such as join gods with Allah, to visit or maintain the mosques of Allah while they witness against their own souls to infidelity. The works of such bear no fruit: In Fire shall they dwell.	It is not for the idolaters to tend Allah's sanctuaries, bearing witness against themselves of disbelief. As for such, their works are vain and in the Fire they will abide.	The idolaters have no right to visit the mosques of Allah while bearing witness to unbelief against themselves, these it is whose doings are null, and in the fire shall they abide.
9 018	The mosques of Allah shall be visited and maintained by such as believe in Allah and the Last Day, establish regular prayers, and practise regular charity, and fear none (at all) except Allah. It is they who are expected to be on true guidance.	He only shall tend Allah's sanctuaries who believeth in Allah and the Last Day and observeth proper worship and payeth the poor-due and feareth none save Allah. For such (only) is it possible that they can be of the rightly guided.	Only he shall visit the mosques of Allah who believes in Allah and the latter day, and keeps up prayer and pays the poor-rate and fears none but Allah; so (as for) these, it may be that they are of the followers of the right course.
9 019	Do ye make the giving of drink to pilgrims, or the maintenance of the Sacred Mosque, equal to (the pious service of) those who believe in Allah and the Last Day, and strive with might and main in the cause of Allah? They are not comparable in the sight of Allah: and Allah guides not those who do wrong.	Count ye the slaking of a pilgrim's thirst and tendance of the Inviolable Place of Worship as (equal to the worth of) him who believeth in Allah and the Last Day, and striveth in the way of Allah? They are not equal in the sight of Allah. Allah guideth not wrongdoing folk.	What! do you make (one who undertakes) the giving of drink to the pilgrims and the guarding of the Sacred Mosque like him who believes in Allah and the latter day and strives hard in Allah's way? They are not equal with Allah; and Allah does not guide the unjust people.
9 020	Those who believe, and suffer exile and strive with might and main, in Allah's cause, with their goods and their persons, have the highest rank in the sight of Allah: they are the people who will achieve (salvation).	Those who believe, and have left their homes and striven with their wealth and their lives in Allah's way are of much greater worth in Allah's sight. These are they who are triumphant.	Those who believed and fled (their homes), and strove hard in Allah's way with their property and their souls, are much higher in rank with Allah; and those are they who are the achievers (of their objects).
9 021	Their Lord doth give them glad tidings of a Mercy from Himself, of His good pleasure, and of gardens for them, wherein are delights that endure:	Their Lord giveth them good tidings of mercy from Him, and acceptance, and Gardens where enduring pleasure will be theirs;	Their Lord gives them good news of mercy from Himself and (His) good pleasure and gardens, wherein lasting blessings shall be theirs;
9 022	They will dwell therein for ever. Verily in Allah's presence is a reward, the greatest (of all).	There they will abide for ever. Lo! with Allah there is immense reward.	Abiding therein for ever; surely Allah has a Mighty reward with Him.
9 023	O ye who believe! take not for protectors your fathers and your brothers if they love infidelity above Faith: if any of you do so, they do wrong.	O ye who believe! Choose not your fathers nor your brethren for friends if they take pleasure in disbelief rather than faith. Whoso of you taketh them for friends, such are wrong-doers.	O you who believe! do not take your fathers and your brothers for guardians if they love unbelief more than belief; and whoever of you takes them for a guardian, these it is that are the unjust.
9 024	Say: If it be that your fathers, your sons, your brothers, your mates, or your kindred; the wealth that ye have gained; the commerce in which ye fear a decline: or the dwellings in which ye delight - are dearer to you than Allah, or His Messenger, or the striving in His cause;- then wait until Allah brings about His decision: and Allah guides not the rebellious.	Say: If your fathers, and your sons, and your brethren, and your wives, and your tribe, and the wealth ye have acquired, and merchandise for which ye fear that there will no sale, and dwellings ye desire are dearer to you than Allah and His messenger and striving in His way: then wait till Allah bringeth His command to pass. Allah guideth not wrongdoing folk.	Say: If your fathers and your sons and your brethren and your mates and your kinsfolk and property which you have acquired, and the slackness of trade which you fear and dwellings which you like, are dearer to you than Allah and His Messenger and striving in His way, then wait till Allah brings about His command: and Allah does not guide the transgressing people.

9 025	Assuredly Allah did help you in many battle-fields and on the day of Hunain: Behold! your great numbers elated you, but they availed you naught: the land, for all that it is wide, did constrain you, and ye turned back in retreat.	Allah hath given you victory on many fields and on the day of Huneyn, when ye exulted in your multitude but it availed you naught, and the earth, vast as it is, was straitened for you; then ye turned back in flight;	Certainly Allah helped you in many battlefields and on the day of Hunain, when your great numbers made you vain, but they availed you nothing and the earth became strait to you notwithstanding its spaciousness, then you turned back retreating.
9 026	But Allah did pour His calm on the Messenger and on the Believers, and sent down forces which ye saw not: He punished the Unbelievers; thus doth He reward those without Faith.	Then Allah sent His peace of reassurance down upon His messenger and upon the believers, and sent down hosts ye could not see, and punished those who disbelieved. Such is the reward of disbelievers.	Then Allah sent down His tranquillity upon His Messenger and upon the believers, and sent down hosts which you did not see, and chastised those who disbelieved, and that is the reward of the unbelievers.
9 027	Again will Allah, after this, turn (in mercy) to whom He will: for Allah is Oft-Forgiving, Most Merciful.	Then afterward Allah will relent toward whom He will; for Allah is Forgiving, Merciful.	Then will Allah after this turn (mercifully) to whom He pleases, and Allah is Forgiving, Merciful.
9 028	O ye who believe! Truly the Pagans are unclean; so let them not, after this year of theirs, approach the Sacred Mosque. And if ye fear poverty, soon will Allah enrich you, if He wills, out of His bounty, for Allah is All-Knowing, All-Wise.	O ye who believe! The idolaters only are unclean. So let them not come near the Inviolable Place of Worship after this their year. If ye fear poverty (from the loss of their merchandise) Allah shall preserve you of His bounty if He will. Lo! Allah is Knower, Wise.	O you who believe! the idolaters are nothing but unclean, so they shall not approach the Sacred Mosque after this year; and if you fear poverty then Allah will enrich you out of His grace if He please; surely Allah is Knowing Wise.
9 029	Fight those who believe not in Allah nor the Last Day, nor hold that forbidden which hath been forbidden by Allah and His Messenger, nor acknowledge the religion of Truth, (even if they are) of the People of the Book, until they pay the Jizya with willing submission, and feel themselves subdued.	Fight against such of those who have been given the Scripture as believe not in Allah nor the Last Day, and forbid not that which Allah hath forbidden by His messenger, and follow not the Religion of Truth, until they pay the tribute readily, being brought low.	Fight those who do not believe in Allah, nor in the latter day, nor do they prohibit what Allah and His Messenger have prohibited, nor follow the religion of truth, out of those who have been given the Book, until they pay the tax in acknowledgment of superiority and they are in a state of subjection.
9 030	The Jews call 'Uzair a son of Allah, and the Christians call Christ the son of Allah. That is a saying from their mouth; (in this) they but imitate what the unbelievers of old used to say. Allah's curse be on them: how they are deluded away from the Truth!	And the Jews say: Ezra is the son of Allah, and the Christians say: The Messiah is the son of Allah. That is their saying with their mouths. They imitate the saying of those who disbelieved of old. Allah (Himself) fighteth against them. How perverse are they!	And the Jews say: Uzair is the son of Allah; and the Christians say: The Messiah is the son of Allah; these are the words of their mouths; they imitate the saying of those who disbelieved before; may Allah destroy them; how they are turned away!
9 031	They take their priests and their anchorites to be their lords in derogation of Allah, and (they take as their Lord) Christ the son of Mary; yet they were commanded to worship but One Allah: there is no god but He. Praise and glory to Him: (Far is He) from having the partners they associate (with Him).	They have taken as lords beside Allah their rabbis and their monks and the Messiah son of Mary, when they were bidden to worship only One Allah. There is no God save Him. Be He Glorified from all that they ascribe as partner (unto Him)!	They have taken their doctors of law and their monks for lords besides Allah, and (also) the Messiah son of Marium and they were enjoined that they should serve one Allah only, there is no god but He; far from His glory be what they set up (with Him).
9 032	Fain would they extinguish Allah's light with their mouths, but Allah will not allow but that His light should be perfected, even though the Unbelievers may detest (it).	Fain would they put out the light of Allah with their mouths, but Allah disdaineth (aught) save that He shall perfect His light, however much the disbelievers are averse.	They desire to put out the light of Allah with their mouths, and Allah will not consent save to perfect His light, though the unbelievers are averse.

9 033	It is He Who hath sent His Messenger with guidance and the Religion of Truth, to proclaim it over all religion, even though the Pagans may detest (it).	He it is Who hath sent His messenger with the guidance and the Religion of Truth, that He may cause it to prevail over all religion, however much the idolaters may be averse.	He it is Who sent His Messenger with guidance and the religion of truth, that He might cause it to prevail over all religions, though the polytheists may be averse.
9 034	O ye who believe! there are indeed many among the priests and anchorites, who in Falsehood devour the substance of men and hinder (them) from the way of Allah. And there are those who bury gold and silver and spend it not in the way of Allah: announce unto them a most grievous penalty-	O ye who believe! Lo! many of the (Jewish) rabbis and the (Christian) monks devour the wealth of mankind wantonly and debar (men) from the way of Allah. They who hoard up gold and silver and spend it not in the way of Allah, unto them give tidings (O Muhammad) of a painful doom,	O you who believe! most surely many of the doctors of law and the monks eat away the property of men falsely, and turn (them) from Allah's way; and (as for) those who hoard up gold and silver and do not spend it in Allah's way, announce to them a painful chastisement,
9 035	On the Day when heat will be produced out of that (wealth) in the fire of Hell, and with it will be branded their foreheads, their flanks, and their backs, their flanks, and their backs.- "This is the (treasure) which ye buried for yourselves: taste ye, then, the (treasures) ye buried!"	On the day when it will (all) be heated in the fire of hell, and their foreheads and their flanks and their backs will be branded therewith (and it will be said unto them): Here is that which ye hoarded for yourselves. Now taste of what ye used to hoard.	On the day when it shall be heated in the fire of hell, then their foreheads and their sides and their backs shall be branded with it; this is what you hoarded up for yourselves, therefore taste what you hoarded.
9 036	The number of months in the sight of Allah is twelve (in a year)- so ordained by Him the day He created the heavens and the earth; of them four are sacred: that is the straight usage. So wrong not yourselves therein, and fight the Pagans all together as they fight you all together. But know that Allah is with those who restrain themselves.	Lo! the number of the months with Allah is twelve months by Allah's ordinance in the day that He created the heavens and the earth. Four of them are sacred: that is the right religion. So wrong not yourselves in them. And wage war on all of the idolaters as they are waging war on all of you. And know that Allah is with those who keep their duty (unto Him).	Surely the number of months with Allah is twelve months in Allah's ordinance since the day when He created the heavens and the earth, of these four being sacred; that is the right reckoning; therefore be not unjust to yourselves regarding them, and fight the polytheists all together as they fight you all together; and know that Allah is with those who guard (against evil).
9 037	Verily the transposing (of a prohibited month) is an addition to Unbelief: the Unbelievers are led to wrong thereby: for they make it lawful one year, and forbidden another year, in order to adjust the number of months forbidden by Allah and make such forbidden ones lawful. The evil of their course seems pleasing to them. But Allah guideth not those who reject Faith.	Postponement (of a sacred month) is only an excess of disbelief whereby those who disbelieve are misled; they allow it one year and forbid it (another) year, that they may make up the number of the months which Allah hath hallowed, so that they allow that which Allah hath forbidden. The evil of their deeds is made fairseeming unto them. Allah guideth not the disbelieving folk.	Postponing (of the sacred month) is only an addition in unbelief, wherewith those who disbelieve are led astray, violating it one year and keeping it sacred another, that they may agree in the number (of months) that Allah has made sacred, and thus violate what Allah has made sacred; the evil of their doings is made fairseeming to them; and Allah does not guide the unbelieving people.
9 038	O ye who believe! what is the matter with you, that, when ye are asked to go forth in the cause of Allah, ye cling heavily to the earth? Do ye prefer the life of this world to the Hereafter? But little is the comfort of this life, as compared with the Hereafter.	O ye who believe! What aileth you that when it is said unto you: Go forth in the way of Allah, ye are bowed down to the ground with heaviness. Take ye pleasure in the life of the world rather than in the Hereafter? The comfort of the life of the world is but little in the Hereafter.	O you who believe! What (excuse) have you that when it is said to you: Go forth in Allah's way, you should incline heavily to earth; are you contented with this world's life instead of the hereafter? But the provision of this world's life compared with the hereafter is but little.

9 039	Unless ye go forth, He will punish you with a grievous penalty, and put others in your place; but Him ye would not harm in the least. For Allah hath power over all things.	If ye go not forth He will afflict you with a painful doom, and will choose instead of you a folk other than you. Ye cannot harm Him at all. Allah is Able to do all things.	If you do not go forth, He will chastise you with a painful chastisement and bring in your place a people other than you, and you will do Him no harm; and Allah has power over all things.
9 040	If ye help not (your leader), (it is no matter): for Allah did indeed help him, when the Unbelievers drove him out: he had no more than one companion; they two were in the cave, and he said to his companion, Have no fear, for Allah is with us: then Allah sent down His peace upon him, and strengthened him with forces which ye saw not, and humbled to the depths the word of the Unbelievers. But the word of Allah is exalted to the heights: for Allah is Exalted in Might, Wise.	If ye help him not, still Allah helped him when those who disbelieve drove him forth, the second of two; when they two were in the cave, when he said unto his comrade: Grieve not. Lo! Allah is with us. Then Allah caused His peace of reassurance to descend upon him and supported him with hosts ye cannot see, and made the word of those who disbelieved the nethermost, while Allah's Word it was that became the uppermost. Allah is Mighty, Wise.	If you will not aid him, Allah certainly aided him when those who disbelieved expelled him, he being the second of the two, when they were both in the cave, when he said to his companion: Grieve not, surely Allah is with us. So Allah sent down His tranquillity upon him and strengthened him with hosts which you did not see, and made lowest the word of those who disbelieved; and the word of Allah, that is the highest; and Allah is Mighty, Wise.
9 041	Go ye forth, (whether equipped) lightly or heavily, and strive and struggle, with your goods and your persons, in the cause of Allah. That is best for you, if ye (but) knew.	Go forth, light-armed and heavy-armed, and strive with your wealth and your lives in the way of Allah! That is best for you if ye but knew.	Go forth light and heavy, and strive hard in Allah's way with your property and your persons; this is better for you, if you know.
9 042	If there had been immediate gain (in sight), and the journey easy, they would (all) without doubt have followed thee, but the distance was long, (and weighed) on them. They would indeed swear by Allah, "If we only could, we should certainly have come out with you": They would destroy their own souls; for Allah doth know that they are certainly lying.	Had it been a near adventure and an easy journey they had followed thee, but the distance seemed too far for them. Yet will they swear by Allah (saying): If we had been able we would surely have set out with you. They destroy their souls, and Allah knoweth that they verily are liars.	Had it been a near advantage and a short journey, they would certainly have followed you, but the tedious journey was too long for them; and they swear by Allah: If we had been able, we would certainly have gone forth with you; they cause their own souls to perish, and Allah knows that they are most surely liars.
9 043	Allah give thee grace! why didst thou grant them exemption until those who told the truth were seen by thee in a clear light, and thou hadst proved the liars?	Allah forgive thee (O Muhammad)! Wherefore didst thou grant them leave ere those who told the truth were manifest to thee and thou didst know the liars?	Allah pardon you! Why did you give them leave until those who spoke the truth had become manifest to you and you had known the liars?
9 044	Those who believe in Allah and the Last Day ask thee for no exemption from fighting with their goods and persons. And Allah knoweth well those who do their duty.	Those who believe in Allah and the Last Day ask no leave of thee lest they should strive with their wealth and their lives. Allah is Aware of those who keep their duty (unto Him).	They do not ask leave of you who believe in Allah and the latter day (to stay away) from striving hard with their property and their persons, and Allah knows those who guard (against evil).
9 045	Only those ask thee for exemption who believe not in Allah and the Last Day, and whose hearts are in doubt, so that they are tossed in their doubts to and fro.	They alone ask leave of thee who believe not in Allah and the Last Day, and whose hearts feel doubt, so in their doubt they waver.	They only ask leave of you who do not believe in Allah and the latter day and their hearts are in doubt, so in their doubt do they waver.
9 046	If they had intended to come out, they would certainly have made some preparation therefor; but Allah was averse to their being sent forth; so He made them lag behind, and they were told, "Sit ye among those who sit (inactive)."	And if they had wished to go forth they would assuredly have made ready some equipment, but Allah was averse to their being sent forth and held them back and it was said (unto them): Sit ye with the sedentary!	And if they had intended to go forth, they would certainly have provided equipment for it, but Allah did not like their going forth, so He withheld them, and it was said (to them): Hold back with those who hold back.

9 047	If they had come out with you, they would not have added to your (strength) but only (made for) disorder, hurrying to and fro in your midst and sowing sedition among you, and there would have been some among you who would have listened to them. But Allah knoweth well those who do wrong.	Had they gone forth among you they had added to you naught save trouble and had hurried to and fro among you, seeking to cause sedition among you; and among you there are some who would have listened to them. Allah is Aware of evil-doers.		Had they gone forth with you, they would not have added to you aught save corruption, and they would certainly have hurried about among you seeking (to sow) dissension among you, and among you there are those who hearken for their sake; and Allah knows the unjust.
9 048	Indeed they had plotted sedition before, and upset matters for thee, until,- the Truth arrived, and the Decree of Allah became manifest much to their disgust.	Aforetime they sought to cause sedition and raised difficulties for thee till the Truth came and the decree of Allah was made manifest, though they were loth.		Certainly they sought (to sow) dissension before, and they meditated plots against you until the truth came, and Allah's commandment prevailed although they were averse (from it).
9 049	Among them is (many) a man who says: "Grant me exemption and draw me not into trial." Have they not fallen into trial already? and indeed Hell surrounds the Unbelievers (on all sides).	Of them is he who saith: Grant me leave (to stay at home) and tempt me not. Surely it is into temptation that they (thus) have fallen. Lo! hell verily is all around the disbelievers.		And among them there is he who says: Allow me and do not try me. Surely into trial have they already tumbled down, and most surely hell encompasses the unbelievers.
9 050	If good befalls thee, it grieves them; but if a misfortune befalls thee, they say, "We took indeed our precautions beforehand," and they turn away rejoicing.	If good befalleth thee (O Muhammad) it afflicteth them, and if calamity befalleth thee, they say: We took precaution, and they turn away well pleased.		If good befalls you, it grieves them, and if hardship afflicts you, they say: Indeed we had taken care of our affair before; and they turn back and are glad.
9 051	Say: "Nothing will happen to us except what Allah has decreed for us: He is our protector": and on Allah let the Believers put their trust.	Say: Naught befalleth us save that which Allah hath decreed for us. He is our Protecting Friend. In Allah let believers put their trust!		Say: Nothing will afflict us save what Allah has ordained for us; He is our Patron; and on Allah let the believers rely.
9 052	Say: "Can you expect for us (any fate) other than one of two glorious things- (Martyrdom or victory)? But we can expect for you either that Allah will send his punishment from Himself, or by our hands. So wait (expectant); we too will wait with you."	Say: Can ye await for us aught save one of two good things (death or victory in Allah's way)? while we await for you that Allah will afflict you with a doom from Him or at our hands. Await then! Lo! We are awaiting with you.		Say: Do you await for us but one of two most excellent things? And we await for you that Allah will afflict you with punishment from Himself or by our hands. So wait; we too will wait with you.
9 053	Say: "Spend (for the cause) willingly or unwillingly: not from you will it be accepted: for ye are indeed a people rebellious and wicked."	Say: Pay (your contribution), willingly or unwillingly, it will not be accepted from you. Lo! ye were ever froward folk.		Say: Spend willingly or unwillingly, it shall not be accepted from you; surely you are a transgressing people.
9 054	The only reasons why their contributions are not accepted are: that they reject Allah and His Messenger; that they come to prayer without earnestness; and that they offer contributions unwillingly.	And naught preventeth that their contributions should be accepted from them save that they have disbelieved in Allah and in His messenger, and they come not to worship save as idlers, and pay not (their contribution) save reluctantly.		And nothing hinders their spendings being accepted from them, except that they disbelieve in Allah and in His Messenger and they do not come to prayer but while they are sluggish, and they do not spend but while they are unwilling.
9 055	Let not their wealth nor their (following in) sons dazzle thee: in reality Allah's plan is to punish them with these things in this life, and that their souls may perish in their (very) denial of Allah.	So let not their riches nor their children please thee (O Muhammad). Allah thereby intendeth but to punish them in the life of the world and that their souls shall pass away while they are disbelievers.		Let not then their property and their children excite your admiration; Allah only wishes to chastise them with these in this world's life and (that) their souls may depart while they are unbelievers.

9 056	They swear by Allah that they are indeed of you; but they are not of you: yet they are afraid (to appear in their true colours).	And they swear by Allah that they are in truth of you, when they are not of you, but they are folk who are afraid.	And they swear by Allah that they are most surely of you, and they are not of you, but they are a people who are afraid (of you).
9 057	If they could find a place to flee to, or caves, or a place of concealment, they would turn straightaway thereto, with an obstinate rush.	Had they but found a refuge, or caverns, or a place to enter, they surely had resorted thither swift as runaways.	If they could find a refuge or cave or a place to enter into, they would certainly have turned thereto, running away in all haste.
9 058	And among them are men who slander thee in the matter of (the distribution of) the alms: if they are given part thereof, they are pleased, but if not, behold! they are indignant!	And of them is he who defameth thee in the matter of the alms. If they are given thereof they are content, and if they are not given thereof, behold! they are enraged.	And of them there are those who blame you with respect to the alms; so if they are given from it they are pleased, and if they are not given from it, lo! they are full of rage.
9 059	If only they had been content with what Allah and His Messenger gave them, and had said, "Sufficient unto us is Allah! Allah and His Messenger will soon give us of His bounty: to Allah do we turn our hopes!" (that would have been the right course).	(How much more seemly) had they been content with that which Allah and His messenger had given them and had said: Allah sufficeth us. Allah will give us of His bounty, and (also) His messenger. Unto Allah we are suppliants.	And if they were content with what Allah and His Messenger gave them, and had said: Allah is sufficient for us; Allah will soon give us (more) out of His grace and His Messenger too; surely to Allah do we make our petition.
9 060	Alms are for the poor and the needy, and those employed to administer the (funds); for those whose hearts have been (recently) reconciled (to Truth); for those in bondage and in debt; in the cause of Allah; and for the wayfarer: (thus is it) ordained by Allah, and Allah is full of knowledge and wisdom.	The alms are only for the poor and the needy, and those who collect them, and those whose hearts are to be reconciled, and to free the captives and the debtors, and for the cause of Allah, and (for) the wayfarer; a duty imposed by Allah. Allah is Knower, Wise.	Alms are only for the poor and the needy, and the officials (appointed) over them, and those whose hearts are made to incline (to truth) and the (ransoming of) captives and those in debts and in the way of Allah and the wayfarer; an ordinance from Allah; and Allah is knowing, Wise.
9 061	Among them are men who molest the Prophet and say, "He is (all) ear." Say, "He listens to what is best for you: he believes in Allah, has faith in the Believers, and is a Mercy to those of you who believe." But those who molest the Messenger will have a grievous penalty.	And of them are those who vex the Prophet and say: He is only a hearer. Say: A hearer of good for you, who believeth in Allah and is true to the believers, and a mercy for such of you as believe. Those who vex the messenger of Allah, for them there is a painful doom.	And there are some of them who molest the Prophet and say: He is one who believes every thing that he hears; say: A hearer of good for you (who) believes in Allah and believes the faithful and a mercy for those of you who believe; and (as for) those who molest the Messenger of Allah, they shall have a painful punishment.
9 062	To you they swear by Allah. In order to please you: But it is more fitting that they should please Allah and His Messenger, if they are Believers.	They swear by Allah to you (Muslims) to please you, but Allah, with His messenger, hath more right that they should please Him if they are believers.	They swear to you by Allah that they might please you and, Allah, as well as His Messenger, has a greater right that they should please Him, if they are believers.
9 063	Know they not that for those who oppose Allah and His Messenger, is the Fire of Hell?- wherein they shall dwell. That is the supreme disgrace.	Know they not that whoso opposeth Allah and His messenger, his verily is fire of hell, to abide therein? That is the extreme abasement.	Do they not know that whoever acts in opposition to Allah and His Messenger, he shall surely have the fire of hell to abide in it? That is the grievous abasement.
9 064	The Hypocrites are afraid lest a Sura should be sent down about them, showing them what is (really passing) in their hearts. Say: "Mock ye! But verily Allah will bring to light all that ye fear (should be revealed)."	The hypocrites fear lest a surah should be revealed concerning them, proclaiming what is in their hearts. Say: Scoff (your fill)! Lo! Allah is disclosing what ye fear.	The hypocrites fear lest a Chapter should be sent down to them telling them plainly of what is in their hearts. Say: Go on mocking, surely Allah will bring forth what you fear.

9 065	If thou dost question them, they declare (with emphasis): "We were only talking idly and in play." Say: "Was it at Allah, and His Signs, and His Messenger, that ye were mocking?"	And if thou ask them (O Muhammad) they will say: We did but talk and jest. Say: Was it at Allah and His revelations and His messenger that ye did scoff?	And if you should question them, they would certainly say: We were only idly discoursing and sporting. Say: Was it at Allah and His communications and His Messenger that you mocked?
9 066	Make ye no excuses: ye have rejected Faith after ye had accepted it. If We pardon some of you, We will punish others amongst you, for that they are in sin.	Make no excuse. Ye have disbelieved after your (confession of) belief. If We forgive a party of you, a party of you We shall punish because they have been guilty.	Do not make excuses; you have denied indeed after you had believed; if We pardon a party of you, We will chastise (another) party because they are guilty.
9 067	The Hypocrites, men and women, (have an understanding) with each other: They enjoin evil, and forbid what is just, and are close with their hands. They have forgotten Allah; so He hath forgotten them. Verily the Hypocrites are rebellious and perverse.	The hypocrites, both men and women, proceed one from another. They enjoin the wrong, and they forbid the right, and they withhold their hands (from spending for the cause of Allah). They forget Allah, so He hath forgotten them. Lo! the hypocrites, they are the transgressors.	The hypocritical men and the hypocritical women are all alike; they enjoin evil and forbid good and withhold their hands; they have forsaken Allah, so He has forsaken them; surely the hypocrites are the transgressors.
9 068	Allah hath promised the Hypocrites men and women, and the rejecters, of Faith, the fire of Hell: Therein shall they dwell: Sufficient is it for them: for them is the curse of Allah, and an enduring punishment,-	Allah promiseth the hypocrites, both men and women, and the disbelievers fire of hell for their abode. It will suffice them. Allah curseth them, and theirs is lasting torment.	Allah has promised the hypocritical men and the hypocritical women and the unbelievers the fire of hell to abide therein; it is enough for them; and Allah has cursed them and they shall have lasting punishment.
9 069	As in the case of those before you: they were mightier than you in power, and more flourishing in wealth and children. They had their enjoyment of their portion: and ye have of yours, as did those before you; and ye indulge in idle talk as they did. They!- their work are fruitless in this world and in the Hereafter, and they will lose (all spiritual good).	Even as those before you who were mightier than you in strength, and more affluent than you in wealth and children. They enjoyed their lot awhile, so ye enjoy your lot awhile even as those before you did enjoy their lot awhile. And ye prate even as they prated. Such are they whose works have perished in the world and the Hereafter. Such are they who are the losers.	Like those before you; they were stronger than you in power and more abundant in wealth and children, so they enjoyed their portion; thus have you enjoyed your portion as those before you enjoyed their portion; and you entered into vain discourses like the vain discourses in which entered those before you. These are they whose works are null in this world and the hereafter, and these are they who are the losers.
9 070	Hath not the story reached them of those before them?- the People of Noah, and 'Ad, and Thamud; the People of Abraham, the men of Midian, and the cities overthrown. To them came their messengers with clear signs. It is not Allah Who wrongs them, but they wrong their own souls.	Hath not the fame of those before them reached them - the folk of Noah, A'ad, Thamud, the folk of Abraham, the dwellers of Midian and the disasters (which befell them)? Their messengers (from Allah) came unto them with proofs (of Allah's Sovereignty). So Allah surely wronged them not, but they did wrong themselves.	Has not the news of those before them come to them; of the people of Nuh and Ad and Samood, and the people of Ibrahim and the dwellers of Madyan and the overthrown cities; their messengers came to them with clear arguments; so it was not Allah Who should do them injustice, but they were unjust to themselves.
9 071	The Believers, men and women, are protectors one of another: they enjoin what is just, and forbid what is evil: they observe regular prayers, practise regular charity, and obey Allah and His Messenger. On them will Allah pour His mercy: for Allah is Exalted in Power, Wise.	And the believers, men and women, are protecting friends one of another; they enjoin the right and forbid the wrong, and they establish worship and they pay the poor-due, and they obey Allah and His messenger. As for these, Allah will have mercy on them. Lo! Allah is Mighty, Wise.	And (as for) the believing men and the believing women, they are guardians of each other; they enjoin good and forbid evil and keep up prayer and pay the poor-rate, and obey Allah and His Messenger; (as for) these, Allah will show mercy to them; surely Allah is Mighty, Wise.

9 072	Allah hath promised to Believers, men and women, gardens under which rivers flow, to dwell therein, and beautiful mansions in gardens of everlasting bliss. But the greatest bliss is the good pleasure of Allah: that is the supreme felicity.	Allah promiseth to the believers, men and women, Gardens underneath which rivers flow, wherein they will abide - blessed dwellings in Gardens of Eden. And - greater (far)! - acceptance from Allah. That is the supreme triumph.	Allah has promised to the believing men and the believing women gardens, beneath which rivers flow, to abide in them, and goodly dwellings in gardens of perpetual abode; and best of all is Allah's goodly pleasure; that is the grand achievement.
9 073	O Prophet! strive hard against the unbelievers and the Hypocrites, and be firm against them. Their abode is Hell,- an evil refuge indeed.	O Prophet! Strive against the disbelievers and the hypocrites! Be harsh with them. Their ultimate abode is hell, a hapless journey's end.	O Prophet! strive hard against the unbelievers and the hypocrites and be unyielding to them; and their abode is hell, and evil is the destination.
9 074	They swear by Allah that they said nothing (evil), but indeed they uttered blasphemy, and they did it after accepting Islam; and they meditated a plot which they were unable to carry out: this revenge of theirs was (their) only return for the bounty with which Allah and His Messenger had enriched them! If they repent, it will be best for them; but if they turn back (to their evil ways), Allah will punish them with a grievous penalty in this life and in the Hereafter: They shall have none on earth to protect or help them.	They swear by Allah that they said nothing (wrong), yet they did say the word of disbelief, and did disbelieve after their Surrender (to Allah). And they purposed that which they could not attain, and they sought revenge only that Allah by His messenger should enrich them of His bounty. If they repent it will be better for them; and if they turn away, Allah will afflict them with a painful doom in the world and the Hereafter, and they have no protecting friend nor helper in the earth.	They swear by Allah that they did not speak, and certainly they did speak, the word of unbelief, and disbelieved after their Islam, and they had determined upon what they have not been able to effect, and they did not find fault except because Allah and His Messenger enriched them out of His grace; therefore if they repent, it will be good for them; and if they turn back, Allah will chastise them with a painful chastisement in this world and the hereafter, and they shall not have in the land any guardian or a helper.
9 075	Amongst them are men who made a covenant with Allah, that if He bestowed on them of His bounty, they would give (largely) in charity, and be truly amongst those who are righteous.	And of them is he who made a covenant with Allah (saying): If He give us of His bounty we will give alms and become of the righteous.	And there are those of them who made a covenant with Allah: If He give us out of His grace, we will certainly give alms and we will certainly be of the good.
9 076	But when He did bestow of His bounty, they became covetous, and turned back (from their covenant), averse (from its fulfilment).	Yet when He gave them of His bounty, they hoarded it and turned away, averse;	But when He gave them out of His grace, they became niggardly of it and they turned back and they withdrew.
9 077	So He hath put as a consequence hypocrisy into their hearts, (to last) till the Day, whereon they shall meet Him: because they broke their covenant with Allah, and because they lied (again and again).	So He hath made the consequence (to be) hypocrisy in their hearts until the day when they shall meet Him, because they broke their word to Allah that they promised Him, and because they lied.	So He made hypocrisy to follow as a consequence into their hearts till the day when they shall meet Him because they failed to perform towards Allah what they had promised with Him and because they told lies.
9 078	Know they not that Allah doth know their secret (thoughts) and their secret counsels, and that Allah knoweth well all things unseen?	Know they not that Allah knoweth both their secret and the thought that they confide, and that Allah is the Knower of Things Hidden?	Do they not know that Allah knows their hidden thoughts and their secret counsels, and that Allah is the great Knower of the unseen things?
9 079	Those who slander such of the believers as give themselves freely to (deeds of) charity, as well as such as can find nothing to give except the fruits of their labour,- and throw ridicule on them,- Allah will throw back their ridicule on them: and they shall have a grievous penalty.	Those who point at such of the believers as give the alms willingly and such as can find naught to give but their endeavours, and deride them - Allah (Himself) derideth them. Theirs will be a painful doom.	They who taunt those of the faithful who give their alms freely, and those who give to the extent of their earnings and scoff at them; Allah will pay them back their scoffing, and they shall have a painful chastisement.

9 080	Whether thou ask for their forgiveness, or not, (their sin is unforgivable): if thou ask seventy times for their forgiveness, Allah will not forgive them: because they have rejected Allah and His Messenger: and Allah guideth not those who are perversely rebellious.	Ask forgiveness for them (O Muhammad), or ask not forgiveness for them; though thou ask forgiveness for them seventy times Allah will not forgive them. That is because they disbelieved in Allah and His messenger, and Allah guideth not wrongdoing folk.	Ask forgiveness for them or do not ask forgiveness for them; even if you ask forgiveness for them seventy times, Allah will not forgive them; this is because they disbelieve in Allah and His Messenger, and Allah does not guide the transgressing people.
9 081	Those who were left behind (in the Tabuk expedition) rejoiced in their inaction behind the back of the Messenger of Allah: they hated to strive and fight, with their goods and their persons, in the cause of Allah: they said, "Go not forth in the heat." Say, "The fire of Hell is fiercer in heat." If only they could understand!	Those who were left behind rejoiced at sitting still behind the messenger of Allah, and were averse to striving with their wealth and their lives in Allah's way. And they said: Go not forth in the heat! Say: The fire of hell is more intense of heat, if they but understood.	Those who were left behind were glad on account of their sitting behind Allah's Messenger and they were averse from striving in Allah's way with their property and their persons, and said: Do not go forth in the heat. Say: The fire of hell is much severe in heat. Would that they understood (it).
9 082	Let them laugh a little: much will they weep: a recompense for the (evil) that they do.	Then let them laugh a little: they will weep much, as the reward of what they used to earn.	Therefore they shall laugh little and weep much as a recompense for what they earned.
9 083	If, then, Allah bring thee back to any of them, and they ask thy permission to come out (with thee), say: "Never shall ye come out with me, nor fight an enemy with me: for ye preferred to sit inactive on the first occasion: Then sit ye (now) with those who lag behind."	If Allah bring thee back (from the campaign) unto a party of them and they ask of thee leave to go out (to fight), then say unto them: Ye shall never more go out with me nor fight with me against a foe. Ye were content with sitting still the first time. So sit still, with the useless.	Therefore if Allah brings you back to a party of them and then they ask your permission to go forth, say: By no means shall you ever go forth with me and by no means shall you fight an enemy with me; surely you chose to sit the first time, therefore sit (now) with those who remain behind.
9 084	Nor do thou ever pray for any of them that dies, nor stand at his grave; for they rejected Allah and His Messenger, and died in a state of perverse rebellion.	And never (O Muhammad) pray for one of them who dieth, nor stand by his grave. Lo! they disbelieved in Allah and His messenger, and they died while they were evil-doers.	And never offer prayer for any one of them who dies and do not stand by his grave; surely they disbelieve in Allah and His Messenger and they shall die in transgression.
9 085	Nor let their wealth nor their (following in) sons dazzle thee: Allah's plan is to punish them with these things in this world, and that their souls may perish in their (very) denial of Allah.	Let not their wealth nor their children please thee! Allah purposeth only to punish them thereby in the world, and that their souls shall pass away while they are disbelievers.	And let not their property and their children excite your admiration; Allah only wishes to chastise them with these in this world and (that) their souls may depart while they are unbelievers.
9 086	When a Sura comes down, enjoining them to believe in Allah and to strive and fight along with His Messenger, those with wealth and influence among them ask thee for exemption, and say: "Leave us (behind): we would be with those who sit (at home)."	And when a surah is revealed (which saith): Believe in Allah and strive along with His messenger, the men of wealth among them still ask leave of thee and say: Suffer us to be with those who sit (at home).	And whenever a Chapter is revealed, saying: Believe in Allah and strive hard along with His Messenger, those having ampleness of means ask permission of you and say: Leave us (behind), that we may be with those who sit.
9 087	They prefer to be with (the women), who remain behind (at home): their hearts are sealed and so they understand not.	They are content that they should be with the useless and their hearts are sealed, so that they apprehend not.	They preferred to be with those who remained behind, and a seal is set on their hearts so they do not understand.

9 088	But the Messenger, and those who believe with him, strive and fight with their wealth and their persons: for them are (all) good things: and it is they who will prosper.	But the messenger and those who believe with him strive with their wealth and their lives. Such are they for whom are the good things. Such are they who are the successful.	But the Messenger and those who believe with him strive hard with their property and their persons; and these it is who shall have the good things and these it is who shall be successful.
9 089	Allah hath prepared for them gardens under which rivers flow, to dwell therein: that is the supreme felicity.	Allah hath made ready for them Gardens underneath which rivers flow, wherein they will abide. That is the supreme triumph.	Allah has prepared for them gardens beneath which rivers flow, to abide in them; that is the great achievement.
9 090	And there were, among the desert Arabs (also), men who made excuses and came to claim exemption; and those who were false to Allah and His Messenger (merely) sat inactive. Soon will a grievous penalty seize the Unbelievers among them.	And those among the wandering Arabs who had an excuse came in order that permission might be granted them. And those who lied to Allah and His messenger sat at home. A painful doom will fall on those of them who disbelieve.	And the defaulters from among the dwellers of the desert came that permission may be given to them and they sat (at home) who lied to Allah and His Messenger; a painful chastisement shall afflict those of them who disbelieved.
9 091	There is no blame on those who are infirm, or ill, or who find no resources to spend (on the cause), if they are sincere (in duty) to Allah and His Messenger: no ground (of complaint) can there be against such as do right: and Allah is Oft-Forgiving, Most Merciful.	Not unto the weak nor unto the sick nor unto those who can find naught to spend is any fault (to be imputed though they stay at home) if they are true to Allah and His messenger. Not unto the good is there any road (of blame). Allah is Forgiving, Merciful.	It shall be no crime in the weak, nor in the sick, nor in those who do not find what they should spend (to stay behind), so long as they are sincere to Allah and His Messenger; there is no way (to blame) against the doers of good; and Allah is Forgiving, Merciful;
9 092	Nor (is there blame) on those who came to thee to be provided with mounts, and when thou saidst, "I can find no mounts for you," they turned back, their eyes streaming with tears of grief that they had no resources wherewith to provide the expenses.	Nor unto those whom, when they came to thee (asking) that thou shouldst mount them, thou didst tell: I cannot find whereon to mount you. They turned back with eyes flowing with tears, for sorrow that they could not find the means to spend.	Nor in those who when they came to you that you might carry them, you said: I cannot find that on which to carry you; they went back while their eyes overflowed with tears on account of grief for not finding that which they should spend.
9 093	The ground (of complaint) is against such as claim exemption while they are rich. They prefer to stay with the (women) who remain behind: Allah hath sealed their hearts; so they know not (What they miss).	The road (of blame) is only against those who ask for leave of thee (to stay at home) when they are rich. They are content to be with the useless. Allah hath sealed their hearts so that they know not.	The way (to blame) is only against those who ask permission of you though they are rich; they have chosen to be with those who remained behind, and Allah has set a seal upon their hearts so they do not know.
9 094	They will present their excuses to you when ye return to them. Say thou: "Present no excuses: we shall not believe you: Allah hath already informed us of the true state of matters concerning you: It is your actions that Allah and His Messenger will observe: in the end will ye be brought back to Him Who knoweth what is hidden and what is open: then will He show you the truth of all that ye did."	They will make excuse to you (Muslims) when ye return unto them. Say: Make no excuse, for we shall not believe you. Allah hath told us tidings of you. Allah and His messenger will see your conduct, and then ye will be brought back unto Him Who knoweth the Invisible as well as the Visible, and He will tell you what ye used to do.	They will excuse themselves to you when you go back to them. Say: Urge no excuse, by no means will we believe you; indeed Allah has informed us of matters relating to you; and now Allah and His Messenger will see your doings, then you shall be brought back to the Knower of the unseen and the seen, then He will inform you of what you did.

9 095	They will swear to you by Allah, when ye return to them, that ye may leave them alone. So leave them alone: For they are an abomination, and Hell is their dwelling-place,-a fitting recompense for the (evil) that they did.	They will swear by Allah unto you, when ye return unto them, that ye may let them be. Let them be, for lo! they are unclean, and their abode is hell as the reward for what they used to earn.	They will swear to you by Allah when you return to them so that you may turn aside from them; so do turn aside from them; surely they are unclean and their abode is hell; a recompense for what they earned.
9 096	They will swear unto you, that ye may be pleased with them but if ye are pleased with them, Allah is not pleased with those who disobey.	They swear unto you, that ye may accept them. Though ye accept them. Allah verily accepteth not wrongdoing folk.	They will swear to you that you may be pleased with them; but if you are pleased with them, yet surely Allah is not pleased with the transgressing people.
9 097	The Arabs of the desert are the worst in Unbelief and hypocrisy, and most fitted to be in ignorance of the command which Allah hath sent down to His Messenger: But Allah is All-Knowing, All-Wise.	The wandering Arabs are more hard in disbelief and hypocrisy, and more likely to be ignorant of the limits which Allah hath revealed unto His messenger. And Allah is Knower, Wise.	The dwellers of the desert are very hard in unbelief and hypocrisy, and more disposed not to know the limits of what Allah has revealed to His Messenger; and Allah is Knowing, Wise.
9 098	Some of the desert Arabs look upon their payments as a fine, and watch for disasters for you: on them be the disaster of evil: for Allah is He That heareth and knoweth (all things).	And of the wandering Arabs there is he who taketh that which he expendeth (for the cause of Allah) as a loss, and awaiteth (evil) turns of fortune for you (that he may be rid of it). The evil turn of fortune will be theirs. Allah is Hearer, Knower.	And of the dwellers of the desert are those who take what they spend to be a fine, and they wait (the befalling of) calamities to you; on them (will be) the evil calamity; and Allah is Hearing, Knowing.
9 099	But some of the desert Arabs believe in Allah and the Last Day, and look on their payments as pious gifts bringing them nearer to Allah and obtaining the prayers of the Messenger. Aye, indeed they bring them nearer (to Him): soon will Allah admit them to His Mercy: for Allah is Oft-Forgiving, Most Merciful.	And of the wandering Arabs there is he who believeth in Allah and the Last Day, and taketh that which he expendeth and also the prayers of the messenger as acceptable offerings in the sight of Allah. Lo! verily it is an acceptable offering for them. Allah will bring them into His mercy. Lo! Allah is Forgiving, Merciful.	And of the dwellers of the desert are those who believe in Allah and the latter day and take what they spend to be (means of) the nearness of Allah and the Messenger's prayers; surely it shall be means of nearness for them; Allah will make them enter into His mercy; surely Allah is Forgiving, Merciful.
9 100	The vanguard (of Islam)- the first of those who forsook (their homes) and of those who gave them aid, and (also) those who follow them in (all) good deeds,- well-pleased is Allah with them, as are they with Him: for them hath He prepared gardens under which rivers flow, to dwell therein for ever: that is the supreme felicity.	And the first to lead the way, of the Muhajirin and the Ansar, and those who followed them in goodness - Allah is well pleased with them and they are well pleased with Him, and He hath made ready for them Gardens underneath which rivers flow, wherein they will abide for ever. That is the supreme triumph.	And (as for) the foremost, the first of the Muhajirs and the Ansars, and those who followed them in goodness, Allah is well pleased with them and they are well pleased with Him, and He has prepared for them gardens beneath which rivers flow, to abide in them for ever; that is the mighty achievement.
9 101	Certain of the desert Arabs round about you are hypocrites, as well as (desert Arabs) among the Medina folk: they are obstinate in hypocrisy: thou knowest them not: We know them: twice shall We punish them: and in addition shall they be sent to a grievous penalty.	And among those around you of the wandering Arabs there are hypocrites, and among the townspeople of Al-Madinah (there are some who) persist in hypocrisy whom thou (O Muhammad) knowest not. We, We know them, and We shall chastise them twice; then they will be relegated to a painful doom.	And from among those who are round about you of the dwellers of the desert there are hypocrites, and from among the people of Medina (also); they are stubborn in hypocrisy; you do not know them; We know them; We will chastise them twice then shall they be turned back to a grievous chastisement.

9 102	Others (there are who) have acknowledged their wrong-doings: they have mixed an act that was good with another that was evil. Perhaps Allah will turn unto them (in Mercy): for Allah is Oft-Forgiving, Most Merciful.	And (there are) others who have acknowledged their faults. They mixed a righteous action with another that was bad. It may be that Allah will relent toward them. Lo! Allah is Forgiving, Merciful.	And others have confessed their faults, they have mingled a good deed and an evil one; may be Allah will turn to them (mercifully); surely Allah is Forgiving, Merciful.
9 103	Of their goods, take alms, that so thou mightest purify and sanctify them; and pray on their behalf. Verily thy prayers are a source of security for them: And Allah is One Who heareth and knoweth.	Take alms of their wealth, wherewith thou mayst purify them and mayst make them grow, and pray for them. Lo! thy prayer is an assuagement for them. Allah is Hearer, Knower.	Take alms out of their property, you would cleanse them and purify them thereby, and pray for them; surely your prayer is a relief to them; and Allah is Hearing, Knowing.
9 104	Know they not that Allah doth accept repentance from His votaries and receives their gifts of charity, and that Allah is verily He, the Oft-Returning, Most Merciful?	Know they not that Allah is He Who accepteth repentance from His bondmen and taketh the alms, and that Allah is He Who is the Relenting, the Merciful.	Do they not know that Allah accepts repentance from His servants and takes the alms, and that Allah is the Oft-returning (to mercy), the Merciful?
9 105	And say: "Work (righteousness): Soon will Allah observe your work, and His Messenger, and the Believers: Soon will ye be brought back to the knower of what is hidden and what is open: then will He show you the truth of all that ye did."	And say (unto them): Act! Allah will behold your actions, and (so will) His messenger and the believers, and ye will be brought back to the Knower of the Invisible and the Visible, and He will tell you what ye used to do.	And say: Work; so Allah will see your work and (so will) His Messenger and the believers; and you shall be brought back to the Knower of the unseen and the seen, then He will inform you of what you did.
9 106	There are (yet) others, held in suspense for the command of Allah, whether He will punish them, or turn in mercy to them: and Allah is All-Knowing, Wise.	And (there are) others who await Allah's decree, whether He will punish them or will forgive them. Allah is Knower, Wise.	And others are made to await Allah's command, whether He chastise them or whether He turn to them (mercifully), and Allah is Knowing, Wise.
9 107	And there are those who put up a mosque by way of mischief and infidelity - to disunite the Believers - and in preparation for one who warred against Allah and His Messenger aforetime. They will indeed swear that their intention is nothing but good; But Allah doth declare that they are certainly liars.	And as for those who chose a place of worship out of opposition and disbelief, and in order to cause dissent among the believers, and as an outpost for those who warred against Allah and His messenger aforetime, they will surely swear: We purposed naught save good. Allah beareth witness that they verily are liars.	And those who built a masjid to cause harm and for unbelief and to cause disunion among the believers and an ambush to him who made war against Allah and His Messenger before; and they will certainly swear: We did not desire aught but good; and Allah bears witness that they are most surely liars.
9 108	Never stand thou forth therein. There is a mosque whose foundation was laid from the first day on piety; it is more worthy of the standing forth (for prayer) therein. In it are men who love to be purified; and Allah loveth those who make themselves pure.	Never stand (to pray) there. A place of worship which was found upon duty (to Allah) from the first day is more worthy that thou shouldst stand (to pray) therein, wherein are men who love to purify themselves. Allah loveth the purifiers.	Never stand in it; certainly a masjid founded on piety from the very first day is more deserving that you should stand in it; in it are men who love that they should be purified; and Allah loves those who purify themselves.
9 109	Which then is best? - he that layeth his foundation on piety to Allah and His good pleasure? - or he that layeth his foundation on an undermined sand-cliff ready to crumble to pieces? and it doth crumble to pieces with him, into the fire of Hell. And Allah guideth not people that do wrong.	Is he who founded his building upon duty to Allah and His good pleasure better; or he who founded his building on the brink of a crumbling, overhanging precipice so that it toppled with him into the fire of hell? Allah guideth not wrongdoing folk.	Is he, therefore, better who lays his foundation on fear of Allah and (His) good pleasure, or he who lays his foundation on the edge of a cracking hollowed bank, so it broke down with him into the fire of hell; and Allah does not guide the unjust people.

9 110	The foundation of those who so build is never free from suspicion and shakiness in their hearts, until their hearts are cut to pieces. And Allah is All-Knowing, Wise.	The building which they built will never cease to be a misgiving in their hearts unless their hearts be torn to pieces. Allah is Knower, Wise.	The building which they have built will ever continue to be a source of disquiet in their hearts, except that their hearts get cut into pieces; and Allah is Knowing, Wise.
9 111	Allah hath purchased of the believers their persons and their goods; for theirs (in return) is the garden (of Paradise): they fight in His cause, and slay and are slain: a promise binding on Him in truth, through the Law, the Gospel, and the Qur'an: and who is more faithful to his covenant than Allah? then rejoice in the bargain which ye have concluded: that is the achievement supreme.	Lo! Allah hath bought from the believers their lives and their wealth because the Garden will be theirs: they shall fight in the way of Allah and shall slay and be slain. It is a promise which is binding on Him in the Torah and the Gospel and the Qur'an. Who fulfilleth His covenant better than Allah? Rejoice then in your bargain that ye have made, for that is the supreme triumph.	Surely Allah has bought of the believers their persons and their property for this, that they shall have the garden; they fight in Allah's way, so they slay and are slain; a promise which is binding on Him in the Taurat and the Injeel and the Quran; and who is more faithful to his covenant than Allah? Rejoice therefore in the pledge which you have made; and that is the mighty achievement.
9 112	Those that turn (to Allah) in repentance; that serve Him, and praise Him; that wander in devotion to the cause of Allah: that bow down and prostrate themselves in prayer; that enjoin good and forbid evil; and observe the limit set by Allah;- (These do rejoice). So proclaim the glad tidings to the Believers.	(Triumphant) are those who turn repentant (to Allah), those who serve (Him), those who praise (Him), those who fast, those who bow down, those who fall prostrate (in worship), those who enjoin the right and who forbid the wrong and those who keep the limits (ordained) of Allah - And give glad tidings to believers!	They who turn (to Allah), who serve (Him), who praise (Him), who fast, who bow down, who prostrate themselves, who enjoin what is good and forbid what is evil, and who keep the limits of Allah; and give good news to the believers.
9 113	It is not fitting, for the Prophet and those who believe, that they should pray for forgiveness for Pagans, even though they be of kin, after it is clear to them that they are companions of the Fire.	It is not for the Prophet, and those who believe, to pray for the forgiveness of idolaters even though they may be near of kin (to them) after it hath become clear that they are people of hell-fire.	It is not (fit) for the Prophet and those who believe that they should ask forgiveness for the polytheists, even though they should be near relatives, after it has become clear to them that they are inmates of the flaming fire.
9 114	And Abraham prayed for his father's forgiveness only because of a promise he had made to him. But when it became clear to him that he was an enemy to Allah, he dissociated himself from him: for Abraham was most tender-hearted, forbearing.	The prayer of Abraham for the forgiveness of his father was only because of a promise he had promised him, but when it had become clear unto him that he (his father) was an enemy to Allah he (Abraham) disowned him. Lo! Abraham was soft of heart, long-suffering.	And Ibrahim asking forgiveness for his sire was only owing to a promise which he had made to him; but when it became clear to him that he was an enemy of Allah, he declared himself to be clear of him; most surely Ibrahim was very tender-hearted forbearing.
9 115	And Allah will not mislead a people after He hath guided them, in order that He may make clear to them what to fear (and avoid)- for Allah hath knowledge of all things.	It was never Allah's (part) that He should send a folk astray after He had guided them until He had made clear unto them what they should avoid. Lo! Allah is Aware of all things.	It is not (attributable to) Allah that He should lead a people astray after He has guided them; He even makes clear to them what they should guard against; surely Allah knows all things.
9 116	Unto Allah belongeth the dominion of the heavens and the earth. He giveth life and He taketh it. Except for Him ye have no protector nor helper.	Lo! Allah! Unto Him belongeth the Sovereignty of the heavens and the earth. He quickeneth and He giveth death. And ye have, instead of Allah, no protecting friend nor helper.	Surely Allah's is the kingdom of the heavens and the earth; He brings to life and causes to die; and there is not for you besides Allah any Guardian or Helper.

9 117	Allah turned with favour to the Prophet, the Muhajirs, and the Ansar,- who followed him in a time of distress, after that the hearts of a part of them had nearly swerved (from duty); but He turned to them (also): for He is unto them Most Kind, Most Merciful.	Allah hath turned in mercy to the Prophet, and to the Muhajirin and the Ansar who followed him in the hour of hardship. After the hearts of a party of them had almost swerved aside, then turned He unto them in mercy. Lo! He is Full of Pity, Merciful for them.	Certainly Allah has turned (mercifully) to the Prophet and those who fled (their homes) and the helpers who followed him in the hour of straitness after the hearts of a part of them were about to deviate, then He turned to them (mercifully); surely to them He is Compassionate, Merciful.
9 118	(He turned in mercy also) to the three who were left behind; (they felt guilty) to such a degree that the earth seemed constrained to them, for all its spaciousness, and their (very) souls seemed straitened to them,- and they perceived that there is no fleeing from Allah (and no refuge) but to Himself. Then He turned to them, that they might repent: for Allah is Oft-Returning, Most Merciful.	And to the three also (did He turn in mercy) who were left behind, when the earth, vast as it is, was straitened for them, and their own souls were straitened for them till they bethought them that there is no refuge from Allah save toward Him. Then turned He unto them in mercy that they (too) might turn (repentant unto Him). Lo! Allah! He is the Relenting, the Merciful.	And to the three who were left behind, until the earth became strait to them notwithstanding its spaciousness and their souls were also straitened to them; and they knew it for certain that there was no refuge from Allah but in Him; then He turned to them (mercifully) that they might turn (to Him); surely Allah is the Oft-returning (to mercy), the Merciful.
9 119	O ye who believe! Fear Allah and be with those who are true (in word and deed).	O ye who believe! Be careful of your duty to Allah, and be with the truthful.	O you who believe! be careful of (your duty to) Allah and be with the true ones.
9 120	It was not fitting for the people of Medina and the Bedouin Arabs of the neighbourhood, to refuse to follow Allah's Messenger, nor to prefer their own lives to his: because nothing could they suffer or do, but was reckoned to their credit as a deed of righteousness,- whether they suffered thirst, or fatigue, or hunger, in the cause of Allah, or trod paths to raise the ire of the Unbelievers, or received any injury whatever from an enemy: for Allah suffereth not the reward to be lost of those who do good;-	It is not for the townsfolk of Al-Madinah and for those around them of the wandering Arabs so stay behind the messenger of Allah and prefer their lives to his life. That is because neither thirst nor toil nor hunger afflicteth them in the way of Allah, nor step they any step that angereth the disbelievers, nor gain they from the enemy a gain, but a good deed is recorded for them therefor. Lo! Allah loseth not the wages of the good.	It did not beseem the people of Medina and those round about them of the dwellers of the desert to remain behind the Messenger of Allah, nor should they desire (anything) for themselves in preference to him; this is because there afflicts them not thirst or fatigue or hunger in Allah's way, nor do they tread a path which enrages the unbelievers, nor do they attain from the enemy what they attain, but a good work is written down to them on account of it; surely Allah does not waste the reward of the doers of good;
9 121	Nor could they spend anything (for the cause) - small or great- nor cut across a valley, but the deed is inscribed to their credit: that Allah may requite their deed with the best (possible reward).	Nor spend they any spending, small or great, nor do they cross a valley, but it is recorded for them, that Allah may repay them the best of what they used to do.	Nor do they spend anything that may be spent, small or great, nor do they traverse a valley, but it is written down to their credit, that Allah may reward them with the best of what they have done.
9 122	Nor should the Believers all go forth together: if a contingent from every expedition remained behind, they could devote themselves to studies in religion, and admonish the people when they return to them,- that thus they (may learn) to guard themselves (against evil).	And the believers should not all go out to fight. Of every troop of them, a party only should go forth, that they (who are left behind) may gain sound knowledge in religion, and that they may warn their folk when they return to them, so that they may beware.	And it does not beseem the believers that they should go forth all together; why should not then a company from every party from among them go forth that they may apply themselves to obtain understanding in religion, and that they may warn their people when they come back to them that they may be cautious?

9	123	O ye who believe! fight the unbelievers who gird you about, and let them find firmness in you: and know that Allah is with those who fear Him.	O ye who believe! Fight those of the disbelievers who are near to you, and let them find harshness in you, and know that Allah is with those who keep their duty (unto Him).	O you who believe! fight those of the unbelievers who are near to you and let them find in you hardness; and know that Allah is with those who guard (against evil).
9	124	Whenever there cometh down a sura, some of them say: "Which of you has had his faith increased by it?" Yea, those who believe,- their faith is increased and they do rejoice.	And whenever a surah is revealed there are some of them who say: Which one of you hath thus increased in faith? As for those who believe, it hath increased them in faith and they rejoice (therefor).	And whenever a Chapter is revealed, there are some of them who say: Which of you has it strengthened in faith? Then as for those who believe, it strengthens them in faith and they rejoice.
9	125	But those in whose hearts is a disease,- it will add doubt to their doubt, and they will die in a state of Unbelief.	But as for those in whose hearts is disease, it only addeth wickedness to their wickedness, and they die while they are disbelievers.	And as for those in whose hearts is a disease, it adds uncleanness to their uncleanness and they die while they are unbelievers.
9	126	See they not that they are tried every year once or twice? Yet they turn not in repentance, and they take no heed.	See they not that they are tested once or twice in every year? Still they turn not in repentance, neither pay they heed.	Do they not see that they are tried once or twice in every year, yet they do not turn (to Allah) nor do they mind.
9	127	Whenever there cometh down a Sura, they look at each other, (saying), Doth anyone see you? Then they turn aside: Allah hath turned their hearts (from the light); for they are a people that understand not.	And whenever a surah is revealed, they look one at another (as who should say): Doth anybody see you? Then they turn away. Allah turneth away their hearts because they are a folk who understand not.	And whenever a Chapter is revealed, they cast glances at one another: Does any one see you? Then they turn away: Allah has turned away their hearts because they are a people who do not understand.
9	128	Now hath come unto you a Messenger from amongst yourselves: it grieves him that ye should perish: ardently anxious is he over you: to the Believers is he most kind and merciful.	There hath come unto you a messenger, (one) of yourselves, unto whom aught that ye are overburdened is grievous, full of concern for you, for the believers full of pity, merciful.	Certainly a Messenger has come to you from among yourselves; grievous to him is your falling into distress, excessively solicitous respecting you; to the believers (he is) compassionate,
9	129	But if they turn away, Say: "Allah sufficeth me: there is no god but He: On Him is my trust,- He the Lord of the Throne (of Glory) Supreme!"	Now, if they turn away (O Muhammad) say: Allah sufficeth me. There is no God save Him. In Him have I put my trust, and He is Lord of the Tremendous Throne.	But if they turn back, say: Allah is sufficient for me, there is no god but He; on Him do I rely, and He is the Lord of mighty power.

Chapter 10:

YUNUS (JONAH)

Total Verses: 109 Revealed At: MAKKA

In the name of Allah, the Most Beneficent, the Most Merciful.

10 001	A.L.R. These are the ayats of the Book of Wisdom.	Alif. Lam. Ra. These are verses of the Wise Scripture.	Alif Lam Ra. These are the verses of the wise Book.
10 002	Is it a matter of wonderment to men that We have sent Our inspiration to a man from among themselves?- that he should warn mankind (of their danger), and give the good news to the Believers that they have before their Lord the lofty rank of truth. (But) say the Unbelievers: "This is indeed an evident sorcerer!"	Is it a wonder for mankind that We have inspired a man among them, saying: Warn mankind and bring unto those who believe the good tidings that they have a sure footing with their Lord? The disbelievers say: Lo! this is a mere wizard.	What! is it a wonder to the people that We revealed to a man from among themselves, saying: Warn the people and give good news to those who believe that theirs is a footing of firmness with their Lord. The unbelievers say: This is most surely a manifest enchanter.
10 003	Verily your Lord is Allah, who created the heavens and the earth in six days, and is firmly established on the throne (of authority), regulating and governing all things. No intercessor (can plead with Him) except after His leave (hath been obtained). This is Allah your Lord; Him therefore serve ye: will ye not receive admonition?	Lo! your Lord is Allah Who created the heavens and the earth in six Days, then He established Himself upon the Throne, directing all things. There is no intercessor (with Him) save after His permission. That is Allah, your Lord, so worship Him. Oh, will ye not remind?	Surely your Lord is Allah, Who created the heavens and the earth in six periods, and He is firm in power, regulating the affair, there is no intercessor except after His permission; this is Allah, your Lord, therefore serve Him; will you not then mind?
10 004	To Him will be your return- of all of you. The promise of Allah is true and sure. It is He Who beginneth the process of creation, and repeateth it, that He may reward with justice those who believe and work righteousness; but those who reject Him will have draughts of boiling fluids, and a penalty grievous, because they did reject Him.	Unto Him is the return of all of you; it is a promise of Allah in truth. Lo! He produceth creation, then reproduceth it, that He may reward those who believe and do good works with equity; while, as for those who disbelieve, theirs will be a boiling drink and painful doom because they disbelieved.	To Him is your return, of all (of you); the promise of Allah (made) in truth; surely He begins the creation in the first instance, then He reproduces it, that He may with justice recompense those who believe and do good; and (as for) those who disbelieve, they shall have a drink of hot water and painful punishment because they disbelieved.
10 005	It is He Who made the sun to be a shining glory and the moon to be a light (of beauty), and measured out stages for her; that ye might know the number of years and the count (of time). Nowise did Allah create this but in truth and righteousness. (Thus) doth He explain His Signs in detail, for those who understand.	He it is Who appointed the sun a splendour and the moon a light, and measured for her stages, that ye might know the number of the years, and the reckoning. Allah created not (all) that save in truth. He detaileth the revelations for people who have knowledge.	He it is Who made the sun a shining brightness and the moon a light, and ordained for it mansions that you might know the computation of years and the reckoning. Allah did not create it but with truth; He makes the signs manifest for a people who know.
10 006	Verily, in the alternation of the night and the day, and in all that Allah hath created, in the heavens and the earth, are signs for those who fear Him.	Lo! in the difference of day and night and all that Allah hath created in the heavens and the earth are portents, verily, for folk who ward off (evil).	Most surely in the variation of the night and the day, and what Allah has created in the heavens and the earth, there are signs for a people who guard (against evil).

10 007	Those who rest not their hope on their meeting with Us, but are pleased and satisfied with the life of the present, and those who heed not Our Signs,-	Lo! those who expect not the meeting with Us but desire the life of the world and feel secure therein, and those who are neglectful of Our revelations,	Surely those who do not hope in Our meeting and are pleased with this world's life and are content with it, and those who are heedless of Our communications:
10 008	Their abode is the Fire, because of the (evil) they earned.	Their home will be the Fire because of what they used to earn.	(As for) those, their abode is the fire because of what they earned.
10 009	Those who believe, and work righteousness,- their Lord will guide them because of their faith: beneath them will flow rivers in gardens of bliss.	Lo! those who believe and do good works, their Lord guideth them by their faith. Rivers will flow beneath them in the Gardens of Delight,	Surely (as for) those who believe and do good, their Lord will guide them by their faith; there shall flow from beneath them rivers in gardens of bliss.
10 010	(This will be) their cry therein: "Glory to Thee, O Allah!" And Peace will be their greeting therein! and the close of their cry will be: "Praise be to Allah, the Cherisher and Sustainer of the worlds!"	Their prayer therein will be: Glory be to Thee, O Allah! and their greeting therein will be: Peace. And the conclusion of their prayer will be: Praise be to Allah, Lord of the Worlds!	Their cry in it shall be: Glory to Thee, O Allah! and their greeting in it shall be: Peace; and the last of their cry shall be: Praise be to Allah, the Lord of the worlds.
10 011	If Allah were to hasten for men the ill (they have earned) as they would fain hasten on the good,- then would their respite be settled at once. But We leave those who rest not their hope on their meeting with Us, in their trespasses, wandering in distraction to and fro.	If Allah were to hasten on for men the ill (that they have earned) as they would hasten on the good, their respite would already have expired. But We suffer those who look not for the meeting with Us to wander blindly on in their contumacy.	And if Allah should hasten the evil to men as they desire the hastening on of good, their doom should certainly have been decreed for them; but We leave those alone who hope not for Our meeting in their inordinacy, blindly wandering on.
10 012	When trouble toucheth a man, He crieth unto Us (in all postures)- lying down on his side, or sitting, or standing. But when We have solved his trouble, he passeth on his way as if he had never cried to Us for a trouble that touched him! thus do the deeds of transgressors seem fair in their eyes!	And if misfortune touch a man he crieth unto Us, (while reclining) on his side, or sitting or standing, but when We have relieved him of the misfortune he goeth his way as though he had not cried unto Us because of a misfortune that afflicted him. Thus is what they do made (seeming) fair unto the prodigal.	And when affliction touches a man, he calls on Us, whether lying on his side or sitting or standing; but when We remove his affliction from him, he passes on as though he had never called on Us on account of an affliction that touched him; thus that which they do is made fair-seeming to the extravagant.
10 013	Generations before you We destroyed when they did wrong: their messengers came to them with clear-signs, but they would not believe! thus do We requite those who sin!	We destroyed the generations before you when they did wrong; and their messengers (from Allah) came unto them with clear proofs (of His Sovereignty) but they would not believe. Thus do We reward the guilty folk.	And certainly We did destroy generations before you when they were unjust, and their messengers had come to them with clear arguments, and they would not believe; thus do We recompense the guilty people.
10 014	Then We made you heirs in the land after them, to see how ye would behave!	Then We appointed you viceroys in the earth after them, that We might see how ye behave.	Then We made you successors in the land after them so that We may see how you act.
10 015	But when Our Clear Signs are rehearsed unto them, those who rest not their hope on their meeting with Us, Say: "Bring us a reading other than this, or change this," Say: "It is not for me, of my own accord, to change it: I follow naught but what is revealed unto me: if I were to disobey my Lord, I should myself fear the penalty of a Great Day (to come)."	And when Our clear revelations are recited unto them, they who look not for the meeting with Us say: Bring a Lecture other than this, or change it. Say (O Muhammad): It is not for me to change it of my accord. I only follow that which is inspired in me. Lo! if I disobey my Lord I fear the retribution of an awful Day.	And when Our clear communications are recited to them, those who hope not for Our meeting say: Bring a Quran other than this or change it. Say: It does not beseem me that I should change it of myself; I follow naught but what is revealed to me; surely I fear, if I disobey my Lord, the punishment of a mighty day.

10 016	Say: "If Allah had so willed, I should not have rehearsed it to you, nor would He have made it known to you. A whole life-time before this have I tarried amongst you: will ye not then understand?"	Say: If Allah had so willed I should not have recited it to you nor would He have made it known to you. I dwelt among you a whole lifetime before it (came to me). Have ye then no sense?	Say: If Allah had desired (otherwise) I would not have recited it to you, nor would He have taught it to you; indeed I have lived a lifetime among you before it; do you not then understand?
10 017	Who doth more wrong than such as forge a lie against Allah, or deny His Signs? But never will prosper those who sin.	Who doeth greater wrong than he who inventeth a lie concerning Allah and denieth His revelations? Lo! the guilty never are successful.	Who is then more unjust than who forges a lie against Allah or (who) gives the lie to His communications? Surely the guilty shall not be successful.
10 018	They serve, besides Allah, things that hurt them not nor profit them, and they say: "These are our intercessors with Allah." Say: "Do ye indeed inform Allah of something He knows not, in the heavens or on earth?- Glory to Him! and far is He above the partners they ascribe (to Him)!"	They worship beside Allah that which neither hurteth them nor profiteth them, and they say: These are our intercessors with Allah. Say: Would ye inform Allah of (something) that He knoweth not in the heavens or in the earth? Praised be He and High Exalted above all that ye associate (with Him)!	And they serve beside Allah what can neither harm them nor profit them, and they say: These are our intercessors with Allah. Say: Do you (presume to) inform Allah of what He knows not in the heavens and the earth? Glory be to Him, and supremely exalted is He above what they set up (with Him).
10 019	Mankind was but one nation, but differed (later). Had it not been for a word that went forth before from thy Lord, their differences would have been settled between them.	Mankind were but one community; then they differed; and had it not been for a word that had already gone forth from thy Lord it had been judged between them in respect of that wherein they differ.	And people are naught but a single nation, so they disagree; and had not a word already gone forth from your Lord, the matter would have certainly been decided between them in respect of that concerning which they disagree.
10 020	They say: "Why is not a sign sent down to him from his Lord?" Say: The Unseen is only for Allah (to know), then wait ye: I too will wait with you."	And they will say: If only a portent were sent down upon him from his Lord! Then say, (O Muhammad): The Unseen belongeth to Allah. So wait! Lo! I am waiting with you.	And they say: Why is not a sign sent to him from his Lord? Say: The unseen is only for Allah; therefore wait-- surely I too, with you am of those who wait.
10 021	When We make mankind taste of some mercy after adversity hath touched them, behold! they take to plotting against Our Signs! Say: "Swifter to plan is Allah!" Verily, Our messengers record all the plots that ye make!	And when We cause mankind to taste of mercy after some adversity which had afflicted them, behold! they have some plot against Our revelations. Say: Allah is more swift in plotting. Lo! Our messengers write down that which ye plot.	And when We make people taste of mercy after an affliction touches them, lo! they devise plans against Our communication. Say: Allah is quicker to plan; surely Our messengers write down what you plan.
10 022	He it is Who enableth you to traverse through land and sea; so that ye even board ships;- they sail with them with a favourable wind, and they rejoice there at; then comes a stormy wind and the waves come to them from all sides, and they think they are being overwhelmed: they cry unto Allah, sincerely offering (their) duty unto Him saying, "If thou dost deliver us from this, we shall truly show our gratitude!"	He it is Who maketh you to go on the land and the sea till, when ye are in the ships and they sail with them with a fair breeze and they are glad therein, a storm-wind reacheth them and the wave cometh unto them from every side and they deem that they are overwhelmed therein; (then) they cry unto Allah, making their faith pure for Him only: If Thou deliver us from this, we truly will be of the thankful.	He it is Who makes you travel by land and sea; until when you are in the ships, and they sail on with them in a pleasant breeze, and they rejoice, a violent wind overtakes them and the billows surge in on them from all sides, and they become certain that they are encompassed about, they pray to Allah, being sincere to Him in obedience: If Thou dost deliver us from this, we will most certainly be of the grateful ones.

10 023	But when He delivereth them, behold! they transgress insolently through the earth in defiance of right! O mankind! your insolence is against your own souls,- an enjoyment of the life of the present: in the end, to Us is your return, and We shall show you the truth of all that ye did.	Yet when He hath delivered them, behold! they rebel in the earth wrongfully. O mankind! Your rebellion is only against yourselves. (Ye have) enjoyment of the life of the world; then unto Us is your return and We shall proclaim unto you what ye used to do.	But when He delivers them, lo! they are unjustly rebellious in the earth. O men! your rebellion is against your own souls-- provision (only) of this world's life-- then to Us shall be your return, so We will inform you of what you did.
10 024	The likeness of the life of the present is as the rain which We send down from the skies: by its mingling arises the produce of the earth- which provides food for men and animals: (It grows) till the earth is clad with its golden ornaments and is decked out (in beauty): the people to whom it belongs think they have all powers of disposal over it: There reaches it Our command by night or by day, and We make it like a harvest clean-mown, as if it had not flourished only the day before! thus do We explain the Signs in detail for those who reflect.	The similitude of the life of the world is only as water which We send down from the sky, then the earth's growth of that which men and cattle eat mingleth with it till, when the earth hath taken on her ornaments and is embellished, and her people deem that they are masters of her, Our commandment cometh by night or by day and We make it as reaped corn as if it had not flourished yesterday. Thus do we expound the revelations for people who reflect.	The likeness of this world's life is only as water which We send down from the cloud, then the herbage of the earth of which men and cattle eat grows luxuriantly thereby, until when the earth puts on its golden raiment and it becomes garnished, and its people think that they have power over it, Our command comes to it, by night or by day, so We render it as reaped seed; produce, as though it had not been in existence yesterday; thus do We make clear the communications for a people who reflect.
10 025	But Allah doth call to the Home of Peace: He doth guide whom He pleaseth to a way that is straight.	And Allah summoneth to the abode of peace, and leadeth whom He will to a straight path.	And Allah invites to the abode of peace and guides whom He pleases into the right path.
10 026	To those who do right is a goodly (reward)- Yea, more (than in measure)! No darkness nor shame shall cover their faces! they are companions of the garden; they will abide therein (for aye)!	For those who do good is the best (reward) and more (thereto). Neither dust nor ignominy cometh near their faces. Such are rightful owners of the Garden; they will abide therein.	For those who do good is good (reward) and more (than this); and blackness or ignominy shall not cover their faces; these are the dwellers of the garden; in it they shall abide.
10 027	But those who have earned evil will have a reward of like evil: ignominy will cover their (faces): No defender will they have from (the wrath of) Allah: Their faces will be covered, as it were, with pieces from the depth of the darkness of night: they are companions of the Fire: they will abide therein (for aye)!	And those who earn ill-deeds, (for them) requital of each ill-deed by the like thereof; and ignominy overtaketh them - They have no protector from Allah - as if their faces had been covered with a cloak of darkest night. Such are rightful owners of the Fire; they will abide therein.	And (as for) those who have earned evil, the punishment of an evil is the like of it, and abasement shall come upon them-- they shall have none to protect them from Allah-- as if their faces had been covered with slices of the dense darkness of night; these are the inmates of the fire; in it they shall abide.
10 028	One day shall We gather them all together. Then shall We say to those who joined gods (with Us): "To your place! ye and those ye joined as 'partners'." We shall separate them, and their 'Partners' shall say: "It was not us that ye worshipped!"	On the day when We gather them all together, then We say unto those who ascribed partners (unto Us): Stand back, ye and your (pretended) partners (of Allah)! And We separate them, the one from the other, and their (pretended) partners say: It was not us ye worshipped.	And on the day when We will gather them all together, then We will say to those who associated others (with Allah): Keep where you are, you and your associates; then We shall separate them widely one from another and their associates would say: It was not us that you served:
10 029	"Enough is Allah for a witness between us and you: we certainly knew nothing of your worship of us!"	Allah sufficeth as a witness between us and you, that we were unaware of your worship.	Therefore Allah is sufficient as a witness between us and you that we were quite unaware of your serving (us).

10 030	There will every soul prove (the fruits of) the deeds it sent before: they will be brought back to Allah their rightful Lord, and their invented falsehoods will leave them in the lurch.	There doth every soul experience that which it did aforetime, and they are returned unto Allah, their rightful Lord, and that which they used to invent hath failed them.	There shall every soul become acquainted with what it sent before, and they shall be brought back to Allah, their true Patron, and what they devised shall escape from them.
10 031	Say: "Who is it that sustains you (in life) from the sky and from the earth? or who is it that has power over hearing and sight? And who is it that brings out the living from the dead and the dead from the living? and who is it that rules and regulates all affairs?" They will soon say, Allah. Say, "will ye not then show piety (to Him)?"	Say (unto them, O Muhammad): Who provideth for you from the sky and the earth, or Who owneth hearing and sight; and Who bringeth forth the living from the dead and bringeth forth the dead from the living; and Who directeth the course? They will say: Allah. Then say: Will ye not then keep your duty (unto Him)?	Say: Who gives you sustenance from the heaven and the earth? Or Who controls the hearing and the sight? And Who brings forth the living from the dead, and brings forth the dead from the living? And Who regulates the affairs? Then they will say: Allah. Say then: Will you not then guard (against evil)?
10 032	Such is Allah, your real Cherisher and Sustainer: apart from truth, what (remains) but error? How then are ye turned away?	Such then is Allah, your rightful Lord. After the Truth what is there saving error? How then are ye turned away!	This then is Allah, your true Lord; and what is there after the truth but error; how are you then turned back?
10 033	Thus is the word of thy Lord proved true against those who rebel: Verily they will not believe.	Thus is the Word of thy Lord justified concerning those who do wrong: that they believe not.	Thus does the word of your Lord prove true against those who transgress that they do not believe.
10 034	Say: "Of your 'partners', can any originate creation and repeat it?" Say: "It is Allah Who originates creation and repeats it: then how are ye deluded away (from the truth)?"	Say: Is there of your partners (whom ye ascribe unto Allah) one that produceth Creation and then reproduceth it? Say: Allah produceth Creation, then reproduceth it. How then, are ye misled!	Say: Is there any one among your associates who can bring into existence the creation in the first instance, then reproduce it? Say: Allah brings the creation into existence, then He reproduces it; how are you then turned away?
10 035	Say: "Of your 'partners' is there any that can give any guidance towards truth?" Say: "It is Allah Who gives guidance towards truth, is then He Who gives guidance to truth more worthy to be followed, or he who finds not guidance (himself) unless he is guided? what then is the matter with you? How judge ye?"	Say: Is there of your partners (whom ye ascribe unto Allah) one that leadeth to the Truth? Say: Allah leadeth to the Truth. Is He Who leadeth to the Truth more deserving that He should be followed, or he who findeth not the way unless he (himself) be guided. What aileth you? How judge ye?	Say: Is there any of your associates who guides to the truth? Say: Allah guides to the truth. Is He then Who guides to the truth more worthy to be followed, or he who himself does not go aright unless he is guided? What then is the matter with you; how do you judge?
10 036	But most of them follow nothing but fancy: truly fancy can be of no avail against truth. Verily Allah is well aware of all that they do.	Most of them follow not but conjecture. Assuredly conjecture can by no means take the place of truth. Lo! Allah is Aware of what they do.	And most of them do not follow (anything) but conjecture; surely conjecture will not avail aught against the truth; surely Allah is cognizant of what they do.
10 037	This Qur'an is not such as can be produced by other than Allah; on the contrary it is a confirmation of (revelations) that went before it, and a fuller explanation of the Book - wherein there is no doubt - from the Lord of the worlds.	And this Qur'an is not such as could ever be invented in despite of Allah; but it is a confirmation of that which was before it and an exposition of that which is decreed for mankind - Therein is no doubt - from the Lord of the Worlds.	And this Quran is not such as could be forged by those besides Allah, but it is a verification of that which is before it and a clear explanation of the book, there is no doubt in it, from the Lord of the worlds.
10 038	Or do they say, "He forged it"? say: "Bring then a Sura like unto it, and call (to your aid) anyone you can besides Allah, if it be ye speak the truth!"	Or say they: He hath invented it? Say: Then bring a surah like unto it, and call (for help) on all ye can besides Allah, if ye are truthful.	Or do they say: He has forged it? Say: Then bring a Chapter like this and invite whom you can besides Allah, if you are truthful.

10 039	Nay, they charge with falsehood that whose knowledge they cannot compass, even before the elucidation thereof hath reached them: thus did those before them make charges of falsehood: but see what was the end of those who did wrong!	Nay, but they denied that, the knowledge whereof they could not compass, and whereof the interpretation (in events) hath not yet come unto them. Even so did those before them deny. Then see what was the consequence for the wrong-doers!	Nay, they reject that of which they have no comprehensive knowledge, and the final sequel of it has not yet come to them; even thus did those before them reject (the truth); see then what was the end of the unjust.
10 040	Of them there are some who believe therein, and some who do not: and thy Lord knoweth best those who are out for mischief.	And of them is he who believeth therein, and of them is he who believeth not therein, and thy Lord is Best Aware of the corrupters.	And of them is he who believes in it, and of them is he who does not believe in it, and your Lord best knows the mischief-makers.
10 041	If they charge thee with falsehood, say: "My work to me, and yours to you! ye are free from responsibility for what I do, and I for what ye do!"	And if they deny thee, say: Unto me my work, and unto you your work. Ye are innocent of what I do, and I am innocent of what ye do.	And if they call you a liar, say: My work is for me and your work for you; you are clear of what I do and I am clear of what you do.
10 042	Among them are some who (pretend to) listen to thee: But canst thou make the deaf to hear,- even though they are without understanding?	And of them are some who listen unto thee. But canst thou make the deaf to hear even though they apprehend not?	And there are those of them who hear you, but can you make the deaf to hear though they will not understand?
10 043	And among them are some who look at thee: but canst thou guide the blind,- even though they will not see?	And of them is he who looketh toward thee. But canst thou guide the blind even though they see not?	And there are those of them who look at you, but can you show the way to the blind though they will not see?
10 044	Verily Allah will not deal unjustly with man in aught: It is man that wrongs his own soul.	Lo! Allah wrongeth not mankind in aught; but mankind wrong themselves.	Surely Allah does not do any injustice to men, but men are unjust to themselves.
10 045	One day He will gather them together: (It will be) as if they had tarried but an hour of a day: they will recognise each other: assuredly those will be lost who denied the meeting with Allah and refused to receive true guidance.	And on the day when He shall gather them together, (when it will seem) as though they had tarried but an hour of the day, recognising one another, those will verily have perished who denied the meeting with Allah and were not guided.	And on the day when He will gather them as though they had not stayed but an hour of the day, they will know each other. They will perish indeed who called the meeting with Allah to be a lie, and they are not followers of the right direction.
10 046	Whether We show thee (realised in thy life-time) some part of what We promise them,- or We take thy soul (to Our Mercy) (Before that),- in any case, to Us is their return: ultimately Allah is witness, to all that they do.	Whether We let thee (O Muhammad) behold something of that which We promise them or (whether We) cause thee to die, still unto Us is their return, and Allah, moreover, is Witness over what they do.	And if We show you something of what We threaten them with, or cause you to die, yet to Us is their return, and Allah is the bearer of witness to what they do.
10 047	To every people (was sent) a messenger: when their messenger comes (before them), the matter will be judged between them with justice, and they will not be wronged.	And for every nation there is a messenger. And when their messenger cometh (on the Day of Judgment) it will be judged between them fairly, and they will not be wronged.	And every nation had a messenger; so when their messenger came, the matter was decided between them with justice and they shall not be dealt with unjustly.
10 048	They say: "When will this promise come to pass,- if ye speak the truth?"	And they say: When will this promise be fulfilled, if ye are truthful?	And they say: When will this threat come about, if you are truthful?

10 049	Say: "I have no power over any harm or profit to myself except as Allah willeth. To every people is a term appointed: when their term is reached, not an hour can they cause delay, nor (an hour) can they advance (it in anticipation)."	Say: I have no power to hurt or benefit myself, save that which Allah willeth. For every nation there is an appointed time. When their time cometh, then they cannot put it off an hour, nor hasten (it).	Say: I do not control for myself any harm, or any benefit except what Allah pleases; every nation has a term; when their term comes, they shall not then remain behind for an hour, nor can they go before (their time).
10 050	Say: "Do ye see,- if His punishment should come to you by night or by day,- what portion of it would the sinners wish to hasten?"	Say: Have ye thought: When His doom cometh unto you as a raid by night, or in the (busy) day; what is there of it that the guilty ones desire to hasten?	Say: Tell me if His punishment overtakes you by night or by day! what then is there of it that the guilty would hasten on?
10 051	"Would ye then believe in it at last, when it actually cometh to pass?" (It will then be said): 'Ah! now? and ye wanted (aforetime) to hasten it on!'	Is it (only) then, when it hath befallen you, that ye will believe? What! (Believe) now, when (until now) ye have been hastening it on (through disbelief)?	And when it comes to pass, will you believe in it? What! now (you believe), and already you wished to have it hastened on.
10 052	"At length will be said to the wrong-doers: 'Taste ye the enduring punishment! ye get but the recompense of what ye earned!'"	Then will it be said unto those who dealt unjustly Taste the torment of eternity. Are ye requited aught save what ye used to earn?	Then it shall be said to those who were unjust: Taste abiding chastisement; you are not requited except for what you earned.
10 053	They seek to be informed by thee: "Is that true?" Say: "Aye! by my Lord! it is the very truth! and ye cannot frustrate it!"	And they ask thee to inform them (saying): Is it true? Say: Yea, by my Lord, verily it is true, and ye cannot escape.	And they ask you: Is that true? Say: Aye! by my Lord! it is most surely the truth, and you will not escape.
10 054	Every soul that hath sinned, if it possessed all that is on earth, would fain give it in ransom: They would declare (their) repentance when they see the penalty: but the judgment between them will be with justice, and no wrong will be done unto them.	And if each soul that doeth wrong had all that is in the earth it would seek to ransom itself therewith; and they will feel remorse within them, when they see the doom. But it hath been judged between them fairly and they are not wronged.	And if every soul that has done injustice had all that is in the earth, it would offer it for ransom, and they will manifest regret when they see the chastisement and the matter shall be decided between them with justice and they shall not be dealt with unjustly.
10 055	Is it not (the case) that to Allah belongeth whatever is in the heavens and on earth? Is it not (the case) that Allah's promise is assuredly true? Yet most of them understand not.	Lo! verily all that is in the heavens and the earth is Allah's. Lo! verily Allah's promise is true. But most of them know not.	Now surely Allah's is what is in the heavens and the earth; now surely Allah's promise is true, but most of them do not know.
10 056	It is He Who giveth life and who taketh it, and to Him shall ye all be brought back.	He quickeneth and giveth death, and unto Him ye will be returned.	He gives life and causes death, and to Him you shall be brought back.
10 057	O mankind! there hath come to you a direction from your Lord and a healing for the (diseases) in your hearts,- and for those who believe, a guidance and a Mercy.	O mankind! There hath come unto you an exhortation from your Lord, a balm for that which is in the breasts, a guidance and a mercy for believers.	O men! there has come to you indeed an admonition from your Lord and a healing for what is in the breasts and a guidance and a mercy for the believers.
10 058	Say: "In the bounty of Allah. And in His Mercy,- in that let them rejoice": that is better than the (wealth) they hoard.	Say: In the bounty of Allah and in His mercy: therein let them rejoice. It is better than what they hoard.	Say: In the grace of Allah and in His mercy-- in that they should rejoice; it is better than that which they gather.
10 059	Say: "See ye what things Allah hath sent down to you for sustenance? Yet ye hold forbidden some things thereof and (some things) lawful." Say: "Hath Allah indeed permitted you, or do ye invent (things) to attribute to Allah?"	Say: Have ye considered what provision Allah hath sent down for you, how ye have made of it lawful and unlawful? Hath Allah permitted you, or do ye invent a lie concerning Allah?	Say: Tell me what Allah has sent down for you of sustenance, then you make (a part) of it unlawful and (a part) lawful. Say: Has Allah commanded you, or do you forge a lie against Allah?

10 060	And what think those who invent lies against Allah, of the Day of Judgment? Verily Allah is full of bounty to mankind, but most of them are ungrateful.	And what think those who invent a lie concerning Allah (will be their plight) upon the Day of Resurrection? Lo! Allah truly is Bountiful toward mankind, but most of them give not thanks.	And what will be the thought of those who forge lies against Allah on the day of resurrection? Most surely Allah is the Lord of grace towards men, but most of them do not give thanks.
10 061	In whatever business thou mayest be, and whatever portion thou mayest be reciting from the Qur'an,- and whatever deed ye (mankind) may be doing,- We are witnesses thereof when ye are deeply engrossed therein. Nor is hidden from thy Lord (so much as) the weight of an atom on the earth or in heaven. And not the least and not the greatest of these things but are recorded in a clear record.	And thou (Muhammad) art not occupied with any business and thou recitest not a Lecture from this (Scripture), and ye (mankind) perform no act, but We are Witness of you when ye are engaged therein. And not an atom's weight in the earth or in the sky escapeth your Lord, nor what is less than that or greater than that, but it is (written) in a clear Book.	And you are not (engaged) in any affair, nor do you recite concerning it any portion of the Quran, nor do you do any work but We are witnesses over you when you enter into it, and there does not lie concealed from your Lord the weight of an atom in the earth or in the heaven, nor any thing less than that nor greater, but it is in a clear book.
10 062	Behold! verily on the friends of Allah there is no fear, nor shall they grieve;	Lo! verily the friends of Allah are (those) on whom fear (cometh) not, nor do they grieve?	Now surely the friends of Allah-- they shall have no fear nor shall they grieve.
10 063	Those who believe and (constantly) guard against evil;-	Those who believe and keep their duty (to Allah).	Those who believe and guarded (against evil):
10 064	For them are glad tidings, in the life of the present and in the Hereafter; no change can there be in the words of Allah. This is indeed the supreme felicity.	Theirs are good tidings in the life of the world and in the Hereafter - There is no changing the Words of Allah - that is the Supreme Triumph.	They shall have good news in this world's life and in the hereafter; there is no changing the words of Allah; that is the mighty achievement.
10 065	Let not their speech grieve thee: for all power and honour belong to Allah: It is He Who heareth and knoweth (all things).	And let not their speech grieve thee (O Muhammad). Lo! power belongeth wholly to Allah. He is the Hearer, the Knower.	And let not their speech grieve you; surely might is wholly Allah's; He is the Hearing, the Knowing.
10 066	Behold! verily to Allah belong all creatures, in the heavens and on earth. What do they follow who worship as His "partners" other than Allah? They follow nothing but fancy, and they do nothing but lie.	Lo! is it not unto Allah that belongeth whosoever is in the heavens and whosoever is in the earth? Those who follow aught instead of Allah follow not (His) partners. They follow only a conjecture, and they do but guess.	Now, surely, whatever is in the heavens and whatever is in the earth is Allah's; and they do not (really) follow any associates, who call on others besides Allah; they do not follow (anything) but conjectures, and they only lie.
10 067	He it is That hath made you the night that ye may rest therein, and the day to make things visible (to you). Verily in this are signs for those who listen (to His Message).	He it is Who hath appointed for you the night that ye should rest therein and the day giving sight. Lo! herein verily are portents for a folk that heed.	He it is Who made for you the night that you might rest in it, and the day giving light; most surely there are signs in it for a people who would hear.
10 068	They say: "Allah hath begotten a son!" - Glory be to Him! He is self-sufficient! His are all things in the heavens and on earth! No warrant have ye for this! say ye about Allah what ye know not?	They say: Allah hath taken (unto Him) a son - Glorified be He! He hath no needs! His is all that is in the heavens and all that is in the earth. Ye have no warrant for this. Tell ye concerning Allah that which ye know not?	They say: Allah has taken a son (to Himself)! Glory be to Him: He is the Self-sufficient: His is what is in the heavens and what is in the earth; you have no authority for this; do you say against Allah what you do not know?
10 069	Say: "Those who invent a lie against Allah will never prosper."	Say: Verily those who invent a lie concerning Allah will not succeed.	Say: Those who forge a lie against Allah shall not be successful.
10 070	A little enjoyment in this world!- and then, to Us will be their return, then shall We make them taste the severest penalty for their blasphemies.	This world's portion (will be theirs), then unto Us is their return. Then We make them taste a dreadful doom because they used to disbelieve.	(It is only) a provision in this world, then to Us shall be their return; then We shall make them taste severe punishment because they disbelieved.

10 071	Relate to them the story of Noah. Behold! he said to his people: O my people, if it be hard on your (mind) that I should stay (with you) and commemorate the signs of Allah,- yet I put my trust in Allah. Get ye then an agreement about your plan and among your partners, so your plan be on to you dark and dubious. Then pass your sentence on me, and give me no respite."	Recite unto them the story of Noah, when he told his people: O my people! If my sojourn (here) and my reminding you by Allah's revelations are an offence unto you, in Allah have I put my trust, so decide upon your course of action you and your partners. Let not your course of action be in doubt for you. Then have at me, give me no respite.	And recite to them the story of Nuh when he said to his people: O my people! if my stay and my reminding (you) by the communications of Allah is hard on you-- yet on Allah do I rely-- then resolve upon your affair and (gather) your associates, then let not your affair remain dubious to you, then have it executed against me and give me no respite:
10 072	"But if ye turn back, (consider): no reward have I asked of you: my reward is only due from Allah, and I have been commanded to be of those who submit to Allah's will (in Islam)."	But if ye are averse I have asked of you no wage. My wage is the concern of Allah only, and I am commanded to be of those who surrender (unto Him).	But if you turn back, I did not ask for any reward from you; my reward is only with Allah, and I am commanded that I should be of those who submit.
10 073	They rejected Him, but We delivered him, and those with him, in the Ark, and We made them inherit (the earth), while We overwhelmed in the flood those who rejected Our Signs. Then see what was the end of those who were warned (but heeded not)!	But they denied him, so We saved him and those with him in the ship, and made them viceroys (in the earth), while We drowned those who denied Our revelations. See then the nature of the consequence for those who had been warned.	But they rejected him, so We delivered him and those with him in the ark, and We made them rulers and drowned those who rejected Our communications; see then what was the end of the (people) warned.
10 074	Then after him We sent (many) messengers to their peoples: they brought them Clear Signs, but they would not believe what they had already rejected beforehand. Thus do We seal the hearts of the transgressors.	Then, after him, We sent messengers unto their folk, and they brought them clear proofs. But they were not ready to believe in that which they before denied. Thus print We on the hearts of the transgressors.	Then did We raise up after him messengers to their people, so they came to them with clear arguments, but they would not believe in what they had rejected before; thus it is that We set seals upon the hearts of those who exceed the limits.
10 075	Then after them sent We Moses and Aaron to Pharaoh and his chiefs with Our Signs. But they were arrogant: they were a people in sin.	Then, after them, We sent Moses and Aaron unto Pharaoh and his chiefs with Our revelations, but they were arrogant and were a guilty folk.	Then did We send up after them Musa and Haroun to Firon and his chiefs with Our signs, but they showed pride and they were a guilty people.
10 076	When the Truth did come to them from Us, they said: "This is indeed evident sorcery!"	And when the Truth from Our presence came unto them, they said: Lo! this is mere magic.	So when the truth came to them from Us they said: This is most surely clear enchantment!
10 077	Said Moses: "Say ye (this) about the truth when it hath (actually) reached you? Is sorcery (like) this? But sorcerers will not prosper."	Moses said: Speak ye (so) of the Truth when it hath come unto you? Is this magic? Now magicians thrive not.	Musa said: Do you say (this) of the truth when it has come to you? Is it magic? And the magicians are not successful.
10 078	They said: "Hast thou come to us to turn us away from the ways we found our fathers following,- in order that thou and thy brother may have greatness in the land? But not we shall believe in you!"	They said: Hast thou come unto us to pervert us from that (faith) in which we found our fathers, and that you two may own the place of greatness in the land? We will not believe you two.	They said: Have you come to us to turn us away from what we found our fathers upon, and (that) greatness in the land should be for you two? And we are not going to believe in you.
10 079	Said Pharaoh: "Bring me every sorcerer well versed."	And Pharaoh said: Bring every cunning wizard unto me.	And Firon said: Bring to me every skillful magician.
10 080	When the sorcerers came, Moses said to them: "Throw ye what ye (wish) to throw!"	And when the wizards came, Moses said unto them: Cast your cast!	And when the magicians came, Musa said to them: Cast down what you have to cast.

10 081	When they had had their throw, Moses said: "What ye have brought is sorcery: Allah will surely make it of no effect: for Allah prospereth not the work of those who make mischief."	And when they had cast, Moses said: That which ye have brought is magic. Lo! Allah will make it vain. Lo! Allah upholdeth not the work of mischief-makers.	So when they cast down, Musa said to them: What you have brought is deception; surely Allah will make it naught; surely Allah does not make the work of mischief-makers to thrive.
10 082	"And Allah by His words doth prove and establish His truth, however much the sinners may hate it!"	And Allah will vindicate the Truth by His words, however much the guilty be averse.	And Allah will show the truth to be the truth by His words, though the guilty may be averse (to it).
10 083	But none believed in Moses except some children of his people, because of the fear of Pharaoh and his chiefs, lest they should persecute them; and certainly Pharaoh was mighty on the earth and one who transgressed all bounds.	But none trusted Moses, save some scions of his people, (and they were) in fear of Pharaoh and their chiefs, that he would persecute them. Lo! Pharaoh was verily a tyrant in the land, and lo! he verily was of the wanton.	But none believed in Musa except the offspring of his people, on account of the fear of Firon and their chiefs, lest he should persecute them; and most surely Firon was lofty in the land; and most surely he was of the extravagant.
10 084	Moses said: "O my people! If ye do (really) believe in Allah, then in Him put your trust if ye submit (your will to His)."	And Moses said: O my people! If ye have believed in Allah then put trust in Him, if ye have indeed surrendered (unto Him)!	And Musa said: O my people! if you believe in Allah, then rely on Him (alone) if you submit (to Allah).
10 085	They said: "In Allah do we put out trust. Our Lord! make us not a trial for those who practise oppression;"	They said: In Allah we put trust. Our Lord! Oh, make us not a lure for the wrongdoing folk;	So they said: On Allah we rely: O our Lord! make us not subject to the persecution of the unjust people:
10 086	"And deliver us by Thy Mercy from those who reject (Thee)."	And, of Thy mercy, save us from the folk that disbelieve.	And do Thou deliver us by Thy mercy from the unbelieving people.
10 087	We inspired Moses and his brother with this Message: "Provide dwellings for your people in Egypt, make your dwellings into places of worship, and establish regular prayers: and give glad tidings to those who believe!"	And We inspired Moses and his brother, (saying): Appoint houses for your people in Egypt and make your houses oratories, and establish worship. And give good news to the believers.	And We revealed to Musa and his brother, saying: Take for your people houses to abide in Egypt and make your houses places of worship and keep up prayer and give good news to the believers.
10 088	Moses prayed: "Our Lord! Thou hast indeed bestowed on Pharaoh and his chiefs splendour and wealth in the life of the present, and so, Our Lord, they mislead (men) from Thy Path. Deface our Lord, the features of their wealth, and send hardness to their hearts, so they will not believe until they see the grievous penalty."	And Moses said: Our Lord! Lo! Thou hast given Pharaoh and his chiefs splendour and riches in the life of the world, Our Lord! that they may lead men astray from Thy way. Our Lord! Destroy their riches and harden their hearts so that they believe not till they see the painful doom.	And Musa said: Our Lord! surely Thou hast given to Firon and his chiefs finery and riches in this world's life, to this end, our Lord, that they lead (people) astray from Thy way: Our Lord! destroy their riches and harden their hearts so that they believe not until they see the painful punishment.
10 089	Allah said: "Accepted is your prayer (O Moses and Aaron)! So stand ye straight, and follow not the path of those who know not."	He said: Your prayer is heard. Do ye twain keep to the straight path, and follow not the road of those who have no knowledge.	He said: The prayer of you both has indeed been accepted, therefore continue in the right way and do not follow the path of those who do not know.
10 090	We took the Children of Israel across the sea: Pharaoh and his hosts followed them in insolence and spite. At length, when overwhelmed with the flood, he said: "I believe that there is no god except Him Whom the Children of Israel believe in: I am of those who submit (to Allah in Islam)."	And We brought the Children of Israel across the sea, and Pharaoh with his hosts pursued them in rebellion and transgression, till, when the (fate of) drowning overtook him, he exclaimed: I believe that there is no God save Him in Whom the Children of Israel believe, and I am of those who surrender (unto Him).	And We made the children of Israel to pass through the sea, then Firon and his hosts followed them for oppression and tyranny; until when drowning overtook him, he said: I believe that there is no god but He in Whom the children of Israel believe and I am of those who submit.

10 091	(It was said to him): "Ah now!- But a little while before, wast thou in rebellion!- and thou didst mischief (and violence)!"	What! Now! When hitherto thou hast rebelled and been of the wrong-doers?	What! now! and indeed you disobeyed before and you were of the mischief-makers.
10 092	"This day shall We save thee in the body, that thou mayest be a sign to those who come after thee! but verily, many among mankind are heedless of Our Signs!"	But this day We save thee in thy body that thou mayst be a portent for those after thee. Lo! most of mankind are heedless of Our portents.	But We will this day deliver you with your body that you may be a sign to those after you, and most surely the majority of the people are heedless to Our communications.
10 093	We settled the Children of Israel in a beautiful dwelling-place, and provided for them sustenance of the best: it was after knowledge had been granted to them, that they fell into schisms. Verily Allah will judge between them as to the schisms amongst them, on the Day of Judgment.	And We verily did allot unto the Children of Israel a fixed abode, and did provide them with good things; and they differed not until the knowledge came unto them. Lo! thy Lord will judge between them on the Day of Resurrection concerning that wherein they used to differ.	And certainly We lodged the children of Israel in a goodly abode and We provided them with good things; but they did not disagree until the knowledge had come to them; surely your Lord will judge between them on the resurrection day concerning that in which they disagreed.
10 094	If thou wert in doubt as to what We have revealed unto thee, then ask those who have been reading the Book from before thee: the Truth hath indeed come to thee from thy Lord: so be in no wise of those in doubt.	And if thou (Muhammad) art in doubt concerning that which We reveal unto thee, then question those who read the Scripture (that was) before thee. Verily the Truth from thy Lord hath come unto thee. So be not thou of the waverers.	But if you are in doubt as to what We have revealed to you, ask those who read the Book before you; certainly the truth has come to you from your Lord, therefore you should not be of the disputers.
10 095	Nor be of those who reject the signs of Allah, or thou shalt be of those who perish.	And be not thou of those who deny the revelations of Allah, for then wert thou of the losers.	And you should not be of those who reject the communications of Allah, (for) then you should be one of the losers.
10 096	Those against whom the word of thy Lord hath been verified would not believe-	Lo! those for whom the word of thy Lord (concerning sinners) hath effect will not believe,	Surely those against whom the word of your Lord has proved true will not believe,
10 097	Even if every Sign was brought unto them,- until they see (for themselves) the penalty grievous.	Though every token come unto them, till they see the painful doom.	Though every sign should come to them, until they witness the painful chastisement.
10 098	Why was there not a single township (among those We warned), which believed,- so its faith should have profited it,- except the people of Jonah? When they believed, We removed from them the penalty of ignominy in the life of the present, and permitted them to enjoy (their life) for a while.	If only there had been a community (of all those that were destroyed of old) that believed and profited by its belief as did the folk of Jonah! When they believed We drew off from them the torment of disgrace in the life of the world and gave them comfort for a while.	And wherefore was there not a town which should believe so that their belief should have profited them but the people of Yunus? When they believed, We removed from them the chastisement of disgrace in this world's life and We gave them provision till a time.
10 099	If it had been thy Lord's will, they would all have believed,- all who are on earth! wilt thou then compel mankind, against their will, to believe!	And if thy Lord willed, all who are in the earth would have believed together. Wouldst thou (Muhammad) compel men until they are believers?	And if your Lord had pleased, surely all those who are in the earth would have believed, all of them; will you then force men till they become believers?
10 100	No soul can believe, except by the will of Allah, and He will place doubt (or obscurity) on those who will not understand.	It is not for any soul to believe save by the permission of Allah. He hath set uncleanness upon those who have no sense.	And it is not for a soul to believe except by Allah's permission; and He casts uncleanness on those who will not understand.
10 101	Say: "Behold all that is in the heavens and on earth"; but neither Signs nor Warners profit those who believe not.	Say: Behold what is in the heavens and the earth! But revelations and warnings avail not folk who will not believe.	Say: Consider what is it that is in the heavens and the earth; and signs and warners do not avail a people who would not believe.

10 102	Do they then expect (any thing) but (what happened in) the days of the men who passed away before them? Say: "Wait ye then: for I, too, will wait with you."	What expect they save the like of the days of those who passed away before them? Say: Expect then! I am with you among the expectant.	What do they wait for then but the like of the days of those who passed away before them? Say: Wait then; surely I too am with you of those who wait.
10 103	In the end We deliver Our messengers and those who believe: Thus is it fitting on Our part that We should deliver those who believe!	Then shall We save Our messengers and the believers, in like manner (as of old). It is incumbent upon Us to save believers.	Then We deliver Our messengers and those who believe-- even so (now), it is binding on Us (that) We deliver the believers.
10 104	Say: "O ye men! If ye are in doubt as to my religion, (behold!) I worship not what ye worship, other than Allah! But I worship Allah - Who will take your souls (at death): I am commanded to be (in the ranks) of the Believers,"	Say (O Muhammad): O mankind! If ye are in doubt of my religion, then (know that) I worship not those whom ye worship instead of Allah, but I worship Allah Who causeth you to die, and I have been commanded to be of the believers.	Say: O people! if you are in doubt as to my religion, then (know that) I do not serve those whom you serve besides Allah but I do serve Allah, Who will cause you to die, and I am commanded that I should be of the believers.
10 105	"And further (thus): 'set thy face towards religion with true piety, and never in any wise be of the Unbelievers;'"	And, (O Muhammad) set thy purpose resolutely for religion, as a man by nature upright, and be not of those who ascribe partners (to Allah).	And that you should keep your course towards the religion uprightly; and you should not be of the polytheists.
10 106	"'Nor call on any, other than Allah;- Such will neither profit thee nor hurt thee: if thou dost, behold! thou shalt certainly be of those who do wrong.'"	And cry not, beside Allah, unto that which cannot profit thee nor hurt thee, for if thou didst so then wert thou of the wrong-doers.	And do not call besides Allah on that which can neither benefit you nor harm you, for if you do then surely you will in that case be of the unjust.
10 107	If Allah do touch thee with hurt, there is none can remove it but He: if He do design some benefit for thee, there is none can keep back His favour: He causeth it to reach whomsoever of His servants He pleaseth. And He is the Oft-Forgiving, Most Merciful.	If Allah afflicteth thee with some hurt, there is none who can remove it save Him; and if He desireth good for thee, there is none who can repel His bounty. He striketh with it whom He will of his bondmen. He is the Forgiving, the Merciful.	And if Allah should afflict you with harm, then there is none to remove it but He; and if He intends good to you there is none to repel His grace; He brings it to whom He pleases of His servants; and He is the Forgiving, the Merciful.
10 108	Say: "O ye men! Now Truth hath reached you from your Lord! those who receive guidance, do so for the good of their own souls; those who stray, do so to their own loss: and I am not (set) over you to arrange your affairs."	Say: O mankind! Now hath the Truth from your Lord come unto you. So whosoever is guided, is guided only for (the good of) his soul, and whosoever erreth erreth only against it. And I am not a warder over you.	Say: O people! indeed there has come to you the truth from your Lord, therefore whoever goes aright, he goes aright only for the good of his own soul, and whoever goes astray, he goes astray only to the detriment of it, and I am not a custodian over you.
10 109	Follow thou the inspiration sent unto thee, and be patient and constant, till Allah do decide: for He is the best to decide.	And (O Muhammad) follow that which is inspired in thee, and forbear until Allah give judgment. And He is the Best of Judges.	And follow what is revealed to you and be patient till Allah should give judgment, and He is the best of the judges.

Chapter 11:

HUD (HUD)

Total Verses: 123 Revealed At: MAKKA

In the name of Allah, the Most Beneficent, the Most Merciful.

11 001	A. L. R. (This is) a Book, with verses basic or fundamental (of established meaning), further explained in detail,- from One Who is Wise and Well-acquainted (with all things):	Alif. Lam. Ra. (This is) a Scripture the revelations whereof are perfected and then expounded. (It cometh) from One Wise, Informed,	Alif Lam Ra (This is) a Book, whose verses are made decisive, then are they made plain, from the Wise, All-aware:
11 002	(It teacheth) that ye should worship none but Allah. (Say): Verily I am (sent) unto you from Him to warn and to bring glad tidings:	(Saying): Serve none but Allah. Lo! I am unto you from Him a warner and a bringer of good tidings.	That you shall not serve (any) but Allah; surely I am a warner for you from Him and a giver of good news,
11 003	"(And to preach thus), 'Seek ye the forgiveness of your Lord, and turn to Him in repentance; that He may grant you enjoyment, good (and true), for a term appointed, and bestow His abounding grace on all who abound in merit! But if ye turn away, then I fear for you the penalty of a great day:'"	And (bidding you): Ask pardon of your Lord and turn to Him repentant. He will cause you to enjoy a fair estate until a time appointed. He giveth His bounty unto every bountiful one. But if ye turn away, lo! (then) I fear for you the retribution of an awful Day.	And you that ask forgiveness of your Lord, then turn to Him; He will provide you with a goodly provision to an appointed term and bestow His grace on every one endowed with grace, and if you turn back, then surely I fear for you the chastisement of a great day.
11 004	"'To Allah is your return, and He hath power over all things.'"	Unto Allah is your return, and He is Able to do all things.	To Allah is your return, and He has power over all things.
11 005	Behold! they fold up their hearts, that they may lie hid from Him! Ah even when they cover themselves with their garments, He knoweth what they conceal, and what they reveal: for He knoweth well the (inmost secrets) of the hearts.	Lo! now they fold up their breasts that they may hide (their thoughts) from Him. At the very moment when they cover themselves with their clothing, Allah knoweth that which they keep hidden and that which they proclaim. Lo! He is Aware of what is in the breasts (of men).	Now surely they fold up their breasts that they may conceal (their enmity) from Him; now surely, when they use their garments as a covering, He knows what they conceal and what they make public; surely He knows what is in the breasts.
11 006	There is no moving creature on earth but its sustenance dependeth on Allah: He knoweth the time and place of its definite abode and its temporary deposit: All is in a clear Record.	And there is not a beast in the earth but the sustenance thereof dependeth on Allah. He knoweth its habitation and its repository. All is in a clear Record.	And there is no animal in the earth but on Allah is the sustenance of it, and He knows its resting place and its depository all (things) are in a manifest book.
11 007	He it is Who created the heavens and the earth in six Days - and His Throne was over the waters - that He might try you, which of you is best in conduct. But if thou wert to say to them, "Ye shall indeed be raised up after death", the Unbelievers would be sure to say, "This is nothing but obvious sorcery!"	And He it is Who created the heavens and the earth in six Days - and His Throne was upon the water - that He might try you, which of you is best in conduct. Yet if thou (O Muhammad) sayest: Lo! ye will be raised again after death! those who disbelieve will surely say: This is naught but mere magic.	And He it is Who created the heavens and the earth in six periods-- and His dominion (extends) on the water-- that He might manifest to you, which of you is best in action, and if you say, surely you shall be raised up after death, those who disbelieve would certainly say: This is nothing but clear magic.

11 008	If We delay the penalty for them for a definite term, they are sure to say, "What keeps it back?" Ah! On the day it (actually) reaches them, nothing will turn it away from them, and they will be completely encircled by that which they used to mock at!	And if We delay for them the doom until a reckoned time, they will surely say: What withholdeth it? Verily on the day when it cometh unto them, it cannot be averted from them, and that which they derided will surround them.	And if We hold back from them the punishment until a stated period of time, they will certainly say: What prevents it? Now surely on the day when it will come to them, it shall not be averted from them and that which they scoffed at shall beset them.
11 009	If We give man a taste of Mercy from Ourselves, and then withdraw it from him, behold! he is despair and (falls into) blasphemy.	And if we cause man to taste some mercy from Us and afterward withdraw it from him, lo! he is despairing, thankless.	And if We make man taste mercy from Us, then take it off from him, most surely he is despairing, ungrateful.
11 010	But if We give him a taste of (Our) favours after adversity hath touched him, he is sure to say, "All evil has departed from me:" Behold! he falls into exultation and pride.	And if We cause him to taste grace after some misfortune that had befallen him, he saith: The ills have gone from me. Lo! he is exultant, boastful;	And if We make him taste a favor after distress has afflicted him, he will certainly say: The evils are gone away from me. Most surely he is exulting, boasting;
11 011	Not so do those who show patience and constancy, and work righteousness; for them is forgiveness (of sins) and a great reward.	Save those who persevere and do good works. Theirs will be forgiveness and a great reward.	Except those who are patient and do good, they shall have forgiveness and a great reward.
11 012	Perchance thou mayest (feel the inclination) to give up a part of what is revealed unto thee, and thy heart feeleth straitened lest they say, "Why is not a treasure sent down unto him, or why does not an angel come down with him?" But thou art there only to warn! It is Allah that arrangeth all affairs!	A likely thing, that thou wouldst forsake aught of that which hath been revealed unto thee, and that thy breast should be straitened for it, because they say: Why hath not a treasure been sent down for him, or an angel come with him? Thou art but a warner, and Allah is in charge of all things.	Then, it may be that you will give up part of what is revealed to you and your breast will become straitened by it because they say: Why has not a treasure been sent down upon him or an angel come with him? You are only a warner; and Allah is custodian over all things.
11 013	Or they may say, "He forged it," Say, "Bring ye then ten suras forged, like unto it, and call (to your aid) whomsoever ye can, other than Allah!- If ye speak the truth!"	Or they say: He hath invented it. Say: Then bring ten surahs, the like thereof, invented, and call on everyone ye can beside Allah, if ye are truthful!	Or, do they say: He has forged it. Say: Then bring ten forged chapters like it and call upon whom you can besides Allah, if you are truthful.
11 014	"If then they (your false gods) answer not your (call), know ye that this revelation is sent down (replete) with the knowledge of Allah, and that there is no god but He! will ye even then submit (to Islam)?"	And if they answer not your prayer, then know that it is revealed only in the knowledge of Allah; and that there is no God save Him. Will ye then be (of) those who surrender?	But if they do not answer you, then know that it is revealed by Allah's knowledge and that there is no god but He; will you then submit?
11 015	Those who desire the life of the present and its glitter,- to them we shall pay (the price of) their deeds therein,- without diminution.	Whoso desireth the life of the world and its pomp, We shall repay them their deeds herein, and therein they will not be wronged.	Whoever desires this world's life and its finery, We will pay them in full their deeds therein, and they shall not be made to suffer loss in respect of them.
11 016	They are those for whom there is nothing in the Hereafter but the Fire: vain are the designs they frame therein, and of no effect and the deeds that they do!	Those are they for whom is naught in the Hereafter save the Fire. (All) that they contrive here is vain and (all) that they are wont to do is fruitless.	These are they for whom there is nothing but fire in the hereafter, and what they wrought in it shall go for nothing, and vain is what they do.

11	017	Can they be (like) those who accept a Clear (Sign) from their Lord, and whom a witness from Himself doth teach, as did the Book of Moses before it,- a guide and a mercy? They believe therein; but those of the Sects that reject it,- the Fire will be their promised meeting-place. Be not then in doubt thereon: for it is the truth from thy Lord: yet many among men do not believe!	Is he (to be counted equal with them) who relieth on a clear proof from his Lord, and a witness from Him reciteth it, and before it was the Book of Moses, an example and a mercy? Such believe therein, and whoso disbelieveth therein of the clans, the Fire is his appointed place. So be not thou in doubt concerning it. Lo! it is the Truth from thy Lord; but most of mankind believe not.	Is he then who has with him clear proof from his Lord, and a witness from Him recites it and before it (is) the Book of Musa, a guide and a mercy? These believe in it; and whoever of the (different) parties disbelieves in it, surely it is the truth from your Lord, but most men do not believe.
11	018	Who doth more wrong than those who invent a lie against Allah? They will be turned back to the presence of their Lord, and the witnesses will say, "These are the ones who lied against their Lord! Behold! the Curse of Allah is on those who do wrong!-"	Who doeth greater wrong than he who inventeth a lie concerning Allah? Such will be brought before their Lord, and the witnesses will say: These are they who lied concerning their Lord. Now the curse of Allah is upon wrong-doers,	And who is more unjust than he who forges a lie against Allah? These shall be brought before their Lord, and the witnesses shall say: These are they who lied against their Lord. Now surely the curse of Allah is on the unjust.
11	019	"Those who would hinder (men) from the path of Allah and would seek in it something crooked: these were they who denied the Hereafter!"	Who debar (men) from the way of Allah and would have it crooked, and who are disbelievers in the Hereafter.	Who turn away from the path of Allah and desire to make it crooked; and they are disbelievers in the hereafter.
11	020	They will in no wise frustrate (His design) on earth, nor have they protectors besides Allah! Their penalty will be doubled! They lost the power to hear, and they did not see!	Such will not escape in the earth, nor have they any protecting friends beside Allah. For them the torment will be double. They could not bear to hear, and they used not to see.	These shall not escape in the earth, nor shall they have any guardians besides Allah; the punishment shall be doubled for them, they could not bear to hear and they did not see.
11	021	They are the ones who have lost their own souls: and the (fancies) they invented have left them in the lurch!	Such are they who have lost their souls, and that which they used to invent hath failed them.	These are they who have lost their souls, and what they forged is gone from them.
11	022	Without a doubt, these are the very ones who will lose most in the Hereafter!	Assuredly in the Hereafter they will be the greatest losers.	Truly in the hereafter they are the greatest losers.
11	023	But those who believe and work righteousness, and humble themselves before their Lord,- They will be companions of the gardens, to dwell therein for aye!	Lo! those who believe and do good works and humble themselves before their Lord: such are rightful owners of the Garden; they will abide therein.	Surely (as to) those who believe and do good and humble themselves to their Lord, these are the dwellers of the garden, in it they will abide.
11	024	These two kinds (of men) may be compared to the blind and deaf, and those who can see and hear well. Are they equal when compared? Will ye not then take heed?	The similitude of the two parties is as the blind and the deaf and the seer and the hearer. Are they equal in similitude? Will ye not then be admonished?	The likeness of the two parties is as the blind and the deaf and the seeing and the hearing: are they equal in condition? Will you not then mind?
11	025	We sent Noah to his people (with a mission): "I have come to you with a Clear Warning:"	And We sent Noah unto his folk (and he said): Lo! I am a plain warner unto you.	And certainly We sent Nuh to his people: Surely I am a plain warner for you:
11	026	"That ye serve none but Allah: Verily I do fear for you the penalty of a grievous day."	That ye serve none, save Allah. Lo! I fear for you the retribution of a painful Day.	That you shall not serve any but Allah, surely I fear for you the punishment of a painful day.

11 027	But the chiefs of the Unbelievers among his people said: "We see (in) thee nothing but a man like ourselves: Nor do we see that any follow thee but the meanest among us, in judgment immature: Nor do we see in you (all) any merit above us: in fact we thing ye are liars!"	The chieftains of his folk, who disbelieved, said: We see thee but a mortal like us, and we see not that any follow thee save the most abject among us, without reflection. We behold in you no merit above us - nay, we deem you liars.		But the chiefs of those who disbelieved from among his people said: We do not consider you but a mortal like ourselves, and we do not see any have followed you but those who are the meanest of us at first thought and we do not see in you any excellence over us; nay, we deem you liars.
11 028	He said: "O my people! See ye if (it be that) I have a Clear Sign from my Lord, and that He hath sent Mercy unto me from His own presence, but that the Mercy hath been obscured from your sight? shall we compel you to accept it when ye are averse to it?"	He said: O my people! Bethink you, if I rely on a clear proof from my Lord and there hath come unto me a mercy from His presence, and it hath been made obscure to you, can we compel you to accept it when ye are averse thereto?		He said: O my people! tell me if I have with me clear proof from my Lord, and He has granted me mercy from Himself and it has been made obscure to you; shall we constrain you to (accept) it while you are averse from it?
11 029	"And O my people! I ask you for no wealth in return: my reward is from none but Allah: But I will not drive away (in contempt) those who believe: for verily they are to meet their Lord, and ye I see are the ignorant ones!"	And O my people! I ask of you no wealth therefor. My reward is the concern only of Allah, and I am not going to thrust away those who believe - Lo! they have to meet their Lord! - but I see you a folk that are ignorant.		And, O my people! I ask you not for wealth in return for it; my reward is only with Allah and I am not going to drive away those who believe; surely they shall meet their Lord, but I consider you a people who are ignorant:
11 030	"And O my people! who would help me against Allah if I drove them away? Will ye not then take heed?"	And, O my people! who would deliver me from Allah if I thrust them away? Will ye not then reflect?		And, O my people! who will help me against Allah if I drive them away? Will you not then mind?
11 031	"I tell you not that with me are the treasures of Allah, nor do I know what is hidden, nor claim I to be an angel. Nor yet do I say, of those whom your eyes do despise that Allah will not grant them (all) that is good: Allah knoweth best what is in their souls: I should, if I did, indeed be a wrong-doer."	I say not unto you: "I have the treasures of Allah" nor "I have knowledge of the Unseen," nor say I: "Lo! I am an angel!" Nor say I unto those whom your eyes scorn that Allah will not give them good - Allah knoweth best what is in their hearts - Lo! then indeed I should be of the wrong-doers.		And I do not say to you that I have the treasures of Allah and I do not know the unseen, nor do I say that I am an angel, nor do I say about those whom your eyes hold in mean estimation (that) Allah will never grant them (any) good-- Allah knows best what is in their souls-- for then most surely I should be of the unjust.
11 032	They said: "O Noah! thou hast disputed with us, and (much) hast thou prolonged the dispute with us: now bring upon us what thou threatenest us with, if thou speakest the truth!"	They said: O Noah! Thou hast disputed with us and multiplied disputation with us; now bring upon us that wherewith thou threatenest us, if thou art of the truthful.		They said: O Nuh! indeed you have disputed with us and lengthened dispute with us, therefore bring to us what you threaten us with, if you are of the truthful ones.
11 033	He said: "Truly, Allah will bring it on you if He wills,- and then, ye will not be able to frustrate it!"	He said: Only Allah will bring it upon you if He will, and ye can by no means escape.		He said: Allah only will bring it to you if He please, and you will not escape:
11 034	"Of no profit will be my counsel to you, much as I desire to give you (good) counsel, if it be that Allah willeth to leave you astray: He is your Lord! and to Him will ye return!"	My counsel will not profit you if I were minded to advise you, if Allah's will is to keep you astray. He is your Lord and unto Him ye will be brought back.		And if I intend to give you good advice, my advice will not profit you if Allah intended that He should leave you to go astray; He is your Lord, and to Him shall you be returned.
11 035	Or do they say, "He has forged it"? Say: "If I had forged it, on me were my sins! and I am free of the sins of which ye are guilty!"	Or say they (again): He hath invented it? Say: If I have invented it, upon me be my crimes, but I am innocent of (all) that ye commit.		Or do they say: He has forged it? Say: If I have forged it, on me is my guilt, and I am clear of that of which you are guilty.

11 036	It was revealed to Noah: "None of thy people will believe except those who have believed already! So grieve no longer over their (evil) deeds."	And it was inspired in Noah, (saying): No-one of thy folk will believe save him who hath believed already. Be not distressed because of what they do.	And it was revealed to Nuh: That none of your people will believe except those who have already believed, therefore do not grieve at what they do:	
11 037	"But construct an Ark under Our eyes and Our inspiration, and address Me no (further) on behalf of those who are in sin: for they are about to be overwhelmed (in the Flood)."	Build the ship under Our eyes and by Our inspiration, and speak not unto Me on behalf of those who do wrong. Lo! they will be drowned.	And make the ark before Our eyes and (according to) Our revelation, and do not speak to Me in respect of those who are unjust; surely they shall be drowned.	
11 038	Forthwith he (starts) constructing the Ark: Every time that the chiefs of his people passed by him, they threw ridicule on him. He said: "If ye ridicule us now, we (in our turn) can look down on you with ridicule likewise!"	And he was building the ship, and every time that chieftains of his people passed him, they made mock of him. He said: Though ye make mock of Us, yet We mock at you even as ye mock;	And he began to make the ark; and whenever the chiefs from among his people passed by him they laughed at him. He said: If you laugh at us, surely we too laugh at you as you laugh (at us).	
11 039	"But soon will ye know who it is on whom will descend a penalty that will cover them with shame,- on whom will be unloosed a penalty lasting:"	And ye shall know to whom a punishment that will confound him cometh, and upon whom a lasting doom will fall.	So shall you know who it is on whom will come a chastisement which will disgrace him, and on whom will lasting chastisement come down.	
11 040	At length, behold! there came Our command, and the fountains of the earth gushed forth! We said: "Embark therein, of each kind two, male and female, and your family - except those against whom the word has already gone forth,- and the Believers." but only a few believed with him.	(Thus it was) till, when Our commandment came to pass and the oven gushed forth water, We said: Load therein two of every kind, a pair (the male and female), and thy household, save him against whom the word hath gone forth already, and those who believe. And but a few were they who believed with him.	Until when Our command came and water came forth from the valley, We said: Carry in it two of all things, a pair, and your own family-- except those against whom the word has already gone forth, and those who believe. And there believed not with him but a few.	
11 041	So he said: "Embark ye on the Ark, In the name of Allah, whether it move or be at rest! For my Lord is, be sure, Oft-Forgiving, Most Merciful!"	And he said: Embark therein! In the name of Allah be its course and its mooring. Lo! my Lord is Forgiving, Merciful.	And he said: Embark in it, in the name of Allah be its sailing and its anchoring; most surely my Lord is Forgiving, Merciful.	
11 042	So the Ark floated with them on the waves (towering) like mountains, and Noah called out to his son, who had separated himself (from the rest): "O my son! embark with us, and be not with the unbelievers!"	And it sailed with them amid waves like mountains, and Noah cried unto his son - and he was standing aloof - O my son! Come ride with us, and be not with the disbelievers.	And it moved on with them amid waves like mountains; and Nuh called out to his son, and he was aloof: O my son! embark with us and be not with the unbelievers.	
11 043	The son replied: "I will betake myself to some mountain: it will save me from the water." Noah said: "This day nothing can save, from the command of Allah, any but those on whom He hath mercy!" And the waves came between them, and the son was among those overwhelmed in the Flood.	He said: I shall betake me to some mountain that will save me from the water. (Noah) said: This day there is none that saveth from the commandment of Allah save him on whom He hath had mercy. And the wave came in between them, so he was among the drowned.	He said: I will betake myself for refuge to a mountain that shall protect me from the water. Nuh said: There is no protector today from Allah's punishment but He Who has mercy; and a wave intervened between them, so he was of the drowned.	

11 044	Then the word went forth: "O earth! swallow up thy water, and O sky! Withhold (thy rain)!" and the water abated, and the matter was ended. The Ark rested on Mount Judi, and the word went forth: "Away with those who do wrong!"	And it was said: O earth! Swallow thy water and, O sky! be cleared of clouds! And the water was made to subside. And the commandment was fulfilled. And it (the ship) came to rest upon (the mount) Al-Judi and it was said: A far removal for wrongdoing folk!	And it was said: O earth, swallow down your water, and O cloud, clear away; and the water was made to abate and the affair was decided, and the ark rested on the Judi, and it was said: Away with the unjust people.
11 045	And Noah called upon his Lord, and said: "O my Lord! surely my son is of my family! and Thy promise is true, and Thou art the Justest of Judges!"	And Noah cried unto his Lord and said: My Lord! Lo! my son is of my household! Surely Thy promise is the truth and Thou are the Most Just of Judges.	And Nuh cried out to his Lord and said: My Lord! surely my son is of my family, and Thy promise is surely true, and Thou art the most just of the judges.
11 046	He said: "O Noah! He is not of thy family: For his conduct is unrighteous. So ask not of Me that of which thou hast no knowledge! I give thee counsel, lest thou act like the ignorant!"	He said: O Noah! Lo! he is not of thy household; lo! he is of evil conduct, so ask not of Me that whereof thou hast no knowledge. I admonish thee lest thou be among the ignorant.	He said: O Nuh! surely he is not of your family; surely he is (the doer of) other than good deeds, therefore ask not of Me that of which you have no knowledge; surely I admonish you lest you may be of the ignorant.
11 047	Noah said: "O my Lord! I do seek refuge with Thee, lest I ask Thee for that of which I have no knowledge. And unless thou forgive me and have Mercy on me, I should indeed be lost!"	He said: My Lord! Lo! in Thee do I seek refuge (from the sin) that I should ask of Thee that whereof I have no knowledge. Unless Thou forgive me and have mercy on me I shall be among the lost.	He said: My Lord! I seek refuge in Thee from asking Thee that of which I have no knowledge; and if Thou shouldst not forgive me and have mercy on me, I should be of the losers.
11 048	The word came: "O Noah! Come down (from the Ark) with peace from Us, and blessing on thee and on some of the peoples (who will spring) from those with thee: but (there will be other) peoples to whom We shall grant their pleasures (for a time), but in the end will a grievous penalty reach them from Us."	It was said (unto him): O Noah! Go thou down (from the mountain) with peace from Us and blessings upon thee and some nations (that will spring) from those with thee. (There will be other) nations unto whom We shall give enjoyment a long while and then a painful doom from Us will overtake them.	It was said: O Nuh! descend with peace from Us and blessings on you and on the people from among those who are with you, and there shall be nations whom We will afford provisions, then a painful punishment from Us shall afflict them.
11 049	Such are some of the stories of the unseen, which We have revealed unto thee: before this, neither thou nor thy people knew them. So persevere patiently: for the End is for those who are righteous.	This is of the tidings of the Unseen which We inspire in thee (Muhammad). Thou thyself knewest it not, nor did thy folk (know it) before this. Then have patience. Lo! the sequel is for those who ward off (evil).	These are announcements relating to the unseen which We reveal to you, you did not know them-- (neither) you nor your people-- before this; therefore be patient; surely the end is for those who guard (against evil).
11 050	To the 'Ad People (We sent) Hud, one of their own brethren. He said: O my people! worship Allah! ye have no other god but Him. (Your other gods) ye do nothing but invent!"	And unto (the tribe of) A'ad (We sent) their brother, Hud. He said: O my people! Serve Allah! Ye have no other Allah save Him. Lo! ye do but invent.	And to Ad (We sent) their brother Hud. He said: O my people! serve Allah, you have no god other than He; you are nothing but forgers (of lies).
11 051	"O my people! I ask of you no reward for this (Message). My reward is from none but Him who created me: Will ye not then understand?"	O my people! I ask of you no reward for it. Lo! my reward is the concern only of Him Who made me. Have ye then no sense?	O my people! I do not ask of you any reward for it; my reward is only with Him Who created me; do you not then understand?

11 052	"And O my people! Ask forgiveness of your Lord, and turn to Him (in repentance): He will send you the skies pouring abundant rain, and add strength to your strength: so turn ye not back in sin!"	And, O my people! Ask forgiveness of your Lord, then turn unto Him repentant; He will cause the sky to rain abundance on you and will add unto you strength to your strength. Turn not away, guilty!	And, O my people! ask forgiveness of your Lord, then turn to Him; He will send on you clouds pouring down abundance of rain and add strength to your strength, and do not turn back guilty.
11 053	They said: "O Hud! No Clear (Sign) that hast thou brought us, and we are not the ones to desert our gods on thy word! Nor shall we believe in thee!"	They said: O Hud! Thou hast brought us no clear proof and we are not going to forsake our gods on thy (mere) saying, and we are not believers in thee.	They said: O Hud! you have not brought to us any clear argument and we are not going to desert our gods for your word, and we are not believers in you:
11 054	"We say nothing but that (perhaps) some of our gods may have seized thee with imbecility." He said: "I call Allah to witness, and do ye bear witness, that I am free from the sin of ascribing, to Him,"	We say naught save that one of our gods hath possessed thee in an evil way. He said: I call Allah to witness, and do ye (too) bear witness, that I am innocent of (all) that ye ascribe as partners (to Allah)	We cannot say aught but that some of our gods have smitten you with evil. He said: Surely I call Allah to witness, and do you bear witness too, that I am clear of what you associate (with Allah).
11 055	"Other gods as partners! so scheme (your worst) against me, all of you, and give me no respite."	Beside Him. So (try to) circumvent me, all of you, give me no respite.	Besides Him, therefore scheme against me all together; then give me no respite:
11 056	"I put my trust in Allah, My Lord and your Lord! There is not a moving creature, but He hath grasp of its forelock. Verily, it is my Lord that is on a straight Path."	Lo! I have put my trust in Allah, my Lord and your Lord. Not an animal but He doth grasp it by the forelock! Lo! my Lord is on a straight path.	Surely I rely on Allah, my Lord and your Lord; there is no living creature but He holds it by its forelock; surely my Lord is on the right path.
11 057	"If ye turn away,- I (at least) have conveyed the Message with which I was sent to you. My Lord will make another people to succeed you, and you will not harm Him in the least. For my Lord hath care and watch over all things."	And if ye turn away, still I have conveyed unto you that wherewith I was sent unto you, and my Lord will set in place of you a folk other than you. Ye cannot injure Him at all. Lo! my Lord is Guardian over all things.	But if you turn back, then indeed I have delivered to you the message with which I have been sent to you, and my Lord will bring another people in your place, and you cannot do Him any harm; surely my Lord is the Preserver of all things.
11 058	So when Our decree issued, We saved Hud and those who believed with him, by (special) Grace from Ourselves: We saved them from a severe penalty.	And when Our commandment came to pass We saved Hud and those who believed with him by a mercy from Us; We saved them from a harsh doom.	And when Our decree came to pass, We delivered Hud and those who believed with him with mercy from Us, and We delivered them from a hard chastisement.
11 059	Such were the 'Ad People: they rejected the Signs of their Lord and Cherisher; disobeyed His messengers; And followed the command of every powerful, obstinate transgressor.	And such were A'ad. They denied the revelations of their Lord and flouted His messengers and followed the command of every froward potentate.	And this was Ad; they denied the communications of their Lord, and disobeyed His messengers and followed the bidding of every insolent opposer (of truth).
11 060	And they were pursued by a Curse in this life,- and on the Day of Judgment. Ah! Behold! for the 'Ad rejected their Lord and Cherisher! Ah! Behold! removed (from sight) were 'Ad the people of Hud!	And a curse was made to follow them in the world and on the Day of Resurrection. Lo! A'ad disbelieved in their Lord. A far removal for A'ad, the folk of Hud!	And they were overtaken by curse in this world and on the resurrection day; now surely Ad disbelieved in their Lord; now surely, away with Ad, the people of Hud.

11 061	To the Thamud People (We sent) Salih, one of their own brethren. He said: "O my people! Worship Allah: ye have no other god but Him. It is He Who hath produced you from the earth and settled you therein: then ask forgiveness of Him, and turn to Him (in repentance): for my Lord is (always) near, ready to answer."	And unto (the tribe of) Thamud (We sent) their brother Salih. He said: O my people! Serve Allah, Ye have no other Allah save Him. He brought you forth from the earth and hath made you husband it. So ask forgiveness of Him and turn unto Him repentant. Lo! my Lord is Nigh, Responsive.	And to Samood (We sent) their brother Salih. He said: O my people! serve Allah, you have no god other than He; He brought you into being from the earth, and made you dwell in it, therefore ask forgiveness of Him, then turn to Him; surely my Lord is Nigh, Answering.
11 062	They said: "O Salih! thou hast been of us! a centre of our hopes hitherto! dost thou (now) forbid us the worship of what our fathers worshipped? But we are really in suspicious (disquieting) doubt as to that to which thou invitest us."	They said: O Salih! Thou hast been among us hitherto as that wherein our hope was placed. Dost thou ask us not to worship what our fathers worshipped? Lo! we verily are in grave doubt concerning that to which thou callest us.	They said: O Salih! surely you were one amongst us in whom great expectations were placed before this; do you (now) forbid us from worshipping what our fathers worshipped? And as to that which you call us to, most surely we are in disquieting doubt.
11 063	He said: "O my people! do ye see? if I have a Clear (Sign) from my Lord and He hath sent Mercy unto me from Himself,- who then can help me against Allah if I were to disobey Him? What then would ye add to my (portion) but perdition?"	He said: O my people! Bethink you: if I am (acting) on clear proof from my Lord and there hath come unto me a mercy from Him, who will save me from Allah if I disobey Him? Ye would add to me naught save perdition.	He said: O my people! tell me if I have clear proof from my Lord and He has granted to me mercy from Himself-- who will then help me against Allah if I disobey Him? Therefore you do not add to me other than loss:
11 064	"And O my people! This she-camel of Allah is a symbol to you: leave her to feed on Allah's (free) earth, and inflict no harm on her, or a swift penalty will seize you!"	O my people! This is the camel of Allah, a token unto you, so suffer her to feed in Allah's earth, and touch her not with harm lest a near torment seize you.	And, O my people! this will be (as) Allah's she-camel for you, a sign; therefore leave her to pasture on Allah's earth and do not touch her with evil, for then a near chastisement will overtake you.
11 065	But they did ham-string her. So he said: "Enjoy yourselves in your homes for three days: (Then will be your ruin): (Behold) there a promise not to be belied!"	But they hamstrung her, and then he said: Enjoy life in your dwelling-place three days! This is a threat that will not be belied.	But they slew her, so he said: Enjoy yourselves in your abode for three days, that is a promise not to be belied.
11 066	When Our Decree issued, We saved Salih and those who believed with him, by (special) Grace from Ourselves - and from the Ignominy of that day. For thy Lord - He is the Strong One, and able to enforce His Will.	So, when Our commandment came to pass, We saved Salih, and those who believed with him, by a mercy from Us, from the ignominy of that day. Lo, thy Lord! He is the Strong, the Mighty.	So when Our decree came to pass, We delivered Salih and those who believed with him by mercy from Us, and (We saved them) from the disgrace of that day; surely your Lord is the Strong, the Mighty.
11 067	The (mighty) Blast overtook the wrong-doers, and they lay prostrate in their homes before the morning,-	And the (awful) Cry overtook those who did wrong, so that morning found them prostrate in their dwellings,	And the rumbling overtook those who were unjust, so they became motionless bodies in their abodes,
11 068	As if they had never dwelt and flourished there. Ah! Behold! for the Thamud rejected their Lord and Cherisher! Ah! Behold! removed (from sight) were the Thamud!	As though they had not dwelt there. Lo! Thamud disbelieved in their Lord. A far removal for Thamud!	As though they had never dwelt in them; now surely did Samood disbelieve in their Lord; now surely, away with Samood.
11 069	There came Our messengers to Abraham with glad tidings. They said, Peace! He answered, "Peace!" and hastened to entertain them with a roasted calf.	And Our messengers came unto Abraham with good news. They said: Peace! He answered: Peace! and delayed not to bring a roasted calf.	And certainly Our messengers came to Ibrahim with good news. They said: Peace. Peace, said he, and he made no delay in bringing a roasted calf.

11 070	But when he saw their hands went not towards the (meal), he felt some mistrust of them, and conceived a fear of them. They said: "Fear not: We have been sent against the people of Lut."	And when he saw their hands reached not to it, he mistrusted them and conceived a fear of them. They said: Fear not! Lo! we are sent unto the folk of Lot.	But when he saw that their hands were not extended towards it, he deemed them strange and conceived fear of them. . They said: Fear not, surely we are sent to Lut's people.
11 071	And his wife was standing (there), and she laughed: But we gave her glad tidings of Isaac, and after him, of Jacob.	And his wife, standing by laughed when We gave her good tidings (of the birth) of Isaac, and, after Isaac, of Jacob.	And his wife was standing (by), so she laughed, then We gave her the good news of Ishaq and after Ishaq of (a son's son) Yaqoub.
11 072	She said: "Alas for me! shall I bear a child, seeing I am an old woman, and my husband here is an old man? That would indeed be a wonderful thing!"	She said: Oh woe is me! Shall I bear a child when I am an old woman, and this my husband is an old man? Lo! this is a strange thing!	She said: O wonder! shall I bear a son when I am an extremely old woman and this my husband an extremely old man? Most surely this is a wonderful thing.
11 073	They said: "Dost thou wonder at Allah's decree? The grace of Allah and His blessings on you, O ye people of the house! for He is indeed worthy of all praise, full of all glory!"	They said: Wonderest thou at the commandment of Allah? The mercy of Allah and His blessings be upon you, O people of the house! Lo! He is Owner of Praise, Owner of Glory!	They said: Do you wonder at Allah's bidding? The mercy of Allah and His blessings are on you, O people of the house, surely He is Praised, Glorious.
11 074	When fear had passed from (the mind of) Abraham and the glad tidings had reached him, he began to plead with us for Lut's people.	And when the awe departed from Abraham, and the glad news reached him, he pleaded with Us on behalf of the folk of Lot.	So when fear had gone away from Ibrahim and good news came to him, he began to plead with Us for Lut's people.
11 075	For Abraham was, without doubt, forbearing (of faults), compassionate, and given to look to Allah.	Lo! Abraham was mild, imploring, penitent.	Most surely Ibrahim was forbearing, tender-hearted, oft-returning (to Allah):
11 076	O Abraham! Seek not this. The decree of thy Lord hath gone forth: for them there cometh a penalty that cannot be turned back!	(It was said) O Abraham! Forsake this! Lo! thy Lord's commandment hath gone forth, and lo! there cometh unto them a doom which cannot be repelled.	O Ibrahim! leave off this, surely the decree of your Lord has come to pass, and surely there must come to them a chastisement that cannot be averted.
11 077	When Our messengers came to Lut, he was grieved on their account and felt himself powerless (to protect) them. He said: "This is a distressful day."	And when Our messengers came unto Lot, he was distressed and knew not how to protect them. He said: This is a distressful day.	And when Our messengers came to Lut, he was grieved for them, and he lacked strength to protect them, and said: This is a hard day.
11 078	And his people came rushing towards him, and they had been long in the habit of practising abominations. He said: "O my people! Here are my daughters: they are purer for you (if ye marry)! Now fear Allah, and cover me not with shame about my guests! Is there not among you a single right-minded man?"	And his people came unto him, running towards him - and before then they used to commit abominations - He said: O my people! Here are my daughters! They are purer for you. Beware of Allah, and degrade me not in (the person of) my guests. Is there not among you any upright man?	And his people came to him, (as if) rushed on towards him, and already they did evil deeds. He said: O my people! these are my daughters-- they are purer for you, so guard against (the punishment of) Allah and do not disgrace me with regard to my guests; is there not among you one right-minded man?
11 079	They said: "Well dost thou know we have no need of thy daughters: indeed thou knowest quite well what we want!"	They said: Well thou knowest that we have no right to thy daughters, and well thou knowest what we want.	They said: Certainly you know that we have no claim on your daughters, and most surely you know what we desire.
11 080	He said: "Would that I had power to suppress you or that I could betake myself to some powerful support."	He said: Would that I had strength to resist you or had some strong support (among you)!	He said: Ah! that I had power to suppress you, rather I shall have recourse to a strong support.

11 081	(The Messengers) said: "O Lut! We are Messengers from thy Lord! By no means shall they reach thee! now travel with thy family while yet a part of the night remains, and let not any of you look back: but thy wife (will remain behind): To her will happen what happens to the people. Morning is their time appointed: Is not the morning nigh?"	(The messengers) said: O Lot! Lo! we are messengers of thy Lord; they shall not reach thee. So travel with thy people in a part of the night, and let not one of you turn round - (all) save thy wife. Lo! that which smiteth them will smite her (also). Lo! their tryst is (for) the morning. Is not the morning nigh?	They said: O Lut! we are the messengers of your Lord; they shall by no means reach you; so remove your followers in a part of the night-- and let none of you turn back-- except your wife, for surely whatsoever befalls them shall befall her; surely their appointed time is the morning; is not the morning nigh?
11 082	When Our Decree issued, We turned (the cities) upside down, and rained down on them brimstones hard as baked clay, spread, layer on layer,-	So when Our commandment came to pass We overthrew (that township) and rained upon it stones of clay, one after another,	So when Our decree came to pass, We turned them upside down and rained down upon them stones, of what had been decreed, one after another.
11 083	Marked as from thy Lord: Nor are they ever far from those who do wrong!	Marked with fire in the providence of thy Lord (for the destruction of the wicked). And they are never far from the wrong-doers.	Marked (for punishment) with your Lord and it is not far off from the unjust.
11 084	To the Madyan People (We sent) Shu'aib, one of their own brethren: he said: "O my people! worship Allah: Ye have no other god but Him. And give not short measure or weight: I see you in prosperity, but I fear for you the penalty of a day that will compass (you) all round."	And unto Midian (We sent) their brother Shu'eyb. He said: O my people! Serve Allah. Ye have no other Allah save Him! And give not short measure and short weight. Lo! I see you well-to-do, and lo! I fear for you the doom of a besetting Day.	And to Madyan (We sent) their brother Shu'aib. He said: O my people! serve Allah, you have no god other than He, and do not give short measure and weight: surely I see you in prosperity and surely I fear for you the punishment of an all-encompassing day.
11 085	"And O my people! give just measure and weight, nor withhold from the people the things that are their due: commit not evil in the land with intent to do mischief."	O my people! Give full measure and full weight in justice, and wrong not people in respect of their goods. And do not evil in the earth, causing corruption.	And, O my people! give full measure and weight fairly, and defraud not men their things, and do not act corruptly in the land, making mischief:
11 086	"That which is left you by Allah is best for you, if ye (but) believed! but I am not set over you to keep watch!"	That which Allah leaveth with you is better for you if ye are believers; and I am not a keeper over you.	What remains with Allah is better for you if you are believers, and I am not a keeper over you.
11 087	They said: "O Shu'aib! Does thy (religion of) prayer command thee that we leave off the worship which our fathers practised, or that we leave off doing what we like with our property? truly, thou art the one that forbeareth with faults and is right-minded!"	They said: O Shu'eyb! Doth thy way of prayer command thee that we should forsake that which our fathers (used to) worship, or that we (should leave off) doing what we will with our own property. Lo! thou art the mild, the guide to right behaviour.	They said: O Shu'aib! does your prayer enjoin you that we should forsake what our fathers worshipped or that we should not do what we please with regard to our property? Forsooth you are the forbearing, the right-directing one.
11 088	He said: "O my people! see ye whether I have a Clear (Sign) from my Lord, and He hath given me sustenance (pure and) good as from Himself? I wish not, in opposition to you, to do that which I forbid you to do. I only desire (your) betterment to the best of my power; and my success (in my task) can only come from Allah. In Him I trust, and unto Him I look."	He said: O my people! Bethink you: if I am (acting) on a clear proof from my Lord and He sustaineth me with fair sustenance from Him (how can I concede aught to you)? I desire not to do behind your backs that which I ask you not to do. I desire naught save reform so far as I am able. My welfare is only in Allah. In Him I trust and unto Him I turn (repentant).	He said: O my people! have you considered if I have a clear proof from my Lord and He has given me a goodly sustenance from Himself, and I do not desire that in opposition to you I should betake myself to that which I forbid you: I desire nothing but reform so far as I am able, and with none but Allah is the direction of my affair to a right issue; on Him do I rely and to Him do I turn:

11 089	"And O my people! let not my dissent (from you) cause you to sin, lest ye suffer a fate similar to that of the people of Noah or of Hud or of Salih, nor are the people of Lut far off from you!"	And, O my people! Let not the schism with me cause you to sin so that there befall you that which befell the folk of Noah and the folk of Hud, and the folk of Salih; and the folk of Lot are not far off from you.	And, O my people! let not opposition to me make you guilty so that there may befall you the like of what befell the people of Nuh, or the people of Hud, or the people of Salih, nor are the people of Lut far off from you;
11 090	"But ask forgiveness of your Lord, and turn unto Him (in repentance): For my Lord is indeed full of mercy and loving-kindness."	Ask pardon of your Lord and then turn unto Him (repentant). Lo! my Lord is Merciful, Loving.	And ask forgiveness of your Lord, then turn to Him; surely my Lord is Merciful, Loving-kind.
11 091	They said: "O Shu'aib! much of what thou sayest we do not understand! In fact among us we see that thou hast no strength! Were it not for thy family, we should certainly have stoned thee! for thou hast among us no great position!"	They said: O Shu'eyb! We understand not much of that thou tellest, and lo! we do behold thee weak among us. But for thy family, we should have stoned thee, for thou art not strong against us.	They said: O Shu'aib! we do not understand much of what you say and most surely we see you to be weak among us, and were it not for your family we would surely stone you, and you are not mighty against us.
11 092	He said: "O my people! is then my family of more consideration with you than Allah? For ye cast Him away behind your backs (with contempt). But verily my Lord encompasseth on all sides all that ye do!"	He said: O my people! Is my family more to be honoured by you than Allah? and ye put Him behind you, neglected! Lo! my Lord surroundeth what ye do.	He said: O my people! is my family more esteemed by you than Allah? And you neglect Him as a thing cast behind your back; surely my Lord encompasses what you do:
11 093	"And O my people! Do whatever ye can: I will do (my part): Soon will ye know who it is on whom descends the penalty of ignominy; and who is a liar! and watch ye! for I too am watching with you!"	And, O my people! Act according to your power, lo! I (too) am acting. Ye will soon know on whom there cometh a doom that will abase him, and who it is that lieth. And watch! Lo! I am a watcher with you.	And, O my people! act according to your ability, I too am acting; you will come to know soon who it is on whom will light the punishment that will disgrace him and who it is that is a liar, and watch, surely I too am watching with you.
11 094	When Our decree issued, We saved Shu'aib and those who believed with him, by (special) mercy from Ourselves: But the (mighty) blast did seize the wrong-doers, and they lay prostrate in their homes by the morning,-	And when Our commandment came to pass We saved Shu'eyb and those who believed with him by a mercy from Us; and the (Awful) Cry seized those who did injustice, and morning found them prostrate in their dwellings,	And when Our decree came to pass We delivered Shu'aib, and those who believed with him by mercy from Us, and the rumbling overtook those who were unjust so they became motionless bodies in their abodes,
11 095	As if they had never dwelt and flourished there! Ah! Behold! How the Madyan were removed (from sight) as were removed the Thamud!	As though they had not dwelt there. A far removal for Midian, even as Thamud had been removed afar!	As though they had never dwelt in them; now surely perdition overtook Madyan as had perished Samood.
11 096	And we sent Moses, with Our Clear (Signs) and an authority manifest,	And verily We sent Moses with Our revelations and a clear warrant	And certainly We sent Musa with Our communications and a clear authority,
11 097	Unto Pharaoh and his chiefs: but they followed the command of Pharaoh and the command of Pharaoh was no right (guide).	Unto Pharaoh and his chiefs, but they did follow the command of Pharaoh, and the command of Pharaoh was no right guide.	To Firon and his chiefs, but they followed the bidding of Firon, and Firon's bidding was not right-directing.
11 098	He will go before his people on the Day of Judgment, and lead them into the Fire (as cattle are led to water): But woeful indeed will be the place to which they are led!	He will go before his people on the Day of Resurrection and will lead them to the Fire for watering-place. Ah, hapless is the watering-place (whither they are) led.	He shall lead his people on the resurrection day, and bring them down to the fire; and evil the place to which they are brought.

11 099	And they are followed by a curse in this (life) and on the Day of Judgment: and woeful is the gift which shall be given (unto them)!	A curse is made to follow them in the world and on the Day of Resurrection. Hapless is the gift (that will be) given (them).	And they are overtaken by curse in this (world), and on the resurrection day, evil the gift which shall be given.
11 100	These are some of the stories of communities which We relate unto thee: of them some are standing, and some have been mown down (by the sickle of time).	That is (something) of the tidings of the townships (which were destroyed of old). We relate it unto thee (Muhammad). Some of them are standing and some (already) reaped.	This is an account of (the fate of) the towns which We relate to you; of them are some that stand and (others) mown down.
11 101	It was not We that wronged them. They wronged their own souls: the deities, other than Allah, whom they invoked, profited them no whit when there issued the decree of thy Lord: Nor did they add aught (to their lot) but perdition!	We wronged them not, but they did wrong themselves; and their gods on whom they call beside Allah availed them naught when came thy Lord's command; they added to them naught save ruin.	And We did not do them injustice, but they were unjust to themselves, so their gods whom they called upon besides Allah did not avail them aught when the decree of your Lord came to pass; and they added but to their ruin.
11 102	Such is the chastisement of thy Lord when He chastises communities in the midst of their wrong: grievous, indeed, and severe is His chastisement.	Even thus is the grasp of thy Lord when He graspeth the townships while they are doing wrong. Lo! His grasp is painful, very strong.	And such is the punishment of your Lord when He punishes the towns while they are unjust; surely His punishment is painful, severe.
11 103	In that is a Sign for those who fear the penalty of the Hereafter: that is a Day for which mankind will be gathered together: that will be a Day of Testimony.	Lo! herein verily there is a portent for those who fear the doom of the Hereafter. That is a day unto which mankind will be gathered, and that is a day that will be witnessed.	Most surely there is a sign in this for him who fears the chastisement of the hereafter; this is a day on which the people shall be gathered together and this is a day that shall be witnessed.
11 104	Nor shall We delay it but for a term appointed.	And We defer it only to a term already reckoned.	And We do not delay it but to an appointed term.
11 105	The day it arrives, no soul shall speak except by His leave: of those (gathered) some will be wretched and some will be blessed.	On the day when it cometh no soul will speak except by His permission; some among them will be wretched, (others) glad.	On the day when it shall come, no soul shall speak except with His permission, then (some) of them shall be unhappy and (others) happy.
11 106	Those who are wretched shall be in the Fire: There will be for them therein (nothing but) the heaving of sighs and sobs:	As for those who will be wretched (on that day) they will be in the Fire; sighing and wailing will be their portion therein,	So as to those who are unhappy, they shall be in the fire; for them shall be sighing and groaning in it:
11 107	They will dwell therein for all the time that the heavens and the earth endure, except as thy Lord willeth: for thy Lord is the (sure) accomplisher of what He planneth.	Abiding there so long as the heavens and the earth endure save for that which thy Lord willeth. Lo! thy Lord is Doer of what He will.	Abiding therein so long as the heavens and the earth endure, except as your Lord please; surely your Lord is the mighty doer of what He intends.
11 108	And those who are blessed shall be in the Garden: They will dwell therein for all the time that the heavens and the earth endure, except as thy Lord willeth: a gift without break.	And as for those who will be glad (that day) they will be in the Garden, abiding there so long as the heavens and the earth endure save for that which thy Lord willeth: a gift unfailing.	And as to those who are made happy, they shall be in the garden, abiding in it as long as the heavens and the earth endure, except as your Lord please; a gift which shall never be cut off.
11 109	Be not then in doubt as to what these men worship. They worship nothing but what their fathers worshipped before (them): but verily We shall pay them back (in full) their portion without (the least) abatement.	So be not thou in doubt concerning that which these (folk) worship. They worship only as their fathers worshipped aforetime. Lo! we shall pay them their whole due unabated.	Therefore be not in doubt as to what these worship; they do not worship but as their fathers worshipped before; and most surely We will pay them back in full their portion undiminished.

11 110	We certainly gave the Book to Moses, but differences arose therein: had it not been that a word had gone forth before from thy Lord, the matter would have been decided between them, but they are in suspicious doubt concerning it.	And we verily gave unto Moses the Scripture, and there was strife thereupon; and had it not been for a Word that had already gone forth from thy Lord, the case would have been judged between them, and lo! they are in grave doubt concerning it.	And certainly We gave the book to Musa, but it was gone against; and had not a word gone forth from your Lord, the matter would surely have been decided between them; and surely they are in a disquieting doubt about it.
11 111	And, of a surety, to all will your Lord pay back (in full the recompense) of their deeds: for He knoweth well all that they do.	And lo! unto each thy Lord will verily repay his works in full. Lo! He is Informed of what they do.	And your Lord will most surely pay back to all their deeds in full; surely He is aware of what they do.
11 112	Therefore stand firm (in the straight Path) as thou art commanded,- thou and those who with thee turn (unto Allah); and transgress not (from the Path): for He seeth well all that ye do.	So tread thou the straight path as thou art commanded, and those who turn (unto Allah) with thee, and transgress not. Lo! He is Seer of what ye do.	Continue then in the right way as you are commanded, as also he who has turned (to Allah) with you, and be not inordinate (O men!), surely He sees what you do.
11 113	And incline not to those who do wrong, or the Fire will seize you; and ye have no protectors other than Allah, nor shall ye be helped.	And incline not toward those who do wrong lest the Fire touch you, and ye have no protecting friends against Allah, and afterward ye would not be helped.	And do not incline to those who are unjust, lest the fire touch you, and you have no guardians besides Allah, then you shall not be helped.
11 114	And establish regular prayers at the two ends of the day and at the approaches of the night: For those things, that are good remove those that are evil: Be that the word of remembrance to those who remember (their Lord):	Establish worship at the two ends of the day and in some watches of the night. Lo! good deeds annul ill-deeds. This is reminder for the mindful.	And keep up prayer in the two parts of the day and in the first hours of the night; surely good deeds take away evil deeds this is a reminder to the mindful.
11 115	And be steadfast in patience; for verily Allah will not suffer the reward of the righteous to perish.	And have patience, (O Muhammad), for lo! Allah loseth not the wages of the good.	And be patient, for surely Allah does not waste the reward of the good-doers.
11 116	Why were there not, among the generations before you, persons possessed of balanced good sense, prohibiting (men) from mischief in the earth - except a few among them whom We saved (from harm)? But the wrong-doers pursued the enjoyment of the good things of life which were given them, and persisted in sin.	If only there had been among the generations before you men possessing a remnant (of good sense) to warn (their people) from corruption in the earth, as did a few of those whom We saved from them! The wrong-doers followed that by which they were made sapless, and were guilty.	But why were there not among the generations before you those possessing understanding, who should have forbidden the making of mischief in the earth, except a few of those whom We delivered from among them? And those who were unjust went after what they are made to enjoy of plenty, and they were guilty.
11 117	Nor would thy Lord be the One to destroy communities for a single wrong-doing, if its members were likely to mend.	In truth thy Lord destroyed not the townships tyrannously while their folk were doing right.	And it did not beseem your Lord to have destroyed the towns tyrannously, while their people acted well.
11 118	If thy Lord had so willed, He could have made mankind one people: but they will not cease to dispute.	And if thy Lord had willed, He verily would have made mankind one nation, yet they cease not differing,	And if your Lord had pleased He would certainly have made people a single nation, and they shall continue to differ.
11 119	Except those on whom thy Lord hath bestowed His Mercy: and for this did He create them: and the Word of thy Lord shall be fulfilled: "I will fill Hell with jinns and men all together."	Save him on whom thy Lord hath mercy; and for that He did create them. And the Word of thy Lord hath been fulfilled: Verily I shall fill hell with the jinn and mankind together.	Except those on whom your Lord has mercy; and for this did He create them; and the word of your Lord is fulfilled: Certainly I will fill hell with the jinn and the men, all together.

11 120	All that we relate to thee of the stories of the messengers,- with it We make firm thy heart: in them there cometh to thee the Truth, as well as an exhortation and a message of remembrance to those who believe.	And all that We relate unto thee of the story of the messengers is in order that thereby We may make firm thy heart. And herein hath come unto thee the Truth and an exhortation and a reminder for believers.	And all we relate to you of the accounts of the messengers is to strengthen your heart therewith; and in this has come to you the truth and an admonition, and a reminder to the believers.
11 121	Say to those who do not believe: "Do what ever ye can: We shall do our part;"	And say unto those who believe not: Act according to your power. Lo! We (too) are acting.	And say to those who do not believe: Act according to your state; surely we too are acting.
11 122	"And wait ye! We too shall wait."	And wait! Lo! We (too) are waiting.	And wait, surely we are waiting also.
11 123	To Allah do belong the unseen (secrets) of the heavens and the earth, and to Him goeth back every affair (for decision): then worship Him, and put thy trust in Him: and thy Lord is not unmindful of aught that ye do.	And Allah's is the Invisible of the heavens and the earth, and unto Him the whole matter will be returned. So worship Him and put thy trust in Him. Lo! thy Lord is not unaware of what ye (mortals) do.	And Allah's is the unseen in the heavens and the earth, and to Him is returned the whole of the affair; therefore serve Him and rely on Him, and your Lord is not heedless of what you do.

Chapter 12:

YUSUF (JOSEPH)

Total Verses: 111 Revealed At: MAKKA

In the name of Allah, the Most Beneficent, the Most Merciful.

12 001	A.L.R. These are the symbols (or Verses) of the perspicuous Book.	Alif. Lam. Ra. These are verse of the Scripture that maketh plain.	Alif Lam Ra. These are the verses of the Book that makes (things) manifest.
12 002	We have sent it down as an Arabic Qur'an, in order that ye may learn wisdom.	Lo! We have revealed it, a Lecture in Arabic, that ye may understand.	Surely We have revealed it-- an Arabic Quran-- that you may understand.
12 003	We do relate unto thee the most beautiful of stories, in that We reveal to thee this (portion of the) Qur'an: before this, thou too was among those who knew it not.	We narrate unto thee (Muhammad) the best of narratives in that We have inspired in thee this Qur'an, though aforetime thou wast of the heedless.	We narrate to you the best of narratives, by Our revealing to you this Quran, though before this you were certainly one of those who did not know.
12 004	Behold! Joseph said to his father: "O my father! I did see eleven stars and the sun and the moon: I saw them prostrate themselves to me!"	When Joseph said unto his father: O my father! Lo! I saw in a dream eleven planets and the sun and the moon, I saw them prostrating themselves unto me.	When Yusuf said to his father: O my father! surely I saw eleven stars and the sun and the moon-- I saw them making obeisance to me.
12 005	Said (the father): "My (dear) little son! relate not thy vision to thy brothers, lest they concoct a plot against thee: for Satan is to man an avowed enemy!"	He said: O my dear son! Tell not thy brethren of thy vision, lest they plot a plot against thee. Lo! Satan is for man an open foe.	He said: O my son! do not relate your vision to your brothers, lest they devise a plan against you; surely the Shaitan is an open enemy to man.

12 006	"Thus will thy Lord choose thee and teach thee the interpretation of stories (and events) and perfect His favour to thee and to the posterity of Jacob - even as He perfected it to thy fathers Abraham and Isaac aforetime! for Allah is full of knowledge and wisdom."	Thus thy Lord will prefer thee and will teach thee the interpretation of events, and will perfect His grace upon thee and upon the family of Jacob as He perfected it upon thy forefathers, Abraham and Isaac. Lo! thy Lord is Knower, Wise.	And thus will your Lord choose you and teach you the interpretation of sayings and make His favor complete to you and to the children of Yaqoub, as He made it complete before to your fathers, Ibrahim and Ishaq; surely your Lord is Knowing, Wise.
12 007	Verily in Joseph and his brethren are signs (or symbols) for seekers (after Truth).	Verily in Joseph and his brethren are signs (of Allah's Sovereignty) for the inquiring.	Certainly in Yusuf and his brothers there are signs for the inquirers.
12 008	They said: "Truly Joseph and his brother are loved more by our father than we: But we are a goodly body! really our father is obviously wandering (in his mind)!"	When they said: Verily Joseph and his brother are dearer to our father than we are, many though we be. Lo! our father is in plain aberration.	When they said: Certainly Yusuf and his brother are dearer to our father than we, though we are a (stronger) company; most surely our father is in manifest error:
12 009	"Slay ye Joseph or cast him out to some (unknown) land, that so the favour of your father may be given to you alone: (there will be time enough) for you to be righteous after that!"	(One said): Kill Joseph or cast him to some (other) land, so that your father's favour may be all for you, and (that) ye may afterward be righteous folk.	Slay Yusuf or cast him (forth) into some land, so that your father's regard may be exclusively for you, and after that you may be a righteous people.
12 010	Said one of them: "Slay not Joseph, but if ye must do something, throw him down to the bottom of the well: he will be picked up by some caravan of travellers."	One among them said: Kill not Joseph but, if ye must be doing, fling him into the depth of the pit; some caravan will find him.	A speaker from among them said: Do not slay Yusuf, and cast him down into the bottom of the pit if you must do (it), (so that) some of the travellers may pick him up.
12 011	They said: "O our father! why dost thou not trust us with Joseph,- seeing we are indeed his sincere well-wishers?"	They said: O our father! Why wilt thou not trust us with Joseph, when lo! we are good friends to him?	They said: O our father! what reason have you that you do not trust in us with respect to Yusuf? And most surely we are his sincere well-wishers:
12 012	"Send him with us tomorrow to enjoy himself and play, and we shall take every care of him."	Send him with us to-morrow that he may enjoy himself and play. And lo! we shall take good care of him.	Send him with us tomorrow that he may enjoy himself and sport, and surely we will guard him well.
12 013	(Jacob) said: "Really it saddens me that ye should take him away: I fear lest the wolf should devour him while ye attend not to him."	He said: Lo! in truth it saddens me that ye should take him with you, and I fear less the wolf devour him while ye are heedless of him.	He said: Surely it grieves me that you should take him off, and I fear lest the wolf devour him while you are heedless of him.
12 014	They said: "If the wolf were to devour him while we are (so large) a party, then should we indeed (first) have perished ourselves!"	They said: If the wolf should devour him when we are (so strong) a band, then surely we should have already perished.	They said: Surely if the wolf should devour him notwithstanding that we are a (strong) company, we should then certainly be losers.
12 015	So they did take him away, and they all agreed to throw him down to the bottom of the well: and We put into his heart (this Message): 'Of a surety thou shalt (one day) tell them the truth of this their affair while they know (thee) not'	Then, when they led him off, and were of one mind that they should place him in the depth of the pit, We inspired in him: Thou wilt tell them of this deed of theirs when they know (thee) not.	So when they had gone off with him and agreed that they should put him down at the bottom of the pit, and We revealed to him: You will most certainly inform them of this their affair while they do not perceive.
12 016	Then they came to their father in the early part of the night, weeping.	And they came weeping to their father in the evening.	And they came to their father at nightfall, weeping.
12 017	They said: "O our father! We went racing with one another, and left Joseph with our things; and the wolf devoured him.... But thou wilt never believe us even though we tell the truth."	Saying: O our father! We went racing one with another, and left Joseph by our things, and the wolf devoured him, and thou believest not our saying even when we speak the truth.	They said: O our father! surely we went off racing and left Yusuf by our goods, so the wolf devoured him, and you will not believe us though we are truthful.

12 018	They stained his shirt with false blood. He said: "Nay, but your minds have made up a tale (that may pass) with you, (for me) patience is most fitting: Against that which ye assert, it is Allah (alone) Whose help can be sought"..	And they came with false blood on his shirt. He said: Nay, but your minds have beguiled you into something. (My course is) comely patience. And Allah it is Whose help is to be sought in that (predicament) which ye describe.	And they brought his shirt with false blood upon it. He said: Nay, your souls have made the matter light for you, but patience is good and Allah is He Whose help is sought for against what you describe.
12 019	Then there came a caravan of travellers: they sent their water-carrier (for water), and he let down his bucket (into the well)...He said. "Ah there! Good news! Here is a (fine) young man!" So they concealed him as a treasure! But Allah knoweth well all that they do!	And there came a caravan, and they sent their waterdrawer. He let down his pail (into the pit). He said: Good luck! Here is a youth. And they hid him as a treasure, and Allah was Aware of what they did.	And there came travellers and they sent their water-drawer and he let down his bucket. He said: O good news! this is a youth; and they concealed him as an article of merchandise, and Allah knew what they did.
12 020	The (Brethren) sold him for a miserable price, for a few dirhams counted out: in such low estimation did they hold him!	And they sold him for a low price, a number of silver coins; and they attached no value to him.	And they sold him for a small price, a few pieces of silver, and they showed no desire for him.
12 021	The man in Egypt who bought him, said to his wife: "Make his stay (among us) honourable: may be he will bring us much good, or we shall adopt him as a son." Thus did We establish Joseph in the land, that We might teach him the interpretation of stories (and events). And Allah hath full power and control over His affairs; but most among mankind know it not.	And he of Egypt who purchased him said unto his wife: Receive him honourably. Perchance he may prove useful to us or we may adopt him as a son. Thus we established Joseph in the land that We might teach him the interpretation of events. And Allah was predominant in His career, but most of mankind know not.	And the Egyptian who bought him said to his wife: Give him an honorable abode, maybe he will be useful to us, or we may adopt him as a son. And thus did We establish Yusuf in the land and that We might teach him the interpretation of sayings; and Allah is the master of His affair, but most people do not know.
12 022	When Joseph attained His full manhood, We gave him power and knowledge: thus do We reward those who do right.	And when he reached his prime We gave him wisdom and knowledge. Thus We reward the good.	And when he had attained his maturity, We gave him wisdom and knowledge: and thus do We reward those who do good.
12 023	But she in whose house he was, sought to seduce him from his (true) self: she fastened the doors, and said: "Now come, thou (dear one)!" He said: "Allah forbid! truly (thy husband) is my lord! he made my sojourn agreeable! truly to no good come those who do wrong!"	And she, in whose house he was, asked of him an evil act. She bolted the doors and said: Come! He said: I seek refuge in Allah! Lo! he is my lord, who hath treated me honourably. Lo! wrong-doers never prosper.	And she in whose house he was sought to make himself yield (to her), and she made fast the doors and said: Come forward. He said: I seek Allah's refuge, surely my Lord made good my abode: Surely the unjust do not prosper.
12 024	And (with passion) did she desire him, and he would have desired her, but that he saw the evidence of his Lord: thus (did We order) that We might turn away from him (all) evil and shameful deeds: for he was one of Our servants, sincere and purified.	She verily desired him, and he would have desired her if it had not been that he saw the argument of his Lord. Thus it was, that We might ward off from him evil and lewdness. Lo! he was of Our chosen slaves.	And certainly she made for him, and he would have made for her, were it not that he had seen the manifest evidence of his Lord; thus (it was) that We might turn away from him evil and indecency, surely he was one of Our sincere servants.
12 025	So they both raced each other to the door, and she tore his shirt from the back: they both found her lord near the door. She said: "What is the (fitting) punishment for one who formed an evil design against thy wife, but prison or a grievous chastisement?"	And they raced with one another to the door, and she tore his shirt from behind, and they met her lord and master at the door. She said: What shall be his reward, who wisheth evil to thy folk, save prison or a painful doom?	And they both hastened to the door, and she rent his shirt from behind and they met her husband at the door. She said: What is the punishment of him who intends evil to your wife except imprisonment or a painful chastisement?

12 026	He said: "It was she that sought to seduce me - from my (true) self." And one of her household saw (this) and bore witness, (thus):- "If it be that his shirt is rent from the front, then is her tale true, and he is a liar!"	(Joseph) said: She it was who asked of me an evil act. And a witness of her own folk testified: If his shirt is torn from before, then she speaketh truth and he is of the liars.	He said: She sought to make me yield (to her); and a witness of her own family bore witness: If his shirt is rent from front, she speaks the truth and he is one of the liars:
12 027	"But if it be that his shirt is torn from the back, then is she the liar, and he is telling the truth!"	And if his shirt is torn from behind, then she hath lied and he is of the truthful.	And if his shirt is rent from behind, she tells a lie and he is one of the truthful.
12 028	So when he saw his shirt,- that it was torn at the back,- (her husband) said: "Behold! It is a snare of you women! truly, mighty is your snare!"	So when he saw his shirt torn from behind, he said: Lo! this is of the guile of you women. Lo! the guile of you is very great.	So when he saw his shirt rent from behind, he said: Surely it is a guile of you women; surely your guile is great:
12 029	"O Joseph, pass this over! (O wife), ask forgiveness for thy sin, for truly thou hast been at fault!"	O Joseph! Turn away from this, and thou, (O woman), ask forgiveness for thy sin. Lo! thou art of the faulty.	O Yusuf! turn aside from this; and (O my wife)! ask forgiveness for your fault, surely you are one of the wrong-doers.
12 030	Ladies said in the City: "The wife of the (great) 'Aziz is seeking to seduce her slave from his (true) self: Truly hath he inspired her with violent love: we see she is evidently going astray."	And women in the city said: The ruler's wife is asking of her slave-boy an ill-deed. Indeed he has smitten her to the heart with love. We behold her in plain aberration.	And women in the city said: The chief's wife seeks her slave to yield himself (to her), surely he has affected her deeply with (his) love; most surely we see her in manifest error.
12 031	When she heard of their malicious talk, she sent for them and prepared a banquet for them: she gave each of them a knife: and she said (to Joseph), "Come out before them." When they saw him, they did extol him, and (in their amazement) cut their hands: they said, "Allah preserve us! no mortal is this! this is none other than a noble angel!"	And when she heard of their sly talk, she sent to them and prepared for them a cushioned couch (to lie on at the feast) and gave to every one of them a knife and said (to Joseph): Come out unto them! And when they saw him they exalted him and cut their hands, exclaiming: Allah Blameless! This is no a human being. This is not other than some gracious angel.	So when she heard of their sly talk she sent for them and prepared for them a repast, and gave each of them a knife, and said (to Yusuf): Come forth to them. So when they saw him, they deemed him great, and cut their hands (in amazement), and said: Remote is Allah (from imperfection); this is not a mortal; this is but a noble angel.
12 032	She said: "There before you is the man about whom ye did blame me! I did seek to seduce him from his (true) self but he did firmly save himself guiltless!.... And now, if he doth not my bidding, he shall certainly be cast into prison, and (what is more) be of the company of the vilest!"	She said: This is he on whose account ye blamed me. I asked of him an evil act, but he proved continent, but if he do not my behest he verily shall be imprisoned, and verily shall be of those brought low.	She said: This is he with respect to whom you blamed me, and certainly I sought his yielding himself (to me), but he abstained, and if he does not do what I bid him, he shall certainly be imprisoned, and he shall certainly be of those who are in a state of ignominy.
12 033	He said: "O my Lord! the prison is more to my liking than that to which they invite me: Unless Thou turn away their snare from me, I should (in my youthful folly) feel inclined towards them and join the ranks of the ignorant."	He said: O my Lord! Prison is more dear than that unto which they urge me, and if Thou fend not off their wiles from me I shall incline unto them and become of the foolish.	He said: My Lord! the prison house is dearer to me than that to which they invite me; and if Thou turn not away their device from me, I will yearn towards them and become (one) of the ignorant.
12 034	So his Lord hearkened to him (in his prayer), and turned away from him their snare: Verily He heareth and knoweth (all things).	So his Lord heard his prayer and fended off their wiles from him. Lo! He is Hearer, Knower.	Thereupon his Lord accepted his prayer and turned away their guile from him; surely He is the Hearing, the Knowing.

12 035	Then it occurred to the men, after they had seen the signs, (that it was best) to imprison him for a time.	And it seemed good to them (the men-folk) after they had seen the signs (of his innocence) to imprison him for a time.	Then it occurred to them after they had seen the signs that they should imprison him till a time.
12 036	Now with him there came into the prison two young men. Said one of them: "I see myself (in a dream) pressing wine." said the other: "I see myself (in a dream) carrying bread on my head, and birds are eating thereof." "Tell us" (they said) "The truth and meaning thereof: for we see thou art one that doth good (to all)."	And two young men went to prison with him. One of them said: I dreamed that I was pressing wine. The other said: I dreamed that I was carrying upon my head bread whereof the birds were eating. Announce unto us the interpretation, for we see thee of those good (at interpretation).	And two youths entered the prison with him. One of them said: I saw myself pressing wine. And the other said: I saw myself carrying bread on my head, of which birds ate. Inform us of its interpretation; surely we see you to be of the doers of good.
12 037	He said: "Before any food comes (in due course) to feed either of you, I will surely reveal to you the truth and meaning of this ere it befall you: that is part of the (duty) which my Lord hath taught me. I have (I assure you) abandoned the ways of a people that believe not in Allah and that (even) deny the Hereafter."	He said: The food which ye are given (daily) shall not come unto you but I shall tell you the interpretation ere it cometh unto you. This is of that which my Lord hath taught me. Lo! I have forsaken the religion of folk who believe not in Allah and are disbelievers in the Hereafter.	He said: There shall not come to you the food with which you are fed, but I will inform you both of its interpretation before it comes to you; this is of what my Lord has taught me; surely I have forsaken the religion of a people who do not believe in Allah, and they are deniers of the hereafter:
12 038	"And I follow the ways of my fathers,- Abraham, Isaac, and Jacob; and never could we attribute any partners whatever to Allah: that (comes) of the grace of Allah to us and to mankind: yet most men are not grateful."	And I have followed the religion of my fathers, Abraham and Isaac and Jacob. It never was for us to attribute aught as partner to Allah. This is of the bounty of Allah unto us (the seed of Abraham) and unto mankind; but most men give not thanks.	And I follow the religion of my fathers, Ibrahim and Ishaq and Yaqoub; it beseems us not that we should associate aught with Allah; this is by Allah's grace upon us and on mankind, but most people do not give thanks:
12 039	"O my two companions of the prison! (I ask you): are many lords differing among themselves better, or the One Allah, Supreme and Irresistible?"	O my fellow-prisoners! Are divers lords better, or Allah the One, Almighty?	O my two mates of the prison! are sundry lords better or Allah the One, the Supreme?
12 040	"If not Him, ye worship nothing but names which ye have named,- ye and your fathers,- for which Allah hath sent down no authority: the command is for none but Allah: He hath commanded that ye worship none but Him: that is the right religion, but most men understand not..."	Those whom ye worship beside Him are but names which ye have named, ye and your fathers. Allah hath revealed no sanction for them. The decision rests with Allah only, Who hath commanded you that ye worship none save Him. This is the right religion, but most men know not.	You do not serve besides Him but names which you have named, you and your fathers; Allah has not sent down any authority for them; judgment is only Allah's; He has commanded that you shall not serve aught but Him; this is the right religion but most people do not know:
12 041	"O my two companions of the prison! As to one of you, he will pour out the wine for his lord to drink: as for the other, he will hang from the cross, and the birds will eat from off his head. (So) hath been decreed that matter whereof ye twain do enquire..."	O my two fellow-prisoners! As for one of you, he will pour out wine for his lord to drink; and as for the other, he will be crucified so that the birds will eat from his head. Thus is the case judged concerning which ye did inquire.	O my two mates of the prison! as for one of you, he shall give his lord to drink wine; and as for the other, he shall be crucified, so that the birds shall eat from his head, the matter is decreed concerning which you inquired.

12 042	And of the two, to that one whom he consider about to be saved, he said: "Mention me to thy lord." But Satan made him forget to mention him to his lord: and (Joseph) lingered in prison a few (more) years.	And he said unto him of the twain who he knew would be released: Mention me in the presence of thy lord. But Satan caused him to forget to mention it to his lord, so he (Joseph) stayed in prison for some years.	And he said to him whom he knew would be delivered of the two: Remember me with your lord; but the Shaitan caused him to forget mentioning (it) to his lord, so he remained in the prison a few years.
12 043	The king (of Egypt) said: "I do see (in a vision) seven fat kine, whom seven lean ones devour, and seven green ears of corn, and seven (others) withered. O ye chiefs! Expound to me my vision if it be that ye can interpret visions."	And the king said: Lo! I saw in a dream seven fat kine which seven lean were eating, and seven green ears of corn and other (seven) dry. O notables! Expound for me my vision, if ye can interpret dreams.	And the king said: Surely I see seven fat kine which seven lean ones devoured; and seven green ears and (seven) others dry: O chiefs! explain to me my dream, if you can interpret the dream.
12 044	They said: "A confused medley of dreams: and we are not skilled in the interpretation of dreams."	They answered: Jumbled dreams! And we are not knowing in interpretation of dreams.	They said: Confused dreams, and we do not know the interpretation of dreams.
12 045	But the man who had been released, one of the two (who had been in prison) and who now bethought him after (so long) a space of time, said: "I will tell you the truth of its interpretation: send ye me (therefore)."	And he of the two who was released, and (now) at length remembered, said: I am going to announce unto you the interpretation, therefore send me forth.	And of the two (prisoners) he who had found deliverance and remembered after a long time said: I will inform you of its interpretation, so let me go:
12 046	"O Joseph!" (he said) "O man of truth! Expound to us (the dream) of seven fat kine whom seven lean ones devour, and of seven green ears of corn and (seven) others withered: that I may return to the people, and that they may understand."	(And when he came to Joseph in the prison, he exclaimed): Joseph! O thou truthful one! Expound for us the seven fat kine which seven lean were eating and the seven green ears of corn and other (seven) dry, that I may return unto the people, so that they may know.	Yusuf! O truthful one! explain to us seven fat kine which seven lean ones devoured, and seven green ears and (seven) others dry, that I may go back to the people so that they may know.
12 047	(Joseph) said: "For seven years shall ye diligently sow as is your wont: and the harvests that ye reap, ye shall leave them in the ear,- except a little, of which ye shall eat."	He said: Ye shall sow seven years as usual, but that which ye reap, leave it in the ear, all save a little which ye eat.	He said: You shall sow for seven years continuously, then what you reap leave it in its ear except a little of which you eat.
12 048	"Then will come after that (period) seven dreadful (years), which will devour what ye shall have laid by in advance for them,- (all) except a little which ye shall have (specially) guarded."	Then after that will come seven hard years which will devour all that ye have prepared for them, save a little of that which ye have stored.	Then there shall come after that seven years of hardship which shall eat away all that you have beforehand laid up in store for them, except a little of what you shall have preserved:
12 049	"Then will come after that (period) a year in which the people will have abundant water, and in which they will press (wine and oil)."	Then, after that, will come a year when the people will have plenteous crops and when they will press (wine and oil).	Then there will come after that a year in which people shall have rain and in which they shall press (grapes).
12 050	So the king said: "Bring ye him unto me." But when the messenger came to him, (Joseph) said: "Go thou back to thy lord, and ask him, 'What is the state of mind of the ladies who cut their hands'? For my Lord is certainly well aware of their snare."	And the king said: Bring him unto me. And when the messenger came unto him, he (Joseph) said: Return unto thy lord and ask him what was the case of the women who cut their hands. Lo! my Lord knoweth their guile.	And the king said: Bring him to me. So when the messenger came to him, he said: Go back to your lord and ask him, what is the case of the women who cut their hands; surely my Lord knows their guile.

12 051	(The king) said (to the ladies): "What was your affair when ye did seek to seduce Joseph from his (true) self?" The ladies said: "Allah preserve us! no evil know we against him!" Said the 'Aziz's wife: "Now is the truth manifest (to all): it was I who sought to seduce him from his (true) self: He is indeed of those who are (ever) true (and virtuous)."	He (the king) (then sent for those women and) said: What happened when ye asked an evil act of Joseph? They answered: Allah Blameless! We know no evil of him. Said the wife of the ruler: Now the truth is out. I asked of him an evil act, and he is surely of the truthful.		He said: How was your affair when you sought Yusuf to yield himself (to you)? They said: Remote is Allah (from imperfection), we knew of no evil on his part. The chief's wife said: Now has the truth become established: I sought him to yield himself (to me), and he is most surely of the truthful ones.
12 052	"This (say I), in order that He may know that I have never been false to him in his absence, and that Allah will never guide the snare of the false ones."	(Then Joseph said: I asked for) this, that he (my lord) may know that I betrayed him not in secret, and that surely Allah guideth not the snare of the betrayers.		This is that he might know that I have not been unfaithful to him in secret and that Allah does not guide the device of the unfaithful.
12 053	"Nor do I absolve my own self (of blame): the (human) soul is certainly prone to evil, unless my Lord do bestow His Mercy: but surely my Lord is Oft-Forgiving, Most Merciful."	I do not exculpate myself. Lo! the (human) soul enjoineth unto evil, save that whereon my Lord hath mercy. Lo! my Lord is Forgiving, Merciful.		And I do not declare myself free, most surely (man's) self is wont to command (him to do) evil, except such as my Lord has had mercy on, surely my Lord is Forgiving, Merciful.
12 054	So the king said: "Bring him unto me; I will take him specially to serve about my own person." Therefore when he had spoken to him, he said: "Be assured this day, thou art, before our own presence, with rank firmly established, and fidelity fully proved!"	And the king said: Bring him unto me that I may attach him to my person. And when he had talked with him he said: Lo! thou art to-day in our presence established and trusted.		And the king said: Bring him to me, I will choose him for myself. So when he had spoken with him, he said: Surely you are in our presence today an honorable, a faithful one.
12 055	(Joseph) said: "Set me over the store-houses of the land: I will indeed guard them, as one that knows (their importance)."	He said: Set me over the storehouses of the land. Lo! I am a skilled custodian.		He said: Place me (in authority) over the treasures of the land, surely I am a good keeper, knowing well.
12 056	Thus did We give established power to Joseph in the land, to take possession therein as, when, or where he pleased. We bestow of our Mercy on whom We please, and We suffer not, to be lost, the reward of those who do good.	Thus gave We power to Joseph in the land. He was the owner of it where he pleased. We reach with Our mercy whom We will. We lose not the reward of the good.		And thus did We give to Yusuf power in the land-- he had mastery in it wherever he liked; We send down Our mercy on whom We please, and We do not waste the reward of those who do good.
12 057	But verily the reward of the Hereafter is the best, for those who believe, and are constant in righteousness.	And the reward of the Hereafter is better, for those who believe and ward off (evil).		And certainly the reward of the hereafter is much better for those who believe and guard (against evil).
12 058	Then came Joseph's brethren: they entered his presence, and he knew them, but they knew him not.	And Joseph's brethren came and presented themselves before him, and he knew them but they knew him not.		And Yusuf's brothers came and went in to him, and he knew them, while they did not recognize him.
12 059	And when he had furnished them forth with provisions (suitable) for them, he said: "Bring unto me a brother ye have, of the same father as yourselves, (but a different mother): see ye not that I pay out full measure, and that I do provide the best hospitality?"	And when he provided them with their provision he said: Bring unto me a brother of yours from your father. See ye not that I fill up the measure and I am the best of hosts?		And when he furnished them with their provision, he said: Bring to me a brother of yours from your father; do you not see that I give full measure and that I am the best of hosts?

12 060	"Now if ye bring him not to me, ye shall have no measure (of corn) from me, nor shall ye (even) come near me."	And if ye bring him not unto me, then there shall be no measure for you with me, nor shall ye draw near.	But if you do not bring him to me, you shall have no measure (of corn) from me, nor shall you come near me.
12 061	They said: "We shall certainly seek to get our wish about him from his father: Indeed we shall do it."	They said: We will try to win him from his father: that we will surely do.	They said: We will strive to make his father yield in respect of him, and we are sure to do (it).
12 062	And (Joseph) told his servants to put their stock-in-trade (with which they had bartered) into their saddle-bags, so they should know it only when they returned to their people, in order that they might come back.	He said unto his young men: Place their merchandise in their saddle-bags, so that they may know it when they go back to their folk, and so will come again.	And he said to his servants: Put their money into their bags that they may recognize it when they go back to their family, so that they may come back.
12 063	Now when they returned to their father, they said: "O our father! No more measure of grain shall we get (unless we take our brother): So send our brother with us, that we may get our measure; and we will indeed take every care of him."	So when they went back to their father they said: O our father! The measure is denied us, so send with us our brother that we may obtain the measure, surely we will guard him well.	So when they returned to their father, they said: O our father, the measure is withheld from us, therefore send with us our brother, (so that) we may get the measure, and we will most surely guard him.
12 064	He said: "Shall I trust you with him with any result other than when I trusted you with his brother aforetime? But Allah is the best to take care (of him), and He is the Most Merciful of those who show mercy!"	He said: Can I entrust him to you save as I entrusted his brother to you aforetime? Allah is better at guarding, and He is the Most Merciful of those who show mercy.	He said: I cannot trust in you with respect to him, except as I trusted in you with respect to his brother before; but Allah is the best Keeper, and He is the most Merciful of the merciful ones.
12 065	Then when they opened their baggage, they found their stock-in-trade had been returned to them. They said: "O our father! What (more) can we desire? this our stock-in-trade has been returned to us: so we shall get (more) food for our family; We shall take care of our brother; and add (at the same time) a full camel's load (of grain to our provisions). This is but a small quantity."	And when they opened their belongings they discovered that their merchandise had been returned to them. They said: O our father! What (more) can we ask? Here is our merchandise returned to us. We shall get provision for our folk and guard our brother, and we shall have the extra measure of a camel (load). This (that we bring now) is a light measure.	And when they opened their goods, they found their money returned to them. They said: O our father! what (more) can we desire? This is our property returned to us, and we will bring corn for our family and guard our brother, and will have in addition the measure of a camel (load); this is an easy measure.
12 066	(Jacob) said: "Never will I send him with you until ye swear a solemn oath to me, in Allah's name, that ye will be sure to bring him back to me unless ye are yourselves hemmed in (and made powerless)." And when they had sworn their solemn oath, he said: "Over all that we say, be Allah the witness and guardian!"	He said: I will not send him with you till ye give me an undertaking in the name of Allah that ye will bring him back to me, unless ye are surrounded. And when they gave him their undertaking he said: Allah is the Warden over what we say.	He said: I will by no means send him with you until you give me a firm covenant in Allah's name that you will most certainly bring him back to me, unless you are completely surrounded. And when they gave him their covenant, he said: Allah is the One in Whom trust is placed as regards what we say.
12 067	Further he said: "O my sons! enter not all by one gate: enter ye by different gates. Not that I can profit you aught against Allah (with my advice): None can command except Allah: On Him do I put my trust: and let all that trust put their trust on Him."	And he said: O my sons! Go not in by one gate; go in by different gates. I can naught avail you as against Allah. Lo! the decision rests with Allah only. In Him do I put my trust, and in Him let all the trusting put their trust.	And he said: O my sons! do not (all) enter by one gate and enter by different gates and I cannot avail you aught against Allah; judgment is only Allah's; on Him do I rely, and on Him let those who are reliant rely.

12 068	And when they entered in the manner their father had enjoined, it did not profit them in the least against (the plan of) Allah: It was but a necessity of Jacob's soul, which he discharged. For he was, by our instruction, full of knowledge (and experience): but most men know not.	And when they entered in the manner which their father had enjoined, it would have naught availed them as against Allah; it was but a need of Jacob's soul which he thus satisfied; and lo! he was a lord of knowledge because We had taught him; but most of mankind know not.	And when they had entered as their father had bidden them, it did not avail them aught against Allah, but (it was only) a desire in the soul of Yaqoub which he satisfied; and surely he was possessed of knowledge because We had given him knowledge, but most people do not know.
12 069	Now when they came into Joseph's presence, he received his (full) brother to stay with him. He said (to him): "Behold! I am thy (own) brother; so grieve not at aught of their doings."	And when they went in before Joseph, he took his brother unto him, saying: Lo! I, even I, am thy brother, therefore sorrow not for what they did.	And when they went in to Yusuf, he lodged his brother with himself, saying: I am your brother, therefore grieve not at what they do.
12 070	At length when he had furnished them forth with provisions (suitable) for them, he put the drinking cup into his brother's saddle-bag. Then shouted out a crier: "O ye (in) the caravan! behold! ye are thieves, without doubt!"	And when he provided them with their provision, he put the drinking-cup in his brother's saddlebag, and then a crier cried: O camel-riders! Lo! ye are surely thieves!	So when he furnished them with their provisions, (someone) placed the drinking cup in his brother's bag. Then a crier cried out: O caravan! you are most surely thieves.
12 071	They said, turning towards them: "What is it that ye miss?"	They cried, coming toward them: What is it ye have lost?	They said while they were facing them: What is it that you miss?
12 072	They said: "We miss the great beaker of the king; for him who produces it, is (the reward of) a camel load; I will be bound by it."	They said: We have lost the king's cup, and he who bringeth it shall have a camel-load, and I (said Joseph) am answerable for it.	They said: We miss the king's drinking cup, and he who shall bring it shall have a camel-load and I am responsible for it.
12 073	(The brothers) said: "By Allah! well ye know that we came not to make mischief in the land, and we are no thieves!"	They said: By Allah, well ye know we came not to do evil in the land, and are no thieves.	They said: By Allah! you know for certain that we have not come to make mischief in the land, and we are not thieves.
12 074	(The Egyptians) said: "What then shall be the penalty of this, if ye are (proved) to have lied?"	They said: And what shall be the penalty for it, if ye prove liars?	They said: But what shall be the requital of this, if you are liars?
12 075	They said: "The penalty should be that he in whose saddle-bag it is found, should be held (as bondman) to atone for the (crime). Thus it is we punish the wrong-doers!"	They said: The penalty for it! He in whose bag (the cup) is found, he is the penalty for it. Thus we requite wrong-doers.	They said: The requital of this is that the person in whose bag it is found shall himself be (held for) the satisfaction thereof; thus do we punish the wrongdoers.
12 076	So he began (the search) with their baggage, before (he came to) the baggage of his brother: at length he brought it out of his brother's baggage. Thus did We plan for Joseph. He could not take his brother by the law of the king except that Allah willed it (so). We raise to degrees (of wisdom) whom We please: but over all endued with knowledge is one, the All-Knowing.	Then he (Joseph) began the search with their bags before his brother's bag, then he produced it from his brother's bag. Thus did We contrive for Joseph. He could not have taken his brother according to the king's law unless Allah willed. We raise by grades (of mercy) whom We will, and over every lord of knowledge there is one more knowing.	So he began with their sacks before the sack of his brother, then he brought it out from his brother's sack. Thus did We plan for Yusuf; it was not (lawful) that he should take his brother under the king's law unless Allah pleased; We raise the degrees of whomsoever We please, and above every one possessed of knowledge is the All-knowing one.
12 077	They said: "If he steals, there was a brother of his who did steal before (him)." But these things did Joseph keep locked in his heart, revealing not the secrets to them. He (simply) said (to himself): "Ye are the worse situated; and Allah knoweth best the truth of what ye assert!"	They said: If he stealeth, a brother of his stole before. But Joseph kept it secret in his soul and revealed it not unto them. He said (within himself): Ye are in worse case, and Allah knoweth best (the truth of) that which ye allege.	They said: If he steal, a brother of his did indeed steal before; but Yusuf kept it secret in his heart and did not disclose it to them. He said: You are in an evil condition and Allah knows best what you state.

12 078	They said: "O exalted one! Behold! he has a father, aged and venerable, (who will grieve for him); so take one of us in his place; for we see that thou art (gracious) in doing good."	They said: O ruler of the land! Lo! he hath a very aged father, so take one of us instead of him. Lo! we behold thee of those who do kindness.	They said: O chief! he has a father, a very old man, therefore retain one of us in his stead; surely we see you to be of the doers of good.
12 079	He said: "Allah forbid that we take other than him with whom we found our property: indeed (if we did so), we should be acting wrongfully."	He said: Allah forbid that we should seize save him with whom we found our property; then truly we should be wrong-doers.	He said: Allah protect us that we should seize other than him with whom we found our property, for then most surely we would be unjust.
12 080	Now when they saw no hope of his (yielding), they held a conference in private. The leader among them said: "Know ye not that your father did take an oath from you in Allah's name, and how, before this, ye did fail in your duty with Joseph? Therefore will I not leave this land until my father permits me, or Allah commands me; and He is the best to command."	So, When they despaired of (moving) him, they conferred together apart. The eldest of them said: Know ye not how your father took an undertaking from you in Allah's name and how ye failed in the case of Joseph aforetime? Therefore I shall not go forth from the land until my father giveth leave or Allah judgeth for me. He is the Best of Judges.	Then when they despaired of him, they retired, conferring privately together. The eldest of them said: Do you not know that your father took from you a covenant in Allah's name, and how you fell short of your duty with respect to Yusuf before? Therefore I will by no means depart from this land until my father permits me or Allah decides for me, and He is the best of the judges:
12 081	"Turn ye back to your father, and say, 'O our father! behold! thy son committed theft! we bear witness only to what we know, and we could not well guard against the unseen!"	Return unto your father and say: O our father! Lo! thy son hath stolen. We testify only to that which we know; we are not guardians of the Unseen.	Go back to your father and say: O our father! surely your son committed theft, and we do not bear witness except to what we have known, and we could not keep watch over the unseen:
12 082	"'Ask at the town where we have been and the caravan in which we returned, and (you will find) we are indeed telling the truth.'"	Ask the township where we were, and the caravan with which we travelled hither. Lo! we speak the truth.	And inquire in the town in which we were and the caravan with which we proceeded, and most surely we are truthful.
12 083	Jacob said: "Nay, but ye have yourselves contrived a story (good enough) for you. So patience is most fitting (for me). Maybe Allah will bring them (back) all to me (in the end). For He is indeed full of knowledge and wisdom."	(And when they came unto their father and had spoken thus to him) he said: Nay, but your minds have beguiled you into something. (My course is) comely patience! It may be that Allah will bring them all unto me. Lo! He, only He, is the Knower, the Wise.	He (Yaqoub) said: Nay, your souls have made a matter light for you, so patience is good; maybe Allah will bring them all together to me; surely He is the Knowing, the Wise.
12 084	And he turned away from them, and said: "How great is my grief for Joseph!" And his eyes became white with sorrow, and he fell into silent melancholy.	And he turned away from them and said: Alas, my grief for Joseph! And his eyes were whitened with the sorrow that he was suppressing.	And he turned away from them, and said: O my sorrow for Yusuf! and his eyes became white on account of the grief, and he was a repressor (of grief).
12 085	They said: "By Allah! (never) wilt thou cease to remember Joseph until thou reach the last extremity of illness, or until thou die!"	They said: By Allah, thou wilt never cease remembering Joseph till thy health is ruined or thou art of those who perish!	They said: By Allah! you will not cease to remember Yusuf until you are a prey to constant disease or (until) you are of those who perish.
12 086	He said: "I only complain of my distraction and anguish to Allah, and I know from Allah that which ye know not..."	He said: I expose my distress and anguish only unto Allah, and I know from Allah that which ye know not.	He said: I only complain of my grief and sorrow to Allah, and I know from Allah what you do not know.

12 087	"O my sons! go ye and enquire about Joseph and his brother, and never give up hope of Allah's Soothing Mercy: truly no one despairs of Allah's Soothing Mercy, except those who have no faith."	Go, O my sons, and ascertain concerning Joseph and his brother, and despair not of the Spirit of Allah. Lo! none despaireth of the Spirit of Allah save disbelieving folk.	O my sons! Go and inquire respecting Yusuf and his brother, and despair not of Allah's mercy; surely none despairs of Allah's mercy except the unbelieving people.
12 088	Then, when they came (back) into (Joseph's) presence they said: "O exalted one! distress has seized us and our family: we have (now) brought but scanty capital: so pay us full measure, (we pray thee), and treat it as charity to us: for Allah doth reward the charitable."	And when they came (again) before him (Joseph) they said: O ruler! Misfortune hath touched us and our folk, and we bring but poor merchandise, so fill for us the measure and be charitable unto us. Lo! Allah will requite the charitable,	So when they came in to him, they said: O chief! distress has afflicted us and our family and we have brought scanty money, so give us full measure and be charitable to us; surely Allah rewards the charitable.
12 089	He said: "Know ye how ye dealt with Joseph and his brother, not knowing (what ye were doing)?"	He said: Know ye what ye did unto Joseph and his brother in your ignorance?	He said: Do you know how you treated Yusuf and his brother when you were ignorant?
12 090	They said: "Art thou indeed Joseph?" He said, "I am Joseph, and this is my brother: Allah has indeed been gracious to us (all): behold, he that is righteous and patient,- never will Allah suffer the reward to be lost, of those who do right."	They said: Is it indeed thou who art Joseph? He said: I am Joseph and this is my brother. Allah hath shown us favour. Lo! he who wardeth off (evil) and endureth (findeth favour); for lo! Allah loseth not the wages of the kindly.	They said: Are you indeed Yusuf? He said: I am Yusuf and this is my brother; Allah has indeed been gracious to us; surely he who guards (against evil) and is patient (is rewarded) for surely Allah does not waste the reward of those who do good.
12 091	They said: "By Allah! indeed has Allah preferred thee above us, and we certainly have been guilty of sin!"	They said: By Allah, verily Allah hath preferred thee above us, and we were indeed sinful.	They said: By Allah! now has Allah certainly chosen you over us, and we were certainly sinners.
12 092	He said: "This day let no reproach be (cast) on you: Allah will forgive you, and He is the Most Merciful of those who show mercy!"	He said: Have no fear this day! May Allah forgive you, and He is the Most Merciful of those who show mercy.	He said: (There shall be) no reproof against you this day; Allah may forgive you, and He is the most Merciful of the merciful.
12 093	"Go with this my shirt, and cast it over the face of my father: he will come to see (clearly). Then come ye (here) to me together with all your family."	Go with this shirt of mine and lay it on my father's face, he will become (again) a seer; and come to me with all your folk.	Take this my shirt and cast it on my father's face, he will (again) be able to see, and come to me with all your families.
12 094	When the caravan left (Egypt), their father said: "I do indeed scent the presence of Joseph: Nay, think me not a dotard."	When the caravan departed their father had said: Truly I am conscious of the breath of Joseph, though ye call me dotard.	And when the caravan had departed, their father said: Most surely I perceive the greatness of Yusuf, unless you pronounce me to be weak in judgment.
12 095	They said: "By Allah! truly thou art in thine old wandering mind."	(Those around him) said: By Allah, lo! thou art in thine old aberration.	They said: By Allah, you are most surely in your old error.
12 096	Then when the bearer of the good news came, He cast (the shirt) over his face, and he forthwith regained clear sight. He said: "Did I not say to you, 'I know from Allah that which ye know not?'"	Then, when the bearer of glad tidings came, he laid it on his face and he became a seer once more. He said: Said I not unto you that I know from Allah that which ye know not?	So when the bearer of good news came he cast it on his face, so forthwith he regained his sight. He said: Did I not say to you that I know from Allah what you do not know?
12 097	They said: "O our father! ask for us forgiveness for our sins, for we were truly at fault."	They said: O our father! Ask forgiveness of our sins for us, for lo! we were sinful.	They said: O our father! ask forgiveness of our faults for us, surely we were sinners.
12 098	He said: "Soon will I ask my Lord for forgiveness for you: for he is indeed Oft-Forgiving, Most Merciful."	He said: I shall ask forgiveness for you of my Lord. Lo! He is the Forgiving, the Merciful.	He said: I will ask for you forgiveness from my Lord; surely He is the Forgiving, the Merciful.

12 099	Then when they entered the presence of Joseph, he provided a home for his parents with himself, and said: "Enter ye Egypt (all) in safety if it please Allah."	And when they came in before Joseph, he took his parents unto him, and said: Come into Egypt safe, if Allah will!	Then when they came in to Yusuf, he took his parents to lodge with him and said: Enter safe into Egypt, if Allah please.
12 100	And he raised his parents high on the throne (of dignity), and they fell down in prostration, (all) before him. He said: "O my father! this is the fulfilment of my vision of old! Allah hath made it come true! He was indeed good to me when He took me out of prison and brought you (all here) out of the desert, (even) after Satan had sown enmity between me and my brothers. Verily my Lord understandeth best the mysteries of all that He planneth to do, for verily He is full of knowledge and wisdom."	And he placed his parents on the dais and they fell down before him prostrate, and he said: O my father! This is the interpretation of my dream of old. My Lord hath made it true, and He hath shown me kindness, since He took me out of the prison and hath brought you from the desert after Satan had made strife between me and my brethren. Lo! my Lord is tender unto whom He will. He is the Knower, the Wise.	And he raised his parents upon the throne and they fell down in prostration before him, and he said: O my father! this is the significance of my vision of old; my Lord has indeed made it to be true; and He was indeed kind to me when He brought me forth from the prison and brought you from the desert after the Shaitan had sown dissensions between me and my brothers, surely my Lord is benignant to whom He pleases; surely He is the Knowing, the Wise.
12 101	"O my Lord! Thou hast indeed bestowed on me some power, and taught me something of the interpretation of dreams and events,- O Thou Creator of the heavens and the earth! Thou art my Protector in this world and in the Hereafter. Take Thou my soul (at death) as one submitting to Thy will (as a Muslim), and unite me with the righteous."	O my Lord! Thou hast given me (something) of sovereignty and hast taught me (something) of the interpretation of events - Creator of the heavens and the earth! Thou art my Protecting Guardian in the world and the Hereafter. Make me to die muslim (unto Thee), and join me to the righteous.	My Lord! Thou hast given me of the kingdom and taught me of the interpretation of sayings: Originator of the heavens and the earth! Thou art my guardian in this world and the hereafter; make me die a muslim and join me with the good.
12 102	Such is one of the stories of what happened unseen, which We reveal by inspiration unto thee; nor wast thou (present) with them then when they concerted their plans together in the process of weaving their plots.	This is of the tidings of the Unseen which We inspire in thee (Muhammad). Thou wast not present with them when they fixed their plan and they were scheming.	This is of the announcements relating to the unseen (which) We reveal to you, and you were not with them when they resolved upon their affair, and they were devising plans.
12 103	Yet no faith will the greater part of mankind have, however ardently thou dost desire it.	And though thou try much, most men will not believe.	And most men will not believe though you desire it eagerly.
12 104	And no reward dost thou ask of them for this: it is no less than a message for all creatures.	Thou askest them no fee for it. It is naught else than a reminder unto the peoples.	And you do not ask them for a reward for this; it is nothing but a reminder for all mankind.
12 105	And how many Signs in the heavens and the earth do they pass by? Yet they turn (their faces) away from them!	How many a portent is there in the heavens and the earth which they pass by with face averted!	And how many a sign in the heavens and the earth which they pass by, yet they turn aside from it.
12 106	And most of them believe not in Allah without associating (other as partners) with Him!	And most of them believe not in Allah except that they attribute partners (unto Him).	And most of them do not believe in Allah without associating others (with Him).
12 107	Do they then feel secure from the coming against them of the covering veil of the wrath of Allah,- or of the coming against them of the (final) Hour all of a sudden while they perceive not?	Deem they themselves secure from the coming on them of a pall of Allah's punishment, or the coming of the Hour suddenly while they are unaware?	Do they then feel secure that there may come to them an extensive chastisement from Allah or (that) the hour may come to them suddenly while they do not perceive?

12 108	Say thou: "This is my way: I do invite unto Allah,- on evidence clear as the seeing with one's eyes,- I and whoever follows me. Glory to Allah! and never will I join gods with Allah!"	Say: This is my Way: I call on Allah with sure knowledge. I and whosoever followeth me - Glory be to Allah! - and I am not of the idolaters.	Say: This is my way: I call to Allah, I and those who follow me being certain, and glory be to Allah, and I am not one of the polytheists.
12 109	Nor did We send before thee (as messengers) any but men, whom we did inspire,- (men) living in human habitations. Do they not travel through the earth, and see what was the end of those before them? But the home of the hereafter is best, for those who do right. Will ye not then understand?	We sent not before thee (any messengers) save men whom We inspired from among the folk of the townships - Have they not travelled in the land and seen the nature of the consequence for those who were before them? And verily the abode of the Hereafter, for those who ward off (evil), is best. Have ye then no sense? -	And We have not sent before you but men from (among) the people of the towns, to whom We sent revelations. Have they not then travelled in the land and seen what was the end of those before them? And certainly the abode of the hereafter is best for those who guard (against evil); do you not then understand?
12 110	(Respite will be granted) until, when the messengers give up hope (of their people) and (come to) think that they were treated as liars, there reaches them Our help, and those whom We will are delivered into safety. But never will be warded off our punishment from those who are in sin.	Till, when the messengers despaired and thought that they were denied, then came unto them Our help, and whom We would was saved. And Our wrath cannot be warded from the guilty.	Until when the messengers despaired and the people became sure that they were indeed told a lie, Our help came to them and whom We pleased was delivered; and Our punishment is not averted from the guilty people.
12 111	There is, in their stories, instruction for men endued with understanding. It is not a tale invented, but a confirmation of what went before it,- a detailed exposition of all things, and a guide and a mercy to any such as believe.	In their history verily there is a lesson for men of understanding. It is no invented story but a confirmation of the existing (Scripture) and a detailed explanation of everything, and a guidance and a mercy for folk who believe.	In their histories there is certainly a lesson for men of understanding. It is not a narrative which could be forged, but a verification of what is before it and a distinct explanation of all things and a guide and a mercy to a people who believe.

Chapter 13:

AL-RAD (THE THUNDER)

Total Verses: 43 Revealed At: MAKKA

In the name of Allah, the Most Beneficent, the Most Merciful.

13 001	A.L.M.R. These are the signs (or verses) of the Book: that which hath been revealed unto thee from thy Lord is the Truth; but most men believe not.	Alif. Lam. Mim. Ra. These are verses of the Scripture. That which is revealed unto thee from thy Lord is the Truth, but most of mankind believe not.	Alif Lam Mim Ra. These are the verses of the Book; and that which is revealed to you from your Lord is the truth, but most people do not believe.
13 002	Allah is He Who raised the heavens without any pillars that ye can see; is firmly established on the throne (of authority); He has subjected the sun and the moon (to his Law)! Each one runs (its course) for a term appointed. He doth regulate all affairs, explaining the signs in detail, that ye may believe with certainty in the meeting with your Lord.	Allah it is Who raised up the heavens without visible supports, then mounted the Throne, and compelled the sun and the moon to be of service, each runneth unto an appointed term; He ordereth the course; He detaileth the revelations, that haply ye may be certain of the meeting with your Lord.	Allah is He Who raised the heavens without any pillars that you see, and He is firm in power and He made the sun and the moon subservient (to you); each one pursues its course to an appointed time; He regulates the affair, making clear the signs that you may be certain of meeting your Lord.
13 003	And it is He who spread out the earth, and set thereon mountains standing firm and (flowing) rivers: and fruit of every kind He made in pairs, two and two: He draweth the night as a veil o'er the Day. Behold, verily in these things there are signs for those who consider!	And He it is Who spread out the earth and placed therein firm hills and flowing streams, and of all fruits He placed therein two spouses (male and female). He covereth the night with the day. Lo! herein verily are portents for people who take thought.	And He it is Who spread the earth and made in it firm mountains and rivers, and of all fruits He has made in it two kinds; He makes the night cover the day; most surely there are signs in this for a people who reflect.
13 004	And in the earth are tracts (diverse though) neighbouring, and gardens of vines and fields sown with corn, and palm trees - growing out of single roots or otherwise: watered with the same water, yet some of them We make more excellent than others to eat. Behold, verily in these things there are signs for those who understand!	And in the Earth are neighbouring tracts, vineyards and ploughed lands, and date-palms, like and unlike, which are watered with one water. And we have made some of them to excel others in fruit. Lo! herein verily are portents for people who have sense.	And in the earth there are tracts side by side and gardens of grapes and corn and palm trees having one root and (others) having distinct roots-- they are watered with one water, and We make some of them excel others in fruit; most surely there are signs in this for a people who understand.
13 005	If thou dost marvel (at their want of faith), strange is their saying: "When we are (actually) dust, shall we indeed then be in a creation renewed?" They are those who deny their Lord! They are those round whose necks will be yokes (of servitude): they will be Companions of the Fire, to dwell therein (for aye)!	And if thou wonderest, then wondrous is their saying: When we are dust, are we then forsooth (to be raised) in a new creation? Such are they who disbelieve in their Lord; such have carcans on their necks; such are rightful owners of the Fire, they will abide therein.	And if you would wonder, then wondrous is their saying: What! when we are dust, shall we then certainly be in a new creation? These are they who disbelieve in their Lord, and these have chains on their necks, and they are the inmates of the fire; in it they shall abide.

13 006	They ask thee to hasten on the evil in preference to the good: Yet have come to pass, before them, (many) exemplary punishments! But verily thy Lord is full of forgiveness for mankind for their wrong-doing, and verily thy Lord is (also) strict in punishment.	And they bid thee hasten on the evil rather than the good, when exemplary punishments have indeed occurred before them. But lo! thy Lord is rich in pardon for mankind despite their wrong, and lo! thy Lord is strong in punishment.	And they ask you to hasten on the evil before the good, and indeed there have been exemplary punishments before them; and most surely your Lord is the Lord of forgiveness to people, notwithstanding their injustice; and most surely your Lord is severe in requiting (evil).
13 007	And the Unbelievers say: "Why is not a sign sent down to him from his Lord?" But thou art truly a warner, and to every people a guide.	Those who disbelieve say: If only some portent were sent down upon him from his Lord! Thou art a warner only, and for every folk a guide.	And those who disbelieve say: Why has not a sign been sent down upon him from his Lord? You are only a warner and (there is) a guide for every people.
13 008	Allah doth know what every female (womb) doth bear, by how much the wombs fall short (of their time or number) or do exceed. Every single thing is before His sight, in (due) proportion.	Allah knoweth that which every female beareth and that which the wombs absorb and that which they grow. And everything with Him is measured.	Allah knows what every female bears, and that of which the wombs fall short of completion and that in which they increase; and there is a measure with Him of everything.
13 009	He knoweth the unseen and that which is open: He is the Great, the Most High.	He is the Knower of the Invisible and the Visible, the Great, the High Exalted.	The knower of the unseen and the seen, the Great, the Most High.
13 010	It is the same (to Him) whether any of you conceal his speech or declare it openly; whether he lie hid by night or walk forth freely by day.	Alike of you is he who hideth the saying and he who noiseth it abroad, he who lurketh in the night and he who goeth freely in the daytime.	Alike (to Him) among you is he who conceals (his) words and he who speaks them openly, and he who hides himself by night and (who) goes forth by day.
13 011	For each (such person) there are (angels) in succession, before and behind him: They guard him by command of Allah. Allah does not change a people's lot unless they change what is in their hearts. But when (once) Allah willeth a people's punishment, there can be no turning it back, nor will they find, besides Him, any to protect.	For him are angels ranged before him and behind him, who guard him by Allah's command. Lo! Allah changeth not the condition of a folk until they (first) change that which is in their hearts; and if Allah willeth misfortune for a folk there is none that can repel it, nor have they a defender beside Him.	For his sake there are angels following one another, before him and behind him, who guard him by Allah's commandment; surely Allah does not change the condition of a people until they change their own condition; and when Allah intends evil to a people, there is no averting it, and besides Him they have no protector.
13 012	It is He Who doth show you the lightning, by way both of fear and of hope: It is He Who doth raise up the clouds, heavy with (fertilising) rain!	He it is Who showeth you the lightning, a fear and a hope, and raiseth the heavy clouds.	He it is Who shows you the lightning causing fear and hope and (Who) brings up the heavy cloud.
13 013	Nay, thunder repeateth His praises, and so do the angels, with awe: He flingeth the loud-voiced thunderbolts, and therewith He striketh whomsoever He will..yet these (are the men) who (dare to) dispute about Allah, with the strength of His power (supreme)!	The thunder hymneth His praise and (so do) the angels for awe of Him. He launcheth the thunderbolts and smiteth with them whom He will while they dispute (in doubt) concerning Allah, and He is mighty in wrath.	And the thunder declares His glory with His praise, and the angels too for awe of Him; and He sends the thunderbolts and smites with them whom He pleases, yet they dispute concerning Allah, and He is mighty in prowess.

13 014	For Him (alone) is prayer in Truth: any others that they call upon besides Him hear them no more than if they were to stretch forth their hands for water to reach their mouths but it reaches them not: for the prayer of those without Faith is nothing but (futile) wandering (in the mind).	Unto Him is the real prayer. Those unto whom they pray beside Allah respond to them not at all, save as (is the response to) one who stretcheth forth his hands toward water (asking) that it may come unto his mouth, and it will never reach it. The prayer of disbelievers goeth (far) astray.	To Him is due the true prayer; and those whom they pray to besides Allah give them no answer, but (they are) like one who stretches forth his two hands towards water that it may reach his mouth, but it will not reach it; and the prayer of the unbelievers is only in error.
13 015	Whatever beings there are in the heavens and the earth do prostrate themselves to Allah (Acknowledging subjection),- with good-will or in spite of themselves: so do their shadows in the morning and evenings.	And unto Allah falleth prostrate whosoever is in the heavens and the earth, willingly or unwillingly, as do their shadows in the morning and the evening hours.	And whoever is in the heavens and the earth makes obeisance to Allah only, willingly and unwillingly, and their shadows too at morn and eve.
13 016	Say: "Who is the Lord and Sustainer of the heavens and the earth?" Say: "(It is) Allah." Say: "Do ye then take (for worship) protectors other than Him, such as have no power either for good or for harm to themselves?" Say: "Are the blind equal with those who see? Or the depths of darkness equal with light?" Or do they assign to Allah partners who have created (anything) as He has created, so that the creation seemed to them similar? Say: "Allah is the Creator of all things: He is the One, the Supreme and Irresistible."	Say (O Muhammad): Who is Lord of the heavens and the earth? Say: Allah. Say: Take ye then (others) beside Him for protectors, which, even for themselves, have neither benefit nor hurt? Say: Is the blind man equal to the seer, or is darkness equal to light? Or assign they unto Allah partners who created the like of His creation so that the creation (which they made and His creation) seemed alike to them? Say: Allah is the Creator of all things, and He is the One, the Almighty.	Say: Who is the Lord of the heavens and the earth?-- Say: Allah. Say: Do you take then besides Him guardians who do not control any profit or harm for themselves? Say: Are the blind and the seeing alike? Or can the darkness and the light be equal? Or have they set up with Allah associates who have created creation like His, so that what is created became confused to them? Say: Allah is the Creator of all things, and He is the One, the Supreme.
13 017	He sends down water from the skies, and the channels flow, each according to its measure: But the torrent bears away to foam that mounts up to the surface. Even so, from that (ore) which they heat in the fire, to make ornaments or utensils therewith, there is a scum likewise. Thus doth Allah (by parables) show forth Truth and Vanity. For the scum disappears like forth cast out; while that which is for the good of mankind remains on the earth. Thus doth Allah set forth parables.	He sendeth down water from the sky, so that valleys flow according to their measure, and the flood beareth (on its surface) swelling foam - from that which they smelt in the fire in order to make ornaments and tools riseth a foam like unto it - thus Allah coineth (the similitude of) the true and the false. Then, as for the foam, it passeth away as scum upon the banks, while, as for that which is of use to mankind, it remaineth in the earth. Thus Allah coineth the similitudes.	He sends down water from the cloud, then watercourses flow (with water) according to their measure, and the torrent bears along the swelling foam, and from what they melt in the fire for the sake of making ornaments or apparatus arises a scum like it; thus does Allah compare truth and falsehood; then as for the scum, it passes away as a worthless thing; and as for that which profits the people, it tarries in the earth; thus does Allah set forth parables.
13 018	For those who respond to their Lord, are (all) good things. But those who respond not to Him,- Even if they had all that is in the heavens and on earth, and as much more, (in vain) would they offer it for ransom. For them will the reckoning be terrible: their abode will be Hell,- what a bed of misery!	For those who answered Allah's call is bliss; and for those who answered not His call, if they had all that is in the earth, and therewith the like thereof, they would proffer it as ransom. Such will have a woeful reckoning, and their habitation will be hell, a dire abode.	For those who respond to their Lord is good; and (as for) those who do not respond to Him, had they all that is in the earth and the like thereof with it they would certainly offer it for a ransom. (As for) those, an evil reckoning shall be theirs and their abode is hell, and evil is the resting-place.

13 019	Is then one who doth know that that which hath been revealed unto thee from thy Lord is the Truth, like one who is blind? It is those who are endued with understanding that receive admonition;-	Is he who knoweth that what is revealed unto thee from thy Lord is the truth like him who is blind? But only men of understanding heed;		Is he then who knows that what has been revealed to you from your Lord is the truth like him who is blind? Only those possessed of understanding will mind,
13 020	Those who fulfil the covenant of Allah and fail not in their plighted word;	Such as keep the pact of Allah, and break not the covenant;		Those who fulfil the promise of Allah and do not break the covenant,
13 021	Those who join together those things which Allah hath commanded to be joined, hold their Lord in awe, and fear the terrible reckoning;	Such as unite that which Allah hath commandeth should be joined, and fear their Lord, and dread a woeful reckoning;		And those who join that which Allah has bidden to be joined and have awe of their Lord and fear the evil reckoning.
13 022	Those who patiently persevere, seeking the countenance of their Lord; Establish regular prayers; spend, out of (the gifts) We have bestowed for their sustenance, secretly and openly; and turn off Evil with good: for such there is the final attainment of the (eternal) home,-	Such as persevere in seeking their Lord's Countenance and are regular in prayer and spend of that which We bestow upon them secretly and openly, and overcome evil with good. Theirs will be the sequel of the (heavenly) Home,		And those who are constant, seeking the pleasure of their Lord, and keep up prayer and spend (benevolently) out of what We have given them secretly and openly and repel evil with good; as for those, they shall have the (happy) issue of the abode,
13 023	Gardens of perpetual bliss: they shall enter there, as well as the righteous among their fathers, their spouses, and their offspring: and angels shall enter unto them from every gate (with the salutation):	Gardens of Eden which they enter, along with all who do right of their fathers and their helpmeets and their seed. The angels enter unto them from every gate,		The gardens of perpetual abode which they will enter along with those who do good from among their parents and their spouses and their offspring; and the angels will enter in upon them from every gate:
13 024	"Peace unto you for that ye persevered in patience! Now how excellent is the final home!"	(Saying): Peace be unto you because ye persevered. Ah, passing sweet will be the sequel of the (heavenly) Home.		Peace be on you because you were constant, how excellent, is then, the issue of the abode.
13 025	But those who break the Covenant of Allah, after having plighted their word thereto, and cut asunder those things which Allah has commanded to be joined, and work mischief in the land;- on them is the curse; for them is the terrible home!	And those who break the covenant of Allah after ratifying it, and sever that which Allah hath commanded should be joined, and make mischief in the earth: theirs is the curse and theirs the ill abode.		And those who break the covenant of Allah after its confirmation and cut asunder that which Allah has ordered to be joined and make mischief in the land; (as for) those, upon them shall be curse and they shall have the evil (issue) of the abode.
13 026	Allah doth enlarge, or grant by (strict) measure, the sustenance (which He giveth) to whomso He pleaseth. (The wordly) rejoice in the life of this world: But the life of this world is but little comfort in the Hereafter.	Allah enlargeth livelihood for whom He will, and straiteneth (it for whom He will); and they rejoice in the life of the world, whereas the life of the world is but brief comfort as compared with the Hereafter.		Allah amplifies and straitens the means of subsistence for whom He pleases; and they rejoice in this world's life, and this world's life is nothing compared with the hereafter but a temporary enjoyment.
13 027	The Unbelievers say: "Why is not a sign sent down to him from his Lord?" Say: "Truly Allah leaveth, to stray, whom He will; But He guideth to Himself those who turn to Him in penitence,-"	Those who disbelieve say: If only a portent were sent down upon him from his Lord! Say: Lo! Allah sendeth whom He will astray, and guideth unto Himself all who turn (unto Him),		And those who disbelieve say: Why is not a sign sent down upon him by his Lord? Say: Surely Allah makes him who will go astray, and guides to Himself those who turn (to Him).

13 028	"Those who believe, and whose hearts find satisfaction in the remembrance of Allah: for without doubt in the remembrance of Allah do hearts find satisfaction."	Who have believed and whose hearts have rest in the remembrance of Allah. Verily in the remembrance of Allah do hearts find rest!	Those who believe and whose hearts are set at rest by the remembrance of Allah; now surely by Allah's remembrance are the hearts set at rest.
13 029	"For those who believe and work righteousness, is (every) blessedness, and a beautiful place of (final) return."	Those who believe and do right: Joy is for them, and bliss (their) journey's end.	(As for) those who believe and do good, a good final state shall be theirs and a goodly return.
13 030	Thus have we sent thee amongst a People before whom (long since) have (other) Peoples (gone and) passed away; in order that thou mightest rehearse unto them what We send down unto thee by inspiration; yet do they reject (Him), the Most Gracious! Say: "He is my Lord! There is no god but He! On Him is my trust, and to Him do I turn!"	Thus We send thee (O Muhammad) unto a nation, before whom other nations have passed away, that thou mayst recite unto them that which We have inspired in thee, while they are disbelievers in the Beneficent. Say: He is my Lord; there is no God save Him. In Him do I put my trust and unto Him is my recourse.	And thus We have sent you among a nation before which other nations have passed away, that you might recite to them what We have revealed to you and (still) they deny the Beneficent Allah. Say: He is my Lord, there is no god but He; on Him do I rely and to Him is my return.
13 031	If there were a Qur'an with which mountains were moved, or the earth were cloven asunder, or the dead were made to speak, (this would be the one!) But, truly, the command is with Allah in all things! Do not the Believers know, that, had Allah (so) willed, He could have guided all mankind (to the right)? But the Unbelievers,- never will disaster cease to seize them for their (ill) deeds, or to settle close to their homes, until the promise of Allah come to pass, for, verily, Allah will not fail in His promise.	Had it been possible for a Lecture to cause the mountains to move, or the earth to be torn asunder, or the dead to speak, (this Qur'an would have done so). Nay, but Allah's is the whole command. Do not those who believe know that, had Allah willed, He could have guided all mankind? As for those who disbelieve, disaster ceaseth not to strike them because of what they do, or it dwelleth near their home until the threat of Allah come to pass. Lo! Allah faileth not to keep the tryst.	And even if there were a Quran with which the mountains were made to pass away, or the earth were travelled over with it, or the dead were made to speak thereby; nay! the commandment is wholly Allah's, Have not yet those who believe known that if Allah please He would certainly guide all the people? And (as for) those who disbelieve, there will not cease to afflict them because of what they do a repelling calamity, or it will alight close by their abodes, until the promise of Allah comes about; surely Allah will not fail in (His) promise.
13 032	Mocked were (many) messengers before thee: but I granted respite to the unbelievers, and finally I punished them: Then how (terrible) was my requital!	And verily messengers (of Allah) were mocked before thee, but long I bore with those who disbelieved. At length I seized them, and how (awful) was My punishment!	And messengers before you were certainly mocked at, but I gave respite to those who disbelieved, then I destroyed them; how then was My requital (of evil)?
13 033	Is then He who standeth over every soul (and knoweth) all that it doth, (like any others)? And yet they ascribe partners to Allah. Say: But name them! is it that ye will inform Him of something he knoweth not on earth, or is it (just) a show of words?" Nay! to those who believe not, their pretence seems pleasing, but they are kept back (thereby) from the path. And those whom Allah leaves to stray, no one can guide.	Is He Who is aware of the deserts of every soul (as he who is aware of nothing)? Yet they ascribe unto Allah partners. Say: Name them. Is it that ye would inform Him of something which He knoweth not in the earth? Or is it but a way of speaking? Nay but their contrivance is made seeming fair for those who disbelieve and they are kept from the right road. He whom Allah sendeth astray, for him there is no guide.	Is He then Who watches every soul as to what it earns? And yet they give associates to Allah! Say: Give them a name; nay, do you mean to inform Him of what He does not know in the earth, or (do you affirm this) by an outward saying? Rather, their plans are made to appear fair-seeming to those who disbelieve, and they are kept back from the path; and whom Allah makes err, he shall have no guide.

13 034	For them is a penalty in the life of this world, but harder, truly, is the penalty of the Hereafter: and defender have they none against Allah.	For them is torment in the life of the world, and verily the doom of the Hereafter is more painful, and they have no defender from Allah.	They shall have chastisement in this world's life, and the chastisement of the hereafter is certainly more grievous, and they shall have no protector against Allah.
13 035	The parable of the Garden which the righteous are promised!- beneath it flow rivers: perpetual is the enjoyment thereof and the shade therein: such is the end of the Righteous; and the end of Unbelievers in the Fire.	A similitude of the Garden which is promised unto those who keep their duty (to Allah): Underneath it rivers flow; its food is everlasting, and its shade; this is the reward of those who keep their duty, while the reward of disbelievers is the Fire.	A likeness of the garden which the righteous are promised; there flow beneath it rivers, its food and shades are perpetual; this is the requital of those who guarded (against evil), and the requital of the unbelievers is the fire.
13 036	Those to whom We have given the Book rejoice at what hath been revealed unto thee: but there are among the clans those who reject a part thereof. Say: "I am commanded to worship Allah, and not to join partners with Him. Unto Him do I call, and unto Him is my return."	Those unto whom We gave the Scripture rejoice in that which is revealed unto thee. And of the clans there are who deny some of it. Say: I am commanded only that I serve Allah and ascribe unto Him no partner. Unto Him I cry, and unto Him is my return.	And those to whom We have given the Book rejoice in that which has been revealed to you, and of the confederates are some who deny a part of it. Say: I am only commanded that I should serve Allah and not associate anything with Him, to Him do I invite (you) and to Him is my return.
13 037	Thus have We revealed it to be a judgment of authority in Arabic. Wert thou to follow their (vain) desires after the knowledge which hath reached thee, then wouldst thou find neither protector nor defender against Allah.	Thus have We revealed it, a decisive utterance in Arabic; and if thou shouldst follow their desires after that which hath come unto thee of knowledge, then truly wouldst thou have from Allah no protecting friend nor defender.	And thus have We revealed it, a true judgment in Arabic, and if you follow their low desires after what has come to you of knowledge, you shall not have against Allah any guardian or a protector.
13 038	We did send messengers before thee, and appointed for them wives and children: and it was never the part of a messenger to bring a sign except as Allah permitted (or commanded). For each period is a Book (revealed).	And verily We sent messengers (to mankind) before thee, and We appointed for them wives and offspring, and it was not (given) to any messenger that he should bring a portent save by Allah's leave. For everything there is a time prescribed.	And certainly We sent messengers before you and gave them wives and children, and it is not in (the power of) a messenger to bring a sign except by Allah's permission; for every term there is an appointment.
13 039	Allah doth blot out or confirm what He pleaseth: with Him is the Mother of the Book.	Allah effaceth what He will, and establisheth (what He will), and with Him is the source of ordinance.	Allah makes to pass away and establishes what He pleases, and with Him is the basis of the Book.
13 040	Whether We shall show thee (within thy life-time) part of what we promised them or take to ourselves thy soul (before it is all accomplished),- thy duty is to make (the Message) reach them: it is our part to call them to account.	Whether We let thee see something of that which We have promised them, or make thee die (before its happening), thine is but conveyance (of the message). Ours the reckoning.	And We will either let you see part of what We threaten them with or cause you to die, for only the delivery of the message is (incumbent) on you, while calling (them) to account is Our (business).
13 041	See they not that We gradually reduce the land (in their control) from its outlying borders? (Where) Allah commands, there is none to put back His Command: and He is swift in calling to account.	See they not how we aim to the land, reducing it of its outlying parts? (When) Allah doometh there is none that can postpone His doom, and He is swift at reckoning.	Do they not see that We are bringing destruction upon the land by curtailing it of its sides? And Allah pronounces a doom-- there is no repeller of His decree, and He is swift to take account.
13 042	Those before them did (also) devise plots; but in all things the masterplanning is Allah's He knoweth the doings of every soul: and soon will the Unbelievers know who gets home in the end.	Those who were before them plotted; but all plotting is Allah's. He knoweth that which each soul earneth. The disbelievers will come to know for whom will be the sequel of the (heavenly) Home.	And those before them did indeed make plans, but all planning is Allah's; He knows what every soul earns, and the unbelievers shall come to know for whom is the (better) issue of the abode.

13 043	The Unbelievers say: "No messenger art thou." Say: "Enough for a witness between me and you is Allah, and such as have knowledge of the Book."	They who disbelieve say: Thou art no messenger (of Allah). Say: Allah, and whosoever hath knowledge of the Scripture, is sufficient witness between me and you.	And those who disbelieve say: You are not a messenger. Say: Allah is sufficient as a witness between me and you and whoever has knowledge of the Book.

Chapter 14:

IBRAHIM (ABRAHAM)

Total Verses: 52 Revealed At: MAKKA

In the name of Allah, the Most Beneficent, the Most Merciful.

14 001	A. L. R. A Book which We have revealed unto thee, in order that thou mightest lead mankind out of the depths of darkness into light - by the leave of their Lord - to the Way of (Him) the Exalted in power, worthy of all praise!-	Alif. Lam. Ra. (This is) a Scripture which We have revealed unto thee (Muhammad) that thereby thou mayst bring forth mankind from darkness unto light, by the permission of their Lord, unto the path of the Mighty, the Owner of Praise,	Alif Lam Ra. (This is) a Book which We have revealed to you that you may bring forth men, by their Lord's permission from utter darkness into light-- to the way of the Mighty, the Praised One,
14 002	Of Allah, to Whom do belong all things in the heavens and on earth! But alas for the Unbelievers for a terrible penalty (their Unfaith will bring them)!-	Allah, unto Whom belongeth whatsoever is in the heavens and whatsoever is in the earth. And woe unto the disbelievers from an awful doom;	(Of) Allah, Whose is whatever is in the heavens and whatever Is in the earth; and woe to the unbelievers on account of the severe chastisement,
14 003	Those who love the life of this world more than the Hereafter, who hinder (men) from the Path of Allah and seek therein something crooked: they are astray by a long distance.	Those who love the life of the world more than the Hereafter, and debar (men) from the way of Allah and would have it crooked: such are far astray.	(To) those who love this world's life more than the hereafter, and turn away from Allah's path and desire to make it crooked; these are in a great error.
14 004	We sent not a messenger except (to teach) in the language of his (own) people, in order to make (things) clear to them. Now Allah leaves straying those whom He pleases and guides whom He pleases: and He is Exalted in power, full of Wisdom.	And We never sent a messenger save with the language of his folk, that he might make (the message) clear for them. Then Allah sendeth whom He will astray, and guideth whom He will. He is the Mighty, the Wise.	And We did not send any messenger but with the language of his people, so that he might explain to them clearly; then Allah makes whom He pleases err and He guides whom He pleases and He is the Mighty, the Wise.
14 005	We sent Moses with Our signs (and the command). "Bring out thy people from the depths of darkness into light, and teach them to remember the Days of Allah." Verily in this there are Signs for such as are firmly patient and constant,- grateful and appreciative.	We verily sent Moses with Our revelations, saying: Bring thy people forth from darkness unto light. And remind them of the days of Allah. Lo! therein are revelations for each steadfast, thankful (heart).	And certainly We sent Musa with Our communications, saying: Bring forth your people from utter darkness into light and remind them of the days of Allah; most surely are signs in this for every patient, grateful one.

14 006	Remember! Moses said to his people: "Call to mind the favour of Allah to you when He delivered you from the people of Pharaoh: they set you hard tasks and punishments, slaughtered your sons, and let your women-folk live: therein was a tremendous trial from your Lord."	And (remind them) how Moses said unto his people: Remember Allah's favour unto you when He delivered you from Pharaoh's folk who were afflicting you with dreadful torment, and were slaying your sons and sparing your women; that was a tremendous trial from your Lord.	And when Musa said to his people: Call to mind Allah's favor to you when He delivered you from Firon's people, who subjected you to severe torment, and slew your sons and spared your women; and in this there was a great trial from your Lord.
14 007	And remember! your Lord caused to be declared (publicly): "If ye are grateful, I will add more (favours) unto you; But if ye show ingratitude, truly My punishment is terrible indeed."	And when your Lord proclaimed: If ye give thanks, I will give you more; but if ye are thankless, lo! My punishment is dire.	And when your Lord made it known: If you are grateful, I would certainly give to you more, and if you are ungrateful, My chastisement is truly severe.
14 008	And Moses said: "If ye show ingratitude, ye and all on earth together, yet is Allah free of all wants, worthy of all praise."	And Moses said: Though ye and all who are in the earth prove thankless, lo! Allah verily is Absolute, Owner of Praise.	And Musa said: If you are ungrateful, you and those on earth all together, most surely Allah is Self-sufficient, Praised;
14 009	Has not the story reached you, (O people!), of those who (went) before you? - of the people of Noah, and 'Ad, and Thamud? - And of those who (came) after them? None knows them but Allah. To them came messengers with Clear (Signs); but they put their hands up to their mouths, and said: "We do deny (the mission) on which ye have been sent, and we are really in suspicious (disquieting) doubt as to that to which ye invite us."	Hath not the history of those before you reached you: the folk of Noah, and (the tribes of) A'ad and Thamud, and those after them? None save Allah knoweth them. Their messengers came unto them with clear proofs, but they thrust their hands into their mouths, and said: Lo! we disbelieve in that wherewith ye have been sent, and lo! we are in grave doubt concerning that to which ye call us.	Has not the account reached you of those before you, of the people of Nuh and Ad and Samood, and those after them? None knows them but Allah. Their messengers come to them with clear arguments, but they thrust their hands into their mouths and said: Surely we deny that with which you are sent, and most surely we are in serious doubt as to that to which you invite us.
14 010	Their messengers said: "Is there a doubt about Allah, The Creator of the heavens and the earth? It is He Who invites you, in order that He may forgive you your sins and give you respite for a term appointed!" They said: "Ah! ye are no more than human, like ourselves! Ye wish to turn us away from the (gods) our fathers used to worship: then bring us some clear authority."	Their messengers said: Can there be doubt concerning Allah, the Creator of the heavens and the earth? He calleth you that He may forgive you your sins and reprieve you unto an appointed term. They said: Ye are but mortals like us, who would fain turn us away from what our fathers used to worship. Then bring some clear warrant.	Their messengers said: Is there doubt about Allah, the Maker of the heavens and the earth? He invites you to forgive you your faults and to respite you till an appointed term. They said: You are nothing but mortals like us; you wish to turn us away from what our fathers used to worship; bring us therefore some clear authority.
14 011	Their messengers said to them: "True, we are human like yourselves, but Allah doth grant His grace to such of his servants as He pleases. It is not for us to bring you an authority except as Allah permits. And on Allah let all men of faith put their trust."	Their messengers said unto them: We are but mortals like you, but Allah giveth grace unto whom He will of His slaves. It is not ours to bring you a warrant unless by the permission of Allah. In Allah let believers put their trust!	Their messengers said to them: We are nothing but mortals like yourselves, but Allah bestows (His) favors on whom He pleases of His servants, and it is not for us that we should bring you an authority except by Allah's permission; and on Allah should the believers rely.
14 012	"No reason have we why we should not put our trust on Allah. Indeed He Has guided us to the Ways we (follow). We shall certainly bear with patience all the hurt you may cause us. For those who put their trust should put their trust on Allah."	How should we not put our trust in Allah when He hath shown us our ways? We surely will endure the hurt ye do us. In Allah let the trusting put their trust.	And what reason have we that we should not rely on Allah? And He has indeed guided us in our ways; and certainly we would bear with patience your persecution of us; and on Allah should the reliant rely.

14 013	And the Unbelievers said to their messengers: "Be sure we shall drive you out of our land, or ye shall return to our religion." But their Lord inspired (this Message) to them: "Verily We shall cause the wrong-doers to perish!"	And those who disbelieved said unto their messengers: Verily we will drive you out from our land, unless ye return to our religion. Then their Lord inspired them, (saying): Verily we shall destroy the wrong-doers,	And those who disbelieved said to their messengers: We will most certainly drive you forth from our land, or else you shall come back into our religion. So their Lord revealed to them: Most certainly We will destroy the unjust.	
14 014	"And verily We shall cause you to abide in the land, and succeed them. This for such as fear the Time when they shall stand before My tribunal,- such as fear the punishment denounced."	And verily We shall make you to dwell in the land after them. This is for him who feareth My Majesty and feareth My threats.	And most certainly We will settle you in the land after them; this is for him who fears standing in My presence and who fears My threat.	
14 015	But they sought victory and decision (there and then), and frustration was the lot of every powerful obstinate transgressor.	And they sought help (from their Lord) and every froward potentate was bought to naught;	And they asked for judgment and every insolent opposer was disappointed:	
14 016	In front of such a one is Hell, and he is given, for drink, boiling fetid water.	Hell is before him, and he is made to drink a festering water,	Hell is before him and he shall be given to drink of festering water:	
14 017	In gulps will he sip it, but never will he be near swallowing it down his throat: death will come to him from every quarter, yet will he not die: and in front of him will be a chastisement unrelenting.	Which he sippeth but can hardly swallow, and death cometh unto him from every side while yet he cannot die, and before him is a harsh doom.	He will drink it little by little and will not be able to swallow it agreeably, and death will come to him from every quarter, but he shall not die; and there shall be vehement chastisement before him.	
14 018	The parable of those who reject their Lord is that their works are as ashes, on which the wind blows furiously on a tempestuous day: No power have they over aught that they have earned: that is the straying far, far (from the goal).	A similitude of those who disbelieve in their Lord: Their works are as ashes which the wind bloweth hard upon a stormy day. They have no control of aught that they have earned. That is the extreme failure.	The parable of those who disbelieve in their Lord: their actions are like ashes on which the wind blows hard on a stormy day; they shall not have power over any thing out of what they have earned; this is the great error.	
14 019	Seest thou not that Allah created the heavens and the earth in Truth? If He so will, He can remove you and put (in your place) a new creation?	Hast thou not seen that Allah hath created the heavens and the earth with truth? If He will, He can remove you and bring (in) some new creation;	Do you not see that Allah created the heavens and the earth with truth? If He please He will take you off and bring a new creation,	
14 020	Nor is that for Allah any great matter.	And that is no great matter for Allah.	And this is not difficult for Allah.	
14 021	They will all be marshalled before Allah together: then will the weak say to those who were arrogant, "For us, we but followed you; can ye then avail us to all against the wrath of Allah?" They will reply, "If we had received the Guidance of Allah, we should have given it to you: to us it makes no difference (now) whether we rage, or bear (these torments) with patience: for ourselves there is no way of escape."	They all come forth unto their Lord. Then those who were despised say unto those who were scornful: We were unto you a following, can ye then avert from us aught of Allah's doom? They say: Had Allah guided us, we should have guided you. Whether we rage or patiently endure is (now) all one for us; we have no place of refuge.	And they shall all come forth before Allah, then the weak shall say to those who were proud: Surely we were your followers, can you therefore avert from us any part of the chastisement of Allah? They would say: If Allah had guided us, we too would have guided you; it is the same to us whether we are impatient (now) or patient, there is no place for us to fly to.	

14 022	And Satan will say when the matter is decided: "It was Allah Who gave you a promise of Truth: I too promised, but I failed in my promise to you. I had no authority over you except to call you but ye listened to me: then reproach not me, but reproach your own souls. I cannot listen to your cries, nor can ye listen to mine. I reject your former act in associating me with Allah. For wrong-doers there must be a grievous penalty."		And Satan saith, when the matter hath been decided: Lo! Allah promised you a promise of truth; and I promised you, then failed you. And I had no power over you save that I called unto you and ye obeyed me. So blame not, but blame yourselves. I cannot help you, nor can ye help me, Lo! I disbelieved in that which ye before ascribed to me. Lo! for wrong-doers is a painful doom.	And the Shaitan shall say after the affair is decided: Surely Allah promised you the promise of truth, and I gave you promises, then failed to keep them to you, and I had no authority over you, except that I called you and you obeyed me, therefore do not blame me but blame yourselves: I cannot be your aider (now) nor can you be my aiders; surely I disbelieved in your associating me with Allah before; surely it is the unjust that shall have the painful punishment.
14 023	But those who believe and work righteousness will be admitted to gardens beneath which rivers flow,- to dwell therein for aye with the leave of their Lord. Their greeting therein will be: "Peace!"		And those who believed and did good works are made to enter Gardens underneath which rivers flow, therein abiding by permission of their Lord, their greeting therein: Peace!	And those who believe and do good are made to enter gardens, beneath which rivers flow, to abide in them by their Lord's permission; their greeting therein is, Peace.
14 024	Seest thou not how Allah sets forth a parable? - A goodly word like a goodly tree, whose root is firmly fixed, and its branches (reach) to the heavens,- of its Lord. So Allah sets forth parables for men, in order that they may receive admonition.		Seest thou not how Allah coineth a similitude: A goodly saying, as a goodly tree, its root set firm, its branches reaching into heaven,	Have you not considered how Allah sets forth a parable of a good word (being) like a good tree, whose root is firm and whose branches are in heaven,
14 025	It brings forth its fruit at all times, by the leave of its Lord. So Allah sets forth parables for men, in order that they may receive admonition.		Giving its fruit at every season by permission of its Lord? Allah coineth the similitudes for mankind in order that they may reflect.	Yielding its fruit in every season by the permission of its Lord? And Allah sets forth parables for men that they may be mindful.
14 026	And the parable of an evil Word is that of an evil tree: It is torn up by the root from the surface of the earth: it has no stability.		And the similitude of a bad saying is as a bad tree, uprooted from upon the earth, possessing no stability.	And the parable of an evil word is as an evil tree pulled up from the earth's surface; it has no stability.
14 027	Allah will establish in strength those who believe, with the word that stands firm, in this world and in the Hereafter; but Allah will leave, to stray, those who do wrong: Allah doeth what He willeth.		Allah confirmeth those who believe by a firm saying in the life of the world and in the Hereafter, and Allah sendeth wrong-doers astray. And Allah doeth what He will.	Allah confirms those who believe with the sure word in this world's life and in the hereafter, and Allah causes the unjust to go astray, and Allah does what He pleases.
14 028	Hast thou not turned thy vision to those who have changed the favour of Allah. Into blasphemy and caused their people to descend to the House of Perdition?-		Hast thou not seen those who gave the grace of Allah in exchange for thanklessness and led their people down to the Abode of Loss,	Have you not seen those who have changed Allah's favor for ungratefulness and made their people to alight into the abode of perdition;
14 029	Into Hell? They will burn therein,- an evil place to stay in!		(Even to) hell? They are exposed thereto. A hapless end!	(Into) hell? They shall enter into it and an evil place it is to settle in.
14 030	And they set up (idols) as equal to Allah, to mislead (men) from the Path! Say: "Enjoy (your brief power)! But verily ye are making straightway for Hell!"		And they set up rivals to Allah that they may mislead (men) from His way. Say: Enjoy life (while ye may) for lo! your journey's end will be the Fire.	And they set up equals with Allah that they may lead (people) astray from His path. Say: Enjoy yourselves, for surely your return is to the fire.

14 031	Speak to my servants who have believed, that they may establish regular prayers, and spend (in charity) out of the sustenance we have given them, secretly and openly, before the coming of a Day in which there will be neither mutual bargaining nor befriending.	Tell My bondmen who believe to establish worship and spend of that which We have given them, secretly and publicly, before a day cometh wherein there will be neither bargaining nor befriending.	Say to My servants who believe that they should keep up prayer and spend out of what We have given them secretly and openly before the coming of the day in which there shall be no bartering nor mutual befriending.
14 032	It is Allah Who hath created the heavens and the earth and sendeth down rain from the skies, and with it bringeth out fruits wherewith to feed you; it is He Who hath made the ships subject to you, that they may sail through the sea by His command; and the rivers (also) hath He made subject to you.	Allah is He Who created the heavens and the earth, and causeth water to descend from the sky, thereby producing fruits as food for you, and maketh the ships to be of service unto you, that they may run upon the sea at His command, and hath made of service unto you the rivers;	Allah is He Who created the heavens and the earth and sent down water from the clouds, then brought forth with it fruits as a sustenance for you, and He has made the ships subservient to you, that they might run their course in the sea by His command, and He has made the rivers subservient to you.
14 033	And He hath made subject to you the sun and the moon, both diligently pursuing their courses; and the night and the day hath he (also) made subject to you.	And maketh the sun and the moon, constant in their courses, to be of service unto you, and hath made of service unto you the night and the day.	And He has made subservient to you the sun and the moon pursuing their courses, and He has made subservient to you the night and the day.
14 034	And He giveth you of all that ye ask for. But if ye count the favours of Allah, never will ye be able to number them. Verily, man is given up to injustice and ingratitude.	And He giveth you of all ye ask of Him, and if ye would count the bounty of Allah ye cannot reckon it. Lo! man is verily a wrong-doer, an ingrate.	And He gives you of all that you ask Him; and if you count Allah's favors, you will not be able to number them; most surely man is very unjust, very ungrateful.
14 035	Remember Abraham said: "O my Lord! make this city one of peace and security: and preserve me and my sons from worshipping idols."	And when Abraham said: My Lord! Make safe this territory, and preserve me and my sons from serving idols.	And when Ibrahim said: My Lord! make this city secure, and save me and my sons from worshipping idols:
14 036	"O my Lord! they have indeed led astray many among mankind; He then who follows my (ways) is of me, and he that disobeys me,- but Thou art indeed Oft-Forgiving, Most Merciful."	My Lord! Lo! they have led many of mankind astray. But whoso followeth me, he verily is of me. And whoso disobeyeth me - Still Thou art Forgiving, Merciful.	My Lord! surely they have led many men astray; then whoever follows me, he is surely of me, and whoever disobeys me, Thou surely arc Forgiving, Merciful:
14 037	"O our Lord! I have made some of my offspring to dwell in a valley without cultivation, by Thy Sacred House; in order, O our Lord, that they may establish regular Prayer: so fill the hearts of some among men with love towards them, and feed them with fruits: so that they may give thanks."	Our Lord! Lo! I have settled some of my posterity in an uncultivable valley near unto Thy holy House, our Lord! that they may establish proper worship; so incline some hearts of men that they may yearn toward them, and provide Thou them with fruits in order that they may be thankful.	O our Lord! surely I have settled a part of my offspring in a valley unproductive of fruit near Thy Sacred House, our Lord! that they may keep up prayer; therefore make the hearts of some people yearn towards them and provide them with fruits; haply they may be grateful:
14 038	"O our Lord! truly Thou dost know what we conceal and what we reveal: for nothing whatever is hidden from Allah, whether on earth or in heaven."	Our Lord! Lo! Thou knowest that which we hide and that which we proclaim. Nothing in the earth or in the heaven is hidden from Allah.	O our Lord! Surely Thou knowest what we hide and what we make public, and nothing in the earth nor any thing in heaven is hidden from Allah:
14 039	"Praise be to Allah, Who hath granted unto me in old age Isma'il and Isaac: for truly my Lord is He, the Hearer of Prayer!"	Praise be to Allah Who hath given me, in my old age, Ishmael and Isaac! Lo! my Lord is indeed the Hearer of Prayer.	Praise be to Allah, Who has given me in old age Ismail and Ishaq; most surely my Lord is the Hearer of prayer:

14 040	O my Lord! make me one who establishes regular Prayer, and also (raise such) among my offspring O our Lord! and accept Thou my Prayer.	My Lord! Make me to establish proper worship, and some of my posterity (also); our Lord! and accept my prayer.	My Lord! make me keep up prayer and from my offspring (too), O our Lord, and accept my prayer:
14 041	"O our Lord! cover (us) with Thy Forgiveness - me, my parents, and (all) Believers, on the Day that the Reckoning will be established!"	Our Lord! Forgive me and my parents and believers on the day when the account is cast.	O our Lord! grant me protection and my parents and the believers on the day when the reckoning shall come to pass!
14 042	Think not that Allah doth not heed the deeds of those who do wrong. He but giveth them respite against a Day when the eyes will fixedly stare in horror,-	Deem not that Allah is unaware of what the wicked do. He but giveth them a respite till a day when eyes will stare (in terror),	And do not think Allah to be heedless of what the unjust do; He only respites them to a day on which the eyes shall be fixedly open,
14 043	They running forward with necks outstretched, their heads uplifted, their gaze returning not towards them, and their hearts a (gaping) void!	As they come hurrying on in fear, their heads upraised, their gaze returning not to them, and their hearts as air.	Hastening forward, their heads upraised, their eyes not reverting to them and their hearts vacant.
14 044	So warn mankind of the Day when the Wrath will reach them: then will the wrong-doers say: "Our Lord! respite us (if only) for a short term: we will answer Thy call, and follow the messengers!" "What! were ye not wont to swear aforetime that ye should suffer no decline?"	And warn mankind of a day when the doom will come upon them, and those who did wrong will say: Our Lord! Reprieve us for a little while. We will obey Thy call and will follow the messengers. (It will be answered): Did ye not swear before that there would be no end for you?	And warn people of the day when the chastisement shall come to them, then those who were unjust will say: O our Lord! respite us to a near term, (so) we shall respond to Thy call and follow the messengers. What! did you not swear before (that) there will be no passing away for you!
14 045	"And ye dwelt in the dwellings of men who wronged their own souls; ye were clearly shown how We dealt with them; and We put forth (many) parables in your behoof!"	And (have ye not) dwelt in the dwellings of those who wronged themselves (of old) and (hath it not) become plain to you how We dealt with them and made examples for you?	And you dwell in the abodes of those who were unjust to themselves, and it is clear to you how We dealt with them and We have made (them) examples to you.
14 046	Mighty indeed were the plots which they made, but their plots were (well) within the sight of Allah, even though they were such as to shake the hills!	Verily they have plotted their plot, and their plot is with Allah, though their plot were one whereby the mountains should be moved.	And they have indeed planned their plan, but their plan is with Allah, though their plan was such that the mountains should pass away thereby.
14 047	Never think that Allah would fail his messengers in His promise: for Allah is Exalted in power, - the Lord of Retribution.	So think not that Allah will fail to keep His promise to His messengers. Lo! Allah is Mighty, Able to Requite (the wrong).	Therefore do not think Allah (to be one) failing in His promise to His messengers; surely Allah is Mighty, the Lord of Retribution.
14 048	One day the earth will be changed to a different earth, and so will be the heavens, and (men) will be marshalled forth, before Allah, the One, the Irresistible;	On the day when the earth will be changed to other than the earth, and the heavens (also will be changed) and they will come forth unto Allah, the One, the Almighty,	On the day when the earth shall be changed into a different earth, and the heavens (as well), and they shall come forth before Allah, the One, the Supreme.
14 049	And thou wilt see the sinners that day bound together in fetters;-	Thou wilt see the guilty on that day linked together in chains,	And you will see the guilty on that day linked together in chains.
14 050	Their garments of liquid pitch, and their faces covered with Fire;	Their raiment of pitch, and the Fire covering their faces,	Their shirts made of pitch and the fire covering their faces
14 051	That Allah may requite each soul according to its deserts; and verily Allah is swift in calling to account.	That Allah may repay each soul what it hath earned. Lo! Allah is swift at reckoning.	That Allah may requite each soul (according to) what it has earned; surely Allah is swift in reckoning.

14 052	Here is a Message for mankind: Let them take warning therefrom, and let them know that He is (no other than) One Allah: let men of understanding take heed.	This is a clear message for mankind in order that they may be warned thereby, and that they may know that He is only One Allah, and that men of understanding may take heed.	This is a sufficient exposition for the people and that they may be warned thereby, and that they may know that He is One Allah and that those possessed of understanding may mind.

Chapter 15:

AL-HIJR (AL-HIJR, STONELAND, ROCK CITY)

Total Verses: 99 Revealed At: MAKKA

In the name of Allah, the Most Beneficent, the Most Merciful.

15 001	A. L. R. These are the Ayats of Revelation,- of a Qur'an that makes things clear.	Alif. Lam. Ra. These are verses of the Scripture and a plain Reading.	Alif Lam Ra. These are the verses of the Book and (of) a Quran that makes (things) clear.
15 002	Again and again will those who disbelieve, wish that they had bowed (to Allah's will) in Islam.	It may be that those who disbelieve wish ardently that they were Muslims.	Often will those who disbelieve wish that they had been Muslims.
15 003	Leave them alone, to enjoy (the good things of this life) and to please themselves: let (false) hope amuse them: soon will knowledge (undeceive them).	Let them eat and enjoy life, and let (false) hope beguile them. They will come to know!	Leave them that they may eat and enjoy themselves and (that) hope may beguile them, for they will soon know.
15 004	Never did We destroy a population that had not a term decreed and assigned beforehand.	And We destroyed no township but there was a known decree for it.	And never did We destroy a town but it had a term made known.
15 005	Neither can a people anticipate its term, nor delay it.	No nation can outstrip its term nor can they lag behind.	No people can hasten on their doom nor can they postpone (it).
15 006	They say: "O thou to whom the Message is being revealed! truly thou art mad (or possessed)!"	And they say: O thou unto whom the Reminder is revealed, lo! thou art indeed a madman!	And they say: O you to whom the Reminder has been revealed! you are most surely insane:
15 007	"Why bringest thou not angels to us if it be that thou hast the Truth?"	Why bringest thou not angels unto us, if thou art of the truthful?	Why do you not bring to us the angels if you are of the truthful ones?
15 008	We send not the angels down except for just cause: if they came (to the ungodly), behold! no respite would they have!	We send not down the angels save with the Fact, and in that case (the disbelievers) would not be tolerated.	We do not send the angels but with truth, and then they would not be respited.
15 009	We have, without doubt, sent down the Message; and We will assuredly guard it (from corruption).	Lo! We, even We, reveal the Reminder, and lo! We verily are its Guardian.	Surely We have revealed the Reminder and We will most surely be its guardian.
15 010	We did send messengers before thee amongst the religious sects of old:	We verily sent (messengers) before thee among the factions of the men of old.	And certainly We sent (messengers) before you among the nations of yore.
15 011	But never came a messenger to them but they mocked him.	And never came there unto them a messenger but they did mock him.	And there never came a messenger to them but they mocked him.
15 012	Even so do we let it creep into the hearts of the sinners -	Thus do We make it traverse the hearts of the guilty:	Thus do We make it to enter into the hearts of the guilty;
15 013	That they should not believe in the (Message); but the ways of the ancients have passed away.	They believe not therein, though the example of the men of old hath gone before.	They do not believe in it, and indeed the example of the former people has already passed.

15 014	Even if We opened out to them a gate from heaven, and they were to continue (all day) ascending therein,	And even if We opened unto them a gate of heaven and they kept mounting through it,	And even if We open to them a gateway of heaven, so that they ascend into it all the while,
15 015	They would only say: "Our eyes have been intoxicated: Nay, we have been bewitched by sorcery."	They would say: Our sight is wrong - nay, but we are folk bewitched.	They would certainly say: Only our eyes have been covered over, rather we are an enchanted people.
15 016	It is We Who have set out the zodiacal signs in the heavens, and made them fair-seeming to (all) beholders;	And verily in the heaven we have set mansions of the stars, and We have beautified it for beholders.	And certainly We have made strongholds in the heaven and We have made it fair seeming to the beholders.
15 017	And (moreover) We have guarded them from every cursed devil:	And We have guarded it from every outcast devil,	And We guard it against every accursed Shaitan,
15 018	But any that gains a hearing by stealth, is pursued by a flaming fire, bright (to see).	Save him who stealeth the hearing, and them doth a clear flame pursue.	But he who steals a hearing, so there follows him a visible flame.
15 019	And the earth We have spread out (like a carpet); set thereon mountains firm and immovable; and produced therein all kinds of things in due balance.	And the earth have We spread out, and placed therein firm hills, and caused each seemly thing to grow therein.	And the earth-- We have spread it forth and made in it firm mountains and caused to grow in it of every suitable thing.
15 020	And We have provided therein means of subsistence,- for you and for those for whose sustenance ye are not responsible.	And we have given unto you livelihoods therein, and unto those for whom ye provide not.	And We have made in it means of subsistence for you and for him for whom you are not the suppliers.
15 021	And there is not a thing but its (sources and) treasures (inexhaustible) are with Us; but We only send down thereof in due and ascertainable measures.	And there is not a thing but with Us are the stores thereof. And we send it not down save in appointed measure.	And there is not a thing but with Us are the treasures of it, and We do not send it down but in a known measure.
15 022	And We send the fecundating winds, then cause the rain to descend from the sky, therewith providing you with water (in abundance), though ye are not the guardians of its stores.	And We send the winds fertilising, and cause water to descend from the sky, and give it you to drink. It is not ye who are the holders of the store thereof.	And We send the winds fertilizing, then send down water from the cloud so We give it to you to drink of, nor is it you who store it up.
15 023	And verily, it is We Who give life, and Who give death: it is We Who remain inheritors (after all else passes away).	Lo! and it is We, even We, Who quicken and give death, and We are the Inheritor.	And most surely We bring to life and cause to die and We are the heirs.
15 024	To Us are known those of you who hasten forward, and those who lag behind.	And verily We know the eager among you and verily We know the laggards.	And certainly We know those of you who have gone before and We certainly know those who shall come later.
15 025	Assuredly it is thy Lord Who will gather them together: for He is perfect in Wisdom and Knowledge.	Lo! thy Lord will gather them together. Lo! He is Wise, Aware.	And surely your Lord will gather them together; surely He is Wise, Knowing.
15 026	We created man from sounding clay, from mud moulded into shape;	Verily We created man of potter's clay of black mud altered,	And certainly We created man of clay that gives forth sound, of black mud fashioned in shape.
15 027	And the jinn race, We had created before, from the fire of a scorching wind.	And the jinn did We create aforetime of essential fire.	And the jinn We created before, of intensely hot fire.
15 028	Behold! thy Lord said to the angels: "I am about to create man, from sounding clay from mud moulded into shape;"	And (remember) when thy Lord said unto the angels: Lo! I am creating a mortal out of potter's clay of black mud altered,	And when your Lord said to the angels: Surely I am going to create a mortal of the essence of black mud fashioned in shape.

15 029	"When I have fashioned him (in due proportion) and breathed into him of My spirit, fall ye down in obeisance unto him."	So, when I have made him and have breathed into him of My Spirit, do ye fall down, prostrating yourselves unto him.	So when I have made him complete and breathed into him of My spirit, fall down making obeisance to him.
15 030	So the angels prostrated themselves, all of them together:	So the angels fell prostrate, all of them together	So the angels made obeisance, all of them together,
15 031	Not so Iblis: he refused to be among those who prostrated themselves.	Save Iblis. He refused to be among the prostrate.	But Iblis (did it not); he refused to be with those who made obeisance.
15 032	(Allah) said: "O Iblis! what is your reason for not being among those who prostrated themselves?"	He said: O Iblis! What aileth thee that thou art not among the prostrate?	He said: O Iblis! what excuse have you that you are not with those who make obeisance?
15 033	(Iblis) said: "I am not one to prostrate myself to man, whom Thou didst create from sounding clay, from mud moulded into shape."	He said: I am not one to prostrate myself unto a mortal whom Thou hast created out of potter's clay of black mud altered!	He said: I am not such that I should make obeisance to a mortal whom Thou hast created of the essence of black mud fashioned in shape.
15 034	(Allah) said: "Then get thee out from here; for thou art rejected, accursed."	He said: Then go thou forth from hence, for lo! thou art outcast.	He said: Then get out of it, for surely you are driven away:
15 035	"And the curse shall be on thee till the day of Judgment."	And lo! the curse shall be upon thee till the Day of Judgment.	And surely on you is curse until the Day of Judgment.
15 036	(Iblis) said: "O my Lord! give me then respite till the Day the (dead) are raised."	He said: My Lord! Reprieve me till the day when they are raised.	He said: My Lord! then respite me till the time when they are raised.
15 037	(Allah) said: "Respite is granted thee-"	He said: Then lo! thou art of those reprieved	He said: So surely you are of the respited ones
15 038	"Till the Day of the Time appointed."	Till the Day of appointed time.	Till the period of the time made known.
15 039	(Iblis) said: "O my Lord! because Thou hast put me in the wrong, I will make (wrong) fair-seeming to them on the earth, and I will put them all in the wrong,-"	He said: My Lord! Because Thou hast sent me astray, I verily shall adorn the path of error for them in the earth, and shall mislead them every one,	He said: My Lord! because Thou hast made life evil to me, I will certainly make (evil) fair-seeming to them on earth, and I will certainly cause them all to deviate,
15 040	"Except Thy servants among them, sincere and purified (by Thy Grace)."	Save such of them as are Thy perfectly devoted slaves.	Except Thy servants from among them, the devoted ones.
15 041	(Allah) said: "This (way of My sincere servants) is indeed a way that leads straight to Me."	He said: This is a right course incumbent upon Me:	He said: This is a right way with Me:
15 042	"For over My servants no authority shalt thou have, except such as put themselves in the wrong and follow thee."	Lo! as for My slaves, thou hast no power over any of them save such of the froward as follow thee,	Surely. as regards My servants, you have no authority over them except those who follow you of the deviators.
15 043	And verily, Hell is the promised abode for them all!	And lo! for all such, hell will be the promised place.	And surely Hell is the promised place of them all:
15 044	To it are seven gates: for each of those gates is a (special) class (of sinners) assigned.	It hath seven gates, and each gate hath an appointed portion.	It has seven gates; for every gate there shall be a separate party of them.
15 045	The righteous (will be) amid gardens and fountains (of clear-flowing water).	Lo! those who ward off (evil) are among gardens and watersprings.	Surely those who guard (against evil) shall be in the midst of gardens and fountains:
15 046	(Their greeting will be): "Enter ye here in peace and security."	(And it is said unto them): Enter them in peace, secure.	Enter them in peace, secure.
15 047	And We shall remove from their hearts any lurking sense of injury: (they will be) brothers (joyfully) facing each other on thrones (of dignity).	And We remove whatever rancour may be in their breasts. As brethren, face to face, (they rest) on couches raised.	And We will root out whatever of rancor is in their breasts-- (they shall be) as brethren, on raised couches, face to face.

15 048	There no sense of fatigue shall touch them, nor shall they (ever) be asked to leave.	Toil cometh not unto them there, nor will they be expelled from thence.	Toil shall not afflict them in it, nor shall they be ever ejected from it.
15 049	Tell My servants that I am indeed the Oft-Forgiving, Most Merciful;	Announce, (O Muhammad) unto My slaves that verily I am the Forgiving, the Merciful,	Inform My servants that I am the Forgiving, the Merciful,
15 050	And that My Penalty will be indeed the most grievous Penalty.	And that My doom is the dolorous doom.	And that My punishment-- that is the painful punishment.
15 051	Tell them about the guests of Abraham.	And tell them of Abraham's guests,	And inform them of the guests of Ibrahim:
15 052	When they entered his presence and said, "Peace!" He said, "We feel afraid of you!"	(How) when they came in unto him, and said: Peace. He said: Lo! we are afraid of you.	When they entered upon him, they said, Peace. He said: Surely we are afraid of you.
15 053	They said: "Fear not! We give thee glad tidings of a son endowed with wisdom."	They said: Be not afraid! Lo! we bring thee good tidings of a boy possessing wisdom.	They said: Be not afraid, surely we give you the good news of a boy, possessing knowledge.
15 054	He said: "Do ye give me glad tidings that old age has seized me? Of what, then, is your good news?"	He said: Bring ye me good tidings (of a son) when old age hath overtaken me? Of what then can ye bring good tidings?	He said: Do you give me good news (of a son) when old age has come upon me?-- Of what then do you give me good news!
15 055	They said: "We give thee glad tidings in truth: be not then in despair!"	They said: We bring thee good tidings in truth. So be not thou of the despairing.	They said: We give you good news with truth, therefore be not of the despairing.
15 056	He said: "And who despairs of the mercy of his Lord, but such as go astray?"	He said: And who despaireth of the mercy of his Lord save those who are astray?	He said: And who despairs of the mercy of his Lord but the erring ones?
15 057	Abraham said: "What then is the business on which ye (have come), O ye messengers (of Allah)?"	He said: And afterward what is your business, O ye messengers (of Allah)?	He said: What is your business then, O messengers?
15 058	They said: "We have been sent to a people (deep) in sin,"	They said: We have been sent unto a guilty folk,	They said: Surely we are sent towards a guilty people,
15 059	"Excepting the adherents of Lut: them we are certainly (charged) to save (from harm),- All -"	(All) save the family of Lot. Them we shall deliver every one,	Except Lut's followers: We will most surely deliver them all,
15 060	"Except his wife, who, We have ascertained, will be among those who will lag behind."	Except his wife, of whom We had decreed that she should be of those who stay behind.	Except his wife; We ordained that she shall surely be of those who remain behind.
15 061	At length when the messengers arrived among the adherents of Lut,	And when the messengers came unto the family of Lot,	So when the messengers came to Lut's followers,
15 062	He said: "Ye appear to be uncommon folk."	He said: Lo! ye are folk unknown (to me).	He said: Surely you are an unknown people.
15 063	They said: "Yea, we have come to thee to accomplish that of which they doubt."	They said: Nay, but we bring thee that concerning which they keep disputing,	They said: Nay, we have come to you with that about which they disputed.
15 064	"We have brought to thee that which is inevitably due, and assuredly we tell the truth."	And bring thee the Truth, and lo! we are truth-tellers.	And we have come to you with the truth, and we are most surely truthful.
15 065	"Then travel by night with thy household, when a portion of the night (yet remains), and do thou bring up the rear: let no one amongst you look back, but pass on whither ye are ordered."	So travel with thy household in a portion of the night, and follow thou their backs. Let none of you turn round, but go whither ye are commanded.	Therefore go forth with your followers in a part of the night and yourself follow their rear, and let not any one of you turn round, and go forth whither you are commanded.
15 066	And We made known this decree to him, that the last remnants of those (sinners) should be cut off by the morning.	And We made plain the case to him, that the root of them (who did wrong) was to be cut off at early morn.	And We revealed to him this decree, that the roots of these shall be cut off in the morning.

15 067	The inhabitants of the city came in (mad) joy (at news of the young men).	And the people of the city came, rejoicing at the news (of new arrivals).	And the people of the town came rejoicing.
15 068	Lut said: "These are my guests: disgrace me not:"	He said: Lo! they are my guests. Affront me not!	He said: Surely these are my guests, therefore do not disgrace me,
15 069	"But fear Allah, and shame me not."	And keep your duty to Allah, and shame me not!	And guard against (the punishment of) Allah and do not put me to shame.
15 070	They said: "Did we not forbid thee (to speak) for all and sundry?"	They said; Have we not forbidden you from (entertaining) anyone?	They said: Have we not forbidden you from (other) people?
15 071	He said: "There are my daughters (to marry), if ye must act (so)."	He said: Here are my daughters, if ye must be doing (so).	He said: These are my daughters, if you will do (aught).
15 072	Verily, by thy life (O Prophet), in their wild intoxication, they wander in distraction, to and fro.	By thy life (O Muhammad) they moved blindly in the frenzy of approaching death.	By your life! they were blindly wandering on in their intoxication.
15 073	But the (mighty) Blast overtook them before morning,	Then the (Awful) Cry overtook them at the sunrise.	So the rumbling overtook them (while) entering upon the time of sunrise;
15 074	And We turned (the cities) upside down, and rained down on them brimstones hard as baked clay.	And We utterly confounded them, and We rained upon them stones of heated clay.	Thus did We turn it upside down, and rained down upon them stones of what had been decreed.
15 075	Behold! in this are Signs for those who by tokens do understand.	Lo! therein verily are portents for those who read the signs.	Surely in this are signs for those who examine.
15 076	And the (cities were) right on the high-road.	And lo! it is upon a road still uneffaced.	And surely it is on a road that still abides.
15 077	Behold! in this is a sign for those who believed.	Lo! therein is indeed a portent for believers.	Most surely there is a sign in this for the believers.
15 078	And the Companions of the Wood were also wrong-doers;	And the dwellers in the wood indeed were evil-doers.	And the dwellers of the thicket also were most surely unjust.
15 079	So We exacted retribution from them. They were both on an open highway, plain to see.	So we took vengeance on them; and lo! they both are on a high-road plain to see.	So We inflicted retribution on them, and they are both, indeed, on an open road (still) pursued.
15 080	The Companions of the Rocky Tract also rejected the messengers:	And the dwellers in Al-Hijr denied (Our) messengers.	And the dwellers of the Rock certainly rejected the messengers;
15 081	We sent them Our Signs, but they persisted in turning away from them.	And we gave them Our revelations, but they were averse to them.	And We gave them Our communications, but they turned aside from them;
15 082	Out of the mountains did they hew (their) edifices, (feeling themselves) secure.	And they used to hew out dwellings from the hills, (wherein they dwelt) secure.	And they hewed houses in the mountains in security.
15 083	But the (mighty) Blast seized them of a morning,	But the (Awful) Cry overtook them at the morning hour,	So the rumbling overtook them in the morning;
15 084	And of no avail to them was all that they did (with such art and care)!	And that which they were wont to count as gain availed them not.	And what they earned did not avail them.
15 085	We created not the heavens, the earth, and all between them, but for just ends. And the Hour is surely coming (when this will be manifest). So overlook (any human faults) with gracious forgiveness.	We created not the heavens and the earth and all that is between them save with truth, and lo! the Hour is surely coming. So forgive, (O Muhammad), with a gracious forgiveness.	And We did not create the heavens and the earth and what is between them two but in truth; and the hour is most surely coming, so turn away with kindly forgiveness.
15 086	For verily it is thy Lord who is the Master-Creator, knowing all things.	Lo! Thy Lord! He is the All-Wise Creator.	Surely your Lord is the Creator of all things, the Knowing.
15 087	And We have bestowed upon thee the Seven oft-repeated (verses) and the Grand Qur'an.	We have given thee seven of the oft-repeated (verses) and the great Qur'an.	And certainly We have given you seven of the oft-repeated (verses) and the grand Quran.

15 088	Strain not thine eyes. (Wistfully) at what We have bestowed on certain classes of them, nor grieve over them: but lower thy wing (in gentleness) to the believers.	Strain not thine eyes toward that which We cause some wedded pairs among them to enjoin, and be not grieved on their account, and lower thy wing (in tenderness) for the believers.	Do not strain your eyes after what We have given certain classes of them to enjoy, and do not grieve for them, and make yourself gentle to the believers.
15 089	And say: "I am indeed he that warneth openly and without ambiguity,"-	And say: Lo! I, even I, am a plain warner,	And say: Surely I am the plain warner.
15 090	(Of just such wrath) as We sent down on those who divided (Scripture into arbitrary parts),-	Such as We send down for those who make division,	Like as We sent down on the dividers
15 091	(So also on such) as have made Qur'an into shreds (as they please).	Those who break the Qur'an into parts.	Those who made the Quran into shreds.
15 092	Therefore, by the Lord, We will, of a surety, call them to account,	Them, by thy Lord, We shall question, every one,	So, by your Lord, We would most certainly question them all,
15 093	For all their deeds.	Of what they used to do.	As to what they did.
15 094	Therefore expound openly what thou art commanded, and turn away from those who join false gods with Allah.	So proclaim that which thou art commanded, and withdraw from the idolaters.	Therefore declare openly what you are bidden and turn aside from the polytheists.
15 095	For sufficient are We unto thee against those who scoff,-	Lo! We defend thee from the scoffers,	Surely We will suffice you against the scoffers
15 096	Those who adopt, with Allah, another god: but soon will they come to know.	Who set some other god along with Allah. But they will come to know.	Those who set up another god with Allah; so they shall soon know.
15 097	We do indeed know how thy heart is distressed at what they say.	Well know We that thy bosom is oppressed by what they say,	And surely We know that your breast straitens at what they say;
15 098	But celebrate the praises of thy Lord, and be of those who prostrate themselves in adoration.	But hymn the praise of thy Lord, and be of those who make prostration (unto Him).	Therefore celebrate the praise of your Lord, and be of those who make obeisance.
15 099	And serve thy Lord until there come unto thee the Hour that is Certain.	And serve thy Lord till the Inevitable cometh unto thee.	And serve your Lord until there comes to you that which is certain.

Chapter 16:

AN-NAHL (THE BEE)

Total Verses: 128 Revealed At: MAKKA

In the name of Allah, the Most Beneficent, the Most Merciful.

16 001	(Inevitable) cometh (to pass) the Command of Allah: seek ye not then to hasten it: Glory to Him, and far is He above having the partners they ascribe unto Him!	The commandment of Allah will come to pass, so seek not ye to hasten it. Glorified and Exalted be He above all that they associate (with Him).	Allah's commandment has come, therefore do not desire to hasten it; glory be to Him, and highly exalted be He above what they associate (with Him).
16 002	He doth send down His angels with inspiration of His Command, to such of His servants as He pleaseth, (saying): "Warn (Man) that there is no god but I: so do your duty unto Me."	He sendeth down the angels with the Spirit of His command unto whom He will of His bondmen, (saying): Warn mankind that there is no God save Me, so keep your duty unto Me.	He sends down the angels with the inspiration by His commandment on whom He pleases of His servants, saying: Give the warning that there is no god but Me, therefore be careful (of your duty) to Me.

16 003	He has created the heavens and the earth for just ends: Far is He above having the partners they ascribe to Him!	He hath created the heavens and the earth with truth. High be He Exalted above all that they associate (with Him).	He created the heavens and the earth with the truth, highly exalted be He above what they associate (with Him).
16 004	He has created man from a sperm-drop; and behold this same (man) becomes an open disputer!	He hath created man from a drop of fluid, yet behold! he is an open opponent.	He created man from a small seed and lo! he is an open contender.
16 005	And cattle He has created for you (men): from them ye derive warmth, and numerous benefits, and of their (meat) ye eat.	And the cattle hath He created, whence ye have warm clothing and uses, and whereof ye eat;	And He created the cattle for you; you have in them warm clothing and (many) advantages, and of them do you eat.
16 006	And ye have a sense of pride and beauty in them as ye drive them home in the evening, and as ye lead them forth to pasture in the morning.	And wherein is beauty for you, when ye bring them home, and when ye take them out to pasture.	And there is beauty in them for you when you drive them back (to home), and when you send them forth (to pasture).
16 007	And they carry your heavy loads to lands that ye could not (otherwise) reach except with souls distressed: for your Lord is indeed Most Kind, Most Merciful,	And they bear your loads for you unto a land ye could not reach save with great trouble to yourselves. Lo! your Lord is Full of Pity, Merciful.	And they carry your heavy loads to regions which you could not reach but with distress of the souls; most surely your Lord is Compassionate, Merciful.
16 008	And (He has created) horses, mules, and donkeys, for you to ride and use for show; and He has created (other) things of which ye have no knowledge.	And horses and mules and asses (hath He created) that ye may ride them, and for ornament. And He createth that which ye know not.	And (He made) horses and mules and asses that you might ride upon them and as an ornament; and He creates what you do not know.
16 009	And unto Allah leads straight the Way, but there are ways that turn aside: if Allah had willed, He could have guided all of you.	And Allah's is the direction of the way, and some (roads) go not straight. And had He willed He would have led you all aright.	And upon Allah it rests to show the right way, and there are some deviating (ways); and if He please He would certainly guide you all aright.
16 010	It is He who sends down rain from the sky: from it ye drink, and out of it (grows) the vegetation on which ye feed your cattle.	He it is Who sendeth down water from the sky, whence ye have drink, and whence are trees on which ye send your beasts to pasture.	He it is Who sends down water from the cloud for you; it gives drink, and by it (grow) the trees upon which you pasture.
16 011	With it He produces for you corn, olives, date-palms, grapes and every kind of fruit: verily in this is a sign for those who give thought.	Therewith He causeth crops to grow for you, and the olive and the date-palm and grapes and all kinds of fruit. Lo! herein is indeed a portent for people who reflect.	He causes to grow for you thereby herbage, and the olives, and the palm trees, and the grapes, and of all the fruits; most surely there is a sign in this for a people who reflect.
16 012	He has made subject to you the Night and the Day; the sun and the moon; and the stars are in subjection by His Command: verily in this are Signs for men who are wise.	And He hath constrained the night and the day and the sun and the moon to be of service unto you, and the stars are made subservient by His command. Lo! herein indeed are portents for people who have sense.	And He has made subservient for you the night and the day and the sun and the moon, and the stars are made subservient by His commandment; most surely there are signs in this for a people who ponder;
16 013	And the things on this earth which He has multiplied in varying colours (and qualities): verily in this is a sign for men who celebrate the praises of Allah (in gratitude).	And whatsoever He hath created for you in the earth of divers hues, lo! therein is indeed a portent for people who take heed.	And what He has created in the earth of varied hues most surely there is a sign in this for a people who are mindful.

16 014	It is He Who has made the sea subject, that ye may eat thereof flesh that is fresh and tender, and that ye may extract therefrom ornaments to wear; and thou seest the ships therein that plough the waves, that ye may seek (thus) of the bounty of Allah and that ye may be grateful.	And He it is Who hath constrained the sea to be of service that ye eat fresh meat from thence, and bring forth from thence ornaments which ye wear. And thou seest the ships ploughing it that ye (mankind) may seek of His bounty and that haply ye may give thanks.	And He it is Who has made the sea subservient that you may eat fresh flesh from it and bring forth from it ornaments which you wear, and you see the ships cleaving through it, and that you might seek of His bounty and that you may give thanks.
16 015	And He has set up on the earth mountains standing firm, lest it should shake with you; and rivers and roads; that ye may guide yourselves;	And He hath cast into the earth firm hills that it quake not with you, and streams and roads that ye may find a way.	And He has cast great mountains in the earth lest it might be convulsed with you, and rivers and roads that you may go aright,
16 016	And marks and sign-posts; and by the stars (men) guide themselves.	And landmarks (too), and by the star they find a way.	And landmarks; and by the stars they find the right way.
16 017	Is then He Who creates like one that creates not? Will ye not receive admonition?	Is He then Who createth as him who createth not? Will ye not then remember?	Is He then Who creates like him who does not create? Do you not then mind?
16 018	If ye would count up the favours of Allah, never would ye be able to number them: for Allah is Oft-Forgiving, Most Merciful.	And if ye would count the favour of Allah ye cannot reckon it. Lo! Allah is indeed Forgiving, Merciful.	And if you would count Allah's favors, you will not be able to number them; most surely Allah is Forgiving, Merciful.
16 019	And Allah doth know what ye conceal, and what ye reveal.	And Allah knoweth that which ye keep hidden and that which ye proclaim.	And Allah knows what you conceal and what you do openly.
16 020	Those whom they invoke besides Allah create nothing and are themselves created.	Those unto whom they cry beside Allah created naught, but are themselves created.	And those whom they call on besides Allah have not created anything while they are themselves created;
16 021	(They are things) dead, lifeless: nor do they know when they will be raised up.	(They are) dead, not living. And they know not when they will be raised.	Dead (are they), not living, and they know not when they shall be raised.
16 022	Your Allah is one Allah: as to those who believe not in the Hereafter, their hearts refuse to know, and they are arrogant.	Your Allah is One Allah. But as for those who believe not in the Hereafter their hearts refuse to know, for they are proud.	Your God is one Allah; so (as for) those who do not believe in the hereafter, their hearts are ignorant and they are proud.
16 023	Undoubtedly Allah doth know what they conceal, and what they reveal: verily He loveth not the arrogant.	Assuredly Allah knoweth that which they keep hidden and that which they proclaim. Lo! He loveth not the proud.	Truly Allah knows what they hide and what they manifest; surely He does not love the proud.
16 024	When it is said to them, "What is it that your Lord has revealed?" they say, "Tales of the ancients!"	And when it is said unto them: What hath your Lord revealed? they say: (Mere) fables of the men of old,	And when it is said to them, what is it that your Lord has revealed? They say: Stories of the ancients;
16 025	Let them bear, on the Day of Judgment, their own burdens in full, and also (something) of the burdens of those without knowledge, whom they misled. Alas, how grievous the burdens they will bear!	That they may bear their burdens undiminished on the Day of Resurrection, with somewhat of the burdens of those whom they mislead without knowledge. Ah! evil is that which they bear!	That they may bear their burdens entirely on the day of resurrection and also of the burdens of those whom they lead astray without knowledge; now surely evil is what they bear.
16 026	Those before them did also plot (against Allah's Way): but Allah took their structures from their foundations, and the roof fell down on them from above; and the Wrath seized them from directions they did not perceive.	Those before them plotted, so Allah struck at the foundations of their building, and then the roof fell down upon them from above them, and the doom came on them whence they knew not;	Those before them did indeed devise plans, but Allah demolished their building from the foundations, so the roof fell down on them from above them, and the punishment came to them from whence they did not perceive.

16 027	Then, on the Day of Judgment, He will cover them with shame, and say: Where are My 'partners' concerning whom ye used to dispute (with the godly)?" Those endued with knowledge will say: "This Day, indeed, are the Unbelievers covered with shame and misery,-"	Then on the Day of Resurrection He will disgrace them and will say: Where are My partners, for whose sake ye opposed (My guidance)? Those who have been given knowledge will say: Disgrace this day and evil are upon the disbelievers,	Then on the resurrection day He will bring them to disgrace and say: Where are the associates you gave Me, for whose sake you became hostile? Those who are given the knowledge will say: Surely the disgrace and the evil are this day upon the unbelievers:
16 028	"(Namely) those whose lives the angels take in a state of wrongdoing to their own souls." Then would they offer submission (with the pretence), "We did no evil (knowingly)." (The angels will reply), "Nay, but verily Allah knoweth all that ye did;"	Whom the angels cause to die while they are wronging themselves. Then will they make full submission (saying): We used not to do any wrong. Nay! Surely Allah is Knower of what ye used to do.	Those whom the angels cause to die while they are unjust to themselves. Then would they offer submission: We used not to do any evil. Aye! surely Allah knows what you did.
16 029	"So enter the gates of Hell, to dwell therein. Thus evil indeed is the abode of the arrogant."	So enter the gates of hell, to dwell therein for ever. Woeful indeed will be the lodging of the arrogant.	Therefore enter the gates of hell, to abide therein; so certainly evil is the dwelling place of the proud.
16 030	To the righteous (when) it is said, "What is it that your Lord has revealed?" they say, "All that is good." To those who do good, there is good in this world, and the Home of the Hereafter is even better and excellent indeed is the Home of the righteous,-	And it is said unto those who ward off (evil): What hath your Lord revealed? They say: Good. For those who do good in this world there is a good (reward) and the home of the Hereafter will be better. Pleasant indeed will be the home of those who ward off (evil) -	And it is said to those who guard (against evil): What is it that your Lord has revealed? They say, Good. For those who do good in this world is good, and certainly the abode of the hereafter is better; and certainly most excellent is the abode of those who guard (against evil);
16 031	Gardens of Eternity which they will enter: beneath them flow (pleasant) rivers: they will have therein all that they wish: thus doth Allah reward the righteous,-	Gardens of Eden which they enter, underneath which rivers flow, wherein they have what they will. Thus Allah repayeth those who ward off (evil),	The gardens of perpetuity, they shall enter them, rivers flowing beneath them; they shall have in them what they please. Thus does Allah reward those who guard (against evil),
16 032	(Namely) those whose lives the angels take in a state of purity, saying (to them), "Peace be on you; enter ye the Garden, because of (the good) which ye did (in the world)."	Those whom the angels cause to die (when they are) good. They say: Peace be unto you! Enter the Garden because of what ye used to do.	Those whom the angels cause to die in a good state, saying: Peace be on you: enter the garden for what you did.
16 033	Do the (ungodly) wait until the angels come to them, or there comes the Command of thy Lord (for their doom)? So did those who went before them. But Allah wronged them not: nay, they wronged their own souls.	Await they aught say that the angels should come unto them or thy Lord's command should come to pass? Even so did those before them. Allah wronged them not, but they did wrong themselves,	They do not wait aught but that the angels should come to them or that the commandment of your Lord should come to pass. Thus did those before them; and Allah was not unjust to them, but they were unjust to themselves.
16 034	But the evil results of their deeds overtook them, and that very (Wrath) at which they had scoffed hemmed them in.	So that the evils of what they did smote them, and that which they used to mock surrounded them.	So the evil (consequences) of what they did shall afflict them and that which they mocked shall encompass them.

16 035	The worshippers of false gods say: "If Allah had so willed, we should not have worshipped aught but Him - neither we nor our fathers,- nor should we have prescribed prohibitions other than His." So did those who went before them. But what is the mission of messengers but to preach the Clear Message?	And the idolaters say: Had Allah willed, we had not worshipped aught beside Him, we and our fathers, nor had we forbidden aught without (command from) Him. Even so did those before them. Are the messengers charged with aught save plain conveyance (of the message)?	And they who give associates (to Allah) say: If Allah had pleased, we would not have served anything besides Allah, (neither) we nor our fathers, nor would we have prohibited anything without (order from) Him. Thus did those before them; is then aught incumbent upon the messengers except a plain delivery (of the message)?
16 036	For We assuredly sent amongst every People a messenger, (with the Command), "Serve Allah, and eschew Evil": of the People were some whom Allah guided, and some on whom error became inevitably (established). So travel through the earth, and see what was the end of those who denied (the Truth).	And verily We have raised in every nation a messenger, (proclaiming): Serve Allah and shun false gods. Then some of them (there were) whom Allah guided, and some of them (there were) upon whom error had just hold. Do but travel in the land and see the nature of the consequence for the deniers!	And certainly We raised in every nation a messenger saying: Serve Allah and shun the Shaitan. So there were some of them whom Allah guided and there were others against whom error was due; therefore travel in the land, then see what was the end of the rejecters.
16 037	If thou art anxious for their guidance, yet Allah guideth not such as He leaves to stray, and there is none to help them.	Even if thou (O Muhammad) desirest their right guidance, still Allah assuredly will not guide him who misleadeth. Such have no helpers.	If you desire for their guidance, yet surely Allah does not guide him who leads astray, nor shall they have any helpers.
16 038	They swear their strongest oaths by Allah, that Allah will not raise up those who die: Nay, but it is a promise (binding) on Him in truth: but most among mankind realise it not.	And they swear by Allah their most binding oaths (that) Allah will not raise up him who dieth. Nay, but it is a promise (binding) upon Him in truth, but most of mankind know not,	And they swear by Allah with the most energetic of their oaths: Allah will not raise up him who dies. Yea! it is a promise binding on Him, quite true, but most people do not know;
16 039	(They must be raised up), in order that He may manifest to them the truth of that wherein they differ, and that the rejecters of Truth may realise that they had indeed (surrendered to) Falsehood.	That He may explain unto them that wherein they differ, and that those who disbelieved may know that they were liars.	So that He might make manifest to them that about which they differ, and that those who disbelieve might know that they were liars.
16 040	For to anything which We have willed, We but say the word, "Be", and it is.	And Our word unto a thing, when We intend it, is only that We say unto it: Be! and it is.	Our word for a thing when We intend it, is only that We say to it, Be, and it is.
16 041	To those who leave their homes in the cause of Allah, after suffering oppression,- We will assuredly give a goodly home in this world; but truly the reward of the Hereafter will be greater. If they only realised (this)!	And those who became fugitives for the cause of Allah after they had been oppressed, We verily shall give them goodly lodging in the world, and surely the reward of the Hereafter is greater, if they but knew;	And those who fly for Allah's sake after they are oppressed, We will most certainly give them a good abode in the world, and the reward of the hereafter is certainly much greater, did they but know;
16 042	(They are) those who persevere in patience, and put their trust on their Lord.	Such as are steadfast and put their trust in Allah.	Those who are patient and on their Lord do they rely.
16 043	And before thee also the messengers We sent were but men, to whom We granted inspiration: if ye realise this not, ask of those who possess the Message.	And We sent not (as Our messengers) before thee other than men whom We inspired - Ask the followers of the Remembrance if ye know not! -	And We did not send before you any but men to whom We sent revelation-- so ask the followers of the Reminder if you do not know--

16 044	(We sent them) with Clear Signs and Books of dark prophecies; and We have sent down unto thee (also) the Message; that thou mayest explain clearly to men what is sent for them, and that they may give thought.	With clear proofs and writings; and We have revealed unto thee the Remembrance that thou mayst explain to mankind that which hath been revealed for them, and that haply they may reflect.	With clear arguments and scriptures; and We have revealed to you the Reminder that you may make clear to men what has been revealed to them, and that haply they may reflect.
16 045	Do then those who devise evil (plots) feel secure that Allah will not cause the earth to swallow them up, or that the Wrath will not seize them from directions they little perceive?-	Are they who plan ill-deeds then secure that Allah will not cause the earth to swallow them, or that the doom will not come on them whence they know not?	Do they then who plan evil (deeds) feel secure (of this) that Allah will not cause the earth to swallow them or that punishment may not overtake them from whence they do not perceive?
16 046	Or that He may not call them to account in the midst of their goings to and fro, without a chance of their frustrating Him?-	Or that He will not seize them in their going to and fro so that there be no escape for them?	Or that He may not seize them in the course of their journeys, then shall they not escape;
16 047	Or that He may not call them to account by a process of slow wastage - for thy Lord is indeed full of kindness and mercy.	Or that He will not seize them with a gradual wasting? Lo! thy Lord is indeed Full of Pity, Merciful.	Or that He may not seize them by causing them to suffer gradual loss, for your Lord is most surely Compassionate, Merciful.
16 048	Do they not look at Allah's creation, (even) among (inanimate) things,- How their (very) shadows turn round, from the right and the left, prostrating themselves to Allah, and that in the humblest manner?	Have they not observed all things that Allah hath created, how their shadows incline to the right and to the left, making prostration unto Allah, and they are lowly?	Do they not consider every thing that Allah has created? Its (very) shadows return from right and left, making obeisance to Allah while they are in utter abasement.
16 049	And to Allah doth obeisance all that is in the heavens and on earth, whether moving (living) creatures or the angels: for none are arrogant (before their Lord).	And unto Allah maketh prostration whatsoever is in the heavens and whatsoever is in the earth of living creatures, and the angels (also) and they are not proud.	And whatever creature that is in the heavens and that is in the earth makes obeisance to Allah (only), and the angels (too) and they do not show pride.
16 050	They all revere their Lord, high above them, and they do all that they are commanded.	They fear their Lord above them, and do what they are bidden.	They fear their Lord above them and do what they are commanded.
16 051	Allah has said: "Take not (for worship) two gods: for He is just One Allah: then fear Me (and Me alone)."	Allah hath said: Choose not two gods. There is only One Allah. So of Me, Me only, be in awe.	And Allah has said: Take not two gods, He is only one Allah; so of Me alone should you be afraid.
16 052	To Him belongs whatever is in the heavens and on earth, and to Him is duty due always: then will ye fear other than Allah?	Unto Him belongeth whatsoever is in the heavens and the earth, and religion is His for ever. Will ye then fear any other than Allah?	And whatever is in the heavens and the earth is His, and to Him should obedience be (rendered) constantly; will you then guard against other than (the punishment of) Allah?
16 053	And ye have no good thing but is from Allah: and moreover, when ye are touched by distress, unto Him ye cry with groans;	And whatever of comfort ye enjoy, it is from Allah. Then, when misfortune reacheth you, unto Him ye cry for help.	And whatever favor is (bestowed) on you it is from Allah; then when evil afflicts you, to Him do you cry for aid.
16 054	Yet, when He removes the distress from you, behold! some of you turn to other gods to join with their Lord-	And afterward, when He hath rid you of the misfortune, behold! a set of you attribute partners to their Lord,	Yet when He removes the evil from you, lo! a party of you associate others with their Lord;
16 055	(As if) to show their ingratitude for the favours we have bestowed on them! then enjoy (your brief day): but soon will ye know (your folly)!	So as to deny that which We have given them. Then enjoy life (while ye may), for ye will come to know.	So that they be ungrateful for what We have given them; then enjoy yourselves; for soon will you know.

16 056	And they (even) assign, to things they do not know, a portion out of that which We have bestowed for their sustenance! By Allah, ye shall certainly be called to account for your false inventions.	And they assign a portion of that which We have given them unto what they know not. By Allah! but ye will indeed be asked concerning (all) that ye used to invent.	And they set apart for what they do not know a portion of what We have given them. By Allah, you shall most certainly be questioned about that which you forged.
16 057	And they assign daughters for Allah! - Glory be to Him! - and for themselves (sons,- the issue) they desire!	And they assign unto Allah daughters - Be He Glorified! - and unto themselves what they desire;	And they ascribe daughters to Allah, glory be to Him; and for themselves (they would have) what they desire.
16 058	When news is brought to one of them, of (the birth of) a female (child), his face darkens, and he is filled with inward grief!	When if one of them receiveth tidings of the birth of a female, his face remaineth darkened, and he is wroth inwardly.	And when a daughter is announced to one of them his face becomes black and he is full of wrath.
16 059	With shame does he hide himself from his people, because of the bad news he has had! Shall he retain it on (sufferance and) contempt, or bury it in the dust? Ah! what an evil (choice) they decide on?	He hideth himself from the folk because of the evil of that whereof he hath had tidings, (asking himself): Shall he keep it in contempt, or bury it beneath the dust. Verily evil is their judgment.	He hides himself from the people because of the evil of that which is announced to him. Shall he keep it with disgrace or bury it (alive) in the dust? Now surely evil is what they judge.
16 060	To those who believe not in the Hereafter, applies the similitude of evil: to Allah applies the highest similitude: for He is the Exalted in Power, full of Wisdom.	For those who believe not in the Hereafter is an evil similitude, and Allah's is the Sublime Similitude. He is the Mighty, the Wise.	For those who do not believe in the hereafter is an evil attribute, and Allah's is the loftiest attribute; and He is the Mighty, the Wise.
16 061	If Allah were to punish men for their wrong-doing, He would not leave, on the (earth), a single living creature: but He gives them respite for a stated Term: When their Term expires, they would not be able to delay (the punishment) for a single hour, just as they would not be able to anticipate it (for a single hour).	If Allah were to take mankind to task for their wrong-doing, he would not leave hereon a living creature, but He reprieveth them to an appointed term, and when their term cometh they cannot put (it) off an hour nor (yet) advance (it).	And if Allah had destroyed men for their iniquity, He would not leave on the earth a single creature, but He respites them till an appointed time; so when their doom will come they shall not be able to delay (it) an hour nor can they bring (it) on (before its time).
16 062	They attribute to Allah what they hate (for themselves), and their tongues assert the falsehood that all good things are for themselves: without doubt for them is the Fire, and they will be the first to be hastened on into it!	And they assign unto Allah that which they (themselves) dislike, and their tongues expound the lie that the better portion will be theirs. Assuredly theirs will be the Fire, and they will be abandoned.	And they ascribe to Allah what they (themselves) hate and their tongues relate the lie that they shall have the good; there is no avoiding it that for them is the fire and that they shall be sent before.
16 063	By Allah, We (also) sent (Our messengers) to Peoples before thee; but Satan made, (to the wicked), their own acts seem alluring: He is also their patron today, but they shall have a most grievous penalty.	By Allah, We verily sent messengers unto the nations before thee, but the devil made their deeds fairseeming unto them. So he is their patron this day, and theirs will be a painful doom.	By Allah, most certainly We sent (messengers) to nations before you, but the Shaitan made their deeds fair-seeming to them, so he is their guardian today, and they shall have a painful punishment.
16 064	And We sent down the Book to thee for the express purpose, that thou shouldst make clear to them those things in which they differ, and that it should be a guide and a mercy to those who believe.	And We have revealed the Scripture unto thee only that thou mayst explain unto them that wherein they differ, and (as) a guidance and a mercy for a people who believe.	And We have not revealed to you the Book except that you may make clear to them that about which they differ, and (as) a guidance and a mercy for a people who believe.
16 065	And Allah sends down rain from the skies, and gives therewith life to the earth after its death: verily in this is a Sign for those who listen.	Allah sendeth down water from the sky and therewith reviveth the earth after her death. Lo! herein is indeed a portent for a folk who hear.	And Allah has sent down water from the cloud and therewith given life to the earth after its death; most surely there is a sign in this for a people who would listen.

16 066	And verily in cattle (too) will ye find an instructive sign. From what is within their bodies between excretions and blood, We produce, for your drink, milk, pure and agreeable to those who drink it.	And lo! in the cattle there is a lesson for you. We give you to drink of that which is in their bellies, from betwixt the refuse and the blood, pure milk palatable to the drinkers.	And most surely there is a lesson for you in the cattle; We give you to drink of what is in their bellies-- from betwixt the feces and the blood-- pure milk, easy and agreeable to swallow for those who drink.
16 067	And from the fruit of the date-palm and the vine, ye get out wholesome drink and food: behold, in this also is a sign for those who are wise.	And of the fruits of the date-palm, and grapes, whence ye derive strong drink and (also) good nourishment. Lo! therein is indeed a portent for people who have sense.	And of the fruits of the palms and the grapes-- you obtain from them intoxication and goodly provision; most surely there is a sign in this for a people who ponder.
16 068	And thy Lord taught the Bee to build its cells in hills, on trees, and in (men's) habitations;	And thy Lord inspired the bee, saying: Choose thou habitations in the hills and in the trees and in that which they thatch;	And your Lord revealed to the bee saying: Make hives in the mountains and in the trees and in what they build:
16 069	Then to eat of all the produce (of the earth), and find with skill the spacious paths of its Lord: there issues from within their bodies a drink of varying colours, wherein is healing for men: verily in this is a Sign for those who give thought.	Then eat of all fruits, and follow the ways of thy Lord, made smooth (for thee). There cometh forth from their bellies a drink divers of hues, wherein is healing for mankind. Lo! herein is indeed a portent for people who reflect.	Then eat of all the fruits and walk in the ways of your Lord submissively. There comes forth from within it a beverage of many colours, in which there is healing for men; most surely there is a sign in this for a people who reflect.
16 070	It is Allah who creates you and takes your souls at death; and of you there are some who are sent back to a feeble age, so that they know nothing after having known (much): for Allah is All-Knowing, All-Powerful.	And Allah createth you, then causeth you to die, and among you is he who is brought back to the most abject stage of life, so that he knoweth nothing after (having had) knowledge. Lo! Allah is Knower, Powerful.	And Allah has created you, then He causes you to die, and of you is he who is brought back to the worst part of life, so that after having knowledge he does not know anything; surely Allah is Knowing, Powerful.
16 071	Allah has bestowed His gifts of sustenance more freely on some of you than on others: those more favoured are not going to throw back their gifts to those whom their right hands possess, so as to be equal in that respect. Will they then deny the favours of Allah?	And Allah hath favoured some of you above others in provision. Now those who are more favoured will by no means hand over their provision to those (slaves) whom their right hands possess, so that they may be equal with them in respect thereof. Is it then the grace of Allah that they deny?	And Allah has made some of you excel others in the means of subsistence, so those who are made to excel do not give away their sustenance to those whom their right hands possess so that they should be equal therein; is it then the favor of Allah which they deny?
16 072	And Allah has made for you mates (and companions) of your own nature, and made for you, out of them, sons and daughters and grandchildren, and provided for you sustenance of the best: will they then believe in vain things, and be ungrateful for Allah's favours?-	And Allah hath given you wives of your own kind, and hath given you, from your wives, sons and grandsons, and hath made provision of good things for you. Is it then in vanity that they believe and in the grace of Allah that they disbelieve?	And Allah has made wives for you from among yourselves, and has given you sons and grandchildren from your wives, and has given you of the good things; is it then in the falsehood that they believe while it is in the favor of Allah that they disbelieve?
16 073	And worship others than Allah,- such as have no power of providing them, for sustenance, with anything in heavens or earth, and cannot possibly have such power?	And they worship beside Allah that which owneth no provision whatsoever for them from the heavens or the earth, nor have they (whom they worship) any power.	And they serve besides Allah that which does not control for them any sustenance at all from the heavens and the earth, nor have they any power.
16 074	Invent not similitudes for Allah: for Allah knoweth, and ye know not.	So coin not similitudes for Allah. Lo! Allah knoweth; ye know not.	Therefore do not give likenesses to Allah; surely Allah knows and you do not know.

16 075	Allah sets forth the Parable (of two men: one) a slave under the dominion of another; He has no power of any sort; and (the other) a man on whom We have bestowed goodly favours from Ourselves, and he spends thereof (freely), privately and publicly: are the two equal? (By no means;) praise be to Allah. But most of them understand not.	Allah coineth a similitude: (on the one hand) a (mere) chattel slave, who hath control of nothing, and (on the other hand) one on whom we have bestowed a fair provision from Us, and he spendeth thereof secretly and openly. Are they equal? Praise be to Allah! But most of them know not.	Allah sets forth a parable: (consider) a slave, the property of another, (who) has no power over anything, and one whom We have granted from Ourselves a goodly sustenance so he spends from it secretly and openly; are the two alike? (All) praise is due to Allah! Nay, most of them do not know.
16 076	Allah sets forth (another) Parable of two men: one of them dumb, with no power of any sort; a wearisome burden is he to his master; whichever way be directs him, he brings no good: is such a man equal with one who commands Justice, and is on a Straight Way?	And Allah coineth a similitude: Two men, one of them dumb, having control of nothing, and he is a burden on his owner; whithersoever he directeth him to go, he bringeth no good. Is he equal with one who enjoineth justice and followeth a straight path (of conduct)?	And Allah sets forth a parable of two men; one of them is dumb, not able to do anything, and he is a burden to his master; wherever he sends him, he brings no good; can he be held equal with him who enjoins what is just, and he (himself) is on the right path?
16 077	To Allah belongeth the Mystery of the heavens and the earth. And the Decision of the Hour (of Judgment) is as the twinkling of an eye, or even quicker: for Allah hath power over all things.	And unto Allah belongeth the Unseen of the heavens and the earth, and the matter of the Hour (of Doom) is but as a twinkling of the eye, or it is nearer still. Lo! Allah is Able to do all things.	And Allah's is the unseen of the heavens and the earth; and the matter of the hour is but as the twinkling of an eye or it is higher still; surely Allah has power over all things.
16 078	It is He Who brought you forth from the wombs of your mothers when ye knew nothing; and He gave you hearing and sight and intelligence and affections: that ye may give thanks (to Allah).	And Allah brought you forth from the wombs of your mothers knowing nothing, and gave you hearing and sight and hearts that haply ye might give thanks.	And Allah has brought you forth from the wombs of your mothers-- you did not know anything-- and He gave you hearing and sight and hearts that you may give thanks.
16 079	Do they not look at the birds, held poised in the midst of (the air and) the sky? Nothing holds them up but (the power of) Allah. Verily in this are signs for those who believe.	Have they not seen the birds obedient in mid-air? None holdeth them save Allah. Lo! herein, verily, are portents for a people who believe.	Do they not see the birds, constrained in the middle of the sky? None withholds them but Allah; most surely there are signs in this for a people who believe.
16 080	It is Allah Who made your habitations homes of rest and quiet for you; and made for you, out of the skins of animals, (tents for) dwellings, which ye find so light (and handy) when ye travel and when ye stop (in your travels); and out of their wool, and their soft fibres (between wool and hair), and their hair, rich stuff and articles of convenience (to serve you) for a time.	And Allah hath given you in your houses an abode, and hath given you (also), of the hides of cattle, houses which ye find light (to carry) on the day of migration and on the day of pitching camp; and of their wool and their fur and their hair, caparison and comfort for a while.	And Allah has given you a place to abide in your houses, and He has given you tents of the skins of cattle which you find light to carry on the day of your march and on the day of your halting, and of their wool and their fur and their hair (He has given you) household stuff and a provision for a time.
16 081	It is Allah Who made out of the things He created, some things to give you shade; of the hills He made some for your shelter; He made you garments to protect you from heat, and coats of mail to protect you from your (mutual) violence. Thus does He complete His favours on you, that ye may bow to His Will (in Islam).	And Allah hath given you, of that which He hath created, shelter from the sun; and hath given you places of refuge in the mountains, and hath given you coats to ward off the heat from you, and coats (of armour) to save you from your own foolhardiness. Thus doth He perfect His favour unto you, in order that ye may surrender (unto Him).	And Allah has made for you of what He has created shelters, and He has given you in the mountains places of retreat, and He has given you garments to preserve you from the heat and coats of mail to preserve you in your fighting; even thus does He complete His favor upon you, that haply you may submit.
16 082	But if they turn away, thy duty is only to preach the clear Message.	Then, if they turn away, thy duty (O Muhammad) is but plain conveyance (of the message).	But if they turn back, then on you devolves only the clear deliverance (of the message).

16 083	They recognise the favours of Allah; then they deny them; and most of them are (creatures) ungrateful.	They know the favour of Allah and then deny it. Most of them are ingrates.	They recognize the favor of Allah, yet they deny it, and most of them are ungrateful.
16 084	One Day We shall raise from all Peoples a Witness: then will no excuse be accepted from Unbelievers, nor will they receive any favours.	And (bethink you of) the day when we raise up of every nation a witness, then there is no leave for disbelievers, nor are they allowed to make amends.	And on the day when We will raise up a witness out of every nation, then shall no permission be given to those who disbelieve, nor shall they be made to solicit favor.
16 085	When the wrong-doers (actually) see the Penalty, then will it in no way be mitigated, nor will they then receive respite.	And when those who did wrong behold the doom, it will not be made light for them, nor will they be reprieved.	And when those who are unjust shall see the chastisement, it shall not be lightened for them, nor shall they be respited. .
16 086	When those who gave partners to Allah will see their "partners", they will say: "Our Lord! these are our 'partners,' those whom we used to invoke besides Thee." But they will throw back their word at them (and say): "Indeed ye are liars!"	And when those who ascribed partners to Allah behold those partners of theirs, they will say: Our Lord! these are our partners unto whom we used to cry instead of Thee. But they will fling to them the saying: Lo! ye verily are liars!	And when those who associate (others with Allah) shall see their associate-gods, they shall say: Our Lord, these are our associate-gods on whom we called besides Thee. But they will give them back the reply: Most surely you are liars.
16 087	That Day shall they (openly) show (their) submission to Allah; and all their inventions shall leave them in the lurch.	And they proffer unto Allah submission on that day, and all that they used to invent hath failed them.	And they shall tender submission to Allah on that day; and what they used to forge shall depart from them.
16 088	Those who reject Allah and hinder (men) from the Path of Allah - for them will We add Penalty to Penalty; for that they used to spread mischief.	For those who disbelieve and debar (men) from the way of Allah, We add doom to doom because they wrought corruption,	(As for) those who disbelieve and turn away from Allah's way, We will add chastisement to their chastisement because they made mischief.
16 089	One day We shall raise from all Peoples a witness against them, from amongst themselves: and We shall bring thee as a witness against these (thy people): and We have sent down to thee the Book explaining all things, a Guide, a Mercy, and Glad Tidings to Muslims.	And (bethink you of) the day when We raise in every nation a witness against them of their own folk, and We bring thee (Muhammad) as a witness against these. And We reveal the Scripture unto thee as an exposition of all things, and a guidance and a mercy and good tidings for those who have surrendered (to Allah).	And on the day when We will raise up in every people a witness against them from among themselves, and bring you as a witness against these-- and We have revealed the Book to you explaining clearly everything, and a guidance and mercy and good news for those who submit.
16 090	Allah commands justice, the doing of good, and liberality to kith and kin, and He forbids all shameful deeds, and injustice and rebellion: He instructs you, that ye may receive admonition.	Lo! Allah enjoineth justice and kindness, and giving to kinsfolk, and forbiddeth lewdness and abomination and wickedness. He exhorteth you in order that ye may take heed.	Surely Allah enjoins the doing of justice and the doing of good (to others) and the giving to the kindred, and He forbids indecency and evil and rebellion; He admonishes you that you may be mindful.
16 091	Fulfil the Covenant of Allah when ye have entered into it, and break not your oaths after ye have confirmed them; indeed ye have made Allah your surety; for Allah knoweth all that ye do.	Fulfil the covenant of Allah when ye have covenanted, and break not your oaths after the asseveration of them, and after ye have made Allah surety over you. Lo! Allah knoweth what ye do.	And fulfill the covenant of Allah when you have made a covenant, and do not break the oaths after making them fast, and you have indeed made Allah a surety for you; surely Allah knows what you do.

16 092	And be not like a woman who breaks into untwisted strands the yarn which she has spun, after it has become strong. Nor take your oaths to practise deception between yourselves, lest one party should be more numerous than another: for Allah will test you by this; and on the Day of Judgment He will certainly make clear to you (the truth of) that wherein ye disagree.	And be not like unto her who unravelleth the thread, after she hath made it strong, to thin filaments, making your oaths a deceit between you because of a nation being more numerous than (another) nation. Allah only trieth you thereby, and He verily will explain to you on the Day of Resurrection that wherein ye differed.	And be not like her who unravels her yarn, disintegrating it into pieces after she has spun it strongly. You make your oaths to be means of deceit between you because (one) nation is more numerous than (another) nation. Allah only tries you by this; and He will most certainly make clear to you on the resurrection day that about which you differed.
16 093	If Allah so willed, He could make you all one people: But He leaves straying whom He pleases, and He guides whom He pleases: but ye shall certainly be called to account for all your actions.	Had Allah willed He could have made you (all) one nation, but He sendeth whom He will astray and guideth whom He will, and ye will indeed be asked of what ye used to do.	And if Allah please He would certainly make you a single nation, but He causes to err whom He pleases and guides whom He pleases; and most certainly you will be questioned as to what you did.
16 094	And take not your oaths, to practise deception between yourselves, with the result that someone's foot may slip after it was firmly planted, and ye may have to taste the evil (consequences) of having hindered (men) from the Path of Allah, and a Mighty Wrath descend on you.	Make not your oaths a deceit between you, lest a foot should slip after being firmly planted and ye should taste evil forasmuch as ye debarred (men) from the way of Allah, and yours should be an awful doom.	And do not make your oaths a means of deceit between you, lest a foot should slip after its stability and you should taste evil because you turned away from Allah's way and grievous punishment be your (lot).
16 095	Nor sell the covenant of Allah for a miserable price: for with Allah is (a prize) far better for you, if ye only knew.	And purchase not a small gain at the price of Allah's covenant. Lo! that which Allah hath is better for you, if ye did but know.	And do not take a small price in exchange for Allah's covenant; surely what is with Allah is better for you, did you but know.
16 096	What is with you must vanish: what is with Allah will endure. And We will certainly bestow, on those who patiently persevere, their reward according to the best of their actions.	That which ye have wasteth away, and that which Allah hath remaineth. And verily We shall pay those who are steadfast a recompense in proportion to the best of what they used to do.	What is with you passes away and what is with Allah is enduring; and We will most certainly give to those who are patient their reward for the best of what they did.
16 097	Whoever works righteousness, man or woman, and has Faith, verily, to him will We give a new Life, a life that is good and pure and We will bestow on such their reward according to the best of their actions.	Whosoever doeth right, whether male or female, and is a believer, him verily we shall quicken with good life, and We shall pay them a recompense in proportion to the best of what they used to do.	Whoever does good whether male or female and he is a believer, We will most certainly make him live a happy life, and We will most certainly give them their reward for the best of what they did.
16 098	When thou dost read the Qur'an, seek Allah's protection from Satan the rejected one.	And when thou recitest the Qur'an, seek refuge in Allah from Satan the outcast.	So when you recite the Quran, seek refuge with Allah from the accursed Shaitan,
16 099	No authority has he over those who believe and put their trust in their Lord.	Lo! he hath no power over those who believe and put trust in their Lord.	Surely he has no authority over those who believe and rely on their Lord.
16 100	His authority is over those only, who take him as patron and who join partners with Allah.	His power is only over those who make a friend of him, and those who ascribe partners unto Him (Allah).	His authority is only over those who befriend him and those who associate others with Him.
16 101	When We substitute one revelation for another,- and Allah knows best what He reveals (in stages),- they say, "Thou art but a forger": but most of them understand not.	And when We put a revelation in place of (another) revelation, - and Allah knoweth best what He revealeth - they say: Lo! thou art but inventing. Most of them know not.	And when We change (one) communication for (another) communication, and Allah knows best what He reveals, they say: You are only a forger. Nay, most of them do not know.

16	102	Say, the Holy Spirit has brought the revelation from thy Lord in Truth, in order to strengthen those who believe, and as a Guide and Glad Tidings to Muslims.	Say: The holy Spirit hath delivered it from thy Lord with truth, that it may confirm (the faith of) those who believe, and as guidance and good tidings for those who have surrendered (to Allah).	Say: The Holy spirit has revealed it from your Lord with the truth, that it may establish those who believe and as a guidance and good news for those who submit.
16	103	We know indeed that they say, "It is a man that teaches him." The tongue of him they wickedly point to is notably foreign, while this is Arabic, pure and clear.	And We know well that they say: Only a man teacheth him. The speech of him at whom they falsely hint is outlandish, and this is clear Arabic speech.	And certainly We know that they say: Only a mortal teaches him. The tongue of him whom they reproach is barbarous, and this is clear Arabic tongue.
16	104	Those who believe not in the Signs of Allah,- Allah will not guide them, and theirs will be a grievous Penalty.	Lo! those who disbelieve the revelations of Allah, Allah guideth them not and theirs will be a painful doom.	(As for) those who do not believe in Allah's communications, surely Allah will not guide them, and they shall have a painful punishment.
16	105	It is those who believe not in the Signs of Allah, that forge falsehood: it is they who lie!	Only they invent falsehood who believe not Allah's revelations, and (only) they are the liars.	Only they forge the lie who do not believe in Allah's communications, and these are the liars.
16	106	Any one who, after accepting faith in Allah, utters Unbelief,- except under compulsion, his heart remaining firm in Faith - but such as open their breast to Unbelief, on them is Wrath from Allah, and theirs will be a dreadful Penalty.	Whoso disbelieveth in Allah after his belief - save him who is forced thereto and whose heart is still content with the Faith - but whoso findeth ease in disbelief: On them is wrath from Allah. Theirs will be an awful doom.	He who disbelieves in Allah after his having believed, not he who is compelled while his heart is at rest on account of faith, but he who opens (his) breast to disbelief-- on these is the wrath of Allah, and they shall have a grievous chastisement.
16	107	This because they love the life of this world better than the Hereafter: and Allah will not guide those who reject Faith.	That is because they have chosen the life of the world rather than the Hereafter, and because Allah guideth not the disbelieving folk.	This is because they love this world's life more than the hereafter, and because Allah does not guide the unbelieving people.
16	108	Those are they whose hearts, ears, and eyes Allah has sealed up, and they take no heed.	Such are they whose hearts and ears and eyes Allah hath sealed. And such are the heedless.	These are they on whose hearts and their hearing and their eyes Allah has set a seal, and these are the heedless ones.
16	109	Without doubt, in the Hereafter they will perish.	Assuredly in the Hereafter they are the losers.	No doubt that in the hereafter they will be the losers.
16	110	But verily thy Lord,- to those who leave their homes after trials and persecutions,- and who thereafter strive and fight for the faith and patiently persevere,- Thy Lord, after all this is Oft-Forgiving, Most Merciful.	Then lo! thy Lord - for those who became fugitives after they had been persecuted, and then fought and were steadfast - lo! thy Lord afterward is (for them) indeed Forgiving, Merciful.	Yet surely your Lord, with respect to those who fly after they are persecuted, then they struggle hard and are patient, most surely your Lord after that is Forgiving, Merciful.
16	111	One Day every soul will come up struggling for itself, and every soul will be recompensed (fully) for all its actions, and none will be unjustly dealt with.	On the Day when every soul will come pleading for itself, and every soul will be repaid what it did, and they will not be wronged.	(Remember) the day when every soul shall come, pleading for itself and every soul shall be paid in full what it has done, and they shall not be dealt with unjustly.
16	112	Allah sets forth a Parable: a city enjoying security and quiet, abundantly supplied with sustenance from every place: Yet was it ungrateful for the favours of Allah: so Allah made it taste of hunger and terror (in extremes) (closing in on it) like a garment (from every side), because of the (evil) which (its people) wrought.	Allah coineth a similitude: a township that dwelt secure and well content, its provision coming to it in abundance from every side, but it disbelieved in Allah's favours, so Allah made it experience the garb of dearth and fear because of what they used to do.	And Allah sets forth a parable: (Consider) a town safe and secure to which its means of subsistence come in abundance from every quarter; but it became ungrateful to Allah's favors, therefore Allah made it to taste the utmost degree of hunger and fear because of what they wrought.

16 113	And there came to them a Messenger from among themselves, but they falsely rejected him; so the Wrath seized them even in the midst of their iniquities.	And verily there had come unto them a messenger from among them, but they had denied him, and so the torment seized them while they were wrong-doers.	And certainly there came to them a Messenger from among them, but they rejected him, so the punishment overtook them while they were unjust.
16 114	So eat of the sustenance which Allah has provided for you, lawful and good; and be grateful for the favours of Allah, if it is He Whom ye serve.	So eat of the lawful and good food which Allah hath provided for you, and thank the bounty of your Lord if it is Him ye serve.	Therefore eat of what Allah has given you, lawful and good (things), and give thanks for Allah's favor if Him do you serve.
16 115	He has only forbidden you dead meat, and blood, and the flesh of swine, and any (food) over which the name of other than Allah has been invoked. But if one is forced by necessity, without wilful disobedience, nor transgressing due limits,- then Allah is Oft-Forgiving, Most Merciful.	He hath forbidden for you only carrion and blood and swineflesh and that which hath been immolated in the name of any other than Allah; but he who is driven thereto, neither craving nor transgressing, lo! then Allah is Forgiving, Merciful.	He has only forbidden you what dies of itself and blood and flesh of swine and that over which any other name than that of Allah has been invoked, but whoever is driven to necessity, not desiring nor exceeding the limit, then surely Allah is Forgiving, Merciful.
16 116	But say not - for any false thing that your tongues may put forth,- This is lawful, and this is forbidden, so as to ascribe false things to Allah. For those who ascribe false things to Allah, will never prosper.	And speak not, concerning that which your own tongues qualify (as clean or unclean), the falsehood: "This is lawful, and this is forbidden," so that ye invent a lie against Allah. Lo! those who invent a lie against Allah will not succeed.	And, for what your tongues describe, do not utter the lie, (saying) This is lawful and this is unlawful, in order to forge a lie against Allah; surely those who forge the lie against Allah shall not prosper.
16 117	(In such falsehood) is but a paltry profit; but they will have a most grievous Penalty.	A brief enjoyment (will be theirs); and theirs a painful doom.	A little enjoyment and they shall have a painful punishment.
16 118	To the Jews We prohibited such things as We have mentioned to thee before: We did them no wrong, but they were used to doing wrong to themselves.	And unto those who are Jews We have forbidden that which We have already related unto thee. And We wronged them not, but they were wont to wrong themselves.	And for those who were Jews We prohibited what We have related to you already, and We did them no injustice, but they were unjust to themselves.
16 119	But verily thy Lord,- to those who do wrong in ignorance, but who thereafter repent and make amends,- thy Lord, after all this, is Oft-Forgiving, Most Merciful.	Then lo! thy Lord - for those who do evil in ignorance and afterward repent and amend - lo! (for them) thy Lord is afterward indeed Forgiving, Merciful.	Yet surely your Lord, with respect to those who do an evil in ignorance, then turn after that and make amends, most surely your Lord after that is Forgiving, Merciful.
16 120	Abraham was indeed a model, devoutly obedient to Allah, (and) true in Faith, and he joined not gods with Allah:	Lo! Abraham was a nation obedient to Allah, by nature upright, and he was not of the idolaters;	Surely Ibrahim was an exemplar, obedient to Allah, upright, and he was not of the polytheists.
16 121	He showed his gratitude for the favours of Allah, who chose him, and guided him to a Straight Way.	Thankful for His bounties; He chose him and He guided him unto a straight path.	Grateful for His favors; He chose him and guided him on the right path.
16 122	And We gave him Good in this world, and he will be, in the Hereafter, in the ranks of the Righteous.	And We gave him good in the world, and in the Hereafter he is among the righteous.	And We gave him good in this world, and in the next he will most surely be among the good.
16 123	So We have taught thee the inspired (Message), "Follow the ways of Abraham the True in Faith, and he joined not gods with Allah."	And afterward We inspired thee (Muhammad, saying): Follow the religion of Abraham, as one by nature upright. He was not of the idolaters.	Then We revealed to you: Follow the faith of Ibrahim, the upright one, and he was not of the polytheists.

16 124	The Sabbath was only made (strict) for those who disagreed (as to its observance); But Allah will judge between them on the Day of Judgment, as to their differences.	The Sabbath was appointed only for those who differed concerning it, and lo! thy Lord will judge between them on the Day of Resurrection concerning that wherein they used to differ.	The Sabbath was ordained only for those who differed about it, and most surely your Lord will judge between them on the resurrection day concerning that about which they differed.
16 125	Invite (all) to the Way of thy Lord with wisdom and beautiful preaching; and argue with them in ways that are best and most gracious: for thy Lord knoweth best, who have strayed from His Path, and who receive guidance.	Call unto the way of thy Lord with wisdom and fair exhortation, and reason with them in the better way. Lo! thy Lord is Best Aware of him who strayeth from His way, and He is Best Aware of those who go aright.	Call to the way of your Lord with wisdom and goodly exhortation, and have disputations with them in the best manner; surely your Lord best knows those who go astray from His path, and He knows best those who follow the right way.
16 126	And if ye do catch them out, catch them out no worse than they catch you out: But if ye show patience, that is indeed the best (course) for those who are patient.	If ye punish, then punish with the like of that wherewith ye were afflicted. But if ye endure patiently, verily it is better for the patient.	And if you take your turn, then retaliate with the like of that with which you were afflicted; but if you are patient, it will certainly be best for those who are patient.
16 127	And do thou be patient, for thy patience is but from Allah; nor grieve over them: and distress not thyself because of their plots.	Endure thou patiently (O Muhammad). Thine endurance is only by (the help of) Allah. Grieve not for them, and be not in distress because of that which they devise.	And be patient and your patience is not but by (the assistance of) Allah, and grieve not for them, and do not distress yourself at what they plan.
16 128	For Allah is with those who restrain themselves, and those who do good.	Lo! Allah is with those who keep their duty unto Him and those who are doers of good.	Surely Allah is with those who guard (against evil) and those who do good (to others).

Chapter 17:

AL-ISRA (ISRA', THE NIGHT JOURNEY, CHILDREN OF ISRAEL)

Total Verses: 111 Revealed At: MAKKA

In the name of Allah, the Most Beneficent, the Most Merciful.

17 001	Glory to (Allah) Who did take His servant for a Journey by night from the Sacred Mosque to the farthest Mosque, whose precincts We did bless,- in order that We might show him some of Our Signs: for He is the One Who heareth and seeth (all things).	Glorified be He Who carried His servant by night from the Inviolable Place of Worship to the Far distant place of worship the neighbourhood whereof We have blessed, that We might show him of Our tokens! Lo! He, only He, is the Hearer, the Seer.	Glory be to Him Who made His servant to go on a night from the Sacred Mosque to the remote mosque of which We have blessed the precincts, so that We may show to him some of Our signs; surely He is the Hearing, the Seeing.
17 002	We gave Moses the Book, and made it a Guide to the Children of Israel, (commanding): "Take not other than Me as Disposer of (your) affairs."	We gave unto Moses the Scripture, and We appointed it a guidance for the children of Israel, saying: Choose no guardian beside Me.	And We gave Musa the Book and made it a guidance to the children of Israel, saying: Do not take a protector besides Me;
17 003	O ye that are sprung from those whom We carried (in the Ark) with Noah! Verily he was a devotee most grateful.	(They were) the seed of those whom We carried (in the ship) along with Noah. Lo! he was a grateful slave.	The offspring of those whom We bore with Nuh; surely he was a grateful servant.

17 004	And We gave (Clear) Warning to the Children of Israel in the Book, that twice would they do mischief on the earth and be elated with mighty arrogance (and twice would they be punished)!	And We decreed for the Children of Israel in the Scripture: Ye verily will work corruption in the earth twice, and ye will become great tyrants.	And We had made known to the children of Israel in the Book: Most certainly you will make mischief in the land twice, and most certainly you will behave insolently with great insolence.
17 005	When the first of the warnings came to pass, We sent against you Our servants given to terrible warfare: They entered the very inmost parts of your homes, and it was a warning (completely) fulfilled.	So when the time for the first of the two came, We roused against you slaves of Ours of great might who ravaged (your) country, and it was a threat performed.	So when the promise for the first of the two came, We sent over you Our servants, of mighty prowess, so they went to and fro among the houses, and it was a promise to be accomplished.
17 006	Then did We grant you the Return as against them: We gave you increase in resources and sons, and made you the more numerous in man-power.	Then we gave you once again your turn against them, and We aided you with wealth and children and made you more in soldiery.	Then We gave you back the turn to prevail against them, and aided you with wealth and children and made you a numerous band.
17 007	If ye did well, ye did well for yourselves; if ye did evil, (ye did it) against yourselves. So when the second of the warnings came to pass, (We permitted your enemies) to disfigure your faces, and to enter your Temple as they had entered it before, and to visit with destruction all that fell into their power.	(Saying): If ye do good, ye do good for your own souls, and if ye do evil, it is for them (in like manner). So, when the time for the second (of the judgments) came (We roused against you others of Our slaves) to ravage you, and to enter the Temple even as they entered it the first time, and to lay waste all that they conquered with an utter wasting.	If you do good, you will do good for your own souls, and if you do evil, it shall be for them. So when the second promise came (We raised another people) that they may bring you to grief and that they may enter the mosque as they entered it the first time, and that they might destroy whatever they gained ascendancy over with utter destruction.
17 008	It may be that your Lord may (yet) show Mercy unto you; but if ye revert (to your sins), We shall revert (to Our punishments): And we have made Hell a prison for those who reject (all Faith).	It may be that your Lord will have mercy on you, but if ye repeat (the crime) We shall repeat (the punishment), and We have appointed hell a dungeon for the disbelievers.	It may be that your Lord will have mercy on you, and if you again return (to disobedience) We too will return (to punishment), and We have made hell a prison for the unbelievers.
17 009	Verily this Qur'an doth guide to that which is most right (or stable), and giveth the Glad Tidings to the Believers who work deeds of righteousness, that they shall have a magnificent reward;	Lo! this Qur'an guideth unto that which is straightest, and giveth tidings unto the believers who do good works that theirs will be a great reward.	Surely this Quran guides to that which is most upright and gives good news to the believers who do good that they shall have a great reward.
17 010	And to those who believe not in the Hereafter, (it announceth) that We have prepared for them a Penalty Grievous (indeed).	And that those who believe not in the Hereafter, for them We have prepared a painful doom.	And that (as for) those who do not believe in the hereafter, We have prepared for them a painful chastisement.
17 011	The prayer that man should make for good, he maketh for evil; for man is given to hasty (deeds).	Man prayeth for evil as he prayeth for good; for man was ever hasty.	And man prays for evil as he ought to pray for good, and man is ever hasty.
17 012	We have made the Night and the Day as two (of Our) Signs: the Sign of the Night have We obscured, while the Sign of the Day We have made to enlighten you; that ye may seek bounty from your Lord, and that ye may know the number and count of the years: all things have We explained in detail.	And We appoint the night and the day two portents. Then We make dark the portent of the night, and We make the portent of the day sight-giving, that ye may seek bounty from your Lord, and that ye may know the computation of the years, and the reckoning; and everything have We expounded with a clear expounding.	And We have made the night and the day two signs, then We have made the sign of the night to pass away and We have made the sign of the day manifest, so that you may seek grace from your Lord, and that you might know the numbering of years and the reckoning; and We have explained everything with distinctness.

17 013	Every man's fate We have fastened on his own neck: On the Day of Judgment We shall bring out for him a scroll, which he will see spread open.	And every man's augury have We fastened to his own neck, and We shall bring forth for him on the Day of Resurrection a book which he will find wide open.	And We have made every man's actions to cling to his neck, and We will bring forth to him on the resurrection day a book which he will find wide open:
17 014	(It will be said to him:) "Read thine (own) record: Sufficient is thy soul this day to make out an account against thee."	(And it will be said unto him): Read thy Book. Thy soul sufficeth as reckoner against thee this day.	Read your book; your own self is sufficient as a reckoner against you this day.
17 015	Who receiveth guidance, receiveth it for his own benefit: who goeth astray doth so to his own loss: No bearer of burdens can bear the burden of another: nor would We visit with Our Wrath until We had sent a messenger (to give warning).	Whosoever goeth right, it is only for (the good of) his own soul that he goeth right, and whosoever erreth, erreth only to its hurt. No laden soul can bear another's load, We never punish until we have sent a messenger.	Whoever goes aright, for his own soul does he go aright; and whoever goes astray, to its detriment only does he go astray: nor can the bearer of a burden bear the burden of another, nor do We chastise until We raise a messenger.
17 016	When We decide to destroy a population, We (first) send a definite order to those among them who are given the good things of this life and yet transgress; so that the word is proved true against them: then (it is) We destroy them utterly.	And when We would destroy a township We send commandment to its folk who live at ease, and afterward they commit abomination therein, and so the Word (of doom) hath effect for it, and we annihilate it with complete annihilation.	And when We wish to destroy a town, We send Our commandment to the people of it who lead easy lives, but they transgress therein; thus the word proves true against it, so We destroy it with utter destruction.
17 017	How many generations have We destroyed after Noah? and enough is thy Lord to note and see the sins of His servants.	How many generations have We destroyed since Noah! And Allah sufficeth as Knower and Beholder of the sins of His slaves.	And how many of the generations did We destroy after Nuh! and your Lord is sufficient as Knowing and Seeing with regard to His servants' faults.
17 018	If any do wish for the transitory things (of this life), We readily grant them - such things as We will, to such person as We will: in the end have We provided Hell for them: they will burn therein, disgraced and rejected.	Whoso desireth that (life) which hasteneth away, We hasten for him therein what We will for whom We please. And afterward We have appointed for him hell; he will endure the heat thereof, condemned, rejected.	Whoever desires this present life, We hasten to him therein what We please for whomsoever We desire, then We assign to him the hell; he shall enter it despised, driven away.
17 019	Those who do wish for the (things of) the Hereafter, and strive therefor with all due striving, and have Faith,- they are the ones whose striving is acceptable (to Allah).	And whoso desireth the Hereafter and striveth for it with the effort necessary, being a believer; for such, their effort findeth favour (with their Lord).	And whoever desires the hereafter and strives for it as he ought to strive and he is a believer; (as for) these, their striving shall surely be accepted.
17 020	Of the bounties of thy Lord We bestow freely on all- These as well as those: The bounties of thy Lord are not closed (to anyone).	Each do We supply, both these and those, from the bounty of thy Lord. And the bounty of thy Lord can never be walled up.	All do We aid-- these as well as those-- out of the bounty of your Lord, and the bounty of your Lord is not confined.
17 021	See how We have bestowed more on some than on others; but verily the Hereafter is more in rank and gradation and more in excellence.	See how We prefer one of them above another, and verily the Hereafter will be greater in degrees and greater in preferment.	See how We have made some of them to excel others, and certainly the hereafter is much superior in respect of excellence.
17 022	Take not with Allah another object of worship; or thou (O man!) wilt sit in disgrace and destitution.	Set not up with Allah any other god (O man) lest thou sit down reproved, forsaken.	Do not associate with Allah any other god, lest you sit down despised, neglected.
17 023	Thy Lord hath decreed that ye worship none but Him, and that ye be kind to parents. Whether one or both of them attain old age in thy life, say not to them a word of contempt, nor repel them, but address them in terms of honour.	Thy Lord hath decreed, that ye worship none save Him, and (that ye show) kindness to parents. If one of them or both of them attain old age with thee, say not "Fie" unto them nor repulse them, but speak unto them a gracious word.	And your Lord has commanded that you shall not serve (any) but Him, and goodness to your parents. If either or both of them reach old age with you, say not to them (so much as) "Ugh" nor chide them, and speak to them a generous word.

17 024	And, out of kindness, lower to them the wing of humility, and say: My Lord! bestow on them thy Mercy even as they cherished me in childhood."	And lower unto them the wing of submission through mercy, and say: My Lord! Have mercy on them both as they did care for me when I was little.	And make yourself submissively gentle to them with compassion, and say: O my Lord! have compassion on them, as they brought me up (when I was) little.
17 025	Your Lord knoweth best what is in your hearts: If ye do deeds of righteousness, verily He is Most Forgiving to those who turn to Him again and again (in true penitence).	Your Lord is Best Aware of what is in your minds. If ye are righteous, then lo! He was ever Forgiving unto those who turn (unto Him).	Your Lord knows best what is in your minds; if you are good, then He is surely Forgiving to those who turn (to Him) frequently.
17 026	And render to the kindred their due rights, as (also) to those in want, and to the wayfarer: But squander not (your wealth) in the manner of a spendthrift.	Give the kinsman his due, and the needy, and the wayfarer, and squander not (thy wealth) in wantonness.	And give to the near of kin his due and (to) the needy and the wayfarer, and do not squander wastefully.
17 027	Verily spendthrifts are brothers of the Evil Ones; and the Evil One is to his Lord (himself) ungrateful.	Lo! the squanderers were ever brothers of the devils, and the devil was ever an ingrate to his Lord.	Surely the squanderers are the fellows of the Shaitans and the Shaitan is ever ungrateful to his Lord.
17 028	And even if thou hast to turn away from them in pursuit of the Mercy from thy Lord which thou dost expect, yet speak to them a word of easy kindness.	But if thou turn away from them, seeking mercy from thy Lord, for which thou hopest, then speak unto them a reasonable word.	And if you turn away from them to seek mercy from your Lord, which you hope for, speak to them a gentle word.
17 029	Make not thy hand tied (like a niggard's) to thy neck, nor stretch it forth to its utmost reach, so that thou become blameworthy and destitute.	And let not thy hand be chained to thy neck nor open it with a complete opening, lest thou sit down rebuked, denuded.	And do not make your hand to be shackled to your neck nor stretch it forth to the utmost (limit) of its stretching forth, lest you should (afterwards) sit down blamed, stripped off.
17 030	Verily thy Lord doth provide sustenance in abundance for whom He pleaseth, and He provideth in a just measure. For He doth know and regard all His servants.	Lo! thy Lord enlargeth the provision for whom He will, and straiteneth (it for whom He will). Lo, He was ever Knower, Seer of His slaves.	Surely your Lord makes plentiful the means of subsistence for whom He pleases and He straitens (them); surely He is ever Aware of, Seeing, His servants.
17 031	Kill not your children for fear of want: We shall provide sustenance for them as well as for you. Verily the killing of them is a great sin.	Slay not your children, fearing a fall to poverty, We shall provide for them and for you. Lo! the slaying of them is great sin.	And do not kill your children for fear of poverty; We give them sustenance and yourselves (too); surely to kill them is a great wrong.
17 032	Nor come nigh to adultery: for it is a shameful (deed) and an evil, opening the road (to other evils).	And come not near unto adultery. Lo! it is an abomination and an evil way.	And go not nigh to fornication; surely it is an indecency and an evil way.
0 033	Nor take life - which Allah has made sacred - except for just cause. And if anyone is slain wrongfully, we have given his heir authority (to demand qisas or to forgive): but let him not exceed bounds in the matter of taking life; for he is helped (by the Law).	And slay not the life which Allah hath forbidden save with right. Whoso is slain wrongfully, We have given power unto his heir, but let him not commit excess in slaying. Lo! he will be helped.	And do not kill any one whom Allah has forbidden, except for a just cause, and whoever is slain unjustly, We have indeed given to his heir authority, so let him not exceed the just limits in slaying; surely he is aided.
17 034	Come not nigh to the orphan's property except to improve it, until he attains the age of full strength; and fulfil (every) engagement, for (every) engagement will be enquired into (on the Day of Reckoning).	Come not near the wealth of the orphan save with that which is better till he come to strength; and keep the covenant. Lo! of the covenant it will be asked.	And draw not near to the property of the orphan except in a goodly way till he attains his maturity and fulfill the promise; surely (every) promise shall be questioned about.

17 035	Give full measure when ye measure, and weigh with a balance that is straight: that is the most fitting and the most advantageous in the final determination.	Fill the measure when ye measure, and weigh with a right balance; that is meet, and better in the end.		And give full measure when you measure out, and weigh with a true balance; this is fair and better in the end.
17 036	And pursue not that of which thou hast no knowledge; for every act of hearing, or of seeing or of (feeling in) the heart will be enquired into (on the Day of Reckoning).	(O man), follow not that whereof thou hast no knowledge. Lo! the hearing and the sight and the heart - of each of these it will be asked.		And follow not that of which you have not the knowledge; surely the hearing and the sight and the heart, all of these, shall be questioned about that.
17 037	Nor walk on the earth with insolence: for thou canst not rend the earth asunder, nor reach the mountains in height.	And walk not in the earth exultant. Lo! thou canst not rend the earth, nor canst thou stretch to the height of the hills.		And do not go about in the land exultingly, for you cannot cut through the earth nor reach the mountains in height.
17 038	Of all such things the evil is hateful in the sight of thy Lord.	The evil of all that is hateful in the sight of thy Lord.		All this-- the evil of it-- is hateful in the sight of your Lord.
17 039	These are among the (precepts of) wisdom, which thy Lord has revealed to thee. Take not, with Allah, another object of worship, lest thou shouldst be thrown into Hell, blameworthy and rejected.	This is (part) of that wisdom wherewith thy Lord hath inspired thee (O Muhammad). And set not up with Allah any other god, lest thou be cast into hell, reproved, abandoned.		This is of what your Lord has revealed to you of wisdom, and do not associate any other god with Allah lest you should be thrown into hell, blamed, cast away.
17 040	Has then your Lord (O Pagans!) preferred for you sons, and taken for Himself daughters among the angels? Truly ye utter a most dreadful saying!	Hath your Lord then distinguished you (O men of Makka) by giving you sons, and hath chosen for Himself females from among the angels? Lo! verily ye speak an awful word!		What! has then your Lord preferred to give you sons, and (for Himself) taken daughters from among the angels? Most surely you utter a grievous saying.
17 041	We have explained (things) in various (ways) in this Qur'an, in order that they may receive admonition, but it only increases their flight (from the Truth)!	We verily have displayed (Our warnings) in this Qur'an that they may take heed, but it increaseth them in naught save aversion.		And certainly We have repeated (warnings) in this Quran that they may be mindful, but it does not add save to their aversion.
17 042	Say: If there had been (other) gods with Him, as they say,- behold, they would certainly have sought out a way to the Lord of the Throne!	Say (O Muhammad, to the disbelievers): If there were other gods along with Him, as they say, then had they sought a way against the Lord of the Throne.		Say: If there were with Him gods as they say, then certainly they would have been able to seek a way to the Lord of power.
17 043	Glory to Him! He is high above all that they say!- Exalted and Great (beyond measure)!	Glorified is He, and High Exalted above what they say!		Glory be to Him and exalted be He in high exaltation above what they say.
17 044	The seven heavens and the earth, and all beings therein, declare His glory: there is not a thing but celebrates His praise; And yet ye understand not how they declare His glory! Verily He is Oft-Forbearing, Most Forgiving!	The seven heavens and the earth and all that is therein praise Him, and there is not a thing but hymneth His praise; but ye understand not their praise. Lo! He is ever Clement, Forgiving.		The seven heavens declare His glory and the earth (too), and those who are in them; and there is not a single thing but glorifies Him with His praise, but you do not understand their glorification; surely He is Forbearing, Forgiving.
17 045	When thou dost recite the Qur'an, We put, between thee and those who believe not in the Hereafter, a veil invisible:	And when thou recitest the Qur'an we place between thee and those who believe not in the Hereafter a hidden barrier;		And when you recite the Quran, We place between you and those who do not believe in the hereafter a hidden barrier;

17 046	And We put coverings over their hearts (and minds) lest they should understand the Qur'an, and deafness into their ears: when thou dost commemorate thy Lord and Him alone in the Qur'an, they turn on their backs, fleeing (from the Truth).	And We place upon their hearts veils lest they should understand it, and in their ears a deafness; and when thou makest mention of thy Lord alone in the Qur'an, they turn their backs in aversion.	And We have placed coverings on their hearts and a heaviness in their ears lest they understand it, and when you mention your Lord alone in the Quran they turn their backs in aversion.
17 047	We know best why it is they listen, when they listen to thee; and when they meet in private conference, behold, the wicked say, "Ye follow none other than a man bewitched!"	We are Best Aware of what they wish to hear when they give ear to thee and when they take secret counsel, when the evil-doers say: Ye follow but a man bewitched.	We know best what they listen to when they listen to you, and when they take counsel secretly, when the unjust say: You follow only a man deprived of reason.
17 048	See what similes they strike for thee: but they have gone astray, and never can they find a way.	See what similitudes they coin for thee, and thus are all astray, and cannot find a road!	See what they liken you to! So they have gone astray and cannot find the way.
17 049	They say: "What! when we are reduced to bones and dust, should we really be raised up (to be) a new creation?"	And they say: When we are bones and fragments, shall we forsooth, be raised up as a new creation?	And they say: What! when we shall have become bones and decayed particles, shall we then certainly be raised up, being a new creation?
17 050	Say: "(Nay!) be ye stones or iron,"	Say: Be ye stones or iron	Say: Become stones or iron,
17 051	"Or created matter which, in your minds, is hardest (to be raised up),- (Yet shall ye be raised up)!" then will they say: "Who will cause us to return?" Say: "He who created you first!" Then will they wag their heads towards thee, and say, "When will that be?" Say, "May be it will be quite soon!"	Or some created thing that is yet greater in your thoughts! Then they will say: Who shall bring us back (to life). Say: He Who created you at the first. Then will they shake their heads at thee, and say: When will it be? Say: It will perhaps be soon;	Or some other creature of those which are too hard (to receive life) in your minds! But they will say: Who will return us? Say: Who created you at first. Still they will shake their heads at you and say: When will it be? Say: Maybe it has drawn nigh.
17 052	"It will be on a Day when He will call you, and ye will answer (His call) with (words of) His praise, and ye will think that ye tarried but a little while!"	A day when He will call you and ye will answer with His praise, and ye will think that ye have tarried but a little while.	On the day when He will call you forth, then shall you obey Him, giving Him praise, and you will think that you tarried but a little (while).
17 053	Say to My servants that they should (only) say those things that are best: for Satan doth sow dissensions among them: For Satan is to man an avowed enemy.	Tell My bondmen to speak that which is kindlier. Lo! the devil soweth discord among them. Lo! the devil is for man an open foe.	And say to My servants (that) they speak that which is best; surely the Shaitan sows dissensions among them; surely the Shaitan is an open enemy to man.
17 054	It is your Lord that knoweth you best: If He please, He granteth you mercy, or if He please, punishment: We have not sent thee to be a disposer of their affairs for them.	Your Lord is Best Aware of you. If He will, He will have mercy on you, or if He will, He will punish you. We have not sent thee (O Muhammad) as a warden over them.	Your Lord knows you best; He will have mercy on you if He pleases, or He will chastise you if He pleases; and We have not sent you as being in charge of them.
17 055	And it is your Lord that knoweth best all beings that are in the heavens and on earth: We did bestow on some prophets more (and other) gifts than on others: and We gave to David (the gift of) the Psalms.	And thy Lord is Best Aware of all who are in the heavens and the earth. And we preferred some of the prophets above others, and unto David We gave the Psalms.	And your Lord best knows those who are in the heavens and the earth; and certainly We have made some of the prophets to excel others, and to Dawood We gave a scripture.
17 056	Say: "Call on those - besides Him - whom ye fancy: they have neither the power to remove your troubles from you nor to change them."	Say: Cry unto those (saints and angels) whom ye assume (to be gods) beside Him, yet they have no power to rid you of misfortune nor to change.	Say: Call on those whom you assert besides Him, so they shall not control the removal of distress from you nor (its) transference.

17 057	Those whom they call upon do desire (for themselves) means of access to their Lord, - even those who are nearest: they hope for His Mercy and fear His Wrath: for the Wrath of thy Lord is something to take heed of.	Those unto whom they cry seek the way of approach to their Lord, which of them shall be the nearest; they hope for His mercy and they fear His doom. Lo! the doom of thy Lord is to be shunned.	Those whom they call upon, themselves seek the means of access to their Lord-- whoever of them is nearest-- and they hope for His mercy and fear His chastisement; surely the chastisement of your Lord is a thing to be cautious of.
17 058	There is not a population but We shall destroy it before the Day of Judgment or punish it with a dreadful Penalty: that is written in the (eternal) Record.	There is not a township but We shall destroy it ere the Day of Resurrection, or punish it with dire punishment. That is set forth in the Book (of Our decrees).	And there is not a town but We will destroy it before the day of resurrection or chastise it with a severe chastisement; this is written in the Divine ordinance.
17 059	And We refrain from sending the signs, only because the men of former generations treated them as false: We sent the she-camel to the Thamud to open their eyes, but they treated her wrongfully: We only send the Signs by way of terror (and warning from evil).	Naught hindereth Us from sending portents save that the folk of old denied them. And We gave Thamud the she-camel - a clear portent save to warn.	And nothing could have hindered Us that We should send signs except that the ancients rejected them; and We gave to Samood the she-camel-- a manifest sign-- but on her account they did injustice, and We do not send signs but to make (men) fear.
17 060	Behold! We told thee that thy Lord doth encompass mankind round about: We granted the vision which We showed thee, but as a trial for men,- as also the Cursed Tree (mentioned) in the Qur'an: We put terror (and warning) into them, but it only increases their inordinate transgression!	And (it was a warning) when we told thee: Lo! thy Lord encompasseth mankind, and We appointed the sight which We showed thee as an ordeal for mankind, and (likewise) the Accursed Tree in the Qur'an. We warn them, but it increaseth them in naught save gross impiety.	And when We said to you: Surely your Lord encompasses men; and We did not make the vision which We showed you but a trial for men and the cursed tree in the Quran as well; and We cause them to fear, but it only adds to their great inordinacy.
17 061	Behold! We said to the angels: "Bow down unto Adam": They bowed down except Iblis: He said, "Shall I bow down to one whom Thou didst create from clay?"	And when We said unto the angels: Fall down prostrate before Adam and they fell prostrate all save Iblis, he said: Shall I fall prostrate before that which Thou hast created of clay?	And when We said to the angels: Make obeisance to Adam; they made obeisance, but Iblis (did it not). He said: Shall I make obeisance to him whom Thou hast created of dust?
17 062	He said: "Seest Thou? this is the one whom Thou hast honoured above me! If Thou wilt but respite me to the Day of Judgment, I will surely bring his descendants under my sway - all but a few!"	He said: Seest Thou this (creature) whom Thou hast honoured above me, if Thou give me grace until the Day of Resurrection I verily will seize his seed, save but a few.	He said: Tell me, is this he whom Thou hast honored above me? If Thou shouldst respite me to the day of resurrection, I will most certainly cause his progeny to perish except a few.
17 063	(Allah) said: "Go thy way; if any of them follow thee, verily Hell will be the recompense of you (all)- an ample recompense."	He said: Go, and whosoever of them followeth thee - lo! hell will be your payment, ample payment.	He said: Be gone! for whoever of them will follow you, then surely hell is your recompense, a full recompense:
17 064	"Lead to destruction those whom thou canst among them, with thy (seductive) voice; make assaults on them with thy cavalry and thy infantry; mutually share with them wealth and children; and make promises to them." But Satan promises them nothing but deceit.	And excite any of them whom thou canst with thy voice, and urge thy horse and foot against them, and be a partner in their wealth and children, and promise them. Satan promiseth them only to deceive.	And beguile whomsoever of them you can with your voice, and collect against them your forces riding and on foot, and share with them in wealth and children, and hold out promises to them; and the Shaitan makes not promises to them but to deceive:
17 065	"As for My servants, no authority shalt thou have over them:" Enough is thy Lord for a Disposer of affairs.	Lo! My (faithful) bondmen - over them thou hast no power, and thy Lord sufficeth as (their) guardian.	Surely (as for) My servants, you have no authority over them; and your Lord is sufficient as a Protector.

17 066	Your Lord is He That maketh the Ship go smoothly for you through the sea, in order that ye may seek of his Bounty. For he is unto you most Merciful.	(O mankind), your Lord is He Who driveth for you the ship upon the sea that ye may seek of His bounty. Lo! He was ever Merciful toward you.		Your Lord is He Who speeds the ships for you in the sea that you may seek of His grace; surely He is ever Merciful to you.
17 067	When distress seizes you at sea, those that ye call upon - besides Himself - leave you in the lurch! but when He brings you back safe to land, ye turn away (from Him). Most ungrateful is man!	And when harm toucheth you upon the sea, all unto whom ye cry (for succour) fail save Him (alone), but when He bringeth you safe to land, ye turn away, for man was ever thankless.		And when distress afflicts you in the sea, away go those whom you call on except He; but when He brings you safe to the land, you turn aside; and man is ever ungrateful.
17 068	Do ye then feel secure that He will not cause you to be swallowed up beneath the earth when ye are on land, or that He will not send against you a violent tornado (with showers of stones) so that ye shall find no one to carry out your affairs for you?	Feel ye then secure that He will not cause a slope of the land to engulf you, or send a sand-storm upon you, and then ye will find that ye have no protector?		What! Do you then feel secure that He will not cause a tract of land to engulf you or send on you a tornado? Then you shall not find a protector for yourselves.
17 069	Or do ye feel secure that He will not send you back a second time to sea and send against you a heavy gale to drown you because of your ingratitude, so that ye find no helper. Therein against Us?	Or feel ye secure that He will not return you to that (plight) a second time, and send against you a hurricane of wind and drown you for your thanklessness, and then ye will not find therein that ye have any avenger against Us?		Or, do you feel secure that He will (not) take you back into it another time, then send on you a fierce gale and thus drown you on account of your ungratefulness? Then you shall not find any aider against Us in the matter.
17 070	We have honoured the sons of Adam; provided them with transport on land and sea; given them for sustenance things good and pure; and conferred on them special favours, above a great part of our creation.	Verily we have honoured the Children of Adam. We carry them on the land and the sea, and have made provision of good things for them, and have preferred them above many of those whom We created with a marked preferment.		And surely We have honored the children of Adam, and We carry them in the land and the sea, and We have given them of the good things, and We have made them to excel by an appropriate excellence over most of those whom We have created.
17 071	One day We shall call together all human beings with their (respective) Imams: those who are given their record in their right hand will read it (with pleasure), and they will not be dealt with unjustly in the least.	On the day when We shall summon all men with their record, whoso is given his book in his right hand - such will read their book and they will not be wronged a shred.		(Remember) the day when We will call every people with their Imam; then whoever is given his book in his right hand, these shall read their book; and they shall not be dealt with a whit unjustly.
17 072	But those who were blind in this world, will be blind in the hereafter, and most astray from the Path.	Whoso is blind here will be blind in the Hereafter, and yet further from the road.		And whoever is blind in this, he shall (also) be blind in the hereafter; and more erring from the way.
17 073	And their purpose was to tempt thee away from that which We had revealed unto thee, to substitute in our name something quite different; (in that case), behold! they would certainly have made thee (their) friend!	And they indeed strove hard to beguile thee (Muhammad) away from that wherewith We have inspired thee, that thou shouldst invent other than it against Us; and then would they have accepted thee as a friend.		And surely they had purposed to turn you away from that which We have revealed to you, that you should forge against Us other than that, and then they would certainly have taken you for a friend.
17 074	And had We not given thee strength, thou wouldst nearly have inclined to them a little.	And if We had not made thee wholly firm thou mightest almost have inclined unto them a little.		And had it not been that We had already established you, you would certainly have been near to incline to them a little;

17 075	In that case We should have made thee taste an equal portion (of punishment) in this life, and an equal portion in death: and moreover thou wouldst have found none to help thee against Us!	Then had we made thee taste a double (punishment) of living and a double (punishment) of dying, then hadst thou found no helper against Us.		In that case We would certainly have made you to taste a double (punishment) in this life and a double (punishment) after death, then you would not have found any helper against Us.
17 076	Their purpose was to scare thee off the land, in order to expel thee; but in that case they would not have stayed (therein) after thee, except for a little while.	And they indeed wished to scare thee from the land that they might drive thee forth from thence, and then they would have stayed (there) but a little after thee.		And surely they purposed to unsettle you from the land that they might expel you from it, and in that case they will not tarry behind you but a little.
17 077	(This was Our) way with the messengers We sent before thee: thou wilt find no change in Our ways.	(Such was Our) method in the case of those whom We sent before thee (to mankind), and thou wilt not find for Our method aught of power to change.		(This is Our) course with regard to those of Our messengers whom We sent before you, and you shall not find a change in Our course.
17 078	Establish regular prayers - at the sun's decline till the darkness of the night, and the morning prayer and reading: for the prayer and reading in the morning carry their testimony.	Establish worship at the going down of the sun until the dark of night, and (the recital of) the Qur'an at dawn. Lo! (the recital of) the Qur'an at dawn is ever witnessed.		Keep up prayer from the declining of the sun till the darkness of the night and the morning recitation; surely the morning recitation is witnessed.
17 079	And pray in the small watches of the morning: (it would be) an additional prayer (or spiritual profit) for thee: soon will thy Lord raise thee to a Station of Praise and Glory!	And some part of the night awake for it, a largess for thee. It may be that thy Lord will raise thee to a praised estate.		And during a part of the night, pray Tahajjud beyond what is incumbent on you; maybe your Lord will raise you to a position of great glory.
17 080	Say: "O my Lord! Let my entry be by the Gate of Truth and Honour, and likewise my exit by the Gate of Truth and Honour; and grant me from Thy Presence an authority to aid (me)."	And say: My Lord! Cause me to come in with a firm incoming and to go out with a firm outgoing. And give me from Thy presence a sustaining Power.		And say: My Lord! make me to enter a goodly entering, and cause me to go forth a goodly going forth, and grant me from near Thee power to assist (me).
17 081	And say: "Truth has (now) arrived, and Falsehood perished: for Falsehood is (by its nature) bound to perish."	And say: Truth hath come and falsehood hath vanished away. Lo! falsehood is ever bound to vanish.		And say: The truth has come and the falsehood has vanished; surely falsehood is a vanishing (thing).
17 082	We send down (stage by stage) in the Qur'an that which is a healing and a mercy to those who believe: to the unjust it causes nothing but loss after loss.	And We reveal of the Qur'an that which is a healing and a mercy for believers though it increase the evil-doers in naught save ruin.		And We reveal of the Quran that which is a healing and a mercy to the believers, and it adds only to the perdition of the unjust.
17 083	Yet when We bestow Our favours on man, he turns away and becomes remote on his side (instead of coming to Us), and when evil seizes him he gives himself up to despair!	And when We make life pleasant unto man, he turneth away and is averse; and when ill toucheth him he is in despair.		And when We bestow favor on man, he turns aside and behaves proudly, and when evil afflicts him, he is despairing.
17 084	Say: "Everyone acts according to his own disposition: But your Lord knows best who it is that is best guided on the Way."	Say: Each one doth according to his rule of conduct, and thy Lord is Best Aware of him whose way is right.		Say: Every one acts according to his manner; but your Lord best knows who is best guided in the path.
17 085	They ask thee concerning the Spirit (of inspiration). Say: "The Spirit (cometh) by command of my Lord: of knowledge it is only a little that is communicated to you, (O men!)"	They are asking thee concerning the Spirit. Say: The Spirit is by command of my Lord, and of knowledge ye have been vouchsafed but little.		And they ask you about the soul. Say: The soul is one of the commands of my Lord, and you are not given aught of knowledge but a little.

17 086	If it were Our Will, We could take away that which We have sent thee by inspiration: then wouldst thou find none to plead thy affair in that matter as against Us,-	And if We willed We could withdraw that which We have revealed unto thee, then wouldst thou find no guardian for thee against Us in respect thereof.	And if We please, We should certainly take away that which We have revealed to you, then you would not find for it any protector against Us.
17 087	Except for Mercy from thy Lord: for his bounty is to thee (indeed) great.	(It is naught) save mercy from thy Lord. Lo! His kindness unto thee was ever great.	But on account of mercy from your Lord-- surely His grace to you is abundant.
17 088	Say: "If the whole of mankind and jinns were to gather together to produce the like of this Qur'an, they could not produce the like thereof, even if they backed up each other with help and support."	Say: Verily, though mankind and the jinn should assemble to produce the like of this Qur'an, they could not produce the like thereof though they were helpers one of another.	Say: If men and jinn should combine together to bring the like of this Quran, they could not bring the like of it, though some of them were aiders of others.
17 089	And We have explained to man, in this Qur'an, every kind of similitude: yet the greater part of men refuse (to receive it) except with ingratitude!	And verily We have displayed for mankind in this Qur'an all kind of similitudes, but most of mankind refuse aught save disbelief.	And certainly We have explained for men in this Quran every kind of similitude, but most men do not consent to aught but denying.
17 090	They say: "We shall not believe in thee, until thou cause a spring to gush forth for us from the earth,"	And they say: We will not put faith in thee till thou cause a spring to gush forth from the earth for us;	And they say: We will by no means believe in you until you cause a fountain to gush forth from the earth for us.
17 091	"Or (until) thou have a garden of date trees and vines, and cause rivers to gush forth in their midst, carrying abundant water;"	Or thou have a garden of date-palms and grapes, and cause rivers to gush forth therein abundantly;	Or you should have a garden of palms and grapes in the midst of which you should cause rivers to flow forth, gushing out.
17 092	"Or thou cause the sky to fall in pieces, as thou sayest (will happen), against us; or thou bring Allah and the angels before (us) face to face:"	Or thou cause the heaven to fall upon us piecemeal, as thou hast pretended, or bring Allah and the angels as a warrant;	Or you should cause the heaven to come down upon us in pieces as you think, or bring Allah and the angels face to face (with us).
17 093	"Or thou have a house adorned with gold, or thou mount a ladder right into the skies. No, we shall not even believe in thy mounting until thou send down to us a book that we could read." Say: "Glory to my Lord! Am I aught but a man,- a messenger?"	Or thou have a house of gold; or thou ascend up into heaven, and even then we will put no faith in thine ascension till thou bring down for us a book that we can read. Say (O Muhammad): My Lord be Glorified! Am I aught save a mortal messenger?	Or you should have a house of gold, or you should ascend into heaven, and we will not believe in your ascending until you bring down to us a book which we may read. Say: Glory be to my Lord; am I aught but a mortal messenger?
17 094	What kept men back from belief when Guidance came to them, was nothing but this: they said, "Has Allah sent a man (like us) to be (His) Messenger?"	And naught prevented mankind from believing when the guidance came unto them save that they said: Hath Allah sent a mortal as (His) messenger?	And nothing prevented people from believing when the guidance came to them except that they said: What! has Allah raised up a mortal to be a messenger?
17 095	Say, "If there were settled, on earth, angels walking about in peace and quiet, We should certainly have sent them down from the heavens an angel for a messenger."	Say: If there were in the earth angels walking secure, We had sent down for them from heaven an angel as messenger.	Say: Had there been in the earth angels walking about as settlers, We would certainly have sent down to them from the heaven an angel as a messenger.
17 096	Say: "Enough is Allah for a witness between me and you: for He is well acquainted with His servants, and He sees (all things)."	Say: Allah sufficeth for a witness between me and you. Lo! He is Knower, Seer of His slaves.	Say: Allah suffices as a witness between me and you; surely He is Aware of His servants, Seeing.

17 097	It is he whom Allah guides, that is on true Guidance; but he whom He leaves astray - for such wilt thou find no protector besides Him. On the Day of Judgment We shall gather, them together, prone on their faces, blind, dumb, and deaf: their abode will be Hell: every time it shows abatement, We shall increase from them the fierceness of the Fire.	And he whom Allah guideth, he is led aright; while, as for him whom He sendeth astray, for them thou wilt find no protecting friends beside Him, and We shall assemble them on the Day of Resurrection on their faces, blind, dumb and deaf; their habitation will be hell; whenever it abateth, We increase the flame for them.	And whomsoever Allah guides, he is the follower of the right way, and whomsoever He causes to err, you shall not find for him guardians besides Him; and We will gather them together on the day of resurrection on their faces, blind and dumb and deaf; their abode is hell; whenever it becomes allayed We will add to their burning.	
17 098	That is their recompense, because they rejected Our signs, and said, When we are reduced to bones and broken dust, should we really be raised up (to be) a new Creation?"	That is their reward because they disbelieved Our revelations and said: When we are bones and fragments shall we, forsooth, be raised up as a new creation?	This is their retribution because they disbelieved in Our communications and said What! when we shall have become bones and decayed particles, shall we then indeed be raised up into a new creation?	
17 099	See they not that Allah, Who created the heavens and the earth, has power to create the like of them (anew)? Only He has decreed a term appointed, of which there is no doubt. But the unjust refuse (to receive it) except with ingratitude.	Have they not seen that Allah Who created the heavens and the earth is Able to create the like of them, and hath appointed for them an end whereof there is no doubt? But the wrong-doers refuse aught save disbelief.	Do they not consider that Allah, Who created the heavens and the earth, is able to create their like, and He has appointed for them a doom about which there is no doubt? But the unjust do not consent to aught but denying.	
17 100	Say: "If ye had control of the Treasures of the Mercy of my Lord, behold, ye would keep them back, for fear of spending them: for man is (every) niggardly!"	Say (unto them): If ye possessed the treasures of the mercy of my Lord, ye would surely hold them back for fear of spending, for man was ever grudging.	Say: If you control the treasures of the mercy of my Lord, then you would withhold (them) from fear of spending, and man is niggardly.	
17 101	To Moses We did give Nine Clear Signs: As the Children of Israel: when he came to them, Pharaoh said to him: "O Moses! I consider thee, indeed, to have been worked upon by sorcery!"	And verily We gave unto Moses nine tokens, clear proofs (of Allah's Sovereignty). Do but ask the Children of Israel how he came unto them, then Pharaoh said unto him: Lo! I deem thee one bewitched, O Moses.	And certainly We gave Musa nine clear signs; so ask the children of Israel. When he came to them, Firon said to him: Most surely I deem you, O Musa, to be a man deprived of reason.	
17 102	Moses said, "Thou knowest well that these things have been sent down by none but the Lord of the heavens and the earth as eye-opening evidence: and I consider thee indeed, O Pharaoh, to be one doomed to destruction!"	He said: In truth thou knowest that none sent down these (portents) save the Lord of the heavens and the earth as proofs, and lo! (for my part) I deem thee lost, O Pharaoh.	He said: Truly you know that none but the Lord of the heavens and the earth has sent down these as clear proof and most surely I believe you, O Firon, to be given over to perdition.	
17 103	So he resolved to remove them from the face of the earth: but We did drown him and all who were with him.	And he wished to scare them from the land, but We drowned him and those with him, all together.	So he desired to destroy them out of the earth, but We drowned him and those with him all together;	
17 104	And We said thereafter to the Children of Israel, "Dwell securely in the land (of promise)": but when the second of the warnings came to pass, We gathered you together in a mingled crowd.	And We said unto the Children of Israel after him: Dwell in the land; but when the promise of the Hereafter cometh to pass We shall bring you as a crowd gathered out of various nations.	And We said to the Israelites after him: Dwell in the land: and when the promise of the next life shall come to pass, we will bring you both together in judgment.	
17 105	We sent down the (Qur'an) in Truth, and in Truth has it descended: and We sent thee but to give Glad Tidings and to warn (sinners).	With truth have We sent it down, and with truth hath it descended. And We have sent thee as naught else save a bearer of good tidings and a warner.	And with truth have We revealed it, and with truth did it come; and We have not sent you but as the giver of good news and as a warner.	

17 106	(It is) a Qur'an which We have divided (into parts from time to time), in order that thou mightest recite it to men at intervals: We have revealed it by stages.	And (it is) a Qur'an that We have divided, that thou mayst recite it unto mankind at intervals, and We have revealed it by (successive) revelation.	And it is a Quran which We have revealed in portions so that you may read it to the people by slow degrees, and We have revealed it, revealing in portions.
17 107	Say: "Whether ye believe in it or not, it is true that those who were given knowledge beforehand, when it is recited to them, fall down on their faces in humble prostration,"	Say: Believe therein or believe not, lo! those who were given knowledge before it, when it is read unto them, fall down prostrate on their faces, adoring,	Say: Believe in it or believe not; surely those who are given the knowledge before it fall down on their faces, making obeisance when it is recited to them.
17 108	"And they say: 'Glory to our Lord! Truly has the promise of our Lord been fulfilled!'"	Saying: Glory to our Lord! Verily the promise of our Lord must be fulfilled.	And they say: Glory be to our Lord! most surely the promise of our Lord was to be fulfilled.
17 109	They fall down on their faces in tears, and it increases their (earnest) humility.	They fall down on their faces, weeping, and it increaseth humility in them.	And they fall down on their faces weeping, and it adds to their humility.
17 110	Say: "Call upon Allah, or call upon Rahman: by whatever name ye call upon Him, (it is well): for to Him belong the Most Beautiful Names. Neither speak thy Prayer aloud, nor speak it in a low tone, but seek a middle course between."	Say (unto mankind): Cry unto Allah, or cry unto the Beneficent, unto whichsoever ye cry (it is the same). His are the most beautiful names. And thou (Muhammad), be not loud-voiced in thy worship nor yet silent therein, but follow a way between.	Say: Call upon Allah or call upon, the Beneficent Allah; whichever you call upon, He has the best names; and do not utter your prayer with a very raised voice nor be silent with regard to it, and seek a way between these.
17 111	Say: "Praise be to Allah, who begets no son, and has no partner in (His) dominion: Nor (needs) He any to protect Him from humiliation: yea, magnify Him for His greatness and glory!"	And say: Praise be to Allah, Who hath not taken unto Himself a son, and Who hath no partner in the Sovereignty, nor hath He any protecting friend through dependence. And magnify Him with all magnificence.	And say: (All) praise is due to Allah, Who has not taken a son and Who has not a partner in the kingdom, and Who has not a helper to save Him from disgrace; and proclaim His greatness magnifying (Him).

Chapter 18:

AL-KAHF (THE CAVE)

Total Verses: 110 Revealed At: MAKKA

In the name of Allah, the Most Beneficent, the Most Merciful.

18 001	Praise be to Allah, Who hath sent to His Servant the Book, and hath allowed therein no Crookedness:	Praise be to Allah Who hath revealed the Scripture unto His slave, and hath not placed therein any crookedness,	(All) praise is due to Allah, Who revealed the Book to His servant and did not make in it any crookedness.
18 002	(He hath made it) Straight (and Clear) in order that He may warn (the godless) of a terrible Punishment from Him, and that He may give Glad Tidings to the Believers who work righteous deeds, that they shall have a goodly Reward,	(But hath made it) straight, to give warning of stern punishment from Him, and to bring unto the believers who do good works the news that theirs will be a fair reward,	Rightly directing, that he might give warning of severe punishment from Him and give good news to the believers who do good that they shall have a goodly reward,
18 003	Wherein they shall remain for ever:	Wherein they will abide for ever;	Staying in it for ever;
18 004	Further, that He may warn those (also) who say, "Allah hath begotten a son":	And to warn those who say: Allah hath chosen a son,	And warn those who say: Allah has taken a son.

18 005	No knowledge have they of such a thing, nor had their fathers. It is a grievous thing that issues from their mouths as a saying what they say is nothing but falsehood!	(A thing) whereof they have no knowledge, nor (had) their fathers, Dreadful is the word that cometh out of their mouths. They speak naught but a lie.	They have no knowledge of it, nor had their fathers; a grievous word it is that comes out of their mouths; they speak nothing but a lie.
18 006	Thou wouldst only, perchance, fret thyself to death, following after them, in grief, if they believe not in this Message.	Yet it may be, if they believe not in this statement, that thou (Muhammad) wilt torment thy soul with grief over their footsteps.	Then maybe you will kill yourself with grief, sorrowing after them, if they do not believe in this announcement.
18 007	That which is on earth we have made but as a glittering show for the earth, in order that We may test them - as to which of them are best in conduct.	Lo! We have placed all that is on the earth as an ornament thereof that We may try them: which of them is best in conduct.	Surely We have made whatever is on the earth an embellishment for it, so that We may try them (as to) which of them is best in works.
18 008	Verily what is on earth we shall make but as dust and dry soil (without growth or herbage).	And lo! We shall make all that is thereon a barren mound.	And most surely We will make what is on it bare ground without herbage.
18 009	Or dost thou reflect that the Companions of the Cave and of the Inscription were wonders among Our Sign?	Or deemest thou that the People of the Cave and the Inscription are a wonder among Our portents?	Or, do you think that the Fellows of the Cave and the Inscription were of Our wonderful signs?
18 010	Behold, the youths betook themselves to the Cave: they said, "Our Lord! bestow on us Mercy from Thyself, and dispose of our affair for us in the right way!"	When the young men fled for refuge to the Cave and said: Our Lord! Give us mercy from Thy presence, and shape for us right conduct in our plight.	When the youths sought refuge in the cave, they said: Our Lord! grant us mercy from Thee, and provide for us a right course in our affair.
18 011	Then We draw (a veil) over their ears, for a number of years, in the Cave, (so that they heard not):	Then We sealed up their hearing in the Cave for a number of years.	So We prevented them from hearing in the cave for a number of years.
18 012	Then We roused them, in order to test which of the two parties was best at calculating the term of years they had tarried!	And afterward We raised them up that We might know which of the two parties would best calculate the time that they had tarried.	Then We raised them up that We might know which of the two parties was best able to compute the time for which they remained.
18 013	We relate to thee their story in truth: they were youths who believed in their Lord, and We advanced them in guidance:	We narrate unto thee their story with truth. Lo! they were young men who believed in their Lord, and We increased them in guidance.	We relate to you their story with the truth; surely they were youths who believed in their Lord and We increased them in guidance.
18 014	We gave strength to their hearts: Behold, they stood up and said: Our Lord is the Lord of the heavens and of the earth: never shall we call upon any god other than Him: if we did, we should indeed have uttered an enormity!"	And We made firm their hearts when they stood forth and said: Our Lord is the Lord of the heavens and the earth. We cry unto no God beside Him, for then should we utter an enormity.	And We strengthened their hearts with patience, when they stood up and said: Our Lord is the Lord of the heavens and the earth; we will by no means call upon any god besides Him, for then indeed we should have said an extravagant thing.
18 015	"These our people have taken for worship gods other than Him: why do they not bring forward an authority clear (and convincing) for what they do? Who doth more wrong than such as invent a falsehood against Allah?"	These, our people, have chosen (other) gods beside Him though they bring no clear warrant (vouchsafed) to them. And who doth greater wrong than he who inventeth a lie concerning Allah?	These our people have taken gods besides Him; why do they not produce any clear authority in their support? Who is then more unjust than he who forges a lie against Allah?

18 016	"When ye turn away from them and the things they worship other than Allah, betake yourselves to the Cave: Your Lord will shower His mercies on you and disposes of your affair towards comfort and ease."	And when ye withdraw from them and that which they worship except Allah, then seek refuge in the Cave; your Lord will spread for you of His mercy and will prepare for you a pillow in your plight.	And when you forsake them and what they worship save Allah, betake yourselves for refuge to the cave; your Lord will extend to you largely of His mercy and provide for you a profitable course in your affair.
18 017	Thou wouldst have seen the sun, when it rose, declining to the right from their Cave, and when it set, turning away from them to the left, while they lay in the open space in the midst of the Cave. Such are among the Signs of Allah: He whom Allah, guides is rightly guided; but he whom Allah leaves to stray,- for him wilt thou find no protector to lead him to the Right Way.	And thou mightest have seen the sun when it rose move away from their cave to the right, and when it set go past them on the left, and they were in the cleft thereof. That was (one) of the portents of Allah. He whom Allah guideth, he indeed is led aright, and he whom He sendeth astray, for him thou wilt not find a guiding friend.	And you might see the sun when it rose, decline from their cave towards the right hand, and when it set, leave them behind on the left while they were in a wide space thereof. This is of the signs of Allah; whomsoever Allah guides, he is the rightly guided one, and whomsoever He causes to err, you shall not find for him any friend to lead (him) aright.
18 018	Thou wouldst have deemed them awake, whilst they were asleep, and We turned them on their right and on their left sides: their dog stretching forth his two fore-legs on the threshold: if thou hadst come up on to them, thou wouldst have certainly turned back from them in flight, and wouldst certainly have been filled with terror of them.	And thou wouldst have deemed them waking though they were asleep, and We caused them to turn over to the right and the left, and their dog stretching out his paws on the threshold. If thou hadst observed them closely thou hadst assuredly turned away from them in flight, and hadst been filled with awe of them.	And you might think them awake while they were asleep and We turned them about to the right and to the left, while their dog (lay) outstretching its paws at the entrance; if you looked at them you would certainly turn back from them in flight, and you would certainly be filled with awe because of them.
18 019	Such (being their state), we raised them up (from sleep), that they might question each other. Said one of them, "How long have ye stayed (here)?" They said, "We have stayed (perhaps) a day, or part of a day." (At length) they (all) said, "Allah (alone) knows best how long ye have stayed here.... Now send ye then one of you with this money of yours to the town: let him find out which is the best food (to be had) and bring some to you, that (ye may) satisfy your hunger therewith: And let him behave with care and courtesy, and let him not inform any one about you."	And in like manner We awakened them that they might question one another. A speaker from among them said: How long have ye tarried? They said: We have tarried a day or some part of a day, (Others) said: Your Lord best knoweth what ye have tarried. Now send one of you with this your silver coin unto the city, and let him see what food is purest there and bring you a supply thereof. Let him be courteous and let no man know of you.	And thus did We rouse them that they might question each other. A speaker among them said: How long have you tarried? They said: We have tarried for a day or a part of a day. (Others) said: Your Lord knows best how long you have tarried. Now send one of you with this silver (coin) of yours to the city, then let him see which of them has purest food, so let him bring you provision from it, and let him behave with gentleness, and by no means make your case known to any one:
18 020	"For if they should come upon you, they would stone you or force you to return to their cult, and in that case ye would never attain prosperity."	For they, if they should come to know of you, will stone you or turn you back to their religion; then ye will never prosper.	For surely if they prevail against you they would stone you to death or force you back to their religion, and then you will never succeed.

18 021	Thus did We make their case known to the people, that they might know that the promise of Allah is true, and that there can be no doubt about the Hour of Judgment. Behold, they dispute among themselves as to their affair. (Some) said, "Construct a building over them": Their Lord knows best about them: those who prevailed over their affair said, "Let us surely build a place of worship over them."	And in like manner We disclosed them (to the people of the city) that they might know that the promise of Allah is true, and that, as for the Hour, there is no doubt concerning it. When (the people of the city) disputed of their case among themselves, they said: Build over them a building; their Lord knoweth best concerning them. Those who won their point said: We verily shall build a place of worship over them.	And thus did We make (men) to get knowledge of them that they might know that Allah's promise is true and that as for the hour there is no doubt about it. When they disputed among themselves about their affair and said: Erect an edifice over them-- their Lord best knows them. Those who prevailed in their affair said: We will certainly raise a masjid over them.
18 022	(Some) say they were three, the dog being the fourth among them; (others) say they were five, the dog being the sixth,- doubtfully guessing at the unknown; (yet others) say they were seven, the dog being the eighth. Say thou: "My Lord knoweth best their number; It is but few that know their (real case)." Enter not, therefore, into controversies concerning them, except on a matter that is clear, nor consult any of them about (the affair of) the Sleepers.	(Some) will say: They were three, their dog the fourth, and (some) say: Five, their dog the sixth, guessing at random; and (some) say: Seven, and their dog the eighth. Say (O Muhammad): My Lord is Best Aware of their number. None knoweth them save a few. So contend not concerning them except with an outward contending, and ask not any of them to pronounce concerning them.	(Some) say: (They are) three, the fourth of them being their dog; and (others) say: Five, the sixth of them being their dog, making conjectures at what is unknown; and (others yet) say: Seven, and the eighth of them is their dog. Say: My Lord best knows their number, none knows them but a few; therefore contend not in the matter of them but with an outward contention, and do not question concerning them any of them.
18 023	Nor say of anything, "I shall be sure to do so and so tomorrow"-	And say not of anything: Lo! I shall do that tomorrow,	And do not say of anything: Surely I will do it tomorrow,
18 024	Without adding, "So please Allah!" and call thy Lord to mind when thou forgettest, and say, "I hope that my Lord will guide me ever closer (even) than this to the right road."	Except if Allah will. And remember thy Lord when thou forgettest, and say: It may be that my Lord guideth me unto a nearer way of truth than this.	Unless Allah pleases; and remember your Lord when you forget and say: Maybe my Lord will guide me to a nearer course to the right than this.
18 025	So they stayed in their Cave three hundred years, and (some) add nine (more)	And (it is said) they tarried in their Cave three hundred years and add nine.	And they remained in their cave three hundred years and (some) add (another) nine.
18 026	Say: "Allah knows best how long they stayed: with Him is (the knowledge of) the secrets of the heavens and the earth: how clearly He sees, how finely He hears (everything)! They have no protector other than Him; nor does He share His Command with any person whatsoever."	Say: Allah is Best Aware how long they tarried. His is the Invisible of the heavens and the earth. How clear of sight is He and keen of hearing! They have no protecting friend beside Him, and He maketh none to share in His government.	Say: Allah knows best how long they remained; to Him are (known) the unseen things of the heavens and the earth; how clear His sight and how clear His hearing! There is none to be a guardian for them besides Him, and He does not make any one His associate in His Judgment.
18 027	And recite (and teach) what has been revealed to thee of the Book of thy Lord: none can change His Words, and none wilt thou find as a refuge other than Him.	And recite that which hath been revealed unto thee of the Scripture of thy Lord. There is none who can change His words, and thou wilt find no refuge beside Him.	And recite what has been revealed to you of the Book of your Lord, there is none who can alter His words; and you shall not find any refuge besides Him.

18 028	And keep thy soul content with those who call on their Lord morning and evening, seeking His Face; and let not thine eyes pass beyond them, seeking the pomp and glitter of this Life; no obey any whose heart We have permitted to neglect the remembrance of Us, one who follows his own desires, whose case has gone beyond all bounds.	Restrain thyself along with those who cry unto their Lord at morn and evening, seeking His Countenance; and let not thine eyes overlook them, desiring the pomp of the life of the world; and obey not him whose heart We have made heedless of Our remembrance, who followeth his own lust and whose case hath been abandoned.	And withhold yourself with those who call on their Lord morning and evening desiring His goodwill, and let not your eyes pass from them, desiring the beauties of this world's life; and do not follow him whose heart We have made unmindful to Our remembrance, and he follows his low desires and his case is one in which due bounds are exceeded.
18 029	Say, "The truth is from your Lord". Let him who will believe, and let him who will, reject (it): for the wrong-doers We have prepared a Fire whose (smoke and flames), like the walls and roof of a tent, will hem them in: if they implore relief they will be granted water like melted brass, that will scald their faces, how dreadful the drink! How uncomfortable a couch to recline on!	Say: (It is) the truth from the Lord of you (all). Then whosoever will, let him believe, and whosoever will, let him disbelieve. Lo! We have prepared for disbelievers Fire. Its tent encloseth them. If they ask for showers, they will be showered with water like to molten lead which burneth the faces. Calamitous the drink and ill the resting-place!	And say: The truth is from your Lord, so let him who please believe, and let him who please disbelieve; surely We have prepared for the iniquitous a fire, the curtains of which shall encompass them about; and if they cry for water, they shall be given water like molten brass which will scald their faces; evil the drink and ill the resting-place.
18 030	As to those who believe and work righteousness, verily We shall not suffer to perish the reward of any who do a (single) righteous deed.	Lo! as for those who believe and do good works - Lo! We suffer not the reward of one whose work is goodly to be lost.	Surely (as for) those who believe and do good, We do not waste the reward of him who does a good work.
18 031	For them will be Gardens of Eternity; beneath them rivers will flow; they will be adorned therein with bracelets of gold, and they will wear green garments of fine silk and heavy brocade: They will recline therein on raised thrones. How good the recompense! How beautiful a couch to recline on!	As for such, theirs will be Gardens of Eden, wherein rivers flow beneath them; therein they will be given armlets of gold and will wear green robes of finest silk and gold embroidery, reclining upon throne therein. Blest the reward, and fair the resting-place!	These it is for whom are gardens of perpetuity beneath which rivers flow, ornaments shall be given to them therein of bracelets of gold, and they shall wear green robes of fine silk and thick silk brocade interwoven with gold, reclining therein on raised couches; excellent the recompense and goodly the resting place.
18 032	Set forth to them the parable of two men: for one of them We provided two gardens of grape-vines and surrounded them with date palms; in between the two We placed corn-fields.	Coin for them a similitude: Two men, unto one of whom We had assigned two gardens of grapes, and We had surrounded both with date-palms and had put between them tillage.	And set forth to them a parable of two men; for one of them We made two gardens of grape vines, and We surrounded them both with palms, and in the midst of them We made cornfields.
18 033	Each of those gardens brought forth its produce, and failed not in the least therein: in the midst of them We caused a river to flow.	Each of the gardens gave its fruit and withheld naught thereof. And We caused a river to gush forth therein.	Both these gardens yielded their fruits, and failed not aught thereof, and We caused a river to gush forth in their midst,
18 034	(Abundant) was the produce this man had: he said to his companion, in the course of a mutual argument: "more wealth have I than you, and more honour and power in (my following of) men."	And he had fruit. And he said unto his comrade, when he spake with him: I am more than thee in wealth, and stronger in respect of men.	And he possessed much wealth; so he said to his companion, while he disputed with him: I have greater wealth than you, and am mightier in followers.
18 035	He went into his garden in a state (of mind) unjust to his soul: He said, "I deem not that this will ever perish,"	And he went into his garden, while he (thus) wronged himself. He said: I think not that all this will ever perish.	And he entered his garden while he was unjust to himself. He said: I do not think that this will ever perish,

18 036	"Nor do I deem that the Hour (of Judgment) will (ever) come: Even if I am brought back to my Lord, I shall surely find (there) something better in exchange."	I think not that the Hour will ever come, and if indeed I am brought back unto my Lord I surely shall find better than this as a resort.	And I do not think the hour will come, and even if I am returned to my Lord I will most certainly find a returning place better than this.
18 037	His companion said to him, in the course of the argument with him: Dost thou deny Him Who created thee out of dust, then out of a sperm-drop, then fashioned thee into a man?"	His comrade, when he (thus) spake with him, exclaimed: Disbelievest thou in Him Who created thee of dust, then of a drop (of seed), and then fashioned thee a man?	His companion said to him while disputing with him: Do you disbelieve in Him Who created you from dust, then from a small seed, then He made you a perfect man?
18 038	"But (I think) for my part that He is Allah, My Lord, and none shall I associate with my Lord."	But He is Allah, my Lord, and I ascribe unto my Lord no partner.	But as for me, He, Allah, is my Lord, and I do not associate anyone with my Lord.
18 039	"Why didst thou not, as thou wentest into thy garden, say: 'Allah's will (be done)! There is no power but with Allah!' If thou dost see me less than thee in wealth and sons,"	If only, when thou enteredst thy garden, thou hadst said: That which Allah willeth (will come to pass)! There is no strength save in Allah! Though thou seest me as less than thee in wealth and children,	And wherefore did you not say when you entered your garden: It is as Allah has pleased, there is no power save in Allah? If you consider me to be inferior to you in wealth and children,
18 040	"It may be that my Lord will give me something better than thy garden, and that He will send on thy garden thunderbolts (by way of reckoning) from heaven, making it (but) slippery sand!-"	Yet it may be that my Lord will give me better than thy garden, and will send on it a bolt from heaven, and some morning it will be a smooth hillside,	Then maybe my Lord will give me what is better than your garden, and send on it a thunderbolt from heaven so that it shall become even ground without plant,
18 041	"Or the water of the garden will run off underground so that thou wilt never be able to find it."	Or some morning the water thereof will be lost in the earth so that thou canst not make search for it.	Or its waters should sink down into the ground so that you are unable to find it.
18 042	So his fruits (and enjoyment) were encompassed (with ruin), and he remained twisting and turning his hands over what he had spent on his property, which had (now) tumbled to pieces to its very foundations, and he could only say, "Woe is me! Would I had never ascribed partners to my Lord and Cherisher!"	And his fruit was beset (with destruction). Then began he to wring his hands for all that he had spent upon it, when (now) it was all ruined on its trellises, and to say: Would that I had ascribed no partner to my Lord!	And his wealth was destroyed; so he began to wring his hands for what he had spent on it, while it lay, having fallen down upon its roofs, and he said: Ah me! would that I had not associated anyone with my Lord.
18 043	Nor had he numbers to help him against Allah, nor was he able to deliver himself.	And he had no troop of men to help him as against Allah, nor could he save himself.	And he had no host to help him besides Allah nor could he defend himself.
18 044	There, the (only) protection comes from Allah, the True One. He is the Best to reward, and the Best to give success.	In this case is protection only from Allah, the True, He is Best for reward, and best for consequence.	Here is protection only Allah's, the True One; He is best in (the giving of) reward and best in requiting.
18 045	Set forth to them the similitude of the life of this world: It is like the rain which we send down from the skies: the earth's vegetation absorbs it, but soon it becomes dry stubble, which the winds do scatter: it is (only) Allah who prevails over all things.	And coin for them the similitude of the life of the world as water which We send down from the sky, and the vegetation of the earth mingleth with it and then becometh dry twigs that the winds scatter. Allah is able to do all things.	And set forth to them parable of the life of this world: like water which We send down from the cloud so the herbage of the earth becomes tangled on account of it, then it becomes dry broken into pieces which the winds scatter; and Allah is the holder of power over all things.

18 046	Wealth and sons are allurements of the life of this world: But the things that endure, good deeds, are best in the sight of thy Lord, as rewards, and best as (the foundation for) hopes.	Wealth and children are an ornament of the life of the world. But the good deeds which endure are better in thy Lord's sight for reward, and better in respect of hope.	Wealth and children are an adornment of the life of this world; and the ever-abiding, the good works, are better with your Lord in reward and better in expectation.
18 047	One Day We shall remove the mountains, and thou wilt see the earth as a level stretch, and We shall gather them, all together, nor shall We leave out any one of them.	And (bethink you of) the Day when we remove the hills and ye see the earth emerging, and We gather them together so as to leave not one of them behind.	And the day on which We will cause the mountains to pass away and you will see the earth a levelled plain and We will gather them and leave not any one of them behind.
18 048	And they will be marshalled before thy Lord in ranks, (with the announcement), "Now have ye come to Us (bare) as We created you first: aye, ye thought We shall not fulfill the appointment made to you to meet (Us)!":	And they are set before thy Lord in ranks (and it is said unto them): Now verily have ye come unto Us as We created you at the first. But ye thought that We had set no tryst for you.	And they shall be brought before your Lord, standing in ranks: Now certainly you have come to Us as We created you at first. Nay, you thought that We had not appointed to you a time of the fulfillment of the promise.
18 049	And the Book (of Deeds) will be placed (before you); and thou wilt see the sinful in great terror because of what is (recorded) therein; they will say, "Ah! woe to us! what a Book is this! It leaves out nothing small or great, but takes account thereof!" They will find all that they did, placed before them: And not one will thy Lord treat with injustice.	And the Book is placed, and thou seest the guilty fearful of that which is therein, and they say: What kind of a Book is this that leaveth not a small thing nor a great thing but hath counted it! And they find all that they did confronting them, and thy Lord wrongeth no-one.	And the Book shall be placed, then you will see the guilty fearing from what is in it, and they will say: Ah! woe to us! what a book is this! it does not omit a small one nor a great one, but numbers them (all); and what they had done they shall find present (there); and your Lord does not deal unjustly with anyone.
18 050	Behold! We said to the angels, "Bow down to Adam": They bowed down except Iblis. He was one of the jinns, and he broke the Command of his Lord. Will ye then take him and his progeny as protectors rather than Me? And they are enemies to you! Evil would be the exchange for the wrong-doers!	And (remember) when We said unto the angels: Fall prostrate before Adam, and they fell prostrate, all save Iblis. He was of the jinn, so he rebelled against his Lord's command. Will ye choose him and his seed for your protecting friends instead of Me, when they are an enemy unto you? Calamitous is the exchange for evil-doers.	And when We said to the angels: Make obeisance to Adam; they made obeisance but Iblis (did it not). He was of the jinn, so he transgressed the commandment of his Lord. What! would you then take him and his offspring for friends rather than Me, and they are your enemies? Evil is (this) change for the unjust.
18 051	I called them not to witness the creation of the heavens and the earth, nor (even) their own creation: nor is it for helpers such as Me to take as lead (men) astray!	I made them not to witness the creation of the heavens and the earth, nor their own creation; nor choose I misleaders for (My) helpers.	I did not make them witnesses of the creation of the heavens and the earth, nor of the creation of their own souls; nor could I take those who lead (others) astray for aiders.
18 052	One Day He will say, "Call on those whom ye thought to be My partners," and they will call on them, but they will not listen to them; and We shall make for them a place of common perdition.	And (be mindful of) the Day when He will say: Call those partners of Mine whom ye pretended. Then they will cry unto them, but they will not hear their prayer, and We shall set a gulf of doom between them.	And on the day when He shall say: Call on those whom you considered to be My associates. So they shall call on them, but they shall not answer them, and We will cause a separation between them.
18 053	And the Sinful shall see the fire and apprehend that they have to fall therein: no means will they find to turn away therefrom.	And the guilty behold the Fire and know that they are about to fall therein, and they find no way of escape thence.	And the guilty shall see the fire, then they shall know that they are going to fall into it, and they shall not find a place to which to turn away from it.

18 054	We have explained in detail in this Qur'an, for the benefit of mankind, every kind of similitude: but man is, in most things, contentious.	And verily We have displayed for mankind in this Qur'an all manner of similitudes, but man is more than anything contentious.	And certainly We have explained in this Quran every kind of example, and man is most of all given to contention.
18 055	And what is there to keep back men from believing, now that Guidance has come to them, nor from praying for forgiveness from their Lord, but that (they ask that) the ways of the ancients be repeated with them, or the Wrath be brought to them face to face?	And naught hindereth mankind from believing when the guidance cometh unto them, and from asking forgiveness of their Lord unless (it be that they wish) that the judgment of the men of old should come upon them or (that) they should be confronted with the Doom.	And nothing prevents men from believing when the guidance comes to them, and from asking forgiveness of their Lord, except that what happened to the ancients should overtake them, or that the chastisement should come face to face with them.
18 056	We only send the messengers to give Glad Tidings and to give warnings: But the unbelievers dispute with vain argument, in order therewith to weaken the truth, and they treat My Signs as a jest, as also the fact that they are warned!	We send not the messengers save as bearers of good news and warners. Those who disbelieve contend with falsehood in order to refute the Truth thereby. And they take Our revelations and that wherewith they are threatened as a jest.	And We do not send messengers but as givers of good news and warning, and those who disbelieve make a false contention that they may render null thereby the truth, and they take My communications and that with which they are warned for a mockery.
18 057	And who doth more wrong than one who is reminded of the Signs of his Lord, but turns away from them, forgetting the (deeds) which his hands have sent forth? Verily We have set veils over their hearts lest they should understand this, and over their ears, deafness, if thou callest them to guidance, even then will they never accept guidance.	And who doth greater wrong than he who hath been reminded of the revelations of his Lord, yet turneth away from them and forgetteth what his hands send forward (to the Judgment)? Lo! on their hearts We have placed coverings so that they understand not, and in their ears a deafness. And though thou call them to the guidance, in that case they can never be led aright.	And who is more unjust than he who is reminded of the communications of his Lord, then he turns away from them and forgets what his two hands have sent before? Surely We have placed veils over their hearts lest they should understand it and a heaviness in their ears; and if you call them to the guidance, they will not ever follow the right course in that case.
18 058	But your Lord is Most Forgiving, Full of Mercy. If He were to call them (at once) to account for what they have earned, then surely He would have hastened their punishment: but they have their appointed time, beyond which they will find no refuge.	Thy Lord is the Forgiver, Full of Mercy. If He took them to task (now) for what they earn, He would hasten on the doom for them; but theirs is an appointed term from which they will find no escape.	And your Lord is Forgiving, the Lord of Mercy; were He to punish them for what they earn, He would certainly have hastened the chastisement for them; but for them there is an appointed time from which they shall not find a refuge.
18 059	Such were the populations we destroyed when they committed iniquities; but we fixed an appointed time for their destruction.	And (all) those townships! We destroyed them when they did wrong, and We appointed a fixed time for their destruction.	And (as for) these towns, We destroyed them when they acted unjustly, and We have appointed a time for their destruction.
18 060	Behold, Moses said to his attendant, "I will not give up until I reach the junction of the two seas or (until) I spend years and years in travel."	And when Moses said unto his servant: I will not give up until I reach the point where the two rivers meet, though I march on for ages.	And when Musa said to his servant: I will not cease until I reach the junction of the two rivers or I will go on for years.
18 061	But when they reached the Junction, they forgot (about) their Fish, which took its course through the sea (straight) as in a tunnel.	And when they reached the point where the two met, they forgot their fish, and it took its way into the waters, being free.	So when they had reached the junction of the two (rivers) they forgot their fish, and it took its way into the sea, going away.
18 062	When they had passed on (some distance), Moses said to his attendant: Bring us our early meal; truly we have suffered much fatigue at this (stage of) our journey."	And when they had gone further, he said unto his servant: Bring us our breakfast. Verily we have found fatigue in this our journey.	But when they had gone farther, he said to his servant: Bring to us our morning meal, certainly we have met with fatigue from this our journey.

18 063	He replied: "Sawest thou (what happened) when we betook ourselves to the rock? I did indeed forget (about) the Fish: none but Satan made me forget to tell (you) about it: it took its course through the sea in a marvellous way!"	He said: Didst thou see, when we took refuge on the rock, and I forgot the fish - and none but Satan caused me to forget to mention it - it took its way into the waters by a marvel.	He said: Did you see when we took refuge on the rock then I forgot the fish, and nothing made me forget to speak of it but the Shaitan, and it took its way into the river; what a wonder!
18 064	Moses said: "That was what we were seeking after:" So they went back on their footsteps, following (the path they had come).	He said: This is that which we have been seeking. So they retraced their steps again.	He said: This is what we sought for; so they returned retracing their footsteps.
18 065	So they found one of Our servants, on whom We had bestowed Mercy from Ourselves and whom We had taught knowledge from Our own Presence.	Then found they one of Our slaves, unto whom We had given mercy from Us, and had taught him knowledge from Our presence.	Then they found one from among Our servants whom We had granted mercy from Us and whom We had taught knowledge from Ourselves.
18 066	Moses said to him: "May I follow thee, on the footing that thou teach me something of the (Higher) Truth which thou hast been taught?"	Moses said unto him: May I follow thee, to the end that thou mayst teach me right conduct of that which thou hast been taught?	Musa said to him: Shall I follow you on condition that you should teach me right knowledge of what you have been taught?
18 067	(The other) said: "Verily thou wilt not be able to have patience with me!"	He said: Lo! thou canst not bear with me.	He said: Surely you cannot have patience with me
18 068	"And how canst thou have patience about things about which thy understanding is not complete?"	How canst thou bear with that whereof thou canst not compass any knowledge?	And how can you have patience in that of which you have not got a comprehensive knowledge?
18 069	Moses said: "Thou wilt find me, if Allah so will, (truly) patient: nor shall I disobey thee in aught."	He said: Allah willing, thou shalt find me patient and I shall not in aught gainsay thee.	He said: If Allah pleases, you will find me patient and I shall not disobey you in any matter.
18 070	The other said: "If then thou wouldst follow me, ask me no questions about anything until I myself speak to thee concerning it."	He said: Well, if thou go with me, ask me not concerning aught till I myself make mention of it unto thee.	He said: If you would follow me, then do not question me about any thing until I myself speak to you about it.
18 071	So they both proceeded: until, when they were in the boat, he scuttled it. Said Moses: "Hast thou scuttled it in order to drown those in it? Truly a strange thing hast thou done!"	So they twain set out till, when they were in the ship, he made a hole therein. (Moses) said: Hast thou made a hole therein to drown the folk thereof? Thou verily hast done a dreadful thing.	So they went (their way) until when they embarked in the boat he made a hole in it. (Musa) said: Have you made a hole in it to drown its inmates? Certainly you have done a grievous thing.
18 072	He answered: "Did I not tell thee that thou canst have no patience with me?"	He said: Did I not tell thee that thou couldst not bear with me?	He said: Did I not say that you will not be able to have patience with me?
18 073	Moses said: "Rebuke me not for forgetting, nor grieve me by raising difficulties in my case."	(Moses) said: Be not wroth with me that I forgot, and be not hard upon me for my fault.	He said: Blame me not for what I forgot, and do not constrain me to a difficult thing in my affair.
18 074	Then they proceeded: until, when they met a young man, he slew him. Moses said: "Hast thou slain an innocent person who had slain none? Truly a foul (unheard of) thing hast thou done!"	So they twain journeyed on till, when they met a lad, he slew him. (Moses) said: What! Hast thou slain an innocent soul who hath slain no man? Verily thou hast done a horrid thing.	So they went on until, when they met a boy, he slew him. (Musa) said: Have you slain an innocent person otherwise than for manslaughter? Certainly you have done an evil thing.
18 075	He answered: "Did I not tell thee that thou canst have no patience with me?"	He said: Did I not tell thee that thou couldst not bear with me?	He said: Did I not say to you that you will not be able to have patience with me?
18 076	(Moses) said: "If ever I ask thee about anything after this, keep me not in thy company: then wouldst thou have received (full) excuse from my side."	(Moses) said: If I ask thee after this concerning aught, keep not company with me. Thou hast received an excuse from me.	He said: If I ask you about anything after this, keep me not in your company; indeed you shall have (then) found an excuse in my case.

18 077	Then they proceeded: until, when they came to the inhabitants of a town, they asked them for food, but they refused them hospitality. They found there a wall on the point of falling down, but he set it up straight. (Moses) said: "If thou hadst wished, surely thou couldst have exacted some recompense for it!"	So they twain journeyed on till, when they came unto the folk of a certain township, they asked its folk for food, but they refused to make them guests. And they found therein a wall upon the point of falling into ruin, and he repaired it. (Moses) said: If thou hadst wished, thou couldst have taken payment for it.	So they went on until when they came to the people of a town, they asked them for food, but they refused to entertain them as guests. Then they found in it a wall which was on the point of falling, so he put it into a right state. (Musa) said: If you had pleased, you might certainly have taken a recompense for it.
18 078	He answered: "This is the parting between me and thee: now will I tell thee the interpretation of (those things) over which thou wast unable to hold patience."	He said: This is the parting between thee and me! I will announce unto thee the interpretation of that thou couldst not bear with patience.	He said: This shall be separation between me and you; now I will inform you of the significance of that with which you could not have patience.
18 079	"As for the boat, it belonged to certain men in dire want: they plied on the water: I but wished to render it unserviceable, for there was after them a certain king who seized on every boat by force."	As for the ship, it belonged to poor people working on the river, and I wished to mar it, for there was a king behind them who is taking every ship by force.	As for the boat, it belonged to (some) poor men who worked on the river and I wished that I should damage it, and there was behind them a king who seized every boat by force.
18 080	"As for the youth, his parents were people of Faith, and we feared that he would grieve them by obstinate rebellion and ingratitude (to Allah and man)."	And as for the lad, his parents were believers and we feared lest he should oppress them by rebellion and disbelief.	And as for the boy, his parents were believers and we feared lest he should make disobedience and ingratitude to come upon them:
18 081	"So we desired that their Lord would give them in exchange (a son) better in purity (of conduct) and closer in affection."	And we intended that their Lord should change him for them for one better in purity and nearer to mercy.	So we desired that their Lord might give them in his place one better than him in purity and nearer to having compassion.
18 082	"As for the wall, it belonged to two youths, orphans, in the Town; there was, beneath it, a buried treasure, to which they were entitled: their father had been a righteous man: So thy Lord desired that they should attain their age of full strength and get out their treasure - a mercy (and favour) from thy Lord. I did it not of my own accord. Such is the interpretation of (those things) over which thou wast unable to hold patience."	And as for the wall, it belonged to two orphan boys in the city, and there was beneath it a treasure belonging to them, and their father had been righteous, and thy Lord intended that they should come to their full strength and should bring forth their treasure as a mercy from their Lord; and I did it not upon my own command. Such is the interpretation of that wherewith thou couldst not bear.	And as for the wall, it belonged to two orphan boys in the city, and there was beneath it a treasure belonging to them, and their father was a righteous man; so your Lord desired that they should attain their maturity and take out their treasure, a mercy from your Lord, and I did not do it of my own accord. This is the significance of that with which you could not have patience.
18 083	They ask thee concerning Zulqarnain. Say, "I will rehearse to you something of his story."	They will ask thee of Dhu'l-Qarneyn. Say: I shall recite unto you a remembrance of him.	And they ask you about Zulqarnain. Say: I will recite to you an account of him.
18 084	Verily We established his power on earth, and We gave him the ways and the means to all ends.	Lo! We made him strong in the land and gave him unto every thing a road.	Surely We established him in the land and granted him means of access to every thing.
18 085	One (such) way he followed,	And he followed a road	So he followed a course.
18 086	Until, when he reached the setting of the sun, he found it set in a spring of murky water: Near it he found a People: We said: "O Zulqarnain! (thou hast authority,) either to punish them, or to treat them with kindness."	Till, when he reached the setting-place of the sun, he found it setting in a muddy spring, and found a people thereabout. We said: O Dhu'l-Qarneyn! Either punish or show them kindness.	Until when he reached the place where the sun set, he found it going down into a black sea, and found by it a people. We said: O Zulqarnain! either give them a chastisement or do them a benefit.

18 087	He said: "Whoever doth wrong, him shall we punish; then shall he be sent back to his Lord; and He will punish him with a punishment unheard-of (before)."	He said: As for him who doeth wrong, we shall punish him, and then he will be brought back unto his Lord, Who will punish him with awful punishment!	He said: As to him who is injust, we will chastise him, then shall he be returned to his Lord, and He will chastise him with an exemplary chastisement:
18 088	"But whoever believes, and works righteousness,- he shall have a goodly reward, and easy will be his task as We order it by our Command."	But as for him who believeth and doeth right, good will be his reward, and We shall speak unto him a mild command.	And as for him who believes and does good, he shall have goodly reward, and We will speak to him an easy word of Our command.
18 089	Then followed he (another) way,	Then he followed a road	Then he followed (another) course.
18 090	Until, when he came to the rising of the sun, he found it rising on a people for whom We had provided no covering protection against the sun.	Till, when he reached the rising-place of the sun, he found it rising on a people for whom We had appointed no shelter therefrom.	Until when he reached the land of the rising of the sun, he found it rising on a people to whom We had given no shelter from It;
18 091	(He left them) as they were: We completely understood what was before him.	So (it was). And We knew all concerning him.	Even so! and We had a full knowledge of what he had.
18 092	Then followed he (another) way,	Then he followed a road	Then he followed (another) course.
18 093	Until, when he reached (a tract) between two mountains, he found, beneath them, a people who scarcely understood a word.	Till, when he came between the two mountains, he found upon their hither side a folk that scarce could understand a saying.	Until when he reached (a place) between the two mountains, he found on that side of them a people who could hardly understand a word.
18 094	They said: "O Zul-qarnain! the Gog and Magog (People) do great mischief on earth: shall we then render thee tribute in order that thou mightest erect a barrier between us and them?"	They said: O Dhu'l-Qarneyn! Lo! Gog and Magog are spoiling the land. So may we pay thee tribute on condition that thou set a barrier between us and them?	They said: O Zulqarnain! surely Gog and Magog make mischief in the land. Shall we then pay you a tribute on condition that you should raise a barrier between us and them.
18 095	He said: "(The power) in which my Lord has established me is better (than tribute): Help me therefore with strength (and labour): I will erect a strong barrier between you and them:"	He said: That wherein my Lord hath established me is better (than your tribute). Do but help me with strength (of men), I will set between you and them a bank.	He said: That in which my Lord has established me is better, therefore you only help me with workers, I will make a fortified barrier between you and them;
18 096	"Bring me blocks of iron." At length, when he had filled up the space between the two steep mountain-sides, He said, "Blow (with your bellows)" Then, when he had made it (red) as fire, he said: "Bring me, that I may pour over it, molten lead."	Give me pieces of iron - till, when he had levelled up (the gap) between the cliffs, he said: Blow! - till, when he had made it a fire, he said: Bring me molten copper to pour thereon.	Bring me blocks of iron; until when he had filled up the space between the two mountain sides, he said: Blow, until when he had made it (as) fire, he said: Bring me molten brass which I may pour over it.
18 097	Thus were they made powerless to scale it or to dig through it.	And (Gog and Magog) were not able to surmount, nor could they pierce (it).	So they were not able to scale it nor could they make a hole in it.
18 098	He said: "This is a mercy from my Lord: But when the promise of my Lord comes to pass, He will make it into dust; and the promise of my Lord is true."	He said: This is a mercy from my Lord; but when the promise of my Lord cometh to pass, He will lay it low, for the promise of my Lord is true.	He said: This is a mercy from my Lord, but when the promise of my Lord comes to pass He will make it level with the ground, and the promise of my Lord is ever true.

18 099	On that day We shall leave them to surge like waves on one another: the trumpet will be blown, and We shall collect them all together.	And on that day we shall let some of them surge against others, and the Trumpet will be blown. Then We shall gather them together in one gathering.	And on that day We will leave a part of them in conflict with another part, and the trumpet will be blown, so We will gather them all together;
18 100	And We shall present Hell that day for Unbelievers to see, all spread out,-	On that day we shall present hell to the disbelievers, plain to view,	And We will bring forth hell, exposed to view, on that day before the unbelievers.
18 101	(Unbelievers) whose eyes had been under a veil from remembrance of Me, and who had been unable even to hear.	Those whose eyes were hoodwinked from My reminder, and who could not bear to hear.	They whose eyes were under a cover from My reminder and they could not even hear.
18 102	Do the Unbelievers think that they can take My servants as protectors besides Me? Verily We have prepared Hell for the Unbelievers for (their) entertainment.	Do the disbelievers reckon that they can choose My bondmen as protecting friends beside Me? Lo! We have prepared hell as a welcome for the disbelievers.	What! do then those who disbelieve think that they can take My servants to be guardians besides Me? Surely We have prepared hell for the entertainment of the unbelievers.
18 103	Say: "Shall we tell you of those who lose most in respect of their deeds?"-	Say: Shall We inform you who will be the greatest losers by their works?	Say: Shall We inform you of the greatest losers in (their) deeds?
18 104	"Those whose efforts have been wasted in this life, while they thought that they were acquiring good by their works?"	Those whose effort goeth astray in the life of the world, and yet they reckon that they do good work.	(These are) they whose labor is lost in this world's life and they think that they are well versed in skill of the work of hands.
18 105	They are those who deny the Signs of their Lord and the fact of their having to meet Him (in the Hereafter): vain will be their works, nor shall We, on the Day of Judgment, give them any weight.	Those are they who disbelieve in the revelations of their Lord and in the meeting with Him. Therefor their works are vain, and on the Day of Resurrection We assign no weight to them.	These are they who disbelieve in the communications of their Lord and His meeting, so their deeds become null, and therefore We will not set up a balance for them on the day of resurrection.
18 106	That is their reward, Hell, because they rejected Faith, and took My Signs and My Messengers by way of jest.	That is their reward: hell, because they disbelieved, and made a jest of Our revelations and Our messengers.	Thus it is that their recompense is hell, because they disbelieved and held My communications and My messengers in mockery.
18 107	As to those who believe and work righteous deeds, they have, for their entertainment, the Gardens of Paradise,	Lo! those who believe and do good works, theirs are the Gardens of Paradise for welcome,	Surely (as for) those who believe and do good deeds, their place of entertainment shall be the gardens of paradise,
18 108	Wherein they shall dwell (for aye): no change will they wish for from them.	Wherein they will abide, with no desire to be removed from thence.	Abiding therein; they shall not desire removal from them.
18 109	Say: "If the ocean were ink (wherewith to write out) the words of my Lord, sooner would the ocean be exhausted than would the words of my Lord, even if we added another ocean like it, for its aid."	Say: Though the sea became ink for the Words of my Lord, verily the sea would be used up before the words of my Lord were exhausted, even though We brought the like thereof to help.	Say: If the sea were ink for the words of my Lord, the sea would surely be consumed before the words of my Lord are exhausted, though We were to bring the like of that (sea) to add thereto.
18 110	Say: "I am but a man like yourselves, (but) the inspiration has come to me, that your Allah is one Allah: whoever expects to meet his Lord, let him work righteousness, and, in the worship of his Lord, admit no one as partner."	Say: I am only a mortal like you. My Lord inspireth in me that your Allah is only One Allah. And whoever hopeth for the meeting with his Lord, let him do righteous work, and make none sharer of the worship due unto his Lord.	Say: I am only a mortal like you; it is revealed to me that your god is one Allah, therefore whoever hopes to meet his Lord, he should do good deeds, and not join any one in the service of his Lord.

Chapter 19:

MARYAM (MARY)

Total Verses: 98 Revealed At: MAKKA

In the name of Allah, the Most Beneficent, the Most Merciful.

19 001	Kaf. Ha. Ya. 'Ain. Sad.	Kaf. Ha. Ya. A'in. Sad.		Kaf Ha Ya Ain Suad.
19 002	(This is) a recital of the Mercy of thy Lord to His servant Zakariya.	A mention of the mercy of thy Lord unto His servant Zachariah.		A mention of the mercy of your Lord to His servant Zakariya.
19 003	Behold! he cried to his Lord in secret,	When he cried unto his Lord a cry in secret,		When he called upon his Lord in a low voice,
19 004	Praying: "O my Lord! infirm indeed are my bones, and the hair of my head doth glisten with grey: but never am I unblest, O my Lord, in my prayer to Thee!"	Saying: My Lord! Lo! the bones of me wax feeble and my head is shining with grey hair, and I have never been unblest in prayer to Thee, my Lord.		He said: My Lord! surely my bones are weakened and my head flares with hoariness, and, my Lord! I have never been unsuccessful in my prayer to Thee:
19 005	"Now I fear (what) my relatives (and colleagues) (will do) after me: but my wife is barren: so give me an heir as from Thyself,"-	Lo! I fear my kinsfolk after me, since my wife is barren. Oh, give me from Thy presence a successor,		And surely I fear my cousins after me, and my wife is barren, therefore grant me from Thyself an heir,
19 006	"(One that) will (truly) represent me, and represent the posterity of Jacob; and make him, O my Lord! one with whom Thou art well-pleased!"	Who shall inherit of me and inherit (also) of the house of Jacob. And make him, my Lord, acceptable (unto Thee).		Who should inherit me and inherit from the children of Yaqoub, and make him, my Lord, one in whom Thou art well pleased.
19 007	(His prayer was answered): "O Zakariya! We give thee good news of a son: His name shall be Yahya: on none by that name have We conferred distinction before."	(It was said unto him): O Zachariah! Lo! We bring thee tidings of a son whose name is John; we have given the same name to none before (him).		O Zakariya! surely We give you good news of a boy whose name shall be Yahya: We have not made before anyone his equal.
19 008	He said: "O my Lord! How shall I have a son, when my wife is barren and I have grown quite decrepit from old age?"	He said: My Lord! How can I have a son when my wife is barren and I have reached infirm old age?		He said: O my Lord! when shall I have a son, and my wife is barren, and I myself have reached indeed the extreme degree of old age?
19 009	He said: "So (it will be) thy Lord saith, 'that is easy for Me: I did indeed create thee before, when thou hadst been nothing!'"	He said: So (it will be). Thy Lord saith: It is easy for Me, even as I created thee before, when thou wast naught.		He said: So shall it be, your Lord says: It is easy to Me, and indeed I created you before, when you were nothing.
19 010	(Zakariya) said: "O my Lord! give me a Sign." "Thy Sign," was the answer, "Shall be that thou shalt speak to no man for three nights, although thou art not dumb."	He said: My Lord! Appoint for me some token. He said: Thy token is that thou, with no bodily defect, shalt not speak unto mankind three nights.		He said: My Lord! give me a sign. He said: Your sign is that you will not be able to speak to the people three nights while in sound health.
19 011	So Zakariya came out to his people from him chamber: He told them by signs to celebrate Allah's praises in the morning and in the evening.	Then he came forth unto his people from the sanctuary, and signified to them: Glorify your Lord at break of day and fall of night.		So he went forth to his people from his place of worship, then he made known to them that they should glorify (Allah) morning and evening.
19 012	(To his son came the command): "O Yahya! take hold of the Book with might": and We gave him Wisdom even as a youth,	(And it was said unto his son): O John! Hold fast the Scripture. And we gave him wisdom when a child,		O Yahya! take hold of the Book with strength, and We granted him wisdom while yet a child,

19 013	And piety (for all creatures) as from Us, and purity: He was devout,	And compassion from Our presence, and purity; and he was devout,	And tenderness from Us and purity, and he was one who guarded (against evil),
19 014	And kind to his parents, and he was not overbearing or rebellious.	And dutiful toward his parents. And he was not arrogant, rebellious.	And dutiful to his parents, and he was not insolent, disobedient.
19 015	So Peace on him the day he was born, the day that he dies, and the day that he will be raised up to life (again)!	Peace on him the day he was born, and the day he dieth and the day he shall be raised alive!	And peace on him on the day he was born, and on the day he dies, and on the day he is raised to life.
19 016	Relate in the Book (the story of) Mary, when she withdrew from her family to a place in the East.	And make mention of Mary in the Scripture, when she had withdrawn from her people to a chamber looking East,	And mention Marium in the Book when she drew aside from her family to an eastern place;
19 017	She placed a screen (to screen herself) from them; then We sent her our angel, and he appeared before her as a man in all respects.	And had chosen seclusion from them. Then We sent unto her Our Spirit and it assumed for her the likeness of a perfect man.	So she took a veil (to screen herself) from them; then We sent to her Our spirit, and there appeared to her a well-made man.
19 018	She said: "I seek refuge from thee to (Allah) Most Gracious: (come not near) if thou dost fear Allah."	She said: Lo! I seek refuge in the Beneficent One from thee, if thou art Allah-fearing.	She said: Surely I fly for refuge from you to the Beneficent Allah, if you are one guarding (against evil).
19 019	He said: "Nay, I am only a messenger from thy Lord, (to announce) to thee the gift of a holy son."	He said: I am only a messenger of thy Lord, that I may bestow on thee a faultless son.	He said: I am only a messenger of your Lord: That I will give you a pure boy.
19 020	She said: "How shall I have a son, seeing that no man has touched me, and I am not unchaste?"	She said: How can I have a son when no mortal hath touched me, neither have I been unchaste?	She said: When shall I have a boy and no mortal has yet touched me, nor have I been unchaste?
19 021	He said: "So (it will be): Thy Lord saith, 'that is easy for Me: and (We wish) to appoint him as a Sign unto men and a Mercy from Us': It is a matter (so) decreed."	He said: So (it will be). Thy Lord saith: It is easy for Me. And (it will be) that We may make of him a revelation for mankind and a mercy from Us, and it is a thing ordained.	He said: Even so; your Lord says: It is easy to Me: and that We may make him a sign to men and a mercy from Us, and it is a matter which has been decreed.
19 022	So she conceived him, and she retired with him to a remote place.	And she conceived him, and she withdrew with him to a far place.	So she conceived him; then withdrew herself with him to a remote place.
19 023	And the pains of childbirth drove her to the trunk of a palm-tree: She cried (in her anguish): "Ah! would that I had died before this! would that I had been a thing forgotten and out of sight!"	And the pangs of childbirth drove her unto the trunk of the palm-tree. She said: Oh, would that I had died ere this and had become a thing of naught, forgotten!	And the throes (of childbirth) compelled her to betake herself to the trunk of a palm tree. She said: Oh, would that I had died before this, and had been a thing quite forgotten!
19 024	But (a voice) cried to her from beneath the (palm-tree): "Grieve not! for thy Lord hath provided a rivulet beneath thee;"	Then (one) cried unto her from below her, saying: Grieve not! Thy Lord hath placed a rivulet beneath thee,	Then (the child) called out to her from beneath her: Grieve not, surely your Lord has made a stream to flow beneath you;
19 025	"And shake towards thyself the trunk of the palm-tree: It will let fall fresh ripe dates upon thee."	And shake the trunk of the palm-tree toward thee, thou wilt cause ripe dates to fall upon thee.	And shake towards you the trunk of the palmtree, it will drop on you fresh ripe dates:
19 026	"So eat and drink and cool (thine) eye. And if thou dost see any man, say, 'I have vowed a fast to (Allah) Most Gracious, and this day will I enter into not talk with any human being'"	So eat and drink and be consoled. And if thou meetest any mortal, say: Lo! I have vowed a fast unto the Beneficent, and may not speak this day to any mortal.	So eat and drink and refresh the eye. Then if you see any mortal, say: Surely I have vowed a fast to the Beneficent Allah, so I shall not speak to any man today.
19 027	At length she brought the (babe) to her people, carrying him (in her arms). They said: "O Mary! truly an amazing thing hast thou brought!"	Then she brought him to her own folk, carrying him. They said: O Mary! Thou hast come with an amazing thing.	And she came to her people with him, carrying him (with her). They said: O Marium! surely you have done a strange thing.

19 028	"O sister of Aaron! Thy father was not a man of evil, nor thy mother a woman unchaste!"	O sister of Aaron! Thy father was not a wicked man nor was thy mother a harlot.		O sister of Haroun! your father was not a bad man, nor, was your mother an unchaste woman.
19 029	But she pointed to the babe. They said: "How can we talk to one who is a child in the cradle?"	Then she pointed to him. They said: How can we talk to one who is in the cradle, a young boy?		But she pointed to him. They said: How should we speak to one who was a child in the cradle?
19 030	He said: "I am indeed a servant of Allah: He hath given me revelation and made me a prophet;"	He spake: Lo! I am the slave of Allah. He hath given me the Scripture and hath appointed me a Prophet,		He said: Surely I am a servant of Allah; He has given me the Book and made me a prophet;
19 031	"And He hath made me blessed wheresoever I be, and hath enjoined on me Prayer and Charity as long as I live;"	And hath made me blessed wheresoever I may be, and hath enjoined upon me prayer and almsgiving so long as I remain alive,		And He has made me blessed wherever I may be, and He has enjoined on me prayer and poor-rate so long as I live;
19 032	"(He) hath made me kind to my mother, and not overbearing or miserable;"	And (hath made me) dutiful toward her who bore me, and hath not made me arrogant, unblest.		And dutiful to my mother, and He has not made me insolent, unblessed;
19 033	"So peace is on me the day I was born, the day that I die, and the day that I shall be raised up to life (again)"!	Peace on me the day I was born, and the day I die, and the day I shall be raised alive!		And peace on me on the day I was born, and on the day I die, and on the day I am raised to life.
19 034	Such (was) Jesus the son of Mary: (it is) a statement of truth, about which they (vainly) dispute.	Such was Jesus, son of Mary: (this is) a statement of the truth concerning which they doubt.		Such is Isa, son of Marium; (this is) the saying of truth about which they dispute.
19 035	It is not befitting to (the majesty of) Allah that He should beget a son. Glory be to Him! when He determines a matter, He only says to it, Be, and it is.	It befitteth not (the Majesty of) Allah that He should take unto Himself a son. Glory be to Him! When He decreeth a thing, He saith unto it only: Be! and it is.		It beseems not Allah that He should take to Himself a son, glory be to Him; when He has decreed a matter He only says to it "Be," and it is.
19 036	Verily Allah is my Lord and your Lord: Him therefore serve ye: this is a Way that is straight.	And lo! Allah is my Lord and your Lord. So serve Him. That is the right path.		And surely Allah is my Lord and your Lord, therefore serve Him; this is the right path.
19 037	But the sects differ among themselves: and woe to the unbelievers because of the (coming) Judgment of a Momentous Day!	The sects among them differ: but woe unto the disbelievers from the meeting of an awful Day.		But parties from among them disagreed with each other, so woe to those who disbelieve, because of presence on a great day.
19 038	How plainly will they see and hear, the Day that they will appear before Us! but the unjust today are in error manifest!	See and hear them on the Day they come unto Us! yet the evil-doers are to-day in error manifest.		How clearly shall they hear and how clearly shall they see on the day when they come to Us; but the unjust this day are in manifest error.
19 039	But warn them of the Day of Distress, when the matter will be determined: for (behold,) they are negligent and they do not believe!	And warn them of the Day of anguish when the case hath been decided. Now they are in a state of carelessness, and they believe not.		And warn them of the day of intense regret, when the matter shall have been decided; and they are (now) in negligence and they do not believe.
19 040	It is We Who will inherit the earth, and all beings thereon: to Us will they all be returned.	Lo! We, only We, inherit the earth and all who are thereon, and unto Us they are returned.		Surely We inherit the earth and all those who are on it, and to Us they shall be returned.
19 041	(Also) mention in the Book (the story of) Abraham: He was a man of Truth, a prophet.	And make mention (O Muhammad) in the Scripture of Abraham. Lo! he was a saint, a prophet.		And mention Ibrahim in the Book; surely he was a truthful man, a prophet.
19 042	Behold, he said to his father: "O my father! why worship that which heareth not and seeth not, and can profit thee nothing?"	When he said unto his father: O my father! Why worshippest thou that which heareth not nor seeth, nor can in aught avail thee?		When he said to his father; O my father! why do you worship what neither hears nor sees, nor does it avail you in the least:

19 043	"O my father! to me hath come knowledge which hath not reached thee: so follow me: I will guide thee to a way that is even and straight."	O my father! Lo! there hath come unto me of knowledge that which came not unto thee. So follow me, and I will lead thee on a right path.	O my father! truly the knowledge has come to me which has not come to you, therefore follow me, I will guide you on a right path:
19 044	"O my father! serve not Satan: for Satan is a rebel against (Allah) Most Gracious."	O my father! Serve not the devil. Lo! the devil is a rebel unto the Beneficent.	O my father! serve not the Shaitan, surely the Shaitan is disobedient to the Beneficent Allah:
19 045	"O my father! I fear lest a Penalty afflict thee from (Allah) Most Gracious, so that thou become to Satan a friend."	O my father! Lo! I fear lest a punishment from the Beneficent overtake thee so that thou become a comrade of the devil.	O my father! surely I fear that a punishment from the Beneficent Allah should afflict you so that you should be a friend of the Shaitan.
19 046	(The father) replied: "Dost thou hate my gods, O Abraham? If thou forbear not, I will indeed stone thee: Now get away from me for a good long while!"	He said: Rejectest thou my gods, O Abraham? If thou cease not, I shall surely stone thee. Depart from me a long while!	He said: Do you dislike my gods, O Ibrahim? If you do not desist I will certainly revile you, and leave me for a time.
19 047	Abraham said: "Peace be on thee: I will pray to my Lord for thy forgiveness: for He is to me Most Gracious."	He said: Peace be unto thee! I shall ask forgiveness of my Lord for thee. Lo! He was ever gracious unto me.	He said: Peace be on you, I will pray to my Lord to forgive you; surely He is ever Affectionate to me:
19 048	"And I will turn away from you (all) and from those whom ye invoke besides Allah: I will call on my Lord: perhaps, by my prayer to my Lord, I shall be not unblest."	I shall withdraw from you and that unto which ye pray beside Allah, and I shall pray unto my Lord. It may be that, in prayer unto my Lord, I shall not be unblest.	And I will withdraw from you and what you call on besides Allah, and I will call upon my Lord; may be I shall not remain unblessed in calling upon my Lord.
19 049	When he had turned away from them and from those whom they worshipped besides Allah, We bestowed on him Isaac and Jacob, and each one of them We made a prophet.	So, when he had withdrawn from them and that which they were worshipping beside Allah, We gave him Isaac and Jacob. Each of them We made a prophet.	So when he withdrew from them and what they worshipped besides Allah, We gave to him Ishaq and Yaqoub, and each one of them We made a prophet.
19 050	And We bestowed of Our Mercy on them, and We granted them lofty honour on the tongue of truth.	And we gave them of Our mercy, and assigned to them a high and true renown.	And We granted to them of Our mercy, and We left (behind them) a truthful mention of eminence for them.
19 051	Also mention in the Book (the story of) Moses: for he was specially chosen, and he was a messenger (and) a prophet.	And make mention in the Scripture of Moses. Lo! he was chosen, and he was a messenger (of Allah), a prophet.	And mention Musa in the Book; surely he was one purified, and he was a messenger, a prophet.
19 052	And we called him from the right side of Mount (Sinai), and made him draw near to Us, for mystic (converse).	We called him from the right slope of the Mount, and brought him nigh in communion.	And We called to him from the blessed side of the mountain, and We made him draw nigh, holding communion (with Us).
19 053	And, out of Our Mercy, We gave him his brother Aaron, (also) a prophet.	And We bestowed upon him of Our mercy his brother Aaron, a prophet (likewise).	And We gave to him out of Our mercy his brother Haroun a prophet.
19 054	Also mention in the Book (the story of) Isma'il: He was (strictly) true to what he promised, and he was a messenger (and) a prophet.	And make mention in the Scripture of Ishmael. Lo! he was a keeper of his promise, and he was a messenger (of Allah), a prophet.	And mention Ismail in the Book; surely he was truthful in (his) promise, and he was a messenger, a prophet.
19 055	He used to enjoin on his people Prayer and Charity, and he was most acceptable in the sight of his Lord.	He enjoined upon his people worship and almsgiving, and was acceptable in the sight of his Lord.	And he enjoined on his family prayer and almsgiving, and was one in whom his Lord was well pleased.
19 056	Also mention in the Book the case of Idris: He was a man of truth (and sincerity), (and) a prophet:	And make mention in the Scripture of Idris. Lo! he was a saint, a prophet;	And mention Idris in the Book; surely he was a truthful man, a prophet,

19 057	And We raised him to a lofty station.	And We raised him to high station.	And We raised him high in Heaven.
19 058	Those were some of the prophets on whom Allah did bestow His Grace,- of the posterity of Adam, and of those who We carried (in the Ark) with Noah, and of the posterity of Abraham and Israel of those whom We guided and chose. Whenever the Signs of (Allah) Most Gracious were rehearsed to them, they would fall down in prostrate adoration and in tears.	These are they unto whom Allah showed favour from among the prophets, of the seed of Adam and of those whom We carried (in the ship) with Noah, and of the seed of Abraham and Israel, and from among those whom We guided and chose. When the revelations of the Beneficent were recited unto them, they fell down, adoring and weeping.	These are they on whom Allah bestowed favors, from among the prophets of the seed of Adam, and of those whom We carried with Nuh, and of the seed of Ibrahim and Israel, and of those whom We guided and chose; when the communications of the Beneficent Allah were recited to them, they fell down making obeisance and weeping.
19 059	But after them there followed a posterity who missed prayers and followed after lusts soon, then, will they face Destruction,-	Now there hath succeeded them a later generation whom have ruined worship and have followed lusts. But they will meet deception.	But there came after them an evil generation, who neglected prayers and followed and sensual desires, so they win meet perdition,
19 060	Except those who repent and believe, and work righteousness: for these will enter the Garden and will not be wronged in the least,-	Save him who shall repent and believe and do right. Such will enter the Garden, and they will not be wronged in aught -	Except such as repent and believe and do good, these shall enter the garden, and they shall not be dealt with unjustly in any way:
19 061	Gardens of Eternity, those which (Allah) Most Gracious has promised to His servants in the Unseen: for His promise must (necessarily) come to pass.	Gardens of Eden, which the Beneficent hath promised to His slaves in the unseen. Lo! His promise is ever sure of fulfilment -	The gardens of perpetuity which the Beneficent Allah has promised to His servants while unseen; surely His promise shall come to pass.
19 062	They will not there hear any vain discourse, but only salutations of Peace: And they will have therein their sustenance, morning and evening.	They hear therein no idle talk, but only Peace; and therein they have food for morn and evening.	They shall not hear therein any vain discourse, but only: Peace, and they shall have their sustenance therein morning and evening.
19 063	Such is the Garden which We give as an inheritance to those of Our servants who guard against Evil.	Such is the Garden which We cause the devout among Our bondmen to inherit.	This is the garden which We cause those of Our servants to inherit who guard (against evil).
19 064	(The angels say:) "We descend not but by command of thy Lord: to Him belongeth what is before us and what is behind us, and what is between: and thy Lord never doth forget,"-	We (angels) come not down save by commandment of thy Lord. Unto Him belongeth all that is before us and all that is behind us and all that is between those two, and thy Lord was never forgetful -	And we do not descend but by the command of your Lord; to Him belongs whatever is before us and whatever is behind us and whatever is between these, and your Lord is not forgetful.
19 065	"Lord of the heavens and of the earth, and of all that is between them; so worship Him, and be constant and patient in His worship: knowest thou of any who is worthy of the same Name as He?"	Lord of the heavens and the earth and all that is between them! Therefor, worship thou Him and be thou steadfast in His service. Knowest thou one that can be named along with Him?	The Lord of the heavens and the earth and what is between them, so serve Him and be patient in His service. Do you know any one equal to Him?
19 066	Man says: "What! When I am dead, shall I then be raised up alive?"	And man saith: When I am dead, shall I forsooth be brought forth alive?	And says man: What! when I am dead shall I truly be brought forth alive?
19 067	But does not man call to mind that We created him before out of nothing?	Doth not man remember that We created him before, when he was naught?	Does not man remember that We created him before, when he was nothing?
19 068	So, by thy Lord, without doubt, We shall gather them together, and (also) the Evil Ones (with them); then shall We bring them forth on their knees round about Hell;	And, by thy Lord, verily We shall assemble them and the devils, then We shall bring them, crouching, around hell.	So by your Lord! We will most certainly gather them together and the Shaitans, then shall We certainly cause them to be present round hell on their knees.

19 069	Then shall We certainly drag out from every sect all those who were worst in obstinate rebellion against (Allah) Most Gracious.	Then We shall pluck out from every sect whichever of them was most stubborn in rebellion to the Beneficent.	Then We will most certainly draw forth from every sect of them him who is most exorbitantly rebellious against the Beneficent Allah.
19 070	And certainly We know best those who are most worthy of being burned therein.	And surely We are Best Aware of those most worthy to be burned therein.	Again We do certainly know best those who deserve most to be burned therein.
19 071	Not one of you but will pass over it: this is, with thy Lord, a Decree which must be accomplished.	There is not one of you but shall approach it. That is a fixed ordinance of thy Lord.	And there is not one of you but shall come to it; this is an unavoidable decree of your Lord.
19 072	But We shall save those who guarded against evil, and We shall leave the wrong-doers therein, (humbled) to their knees.	Then We shall rescue those who kept from evil, and leave the evil-doers crouching there.	And We will deliver those who guarded (against evil), and We will leave the unjust therein on their knees.
19 073	When Our Clear Signs are rehearsed to them, the Unbelievers say to those who believe, "Which of the two sides is best in point of position? Which makes the best show in council?"	And when Our clear revelations are recited unto them, those who disbelieve say unto those who believe: Which of the two parties (yours or ours) is better in position, and more imposing as an army?	And when Our clear communications are recited to them, those who disbelieve say to those who believe: Which of the two parties is best in abiding and best in assembly?
19 074	But how many (countless) generations before them have we destroyed, who were even better in equipment and in glitter to the eye?	How many a generation have We destroyed before them, who were more imposing in respect of gear and outward seeming!	And how many of the generations have We destroyed before them who were better in respect of goods and outward appearance!
19 075	Say: "If any men go astray, (Allah) Most Gracious extends (the rope) to them, until, when they see the warning of Allah (being fulfilled) - either in punishment or in (the approach of) the Hour,- they will at length realise who is worst in position, and (who) weakest in forces!"	Say: As for him who is in error, the Beneficent will verily prolong his span of life until, when they behold that which they were promised, whether it be punishment (in the world), or the Hour (of doom), they will know who is worse in position and who is weaker as an army.	Say: As for him who remains in error, the Beneficent Allah will surely prolong his length of days, until they see what they were threatened with, either the punishment or the hour; then they shall know who is in more evil plight and weaker in forces.
19 076	"And Allah doth advance in guidance those who seek guidance: and the things that endure, Good Deeds, are best in the sight of thy Lord, as rewards, and best in respect of (their) eventual return."	Allah increaseth in right guidance those who walk aright, and the good deeds which endure are better in thy Lord's sight for reward, and better for resort.	And Allah increases in guidance those who go aright; and ever-abiding good works are with your Lord best in recompense and best in yielding fruit.
19 077	Hast thou then seen the (sort of) man who rejects Our Signs, yet says: "I shall certainly be given wealth and children?"	Hast thou seen him who disbelieveth in Our revelations and saith: Assuredly I shall be given wealth and children?	Have you, then, seen him who disbelieves in Our communications and says: I shall certainly be given wealth and children?
19 078	Has he penetrated to the Unseen, or has he taken a contract with (Allah) Most Gracious?	Hath he perused the Unseen, or hath he made a pact with the Beneficent?	Has he gained knowledge of the unseen, or made a covenant with the Beneficent Allah?
19 079	Nay! We shall record what he says, and We shall add and add to his punishment.	Nay, but We shall record that which he saith and prolong for him a span of torment.	By no means! We write down what he says, and We will lengthen to him the length of the chastisement,
19 080	To Us shall return all that he talks of and he shall appear before Us bare and alone.	And We shall inherit from him that whereof he spake, and he will come unto Us, alone (without his wealth and children).	And We will inherit of him what he says, and he shall come to Us alone.
19 081	And they have taken (for worship) gods other than Allah, to give them power and glory!	And they have chosen (other) gods beside Allah that they may be a power for them.	And they have taken gods besides Allah, that they should be to them a source of strength;
19 082	Instead, they shall reject their worship, and become adversaries against them.	Nay, but they will deny their worship of them, and become opponents unto them.	By no means! They shall soon deny their worshipping them, and they shall be adversaries to them.

19 083	Seest thou not that We have set the Evil Ones on against the unbelievers, to incite them with fury?	Seest thou not that We have set the devils on the disbelievers to confound them with confusion?	Do you not see that We have sent the Shaitans against the unbelievers, inciting them by incitement?
19 084	So make no haste against them, for We but count out to them a (limited) number (of days).	So make no haste against them (O Muhammad). We do but number unto them a sum (of days).	Therefore be not in haste against them, We only number out to them a number (of days).
19 085	The day We shall gather the righteous to (Allah) Most Gracious, like a band presented before a king for honours,	On the day when We shall gather the righteous unto the Beneficent, a goodly company.	The day on which We will gather those who guard (against evil) to the Beneficent Allah to receive honors,
19 086	And We shall drive the sinners to Hell, like thirsty cattle driven down to water,-	And drive the guilty unto hell, a weary herd,	And We will drive the guilty to hell thirsty
19 087	None shall have the power of intercession, but such a one as has received permission (or promise) from (Allah) Most Gracious.	They will have no power of intercession, save him who hath made a covenant with his Lord.	They shall not control intercession, save he who has made a covenant with the Beneficent Allah.
19 088	They say: "(Allah) Most Gracious has begotten a son!"	And they say: The Beneficent hath taken unto Himself a son.	And they say: The Beneficent Allah has taken (to Himself) a son.
19 089	Indeed ye have put forth a thing most monstrous!	Assuredly ye utter a disastrous thing	Certainly you have made an abominable assertion
19 090	At it the skies are ready to burst, the earth to split asunder, and the mountains to fall down in utter ruin,	Whereby almost the heavens are torn, and the earth is split asunder and the mountains fall in ruins,	The heavens may almost be rent thereat, and the earth cleave asunder, and the mountains fall down in pieces,
19 091	That they should invoke a son for (Allah) Most Gracious.	That ye ascribe unto the Beneficent a son,	That they ascribe a son to the Beneficent Allah.
19 092	For it is not consonant with the majesty of (Allah) Most Gracious that He should beget a son.	When it is not meet for (the Majesty of) the Beneficent that He should choose a son.	And it is not worthy of the Beneficent Allah that He should take (to Himself) a son.
19 093	Not one of the beings in the heavens and the earth but must come to (Allah) Most Gracious as a servant.	There is none in the heavens and the earth but cometh unto the Beneficent as a slave.	There is no one in the heavens and the earth but will come to the Beneficent Allah as a servant.
19 094	He does take an account of them (all), and hath numbered them (all) exactly.	Verily He knoweth them and numbereth them with (right) numbering.	Certainly He has a comprehensive knowledge of them and He has numbered them a (comprehensive) numbering.
19 095	And everyone of them will come to Him singly on the Day of Judgment.	And each one of them will come unto Him on the Day of Resurrection, alone.	And every one of them will come to Him on the day of resurrection alone.
19 096	On those who believe and work deeds of righteousness, will (Allah) Most Gracious bestow love.	Lo! those who believe and do good works, the Beneficent will appoint for them love.	Surely (as for) those who believe and do good deeds for them will Allah bring about love.
19 097	So have We made the (Qur'an) easy in thine own tongue, that with it thou mayest give Glad Tidings to the righteous, and warnings to people given to contention.	And We make (this Scripture) easy in thy tongue, (O Muhammad) only that thou mayst bear good tidings therewith unto those who ward off (evil), and warn therewith the froward folk.	So We have only made it easy in your tongue that you may give good news thereby to those who guard (against evil) and warn thereby a vehemently contentious people.
19 098	But how many (countless) generations before them have We destroyed? Canst thou find a single one of them (now) or hear (so much as) a whisper of them?	And how many a generation before them have We destroyed! Canst thou (Muhammad) see a single man of them, or hear from them the slightest sound?	And how many a generation have We destroyed before them! Do you see any one of them or hear a sound of them?

Chapter 20:

TA-HA (TA-HA)

Total Verses: 135 Revealed At: MAKKA

In the name of Allah, the Most Beneficent, the Most Merciful.

20 001	Ta-Ha.	Ta. Ha.	Ta Ha.
20 002	We have not sent down the Qur'an to thee to be (an occasion) for thy distress,	We have not revealed unto thee (Muhammad) this Qur'an that thou shouldst be distressed,	We have not revealed the Quran to you that you may be unsuccessful.
20 003	But only as an admonition to those who fear (Allah),-	But as a reminder unto him who feareth,	Nay, it is a reminder to him who fears:
20 004	A revelation from Him Who created the earth and the heavens on high.	A revelation from Him Who created the earth and the high heavens,	A revelation from Him Who created the earth and the high heavens.
20 005	(Allah) Most Gracious is firmly established on the throne (of authority).	The Beneficent One, Who is established on the Throne.	The Beneficent Allah is firm in power.
20 006	To Him belongs what is in the heavens and on earth, and all between them, and all beneath the soil.	Unto Him belongeth whatsoever is in the heavens and whatsoever is in the earth, and whatsoever is between them, and whatsoever is beneath the sod.	His is what is in the heavens and what is in the earth and what is between them two and what is beneath the ground.
20 007	If thou pronounce the word aloud, (it is no matter): for verily He knoweth what is secret and what is yet more hidden.	And if thou speakest aloud, then lo! He knoweth the secret (thought) and (that which is yet) more hidden.	And if you utter the saying aloud, then surely He knows the secret, and what is yet more hidden.
20 008	Allah! there is no god but He! To Him belong the most Beautiful Names.	Allah! There is no God save Him. His are the most beautiful names.	Allah-- there is no god but He; His are the very best names.
20 009	Has the story of Moses reached thee?	Hath there come unto thee the story of Moses?	And has the story of Musa come to you?
20 010	Behold, he saw a fire: So he said to his family, "Tarry ye; I perceive a fire; perhaps I can bring you some burning brand therefrom, or find some guidance at the fire."	When he saw a fire and said unto his folk: Lo! Wait! I see a fire afar off. Peradventure I may bring you a brand therefrom or may find guidance at the fire.	When he saw fire, he said to his family: Stop, for surely I see a fire, haply I may bring to you therefrom a live coal or find a guidance at the fire.
20 011	But when he came to the fire, a voice was heard: "O Moses!"	And when he reached it, he was called by name: O Moses!	So when he came to it, a voice was uttered: O Musa:
20 012	"Verily I am thy Lord! therefore (in My presence) put off thy shoes: thou art in the sacred valley Tuwa.	Lo! I, even I, am thy Lord. So take off thy shoes, for lo! thou art in the holy valley of Tuwa.	Surely I am your Lord, therefore put off your shoes; surely you are in the sacred valley, Tuwa,
20 013	"I have chosen thee: listen, then, to the inspiration (sent to thee)."	And I have chosen thee, so hearken unto that which is inspired.	And I have chosen you, so listen to what is revealed:
20 014	"Verily, I am Allah: There is no god but I: So serve thou Me (only), and establish regular prayer for celebrating My praise."	Lo! I, even I, am Allah, There is no God save Me. So serve Me and establish worship for My remembrance.	Surely I am Allah, there is no god but I, therefore serve Me and keep up prayer for My remembrance:
20 015	"Verily the Hour is coming - My design is to keep it hidden - for every soul to receive its reward by the measure of its Endeavour."	Lo! the Hour is surely coming. But I will to keep it hidden, that every soul may be rewarded for that which it striveth (to achieve).	Surely the hour is coming-- I am about to make it manifest-- so that every soul may be rewarded as it strives:

20 016	"Therefore let not such as believe not therein but follow their own lusts, divert thee therefrom, lest thou perish!"..	Therefor, let not him turn thee aside from (the thought of) it who believeth not therein but followeth his own desire, lest thou perish.	Therefore let not him who believes not in it and follows his low desires turn you away from it so that you should perish;
20 017	"And what is that in the right hand, O Moses?"	And what is that in thy right hand, O Moses?	And what is this in your right hand, O Musa!
20 018	He said, "It is my rod: on it I lean; with it I beat down fodder for my flocks; and in it I find other uses."	He said: This is my staff whereon I lean, and wherewith I bear down branches for my sheep, and wherein I find other uses.	He said: This is my staff: I recline on it and I beat the leaves with it to make them fall upon my sheep, and I have other uses for it.
20 019	(Allah) said, "Throw it, O Moses!"	He said: Cast it down, O Moses!	He said: Cast it down, O Musa!
20 020	He threw it, and behold! It was a snake, active in motion.	So he cast it down, and lo! it was a serpent, gliding.	So he cast it down; and lo! it was a serpent running.
20 021	(Allah) said, "Seize it, and fear not: We shall return it at once to its former condition"..	He said: Grasp it and fear not. We shall return it to its former state.	He said: Take hold of it and fear not; We will restore it to its former state:
20 022	"Now draw thy hand close to thy side: It shall come forth white (and shining), without harm (or stain),- as another Sign,"-	And thrust thy hand within thine armpit, it will come forth white without hurt. (That will be) another token.	And press your hand to your side, it shall come out white without evil: another sign:
20 023	"In order that We may show thee (two) of our Greater Signs."	That We may show thee (some) of Our greater portents,	That We may show you of Our greater signs:
20 024	"Go thou to Pharaoh, for he has indeed transgressed all bounds."	Go thou unto Pharaoh! Lo! he hath transgressed (the bounds).	Go to Firon, surely he has exceeded all limits.
20 025	(Moses) said: "O my Lord! expand me my breast;"	(Moses) said: My Lord! relieve my mind	He said: O my Lord! Expand my breast for me,
20 026	"Ease my task for me;"	And ease my task for me;	And make my affair easy to me,
20 027	"And remove the impediment from my speech,"	And loose a knot from my tongue,	And loose the knot from my tongue,
20 028	"So they may understand what I say:"	That they may understand my saying.	(That) they may understand my word;
20 029	"And give me a Minister from my family,"	Appoint for me a henchman from my folk,	And give to me an aider from my family:
20 030	"Aaron, my brother;"	Aaron, my brother.	Haroun, my brother,
20 031	"Add to my strength through him,"	Confirm my strength with him	Strengthen my back by him,
20 032	"And make him share my task:"	And let him share my task,	And associate him (with me) in my affair,
20 033	"That we may celebrate Thy praise without stint,"	That we may glorify Thee much	So that we should glorify Thee much,
20 034	"And remember Thee without stint:"	And much remember Thee.	And remember Thee oft.
20 035	"For Thou art He that (ever) regardeth us."	Lo! Thou art ever Seeing us.	Surely, Thou art seeing us.
20 036	(Allah) said: "Granted is thy prayer, O Moses!"	He said: Thou art granted thy request, O Moses.	He said: You are indeed granted your petition, O Musa
20 037	"And indeed We conferred a favour on thee another time (before)."	And indeed, another time, already We have shown thee favour,	And certainly We bestowed on you a favor at another time;
20 038	"Behold! We sent to thy mother, by inspiration, the message:"	When we inspired in thy mother that which is inspired,	When We revealed to your mother what was revealed;

20 039	"'Throw (the child) into the chest, and throw (the chest) into the river: the river will cast him up on the bank, and he will be taken up by one who is an enemy to Me and an enemy to him': But I cast (the garment of) love over thee from Me: and (this) in order that thou mayest be reared under Mine eye."	Saying: Throw him into the ark, and throw it into the river, then the river shall throw it on to the bank, and there an enemy to Me and an enemy to him shall take him. And I endued thee with love from Me that thou mightest be trained according to My will,	Saying: Put him into a chest, then cast it down into the river, then the river shall throw him on the shore; there shall take him up one who is an enemy to Me and enemy to him, and I cast down upon you love from Me, and that you might be brought up before My eyes;
20 040	"Behold! thy sister goeth forth and saith, 'shall I show you one who will nurse and rear the (child)?' So We brought thee back to thy mother, that her eye might be cooled and she should not grieve. Then thou didst slay a man, but We saved thee from trouble, and We tried thee in various ways. Then didst thou tarry a number of years with the people of Midian. Then didst thou come hither as ordained, O Moses!"	When thy sister went and said: Shall I show you one who will nurse him? and we restored thee to thy mother that her eyes might be refreshed and might not sorrow. And thou didst kill a man and We delivered thee from great distress, and tried thee with a heavy trial. And thou didst tarry years among the folk of Midian. Then camest thou (hither) by (My) providence, O Moses,	When your sister went and said: Shall I direct you to one who will take charge of him? So We brought you back to your mother, that her eye might be cooled and she should not grieve and you killed a man, then We delivered you from the grief, and We tried you with (a severe) trying. Then you stayed for years among the people of Madyan; then you came hither as ordained, O Musa.
20 041	"And I have prepared thee for Myself (for service")..	And I have attached thee to Myself.	And I have chosen you for Myself:
20 042	"Go, thou and thy brother, with My Signs, and slacken not, either of you, in keeping Me in remembrance."	Go, thou and thy brother, with My tokens, and be not faint in remembrance of Me.	Go you and your brother with My communications and be not remiss in remembering Me;
20 043	"Go, both of you, to Pharaoh, for he has indeed transgressed all bounds;"	Go, both of you, unto Pharaoh. Lo! he hath transgressed (the bounds).	Go both to Firon, surely he has become inordinate;
20 044	"But speak to him mildly; perchance he may take warning or fear (Allah)."	And speak unto him a gentle word, that peradventure he may heed or fear.	Then speak to him a gentle word haply he may mind or fear.
20 045	They (Moses and Aaron) said: "Our Lord! We fear lest he hasten with insolence against us, or lest he transgress all bounds."	They said: Our Lord! Lo! we fear that he may be beforehand with us or that he may play the tyrant.	Both said: O our Lord! Surely we fear that he may hasten to do evil to us or that he may become inordinate.
20 046	He said: "Fear not: for I am with you: I hear and see (everything)."	He said: Fear not. Lo! I am with you twain, Hearing and Seeing.	He said: Fear not, surely I am with you both: I do hear and see.
20 047	"So go ye both to him, and say, 'Verily we are messengers sent by thy Lord: Send forth, therefore, the Children of Israel with us, and afflict them not: with a Sign, indeed, have we come from thy Lord! and peace to all who follow guidance!"	So go ye unto him and say: Lo! we are two messengers of thy Lord. So let the children of Israel go with us, and torment them not. We bring thee a token from thy Lord. And peace will be for him who followeth right guidance.	So go you both to him and say: Surely we are two messengers of your Lord; therefore send the children of Israel with us and do not torment them! Indeed we have brought to you a communication from your Lord, and peace is on him who follows the guidance;
20 048	"'Verily it has been revealed to us that the Penalty (awaits) those who reject and turn away.'"	Lo! it hath been revealed unto us that the doom will be for him who denieth and turneth away.	Surely it has been revealed to us that the chastisement will surely come upon him who rejects and turns back.
20 049	(When this message was delivered), (Pharaoh) said: "Who, then, O Moses, is the Lord of you two?"	(Pharaoh) said: Who then is the Lord of you twain, O Moses?	(Firon) said: And who is your Lord, O Musa?
20 050	He said: "Our Lord is He Who gave to each (created) thing its form and nature, and further, gave (it) guidance."	He said: Our Lord is He Who gave unto everything its nature, then guided it aright.	He said: Our Lord is He Who gave to everything its creation, then guided it (to its goal).

20 051	(Pharaoh) said: "What then is the condition of previous generations?"	He said: What then is the state of the generations of old?		He said: Then what is the state of the former generations?
20 052	He replied: "The knowledge of that is with my Lord, duly recorded: my Lord never errs, nor forgets,"-	He said: The knowledge thereof is with my Lord in a Record. My Lord neither erreth nor forgetteth,		He said: The knowledge thereof is with my Lord in a book, my Lord errs not, nor does He forget;
20 053	"He Who has, made for you the earth like a carpet spread out; has enabled you to go about therein by roads (and channels); and has sent down water from the sky." With it have We produced diverse pairs of plants each separate from the others.	Who hath appointed the earth as a bed and hath threaded roads for you therein and hath sent down water from the sky and thereby We have brought forth divers kinds of vegetation,		Who made the earth for you an expanse and made for you therein paths and sent down water from the cloud; then thereby We have brought forth many species of various herbs.
20 054	Eat (for yourselves) and pasture your cattle: verily, in this are Signs for men endued with understanding.	(Saying): Eat ye and feed your cattle. Lo! herein verily are portents for men of thought.		Eat and pasture your cattle; most surely there are signs in this for those endowed with understanding.
20 055	From the (earth) did We create you, and into it shall We return you, and from it shall We bring you out once again.	Thereof We created you, and thereunto We return you, and thence We bring you forth a second time.		From it We created you and into it We shall send you back and from it will We raise you a second time.
20 056	And We showed Pharaoh all Our Signs, but he did reject and refuse.	And We verily did show him all Our tokens, but he denied them and refused.		And truly We showed him Our signs, all of them, but he rejected and refused.
20 057	He said: "Hast thou come to drive us out of our land with thy magic, O Moses?"	He said: Hast come to drive us out from our land by thy magic, O Moses?		Said he: Have you come to us that you should turn us out of our land by your magic, O Musa?
20 058	"But we can surely produce magic to match thine! So make a tryst between us and thee, which we shall not fail to keep - neither we nor thou - in a place where both shall have even chances."	But we surely can produce for thee magic the like thereof; so appoint a tryst between us and you, which neither we nor thou shall fail to keep, at a place convenient (to us both).		So we too will produce before you magic like it, therefore make between us and you an appointment, which we should not break, (neither) we nor you, (in) a central place.
20 059	Moses said: "Your tryst is the Day of the Festival, and let the people be assembled when the sun is well up."	(Moses) said: Your tryst shall be the day of the feast, and let the people assemble when the sun hath risen high.		(Musa) said: Your appointment is the day of the Festival and let the people be gathered together in the early forenoon.
20 060	So Pharaoh withdrew: He concerted his plan, and then came (back).	Then Pharaoh went and gathered his strength, then came (to the appointed tryst).		So Firon turned his back and settled his plan, then came.
20 061	Moses said to him: "Woe to you! Forge not ye a lie against Allah, lest He destroy you (at once) utterly by chastisement: the forger must suffer frustration!"	Moses said unto them: Woe unto you! Invent not a lie against Allah, lest He extirpate you by some punishment. He who lieth faileth miserably.		Musa said to them: Woe to you! do not forge a lie against Allah, lest He destroy you by a punishment, and he who forges (a lie) indeed fails to attain (his desire).
20 062	So they disputed, one with another, over their affair, but they kept their talk secret.	Then they debated one with another what they must do, and they kept their counsel secret.		So they disputed with one another about their affair and kept the discourse secret.
20 063	They said: "These two are certainly (expert) magicians: their object is to drive you out from your land with their magic, and to do away with your most cherished institutions".	They said: Lo! these are two wizards who would drive you out from your country by their magic, and destroy your best traditions;		They said: These are most surely two magicians who wish to turn you out from your land by their magic and to take away your best traditions.
20 064	"Therefore concert your plan, and then assemble in (serried) ranks: He wins (all along) today who gains the upper hand."	So arrange your plan, and come in battle line. Whoso is uppermost this day will be indeed successful.		Therefore settle your plan, then come standing in ranks and he will prosper indeed this day who overcomes.

20 065	They said: "O Moses! whether wilt thou that thou throw (first) or that we be the first to throw?"	They said: O Moses! Either throw first, or let us be the first to throw?	They said: O Musa! will you cast, or shall we be the first who cast down?
20 066	He said, "Nay, throw ye first!" Then behold their ropes and their rods-so it seemed to him on account of their magic - began to be in lively motion!	He said: Nay, do ye throw! Then lo! their cords and their staves, by their magic, appeared to him as though they ran.	He said: Nay! cast down. Then lo! their cords and their rods-- it was imaged to him on account of their magic as if they were running.
20 067	So Moses conceived in his mind a (sort of) fear.	And Moses conceived a fear in his mind.	So Musa conceived in his mind a fear.
20 068	We said: "Fear not! for thou hast indeed the upper hand:"	We said: Fear not! Lo! thou art the higher.	We said: Fear not, surely you shall be the uppermost,
20 069	"Throw that which is in thy right hand: Quickly will it swallow up that which they have faked what they have faked is but a magician's trick: and the magician thrives not, (no matter) where he goes."	Throw that which is in thy right hand! It will eat up that which they have made. Lo! that which they have made is but a wizard's artifice, and a wizard shall not be successful to whatever point (of skill) he may attain.	And cast down what is in your right hand; it shall devour what they have wrought; they have wrought only the plan of a magician, and the magician shall not be successful wheresoever he may come from.
20 070	So the magicians were thrown down to prostration: they said, "We believe in the Lord of Aaron and Moses".	Then the wizards were (all) flung down prostrate, crying: We believe in the Lord of Aaron and Moses.	And the magicians were cast down making obeisance; they said: We believe in the Lord of Haroun and Musa.
20 071	(Pharaoh) said: "Believe ye in Him before I give you permission? Surely this must be your leader, who has taught you magic! be sure I will cut off your hands and feet on opposite sides, and I will have you crucified on trunks of palm-trees: so shall ye know for certain, which of us can give the more severe and the more lasting punishment!"	(Pharaoh) said: Ye put faith in him before I give you leave. Lo! he is your chief who taught you magic. Now surely I shall cut off your hands and your feet alternately, and I shall crucify you on the trunks of palm trees, and ye shall know for certain which of us hath sterner and more lasting punishment.	(Firon) said: You believe in him before I give you leave; most surely he is the chief of you who taught you enchantment, therefore I will certainly cut off your hands and your feet on opposite sides, and I will certainly crucify you on the trunks of the palm trees, and certainly you will come to know which of us is the more severe and the more abiding in chastising.
20 072	They said: "Never shall we regard thee as more than the Clear Signs that have come to us, or than Him Who created us! so decree whatever thou desirest to decree: for thou canst only decree (touching) the life of this world."	They said: We choose thee not above the clear proofs that have come unto us, and above Him Who created us. So decree what thou wilt decree. Thou wilt end for us only this life of the world.	They said: We do not prefer you to what has come to us of clear arguments and to He Who made us, therefore decide what you are going to decide; you can only decide about this world's life.
20 073	"For us, we have believed in our Lord: may He forgive us our faults, and the magic to which thou didst compel us: for Allah is Best and Most Abiding."	Lo! we believe in our Lord, that He may forgive us our sins and the magic unto which thou didst force us. Allah is better and more lasting.	Surely we believe in our Lord that He may forgive us our sins and the magic to which you compelled us; and Allah is better and more abiding.
20 074	Verily he who comes to his Lord as a sinner (at Judgment),- for him is Hell: therein shall he neither die nor live.	Lo! whoso cometh guilty unto his Lord, verily for him is hell. There he will neither die nor live.	Whoever comes to his Lord (being) guilty, for him is surely hell; he shall not die therein, nor shall he live.
20 075	But such as come to Him as Believers who have worked righteous deeds,- for them are ranks exalted,-	But whoso cometh unto Him a believer, having done good works, for such are the high stations;	And whoever comes to Him a believer (and) he has done good deeds indeed, these it is who shall have the high ranks,
20 076	Gardens of Eternity, beneath which flow rivers: they will dwell therein for aye: such is the reward of those who purify themselves (from evil).	Gardens of Eden underneath which rivers flow, wherein they will abide for ever. That is the reward of him who groweth.	The gardens of perpetuity, beneath which rivers flow, to abide therein; and this is the reward of him who has purified himself.

20 077	We sent an inspiration to Moses: "Travel by night with My servants, and strike a dry path for them through the sea, without fear of being overtaken (by Pharaoh) and without (any other) fear."	And verily We inspired Moses, saying: Take away My slaves by night and strike for them a dry path in the sea, fearing not to be overtaken, neither being afraid (of the sea).	And certainly We revealed to Musa, saying: Travel by night with My servants, then make for them a dry path in the sea, not fearing to be overtaken, nor being afraid.
20 078	Then Pharaoh pursued them with his forces, but the waters completely overwhelmed them and covered them up.	Then Pharaoh followed them with his hosts and there covered them that which did cover them of the sea.	And Firon followed them with his armies, so there came upon them of the sea that which came upon them.
20 079	Pharaoh led his people astray instead of leading them aright.	And Pharaoh led his folk astray, he did not guide them.	And Firon led astray his people and he did not guide (them) aright.
20 080	O ye Children of Israel! We delivered you from your enemy, and We made a Covenant with you on the right side of Mount (Sinai), and We sent down to you Manna and quails:	O Children of Israel! We delivered you from your enemy, and we made a covenant with you on the holy mountain's side, and sent down on you the manna and the quails,	O children of Israel! indeed We delivered you from your enemy, and We made a covenant with you on the blessed side of the mountain, and We sent to you the manna and the quails.
20 081	(Saying): "Eat of the good things We have provided for your sustenance, but commit no excess therein, lest My Wrath should justly descend on you: and those on whom descends My Wrath do perish indeed!"	(Saying): Eat of the good things wherewith We have provided you, and transgress not in respect thereof lest My wrath come upon you: and he on whom My wrath cometh, he is lost indeed.	Eat of the good things We have given you for sustenance, and be not inordinate with respect to them, lest My wrath should be due to you, and to whomsoever My wrath is due be shall perish indeed.
20 082	"But, without doubt, I am (also) He that forgives again and again, to those who repent, believe, and do right, who,- in fine, are ready to receive true guidance."	And lo! verily I am Forgiving toward him who repenteth and believeth and doeth good, and afterward walketh aright.	And most surely I am most Forgiving to him who repents and believes and does good, then continues to follow the right direction.
20 083	(When Moses was up on the Mount, Allah said:) "What made thee hasten in advance of thy people, O Moses?"	And (it was said): What hath made thee hasten from thy folk, O Moses?	And what caused you to hasten from your people, O Musa?
20 084	He replied: "Behold, they are close on my footsteps: I hastened to thee, O my Lord, to please thee."	He said: They are close upon my track. I hastened unto Thee, my Lord, that Thou mightest be well pleased.	He said: They are here on my track and I hastened on to Thee, my Lord, that Thou mightest be pleased.
20 085	(Allah) said: "We have tested thy people in thy absence: the Samiri has led them astray."	He said: Lo! We have tried thy folk in thine absence, and As-Samiri hath misled them.	He said: So surely We have tried your people after you, and the Samiri has led them astray.
20 086	So Moses returned to his people in a state of indignation and sorrow. He said: "O my people! did not your Lord make a handsome promise to you? Did then the promise seem to you long (in coming)? Or did ye desire that Wrath should descend from your Lord on you, and so ye broke your promise to me?"	Then Moses went back unto his folk, angry and sad. He said: O my people! Hath not your Lord promised you a fair promise? Did the time appointed then appear too long for you, or did ye wish that wrath from your Lord should come upon you, that ye broke tryst with me?	So Musa returned to his people wrathful, sorrowing. Said he: O my people! did not your Lord promise you a goodly promise: did then the time seem long to you, or did you wish that displeasure from your Lord should be due to you, so that you broke (your) promise to me?
20 087	They said: "We broke not the promise to thee, as far as lay in our power: but we were made to carry the weight of the ornaments of the (whole) people, and we threw them (into the fire), and that was what the Samiri suggested."	They said: We broke not tryst with thee of our own will, but we were laden with burdens of ornaments of the folk, then cast them (in the fire), for thus As-Samiri proposed.	They said: We did not break (our) promise to you of our own accord, but we were made to bear the burdens of the ornaments of the people, then we made a casting of them, and thus did the Samiri suggest.

20 088	"Then he brought out (of the fire) before the (people) the image of a calf: It seemed to low: so they said: This is your god, and the god of Moses, but (Moses) has forgotten!"	Then he produced for them a calf, of saffron hue, which gave forth a lowing sound. And they cried: This is your god and the god of Moses, but he hath forgotten.	So he brought forth for them a calf, a (mere) body, which had a mooing sound, so they said: This is your god and the god of Musa, but he forgot.
20 089	Could they not see that it could not return them a word (for answer), and that it had no power either to harm them or to do them good?	See they not, then, that it returneth no saying unto them and possesseth for them neither hurt nor use?	What! could they not see that it did not return to them a reply, and (that) it did not control any harm or benefit for them?
20 090	Aaron had already, before this said to them: "O my people! ye are being tested in this: for verily your Lord is (Allah) Most Gracious; so follow me and obey my command."	And Aaron indeed had told them beforehand: O my people! Ye are but being seduced therewith, for lo! your Lord is the Beneficent, so follow me and obey my order.	And certainly Haroun had said to them before: O my people! you are only tried by it, and surely your Lord is the Beneficent Allah, therefore follow me and obey my order.
20 091	They had said: "We will not abandon this cult, but we will devote ourselves to it until Moses returns to us."	They said: We shall by no means cease to be its votaries till Moses return unto us.	They said: We will by no means cease to keep to its worship until Musa returns to us.
20 092	(Moses) said: "O Aaron! what kept thee back, when thou sawest them going wrong,"	He (Moses) said: O Aaron! What held thee back when thou didst see them gone astray,	(Musa) said: O Haroun! what prevented you, when you saw them going astray,
20 093	"From following me? Didst thou then disobey my order?"	That thou followedst me not? Hast thou then disobeyed my order?	So that you did not follow me? Did you then disobey my order?
20 094	(Aaron) replied: "O son of my mother! Seize (me) not by my beard nor by (the hair of) my head! Truly I feared lest thou shouldst say, 'Thou has caused a division among the children of Israel, and thou didst not respect my word!'"	He said: O son of my mother! Clutch not my beard nor my head! I feared lest thou shouldst say: Thou hast caused division among the Children of Israel, and hast not waited for my word.	He said: O son of my mother! seize me not by my beard nor by my head; surely I was afraid lest you should say: You have caused a division among the children of Israel and not waited for my word.
20 095	(Moses) said: "What then is thy case, O Samiri?"	(Moses) said: And what hast thou to say, O Samiri?	He said: What was then your object, O Samiri?
20 096	He replied: "I saw what they saw not: so I took a handful (of dust) from the footprint of the Messenger, and threw it (into the calf): thus did my soul suggest to me."	He said: I perceived what they perceive not, so I seized a handful from the footsteps of the messenger, and then threw it in. Thus my soul commended to me.	He said: I saw (Jibreel) what they did not see, so I took a handful (of the dust) from the footsteps of the messenger, then I threw it in the casting; thus did my soul commend to me.
20 097	(Moses) said: "Get thee gone! but thy (punishment) in this life will be that thou wilt say, 'touch me not'; and moreover (for a future penalty) thou hast a promise that will not fail: Now look at thy god, of whom thou hast become a devoted worshipper: We will certainly (melt) it in a blazing fire and scatter it broadcast in the sea!"	(Moses) said: Then go! and lo! in this life it is for thee to say: Touch me not! and lo! there is for thee a tryst thou canst not break. Now look upon thy god of which thou hast remained a votary. Verily we will burn it and will scatter its dust over the sea.	He said: Begone then, surely for you it will be in this life to say, Touch (me) not; and surely there is a threat for you, which shall not be made to fail to you, and look at your god to whose worship you kept (so long); we will certainly burn it, then we will certainly scatter it a (wide) scattering in the sea.
20 098	But the god of you all is the One Allah: there is no god but He: all things He comprehends in His knowledge.	Your God is only Allah, than Whom there is no other God. He embraceth all things in His knowledge.	Your God is only Allah, there is no god but He; He comprehends all things in (His) knowledge.
20 099	Thus do We relate to thee some stories of what happened before: for We have sent thee a Message from Our own Presence.	Thus relate We unto thee (Muhammad) some tidings of that which happened of old, and We have given thee from Our presence a reminder.	Thus do We relate to you (some) of the news of what has gone before; and indeed We have given to you a Reminder from Ourselves.

20 100	If any do turn away therefrom, verily they will bear a burden on the Day of judgment;	Whoso turneth away from it, he verily will bear a burden on the Day of Resurrection,	Whoever turns aside from it, he shall surely bear a burden on the day of resurrection,
20 101	They will abide in this (state): and grievous will the burden be to them on that Day,-	Abiding under it - an evil burden for them on the Day of Resurrection,	Abiding in this (state), and evil will it be for them to bear on the day of resurrection;
20 102	The Day when the Trumpet will be sounded: that Day, We shall gather the sinful, blear-eyed (with terror).	The day when the Trumpet is blown. On that day we assemble the guilty white-eyed (with terror),	On the day when the trumpet shall be blown, and We will gather the guilty, blue-eyed, on that day;
20 103	In whispers will they consult each other: "Yet tarried not longer than ten (Days);"	Murmuring among themselves: Ye have tarried but ten (days).	They shall consult together secretly. You did tarry but ten (centuries).
20 104	We know best what they will say, when their leader most eminent in conduct will say: "Ye tarried not longer than a day!"	We are Best Aware of what they utter when their best in conduct say: Ye have tarried but a day.	We know best what they say, when the fairest of them in course would say: You tarried but a day.
20 105	They ask thee concerning the Mountains: say, "My Lord will uproot them and scatter them as dust;"	They will ask thee of the mountains (on that day). Say: My Lord will break them into scattered dust.	And they ask you about the mountains. Say: My Lord will carry them away from the roots.
20 106	"He will leave them as plains smooth and level;"	And leave it as an empty plain,	Then leave it a plain, smooth level
20 107	"Nothing crooked or curved wilt thou see in their place."	Wherein thou seest neither curve nor ruggedness.	You shall not see therein any crookedness or unevenness.
20 108	On that Day will they follow the Caller (straight): no crookedness (can they show) him: all sounds shall humble themselves in the Presence of (Allah) Most Gracious: nothing shalt thou hear but the tramp of their feet (as they march).	On that day they follow the summoner who deceiveth not, and voices are hushed for the Beneficent, and thou hearest but a faint murmur.	On that day they shall follow the inviter, there is no crookedness in him, and the voices shall be low before the Beneficent Allah so that you shall not hear aught but a soft sound.
20 109	On that Day shall no intercession avail except for those for whom permission has been granted by (Allah) Most Gracious and whose word is acceptable to Him.	On that day no intercession availeth save (that of) him unto whom the Beneficent hath given leave and whose word He accepteth.	On that day shall no intercession avail except of him whom the Beneficent Allah allows and whose word He is pleased with.
20 110	He knows what (appears to His creatures as) before or after or behind them: but they shall not compass it with their knowledge.	He knoweth (all) that is before them and (all) that is behind them, while they cannot compass it in knowledge.	He knows what is before them and what is behind them, while they do not comprehend it in knowledge.
20 111	(All) faces shall be humbled before (Him) - the Living, the Self-Subsisting, Eternal: hopeless indeed will be the man that carries iniquity (on his back).	And faces humble themselves before the Living, the Eternal. And he who beareth (a burden of) wrongdoing is indeed a failure (on that day).	And the faces shall be humbled before the Living, the Self-subsistent Allah, and he who bears iniquity is indeed a failure.
20 112	But he who works deeds of righteousness, and has faith, will have no fear of harm nor of any curtailment (of what is his due).	And he who hath done some good works, being a believer, he feareth not injustice nor begrudging (of his wage).	And whoever does good works and he is a believer, he shall have no fear of injustice nor of the withholding of his due.
20 113	Thus have We sent this down - an Arabic Qur'an - and explained therein in detail some of the warnings, in order that they may fear Allah, or that it may cause their remembrance (of Him).	Thus we have revealed it as a Lecture in Arabic, and have displayed therein certain threats, that peradventure they may keep from evil or that it may cause them to take heed.	And thus have We sent it down an Arabic Quran, and have distinctly set forth therein of threats that they may guard (against evil) or that it may produce a reminder for them.

20 114	High above all is Allah, the King, the Truth! Be not in haste with the Qur'an before its revelation to thee is completed, but say, "O my Lord! advance me in knowledge."	Then exalted be Allah, the True King! And hasten not (O Muhammad) with the Qur'an ere its revelation hath been perfected unto thee, and say: My Lord! Increase me in knowledge.	Supremely exalted is therefore Allah, the King, the Truth, and do not make haste with the Quran before its revelation is made complete to you and say: O my Lord! increase me in knowledge.
20 115	We had already, beforehand, taken the covenant of Adam, but he forgot: and We found on his part no firm resolve.	And verily We made a covenant of old with Adam, but he forgot, and We found no constancy in him.	And certainly We gave a commandment to Adam before, but he forgot; and We did not find in him any determination.
20 116	When We said to the angels, "Prostrate yourselves to Adam", they prostrated themselves, but not Iblis: he refused.	And when We said unto the angels: Fall prostrate before Adam, they fell prostrate (all) save Iblis; he refused.	And when We said to the angels: Make obeisance to Adam, they made obeisance, but Iblis (did it not); he refused.
20 117	Then We said: "O Adam! verily, this is an enemy to thee and thy wife: so let him not get you both out of the Garden, so that thou art landed in misery."	Therefor we said: O Adam! This is an enemy unto thee and unto thy wife, so let him not drive you both out of the Garden so that thou come to toil.	So We said: O Adam! This is an enemy to you and to your wife; therefore let him not drive you both forth from the garden so that you should be unhappy;
20 118	"There is therein (enough provision) for thee not to go hungry nor to go naked,"	It is (vouchsafed) unto thee that thou hungerest not therein nor art naked,	Surely it is (ordained) for you that you shall not be hungry therein nor bare of clothing;
20 119	"Nor to suffer from thirst, nor from the sun's heat."	And that thou thirstest not therein nor art exposed to the sun's heat.	And that you shall not be thirsty therein nor shall you feel the heat of the sun.
20 120	But Satan whispered evil to him: he said, "O Adam! shall I lead thee to the Tree of Eternity and to a kingdom that never decays?"	But the devil whispered to him, saying: O Adam! Shall I show thee the tree of immortality and power that wasteth not away?	But the Shaitan made an evil suggestion to him; he said: O Adam! Shall I guide you to the tree of immortality and a kingdom which decays not?
20 121	In the result, they both ate of the tree, and so their nakedness appeared to them: they began to sew together, for their covering, leaves from the Garden: thus did Adam disobey his Lord, and allow himself to be seduced.	Then they twain ate thereof, so that their shame became apparent unto them, and they began to hide by heaping on themselves some of the leaves of the Garden. And Adam disobeyed his Lord, so went astray.	Then they both ate of it, so their evil inclinations became manifest to them, and they both began to cover themselves with leaves of the garden, and Adam disobeyed his Lord, so his life became evil (to him).
20 122	But his Lord chose him (for His Grace): He turned to him, and gave him Guidance.	Then his Lord chose him, and relented toward him, and guided him.	Then his Lord chose him, so He turned to him and guided (him).
20 123	He said: "Get ye down, both of you,- all together, from the Garden, with enmity one to another: but if, as is sure, there comes to you Guidance from Me, whosoever follows My Guidance, will not lose his way, nor fall into misery."	He said: Go down hence, both of you, one of you a foe unto the other. But when there come unto you from Me a guidance, then whoso followeth My guidance, he will not go astray nor come to grief.	He said: Get forth you two therefrom, all (of you), one of you (is) enemy to another. So there will surely come to you guidance from Me, then whoever follows My guidance, he shall not go astray nor be unhappy;
20 124	"But whosoever turns away from My Message, verily for him is a life narrowed down, and We shall raise him up blind on the Day of Judgment."	But he who turneth away from remembrance of Me, his will be a narrow life, and I shall bring him blind to the assembly on the Day of Resurrection.	And whoever turns away from My reminder, his shall be a straitened life, and We will raise him on the day of resurrection, blind.
20 125	He will say: "O my Lord! why hast Thou raised me up blind, while I had sight (before)?"	He will say: My Lord! Wherefor hast Thou gathered me (hither) blind, when I was wont to see?	He shall say: My Lord! why hast Thou raised me blind and I was a seeing one indeed?
20 126	(Allah) will say: "Thus didst Thou, when Our Signs came unto thee, disregard them: so wilt thou, this day, be disregarded."	He will say: So (it must be). Our revelations came unto thee but thou didst forget them. In like manner thou art forgotten this Day.	He will say: Even so, Our communications came to you but you neglected them; even thus shall you be forsaken this day.

20	127	And thus do We recompense him who transgresses beyond bounds and believes not in the Signs of his Lord: and the Penalty of the Hereafter is far more grievous and more enduring.	Thus do We reward him who is prodigal and believeth not the revelations of his Lord; and verily the doom of the Hereafter will be sterner and more lasting.	And thus do We recompense him who is extravagant and does not believe in the communications of his Lord, and certainly the chastisement of the hereafter is severer and more lasting.
20	128	Is it not a warning to such men (to call to mind) how many generations before them We destroyed, in whose haunts they (now) move? Verily, in this are Signs for men endued with understanding.	Is it not a guidance for them (to know) how many a generation We destroyed before them, amid whose dwellings they walk? Lo! therein verily are signs for men of thought.	Does it not then direct them aright how many of the generations in whose dwelling-places they go about We destroyed before them? Most surely there are signs in this for those endowed with understanding.
20	129	Had it not been for a Word that went forth before from thy Lord, (their punishment) must necessarily have come; but there is a Term appointed (for respite).	And but for a decree that had already gone forth from thy Lord, and a term already fixed, the judgment would have been inevitable (in this world).	And had there not been a word (that had) already gone forth from your Lord and an appointed term, it would surely have been made to cleave (to them).
20	130	Therefore be patient with what they say, and celebrate (constantly) the praises of thy Lord, before the rising of the sun, and before its setting; yea, celebrate them for part of the hours of the night, and at the sides of the day: that thou mayest have (spiritual) joy.	Therefor (O Muhammad), bear with what they say, and celebrate the praise of thy Lord ere the rising of the sun and ere the going down thereof. And glorify Him some hours of the night and at the two ends of the day, that thou mayst find acceptance.	Bear then patiently what they say, and glorify your Lord by the praising of Him before the rising of the sun and before its setting, and during hours of the night do also glorify (Him) and during parts of the day, that you may be well pleased.
20	131	Nor strain thine eyes in longing for the things We have given for enjoyment to parties of them, the splendour of the life of this world, through which We test them: but the provision of thy Lord is better and more enduring.	And strain not thine eyes toward that which We cause some wedded pairs among them to enjoy, the flower of the life of the world, that We may try them thereby. The provision of thy Lord is better and more lasting.	And do not stretch your eyes after that with which We have provided different classes of them, (of) the splendor of this world's life, that We may thereby try them; and the sustenance (given) by your Lord is better and more abiding.
20	132	Enjoin prayer on thy people, and be constant therein. We ask thee not to provide sustenance: We provide it for thee. But the (fruit of) the Hereafter is for righteousness.	And enjoin upon thy people worship, and be constant therein. We ask not of thee a provision: We provided for thee. And the sequel is for righteousness.	And enjoin prayer on your followers, and steadily adhere to it; We do not ask you for subsistence; We do give you subsistence, and the (good) end is for guarding (against evil).
20	133	They say: "Why does he not bring us a sign from his Lord?" Has not a Clear Sign come to them of all that was in the former Books of revelation?	And they say: If only he would bring us a miracle from his Lord! Hath there not come unto them the proof of what is in the former scriptures?	And they say: Why does he not bring to us a sign from his Lord? Has not there come to them a clear evidence of what is in the previous books?
20	134	And if We had inflicted on them a penalty before this, they would have said: "Our Lord! If only Thou hadst sent us a messenger, we should certainly have followed Thy Signs before we were humbled and put to shame."	And if we had destroyed them with some punishment before it, they would assuredly have said: Our Lord! If only Thou hadst sent unto us a messenger, so that we might have followed Thy revelations before we were (thus) humbled and disgraced!	And had We destroyed them with chastisement before this, they would certainly have said: O our Lord! why didst Thou not send to us a messenger, for then we should have followed Thy communications before that we met disgrace and shame.
20	135	Say: "Each one (of us) is waiting: wait ye, therefore, and soon shall ye know who it is that is on the straight and even way, and who it is that has received Guidance."	Say: Each is awaiting; so await ye! Ye will come to know who are the owners of the path of equity, and who is right.	Say: Every one (of us) is awaiting, therefore do await: So you will come to know who is the follower of the even path and who goes aright.

Chapter 21:

AL-ANBIYA (THE PROPHETS)

Total Verses: 112 Revealed At: MAKKA

In the name of Allah, the Most Beneficent, the Most Merciful.

21 001	Closer and closer to mankind comes their Reckoning: yet they heed not and they turn away.	Their reckoning draweth nigh for mankind, while they turn away in heedlessness.		Their reckoning has drawn near to men, and in heedlessness are they turning aside.
21 002	Never comes (aught) to them of a renewed Message from their Lord, but they listen to it as in jest,-	Never cometh there unto them a new reminder from their Lord but they listen to it while they play,		There comes not to them a new reminder from their Lord but they hear it while they sport,
21 003	Their hearts toying as with trifles. The wrong-doers conceal their private counsels, (saying), "Is this (one) more than a man like yourselves? Will ye go to witchcraft with your eyes open?"	With hearts preoccupied. And they confer in secret. The wrong-doers say: Is this other than a mortal like you? Will ye then succumb to magic when ye see (it)?		Their hearts trifling; and those who are unjust counsel together in secret: He is nothing but a mortal like yourselves; what! will you then yield to enchantment while you see?
21 004	Say: "My Lord knoweth (every) word (spoken) in the heavens and on earth: He is the One that heareth and knoweth (all things)."	He saith: My Lord knoweth what is spoken in the heaven and the earth. He is the Hearer, the Knower.		He said: My Lord knows what is spoken in the heaven and the earth, and He is the Hearing, the Knowing.
21 005	"Nay," they say, "(these are) medleys of dream! - Nay, He forged it! - nay, He is (but) a poet!Let him then bring us a Sign like the ones that were sent to (Prophets) of old!"	Nay, say they, (these are but) muddled dreams; nay, he hath but invented it; nay, he is but a poet. Let him bring us a portent even as those of old (who were Allah's messengers) were sent (with portents).		Nay! say they: Medleys of dreams; nay! he has forged it; nay! he is a poet; so let him bring to us a sign as the former (prophets) were sent (with).
21 006	(As to those) before them, not one of the populations which We destroyed believed: will these believe?	Not a township believed of those which We destroyed before them (though We sent them portents): would they then believe?		There did not believe before them any town which We destroyed, will they then believe?
21 007	Before thee, also, the messengers We sent were but men, to whom We granted inspiration: If ye realise this not, ask of those who possess the Message.	And We sent not (as Our messengers) before thee other than men, whom We inspired. Ask the followers of the Reminder if ye know not?		And We did not send before you any but men to whom We sent revelation, so ask the followers of the reminder if you do not know.
21 008	Nor did We give them bodies that ate no food, nor were they exempt from death.	We gave them not bodies that would not eat food, nor were they immortals.		And We did not make them bodies not eating the food, and they were not to abide (forever).
21 009	In the end We fulfilled to them Our Promise, and We saved them and those whom We pleased, but We destroyed those who transgressed beyond bounds.	Then we fulfilled the promise unto them. So we delivered them and whom We would, and We destroyed the prodigals.		Then We made Our promise good to them, so We delivered them and those whom We pleased, and We destroyed the extravagant.
21 010	We have revealed for you (O men!) a book in which is a Message for you: will ye not then understand?	Now We have revealed unto you a Scripture wherein is your Reminder. Have ye then no sense?		Certainly We have revealed to you a Book in which is your good remembrance; what! do you not then understand?

21 011	How many were the populations We utterly destroyed because of their iniquities, setting up in their places other peoples?	How many a community that dealt unjustly have We shattered, and raised up after them another folk!		And how many a town which was iniquitous did We demolish, and We raised up after it another people!
21 012	Yet, when they felt Our Punishment (coming), behold, they (tried to) flee from it.	And, when they felt Our might, behold them fleeing from it!		So when they felt Our punishment, lo! they began to fly
21 013	Flee not, but return to the good things of this life which were given you, and to your homes in order that ye may be called to account.	(But it was said unto them): Flee not, but return to that (existence) which emasculated you and to your dwellings, that ye may be questioned.		Do not fly (now) and come back to what you were made to lead easy lives in and to your dwellings, haply you will be questioned.
21 014	They said: "Ah! woe to us! We were indeed wrong-doers!"	They cried: Alas for us! we were wrong-doers.		They said: O woe to us! surely we were unjust.
21 015	And that cry of theirs ceased not, till We made them as a field that is mown, as ashes silent and quenched.	And this their crying ceased not till We made them as reaped corn, extinct.		And this ceased not to be their cry till We made them cut
21 016	Not for (idle) sport did We create the heavens and the earth and all that is between!	We created not the heaven and the earth and all that is between them in play.		And We did not create the heaven and the earth and what is between them for sport.
21 017	If it had been Our wish to take (just) a pastime, We should surely have taken it from the things nearest to Us, if We would do (such a thing)!	If We had wished to find a pastime, We could have found it in Our presence - if We ever did.		Had We wished to make a diversion, We would have made it from before Ourselves: by no means would We do (it).
21 018	Nay, We hurl the Truth against falsehood, and it knocks out its brain, and behold, falsehood doth perish! Ah! woe be to you for the (false) things ye ascribe (to Us).	Nay, but We hurl the true against the false, and it doth break its head and lo! it vanisheth. And yours will be woe for that which ye ascribe (unto Him).		Nay! We cast the truth against the falsehood, so that it breaks its head, and lo! it vanishes; and woe to you for what you describe;
21 019	To Him belong all (creatures) in the heavens and on earth: Even those who are in His (very) Presence are not too proud to serve Him, nor are they (ever) weary (of His service):	Unto Him belongeth whosoever is in the heavens and the earth. And those who dwell in His presence are not too proud to worship Him, nor do they weary;		And whoever is in the heavens and the earth is His; and those who are with Him are not proud to serve Him, nor do they grow weary.
21 020	They celebrate His praises night and day, nor do they ever flag or intermit.	They glorify (Him) night and day; they flag not.		They glorify (Him) by night and day; they are never languid.
21 021	Or have they taken (for worship) gods from the earth who can raise (the dead)?	Or have they chosen gods from the earth who raise the dead?		Or have they taken gods from the earth who raise (the dead).
21 022	If there were, in the heavens and the earth, other gods besides Allah, there would have been confusion in both! but glory to Allah, the Lord of the Throne: (High is He) above what they attribute to Him!	If there were therein gods beside Allah, then verily both (the heavens and the earth) had been disordered. Glorified be Allah, the Lord of the Throne, from all that they ascribe (unto Him).		If there had been in them any gods except Allah, they would both have certainly been in a state of disorder; therefore glory be to Allah, the Lord of the dominion, above what they attribute (to Him).
21 023	He cannot be questioned for His acts, but they will be questioned (for theirs).	He will not be questioned as to that which He doeth, but they will be questioned.		He cannot be questioned concerning what He does and they shall be questioned.
21 024	Or have they taken for worship (other) gods besides him? Say, Bring your convincing proof: this is the Message of those with me and the Message of those before me." But most of them know not the Truth, and so turn away.	Or have they chosen other gods beside Him? say: Bring your proof (of their godhead). This is the Reminder of those with me and those before me, but most of them know not the Truth and so they are averse.		Or, have they taken gods besides Him? Say: Bring your proof; this is the reminder of those with me and the reminder of those before me. Nay! most of them do not know the truth, so they turn aside.

21 025	Not a messenger did We send before thee without this inspiration sent by Us to him: that there is no god but I; therefore worship and serve Me.	And We sent no messenger before thee but We inspired him, (saying): There is no God save Me (Allah), so worship Me.	And We did not send before you any messenger but We revealed to him that there is no god but Me, therefore serve Me.
21 026	And they say: "(Allah) Most Gracious has begotten offspring." Glory to Him! they are (but) servants raised to honour.	And they say: The Beneficent hath taken unto Himself a son. Be He Glorified! Nay, but (those whom they call sons) are honoured slaves;	And they say: The Beneficent Allah has taken to Himself a son. Glory be to Him. Nay! they are honored servants;
21 027	They speak not before He speaks, and they act (in all things) by His Command.	They speak not until He hath spoken, and they act by His command.	They do not precede Him in speech and (only) according to His commandment do they act.
21 028	He knows what is before them, and what is behind them, and they offer no intercession except for those who are acceptable, and they stand in awe and reverence of His (Glory).	He knoweth what is before them and what is behind them, and they cannot intercede except for him whom He accepteth, and they quake for awe of Him.	He knows what is before them and what is behind them, and they do not intercede except for him whom He approves and for fear of Him they tremble.
21 029	If any of them should say, "I am a god besides Him", such a one We should reward with Hell: thus do We reward those who do wrong.	And one of them who should say: Lo! I am a god beside Him, that one We should repay with hell. Thus We Repay wrong-doers.	And whoever of them should say: Surely I am a god besides Him, such a one do We recompense with hell; thus do, We recompense the unjust.
21 030	Do not the Unbelievers see that the heavens and the earth were joined together (as one unit of creation), before we clove them asunder? We made from water every living thing. Will they not then believe?	Have not those who disbelieve known that the heavens and the earth were of one piece, then We parted them, and we made every living thing of water? Will they not then believe?	Do not those who disbelieve see that the heavens and the earth were closed up, but We have opened them; and We have made of water everything living, will they not then believe?
21 031	And We have set on the earth mountains standing firm, lest it should shake with them, and We have made therein broad highways (between mountains) for them to pass through: that they may receive Guidance.	And We have placed in the earth firm hills lest it quake with them, and We have placed therein ravines as roads that haply they may find their way.	And We have made great mountains in the earth lest it might be convulsed with them, and We have made in it wide ways that they may follow a right direction.
21 032	And We have made the heavens as a canopy well guarded: yet do they turn away from the Signs which these things (point to)!	And we have made the sky a roof withheld (from them). Yet they turn away from its portents.	And We have made the heaven a guarded canopy and (yet) they turn aside from its signs.
21 033	It is He Who created the Night and the Day, and the sun and the moon: all (the celestial bodies) swim along, each in its rounded course.	And He it is Who created the night and the day, and the sun and the moon. They float, each in an orbit.	And He it is Who created the night and the day and the sun and the moon; all (orbs) travel along swiftly in their celestial spheres.
21 034	We granted not to any man before thee permanent life (here): if then thou shouldst die, would they live permanently?	We appointed immortality for no mortal before thee. What! if thou diest, can they be immortal!	And We did not ordain abiding for any mortal before you. What! Then if you die, will they abide?
21 035	Every soul shall have a taste of death: And We test you by evil and by good by way of trial: To Us must ye return.	Every soul must taste of death, and We try you with evil and with good, for ordeal. And unto Us ye will be returned.	Every soul must taste of death and We try you by evil and good by way of probation; and to Us you shall be brought back.
21 036	When the Unbelievers see thee, they treat thee not except with ridicule. "Is this," (they say), "the one who talks of your gods?" and they blaspheme at the mention of (Allah) Most Gracious!	And when those who disbelieve behold thee, they but choose thee out for mockery, (saying): Is this he who maketh mention of your gods? And they would deny all mention of the Beneficent.	And when those who disbelieve see you, they do not take you but for one to be scoffed at: Is this he who speaks of your gods? And they are deniers at the mention of the Beneficent Allah.

21 037	Man is a creature of haste: soon (enough) will I show you My Signs; then ye will not ask Me to hasten them!	Man is made of haste. I shall show you My portents, but ask Me not to hasten.	Man is created of haste; now will I show to you My signs, therefore do not ask Me to hasten (them) on.
21 038	They say: "When will this promise come to pass, if ye are telling the truth?"	And they say: When will this promise (be fulfilled), if ye are truthful?	And they say: When will this threat come to pass if you are truthful?
21 039	If only the Unbelievers knew (the time) when they will not be able to ward off the fire from their faces, nor yet from their backs, and (when) no help can reach them!	If those who disbelieved but knew the time when they will not be able to drive off the fire from their faces and from their backs, and they will not be helped!	Had those who disbelieve but known (of the time) when they shall not be able to ward off the fire from their faces nor from their backs, nor shall they be helped.
21 040	Nay, it may come to them all of a sudden and confound them: no power will they have then to avert it, nor will they (then) get respite.	Nay, but it will come upon them unawares so that it will stupefy them, and they will be unable to repel it, neither will they be reprieved.	Nay, it shall come on them all of a sudden and cause them to become confounded, so they shall not have the power to avert it, nor shall they be respited.
21 041	Mocked were (many) messenger before thee; But their scoffers were hemmed in by the thing that they mocked.	Messengers before thee, indeed, were mocked, but that whereat they mocked surrounded those who scoffed at them.	And certainly messengers before you were scoffed at, then there befell those of them who scoffed that at which they had scoffed.
21 042	Say: "Who can keep you safe by night and by day from (the Wrath of) (Allah) Most Gracious?" Yet they turn away from the mention of their Lord.	Say: Who guardeth you in the night or in the day from the Beneficent? Nay, but they turn away from mention of their Lord!	Say: Who guards you by night and by day from the Beneficent Allah? Nay, they turn aside at the mention of their Lord.
21 043	Or have they gods that can guard them from Us? They have no power to aid themselves, nor can they be defended from Us.	Or have they gods who can shield them from Us? They cannot help themselves nor can they be defended from Us.	Or, have they gods who can defend them against Us? They shall not be able to assist themselves, nor shall they be defended from Us.
21 044	Nay, We gave the good things of this life to these men and their fathers until the period grew long for them; See they not that We gradually reduce the land (in their control) from its outlying borders? Is it then they who will win?	Nay, but We gave these and their fathers ease until life grew long for them. See they not how we aim to the land, reducing it of its outlying parts? Can they then be the victors?	Nay, We gave provision to these and their fathers until life was prolonged to them. Do they not then see that We are visiting the land, curtailing it of its sides? Shall they then prevail?
21 045	Say, "I do but warn you according to revelation": But the deaf will not hear the call, (even) when they are warned!	Say (O Muhammad, unto mankind): I warn you only by the Inspiration. But the deaf hear not the call when they are warned.	Say: I warn you only by revelation; and the deaf do not hear the call whenever they are warned.
21 046	If but a breath of the Wrath of thy Lord do touch them, they will then say, "Woe to us! we did wrong indeed!"	And if a breath of thy Lord's punishment were to touch them, they assuredly would say: Alas for us! Lo! we were wrong-doers.	And if a blast of the chastisement of your Lord were to touch them, they will certainly say: O woe to us! surely we were unjust.
21 047	We shall set up scales of justice for the Day of Judgment, so that not a soul will be dealt with unjustly in the least, and if there be (no more than) the weight of a mustard seed, We will bring it (to account): and enough are We to take account.	And We set a just balance for the Day of Resurrection so that no soul is wronged in aught. Though it be of the weight of a grain of mustard seed, We bring it. And We suffice for reckoners.	And We will set up a just balance on the day of resurrection, so no soul shall be dealt with unjustly in the least; and though there be the weight of a grain of mustard seed, (yet) will We bring it, and sufficient are We to take account.
21 048	In the past We granted to Moses and Aaron the criterion (for judgment), and a Light and a Message for those who would do right,-	And We verily gave Moses and Aaron the Criterion (of right and wrong) and a light and a Reminder for those who keep from evil,	And certainly We gave to Musa and Haroun the Furqan and a light and a reminder for those who would guard (against evil).
21 049	Those who fear their Lord in their most secret thoughts, and who hold the Hour (of Judgment) in awe.	Those who fear their Lord in secret and who dread the Hour (of doom).	(For) those who fear their Lord in secret and they are fearful of the hour.

21 050	And this is a blessed Message which We have sent down: will ye then reject it?	This is a blessed Reminder that we have revealed: Will ye then reject it?	And this is a blessed Reminder which We have revealed; will you then deny it?
21 051	We bestowed aforetime on Abraham his rectitude of conduct, and well were We acquainted with him.	And We verily gave Abraham of old his proper course, and We were Aware of him,	And certainly We gave to Ibrahim his rectitude before, and We knew him fully well.
21 052	Behold! he said to his father and his people, "What are these images, to which ye are (so assiduously) devoted?"	When he said unto his father and his folk: What are these images unto which ye pay devotion?	When he said to his father and his people: What are these images to whose worship you cleave?
21 053	They said, "We found our fathers worshipping them."	They said: We found our fathers worshippers of them.	They said: We found our fathers worshipping them.
21 054	He said, "Indeed ye have been in manifest error - ye and your fathers."	He said: Verily ye and your fathers were in plain error.	He said: Certainly you have been, (both) you and your fathers, in manifest error.
21 055	They said, "Have you brought us the Truth, or are you one of those who jest?"	They said: Bringest thou unto us the truth, or art thou some jester?	They said: Have you brought to us the truth, or are you one of the triflers?
21 056	He said, "Nay, your Lord is the Lord of the heavens and the earth, He Who created them (from nothing): and I am a witness to this (Truth)."	He said: Nay, but your Lord is the Lord of the heavens and the earth, Who created them; and I am of those who testify unto that.	He said: Nay! your Lord is the Lord of the heavens and the earth, Who brought them into existence, and I am of those who bear witness to this:
21 057	"And by Allah, I have a plan for your idols - after ye go away and turn your backs"..	And, by Allah, I shall circumvent your idols after ye have gone away and turned your backs.	And, by Allah! I will certainly do something against your idols after you go away, turning back.
21 058	So he broke them to pieces, (all) but the biggest of them, that they might turn (and address themselves) to it.	Then he reduced them to fragments, all save the chief of them, that haply they might have recourse to it.	So he broke them into pieces, except the chief of them, that haply they may return to it.
21 059	They said, "Who has done this to our gods? He must indeed be some man of impiety!"	They said: Who hath done this to our gods? Surely it must be some evil-doer.	They said: Who has done this to our gods? Most surely he is one of the unjust.
21 060	They said, "We heard a youth talk of them: He is called Abraham."	They said: We heard a youth make mention of them, who is called Abraham.	They said: We heard a youth called Ibrahim speak of them.
21 061	They said, "Then bring him before the eyes of the people, that they may bear witness."	They said: Then bring him (hither) before the people's eyes that they may testify.	Said they: Then bring him before the eyes of the people, perhaps they may bear witness.
21 062	They said, "Art thou the one that did this with our gods, O Abraham?"	They said: Is it thou who hast done this to our gods, O Abraham?	They said: Have you done this to our gods, O Ibrahim?
21 063	He said: "Nay, this was done by - this is their biggest one! ask them, if they can speak intelligently!"	He said: But this, their chief hath done it. So question them, if they can speak.	He said: Surely (some doer) has done it; the chief of them is this, therefore ask them, if they can speak.
21 064	So they turned to themselves and said, "Surely ye are the ones in the wrong!"	Then gathered they apart and said: Lo! ye yourselves are the wrong-doers.	Then they turned to themselves and said: Surely you yourselves are the unjust;
21 065	Then were they confounded with shame: (they said), "Thou knowest full well that these (idols) do not speak!"	And they were utterly confounded, and they said: Well thou knowest that these speak not.	Then they were made to hang down their heads: Certainly you know that they do not speak.
21 066	(Abraham) said, "Do ye then worship, besides Allah, things that can neither be of any good to you nor do you harm?"	He said: Worship ye then instead of Allah that which cannot profit you at all, nor harm you?	He said: What! do you then serve besides Allah what brings you not any benefit at all, nor does it harm you?

21 067	"Fie upon you, and upon the things that ye worship besides Allah! Have ye no sense?"..	Fie on you and all that ye worship instead of Allah! Have ye then no sense?	Fie on you and on what you serve besides Allah; what! do you not then understand?
21 068	They said, "Burn him and protect your gods, if ye do (anything at all)!"	They cried: Burn him and stand by your gods, if ye will be doing.	They said: Burn him and help your gods, if you are going to do (anything).
21 069	We said, "O Fire! be thou cool, and (a means of) safety for Abraham!"	We said: O fire, be coolness and peace for Abraham,	We said: O fire! be a comfort and peace to Ibrahim;
21 070	Then they sought a stratagem against him: but We made them the ones that lost most!	And they wished to set a snare for him, but We made them the greater losers.	And they desired a war on him, but We made them the greatest losers.
21 071	But We delivered him and (his nephew) Lut (and directed them) to the land which We have blessed for the nations.	And We rescued him and Lot (and brought them) to the land which We have blessed for (all) peoples.	And We delivered him as well as Lut (removing them) to the land which We had blessed for all people.
21 072	And We bestowed on him Isaac and, as an additional gift, (a grandson), Jacob, and We made righteous men of every one (of them).	And We bestowed upon him Isaac, and Jacob as a grandson. Each of them We made righteous.	And We gave him Ishaq and Yaqoub, a son's son, and We made (them) all good.
21 073	And We made them leaders, guiding (men) by Our Command, and We sent them inspiration to do good deeds, to establish regular prayers, and to practise regular charity; and they constantly served Us (and Us only).	And We made them chiefs who guide by Our command, and We inspired in them the doing of good deeds and the right establishment of worship and the giving of alms, and they were worshippers of Us (alone).	And We made them Imams who guided (people) by Our command, and We revealed to them the doing of good and the keeping up of prayer and the giving of the alms, and Us (alone) did they serve;
21 074	And to Lut, too, We gave Judgment and Knowledge, and We saved him from the town which practised abominations: truly they were a people given to Evil, a rebellious people.	And unto Lot we gave judgment and knowledge, and We delivered him from the community that did abominations. Lo! they were folk of evil, lewd.	And (as for) Lut, We gave him wisdom and knowledge, and We delivered him from the town which wrought abominations; surely they were an evil people, transgressors;
21 075	And We admitted him to Our Mercy: for he was one of the Righteous.	And We brought him in unto Our mercy. Lo! he was of the righteous.	And We took him into Our mercy; surely he was of the good.
21 076	(Remember) Noah, when he cried (to Us) aforetime: We listened to his (prayer) and delivered him and his family from great distress.	And Noah, when he cried of old, We heard his prayer and saved him and his household from the great affliction.	And Nuh, when he cried aforetime, so We answered him, and delivered him and his followers from the great calamity.
21 077	We helped him against people who rejected Our Signs: truly they were a people given to Evil: so We drowned them (in the Flood) all together.	And delivered him from the people who denied Our revelations. Lo! they were folk of evil, therefor did We drown them all.	And We helped him against the people who rejected Our communications; surely they were an evil people, so We drowned them all.
21 078	And remember David and Solomon, when they gave judgment in the matter of the field into which the sheep of certain people had strayed by night: We did witness their judgment.	And David and Solomon, when they gave judgment concerning the field, when people's sheep had strayed and browsed therein by night; and We were witnesses to their judgment.	And Dawood and Sulaiman when they gave judgment concerning the field when the people's sheep pastured therein by night, and We were bearers of witness to their judgment.
21 079	To Solomon We inspired the (right) understanding of the matter: to each (of them) We gave Judgment and Knowledge; it was Our power that made the hills and the birds celebrate Our praises, with David: it was We Who did (all these things).	And We made Solomon to understand (the case); and unto each of them We gave judgment and knowledge. And we subdued the hills and the birds to hymn (His) praise along with David. We were the doers (thereof).	So We made Sulaiman to understand it; and to each one We gave wisdom and knowledge; and We made the mountains, and the birds to celebrate Our praise with Dawood; and We were the doers.

21 080	It was We Who taught him the making of coats of mail for your benefit, to guard you from each other's violence: will ye then be grateful?	And We taught him the art of making garments (of mail) to protect you in your daring. Are ye then thankful?	And We taught him the making of coats of mail for you, that they might protect you in your wars; will you then be grateful?
21 081	(It was Our power that made) the violent (unruly) wind flow (tamely) for Solomon, to his order, to the land which We had blessed: for We do know all things.	And unto Solomon (We subdued) the wind in its raging. It set by his command toward the land which We had blessed. And of everything We are Aware.	And (We made subservient) to Sulaiman the wind blowing violent, pursuing its course by his command to the land which We had blessed, and We are knower of all things.
21 082	And of the evil ones, were some who dived for him, and did other work besides; and it was We Who guarded them.	And of the evil ones (subdued We unto him) some who dived (for pearls) for him and did other work, and We were warders unto them.	And of the rebellious people there were those who dived for him and did other work besides that, and We kept guard over them;
21 083	And (remember) Job, when He cried to his Lord, "Truly distress has seized me, but Thou art the Most Merciful of those that are merciful."	And Job, when he cried unto his Lord, (saying): Lo! adversity afflicteth me, and Thou art Most Merciful of all who show mercy.	And Ayub, when he cried to his Lord, (saying): Harm has afflicted me, and Thou art the most Merciful of the merciful.
21 084	So We listened to him: We removed the distress that was on him, and We restored his people to him, and doubled their number,- as a Grace from Ourselves, and a thing for commemoration, for all who serve Us.	Then We heard his prayer and removed that adversity from which he suffered, and We gave him his household (that he had lost) and the like thereof along with them, a mercy from Our store, and a remembrance for the worshippers;	Therefore We responded to him and took off what harm he had, and We gave him his family and the like of them with them: a mercy from Us and a reminder to the worshippers.
21 085	And (remember) Isma'il, Idris, and Zul-kifl, all (men) of constancy and patience;	And (mention) Ishmael, and Idris, and Dhu'l-Kifl. All were of the steadfast.	And Ismail and Idris and Zulkifl; all were of the patient ones;
21 086	We admitted them to Our mercy: for they were of the righteous ones.	And We brought them in unto Our mercy. Lo! they are among the righteous.	And We caused them to enter into Our mercy, surely they were of the good ones.
21 087	And remember Zun-nun, when he departed in wrath: He imagined that We had no power over him! But he cried through the depths of darkness, There is no god but Thou: glory to Thee: I was indeed wrong!	And (mention) Dhu'n-Nun, when he went off in anger and deemed that We had no power over him, but he cried out in the darkness, saying: There is no God save Thee. Be Thou Glorified! Lo! I have been a wrong-doer.	And Yunus, when he went away in wrath, so he thought that We would not straiten him, so he called out among afflictions: There is no god but Thou, glory be to Thee; surely I am of those who make themselves to suffer loss.
21 088	So We listened to him: and delivered him from distress: and thus do We deliver those who have faith.	Then we heard his prayer and saved him from the anguish. Thus we save believers.	So We responded to him and delivered him from the grief and thus do We deliver the believers.
21 089	And (remember) Zakariya, when he cried to his Lord: "O my Lord! leave me not without offspring, though thou art the best of inheritors."	And Zachariah, when he cried unto his Lord: My Lord! Leave me not childless, though Thou art the Best of inheritors.	And Zakariya, when he cried to his Lord: O my Lord leave me not alone; and Thou art the best of inheritors.
21 090	So We listened to him: and We granted him Yahya: We cured his wife's (Barrenness) for him. These (three) were ever quick in emulation in good works; they used to call on Us with love and reverence, and humble themselves before Us.	Then We heard his prayer, and bestowed upon him John, and adjusted his wife (to bear a child) for him. Lo! they used to vie one with the other in good deeds, and they cried unto Us in longing and in fear, and were submissive unto Us.	So We responded to him and gave him Yahya and made his wife fit for him; surely they used to hasten, one with another, in deeds of goodness and to call upon Us, hoping and fearing; and they were humble before Us.

21 091	And (remember) her who guarded her chastity: We breathed into her of Our spirit, and We made her and her son a sign for all peoples.	And she who was chaste, therefor We breathed into her (something) of Our Spirit and made her and her son a token for (all) peoples.	And she who guarded her chastity, so We breathed into her of Our inspiration and made her and her son a sign for the nations.
21 092	Verily, this brotherhood of yours is a single brotherhood, and I am your Lord and Cherisher: therefore serve Me (and no other).	Lo! this, your religion, is one religion, and I am your Lord, so worship Me.	Surely this Islam is your religion, one religion (only), and I am your Lord, therefore serve Me.
21 093	But (later generations) cut off their affair (of unity), one from another: (yet) will they all return to Us.	And they have broken their religion (into fragments) among them, (yet) all are returning unto Us.	And they broke their religion (into sects) between them: to Us shall all come back.
21 094	Whoever works any act of righteousness and has faith,- his endeavour will not be rejected: We shall record it in his favour.	Then whoso doeth some good works and is a believer, there will be no rejection of his effort. Lo! We record (it) for him.	Therefore whoever shall do of good deeds and he is a believer, there shall be no denying of his exertion, and surely We will write (It) down for him.
21 095	But there is a ban on any population which We have destroyed: that they shall not return,	And there is a ban upon any community which We have destroyed: that they shall not return.	And it is binding on a town which We destroy that they shall not return.
21 096	Until the Gog and Magog (people) are let through (their barrier), and they swiftly swarm from every hill.	Until, when Gog and Magog are let loose, and they hasten out of every mound,	Even when Gog and Magog are let loose and they shall break forth from every elevated place.
21 097	Then will the true promise draw nigh (of fulfilment): then behold! the eyes of the Unbelievers will fixedly stare in horror: "Ah! Woe to us! we were indeed heedless of this; nay, we truly did wrong!"	And the True Promise draweth nigh; then behold them, staring wide (in terror), the eyes of those who disbelieve! (They say): Alas for us! We (lived) in forgetfulness of this. Ah, but we were wrongdoers!	And the true promise shall draw nigh, then lo! the eyes of those who disbelieved shall be fixedly open: O woe to us! surely we were in a state of heedlessness as to this; nay, we were unjust.
21 098	Verily ye, (unbelievers), and the (false) gods that ye worship besides Allah, are (but) fuel for Hell! to it will ye (surely) come!	Lo! ye (idolaters) and that which ye worship beside Allah are fuel of hell. Thereunto ye will come.	Surely you and what you worship besides Allah are the firewood of hell; to it you shall come.
21 099	If these had been gods, they would not have got there! but each one will abide therein.	If these had been gods they would not have come thither, but all will abide therein.	Had these been gods, they would not have come to it and all shall abide therein.
21 100	There, sobbing will be their lot, nor will they there hear (aught else).	Therein wailing is their portion, and therein they hear not.	For them therein shall be groaning and therein they shall not hear.
21 101	Those for whom the good (record) from Us has gone before, will be removed far therefrom.	Lo! those unto whom kindness hath gone forth before from Us, they will be far removed from thence.	Surely (as for) those for whom the good has already gone forth from Us, they shall be kept far off from it;
21 102	Not the slightest sound will they hear of Hell: what their souls desired, in that will they dwell.	They will not hear the slightest sound thereof, while they abide in that which their souls desire.	They will not hear its faintest sound, and they shall abide in that which their souls long for.
21 103	The Great Terror will bring them no grief: but the angels will meet them (with mutual greetings): "This is your Day,- (the Day) that ye were promised."	The Supreme Horror will not grieve them, and the angels will welcome them, (saying): This is your Day which ye were promised;	The great fearful event shall not grieve them, and the angels shall meet them: This is your day which you were promised.
21 104	The Day that We roll up the heavens like a scroll rolled up for books (completed),- even as We produced the first creation, so shall We produce a new one: a promise We have undertaken: truly shall We fulfil it.	The Day when We shall roll up the heavens as a recorder rolleth up a written scroll. As We began the first creation, We shall repeat it. (It is) a promise (binding) upon Us. Lo! We are to perform it.	On the day when We will roll up heaven like the rolling up of the scroll for writings, as We originated the first creation, (so) We shall reproduce it; a promise (binding on Us); surely We will bring it about.

21 105	Before this We wrote in the Psalms, after the Message (given to Moses): "My servants the righteous, shall inherit the earth."	And verily we have written in the Scripture, after the Reminder: My righteous slaves will inherit the earth:	And certainly We wrote in the Book after the reminder that (as for) the land, My righteous servants shall inherit it.
21 106	Verily in this (Qur'an) is a Message for people who would (truly) worship Allah.	Lo! there is a plain statement for folk who are devout.	Most surely in this is a message to a people who serve
21 107	We sent thee not, but as a Mercy for all creatures.	We sent thee not save as a mercy for the peoples.	And We have not sent you but as a mercy to the worlds.
21 108	Say: "What has come to me by inspiration is that your Allah is One Allah: will ye therefore bow to His Will (in Islam)?"	Say: It is only inspired in me that your Allah is One Allah. Will ye then surrender (unto Him)?	Say: It is only revealed to me that your Allah is one Allah; will you then submit?
21 109	But if they turn back, say: "I have proclaimed the Message to you all alike and in truth; but I know not whether that which ye are promised is near or far."	But if they are averse, then say: I have warned you all alike, although I know not whether nigh or far is that which ye are promised.	But if they turn back, say: I have given you warning in fairness and I do not know whether what you are threatened with is near or far:
21 110	"It is He Who knows what is open in speech and what ye hide (in your hearts)."	Lo! He knoweth that which is said openly, and that which ye conceal.	Surely He knows what is spoken openly and He knows what you hide:
21 111	"I know not but that it may be a trial for you, and a grant of (worldly) livelihood (to you) for a time."	And I know not but that this may be a trial for you, and enjoyment for a while.	And I do not know if this may be a trial for you and a provision till a time.
21 112	Say: "O my Lord! judge Thou in truth!" "Our Lord Most Gracious is the One Whose assistance should be sought against the blasphemies ye utter!"	He saith: My Lord! Judge Thou with truth. Our Lord is the Beneficent, Whose help is to be implored against that which ye ascribe (unto Him).	He said: O my Lord! judge Thou with truth; and our Lord is the Beneficent Allah, Whose help is sought against what you ascribe (to Him).

Chapter 22:

AL-HAJJ (THE PILGRIMAGE)

Total Verses: 78 Revealed At: MADINA

In the name of Allah, the Most Beneficent, the Most Merciful.

22 001	O mankind! fear your Lord! for the convulsion of the Hour (of Judgment) will be a thing terrible!	O mankind! Fear your Lord. Lo! the earthquake of the Hour (of Doom) is a tremendous thing.	O people! guard against (the punishment from) your Lord; surely the violence of the hour is a grievous thing.
22 002	The Day ye shall see it, every mother giving suck shall forget her suckling-babe, and every pregnant female shall drop her load (unformed): thou shalt see mankind as in a drunken riot, yet not drunk: but dreadful will be the Wrath of Allah.	On the day when ye behold it, every nursing mother will forget her nursling and every pregnant one will be delivered of her burden, and thou (Muhammad) wilt see mankind as drunken, yet they will not be drunken, but the Doom of Allah will be strong (upon them).	On the day when you shall see it, every woman giving suck shall quit in confusion what she suckled, and every pregnant woman shall lay down her burden, and you shall see men intoxicated, and they shall not be intoxicated but the chastisement of Allah will be severe.
22 003	And yet among men there are such as dispute about Allah, without knowledge, and follow every evil one obstinate in rebellion!	Among mankind is he who disputeth concerning Allah without knowledge, and followeth each froward devil;	And among men there is he who disputes about Allah without knowledge and follows every rebellious Shaitan;

22 004	About the (Evil One) it is decreed that whoever turns to him for friendship, him will he lead astray, and he will guide him to the Penalty of the Fire.	For him it is decreed that whoso taketh him for friend, he verily will mislead him and will guide him to the punishment of the Flame.	Against him it is written down that whoever takes him for a friend, he shall lead him astray and conduct him to the chastisement of the burning fire.
22 005	O mankind! if ye have a doubt about the Resurrection, (consider) that We created you out of dust, then out of sperm, then out of a leech-like clot, then out of a morsel of flesh, partly formed and partly unformed, in order that We may manifest (our power) to you; and We cause whom We will to rest in the wombs for an appointed term, then do We bring you out as babes, then (foster you) that ye may reach your age of full strength; and some of you are called to die, and some are sent back to the feeblest old age, so that they know nothing after having known (much), and (further), thou seest the earth barren and lifeless, but when We pour down rain on it, it is stirred (to life), it swells, and it puts forth every kind of beautiful growth (in pairs).	O mankind! if ye are in doubt concerning the Resurrection, then lo! We have created you from dust, then from a drop of seed, then from a clot, then from a little lump of flesh shapely and shapeless, that We may make (it) clear for you. And We cause what We will to remain in the wombs for an appointed time, and afterward We bring you forth as infants, then (give you growth) that ye attain your full strength. And among you there is he who dieth (young), and among you there is he who is brought back to the most abject time of life, so that, after knowledge, he knoweth naught. And thou (Muhammad) seest the earth barren, but when We send down water thereon, it doth thrill and swell and put forth every lovely kind (of growth).	O people! if you are in doubt about the raising, then surely We created you from dust, then from a small seed, then from a clot, then from a lump of flesh, complete in make and incomplete, that We may make clear to you; and We cause what We please to stay in the wombs till an appointed time, then We bring you forth as babies, then that you may attain your maturity; and of you is he who is caused to die, and of you is he who is brought back to the worst part of life, so that after having knowledge he does not know anything; and you see the earth sterile land, but when We send down on it the water, it stirs and swells and brings forth of every kind a beautiful herbage.
22 006	This is so, because Allah is the Reality: it is He Who gives life to the dead, and it is He Who has power over all things.	That is because Allah, He is the Truth and because He quickeneth the dead, and because He is Able to do all things;	This is because Allah is the Truth and because He gives life to the dead and because He has power over all things,
22 007	And verily the Hour will come: there can be no doubt about it, or about (the fact) that Allah will raise up all who are in the graves.	And because the Hour will come, there is no doubt thereof; and because Allah will raise those who are in the graves.	And because the hour is coming, there is no doubt about it; and because Allah shall raise up those who are in the graves.
22 008	Yet there is among men such a one as disputes about Allah, without Knowledge, without Guidance, and without a Book of Enlightenment,-	And among mankind is he who disputeth concerning Allah without knowledge or guidance or a scripture giving light,	And among men there is he who disputes about Allah without knowledge and without guidance and without an illuminating book,
22 009	(Disdainfully) bending his side, in order to lead (men) astray from the Path of Allah: for him there is disgrace in this life, and on the Day of Judgment We shall make him taste the Penalty of burning (Fire).	Turning away in pride to beguile (men) from the way of Allah. For him in this world is ignominy, and on the Day of Resurrection We make him taste the doom of burning.	Turning away haughtily that he may lead (others) astray from the way of Allah; for him is disgrace in this world, and on the day of resurrection We will make him taste the punishment of burning:
22 010	(It will be said): "This is because of the deeds which thy hands sent forth, for verily Allah is not unjust to His servants."	(And unto him it will be said): This is for that which thy two hands have sent before, and because Allah is no oppressor of His slaves.	This is due to what your two hands have sent before, and because Allah is not in the least unjust to the servants.
22 011	There are among men some who serve Allah, as it were, on the verge: if good befalls them, they are, therewith, well content; but if a trial comes to them, they turn on their faces: they lose both this world and the Hereafter: that is loss for all to see!	And among mankind is he who worshippeth Allah upon a narrow marge so that if good befalleth him he is content therewith, but if a trial befalleth him, he falleth away utterly. He loseth both the world and the Hereafter. That is the sheer loss.	And among men is he who serves Allah (standing) on the verge, so that if good befalls him he is satisfied therewith, but if a trial afflict him he turns back headlong; he loses this world as well as the hereafter; that is a manifest loss.

22	012	They call on such deities, besides Allah, as can neither hurt nor profit them: that is straying far indeed (from the Way)!	He calleth, beside Allah, unto that which hurteth him not nor benefiteth him. That is the far error.	He calls besides Allah upon that which does not harm him and that which does not profit him, that is the great straying.
22	013	(Perhaps) they call on one whose hurt is nearer than his profit: evil, indeed, is the patron, and evil the companion (or help)!	He calleth unto him whose harm is nearer than his benefit; verily an evil patron and verily an evil friend!	He calls upon him whose harm is nearer than his profit; evil certainly is the guardian and evil certainly is the associate.
22	014	Verily Allah will admit those who believe and work righteous deeds, to Gardens, beneath which rivers flow: for Allah carries out all that He plans.	Lo! Allah causeth those who believe and do good works to enter Gardens underneath which rivers flow. Lo! Allah doth what He intendeth.	Surely Allah will cause those who believe and do good deeds to enter gardens beneath which rivers flow, surely Allah does what He pleases.
22	015	If any think that Allah will not help him (His Messenger) in this world and the Hereafter, let him stretch out a rope to the ceiling and cut (himself) off: then let him see whether his plan will remove that which enrages (him)!	Whoso is wont to think (through envy) that Allah will not give him (Muhammad) victory in the world and the Hereafter (and is enraged at the thought of his victory), let him stretch a rope up to the roof (of his dwelling), and let him hang himself. Then let him see whether his strategy dispelleth that whereat he rageth!	Whoever thinks that Allah will not assist him in this life and the hereafter, let him stretch a rope to the ceiling, then let him cut (it) off, then let him see if his struggle will take away that at which he is enraged.
22	016	Thus have We sent down Clear Signs; and verily Allah doth guide whom He will!	Thus We reveal it as plain revelations, and verily Allah guideth whom He will.	And thus have We revealed it, being clear arguments, and because Allah guides whom He intends.
22	017	Those who believe (in the Qur'an), those who follow the Jewish (scriptures), and the Sabians, Christians, Magians, and Polytheists,- Allah will judge between them on the Day of Judgment: for Allah is witness of all things.	Lo! those who believe (this revelation), and those who are Jews, and the Sabaeans and the Christians and the Magians and the idolaters - Lo! Allah will decide between them on the Day of Resurrection. Lo! Allah is Witness over all things.	Surely those who believe and those who are Jews and the Sabeans and the Christians and the Magians and those who associate (others with Allah)-- surely Allah will decide between them on the day of resurrection; surely Allah is a witness over all things.
22	018	Seest thou not that to Allah bow down in worship all things that are in the heavens and on earth,- the sun, the moon, the stars; the hills, the trees, the animals; and a great number among mankind? But a great number are (also) such as are fit for Punishment: and such as Allah shall disgrace,- None can raise to honour: for Allah carries out all that He wills.	Hast thou not seen that unto Allah payeth adoration whosoever is in the heavens and whosoever is in the earth, and the sun, and the moon, and the stars, and the hills, and the trees, and the beasts, and many of mankind, while there are many unto whom the doom is justly due. He whom Allah scorneth, there is none to give him honour. Lo! Allah doeth what He will.	Do you not see that Allah is He, Whom obeys whoever is in the heavens and whoever is in the earth, and the sun and the moon and the stars, and the mountains and the trees, and the animals and many of the people; and many there are against whom chastisement has become necessary; and whomsoever Allah abases, there is none who can make him honorable; surely Allah does what He pleases.
22	019	These two antagonists dispute with each other about their Lord: But those who deny (their Lord),- for them will be cut out a garment of Fire: over their heads will be poured out boiling water.	These twain (the believers and the disbelievers) are two opponents who contend concerning their Lord. But as for those who disbelieve, garments of fire will be cut out for them; boiling fluid will be poured down on their heads,	These are two adversaries who dispute about their Lord; then (as to) those who disbelieve, for them are cut out garments of fire, boiling water shall be poured over their heads.
22	020	With it will be scalded what is within their bodies, as well as (their) skins.	Whereby that which is in their bellies, and their skins too, will be melted;	With it shall be melted what is in their bellies and (their) skins as well.
22	021	In addition there will be maces of iron (to punish) them.	And for them are hooked rods of iron.	And for them are whips of iron.

22 022	Every time they wish to get away therefrom, from anguish, they will be forced back therein, and (it will be said), "Taste ye the Penalty of Burning!"	Whenever, in their anguish, they would go forth from thence they are driven back therein and (it is said unto them): Taste the doom of burning.	Whenever they will desire to go forth from it, from grief, they shall be turned back into it, and taste the chastisement of burning.
22 023	Allah will admit those who believe and work righteous deeds, to Gardens beneath which rivers flow: they shall be adorned therein with bracelets of gold and pearls; and their garments there will be of silk.	Lo! Allah will cause those who believe and do good works to enter Gardens underneath which rivers flow, wherein they will be allowed armlets of gold, and pearls, and their raiment therein will be silk.	Surely Allah will make those who believe and do good deeds enter gardens beneath which rivers flow; they shall be adorned therein with bracelets of gold and (with) pearls, and their garments therein shall be of silk.
22 024	For they have been guided (in this life) to the purest of speeches; they have been guided to the Path of Him Who is Worthy of (all) Praise.	They are guided unto gentle speech; they are guided unto the path of the Glorious One.	And they are guided to goodly words and they are guided into the path of the Praised One.
22 025	As to those who have rejected (Allah), and would keep back (men) from the Way of Allah, and from the Sacred Mosque, which We have made (open) to (all) men - equal is the dweller there and the visitor from the country - and any whose purpose therein is profanity or wrong-doing - them will We cause to taste of a most Grievous Penalty.	Lo! those who disbelieve and bar (men) from the way of Allah and from the Inviolable Place of Worship, which We have appointed for mankind together, the dweller therein and the nomad: whosoever seeketh wrongful partiality therein, him We shall cause to taste a painful doom.	Surely (as for) those who disbelieve, and hinder (men) from Allah's way and from the Sacred Mosque which We have made equally for all men, (for) the dweller therein and (for) the visitor, and whoever shall incline therein to wrong unjustly, We will make him taste of a painful chastisement.
22 026	Behold! We gave the site, to Abraham, of the (Sacred) House, (saying): "Associate not anything (in worship) with Me; and sanctify My House for those who compass it round, or stand up, or bow, or prostrate themselves (therein in prayer)."	And (remember) when We prepared for Abraham the place of the (holy) House, saying: Ascribe thou no thing as partner unto Me, and purify My House for those who make the round (thereof) and those who stand and those who bow and make prostration.	And when We assigned to Ibrahim the place of the House, saying: Do not associate with Me aught, and purify My House for those who make the circuit and stand to pray and bow and prostrate themselves.
22 027	"And proclaim the Pilgrimage among men: they will come to thee on foot and (mounted) on every kind of camel, lean on account of journeys through deep and distant mountain highways;"	And proclaim unto mankind the pilgrimage. They will come unto thee on foot and on every lean camel; they will come from every deep ravine,	And proclaim among men the Pilgrimage: they will come to you on foot and on every lean camel, coming from every remote path,
22 028	"That they may witness the benefits (provided) for them, and celebrate the name of Allah, through the Days appointed, over the cattle which He has provided for them (for sacrifice): then eat ye thereof and feed the distressed ones in want."	That they may witness things that are of benefit to them, and mention the name of Allah on appointed days over the beast of cattle that He hath bestowed upon them. Then eat thereof and feed therewith the poor unfortunate.	That they may witness advantages for them and mention the name of Allah during stated days over what He has given them of the cattle quadrupeds, then eat of them and feed the distressed one, the needy.
22 029	"Then let them complete the rites prescribed for them, perform their vows, and (again) circumambulate the Ancient House."	Then let them make an end of their unkemptness and pay their vows and go around the ancient House.	Then let them accomplish their needful acts of shaving and cleansing, and let them fulfil their vows and let them go round the Ancient House.

22 030	Such (is the Pilgrimage): whoever honours the sacred rites of Allah, for him it is good in the Sight of his Lord. Lawful to you (for food in Pilgrimage) are cattle, except those mentioned to you (as exception): but shun the abomination of idols, and shun the word that is false,-	That (is the command). And whoso magnifieth the sacred things of Allah, it will be well for him in the sight of his Lord. The cattle are lawful unto you save that which hath been told you. So shun the filth of idols, and shun lying speech,	That (shall be so); and whoever respects the sacred ordinances of Allah, it is better for him with his Lord; and the cattle are made lawful for you, except that which is recited to you, therefore avoid the uncleanness of the idols and avoid false words,
22 031	Being true in faith to Allah, and never assigning partners to Him: if anyone assigns partners to Allah, is as if he had fallen from heaven and been snatched up by birds, or the wind had swooped (like a bird on its prey) and thrown him into a far-distant place.	Turning unto Allah (only), not ascribing partners unto Him; for whoso ascribeth partners unto Allah, it is as if he had fallen from the sky and the birds had snatched him or the wind had blown him to a far-off place.	Being upright for Allah, not associating aught with Him and whoever associates (others) with Allah, it is as though he had fallen from on high, then the birds snatch him away or the wind carries him off to a far-distant place.
22 032	Such (is his state): and whoever holds in honour the symbols of Allah, (in the sacrifice of animals), such (honour) should come truly from piety of heart.	That (is the command). And whoso magnifieth the offerings consecrated to Allah, it surely is from devotion of the hearts,	That (shall be so); and whoever respects the signs of Allah, this surely is (the outcome) of the piety of hearts.
22 033	In them ye have benefits for a term appointed: in the end their place of sacrifice is near the Ancient House.	Therein are benefits for you for an appointed term; and afterward they are brought for sacrifice unto the ancient House.	You have advantages in them till a fixed time, then their place of sacrifice is the Ancient House.
22 034	To every people did We appoint rites (of sacrifice), that they might celebrate the name of Allah over the sustenance He gave them from animals (fit for food). But your Allah is One Allah: submit then your wills to Him (in Islam): and give thou the good news to those who humble themselves,-	And for every nation have We appointed a ritual, that they may mention the name of Allah over the beast of cattle that He hath given them for food; and your Allah is One Allah, therefor surrender unto Him. And give good tidings (O Muhammad) to the humble,	And to every nation We appointed acts of devotion that they may mention the name of Allah on what He has given them of the cattle quadrupeds; so your Allah is One Allah, therefore to Him should you submit, and give good news to the humble,
22 035	To those whose hearts when Allah is mentioned, are filled with fear, who show patient perseverance over their afflictions, keep up regular prayer, and spend (in charity) out of what We have bestowed upon them.	Whose hearts fear when Allah is mentioned, and the patient of whatever may befall them, and those who establish worship and who spend of that We have bestowed on them.	(To) those whose hearts tremble when Allah is mentioned, and those who are patient under that which afflicts them, and those who keep up prayer, and spend (benevolently) out of what We have given them.
22 036	The sacrificial camels we have made for you as among the symbols from Allah: in them is (much) good for you: then pronounce the name of Allah over them as they line up (for sacrifice): when they are down on their sides (after slaughter), eat ye thereof, and feed such as (beg not but) live in contentment, and such as beg with due humility: thus have We made animals subject to you, that ye may be grateful.	And the camels! We have appointed them among the ceremonies of Allah. Therein ye have much good. So mention the name of Allah over them when they are drawn up in lines. Then when their flanks fall (dead), eat thereof and feed the beggar and the suppliant. Thus have We made them subject unto you, that haply ye may give thanks.	And (as for) the camels, We have made them of the signs of the religion of Allah for you; for you therein is much good; therefore mention the name of Allah on them as they stand in a row, then when they fall down eat of them and feed the poor man who is contented and the beggar; thus have We made them subservient to you, that you may be grateful.

22 037	It is not their meat nor their blood, that reaches Allah: it is your piety that reaches Him: He has thus made them subject to you, that ye may glorify Allah for His Guidance to you and proclaim the good news to all who do right.	Their flesh and their food reach not Allah, but the devotion from you reacheth Him. Thus have We made them subject unto you that ye may magnify Allah that He hath guided you. And give good tidings (O Muhammad) to the good.	There does not reach Allah their flesh nor their blood, but to Him is acceptable the guarding (against evil) on your part; thus has He made them subservient to you, that you may magnify Allah because He has guided you aright; and give good news to those who do good (to others).
22 038	Verily Allah will defend (from ill) those who believe: verily, Allah loveth not any that is a traitor to faith, or show ingratitude.	Lo! Allah defendeth those who are true. Lo! Allah loveth not each treacherous ingrate.	Surely Allah will defend those who believe; surely Allah does not love any one who is unfaithful, ungrateful.
22 039	To those against whom war is made, permission is given (to fight), because they are wronged;- and verily, Allah is most powerful for their aid;-	Sanction is given unto those who fight because they have been wronged; and Allah is indeed Able to give them victory;	Permission (to fight) is given to those upon whom war is made because they are oppressed, and most surely Allah is well able to assist them;
22 040	(They are) those who have been expelled from their homes in defiance of right,- (for no cause) except that they say, "Our Lord is Allah". Did not Allah check one set of people by means of another, there would surely have been pulled down monasteries, churches, synagogues, and mosques, in which the name of Allah is commemorated in abundant measure. Allah will certainly aid those who aid his (cause);- for verily Allah is full of Strength, Exalted in Might, (able to enforce His Will).	Those who have been driven from their homes unjustly only because they said: Our Lord is Allah - For had it not been for Allah's repelling some men by means of others, cloisters and churches and oratories and mosques, wherein the name of Allah is oft mentioned, would assuredly have been pulled down. Verily Allah helpeth one who helpeth Him. Lo! Allah is Strong, Almighty -	Those who have been expelled from their homes without a just cause except that they say: Our Lord is Allah. And had there not been Allah's repelling some people by others, certainly there would have been pulled down cloisters and churches and synagogues and mosques in which Allah's name is much remembered; and surely Allah will help him who helps His cause; most surely Allah is Strong, Mighty.
22 041	(They are) those who, if We establish them in the land, establish regular prayer and give regular charity, enjoin the right and forbid wrong: with Allah rests the end (and decision) of (all) affairs.	Those who, if We give them power in the land, establish worship and pay the poor-due and enjoin kindness and forbid iniquity. And Allah's is the sequel of events.	Those who, should We establish them in the land, will keep up prayer and pay the poor-rate and enjoin good and forbid evil; and Allah's is the end of affairs.
22 042	If they treat thy (mission) as false, so did the peoples before them (with their prophets),- the People of Noah, and 'Ad and Thamud;	If they deny thee (Muhammad), even so the folk of Noah, and (the tribes of) A'ad and Thamud, before thee, denied (Our messengers);	And if they reject you, then already before you did the people of Nuh and Ad and Samood reject (prophets).
22 043	Those of Abraham and Lut;	And the folk of Abraham and the folk of Lot;	And the people of Ibrahim and the people of Lut,
22 044	And the Companions of the Madyan People; and Moses was rejected (in the same way). But I granted respite to the Unbelievers, and (only) after that did I punish them: but how (terrible) was my rejection (of them)!	(And) the dwellers in Midian. And Moses was denied; but I indulged the disbelievers a long while, then I seized them, and how (terrible) was My abhorrence!	As well as those of Madyan and Musa (too) was rejected, but I gave respite to the unbelievers, then did I overtake them, so how (severe) was My disapproval.
22 045	How many populations have We destroyed, which were given to wrong-doing? They tumbled down on their roofs. And how many wells are lying idle and neglected, and castles lofty and well-built?	How many a township have We destroyed while it was sinful, so that it lieth (to this day) in ruins, and (how many) a deserted well and lofty tower!	So how many a town did We destroy while it was unjust, so it was fallen down upon its roofs, and (how many a) deserted well and palace raised high.

22 046	Do they not travel through the land, so that their hearts (and minds) may thus learn wisdom and their ears may thus learn to hear? Truly it is not their eyes that are blind, but their hearts which are in their breasts.	Have they not travelled in the land, and have they hearts wherewith to feel and ears wherewith to hear? For indeed it is not the eyes that grow blind, but it is the hearts, which are within the bosoms, that grow blind.	Have they not travelled in the land so that they should have hearts with which to understand, or ears with which to hear? For surely it is not the eyes that are blind, but blind are the hearts which are in the breasts.
22 047	Yet they ask thee to hasten on the Punishment! But Allah will not fail in His Promise. Verily a Day in the sight of thy Lord is like a thousand years of your reckoning.	And they will bid thee hasten on the Doom, and Allah faileth not His promise, but lo! a Day with Allah is as a thousand years of what ye reckon.	And they ask you to hasten on the punishment, and Allah will by no means fail in His promise, and surely a day with your Lord is as a thousand years of what you number.
22 048	And to how many populations did I give respite, which were given to wrong-doing? in the end I punished them. To me is the destination (of all).	And how many a township did I suffer long though it was sinful! Then I grasped it. Unto Me is the return.	And how many a town to which I gave respite while it was unjust, then I overtook it, and to Me is the return.
22 049	Say: "O men! I am (sent) to you only to give a Clear Warning:"	Say: O mankind! I am only a plain warner unto you.	Say: O people! I am only a plain warner to you.
22 050	"Those who believe and work righteousness, for them is forgiveness and a sustenance most generous."	Those who believe and do good works, for them is pardon and a rich provision;	Then (as for) those who believe and do good, they shall have forgiveness and an honorable sustenance.
22 051	"But those who strive against Our Signs, to frustrate them,- they will be Companions of the Fire."	While those who strive to thwart Our revelations, such are rightful owners of the Fire.	And (as for) those who strive to oppose Our communications, they shall be the inmates of the flaming fire.
22 052	Never did We send a messenger or a prophet before thee, but, when he framed a desire, Satan threw some (vanity) into his desire: but Allah will cancel anything (vain) that Satan throws in, and Allah will confirm (and establish) His Signs: for Allah is full of Knowledge and Wisdom:	Never sent We a messenger or a prophet before thee but when He recited (the message) Satan proposed (opposition) in respect of that which he recited thereof. But Allah abolisheth that which Satan proposeth. Then Allah establisheth His revelations. Allah is Knower, Wise;	And We did not send before you any messenger or prophet, but when he desired, the Shaitan made a suggestion respecting his desire; but Allah annuls that which the Shaitan casts, then does Allah establish His communications, and Allah is Knowing, Wise,
22 053	That He may make the suggestions thrown in by Satan, but a trial for those in whose hearts is a disease and who are hardened of heart: verily the wrong-doers are in a schism far (from the Truth):	That He may make that which the devil proposeth a temptation for those in whose hearts is a disease, and those whose hearts are hardened - Lo! the evil-doers are in open schism -	So that He may make what the Shaitan casts a trial for those in whose hearts is disease and those whose hearts are hard; and most surely the unjust are in a great opposition,
22 054	And that those on whom knowledge has been bestowed may learn that the (Qur'an) is the Truth from thy Lord, and that they may believe therein, and their hearts may be made humbly (open) to it: for verily Allah is the Guide of those who believe, to the Straight Way.	And that those who have been given knowledge may know that it is the truth from thy Lord, so that they may believe therein and their hearts may submit humbly unto Him. Lo! Allah verily is guiding those who believe unto a right path.	And that those who have been given the knowledge may know that it is the truth from your Lord, so they may believe in it and their hearts may be lowly before it; and most surely Allah is the Guide of those who believe into a right path.
22 055	Those who reject Faith will not cease to be in doubt concerning (Revelation) until the Hour (of Judgment) comes suddenly upon them, or there comes to them the Penalty of a Day of Disaster.	And those who disbelieve will not cease to be in doubt thereof until the Hour come upon them unawares, or there come unto them the doom of a disastrous day.	And those who disbelieve shall not cease to be in doubt concerning it until the hour overtakes them suddenly, or there comes on them the chastisement of a destructive day.

22 056	On that Day of Dominion will be that of Allah: He will judge between them: so those who believe and work righteous deeds will be in Gardens of Delight.	The Sovereignty on that day will be Allah's, He will judge between them. Then those who believed and did good works will be in Gardens of Delight,	The kingdom on that day shall be Allah's; He will judge between them; so those who believe and do good will be in gardens of bliss.
22 057	And for those who reject Faith and deny our Signs, there will be a humiliating Punishment.	While those who disbelieved and denied Our revelations, for them will be a shameful doom.	And (as for) those who disbelieve in and reject Our communications, these it is who shall have a disgraceful chastisement.
22 058	Those who leave their homes in the cause of Allah, and are then slain or die,- On them will Allah bestow verily a goodly Provision: Truly Allah is He Who bestows the best provision.	Those who fled their homes for the cause of Allah and then were slain or died, Allah verily will provide for them a good provision. Lo! Allah, He verily is Best of all who make provision.	And (as for) those who fly in Allah's way and are then slain or die, Allah will most certainly grant them a goodly sustenance, and most surely Allah is the best Giver of sustenance.
22 059	Verily He will admit them to a place with which they shall be well pleased: for Allah is All-Knowing, Most Forbearing.	Assuredly He will cause them to enter by an entry that they will love. Lo! Allah verily is Knower, Indulgent.	He will certainly cause them to enter a place of entrance which they shall be well pleased with, and most surely Allah is Knowing, Forbearing.
22 060	That (is so). And if one has retaliated to no greater extent than the injury he received, and is again set upon inordinately, Allah will help him: for Allah is One that blots out (sins) and forgives (again and again).	That (is so). And whoso hath retaliated with the like of that which he was made to suffer and then hath (again) been wronged, Allah will succour him. Lo! Allah verily is Mild, Forgiving.	That (shall be so); and he who retaliates with the like of that with which he has been afflicted and he has been oppressed, Allah will most certainly aid him; most surely Allah is Pardoning, Forgiving.
22 061	That is because Allah merges night into day, and He merges day into night, and verily it is Allah Who hears and sees (all things).	That is because Allah maketh the night to pass into the day and maketh the day to pass into the night, and because Allah is Hearer, Seer.	That is because Allah causes the night to enter into the day and causes the day to enter into the night, and because Allah is Hearing, Seeing.
22 062	That is because Allah - He is the Reality; and those besides Him whom they invoke,- they are but vain Falsehood: verily Allah is He, Most High, Most Great.	That is because Allah, He is the True, and that whereon they call instead of Him, it is the false, and because Allah, He is the High, the Great.	That is because Allah is the Truth, and that what they call upon besides Him-- that is the falsehood, and because Allah is the High, the Great.
22 063	Seest thou not that Allah sends down rain from the sky, and forthwith the earth becomes clothed with green? for Allah is He Who understands the finest mysteries, and is well-acquainted (with them).	Seest thou not how Allah sendeth down water from the sky and then the earth becometh green upon the morrow? Lo! Allah is Subtile, Aware.	Do you not see that Allah sends down water from the cloud so the earth becomes green? Surely Allah is Benignant, Aware.
22 064	To Him belongs all that is in the heavens and on earth: for verily Allah,- He is free of all wants, Worthy of all Praise.	Unto Him belongeth all that is in the heavens and all that is in the earth. Lo! Allah, He verily is the Absolute, the Owner of Praise.	His is whatsoever is in the heavens and whatsoever is in the earth; and most surely Allah is the Self-sufficient, the Praised.
22 065	Seest thou not that Allah has made subject to you (men) all that is on the earth, and the ships that sail through the sea by His Command? He withholds the sky (rain) from failing on the earth except by His leave: for Allah is Most Kind and Most Merciful to man.	Hast thou not seen how Allah hath made all that is in the earth subservient unto you? And the ship runneth upon the sea by His command, and He holdeth back the heaven from falling on the earth unless by His leave. Lo! Allah is, for mankind, Full of Pity, Merciful.	Do you not see that Allah has made subservient to you whatsoever is in the earth and the ships running in the sea by His command? And He withholds the heaven from falling on the earth except with His permission; most surely Allah is Compassionate, Merciful to men.
22 066	It is He Who gave you life, will cause you to die, and will again give you life: Truly man is a most ungrateful creature!	And He it is Who gave you life, then He will cause you to die, and then will give you life (again). Lo! man is verily an ingrate.	And He it is Who has brought you to life, then He will cause you to die, then bring you to life (again); most surely man is ungrateful.

22 067	To every People have We appointed rites and ceremonies which they must follow: let them not then dispute with thee on the matter, but do thou invite (them) to thy Lord: for thou art assuredly on the Right Way.	Unto each nation have We given sacred rites which they are to perform; so let them not dispute with thee of the matter, but summon thou unto thy Lord. Lo! thou indeed followest right guidance.	To every nation We appointed acts of devotion which they observe, therefore they should not dispute with you about the matter and call to your Lord; most surely you are on a right way.
22 068	If they do wrangle with thee, say, "Allah knows best what it is ye are doing."	And if they wrangle with thee, say: Allah is Best Aware of what ye do.	And if they contend with you, say: Allah best knows what you do.
22 069	"Allah will judge between you on the Day of Judgment concerning the matters in which ye differ."	Allah will judge between you on the Day of Resurrection concerning that wherein ye used to differ.	Allah will judge between you on the day of resurrection respecting that in which you differ.
22 070	Knowest thou not that Allah knows all that is in heaven and on earth? Indeed it is all in a Record, and that is easy for Allah.	Hast thou not known that Allah knoweth all that is in the heaven and the earth? Lo! it is in a record. Lo! that is easy for Allah.	Do you not know that Allah knows what is in the heaven and the earth? Surely this is in a book; surely this is easy to Allah.
22 071	Yet they worship, besides Allah, things for which no authority has been sent down to them, and of which they have (really) no knowledge: for those that do wrong there is no helper.	And they worship instead of Allah that for which He hath sent down no warrant, and that whereof they have no knowledge. For evil-doers there is no helper.	And they serve besides Allah that for which He has not sent any authority, and that of which they have no knowledge; and for the unjust there shall be no helper.
22 072	When Our Clear Signs are rehearsed to them, thou wilt notice a denial on the faces of the Unbelievers! they nearly attack with violence those who rehearse Our Signs to them. Say, "Shall I tell you of something (far) worse than these Signs? It is the Fire (of Hell)! Allah has promised it to the Unbelievers! and evil is that destination!"	And when Our revelations are recited unto them, thou knowest the denial in the faces of those who disbelieve; they all but attack those who recite Our revelations unto them. Say: Shall I proclaim unto you worse than that? The Fire! Allah hath promised it for those who disbelieve. A hapless journey's end!	And when Our clear communications are recited to them you will find denial on the faces of those who disbelieve; they almost spring upon those who recite to them Our communications. Say: Shall I inform you of what is worse than this? The fire; Allah has promised it to those who disbelieve; and how evil the resort!
22 073	O men! Here is a parable set forth! listen to it! Those on whom, besides Allah, ye call, cannot create (even) a fly, if they all met together for the purpose! and if the fly should snatch away anything from them, they would have no power to release it from the fly. Feeble are those who petition and those whom they petition!	O mankind! A similitude is coined, so pay ye heed to it: Lo! those on whom ye call beside Allah will never create a fly though they combine together for the purpose. And if the fly took something from them, they could not rescue it from it. So weak are (both) the seeker and the sought!	O people! a parable is set forth, therefore listen to it: surely those whom you call upon besides Allah cannot create fly, though they should all gather for it, and should the fly snatch away anything from them, they could not take it back from it; weak are the invoker and the invoked.
22 074	No just estimate have they made of Allah: for Allah is He Who is strong and able to Carry out His Will.	They measure not Allah His rightful measure. Lo! Allah is Strong, Almighty.	They have not estimated Allah with the estimation that is due to Him; most surely Allah is Strong, Mighty.
22 075	Allah chooses messengers from angels and from men for Allah is He Who hears and sees (all things).	Allah chooseth from the angels messengers, and (also) from mankind. Lo! Allah is Hearer, Seer.	Allah chooses messengers from among the angels and from among the men; surely Allah is Hearing, Seeing.
22 076	He knows what is before them and what is behind them: and to Allah go back all questions (for decision).	He knoweth all that is before them and all that is behind them, and unto Allah all things are returned.	He knows what is before them and what is behind them and to Allah are all affairs turned back.
22 077	O ye who believe! bow down, prostrate yourselves, and adore your Lord; and do good; that ye may prosper.	O ye who believe! Bow down and prostrate yourselves, and worship your Lord, and do good, that haply ye may prosper.	O you who believe! bow down and prostrate yourselves and serve your Lord, and do good that you may succeed.

22 078	And strive in His cause as ye ought to strive, (with sincerity and under discipline). He has chosen you, and has imposed no difficulties on you in religion; it is the cult of your father Abraham. It is He Who has named you Muslims, both before and in this (Revelation); that the Messenger may be a witness for you, and ye be witnesses for mankind! So establish regular Prayer, give regular Charity, and hold fast to Allah! He is your Protector - the Best to protect and the Best to help!	And strive for Allah with the endeavour which is His right. He hath chosen you and hath not laid upon you in religion any hardship; the faith of your father Abraham (is yours). He hath named you Muslims of old time and in this (Scripture), that the messenger may be a witness against you, and that ye may be witnesses against mankind. So establish worship, pay the poor-due, and hold fast to Allah. He is your Protecting friend. A blessed Patron and a blessed Helper!	And strive hard in (the way of) Allah, (such) a striving a is due to Him; He has chosen you and has not laid upon you an hardship in religion; the faith of your father Ibrahim; He named you Muslims before and in this, that the Messenger may be a bearer of witness to you, and you may be bearers of witness to the people; therefore keep up prayer and pay the poor rate and hold fast by Allah; He is your Guardian; how excellent the Guardian and how excellent the Helper!

Chapter 23:

AL-MUMENOON (THE BELIEVERS)

Total Verses: 118 Revealed At: MAKKA

In the name of Allah, the Most Beneficent, the Most Merciful.

23 001	The believers must (eventually) win through,-	Successful indeed are the believers	Successful indeed are the believers,
23 002	Those who humble themselves in their prayers;	Who are humble in their prayers,	Who are humble in their prayers,
23 003	Who avoid vain talk;	And who shun vain conversation,	And who keep aloof from what is vain,
23 004	Who are active in deeds of charity;	And who are payers of the poor-due;	And who are givers of poor-rate,
23 005	Who abstain from sex,	And who guard their modesty -	And who guard their private parts,
23 006	Except with those joined to them in the marriage bond, or (the captives) whom their right hands possess,- for (in their case) they are free from blame,	Save from their wives or the (slaves) that their right hands possess, for then they are not blameworthy,	Except before their mates or those whom their right hands possess, for they surely are not blameable,
23 007	But those whose desires exceed those limits are transgressors;-	But whoso craveth beyond that, such are transgressors -	But whoever seeks to go beyond that, these are they that exceed the limits;
23 008	Those who faithfully observe their trusts and their covenants;	And who are shepherds of their pledge and their covenant,	And those who are keepers of their trusts and their covenant,
23 009	And who (strictly) guard their prayers;-	And who pay heed to their prayers.	And those who keep a guard on their prayers;
23 010	These will be the heirs,	These are the heirs	These are they who are the heirs,
23 011	Who will inherit Paradise: they will dwell therein (for ever).	Who will inherit paradise. There they will abide.	Who shall inherit the Paradise; they shall abide therein.
23 012	Man We did create from a quintessence (of clay);	Verily We created man from a product of wet earth;	And certainly We created man of an extract of clay,
23 013	Then We placed him as (a drop of) sperm in a place of rest, firmly fixed;	Then placed him as a drop (of seed) in a safe lodging;	Then We made him a small seed in a firm resting-place,

23 014	Then We made the sperm into a clot of congealed blood; then of that clot We made a (foetus) lump; then we made out of that lump bones and clothed the bones with flesh; then we developed out of it another creature. So blessed be Allah, the best to create!	Then fashioned We the drop a clot, then fashioned We the clot a little lump, then fashioned We the little lump bones, then clothed the bones with flesh, and then produced it as another creation. So blessed be Allah, the Best of creators!		Then We made the seed a clot, then We made the clot a lump of flesh, then We made (in) the lump of flesh bones, then We clothed the bones with flesh, then We caused it to grow into another creation, so blessed be Allah, the best of the creators.
23 015	After that, at length ye will die.	Then lo! after that ye surely die.		Then after that you will most surely die.
23 016	Again, on the Day of Judgment, will ye be raised up.	Then lo! on the Day of Resurrection ye are raised (again).		Then surely on the day of resurrection you shall be raised.
23 017	And We have made, above you, seven tracts; and We are never unmindful of (our) Creation.	And We have created above you seven paths, and We are never unmindful of creation.		And certainly We made above you seven heavens; and never are We heedless of creation.
23 018	And We send down water from the sky according to (due) measure, and We cause it to soak in the soil; and We certainly are able to drain it off (with ease).	And we send down from the sky water in measure, and We give it lodging in the earth, and lo! We are Able to withdraw it.		And We send down water from the cloud according to a measure, then We cause it to settle in the earth, and most surely We are able to carry it away.
23 019	With it We grow for you gardens of date-palms and vines: in them have ye abundant fruits: and of them ye eat (and have enjoyment),-	Then We produce for you therewith gardens of date-palms and grapes, wherein is much fruit for you and whereof ye eat;		Then We cause to grow thereby gardens of palm trees and grapes for you; you have in them many fruits and from them do you eat;
23 020	Also a tree springing out of Mount Sinai, which produces oil, and relish for those who use it for food.	And a tree that springeth forth from Mount Sinai that groweth oil and relish for the eaters.		And a tree that grows out of Mount Sinai which produces oil and a condiment for those who eat.
23 021	And in cattle (too) ye have an instructive example: from within their bodies We produce (milk) for you to drink; there are, in them, (besides), numerous (other) benefits for you; and of their (meat) ye eat;	And lo! in the cattle there is verily a lesson for you. We give you to drink of that which is in their bellies, and many uses have ye in them, and of them do ye eat;		And most surely there is a lesson for you in the cattle: We make you to drink of what is in their bellies, and you have in them many advantages and of them you eat,
23 022	An on them, as well as in slips, ye side.	And on them and on the ship ye are carried.		And on them and on the ships you are borne.
23 023	(Further, We sent a long line of prophets for your instruction). We sent Noah to his people: He said, "O my people! worship Allah! Ye have no other god but Him. Will ye not fear (Him)?"	And We verily sent Noah unto his folk, and he said: O my people! Serve Allah. Ye have no other Allah save Him. Will ye not ward off (evil)?		And certainly We sent Nuh to his people, and he said: O my people! serve Allah, you have no god other than Him; will you not then guard (against evil)?
23 024	The chiefs of the Unbelievers among his people said: "He is no more than a man like yourselves: his wish is to assert his superiority over you: if Allah had wished (to send messengers), He could have sent down angels; never did we hear such a thing (as he says), among our ancestors of old."	But the chieftains of his folk, who disbelieved, said: This is only a mortal like you who would make himself superior to you. Had Allah willed, He surely could have sent down angels. We heard not of this in the case of our fathers of old.		And the chiefs of those who disbelieved from among his people said: He is nothing but a mortal like yourselves who desires that he may have superiority over you, and if Allah had pleased, He could certainly have sent down angels. We have not heard of this among our fathers of yore:
23 025	(And some said): "He is only a man possessed: wait (and have patience) with him for a time."	He is only a man in whom is a madness, so watch him for a while.		He is only a madman, so bear with him for a time.
23 026	(Noah) said: "O my Lord! help me: for that they accuse me of falsehood!"	He said: My Lord! Help me because they deny me.		He said: O my Lord! help me against their calling me a liar.

23 027	So We inspired him (with this message): "Construct the Ark within Our sight and under Our guidance: then when comes Our Command, and the fountains of the earth gush forth, take thou on board pairs of every species, male and female, and thy family- except those of them against whom the Word has already gone forth: And address Me not in favour of the wrong doers; for they shall be drowned (in the Flood)."	Then We inspired in him, saying: Make the ship under Our eyes and Our inspiration. Then, when Our command cometh and the oven gusheth water, introduce therein of every (kind) two spouses, and thy household save him thereof against whom the Word hath already gone forth. And plead not with Me on behalf of those who have done wrong. Lo! they will be drowned.	So We revealed to him, saying: Make the ark before Our eyes and (according to) Our revelation; and when Our command is given and the valley overflows, take into it of every kind a pair, two, and your followers, except those among them against whom the word has gone forth, and do not speak to Me in respect of those who are unjust; surely they shall be drowned.
23 028	And when thou hast embarked on the Ark - thou and those with thee,- say: "Praise be to Allah, Who has saved us from the people who do wrong."	And when thou art on board the ship, thou and whoso is with thee, then say: Praise be to Allah Who hath saved us from the wrongdoing folk!	And when you are firmly seated, you and those with you, in the ark, say: All praise is due to Allah who delivered us from the unjust people:
23 029	And say: "O my Lord! enable me to disembark with thy blessing: for Thou art the Best to enable (us) to disembark."	And say: My Lord! Cause me to land at a blessed landing-place, for Thou art Best of all who bring to land.	And say: O my Lord! cause me to disembark a blessed alighting, and Thou art the best to cause to alight.
23 030	Verily in this there are Signs (for men to understand); (thus) do We try (men).	Lo! herein verily are portents, for lo! We are ever putting (mankind) to the test.	Most surely there are signs in this, and most surely We are ever trying (men).
23 031	Then We raised after them another generation.	Then, after them, We brought forth another generation;	Then We raised up after them another generation.
23 032	And We sent to them a messenger from among themselves, (saying), Worship Allah! ye have no other god but Him. Will ye not fear (Him)?	And we sent among them a messenger of their own, saying: Serve Allah, Ye have no other Allah save Him. Will ye not ward off (evil)?	So We sent among them a messenger from among them, saying: Serve Allah, you have no god other than Him; will you not then guard (against evil)?
23 033	And the chiefs of his people, who disbelieved and denied the Meeting in the Hereafter, and on whom We had bestowed the good things of this life, said: "He is no more than a man like yourselves: he eats of that of which ye eat, and drinks of what ye drink."	And the chieftains of his folk, who disbelieved and denied the meeting of the Hereafter, and whom We had made soft in the life of the world, said: This is only a mortal like you, who eateth of that whereof ye eat and drinketh of that ye drink.	And the chiefs of his people who disbelieved and called the meeting of the hereafter a lie, and whom We had given plenty to enjoy in this world's life, said: This is nothing but a mortal like yourselves, eating of what you eat from and drinking of what you drink.
23 034	"If ye obey a man like yourselves, behold, it is certain ye will be lost."	If ye were to obey a mortal like yourselves, then, lo! ye surely would be losers.	And if you obey a mortal like yourselves, then most surely you will be losers:
23 035	"Does he promise that when ye die and become dust and bones, ye shall be brought forth (again)?"	Doth he promise you that you, when ye are dead and have become dust and bones, will (again) be brought forth?	What! does he threaten you that when you are dead and become dust and bones that you shall then be brought forth?
23 036	"Far, very far is that which ye are promised!"	Begone, begone, with that which ye are promised!	Far, far is that which you are threatened with.
23 037	"There is nothing but our life in this world! We shall die and we live! But we shall never be raised up again!"	There is naught but our life of the world; we die and we live, and we shall not be raised (again).	There is naught but our life in this world; we die and we live and we shall not be raised again.
23 038	"He is only a man who invents a lie against Allah, but we are not the ones to believe in him!"	He is only a man who hath invented a lie about Allah. We are not going to put faith in him.	He is naught but a man who has forged a lie against Allah, and we are not going to believe in him.
23 039	(The prophet) said: "O my Lord! help me: for that they accuse me of falsehood."	He said: My Lord! Help me because they deny me.	He said: O my Lord! help me against their calling me a liar.

23 040	(Allah) said: "In but a little while, they are sure to be sorry!"	He said: In a little while they surely will become repentant.		He said: In a little while they will most certainly be repenting.
23 041	Then the Blast overtook them with justice, and We made them as rubbish of dead leaves (floating on the stream of Time)! So away with the people who do wrong!	So the (Awful) Cry overtook them rightfully, and We made them like as wreckage (that a torrent hurleth). A far removal for wrongdoing folk!		So the punishment overtook them in justice, and We made them as rubbish; so away with the unjust people.
23 042	Then We raised after them other generations.	Then after them We brought forth other generations.		Then We raised after them other generations.
23 043	No people can hasten their term, nor can they delay (it).	No nation can outstrip its term, nor yet postpone it.		No people can hasten on their doom nor can they postpone (it).
23 044	Then sent We our messengers in succession: every time there came to a people their messenger, they accused him of falsehood: so We made them follow each other (in punishment): We made them as a tale (that is told): So away with a people that will not believe!	Then We sent our messengers one after another. Whenever its messenger came unto a nation they denied him; so We caused them to follow one another (to disaster) and We made them bywords. A far removal for folk who believe not!		Then We sent Our messengers one after another; whenever there came to a people their messenger, they called him a liar, so We made some of them follow others and We made them stories; so away with a people who do not believe!
23 045	Then We sent Moses and his brother Aaron, with Our Signs and authority manifest,	Then We sent Moses and his brother Aaron with Our tokens and a clear warrant,		Then We sent Musa and his brother Haroun, with Our communications and a clear authority,
23 046	To Pharaoh and his Chiefs: But these behaved insolently: they were an arrogant people.	Unto Pharaoh and his chiefs, but they scorned (them) and they were despotic folk.		To Firon and his chiefs, but they behaved haughtily and they were an insolent people.
23 047	They said: "Shall we believe in two men like ourselves? And their people are subject to us!"	And they said: Shall we put faith in two mortals like ourselves, and whose folk are servile unto us?		And they said: What! shall we believe in two mortals like ourselves while their people serve us?
23 048	So they accused them of falsehood, and they became of those who were destroyed.	So they denied them, and became of those who were destroyed.		So they rejected them and became of those who were destroyed.
23 049	And We gave Moses the Book, in order that they might receive guidance.	And We verily gave Moses the Scripture, that haply they might go aright.		And certainly We gave Musa the Book that they may follow a right direction.
23 050	And We made the son of Mary and his mother as a Sign: We gave them both shelter on high ground, affording rest and security and furnished with springs.	And We made the son of Mary and his mother a portent, and We gave them refuge on a height, a place of flocks and watersprings.		And We made the son of Marium and his mother a sign, and We gave them a shelter on a lofty ground having meadows and springs.
23 051	O ye messengers! enjoy (all) things good and pure, and work righteousness: for I am well-acquainted with (all) that ye do.	O ye messengers! Eat of the good things, and do right. Lo! I am Aware of what ye do.		O messengers! eat of the good things and do good; surely I know what you do.
23 052	And verily this Brotherhood of yours is a single Brotherhood, and I am your Lord and Cherisher: therefore fear Me (and no other).	And lo! this your religion is one religion and I am your Lord, so keep your duty unto Me.		And surely this your religion is one religion and I am your Lord, therefore be careful (of your duty) to Me.
23 053	But people have cut off their affair (of unity), between them, into sects: each party rejoices in that which is with itself.	But they (mankind) have broken their religion among them into sects, each group rejoicing in its tenets.		But they cut off their religion among themselves into sects, each part rejoicing in that which is with them.
23 054	But leave them in their confused ignorance for a time.	So leave them in their error till a time.		Therefore leave them in their overwhelming ignorance till
23 055	Do they think that because We have granted them abundance of wealth and sons,	Think they that in the wealth and sons wherewith We provide them		Do they think that by what We aid them with of wealth and children,
23 056	We would hasten them on in every good? Nay, they do not understand.	We hasten unto them with good things? Nay, but they perceive not.		We are hastening to them of good things? Nay, they do not perceive.

23 057	Verily those who live in awe for fear of their Lord;	Lo! those who go in awe for fear of their Lord.	Surely they who from fear of their Lord are cautious,
23 058	Those who believe in the Signs of their Lord;	And those who believe in the revelations of their Lord,	And those who believe in the communications of their Lord,
23 059	Those who join not (in worship) partners with their Lord;	And those who ascribe not partners unto their Lord,	And those who do not associate (aught) with their Lord,
23 060	And those who dispense their charity with their hearts full of fear, because they will return to their Lord;-	And those who give that which they give with hearts afraid because they are about to return unto their Lord,	And those who give what they give (in alms) while their hearts are full of fear that to their Lord they must return,
23 061	It is those who hasten in every good work, and these who are foremost in them.	These race for the good things, and they shall win them in the race.	These hasten to good things and they are foremost in (attaining) them.
23 062	On no soul do We place a burden greater than it can bear: before Us is a record which clearly shows the truth: they will never be wronged.	And we task not any soul beyond its scope, and with Us is a Record which speaketh the truth, and they will not be wronged.	And We do not lay on any soul a burden except to the extent of its ability, and with Us is a book which speaks the truth, and they shall not be dealt with unjustly.
23 063	But their hearts are in confused ignorance of this; and there are, besides that, deeds of theirs, which they will (continue) to do,-	Nay, but their hearts are in ignorance of this (Qur'an), and they have other works, besides, which they are doing;	Nay, their hearts are in overwhelming ignorance with respect to it and they have besides this other deeds which they do.
23 064	Until, when We seize in Punishment those of them who received the good things of this world, behold, they will groan in supplication!	Till when We grasp their luxurious ones with the punishment, behold! they supplicate.	Until when We overtake those who lead easy lives among them with punishment, lo! they cry for succor.
23 065	(It will be said): "Groan not in supplication this day: for ye shall certainly not be helped by Us."	Supplicate not this day! Assuredly ye will not be helped by Us.	Cry not for succor this day; surely you shall not be given help from Us.
23 066	"My Signs used to be rehearsed to you, but ye used to turn back on your heels"-	My revelations were recited unto you, but ye used to turn back on your heels,	My communications were indeed recited to you, but you used to turn back on your heels,
23 067	"In arrogance: talking nonsense about the (Qur'an), like one telling fables by night."	In scorn thereof. Nightly did ye rave together.	In arrogance; talking nonsense about the Quran, and left him like one telling fables by night.
23 068	Do they not ponder over the Word (of Allah), or has anything (new) come to them that did not come to their fathers of old?	Have they not pondered the Word, or hath that come unto them which came not unto their fathers of old?	Is it then that they do not ponder over what is said, or is it that there has come to them that which did not come to their fathers of old?
23 069	Or do they not recognise their Messenger, that they deny him?	Or know they not their messenger, and so reject him?	Or is it that they have not recognized their Messenger, so that they deny him?
23 070	Or do they say, "He is possessed"? Nay, he has brought them the Truth, but most of them hate the Truth.	Or say they: There is a madness in him? Nay, but he bringeth them the Truth; and most of them are haters of the Truth.	Or do they say: There is madness in him? Nay! he has brought them the truth, and most of them are averse from the truth.
23 071	If the Truth had been in accord with their desires, truly the heavens and the earth, and all beings therein would have been in confusion and corruption! Nay, We have sent them their admonition, but they turn away from their admonition.	And if the Truth had followed their desires, verily the heavens and the earth and whosoever is therein had been corrupted. Nay, We have brought them their Reminder, but from their Reminder they now turn away.	And should the truth follow their low desires, surely the heavens and the earth and all those who are therein would have perished. Nay! We have brought to them their reminder, but from their reminder they turn aside.
23 072	Or is it that thou askest them for some recompense? But the recompense of thy Lord is best: He is the Best of those who give sustenance.	Or dost thou ask of them (O Muhammad) any tribute? But the bounty of thy Lord is better, for He is Best of all who make provision.	Or is it that you ask them a recompense? But the recompense of your Lord is best, and He is the best of those who provide sustenance.

23 073	But verily thou callest them to the Straight Way;	And lo! thou summonest them indeed unto a straight path.	And most surely you invite them to a right way.
23 074	And verily those who believe not in the Hereafter are deviating from that Way.	And lo! those who believe not in the Hereafter are indeed astray from the path.	And most surely those who do not believe in the hereafter are deviating from the way.
23 075	If We had mercy on them and removed the distress which is on them, they would obstinately persist in their transgression, wandering in distraction to and fro.	Though We had mercy on them and relieved them of the harm afflicting them, they still would wander blindly on in their contumacy.	And if We show mercy to them and remove the distress they have, they would persist in their inordinacy, blindly wandering on.
23 076	We inflicted Punishment on them, but they humbled not themselves to their Lord, nor do they submissively entreat (Him)!-	Already have We grasped them with punishment, but they humble not themselves unto their Lord, nor do they pray,	And already We overtook them with chastisement, but they were not submissive to their Lord, nor do they humble themselves.
23 077	Until We open on them a gate leading to a severe Punishment: then Lo! they will be plunged in despair therein!	Until, when We open for them the gate of extreme punishment, behold! they are aghast thereat.	Until when We open upon them a door of severe chastisement, lo! they are in despair at it.
23 078	It is He Who has created for you (the faculties of) hearing, sight, feeling and understanding: little thanks it is ye give!	He it is Who hath created for you ears and eyes and hearts. Small thanks give ye!	And He it is Who made for you the ears and the eyes and the hearts; little is it that you give thanks.
23 079	And He has multiplied you through the earth, and to Him shall ye be gathered back.	And He it is Who hath sown you broadcast in the earth, and unto Him ye will be gathered.	And He it is Who multiplied you in the earth, and to Him you shall be gathered.
23 080	It is He Who gives life and death, and to Him (is due) the alternation of Night and Day: will ye not then understand?	And He it is Who giveth life and causeth death, and His is the difference of night and day. Have ye then no sense?	And He it is Who gives life and causes death, and (in) His (control) is the alternation of the night and the day; do you not then understand?
23 081	On the contrary they say things similar to what the ancients said.	Nay, but they say the like of that which said the men of old;	Nay, they say the like of what the ancients said:
23 082	They say: "What! when we die and become dust and bones, could we really be raised up again?"	They say: When we are dead and have become (mere) dust and bones, shall we then, forsooth, be raised again?	They say: What! When we are dead and become dust and bones, shall we then be raised?
23 083	"Such things have been promised to us and to our fathers before! they are nothing but tales of the ancients!"	We were already promised this, we and our forefathers. Lo! this is naught but fables of the men of old.	Certainly we are promised this, and (so were) our fathers aforetime; this is naught but stories of those of old.
23 084	Say: "To whom belong the earth and all beings therein? (say) if ye know!"	Say: Unto Whom (belongeth) the earth and whosoever is therein, if ye have knowledge?	Say: Whose is the earth, and whoever is therein, if you know?
23 085	They will say, "To Allah!" say: "Yet will ye not receive admonition?"	They will say: Unto Allah. Say: Will ye not then remember?	They will say: Allah's. Say: Will you not then mind?
23 086	Say: "Who is the Lord of the seven heavens, and the Lord of the Throne (of Glory) Supreme?"	Say: Who is Lord of the seven heavens, and Lord of the Tremendous Throne?	Say: Who is the Lord of the seven heavens and the Lord of the mighty dominion?
23 087	They will say, "(They belong) to Allah." Say: "Will ye not then be filled with awe?"	They will say: Unto Allah (all that belongeth). Say: Will ye not then keep duty (unto Him)?	They will say: (This is) Allah's. Say: Will you not then guard (against evil)?
23 088	Say: "Who is it in whose hands is the governance of all things,- who protects (all), but is not protected (of any)? (say) if ye know."	Say: In Whose hand is the dominion over all things and He protecteth, while against Him there is no protection, if ye have knowledge?	Say: Who is it in Whose hand is the kingdom of all things and Who gives succor, but against Him Succor is not given, if you do but know?

23 089	They will say, "(It belongs) to Allah." Say: "Then how are ye deluded?"	They will say: Unto Allah (all that belongeth). Say: How then are ye bewitched?	They will say: (This is) Allah's. Say: From whence are you then deceived?
23 090	We have sent them the Truth: but they indeed practise falsehood!	Nay, but We have brought them the Truth, and lo! they are liars.	Nay! We have brought to them the truth, and most surely they are liars.
23 091	No son did Allah beget, nor is there any god along with Him: (if there were many gods), behold, each god would have taken away what he had created, and some would have lorded it over others! Glory to Allah! (He is free) from the (sort of) things they attribute to Him!	Allah hath not chosen any son, nor is there any god along with Him; else would each god have assuredly championed that which he created, and some of them would assuredly have overcome others. Glorified be Allah above all that they allege.	Never did Allah take to Himself a son, and never was there with him any (other) god-- in that case would each god have certainly taken away what he created, and some of them would certainly have overpowered others; glory be to Allah above what they describe!
23 092	He knows what is hidden and what is open: too high is He for the partners they attribute to Him!	Knower of the invisible and the visible! and exalted be He over all that they ascribe as partners (unto Him)!	The Knower of the unseen and the seen, so may He be exalted above what they associate (with Him).
23 093	Say: "O my Lord! if Thou wilt show me (in my lifetime) that which they are warned against,"-	Say: My Lord! If Thou shouldst show me that which they are promised.	Say: O my Lord! if Thou shouldst make me see what they are threatened with:
23 094	"Then, O my Lord! put me not amongst the people who do wrong!"	My Lord! then set me not among the wrongdoing folk.	My Lord! then place me not with the unjust.
23 095	And We are certainly able to show thee (in fulfilment) that against which they are warned.	And verily We are Able to show thee that which We have promised them.	And most surely We are well able to make you see what We threaten them with.
23 096	Repel evil with that which is best: We are well acquainted with the things they say.	Repel evil with that which is better. We are Best Aware of that which they allege.	Repel evil by what is best; We know best what they describe.
23 097	And say "O my Lord! I seek refuge with Thee from the suggestions of the Evil Ones."	And say: My Lord! I seek refuge in Thee from suggestions of the evil ones,	And say: O my Lord! I seek refuge in Thee from the evil suggestions of the Shaitans;
23 098	"And I seek refuge with Thee O my Lord! lest they should come near me."	And I seek refuge in Thee, my Lord, lest they be present with me,	And I seek refuge in Thee! O my Lord! from their presence.
23 099	(In Falsehood will they be) Until, when death comes to one of them, he says: "O my Lord! send me back (to life),"-	Until, when death cometh unto one of them, he saith: My Lord! Send me back,	Until when death overtakes one of them, he says: Send me back, my Lord, send me back;
23 100	"In order that I may work righteousness in the things I neglected." - By no means! It is but a word he says.- Before them is a Partition till the Day they are raised up.	That I may do right in that which I have left behind! But nay! It is but a word that he speaketh; and behind them is a barrier until the day when they are raised.	Haply I may do good in that which I have left. By no means! it is a (mere) word that he speaks; and before them is a barrier until the day they are raised.
23 101	Then when the Trumpet is blown, there will be no more relationships between them that day, nor will one ask after another!	And when the trumpet is blown there will be no kinship among them that day, nor will they ask of one another.	So when the trumpet is blown, there shall be no ties of relationship between them on that day, nor shall they ask of each other.
23 102	Then those whose balance (of good deeds) is heavy,- they will attain salvation:	Then those whose scales are heavy, they are the successful.	Then as for him whose good deeds are preponderant, these are the successful.
23 103	But those whose balance is light, will be those who have lost their souls, in Hell will they abide.	And those whose scales are light are those who lose their souls, in hell abiding.	And as for him whose good deeds are light, these are they who shall have lost their souls, abiding in hell.
23 104	The Fire will burn their faces, and they will therein grin, with their lips displaced.	The fire burneth their faces, and they are glum therein.	The fire shall scorch their faces, and they therein shall be in severe affliction.

23	105	"Were not My Signs rehearsed to you, and ye did but treat them as falsehood?"	(It will be said): Were not My revelations recited unto you, and then ye used to deny them?	Were not My communications recited to you? But you used to reject them.
23	106	They will say: "Our Lord! Our misfortune overwhelmed us, and we became a people astray!"	They will say: Our Lord! Our evil fortune conquered us, and we were erring folk.	They shall say: O our Lord! our adversity overcame us and we were an erring people:
23	107	"Our Lord! bring us out of this: if ever we return (to Evil), then shall we be wrong-doers indeed!"	Our Lord! Oh, bring us forth from hence! If we return (to evil) then indeed we shall be wrong-doers.	O our Lord! Take us out of it; then if we return (to evil) surely we shall be unjust.
23	108	He will say: "Be ye driven into it (with ignominy)! And speak ye not to Me!"	He saith: Begone therein, and speak not unto Me.	He shall say: Go away into it and speak not to Me;
23	109	"A part of My servants there was, who used to pray 'our Lord! we believe; then do Thou forgive us, and have mercy upon us: For Thou art the Best of those who show mercy!"	Lo! there was a party of My slaves who said: Our Lord! We believe, therefor forgive us and have mercy on us for Thou art Best of all who show mercy;	Surely there was a party of My servants who said: O our Lord! we believe, so do Thou forgive us and have mercy on us, and Thou art the best of the Merciful ones.
23	110	"But ye treated them with ridicule, so much so that (ridicule of) them made you forget My Message while ye were laughing at them!"	But ye chose them for a laughing-stock until they caused you to forget remembrance of Me, while ye laughed at them.	But you took them for a mockery until they made you forget My remembrance and you used to laugh at them.
23	111	"I have rewarded them this Day for their patience and constancy: they are indeed the ones that have achieved Bliss..."	Lo! I have rewarded them this day forasmuch as they were steadfast; and they surely are the triumphant.	Surely I have rewarded them this day because they were patient, that they are the achievers.
23	112	He will say: "What number of years did ye stay on earth?"	He will say: How long tarried ye in the earth, counting by years?	He will say: How many years did you tarry in the earth?
23	113	They will say: "We stayed a day or part of a day: but ask those who keep account."	They will say: We tarried by a day or part of a day. Ask of those who keep count!	They will say: We tarried a day or part of a day, but ask those who keep account.
23	114	He will say: "Ye stayed not but a little,- if ye had only known!"	He will say: Ye tarried but a little if ye only knew.	He will say: You did tarry but a little-- had you but known (it):
23	115	"Did ye then think that We had created you in jest, and that ye would not be brought back to Us (for account)?"	Deemed ye then that We had created you for naught, and that ye would not be returned unto Us?	What! did you then think that We had created you in vain and that you shall not be returned to Us?
23	116	Therefore exalted be Allah, the King, the Reality: there is no god but He, the Lord of the Throne of Honour!	Now Allah be Exalted, the True King! There is no God save Him, the Lord of the Throne of Grace.	So exalted be Allah, the True King; no god is there but He, the Lord of the honorable dominion.
23	117	If anyone invokes, besides Allah, any other god, he has no authority therefor; and his reckoning will be only with his Lord! and verily the Unbelievers will fail to win through!	He who crieth unto any other god along with Allah hath no proof thereof. His reckoning is only with his Lord. Lo! disbelievers will not be successful.	And whoever invokes with Allah another god-- he has no proof of this-- his reckoning is only with his Lord; surely the unbelievers shall not be successful.
23	118	So say: "O my Lord! grant Thou forgiveness and mercy for Thou art the Best of those who show mercy!"	And (O Muhammad) say: My Lord! Forgive and have mercy, for Thou art best of all who show mercy.	And say: O my Lord! forgive and have mercy, and Thou art the best of the Merciful ones.

Chapter 24:

AL-NOOR (THE LIGHT)

Total Verses: 64 Revealed At: MADINA

In the name of Allah, the Most Beneficent, the Most Merciful.

24 001	A sura which We have sent down and which We have ordained in it have We sent down Clear Signs, in order that ye may receive admonition.	(Here is) a surah which We have revealed and enjoined, and wherein We have revealed plain tokens, that haply ye may take heed.	(This is) a Chapter which We have revealed and made obligatory and in which We have revealed clear communications that you may be mindful.
24 002	The woman and the man guilty of adultery or fornication,- flog each of them with a hundred stripes: Let not compassion move you in their case, in a matter prescribed by Allah, if ye believe in Allah and the Last Day: and let a party of the Believers witness their punishment.	The adulterer and the adulteress, scourge ye each one of them (with) a hundred stripes. And let not pity for the twain withhold you from obedience to Allah, if ye believe in Allah and the Last Day. And let a party of believers witness their punishment.	(As for) the fornicatress and the fornicator, flog each of them, (giving) a hundred stripes, and let not pity for them detain you in the matter of obedience to Allah, if you believe in Allah and the last day, and let a party of believers witness their chastisement.
24 003	Let no man guilty of adultery or fornication marry and but a woman similarly guilty, or an Unbeliever: nor let any but such a man or an unbeliever marry such a woman: to the Believers such a thing is forbidden.	The adulterer shall not marry save an adulteress or an idolatress, and the adulteress none shall marry save an adulterer or an idolater. All that is forbidden unto believers.	The fornicator shall not marry any but a fornicatress or idolatress, and (as for) the fornicatress, none shall marry her but a fornicator or an idolater; and it is forbidden to the believers.
24 004	And those who launch a charge against chaste women, and produce not four witnesses (to support their allegations),- flog them with eighty stripes; and reject their evidence ever after: for such men are wicked transgressors;-	And those who accuse honourable women but bring not four witnesses, scourge them (with) eighty stripes and never (afterward) accept their testimony - They indeed are evil-doers -	And those who accuse free women then do not bring four witnesses, flog them, (giving) eighty stripes, and do not admit any evidence from them ever; and these it is that are the transgressors,
24 005	Unless they repent thereafter and mend (their conduct); for Allah is Oft-Forgiving, Most Merciful.	Save those who afterward repent and make amends. (For such) lo! Allah is Forgiving, Merciful.	Except those who repent after this and act aright, for surely Allah is Forgiving, Merciful.
24 006	And for those who launch a charge against their spouses, and have (in support) no evidence but their own,- their solitary evidence (can be received) if they bear witness four times (with an oath) by Allah that they are solemnly telling the truth;	As for those who accuse their wives but have no witnesses except themselves; let the testimony of one of them be four testimonies, (swearing) by Allah that he is of those who speak the truth;	And (as for) those who accuse their wives and have no witnesses except themselves, the evidence of one of these (should be taken) four times, bearing Allah to witness that he is most surely of the truthful ones.
24 007	And the fifth (oath) (should be) that they solemnly invoke the curse of Allah on themselves if they tell a lie.	And yet a fifth, invoking the curse of Allah on him if he is of those who lie.	And the fifth (time) that the curse of Allah be on him if he is one of the liars.
24 008	But it would avert the punishment from the wife, if she bears witness four times (with an oath) By Allah, that (her husband) is telling a lie;	And it shall avert the punishment from her if she bear witness before Allah four times that the thing he saith is indeed false,	And it shall avert the chastisement from her if she testify four times, bearing Allah to witness that he is most surely one of the liars;

24 009	And the fifth (oath) should be that she solemnly invokes the wrath of Allah on herself if (her accuser) is telling the truth.	And a fifth (time) that the wrath of Allah be upon her if he speaketh truth.	And the fifth (time) that the wrath of Allah be on her if he is one of the truthful.
24 010	If it were not for Allah's grace and mercy on you, and that Allah is Oft-Returning, Full of Wisdom,- (Ye would be ruined indeed).	And had it not been for the grace of Allah and His mercy unto you, and that Allah is Clement, Wise, (ye had been undone).	And were it not for Allah's grace upon you and His mercy-- and that Allah is Oft-returning (to mercy), Wise!
24 011	Those who brought forward the lie are a body among yourselves: think it not to be an evil to you; On the contrary it is good for you: to every man among them (will come the punishment) of the sin that he earned, and to him who took on himself the lead among them, will be a penalty grievous.	Lo! they who spread the slander are a gang among you. Deem it not a bad thing for you; nay, it is good for you. Unto every man of them (will be paid) that which he hath earned of the sin; and as for him among them who had the greater share therein, his will be an awful doom.	Surely they who concocted the lie are a party from among you. Do not regard it an evil to you; nay, it is good for you. Every man of them shall have what he has earned of sin; and (as for) him who took upon himself the main part thereof, he shall have a grievous chastisement.
24 012	Why did not the believers - men and women - when ye heard of the affair,- put the best construction on it in their own minds and say, This (charge) is an obvious lie?	Why did not the believers, men and women, when ye heard it, think good of their own folk, and say: It is a manifest untruth?	Why did not the believing men and the believing women, when you heard it, think well of their own people, and say: This is an evident falsehood?
24 013	Why did they not bring four witnesses to prove it? When they have not brought the witnesses, such men, in the sight of Allah, (stand forth) themselves as liars!	Why did they not produce four witnesses? Since they produce not witnesses, they verily are liars in the sight of Allah.	Why did they not bring four witnesses of it? But as they have not brought witnesses they are liars before Allah.
24 014	Were it not for the grace and mercy of Allah on you, in this world and the Hereafter, a grievous penalty would have seized you in that ye rushed glibly into this affair.	Had it not been for the grace of Allah and His mercy unto you in the world and the Hereafter an awful doom had overtaken you for that whereof ye murmured.	And were it not for Allah's grace upon you and His mercy in this world and the hereafter, a grievous chastisement would certainly have touched you on account of the discourse which you entered into.
24 015	Behold, ye received it on your tongues, and said out of your mouths things of which ye had no knowledge; and ye thought it to be a light matter, while it was most serious in the sight of Allah.	When ye welcomed it with your tongues, and uttered with your mouths that whereof ye had no knowledge, ye counted it a trifle. In the sight of Allah it is very great.	When you received it with your tongues and spoke with your mouths what you had no knowledge of, and you deemed it an easy matter while with Allah it was grievous.
24 016	And why did ye not, when ye heard it, say? - "It is not right of us to speak of this: Glory to Allah! this is a most serious slander!"	Wherefor, when ye heard it, said ye not: It is not for us to speak of this. Glory be to Thee (O Allah)! This is awful calumny.	And why did you not, when you heard it, say: It does not beseem us that we should talk of it; glory be to Thee! this is a great calumny?
24 017	Allah doth admonish you, that ye may never repeat such (conduct), if ye are (true) Believers.	Allah admonisheth you that ye repeat not the like thereof ever, if ye are (in truth) believers.	Allah admonishes you that you should not return to the like of it ever again if you are believers.
24 018	And Allah makes the Signs plain to you: for Allah is full of knowledge and wisdom.	And He expoundeth unto you the revelations. Allah is Knower, Wise.	And Allah makes clear to you the communications; and Allah is Knowing, Wise.
24 019	Those who love (to see) scandal published broadcast among the Believers, will have a grievous Penalty in this life and in the Hereafter: Allah knows, and ye know not.	Lo! those who love that slander should be spread concerning those who believe, theirs will be a painful punishment in the world and the Hereafter. Allah knoweth. Ye know not.	Surely (as for) those who love that scandal should circulate respecting those who believe, they shall have a grievous chastisement in this world and the hereafter; and Allah knows, while you do not know.
24 020	Were it not for the grace and mercy of Allah on you, and that Allah is full of kindness and mercy, (ye would be ruined indeed).	Had it not been for the grace of Allah and His mercy unto you, and that Allah is Clement, Merciful, (ye had been undone).	And were it not for Allah's grace on you and His mercy, and that Allah is Compassionate, Merciful.

24 021	O ye who believe! follow not Satan's footsteps: if any will follow the footsteps of Satan, he will (but) command what is shameful and wrong: and were it not for the grace and mercy of Allah on you, not one of you would ever have been pure: but Allah doth purify whom He pleases: and Allah is One Who hears and knows (all things).	O ye who believe! Follow not the footsteps of the devil. Unto whomsoever followeth the footsteps of the devil, lo! he commandeth filthiness and wrong. Had it not been for the grace of Allah and His mercy unto you, not one of you would ever have grown pure. But Allah causeth whom He will to grow. And Allah is Hearer, Knower.		O you who believe! do not follow the footsteps of the Shaitan, and whoever follows the footsteps of the Shaitan, then surely he bids the doing of indecency and evil; and were it not for Allah's grace upon you and His mercy, not one of you would have ever been pure, but Allah purifies whom He pleases; and Allah is Hearing, Knowing.
24 022	Let not those among you who are endued with grace and amplitude of means resolve by oath against helping their kinsmen, those in want, and those who have left their homes in Allah's cause: let them forgive and overlook, do you not wish that Allah should forgive you? For Allah is Oft-Forgiving, Most Merciful.	And let not those who possess dignity and ease among you swear not to give to the near of kin and to the needy, and to fugitives for the cause of Allah. Let them forgive and show indulgence. Yearn ye not that Allah may forgive you? Allah is Forgiving, Merciful.		And let not those of you who possess grace and abundance swear against giving to the near of kin and the poor and those who have fled in Allah's way, and they should pardon and turn away. Do you not love that Allah should forgive you? And Allah is Forgiving, Merciful.
24 023	Those who slander chaste women, indiscreet but believing, are cursed in this life and in the Hereafter: for them is a grievous Penalty,-	Lo! as for those who traduce virtuous, believing women (who are) careless, cursed are they in the world and the Hereafter. Theirs will be an awful doom.		Surely those who accuse chaste believing women, unaware (of the evil), are cursed in this world and the hereafter, and they shall have a grievous chastisement.
24 024	On the Day when their tongues, their hands, and their feet will bear witness against them as to their actions.	On the day when their tongues and their hands and their feet testify against them as to what they used to do,		On the day when their tongues and their hands and their feet shall bear witness against them as to what they did.
24 025	On that Day Allah will pay them back (all) their just dues, and they will realise that Allah is the (very) Truth, that makes all things manifest.	On that day Allah will pay them their just due, and they will know that Allah, He is the Manifest Truth.		On that day Allah will pay back to them in full their just reward, and they shall know that Allah is the evident Truth.
24 026	Women impure are for men impure, and men impure for women impure and women of purity are for men of purity, and men of purity are for women of purity: these are not affected by what people say: for them there is forgiveness, and a provision honourable.	Vile women are for vile men, and vile men for vile women. Good women are for good men, and good men for good women; such are innocent of that which people say: For them is pardon and a bountiful provision.		Unclean things are for unclean ones and unclean ones are for unclean things, and the good things are for good ones and the good ones are for good things; these are free from what they say; they shall have forgiveness and an honorable sustenance.
24 027	O ye who believe! enter not houses other than your own, until ye have asked permission and saluted those in them: that is best for you, in order that ye may heed (what is seemly).	O ye who believe! Enter not houses other than your own without first announcing your presence and invoking peace upon the folk thereof. That is better for you, that ye may be heedful.		O you who believe! Do not enter houses other than your own houses until you have asked permission and saluted their inmates; this is better for you, that you may be mindful.
24 028	If ye find no one in the house, enter not until permission is given to you: if ye are asked to go back, go back: that makes for greater purity for yourselves: and Allah knows well all that ye do.	And if ye find no-one therein, still enter not until permission hath been given. And if it be said unto you: Go away again, then go away, for it is purer for you. Allah knoweth what ye do.		But if you do not find any one therein, then do not enter them until permission is given to you; and if it is said to you: Go back, then go back; this is purer for you; and Allah is Cognizant of what you do.
24 029	It is no fault on your part to enter houses not used for living in, which serve some (other) use for you: And Allah has knowledge of what ye reveal and what ye conceal.	(It is) no sin for you to enter uninhabited houses wherein is comfort for you. Allah knoweth what ye proclaim and what ye hide.		It is no sin in you that you enter uninhabited houses wherein you have your necessaries; and Allah knows what you do openly and what you hide.

24 030	Say to the believing men that they should lower their gaze and guard their modesty: that will make for greater purity for them: And Allah is well acquainted with all that they do.	Tell the believing men to lower their gaze and be modest. That is purer for them. Lo! Allah is aware of what they do.	Say to the believing men that they cast down their looks and guard their private parts; that is purer for them; surely Allah is Aware of what they do.
24 031	And say to the believing women that they should lower their gaze and guard their modesty; that they should not display their beauty and ornaments except what (must ordinarily) appear thereof; that they should draw their veils over their bosoms and not display their beauty except to their husbands, their fathers, their husband's fathers, their sons, their husbands' sons, their brothers or their brothers' sons, or their sisters' sons, or their women, or the slaves whom their right hands possess, or male servants free of physical needs, or small children who have no sense of the shame of sex; and that they should not strike their feet in order to draw attention to their hidden ornaments. And O ye Believers! turn ye all together towards Allah, that ye may attain Bliss.	And tell the believing women to lower their gaze and be modest, and to display of their adornment only that which is apparent, and to draw their veils over their bosoms, and not to reveal their adornment save to their own husbands or fathers or husbands' fathers, or their sons or their husbands' sons, or their brothers or their brothers' sons or sisters' sons, or their women, or their slaves, or male attendants who lack vigour, or children who know naught of women's nakedness. And let them not stamp their feet so as to reveal what they hide of their adornment. And turn unto Allah together, O believers, in order that ye may succeed.	And say to the believing women that they cast down their looks and guard their private parts and do not display their ornaments except what appears thereof, and let them wear their head-coverings over their bosoms, and not display their ornaments except to their husbands or their fathers, or the fathers of their husbands, or their sons, or the sons of their husbands, or their brothers, or their brothers' sons, or their sisters' sons, or their women, or those whom their right hands possess, or the male servants not having need (of women), or the children who have not attained knowledge of what is hidden of women; and let them not strike their feet so that what they hide of their ornaments may be known; and turn to Allah all of you, O believers! so that you may be successful.
24 032	Marry those among you who are single, or the virtuous ones among yourselves, male or female: if they are in poverty, Allah will give them means out of His grace: for Allah encompasseth all, and he knoweth all things.	And marry such of you as are solitary and the pious of your slaves and maid-servants. If they be poor, Allah will enrich them of His bounty. Allah is of ample means, Aware.	And marry those among you who are single and those who are fit among your male slaves and your female slaves; if they are needy, Allah will make them free from want out of His grace; and Allah is Ample-giving, Knowing.
24 033	Let those who find not the wherewithal for marriage keep themselves chaste, until Allah gives them means out of His grace. And if any of your slaves ask for a deed in writing (to enable them to earn their freedom for a certain sum), give them such a deed if ye know any good in them: yea, give them something yourselves out of the means which Allah has given to you. But force not your maids to prostitution when they desire chastity, in order that ye may make a gain in the goods of this life. But if anyone compels them, yet, after such compulsion, is Allah, Oft-Forgiving, Most Merciful (to them),	And let those who cannot find a match keep chaste till Allah give them independence by His grace. And such of your slaves as seek a writing (of emancipation), write it for them if ye are aware of aught of good in them, and bestow upon them of the wealth of Allah which He hath bestowed upon you. Force not your slave-girls to whoredom that ye may seek enjoyment of the life of the world, if they would preserve their chastity. And if one force them, then (unto them), after their compulsion, lo! Allah will be Forgiving, Merciful.	And let those who do not find the means to marry keep chaste until Allah makes them free from want out of His grace. And (as for) those who ask for a writing from among those whom your right hands possess, give them the writing if you know any good in them, and give them of the wealth of Allah which He has given you; and do not compel your slave girls to prostitution, when they desire to keep chaste, in order to seek the frail good of this world's life; and whoever compels them, then surely after their compulsion Allah is Forgiving, Merciful.

24 034	We have already sent down to you verses making things clear, an illustration from (the story of) people who passed away before you, and an admonition for those who fear (Allah).	And verily We have sent down for you revelations that make plain, and the example of those who passed away before you. An admonition unto those who ward off (evil).	And certainly We have sent to you clear communications and a description of those who have passed away before you, and an admonition to those who guard (against evil).
24 035	Allah is the Light of the heavens and the earth. The Parable of His Light is as if there were a Niche and within it a Lamp: the Lamp enclosed in Glass: the glass as it were a brilliant star: Lit from a blessed Tree, an Olive, neither of the east nor of the west, whose oil is well-nigh luminous, though fire scarce touched it: Light upon Light! Allah doth guide whom He will to His Light: Allah doth set forth Parables for men: and Allah doth know all things.	Allah is the Light of the heavens and the earth. The similitude of His light is as a niche wherein is a lamp. The lamp is in a glass. The glass is as it were a shining star. (This lamp is) kindled from a blessed tree, an olive neither of the East nor of the West, whose oil would almost glow forth (of itself) though no fire touched it. Light upon light. Allah guideth unto His light whom He will. And Allah speaketh to mankind in allegories, for Allah is Knower of all things.	Allah is the light of the heavens and the earth; a likeness of His light is as a niche in which is a lamp, the lamp is in a glass, (and) the glass is as it were a brightly shining star, lit from a blessed olive-tree, neither eastern nor western, the oil whereof almost gives light though fire touch it not-- light upon light-- Allah guides to His light whom He pleases, and Allah sets forth parables for men, and Allah is Cognizant of all things.
24 036	(Lit is such a Light) in houses, which Allah hath permitted to be raised to honour; for the celebration, in them, of His name: In them is He glorified in the mornings and in the evenings, (again and again),-	(This lamp is found) in houses which Allah hath allowed to be exalted and that His name shall be remembered therein. Therein do offer praise to Him at morn and evening.	In houses which Allah has permitted to be exalted and that His name may be remembered in them; there glorify Him therein in the mornings and the evenings,
24 037	By men whom neither traffic nor merchandise can divert from the Remembrance of Allah, nor from regular Prayer, nor from the practice of regular Charity: Their (only) fear is for the Day when hearts and eyes will be transformed (in a world wholly new),-	Men whom neither merchandise nor sale beguileth from remembrance of Allah and constancy in prayer and paying to the poor their due; who fear a day when hearts and eyeballs will be overturned;	Men whom neither merchandise nor selling diverts from the remembrance of Allah and the keeping up of prayer and the giving of poor-rate; they fear a day in which the hearts and eyes shall turn about;
24 038	That Allah may reward them according to the best of their deeds, and add even more for them out of His Grace: for Allah doth provide for those whom He will, without measure.	That Allah may reward them with the best of what they did, and increase reward for them of His bounty. Allah giveth blessings without stint to whom He will.	That Allah may give them the best reward of what they have done, and give them more out of His grace; and Allah gives sustenance to whom He pleases without measure.
24 039	But the Unbelievers,- their deeds are like a mirage in sandy deserts, which the man parched with thirst mistakes for water; until when he comes up to it, he finds it to be nothing: But he finds Allah (ever) with him, and Allah will pay him his account: and Allah is swift in taking account.	As for those who disbelieve, their deeds are as a mirage in a desert. The thirsty one supposeth it to be water till he cometh unto it and findeth it naught, and findeth, in the place thereof, Allah Who payeth him his due; and Allah is swift at reckoning.	And (as for) those who disbelieve, their deeds are like the mirage in a desert, which the thirsty man deems to be water; until when he comes to it he finds it to be naught, and there he finds Allah, so He pays back to him his reckoning in full; and Allah is quick in reckoning;
24 040	Or (the Unbelievers' state) is like the depths of darkness in a vast deep ocean, overwhelmed with billow topped by billow, topped by (dark) clouds: depths of darkness, one above another: if a man stretches out his hands, he can hardly see it! for any to whom Allah giveth not light, there is no light!	Or as darkness on a vast, abysmal sea. There covereth him a wave, above which is a wave, above which is a cloud. Layer upon layer of darkness. When he holdeth out his hand he scarce can see it. And he for whom Allah hath not appointed light, for him there is no light.	Or like utter darkness in the deep sea: there covers it a wave above which is another wave, above which is a cloud, (layers of) utter darkness one above another; when he holds out his hand, he is almost unable to see it; and to whomsoever Allah does not give light, he has no light.

24 041	Seest thou not that it is Allah Whose praises all beings in the heavens and on earth do celebrate, and the birds (of the air) with wings outspread? Each one knows its own (mode of) prayer and praise. And Allah knows well all that they do.	Hast thou not seen that Allah, He it is Whom all who are in the heavens and the earth praise, and the birds in their flight? Of each He knoweth verily the worship and the praise; and Allah is Aware of what they do.	Do you not see that Allah is He Whom do glorify all those who are in the heavens and the earth, and the (very) birds with expanded wings? He knows the prayer of each one and its glorification, and Allah is Cognizant of what they do.
24 042	Yea, to Allah belongs the dominion of the heavens and the earth; and to Allah is the final goal (of all).	And unto Allah belongeth the Sovereignty of the heavens and the earth, and unto Allah is the journeying.	And Allah's is the kingdom of the heavens and the earth, and to Allah is the eventual coming.
24 043	Seest thou not that Allah makes the clouds move gently, then joins them together, then makes them into a heap? - then wilt thou see rain issue forth from their midst. And He sends down from the sky mountain masses (of clouds) wherein is hail: He strikes therewith whom He pleases and He turns it away from whom He pleases, the vivid flash of His lightning well-nigh blinds the sight.	Hast thou not seen how Allah wafteth the clouds, then gathereth them, then maketh them layers, and thou seest the rain come forth from between them; He sendeth down from the heaven mountains wherein is hail, and smiteth therewith whom He will, and averteth it from whom He will. The flashing of His lightning all but snatcheth away the sight.	Do you not see that Allah drives along the clouds, then gathers them together, then piles them up, so that you see the rain coming forth from their midst? And He sends down of the clouds that are (like) mountains wherein is hail, afflicting therewith whom He pleases and turning it away from whom He pleases; the flash of His lightning almost takes away the sight.
24 044	It is Allah Who alternates the Night and the Day: verily in these things is an instructive example for those who have vision!	Allah causeth the revolution of the day and the night. Lo! herein is indeed a lesson for those who see.	Allah turns over the night and the day; most surely there is a lesson in this for those who have sight.
24 045	And Allah has created every animal from water: of them there are some that creep on their bellies; some that walk on two legs; and some that walk on four. Allah creates what He wills for verily Allah has power over all things.	Allah hath created every animal of water. Of them is (a kind) that goeth upon its belly and (a kind) that goeth upon two legs and (a kind) that goeth upon four. Allah createth what He will. Lo! Allah is Able to do all things.	And Allah has created from water every living creature: so of them is that which walks upon its belly, and of them is that which walks upon two feet, and of them is that which walks upon four; Allah creates what He pleases; surely Allah has power over all things.
24 046	We have indeed sent down signs that make things manifest: and Allah guides whom He wills to a way that is straight.	Verily We have sent down revelations and explained them. Allah guideth whom He will unto a straight path.	Certainly We have revealed clear communications, and Allah guides whom He pleases to the right way.
24 047	They say, "We believe in Allah and in the messenger, and we obey": but even after that, some of them turn away: they are not (really) Believers.	And they say: We believe in Allah and the messenger, and we obey; then after that a faction of them turn away. Such are not believers.	And they say: We believe in Allah and in the messenger and we obey; then a party of them turn back after this, and these are not believers.
24 048	When they are summoned to Allah and His messenger, in order that He may judge between them, behold some of them decline (to come).	And when they appeal unto Allah and His messenger to judge between them, lo! a faction of them are averse;	And when they are called to Allah and His Messenger that he may judge between them, lo! a party of them turn aside.
24 049	But if the right is on their side, they come to him with all submission.	But if right had been with them they would have come unto him willingly.	And if the truth be on their side, they come to him quickly, obedient.
24 050	Is it that there is a disease in their hearts? or do they doubt, or are they in fear, that Allah and His Messenger will deal unjustly with them? Nay, it is they themselves who do wrong.	Is there in their hearts a disease, or have they doubts, or fear they lest Allah and His messenger should wrong them in judgment? Nay, but such are evil-doers.	Is there in their hearts a disease, or are they in doubt, or do they fear that Allah and His Messenger will act wrongfully towards them? Nay! they themselves are the unjust.

24 051	The answer of the Believers, when summoned to Allah and His Messenger, in order that He may judge between them, is no other than this: they say, "We hear and we obey": it is such as these that will attain felicity.	The saying of (all true) believers when they appeal unto Allah and His messenger to judge between them is only that they say: We hear and we obey. And such are the successful.	The response of the believers, when they are invited to Allah and His Messenger that he may judge between them, is only to say: We hear and we obey; and these it is that are the successful.
24 052	It is such as obey Allah and His Messenger, and fear Allah and do right, that will win (in the end),	He who obeyeth Allah and His messenger, and feareth Allah, and keepeth duty (unto Him): such indeed are the victorious.	And he who obeys Allah and His Messenger, and fears Allah, and is careful of (his duty to) Him, these it is that are the achievers.
24 053	They swear their strongest oaths by Allah that, if only thou wouldst command them, they would leave (their homes). Say: "Swear ye not; Obedience is (more) reasonable; verily, Allah is well acquainted with all that ye do."	They swear by Allah solemnly that, if thou order them, they will go forth. Say: Swear not; known obedience (is better). Lo! Allah is Informed of what ye do.	And they swear by Allah with the most energetic of their oaths that if you command them they would certainly go forth. Say: Swear not; reasonable obedience (is desired); surely Allah is aware of what you do.
24 054	Say: "Obey Allah, and obey the Messenger: but if ye turn away, he is only responsible for the duty placed on him and ye for that placed on you. If ye obey him, ye shall be on right guidance. The Messenger's duty is only to preach the clear (Message)."	Say: Obey Allah and obey the messenger. But if ye turn away, then (it is) for him (to do) only that wherewith he hath been charged, and for you (to do) only that wherewith ye have been charged. If ye obey him, ye will go aright. But the messenger hath no other charge than to convey (the message) plainly.	Say: Obey Allah and obey the Messenger; but if you turn back, then on him rests that which is imposed on him and on you rests that which is imposed on you; and if you obey him, you are on the right way; and nothing rests on the Messenger but clear delivering (of the message).
24 055	Allah has promised, to those among you who believe and work righteous deeds, that He will, of a surety, grant them in the land, inheritance (of power), as He granted it to those before them; that He will establish in authority their religion - the one which He has chosen for them; and that He will change (their state), after the fear in which they (lived), to one of security and peace: 'They will worship Me (alone) and not associate aught with Me. 'If any do reject Faith after this, they are rebellious and wicked.	Allah hath promised such of you as believe and do good work that He will surely make them to succeed (the present rulers) in the earth even as He caused those who were before them to succeed (others); and that He will surely establish for them their religion which He hath approved for them, and will give them in exchange safety after their fear. They serve Me. They ascribe no thing as partner unto Me. Those who disbelieve henceforth, they are the miscreants.	Allah has promised to those of you who believe and do good that He will most certainly make them rulers in the earth as He made rulers those before them, and that He will most certainly establish for them their religion which He has chosen for them, and that He will most certainly, after their fear, give them security in exchange; they shall serve Me, not associating aught with Me; and whoever is ungrateful after this, these it is who are the transgressors.
24 056	So establish regular Prayer and give regular Charity; and obey the Messenger; that ye may receive mercy.	Establish worship and pay the poor-due and obey the messenger, that haply ye may find mercy.	And keep up prayer and pay the poor-rate and obey the Messenger, so that mercy may be shown to you.
24 057	Never think thou that the Unbelievers are going to frustrate (Allah's Plan) on earth: their abode is the Fire,- and it is indeed an evil refuge!	Think not that the disbelievers can escape in the land. Fire will be their home - a hapless journey's end!	Think not that those who disbelieve shall escape in the earth, and their abode is the fire; and certainly evil is the resort!

24 058 — O ye who believe! let those whom your right hands possess, and the (children) among you who have not come of age ask your permission (before they come to your presence), on three occasions: before morning prayer; the while ye doff your clothes for the noonday heat; and after the late-night prayer: these are your three times of undress: outside those times it is not wrong for you or for them to move about attending to each other: Thus does Allah make clear the Signs to you: for Allah is full of knowledge and wisdom.

24 059 — But when the children among you come of age, let them (also) ask for permission, as do those senior to them (in age): Thus does Allah make clear His Signs to you: for Allah is full of knowledge and wisdom.

24 060 — Such elderly women as are past the prospect of marriage,- there is no blame on them if they lay aside their (outer) garments, provided they make not a wanton display of their beauty: but it is best for them to be modest: and Allah is One Who sees and knows all things.

24 061 — It is no fault in the blind nor in one born lame, nor in one afflicted with illness, nor in yourselves, that ye should eat in your own houses, or those of your fathers, or your mothers, or your brothers, or your sisters, or your father's brothers or your father's sisters, or your mother's brothers, or your mother's sisters, or in houses of which the keys are in your possession, or in the house of a sincere friend of yours: there is no blame on you, whether ye eat in company or separately. But if ye enter houses, salute each other - a greeting of blessing and purity as from Allah. Thus does Allah make clear the signs to you: that ye may understand.

O ye who believe! Let your slaves, and those of you who have not come to puberty, ask leave of you at three times (before they come into your presence): Before the prayer of dawn, and when ye lay aside your raiment for the heat of noon, and after the prayer of night. Three times of privacy for you. It is no sin for them or for you at other times, when some of you go round attendant upon others (if they come into your presence without leave). Thus Allah maketh clear the revelations for you. Allah is Knower, Wise.

And when the children among you come to puberty then let them ask leave even as those before them used to ask it. Thus Allah maketh clear His revelations for you. Allah is Knower, Wise.

As for women past child-bearing, who have no hope of marriage, it is no sin for them if they discard their (outer) clothing in such a way as not to show adornment. But to refrain is better for them. Allah is Hearer, Knower.

No blame is there upon the blind nor any blame upon the lame nor any blame upon the sick nor on yourselves if ye eat from your houses, or the houses of your fathers, or the houses of your mothers, or the houses of your brothers, or the houses of your sisters, or the houses of your fathers' brothers, or the houses of your fathers' sisters, or the houses of your mothers' brothers, or the houses of your mothers' sisters, or (from that) whereof ye hold the keys, or (from the house) of a friend. No sin shall it be for you whether ye eat together or apart. But when ye enter houses, salute one another with a greeting from Allah, blessed and sweet. Thus Allah maketh clear His revelations for you, that haply ye may understand.

O you who believe! let those whom your right hands possess and those of you who have not attained to puberty ask permission of you three times; before the morning prayer, and when you put off your clothes at midday in summer, and after the prayer of the nightfall; these are three times of privacy for you; neither is it a sin for you nor for them besides these, some of you must go round about (waiting) upon others; thus does Allah make clear to you the communications, and Allah is Knowing, Wise.

And when the children among you have attained to puberty, let them seek permission as those before them sought permission; thus does Allah make clear to you His communications, and Allah is knowing, Wise.

And (as for) women advanced in years who do not hope for a marriage, it is no sin for them if they put off their clothes without displaying their ornaments; and if they restrain themselves it is better for them; and Allah is Hearing, Knowing.

There is no blame on the blind man, nor is there blame on the lame, nor is there blame on the sick, nor on yourselves that you eat from your houses, or your fathers' houses or your mothers' houses, or your brothers' houses, or your sisters' houses, or your paternal uncles' houses, or your paternal aunts' houses, or your maternal uncles' houses, or your maternal aunts' houses, or what you possess the keys of, or your friends' (houses). It is no sin in you that you eat together or separately. So when you enter houses, greet your people with a salutation from Allah, blessed (and) goodly; thus does Allah make clear to you the communications that you may understand.

24 062	Only those are believers, who believe in Allah and His Messenger: when they are with him on a matter requiring collective action, they do not depart until they have asked for his leave; those who ask for thy leave are those who believe in Allah and His Messenger; so when they ask for thy leave, for some business of theirs, give leave to those of them whom thou wilt, and ask Allah for their forgiveness: for Allah is Oft-Forgiving, Most Merciful.	They only are the true believers who believe in Allah and His messenger and, when they are with him on some common errand, go not away until they have asked leave of him. Lo! those who ask leave of thee, those are they who believe in Allah and His messenger. So, if they ask thy leave for some affair of theirs, give leave to whom thou wilt of them, and ask for them forgiveness of Allah. Lo! Allah is Forgiving, Merciful.	Only those are believers who believe in Allah and His Messenger, and when they are with him on a momentous affair they go not away until they have asked his permission; surely they who ask your permission are they who believe in Allah and His Messenger; so when they ask your permission for some affair of theirs, give permission to whom you please of them and ask forgiveness for them from Allah; surely Allah is Forgiving, Merciful.
24 063	Deem not the summons of the Messenger among yourselves like the summons of one of you to another: Allah doth know those of you who slip away under shelter of some excuse: then let those beware who withstand the Messenger's order, lest some trial befall them, or a grievous penalty be inflicted on them.	Make not the calling of the messenger among you as your calling one of another. Allah knoweth those of you who steal away, hiding themselves. And let those who conspire to evade orders beware lest grief or painful punishment befall them.	Do not hold the Messenger's calling (you) among you to be like your calling one to the other; Allah indeed knows those who steal away from among you, concealing themselves; therefore let those beware who go against his order lest a trial afflict them or there befall them a painful chastisement.
24 064	Be quite sure that to Allah doth belong whatever is in the heavens and on earth. Well doth He know what ye are intent upon: and one day they will be brought back to Him, and He will tell them the truth of what they did: for Allah doth know all things.	Lo! verily unto Allah belongeth whatsoever is in the heavens and the earth. He knoweth your condition. And (He knoweth) the Day when they are returned unto Him so that He may inform them of what they did. Allah is Knower of all things.	Now surely Allah's is whatever is in the heavens and the earth; He knows indeed that to which you are conforming yourselves; and on the day on which they are returned to Him He will inform them of what they did; and Allah is Cognizant of all things.

Chapter 25:

AL-FURQAN (THE CRITERION, THE STANDARD)

Total Verses: 77 Revealed At: MAKKA

In the name of Allah, the Most Beneficent, the Most Merciful.

25 001	Blessed is He who sent down the criterion to His servant, that it may be an admonition to all creatures;-	Blessed is He Who hath revealed unto His slave the Criterion (of right and wrong), that he may be a warner to the peoples.	Blessed is He Who sent down the Furqan upon His servant that he may be a warner to the nations;
25 002	He to Whom belongs the dominion of the heavens and the earth: no son has He begotten, nor has He a partner in His dominion: it is He who created all things, and ordered them in due proportions.	He unto Whom belongeth the Sovereignty of the heavens and the earth, He hath chosen no son nor hath He any partner in the Sovereignty. He hath created everything and hath meted out for it a measure.	He, Whose is the kingdom of the heavens and the earth, and Who did not take to Himself a son, and Who has no associate in the kingdom, and Who created everything, then ordained for it a measure.

25 003	Yet have they taken, besides him, gods that can create nothing but are themselves created; that have no control of hurt or good to themselves; nor can they control death nor life nor resurrection.	Yet they choose beside Him other gods who create naught but are themselves created, and possess not hurt nor profit for themselves, and possess not death nor life, nor power to raise the dead.	And they have taken besides Him gods, who do not create anything while they are themselves created, and they control not for themselves any harm or profit, and they control not death nor life, nor raising (the dead) to life.
25 004	But the misbelievers say: "Naught is this but a lie which he has forged, and others have helped him at it." In truth it is they who have put forward an iniquity and a falsehood.	Those who disbelieve say: This is naught but a lie that he hath invented, and other folk have helped him with it, so that they have produced a slander and a lie.	And those who disbelieve say: This is nothing but a lie which he has forged, and other people have helped him at it; so indeed they have done injustice and (uttered) a falsehood.
25 005	And they say: "Tales of the ancients, which he has caused to be written: and they are dictated before him morning and evening."	And they say: Fables of the men of old which he hath had written down so that they are dictated to him morn and evening.	And they say: The stories of the ancients-- he has got them written-- so these are read out to him morning and evening.
25 006	Say: "The (Qur'an) was sent down by Him who knows the mystery (that is) in the heavens and the earth: verily He is Oft-Forgiving, Most Merciful."	Say (unto them, O Muhammad): He who knoweth the secret of the heavens and the earth hath revealed it. Lo! He ever is Forgiving, Merciful.	Say: He has revealed it Who knows the secret in the heavens and the earth; surely He is ever Forgiving, Merciful.
25 007	And they say: "What sort of a messenger is this, who eats food, and walks through the streets? Why has not an angel been sent down to him to give admonition with him?"	And they say: What aileth this messenger (of Allah) that he eateth food and walketh in the markets? Why is not an angel sent down unto him, to be a warner with him.	And they say: What is the matter with this Messenger that he eats food and goes about in the markets; why has not an angel been sent down to him, so that he should have been a warner with him?
25 008	"Or (Why) has not a treasure been bestowed on him, or why has he (not) a garden for enjoyment?" The wicked say: "Ye follow none other than a man bewitched."	Or (why is not) treasure thrown down unto him, or why hath he not a paradise from whence to eat? And the evil-doers say: Ye are but following a man bewitched.	Or (why is not) a treasure sent down to him, or he is made to have a garden from which he should eat? And the unjust say: You do not follow any but a man deprived of reason.
25 009	See what kinds of comparisons they make for thee! But they have gone astray, and never a way will they be able to find!	See how they coin similitudes for thee, so that they are all astray and cannot find a road!	See what likenesses do they apply to you, so they have gone astray, therefore they shall not be able to find a way.
25 010	Blessed is He who, if that were His will, could give thee better (things) than those,- Gardens beneath which rivers flow; and He could give thee palaces (secure to dwell in).	Blessed is He Who, if He will, will assign thee better than (all) that - Gardens underneath which rivers flow - and will assign thee mansions.	Blessed is He Who, if He please, will give you what is better than this, gardens beneath which rivers flow, and He will give you palaces.
25 011	Nay they deny the hour (of the judgment to come): but We have prepared a blazing fire for such as deny the hour:	Nay, but they deny (the coming of) the Hour, and for those who deny (the coming of) the Hour We have prepared a flame.	But they reject the hour, and We have prepared a burning fire for him who rejects the hour.
25 012	When it sees them from a place far off, they will hear its fury and its ranging sigh.	When it seeth them from afar, they hear the crackling and the roar thereof.	When it shall come into their sight from a distant place, they shall hear its vehement raging and roaring.
25 013	And when they are cast, bound together into a constricted place therein, they will plead for destruction there and then!	And when they are flung into a narrow place thereof, chained together, they pray for destruction there.	And when they are cast into a narrow place in it, bound, they shall there call out for destruction.
25 014	"This day plead not for a single destruction: plead for destruction oft-repeated!"	Pray not that day for one destruction, but pray for many destructions!	Call not this day for one destruction, but call for destructions many.

25 015	Say: "Is that best, or the eternal garden, promised to the righteous? for them, that is a reward as well as a goal (of attainment)."	Say: Is that (doom) better or the Garden of Immortality which is promised unto those who ward off (evil)? It will be their reward and journey's end.	Say: Is this better or the abiding garden which those who guard (against evil) are promised? That shall be a reward and a resort for them.
25 016	"For them there will be therein all that they wish for: they will dwell (there) for aye: A promise to be prayed for from thy Lord."	Therein abiding, they have all that they desire. It is for thy Lord a promise that must be fulfilled.	They shall have therein what they desire abiding (in it); it is a promise which it is proper to be prayed for from your Lord.
25 017	The day He will gather them together as well as those whom they worship besides Allah, He will ask: "Was it ye who let these My servants astray, or did they stray from the Path themselves?"	And on the day when He will assemble them and that which they worship instead of Allah and will say: Was it ye who misled these My slaves or did they (themselves) wander from the way?	And on the day when He shall gather them, and whatever they served besides Allah, He shall say: Was it you who led astray these My servants, or did they themselves go astray from the path?
25 018	They will say: "Glory to Thee! not meet was it for us that we should take for protectors others besides Thee: But Thou didst bestow, on them and their fathers, good things (in life), until they forgot the Message: for they were a people (worthless and) lost."	They will say: Be Thou Glorified! it was not for us to choose any protecting friends beside thee; but Thou didst give them and their fathers ease till they forgot the warning and became lost folk.	They shall say: Glory be to Thee; it was not beseeming for us that we should take any guardians besides Thee, but Thou didst make them and their fathers to enjoy until they forsook the reminder, and they were a people in perdition,
25 019	(Allah will say): "Now have they proved you liars in what ye say: so ye cannot avert (your penalty) nor (get) help." And whoever among you does wrong, him shall We cause to taste of a grievous Penalty.	Thus they will give you the lie regarding what ye say, then ye can neither avert (the doom) nor obtain help. And whoso among you doeth wrong, We shall make him taste great torment.	So they shall indeed give you the lie in what you say, then you shall not be able to ward off or help, and whoever among you is unjust, We will make him taste a great chastisement.
25 020	And the messengers whom We sent before thee were all (men) who ate food and walked through the streets: We have made some of you as a trial for others: will ye have patience? for Allah is One Who sees (all things).	We never sent before thee any messengers but lo! they verily ate food and walked in the markets. And We have appointed some of you a test for others: Will ye be steadfast? And thy Lord is ever Seer.	And We have not sent before you any messengers but they most surely ate food and went about in the markets; and We have made some of you a trial for others; will you bear patiently? And your Lord is ever Seeing.
25 021	Such as fear not the meeting with Us (for Judgment) say: "Why are not the angels sent down to us, or (why) do we not see our Lord?" Indeed they have an arrogant conceit of themselves, and mighty is the insolence of their impiety!	And those who look not for a meeting with Us say: Why are angels not sent down unto us and (Why) do we not see our Lord! Assuredly they think too highly of themselves and are scornful with great pride.	And those who do not hope for Our meeting, say: Why have not angels been sent down upon us, or (why) do we not see our Lord? Now certainly they are too proud of themselves and have revolted in great revolt.
25 022	The Day they see the angels,- no joy will there be to the sinners that Day: The (angels) will say: "There is a barrier forbidden (to you) altogether!"	On the day when they behold the angels, on that day there will be no good tidings for the guilty; and they will cry: A forbidding ban!	On the day when they shall see the angels, there shall be no joy on that day for the guilty, and they shall say: It is a forbidden thing totally prohibited.
25 023	And We shall turn to whatever deeds they did (in this life), and We shall make such deeds as floating dust scattered about.	And We shall turn unto the work they did and make it scattered motes.	And We will proceed to what they have done of deeds, so We shall render them as scattered floating dust.
25 024	The Companions of the Garden will be well, that Day, in their abode, and have the fairest of places for repose.	Those who have earned the Garden on that day will be better in their home and happier in their place of noonday rest;	The dwellers of the garden shall on that day be in a better abiding-place and a better resting-place.

25 025	The Day the heaven shall be rent asunder with clouds, and angels shall be sent down, descending (in ranks),-	A day when the heaven with the clouds will be rent asunder and the angels will be sent down, a grand descent.	And on the day when the heaven shall burst asunder with the clouds, and the angels shall be sent down descending (in ranks).
25 026	That Day, the dominion as of right and truth, shall be (wholly) for (Allah) Most Merciful: it will be a Day of dire difficulty for the Misbelievers.	The Sovereignty on that day will be the True (Sovereignty) belonging to the Beneficent One, and it will be a hard day for disbelievers.	The kingdom on that day shall rightly belong to the Beneficent Allah, and a hard day shall it be for the unbelievers.
25 027	The Day that the wrong-doer will bite at his hands, he will say, Oh! would that I had taken a (straight) path with the Messenger!	On the day when the wrong-doer gnaweth his hands, he will say: Ah, would that I had chosen a way together with the messenger (of Allah)!	And the day when the unjust one shall bite his hands saying: O! would that I had taken a way with the Messenger;
25 028	"Ah! woe is me! Would that I had never taken such a one for a friend!"	Alas for me! Ah, would that I had never taken such a one for friend!	O woe is me! would that I had not taken such a one for a friend!
25 029	"He did lead me astray from the Message (of Allah) after it had come to me! Ah! the Evil One is but a traitor to man!"	He verily led me astray from the Reminder after it had reached me. Satan was ever man's deserter in the hour of need.	Certainly he led me astray from the reminder after it had come to me; and the Shaitan fails to aid man.
25 030	Then the Messenger will say: "O my Lord! Truly my people took this Qur'an for just foolish nonsense."	And the messenger saith: O my Lord! Lo! mine own folk make this Qur'an of no account.	And the Messenger cried out: O my Lord! surely my people have treated this Quran as a forsaken thing.
25 031	Thus have We made for every prophet an enemy among the sinners: but enough is thy Lord to guide and to help.	Even so have We appointed unto every prophet an opponent from among the guilty; but Allah sufficeth for a Guide and Helper.	And thus have We made for every prophet an enemy from among the sinners and sufficient is your Lord as a Guide and a Helper.
25 032	Those who reject Faith say: "Why is not the Qur'an revealed to him all at once? Thus (is it revealed), that We may strengthen thy heart thereby, and We have rehearsed it to thee in slow, well-arranged stages, gradually."	And those who disbelieve say: Why is the Qur'an not revealed unto him all at once? (It is revealed) thus that We may strengthen thy heart therewith; and We have arranged it in right order.	And those who disbelieve say: Why has not the Quran been revealed to him all at once? Thus, that We may strengthen your heart by it and We have arranged it well in arranging.
25 033	And no question do they bring to thee but We reveal to thee the truth and the best explanation (thereof).	And they bring thee no similitude but We bring thee the Truth (as against it), and better (than their similitude) as argument.	And they shall not bring to you any argument, but We have brought to you (one) with truth and best in significance.
25 034	Those who will be gathered to Hell (prone) on their faces,- they will be in an evil plight, and, as to Path, most astray.	Those who will be gathered on their faces unto hell: such are worse in plight and further from the right road.	(As for) those who shall be gathered upon their faces to hell, they are in a worse plight and straying farther away from the path.
25 035	(Before this,) We sent Moses The Book, and appointed his brother Aaron with him as minister;	We verily gave Moses the Scripture and placed with him his brother Aaron as henchman.	And certainly We gave Musa the Book and We appointed with him his brother Haroun an aider.
25 036	And We command: "Go ye both, to the people who have rejected our Signs:" And those (people) We destroyed with utter destruction.	Then We said: Go together unto the folk who have denied Our revelations. Then We destroyed them, a complete destruction.	Then We said: Go you both to the people who rejected Our communications; so We destroyed them with utter destruction.
25 037	And the people of Noah,- when they rejected the messengers, We drowned them, and We made them as a Sign for mankind; and We have prepared for (all) wrong-doers a grievous Penalty;-	And Noah's folk, when they denied the messengers, We drowned them and made of them a portent for mankind. We have prepared a painful doom for evil-doers.	And the people of Nuh, when they rejected the messengers, We drowned them, and made them a sign for men, and We have prepared a painful punishment for the unjust;

25 038	As also 'Ad and Thamud, and the Companions of the Rass, and many a generation between them.	And (the tribes of) A'ad and Thamud, and the dwellers in Ar-Rass, and many generations in between.	And Ad and Samood and the dwellers of the Rass and many generations between them.
25 039	To each one We set forth Parables and examples; and each one We broke to utter annihilation (for their sins).	Each (of them) We warned by examples, and each (of them) We brought to utter ruin.	And to every one We gave examples and every one did We destroy with utter destruction.
25 040	And the (Unbelievers) must indeed have passed by the town on which was rained a shower of evil: did they not then see it (with their own eyes)? But they fear not the Resurrection.	And indeed they have passed by the township whereon was rained the fatal rain. Can it be that they have not seen it? Nay, but they hope for no resurrection.	And certainly they have (often) passed by the town on which was rained an evil rain, did they not then see it? Nay! they did not hope to be raised again.
25 041	When they see thee, they treat thee no otherwise than in mockery: Is this the one whom Allah has sent as a messenger?	And when they see thee (O Muhammad) they treat thee only as a jest (saying): Is this he whom Allah sendeth as a messenger?	And when they see you, they do not take you for aught but a mockery: Is this he whom Allah has raised to be a messenger?
25 042	"He indeed would well-nigh have misled us from our gods, had it not been that we were constant to them!" - Soon will they know, when they see the Penalty, who it is that is most misled in Path!	He would have led us far away from our gods if we had not been staunch to them. They will know, when they behold the doom, who is more astray as to the road.	He had well-nigh led us astray from our gods had we not adhered to them patiently! And they will know, when they see the punishment, who is straying farther off from the path.
25 043	Seest thou such a one as taketh for his god his own passion (or impulse)? Couldst thou be a disposer of affairs for him?	Hast thou seen him who chooseth for his god his own lust? Wouldst thou then be guardian over him?	Have you seen him who takes his low desires for his god? Will you then be a protector over him?
25 044	Or thinkest thou that most of them listen or understand? They are only like cattle;- nay, they are worse astray in Path.	Or deemest thou that most of them hear or understand? They are but as the cattle - nay, but they are farther astray?	Or do you think that most of them do hear or understand? They are nothing but as cattle; nay, they are straying farther off from the path.
25 045	Hast thou not turned thy vision to thy Lord?- How He doth prolong the shadow! If He willed, He could make it stationary! then do We make the sun its guide;	Hast thou not seen how thy Lord hath spread the shade - And if He willed He could have made it still - then We have made the sun its pilot;	Have you not considered (the work of) your Lord, how He extends the shade? And if He had pleased He would certainly have made it stationary; then We have made the sun an indication of it;
25 046	Then We draw it in towards Ourselves,- a contraction by easy stages.	Then We withdraw it unto Us, a gradual withdrawal?	Then We take it to Ourselves, taking little by little.
25 047	And He it is Who makes the Night as a Robe for you, and Sleep as Repose, and makes the Day (as it were) a Resurrection.	And He it is Who maketh night a covering for you, and sleep repose, and maketh day a resurrection.	And He it is Who made the night a covering for you, and the sleep a rest, and He made the day to rise up again.
25 048	And He it is Who sends the winds as heralds of glad tidings, going before His mercy, and We send down pure water from the sky,-	And He it is Who sendeth the winds, glad tidings heralding His mercy, and We send down purifying water from the sky,	And He it is Who sends the winds as good news before His mercy; and We send down pure water from the cloud,
25 049	That with it We may give life to a dead land, and slake the thirst of things We have created,- cattle and men in great numbers.	That We may give life thereby to a dead land, and We give many beasts and men that We have created to drink thereof.	That We may give life thereby to a dead land and give it for drink, out of what We have created, to cattle and many people.
25 050	And We have distributed the (water) amongst them, in order that they may celebrate (our) praises, but most men are averse (to aught) but (rank) ingratitude.	And verily We have repeated it among them that they may remember, but most of mankind begrudge aught save ingratitude.	And certainly We have repeated this to them that they may be mindful, but the greater number of men do not consent to aught except denying.

25 051	Had it been Our Will, We could have sent a warner to every centre of population.	If We willed, We could raise up a warner in every village.	And if We had pleased We would certainly have raised a warner in every town.
25 052	Therefore listen not to the Unbelievers, but strive against them with the utmost strenuousness, with the (Qur'an).	So obey not the disbelievers, but strive against them herewith with a great endeavour.	So do not follow the unbelievers, and strive against them a mighty striving with it.
25 053	It is He Who has let free the two bodies of flowing water: One palatable and sweet, and the other salt and bitter; yet has He made a barrier between them, a partition that is forbidden to be passed.	And He it is Who hath given independence to the two seas (though they meet); one palatable, sweet, and the other saltish, bitter; and hath set a bar and a forbidding ban between them.	And He it is Who has made two seas to flow freely, the one sweet that subdues thirst by its sweetness, and the other salt that burns by its saltness; and between the two He has made a barrier and inviolable obstruction.
25 054	It is He Who has created man from water: then has He established relationships of lineage and marriage: for thy Lord has power (over all things).	And He it is Who hath created man from water, and hath appointed for him kindred by blood and kindred by marriage; for thy Lord is ever Powerful.	And He it is Who has created man from the water, then He has made for him blood relationship and marriage relationship, and your Lord is powerful.
25 055	Yet do they worship, besides Allah, things that can neither profit them nor harm them: and the Misbeliever is a helper (of Evil), against his own Lord!	Yet they worship instead of Allah that which can neither benefit them nor hurt them. The disbeliever was ever a partisan against his Lord.	And they serve besides Allah that which neither profits them nor causes them harm; and the unbeliever is a partisan against his Lord.
25 056	But thee We only sent to give glad tidings and admonition.	And We have sent thee (O Muhammad) only as a bearer of good tidings and a warner.	And We have not sent you but as a giver of good news and as a warner.
25 057	Say: "No reward do I ask of you for it but this: that each one who will may take a (straight) Path to his Lord."	Say: I ask of you no reward for this, save that whoso will may choose a way unto his Lord.	Say: I do not ask you aught in return except that he who will, may take the way to his Lord.
25 058	And put thy trust in Him Who lives and dies not; and celebrate his praise; and enough is He to be acquainted with the faults of His servants;-	And trust thou in the Living One Who dieth not, and hymn His praise. He sufficeth as the Knower of His bondmen's sins,	And rely on the Ever-living Who dies not, and celebrate His praise; and Sufficient is He as being aware of the faults of His servants,
25 059	He Who created the heavens and the earth and all that is between, in six days, and is firmly established on the Throne (of Authority): Allah Most Gracious: ask thou, then, about Him of any acquainted (with such things).	Who created the heavens and the earth and all that is between them in six Days, then He mounted the Throne. The Beneficent! Ask anyone informed concerning Him!	Who created the heavens and the earth and what is between them in six periods, and He is firmly established on the throne of authority; the Beneficent Allah, so ask respecting it one aware.
25 060	When it is said to them, "Prostrate to (Allah) Most Gracious!", they say, "And what is (Allah) Most Gracious? Shall we prostrate to that which thou commandest us?" And it increases their flight (from the Truth).	And when it is said unto them: Prostrate to the Beneficent! they say: And what is the Beneficent? Are we to prostrate to whatever thou (Muhammad) biddest us? And it increaseth aversion in them.	And when it is said to them: Prostrate to the Beneficent Allah, they say: And what is the Allah of beneficence? Shall we prostrate to what you bid us? And it adds to their aversion.
25 061	Blessed is He Who made constellations in the skies, and placed therein a Lamp and a Moon giving light;	Blessed be He Who hath placed in the heaven mansions of the stars, and hath placed therein a great lamp and a moon giving light!	Blessed is He Who made the constellations in the heavens and made therein a lamp and a shining moon.
25 062	And it is He Who made the Night and the Day to follow each other: for such as have the will to celebrate His praises or to show their gratitude.	And He it is Who hath appointed night and day in succession, for him who desireth to remember, or desireth thankfulness.	And He it is Who made the night and the day to follow each other for him who desires to be mindful or desires to be thankful.

25 063	And the servants of (Allah) Most Gracious are those who walk on the earth in humility, and when the ignorant address them, they say, Peace!;	The (faithful) slaves of the Beneficent are they who walk upon the earth modestly, and when the foolish ones address them answer: Peace;	And the servants of the Beneficent Allah are they who walk on the earth in humbleness, and when the ignorant address them, they say: Peace.
25 064	Those who spend the night in adoration of their Lord prostrate and standing;	And who spend the night before their Lord, prostrate and standing,	And they who pass the night prostrating themselves before their Lord and standing.
25 065	Those who say, "Our Lord! avert from us the Wrath of Hell, for its Wrath is indeed an affliction grievous,"-	And who say: Our Lord! Avert from us the doom of hell; lo! the doom thereof is anguish;	And they who say: O our Lord! turn away from us the punishment of hell, surely the punishment thereof is a lasting evil.
25 066	"Evil indeed is it as an abode, and as a place to rest in";	Lo! it is wretched as abode and station;	Surely it is an evil abode and (evil) place to stay.
25 067	Those who, when they spend, are not extravagant and not niggardly, but hold a just (balance) between those (extremes);	And those who, when they spend, are neither prodigal nor grudging; and there is ever a firm station between the two;	And they who when they spend, are neither extravagant nor parsimonious, and (keep) between these the just mean.
25 068	Those who invoke not, with Allah, any other god, nor slay such life as Allah has made sacred except for just cause, nor commit fornication; - and any that does this (not only) meets punishment,	And those who cry not unto any other god along with Allah, nor take the life which Allah hath forbidden save in (course of) justice, nor commit adultery - and whoso doeth this shall pay the penalty;	And they who do not call upon another god with Allah and do not slay the soul, which Allah has forbidden except in the requirements of justice, and (who) do not commit fornication and he who does this shall find a requital of sin;
25 069	(But) the Penalty on the Day of Judgment will be doubled to him, and he will dwell therein in ignominy,-	The doom will be doubled for him on the Day of Resurrection, and he will abide therein disdained for ever;	The punishment shall be doubled to him on the day of resurrection, and he shall abide therein in abasement;
25 070	Unless he repents, believes, and works righteous deeds, for Allah will change the evil of such persons into good, and Allah is Oft-Forgiving, Most Merciful,	Save him who repenteth and believeth and doth righteous work; as for such, Allah will change their evil deeds to good deeds. Allah is ever Forgiving, Merciful.	Except him who repents and believes and does a good deed; so these are they of whom Allah changes the evil deeds to good ones; and Allah is Forgiving, Merciful.
25 071	And whoever repents and does good has truly turned to Allah with an (acceptable) conversion;-	And whosoever repenteth and doeth good, he verily repenteth toward Allah with true repentance -	And whoever repents and does good, he surely turns to Allah a (goodly) turning.
25 072	Those who witness no falsehood, and, if they pass by futility, they pass by it with honourable (avoidance);	And those who will not witness vanity, but when they pass near senseless play, pass by with dignity.	And they who do not bear witness to what is false, and when they pass by what is vain, they pass by nobly.
25 073	Those who, when they are admonished with the Signs of their Lord, droop not down at them as if they were deaf or blind;	And those who, when they are reminded of the revelations of their Lord, fall not deaf and blind thereat.	And they who, when reminded of the communications of their Lord, do not fall down thereat deaf and blind.
25 074	And those who pray, "Our Lord! Grant unto us wives and offspring who will be the comfort of our eyes, and give us (the grace) to lead the righteous."	And who say: Our Lord! Vouchsafe us comfort of our wives and of our offspring, and make us patterns for (all) those who ward off (evil).	And they who say: O our Lord! grant us in our wives and our offspring the joy of our eyes, and make us guides to those who guard (against evil).
25 075	Those are the ones who will be rewarded with the highest place in heaven, because of their patient constancy: therein shall they be met with salutations and peace,	They will be awarded the high place forasmuch as they were steadfast, and they will meet therein with welcome and the ward of peace,	These shall be rewarded with high places because they were patient, and shall be met therein with greetings and salutations.
25 076	Dwelling therein;- how beautiful an abode and place of rest!	Abiding there for ever. Happy is it as abode and station!	Abiding therein; goodly the abode and the resting-place.

25 077	Say (to the Rejecters): "My Lord is not uneasy because of you if ye call not on Him: But ye have indeed rejected (Him), and soon will come the inevitable (punishment)!"	Say (O Muhammad, unto the disbelievers): My Lord would not concern Himself with you but for your prayer. But now ye have denied (the Truth), therefor there will be judgment.	Say: My Lord would not care for you were it not for your prayer; but you have indeed rejected (the truth), so that which shall cleave shall come.

Chapter 26:

AL-SHUARA (THE POETS)

Total Verses: 227 Revealed At: MAKKA

In the name of Allah, the Most Beneficent, the Most Merciful.

26 001	Ta. Sin. Mim.	Ta. Sin. Mim.	Ta Sin Mim.
26 002	These are verses of the Book that makes (things) clear.	These are revelations of the Scripture that maketh plain.	These are the verses of the Book that makes (things) clear.
26 003	It may be thou frettest thy soul with grief, that they do not become Believers.	It may be that thou tormentest thyself (O Muhammad) because they believe not.	Perhaps you will kill yourself with grief because they do not believe.
26 004	If (such) were Our Will, We could send down to them from the sky a Sign, to which they would bend their necks in humility.	If We will, We can send down on them from the sky a portent so that their necks would remain bowed before it.	If We please, We should send down upon them a sign from the heaven so that their necks should stoop to it.
26 005	But there comes not to them a newly-revealed Message from (Allah) Most Gracious, but they turn away therefrom.	Never cometh there unto them a fresh reminder from the Beneficent One, but they turn away from it.	And there does not come to them a new reminder from the Beneficent Allah but they turn aside from it.
26 006	They have indeed rejected (the Message): so they will know soon (enough) the truth of what they mocked at!	Now they have denied (the Truth); but there will come unto them tidings of that whereat they used to scoff.	So they have indeed rejected (the truth), therefore the news of that which they mock shall soon come to them.
26 007	Do they not look at the earth,- how many noble things of all kinds We have produced therein?	Have they not seen the earth, how much of every fruitful kind We make to grow therein?	Do they not see the earth, how many of every noble kind We have caused to grow in it?
26 008	Verily, in this is a Sign: but most of them do not believe.	Lo! herein is indeed a portent; yet most of them are not believers.	Most surely there is a sign in that, but most of them will not believe.
26 009	And verily, thy Lord is He, the Exalted in Might, Most Merciful.	And lo! thy Lord! He is indeed the Mighty, the Merciful.	And most surely your Lord is the Mighty, the Merciful.
26 010	Behold, thy Lord called Moses: "Go to the people of iniquity,"-	And when thy Lord called Moses, saying: Go unto the wrongdoing folk,	And when your Lord called out to Musa, saying: Go to the unjust people,
26 011	"The people of the Pharaoh: will they not fear Allah?"	The folk of Pharaoh. Will they not ward off (evil)?	The people of Firon: Will they not guard (against evil)?
26 012	He said: "O my Lord! I do fear that they will charge me with falsehood:"	He said: My Lord! Lo! I fear that they will deny me,	He said: O my Lord! surely I fear that they will reject me;
26 013	"My breast will be straitened. And my speech may not go (smoothly): so send unto Aaron."	And I shall be embarrassed, and my tongue will not speak plainly, therefor send for Aaron (to help me).	And by breast straitens, and my tongue is not eloquent, therefore send Thou to Haroun (to help me);
26 014	"And (further), they have a charge of crime against me; and I fear they may slay me."	And they have a crime against me, so I fear that they will kill me.	And they have a crime against me, therefore I fear that they may slay me.

26 015	Allah said: "By no means! proceed then, both of you, with Our Signs; We are with you, and will listen (to your call)."	He said: Nay, verily. So go ye twain with Our tokens. Lo! We shall be with you, Hearing.	He said: By no means, so go you both with Our signs; surely We are with you, hearing;
26 016	"So go forth, both of you, to Pharaoh, and say: 'We have been sent by the Lord and Cherisher of the worlds;'"	And come together unto Pharaoh and say: Lo! we bear a message of the Lord of the Worlds,	Then come to Firon and say: Surely we are the messengers of the Lord of the worlds:
26 017	"'Send thou with us the Children of Israel.'"	(Saying): Let the Children of Israel go with us.	Then send with us the children of Israel.
26 018	(Pharaoh) said: "Did we not cherish thee as a child among us, and didst thou not stay in our midst many years of thy life?"	(Pharaoh) said (unto Moses): Did we not rear thee among us as a child? And thou didst dwell many years of thy life among us,	(Firon) said: Did we not bring you up as a child among us, and you tarried among us for (many) years of your life?
26 019	"And thou didst a deed of thine which (thou knowest) thou didst, and thou art an ungrateful (wretch)!"	And thou didst that thy deed which thou didst, and thou wast one of the ingrates.	And you did (that) deed of yours which you did, and you are one of the ungrateful.
26 020	Moses said: "I did it then, when I was in error."	He said: I did it then, when I was of those who are astray.	He said: I did it then while I was of those unable to see the right course;
26 021	"So I fled from you (all) when I feared you; but my Lord has (since) invested me with judgment (and wisdom) and appointed me as one of the messengers."	Then I fled from you when I feared you, and my Lord vouchsafed me a command and appointed me (of the number) of those sent (by Him).	So I fled from you when I feared you, then my Lord granted me wisdom and made me of the messengers;
26 022	"And this is the favour with which thou dost reproach me,- that thou hast enslaved the Children of Israel!"	And this is the past favour wherewith thou reproachest me: that thou hast enslaved the Children of Israel.	And is it a favor of which you remind me that you have enslaved the children of Israel?
26 023	Pharaoh said: "And what is the 'Lord and Cherisher of the worlds'?"	Pharaoh said: And what is the Lord of the Worlds?	Firon said: And what is the Lord of the worlds?
26 024	(Moses) said: "The Lord and Cherisher of the heavens and the earth, and all between,- if ye want to be quite sure."	(Moses) said: Lord of the heavens and the earth and all that is between them, if ye had but sure belief.	He said: The Lord of the heavens and the earth and what is between them, if you would be sure.
26 025	(Pharaoh) said to those around: "Did ye not listen (to what he says)?"	(Pharaoh) said unto those around him: Hear ye not?	(Firon) said to those around him: Do you not hear?
26 026	(Moses) said: "Your Lord and the Lord of your fathers from the beginning!"	He said: Your Lord and the Lord of your fathers.	He said: Your Lord and the Lord of your fathers of old.
26 027	(Pharaoh) said: "Truly your messenger who has been sent to you is a veritable madman!"	(Pharaoh) said: Lo! your messenger who hath been sent unto you is indeed a madman!	Said he: Most surely your Messenger who is sent to you is mad.
26 028	(Moses) said: "Lord of the East and the West, and all between! if ye only had sense!"	He said: Lord of the East and the West and all that is between them, if ye did but understand.	He said: The Lord of the east and the west and what is between them, if you understand.
26 029	(Pharaoh) said: "If thou dost put forward any god other than me, I will certainly put thee in prison!"	(Pharaoh) said: If thou choosest a god other than me, I assuredly shall place thee among the prisoners.	Said he: If you will take a god besides me, I will most certainly make you one of the imprisoned.
26 030	(Moses) said: "Even if I showed you something clear (and) convincing?"	He said: Even though I show thee something plain?	He said: What! even if I bring to you something manifest?
26 031	(Pharaoh) said: "Show it then, if thou tellest the truth!"	(Pharaoh) said: Produce it then, if thou art of the truthful!	Said he: Bring it then, if you are of the truthful ones.
26 032	So (Moses) threw his rod, and behold, it was a serpent, plain (for all to see)!	Then he flung down his staff and it became a serpent manifest,	So he cast down his rod, and lo! it was an obvious serpent,

26 033	And he drew out his hand, and behold, it was white to all beholders!	And he drew forth his hand and lo! it was white to the beholders.	And he drew forth his hand, and lo! it appeared white to the onlookers.
26 034	(Pharaoh) said to the Chiefs around him: "This is indeed a sorcerer well-versed:"	(Pharaoh) said unto the chiefs about him: Lo! this is verily a knowing wizard,	(Firon) said to the chiefs around him: Most surely this is a skillful magician,
26 035	"His plan is to get you out of your land by his sorcery; then what is it ye counsel?"	Who would drive you out of your land by his magic. Now what counsel ye?	Who desires to turn you out of your land with his magic; what is it then that you advise?
26 036	They said: "Keep him and his brother in suspense (for a while), and dispatch to the Cities heralds to collect-"	They said: Put him off, (him) and his brother, and send into the cities summoners,	They said: Give him and his brother respite and send heralds into the cities;
26 037	"And bring up to thee all (our) sorcerers well-versed."	Who shall bring unto thee every knowing wizard.	That they should bring to you every skillful magician.
26 038	So the sorcerers were got together for the appointment of a day well-known,	So the wizards were gathered together at a set time on a day appointed.	So the magicians were gathered together at the appointed time on the fixed day,
26 039	And the people were told: "Are ye (now) assembled?"-	And it was said unto the people: Are ye (also) gathering?	And it was said to the people: Will you gather together?
26 040	"That we may follow the sorcerers (in religion) if they win?"	(They said): Aye, so that we may follow the wizards if they are the winners.	Haply we may follow the magicians, if they are the vanquishers.
26 041	So when the sorcerers arrived, they said to Pharaoh: "Of course - shall we have a (suitable) reward if we win?"	And when the wizards came they said unto Pharaoh: Will there surely be a reward for us if we are the winners?	And when the magicians came, they said to Firon: Shall we get a reward if we are the vanquishers?
26 042	He said: "Yea, (and more),- for ye shall in that case be (raised to posts) nearest (to my person)."	He said: Aye, and ye will then surely be of those brought near (to me).	He said: Yes, and surely you will then be of those who are made near.
26 043	Moses said to them: "Throw ye - that which ye are about to throw!"	Moses said unto them: Throw what ye are going to throw!	Musa said to them: Cast what you are going to cast.
26 044	So they threw their ropes and their rods, and said: "By the might of Pharaoh, it is we who will certainly win!"	Then they threw down their cords and their staves and said: By Pharaoh's might, lo! we verily are the winners.	So they cast down their cords and their rods and said: By Firon's power, we shall most surely be victorious.
26 045	Then Moses threw his rod, when, behold, it straightway swallows up all the falsehoods which they fake!	Then Moses threw his staff and lo! it swallowed that which they did falsely show.	Then Musa cast down his staff and lo! it swallowed up the lies they told.
26 046	Then did the sorcerers fall down, prostrate in adoration,	And the wizards were flung prostrate,	And the magicians were thrown down prostrate;
26 047	Saying: "We believe in the Lord of the Worlds,"	Crying: We believe in the Lord of the Worlds,	They said: We believe in the Lord of the worlds:
26 048	"The Lord of Moses and Aaron."	The Lord of Moses and Aaron.	The Lord of Musa and Haroun.
26 049	Said (Pharaoh): "Believe ye in Him before I give you permission? surely he is your leader, who has taught you sorcery! but soon shall ye know!" - "Be sure I will cut off your hands and your feet on opposite sides, and I will cause you all to die on the cross!"	(Pharaoh) said: Ye put your faith in him before I give you leave. Lo! he doubtless is your chief who taught you magic! But verily ye shall come to know. Verily I will cut off your hands and your feet alternately, and verily I will crucify you every one.	Said he: You believe in him before I give you permission; most surely he is the chief of you who taught you the magic, so you shall know: certainly I will cut off your hands and your feet on opposite sides, and certainly I will crucify you all.
26 050	They said: "No matter! for us, we shall but return to our Lord!"	They said: It is no hurt, for lo! unto our Lord we shall return.	They said: No harm; surely to our Lord we go back;
26 051	"Only, our desire is that our Lord will forgive us our faults, that we may become foremost among the believers!"	Lo! we ardently hope that our Lord will forgive us our sins because we are the first of the believers.	Surely we hope that our Lord will forgive us our wrongs because we are the first of the believers.

26 052	By inspiration we told Moses: "Travel by night with my servants; for surely ye shall be pursued."	And We inspired Moses, saying: Take away My slaves by night, for ye will be pursued.	And We revealed to Musa, saying: Go away with My servants travelling by night, surely you will be pursued.
26 053	Then Pharaoh sent heralds to (all) the Cities,	Then Pharaoh sent into the cities summoners,	So Firon sent heralds into the cities;
26 054	(Saying): "These (Israelites) are but a small band,"	(Who said): Lo! these indeed are but a little troop,	Most surely these are a small company;
26 055	"And they are raging furiously against us;"	And lo! they are offenders against us.	And most surely they have enraged us;
26 056	"But we are a multitude amply fore-warned."	And lo! we are a ready host.	And most surely we are a vigilant multitude.
26 057	So We expelled them from gardens, springs,	Thus did We take them away from gardens and watersprings,	So We turned them out of gardens and springs,
26 058	Treasures, and every kind of honourable position;	And treasures and a fair estate.	And treasures and goodly dwellings,
26 059	Thus it was, but We made the Children of Israel inheritors of such things.	Thus (were those things taken from them) and We caused the Children of Israel to inherit them.	Even so. And We gave them as a heritage to the children of Israel.
26 060	So they pursued them at sunrise.	And they overtook them at sunrise.	Then they pursued them at sunrise.
26 061	And when the two bodies saw each other, the people of Moses said: We are sure to be overtaken.	And when the two hosts saw each other, those with Moses said: Lo! we are indeed caught.	So when the two hosts saw each other, the companions of Musa cried out: Most surely we are being overtaken.
26 062	(Moses) said: "By no means! my Lord is with me! Soon will He guide me!"	He said: Nay, verily! for lo! my Lord is with me. He will guide me.	He said: By no means; surely my Lord is with me: He will show me a way out.
26 063	Then We told Moses by inspiration: "Strike the sea with thy rod." So it divided, and each separate part became like the huge, firm mass of a mountain.	Then We inspired Moses, saying: Smite the sea with thy staff. And it parted, and each part was as a mountain vast.	Then We revealed to Musa: Strike the sea with your staff. So it had cloven asunder, and each part was like a huge mound.
26 064	And We made the other party approach thither.	Then brought We near the others to that place.	And We brought near, there, the others.
26 065	We delivered Moses and all who were with him;	And We saved Moses and those with him, every one;	And We saved Musa and those with him, all of them.
26 066	But We drowned the others.	And We drowned the others.	Then We drowned the others.
26 067	Verily in this is a Sign: but most of them do not believe.	Lo! herein is indeed a portent, yet most of them are not believers.	Most surely there is a sign in this, but most of them do not believe.
26 068	And verily thy Lord is He, the Exalted in Might, Most Merciful.	And lo, thy Lord! He is indeed the Mighty, the Merciful.	And most surely your Lord is the Mighty, the Merciful.
26 069	And rehearse to them (something of) Abraham's story.	Recite unto them the story of Abraham:	And recite to them the story of Ibrahim.
26 070	Behold, he said to his father and his people: "What worship ye?"	When he said unto his father and his folk: What worship ye?	When he said to his father and his people: What do you worship?
26 071	They said: "We worship idols, and we remain constantly in attendance on them."	They said: We worship idols, and are ever devoted unto them.	They said: We worship idols, so we shall be their votaries.
26 072	He said: "Do they listen to you when ye call (on them),"	He said: Do they hear you when ye cry?	He said: Do they hear you when you call?
26 073	"Or do you good or harm?"	Or do they benefit or harm you?	Or do they profit you or cause you harm?
26 074	They said: "Nay, but we found our fathers doing thus (what we do)."	They said: Nay, but we found our fathers acting on this wise.	They said: Nay, we found our fathers doing so.
26 075	He said: "Do ye then see whom ye have been worshipping,"-	He said: See now that which ye worship,	He said: Have you then considered what you have been worshipping:

26 076	"Ye and your fathers before you?"-	Ye and your forefathers!		You and your ancient sires.
26 077	"For they are enemies to me; not so the Lord and Cherisher of the Worlds;"	Lo! they are (all) an enemy unto me, save the Lord of the Worlds,		Surely they are enemies to me, but not (so) the Lord of the worlds;
26 078	"Who created me, and it is He Who guides me;"	Who created me, and He doth guide me,		Who created me, then He has shown me the way:
26 079	"Who gives me food and drink,"	And Who feedeth me and watereth me.		And He Who gives me to eat and gives me to drink:
26 080	"And when I am ill, it is He Who cures me;"	And when I sicken, then He healeth me,		And when I am sick, then He restores me to health
26 081	"Who will cause me to die, and then to life (again);"	And Who causeth me to die, then giveth me life (again),		And He Who will cause me to die, then give me life;
26 082	"And Who, I hope, will forgive me my faults on the Day of Judgment...."	And Who, I ardently hope, will forgive me my sin on the Day of Judgment.		And Who, I hope, will forgive me my mistakes on the Day of Judgment.
26 083	"O my Lord! bestow wisdom on me, and join me with the righteous;"	My Lord! Vouchsafe me wisdom and unite me to the righteous.		My Lord: Grant me wisdom, and join me with the good
26 084	"Grant me honourable mention on the tongue of truth among the latest (generations);"	And give unto me a good report in later generations.		And ordain for me a goodly mention among posterity
26 085	"Make me one of the inheritors of the Garden of Bliss;"	And place me among the inheritors of the Garden of Delight,		And make me of the heirs of the garden of bliss
26 086	"Forgive my father, for that he is among those astray;"	And forgive my father. Lo! he is of those who err.		And forgive my father, for surely he is of those who have gone astray;
26 087	"And let me not be in disgrace on the Day when (men) will be raised up;"-	And abase me not on the day when they are raised,		And disgrace me not on the day when they are raised
26 088	"The Day whereon neither wealth nor sons will avail,"	The day when wealth and sons avail not (any man)		The day on which property will not avail, nor sons
26 089	"But only he (will prosper) that brings to Allah a sound heart;"	Save him who bringeth unto Allah a whole heart.		Except him who comes to Allah with a heart free (from evil).
26 090	"To the righteous, the Garden will be brought near,"	And the Garden will be brought nigh for those who ward off (evil).		And the garden shall be brought near for those who guard (against evil),
26 091	"And to those straying in Evil, the Fire will be placed in full view;"	And hell will appear plainly to the erring.		And the hell shall be made manifest to the erring ones,
26 092	"And it shall be said to them: 'Where are the (gods) ye worshipped-'"	And it will be said unto them: Where is (all) that ye used to worship		And it shall be said to them: Where are those that you used to worship;
26 093	"'Besides Allah? Can they help you or help themselves?'"	Instead of Allah? Can they help you or help themselves?		Besides Allah? Can they help you or yet help themselves?
26 094	"Then they will be thrown headlong into the (Fire),- they and those straying in Evil,"	Then will they be hurled therein, they and the seducers		So they shall be thrown down into it, they and the erring ones,
26 095	"And the whole hosts of Iblis together."	And the hosts of Iblis, together.		And the hosts of the Shaitan, all.
26 096	"They will say there in their mutual bickerings:"	And they will say, when they are quarrelling therein:		They shall say while they contend therein:
26 097	"'By Allah, we were truly in an error manifest,"	By Allah, of a truth we were in error manifest		By Allah! we were certainly in manifest error,
26 098	"'When we held you as equals with the Lord of the Worlds;"	When we made you equal with the Lord of the Worlds.		When we made you equal to the Lord of the worlds;
26 099	"'And our seducers were only those who were steeped in guilt."	It was but the guilty who misled us.		And none but the guilty led us astray;
26 100	"'Now, then, we have none to intercede (for us),'"	Now we have no intercessors		So we have no intercessors,

26 101	"'Nor a single friend to feel (for us).'"	Nor any loving friend.	Nor a true friend;
26 102	"'Now if we only had a chance of return we shall truly be of those who believe!'"	Oh, that we had another turn (on earth), that we might be of the believers!	But if we could but once return, we would be of the believers.
26 103	Verily in this is a Sign but most of them do not believe.	Lo! herein is indeed a portent, yet most of them are not believers!	Most surely there is a sign in this, but most of them do not believe.
26 104	And verily thy Lord is He, the Exalted in Might, Most Merciful.	And lo, thy Lord! He is indeed the Mighty, the Merciful.	And most surely your Lord is the Mighty, the Merciful.
26 105	The people of Noah rejected the messengers.	Noah's folk denied the messengers (of Allah),	The people of Nuh rejected the messengers.
26 106	Behold, their brother Noah said to them: "Will ye not fear (Allah)?"	When their brother Noah said unto them: Will ye not ward off (evil)?	When their brother Nuh said to them: Will you not guard (against evil)?
26 107	"I am to you a messenger worthy of all trust:"	Lo! I am a faithful messenger unto you,	Surely I am a faithful messenger to you;
26 108	"So fear Allah, and obey me."	So keep your duty to Allah, and obey me.	Therefore guard against (the punishment of) Allah and obey me
26 109	"No reward do I ask of you for it: my reward is only from the Lord of the Worlds:"	And I ask of you no wage therefor; my wage is the concern only of the Lord of the Worlds.	And I do not ask you any reward for it; my reward is only with the Lord of the worlds:
26 110	"So fear Allah, and obey me."	So keep your duty to Allah, and obey me.	So guard against (the punishment of) Allah and obey me.
26 111	They said: "Shall we believe in thee when it is the meanest that follow thee?"	They said: Shall we put faith in thee, when the lowest (of the people) follow thee?	They said: Shall we believe in you while the meanest follow you?
26 112	He said: "And what do I know as to what they do?"	He said: And what knowledge have I of what they may have been doing (in the past)?	He said: And what knowledge have I of what they do?
26 113	"Their account is only with my Lord, if ye could (but) understand."	Lo! their reckoning is my Lord's concern, if ye but knew;	Their account is only with my Lord, if you could perceive
26 114	"I am not one to drive away those who believe."	And I am not (here) to repulse believers.	And I am not going to drive away the believers;
26 115	"I am sent only to warn plainly in public."	I am only a plain warner.	I am naught but a plain warner.
26 116	They said: "If thou desist not, O Noah! thou shalt be stoned (to death)."	They said: If thou cease not, O Noah, thou wilt surely be among those stoned (to death).	They said: If you desist not, O Nuh, you shall most certainly be of those stoned to death.
26 117	He said: "O my Lord! truly my people have rejected me."	He said: My Lord! Lo! my own folk deny me.	He said: My Lord! Surely my people give me the lie!
26 118	"Judge Thou, then, between me and them openly, and deliver me and those of the Believers who are with me."	Therefor judge Thou between us, a (conclusive) judgment, and save me and those believers who are with me.	Therefore judge Thou between me and them with a (just) judgment, and deliver me and those who are with me of the believers.
26 119	So We delivered him and those with him, in the Ark filled (with all creatures).	And We saved him and those with him in the laden ship.	So We delivered him and those with him in the laden ark.
26 120	Thereafter We drowned those who remained behind.	Then afterward We drowned the others.	Then We drowned the rest afterwards
26 121	Verily in this is a Sign: but most of them do not believe.	Lo! herein is indeed a portent, yet most of them are not believers.	Most surely there is a sign in this, but most of them do not believe.
26 122	And verily thy Lord is He, the Exalted in Might, Most Merciful.	And lo, thy Lord, He is indeed the Mighty, the Merciful.	And most surely your Lord is the Mighty, the Merciful.
26 123	The 'Ad (people) rejected the messengers.	(The tribe of) A'ad denied the messengers (of Allah).	Ad gave the lie to the messengers.
26 124	Behold, their brother Hud said to them: "Will ye not fear (Allah)?"	When their brother Hud said unto them: Will ye not ward off (evil)?	When their brother Hud said to them: Will you not guard (against evil)?

26 125	"I am to you a messenger worthy of all trust:"	Lo! I am a faithful messenger unto you,		Surely I am a faithful messenger to you;
26 126	"So fear Allah and obey me."	So keep your duty to Allah and obey me.		Therefore guard against (the punishment of) Allah and obey me:
26 127	"No reward do I ask of you for it: my reward is only from the Lord of the Worlds."	And I ask of you no wage therefor; my wage is the concern only of the Lord of the Worlds.		And I do not ask you any reward for it; surely my reward is only with the Lord of the worlds;
26 128	"Do ye build a landmark on every high place to amuse yourselves?"	Build ye on every high place a monument for vain delight?		Do you build on every height a monument? Vain is it that you do:
26 129	"And do ye get for yourselves fine buildings in the hope of living therein (for ever)?"	And seek ye out strongholds, that haply ye may last for ever?		And you make strong fortresses that perhaps you may
26 130	"And when ye exert your strong hand, do ye do it like men of absolute power?"	And if ye seize by force, seize ye as tyrants?		And when you lay hands (on men) you lay hands (like) tyrants;
26 131	"Now fear Allah, and obey me."	Rather keep your duty to Allah, and obey me.		So guard against (the punishment of) Allah and obey me
26 132	"Yea, fear Him Who has bestowed on you freely all that ye know."	Keep your duty toward Him Who hath aided you with (the good things) that ye know,		And be careful of (your duty to) Him Who has given you abundance of what you know.
26 133	"Freely has He bestowed on you cattle and sons,"-	Hath aided you with cattle and sons.		He has given you abundance of cattle and children
26 134	"And Gardens and Springs."	And gardens and watersprings.		And gardens and fountains;
26 135	"Truly I fear for you the Penalty of a Great Day."	Lo! I fear for you the retribution of an awful day.		Surely I fear for you the chastisement of a grievous day
26 136	They said: "It is the same to us whether thou admonish us or be not among (our) admonishers!"	They said: It is all one to us whether thou preachest or art not of those who preach;		They said: It is the same to us whether you admonish or are not one of the admonishers;
26 137	"This is no other than a customary device of the ancients,"	This is but a fable of the men of old,		This is naught but a custom of the ancients;
26 138	"And we are not the ones to receive Pains and Penalties!"	And we shall not be doomed.		And we are not going to be punished.
26 139	So they rejected him, and We destroyed them. Verily in this is a Sign: but most of them do not believe.	And they denied him; therefor We destroyed them. Lo! herein is indeed a portent, yet most of them are not believers.		So they gave him the lie, then We destroyed them. Most surely there is a sign in this, but most of them do not believe.
26 140	And verily thy Lord is He, the Exalted in Might, Most Merciful.	And lo! thy Lord, He is indeed the Mighty, the Merciful.		And most surely your Lord is the Mighty, the Merciful.
26 141	The Thamud (people) rejected the messengers.	(The tribe of) Thamud denied the messengers (of Allah)		Samood gave the lie to the messengers
26 142	Behold, their brother Salih said to them: "Will you not fear (Allah)?"	When their brother Salih said unto them: Will ye not ward off (evil)?		When their brother Salih said to them: Will you not guard (against evil)?
26 143	"I am to you a messenger worthy of all trust."	Lo! I am a faithful messenger unto you,		Surely I am a faithful messenger to you
26 144	"So fear Allah, and obey me."	So keep your duty to Allah and obey me.		Therefore guard against (the punishment of) Allah and obey me:
26 145	"No reward do I ask of you for it: my reward is only from the Lord of the Worlds."	And I ask of you no wage therefor; my wage is the concern only of the Lord of the Worlds.		And I do not ask you any reward for it; my reward is only with the Lord of the worlds:
26 146	"Will ye be left secure, in (the enjoyment of) all that ye have here?"-	Will ye be left secure in that which is here before us,		Will you be left secure in what is here;
26 147	"Gardens and Springs,"	In gardens and watersprings.		In gardens and fountains,
26 148	"And corn-fields and date-palms with spathes near breaking (with the weight of fruit)?"	And tilled fields and heavy-sheathed palm-trees,		And cornfields and palm-trees having fine spadices?

26 149	"And ye carve houses out of (rocky) mountains with great skill."	Though ye hew out dwellings in the mountain, being skilful?	And you hew houses out of the mountains exultingly;
26 150	"But fear Allah and obey me;"	Therefor keep your duty to Allah and obey me,	Therefore guard against (the punishment of) Allah and obey me;
26 151	"And follow not the bidding of those who are extravagant,"-	And obey not the command of the prodigal,	And do not obey the bidding of the extravagant,
26 152	"Who make mischief in the land, and mend not (their ways)."	Who spread corruption in the earth, and reform not.	Who make mischief in the land and do not act aright.
26 153	They said: "Thou art only one of those bewitched!"	They said: Thou art but one of the bewitched;	They said: You are only of the deluded ones;
26 154	"Thou art no more than a mortal like us: then bring us a Sign, if thou tellest the truth!"	Thou art but a mortal like us. So bring some token if thou art of the truthful.	You are naught but a mortal like ourselves; so bring a sign if you are one of the truthful.
26 155	He said: "Here is a she-camel: she has a right of watering, and ye have a right of watering, (severally) on a day appointed."	He said: (Behold) this she-camel. She hath the right to drink (at the well), and ye have the right to drink, (each) on an appointed day.	He said: This is a she-camel; she shall have her portion of water, and you have your portion of water on an appointed time;
26 156	"Touch her not with harm, lest the Penalty of a Great Day seize you."	And touch her not with ill lest there come on you the retribution of an awful day.	And do not touch her with evil, lest the punishment of a grievous day should overtake you.
26 157	But they ham-strung her: then did they become full of regrets.	But they hamstrung her, and then were penitent.	But they hamstrung her, then regretted;
26 158	But the Penalty seized them. Verily in this is a Sign: but most of them do not believe.	So the retribution came on them. Lo! herein is indeed a portent, yet most of them are not believers.	So the punishment overtook them. Most surely there is a sign in this, but most of them do not believe.
26 159	And verily thy Lord is He, the Exalted in Might, Most Merciful.	And lo! thy Lord! He is indeed the Mighty, the Merciful.	And most surely your Lord is the Mighty, the Merciful.
26 160	The people of Lut rejected the messengers.	The folk of Lot denied the messengers (of Allah),	The people of Lut gave the lie to the messengers.
26 161	Behold, their brother Lut said to them: "Will ye not fear (Allah)?"	When their brother Lot said unto them: Will ye not ward off (evil)?	When their brother Lut said to them: Will you not guard (against evil)?
26 162	"I am to you a messenger worthy of all trust."	Lo! I am a faithful messenger unto you,	Surely I am a faithful messenger to you;
26 163	"So fear Allah and obey me."	So keep your duty to Allah and obey me.	Therefore guard against (the punishment of) Allah and obey me:
26 164	"No reward do I ask of you for it: my reward is only from the Lord of the Worlds."	And I ask of you no wage therefor; my wage is the concern only of the Lord of the Worlds.	And I do not ask you any reward for it; my reward is only with the Lord of the worlds;
26 165	"Of all the creatures in the world, will ye approach males,"	What! Of all creatures do ye come unto the males,	What! do you come to the males from among the creatures
26 166	"And leave those whom Allah has created for you to be your mates? Nay, ye are a people transgressing (all limits)!"	And leave the wives your Lord created for you? Nay, but ye are froward folk.	And leave what your Lord has created for you of your wives? Nay, you are a people exceeding limits.
26 167	They said: "If thou desist not, O Lut! thou wilt assuredly be cast out!"	They said: If thou cease not, O Lot, thou wilt soon be of the outcast.	They said: If you desist not, O Lut! you shall surely be of those who are expelled.
26 168	He said: "I do detest your doings."	He said: I am in truth of those who hate your conduct.	He said: Surely I am of those who utterly abhor your doing;
26 169	"O my Lord! deliver me and my family from such things as they do!"	My Lord! Save me and my household from what they do.	My Lord! deliver me and my followers from what they do.
26 170	So We delivered him and his family,- all,	So We saved him and his household, every one,	So We delivered him and his followers all,
26 171	Except an old woman who lingered behind.	Save an old woman among those who stayed behind.	Except an old woman, among those who remained behind.
26 172	But the rest We destroyed utterly.	Then afterward We destroyed the others.	Then We utterly destroyed the others.

26 173	We rained down on them a shower (of brimstone): and evil was the shower on those who were admonished (but heeded not)!	And We rained on them a rain. And dreadful is the rain of those who have been warned.	And We rained down upon them a rain, and evil was the rain on those warned.
26 174	Verily in this is a Sign: but most of them do not believe.	Lo! herein is indeed a portent, yet most of them are not believers.	Most surely there is a sign in this, but most of them do not believe.
26 175	And verily thy Lord is He, the Exalted in Might Most Merciful.	And lo! thy Lord, He is indeed the Mighty, the Merciful.	And most surely your Lord is the Mighty, the Merciful.
26 176	The Companions of the Wood rejected the messengers.	The dwellers in the wood (of Midian) denied the messengers (of Allah),	The dwellers of the thicket gave the lie to the messengers.
26 177	Behold, Shu'aib said to them: "Will ye not fear (Allah)?"	When Shu'eyb said unto them: Will ye not ward off (evil)?	When Shu'aib said to them: Will you not guard (against evil)?
26 178	"I am to you a messenger worthy of all trust."	Lo! I am a faithful messenger unto you,	Surely I am a faithful messenger to you;
26 179	"So fear Allah and obey me."	So keep your duty to Allah and obey me.	Therefore guard against (the punishment of) Allah and obey me:
26 180	"No reward do I ask of you for it: my reward is only from the Lord of the Worlds."	And I ask of you no wage for it; my wage is the concern only of the Lord of the Worlds.	And I do not ask you any reward for it, my reward is only with the Lord of the worlds;
26 181	"Give just measure, and cause no loss (to others by fraud)."	Give full measure, and be not of those who give less (than the due).	Give a full measure and be not of those who diminish;
26 182	"And weigh with scales true and upright."	And weigh with the true balance.	And weigh (things) with a right balance,
26 183	"And withhold not things justly due to men, nor do evil in the land, working mischief."	Wrong not mankind in their goods, and do not evil, making mischief, in the earth.	And do not wrong men of their things, and do not act corruptly in the earth, making mischief.
26 184	"And fear Him Who created you and (who created) the generations before (you)."	And keep your duty unto Him Who created you and the generations of the men of old.	And guard against (the punishment of) Him who created you and the former nations.
26 185	They said: "Thou art only one of those bewitched!"	They said: Thou art but one of the bewitched;	They said: You are only of those deluded;
26 186	"Thou art no more than a mortal like us, and indeed we think thou art a liar!"	Thou art but a mortal like us, and lo! we deem thee of the liars.	And you are naught but a mortal like ourselves, and we know you to be certainly of the liars.
26 187	"Now cause a piece of the sky to fall on us, if thou art truthful!"	Then make fragments of the heaven fall upon us, if thou art of the truthful.	Therefore cause a portion of the heaven to come down upon us, if you are one of the truthful.
26 188	He said: "My Lord knows best what ye do."	He said: My Lord is Best Aware of what ye do.	He said: My Lord knows best what you do.
26 189	But they rejected him. Then the punishment of a day of overshadowing gloom seized them, and that was the Penalty of a Great Day.	But they denied him, so there came on them the retribution of the day of gloom. Lo! it was the retribution of an awful day.	But they called him a liar, so the punishment of the day of covering overtook them; surely it was the punishment of a grievous day.
26 190	Verily in that is a Sign: but most of them do not believe.	Lo! herein is indeed a portent; yet most of them are not believers.	Most surely there is a sign in this, but most of them do not believe.
26 191	And verily thy Lord is He, the Exalted in Might, Most Merciful.	And lo! thy Lord! He is indeed the Mighty, the Merciful.	And most surely your Lord is Mighty, the Merciful.
26 192	Verily this is a Revelation from the Lord of the Worlds:	And lo! it is a revelation of the Lord of the Worlds,	And most surely this is a revelation from the Lord of the worlds.
26 193	With it came down the spirit of Faith and Truth-	Which the True Spirit hath brought down	The Faithful Spirit has descended with it,
26 194	To thy heart and mind, that thou mayest admonish.	Upon thy heart, that thou mayst be (one) of the warners,	Upon your heart that you may be of the warners
26 195	In the perspicuous Arabic tongue.	In plain Arabic speech.	In plain Arabic language.
26 196	Without doubt it is (announced) in the mystic Books of former peoples.	And lo! it is in the Scriptures of the men of old.	And most surely the same is in the scriptures of the ancients.

26 197	Is it not a Sign to them that the Learned of the Children of Israel knew it (as true)?	Is it not a token for them that the doctors of the Children of Israel know it?	Is it not a sign to them that the learned men of the Israelites know it?
26 198	Had We revealed it to any of the non-Arabs,	And if We had revealed it unto one of any other nation than the Arabs,	And if we had revealed it to any of the foreigners
26 199	And had he recited it to them, they would not have believed in it.	And he had read it unto them, they would not have believed in it.	So that he should have recited it to them, they would not have believed therein.
26 200	Thus have We caused it to enter the hearts of the sinners.	Thus do We make it traverse the hearts of the guilty.	Thus have We caused it to enter into the hearts of the guilty.
26 201	They will not believe in it until they see the grievous Penalty;	They will not believe in it till they behold the painful doom,	They will not believe in it until they see the painful punishment.
26 202	But the (Penalty) will come to them of a sudden, while they perceive it not;	So that it will come upon them suddenly, when they perceive not.	And it shall come to them all of a sudden, while they shall not perceive;
26 203	Then they will say: "Shall we be respited?"	Then they will say: Are we to be reprieved?	Then they will say: Shall we be respited?
26 204	Do they then ask for Our Penalty to be hastened on?	Would they (now) hasten on Our doom?	What! do they still seek to hasten on Our punishment?
26 205	Seest thou? If We do let them enjoy (this life) for a few years,	Hast thou then seen, if We content them for (long) years,	Have you then considered if We let them enjoy themselves for years,
26 206	Yet there comes to them at length the (Punishment) which they were promised!	And then cometh that which they were promised,	Then there comes to them that with which they are threatened,
26 207	It will profit them not that they enjoyed (this life)!	(How) that wherewith they were contented naught availeth them?	That which they were made to enjoy shall not avail them?
26 208	Never did We destroy a population, but had its warners -	And We destroyed no township but it had its warners	And We did not destroy any town but it had (its) warners,
26 209	By way of reminder; and We never are unjust.	For reminder, for We never were oppressors.	To remind, and We are never unjust.
26 210	No evil ones have brought down this (Revelation):	The devils did not bring it down.	And the Shaitans have not come down with it.
26 211	It would neither suit them nor would they be able (to produce it).	It is not meet for them, nor is it in their power,	And it behoves them not, and they have not the power to do (it).
26 212	Indeed they have been removed far from even (a chance of) hearing it.	Lo! verily they are banished from the hearing.	Most surely they are far removed from the hearing of it.
26 213	So call not on any other god with Allah, or thou wilt be among those under the Penalty.	Therefor invoke not with Allah another god, lest thou be one of the doomed.	So call not upon another god with Allah, lest you be of those who are punished.
26 214	And admonish thy nearest kinsmen,	And warn thy tribe of near kindred,	And warn your nearest relations,
26 215	And lower thy wing to the Believers who follow thee.	And lower thy wing (in kindness) unto those believers who follow thee.	And be kind to him who follows you of the believers.
26 216	Then if they disobey thee, say: "I am free (of responsibility) for what ye do!"	And if they (thy kinsfolk) disobey thee, say: Lo! I am innocent of what they do.	But if they disobey you, then say: Surely I am clear of what you do.
26 217	And put thy trust on the Exalted in Might, the Merciful,-	And put thy trust in the Mighty, the Merciful.	And rely on the Mighty, the Merciful,
26 218	Who seeth thee standing forth (in prayer),	Who seeth thee when thou standest up (to pray)	Who sees you when you stand up.
26 219	And thy movements among those who prostrate themselves,	And (seeth) thine abasement among those who fall prostrate (in worship).	And your turning over and over among those who prostrate themselves before Allah.
26 220	For it is He Who heareth and knoweth all things.	Lo! He, only He, is the Hearer, the Knower.	Surely He is the Hearing, the Knowing.
26 221	Shall I inform you, (O people!), on whom it is that the evil ones descend?	Shall I inform you upon whom the devils descend?	Shall I inform you (of him) upon whom the Shaitans descend?

26 222	They descend on every lying, wicked person,	They descend on every sinful, false one.	They descend upon every lying, sinful one,
26 223	(Into whose ears) they pour hearsay vanities, and most of them are liars.	They listen eagerly, but most of them are liars.	They incline their ears, and most of them are liars.
26 224	And the Poets,- It is those straying in Evil, who follow them:	As for poets, the erring follow them.	And as to the poets, those who go astray follow them.
26 225	Seest thou not that they wander distracted in every valley?-	Hast thou not seen how they stray in every valley,	Do you not see that they wander about bewildered in every valley?
26 226	And that they say what they practise not?-	And how they say that which they do not?	And that they say that which they do not do,
26 227	Except those who believe, work righteousness, engage much in the remembrance of Allah, and defend themselves only after they are unjustly attacked. And soon will the unjust assailants know what vicissitudes their affairs will take!	Save those who believe and do good works, and remember Allah much, and vindicate themselves after they have been wronged. Those who do wrong will come to know by what a (great) reverse they will be overturned!	Except those who believe and do good and remember Allah much, and defend themselves after they are oppressed; and they who act unjustly shall know to what final place of turning they shall turn back.

Chapter 27:

AL-NAML (THE ANT, THE ANTS)

Total Verses: 93 Revealed At: MAKKA

In the name of Allah, the Most Beneficent, the Most Merciful.

27 001	These are verses of the Qur'an,-a book that makes (things) clear;	Ta. Sin. These are revelations of the Qur'an and a Scripture that maketh plain;	Ta Sin! These are the verses of the Quran and the Book that makes (things) clear,
27 002	A guide: and glad tidings for the believers,-	A guidance and good tidings for believers	A guidance and good news for the believers,
27 003	Those who establish regular prayers and give in regular charity, and also have (full) assurance of the hereafter.	Who establish worship and pay the poor-due and are sure of the Hereafter.	Who keep up prayer and pay the poor-rate, and of the hereafter, they are sure.
27 004	As to those who believe not in the Hereafter, We have made their deeds pleasing in their eyes; and so they wander about in distraction.	Lo! as for those who believe not in the Hereafter, We have made their works fairseeming unto them so that they are all astray.	As to those who do not believe in the hereafter, We have surely made their deeds fair-seeming to them, but they blindly wander on.
27 005	Such are they for whom a grievous Penalty is (waiting); and in the Hereafter theirs will be the greatest loss.	Those are they for whom is the worst of punishment, and in the Hereafter they will be the greatest losers.	These are they who shall have an evil punishment, and in the hereafter they shall be the greatest losers.
27 006	As to thee, the Qur'an is bestowed upon thee from the presence of one Who is Wise and All-Knowing.	Lo! as for thee (Muhammad), thou verily receivest the Qur'an from the presence of One Wise, Aware.	And most surely you are made to receive the Quran from the Wise, the Knowing Allah.
27 007	Behold! Moses said to his family: "I perceive a fire; soon will I bring you from there some information, or I will bring you a burning brand to light our fuel, that ye may warm yourselves."	(Remember) when Moses said unto his household: Lo! I spy afar off a fire; I will bring you tidings thence, or bring to you a borrowed flame that ye may warm yourselves.	When Musa said to his family: Surely I see fire; I will bring to you from it some news, or I will bring to you therefrom a burning firebrand so that you may warm yourselves.

27	008	But when he came to the (fire), a voice was heard: "Blessed are those in the fire and those around: and Glory to Allah, the Lord of the Worlds!"	But when he reached it, he was called, saying: Blessed is Whosoever is in the fire and Whosoever is round about it! And Glorified be Allah, the Lord of the Worlds!	So when he came to it a voice was uttered saying: Blessed is Whoever is in the fire and whatever is about it; and glory be to Allah, the Lord of the worlds;
27	009	"O Moses! verily, I am Allah, the Exalted in Might, the Wise!..."	O Moses! Lo! it is I, Allah, the Mighty, the Wise.	O Musa! surely I am Allah, the Mighty, the Wise;
27	010	"Now do thou throw thy rod!" But when he saw it moving (of its own accord) as if it had been a snake, he turned back in retreat, and retraced not his steps: "O Moses!" (it was said), "Fear not: truly, in My presence, those called as messengers have no fear,"-	And throw down thy staff! But when he saw it writhing as it were a demon, he turned to flee headlong; (but it was said unto him): O Moses! Fear not! the emissaries fear not in My presence,	And cast down your staff. So when he saw it in motion as if it were a serpent, he turned back retreating and did not return: O Musa! fear not; surely the messengers shall not fear in My presence;
27	011	"But if any have done wrong and have thereafter substituted good to take the place of evil, truly, I am Oft-Forgiving, Most Merciful."	Save him who hath done wrong and afterward hath changed evil for good. And lo! I am Forgiving, Merciful.	Neither he who has been unjust, then he does good instead after evil, for surely I am the Forgiving, the Merciful:
27	012	"Now put thy hand into thy bosom, and it will come forth white without stain (or harm): (these are) among the nine Signs (thou wilt take) to Pharaoh and his people: for they are a people rebellious in transgression."	And put thy hand into the bosom of thy robe, it will come forth white but unhurt. (This will be one) among nine tokens unto Pharaoh and his people Lo! they were ever evil-living folk.	And enter your hand into the opening of your bosom, it shall come forth white without evil; among nine signs to Firon and his people, surely they are a transgressing people.
27	013	But when Our Signs came to them, that should have opened their eyes, they said: "This is sorcery manifest!"	But when Our tokens came unto them, plain to see, they said: This is mere magic,	So when Our clear signs came to them, they said: This is clear enchantment.
27	014	And they rejected those Signs in iniquity and arrogance, though their souls were convinced thereof: so see what was the end of those who acted corruptly!	And they denied them, though their souls acknowledged them, for spite and arrogance. Then see the nature of the consequence for the wrong-doers!	And they denied them unjustly and proudly while their soul had been convinced of them; consider, then how was the end of the mischief-makers.
27	015	We gave (in the past) knowledge to David and Solomon: And they both said: "Praise be to Allah, Who has favoured us above many of his servants who believe!"	And We verily gave knowledge unto David and Solomon, and they said: Praise be to Allah, Who hath preferred us above many of His believing slaves!	And certainly We gave knowledge to Dawood and Sulaiman, and they both said: Praise be to Allah, Who has made us to excel many of His believing servants.
27	016	And Solomon was David's heir. He said: "O ye people! We have been taught the speech of birds, and on us has been bestowed (a little) of all things: this is indeed Grace manifest (from Allah.)"	And Solomon was David's heir. And he said: O mankind! Lo! we have been taught the language of birds, and have been given (abundance) of all things. This surely is evident favour.	And Sulaiman was Dawood's heir, and he said: O men! we have been taught the language of birds, and we have been given all things; most surely this is manifest grace.
27	017	And before Solomon were marshalled his hosts,- of jinns and men and birds, and they were all kept in order and ranks.	And there were gathered together unto Solomon his armies of the jinn and humankind, and of the birds, and they were set in battle order;	And his hosts of the jinn and men and the birds were gathered to him, and they were formed into groups.
27	018	At length, when they came to a (lowly) valley of ants, one of the ants said: "O ye ants, get into your habitations, lest Solomon and his hosts crush you (under foot) without knowing it."	Till, when they reached the Valley of the Ants, an ant exclaimed: O ants! Enter your dwellings lest Solomon and his armies crush you, unperceiving.	Until when they came to the valley of the Naml, a Namlite said: O Naml! enter your houses, (that) Sulaiman and his hosts may not crush you while they do not know.

27 019	So he smiled, amused at her speech; and he said: "O my Lord! so order me that I may be grateful for Thy favours, which thou hast bestowed on me and on my parents, and that I may work the righteousness that will please Thee: And admit me, by Thy Grace, to the ranks of Thy righteous Servants."	And (Solomon) smiled, laughing at her speech, and said: My Lord, arouse me to be thankful for Thy favour wherewith Thou hast favoured me and my parents, and to do good that shall be pleasing unto Thee, and include me in (the number of) Thy righteous slaves.	So he smiled, wondering at her word, and said: My Lord! grant me that I should be grateful for Thy favor which Thou hast bestowed on me and on my parents, and that I should do good such as Thou art pleased with, and make me enter, by Thy mercy, into Thy servants, the good ones.
27 020	And he took a muster of the Birds; and he said: "Why is it I see not the Hoopoe? Or is he among the absentees?"	And he sought among the birds and said: How is it that I see not the hoopoe, or is he among the absent?	And he reviewed the birds, then said: How is it I see not the hoopoe or is it that he is of the absentees?
27 021	"I will certainly punish him with a severe penalty, or execute him, unless he bring me a clear reason (for absence)."	I verily will punish him with hard punishment or I verily will slay him, or he verily shall bring me a plain excuse.	I will most certainly punish him with a severe punishment, or kill him, or he shall bring to me a clear plea.
27 022	But the Hoopoe tarried not far: he (came up and) said: "I have compassed (territory) which thou hast not compassed, and I have come to thee from Saba with tidings true."	But he was not long in coming, and he said: I have found out (a thing) that thou apprehendest not, and I come unto thee from Sheba with sure tidings.	And he tarried not long, then said: I comprehend that which you do not comprehend and I have brought to you a sure information from Sheba.
27 023	"I found (there) a woman ruling over them and provided with every requisite; and she has a magnificent throne."	Lo! I found a woman ruling over them, and she hath been given (abundance) of all things, and hers is a mighty throne.	Surely I found a woman ruling over them, and she has been given abundance and she has a mighty throne:
27 024	"I found her and her people worshipping the sun besides Allah: Satan has made their deeds seem pleasing in their eyes, and has kept them away from the Path,- so they receive no guidance,"-	I found her and her people worshipping the sun instead of Allah; and Satan maketh their works fairseeming unto them, and debarreth them from the way (of Truth), so that they go not aright;	I found her and her people adoring the sun instead of Allah, and the Shaitan has made their deeds fair-seeming to them and thus turned them from the way, so they do not go aright;
27 025	"(Kept them away from the Path), that they should not worship Allah, Who brings to light what is hidden in the heavens and the earth, and knows what ye hide and what ye reveal."	So that they worship not Allah, Who bringeth forth the hidden in the heavens and the earth, and knoweth what ye hide and what ye proclaim,	That they do not make obeisance to Allah, Who brings forth what is hidden in the heavens and the earth and knows what you hide and what you make manifest:
27 026	"Allah!- there is no god but He!- Lord of the Throne Supreme!"	Allah; there is no God save Him, the Lord of the Tremendous Throne.	Allah, there is no god but He: He is the Lord of mighty power.
27 027	(Solomon) said: "Soon shall we see whether thou hast told the truth or lied!"	(Solomon) said: We shall see whether thou speakest truth or whether thou art of the liars.	He said: We will see whether you have told the truth or whether you are of the liars:
27 028	"Go thou, with this letter of mine, and deliver it to them: then draw back from them, and (wait to) see what answer they return"...	Go with this my letter and throw it down unto them; then turn away and see what (answer) they return,	Take this my letter and hand it over to them, then turn away from them and see what (answer) they return.
27 029	(The queen) said: "Ye chiefs! here is delivered to me - a letter worthy of respect."	(The Queen of Sheba) said (when she received the letter): O chieftains! Lo! there hath been thrown unto me a noble letter.	She said: O chief! surely an honorable letter has been delivered to me
27 030	"It is from Solomon, and is (as follows): 'In the name of Allah, Most Gracious, Most Merciful:'"	Lo! it is from Solomon, and lo! it is: In the name of Allah, the Beneficent, the Merciful;	Surely it is from Sulaiman, and surely it is in the name of Allah, the Beneficent, the Merciful;
27 031	"'Be ye not arrogant against me, but come to me in submission (to the true Religion).'"	Exalt not yourselves against me, but come unto me as those who surrender.	Saying: exalt not yourselves against me and come to me in submission.

27 032	She said: "Ye chiefs! advise me in (this) my affair: no affair have I decided except in your presence."	She said: O chieftains! Pronounce for me in my case. I decide no case till ye are present with me.	She said: O chiefs! give me advice respecting my affair: I never decide an affair until you are in my presence.
27 033	They said: "We are endued with strength, and given to vehement war: but the command is with thee; so consider what thou wilt command."	They said: We are lords of might and lords of great prowess, but it is for thee to command; so consider what thou wilt command.	They said: We are possessors of strength and possessors of mighty prowess, and the command is yours, therefore see what you will command.
27 034	She said: "Kings, when they enter a country, despoil it, and make the noblest of its people its meanest thus do they behave."	She said: Lo! kings, when they enter a township, ruin it and make the honour of its people shame. Thus will they do.	She said: Surely the kings, when they enter a town, ruin it and make the noblest of its people to be low, and thus they (always) do;
27 035	"But I am going to send him a present, and (wait) to see with what (answer) return (my) ambassadors."	But lo! I am going to send a present unto them, and to see with what (answer) the messengers return.	And surely I am going to send a present to them, and shall wait to see what (answer) do the messengers bring back.
27 036	Now when (the embassy) came to Solomon, he said: "Will ye give me abundance in wealth? But that which Allah has given me is better than that which He has given you! Nay it is ye who rejoice in your gift!"	So when (the envoy) came unto Solomon, (the King) said: What! Would ye help me with wealth? But that which Allah hath given me is better than that which He hath given you. Nay it is ye (and not I) who exult in your gift.	So when he came to Sulaiman, he said: What! will you help me with wealth? But what Allah has given me is better than what He has given you. Nay, you are exultant because of your present;
27 037	"Go back to them, and be sure we shall come to them with such hosts as they will never be able to meet: We shall expel them from there in disgrace, and they will feel humbled (indeed)."	Return unto them. We verily shall come unto them with hosts that they cannot resist, and we shall drive them out from thence with shame, and they will be abased.	Go back to them, so we will most certainly come to them with hosts which they shall have no power to oppose, and we will most certainly expel them therefrom in abasement, and they shall be in a state of ignominy.
27 038	He said (to his own men): "Ye chiefs! which of you can bring me her throne before they come to me in submission?"	He said: O chiefs! Which of you will bring me her throne before they come unto me, surrendering?	He said: O chiefs! which of you can bring to me her throne before they come to me in submission?
27 039	Said an 'Ifrit, of the jinns: "I will bring it to thee before thou rise from thy council: indeed I have full strength for the purpose, and may be trusted."	A stalwart of the jinn said: I will bring it thee before thou canst rise from thy place. Lo! I verily am strong and trusty for such work.	One audacious among the jinn said: I will bring it to you before you rise up from your place; and most surely I am strong (and) trusty for it.
27 040	Said one who had knowledge of the Book: "I will bring it to thee within the twinkling of an eye!" Then when (Solomon) saw it placed firmly before him, he said: "This is by the Grace of my Lord!- to test me whether I am grateful or ungrateful! and if any is grateful, truly his gratitude is (a gain) for his own soul; but if any is ungrateful, truly my Lord is Free of all Needs, Supreme in Honour !"	One with whom was knowledge of the Scripture said: I will bring it thee before thy gaze returneth unto thee. And when he saw it set in his presence, (Solomon) said: This is of the bounty of my Lord, that He may try me whether I give thanks or am ungrateful. Whosoever giveth thanks he only giveth thanks for (the good of) his own soul; and whosoever is ungrateful (is ungrateful only to his own soul's hurt). For lo! my Lord is Absolute in independence, Bountiful.	One who had the knowledge of the Book said: I will bring it to you in the twinkling of an eye. Then when he saw it settled beside him, he said: This is of the grace of my Lord that He may try me whether I am grateful or ungrateful; and whoever is grateful, he is grateful only for his own soul, and whoever is ungrateful, then surely my Lord is Self-sufficient, Honored.
27 041	He said: "Transform her throne out of all recognition by her: let us see whether she is guided (to the truth) or is one of those who receive no guidance."	He said: Disguise her throne for her that we may see whether she will go aright or be of those not rightly guided.	He said: Alter her throne for her, we will see whether she follows the right way or is of those who do not go aright.

27 042	So when she arrived, she was asked, "Is this thy throne?" She said, It was just like this; and knowledge was bestowed on us in advance of this, and we have submitted to Allah (in Islam)."	So, when she came, it was said (unto her): Is thy throne like this? She said: (It is) as though it were the very one. And (Solomon said): We were given the knowledge before her and we had surrendered (to Allah).	So when she came, it was said: Is your throne like this? She said: It is as it were the same, and we were given the knowledge before it, and we were submissive.
27 043	And he diverted her from the worship of others besides Allah: for she was (sprung) of a people that had no faith.	And (all) that she was wont to worship instead of Allah hindered her, for she came of disbelieving folk.	And what she worshipped besides Allah prevented her, surely she was of an unbelieving people.
27 044	She was asked to enter the lofty Palace: but when she saw it, she thought it was a lake of water, and she (tucked up her skirts), uncovering her legs. He said: "This is but a palace paved smooth with slabs of glass." She said: "O my Lord! I have indeed wronged my soul: I do (now) submit (in Islam), with Solomon, to the Lord of the Worlds."	It was said unto her: Enter the hall. And when she saw it she deemed it a pool and bared her legs. (Solomon) said: Lo! it is a hall, made smooth, of glass. She said: My Lord! Lo! I have wronged myself, and I surrender with Solomon unto Allah, the Lord of the Worlds.	It was said to her: Enter the palace; but when she saw it she deemed it to be a great expanse of water, and bared her legs. He said: Surely it is a palace made smooth with glass. She said: My Lord! surely I have been unjust to myself, and I submit with Sulaiman to Allah, the Lord of the worlds.
27 045	We sent (aforetime), to the Thamud, their brother Salih, saying, Serve Allah: But behold, they became two factions quarrelling with each other.	And We verily sent unto Thamud their brother Salih, saying: Worship Allah. And lo! they (then) became two parties quarrelling.	And certainly We sent to Samood their brother Salih, saying: Serve Allah; and lo! they became two sects quarrelling with each other.
27 046	He said: "O my people! why ask ye to hasten on the evil in preference to the good? If only ye ask Allah for forgiveness, ye may hope to receive mercy."	He said: O my people! Why will ye hasten on the evil rather than the good? Why will ye not ask pardon of Allah, that ye may receive mercy.	He said: O my people! why do you seek to hasten on the evil before the good? Why do you not ask forgiveness of Allah so that you may be dealt with mercifully?
27 047	They said: "Ill omen do we augur from thee and those that are with thee". He said: "Your ill omen is with Allah; yea, ye are a people under trial."	They said: We augur evil of thee and those with thee. He said: Your evil augury is with Allah. Nay, but ye are folk that are being tested.	They said: We have met with ill luck on account of you and on account of those with you. He said: The cause of your evil fortune is with Allah; nay, you are a people who are tried.
27 048	There were in the city nine men of a family, who made mischief in the land, and would not reform.	And there were in the city nine persons who made mischief in the land and reformed not.	And there were in the city nine persons who made mischief in the land and did not act aright.
27 049	They said: "Swear a mutual oath by Allah that we shall make a secret night attack on him and his people, and that we shall then say to his heir (when he seeks vengeance): 'We were not present at the slaughter of his people, and we are positively telling the truth.'"	They said: Swear one to another by Allah that we verily will attack him and his household by night, and afterward we will surely say unto his friend: We witnessed not the destruction of his household. And lo! we are truthtellers.	They said: Swear to each other by Allah that we will certainly make a sudden attack on him and his family by night, then we will say to his heir: We did not witness the destruction of his family, and we are most surely truthful.
27 050	They plotted and planned, but We too planned, even while they perceived it not.	So they plotted a plot: and We plotted a plot, while they perceived not.	And they planned a plan, and We planned a plan while they perceived not.
27 051	Then see what was the end of their plot!- this, that We destroyed them and their people, all (of them).	Then see the nature of the consequence of their plotting, for lo! We destroyed them and their people, every one.	See, then, how was the end of their plan that We destroyed them and their people, all (of them).

27	052	Now such were their houses, - in utter ruin, - because they practised wrong-doing. Verily in this is a Sign for people of knowledge.	See, yonder are their dwellings empty and in ruins because they did wrong. Lo! herein is indeed a portent for a people who have knowledge.	So those are their houses fallen down because they were unjust, most surely there is a sign in this for a people who know.
27	053	And We saved those who believed and practised righteousness.	And we saved those who believed and used to ward off (evil).	And We delivered those who believed and who guarded (against evil).
27	054	(We also sent) Lut (as a messenger): behold, He said to his people, Do ye do what is shameful though ye see (its iniquity)?	And Lot! when he said unto his folk: Will ye commit abomination knowingly?	And (We sent) Lut, when he said to his people: What! do you commit indecency while you see?
27	055	Would ye really approach men in your lusts rather than women? Nay, ye are a people (grossly) ignorant!	Must ye seek lust after men instead of women? Nay, but ye are folk who act senselessly.	What! do you indeed approach men lustfully rather than women? Nay, you are a people who act ignorantly.
27	056	But his people gave no other answer but this: they said, "Drive out the followers of Lut from your city: these are indeed men who want to be clean and pure!"	But the answer of his folk was naught save that they said: Expel the household of Lot from your township, for they (forsooth) are folk who would keep clean!	But the answer of his people was no other except that they said: Turn out Lut's followers from your town; surely they are a people who would keep pure!
27	057	But We saved him and his family, except his wife; her We destined to be of those who lagged behind.	Then We saved him and his household save his wife; We destined her to be of those who stayed behind.	But We delivered him and his followers except his wife; We ordained her to be of those who remained behind.
27	058	And We rained down on them a shower (of brimstone): and evil was the shower on those who were admonished (but heeded not)!	And We rained a rain upon them. Dreadful is the rain of those who have been warned.	And We rained on them a rain, and evil was the rain of those who had been warned.
27	059	Say: Praise be to Allah, and Peace on his servants whom He has chosen (for his Message). (Who) is better?- Allah or the false gods they associate (with Him)?	Say (O Muhammad): Praise be to Allah, and peace be on His slaves whom He hath chosen! Is Allah best, or (all) that ye ascribe as partners (unto Him)?	Say: Praise be to Allah and peace on His servants whom He has chosen: is Allah better, or what they associate (with Him)?
27	060	Or, Who has created the heavens and the earth, and Who sends you down rain from the sky? Yea, with it We cause to grow well-planted orchards full of beauty of delight: it is not in your power to cause the growth of the trees in them. (Can there be another) god besides Allah? Nay, they are a people who swerve from justice.	Is not He (best) Who created the heavens and the earth, and sendeth down for you water from the sky wherewith We cause to spring forth joyous orchards, whose trees it never hath been yours to cause to grow. Is there any Allah beside Allah? Nay, but they are folk who ascribe equals (unto Him)!	Nay, He Who created the heavens and the earth, and sent down for you water from the cloud; then We cause to grow thereby beautiful gardens; it is not possible for you that you should make the trees thereof to grow. Is there a god with Allah? Nay! they are people who deviate.
27	061	Or, Who has made the earth firm to live in; made rivers in its midst; set thereon mountains immovable; and made a separating bar between the two bodies of flowing water? (can there be another) god besides Allah? Nay, most of them know not.	Is not He (best) Who made the earth a fixed abode, and placed rivers in the folds thereof, and placed firm hills therein, and hath set a barrier between the two seas? Is there any Allah beside Allah? Nay, but most of them know not!	Or, Who made the earth a resting-place, and made in it rivers, and raised on it mountains and placed between the two seas a barrier. Is there a god with Allah? Nay! most of them do not know!
27	062	Or, Who listens to the (soul) distressed when it calls on Him, and Who relieves its suffering, and makes you (mankind) inheritors of the earth? (Can there be another) god besides Allah? Little it is that ye heed!	Is not He (best) Who answereth the wronged one when he crieth unto Him and removeth the evil, and hath made you viceroys of the earth? Is there any God beside Allah? Little do they reflect!	Or, Who answers the distressed one when he calls upon Him and removes the evil, and He will make you successors in the earth. Is there a god with Allah? Little is it that you mind!

27 063	Or, Who guides you through the depths of darkness on land and sea, and Who sends the winds as heralds of glad tidings, going before His Mercy? (Can there be another) god besides Allah?- High is Allah above what they associate with Him!	Is not He (best) Who guideth you in the darkness of the land and the sea, He Who sendeth the winds as heralds of His mercy? Is there any God beside Allah? High Exalted be Allah from all that they ascribe as partner (unto Him)!	Or, Who guides you in utter darkness of the land and the sea, and Who sends the winds as good news before His mercy. Is there a god with Allah? Exalted by Allah above what they associate (with Him).
27 064	Or, Who originates creation, then repeats it, and who gives you sustenance from heaven and earth? (Can there be another) god besides Allah? Say, "Bring forth your argument, if ye are telling the truth!"	Is not He (best) Who produceth creation, then reproduceth it, and Who provideth for you from the heaven and the earth? Is there any God beside Allah? Say: Bring your proof, if ye are truthful!	Or, Who originates the creation, then reproduces it and Who gives you sustenance from the heaven and the earth. Is there a god With Allah? Say: Bring your proof if you are truthful.
27 065	Say: None in the heavens or on earth, except Allah, knows what is hidden: nor can they perceive when they shall be raised up (for Judgment).	Say (O Muhammad): None in the heavens and the earth knoweth the Unseen save Allah; and they know not when they will be raised (again).	Say: No one in the heavens and the earth knows the unseen but Allah; and they do not know when they shall be raised.
27 066	Still less can their knowledge comprehend the Hereafter: Nay, they are in doubt and uncertainty thereanent; nay, they are blind thereunto!	Nay, but doth their knowledge reach to the Hereafter? Nay, for they are in doubt concerning it. Nay, for they cannot see it.	Nay, their knowledge respecting the hereafter is slight and hasty; nay, they are in doubt about it; nay, they are quite blind to it.
27 067	The Unbelievers say: "What! when we become dust,- we and our fathers,- shall we really be raised (from the dead)?"	Yet those who disbelieve say: When we have become dust like our fathers, shall we verily be brought forth (again)?	And those who disbelieve say: What! when we have become dust and our fathers (too), shall we certainly be brought forth?
27 068	"It is true we were promised this,- we and our fathers before (us): these are nothing but tales of the ancients."	We were promised this, forsooth, we and our fathers. (All) this is naught but fables of the men of old.	We have certainly been promised this, we and our fathers before; these are naught but stories of the ancients.
27 069	Say: "Go ye through the earth and see what has been the end of those guilty (of sin)."	Say (unto them, O Muhammad): Travel in the land and see the nature of the sequel for the guilty!	Say: Travel in the earth, then see how was the end of the guilty.
27 070	But grieve not over them, nor distress thyself because of their plots.	And grieve thou not for them, nor be in distress because of what they plot (against thee).	And grieve not for them and be not distressed because of what they plan.
27 071	They also say: "When will this promise (come to pass)? (Say) if ye are truthful."	And they say: When (will) this promise (be fulfilled), if ye are truthful?	And they say: When will this threat come to pass, if you are truthful?
27 072	Say: "It may be that some of the events which ye wish to hasten on may be (close) in your pursuit!"	Say: It may be that a part of that which ye would hasten on is close behind you.	Say: Maybe there may have drawn near to you somewhat of that which you seek to hasten on.
27 073	But verily thy Lord is full of grace to mankind: Yet most of them are ungrateful.	Lo! thy Lord is full of bounty for mankind, but most of them do not give thanks.	And surely your Lord is the Lord of grace to men, but most of them are not grateful.
27 074	And verily thy Lord knoweth all that their hearts do hide. As well as all that they reveal.	Lo! thy Lord knoweth surely all that their bosoms hide, and all that they proclaim.	And most surely your Lord knows what their breasts conceal and what they manifest.
27 075	Nor is there aught of the unseen, in heaven or earth, but is (recorded) in a clear record.	And there is nothing hidden in the heaven or the earth but it is in a clear Record.	And there is nothing concealed in the heaven and the earth but it is in a clear book.
27 076	Verily this Qur'an doth explain to the Children of Israel most of the matters in which they disagree.	Lo! this Qur'an narrateth unto the Children of Israel most of that concerning which they differ.	Surely this Quran declares to the children of Israel most of what they differ in.
27 077	And it certainly is a Guide and a Mercy to those who believe.	And lo! it is a guidance and a mercy for believers.	And most surely it is a guidance and a mercy for the believers.

27 078	Verily thy Lord will decide between them by His Decree: and He is Exalted in Might, All-Knowing.	Lo! thy Lord will judge between them of His wisdom, and He is the Mighty, the Wise.	Surely your Lord will judge between them by his judgment, and He is the Mighty, the Knowing.
27 079	So put thy trust in Allah: for thou art on (the path of) manifest Truth.	Therefor (O Muhammad) put thy trust in Allah, for thou (standest) on the plain Truth.	Therefore rely on Allah; surely you are on the clear truth.
27 080	Truly thou canst not cause the dead to listen, nor canst thou cause the deaf to hear the call, (especially) when they turn back in retreat.	Lo! thou canst not make the dead to hear, nor canst thou make the deaf to hear the call when they have turned to flee;	Surely you do not make the dead to hear, and you do not make the deaf to hear the call when they go back retreating.
27 081	Nor canst thou be a guide to the blind, (to prevent them) from straying: only those wilt thou get to listen who believe in Our Signs, and they will bow in Islam.	Nor canst thou lead the blind out of their error. Thou canst make none to hear, save those who believe Our revelations and who have surrendered.	Nor can you be a guide to the blind out of their error; you cannot make to bear (any one) except those who believe in Our communications, so they submit.
27 082	And when the Word is fulfilled against them (the unjust), we shall produce from the earth a beast to (face) them: He will speak to them, for that mankind did not believe with assurance in Our Signs.	And when the word is fulfilled concerning them, We shall bring forth a beast of the earth to speak unto them because mankind had not faith in Our revelations.	And when the word shall come to pass against them, We shall bring forth for them a creature from the earth that shall wound them, because people did not believe in Our communications.
27 083	One day We shall gather together from every people a troop of those who reject our Signs, and they shall be kept in ranks,-	And (remind them of) the Day when We shall gather out of every nation a host of those who denied Our revelations, and they will be set in array;	And on the day when We will gather from every nation a party from among those who rejected Our communications, then they shall be formed into groups.
27 084	Until, when they come (before the Judgment-seat), (Allah) will say: Did ye reject My Signs, though ye comprehended them not in knowledge, or what was it ye did?"	Till, when they come (before their Lord), He will say: Did ye deny My revelations when ye could not compass them in knowledge, or what was it that ye did?	Until when they come, He will say: Did you reject My communications while you had no comprehensive knowledge of them? Or what was it that you did?
27 085	And the Word will be fulfilled against them, because of their wrong-doing, and they will be unable to speak (in plea).	And the Word will be fulfilled concerning them because they have done wrong, and they will not speak.	And the word shall come to pass against them because they were unjust, so they shall not speak.
27 086	See they not that We have made the Night for them to rest in and the Day to give them light? Verily in this are Signs for any people that believe!	Have they not seen how We have appointed the night that they may rest therein, and the day sight-giving? Lo! therein verily are portents for a people who believe.	Do they not consider that We have made the night that they may rest therein, and the day to give light? Most surely there are signs in this for a people who believe.
27 087	And the Day that the Trumpet will be sounded - then will be smitten with terror those who are in the heavens, and those who are on earth, except such as Allah will please (to exempt): and all shall come to His (Presence) as beings conscious of their lowliness.	And (remind them of) the Day when the Trumpet will be blown, and all who are in the heavens and the earth will start in fear, save him whom Allah willeth. And all come unto Him, humbled.	And on the day when the trumpet shall be blown, then those who are in the heavens and those who are in the earth shall be terrified except such as Allah please, and all shall come to him abased.
27 088	Thou seest the mountains and thinkest them firmly fixed: but they shall pass away as the clouds pass away: (such is) the artistry of Allah, who disposes of all things in perfect order: for he is well acquainted with all that ye do.	And thou seest the hills thou deemest solid flying with the flight of clouds: the doing of Allah Who perfecteth all things. Lo! He is Informed of what ye do.	And you see the mountains, you think them to be solid, and they shall pass away as the passing away of the cloud-- the handiwork of Allah Who has made every thing thoroughly; surely He is Aware of what you do.
27 089	If any do good, good will (accrue) to them therefrom; and they will be secure from terror that Day.	Whoso bringeth a good deed will have better than its worth; and such are safe from fear that Day.	Whoever brings good, he shall have better than it; and they shall be secure from terror on the day.

27 090	And if any do evil, their faces will be thrown headlong into the Fire: "Do ye receive a reward other than that which ye have earned by your deeds?"	And whoso bringeth an ill-deed, such will be flung down on their faces in the Fire. Are ye rewarded aught save what ye did?		And whoever brings evil, these shall be thrown down on their faces into the fire; shall you be rewarded (for) aught except what you did?
27 091	For me, I have been commanded to serve the Lord of this city, Him Who has sanctified it and to Whom (belong) all things: and I am commanded to be of those who bow in Islam to Allah's Will,-	(Say): I (Muhammad) am commanded only to serve the Lord of this land which He hath hallowed, and unto Whom all things belong. And I am commanded to be of those who surrender (unto Him),		I am commanded only that I should serve the Lord of this city, Who has made it sacred, and His are all things; and I am commanded that I should be of these who submit;
27 092	And to rehearse the Qur'an: and if any accept guidance, they do it for the good of their own souls, and if any stray, say: "I am only a Warner".	And to recite the Qur'an. And whoso goeth right, goeth right only for (the good of) his own soul; and as for him who goeth astray - (Unto him) say: Lo! I am only a warner.		And that I should recite the Quran. Therefore whoever goes aright, he goes aright for his own soul, and whoever goes astray, then say: I am only one of the warners.
27 093	And say: "Praise be to Allah, Who will soon show you His Signs, so that ye shall know them"; and thy Lord is not unmindful of all that ye do.	And say: Praise be to Allah Who will show you His portents so that ye shall know them. And thy Lord is not unaware of what ye (mortals) do.		And say: Praise be to Allah, He will show you His signs so that you shall recognize them; nor is your Lord heedless of what you do.

Chapter 28:

AL-QASAS (THE STORY, STORIES)

Total Verses: 88 Revealed At: MAKKA

In the name of Allah, the Most Beneficent, the Most Merciful.

28 001	Ta. Sin. Mim.	Ta. Sin. Mim.		Ta sin Mim.
28 002	These are Verses of the Book that makes (things) clear.	These are revelations of the Scripture that maketh plain.		These are the verses of the Book that makes (things) clear.
28 003	We rehearse to thee some of the story of Moses and Pharaoh in Truth, for people who believe.	We narrate unto thee (somewhat) of the story of Moses and Pharaoh with truth, for folk who believe.		We recite to you from the account of Musa and Firon with truth for people who believe.
28 004	Truly Pharaoh elated himself in the land and broke up its people into sections, depressing a small group among them: their sons he slew, but he kept alive their females: for he was indeed a maker of mischief.	Lo! Pharaoh exalted himself in the earth and made its people castes. A tribe among them he oppressed, killing their sons and sparing their women. Lo! he was of those who work corruption.		Surely Firon exalted himself in the land and made its people into parties, weakening one party from among them; he slaughtered their sons and let their women live; surely he was one of the mischiefmakers.
28 005	And We wished to be Gracious to those who were being depressed in the land, to make them leaders (in Faith) and make them heirs,	And We desired to show favour unto those who were oppressed in the earth, and to make them examples and to make them the inheritors,		And We desired to bestow a favor upon those who were deemed weak in the land, and to make them the Imams, and to make them the heirs,
28 006	To establish a firm place for them in the land, and to show Pharaoh, Haman, and their hosts, at their hands, the very things against which they were taking precautions.	And to establish them in the earth, and to show Pharaoh and Haman and their hosts that which they feared from them.		And to grant them power in the land, and to make Firon and Haman and their hosts see from them what they feared.

28 007	So We sent this inspiration to the mother of Moses: "Suckle (thy child), but when thou hast fears about him, cast him into the river, but fear not nor grieve: for We shall restore him to thee, and We shall make him one of Our messengers."	And We inspired the mother of Moses, saying: Suckle him and, when thou fearest for him, then cast him into the river and fear not nor grieve. Lo! We shall bring him back unto thee and shall make him (one) of Our messengers.	And We revealed to Musa's mothers, saying: Give him suck, then when you fear for him, cast him into the river and do not fear nor grieve; surely We will bring him back to you and make him one of the messengers.
28 008	Then the people of Pharaoh picked him up (from the river): (It was intended) that (Moses) should be to them an adversary and a cause of sorrow: for Pharaoh and Haman and (all) their hosts were men of sin.	And the family of Pharaoh took him up, that he might become for them an enemy and a sorrow, Lo! Pharaoh and Haman and their hosts were ever sinning.	And Firon's family took him up that he might be an enemy and a grief for them; surely Firon and Haman and their hosts were wrongdoers.
28 009	The wife of Pharaoh said: "(Here is) joy of the eye, for me and for thee: slay him not. It may be that he will be use to us, or we may adopt him as a son." And they perceived not (what they were doing)!	And the wife of Pharaoh said: (He will be) a consolation for me and for thee. Kill him not. Peradventure he may be of use to us, or we may choose him for a son. And they perceived not.	And Firon's wife said: A refreshment of the eye to me and to you; do not slay him; maybe he will be useful to us, or we may take him for a son; and they did not perceive.
28 010	But there came to be a void in the heart of the mother of Moses: She was going almost to disclose his (case), had We not strengthened her heart (with faith), so that she might remain a (firm) believer.	And the heart of the mother of Moses became void, and she would have betrayed him if We had not fortified her heart, that she might be of the believers.	And the heart of Musa's mother was free (from anxiety) she would have almost disclosed it had We not strengthened her heart so that she might be of the believers.
28 011	And she said to the sister of (Moses), "Follow him" so she (the sister) watched him in the character of a stranger. And they knew not.	And she said unto his sister: Trace him. So she observed him from afar, and they perceived not.	And she said to his sister: Follow him up. So she watched him from a distance while they did not perceive,
28 012	And we ordained that he refused suck at first, until (His sister came up and) said: "Shall I point out to you the people of a house that will nourish and bring him up for you and be sincerely attached to him?"...	And We had before forbidden foster-mothers for him, so she said: Shall I show you a household who will rear him for you and take care of him?	And We ordained that he refused to suck any foster mother before, so she said: Shall I point out to you the people of a house who will take care of him for you, and they will be benevolent to him?
28 013	Thus did We restore him to his mother, that her eye might be comforted, that she might not grieve, and that she might know that the promise of Allah is true: but most of them do not understand.	So We restored him to his mother that she might be comforted and not grieve, and that she might know that the promise of Allah is true. But most of them know not.	So We gave him back to his mother that her eye might be refreshed, and that she might no grieve, and that she might know that the promise of Allah is true, but most of them do not know.
28 014	When he reached full age, and was firmly established (in life), We bestowed on him wisdom and knowledge: for thus do We reward those who do good.	And when he reached his full strength and was ripe, We gave him wisdom and knowledge. Thus do We reward the good.	And when he attained his maturity and became full grown, We granted him wisdom and knowledge; and thus do We reward those who do good (to others).

28 015	And he entered the city at a time when its people were not watching: and he found there two men fighting,- one of his own religion, and the other, of his foes. Now the man of his own religion appealed to him against his foe, and Moses struck him with his fist and made an end of him. He said: "This is a work of Evil (Satan): for he is an enemy that manifestly misleads!"	And he entered the city at a time of carelessness of its folk, and he found therein two men fighting, one of his own caste, and the other of his enemies; and he who was of his caste asked him for help against him who was of his enemies. So Moses struck him with his fist and killed him. He said: This is of the devil's doing. Lo! he is an enemy, a mere misleader.	And he went into the city at a time of unvigilance on the part of its people, so he found therein two men fighting, one being of his party and the other of his foes, and he who was of his party cried out to him for help against him who was of his enemies, so Musa struck him with his fist and killed him. He said: This is on account of the Shaitan's doing; surely he is an enemy, openly leading astray.
28 016	He prayed: "O my Lord! I have indeed wronged my soul! Do Thou then forgive me!" So (Allah) forgave him: for He is the Oft-Forgiving, Most Merciful.	He said: My Lord! Lo! I have wronged my soul, so forgive me. Then He forgave him. Lo! He is the Forgiving, the Merciful.	He said: My Lord! surely I have done harm to myself, so do Thou protect me. So He protected him; surely He is the Forgiving, the Merciful.
28 017	He said: "O my Lord! For that Thou hast bestowed Thy Grace on me, never shall I be a help to those who sin!"	He said: My Lord! Forasmuch as Thou hast favoured me, I will nevermore be a supporter of the guilty.	He said: My Lord! because Thou hast bestowed a favor on me, I shall never be a backer of the guilty.
28 018	So he saw the morning in the city, looking about, in a state of fear, when behold, the man who had, the day before, sought his help called aloud for his help (again). Moses said to him: "Thou art truly, it is clear, a quarrelsome fellow!"	And morning found him in the city, fearing, vigilant, when behold! he who had appealed to him the day before cried out to him for help. Moses said unto him: Lo! thou art indeed a mere hothead.	And he was in the city, fearing, awaiting, when lo! he who had asked his assistance the day before was crying out to him for aid. Musa said to him: You are most surely one erring manifestly.
28 019	Then, when he decided to lay hold of the man who was an enemy to both of them, that man said: "O Moses! Is it thy intention to slay me as thou slewest a man yesterday? Thy intention is none other than to become a powerful violent man in the land, and not to be one who sets things right!"	And when he would have fallen upon the man who was an enemy unto them both, he said: O Moses! Wouldst thou kill me as thou didst kill a person yesterday. Thou wouldst be nothing but a tyrant in the land, thou wouldst not be of the reformers.	So when he desired to seize him who was an enemy to them both, he said: O Musa! do you intend to kill me as you killed a person yesterday? You desire nothing but that you should be a tyrant in the land, and you do not desire to be of those who act aright.
28 020	And there came a man, running, from the furthest end of the City. He said: "O Moses! the Chiefs are taking counsel together about thee, to slay thee: so get thee away, for I do give thee sincere advice."	And a man came from the uttermost part of the city, running. He said: O Moses! Lo! the chiefs take counsel against thee to slay thee; therefor escape. Lo! I am of those who give thee good advice.	And a man came running from the remotest part of the city. He said: O Musa! surely the chiefs are consulting together to slay you, therefore depart (at once); surely I am of those who wish well to you.
28 021	He therefore got away therefrom, looking about, in a state of fear. He prayed "O my Lord! save me from people given to wrong-doing."	So he escaped from thence, fearing, vigilant. He said: My Lord! Deliver me from the wrongdoing folk.	So he went forth therefrom, fearing, awaiting, (and) he said: My Lord! deliver me from the unjust people.
28 022	Then, when he turned his face towards (the land of) Madyan, he said: I do hope that my Lord will show me the smooth and straight Path.	And when he turned his face toward Midian, he said: Peradventure my Lord will guide me in the right road.	And when he turned his face towards Madyan, he said: Maybe my Lord will guide me in the right path.

28 023	And when he arrived at the watering (place) in Madyan, he found there a group of men watering (their flocks), and besides them he found two women who were keeping back (their flocks). He said: "What is the matter with you?" They said: "We cannot water (our flocks) until the shepherds take back (their flocks): And our father is a very old man."	And when he came unto the water of Midian he found there a whole tribe of men, watering. And he found apart from them two women keeping back (their flocks). He said: What aileth you? The two said: We cannot give (our flocks) to drink till the shepherds return from the water; and our father is a very old man.	And when he came to the water of Madyan, he found on it a group of men watering, and he found besides them two women keeping back (their flocks). He said: What is the matter with you? They said: We cannot water until the shepherds take away (their sheep) from the water, and our father is a very old man.
28 024	So he watered (their flocks) for them; then he turned back to the shade, and said: "O my Lord! truly am I in (desperate) need of any good that Thou dost send me!"...	So he watered (their flock) for them. Then he turned aside into the shade, and said: My Lord! I am needy of whatever good Thou sendest down for me.	So he watered (their sheep) for them, then went back to the shade and said: My Lord! surely I stand in need of whatever good Thou mayest send down to me.
28 025	Afterwards one of the (damsels) came (back) to him, walking bashfully. She said: "My father invites thee that he may reward thee for having watered (our flocks) for us." So when he came to him and narrated the story, he said: "Fear thou not: (well) hast thou escaped from unjust people."	Then there came unto him one of the two women, walking shyly. She said: Lo! my father biddeth thee, that he may reward thee with a payment for that thou didst water (the flock) for us. Then, when he came unto him and told him the (whole) story, he said: Fear not! Thou hast escaped from the wrong-doing folk.	Then one of the two women came to him walking bashfully. She said: My father invites you that he may give you the reward of your having watered for us. So when he came to him and gave to him the account, he said: Fear not, you are secure from the unjust people.
28 026	Said one of the (damsels): "O my (dear) father! engage him on wages: truly the best of men for thee to employ is the (man) who is strong and trusty"....	One of the two women said: O my father! Hire him! For the best (man) that thou canst hire in the strong, the trustworthy.	Said one of them: O my father! employ him, surely the best of those that you can employ is the strong man, the faithful one.
28 027	He said: "I intend to wed one of these my daughters to thee, on condition that thou serve me for eight years; but if thou complete ten years, it will be (grace) from thee. But I intend not to place thee under a difficulty: thou wilt find me, indeed, if Allah wills, one of the righteous."	He said: Lo! I fain would marry thee to one of these two daughters of mine on condition that thou hirest thyself to me for (the term of) eight pilgrimages. Then if thou completest ten it will be of thine own accord, for I would not make it hard for thee. Allah willing, thou wilt find me of the righteous.	He said: I desire to marry one of these two daughters of mine to you on condition that you should serve me for eight years; but if you complete ten, it will be of your own free will, and I do not wish to be hard to you; if Allah please, you will find me one of the good.
28 028	He said: "Be that (the agreement) between me and thee: whichever of the two terms I fulfil, let there be no ill-will to me. Be Allah a witness to what we say."	He said: That (is settled) between thee and me. Whichever of the two terms I fulfil, there will be no injustice to me, and Allah is Surety over what we say.	He said: This shall be (an agreement) between me and you; whichever of the two terms I fulfill, there shall be no wrongdoing to me; and Allah is a witness of what we say.
28 029	Now when Moses had fulfilled the term, and was travelling with his family, he perceived a fire in the direction of Mount Tur. He said to his family: "Tarry ye; I perceive a fire; I hope to bring you from there some information, or a burning firebrand, that ye may warm yourselves."	Then, when Moses had fulfilled the term, and was travelling with his housefolk, he saw in the distance a fire and said unto his housefolk: Bide ye (here). Lo! I see in the distance a fire; peradventure I shall bring you tidings thence, or a brand from the fire that ye may warm yourselves.	So when Musa had fulfilled the term, and he journeyed with his family, he perceived on this side of the mountain a fire. He said to his family: Wait, I have seen a fire, maybe I will bring to you from it some news or a brand of fire, so that you may warm yourselves.

28 030	But when he came to the (fire), a voice was heard from the right bank of the valley, from a tree in hallowed ground: "O Moses! Verily I am Allah, the Lord of the Worlds...."	And when he reached it, he was called from the right side of the valley in the blessed field, from the tree: O Moses! Lo! I, even I, am Allah, the Lord of the Worlds;	And when he came to it, a voice was uttered from the right side of the valley in the blessed spot of the bush, saying: O Musa! surely I am Allah, the Lord of the worlds.
28 031	"Now do thou throw thy rod!" but when he saw it moving (of its own accord) as if it had been a snake, he turned back in retreat, and retraced not his steps: "O Moses!" (It was said), "Draw near, and fear not: for thou art of those who are secure."	Throw down thy staff. And when he saw it writhing as it had been a demon, he turned to flee headlong, (and it was said unto him): O Moses! Draw nigh and fear not. Lo! thou art of those who are secure.	And saying: Cast down you staff. So when he saw it in motion as if it were a serpent, he turned back retreating, and did not return. O Musa! come forward and fear not; surely you are of those who are secure;
28 032	"Move thy hand into thy bosom, and it will come forth white without stain (or harm), and draw thy hand close to thy side (to guard) against fear. Those are the two credentials from thy Lord to Pharaoh and his Chiefs: for truly they are a people rebellious and wicked."	Thrust thy hand into the bosom of thy robe it will come forth white without hurt. And guard thy heart from fear. Then these shall be two proofs from your Lord unto Pharaoh and his chiefs. Lo! they are evil-living folk.	Enter your hand into the opening of your bosom, it will come forth white without evil, and draw your hand to yourself to ward off fear: so these two shall be two arguments from your Lord to Firon and his chiefs, surely they are a transgressing people.
28 033	He said: "O my Lord! I have slain a man among them, and I fear lest they slay me."	He said: My Lord! Lo! I killed a man among them and I fear that they will kill me.	He said: My Lord! surely I killed one of them, so I fear lest they should slay me;
28 034	"And my brother Aaron - He is more eloquent in speech than I: so send him with me as a helper, to confirm (and strengthen) me: for I fear that they may accuse me of falsehood."	My brother Aaron is more eloquent than me in speech. Therefor send him with me as a helper to confirm me. Lo! I fear that they will give the lie to me.	And my brother, Haroun, he is more eloquent of tongue than I, therefore send him with me as an aider, verifying me: surely I fear that they would reject me.
28 035	He said: "We will certainly strengthen thy arm through thy brother, and invest you both with authority, so they shall not be able to touch you: with Our Sign shall ye triumph,- you two as well as those who follow you."	He said: We will strengthen thine arm with thy brother, and We will give unto you both power so that they cannot reach you for Our portents. Ye twain, and those who follow you, will be the winners.	He said: We will strengthen your arm with your brother, and We will give you both an authority, so that they shall not reach you; (go) with Our signs; you two and those who follow you shall be uppermost.
28 036	When Moses came to them with Our clear signs, they said: "This is nothing but sorcery faked up: never did we head the like among our fathers of old!"	But when Moses came unto them with Our clear tokens, they said: This is naught but invented magic. We never heard of this among our fathers of old.	So when Musa came to them with Our clear signs, they said: This is nothing but forged enchantment, and we never heard of it amongst our fathers of old.
28 037	Moses said: "My Lord knows best who it is that comes with guidance from Him and whose end will be best in the Hereafter: certain it is that the wrong-doers will not prosper."	And Moses said: My Lord is Best Aware of him who bringeth guidance from His presence, and whose will be the sequel of the Home (of bliss). Lo! wrong-doers will not be successful.	And Musa said: My Lord knows best who comes with guidance from Him, and whose shall be the good end of the abode; surely the unjust shall not be successful.
28 038	Pharaoh said: "O Chiefs! no god do I know for you but myself: therefore, O Haman! light me a (kiln to bake bricks) out of clay, and build me a lofty palace, that I may mount up to the god of Moses: but as far as I am concerned, I think (Moses) is a liar!"	And Pharaoh said: O chiefs! I know not that ye have a god other than me, so kindle for me (a fire), O Haman, to bake the mud; and set up for me a lofty tower in order that I may survey the god of Moses; and lo! I deem him of the liars.	And Firon said: O chiefs! I do not know of any god for you besides myself; therefore kindle a fire for me, O Haman, for brick, then prepare for me a lofty building so that I may obtain knowledge of Musa's god, and most surely I think him to be one of the liars.

28 039	And he was arrogant and insolent in the land, beyond reason,- He and his hosts: they thought that they would not have to return to Us!	And he and his hosts were haughty in the land without right, and deemed that they would never be brought back to Us.	And he was unjustly proud in the land, he and his hosts, and they deemed that they would not be brought back to Us.
28 040	So We seized him and his hosts, and We flung them into the sea: Now behold what was the end of those who did wrong!	Therefor We seized him and his hosts, and abandoned them unto the sea. Behold the nature of the consequence for evil-doers!	So We caught hold of him and his hosts, then We cast them into the sea, and see how was the end of the unjust.
28 041	And we made them (but) leaders inviting to the Fire; and on the Day of Judgment no help shall they find.	And We made them patterns that invite unto the Fire, and on the Day of Resurrection they will not be helped.	And We made them Imams who call to the fire, and on the day of resurrection they shall not be assisted.
28 042	in this world We made a curse to follow them and on the Day of Judgment they will be among the loathed (and despised).	And We made a curse to follow them in this world, and on the Day of Resurrection they will be among the hateful.	And We caused a curse to follow them in this world, and on the day of resurrection they shall be of those made to appear hideous.
28 043	We did reveal to Moses the Book after We had destroyed the earlier generations, (to give) Insight to men, and guidance and Mercy, that they might receive admonition.	And We verily gave the Scripture unto Moses after We had destroyed the generations of old: clear testimonies for mankind, and a guidance and a mercy, that haply they might reflect.	And certainly We gave Musa the Book after We had destroyed the former generations, clear arguments for men and a guidance and a mercy, that they may be mindful.
28 044	Thou wast not on the Western side when We decreed the Commission to Moses, nor wast thou a witness (of those events).	And thou (Muhammad) wast not on the western side (of the Mount) when We expounded unto Moses the commandment, and thou wast not among those present;	And you were not on the western side when We revealed to Musa the commandment, and you were not among the witnesses;
28 045	But We raised up (new) generations, and long were the ages that passed over them; but thou wast not a dweller among the people of Madyan, rehearsing Our Signs to them; but it is We Who send messengers (with inspiration).	But We brought forth generations, and their lives dragged on for them. And thou wast not a dweller in Midian, reciting unto them Our revelations, but We kept sending (messengers to men).	But We raised up generations, then life became prolonged to them; and you were not dwelling among the people of Madyan, reciting to them Our communications, but We were the senders.
28 046	Nor wast thou at the side of (the Mountain of) Tur when we called (to Moses). Yet (art thou sent) as Mercy from thy Lord, to give warning to a people to whom no warner had come before thee: in order that they may receive admonition.	And thou was not beside the Mount when We did call; but (the knowledge of it is) a mercy from thy Lord that thou mayst warn a folk unto whom no warner came before thee, that haply they may give heed.	And you were not on this side of the mountain when We called, but a mercy from your Lord that you may warn a people to whom no warner came before you, that they may be mindful.
28 047	If (We had) not (sent thee to the Quraish),- in case a calamity should seize them for (the deeds) that their hands have sent forth, they might say: "Our Lord! why didst Thou not sent us a messenger? We should then have followed Thy Signs and been amongst those who believe!"	Otherwise, if disaster should afflict them because of that which their own hands have sent before (them), they might say: Our Lord! Why sentest Thou no messenger unto us, that we might have followed Thy revelations and been of the believers?	And were it not that there should befall them a disaster for what their hands have sent before, then they should say: Our Lord! why didst Thou not send to us a messenger so that we should have followed Thy communications and been of the believers!

28 048	But (now), when the Truth has come to them from Ourselves, they say, Why are not (Signs) sent to him, like those which were sent to Moses? Do they not then reject (the Signs) which were formerly sent to Moses? They say: "Two kinds of sorcery, each assisting the other!" And they say: "For us, we reject all (such things)!"	But when there came unto them the Truth from Our presence, they said: Why is he not given the like of what was given unto Moses? Did they not disbelieve in that which was given unto Moses of old? They say: Two magics that support each other; and they say: Lo! in both we are disbelievers.	But (now) when the truth has come to them from Us, they say: Why is he not given the like of what was given to Musa? What! did they not disbelieve in what Musa was given before? They say: Two magicians backing up each other; and they say: Surely we are unbelievers in all.
28 049	Say: "Then bring ye a Book from Allah, which is a better guide than either of them, that I may follow it! (do), if ye are truthful!"	Say (unto them, O Muhammad): Then bring a scripture from the presence of Allah that giveth clearer guidance than these two (that) I may follow it, if ye are truthful.	Say: Then bring some (other) book from Allah which is a better guide than both of them, (that) I may follow it, if you are truthful.
28 050	But if they hearken not to thee, know that they only follow their own lusts: and who is more astray than one who follow his own lusts, devoid of guidance from Allah? for Allah guides not people given to wrong-doing.	And if they answer thee not, then know that what they follow is their lusts. And who goeth farther astray than he who followeth his lust without guidance from Allah. Lo! Allah guideth not wrongdoing folk.	But if they do not answer you, then know that they only follow their low desires; and who is more erring than he who follows his low desires without any guidance from Allah? Surely Allah does not guide the unjust people.
28 051	Now have We caused the Word to reach them themselves, in order that they may receive admonition.	And now verily We have caused the Word to reach them, that haply they may give heed.	And certainly We have made the word to reach them so that they may be mindful.
28 052	Those to whom We sent the Book before this,- they do believe in this (revelation):	Those unto whom We gave the Scripture before it, they believe in it,	(As to) those whom We gave the Book before it, they are believers in it.
28 053	And when it is recited to them, they say: "We believe therein, for it is the Truth from our Lord: indeed we have been Muslims (bowing to Allah's Will) from before this."	And when it is recited unto them, they say: We believe in it. Lo! it is the Truth from our Lord. Lo! even before it we were of those who surrender (unto Him).	And when it is recited to them they say: We believe in it surely it is the truth from our Lord; surely we were submitters before this.
28 054	Twice will they be given their reward, for that they have persevered, that they avert Evil with Good, and that they spend (in charity) out of what We have given them.	These will be given their reward twice over, because they are steadfast and repel evil with good, and spend of that wherewith We have provided them,	These shall be granted their reward twice, because they are steadfast and they repel evil with good and spend out of what We have given them.
28 055	And when they hear vain talk, they turn away therefrom and say: To us our deeds, and to you yours; peace be to you: we seek not the ignorant."	And when they hear vanity they withdraw from it and say: Unto us our works and unto you your works. Peace be unto you! We desire not the ignorant.	And when they hear idle talk they turn aside from it and say: We shall have our deeds and you shall have your deeds; peace be on you, we do not desire the ignorant.
28 056	It is true thou wilt not be able to guide every one, whom thou lovest; but Allah guides those whom He will and He knows best those who receive guidance.	Lo! thou (O Muhammad) guidest not whom thou lovest, but Allah guideth whom He will. And He is Best Aware of those who walk aright.	Surely you cannot guide whom you love, but Allah guides whom He pleases, and He knows best the followers of the right way.
28 057	They say: "If we were to follow the guidance with thee, we should be snatched away from our land." Have We not established for them a secure sanctuary, to which are brought as tribute fruits of all kinds,- a provision from Ourselves? but most of them understand not.	And they say: If we were to follow the Guidance with thee we should be torn out of our land. Have We not established for them a sure sanctuary, whereunto the produce of all things is brought (in trade), a provision from Our presence? But most of them know not.	And they say: If we follow the guidance with you, we shall be carried off from our country. What! have We not settled them in a safe, sacred territory to which fruits of every kind shall be drawn?-- a sustenance from Us; but most of them do not know.

28 058	And how many populations We destroyed, which exulted in their life (of ease and plenty)! now those habitations of theirs, after them, are deserted,- All but a (miserable) few! and We are their heirs!	And how many a community have We destroyed that was thankless for its means of livelihood! And yonder are their dwellings, which have not been inhabited after them save a little. And We, even We, were the inheritors.	And how many a town have We destroyed which exulted in its means of subsistence, so these are their abodes, they have not been dwelt in after them except a little, and We are the inheritors,
28 059	Nor was thy Lord the one to destroy a population until He had sent to its centre a messenger, rehearsing to them Our Signs; nor are We going to destroy a population except when its members practise iniquity.	And never did thy Lord destroy the townships, till He had raised up in their mother(-town) a messenger reciting unto them Our revelations. And never did We destroy the townships unless the folk thereof were evil-doers.	And your Lord never destroyed the towns until He raised in their metropolis a messenger, reciting to them Our communications, and We never destroyed the towns except when their people were unjust.
28 060	The (material) things which ye are given are but the conveniences of this life and the glitter thereof; but that which is with Allah is better and more enduring: will ye not then be wise?	And whatsoever ye have been given is a comfort of the life of the world and an ornament thereof; and that which Allah hath is better and more lasting. Have ye then no sense?	And whatever things you have been given are only a provision of this world's life and its adornment, and whatever is with Allah is better and more lasting; do you not then understand?
28 061	Are (these two) alike?- one to whom We have made a goodly promise, and who is going to reach its (fulfilment), and one to whom We have given the good things of this life, but who, on the Day of Judgment, is to be among those brought up (for punishment)?	Is he whom We have promised a fair promise which he will find (true) like him whom We suffer to enjoy awhile the comfort of the life of the world, then on the Day of Resurrection he will be of those arraigned?	Is he to whom We have promised a goodly promise which he shall meet with like him whom We have provided with the provisions of this world's life, then on the day of resurrection he shall be of those who are brought up?
28 062	That Day (Allah) will call to them, and say "Where are my 'partners'?- whom ye imagined (to be such)?"	On the day when He will call unto them and say: Where are My partners whom ye imagined?	And on the day when He will call them and say: Where are those whom you deemed to be My associates?
28 063	Those against whom the charge will be proved, will say: "Our Lord! These are the ones whom we led astray: we led them astray, as we were astray ourselves: we free ourselves (from them) in Thy presence: it was not us they worshipped."	Those concerning whom the Word will have come true will say: Our Lord! These are they whom we led astray. We led them astray even as we ourselves were astray. We declare our innocence before Thee: us they never worshipped.	Those against whom the sentence has become confirmed will say: Our Lord! these are they whom we caused to err; we caused them to err as we ourselves did err; to Thee we declare ourselves to be clear (of them); they never served Us.
28 064	It will be said (to them): "Call upon your 'partners' (for help)": they will call upon them, but they will not listen to them; and they will see the Penalty (before them); (how they will wish) 'if only they had been open to guidance!'	And it will be said: Cry unto your (so-called) partners (of Allah). And they will cry unto them, and they will give no answer unto them, and they will see the Doom. Ah, if they had but been guided!	And it will be said: Call your associate-gods. So they will call upon them, but they will not answer them, and they shall see the punishment; would that they had followed the right way!
28 065	That Day (Allah) will call to them, and say: "What was the answer ye gave to the messengers?"	And on the Day when He will call unto them and say: What answer gave ye to the messengers?	And on the day when He shall call them and say: What was the answer you gave to the messengers?
28 066	Then the (whole) story that Day will seem obscure to them (like light to the blind) and they will not be able (even) to question each other.	On that day (all) tidings will be dimmed for them, nor will they ask one of another,	Then the pleas shall become obscure to them on that day, so they shall not ask each other.

28 067	But any that (in this life) had repented, believed, and worked righteousness, will have hopes to be among those who achieve salvation.	But as for him who shall repent and believe and do right, he haply may be one of the successful.	But as to him who repents and believes and does good, maybe he will be among the successful:
28 068	Thy Lord does create and choose as He pleases: no choice have they (in the matter): Glory to Allah! and far is He above the partners they ascribe (to Him)!	Thy Lord bringeth to pass what He willeth and chooseth. They have never any choice. Glorified be Allah and Exalted above all that they associate (with Him)!	And your Lord creates and chooses whom He pleases; to choose is not theirs; glory be to Allah, and exalted be He above what they associate (with Him).
28 069	And thy Lord knows all that their hearts conceal and all that they reveal.	And thy Lord knoweth what their breasts conceal, and what they publish.	And your Lord knows what their breasts conceal and what they manifest.
28 070	And He is Allah: There is no god but He. To Him be praise, at the first and at the last: for Him is the Command, and to Him shall ye (all) be brought back.	And He is Allah; there is no God save Him. His is all praise in the former and the latter (state), and His is the command, and unto Him ye will be brought back.	And He is Allah, there is no god but He! All praise is due to Him in this (life) and the hereafter, and His is the judgment, and to Him you shall be brought back.
28 071	Say: See ye? If Allah were to make the night perpetual over you to the Day of Judgment, what god is there other than Allah, who can give you enlightenment? Will ye not then hearken?	Say: Have ye thought, if Allah made night everlasting for you till the Day of Resurrection, who is a god beside Allah who could bring you light? Will ye not then hear?	Say: Tell me, if Allah were to make the night to continue incessantly on you till the day of resurrection, who is the god besides Allah that could bring you light? Do you not then hear?
28 072	Say: See ye? If Allah were to make the day perpetual over you to the Day of Judgment, what god is there other than Allah, who can give you a night in which ye can rest? Will ye not then see?	Say: Have ye thought, if Allah made day everlasting for you till the Day of Resurrection, who is a god beside Allah who could bring you night wherein ye rest? Will ye not then see?	Say: Tell me, if Allah were to make the day to continue incessantly on you till the day of resurrection, who is the god besides Allah that could bring you the night in which you take rest? Do you not then see?
28 073	It is out of His Mercy that He has made for you Night and Day,- that ye may rest therein, and that ye may seek of his Grace;- and in order that ye may be grateful.	Of His mercy hath He appointed for you night and day, that therein ye may rest, and that ye may seek His bounty, and that haply ye may be thankful.	And out of His mercy He has made for you the night and the day, that you may rest therein, and that you may seek of His grace, and that you may give thanks.
28 074	The Day that He will call on them, He will say: "Where are my 'partners'? whom ye imagined (to be such)?"	And on the Day when He shall call unto them and say: Where are My partners whom ye pretended?	And on the day when He shall call them and say: Where are those whom you deemed to be My associates?
28 075	And from each people shall We draw a witness, and We shall say: Produce your Proof: then shall they know that the Truth is in Allah (alone), and the (lies) which they invented will leave them in lurch.	And We shall take out from every nation a witness and We shall say: Bring your proof. Then they will know that Allah hath the Truth, and all that they invented will have failed them.	And We will draw forth from among every nation a witness and say: Bring your proof; then shall they know that the truth is Allah's, and that which they forged shall depart from them.
28 076	Qarun was doubtless, of the people of Moses; but he acted insolently towards them: such were the treasures We had bestowed on him that their very keys would have been a burden to a body of strong men, behold, his people said to him: "Exult not, for Allah loveth not those who exult (in riches)."	Now Korah was of Moses' folk, but he oppressed them; and We gave him so much treasure that the stores thereof would verily have been a burden for a troop of mighty men. When his own folk said unto him: Exult not; lo! Allah loveth not the exultant;	Surely Qaroun was of the people of Musa, but he rebelled against them, and We had given him of the treasures, so much so that his hoards of wealth would certainly weigh down a company of men possessed of great strength. When his people said to him: Do not exult, surely Allah does not love the exultant;

28 077	"But seek, with the (wealth) which Allah has bestowed on thee, the Home of the Hereafter, nor forget thy portion in this world: but do thou good, as Allah has been good to thee, and seek not (occasions for) mischief in the land: for Allah loves not those who do mischief."	But seek the abode of the Hereafter in that which Allah hath given thee and neglect not thy portion of the world, and be thou kind even as Allah hath been kind to thee, and seek not corruption in the earth; lo! Allah loveth not corrupters,	And seek by means of what Allah has given you the future abode, and do not neglect your portion of this world, and do good (to others) as Allah has done good to you, and do not seek to make mischief in the land, surely Allah does not love the mischief-makers.
28 078	He said: "This has been given to me because of a certain knowledge which I have." Did he not know that Allah had destroyed, before him, (whole) generations,- which were superior to him in strength and greater in the amount (of riches) they had collected? but the wicked are not called (immediately) to account for their sins.	He said: I have been given it only on account of knowledge I possess. Knew he not that Allah had destroyed already of the generations before him men who were mightier than him in strength and greater in respect of following? The guilty are not questioned of their sins.	He said: I have been given this only on account of the knowledge I have. Did he not know that Allah had destroyed before him of the generations those who were mightier in strength than he and greater in assemblage? And the guilty shall not be asked about their faults.
28 079	So he went forth among his people in the (pride of his wordly) glitter. Said those whose aim is the Life of this World: "Oh! that we had the like of what Qarun has got! for he is truly a lord of mighty good fortune!"	Then went he forth before his people in his pomp. Those who were desirous of the life of the world said: Ah, would that we had the like of what hath been given unto Korah! Lo! he is lord of rare good fortune.	So he went forth to his people in his finery. Those who desire this world's life said: O would that we had the like of what Qaroun is given; most surely he is possessed of mighty good fortune.
28 080	But those who had been granted (true) knowledge said: "Alas for you! The reward of Allah (in the Hereafter) is best for those who believe and work righteousness: but this none shall attain, save those who steadfastly persevere (in good)."	But those who had been given knowledge said: Woe unto you! The reward of Allah for him who believeth and doeth right is better, and only the steadfast will obtain it.	And those who were given the knowledge said: Woe to you! Allah's reward is better for him who believes and does good, and none is made to receive this except the patient.
28 081	Then We caused the earth to swallow up him and his house; and he had not (the least little) party to help him against Allah, nor could he defend himself.	So We caused the earth to swallow him and his dwelling-place. Then he had no host to help him against Allah, nor was he of those who can save themselves.	Thus We made the earth to swallow up him and his abode; so he had no body of helpers to assist him against Allah nor was he of those who can defend themselves.
28 082	And those who had envied his position the day before began to say on the morrow: "Ah! it is indeed Allah Who enlarges the provision or restricts it, to any of His servants He pleases! had it not been that Allah was gracious to us, He could have caused the earth to swallow us up! Ah! those who reject Allah will assuredly never prosper."	And morning found those who had coveted his place but yesterday crying: Ah, welladay! Allah enlargeth the provision for whom He will of His slaves and straiteneth it (for whom He will). If Allah had not been gracious unto us He would have caused it to swallow us (also). Ah, welladay! the disbelievers never prosper.	And those who yearned for his place only the day before began to say: Ah! (know) that Allah amplifies and straitens the means of subsistence for whom He pleases of His servants; had not Allah been gracious to us, He would most surely have abased us; ah! (know) that the ungrateful are never successful.
28 083	That Home of the Hereafter We shall give to those who intend not high-handedness or mischief on earth: and the end is (best) for the righteous.	As for that Abode of the Hereafter We assign it unto those who seek not oppression in the earth, nor yet corruption. The sequel is for those who ward off (evil).	(As for) that future abode, We assign it to those who have no desire to exalt themselves in the earth nor to make mischief and the good end is for those who guard (against evil)
28 084	If any does good, the reward to him is better than his deed; but if any does evil, the doers of evil are only punished (to the extent) of their deeds.	Whoso bringeth a good deed, he will have better than the same; while as for him who bringeth an ill-deed, those who do ill-deeds will be requited only what they did.	Whoever brings good, he shall have better than it, and whoever brings evil, those who do evil shall not be rewarded (for) aught except what they did.

28 085	Verily He Who ordained the Qur'an for thee, will bring thee back to the Place of Return. Say: "My Lord knows best who it is that brings true guidance, and who is in manifest error."	Lo! He Who hath given thee the Qur'an for a law will surely bring thee home again. Say: My Lord is Best Aware of him who bringeth guidance and him who is in error manifest.	Most surely He Who has made the Quran binding on you will bring you back to the destination. Say: My Lord knows best him who has brought the guidance and him who is in manifest error.
28 086	And thou hadst not expected that the Book would be sent to thee except as a Mercy from thy Lord: Therefore lend not thou support in any way to those who reject (Allah's Message).	Thou hadst no hope that the Scripture would be inspired in thee; but it is a mercy from thy Lord, so never be a helper to the disbelievers.	And you did not expect that the Book would be inspired to you, but it is a mercy from your Lord, therefore be not a backer-up of the unbelievers.
28 087	And let nothing keep thee back from the Signs of Allah after they have been revealed to thee: and invite (men) to thy Lord, and be not of the company of those who join gods with Allah.	And let them not divert thee from the revelations of Allah after they have been sent down unto thee; but call (mankind) unto thy Lord, and be not of those who ascribe partners (unto Him).	And let them not turn you aside from the communications of Allah after they have been revealed to you, and call (men) to your Lord and be not of the polytheists.
28 088	And call not, besides Allah, on another god. There is no god but He. Everything (that exists) will perish except His own Face. To Him belongs the Command, and to Him will ye (all) be brought back.	And cry not unto any other god along with Allah. There is no God save Him. Everything will perish save His countenance. His is the command, and unto Him ye will be brought back.	And call not with Allah any other god; there is no god but He, every thing is perishable but He; His is the judgment, and to Him you shall be brought back.

Chapter 29:

AL-ANKABOOT (THE SPIDER)

Total Verses: 69 Revealed At: MAKKA

In the name of Allah, the Most Beneficent, the Most Merciful.

29 001	A.L.M.	Alif. Lam. Mim.	Alif Lam Mim.
29 002	Do men think that they will be left alone on saying, "We believe", and that they will not be tested?	Do men imagine that they will be left (at ease) because they say, We believe, and will not be tested with affliction?	Do men think that they will be left alone on saying, We believe, and not be tried?
29 003	We did test those before them, and Allah will certainly know those who are true from those who are false.	Lo! We tested those who were before you. Thus Allah knoweth those who are sincere, and knoweth those who feign.	And certainly We tried those before them, so Allah will certainly know those who are true and He will certainly know the liars.
29 004	Do those who practise evil think that they will get the better of Us? Evil is their judgment!	Or do those who do ill-deeds imagine that they can outstrip Us? Evil (for them) is that which they decide.	Or do they who work evil think that they will escape Us? Evil is it that they judge!
29 005	For those whose hopes are in the meeting with Allah (in the Hereafter, let them strive); for the term (appointed) by Allah is surely coming and He hears and knows (all things).	Whoso looketh forward to the meeting with Allah (let him know that) Allah's reckoning is surely nigh, and He is the Hearer, the Knower.	Whoever hopes to meet Allah, the term appointed by Allah will then most surely come; and He is the Hearing, the Knowing.

29 006	And if any strive (with might and main), they do so for their own souls: for Allah is free of all needs from all creation.	And whosoever striveth, striveth only for himself, for lo! Allah is altogether Independent of (His) creatures.	And whoever strives hard, he strives only for his own soul; most surely Allah is Self-sufficient, above (need of) the worlds.
29 007	Those who believe and work righteous deeds,- from them shall We blot out all evil (that may be) in them, and We shall reward them according to the best of their deeds.	And as for those who believe and do good works, We shall remit from them their evil deeds and shall repay them the best that they did.	And (as for) those who believe and do good, We will most certainly do away with their evil deeds and We will most certainly reward them the best of what they did.
29 008	We have enjoined on man kindness to parents: but if they (either of them) strive (to force) thee to join with Me (in worship) anything of which thou hast no knowledge, obey them not. Ye have (all) to return to me, and I will tell you (the truth) of all that ye did.	We have enjoined on man kindness to parents; but if they strive to make thee join with Me that of which thou hast no knowledge, then obey them not. Unto Me is your return and I shall tell you what ye used to do.	And We have enjoined on man goodness to his parents, and if they contend with you that you should associate (others) with Me, of which you have no knowledge, do not obey them, to Me is your return, so I will inform you of what you did.
29 009	And those who believe and work righteous deeds,- them shall We admit to the company of the Righteous.	And as for those who believe and do good works, We verily shall make them enter in among the righteous.	And (as for) those who believe and do good, We will most surely cause them to enter among the good.
29 010	Then there are among men such as say, "We believe in Allah"; but when they suffer affliction in (the cause of) Allah, they treat men's oppression as if it were the Wrath of Allah! And if help comes (to thee) from thy Lord, they are sure to say, "We have (always) been with you!" Does not Allah know best all that is in the hearts of all creation?	Of mankind is he who saith: We believe in Allah, but, if he be made to suffer for the sake of Allah, he mistaketh the persecution of mankind for Allah's punishment; and then, if victory cometh from thy Lord, will say: Lo! we were with you (all the while). Is not Allah Best Aware of what is in the bosoms of (His) creatures?	And among men is he who says: We believe in Allah; but when he is persecuted in (the way of) Allah he thinks the persecution of men to be as the chastisement of Allah; and if there come assistance from your Lord, they would most certainly say: Surely we were with you. What! is not Allah the best knower of what is in the breasts of mankind.
29 011	And Allah most certainly knows those who believe, and as certainly those who are Hypocrites.	Verily Allah knoweth those who believe, and verily He knoweth the hypocrites.	And most certainly Allah will know those who believe and most certainly He will know the hypocrites.
29 012	And the Unbelievers say to those who believe: "Follow our path, and we will bear (the consequences) of your faults." Never in the least will they bear their faults: in fact they are liars!	Those who disbelieve say unto those who believe: Follow our way (of religion) and we verily will bear your sins (for you). They cannot bear aught of their sins. Lo! they verily are liars.	And those who disbelieve say to those who believe: Follow our path and we will bear your wrongs. And never shall they be the bearers of any of their wrongs; most surely they are liars.
29 013	They will bear their own burdens, and (other) burdens along with their own, and on the Day of Judgments they will be called to account for their falsehoods.	But they verily will bear their own loads and other loads beside their own, and they verily will be questioned on the Day of Resurrection concerning that which they invented.	And most certainly they shall carry their own burdens, and other burdens with their own burdens, and most certainly they shall be questioned on the resurrection day as to what they forged.
29 014	We (once) sent Noah to his people, and he tarried among them a thousand years less fifty: but the Deluge overwhelmed them while they (persisted in) sin.	And verily we sent Noah (as Our messenger) unto his folk, and he continued with them for a thousand years save fifty years; and the flood engulfed them, for they were wrong-doers.	And certainly We sent Nuh to his people, so he remained among them a thousand years save fifty years. And the deluge overtook them, while they were unjust.
29 015	But We saved him and the companions of the Ark, and We made the (Ark) a Sign for all peoples!	And We rescued him and those with him in the ship, and made of it a portent for the peoples.	So We delivered him and the inmates of the ark, and made it a sign to the nations.

29 016	And (We also saved) Abraham: behold, he said to his people, "Serve Allah and fear Him: that will be best for you- if ye understand!"	And Abraham! (Remember) when he said unto his folk: Serve Allah, and keep your duty unto Him; that is better for you if ye did but know.	And (We sent) Ibrahim, when he said to his people: Serve Allah and be careful of (your duty to) Him; this is best for you, if you did but know:
29 017	"For ye do worship idols besides Allah, and ye invent falsehood. The things that ye worship besides Allah have no power to give you sustenance: then seek ye sustenance from Allah, serve Him, and be grateful to Him: to Him will be your return."	Ye serve instead of Allah only idols, and ye only invent a lie. Lo! those whom ye serve instead of Allah own no provision for you. So seek your provision from Allah, and serve Him, and give thanks unto Him, (for) unto Him ye will be brought back.	You only worship idols besides Allah and you create a lie surely they whom you serve besides Allah do not control for you any sustenance, therefore seek the sustenance from Allah and serve Him and be grateful to Him; to Him you shall be brought back.
29 018	"And if ye reject (the Message), so did generations before you: and the duty of the messenger is only to preach publicly (and clearly)."	But if ye deny, then nations have denied before you. The messenger is only to convey (the message) plainly.	And if you reject (the truth), nations before you did indeed reject (the truth); and nothing is incumbent on the messenger but a plain delivering (of the message).
29 019	See they not how Allah originates creation, then repeats it: truly that is easy for Allah.	See they not how Allah produceth creation, then reproduceth it? Lo! for Allah that is easy.	What! do they not consider how Allah originates the creation, then reproduces it? Surely that is easy to Allah.
29 020	Say: "Travel through the earth and see how Allah did originate creation; so will Allah produce a later creation: for Allah has power over all things."	Say (O Muhammad): Travel in the land and see how He originated creation, then Allah bringeth forth the later growth. Lo! Allah is Able to do all things.	Say: Travel in the earth and see how He makes the first creation, then Allah creates the latter creation; surely Allah has power over all things.
29 021	"He punishes whom He pleases, and He grants Mercy to whom He pleases, and towards Him are ye turned."	He punisheth whom He will and showeth mercy unto whom He will, and unto Him ye will be turned.	He punishes whom He pleases and has mercy on whom He pleases, and to Him you shall be turned back.
29 022	"Not on earth nor in heaven will ye be able (fleeing) to frustrate (his Plan), nor have ye, besides Allah, any protector or helper."	Ye cannot escape (from Him) in the earth or in the sky, and beside Allah there is for you no friend or helper.	And you shall not escape in the earth nor in the heaven, and you have neither a protector nor a helper besides Allah.
29 023	Those who reject the Signs of Allah and the Meeting with Him (in the Hereafter),- it is they who shall despair of My Mercy: it is they who will (suffer) a most grievous Penalty.	Those who disbelieve in the revelations of Allah and in (their) Meeting with Him, such have no hope of My mercy. For such there is a painful doom.	And (as to) those who disbelieve in the communications of Allah and His meeting, they have despaired of My mercy, and these it is that shall have a painful punishment.
29 024	So naught was the answer of (Abraham's) people except that they said: Slay him or burn him. But Allah did save him from the Fire. Verily in this are Signs for people who believe.	But the answer of his folk was only that they said: "Kill him" or Burn him. Then Allah saved him from the Fire. Lo! herein verily are portents for folk who believe.	So naught was the answer of his people except that they said: Slay him or burn him; then Allah delivered him from the fire; most surely there are signs in this for a people who believe.
29 025	And he said: "For you, ye have taken (for worship) idols besides Allah, out of mutual love and regard between yourselves in this life; but on the Day of Judgment ye shall disown each other and curse each other: and your abode will be the Fire, and ye shall have none to help."	He said: Ye have chosen only idols instead of Allah. The love between you is only in the life of the world. Then on the Day of Resurrection ye will deny each other and curse each other, and your abode will be the Fire, and ye will have no helpers.	And he said: You have only taken for yourselves idols besides Allah by way of friendship between you in this world's life, then on the resurrection day some of you shall deny others, and some of you curse others, and your abode is the fire, and you shall not have any helpers.

29 026	But Lut had faith in Him: He said: "I will leave home for the sake of my Lord: for He is Exalted in Might, and Wise."	And Lot believed him, and said: Lo! I am a fugitive unto my Lord. Lo! He, only He, is the Mighty, the Wise.	And Lut believed in Him, and he said: I am fleeing to my Lord, surely He is the Mighty, the Wise.
29 027	And We gave (Abraham) Isaac and Jacob, and ordained among his progeny Prophethood and Revelation, and We granted him his reward in this life; and he was in the Hereafter (of the company) of the Righteous.	And We bestowed on him Isaac and Jacob, and We established the prophethood and the Scripture among his seed, and We gave him his reward in the world, and lo! in the Hereafter he verily is among the righteous.	And We granted him Ishaq and Yaqoub, and caused the prophethood and the book to remain in his seed, and We gave him his reward in this world, and in the hereafter he will most surely be among the good.
29 028	And (remember) Lut: behold, he said to his people: "Ye do commit lewdness, such as no people in Creation (ever) committed before you."	And Lot! (Remember) when he said unto his folk: Lo! ye commit lewdness such as no creature did before you.	And (We sent) Lut when he said to his people: Most surely you are guilty of an indecency which none of the nations has ever done before you;
29 029	"Do ye indeed approach men, and cut off the highway?- and practise wickedness (even) in your councils?" But his people gave no answer but this: they said: "Bring us the Wrath of Allah if thou tellest the truth."	For come ye not in unto males, and cut ye not the road (for travellers), and commit ye not abomination in your meetings? But the answer of his folk was only that they said: Bring Allah's doom upon us if thou art a truthteller!	What! do you come to the males and commit robbery on the highway, and you commit evil deeds in your assemblies? But nothing was the answer of his people except that they said: Bring on us Allah's punishment, if you are one of the truthful.
29 030	He said: "O my Lord! help Thou me against people who do mischief!"	He said: My Lord! Give me victory over folk who work corruption.	He said: My Lord! help me against the mischievous people.
29 031	When Our Messengers came to Abraham with the good news, they said: We are indeed going to destroy the people of this township: for truly they are (addicted to) crime."	And when Our messengers brought Abraham the good news, they said: Lo! we are about to destroy the people of that township, for its people are wrong-doers.	And when Our messengers came to Ibrahim with the good news, they said: Surely we are going to destroy the people of this town, for its people are unjust.
29 032	He said: "But there is Lut there." They said: "Well do we know who is there: we will certainly save him and his following,- except his wife: she is of those who lag behind!"	He said: Lo! Lot is there. They said: We are best aware of who is there. We are to deliver him and his household, all save his wife, who is of those who stay behind.	He said: Surely in it is Lut. They said: We know well who is in it; we shall certainly deliver him and his followers, except his wife; she shall be of those who remain behind.
29 033	And when Our Messengers came to Lut, he was grieved on their account, and felt himself powerless (to protect) them: but they said: "Fear thou not, nor grieve: we are (here) to save thee and thy following, except thy wife: she is of those who lag behind."	And when Our messengers came unto Lot, he was troubled upon their account, for he could not protect them; but they said: Fear not, nor grieve! Lo! we are to deliver thee and thy household, (all) save thy wife, who is of those who stay behind.	And when Our messengers came to Lut he was grieved on account of them, and he felt powerless (to protect) them; and they said: Fear not, nor grieve; surely we will deliver you and your followers, except your wife; she shall be of those who remain behind.
29 034	"For we are going to bring down on the people of this township a Punishment from heaven, because they have been wickedly rebellious."	Lo! We are about to bring down upon the folk of this township a fury from the sky because they are evil-livers.	Surely We will cause to come down upon the people of this town a punishment from heaven, because they transgressed.
29 035	And We have left thereof an evident Sign, for any people who (care to) understand.	And verily of that We have left a clear sign for people who have sense.	And certainly We have left a clear sign of it for a people who understand.

29 036	To the Madyan (people) (We sent) their brother Shu'aib. Then he said: O my people! serve Allah, and fear the Last Day: nor commit evil on the earth, with intent to do mischief."	And unto Midian We sent Shu'eyb, their brother. He said: O my people! Serve Allah, and look forward to the Last Day, and do not evil, making mischief, in the earth.	And to Madyan (We sent) their brother Shuaib, so he said: O my people! serve Allah and fear the latter day and do not act corruptly in the land, making mischief.
29 037	But they rejected him: Then the mighty Blast seized them, and they lay prostrate in their homes by the morning.	But they denied him, and the dreadful earthquake took them, and morning found them prostrate in their dwelling place.	But they rejected him, so a severe earthquake overtook them, and they became motionless bodies in their abode.
29 038	(Remember also) the 'Ad and the Thamud (people): clearly will appear to you from (the traces) of their buildings (their fate): the Evil One made their deeds alluring to them, and kept them back from the Path, though they were gifted with intelligence and skill.	And (the tribes of) A'ad and Thamud! (Their fate) is manifest unto you from their (ruined and deserted) dwellings. Satan made their deeds seem fair unto them and so debarred them from the Way, though they were keen observers.	And (We destroyed) Ad and Samood, and from their dwellings (this) is apparent to you indeed; and the Shaitan made their deeds fair-seeming to them, so he kept them back from the path, though they were endowed with intelligence and skill,
29 039	(Remember also) Qarun, Pharaoh, and Haman: there came to them Moses with Clear Signs, but they behaved with insolence on the earth; yet they could not overreach (Us).	And Korah, Pharaoh and Haman! Moses came unto them with clear proofs (of Allah's Sovereignty), but they were boastful in the land. And they were not winners (in the race).	And (We destroyed) Qaroun and Firon and Haman; and certainly Musa came to them with clear arguments, but they behaved haughtily in the land; yet they could not outstrip (Us).
29 040	Each one of them We seized for his crime: of them, against some We sent a violent tornado (with showers of stones); some were caught by a (mighty) Blast; some We caused the earth to swallow up; and some We drowned (in the waters): It was not Allah Who injured (or oppressed) them: They injured (and oppressed) their own souls.	So We took each one in his sin; of them was he on whom We sent a hurricane, and of them was he who was overtaken by the (Awful) Cry, and of them was he whom We caused the earth to swallow, and of them was he whom We drowned. It was not for Allah to wrong them, but they wronged themselves.	So each We punished for his sin; of them was he on whom We sent down a violent storm, and of them was he whom the rumbling overtook, and of them was he whom We made to be swallowed up by the earth, and of them was he whom We drowned; and it did not beseem Allah that He should be unjust to them, but they were unjust to their own souls.
29 041	The parable of those who take protectors other than Allah is that of the spider, who builds (to itself) a house; but truly the flimsiest of houses is the spider's house;- if they but knew.	The likeness of those who choose other patrons than Allah is as the likeness of the spider when she taketh unto herself a house, and lo! the frailest of all houses is the spider's house, if they but knew.	The parable of those who take guardians besides Allah is as the parable of the spider that makes for itself a house; and most surely the frailest of the houses is the spider's house did they but know.
29 042	Verily Allah doth know of (every) thing whatever that they call upon besides Him: and He is Exalted (in power), Wise.	Lo! Allah knoweth what thing they invoke instead of Him. He is the Mighty, the Wise.	Surely Allah knows whatever thing they call upon besides Him; and He is the Mighty, the Wise.
29 043	And such are the Parables We set forth for mankind, but only those understand them who have knowledge.	As for these similitudes, We coin them for mankind, but none will grasp their meaning save the wise.	And (as for) these examples, We set them forth for men, and none understand them but the learned.
29 044	Allah created the heavens and the earth in true (proportions): verily in that is a Sign for those who believe.	Allah created the heavens and the earth with truth. Lo! therein is indeed a portent for believers.	Allah created the heavens and the earth with truth; most surely there is a sign in this for the believers.

29 045	Recite what is sent of the Book by inspiration to thee, and establish regular Prayer: for Prayer restrains from shameful and unjust deeds; and remembrance of Allah is the greatest (thing in life) without doubt. And Allah knows the (deeds) that ye do.	Recite that which hath been inspired in thee of the Scripture, and establish worship. Lo! worship preserveth from lewdness and iniquity, but verily remembrance of Allah is more important. And Allah knoweth what ye do.	Recite that which has been revealed to you of the Book and keep up prayer; surely prayer keeps (one) away from indecency and evil, and certainly the remembrance of Allah is the greatest, and Allah knows what you do.
29 046	And dispute ye not with the People of the Book, except with means better (than mere disputation), unless it be with those of them who inflict wrong (and injury): but say, "We believe in the revelation which has come down to us and in that which came down to you; Our Allah and your Allah is one; and it is to Him we bow (in Islam)."	And argue not with the People of the Scripture unless it be in (a way) that is better, save with such of them as do wrong; and say: We believe in that which hath been revealed unto us and revealed unto you; our Allah and your Allah is One, and unto Him we surrender.	And do not dispute with the followers of the Book except by what is best, except those of them who act unjustly, and say: We believe in that which has been revealed to us and revealed to you, and our Allah and your Allah is One, and to Him do we submit.
29 047	And thus (it is) that We have sent down the Book to thee. So the People of the Book believe therein, as also do some of these (pagan Arabs): and none but Unbelievers reject our signs.	In like manner We have revealed unto thee the Scripture, and those unto whom We gave the Scripture aforetime will believe therein; and of these (also) there are some who believe therein. And none deny Our revelations save the disbelievers.	And thus have We revealed the Book to you. So those whom We have given the Book believe in it, and of these there are those who believe in it, and none deny Our communications except the unbelievers.
29 048	And thou wast not (able) to recite a Book before this (Book came), nor art thou (able) to transcribe it with thy right hand: In that case, indeed, would the talkers of vanities have doubted.	And thou (O Muhammad) wast not a reader of any scripture before it, nor didst thou write it with thy right hand, for then might those have doubted, who follow falsehood.	And you did not recite before it any book, nor did you transcribe one with your right hand, for then could those who say untrue things have doubted.
29 049	Nay, here are Signs self-evident in the hearts of those endowed with knowledge: and none but the unjust reject Our Signs.	But it is clear revelations in the hearts of those who have been given knowledge, and none deny Our revelations save wrong-doers.	Nay! these are clear communications in the breasts of those who are granted knowledge; and none deny Our communications except the unjust.
29 050	Ye they say: "Why are not Signs sent down to him from his Lord?" Say: The signs are indeed with Allah: and I am indeed a clear Warner.	And they say: Why are not portents sent down upon him from his Lord? Say: Portents are with Allah only, and I am but a plain warner.	And they say: Why are not signs sent down upon him from his Lord? Say: The signs are only with Allah, and I am only a plain warner.
29 051	And is it not enough for them that we have sent down to thee the Book which is rehearsed to them? Verily, in it is Mercy and a Reminder to those who believe.	Is it not enough for them that We have sent down unto thee the Scripture which is read unto them? Lo! herein verily is mercy, and a reminder for folk who believe.	Is it not enough for them that We have revealed to you the Book which is recited to them? Most surely there is mercy in this and a reminder for a people who believe.
29 052	Say: "Enough is Allah for a witness between me and you: He knows what is in the heavens and on earth." And it is those who believe in vanities and reject Allah, that will perish (in the end).	Say (unto them, O Muhammad): Allah sufficeth for witness between me and you. He knoweth whatsoever is in the heavens and the earth. And those who believe in vanity and disbelieve in Allah, they it is who are the losers.	Say: Allah is sufficient as a witness between me and you; He knows what is in the heavens and the earth. And (as for) those who believe in the falsehood and disbelieve in Allah, these it is that are the losers.

29 053	They ask thee to hasten on the Punishment (for them): had it not been for a term (of respite) appointed, the Punishment would certainly have come to them: and it will certainly reach them,- of a sudden, while they perceive not!	They bid thee hasten on the doom (of Allah). And if a term had not been appointed, the doom would assuredly have come unto them (ere now). And verily it will come upon them suddenly when they perceive not.	And they ask you to hasten on the chastisement; and had not a term been appointed, the chastisement would certainly have come to them; and most certainly it will come to them all of a sudden while they will not perceive.
29 054	They ask thee to hasten on the Punishment: but, of a surety, Hell will encompass the Rejecters of Faith!-	They bid thee hasten on the doom, when lo! hell verily will encompass the disbelievers.	They ask you to hasten on the chastisement, and most surely hell encompasses the unbelievers;
29 055	On the Day that the Punishment shall cover them from above them and from below them, and (a Voice) shall say: "Taste ye (the fruits) of your deeds!"	On the day when the doom will overwhelm them from above them and from underneath their feet, and He will say: Taste what ye used to do!	On the day when the chastisement shall cover them from above them, and from beneath their feet; and He shall say: Taste what you did.
29 056	O My servants who believe! truly, spacious is My Earth: therefore serve ye Me - (and Me alone)!	O my bondmen who believe! Lo! My earth is spacious. Therefor serve Me only.	O My servants who believe! surely My earth is vast, therefore Me alone should you serve.
29 057	Every soul shall have a taste of death: In the end to Us shall ye be brought back.	Every soul will taste of death. Then unto Us ye will be returned.	Every soul must taste of death, then to Us you shall be brought back.
29 058	But those who believe and work deeds of righteousness - to them shall We give a Home in Heaven,- lofty mansions beneath which flow rivers,- to dwell therein for aye;- an excellent reward for those who do (good)!-	Those who believe and do good works, them verily We shall house in lofty dwellings of the Garden underneath which rivers flow. There they will dwell secure. How sweet the guerdon of the toilers,	And (as for) those who believe and do good, We will certainly give them abode in the high places in gardens beneath which rivers flow, abiding therein; how good the reward of the workers:
29 059	Those who persevere in patience, and put their trust, in their Lord and Cherisher.	Who persevere, and put their trust in their Lord!	Those who are patient, and on their Lord do they rely.
29 060	How many are the creatures that carry not their own sustenance? It is Allah who feeds (both) them and you: for He hears and knows (all things).	And how many an animal there is that beareth not its own provision! Allah provideth for it and for you. He is the Hearer, the Knower.	And how many a living creature that does not carry its sustenance: Allah sustains it and yourselves; and He is the Hearing, the Knowing.
29 061	If indeed thou ask them who has created the heavens and the earth and subjected the sun and the moon (to his Law), they will certainly reply, Allah. How are they then deluded away (from the truth)?	And if thou wert to ask them: Who created the heavens and the earth, and constrained the sun and the moon (to their appointed work)? they would say: Allah. How then are they turned away?	And if you ask them, Who created the heavens and the earth and made the sun and the moon subservient, they will certainly say, Allah. Whence are they then turned away?
29 062	Allah enlarges the sustenance (which He gives) to whichever of His servants He pleases; and He (similarly) grants by (strict) measure, (as He pleases): for Allah has full knowledge of all things.	Allah maketh the provision wide for whom He will of His bondmen, and straiteneth it for whom (He will). Lo! Allah is Aware of all things.	Allah makes abundant the means of subsistence for whom He pleases of His servants, and straitens them for whom (He pleases) surely Allah is Cognizant of all things.
29 063	And if indeed thou ask them who it is that sends down rain from the sky, and gives life therewith to the earth after its death, they will certainly reply, "Allah!" Say, "Praise be to Allah!" But most of them understand not.	And if thou wert to ask them: Who causeth water to come down from the sky, and therewith reviveth the earth after its death? they verily would say: Allah. Say: Praise be to Allah! But most of them have no sense.	And if you ask them Who is it that sends down water from the clouds, then gives life to the earth with it after its death, they will certainly say, Allah. Say: All praise is due to Allah. Nay, most of them do not understand.
29 064	What is the life of this world but amusement and play? but verily the Home in the Hereafter,- that is life indeed, if they but knew.	This life of the world is but a pastime and a game. Lo! the home of the Hereafter - that is Life, if they but knew.	And this life of the world is nothing but a sport and a play; and as for the next abode, that most surely is the life-- did they but know!

29 065	Now, if they embark on a boat, they call on Allah, making their devotion sincerely (and exclusively) to Him; but when He has delivered them safely to (dry) land, behold, they give a share (of their worship to others)!-	And when they mount upon the ships they pray to Allah, making their faith pure for Him only, but when He bringeth them safe to land, behold! they ascribe partners (unto Him),	So when they ride in the ships they call upon Allah, being sincerely obedient to Him, but when He brings them safe to the land, lo! they associate others (with Him);
29 066	Disdaining ungratefully Our gifts, and giving themselves up to (worldly) enjoyment! But soon will they know.	That they may disbelieve in that which We have given them, and that they may take their ease. But they will come to know.	Thus they become ungrateful for what We have given them, so that they may enjoy; but they shall soon know.
29 067	Do they not then see that We have made a sanctuary secure, and that men are being snatched away from all around them? Then, do they believe in that which is vain, and reject the Grace of Allah?	Have they not seen that We have appointed a sanctuary immune (from violence), while mankind are ravaged all around them? Do they then believe in falsehood and disbelieve in the bounty of Allah?	Do they not see that We have made a sacred territory secure, while men are carried off by force from around them? Will they still believe in the falsehood and disbelieve in the favour of Allah?
29 068	And who does more wrong than he who invents a lie against Allah or rejects the Truth when it reaches him? Is there not a home in Hell for those who reject Faith?	Who doeth greater wrong than he who inventeth a lie concerning Allah, or denieth the truth when it cometh unto him? Is not there a home in hell for disbelievers?	And who is more unjust than one who forges a lie against Allah, or gives the lie to the truth when it has come to him? Will not in hell be the abode of the unbelievers?
29 069	And those who strive in Our (cause),- We will certainly guide them to our Paths: For verily Allah is with those who do right.	As for those who strive in Us, We surely guide them to Our paths, and lo! Allah is with the good.	And (as for) those who strive hard for Us, We will most certainly guide them in Our ways; and Allah is most surely with the doers of good.

Chapter 30:

AL-ROOM (THE ROMANS, THE BYZANTINES)

Total Verses: 60 Revealed At: MAKKA

In the name of Allah, the Most Beneficent, the Most Merciful.

30 001	A. L. M.	Alif. Lam. Mim.	Alif Lam Mim.
30 002	The Roman Empire has been defeated-	The Romans have been defeated,	The Romans are vanquished,
30 003	In a land close by; but they, (even) after (this) defeat of theirs, will soon be victorious-	In the nearer land, and they, after their defeat will be victorious,	In a near land, and they, after being vanquished, shall overcome,
30 004	Within a few years. With Allah is the Decision, in the past and in the Future: on that Day shall the Believers rejoice-	Within ten years - Allah's is the command in the former case and in the latter - and in that day believers will rejoice,	Within a few years. Allah's is the command before and after; and on that day the believers shall rejoice,
30 005	With the help of Allah. He helps whom He will, and He is Exalted in Might, most Merciful.	In Allah's help to victory. He helpeth to victory whom He will. He is the Mighty, the Merciful.	With the help of Allah; He helps whom He pleases; and He is the Mighty, the Merciful;
30 006	(It is) the promise of Allah. Never does Allah depart from His promise: but most men understand not.	It is a promise of Allah. Allah faileth not His promise, but most of mankind know not.	(This is) Allah's promise! Allah will not fail His promise, but most people do not know.
30 007	They know but the outer (things) in the life of this world: but of the End of things they are heedless.	They know only some appearance of the life of the world, and are heedless of the Hereafter.	They know the outward of this world's life, but of the hereafter they are absolutely heedless.

30	008	Do they not reflect in their own minds? Not but for just ends and for a term appointed, did Allah create the heavens and the earth, and all between them: yet are there truly many among men who deny the meeting with their Lord (at the Resurrection)!	Have they not pondered upon themselves? Allah created not the heavens and the earth, and that which is between them, save with truth and for a destined end. But truly many of mankind are disbelievers in the meeting with their Lord.	Do they not reflect within themselves: Allah did not create the heavens and the earth and what is between them two but with truth, and (for) an appointed term? And most surely most of the people are deniers of the meeting of their Lord.
30	009	Do they not travel through the earth, and see what was the end of those before them? They were superior to them in strength: they tilled the soil and populated it in greater numbers than these have done: there came to them their messengers with Clear (Signs). (Which they rejected, to their own destruction): It was not Allah Who wronged them, but they wronged their own souls.	Have they not travelled in the land and seen the nature of the consequence for those who were before them? They were stronger than these in power, and they dug the earth and built upon it more than these have built. Messengers of their own came unto them with clear proofs (of Allah's Sovereignty). Surely Allah wronged them not, but they did wrong themselves.	Have they not travelled in the earth and seen how was the end of those before them? They were stronger than these in prowess, and dug up the earth, and built on it in greater abundance than these have built on it, and there came to them their messengers with clear arguments; so it was not beseeming for Allah that He should deal with them unjustly, but they dealt unjustly with their own souls.
30	010	In the long run evil in the extreme will be the End of those who do evil; for that they rejected the Signs of Allah, and held them up to ridicule.	Then evil was the consequence to those who dealt in evil, because they denied the revelations of Allah and made a mock of them.	Then evil was the end of those who did evil, because they | rejected the communications of Allah and used to mock them.
30	011	It is Allah Who begins (the process of) creation; then repeats it; then shall ye be brought back to Him.	Allah produceth creation, then He reproduceth it, then unto Him ye will be returned.	Allah originates the creation, then reproduces it, then to Him you shall be brought back.
30	012	On the Day that the Hour will be established, the guilty will be struck dumb with despair.	And in the day when the Hour riseth the unrighteous will despair.	And at the time when the hour shall come the guilty shall be in despair.
30	013	No intercessor will they have among their "Partners" and they will (themselves) reject their "Partners".	There will be none to intercede for them of those whom they made equal with Allah. And they will reject their partners (whom they ascribed unto Him).	And they shall not have any intercessors from among their gods they have joined with Allah, and they shall be deniers of their associate-gods.
30	014	On the Day that the Hour will be established,- that Day shall (all men) be sorted out.	In the day when the Hour cometh, in that day they will be sundered.	And at the time when the hour shall come, at that time they shall become separated one from the other.
30	015	Then those who have believed and worked righteous deeds, shall be made happy in a Mead of Delight.	As for those who believed and did good works, they will be made happy in a Garden.	Then as to those who believed and did good, they shall be made happy in a garden.
30	016	And those who have rejected Faith and falsely denied our Signs and the meeting of the Hereafter,- such shall be brought forth to Punishment.	But as for those who disbelieved and denied Our revelations, and denied the meeting of the Hereafter, such will be brought to doom.	And as to those who disbelieved and rejected Our communications and the meeting of the hereafter, these shall be brought over to the chastisement.
30	017	So (give) glory to Allah, when ye reach eventide and when ye rise in the morning;	So glory be to Allah when ye enter the night and when ye enter the morning -	Therefore glory be to Allah when you enter upon the time of the evening and when you enter upon the time of the morning.
30	018	Yea, to Him be praise, in the heavens and on earth; and in the late afternoon and when the day begins to decline.	Unto Him be praise in the heavens and the earth! - and at the sun's decline and in the noonday.	And to Him belongs praise in the heavens and the earth, and at nightfall and when you are at midday.

30	019	It is He Who brings out the living from the dead, and brings out the dead from the living, and Who gives life to the earth after it is dead: and thus shall ye be brought out (from the dead).	He bringeth forth the living from the dead, and He bringeth forth the dead from the living, and He reviveth the earth after her death. And even so will ye be brought forth.	He brings forth the living from the dead and brings forth the dead from the living, and gives life to the earth after its death, and thus shall you be brought forth.
30	020	Among His Signs in this, that He created you from dust; and then,- behold, ye are men scattered (far and wide)!	And of His signs is this: He created you of dust, and behold you human beings, ranging widely!	And one of His signs is that He created you from dust, then lo! you are mortals (who) scatter.
30	021	And among His Signs is this, that He created for you mates from among yourselves, that ye may dwell in tranquillity with them, and He has put love and mercy between your (hearts): verily in that are Signs for those who reflect.	And of His signs is this: He created for you helpmeets from yourselves that ye might find rest in them, and He ordained between you love and mercy. Lo! herein indeed are portents for folk who reflect.	And one of His signs is that He created mates for you from yourselves that you may find rest in them, and He put between you love and compassion; most surely there are signs in this for a people who reflect.
30	022	And among His Signs is the creation of the heavens and the earth, and the variations in your languages and your colours: verily in that are Signs for those who know.	And of His signs is the creation of the heavens and the earth, and the difference of your languages and colours. Lo! herein indeed are portents for men of knowledge.	And one of His signs is the creation of the heavens and the earth and the diversity of your tongues and colors; most surely there are signs in this for the learned.
30	023	And among His Signs is the sleep that ye take by night and by day, and the quest that ye (make for livelihood) out of His Bounty: verily in that are signs for those who hearken.	And of His signs is your slumber by night and by day, and your seeking of His bounty. Lo! herein indeed are portents for folk who heed.	And one of His signs is your sleeping and your seeking of His grace by night and (by) day; most surely there are signs in this for a people who would hear.
30	024	And among His Signs, He shows you the lightning, by way both of fear and of hope, and He sends down rain from the sky and with it gives life to the earth after it is dead: verily in that are Signs for those who are wise.	And of His signs is this: He showeth you the lightning for a fear and for a hope, and sendeth down water from the sky, and thereby quickeneth the earth after her death. Lo! herein indeed are portents for folk who understand.	And one of His signs is that He shows you the lightning for fear and for hope, and sends down water from the clouds then gives life therewith to the earth after its death; most surely there are signs in this for a people who understand.
30	025	And among His Signs is this, that heaven and earth stand by His Command: then when He calls you, by a single call, from the earth, behold, ye (straightway) come forth.	And of His signs is this: The heavens and the earth stand fast by His command, and afterward, when He calleth you, lo! from the earth ye will emerge.	And one of His signs is that the heaven and the earth subsist by His command, then when He calls you with a (single) call from out of the earth, lo! you come forth.
30	026	To Him belongs every being that is in the heavens and on earth: all are devoutly obedient to Him.	Unto Him belongeth whosoever is in the heavens and the earth. All are obedient unto Him.	And His is whosoever is in the heavens and the earth; all are obedient to Him.
30	027	It is He Who begins (the process of) creation; then repeats it; and for Him it is most easy. To Him belongs the loftiest similitude (we can think of) in the heavens and the earth: for He is Exalted in Might, full of Wisdom.	He it is Who produceth creation, then reproduceth it, and it is easier for Him. His is the Sublime Similitude in the heavens and the earth. He is the Mighty, the Wise.	And He it is Who originates the creation, then reproduces it, and it is easy to Him; and His are the most exalted attributes in the heavens and the earth, and He is the Mighty, the Wise.

30 028	He does propound to you a similitude from your own (experience): do ye have partners among those whom your right hands possess, to share as equals in the wealth We have bestowed on you? Do ye fear them as ye fear each other? Thus do we explain the Signs in detail to a people that understand.	He coineth for you a similitude of yourselves. Have ye, from among those whom your right hands possess, partners in the wealth We have bestowed upon you, equal with you in respect thereof, so that ye fear them as ye fear each other (that ye ascribe unto Us partners out of that which We created)? Thus We display the revelations for people who have sense.	He sets forth to you a parable relating to yourselves: Have you among those whom your right hands possess partners in what We have given you for sustenance, so that with respect to it you are alike; you fear them as you fear each other? Thus do We make the communications distinct for a people who understand.
30 029	Nay, the wrong-doers (merely) follow their own lusts, being devoid of knowledge. But who will guide those whom Allah leaves astray? To them there will be no helpers.	Nay, but those who do wrong follow their own lusts without knowledge. Who is able to guide him whom Allah hath sent astray? For such there are no helpers.	Nay! those who are unjust follow their low desires without any knowledge; so who can guide him whom Allah makes err? And they shall have no helpers.
30 030	So set thou thy face steadily and truly to the Faith: (establish) Allah's handiwork according to the pattern on which He has made mankind: no change (let there be) in the work (wrought) by Allah: that is the standard Religion: but most among mankind understand not.	So set thy purpose (O Muhammad) for religion as a man by nature upright - the nature (framed) of Allah, in which He hath created man. There is no altering (the laws of) Allah's creation. That is the right religion, but most men know not -	Then set your face upright for religion in the right state-- the nature made by Allah in which He has made men; there is no altering of Allah's creation; that is the right religion, but most people do not know--
30 031	Turn ye back in repentance to Him, and fear Him: establish regular prayers, and be not ye among those who join gods with Allah,-	Turning unto Him (only); and be careful of your duty unto Him and establish worship, and be not of those who ascribe partners (unto Him);	Turning to Him, and be careful of (your duty to) Him and keep up prayer and be not of the polytheists,
30 032	Those who split up their Religion, and become (mere) Sects,- each party rejoicing in that which is with itself!	Of those who split up their religion and became schismatics, each sect exulting in its tenets.	Of those who divided their religion and became sects, every sect rejoicing in what they had with them.
30 033	When trouble touches men, they cry to their Lord, turning back to Him in repentance: but when He gives them a taste of Mercy as from Himself, behold, some of them pay part-worship to other god's besides their Lord,-	And when harm toucheth men they cry unto their Lord, turning to Him in repentance; then, when they have tasted of His mercy, behold! some of them attribute partners to their Lord.	And when harm afflicts men, they call upon their Lord, turning to Him, then when He makes them taste of mercy from Him, lo! some of them begin to associate (others) with their Lord,
30 034	(As if) to show their ingratitude for the (favours) We have bestowed on them! Then enjoy (your brief day); but soon will ye know (your folly).	So as to disbelieve in that which We have given them. (Unto such it is said): Enjoy yourselves awhile, but ye will come to know.	So as to be ungrateful for what We have given them; but enjoy yourselves (for a while), for you shall soon come to know.
30 035	Or have We sent down authority to them, which points out to them the things to which they pay part-worship?	Or have We revealed unto them any warrant which speaketh of that which they associate with Him?	Or, have We sent down upon them an authority so that it speaks of that which they associate with Him?
30 036	When We give men a taste of Mercy, they exult thereat: and when some evil afflicts them because of what their (own) hands have sent forth, behold, they are in despair!	And when We cause mankind to taste of mercy they rejoice therein; but if an evil thing befall them as the consequence of their own deeds, lo! they are in despair!	And when We make people taste of mercy they rejoice in it, and if an evil befall them for what their hands have already wrought, lo! they are in despair.

30 037	See they not that Allah enlarges the provision and restricts it, to whomsoever He pleases? Verily in that are Signs for those who believe.	See they not that Allah enlargeth the provision for whom He will, and straiteneth (it for whom He will). Lo! herein indeed are portents for folk who believe.	Do they not see that Allah makes ample provision for whom He pleases, or straitens? Most surely there are signs in this for a people who believe.
30 038	So give what is due to kindred, the needy, and the wayfarer. That is best for those who seek the Countenance, of Allah, and it is they who will prosper.	So give to the kinsman his due, and to the needy, and to the wayfarer. That is best for those who seek Allah's Countenance. And such are they who are successful.	Then give to the near of kin his due, and to the needy and the wayfarer; this is best for those who desire Allah's pleasure, and these it is who are successful.
30 039	That which ye lay out for increase through the property of (other) people, will have no increase with Allah: but that which ye lay out for charity, seeking the Countenance of Allah, (will increase): it is these who will get a recompense multiplied.	That which ye give in usury in order that it may increase on (other) people's property hath no increase with Allah; but that which ye give in charity, seeking Allah's Countenance, hath increase manifold.	And whatever you lay out as usury, so that it may increase in the property of men, it shall not increase with Allah; and whatever you give in charity, desiring Allah's pleasure-- it is these (persons) that shall get manifold.
30 040	It is Allah Who has created you: further, He has provided for your sustenance; then He will cause you to die; and again He will give you life. Are there any of your (false) "Partners" who can do any single one of these things? Glory to Him! and high is He above the partners they attribute (to him)!	Allah is He Who created you and then sustained you, then causeth you to die, then giveth life to you again. Is there any of your (so-called) partners (of Allah) that doeth aught of that? Praised and Exalted be He above what they associate (with Him)!	Allah is He Who created you, then gave you sustenance, then He causes you to die, then brings you to life. Is there any of your associate-gods who does aught of it? Glory be to Him, and exalted be He above what they associate (with Him).
30 041	Mischief has appeared on land and sea because of (the meed) that the hands of men have earned, that (Allah) may give them a taste of some of their deeds: in order that they may turn back (from Evil).	Corruption doth appear on land and sea because of (the evil) which men's hands have done, that He may make them taste a part of that which they have done, in order that they may return.	Corruption has appeared in the land and the sea on account of what the hands of men have wrought, that He may make them taste a part of that which they have done, so that they may return.
30 042	Say: "Travel through the earth and see what was the end of those before (you): Most of them worshipped others besides Allah."	Say (O Muhammad, to the disbelievers): Travel in the land, and see the nature of the consequence for those who were before you! Most of them were idolaters.	Say: Travel in the land, then see how was the end of those before; most of them were polytheists.
30 043	But set thou thy face to the right Religion before there come from Allah the Day which there is no chance of averting: on that Day shall men be divided (in two).	So set thy purpose resolutely for the right religion, before the inevitable day cometh from Allah. On that day mankind will be sundered-	Then turn thy face straight to the right religion before there come from Allah the day which cannot be averted; on that day they shall become separated.
30 044	Those who reject Faith will suffer from that rejection: and those who work righteousness will spread their couch (of repose) for themselves (in heaven):	Whoso disbelieveth must (then) bear the consequences of his disbelief, while those who do right make provision for themselves -	Whoever disbelieves, he shall be responsible for his disbelief, and whoever does good, they prepare (good) for their own souls,
30 045	That He may reward those who believe and work righteous deeds, out of his Bounty. For He loves not those who reject Faith.	That He may reward out of His bounty those who believe and do good works. Lo! He loveth not the disbelievers (in His guidance).	That He may reward those who believe and do good out of His grace; surely He does not love the unbelievers.

30 046	Among His Signs is this, that He sends the Winds, as heralds of Glad Tidings, giving you a taste of His (Grace and) Mercy,- that the ships may sail (majestically) by His Command and that ye may seek of His Bounty: in order that ye may be grateful.	And of His signs is this: He sendeth herald winds to make you taste His mercy, and that the ships may sail at His command, and that ye may seek his favour, and that haply ye may be thankful.	And one of His signs is that He sends forth the winds bearing good news, and that He may make your taste of His mercy, and that the ships may run by His command, and that you may seek of His grace, and that you may be grateful.
30 047	We did indeed send, before thee, messengers to their (respective) peoples, and they came to them with Clear Signs: then, to those who transgressed, We meted out Retribution: and it was due from Us to aid those who believed.	Verily We sent before thee (Muhammad) messengers to their own folk. Then we took vengeance upon those who were guilty (in regard to them). To help believers is ever incumbent upon Us.	And certainly We sent before you messengers to their people, so they came to them with clear arguments, then We gave the punishment to those who were guilty; and helping the believers is ever incumbent on Us.
30 048	It is Allah Who sends the Winds, and they raise the Clouds: then does He spread them in the sky as He wills, and break them into fragments, until thou seest raindrops issue from the midst thereof: then when He has made them reach such of his servants as He wills behold, they do rejoice!-	Allah is He Who sendeth the winds so that they raise clouds, and spreadeth them along the sky as pleaseth Him, and causeth them to break and thou seest the rain downpouring from within them. And when He maketh it to fall on whom He will of His bondmen, lo! they rejoice;	Allah is he Who sends forth the winds so they raise a cloud, then He spreads it forth in the sky as He pleases, and He breaks it up so that you see the rain coming forth from inside it; then when He causes it to fall upon whom He pleases of His servants, lo! they are joyful,
30 049	Even though, before they received (the rain) - just before this - they were dumb with despair!	Though before that, even before it was sent down upon them, they were in despair.	Though they were before this, before it was sent down upon them, confounded in sure despair.
30 050	Then contemplate (O man!) the memorials of Allah's Mercy!- how He gives life to the earth after its death: verily the same will give life to the men who are dead: for He has power over all things.	Look, therefore, at the prints of Allah's mercy (in creation): how He quickeneth the earth after her death. Lo! He verily is the Quickener of the Dead, and He is Able to do all things.	Look then at the signs of Allah's mercy, how He gives life to the earth after its death, most surely He will raise the dead to life; and He has power over all things.
30 051	And if We (but) send a Wind from which they see (their tilth) turn yellow,- behold, they become, thereafter, Ungrateful (Unbelievers)!	And if We sent a wind and they beheld it yellow, they verily would still continue in their disbelief.	And if We send a wind and they see it to be yellow, they would after that certainly continue to disbelieve,
30 052	So verily thou canst not make the dead to hear, nor canst thou make the deaf to hear the call, when they show their backs and turn away.	For verily thou (Muhammad) canst not make the dead to hear, nor canst thou make the deaf to hear the call when they have turned to flee.	For surely you cannot, make the dead to hear and you cannot make the deaf to hear the call, when they turn back and flee.
30 053	Nor canst thou lead back the blind from their straying: only those wilt thou make to hear, who believe in Our signs and submit (their wills in Islam).	Nor canst thou guide the blind out of their error. Thou canst make none to hear save those who believe in Our revelations so that they surrender (unto Him).	Nor can you lead away the blind out of their error. You cannot make to hear any but those who believe in Our communications so they shall submit.
30 054	It is Allah Who created you in a state of (helpless) weakness, then gave (you) strength after weakness, then, after strength, gave (you) weakness and a hoary head: He creates as He wills, and it is He Who has all knowledge and power.	Allah is He Who shaped you out of weakness, then appointed after weakness strength, then, after strength, appointed weakness and grey hair. He createth what He will. He is the Knower, the Mighty.	Allah is He Who created you from a state of weakness then He gave strength after weakness, then ordained weakness and hoary hair after strength; He creates what He pleases, and He is the Knowing, the Powerful.

30 055	On the Day that the Hour (of Reckoning) will be established, the transgressors will swear that they tarried not but an hour: thus were they used to being deluded!	And on the day when the Hour riseth the guilty will vow that they did tarry but an hour - thus were they ever deceived.	And at the time when the hour shall come, the guilty shall swear (that) they did not tarry but an hour; thus are they ever turned away.
30 056	But those endued with knowledge and faith will say: "Indeed ye did tarry, within Allah's Decree, to the Day of Resurrection, and this is the Day of Resurrection: but ye - ye were not aware!"	But those to whom knowledge and faith are given will say: The truth is, ye have tarried, by Allah's decree, until the Day of Resurrection. This is the Day of Resurrection, but ye used not to know.	And those who are given knowledge and faith will say: Certainly you tarried according to the ordinance of Allah till the day of resurrection, so this is the day of resurrection, but you did not know.
30 057	So on that Day no excuse of theirs will avail the transgressors, nor will they be invited (then) to seek grace (by repentance).	In that day their excuses will not profit those who did injustice, nor will they be allowed to make amends.	But on that day their excuse shall not profit those who were unjust, nor shall they be regarded with goodwill.
30 058	verily We have propounded for men, in this Qur'an every kind of Parable: But if thou bring to them any Sign, the Unbelievers are sure to say, "Ye do nothing but talk vanities."	Verily We have coined for mankind in this Qur'an all kinds of similitudes; and indeed if thou camest unto them with a miracle, those who disbelieve would verily exclaim: Ye are but tricksters!	And certainly We have set forth for men every kind of example in this Quran; and if you should bring them a communication, those who disbelieve would certainly say: You are naught but false claimants.
30 059	Thus does Allah seal up the hearts of those who understand not.	Thus doth Allah seal the hearts of those who know not.	Thus does Allah set a seal on the hearts of those who do not know.
30 060	So patiently persevere: for verily the promise of Allah is true: nor let those shake thy firmness, who have (themselves) no certainty of faith.	So have patience (O Muhammad)! Allah's promise is the very truth, and let not those who have no certainty make thee impatient.	Therefore be patient; surely the promise of Allah is true and let not those who have no certainty hold you in light estimation.

Chapter 31:

LUQMAN (LUQMAN)

Total Verses: 34 Revealed At: MAKKA

In the name of Allah, the Most Beneficent, the Most Merciful.

31 001	A. L. M.	Alif. Lam. Mim.	Alif Lam Mim.
31 002	These are Verses of the Wise Book,-	These are revelations of the wise Scripture,	These are verses of the Book of Wisdom
31 003	A Guide and a Mercy to the Doers of Good,-	A guidance and a mercy for the good,	A guidance and a mercy for the doers of goodness,
31 004	Those who establish regular Prayer, and give regular Charity, and have (in their hearts) the assurance of the Hereafter.	Those who establish worship and pay the poor-due and have sure faith in the Hereafter.	Those who keep up prayer and pay the poor-rate and they are certain of the hereafter.
31 005	These are on (true) guidance from their Lord: and these are the ones who will prosper.	Such have guidance from their Lord. Such are the successful.	These are on a guidance from their Lord, and these are they who are successful:
31 006	But there are, among men, those who purchase idle tales, without knowledge (or meaning), to mislead (men) from the Path of Allah and throw ridicule (on the Path): for such there will be a Humiliating Penalty.	And of mankind is he who payeth for mere pastime of discourse, that he may mislead from Allah's way without knowledge, and maketh it the butt of mockery. For such there is a shameful doom.	And of men is he who takes instead frivolous discourse to lead astray from Allah's path without knowledge, and to take it for a mockery; these shall have an abasing chastisement.

31 007	When Our Signs are rehearsed to such a one, he turns away in arrogance, as if he heard them not, as if there were deafness in both his ears: announce to him a grievous Penalty.	And when Our revelations are recited unto him he turneth away in pride as if he heard them not, as if there were a deafness in his ears. So give him tidings of a painful doom.	And when Our communications are recited to him, he turns back proudly, as if he had not heard them, as though in his ears were a heaviness, therefore announce to him a painful chastisement.
31 008	For those who believe and work righteous deeds, there will be Gardens of Bliss,-	Lo! those who believe and do good works, for them are the gardens of delight,	(As for) those who believe and do good, they shall surely have gardens of bliss,
31 009	To dwell therein. The promise of Allah is true: and He is Exalted in Power, Wise.	Wherein they will abide. It is a promise of Allah in truth. He is the Mighty, the Wise.	Abiding in them; the promise of Allah; (a) true (promise), and He is the Mighty, the Wise.
31 010	He created the heavens without any pillars that ye can see; He set on the earth mountains standing firm, lest it should shake with you; and He scattered through it beasts of all kinds. We send down rain from the sky, and produce on the earth every kind of noble creature, in pairs.	He hath created the heavens without supports that ye can see, and hath cast into the earth firm hills, so that it quake not with you; and He hath dispersed therein all kinds of beasts. And We send down water from the sky and We cause (plants) of every goodly kind to grow therein.	He created the heavens without pillars as you see them, and put mountains upon the earth lest it might convulse with you, and He spread in it animals of every kind; and We sent down water from the cloud, then caused to grow therein (vegetation) of every noble kind.
31 011	Such is the Creation of Allah: now show Me what is there that others besides Him have created: nay, but the Transgressors are in manifest error.	This is the Creation of Allah. Now show me that which those (ye worship) beside Him have created. Nay, but the wrong-doers are in error manifest!	This is Allah's creation, but show Me what those besides Him have created. Nay, the unjust are in manifest error.
31 012	We bestowed (in the past) Wisdom on Luqman: "Show (thy) gratitude to Allah." Any who is (so) grateful does so to the profit of his own soul: but if any is ungrateful, verily Allah is free of all wants, Worthy of all praise.	And verily We gave Luqman wisdom, saying: Give thanks unto Allah; and whosoever giveth thanks, he giveth thanks for (the good of) his soul. And whosoever refuseth - Lo! Allah is Absolute, Owner of Praise.	And certainly We gave wisdom to Luqman, saying: Be grateful to Allah. And whoever is grateful, he is only grateful for his own soul; and whoever is ungrateful, then surely Allah is Self-sufficient, Praised.
31 013	Behold, Luqman said to his son by way of instruction: "O my son! join not in worship (others) with Allah: for false worship is indeed the highest wrong-doing."	And (remember) when Luqman said unto his son, when he was exhorting him: O my dear son! Ascribe no partners unto Allah. Lo! to ascribe partners (unto Him) is a tremendous wrong -	And when Luqman said to his son while he admonished him: O my son! do not associate aught with Allah; most surely polytheism is a grievous iniquity-
31 014	And We have enjoined on man (to be good) to his parents: in travail upon travail did his mother bear him, and in years twain was his weaning: (hear the command), "Show gratitude to Me and to thy parents: to Me is (thy final) Goal."	And We have enjoined upon man concerning his partners - His mother beareth him in weakness upon weakness, and his weaning is in two years - give thanks unto Me and unto thy parents. unto Me is the journeying.	And We have enjoined man in respect of his parents-- his mother bears him with faintings upon faintings and his weaning takes two years-- saying: Be grateful to Me and to both your parents; to Me is the eventual coming.
31 015	"But if they strive to make thee join in worship with Me things of which thou hast no knowledge, obey them not; yet bear them company in this life with justice (and consideration), and follow the way of those who turn to me (in love): in the end the return of you all is to Me, and I will tell you the truth (and meaning) of all that ye did."	But if they strive with thee to make thee ascribe unto Me as partner that of which thou hast no knowledge, then obey them not. Consort with them in the world kindly, and follow the path of him who repenteth unto Me. Then unto Me will be your return, and I shall tell you what ye used to do -	And if they contend with you that you should associate with Me what you have no knowledge of, do not obey them, and keep company with them in this world kindly, and follow the way of him who turns to Me, then to Me is your return, then will I inform you of what you did--

31 016	"O my son!" (said Luqman), "If there be (but) the weight of a mustard-seed and it were (hidden) in a rock, or (anywhere) in the heavens or on earth, Allah will bring it forth: for Allah understands the finest mysteries, (and) is well-acquainted (with them)."	O my dear son! Lo! though it be but the weight of a grain of mustard-seed, and though it be in a rock, or in the heavens, or in the earth, Allah will bring it forth. Lo! Allah is Subtile, Aware.	O my son! surely if it is the very weight of the grain of a mustard-seed, even though it is in (the heart of) rock, or (high above) in the heaven or (deep down) in the earth, Allah will bring it (to light); surely Allah is Knower of subtleties, Aware;
31 017	"O my son! establish regular prayer, enjoin what is just, and forbid what is wrong. and bear with patient constancy whatever betide thee; for this is firmness (of purpose) in (the conduct of) affairs."	O my dear son! Establish worship and enjoin kindness and forbid iniquity, and persevere whatever may befall thee. Lo! that is of the steadfast heart of things.	O my son! keep up prayer and enjoin the good and forbid the evil, and bear patiently that which befalls you; surely these acts require courage;
31 018	"And swell not thy cheek (for pride) at men, nor walk in insolence through the earth; for Allah loveth not any arrogant boaster."	Turn not thy cheek in scorn toward folk, nor walk with pertness in the land. Lo! Allah loveth not each braggart boaster.	And do not turn your face away from people in contempt, nor go about in the land exulting overmuch; surely Allah does not love any self-conceited boaster;
31 019	"And be moderate in thy pace, and lower thy voice; for the harshest of sounds without doubt is the braying of the ass."	Be modest in thy bearing and subdue thy voice. Lo! the harshest of all voices is the voice of the ass.	And pursue the right course in your going about and lower your voice; surely the most hateful of voices is braying of the asses.
31 020	Do ye not see that Allah has subjected to your (use) all things in the heavens and on earth, and has made his bounties flow to you in exceeding measure, (both) seen and unseen? Yet there are among men those who dispute about Allah, without knowledge and without guidance, and without a Book to enlighten them!	See ye not how Allah hath made serviceable unto you whatsoever is in the skies and whatsoever is in the earth and hath loaded you with His favours both without and within? Yet of mankind is he who disputeth concerning Allah, without knowledge or guidance or a scripture giving light.	Do you not see that Allah has made what is in the heavens and what is in the earth subservient to you, and made complete to you His favors outwardly and inwardly? And among men is he who disputes in respect of Allah though having no knowledge nor guidance, nor a book giving light.
31 021	When they are told to follow the (Revelation) that Allah has sent down, they say: "Nay, we shall follow the ways that we found our fathers (following)." What! even if it is Satan beckoning them to the Penalty of the (Blazing) Fire?	And if it be said unto them: Follow that which Allah hath revealed, they say: Nay, but we follow that wherein we found our fathers. What! Even though the devil were inviting them unto the doom of flame?	And when it is said to them: Follow what Allah has revealed, they say: Nay, we follow that on which we found our fathers. What! though the Shaitan calls them to the chastisement of the burning fire!
31 022	Whoever submits his whole self to Allah, and is a doer of good, has grasped indeed the most trustworthy hand-hold: and with Allah rests the End and Decision of (all) affairs.	Whosoever surrendereth his purpose to Allah while doing good, he verily hath grasped the firm handhold. Unto Allah belongeth the sequel of all things.	And whoever submits himself wholly to Allah and he is the doer of good (to others), he indeed has taken hold of the firmest thing upon which one can lay hold; and Allah's is the end of affairs.
31 023	But if any reject Faith, let not his rejection grieve thee: to Us is their return, and We shall tell them the truth of their deeds: for Allah knows well all that is in (men's) hearts.	And whosoever disbelieveth, let not his disbelief afflict thee (O Muhammad). Unto Us is their return, and We shall tell them what they did. Lo! Allah is Aware of what is in the breasts (of men).	And whoever disbelieves, let not his disbelief grieve you; to Us is their return, then will We inform them of what they did surely Allah is the Knower of what is in the breasts.
31 024	We grant them their pleasure for a little while: in the end shall We drive them to a chastisement unrelenting.	We give them comfort for a little, and then We drive them to a heavy doom.	We give them to enjoy a little, then will We drive them to a severe chastisement.

31 025	If thou ask them, who it is that created the heavens and the earth. They will certainly say, "Allah". Say: "Praise be to Allah!" But most of them understand not.	If thou shouldst ask them: Who created the heavens and the earth? they would answer: Allah. Say: Praise be to Allah! But most of them know not.	And if you ask them who created the heavens and the earth, they will certainly say: Allah. Say: (All) praise is due to Allah; nay! most of them do not know.
31 026	To Allah belong all things in heaven and earth: verily Allah is He (that is) free of all wants, worthy of all praise.	Unto Allah belongeth whatsoever is in the heavens and the earth. Lo! Allah, He is the Absolute, the Owner of Praise.	What is in the heavens and the earth is Allah's; surely Allah is the Self-sufficient, the Praised.
31 027	And if all the trees on earth were pens and the ocean (were ink), with seven oceans behind it to add to its (supply), yet would not the words of Allah be exhausted (in the writing): for Allah is Exalted in Power, full of Wisdom.	And if all the trees in the earth were pens, and the sea, with seven more seas to help it, (were ink), the words of Allah could not be exhausted. Lo! Allah is Mighty, Wise.	And were every tree that is in the earth (made into) pens and the sea (to supply it with ink), with seven more seas to increase it, the words of Allah would not come to an end; surely Allah is Mighty, Wise.
31 028	And your creation or your resurrection is in no wise but as an individual soul: for Allah is He Who hears and sees (all things).	Your creation and your raising (from the dead) are only as (the creation and the raising of) a single soul. Lo! Allah is Hearer, Knower.	Neither your creation nor your raising is anything but as a single soul; surely Allah is Hearing, Seeing.
31 029	Seest thou not that Allah merges Night into Day and he merges Day into Night; that He has subjected the sun, and the moon (to his Law), each running its course for a term appointed; and that Allah is well-acquainted with all that ye do?	Hast thou not seen how Allah causeth the night to pass into the day and causeth the day to pass into the night, and hath subdued the sun and the moon (to do their work), each running unto an appointed term; and that Allah is Informed of what ye do?	Do you not see that Allah makes the night to enter into the day, and He makes the day to enter into the night, and He has made the sun and the moon subservient (to you); each pursues its course till an appointed time; and that Allah is Aware of what you do?
31 030	That is because Allah is the (only) Reality, and because whatever else they invoke besides Him is Falsehood; and because Allah,- He is the Most High, Most Great.	That (is so) because Allah, He is the True, and that which they invoke beside Him is the False, and because Allah, He is the Sublime, the Great.	This is because Allah is the Truth, and that which they call upon besides Him is the falsehood, and that Allah is the High, the Great.
31 031	Seest thou not that the ships sail through the ocean by the Grace of Allah?- that He may show you of His Signs? Verily in this are Signs for all who constantly persevere and give thanks.	Hast thou not seen how the ships glide on the sea by Allah's grace, that He may show you of His wonders? Lo! therein indeed are portents for every steadfast, grateful (heart).	Do you not see that the ships run on in the sea by Allah's favor that He may show you of His signs? Most surely there are signs in this for every patient endurer, grateful one.
31 032	When a wave covers them like the canopy (of clouds), they call to Allah, offering Him sincere devotion. But when He has delivered them safely to land, there are among them those that halt between (right and wrong). But none reject Our Signs except only a perfidious ungrateful (wretch)!	And if a wave enshroudeth them like awnings, they cry unto Allah, making their faith pure for Him only. But when He bringeth them safe to land, some of them compromise. None denieth Our signs save every traitor ingrate.	And when a wave like mountains covers them they call upon Allah, being sincere to Him in obedience, but when He brings them safe to the land, some of them follow the middle course; and none denies Our signs but every perfidious, ungrateful one.
31 033	O mankind! do your duty to your Lord, and fear (the coming of) a Day when no father can avail aught for his son, nor a son avail aught for his father. Verily, the promise of Allah is true: let not then this present life deceive you, nor let the chief Deceiver deceive you about Allah.	O mankind! Keep your duty to your Lord and fear a Day when the parent will not be able to avail the child in aught, nor the child to avail the parent. Lo! Allah's promise is the very truth. Let not the life of the world beguile you, nor let the deceiver beguile you, in regard to Allah.	O people! guard against (the punishment of) your Lord and dread the day when a father shall not make any satisfaction for his son, nor shall the child be the maker of any satisfaction for his father; surely the promise of Allah is true, therefore let not this world's life deceive you, nor let the arch-deceiver deceive you in respect of Allah.

31 034	Verily the knowledge of the Hour is with Allah (alone). It is He Who sends down rain, and He Who knows what is in the wombs. Nor does any one know what it is that he will earn on the morrow: Nor does any one know in what land he is to die. Verily with Allah is full knowledge and He is acquainted (with all things).	Lo! Allah! With Him is knowledge of the Hour. He sendeth down the rain, and knoweth that which is in the wombs. No soul knoweth what it will earn to-morrow, and no soul knoweth in what land it will die. Lo! Allah is Knower, Aware.		Surely Allah is He with Whom is the knowledge of the hour, and He sends down the rain and He knows what is in the wombs; and no one knows what he shall earn on the morrow; and no one knows in what land he shall die; surely Allah is Knowing, Aware.

Chapter 32:

AS-SAJDA (THE PROSTRATION, WORSHIP, ADORATION)

Total Verses: 30 Revealed At: MAKKA

In the name of Allah, the Most Beneficent, the Most Merciful.

32 001	A. L. M.	Alif. Lam. Mim	Alif Lam Mim.
32 002	(This is) the Revelation of the Book in which there is no doubt,- from the Lord of the Worlds.	The revelation of the Scripture whereof there is no doubt is from the Lord of the Worlds.	The revelation of the Book, there is no doubt in it, is from the Lord of the worlds.
32 003	Or do they say, "He has forged it"? Nay, it is the Truth from thy Lord, that thou mayest admonish a people to whom no warner has come before thee: in order that they may receive guidance.	Or say they: He hath invented it? Nay, but it is the Truth from thy Lord, that thou mayst warn a folk to whom no warner came before thee, that haply they may walk aright.	Or do they say: He has forged it? Nay! it is the truth from your Lord that you may warn a people to whom no warner has come before you, that they may follow the right direction.
32 004	It is Allah Who has created the heavens and the earth, and all between them, in six Days, and is firmly established on the Throne (of Authority): ye have none, besides Him, to protect or intercede (for you): will ye not then receive admonition?	Allah it is Who created the heavens and the earth, and that which is between them, in six Days. Then He mounted the Throne. Ye have not, beside Him, a protecting friend or mediator. Will ye not then remember?	Allah is He Who created the heavens and the earth and what is between them in six periods, and He mounted the throne (of authority); you have not besides Him any guardian or any intercessor, will you not then mind?
32 005	He rules (all) affairs from the heavens to the earth: in the end will (all affairs) go up to Him, on a Day, the space whereof will be (as) a thousand years of your reckoning.	He directeth the ordinance from the heaven unto the earth; then it ascendeth unto Him in a Day, whereof the measure is a thousand years of that ye reckon.	He regulates the affair from the heaven to the earth; then shall it ascend to Him in a day the measure of which is a thousand years of what you count.
32 006	Such is He, the Knower of all things, hidden and open, the Exalted (in power), the Merciful;-	Such is the Knower of the Invisible and the Visible, the Mighty, the Merciful,	This is the Knower of the unseen and the seen, the Mighty the Merciful,
32 007	He Who has made everything which He has created most good: He began the creation of man with (nothing more than) clay,	Who made all things good which He created, and He began the creation of man from clay;	Who made good everything that He has created, and He began the creation of man from dust.
32 008	And made his progeny from a quintessence of the nature of a fluid despised:	Then He made his seed from a draught of despised fluid;	Then He made his progeny of an extract, of water held in light estimation.

32 009	But He fashioned him in due proportion, and breathed into him something of His spirit. And He gave you (the faculties of) hearing and sight and feeling (and understanding): little thanks do ye give!	Then He fashioned him and breathed into him of His Spirit; and appointed for you hearing and sight and hearts. Small thanks give ye!	Then He made him complete and breathed into him of His spirit, and made for you the ears and the eyes and the hearts; little is it that you give thanks.
32 010	And they say: "What! when we lie, hidden and lost, in the earth, shall we indeed be in a Creation renewed? Nay, they deny the Meeting with their Lord."	And they say: When we are lost in the earth, how can we then be re-created? Nay but they are disbelievers in the meeting with their Lord.	And they say: What! when we have become lost in the earth, shall we then certainly be in a new creation? Nay! they are disbelievers in the meeting of their Lord.
32 011	Say: "The Angel of Death, put in charge of you, will (duly) take your souls: then shall ye be brought back to your Lord."	Say: The angel of death, who hath charge concerning you, will gather you, and afterward unto your Lord ye will be returned.	Say: The angel of death who is given charge of you shall cause you to die, then to your Lord you shall be brought back.
32 012	If only thou couldst see when the guilty ones will bend low their heads before their Lord, (saying:) "Our Lord! We have seen and we have heard: Now then send us back (to the world): we will work righteousness: for we do indeed (now) believe."	Couldst thou but see when the guilty hang their heads before their Lord, (and say): Our Lord! We have now seen and heard, so send us back; we will do right, now we are sure.	And could you but see when the guilty shall hang down their heads before their Lord: Our Lord! we have seen and we have heard, therefore send us back, we will do good; surely (now) we are certain.
32 013	If We had so willed, We could certainly have brought every soul its true guidance: but the Word from Me will come true, "I will fill Hell with jinns and men all together."	And if We had so willed, We could have given every soul its guidance, but the word from Me concerning evildoers took effect: that I will fill hell with the jinn and mankind together.	And if We had pleased We would certainly have given to every soul its guidance, but the word (which had gone forth) from Me was just: I will certainly fill hell with the jinn and men together.
32 014	"Taste ye then - for ye forgot the Meeting of this Day of yours, and We too will forget you - taste ye the Penalty of Eternity for your (evil) deeds!"	So taste (the evil of your deeds). Forasmuch as ye forgot the meeting of this your day, lo! We forget you. Taste the doom of immortality because of what ye used to do.	So taste, because you neglected the meeting of this day of yours; surely We forsake you; and taste the abiding chastisement for what you did.
32 015	Only those believe in Our Signs, who, when they are recited to them, fall down in prostration, and celebrate the praises of their Lord, nor are they (ever) puffed up with pride.	Only those believe in Our revelations who, when they are reminded of them, fall down prostrate and hymn the praise of their Lord, and they are not scornful,	Only they believe in Our communications who, when they are reminded of them, fall down in prostration and celebrate the praise of their Lord, and they are not proud.
32 016	Their limbs do forsake their beds of sleep, the while they call on their Lord, in Fear and Hope: and they spend (in charity) out of the sustenance which We have bestowed on them.	Who forsake their beds to cry unto their Lord in fear and hope, and spend of that We have bestowed on them.	Their sides draw away from (their) beds, they call upon their Lord in fear and in hope, and they spend (benevolently) out of what We have given them.
32 017	Now no person knows what delights of the eye are kept hidden (in reserve) for them - as a reward for their (good) deeds.	No soul knoweth what is kept hid for them of joy, as a reward for what they used to do.	So no soul knows what is hidden for them of that which will refresh the eyes; a reward for what they did.
32 018	Is then the man who believes no better than the man who is rebellious and wicked? Not equal are they.	Is he who is a believer like unto him who is an evil-liver? They are not alike.	Is he then who is a believer like him who is a transgressor? They are not equal.
32 019	For those who believe and do righteous deeds are Gardens as hospitable homes, for their (good) deeds.	But as for those who believe and do good works, for them are the Gardens of Retreat - a welcome (in reward) for what they used to do.	As for those who believe and do good, the gardens are their abiding-place; an entertainment for what they did.

32 020	As to those who are rebellious and wicked, their abode will be the Fire: every time they wish to get away therefrom, they will be forced thereinto, and it will be said to them: "Taste ye the Penalty of the Fire, the which ye were wont to reject as false."	And as for those who do evil, their retreat is the Fire. Whenever they desire to issue forth from thence, they are brought back thither. Unto them it is said: Taste the torment of the Fire which ye used to deny.		And as for those who transgress, their abode is the fire; whenever they desire to go forth from it they shall be brought back into it, and it will be said to them: Taste the chastisement of the fire which you called a lie.
32 021	And indeed We will make them taste of the Penalty of this (life) prior to the supreme Penalty, in order that they may (repent and) return.	And verily We make them taste the lower punishment before the greater, that haply they may return.		And most certainly We will make them taste of the nearer chastisement before the greater chastisement that haply they may turn.
32 022	And who does more wrong than one to whom are recited the Signs of his Lord, and who then turns away therefrom? Verily from those who transgress We shall exact (due) Retribution.	And who doth greater wrong than he who is reminded of the revelations of his Lord, then turneth from them. Lo! We shall requite the guilty.		And who is more unjust than he who is reminded of the communications of his Lord, then he turns away from them? Surely We will give punishment to the guilty.
32 023	We did indeed aforetime give the Book to Moses: be not then in doubt of its reaching (thee): and We made it a guide to the Children of Israel.	We verily gave Moses the Scripture; so be not ye in doubt of his receiving it; and We appointed it a guidance for the Children of Israel.		And certainly We gave the Book to Musa, so be not in doubt concerning the receiving of it, and We made it a guide for the children of Israel.
32 024	And We appointed, from among them, leaders, giving guidance under Our command, so long as they persevered with patience and continued to have faith in Our Signs.	And when they became steadfast and believed firmly in Our revelations, We appointed from among them leaders who guided by Our command.		And We made of them Imams to guide by Our command when they were patient, and they were certain of Our communications.
32 025	Verily thy Lord will judge between them on the Day of Judgment, in the matters wherein they differ (among themselves)	Lo! thy Lord will judge between them on the Day of Resurrection concerning that wherein they used to differ.		Surely your Lord will judge between them on the day of resurrection concerning that wherein they differ.
32 026	Does it not teach them a lesson, how many generations We destroyed before them, in whose dwellings they (now) go to and fro? Verily in that are Signs: Do they not then listen?	Is it not a guidance for them (to observe) how many generations We destroyed before them, amid whose dwelling places they do walk? Lo! therein verily are portents! Will they not then heed?		Does it not point out to them the right way, how many of the generations, in whose abodes they go about, did We destroy before them? Most surely there are signs in this; will they not then hear?
32 027	And do they not see that We do drive rain to parched soil (bare of herbage), and produce therewith crops, providing food for their cattle and themselves? Have they not the vision?	Have they not seen how We lead the water to the barren land and therewith bring forth crops whereof their cattle eat, and they themselves? Will they not then see?		Do they not see that We drive the water to a land having no herbage, then We bring forth thereby seed-produce of which their cattle and they themselves eat; will they not then see?
32 028	They say: "When will this decision be, if ye are telling the truth?"	And they say: When cometh this victory (of yours) if ye are truthful?		And they say: When will this judgment take place, if you are truthful?
32 029	Say: "On the Day of Decision, no profit will it be to Unbelievers if they (then) believe! nor will they be granted a respite."	Say (unto them): On the day of the victory the faith of those who disbelieve (and who then will believe) will not avail them, neither will they be reprieved.		Say: On the Day of Judgment the faith of those who (now) disbelieve will not profit them, nor will they be respited.
32 030	So turn away from them, and wait: they too are waiting.	So withdraw from them (O Muhammad), and await (the event). Lo! they (also) are awaiting (it).		Therefore turn away from them and wait, surely they too are waiting.

Chapter 33:

AL-AHZAB (THE CLANS, THE COALITION, THE COMBINED FORCES)

Total Verses: 73 Revealed At: MADINA

In the name of Allah, the Most Beneficent, the Most Merciful.

33 001	O Prophet! Fear Allah, and hearken not to the Unbelievers and the Hypocrites: verily Allah is full of Knowledge and Wisdom.	O Prophet! Keep thy duty to Allah and obey not the disbelievers and the hypocrites. Lo! Allah is Knower, Wise.	O Prophet! be careful of (your duty to) Allah and do not comply with (the wishes of) the unbelievers and the hypocrites; surely Allah is Knowing, Wise;
33 002	But follow that which comes to thee by inspiration from thy Lord: for Allah is well acquainted with (all) that ye do.	And follow that which is inspired in thee from thy Lord. Lo! Allah is Aware of what ye do.	And follow what is revealed to you from your Lord; surely Allah is Aware of what you do;
33 003	And put thy trust in Allah, and enough is Allah as a disposer of affairs.	And put thy trust in Allah, for Allah is sufficient as Trustee.	And rely on Allah; and Allah is sufficient for a Protector.
33 004	Allah has not made for any man two hearts in his (one) body: nor has He made your wives whom ye divorce by Zihar your mothers: nor has He made your adopted sons your sons. Such is (only) your (manner of) speech by your mouths. But Allah tells (you) the Truth, and He shows the (right) Way.	Allah hath not assigned unto any man two hearts within his body, nor hath He made your wives whom ye declare (to be your mothers) your mothers, nor hath He made those whom ye claim (to be your sons) your sons. This is but a saying of your mouths. But Allah saith the truth and He showeth the way.	Allah has not made for any man two hearts within him; nor has He made your wives whose backs you liken to the backs of your mothers as your mothers, nor has He made those whom you assert to be your sons your real sons; these are the words of your mouths; and Allah speaks the truth and He guides to the way.
33 005	Call them by (the names of) their fathers: that is juster in the sight of Allah. But if ye know not their father's (names, call them) your Brothers in faith, or your maulas. But there is no blame on you if ye make a mistake therein: (what counts is) the intention of your hearts: and Allah is Oft-Returning, Most Merciful.	Proclaim their real parentage. That will be more equitable in the sight of Allah. And if ye know not their fathers, then (they are) your brethren in the faith, and your clients. And there is no sin for you in the mistakes that ye make unintentionally, but what your hearts purpose (that will be a sin for you). Allah is ever Forgiving, Merciful.	Assert their relationship to their fathers; this is more equitable with Allah; but if you do not know their fathers, then they are your brethren in faith and your friends; and there is no blame on you concerning that in which you made a mistake, but (concerning) that which your hearts do purposely (blame may rest on you), and Allah is Forgiving, Merciful.
33 006	The Prophet is closer to the Believers than their own selves, and his wives are their mothers. Blood-relations among each other have closer personal ties, in the Decree of Allah. Than (the Brotherhood of) Believers and Muhajirs: nevertheless do ye what is just to your closest friends: such is the writing in the Decree (of Allah).	The Prophet is closer to the believers than their selves, and his wives are (as) their mothers. And the owners of kinship are closer one to another in the ordinance of Allah than (other) believers and the fugitives (who fled from Mecca), except that ye should do kindness to your friends. This is written in the Book (of nature).	The Prophet has a greater claim on the faithful than they have on themselves, and his wives are (as) their mothers; and the possessors of relationship have the better claim in the ordinance of Allah to inheritance, one with respect to another, than (other) believers, and (than) those who have fled (their homes), except that you do some good to your friends; this is written in the Book.

33 007	And remember We took from the prophets their covenant: As (We did) from thee: from Noah, Abraham, Moses, and Jesus the son of Mary: We took from them a solemn covenant:	And when We exacted a covenant from the prophets, and from thee (O Muhammad) and from Noah and Abraham and Moses and Jesus son of Mary. We took from them a solemn covenant;	And when We made a covenant with the prophets and with you, and with Nuh and Ibrahim and Musa and Isa, son of Marium, and We made with them a strong covenant,	
33 008	That (Allah) may question the (custodians) of Truth concerning the Truth they (were charged with): And He has prepared for the Unbelievers a grievous Penalty.	That He may ask the loyal of their loyalty. And He hath prepared a painful doom for the unfaithful.	That He may question the truthful of their truth, and He has prepared for the unbelievers a painful punishment.	
33 009	O ye who believe! Remember the Grace of Allah, (bestowed) on you, when there came down on you hosts (to overwhelm you): But We sent against them a hurricane and forces that ye saw not: but Allah sees (clearly) all that ye do.	O ye who believe! Remember Allah's favour unto you when there came against you hosts, and We sent against them a great wind and hosts ye could not see. And Allah is ever Seer of what ye do.	O you who believe! call to mind the favor of Allah to you when there came down upon you hosts, so We sent against them a strong wind and hosts, that you saw not, and Allah is Seeing what you do.	
33 010	Behold! they came on you from above you and from below you, and behold, the eyes became dim and the hearts gaped up to the throats, and ye imagined various (vain) thoughts about Allah!	When they came upon you from above you and from below you, and when eyes grew wild and hearts reached to the throats, and ye were imagining vain thoughts concerning Allah.	When they came upon you from above you and from below you, and when the eyes turned dull, and the hearts rose up to the throats, and you began to think diverse thoughts of Allah.	
33 011	In that situation were the Believers tried: they were shaken as by a tremendous shaking.	There were the believers sorely tried, and shaken with a mighty shock.	There the believers were tried and they were shaken with severe shaking.	
33 012	And behold! The Hypocrites and those in whose hearts is a disease (even) say: "Allah and His Messenger promised us nothing but delusion!"	And when the hypocrites, and those in whose hearts is a disease, were saying: Allah and His messenger promised us naught but delusion.	And when the hypocrites and those in whose hearts was a disease began to say: Allah and His Messenger did not promise us (victory) but only to deceive.	
33 013	Behold! A party among them said: "Ye men of Yathrib! ye cannot stand (the attack)! therefore go back!" And a band of them ask for leave of the Prophet, saying, "Truly our houses are bare and exposed," though they were not exposed they intended nothing but to run away.	And when a party of them said: O folk of Yathrib! There is no stand (possible) for you, therefor turn back. And certain of them (even) sought permission of the Prophet, saying: Our homes lie open (to the enemy). And they lay not open. They but wished to flee.	And when a party of them said: O people of Yasrib! there IS no place to stand for you (here), therefore go back; and a party of them asked permission of the prophet, saying. Surely our houses are exposed; and they were not exposed; they only desired to fly away.	
33 014	And if an entry had been effected to them from the sides of the (city), and they had been incited to sedition, they would certainly have brought it to pass, with none but a brief delay!	If the enemy had entered from all sides and they had been exhorted to treachery, they would have committed it, and would have hesitated thereupon but little.	And if an entry were made upon them from the outlying parts of it, then they were asked to wage war, they would certainly have done it, and they would not have stayed in it but a little while.	
33 015	And yet they had already covenanted with Allah not to turn their backs, and a covenant with Allah must (surely) be answered for.	And verily they had already sworn unto Allah that they would not turn their backs (to the foe). An oath to Allah must be answered for.	And certainly they had made a covenant with Allah before, (that) they would not turn (their) backs; and Allah's covenant shall be inquired of.	
33 016	Say: "Running away will not profit you if ye are running away from death or slaughter; and even if (ye do escape), no more than a brief (respite) will ye be allowed to enjoy!"	Say: Flight will not avail you if ye flee from death or killing, and then ye dwell in comfort but a little while.	Say: Flight shall not do you any good if you fly from death or slaughter, and in that case you will not be allowed to enjoy yourselves but a little.	

33 017	Say: "Who is it that can screen you from Allah if it be His wish to give you punishment or to give you Mercy?" Nor will they find for themselves, besides Allah, any protector or helper.	Say: Who is he who can preserve you from Allah if He intendeth harm for you, or intendeth mercy for you. They will not find that they have any friend or helper other than Allah.	Say: Who is it that can withhold you from Allah if He intends to do you evil, rather He intends to show you mercy? And they will not find for themselves besides Allah any guardian or a helper.
33 018	Verily Allah knows those among you who keep back (men) and those who say to their brethren, "Come along to us", but come not to the fight except for just a little while.	Allah already knoweth those of you who hinder, and those who say unto their brethren: "Come ye hither unto us!" and they come not to the stress of battle save a little,	Allah knows indeed those among you who hinder others and those who say to their brethren: Come to us; and they come not to the fight but a little,
33 019	Covetous over you. Then when fear comes, thou wilt see them looking to thee, their eyes revolving, like (those of) one over whom hovers death: but when the fear is past, they will smite you with sharp tongues, covetous of goods. Such men have no faith, and so Allah has made their deeds of none effect: and that is easy for Allah.	Being sparing of their help to you (believers). But when the fear cometh, then thou (Muhammad) seest them regarding thee with rolling eyes like one who fainteth unto death. Then, when the fear departeth, they scald you with sharp tongues in their greed for wealth (from the spoil). Such have not believed. Therefor Allah maketh their deeds fruitless. And that is easy for Allah.	Being niggardly with respect to you; but when fear comes, you will see them looking to you, their eyes rolling like one swooning because of death; but when the fear is gone they smite you with sharp tongues, being niggardly of the good things. These have not believed, therefore Allah has made their doing naught; and this is easy to Allah.
33 020	They think that the Confederates have not withdrawn; and if the Confederates should come (again), they would wish they were in the deserts (wandering) among the Bedouins, and seeking news about you (from a safe distance); and if they were in your midst, they would fight but little.	They hold that the clans have not retired (for good); and if the clans should advance (again), they would fain be in the desert with the wandering Arabs, asking for the news of you; and if they were among you, they would not give battle, save a little.	They think the allies are not gone, and if the allies should come (again) they would fain be in the deserts with the desert Arabs asking for news about you, and if they were among you they would not fight save a little.
33 021	Ye have indeed in the Messenger of Allah a beautiful pattern (of conduct) for any one whose hope is in Allah and the Final Day, and who engages much in the Praise of Allah.	Verily in the messenger of Allah ye have a good example for him who looketh unto Allah and the Last Day, and remembereth Allah much.	Certainly you have in the Messenger of Allah an excellent exemplar for him who hopes in Allah and the latter day and remembers Allah much.
33 022	When the Believers saw the Confederate forces, they said: "This is what Allah and his Messenger had promised us, and Allah and His Messenger told us what was true." And it only added to their faith and their zeal in obedience.	And when the true believers saw the clans, they said: This is that which Allah and His messenger promised us. Allah and His messenger are true. It did but confirm them in their faith and resignation.	And when the believers saw the allies, they said: This is what Allah and His Messenger promised us, and Allah and His Messenger spoke the truth; and it only increased them in faith and submission.
33 023	Among the Believers are men who have been true to their covenant with Allah: of them some have completed their vow (to the extreme), and some (still) wait: but they have never changed (their determination) in the least:	Of the believers are men who are true to that which they covenanted with Allah. Some of them have paid their vow by death (in battle), and some of them still are waiting; and they have not altered in the least;	Of the believers are men who are true to the covenant which they made with Allah: so of them is he who accomplished his vow, and of them is he who yet waits, and they have not changed in the least;
33 024	That Allah may reward the men of Truth for their Truth, and punish the Hypocrites if that be His Will, or turn to them in Mercy: for Allah is Oft-Forgiving, Most Merciful.	That Allah may reward the true men for their truth, and punish the hypocrites if He will, or relent toward them (if He will). Lo! Allah is Forgiving, Merciful.	That Allah may reward the truthful for their truth, and punish the hypocrites if He please or turn to them (mercifully); surely Allah is Forgiving, Merciful.

33 025	And Allah turned back the Unbelievers for (all) their fury: no advantage did they gain; and enough is Allah for the believers in their fight. And Allah is full of Strength, able to enforce His Will.	And Allah repulsed the disbelievers in their wrath; they gained no good. Allah averted their attack from the believers. Allah is ever Strong, Mighty.	And Allah turned back the unbelievers in their rage; they did not obtain any advantage, and Allah sufficed the believers in fighting; and Allah is Strong, Mighty.
33 026	And those of the People of the Book who aided them - Allah did take them down from their strongholds, and cast terror into their hearts. (So that) some ye slew, and some ye made prisoners.	And He brought those of the People of the Scripture who supported them down from their strongholds, and cast panic into their hearts. Some ye slew, and ye made captive some.	And He drove down those of the followers of the Book who backed them from their fortresses and He cast awe into their hearts; some you killed and you took captive another part.
33 027	And He made you heirs of their lands, their houses, and their goods, and of a land which ye had not frequented (before). And Allah has power over all things.	And He caused you to inherit their land and their houses and their wealth, and land ye have not trodden. Allah is ever Able to do all things.	And He made you heirs to their land and their dwellings and their property, and (to) a land which you have not yet trodden, and Allah has power over all things.
33 028	O Prophet! Say to thy Consorts: "If it be that ye desire the life of this World, and its glitter,- then come! I will provide for your enjoyment and set you free in a handsome manner."	O Prophet! Say unto thy wives: If ye desire the world's life and its adornment, come! I will content you and will release you with a fair release.	O Prophet! say to your wives: If you desire this world's life and its adornment, then come, I will give you a provision and allow you to depart a goodly departing;
33 029	But if ye seek Allah and His Messenger, and the Home of the Hereafter, verily Allah has prepared for the well-doers amongst you a great reward.	But if ye desire Allah and His messenger and the abode of the Hereafter, then lo! Allah hath prepared for the good among you an immense reward.	And if you desire Allah and His Messenger and the latter abode, then surely Allah has prepared for the doers of good among you a mighty reward.
33 030	O Consorts of the Prophet! If any of you were guilty of evident unseemly conduct, the Punishment would be doubled to her, and that is easy for Allah.	O ye wives of the Prophet! Whosoever of you committeth manifest lewdness, the punishment for her will be doubled, and that is easy for Allah.	O wives of the prophet! whoever of you commits an open indecency, the punishment shall be increased to her doubly; and this IS easy to Allah.
33 031	But any of you that is devout in the service of Allah and His Messenger, and works righteousness,- to her shall We grant her reward twice: and We have prepared for her a generous Sustenance.	And whosoever of you is submissive unto Allah and His messenger and doeth right, We shall give her reward twice over, and We have prepared for her a rich provision.	And whoever of you is obedient to Allah and His Messenger and does good, We will give to her her reward doubly, and We have prepared for her an honorable sustenance.
33 032	O Consorts of the Prophet! Ye are not like any of the (other) women: if ye do fear (Allah), be not too complacent of speech, lest one in whose heart is a disease should be moved with desire: but speak ye a speech (that is) just.	O ye wives of the Prophet! Ye are not like any other women. If ye keep your duty (to Allah), then be not soft of speech, lest he in whose heart is a disease aspire (to you), but utter customary speech.	O wives of the Prophet! you are not like any other of the women; If you will be on your guard, then be not soft in (your) speech, lest he in whose heart is a disease yearn; and speak a good word.
33 033	And stay quietly in your houses, and make not a dazzling display, like that of the former Times of Ignorance; and establish regular Prayer, and give regular Charity; and obey Allah and His Messenger. And Allah only wishes to remove all abomination from you, ye Members of the Family, and to make you pure and spotless.	And stay in your houses. Bedizen not yourselves with the bedizenment of the Time of Ignorance. Be regular in prayer, and pay the poor-due, and obey Allah and His messenger. Allah's wish is but to remove uncleanness far from you, O Folk of the Household, and cleanse you with a thorough cleansing.	And stay in your houses and do not display your finery like the displaying of the ignorance of yore; and keep up prayer, and pay the poor-rate, and obey Allah and His Messenger. Allah only desires to keep away the uncleanness from you, O people of the House! and to purify you a (thorough) purifying.

33 034	And recite what is rehearsed to you in your homes, of the Signs of Allah and His Wisdom: for Allah understands the finest mysteries and is well-acquainted (with them).	And bear in mind that which is recited in your houses of the revelations of Allah and wisdom. Lo! Allah is Subtile, Aware.	And keep to mind what is recited in your houses of the communications of Allah and the wisdom; surely Allah is Knower of subtleties, Aware.
33 035	For Muslim men and women,- for believing men and women, for devout men and women, for true men and women, for men and women who are patient and constant, for men and women who humble themselves, for men and women who give in Charity, for men and women who fast (and deny themselves), for men and women who guard their chastity, and for men and women who engage much in Allah's praise,- for them has Allah prepared forgiveness and great reward.	Lo! men who surrender unto Allah, and women who surrender, and men who believe and women who believe, and men who obey and women who obey, and men who speak the truth and women who speak the truth, and men who persevere (in righteousness) and women who persevere, and men who are humble and women who are humble, and men who give alms and women who give alms, and men who fast and women who fast, and men who guard their modesty and women who guard (their modesty), and men who remember Allah much and women who remember - Allah hath prepared for them forgiveness and a vast reward.	Surely the men who submit and the women who submit, and the believing men and the believing women, and the obeying men and the obeying women, and the truthful men and the truthful women, and the patient men and the patient women and the humble men and the humble women, and the almsgiving men and the almsgiving women, and the fasting men and the fasting women, and the men who guard their private parts and the women who guard, and the men who remember Allah much and the women who remember-- Allah has prepared for them forgiveness and a mighty reward.
33 036	It is not fitting for a Believer, man or woman, when a matter has been decided by Allah and His Messenger to have any option about their decision: if any one disobeys Allah and His Messenger, he is indeed on a clearly wrong Path.	And it becometh not a believing man or a believing woman, when Allah and His messenger have decided an affair (for them), that they should (after that) claim any say in their affair; and whoso is rebellious to Allah and His messenger, he verily goeth astray in error manifest.	And it behoves not a believing man and a believing woman that they should have any choice in their matter when Allah and His Messenger have decided a matter; and whoever disobeys Allah and His Messenger, he surely strays off a manifest straying.
33 037	Behold! Thou didst say to one who had received the grace of Allah and thy favour: "Retain thou (in wedlock) thy wife, and fear Allah." But thou didst hide in thy heart that which Allah was about to make manifest: thou didst fear the people, but it is more fitting that thou shouldst fear Allah. Then when Zaid had dissolved (his marriage) with her, with the necessary (formality), We joined her in marriage to thee: in order that (in future) there may be no difficulty to the Believers in (the matter of) marriage with the wives of their adopted sons, when the latter have dissolved with the necessary (formality) (their marriage) with them. And Allah's command must be fulfilled.	And when thou saidst unto him on whom Allah hath conferred favour and thou hast conferred favour: Keep thy wife to thyself, and fear Allah. And thou didst hide in thy mind that which Allah was to bring to light, and thou didst fear mankind whereas Allah hath a better right that thou shouldst fear Him. So when Zeyd had performed that necessary formality (of divorce) from her, We gave her unto thee in marriage, so that (henceforth) there may be no sin for believers in respect of wives of their adopted sons, when the latter have performed the necessary formality (of release) from them. The commandment of Allah must be fulfilled.	And when you said to him to whom Allah had shown favor and to whom you had shown a favor: Keep your wife to yourself and be careful of (your duty to) Allah; and you concealed in your soul what Allah would bring to light, and you feared men, and Allah had a greater right that you should fear Him. But when Zaid had accomplished his want of her, We gave her to you as a wife, so that there should be no difficulty for the believers in respect of the wives of their adopted sons, when they have accomplished their want of them; and Allah's command shall be performed.

33 038	There can be no difficulty to the Prophet in what Allah has indicated to him as a duty. It was the practice (approved) of Allah amongst those of old that have passed away. And the command of Allah is a decree determined.	There is no reproach for the Prophet in that which Allah maketh his due. That was Allah's way with those who passed away of old - and the commandment of Allah is certain destiny -	There is no harm in the Prophet doing that which Allah has ordained for him; such has been the course of Allah with respect to those who have gone before; and the command of Allah is a decree that is made absolute:
33 039	(It is the practice of those) who preach the Messages of Allah, and fear Him, and fear none but Allah. And enough is Allah to call (men) to account.	Who delivered the messages of Allah and feared Him, and feared none save Allah. Allah keepeth good account.	Those who deliver the messages of Allah and fear Him, and do not fear any one but Allah; and Allah is sufficient to take account.
33 040	Muhammad is not the father of any of your men, but (he is) the Messenger of Allah, and the Seal of the Prophets: and Allah has full knowledge of all things.	Muhammad is not the father of any man among you, but he is the messenger of Allah and the Seal of the Prophets; and Allah is ever Aware of all things.	Muhammad is not the father of any of your men, but he is the Messenger of Allah and the Last of the prophets; and Allah is cognizant of all things.
33 041	O ye who believe! Celebrate the praises of Allah, and do this often;	O ye who believe! Remember Allah with much remembrance.	O you who believe! remember Allah, remembering frequently,
33 042	And glorify Him morning and evening.	And glorify Him early and late.	And glorify Him morning and evening.
33 043	He it is Who sends blessings on you, as do His angels, that He may bring you out from the depths of Darkness into Light: and He is Full of Mercy to the Believers.	He it is Who blesseth you, and His angels (bless you), that He may bring you forth from darkness unto light; and He is ever Merciful to the believers.	He it is Who sends His blessings on you, and (so do) His angels, that He may bring you forth out of utter darkness into the light; and He is Merciful to the believers.
33 044	Their salutation on the Day they meet Him will be "Peace!"; and He has prepared for them a generous Reward.	Their salutation on the day when they shall meet Him will be: Peace. And He hath prepared for them a goodly recompense.	Their salutation on the day that they meet Him shall be, Peace, and He has prepared for them an honourable reward.
33 045	O Prophet! Truly We have sent thee as a Witness, a Bearer of Glad Tidings, and Warner,-	O Prophet! Lo! We have sent thee as a witness and a bringer of good tidings and a warner.	O Prophet! surely We have sent you as a witness, and as a bearer of good news and as a warner,
33 046	And as one who invites to Allah's (grace) by His leave, and as a lamp spreading light.	And as a summoner unto Allah by His permission, and as a lamp that giveth light.	And as one inviting to Allah by His permission, and as a light-giving torch.
33 047	Then give the Glad Tidings to the Believers, that they shall have from Allah a very great Bounty.	And announce unto the believers the good tidings that they will have great bounty from Allah.	And give to the believers the good news that they shall have a great grace from Allah.
33 048	And obey not (the behests) of the Unbelievers and the Hypocrites, and heed not their annoyances, but put thy Trust in Allah. For enough is Allah as a Disposer of affairs.	And incline not to the disbelievers and the hypocrites. Disregard their noxious talk, and put thy trust in Allah. Allah is sufficient as Trustee.	And be not compliant to the unbelievers and the hypocrites, and leave unregarded their annoying talk, and rely on Allah; and Allah is sufficient as a Protector.
33 049	O ye who believe! When ye marry believing women, and then divorce them before ye have touched them, no period of 'Iddat have ye to count in respect of them: so give them a present. And set them free in a handsome manner.	O ye who believe! If ye wed believing women and divorce them before ye have touched them, then there is no period that ye should reckon. But content them and release them handsomely.	O you who believe! when you marry the believing women, then divorce them before you touch them, you have in their case no term which you should reckon; so make some provision for them and send them forth a goodly sending forth.

33 050	O Prophet! We have made lawful to thee thy wives to whom thou hast paid their dowers; and those whom thy right hand possesses out of the prisoners of war whom Allah has assigned to thee; and daughters of thy paternal uncles and aunts, and daughters of thy maternal uncles and aunts, who migrated (from Makka) with thee; and any believing woman who dedicates her soul to the Prophet if the Prophet wishes to wed her;- this only for thee, and not for the Believers (at large); We know what We have appointed for them as to their wives and the captives whom their right hands possess;- in order that there should be no difficulty for thee. And Allah is Oft-Forgiving, Most Merciful.	O Prophet! Lo! We have made lawful unto thee thy wives unto whom thou hast paid their dowries, and those whom thy right hand possesseth of those whom Allah hath given thee as spoils of war, and the daughters of thine uncle on the father's side and the daughters of thine aunts on the father's side, and the daughters of thine uncle on the mother's side and the daughters of thine aunts on the mother's side who emigrated with thee, and a believing woman if she give herself unto the Prophet and the Prophet desire to ask her in marriage - a privilege for thee only, not for the (rest of) believers - We are Aware of that which We enjoined upon them concerning their wives and those whom their right hands possess - that thou mayst be free from blame, for Allah is ever Forgiving, Merciful.	O Prophet! surely We have made lawful to you your wives whom you have given their dowries, and those whom your right hand possesses out of those whom Allah has given to you as prisoners of war, and the daughters of your paternal uncles and the daughters of your paternal aunts, and the daughters of your maternal uncles and the daughters of your maternal aunts who fled with you; and a believing woman if she gave herself to the Prophet, if the Prophet desired to marry her-- specially for you, not for the (rest of) believers; We know what We have ordained for them concerning their wives and those whom their right hands possess in order that no blame may attach to you; and Allah is Forgiving, Merciful.
33 051	Thou mayest defer (the turn of) any of them that thou pleasest, and thou mayest receive any thou pleasest: and there is no blame on thee if thou invite one whose (turn) thou hadst set aside. This were nigher to the cooling of their eyes, the prevention of their grief, and their satisfaction - that of all of them - with that which thou hast to give them: and Allah knows (all) that is in your hearts: and Allah is All-Knowing, Most Forbearing.	Thou canst defer whom thou wilt of them and receive unto thee whom thou wilt, and whomsoever thou desirest of those whom thou hast set aside (temporarily), it is no sin for thee (to receive her again); that is better; that they may be comforted and not grieve, and may all be pleased with what thou givest them. Allah knoweth what is in your hearts (O men), and Allah is ever Forgiving, Clement.	You may put off whom you please of them, and you may take to you whom you please, and whom you desire of those whom you had separated provisionally; no blame attaches to you; this is most proper, so that their eyes may be cool and they may not grieve, and that they should be pleased, all of them with what you give them, and Allah knows what is in your hearts; and Allah is Knowing, Forbearing.
33 052	It is not lawful for thee (to marry more) women after this, nor to change them for (other) wives, even though their beauty attract thee, except any thy right hand should possess (as handmaidens): and Allah doth watch over all things.	It is not allowed thee to take (other) women henceforth, nor that thou shouldst change them for other wives even though their beauty pleased thee, save those whom thy right hand possesseth. And Allah is ever Watcher over all things.	It is not allowed to you to take women afterwards, nor that you should change them for other wives, though their beauty be pleasing to you, except what your right hand possesses and Allah is Watchful over all things.

33 053	O ye who believe! Enter not the Prophet's houses,- until leave is given you,- for a meal, (and then) not (so early as) to wait for its preparation: but when ye are invited, enter; and when ye have taken your meal, disperse, without seeking familiar talk. Such (behaviour) annoys the Prophet: he is ashamed to dismiss you, but Allah is not ashamed (to tell you) the truth. And when ye ask (his ladies) for anything ye want, ask them from before a screen: that makes for greater purity for your hearts and for theirs. Nor is it right for you that ye should annoy Allah's Messenger, or that ye should marry his widows after him at any time. Truly such a thing is in Allah's sight an enormity.	O Ye who believe! Enter not the dwellings of the Prophet for a meal without waiting for the proper time, unless permission be granted you. But if ye are invited, enter, and, when your meal is ended, then disperse. Linger not for conversation. Lo! that would cause annoyance to the Prophet, and he would be shy of (asking) you (to go); but Allah is not shy of the truth. And when ye ask of them (the wives of the Prophet) anything, ask it of them from behind a curtain. That is purer for your hearts and for their hearts. And it is not for you to cause annoyance to the messenger of Allah, nor that ye should ever marry his wives after him. Lo! that in Allah's sight would be an enormity.	O you who believe! do not enter the houses of the Prophet unless permission is given to you for a meal, not waiting for its cooking being finished-- but when you are invited, enter, and when you have taken the food, then disperse-- not seeking to listen to talk; surely this gives the Prophet trouble, but he forbears from you, and Allah does not forbear from the truth. And when you ask of them any goods, ask of them from behind a curtain; this is purer for your hearts and (for) their hearts; and it does not behove you that you should give trouble to the Messenger of Allah, nor that you should marry his wives after him ever; surely this is grievous in the sight of Allah.
33 054	Whether ye reveal anything or conceal it, verily Allah has full knowledge of all things.	Whether ye divulge a thing or keep it hidden, lo! Allah is ever Knower of all things.	If you do a thing openly or do it in secret, then surely Allah is Cognizant of all things.
33 055	There is no blame (on these ladies if they appear) before their fathers or their sons, their brothers, or their brother's sons, or their sisters' sons, or their women, or the (slaves) whom their right hands possess. And, (ladies), fear Allah; for Allah is Witness to all things.	It is no sin for them (thy wives) (to converse freely) with their fathers, or their sons, or their brothers, or their brothers' sons, or the sons of their sisters or of their own women, or their slaves. O women! Keep your duty to Allah. Lo! Allah is ever Witness over all things.	There is no blame on them in respect of their fathers, nor their brothers, nor their brothers' sons, nor their sisters' sons nor their own women, nor of what their right hands possess; and be careful of (your duty to) Allah; surely Allah is a witness of all things.
33 056	Allah and His angels send blessings on the Prophet: O ye that believe! Send ye blessings on him, and salute him with all respect.	Lo! Allah and His angels shower blessings on the Prophet. O ye who believe! Ask blessings on him and salute him with a worthy salutation.	Surely Allah and His angels bless the Prophet; O you who believe! call for (Divine) blessings on him and salute him with a (becoming) salutation.
33 057	Those who annoy Allah and His Messenger - Allah has cursed them in this World and in the Hereafter, and has prepared for them a humiliating Punishment.	Lo! those who malign Allah and His messenger, Allah hath cursed them in the world and the Hereafter, and hath prepared for them the doom of the disdained.	Surely (as for) those who speak evil things of Allah and His Messenger, Allah has cursed them in this world and the here after, and He has prepared for them a chastisement bringing disgrace.
33 058	And those who annoy believing men and women undeservedly, bear (on themselves) a calumny and a glaring sin.	And those who malign believing men and believing women undeservedly, they bear the guilt of slander and manifest sin.	And those who speak evil things of the believing men and the believing women without their having earned (it), they are guilty indeed of a false accusation and a manifest sin.
33 059	O Prophet! Tell thy wives and daughters, and the believing women, that they should cast their outer garments over their persons (when abroad): that is most convenient, that they should be known (as such) and not molested. And Allah is Oft-Forgiving, Most Merciful.	O Prophet! Tell thy wives and thy daughters and the women of the believers to draw their cloaks close round them (when they go abroad). That will be better, so that they may be recognised and not annoyed. Allah is ever Forgiving, Merciful.	O Prophet! say to your wives and your daughters and the women of the believers that they let down upon them their over-garments; this will be more proper, that they may be known, and thus they will not be given trouble; and Allah is Forgiving, Merciful.

33 060	Truly, if the Hypocrites, and those in whose hearts is a disease, and those who stir up sedition in the City, desist not, We shall certainly stir thee up against them: Then will they not be able to stay in it as thy neighbours for any length of time:		If the hypocrites, and those in whose hearts is a disease, and the alarmists in the city do not cease, We verily shall urge thee on against them, then they will be your neighbours in it but a little while.	If the hypocrites and those in whose hearts is a disease and the agitators in the city do not desist, We shall most certainly set you over them, then they shall not be your neighbors in it but for a little while;
33 061	They shall have a curse on them: whenever they are found, they shall be seized and slain (without mercy).		Accursed, they will be seized wherever found and slain with a (fierce) slaughter.	Cursed: wherever they are found they shall be seized and murdered, a (horrible) murdering.
33 062	(Such was) the practice (approved) of Allah among those who lived aforetime: No change wilt thou find in the practice (approved) of Allah.		That was the way of Allah in the case of those who passed away of old; thou wilt not find for the way of Allah aught of power to change.	(Such has been) the course of Allah with respect to those who have gone before; and you shall not find any change in the course of Allah.
33 063	Men ask thee concerning the Hour: Say, "The knowledge thereof is with Allah (alone)": and what will make thee understand?- perchance the Hour is nigh!		Men ask thee of the Hour. Say: The knowledge of it is with Allah only. What can convey (the knowledge) unto thee? It may be that the Hour is nigh.	Men ask you about the hour; say: The knowledge of it is only with Allah, and what will make you comprehend that the hour may be nigh.
33 064	Verily Allah has cursed the Unbelievers and prepared for them a Blazing Fire,-		Lo! Allah hath cursed the disbelievers, and hath prepared for them a flaming fire,	Surely Allah has cursed the unbelievers and has prepared for them a burning fire,
33 065	To dwell therein for ever: no protector will they find, nor helper.		Wherein they will abide for ever. They will find (then) no protecting friend nor helper.	To abide therein for a long time; they shall not find a protector or a helper.
33 066	The Day that their faces will be turned upside down in the Fire, they will say: "Woe to us! Would that we had obeyed Allah and obeyed the Messenger!"		On the day when their faces are turned over in the Fire, they say: Oh, would that we had obeyed Allah and had obeyed His messenger!	On the day when their faces shall be turned back into the fire, they shall say: O would that we had obeyed Allah and obeyed the Messenger!
33 067	And they would say: "Our Lord! We obeyed our chiefs and our great ones, and they misled us as to the (right) Path."		And they say: Our Lord! Lo! we obeyed our princes and great men, and they misled us from the Way.	And they shall say: O our Lord! surely we obeyed our leaders and our great men, so they led us astray from the path;
33 068	"Our Lord! Give them double Penalty and curse them with a very great Curse!"		Our Lord! Oh, give them double torment and curse them with a mighty curse.	O our Lord! give them a double punishment and curse them with a great curse.
33 069	O ye who believe! Be ye not like those who vexed and insulted Moses, but Allah cleared him of the (calumnies) they had uttered: and he was honourable in Allah's sight.		O ye who believe! Be not as those who slandered Moses, but Allah proved his innocence of that which they alleged, and he was well esteemed in Allah's sight.	O you who believe! be not like those who spoke evil things of Musa, but Allah cleared him of what they said, and he was worthy of regard with Allah.
33 070	O ye who believe! Fear Allah, and (always) say a word directed to the Right:		O ye who believe! Guard your duty to Allah, and speak words straight to the point;	O you who believe! be careful of (your duty to) Allah and speak the right word,
33 071	That He may make your conduct whole and sound and forgive you your sins: He that obeys Allah and His Messenger, has already attained the highest achievement.		He will adjust your works for you and will forgive you your sins. Whosoever obeyeth Allah and His messenger, he verily hath gained a signal victory.	He will put your deeds into a right state for you, and forgive you your faults; and whoever obeys Allah and His Messenger, he indeed achieves a mighty success.
33 072	We did indeed offer the Trust to the Heavens and the Earth and the Mountains; but they refused to undertake it, being afraid thereof: but man undertook it;- He was indeed unjust and foolish;-		Lo! We offered the trust unto the heavens and the earth and the hills, but they shrank from bearing it and were afraid of it. And man assumed it. Lo! he hath proved a tyrant and a fool.	Surely We offered the trust to the heavens and the earth and the mountains, but they refused to be unfaithful to it and feared from it, and man has turned unfaithful to it; surely he is unjust, ignorant;

33 073	(With the result) that Allah has to punish the Hypocrites, men and women, and the Unbelievers, men and women, and Allah turns in Mercy to the Believers, men and women: for Allah is Oft-Forgiving, Most Merciful.	So Allah punisheth hypocritical men and hypocritical women, and idolatrous men and idolatrous women. But Allah pardoneth believing men and believing women, and Allah is ever Forgiving, Merciful.	So Allah will chastise the hypocritical men and the hypocritical women and the polytheistic men and the polytheistic women, and Allah will turn (mercifully) to the believing women, and Allah is Forgiving, Merciful.

Chapter 34:

SABA (SABA, SHEBA)

Total Verses: 54 Revealed At: MAKKA

In the name of Allah, the Most Beneficent, the Most Merciful.

34 001	Praise be to Allah, to Whom belong all things in the heavens and on earth: to Him be Praise in the Hereafter: and He is Full of Wisdom, acquainted with all things.	Praise be to Allah, unto Whom belongeth whatsoever is in the heavens and whatsoever is in the earth. His is the praise in the Hereafter, and He is the Wise, the Aware.	(All) praise is due to Allah, Whose is what is in the heavens and what is in the earth, and to Him is due (all) praise in the hereafter; and He is the Wise, the Aware.
34 002	He knows all that goes into the earth, and all that comes out thereof; all that comes down from the sky and all that ascends thereto and He is the Most Merciful, the Oft-Forgiving.	He knoweth that which goeth into the earth and that which cometh forth from it, and that descendeth from the heaven and that which ascendeth into it. He is the Merciful, the Forgiving.	He knows that which goes down into the earth and that which comes out of it, and that which comes down from the heaven and that which goes up to it; and He is the Merciful, the Forgiving.
34 003	The Unbelievers say, "Never to us will come the Hour": Say, "Nay! but most surely, by my Lord, it will come upon you;- by Him Who knows the unseen,- from Whom is not hidden the least little atom in the heavens or on earth: Nor is there anything less than that, or greater, but is in the Record Perspicuous:"	Those who disbelieve say: The Hour will never come unto us. Say: Nay, by my Lord, but it is coming unto you surely. (He is) the Knower of the Unseen. Not an atom's weight, or less than that or greater, escapeth Him in the heavens or in the earth, but it is in a clear Record,	And those who disbelieve say: The hour shall not come upon us. Say: Yea! by my Lord, the Knower of the unseen, it shall certainly come upon you; not the weight of an atom becomes absent from Him, in the heavens or in the earth, and neither less than that nor greater, but (all) is in a clear book,
34 004	"That He may reward those who believe and work deeds of righteousness: for such is Forgiveness and a Sustenance Most Generous."	That He may reward those who believe and do good works. For them is pardon and a rich provision.	That He may reward those who believe and do good; these it is for whom is forgiveness and an honorable sustenance.
34 005	But those who strive against Our Signs, to frustrate them,- for such will be a Penalty,- a Punishment most humiliating.	But those who strive against Our revelations, challenging (Us), theirs will be a painful doom of wrath.	And (as for) those who strive hard in opposing Our communications, these it is for whom is a painful chastisement of an evil kind.
34 006	And those to whom knowledge has come see that the (Revelation) sent down to thee from thy Lord - that is the Truth, and that it guides to the Path of the Exalted (in might), Worthy of all praise.	Those who have been given knowledge see that what is revealed unto thee from thy Lord is the truth and leadeth unto the path of the Mighty, the Owner of Praise.	And those to whom the knowledge has been given see that which has been revealed to you from your Lord, that is the truth, and it guides into the path of the Mighty, the Praised.

34 007	The Unbelievers say (in ridicule): "Shall we point out to you a man that will tell you, when ye are all scattered to pieces in disintegration, that ye shall (then be raised) in a New Creation?"	Those who disbelieve say: Shall we show you a man who will tell you (that) when ye have become dispersed in dust with most complete dispersal still, even then, ye will be created anew?	And those who disbelieve say: Shall we point out to you a man who informs you that when you are scattered the utmost scattering you shall then be most surely (raised) in (to) a new creation?
34 008	"Has he invented a falsehood against Allah, or has a spirit (seized) him?"- Nay, it is those who believe not in the Hereafter, that are in (real) Penalty, and in farthest error.	Hath he invented a lie concerning Allah, or is there in him a madness? Nay, but those who disbelieve in the Hereafter are in torment and far error.	He has forged a lie against Allah or there is madness in him. Nay! those who do not believe in the hereafter are in torment and in great error.
34 009	See they not what is before them and behind them, of the sky and the earth? If We wished, We could cause the earth to swallow them up, or cause a piece of the sky to fall upon them. Verily in this is a Sign for every devotee that turns to Allah (in repentance).	Have they not observed what is before them and what is behind them of the sky and the earth? If We will, We can make the earth swallow them, or cause obliteration from the sky to fall on them. Lo! herein surely is a portent for every slave who turneth (to Allah) repentant.	Do they not then consider what is before them and what is behind them of the heaven and the earth? If We please We will make them disappear in the land or bring down upon them a portion from the heaven; most surely there is a sign in this for every servant turning (to Allah).
34 010	We bestowed Grace aforetime on David from ourselves: "O ye Mountains! Sing ye back the Praises of Allah with him! and ye birds (also)! And We made the iron soft for him;"-	And assuredly We gave David grace from Us, (saying): O ye hills and birds, echo his psalms of praise! And We made the iron supple unto him,	And certainly We gave to Dawood excellence from Us: O mountains! sing praises with him, and the birds; and We made the iron pliant to him,
34 011	(Commanding), "Make thou coast of mail, balancing well the rings of chain armour, and work ye righteousness; for be sure I see (clearly) all that ye do."	Saying: Make thou long coats of mail and measure the links (thereof). And do ye right. Lo! I am Seer of what ye do.	Saying: Make ample (coats of mail), and assign a time to the making of coats of mail and do good; surely I am Seeing what you do.
34 012	And to Solomon (We made) the Wind (obedient): Its early morning (stride) was a month's (journey), and its evening (stride) was a month's (journey); and We made a Font of molten brass to flow for him; and there were jinns that worked in front of him, by the leave of his Lord, and if any of them turned aside from Our command, We made him taste of the Penalty of the Blazing Fire.	And unto Solomon (We gave) the wind, whereof the morning course was a month's journey and the evening course a month's journey, and We caused the fount of copper to gush forth for him, and (We gave him) certain of the jinn who worked before him by permission of his Lord. And such of them as deviated from Our command, them We caused to taste the punishment of flaming fire.	And (We made) the wind (subservient) to Sulaiman, which made a month's journey in the morning and a month's journey in the evening, and We made a fountain of molten copper to flow out for him, and of the jinn there were those who worked before him by the command of his Lord; and whoever turned aside from Our command from among them, We made him taste of the punishment of burning.
34 013	They worked for him as he desired, (making) Arches, Images, Basons as large as Reservoirs, and (cooking) Cauldrons fixed (in their places): Work ye, sons of David, with thanks! but few of My servants are grateful!"	They made for him what he willed: synagogues and statues, basins like wells and boilers built into the ground. Give thanks, O House of David! Few of My bondmen are thankful.	They made for him what he pleased of fortresses and images, and bowls (large) as watering-troughs and cooking-pots that will not move from their place; give thanks, O family of Dawood! and very few of My servants are grateful.

34 014	Then, when We decreed (Solomon's) death, nothing showed them his death except a little worm of the earth, which kept (slowly) gnawing away at his staff: so when he fell down, the jinns saw plainly that if they had known the unseen, they would not have tarried in the humiliating Penalty (of their Task).	And when We decreed death for him, nothing showed his death to them save a creeping creature of the earth which gnawed away his staff. And when he fell the jinn saw clearly how, if they had known the Unseen, they would not have continued in despised toil.	But when We decreed death for him, naught showed them his death but a creature of the earth that ate away his staff; and when it fell down, the jinn came to know plainly that if they had known the unseen, they would not have tarried in abasing torment.
34 015	There was, for Saba, aforetime, a Sign in their home-land - two Gardens to the right and to the left. "Eat of the Sustenance (provided) by your Lord, and be grateful to Him: a territory fair and happy, and a Lord Oft-Forgiving!"	There was indeed a sign for Sheba in their dwelling-place: Two gardens on the right hand and the left (as who should say): Eat of the provision of your Lord and render thanks to Him. A fair land and an indulgent Lord!	Certainly there was a sign for Saba in their abode; two gardens on the right and the left; eat of the sustenance of your Lord and give thanks to Him: a good land and a Forgiving Lord!
34 016	But they turned away (from Allah), and We sent against them the Flood (released) from the dams, and We converted their two garden (rows) into gardens producing bitter fruit, and tamarisks, and some few (stunted) Lote-trees.	But they were froward, so We sent on them the flood of 'Iram, and in exchange for their two gardens gave them two gardens bearing bitter fruit, the tamarisk and here and there a lote-tree.	But they turned aside, so We sent upon them a torrent of which the rush could not be withstood, and in place of their two gardens We gave to them two gardens yielding bitter fruit and (growing) tamarisk and a few lote-trees.
34 017	That was the Requital We gave them because they ungratefully rejected Faith: and never do We give (such) requital except to such as are ungrateful rejecters.	This We awarded them because of their ingratitude. Punish We ever any save the ingrates?	This We requited them with because they disbelieved; and We do not punish any but the ungrateful.
34 018	Between them and the Cities on which We had poured our blessings, We had placed Cities in prominent positions, and between them We had appointed stages of journey in due proportion: "Travel therein, secure, by night and by day."	And We set, between them and the towns which We had blessed, towns easy to be seen, and We made the stage between them easy, (saying): Travel in them safely both by night and day.	And We made between them and the towns which We had blessed (other) towns to be easily seen, and We apportioned the journey therein: Travel through them nights and days, secure.
34 019	But they said: "Our Lord! Place longer distances between our journey-stages": but they wronged themselves (therein). At length We made them as a tale (that is told), and We dispersed them all in scattered fragments. Verily in this are Signs for every (soul that is) patiently constant and grateful.	But they said: Our Lord! Make the stage between our journeys longer. And they wronged themselves, therefore We made them bywords (in the land) and scattered them abroad, a total scattering. Lo! herein verily are portents for each steadfast, grateful (heart).	And they said: O our Lord! make spaces to be longer between our journeys; and they were unjust to themselves so We made them stories and scattered them with an utter scattering; most surely there are signs in this for every patient, grateful one.
34 020	And on them did Satan prove true his idea, and they followed him, all but a party that believed.	And Satan indeed found his calculation true concerning them, for they follow him, all save a group of true believers.	And certainly the Shaitan found true his conjecture concerning them, so they follow him, except a party of the believers.
34 021	But he had no authority over them,- except that We might test the man who believes in the Hereafter from him who is in doubt concerning it: and thy Lord doth watch over all things.	And he had no warrant whatsoever against them, save that We would know him who believeth in the Hereafter from him who is in doubt thereof; and thy Lord (O Muhammad) taketh note of all things.	And he has no authority over them, but that We may distinguish him who believes in the hereafter from him who is in doubt concerning it; and your Lord is the Preserver of all things.

34 022	Say: "Call upon other (gods) whom ye fancy, besides Allah: They have no power,- not the weight of an atom,- in the heavens or on earth: No (sort of) share have they therein, nor is any of them a helper to Allah."	Say (O Muhammad): Call upon those whom ye set up beside Allah! They possess not an atom's weight either in the heavens or in the earth, nor have they any share in either, nor hath He an auxiliary among them.	Say: Call upon those whom you assert besides Allah; they do not control the weight of an atom in the heavens or in the earth nor have they any partnership in either, nor has He among them any one to back (Him) up.
34 023	"No intercession can avail in His Presence, except for those for whom He has granted permission. So far (is this the case) that, when terror is removed from their hearts (at the Day of Judgment, then) will they say, 'What is it that your Lord commanded?' they will say, 'That which is true and just'; and He is the Most High, Most Great."	No intercession availeth with Him save for him whom He permitteth. Yet, when fear is banished from their hearts, they say: What was it that your Lord said? They say: The Truth. And He is the Sublime, the Great.	And intercession will not avail aught with Him save of him whom He permits. Until when fear shall be removed from their hearts, they shall say: What is it that your Lord said? They shall say: The truth. And He is the Most High, the Great.
34 024	Say: "Who gives you sustenance, from the heavens and the earth?" Say: It is Allah; and certain it is that either we or ye are on right guidance or in manifest error!"	Say: Who giveth you provision from the sky and the earth? Say: Allah, Lo! we or you assuredly are rightly guided or in error manifest.	Say: Who gives you the sustenance from the heavens and the earth? Say: Allah. And most surely we or you are on a right way or in manifest error.
34 025	Say: "Ye shall not be questioned as to our sins, nor shall we be questioned as to what ye do."	Say: Ye will not be asked of what we committed, nor shall we be asked of what ye do.	Say: You will not be questioned as to what we are guilty of, nor shall we be questioned as to what you do.
34 026	Say: "Our Lord will gather us together and will in the end decide the matter between us (and you) in truth and justice: and He is the one to decide, the One Who knows all."	Say: Our Lord will bring us all together, then He will judge between us with truth. He is the All-knowing Judge.	Say: Our Lord will gather us together, then will He judge between us with the truth; and He is the greatest Judge, the All-knowing.
34 027	Say: "Show me those whom ye have joined with Him as partners: by no means (can ye). Nay, He is Allah, the Exalted in Power, the Wise."	Say: Show me those whom ye have joined unto Him as partners. Nay (ye dare not)! For He is Allah, the Mighty, the Wise.	Say: Show me those whom you have joined with Him as associates; by no means (can you do it). Nay! He is Allah, the Mighty, the Wise.
34 028	We have not sent thee but as a universal (Messenger) to men, giving them glad tidings, and warning them (against sin), but most men understand not.	And We have not sent thee (O Muhammad) save as a bringer of good tidings and a warner unto all mankind; but most of mankind know not.	And We have not sent you but to all the men as a bearer of good news and as a warner, but most men do not know.
34 029	They say: "When will this promise (come to pass) if ye are telling the truth?"	And they say: When is this promise (to be fulfilled) if ye are truthful?	And they say: When will this promise be (fulfilled) if you are truthful?
34 030	Say: "The appointment to you is for a Day, which ye cannot put back for an hour nor put forward."	Say (O Muhammad): Yours is the promise of a Day which ye cannot postpone nor hasten by an hour.	Say: You have the appointment of a day from which you cannot hold back any while, nor can you bring it on.
34 031	The Unbelievers say: "We shall neither believe in this scripture nor in (any) that (came) before it." Couldst thou but see when the wrong-doers will be made to stand before their Lord, throwing back the word (of blame) on one another! Those who had been despised will say to the arrogant ones: "Had it not been for you, we should certainly have been believers!"	And those who disbelieve say: We believe not in this Qur'an nor in that which was before it; but oh, if thou couldst see, when the wrong-doers are brought up before their Lord, how they cast the blame one to another; how those who were despised (in the earth) say unto those who were proud: But for you, we should have been believers.	And those who disbelieve say: By no means will we believe in this Quran, nor in that which is before it; and could you see when the unjust shall be made to stand before their Lord, bandying words one with another! Those who were reckoned weak shall say to those who were proud: Had it not been for you we would certainly have been believers.

34	032	The arrogant ones will say to those who had been despised: "Was it we who kept you back from Guidance after it reached you? Nay, rather, it was ye who transgressed."	Those who were proud say unto those who were despised: Did we drive you away from the guidance after it had come unto you? Nay, but ye were guilty.	Those who were proud shall say to those who were deemed weak: Did we turn you away from the guidance after it had come to you? Nay, you (yourselves) were guilty.
34	033	Those who had been despised will say to the arrogant ones: "Nay! it was a plot (of yours) by day and by night: Behold! Ye (constantly) ordered us to be ungrateful to Allah and to attribute equals to Him!" They will declare (their) repentance when they see the Penalty: We shall put yokes on the necks of the Unbelievers: It would only be a requital for their (ill) Deeds.	Those who were despised say unto those who were proud: Nay but (it was your) scheming night and day, when ye commanded us to disbelieve in Allah and set up rivals unto Him. And they are filled with remorse when they behold the doom; and We place carcans on the necks of those who disbelieved. Are they requited aught save what they used to do?	And those who were deemed weak shall say to those who were proud. Nay, (it was) planning by night and day when you told us to disbelieve in Allah and to set up likes with Him. And they shall conceal regret when they shall see the punishment; and We will put shackles on the necks of those who disbelieved; they shall not be requited but what they did.
34	034	Never did We send a warner to a population, but the wealthy ones among them said: "We believe not in the (Message) with which ye have been sent."	And We sent not unto any township a warner, but its pampered ones declared: Lo! we are disbelievers in that wherewith ye have been sent.	And We never sent a warner to a town but those who led lives in ease in it said: We are surely disbelievers in what you are sent with.
34	035	They said: "We have more in wealth and in sons, and we cannot be punished."	And they say: We are more (than you) in wealth and children. We are not the punished!	And they say: We have more wealth and children, and we shall not be punished.
34	036	Say: "Verily my Lord enlarges and restricts the Provision to whom He pleases, but most men understand not."	Say (O Muhammad): Lo! my Lord enlargeth the provision for whom He will and narroweth it (for whom He will). But most of mankind know not.	Say: Surely my Lord amplifies the means of subsistence for whom He pleases and straitens (for whom He pleases), but most men do not know.
34	037	It is not your wealth nor your sons, that will bring you nearer to Us in degree: but only those who believe and work righteousness - these are the ones for whom there is a multiplied Reward for their deeds, while secure they (reside) in the dwellings on high!	And it is not your wealth nor your children that will bring you near unto Us, but he who believeth and doeth good (he draweth near). As for such, theirs will be twofold reward for what they did and they will dwell secure in lofty halls.	And not your wealth nor your children, are the things which bring you near Us in station, but whoever believes and does good, these it is for whom is a double reward for what they do, and they shall be secure in the highest places.
34	038	Those who strive against Our Signs, to frustrate them, will be given over into Punishment.	And as for those who strive against Our revelations, challenging, they will be brought to the doom.	And (as for) those who strive in opposing Our communications, they shall be caused to be brought to the chastisement.
34	039	Say: "Verily my Lord enlarges and restricts the Sustenance to such of his servants as He pleases: and nothing do ye spend in the least (in His cause) but He replaces it: for He is the Best of those who grant Sustenance."	Say: Lo! my Lord enlargeth the provision for whom He will of His bondmen, and narroweth (it) for him. And whatsoever ye spend (for good) He replaceth it. And He is the Best of Providers.	Say: Surely my Lord amplifies the means of subsistence for whom He pleases of His servants and straitens (them) for whom (He pleases), and whatever thing you spend, He exceeds it in reward, and He is the best of Sustainers.
34	040	One Day He will gather them all together, and say to the angels, Was it you that these men used to worship?	And on the day when He will gather them all together, He will say unto the angels: Did these worship you?	And on the day when He will gather them all together, then will He say to the angels: Did these worship you?
34	041	They will say, "Glory to Thee! our (tie) is with Thee - as Protector - not with them. nay, but they worshipped the jinns: most of them believed in them."	They will say: Be Thou Glorified. Thou (alone) art our Guardian, not them! Nay, but they worshipped the jinn; most of them were believers in them.	They shall say: Glory be to Thee! Thou art our Guardian, not they; nay! they worshipped the jinn; most of them were believers in them.

34 042	So on that Day no power shall they have over each other, for profit or harm: and We shall say to the wrong-doers, "Taste ye the Penalty of the Fire,- the which ye were wont to deny!"	That day ye will possess no use nor hurt one for another. And We shall say unto those who did wrong: Taste the doom of the Fire which ye used to deny.	So on that day one of you shall not control profit or harm for another, and We will say to those who were unjust: Taste the chastisement of the fire which you called a lie.
34 043	When Our Clear Signs are rehearsed to them, they say, "This is only a man who wishes to hinder you from the (worship) which your fathers practised." And they say, "This is only a falsehood invented!" and the Unbelievers say of the Truth when it comes to them, "This is nothing but evident magic!"	And if Our revelations are recited unto them in plain terms, they say: This is naught else than a man who would turn you away from what your fathers used to worship; and they say: This is naught else than an invented lie. Those who disbelieve say of the truth when it reacheth them: This is naught else than mere magic.	And when Our clear communications are recited to them, they say: This is naught but a man who desires to turn you away from that which your fathers worshipped. And they say: This is naught but a lie that is forged. And those who disbelieve say of the truth when it comes to them: This is only clear enchantment.
34 044	But We had not given them Books which they could study, nor sent messengers to them before thee as Warners.	And We have given them no scriptures which they study, nor sent We unto them, before thee, any warner.	And We have not given them any books which they read, nor did We send to them before you a warner.
34 045	And their predecessors rejected (the Truth); these have not received a tenth of what We had granted to those: yet when they rejected My messengers, how (terrible) was My rejection (of them)!	Those before them denied, and these have not attained a tithe of that which We bestowed on them (of old); yet they denied My messengers. How intense then was My abhorrence (of them)!	And those before them rejected (the truth), and these have not yet attained a tenth of what We gave them, but they gave the lie to My messengers, then how was the manifestation of My disapproval?
34 046	Say: "I do admonish you on one point: that ye do stand up before Allah,- (It may be) in pairs, or (it may be) singly,- and reflect (within yourselves): your Companion is not possessed: he is no less than a warner to you, in face of a terrible Penalty."	Say (unto them, O Muhammad): I exhort you unto one thing only: that ye awake, for Allah's sake, by twos and singly, and then reflect: There is no madness in your comrade. He is naught else than a warner unto you in face of a terrific doom.	Say: I exhort you only to one thing, that rise up for Allah's sake in twos and singly, then ponder: there is no madness in your fellow-citizen; he is only a warner to you before a severe chastisement.
34 047	Say: "No reward do I ask of you: it is (all) in your interest: my reward is only due from Allah: And He is witness to all things."	Say: Whatever reward I might have asked of you is yours. My reward is the affair of Allah only. He is Witness over all things.	Say: Whatever reward I have asked of you, that is only for yourselves; my reward is only with Allah, and He is a witness of all things.
34 048	Say: "Verily my Lord doth cast the (mantle of) Truth (over His servants),- He that has full knowledge of (all) that is hidden."	Say: Lo! my Lord hurleth the truth. (He is) the Knower of Things Hidden.	Say: Surely my Lord utters the truth, the great Knower of the unseen.
34 049	Say: "The Truth has arrived, and Falsehood neither creates anything new, nor restores anything."	Say: The Truth hath come, and falsehood showeth not its face and will not return.	Say: The truth has come, and the falsehood shall vanish and shall not come back.
34 050	Say: "If I am astray, I only stray to the loss of my own soul: but if I receive guidance, it is because of the inspiration of my Lord to me: it is He Who hears all things, and is (ever) near."	Say: If I err, I err only to my own loss, and if I am rightly guided it is because of that which my Lord hath revealed unto me. Lo! He is Hearer, Nigh.	Say: If I err, I err only against my own soul, and if I follow a right direction, it is because of what my Lord reveals to me; surely He is Hearing, Nigh.
34 051	If thou couldst but see when they will quake with terror; but then there will be no escape (for them), and they will be seized from a position (quite) near.	Couldst thou but see when they are terrified with no escape, and are seized from near at hand,	And could you see when they shall become terrified, but (then) there shall be no escape and they shall be seized upon from a near place,

34 052	And they will say, "We do believe (now) in the (Truth)"; but how could they receive (Faith) from a position (so) far off,-	And say: We (now) believe therein. But how can they reach (faith) from afar off,	And they shall say: We believe in it. And how shall the attaining (of faith) be possible to them from a distant place?
34 053	Seeing that they did reject Faith (entirely) before, and that they (continually) cast (slanders) on the unseen from a position far off?	When they disbelieved in it of yore. They aim at the unseen from afar off.	And they disbelieved in it before, and they utter conjectures with regard to the unseen from a distant place.
34 054	And between them and their desires, is placed a barrier, as was done in the past with their partisans: for they were indeed in suspicious (disquieting) doubt.	And a gulf is set between them and that which they desire, as was done for people of their kind of old. Lo! they were in hopeless doubt.	And a barrier shall be placed between them and that which they desire, as was done with the likes of them before: surely they are in a disquieting doubt.

Chapter 35:

FATIR (THE ANGELS, ORIGINATOR)

Total Verses: 45 Revealed At: MAKKA

In the name of Allah, the Most Beneficent, the Most Merciful.

35 001	Praise be to Allah, Who created (out of nothing) the heavens and the earth, Who made the angels, messengers with wings,- two, or three, or four (pairs): He adds to Creation as He pleases: for Allah has power over all things.	Praise be to Allah, the Creator of the heavens and the earth, Who appointeth the angels messengers having wings two, three and four. He multiplieth in creation what He will. Lo! Allah is Able to do all things.	All praise is due to Allah, the Originator of the heavens and the earth, the Maker of the angels, messengers flying on wings, two, and three, and four; He increases in creation what He pleases; surely Allah has power over all things.
35 002	What Allah out of his Mercy doth bestow on mankind there is none can withhold: what He doth withhold, there is none can grant, apart from Him: and He is the Exalted in Power, full of Wisdom.	That which Allah openeth unto mankind of mercy none can withhold it; and that which He withholdeth none can release thereafter. He is the Mighty, the Wise.	Whatever Allah grants to men of (His) mercy, there is none to withhold it, and what He withholds there is none to send it forth after that, and He is the Mighty, the Wise.
35 003	O men! Call to mind the grace of Allah unto you! is there a creator, other than Allah, to give you sustenance from heaven or earth? There is no god but He: how then are ye deluded away from the Truth?	O mankind! Remember Allah's grace toward you! Is there any creator other than Allah who provideth for you from the sky and the earth? There is no God save Him. Whither then are ye turned?	O men! call to mind the favor of Allah on you; is there any creator besides Allah who gives you sustenance from the heaven and the earth? There is no god but He; whence are you then turned away?
35 004	And if they reject thee, so were messengers rejected before thee: to Allah go back for decision all affairs.	And if they deny thee, (O Muhammad), messengers (of Allah) were denied before thee. Unto Allah all things are brought back.	And if they call you a liar, truly messengers before you were called liars, and to Allah are all affairs returned.
35 005	O men! Certainly the promise of Allah is true. Let not then this present life deceive you, nor let the Chief Deceiver deceive you about Allah.	O mankind! Lo! the promise of Allah is true. So let not the life of the world beguile you, and let not the (avowed) beguiler beguile you with regard to Allah.	O men! surely the promise of Allah is true, therefore let not the life of this world deceive you, and let not the archdeceiver deceive you respecting Allah.
35 006	Verily Satan is an enemy to you: so treat him as an enemy. He only invites his adherents, that they may become Companions of the Blazing Fire.	Lo! the devil is an enemy for you, so treat him as an enemy. He only summoneth his faction to be owners of the flaming Fire.	Surely the Shaitan is your enemy, so take him for an enemy; he only invites his party that they may be inmates of the burning fire.

35 007	For those who reject Allah, is a terrible Penalty: but for those who believe and work righteous deeds, is Forgiveness, and a magnificent Reward.	Those who disbelieve, theirs will be an awful doom; and those who believe and do good works, theirs will be forgiveness and a great reward.	(As for) those who disbelieve, they shall have a severe punishment, and (as for) those who believe and do good, they shall have forgiveness and a great reward.
35 008	Is he, then, to whom the evil of his conduct is made alluring, so that he looks upon it as good, (equal to one who is rightly guided)? For Allah leaves to stray whom He wills, and guides whom He wills. So let not thy soul go out in (vainly) sighing after them: for Allah knows well all that they do!	Is he, the evil of whose deeds is made fairseeming unto him so that he deemeth it good, (other than Satan's dupe)? Allah verily sendeth whom He will astray, and guideth whom He will; so let not thy soul expire in sighings for them. Lo! Allah is Aware of what they do!	What! is he whose evil deed is made fairseeming to him so much so that he considers it good? Now surely Allah makes err whom He pleases and guides aright whom He pleases, so let not your soul waste away in grief for them; surely Allah is Cognizant of what they do.
35 009	It is Allah Who sends forth the Winds, so that they raise up the Clouds, and We drive them to a land that is dead, and revive the earth therewith after its death: even so (will be) the Resurrection!	And Allah it is Who sendeth the winds and they raise a cloud; then We lead it unto a dead land and revive therewith the earth after its death. Such is the Resurrection.	And Allah is He Who sends the winds so they raise a cloud, then We drive it on to a dead country, and therewith We give life to the earth after its death; even so is the quickening.
35 010	If any do seek for glory and power,- to Allah belong all glory and power. To Him mount up (all) Words of Purity: It is He Who exalts each Deed of Righteousness. Those that lay Plots of Evil,- for them is a Penalty terrible; and the plotting of such will be void (of result).	Whoso desireth power (should know that) all power belongeth to Allah. Unto Him good words ascend, and the pious deed doth He exalt; but those who plot iniquities, theirs will be an awful doom; and the plotting of such (folk) will come to naught.	Whoever desires honor, then to Allah belongs the honor wholly. To Him do ascend the good words; and the good deeds, lift them up, and (as for) those who plan evil deeds, they shall have a severe chastisement; and (as for) their plan, it shall perish.
35 011	And Allah did create you from dust; then from a sperm-drop; then He made you in pairs. And no female conceives, or lays down (her load), but with His knowledge. Nor is a man long-lived granted length of days, nor is a part cut off from his life, but is in a Decree (ordained). All this is easy to Allah.	Allah created you from dust, then from a little fluid, then He made you pairs (the male and female). No female beareth or bringeth forth save with His knowledge. And noone groweth old who groweth old, nor is aught lessened of his life, but it is recorded in a Book, Lo! that is easy for Allah.	And Allah created you of dust, then of the life-germ, then He made you pairs; and no female bears, nor does she bring forth, except with His knowledge; and no one whose life is lengthened has his life lengthened, nor is aught diminished of one's life, but it is all in a book; surely this is easy to Allah.
35 012	Nor are the two bodies of flowing water alike,- the one palatable, sweet, and pleasant to drink, and the other, salt and bitter. Yet from each (kind of water) do ye eat flesh fresh and tender, and ye extract ornaments to wear; and thou seest the ships therein that plough the waves, that ye may seek (thus) of the Bounty of Allah that ye may be grateful.	And the two seas are not alike: this, fresh, sweet, good to drink, this (other) bitter, salt. And from them both ye eat fresh meat and derive the ornament that ye wear. And thou seest the ship cleaving them with its prow that ye may seek of His bounty, and that haply ye may give thanks.	And the two seas are not alike: the one sweet, that subdues thirst by its excessive sweetness, pleasant to drink; and the other salt, that burns by its saltness; yet from each of them you eat fresh flesh and bring forth ornaments which you wear; and you see the ships cleave through it that you may seek of His bounty and that you may be grateful.
35 013	He merges Night into Day, and he merges Day into Night, and he has subjected the sun and the moon (to his Law): each one runs its course for a term appointed. Such is Allah your Lord: to Him belongs all Dominion. And those whom ye invoke besides Him have not the least power.	He maketh the night to pass into the day and He maketh the day to pass into the night. He hath subdued the sun and moon to service. Each runneth unto an appointed term. Such is Allah, your Lord; His is the Sovereignty; and those unto whom ye pray instead of Him own not so much as the white spot on a date-stone.	He causes the night to enter in upon the day, and He causes the day to enter in upon the night, and He has made subservient (to you) the sun and the moon; each one follows its course to an appointed time; this is Allah, your Lord, His is the kingdom; and those whom you call upon besides Him do not control a straw.

35 014	If ye invoke them, they will not listen to your call, and if they were to listen, they cannot answer your (prayer). On the Day of Judgment they will reject your "Partnership". and none, (O man!) can tell thee (the Truth) like the One Who is acquainted with all things.	If ye pray unto them they hear not your prayer, and if they heard they could not grant it you. On the Day of Resurrection they will disown association with you. None can inform you like Him Who is Aware.	If you call on them they shall not hear your call, and even if they could hear they shall not answer you; and on the resurrection day they will deny your associating them (with Allah); and none can inform you like the One Who is Aware.
35 015	O ye men! It is ye that have need of Allah: but Allah is the One Free of all wants, worthy of all praise.	O mankind! Ye are the poor in your relation to Allah. And Allah! He is the Absolute, the Owner of Praise.	O men! you are they who stand in need of Allah, and Allah is He Who is the Self-sufficient, the Praised One.
35 016	If He so pleased, He could blot you out and bring in a New Creation.	If He will, He can be rid of you and bring (instead of you) some new creation.	If He please, He will take you off and bring a new generation.
35 017	Nor is that (at all) difficult for Allah.	That is not a hard thing for Allah.	And this is not hard to Allah.
35 018	Nor can a bearer of burdens bear another's burdens if one heavily laden should call another to (bear) his load. Not the least portion of it can be carried (by the other). Even though he be nearly related. Thou canst but admonish such as fear their Lord unseen and establish regular Prayer. And whoever purifies himself does so for the benefit of his own soul; and the destination (of all) is to Allah.	And no burdened soul can bear another's burden, and if one heavy laden crieth for (help with) his load, naught of it will be lifted even though he (unto whom he crieth) be of kin. Thou warnest only those who fear their Lord in secret, and have established worship. He who groweth (in goodness), groweth only for himself, (he cannot by his merit redeem others). Unto Allah is the journeying.	And a burdened soul cannot bear the burden of another and if one weighed down by burden should cry for (another to carry) its burden, not aught of it shall be carried, even though he be near of kin. You warn only those who fear their Lord in secret and keep up prayer; and whoever purifies himself, he purifies himself only for (the good of) his own soul; and to Allah is the eventual coming.
35 019	The blind and the seeing are not alike;	The blind man is not equal with the seer;	And the blind and the seeing are not alike
35 020	Nor are the depths of Darkness and the Light;	Nor is darkness (tantamount to) light;	Nor the darkness and the light,
35 021	Nor are the (chilly) shade and the (genial) heat of the sun:	Nor is the shadow equal with the sun's full heat;	Nor the shade and the heat,
35 022	Nor are alike those that are living and those that are dead. Allah can make any that He wills to hear; but thou canst not make those to hear who are (buried) in graves.	Nor are the living equal with the dead. Lo! Allah maketh whom He will to hear. Thou canst not reach those who are in the graves.	Neither are the living and the dead alike. Surely Allah makes whom He pleases hear, and you cannot make those hear who are in the graves.
35 023	Thou art no other than a warner.	Thou art but a warner.	You are naught but a warner.
35 024	Verily We have sent thee in truth, as a bearer of glad tidings, and as a warner: and there never was a people, without a warner having lived among them (in the past).	Lo! We have sent thee with the Truth, a bearer of glad tidings and a warner; and there is not a nation but a warner hath passed among them.	Surely We have sent you with the truth as a bearer of good news and a warner; and there is not a people but a warner has gone among them.
35 025	And if they reject thee, so did their predecessors, to whom came their messengers with Clear Signs, Books of dark prophecies, and the Book of Enlightenment.	And if they deny thee, those before them also denied. Their messengers came unto them with clear proofs (of Allah's Sovereignty), and with the Psalms and the Scripture giving light.	And if they call you a liar, so did those before them indeed call (their messengers) liars; their messengers had come to them with clear arguments, and with scriptures, and with the illuminating book.
35 026	In the end did I punish those who rejected Faith: and how (terrible) was My rejection (of them)!	Then seized I those who disbelieved, and how intense was My abhorrence!	Then did I punish those who disbelieved, so how was the manifestation of My disapproval?

35 027	Seest thou not that Allah sends down rain from the sky? With it We then bring out produce of various colours. And in the mountains are tracts white and red, of various shades of colour, and black intense in hue.	Hast thou not seen that Allah causeth water to fall from the sky, and We produce therewith fruit of divers hues; and among the hills are streaks white and red, of divers hues, and (others) raven-black;		Do you not see that Allah sends down water from the cloud, then We bring forth therewith fruits of various colors; and in the mountains are streaks, white and red, of various hues and (others) intensely black?
35 028	And so amongst men and crawling creatures and cattle, are they of various colours. Those truly fear Allah, among His Servants, who have knowledge: for Allah is Exalted in Might, Oft-Forgiving.	And of men and beasts and cattle, in like manner, divers hues? The erudite among His bondmen fear Allah alone. Lo! Allah is Mighty, Forgiving.		And of men and beasts and cattle are various species of it likewise; those of His servants only who are possessed of knowledge fear Allah; surely Allah is Mighty, Forgiving.
35 029	Those who rehearse the Book of Allah, establish regular Prayer, and spend (in Charity) out of what We have provided for them, secretly and openly, hope for a commerce that will never fail:	Lo! those who read the Scripture of Allah, and establish worship, and spend of that which We have bestowed on them secretly and openly, they look forward to imperishable gain,		Surely they who recite the Book of Allah and keep up prayer and spend out of what We have given them secretly and openly, hope for a gain which will not perish.
35 030	For He will pay them their meed, nay, He will give them (even) more out of His Bounty: for He is Oft-Forgiving, Most Ready to appreciate (service).	That He will pay them their wages and increase them of His grace. Lo! He is Forgiving, Responsive.		That He may pay them back fully their rewards and give them more out of His grace: surely He is Forgiving, Multiplier of rewards.
35 031	That which We have revealed to thee of the Book is the Truth,- confirming what was (revealed) before it: for Allah is assuredly- with respect to His Servants - well acquainted and Fully Observant.	As for that which We inspire in thee of the Scripture, it is the Truth confirming that which was (revealed) before it. Lo! Allah is indeed Observer, Seer of His slaves.		And that which We have revealed to you of the Book, that is the truth verifying that which is before it; most surely with respect to His servants Allah is Aware, Seeing.
35 032	Then We have given the Book for inheritance to such of Our Servants as We have chosen: but there are among them some who wrong their own souls; some who follow a middle course; and some who are, by Allah's leave, foremost in good deeds that is the highest Grace.	Then We gave the Scripture as inheritance unto those whom We elected of Our bondmen. But of them are some who wrong themselves and of them are some who are lukewarm, and of them are some who outstrip (others) through good deeds, by Allah's leave. That is the great favour!		Then We gave the Book for an inheritance to those whom We chose from among Our servants; but of them is he who makes his soul to suffer a loss, and of them is he who takes a middle course, and of them is he who is foremost in deeds of goodness by Allah's permission; this is the great excellence.
35 033	Gardens of Eternity will they enter: therein will they be adorned with bracelets of gold and pearls; and their garments there will be of silk.	Gardens of Eden! They enter them wearing armlets of gold and pearl and their raiment therein is silk.		Gardens of perpetuity, they shall enter therein; they shad be made to wear therein bracelets of gold and pearls, and their dress therein shall be silk.
35 034	And they will say: "Praise be to Allah, Who has removed from us (all) sorrow: for our Lord is indeed Oft-Forgiving Ready to appreciate (service):"	And they say: Praise be to Allah Who hath put grief away from us. Lo! Our Lord is Forgiving, Bountiful,		And they shall say: (All) praise is due to Allah, Who has made grief to depart from us; most surely our Lord is Forgiving, Multiplier of rewards,
35 035	"Who has, out of His Bounty, settled us in a Home that will last: no toil nor sense of weariness shall touch us therein."	Who, of His grace, hath installed us in the mansion of eternity, where toil toucheth us not nor can weariness affect us.		Who has made us alight in a house abiding for ever out of His grace; toil shall not touch us therein, nor shall fatigue therein afflict us.

35	036	But those who reject (Allah) - for them will be the Fire of Hell: No term shall be determined for them, so they should die, nor shall its Penalty be lightened for them. Thus do We reward every ungrateful one!	But as for those who disbelieve, for them is fire of hell; it taketh not complete effect upon them so that they can die, nor is its torment lightened for them. Thus We punish every ingrate.	And (as for) those who disbelieve, for them is the fire of hell; it shall not be finished with them entirely so that they should die, nor shall the chastisement thereof be lightened to them: even thus do We retribute every ungrateful one.
35	037	Therein will they cry aloud (for assistance): "Our Lord! Bring us out: we shall work righteousness, not the (deeds) we used to do!" - Did We not give you long enough life so that he that would should receive admonition? and (moreover) the warner came to you. So taste ye (the fruits of your deeds): for the wrong-doers there is no helper."	And they cry for help there, (saying): Our Lord! Release us; we will do right, not (the wrong) that we used to do. Did not We grant you a life long enough for him who reflected to reflect therein? And the warner came unto you. Now taste (the flavour of your deeds), for evil-doers have no helper.	And they shall cry therein for succour: O our Lord! take us out, we will do good deeds other than those which we used to do. Did We not preserve you alive long enough, so that he who would be mindful in it should mind? And there came to you the warner; therefore taste; because for the unjust, there is no helper.
35	038	Verily Allah knows (all) the hidden things of the heavens and the earth: verily He has full knowledge of all that is in (men's) hearts.	Lo! Allah is the Knower of the Unseen of the heavens and the earth. Lo! He is Aware of the secret of (men's) breasts.	Surely Allah is the Knower of what is unseen in the heavens and earth; surely He is Cognizant of what is in the hearts.
35	039	He it is that has made you inheritors in the earth: if, then, any do reject (Allah), their rejection (works) against themselves: their rejection but adds to the odium for the Unbelievers in the sight of their Lord: their rejection but adds to (their own) undoing.	He it is Who hath made you regents in the earth; so he who disbelieveth, his disbelief be on his own head. Their disbelief increaseth for the disbelievers, in their Lord's sight, naught save abhorrence. Their disbelief increaseth for the disbelievers naught save loss.	He it is Who made you rulers in the land; therefore whoever disbelieves, his unbelief is against himself; and their unbelief does not increase the disbelievers with their Lord in anything except hatred; and their unbelief does not increase the disbelievers in anything except loss.
35	040	Say: "Have ye seen (these) 'Partners' of yours whom ye call upon besides Allah? Show Me what it is they have created in the (wide) earth. Or have they a share in the heavens? Or have We given them a Book from which they (can derive) clear (evidence)?- Nay, the wrong-doers promise each other nothing but delusions."	Say: Have ye seen your partner-gods to whom ye pray beside Allah? Show me what they created of the earth! Or have they any portion in the heavens? Or have We given them a scripture so they act on clear proof therefrom? Nay, the evil-doers promise one another only to deceive.	Say: Have you considered your associates which you call upon besides Allah? Show me what part of the earth they have created, or have they any share in the heavens; or, have We given them a book so that they follow a clear argument thereof? Nay, the unjust do not hold out promises one to another but only to deceive.
35	041	It is Allah Who sustains the heavens and the earth, lest they cease (to function): and if they should fail, there is none - not one - can sustain them thereafter: Verily He is Most Forbearing, Oft-Forgiving.	Lo! Allah graspeth the heavens and the earth that they deviate not, and if they were to deviate there is not one that could grasp them after Him. Lo! He is ever Clement, Forgiving.	Surely Allah upholds the heavens and the earth lest they come to naught; and if they should come to naught, there is none who can uphold them after Him; surely He is the Forbearing, the Forgiving.
35	042	They swore their strongest oaths by Allah that if a warner came to them, they would follow his guidance better than any (other) of the Peoples: But when a warner came to them, it has only increased their flight (from righteousness),-	And they swore by Allah, their most binding oath, that if a warner came unto them they would be more tractable than any of the nations; yet, when a warner came unto them it aroused in them naught save repugnance,	And they swore by Allah with the strongest of their oaths that if there came to them a warner they would be better guided than any of the nations; but when there came to them a warner it increased them in naught but aversion.

35 043	On account of their arrogance in the land and their plotting of Evil, but the plotting of Evil will hem in only the authors thereof. Now are they but looking for the way the ancients were dealt with? But no change wilt thou find in Allah's way (of dealing): no turning off wilt thou find in Allah's way (of dealing).	(Shown in their) behaving arrogantly in the land and plotting evil; and the evil plot encloseth but the men who make it. Then, can they expect aught save the treatment of the folk of old? Thou wilt not find for Allah's way of treatment any substitute, nor wilt thou find for Allah's way of treatment aught of power to change.	(In) behaving proudly in the land and in planning evil; and the evil plans shall not beset any save the authors of it. Then should they wait for aught except the way of the former people? For you shall not find any alteration in the course of Allah; and you shall not find any change in the course of Allah.	
35 044	Do they not travel through the earth, and see what was the End of those before them,- though they were superior to them in strength? Nor is Allah to be frustrated by anything whatever in the heavens or on earth: for He is All-Knowing. All-Powerful.	Have they not travelled in the land and seen the nature of the consequence for those who were before them, and they were mightier than these in power? Allah is not such that aught in the heavens or in the earth escapeth Him. Lo! He is the Wise, the Mighty.	Have they not travelled in the land and seen how was the end of those before them while they were stronger than these in power? And Allah is not such that any thing in the heavens or in the earth should escape Him; surely He is Knowing, Powerful.	
35 045	If Allah were to punish men according to what they deserve. He would not leave on the back of the (earth) a single living creature: but He gives them respite for a stated Term: when their Term expires, verily Allah has in His sight all His Servants.	If Allah took mankind to task by that which they deserve, He would not leave a living creature on the surface of the earth; but He reprieveth them unto an appointed term, and when their term cometh - then verily (they will know that) Allah is ever Seer of His slaves.	And were Allah to punish men for what they earn, He would not leave on the back of it any creature, but He respites them till an appointed term; so when their doom shall come, then surely Allah is Seeing with respect to His servants.	

Chapter 36:

YA-SEEN (YA-SEEN)

Total Verses: 83 Revealed At: MAKKA

In the name of Allah, the Most Beneficent, the Most Merciful.

36 001	Ya Sin.	Ya Sin.	Ya Seen.
36 002	By the Qur'an, full of Wisdom,-	By the wise Qur'an,	I swear by the Quran full of wisdom
36 003	Thou art indeed one of the messengers,	Lo! thou art of those sent	Most surely you are one of the messengers
36 004	On a Straight Way.	On a straight path,	On a right way.
36 005	It is a Revelation sent down by (Him), the Exalted in Might, Most Merciful.	A revelation of the Mighty, the Merciful,	A revelation of the Mighty, the Merciful.
36 006	In order that thou mayest admonish a people, whose fathers had received no admonition, and who therefore remain heedless (of the Signs of Allah).	That thou mayst warn a folk whose fathers were not warned, so they are heedless.	That you may warn a people whose fathers were not warned, so they are heedless.
36 007	The Word is proved true against the greater part of them: for they do not believe.	Already hath the judgment, (for their infidelity) proved true of most of them, for they believe not.	Certainly the word has proved true of most of them, so they do not believe.

36 008	We have put yokes round their necks right up to their chins, so that their heads are forced up (and they cannot see).	Lo! We have put on their necks carcans reaching unto the chins, so that they are made stiff-necked.	Surely We have placed chains on their necks, and these reach up to their chins, so they have their heads raised aloft.
36 009	And We have put a bar in front of them and a bar behind them, and further, We have covered them up; so that they cannot see.	And We have set a bar before them and a bar behind them, and (thus) have covered them so that they see not.	And We have made before them a barrier and a barrier behind them, then We have covered them over so that they do not see.
36 010	The same is it to them whether thou admonish them or thou do not admonish them, they will not believe.	Whether thou warn them or thou warn them not, it is alike for them, for they believe not.	And it is alike to them whether you warn them or warn them not: they do not believe.
36 011	Thou canst but admonish such a one as follows the Message and fears the (Lord) Most Gracious, unseen: give such a one, therefore, good tidings, of Forgiveness and a Reward most generous.	Thou warnest only him who followeth the Reminder and feareth the Beneficent in secret. To him bear tidings of forgiveness and a rich reward.	You can only warn him who follows the reminder and fears the Beneficent Allah in secret; so announce to him forgiveness and an honorable reward.
36 012	Verily We shall give life to the dead, and We record that which they send before and that which they leave behind, and of all things have We taken account in a clear Book (of evidence).	Lo! We it is Who bring the dead to life. We record that which they send before (them), and their footprints. And all things We have kept in a clear Register.	Surely We give life to the dead, and We write down what they have sent before and their footprints, and We have recorded everything in a clear writing.
36 013	Set forth to them, by way of a parable, the (story of) the Companions of the City. Behold, there came messengers to it.	Coin for them a similitude: The people of the city when those sent (from Allah) came unto them;	And set out to them an example of the people of the town, when the messengers came to it.
36 014	When We (first) sent to them two messengers, they rejected them: But We strengthened them with a third: they said, "Truly, we have been sent on a mission to you."	When We sent unto them twain, and they denied them both, so We reinforced them with a third, and they said: Lo! we have been sent unto you.	When We sent to them two, they rejected both of them, then We strengthened (them) with a third, so they said: Surely we are messengers to you.
36 015	The (people) said: "Ye are only men like ourselves; and (Allah) Most Gracious sends no sort of revelation: ye do nothing but lie."	They said: Ye are but mortals like unto us. The Beneficent hath naught revealed. Ye do but lie!	They said: You are naught but mortals like ourselves, nor has the Beneficent Allah revealed anything; you only lie.
36 016	They said: "Our Lord doth know that we have been sent on a mission to you:"	They answered: Our Lord knoweth that we are indeed sent unto you,	They said: Our Lord knows that we are most surely messengers to you.
36 017	"And our duty is only to proclaim the clear Message."	And our duty is but plain conveyance (of the message).	And nothing devolves on us but a clear deliverance (of the message).
36 018	The (people) said: "for us, we augur an evil omen from you: if ye desist not, we will certainly stone you. And a grievous punishment indeed will be inflicted on you by us."	(The people of the city) said: We augur ill of you. If ye desist not, we shall surely stone you, and grievous torture will befall you at our hands.	They said: Surely we augur evil from you; if you do not desist, we will certainly stone you, and there shall certainly afflict you a painful chastisement from us.
36 019	They said: "Your evil omens are with yourselves: (deem ye this an evil omen). If ye are admonished? Nay, but ye are a people transgressing all bounds!"	They said: Your evil augury be with you! Is it because ye are reminded (of the truth)? Nay, but ye are froward folk!	They said: Your evil fortune is with you; what! if you are reminded! Nay, you are an extravagant people.
36 020	Then there came running, from the farthest part of the City, a man, saying, "O my people! Obey the messengers:"	And there came from the uttermost part of the city a man running. He cried: O my people! Follow those who have been sent!	And from the remote part of the city there came a man running, he said: O my people! follow the messengers;
36 021	"Obey those who ask no reward of you (for themselves), and who have themselves received Guidance."	Follow those who ask of you no fee, and who are rightly guided.	Follow him who does not ask you for reward, and they are the followers of the right course;

36 022	"It would not be reasonable in me if I did not serve Him Who created me, and to Whom ye shall (all) be brought back."	For what cause should I not serve Him Who hath created me, and unto Whom ye will be brought back?	And what reason have I that I should not serve Him Who brought me into existence? And to Him you shall be brought back;
36 023	"Shall I take (other) gods besides Him? If (Allah) Most Gracious should intend some adversity for me, of no use whatever will be their intercession for me, nor can they deliver me."	Shall I take (other) gods in place of Him when, if the Beneficent should wish me any harm, their intercession will avail me naught, nor can they save?	What! shall I take besides Him gods whose intercession, if the Beneficent Allah should desire to afflict me with a harm, shall not avail me aught, nor shall they be able to deliver me?
36 024	"I would indeed, if I were to do so, be in manifest Error."	Then truly I should be in error manifest.	In that case I shall most surely be in clear error:
36 025	"For me, I have faith in the Lord of you (all): listen, then, to me!"	Lo! I have believed in your Lord, so hear me!	Surely I believe in your Lord, therefore hear me.
36 026	It was said: "Enter thou the Garden." He said: "Ah me! Would that my People knew (what I know)!"-	It was said (unto him): Enter paradise. He said: Would that my people knew,	It was said: Enter the garden. He said: O would that my people had known,
36 027	"For that my Lord has granted me Forgiveness and has enrolled me among those held in honour!"	With what (munificence) my Lord hath pardoned me and made me of the honoured ones!	Of that on account of which my Lord has forgiven me and made me of the honored ones!
36 028	And We sent not down against his People, after him, any hosts from heaven, nor was it needful for Us so to do.	We sent not down against his people after him a host from heaven, nor do We ever send.	And We did not send down upon his people after him any hosts from heaven, nor do We ever send down.
36 029	It was no more than a single mighty Blast, and behold! they were (like ashes) quenched and silent.	It was but one Shout, and lo! they were extinct.	It was naught but a single cry, and lo! they were still.
36 030	Ah! Alas for (My) Servants! There comes not a messenger to them but they mock him!	Ah, the anguish for the bondmen! Never came there unto them a messenger but they did mock him!	Alas for the servants! there comes not to them a messenger but they mock at him.
36 031	See they not how many generations before them we destroyed? Not to them will they return:	Have they not seen how many generations We destroyed before them, which indeed returned not unto them;	Do they not consider how many of the generations have We destroyed before them, because they do not turn to them?
36 032	But each one of them all - will be brought before Us (for judgment).	But all, without exception, will be brought before Us.	And all of them shall surely be brought before Us.
36 033	A Sign for them is the earth that is dead: We do give it life, and produce grain therefrom, of which ye do eat.	A token unto them is the dead earth. We revive it, and We bring forth from it grain so that they eat thereof;	And a sign to them is the dead earth: We give life to it and bring forth from it grain SQ they eat of it.
36 034	And We produce therein orchard with date-palms and vines, and We cause springs to gush forth therein:	And We have placed therein gardens of the date-palm and grapes, and We have caused springs of water to gush forth therein,	And We make therein gardens of palms and grapevines and We make springs to flow forth in it,
36 035	That they may enjoy the fruits of this (artistry): It was not their hands that made this: will they not then give thanks?	That they may eat of the fruit thereof, and their hands made it not. Will they not, then, give thanks?	That they may eat of the fruit thereof, and their hands did not make it; will they not then be grateful?
36 036	Glory to Allah, Who created in pairs all things that the earth produces, as well as their own (human) kind and (other) things of which they have no knowledge.	Glory be to Him Who created all the sexual pairs, of that which the earth groweth, and of themselves, and of that which they know not!	Glory be to Him Who created pairs of all things, of what the earth grows, and of their kind and of what they do not know.
36 037	And a Sign for them is the Night: We withdraw therefrom the Day, and behold they are plunged in darkness;	A token unto them is night. We strip it of the day, and lo! they are in darkness.	And a sign to them is the night: We draw forth from it the day, then lo! they are in the dark;

36 038	And the sun runs his course for a period determined for him: that is the decree of (Him), the Exalted in Might, the All-Knowing.	And the sun runneth on unto a resting-place for him. That is the measuring of the Mighty, the Wise.	And the sun runs on to a term appointed for it; that is the ordinance of the Mighty, the Knowing.
36 039	And the Moon,- We have measured for her mansions (to traverse) till she returns like the old (and withered) lower part of a date-stalk.	And for the moon We have appointed mansions till she return like an old shrivelled palm-leaf.	And (as for) the moon, We have ordained for it stages till it becomes again as an old dry palm branch.
36 040	It is not permitted to the Sun to catch up the Moon, nor can the Night outstrip the Day. Each (just) swims along in (its own) orbit (according to Law).	It is not for the sun to overtake the moon, nor doth the night outstrip the day. They float each in an orbit.	Neither is it allowable to the sun that it should overtake the moon, nor can the night outstrip the day; and all float on in a sphere.
36 041	And a Sign for them is that We bore their race (through the Flood) in the loaded Ark;	And a token unto them is that We bear their offspring in the laden ship,	And a sign to them is that We bear their offspring in the laden ship.
36 042	And We have created for them similar (vessels) on which they ride.	And have created for them of the like thereof whereon they ride.	And We have created for them the like of it, what they will ride on.
36 043	If it were Our Will, We could drown them: then would there be no helper (to hear their cry), nor could they be delivered,	And if We will, We drown them, and there is no help for them, neither can they be saved;	And if We please, We can drown them, then there shall be no succorer for them, nor shall they be rescued,
36 044	Except by way of Mercy from Us, and by way of (world) convenience (to serve them) for a time.	Unless by mercy from Us and as comfort for a while.	But (by) mercy from Us and for enjoyment till a time.
36 045	When they are told, "Fear ye that which is before you and that which will be after you, in order that ye may receive Mercy," (they turn back).	When it is said unto them: Beware of that which is before you and that which is behind you, that haply ye may find mercy (they are heedless).	And when it is said to them: Guard against what is before you and what is behind you, that mercy may be had on you.
36 046	Not a Sign comes to them from among the Signs of their Lord, but they turn away therefrom.	Never came a token of the tokens of their Lord to them, but they did turn away from it!	And there comes not to them a communication of the communications of their Lord but they turn aside from it.
36 047	And when they are told, "Spend ye of (the bounties) with which Allah has provided you," the Unbelievers say to those who believe: "Shall we then feed those whom, if Allah had so willed, He would have fed, (Himself)?- Ye are in nothing but manifest error."	And when it is said unto them: Spend of that wherewith Allah hath provided you, those who disbelieve say unto those who believe: Shall we feed those whom Allah, if He willed, would feed? Ye are in naught else than error manifest.	And when it is said to them: Spend out of what Allah has given you, those who disbelieve say to those who believe: Shall we feed him whom, if Allah please, He could feed? You are in naught but clear error.
36 048	Further, they say, "When will this promise (come to pass), if what ye say is true?"	And they say: When will this promise be fulfilled, if ye are truthful?	And they say: When will this threat come to pass, if you are truthful?
36 049	They will not (have to) wait for aught but a single Blast: it will seize them while they are yet disputing among themselves!	They await but one Shout, which will surprise them while they are disputing.	They wait not for aught but a single cry which will overtake them while they yet contend with one another.
36 050	No (chance) will they then have, by will, to dispose (of their affairs), nor to return to their own people!	Then they cannot make bequest, nor can they return to their own folk.	So they shall not be able to make a bequest, nor shall they return to their families.
36 051	The trumpet shall be sounded, when behold! from the sepulchres (men) will rush forth to their Lord!	And the trumpet is blown and lo! from the graves they hie unto their Lord,	And the trumpet shall be blown, when lo! from their graves they shall hasten on to their Lord.

36 052	They will say: "Ah! Woe unto us! Who hath raised us up from our beds of repose?"... (A voice will say:) "This is what (Allah) Most Gracious had promised. And true was the word of the messengers!"	Crying: Woe upon us! Who hath raised us from our place of sleep? This is that which the Beneficent did promise, and the messengers spoke truth.	They shall say: O woe to us! who has raised us up from our sleeping-place? This is what the Beneficent Allah promised and the messengers told the truth.
36 053	It will be no more than a single Blast, when lo! they will all be brought up before Us!	It is but one Shout, and behold them brought together before Us!	There would be naught but a single cry, when lo! they shall all be brought before Us.
36 054	Then, on that Day, not a soul will be wronged in the least, and ye shall but be repaid the meeds of your past Deeds.	This day no soul is wronged in aught; nor are ye requited aught save what ye used to do.	So this day no soul shall be dealt with unjustly in the least; and you shall not be rewarded aught but that which you did.
36 055	Verily the Companions of the Garden shall that Day have joy in all that they do;	Lo! those who merit paradise this day are happily employed,	Surely the dwellers of the garden shall on that day be in an occupation quite happy.
36 056	They and their associates will be in groves of (cool) shade, reclining on Thrones (of dignity);	They and their wives, in pleasant shade, on thrones reclining;	They and their wives shall be in shades, reclining on raised couches.
36 057	(Every) fruit (enjoyment) will be there for them; they shall have whatever they call for;	Theirs the fruit (of their good deeds) and theirs (all) that they ask;	They shall have fruits therein, and they shall have whatever they desire.
36 058	"Peace!" - a word (of salutation) from a Lord Most Merciful!	The word from a Merciful Lord (for them) is: Peace!	Peace: a word from a Merciful Lord.
36 059	"And O ye in sin! Get ye apart this Day!"	But avaunt ye, O ye guilty, this day!	And get aside today, O guilty ones!
36 060	"Did I not enjoin on you, O ye Children of Adam, that ye should not worship Satan; for that he was to you an enemy avowed?"-	Did I not charge you, O ye sons of Adam, that ye worship not the devil - Lo! he is your open foe!	Did I not charge you, O children of Adam! that you should not serve the Shaitan? Surely he is your open enemy,
36 061	"And that ye should worship Me, (for that) this was the Straight Way?"	But that ye worship Me? That was the right path.	And that you should serve Me; this is the right way.
36 062	"But he did lead astray a great multitude of you. Did ye not, then, understand?"	Yet he hath led astray of you a great multitude. Had ye then no sense?	And certainly he led astray numerous people from among you. What! could you not then understand?
36 063	"This is the Hell of which ye were (repeatedly) warned!"	This is hell which ye were promised (if ye followed him).	This is the hell with which you were threatened.
36 064	"Embrace ye the (fire) this Day, for that ye (persistently) rejected (Truth)."	Burn therein this day for that ye disbelieved.	Enter into it this day because you disbelieved.
36 065	That Day shall We set a seal on their mouths. But their hands will speak to us, and their feet bear witness, to all that they did.	This day We seal up their mouths, and their hands speak out to Us and their feet bear witness as to what they used to earn.	On that day We will set a seal upon their mouths, and their hands shall speak to Us, and their feet shall bear witness of what they earned.
36 066	If it had been our Will, We could surely have blotted out their eyes; then should they have run about groping for the Path, but how could they have seen?	And had We willed, We verily could have quenched their eyesight so that they should struggle for the way. Then how could they have seen?	And if We please We would certainly put out their eyes, then they would run about groping for the way, but how should they see?
36 067	And if it had been Our Will, We could have transformed them (to remain) in their places; then should they have been unable to move about, nor could they have returned (after error).	And had We willed, We verily could have fixed them in their place, making them powerless to go forward or turn back.	And if We please We would surely transform them in their place, then they would not be able to go on, nor will they return.

36 068	If We grant long life to any, We cause him to be reversed in nature: Will they not then understand?	He whom we bring unto old age, We reverse him in creation (making him go back to weakness after strength). Have ye then no sense?	And whomsoever We cause to live long, We reduce (him) to an abject state in constitution; do they not then understand?
36 069	We have not instructed the (Prophet) in Poetry, nor is it meet for him: this is no less than a Message and a Qur'an making things clear:	And We have not taught him (Muhammad) poetry, nor is it meet for him. This is naught else than a Reminder and a Lecture making plain,	And We have not taught him poetry, nor is it meet for him; it is nothing but a reminder and a plain Quran,
36 070	That it may give admonition to any (who are) alive, and that the charge may be proved against those who reject (Truth).	To warn whosoever liveth, and that the word may be fulfilled against the disbelievers.	That it may warn him who would have life, and (that) the word may prove true against the unbelievers.
36 071	See they not that it is We Who have created for them - among the things which Our hands have fashioned - cattle, which are under their dominion?-	Have they not seen how We have created for them of Our handiwork the cattle, so that they are their owners,	Do they not see that We have created cattle for them, out of what Our hands have wrought, so they are their masters?
36 072	And that We have subjected them to their (use)? of them some do carry them and some they eat:	And have subdued them unto them, so that some of them they have for riding, some for food?	And We have subjected them to them, so some of them they have to ride upon, and some of them they eat.
36 073	And they have (other) profits from them (besides), and they get (milk) to drink. Will they not then be grateful?	Benefits and (divers) drinks have they from them. Will they not then give thanks?	And therein they have advantages and drinks; will they not then be grateful?
36 074	Yet they take (for worship) gods other than Allah, (hoping) that they might be helped!	And they have taken (other) gods beside Allah, in order that they may be helped.	And they have taken gods besides Allah that they may be helped.
36 075	They have not the power to help them: but they will be brought up (before Our Judgment-seat) as a troop (to be condemned).	It is not in their power to help them; but they (the worshippers) are unto them a host in arms.	(But) they shall not be able to assist them, and they shall be a host brought up before them.
36 076	Let not their speech, then, grieve thee. Verily We know what they hide as well as what they disclose.	So let not their speech grieve thee (O Muhammad). Lo! We know what they conceal and what proclaim.	Therefore let not their speech grieve you; surely We know what they do in secret and what they do openly.
36 077	Doth not man see that it is We Who created him from sperm? yet behold! he (stands forth) as an open adversary!	Hath not man seen that We have created him from a drop of seed? Yet lo! he is an open opponent.	Does not man see that We have created him from the small seed? Then lo! he is an open disputant.
36 078	And he makes comparisons for Us, and forgets his own (origin and) Creation: He says, "Who can give life to (dry) bones and decomposed ones (at that)?"	And he hath coined for Us a similitude, and hath forgotten the fact of his creation, saying: Who will revive these bones when they have rotted away?	And he strikes out a likeness for Us and forgets his own creation. Says he: Who will give life to the bones when they are rotten?
36 079	Say, "He will give them life Who created them for the first time! for He is Well-versed in every kind of creation!"-	Say: He will revive them Who produced them at the first, for He is Knower of every creation,	Say: He will give life to them Who brought them into existence at first, and He is cognizant of all creation,
36 080	"The same Who produces for you fire out of the green tree, when behold! ye kindle therewith (your own fires)!"	Who hath appointed for you fire from the green tree, and behold! ye kindle from it.	He Who has made for you the fire (to burn) from the green tree, so that with it you kindle (fire).
36 081	"Is not He Who created the heavens and the earth able to create the like thereof?" - Yea, indeed! for He is the Creator Supreme, of skill and knowledge (infinite)!	Is not He Who created the heavens and the earth Able to create the like of them? Aye, that He is! for He is the All-Wise Creator,	Is not He Who created the heavens and the earth able to create the like of them? Yea! and He is the Creator (of all), the Knower.

36 082	Verily, when He intends a thing, His Command is, "be", and it is!	But His command, when He intendeth a thing, is only that He saith unto it: Be! and it is.	His command, when He intends anything, is only to say to it: Be, so it is.
36 083	So glory to Him in Whose hands is the dominion of all things: and to Him will ye be all brought back.	Therefor Glory be to Him in Whose hand is the dominion over all things! Unto Him ye will be brought back.	Therefore glory be to Him in Whose hand is the kingdom of all things, and to Him you shall be brought back.

Chapter 37:

AS-SAAFFAT (THOSE WHO SET THE RANKS, DRAWN UP IN RANKS)

Total Verses: 182 Revealed At: MAKKA

In the name of Allah, the Most Beneficent, the Most Merciful.

37 001	By those who range themselves in ranks,	By those who set the ranks in battle order	I swear by those who draw themselves out in ranks
37 002	And so are strong in repelling (evil),	And those who drive away (the wicked) with reproof	Then those who drive away with reproof,
37 003	And thus proclaim the Message (of Allah)!	And those who read (the Word) for a reminder,	Then those who recite, being mindful,
37 004	Verily, verily, your Allah is one!-	Lo! thy Lord is surely One;	Most surely your Allah is One:
37 005	Lord of the heavens and of the earth and all between them, and Lord of every point at the rising of the sun!	Lord of the heavens and of the earth and all that is between them, and Lord of the sun's risings.	The Lord of the heavens and the earth and what is between them, and Lord of the easts.
37 006	We have indeed decked the lower heaven with beauty (in) the stars,-	Lo! We have adorned the lowest heaven with an ornament, the planets;	Surely We have adorned the nearest heaven with an adornment, the stars,
37 007	(For beauty) and for guard against all obstinate rebellious evil spirits,	With security from every froward devil.	And (there is) a safeguard against every rebellious Shaitan.
37 008	(So) they should not strain their ears in the direction of the Exalted Assembly but be cast away from every side,	They cannot listen to the Highest Chiefs for they are pelted from every side,	They cannot listen to the exalted assembly and they are thrown at from every side,
37 009	Repulsed, for they are under a perpetual penalty,	Outcast, and theirs is a perpetual torment;	Being driven off, and for them is a perpetual chastisement,
37 010	Except such as snatch away something by stealth, and they are pursued by a flaming fire, of piercing brightness.	Save him who snatcheth a fragment, and there pursueth him a piercing flame.	Except him who snatches off but once, then there follows him a brightly shining flame.
37 011	Just ask their opinion: are they the more difficult to create, or the (other) beings We have created? Them have We created out of a sticky clay!	Then ask them (O Muhammad): Are they stronger as a creation, or those (others) whom we have created? Lo! We created them of plastic clay.	Then ask them whether they are stronger in creation or those (others) whom We have created. Surely We created them of firm clay.
37 012	Truly dost thou marvel, while they ridicule,	Nay, but thou dost marvel when they mock	Nay! you wonder while they mock,
37 013	And, when they are admonished, pay no heed,-	And heed not when they are reminded,	And when they are reminded, they mind not,
37 014	And, when they see a Sign, turn it to mockery,	And seek to scoff when they behold a portent.	And when they see a sign they incite one another to scoff,
37 015	And say, "This is nothing but evident sorcery!"	And they say: Lo! this is mere magic;	And they say: This is nothing but clear magic:

37 016	"What! when we die, and become dust and bones, shall we (then) be raised up (again)?"	When we are dead and have become dust and bones, shall we then, forsooth, be raised (again)?	What! when we are dead and have become dust and bones, shall we then certainly be raised,
37 017	"And also our fathers of old?"	And our forefathers?	Or our fathers of yore?
37 018	Say thou: "Yea, and ye shall then be humiliated (on account of your evil)."	Say (O Muhammad): Ye, in truth; and ye will be brought low.	Say: Aye! and you shall be abject.
37 019	Then it will be a single (compelling) cry; and behold, they will begin to see!	There is but one Shout, and lo! they behold,	So it shall only be a single cry, when lo! they shall see.
37 020	They will say, "Ah! Woe to us! This is the Day of Judgment!"	And say: Ah, woe for us! This is the Day of Judgment.	And they shall say: O woe to us! this is the day of requital.
37 021	(A voice will say,) "This is the Day of Sorting Out, whose truth ye (once) denied!"	This is the Day of Separation, which ye used to deny.	This is the day of the judgment which you called a lie.
37 022	"Bring ye up", it shall be said, "The wrong-doers and their wives, and the things they worshipped-"	(And it is said unto the angels): Assemble those who did wrong, together with their wives and what they used to worship	Gather together those who were unjust and their associates, and what they used to worship
37 023	"Besides Allah, and lead them to the Way to the (Fierce) Fire!"	Instead of Allah, and lead them to the path to hell;	Besides Allah, then lead them to the way to hell.
37 024	"But stop them, for they must be asked:"	And stop them, for they must be questioned.	And stop them, for they shall be questioned:
37 025	"'What is the matter with you that ye help not each other?'"	What aileth you that ye help not one another?	What is the matter with you that you do not help each other?
37 026	Nay, but that day they shall submit (to Judgment);	Nay, but this day they make full submission.	Nay! on that day they shall be submissive.
37 027	And they will turn to one another, and question one another.	And some of them draw near unto others, mutually questioning.	And some of them shall advance towards others, questioning each other.
37 028	They will say: "It was ye who used to come to us from the right hand (of power and authority)!"	They say: Lo! ye used to come unto us, imposing, (swearing that ye spoke the truth).	They shall say: Surely you used to come to us from the right side.
37 029	They will reply: "Nay, ye yourselves had no Faith!"	They answer: Nay, but ye (yourselves) were not believers.	They shall say: Nay, you (yourselves) were not believers;
37 030	"Nor had we any authority over you. Nay, it was ye who were a people in obstinate rebellion!"	We had no power over you, but ye were wayward folk.	And we had no authority over you, but you were an inordinate people;
37 031	"So now has been proved true, against us, the word of our Lord that we shall indeed (have to) taste (the punishment of our sins)."	Now the Word of our Lord hath been fulfilled concerning us. Lo! we are about to taste (the doom).	So the sentence of our Lord has come to pass against us: (now) we shall surely taste;
37 032	"We led you astray: for truly we were ourselves astray."	Thus we misled you. Lo! we were (ourselves) astray.	So we led you astray, for we ourselves were erring.
37 033	Truly, that Day, they will (all) share in the Penalty.	Then lo! this day they (both) are sharers in the doom.	So they shall on that day be sharers in the chastisement one with another.
37 034	Verily that is how We shall deal with Sinners.	Lo! thus deal We with the guilty.	Surely thus do We deal with the guilty.
37 035	For they, when they were told that there is no god except Allah, would puff themselves up with Pride,	For when it was said unto them, There is no God save Allah, they were scornful	Surely they used to behave proudly when it was said to them: There is no god but Allah;
37 036	And say: "What! shall we give up our gods for the sake of a Poet possessed?"	And said: Shall we forsake our gods for a mad poet?	And to say: What! shall we indeed give up our gods for the sake of a mad poet?

37 037	Nay! he has come with the (very) Truth, and he confirms (the Message of) the messengers (before him).	Nay, but he brought the Truth, and he confirmed those sent (before him).	Nay: he has come with the truth and verified the messengers.
37 038	Ye shall indeed taste of the Grievous Penalty;-	Lo! (now) verily ye taste the painful doom -	Most surely you will taste the painful punishment.
37 039	But it will be no more than the retribution of (the Evil) that ye have wrought;-	Ye are requited naught save what ye did -	And you shall not be rewarded except (for) what you did.
37 040	But the sincere (and devoted) Servants of Allah,-	Save single-minded slaves of Allah;	Save the servants of Allah, the purified ones.
37 041	For them is a Sustenance determined,	For them there is a known provision,	For them is a known sustenance,
37 042	Fruits (Delights); and they (shall enjoy) honour and dignity,	Fruits. And they will be honoured	Fruits, and they shall be highly honored,
37 043	In Gardens of Felicity,	In the Gardens of delight,	In gardens of pleasure,
37 044	Facing each other on Thrones (of Dignity):	On couches facing one another;	On thrones, facing each other.
37 045	Round will be passed to them a Cup from a clear-flowing fountain,	A cup from a gushing spring is brought round for them,	A bowl shall be made to go round them from water running out of springs,
37 046	Crystal-white, of a taste delicious to those who drink (thereof),	White, delicious to the drinkers,	White, delicious to those who drink.
37 047	Free from headiness; nor will they suffer intoxication therefrom.	Wherein there is no headache nor are they made mad thereby.	There shall be no trouble in it, nor shall they be exhausted therewith.
37 048	And besides them will be chaste women, restraining their glances, with big eyes (of wonder and beauty).	And with them are those of modest gaze, with lovely eyes,	And with them shall be those who restrain the eyes, having beautiful eyes;
37 049	As if they were (delicate) eggs closely guarded.	(Pure) as they were hidden eggs (of the ostrich).	As if they were eggs carefully protected.
37 050	Then they will turn to one another and question one another.	And some of them draw near unto others, mutually questioning.	Then shall some of them advance to others, questioning each other.
37 051	One of them will start the talk and say: "I had an intimate companion (on the earth),"	A speaker of them saith: Lo! I had a comrade	A speaker from among them shall say: Surely I had a comrade of mine,
37 052	"Who used to say, 'what! art thou amongst those who bear witness to the Truth (of the Message)?"	Who used to say: Art thou in truth of those who put faith (in his words)?	Who said: What! are you indeed of those who accept (the truth)?
37 053	"'When we die and become dust and bones, shall we indeed receive rewards and punishments?'"	Can we, when we are dead and have become mere dust and bones - can we (then) verily be brought to book?	What! when we are dead and have become dust and bones, shall we then be certainly brought to judgment?
37 054	(A voice) said: "Would ye like to look down?"	He saith: Will ye look?	He shall say: Will you look on?
37 055	He looked down and saw him in the midst of the Fire.	Then looketh he and seeth him in the depth of hell.	Then he looked down and saw him in the midst of hell.
37 056	He said: "By Allah! thou wast little short of bringing me to perdition!"	He saith: By Allah, thou verily didst all but cause my ruin,	He shall say: By Allah! you had almost caused me to perish;
37 057	"Had it not been for the Grace of my Lord, I should certainly have been among those brought (there)!"	And had it not been for the favour of my Lord, I too had been of those haled forth (to doom).	And had it not been for the favor of my Lord, I would certainly have been among those brought up.
37 058	"Is it (the case) that we shall not die,"	Are we then not to die	Is it then that we are not going to die,
37 059	"Except our first death, and that we shall not be punished?"	Saving our former death, and are we not to be punished?	Except our previous death? And we shall not be chastised?
37 060	Verily this is the supreme achievement!	Lo! this is the supreme triumph.	Most surely this is the mighty achievement.

37 061	For the like of this let all strive, who wish to strive.	For the like of this, then, let the workers work.	For the like of this then let the workers work.
37 062	Is that the better entertainment or the Tree of Zaqqum?	Is this better as a welcome, or the tree of Zaqqum?	Is this better as an entertainment or the tree of Zaqqum?
37 063	For We have truly made it (as) a trial for the wrong-doers.	Lo! We have appointed it a torment for wrong-doers.	Surely We have made it to be a trial to the unjust.
37 064	For it is a tree that springs out of the bottom of Hell-Fire:	Lo! it is a tree that springeth in the heart of hell.	Surely it is a tree that grows in the bottom of the hell;
37 065	The shoots of its fruit-stalks are like the heads of devils:	Its crop is as it were the heads of devils	Its produce is as it were the heads of the serpents.
37 066	Truly they will eat thereof and fill their bellies therewith.	And lo! they verily must eat thereof, and fill (their) bellies therewith.	Then most surely they shall eat of it and fill (their) bellies with it.
37 067	Then on top of that they will be given a mixture made of boiling water.	And afterward, lo! thereupon they have a drink of boiling water	Then most surely they shall have after it to drink of a mixture prepared in boiling water.
37 068	Then shall their return be to the (Blazing) Fire.	And afterward, lo! their return is surely unto hell.	Then most surely their return shall be to hell.
37 069	Truly they found their fathers on the wrong Path;	They indeed found their fathers astray,	Surely they found their fathers going astray,
37 070	So they (too) were rushed down on their footsteps!	But they make haste (to follow) in their footsteps.	So in their footsteps they are being hastened on.
37 071	And truly before them, many of the ancients went astray;-	And verily most of the men of old went astray before them,	And certainly most of the ancients went astray before them,
37 072	But We sent aforetime, among them, (messengers) to admonish them;-	And verily We sent among them warners.	And certainly We sent among them warners.
37 073	Then see what was the end of those who were admonished (but heeded not),-	Then see the nature of the consequence for those warned,	Then see how was the end of those warned,
37 074	Except the sincere (and devoted) Servants of Allah.	Save single-minded slaves of Allah.	Except the servants of Allah, the purified ones.
37 075	(In the days of old), Noah cried to Us, and We are the best to hear prayer.	And Noah verily prayed unto Us, and gracious was the Hearer of his prayer.	And Nuh did certainly call upon Us, and most excellent answerer of prayer are We.
37 076	And We delivered him and his people from the Great Calamity,	And We saved him and his household from the great distress,	And We delivered him and his followers from the mighty distress.
37 077	And made his progeny to endure (on this earth);	And made his seed the survivors,	And We made his offspring the survivors.
37 078	And We left (this blessing) for him among generations to come in later times:	And left for him among the later folk (the salutation):	And We perpetuated to him (praise) among the later generations.
37 079	"Peace and salutation to Noah among the nations!"	Peace be unto Noah among the peoples!	Peace and salutation to Nuh among the nations.
37 080	Thus indeed do we reward those who do right.	Lo! thus do We reward the good.	Thus do We surely reward the doers of good.
37 081	For he was one of our believing Servants.	Lo! he is one of Our believing slaves.	Surely he was of Our believing servants.
37 082	Then the rest we overwhelmed in the Flood.	Then We did drown the others.	Then We drowned the others
37 083	Verily among those who followed his Way was Abraham.	And lo! of his persuasion verily was Abraham	And most surely Ibrahim followed his way.
37 084	Behold! he approached his Lord with a sound heart.	When he came unto his Lord with a whole heart;	When he came to his Lord with a free heart,
37 085	Behold! he said to his father and to his people, "What is that which ye worship?"	When he said unto his father and his folk: What is it that ye worship?	When he said to his father and his people: What is it that you worship?
37 086	"Is it a falsehood- gods other than Allah- that ye desire?"	Is it a falsehood - gods beside Allah - that ye desire?	A lie-- gods besides Allah-- do you desire?

37 087	"Then what is your idea about the Lord of the worlds?"	What then is your opinion of the Lord of the Worlds?	What is then your idea about the Lord of the worlds?
37 088	Then did he cast a glance at the Stars.	And he glanced a glance at the stars	Then he looked at the stars, looking up once,
37 089	And he said, "I am indeed sick (at heart)!"	Then said: Lo! I feel sick!	Then he said: Surely I am sick (of your worshipping these).
37 090	So they turned away from him, and departed.	And they turned their backs and went away from him.	So they went away from him, turning back.
37 091	Then did he turn to their gods and said, "Will ye not eat (of the offerings before you)?..."	Then turned he to their gods and said: Will ye not eat?	Then he turned aside to their gods secretly and said: What! do you not eat?
37 092	"What is the matter with you that ye speak not (intelligently)?"	What aileth you that ye speak not?	What is the matter with you that you do not speak?
37 093	Then did he turn upon them, striking (them) with the right hand.	Then he attacked them, striking with his right hand.	Then he turned against them secretly, smiting them with the right hand.
37 094	Then came (the worshippers) with hurried steps, and faced (him).	And (his people) came toward him, hastening.	So they (people) advanced towards him, hastening.
37 095	He said: "Worship ye that which ye have (yourselves) carved?"	He said: Worship ye that which ye yourselves do carve	Said he: What! do you worship what you hew out?
37 096	"But Allah has created you and your handwork!"	When Allah hath created you and what ye make?	And Allah has created you and what you make.
37 097	They said, "Build him a furnace, and throw him into the blazing fire!"	They said: Build for him a building and fling him in the red-hotfire.	They said: Build for him a furnace, then cast him into the burning fire.
37 098	(This failing), they then sought a stratagem against him, but We made them the ones most humiliated!	And they designed a snare for him, but We made them the undermost.	And they desired a war against him, but We brought them low.
37 099	He said: "I will go to my Lord! He will surely guide me!"	And he said: Lo! I am going unto my Lord Who will guide me.	And he said: Surely I fly to my lord; He will guide me.
37 100	"O my Lord! Grant me a righteous (son)!"	My Lord! Vouchsafe me of the righteous.	My Lord! grant me of the doers of good deeds.
37 101	So We gave him the good news of a boy ready to suffer and forbear.	So We gave him tidings of a gentle son.	So We gave him the good news of a boy, possessing forbearance.
37 102	Then, when (the son) reached (the age of) (serious) work with him, he said: "O my son! I see in vision that I offer thee in sacrifice: Now see what is thy view!" (The son) said: "O my father! Do as thou art commanded: thou will find me, if Allah so wills one practising Patience and Constancy!"	And when (his son) was old enough to walk with him, (Abraham) said: O my dear son, I have seen in a dream that I must sacrifice thee. So look, what thinkest thou? He said: O my father! Do that which thou art commanded. Allah willing, thou shalt find me of the steadfast.	And when he attained to working with him, he said: O my son! surely I have seen in a dream that I should sacrifice you; consider then what you see. He said: O my father! do what you are commanded; if Allah please, you will find me of the patient ones.
37 103	So when they had both submitted their wills (to Allah), and he had laid him prostrate on his forehead (for sacrifice),	Then, when they had both surrendered (to Allah), and he had flung him down upon his face,	So when they both submitted and he threw him down upon his forehead,
37 104	We called out to him "O Abraham!"	We called unto him: O Abraham!	And We called out to him saying: O Ibrahim!
37 105	"Thou hast already fulfilled the vision!" - thus indeed do We reward those who do right.	Thou hast already fulfilled the vision. Lo! thus do We reward the good.	You have indeed shown the truth of the vision; surely thus do We reward the doers of good:
37 106	For this was obviously a trial-	Lo! that verily was a clear test.	Most surely this is a manifest trial.
37 107	And We ransomed him with a momentous sacrifice:	Then We ransomed him with a tremendous victim.	And We ransomed him with a Feat sacrifice.

37	108	And We left (this blessing) for him among generations (to come) in later times:	And We left for him among the later folk (the salutation):	And We perpetuated (praise) to him among the later generations.
37	109	"Peace and salutation to Abraham!"	Peace be unto Abraham!	Peace be on Ibrahim.
37	110	Thus indeed do We reward those who do right.	Thus do We reward the good.	Thus do We reward the doers of good.
37	111	For he was one of our believing Servants.	Lo! he is one of Our believing slaves.	Surely he was one of Our believing servants.
37	112	And We gave him the good news of Isaac - a prophet,- one of the Righteous.	And we gave him tidings of the birth of Isaac, a prophet of the righteous.	And We gave him the good news of Ishaq, a prophet among the good ones.
37	113	We blessed him and Isaac: but of their progeny are (some) that do right, and (some) that obviously do wrong, to their own souls.	And We blessed him and Isaac. And of their seed are some who do good, and some who plainly wrong themselves.	And We showered Our blessings on him and on Ishaq; and of their offspring are the doers of good, and (also) those who are clearly unjust to their own souls.
37	114	Again (of old) We bestowed Our favour on Moses and Aaron,	And We verily gave grace unto Moses and Aaron,	And certainly We conferred a favor on Musa and Haroun.
37	115	And We delivered them and their people from (their) Great Calamity;	And saved them and their people from the great distress,	And We delivered them both and their people from the mighty distress.
37	116	And We helped them, so they overcame (their troubles);	And helped them so that they became the victors.	And We helped them, so they were the vanquishers.
37	117	And We gave them the Book which helps to make things clear;	And We gave them the clear Scripture	And We gave them both the Book that made (things) clear.
37	118	And We guided them to the Straight Way.	And showed them the right path.	And We guided them both on the right way.
37	119	And We left (this blessing) for them among generations (to come) in later times:	And We left for them among the later folk (the salutation):	And We perpetuated (praise) to them among the later generations.
37	120	"Peace and salutation to Moses and Aaron!"	Peace be unto Moses and Aaron!	Peace be on Musa and Haroun.
37	121	Thus indeed do We reward those who do right.	Lo! thus do We reward the good.	Even thus do We reward the doers of good.
37	122	For they were two of our believing Servants.	Lo! they are two of Our believing slaves.	Surely they were both of Our believing servants.
37	123	So also was Elias among those sent (by Us).	And lo! Elias was of those sent (to warn),	And Ilyas was most surely of the messengers.
37	124	Behold, he said to his people, "Will ye not fear (Allah)?"	When he said unto his folk: Will ye not ward off (evil)?	When he said to his people: Do you not guard (against evil)?
37	125	"Will ye call upon Baal and forsake the Best of Creators,"-	Will ye cry unto Baal and forsake the Best of creators,	What! do you call upon Ba'l and forsake the best of the creators,
37	126	"Allah, your Lord and Cherisher and the Lord and Cherisher of your fathers of old?"	Allah, your Lord and Lord of your forefathers?	Allah, your Lord and the Lord of your fathers of yore?
37	127	But they rejected him, and they will certainly be called up (for punishment),-	But they denied him, so they surely will be haled forth (to the doom)	But they called him a liar, therefore they shall most surely be brought up.
37	128	Except the sincere and devoted Servants of Allah (among them).	Save single-minded slaves of Allah.	But not the servants of Allah, the purified ones.
37	129	And We left (this blessing) for him among generations (to come) in later times:	And we left for him among the later folk (the salutation):	And We perpetuated to him (praise) among the later generations.
37	130	"Peace and salutation to such as Elias!"	Peace be unto Elias!	Peace be on Ilyas.
37	131	Thus indeed do We reward those who do right.	Lo! thus do We reward the good.	Even thus do We reward the doers of good.

37	132	For he was one of our believing Servants.	Lo! he is one of our believing slaves.	Surely he was one of Our believing servants.
37	133	So also was Lut among those sent (by Us).	And lo! Lot verily was of those sent (to warn).	And Lut was most surely of the messengers.
37	134	Behold, We delivered him and his adherents, all	When We saved him and his household, every one,	When We delivered him and his followers, all--
37	135	Except an old woman who was among those who lagged behind:	Save an old woman among those who stayed behind;	Except an old woman (who was) amongst those who tarried.
37	136	Then We destroyed the rest.	Then We destroyed the others.	Then We destroyed the others.
37	137	Verily, ye pass by their (sites), by day-	And lo! ye verily pass by (the ruin of) them in the morning	And most surely you pass by them in the morning,
37	138	And by night: will ye not understand?	And at night-time; have ye then no sense?	And at night; do you not then understand?
37	139	So also was Jonah among those sent (by Us).	And lo! Jonah verily was of those sent (to warn)	And Yunus was most surely of the messengers.
37	140	When he ran away (like a slave from captivity) to the ship (fully) laden,	When he fled unto the laden ship,	When he ran away to a ship completely laden,
37	141	He (agreed to) cast lots, and he was condemned:	And then drew lots and was of those rejected;	So he shared (with them), but was of those who are cast off.
37	142	Then the big Fish did swallow him, and he had done acts worthy of blame.	And the fish swallowed him while he was blameworthy;	So the fish swallowed him while he did that for which he blamed himself.
37	143	Had it not been that he (repented and) glorified Allah,	And had he not been one of those who glorify (Allah)	But had it not been that he was of those who glorify (Us),
37	144	He would certainly have remained inside the Fish till the Day of Resurrection.	He would have tarried in its belly till the day when they are raised;	He would certainly have tarried in its belly to the day when they are raised.
37	145	But We cast him forth on the naked shore in a state of sickness,	Then We cast him on a desert shore while he was sick;	Then We cast him on to the vacant surface of the earth while he was sick.
37	146	And We caused to grow, over him, a spreading plant of the gourd kind.	And We caused a tree of gourd to grow above him;	And We caused to grow up for him a gourdplant.
37	147	And We sent him (on a mission) to a hundred thousand (men) or more.	And We sent him to a hundred thousand (folk) or more	And We sent him to a hundred thousand, rather they exceeded.
37	148	And they believed; so We permitted them to enjoy (their life) for a while.	And they believed, therefor We gave them comfort for a while.	And they believed, so We gave them provision till a time.
37	149	Now ask them their opinion: Is it that thy Lord has (only) daughters, and they have sons?-	Now ask them (O Muhammad): Hath thy Lord daughters whereas they have sons?	Then ask them whether your Lord has daughters and they have sons.
37	150	Or that We created the angels female, and they are witnesses (thereto)?	Or created We the angels females while they were present?	Or did We create the angels females while they were witnesses?
37	151	Is it not that they say, from their own invention,	Lo! it is of their falsehood that they say:	Now surely it is of their own lie that they say:
37	152	"Allah has begotten children"? but they are liars!	Allah hath begotten. Allah! verily they tell a lie.	Allah has begotten; and most surely they are liars.
37	153	Did He (then) choose daughters rather than sons?	(And again of their falsehood): He hath preferred daughters to sons.	Has He chosen daughters in preference to sons?
37	154	What is the matter with you? How judge ye?	What aileth you? How judge ye?	What is the matter with you, how is it that you judge?
37	155	Will ye not then receive admonition?	Will ye not then reflect?	Will you not then mind?
37	156	Or have ye an authority manifest?	Or have ye a clear warrant?	Or have you a clear authority?
37	157	Then bring ye your Book (of authority) if ye be truthful!	Then produce your writ, if ye are truthful.	Then bring your book, if you are truthful.

37 158	And they have invented a blood-relationship between Him and the jinns: but the jinns know (quite well) that they have indeed to appear (before his Judgment-Seat)!	And they imagine kinship between him and the jinn, whereas the jinn know well that they will be brought before (Him).	And they assert a relationship between Him and the jinn; and certainly the jinn do know that they shall surely be brought up;
37 159	Glory to Allah! (He is free) from the things they ascribe (to Him)!	Glorified be Allah from that which they attribute (unto Him),	Glory be to Allah (for freedom) from what they describe;
37 160	Not (so do) the Servants of Allah, sincere and devoted.	Save single-minded slaves of Allah.	But not so the servants of Allah, the purified ones.
37 161	For, verily, neither ye nor those ye worship-	Lo! verily, ye and that which ye worship,	So surely you and what you worship,
37 162	Can lead (any) into temptation concerning Allah,	Ye cannot excite (anyone) against Him.	Not against Him can you cause (any) to fall into trial,
37 163	Except such as are (themselves) going to the blazing Fire!	Save him who is to burn in hell.	Save him who will go to hell.
37 164	(Those ranged in ranks say): "Not one of us but has a place appointed;"	There is not one of us but hath his known position.	And there is none of us but has an assigned place,
37 165	"And we are verily ranged in ranks (for service);"	Lo! we, even we are they who set the ranks,	And most surely we are they who draw themselves out in ranks,
37 166	"And we are verily those who declare (Allah's) glory!"	Lo! we, even we are they who hymn His praise	And we are most surely they who declare the glory (of Allah).
37 167	And there were those who said,	And indeed they used to say:	And surely they used to say:
37 168	"If only we had had before us a Message from those of old,"	If we had but a reminder from the men of old	Had we a reminder from those of yore,
37 169	"We should certainly have been Servants of Allah, sincere (and devoted)!"	We would be single-minded slaves of Allah.	We would certainly have been the servants of Allah-- the purified ones.
37 170	But (now that the Qur'an has come), they reject it: But soon will they know!	Yet (now that it is come) they disbelieve therein; but they will come to know.	But (now) they disbelieve in it, so they will come to know.
37 171	Already has Our Word been passed before (this) to our Servants sent (by Us),	And verily Our word went forth of old unto Our bondmen sent (to warn)	And certainly Our word has already gone forth in respect of Our servants, the messengers:
37 172	That they would certainly be assisted,	That they verily would be helped,	Most surely they shall be the assisted ones
37 173	And that Our forces,- they surely must conquer.	And that Our host, they verily would be the victors.	And most surely Our host alone shall be the victorious ones.
37 174	So turn thou away from them for a little while,	So withdraw from them (O Muhammad) awhile,	Therefore turn away from them till a time,
37 175	And watch them (how they fare), and they soon shall see (how thou farest)!	And watch, for they will (soon) see.	And (then) see them, so they too shall see.
37 176	Do they wish (indeed) to hurry on our Punishment?	Would they hasten on Our doom?	What! would they then hasten on Our chastisement?
37 177	But when it descends into the open space before them, evil will be the morning for those who were warned (and heeded not)!	But when it cometh home to them, then it will be a hapless morning for those who have been warned.	But when it shall descend in their court, evil shall then be the morning of the warned ones.
37 178	So turn thou away from them for a little while,	Withdraw from them awhile	And turn away from them till a time
37 179	And watch (how they fare) and they soon shall see (how thou farest)!	And watch, for they will (soon) see.	And (then) see, for they too shall see.
37 180	Glory to thy Lord, the Lord of Honour and Power! (He is free) from what they ascribe (to Him)!	Glorified be thy Lord, the Lord of Majesty, from that which they attribute (unto Him)	Glory be to your Lord, the Lord of Honor, above what they describe.

37 181	And Peace on the messengers!	And peace be unto those sent (to warn).	And peace be on the messengers.
37 182	And Praise to Allah, the Lord and Cherisher of the Worlds.	And praise be to Allah, Lord of the Worlds!	And all praise is due to Allah, the Lord of the worlds.

Chapter 38:

SAD (THE LETTER SAD)

Total Verses: 88 Revealed At: MAKKA

In the name of Allah, the Most Beneficent, the Most Merciful.

38 001	Sad: By the Qur'an, Full of Admonition: (This is the Truth).	Sad. By the renowned Qur'an,	Suad, I swear by the Quran, full of admonition.
38 002	But the Unbelievers (are steeped) in self-glory and Separatism.	Nay, but those who disbelieve are in false pride and schism.	Nay! those who disbelieve are in self-exaltation and opposition.
38 003	How many generations before them did We destroy? In the end they cried (for mercy)- when there was no longer time for being saved!	How many a generation We destroyed before them, and they cried out when it was no longer the time for escape!	How many did We destroy before them of the generations, then they cried while the time of escaping had passed away.
38 004	So they wonder that a Warner has come to them from among themselves! and the Unbelievers say, "This is a sorcerer telling lies!"	And they marvel that a warner from among themselves hath come unto them, and the disbelievers say: This is a wizard, a charlatan.	And they wonder that there has come to them a warner from among themselves, and the disbelievers say: This IS an enchanter, a liar.
38 005	"Has he made the gods (all) into one Allah? Truly this is a wonderful thing!"	Maketh he the gods One Allah? Lo! that is an astounding thing.	What! makes he the gods a single Allah? A strange thing is this, to be sure!
38 006	And the leader among them go away (impatiently), (saying), "Walk ye away, and remain constant to your gods! For this is truly a thing designed (against you)!"	The chiefs among them go about, exhorting: Go and be staunch to your gods! Lo! this is a thing designed.	And the chief persons of them break forth, saying: Go and steadily adhere to your gods; this is most surely a thing sought after.
38 007	"We never heard (the like) of this among the people of these latter days: this is nothing but a made-up tale!"	We have not heard of this in later religion. This is naught but an invention.	We never heard of this in the former faith; this is nothing but a forgery:
38 008	"What! has the Message been sent to him - (Of all persons) among us?"...but they are in doubt concerning My (Own) Message! Nay, they have not yet tasted My Punishment!	Hath the reminder been unto him (alone) among us? Nay, but they are in doubt concerning My reminder; nay but they have not yet tasted My doom.	Has the reminder been revealed to him from among us? Nay! they are in doubt as to My reminder. Nay! they have not yet tasted My chastisement!
38 009	Or have they the treasures of the mercy of thy Lord,- the Exalted in Power, the Grantor of Bounties without measure?	Or are theirs the treasures of the mercy of thy Lord, the Mighty, the Bestower?	Or is it that they have the treasures of the mercy of your Lord, the Mighty, the great Giver?
38 010	Or have they the dominion of the heavens and the earth and all between? If so, let them mount up with the ropes and means (to reach that end)!	Or is the kingdom of the heavens and the earth and all that is between them theirs? Then let them ascend by ropes!	Or is it that theirs is the kingdom of the heavens and the earth and what is between them? Then let them ascend by any means.
38 011	But there - will be put to flight even a host of confederates.	A defeated host are (all) the factions that are there.	A host of deserters of the allies shall be here put to flight.

38 012	Before them (were many who) rejected messengers,- the people of Noah, and 'Ad, and Pharaoh, the Lord of Stakes,	The folk of Noah before them denied (their messenger) and (so did the tribe of) A'ad, and Pharaoh firmly planted,	The people of Nuh and Ad, and Firon, the lord of spikes, rejected (messengers) before them.
38 013	And Thamud, and the people of Lut, and the Companions of the Wood; - such were the Confederates.	And (the tribe of) Thamud, and the folk of Lot, and the dwellers in the wood: these were the factions.	And Samood and the people of Lut and the dwellers of the thicket; these were the parties.
38 014	Not one (of them) but rejected the messengers, but My punishment came justly and inevitably (on them).	Not one of them but did deny the messengers, therefor My doom was justified,	There was none of them but called the messengers liars, so just was My retribution.
38 015	These (today) only wait for a single mighty Blast, which (when it comes) will brook no delay.	These wait for but one Shout, there will be no second thereto.	Nor do these await aught but a single cry, there being no delay in it.
38 016	They say: "Our Lord! hasten to us our sentence (even) before the Day of Account!"	They say: Our Lord! Hasten on for us our fate before the Day of Reckoning.	And they say: O our Lord! hasten on to us our portion before the day of reckoning.
38 017	Have patience at what they say, and remember our servant David, the man of strength: for he ever turned (to Allah).	Bear with what they say, and remember Our bondman David, lord of might, Lo! he was ever turning in repentance (toward Allah).	Bear patiently what they say, and remember Our servant Dawood, the possessor of power; surely he was frequent in returning (to Allah).
38 018	It was We that made the hills declare, in unison with him, Our Praises, at eventide and at break of day,	Lo! We subdued the hills to hymn the praises (of their Lord) with him at nightfall and sunrise,	Surely We made the mountains to sing the glory (of Allah) in unison with him at the evening and the sunrise,
38 019	And the birds gathered (in assemblies): all with him did turn (to Allah).	And the birds assembled; all were turning unto Him.	And the birds gathered together; all joined in singing with him.
38 020	We strengthened his kingdom, and gave him wisdom and sound judgment in speech and decision.	We made his kingdom strong and gave him wisdom and decisive speech.	And We strengthened his kingdom and We gave him wisdom and a clear judgment.
38 021	Has the Story of the Disputants reached thee? Behold, they climbed over the wall of the private chamber;	And hath the story of the litigants come unto thee? How they climbed the wall into the royal chamber;	And has there come to you the story of the litigants, when they made an entry into the private chamber by ascending over the walls?
38 022	When they entered the presence of David, and he was terrified of them, they said: "Fear not: we are two disputants, one of whom has wronged the other: Decide now between us with truth, and treat us not with injustice, but guide us to the even Path..."	How they burst in upon David, and he was afraid of them. They said: Be not afraid! (We are) two litigants, one of whom hath wronged the other, therefor judge aright between us; be not unjust; and show us the fair way.	When they entered in upon Dawood and he was frightened at them, they said: Fear not; two litigants, of whom one has acted wrongfully towards the other, therefore decide between us with justice, and do not act unjustly, and guide us to the right way.
38 023	"This man is my brother: He has nine and ninety ewes, and I have (but) one: Yet he says, 'commit her to my care,' and is (moreover) harsh to me in speech."	Lo! this my brother hath ninety and nine ewes while I had one ewe; and he said: Entrust it to me, and he conquered me in speech.	Surely this is my brother; he has ninety-nine ewes and I have a single ewe; but he said: Make it over to me, and he has prevailed against me in discourse.

38 024	(David) said: "He has undoubtedly wronged thee in demanding thy (single) ewe to be added to his (flock of) ewes: truly many are the partners (in business) who wrong each other: Not so do those who believe and work deeds of righteousness, and how few are they?"...and David gathered that We had tried him: he asked forgiveness of his Lord, fell down, bowing (in prostration), and turned (to Allah in repentance).	(David) said: He hath wronged thee in demanding thine ewe in addition to his ewes, and lo! many partners oppress one another, save such as believe and do good works, and they are few. And David guessed that We had tried him, and he sought forgiveness of his Lord, and he bowed himself and fell down prostrate and repented.	He said: Surely he has been unjust to you in demanding your ewe (to add) to his own ewes; and most surely most of the partners act wrongfully towards one another, save those who believe and do good, and very few are they; and Dawood was sure that We had tried him, so he sought the protection of his Lord and he fell down bowing and turned time after time (to Him).
38 025	So We forgave him this (lapse): he enjoyed, indeed, a Near Approach to Us, and a beautiful place of (Final) Return.	So We forgave him that; and lo! he had access to Our presence and a happy journey's end.	Therefore We rectified for him this, and most surely he had a nearness to Us and an excellent resort.
38 026	O David! We did indeed make thee a vicegerent on earth: so judge thou between men in truth (and justice): Nor follow thou the lusts (of thy heart), for they will mislead thee from the Path of Allah: for those who wander astray from the Path of Allah, is a Penalty Grievous, for that they forget the Day of Account.	(And it was said unto him): O David! Lo! We have set thee as a viceroy in the earth; therefor judge aright between mankind, and follow not desire that it beguile thee from the way of Allah. Lo! those who wander from the way of Allah have an awful doom, forasmuch as they forgot the Day of Reckoning.	O Dawood! surely We have made you a ruler in the land; so judge between men with justice and do not follow desire, lest it should lead you astray from the path of Allah; (as for) those who go astray from the path of Allah, they shall surely have a severe punishment because they forgot the day of reckoning.
38 027	Not without purpose did We create heaven and earth and all between! that were the thought of Unbelievers! but woe to the Unbelievers because of the Fire (of Hell)!	And We created not the heaven and the earth and all that is between them in vain. That is the opinion of those who disbelieve. And woe unto those who disbelieve, from the Fire!	And We did not create the heaven and the earth and what is between them in vain; that is the opinion of those who disbelieve then woe to those who disbelieve on account of the fire.
38 028	Shall We treat those who believe and work deeds of righteousness, the same as those who do mischief on earth? Shall We treat those who guard against evil, the same as those who turn aside from the right?	Shall We treat those who believe and do good works as those who spread corruption in the earth; or shall We treat the pious as the wicked?	Shall We treat those who believe and do good like the mischief-makers in the earth? Or shall We make those who guard (against evil) like the wicked?
38 029	(Here is) a Book which We have sent down unto thee, full of blessings, that they may mediate on its Signs, and that men of understanding may receive admonition.	(This is) a Scripture that We have revealed unto thee, full of blessing, that they may ponder its revelations, and that men of understanding may reflect.	(It is) a Book We have revealed to you abounding in good that they may ponder over its verses, and that those endowed with understanding may be mindful.
38 030	To David We gave Solomon (for a son),- How excellent in Our service! Ever did he turn (to Us)!	And We bestowed on David, Solomon. How excellent a slave! Lo! he was ever turning in repentance (toward Allah).	And We gave to Dawood Sulaiman, most excellent the servant! Surely he was frequent in returning (to Allah).
38 031	Behold, there were brought before him, at eventide coursers of the highest breeding, and swift of foot;	When there were shown to him at eventide lightfooted coursers	When there were brought to him in the evening (horses) still when standing, swift when running--
38 032	And he said, "Truly do I love the love of good, with a view to the glory of my Lord,"- until (the sun) was hidden in the veil (of night):	And he said: Lo! I have preferred the good things (of the world) to the remembrance of my Lord; till they were taken out of sight behind the curtain.	Then he said: Surely I preferred the good things to the remembrance of my Lord-- until the sun set and time for Asr prayer was over, (he said):

38 033	"Bring them back to me." then began he to pass his hand over (their) legs and their necks.	(Then he said): Bring them back to me, and fell to slashing (with his sword their) legs and necks.	Bring them back to me; so he began to slash (their) legs and necks.
38 034	And We did try Solomon: We placed on his throne a body (without life); but he did turn (to Us in true devotion):	And verily We tried Solomon, and set upon his throne a (mere) body. Then did he repent.	And certainly We tried Sulaiman, and We put on his throne a (mere) body, so he turned (to Allah).
38 035	He said, "O my Lord! Forgive me, and grant me a kingdom which, (it may be), suits not another after me: for Thou art the Grantor of Bounties (without measure)."	He said: My Lord! Forgive me and bestow on me sovereignty such as shall not belong to any after me. Lo! Thou art the Bestower.	He said: My Lord! do Thou forgive me and grant me a kingdom which is not fit for (being inherited by) anyone after me;
38 036	Then We subjected the wind to his power, to flow gently to his order, Whithersoever he willed,-	So We made the wind subservient unto him, setting fair by his command whithersoever he intended.	Then We made the wind subservient to him; it made his command to run gently wherever he desired,
38 037	As also the evil ones, (including) every kind of builder and diver,-	And the unruly, every builder and diver (made We subservient),	And the shaitans, every builder and diver,
38 038	As also others bound together in fetters.	And others linked together in chains,	And others fettered in chains.
38 039	"Such are Our Bounties: whether thou bestow them (on others) or withhold them, no account will be asked."	(Saying): This is Our gift, so bestow thou, or withhold, without reckoning.	This is Our free gift, therefore give freely or withhold, without reckoning.
38 040	And he enjoyed, indeed, a Near Approach to Us, and a beautiful Place of (Final) Return.	And lo! he hath favour with Us, and a happy journey's end.	And most surely he had a nearness to Us and an excellent resort.
38 041	Commemorate Our Servant Job. Behold he cried to his Lord: "The Evil One has afflicted me with distress and suffering!"	And make mention (O Muhammad) of Our bondman Job, when he cried unto his Lord (saying): Lo! the devil doth afflict me with distress and torment.	And remember Our servant Ayyub, when he called upon his Lord: The Shaitan has afflicted me with toil and torment.
38 042	(The command was given:) "Strike with thy foot: here is (water) wherein to wash, cool and refreshing, and (water) to drink."	(And it was said unto him): Strike the ground with thy foot. This (spring) is a cool bath and a refreshing drink.	Urge with your foot; here is a cool washing-place and a drink.
38 043	And We gave him (back) his people, and doubled their number,- as a Grace from Ourselves, and a thing for commemoration, for all who have Understanding.	And We bestowed on him (again) his household and therewith the like thereof, a mercy from Us, and a memorial for men of understanding.	And We gave him his family and the like of them with them, as a mercy from Us, and as a reminder to those possessed of understanding.
38 044	"And take in thy hand a little grass, and strike therewith: and break not (thy oath)." Truly We found him full of patience and constancy. How excellent in Our service! ever did he turn (to Us)!	And (it was said unto him): Take in thine hand a branch and smite therewith, and break not thine oath. Lo! We found him steadfast, how excellent a slave! Lo! he was ever turning in repentance (to his Lord).	And take in your hand a green branch and beat her with it and do not break your oath; surely We found him patient; most excellent the servant! Surely he was frequent in returning (to Allah).
38 045	And commemorate Our Servants Abraham, Isaac, and Jacob, possessors of Power and Vision.	And make mention of Our bondmen, Abraham, Isaac and Jacob, men of parts and vision.	And remember Our servants Ibrahim and Ishaq and Yaqoub, men of power and insight.
38 046	Verily We did choose them for a special (purpose)- proclaiming the Message of the Hereafter.	Lo! We purified them with a pure thought, remembrance of the Home (of the Hereafter).	Surely We purified them by a pure quality, the keeping in mind of the (final) abode.
38 047	They were, in Our sight, truly, of the company of the Elect and the Good.	Lo! in Our sight they are verily of the elect, the excellent.	And most surely they were with Us, of the elect, the best.
38 048	And commemorate Isma'il, Elisha, and Zul-Kifl: Each of them was of the Company of the Good.	And make mention of Ishmael and Elisha and Dhu'l-Kifl. All are of the chosen.	And remember Ismail and Al-Yasha and Zulkifl; and they were all of the best.

38 049	This is a Message (of admonition): and verily, for the righteous, is a beautiful Place of (Final) Return,-	This is a reminder. And lo! for those who ward off (evil) is a happy journey's end,	This is a reminder; and most surely there is an excellent resort for those who guard (against evil),
38 050	Gardens of Eternity, whose doors will (ever) be open to them;	Gardens of Eden, whereof the gates are opened for them,	The gardens of perpetuity, the doors are opened for them.
38 051	Therein will they recline (at ease): Therein can they call (at pleasure) for fruit in abundance, and (delicious) drink;	Wherein, reclining, they call for plenteous fruit and cool drink (that is) therein.	Reclining therein, calling therein for many fruits and drink.
38 052	And beside them will be chaste women restraining their glances, (companions) of equal age.	And with them are those of modest gaze, companions.	And with them shall be those restraining their eyes, equals in age.
38 053	Such is the Promise made, to you for the Day of Account!	This it is that ye are promised for the Day of Reckoning.	This is what you are promised for the day of reckoning.
38 054	Truly such will be Our Bounty (to you); it will never fail;-	Lo! this in truth is Our provision, which will never waste away.	Most surely this is Our sustenance; it shall never come to an end;
38 055	Yea, such! but - for the wrong-doers will be an evil place of (Final) Return!-	This (is for the righteous). And lo! for the transgressors there will be an evil journey's end,	This (shall be so); and most surely there is an evil resort for the inordinate ones;
38 056	Hell!- they will burn therein, - an evil bed (indeed, to lie on)!-	Hell, where they will burn, an evil resting-place.	Hell; they shall enter it, so evil is the resting-place.
38 057	Yea, such! - then shall they taste it,- a boiling fluid, and a fluid dark, murky, intensely cold!-	Here is a boiling and an ice-cold draught, so let them taste it,	This (shall be so); so let them taste it, boiling and intensely cold (drink).
38 058	And other Penalties of a similar kind, to match them!	And other (torment) of the kind in pairs (the two extremes)!	And other (punishment) of the same kind-- of various sorts.
38 059	Here is a troop rushing headlong with you! No welcome for them! truly, they shall burn in the Fire!	Here is an army rushing blindly with you. (Those who are already in the Fire say): No word of welcome for them. Lo! they will roast at the Fire.	This is an army plunging in without consideration along with you; no welcome for them, surely they shall enter fire.
38 060	(The followers shall cry to the misleaders:) "Nay, ye (too)! No welcome for you! It is ye who have brought this upon us! Now evil is (this) place to stay in!"	They say: Nay, but you (misleaders), for you there is no word of welcome. Ye prepared this for us (by your misleading). Now hapless is the plight.	They shall say: Nay! you-- no welcome to you: you did proffer it to us, so evil is the resting-place.
38 061	They will say: "Our Lord! whoever brought this upon us,- Add to him a double Penalty in the Fire!"	They say: Our Lord! Whoever did prepare this for us, oh, give him double portion of the Fire!	They shall say: Our Lord! whoever prepared it first for us, add Thou to him a double chastisement in the fire.
38 062	And they will say: "What has happened to us that we see not men whom we used to number among the bad ones?"	And they say: What aileth us that we behold not men whom we were wont to count among the wicked?	And they shall say: What is the matter with us that we do not see men whom we used to count among the vicious?
38 063	"Did we treat them (as such) in ridicule, or have (our) eyes failed to perceive them?"	Did we take them (wrongly) for a laughing-stock, or have our eyes missed them?	Was it that we (only) took them in scorn, or have our eyes (now) turned aside from them?
38 064	Truly that is just and fitting,- the mutual recriminations of the People of the Fire!	Lo! that is very truth: the wrangling of the dwellers in the Fire.	That most surely is the truth: the contending one with another of the inmates of the fire.
38 065	Say: "Truly am I a Warner: no god is there but the one Allah, Supreme and Irresistible,"-	Say (unto them, O Muhammad): I am only a warner, and there is no Allah save Allah, the One, the Absolute,	Say: I am only a warner, and there is no god but Allah, the One, the Subduer (of all):
38 066	"The Lord of the heavens and the earth, and all between,- Exalted in Might, able to enforce His Will, forgiving again and again."	Lord of the heavens and the earth and all that is between them, the Mighty, the Pardoning.	The Lord of the heavens and the earth and what is between them, the Mighty, the most Forgiving.

38 067	Say: "That is a Message Supreme (above all),"-	Say: It is tremendous tidings		Say: It is a message of importance,
38 068	"From which ye do turn away!"	Whence ye turn away!		(And) you are turning aside from it:
38 069	"No knowledge have I of the Chiefs on high, when they discuss (matters) among themselves."	I had no knowledge of the Highest Chiefs when they disputed;		I had no knowledge of the exalted chiefs when they contended:
38 070	"Only this has been revealed to me: that I am to give warning plainly and publicly."	It is revealed unto me only that I may be a plain warner.		Naught is revealed to me save that I am a plain warner.
38 071	Behold, thy Lord said to the angels, "I am about to create man from clay:"	When thy Lord said unto the angels: Lo! I am about to create a mortal out of mire,		When your Lord said to the angels; Surely I am going to create a mortal from dust:
38 072	"When I have fashioned him (in due proportion) and breathed into him of My spirit, fall ye down in obeisance unto him."	And when I have fashioned him and breathed into him of My Spirit, then fall down before him prostrate,		So when I have made him complete and breathed into him of My spirit, then fall down making obeisance to him.
38 073	So the angels prostrated themselves, all of them together:	The angels fell down prostrate, every one,		And the angels did obeisance, all of them,
38 074	Not so Iblis: he was haughty, and became one of those who reject Faith.	Saving Iblis; he was scornful and became one of the disbelievers.		But not Iblis: he was proud and he was one of the unbelievers.
38 075	(Allah) said: "O Iblis! What prevents thee from prostrating thyself to one whom I have created with my hands? Art thou haughty? Or art thou one of the high (and mighty) ones?"	He said: O Iblis! What hindereth thee from falling prostrate before that which I have created with both My hands? Art thou too proud or art thou of the high exalted?		He said: O Iblis! what prevented you that you should do obeisance to him whom I created with My two hands? Are you proud or are you of the exalted ones?
38 076	(Iblis) said: "I am better than he: thou createdst me from fire, and him thou createdst from clay."	He said: I am better than him. Thou createdst me of fire, whilst him Thou didst create of clay.		He said: I am better than he; Thou hast created me of fire, and him Thou didst create of dust.
38 077	(Allah) said: "Then get thee out from here: for thou art rejected, accursed."	He said: Go forth from hence, for lo! thou art outcast,		He said: Then get out of it, for surely you are driven away:
38 078	"And My curse shall be on thee till the Day of Judgment."	And lo! My curse is on thee till the Day of Judgment.		And surely My curse is on you to the Day of Judgment.
38 079	(Iblis) said: "O my Lord! Give me then respite till the Day the (dead) are raised."	He said: My Lord! Reprieve me till the day when they are raised.		He said: My Lord! then respite me to the day that they are raised.
38 080	(Allah) said: "Respite then is granted thee-"	He said: Lo! thou art of those reprieved		He said: Surely you are of the respited ones,
38 081	"Till the Day of the Time Appointed."	Until the day of the time appointed.		Till the period of the time made known.
38 082	(Iblis) said: "Then, by Thy power, I will put them all in the wrong,"-	He said: Then, by Thy might, I surely will beguile them every one,		He said: Then by Thy Might I will surely make them live an evil life, all,
38 083	"Except Thy Servants amongst them, sincere and purified (by Thy Grace)."	Save Thy single-minded slaves among them.		Except Thy servants from among them, the purified ones.
38 084	(Allah) said: "Then it is just and fitting- and I say what is just and fitting-"	He said: The Truth is, and the Truth I speak,		He said: The truth then is and the truth do I speak:
38 085	"That I will certainly fill Hell with thee and those that follow thee,- every one."	That I shall fill hell with thee and with such of them as follow thee, together.		That I will most certainly fill hell with you and with those among them who follow you, all.
38 086	Say: "No reward do I ask of you for this (Qur'an), nor am I a pretender."	Say (O Muhammad, unto mankind): I ask of you no fee for this, and I am no simulating.		Say: I do not ask you for any reward for it; nor am I of those who affect:

38 087	"This is no less than a Message to (all) the Worlds."	Lo! it is naught else than a reminder for all peoples	It is nothing but a reminder to the nations;
38 088	"And ye shall certainly know the truth of it (all) after a while."	And ye will come in time to know the truth thereof.	And most certainly you will come to know about it after a time.

Chapter 39:

AZ-ZUMAR (THE TROOPS, THRONGS)

Total Verses: 75   Revealed At: MAKKA

In the name of Allah, the Most Beneficent, the Most Merciful.

39 001	The revelation of this Book is from Allah, the Exalted in Power, full of Wisdom.	The revelation of the Scripture is from Allah, the Mighty, the Wise.	The revelation of the Book is from Allah, the Mighty, the Wise.
39 002	Verily it is We Who have revealed the Book to thee in Truth: so serve Allah, offering Him sincere devotion.	Lo! We have revealed the Scripture unto thee (Muhammad) with truth; so worship Allah, making religion pure for Him (only).	Surely We have revealed to you the Book with the truth, therefore serve Allah, being sincere to Him in obedience.
39 003	Is it not to Allah that sincere devotion is due? But those who take for protectors other than Allah (say): "We only serve them in order that they may bring us nearer to Allah." Truly Allah will judge between them in that wherein they differ. But Allah guides not such as are false and ungrateful.	Surely pure religion is for Allah only. And those who choose protecting friends beside Him (say): We worship them only that they may bring us near unto Allah. Lo! Allah will judge between them concerning that wherein they differ. Lo! Allah guideth not him who is a liar, an ingrate.	Now, surely, sincere obedience is due to Allah (alone) and (as for) those who take guardians besides Him, (saying), We do not serve them save that they may make us nearer to Allah, surely Allah will judge between them in that in which they differ; surely Allah does not guide him aright who is a liar, ungrateful.
39 004	Had Allah wished to take to Himself a son, He could have chosen whom He pleased out of those whom He doth create: but Glory be to Him! (He is above such things.) He is Allah, the One, the Irresistible.	If Allah had willed to choose a son, He could have chosen what He would of that which He hath created. Be He Glorified! He is Allah, the One, the Absolute.	If Allah desire to take a son to Himself, He will surely choose those He pleases from what He has created. Glory be to Him: He is Allah, the One, the Subduer (of all).
39 005	He created the heavens and the earth in true (proportions): He makes the Night overlap the Day, and the Day overlap the Night: He has subjected the sun and the moon (to His law): Each one follows a course for a time appointed. Is not He the Exalted in Power - He Who forgives again and again?	He hath created the heavens and the earth with truth. He maketh night to succeed day, and He maketh day to succeed night, and He constraineth the sun and the moon to give service, each running on for an appointed term. Is not He the Mighty, the Forgiver?	He has created the heavens and the earth with the truth; He makes the night cover the day and makes the day overtake the night, and He has made the sun and the moon subservient; each one runs on to an assigned term; now surely He is the Mighty, the great Forgiver.

39 006	He created you (all) from a single person: then created, of like nature, his mate; and he sent down for you eight head of cattle in pairs: He makes you, in the wombs of your mothers, in stages, one after another, in three veils of darkness. Such is Allah, your Lord and Cherisher: to Him belongs (all) dominion. There is no god but He: then how are ye turned away (from your true Centre)?	He created you from one being, then from that (being) He made its mate; and He hath provided for you of cattle eight kinds. He created you in the wombs of your mothers, creation after creation, in a threefold gloom. Such is Allah, your Lord. His is the Sovereignty. There is no God save Him. How then are ye turned away?	He has created you from a single being, then made its mate of the same (kind), and He has made for you eight of the cattle in pairs. He creates you in the wombs of your mothers-- a creation after a creation-- in triple darkness; that is Allah your Lord, His is the kingdom; there is no god but He; whence are you then turned away?
39 007	If ye reject (Allah), Truly Allah hath no need of you; but He liketh not ingratitude from His servants: if ye are grateful, He is pleased with you. No bearer of burdens can bear the burden of another. In the end, to your Lord is your Return, when He will tell you the truth of all that ye did (in this life). For He knoweth well all that is in (men's) hearts.	If ye are thankless, yet Allah is Independent of you, though He is not pleased with thanklessness for His bondmen; and if ye are thankful He is pleased therewith for you. No laden soul will bear another's load. Then unto your Lord is your return; and He will tell you what ye used to do. Lo! He knoweth what is in the breasts (of men).	If you are ungrateful, then surely Allah is Self-sufficient above all need of you; and He does not like ungratefulness in His servants; and if you are grateful, He likes it in you; and no bearer of burden shall bear the burden of another; then to your Lord is your return, then will He inform you of what you did; surely He is Cognizant of what is in the breasts.
39 008	When some trouble toucheth man, he crieth unto his Lord, turning to Him in repentance: but when He bestoweth a favour upon him as from Himself, (man) doth forget what he cried and prayed for before, and he doth set up rivals unto Allah, thus misleading others from Allah's Path. Say, "Enjoy thy blasphemy for a little while: verily thou art (one) of the Companions of the Fire!"	And when some hurt toucheth man, he crieth unto his Lord, turning unto Him (repentant). Then, when He granteth him a boon from Him he forgetteth that for which he cried unto Him before, and setteth up rivals to Allah that he may beguile (men) from his way. Say (O Muhammad, unto such a one): Take pleasure in thy disbelief a while. Lo! thou art of the owners of the Fire.	And when distress afflicts a man he calls upon his Lord turning to Him frequently; then when He makes him possess a favor from Him, he forgets that for which he called upon Him before, and sets up rivals to Allah that he may cause (men) to stray off from His path. Say: Enjoy yourself in your ungratefulness a little, surely you are of the inmates of the fire.
39 009	Is one who worships devoutly during the hour of the night prostrating himself or standing (in adoration), who takes heed of the Hereafter, and who places his hope in the Mercy of his Lord - (like one who does not)? Say: "Are those equal, those who know and those who do not know? It is those who are endued with understanding that receive admonition."	Is he who payeth adoration in the watches of the night, prostrate and standing, bewaring of the Hereafter and hoping for the mercy of his Lord, (to be accounted equal with a disbeliever)? Say (unto them, O Muhammad): Are those who know equal with those who know not? But only men of understanding will pay heed.	What! he who is obedient during hours of the night, prostrating himself and standing, takes care of the hereafter and hopes for the mercy of his Lord! Say: Are those who know and those who do not know alike? Only the men of understanding are mindful.
39 010	Say: "O ye my servants who believe! Fear your Lord, good is (the reward) for those who do good in this world. Spacious is Allah's earth! those who patiently persevere will truly receive a reward without measure!"	Say: O My bondmen who believe! Observe your duty to your Lord. For those who do good in this world there is good, and Allah's earth is spacious. Verily the steadfast will be paid their wages without stint.	Say: O my servants who believe! be careful of (your duty to) your Lord; for those who do good in this world is good, and Allah's earth is spacious; only the patient will be paid back their reward in full without measure.
39 011	Say: "Verily, I am commanded to serve Allah with sincere devotion;"	Say (O Muhammad): Lo! I am commanded to worship Allah, making religion pure for Him (only).	Say: I am commanded that I should serve Allah, being sincere to Him in obedience.

39 012	"And I am commanded to be the first of those who bow to Allah in Islam."	And I am commanded to be the first of those who are Muslims (surrender unto Him).	And I am commanded that I shall be the first of those who submit.
39 013	Say: "I would, if I disobeyed my Lord, indeed have fear of the Penalty of a Mighty Day."	Say: Lo! if I should disobey my Lord, I fear the doom of a tremendous Day.	Say: I fear, if I disobey my Lord, the chastisement of a grievous day.
39 014	Say: "It is Allah I serve, with my sincere (and exclusive) devotion:"	Say: Allah I worship, making my religion pure for Him (only).	Say: Allah (it is Whom) I serve, being sincere to Him in my obedience:
39 015	"Serve ye what ye will besides him." Say: "Truly, those in loss are those who lose their own souls and their People on the Day of Judgment: Ah! that is indeed the (real and) evident Loss!"	Then worship what ye will beside Him. Say: The losers will be those who lose themselves and their housefolk on the Day of Resurrection. Ah, that will be the manifest loss!	Serve then what you like besides Him. Say: The losers surely are those who shall have lost themselves and their families on the day of resurrection; now surely that is the clear loss.
39 016	They shall have Layers of Fire above them, and Layers (of Fire) below them: with this doth Allah warn off his servants: "O My Servants! then fear ye Me!"	They have an awning of fire above them and beneath them a dais (of fire). With this doth Allah appall His bondmen. O My bondmen, therefor fear Me!	They shall have coverings of fire above them and coverings beneath them; with that Allah makes His servants to fear, so be careful of (your duty to) Me, O My servants!
39 017	Those who eschew Evil,- and fall not into its worship,- and turn to Allah (in repentance),- for them is Good News: so announce the Good News to My Servants,-	And those who put away false gods lest they should worship them and turn to Allah in repentance, for them there are glad tidings. Therefore give good tidings (O Muhammad) to My bondmen	And (as for) those who keep off from the worship of the idols and turn to Allah, they shall have good news, therefore give good news to My servants,
39 018	Those who listen to the Word, and follow the best (meaning) in it: those are the ones whom Allah has guided, and those are the ones endued with understanding.	Who hear advice and follow the best thereof. Such are those whom Allah guideth, and such are men of understanding.	Those who listen to the word, then follow the best of it; those are they whom Allah has guided, and those it is who are the men of understanding.
39 019	Is, then, one against whom the decree of Punishment is justly due (equal to one who eschews Evil)? Wouldst thou, then, deliver one (who is) in the Fire?	Is he on whom the word of doom is fulfilled (to be helped), and canst thou (O Muhammad) rescue him who is in the Fire?	What! as for him then against whom the sentence of chastisement is due: What! can you save him who is in the fire?
39 020	But it is for those who fear their Lord. That lofty mansions, one above another, have been built: beneath them flow rivers (of delight): (such is) the Promise of Allah: never doth Allah fail in (His) promise.	But those who keep their duty to their Lord, for them are lofty halls with lofty halls above them, built (for them), beneath which rivers flow. (It is) a promise of Allah. Allah faileth not His promise.	But (as for) those who are careful of (their duty to) their Lord, they shall have high places, above them higher places, built (for them), beneath which flow rivers; (this is) the promise of Allah: Allah will not fail in (His) promise.
39 021	Seest thou not that Allah sends down rain from the sky, and leads it through springs in the earth? Then He causes to grow, therewith, produce of various colours: then it withers; thou wilt see it grow yellow; then He makes it dry up and crumble away. Truly, in this, is a Message of remembrance to men of understanding.	Hast thou not seen how Allah hath sent down water from the sky and hath caused it to penetrate the earth as watersprings, and afterward thereby produceth crops of divers hues; and afterward they wither and thou seest them turn yellow; then He maketh them chaff. Lo! herein verily is a reminder for men of understanding.	Do you not see that Allah sends down water from the cloud, then makes it go along in the earth in springs, then brings forth therewith herbage of various colors, then it withers so that you see it becoming yellow, then He makes it a thing crushed and broken into pieces? Most surely there is a reminder in this for the men of understanding.

39 022	Is one whose heart Allah has opened to Islam, so that he has received Enlightenment from Allah, (no better than one hard-hearted)? Woe to those whose hearts are hardened against celebrating the praises of Allah! they are manifestly wandering (in error)!	Is he whose bosom Allah hath expanded for Al-Islam, so that he followeth a light from his Lord, (as he who disbelieveth)? Then woe unto those whose hearts are hardened against remembrance of Allah. Such are in plain error.	What! is he whose heart Allah has opened for Islam so that he is in a light from his Lord (like the hard-hearted)? Nay, woe to those whose hearts are hard against the remembrance of Allah; those are in clear error.
39 023	Allah has revealed (from time to time) the most beautiful Message in the form of a Book, consistent with itself, (yet) repeating (its teaching in various aspects): the skins of those who fear their Lord tremble thereat; then their skins and their hearts do soften to the celebration of Allah's praises. Such is the guidance of Allah: He guides therewith whom He pleases, but such as Allah leaves to stray, can have none to guide.	Allah hath (now) revealed the fairest of statements, a Scripture consistent, (wherein promises of reward are) paired (with threats of punishment), whereat doth creep the flesh of those who fear their Lord, so that their flesh and their hearts soften to Allah's reminder. Such is Allah's guidance, wherewith He guideth whom He will. And him whom Allah sendeth astray, for him there is no guide.	Allah has revealed the best announcement, a book conformable in its various parts, repeating, whereat do shudder the skins of those who fear their Lord, then their skins and their hearts become pliant to the remembrance of Allah; this is Allah's guidance, He guides with it whom He pleases; and (as for) him whom Allah makes err, there is no guide for him.
39 024	Is, then, one who has to fear the brunt of the Penalty on the Day of Judgment (and receive it) on his face, (like one guarded therefrom)? It will be said to the wrong-doers: "Taste ye (the fruits of) what ye earned!"	Is he then, who will strike his face against the awful doom upon the Day of Resurrection (as he who doeth right)? And it will be said unto the wrong-doers: Taste what ye used to earn.	Is he then who has to guard himself with his own person against the evil chastisement on the resurrection day? And it will be said to the unjust: Taste what you earned.
39 025	Those before them (also) rejected (revelation), and so the Punishment came to them from directions they did not perceive.	Those before them denied, and so the doom came on them whence they knew not.	Those before them rejected (prophets), therefore there came to them the chastisement from whence they perceived not.
39 026	So Allah gave them a taste of humiliation in the present life, but greater is the punishment of the Hereafter, if they only knew!	Thus Allah made them taste humiliation in the life of the world, and verily the doom of the Hereafter will be greater if they did but know.	So Allah made them taste the disgrace in this world's life, and certainly the punishment of the hereafter is greater; did they but know!
39 027	We have put forth for men, in this Qur'an every kind of Parable, in order that they may receive admonition.	And verily We have coined for mankind in this Qur'an all kinds of similitudes, that haply they may reflect;	And certainly We have set forth to men in this Quran similitudes of every sort that they may mind.
39 028	(It is) a Qur'an in Arabic, without any crookedness (therein): in order that they may guard against Evil.	A Lecture in Arabic, containing no crookedness, that haply they may ward off (evil).	An Arabic Quran without any crookedness, that they may guard (against evil).
39 029	Allah puts forth a Parable a man belonging to many partners at variance with each other, and a man belonging entirely to one master: are those two equal in comparison? Praise be to Allah! but most of them have no knowledge.	Allah coineth a similitude: A man in relation to whom are several part-owners, quarrelling, and a man belonging wholly to one man. Are the two equal in similitude? Praise be to Allah! But most of them know not.	Allah sets forth an example: There is a slave in whom are (several) partners differing with one another, and there is another slave wholly owned by one man. Are the two alike in condition? (All) praise is due to Allah. Nay! most of them do not know.
39 030	Truly thou wilt die (one day), and truly they (too) will die (one day).	Lo! thou wilt die, and lo! they will die;	Surely you shall die and they (too) shall surely die.
39 031	In the end will ye (all), on the Day of Judgment, settle your disputes in the presence of your Lord.	Then lo! on the Day of Resurrection, before your Lord ye will dispute.	Then surely on the day of resurrection you will contend one with another before your Lord.

39 032	Who, then, doth more wrong than one who utters a lie concerning Allah, and rejects the Truth when it comes to him; is there not in Hell an abode for blasphemers?	And who doth greater wrong than he who telleth a lie against Allah, and denieth the truth when it reacheth him? Will not the home of disbelievers be in hell?	Who is then more unjust than he who utters a lie against Allah and (he who) gives the lie to the truth when it comes to him; is there not in hell an abode for the unbelievers?
39 033	And he who brings the Truth and he who confirms (and supports) it - such are the men who do right.	And whoso bringeth the truth and believeth therein - Such are the dutiful.	And he who brings the truth and (he who) accepts it as the truth-- these are they that guard (against evil).
39 034	They shall have all that they wish for, in the presence of their Lord: such is the reward of those who do good:	They shall have what they will of their Lord's bounty. That is the reward of the good:	They shall have with their Lord what they please; that is the reward of the doers of good;
39 035	So that Allah will turn off from them (even) the worst in their deeds and give them their reward according to the best of what they have done.	That Allah will remit from them the worst of what they did, and will pay them for reward the best they used to do.	So that Allah will do away with the worst of what they did and give them their reward for the best of what they do.
39 036	Is not Allah enough for his Servant? But they try to frighten thee with other (gods) besides Him! for such as Allah leaves to stray, there can be no guide.	Will not Allah defend His slave? Yet they would frighten thee with those beside Him. He whom Allah sendeth astray, for him there is no guide.	Is not Allah sufficient for His servant? And they seek to frighten you with those besides Him; and whomsoever Allah makes err, there is no guide for him.
39 037	And such as Allah doth guide there can be none to lead astray. Is not Allah Exalted in Power, (Able to enforce His Will), Lord of Retribution?	And he whom Allah guideth, for him there can be no misleader. Is not Allah Mighty, Able to Requite (the wrong)?	And whom Allah guides, there is none that can lead him astray; is not Allah Mighty, the Lord of retribution?
39 038	If indeed thou ask them who it is that created the heavens and the earth, they would be sure to say, "Allah". Say: "See ye then? the things that ye invoke besides Allah,- can they, if Allah wills some Penalty for me, remove His Penalty?- Or if He wills some Grace for me, can they keep back his Grace?" Say: "Sufficient is Allah for me! In Him trust those who put their trust."	And verily, if thou shouldst ask them: Who created the heavens and the earth? they will say: Allah. Say: Bethink you then of those ye worship beside Allah, if Allah willed some hurt for me, could they remove from me His hurt; or if He willed some mercy for me, could they restrain His mercy? Say: Allah is my all. In Him do (all) the trusting put their trust.	And should you ask them, Who created the heavens and the earth? They would most certainly say: Allah. Say: Have you then considered that what you call upon besides Allah, would they, if Allah desire to afflict me with harm, be the removers of His harm, or (would they), if Allah desire to show me mercy, be the withholders of His mercy? Say: Allah is sufficient for me; on Him do the reliant rely.
39 039	Say: "O my People! Do whatever ye can: I will do (my part): but soon will ye know-"	Say: O my people! Act in your manner. Lo! I (too) am acting. Thus ye will come to know	Say: O my people! work in your place, surely I am a worker, so you will come to know.
39 040	"Who it is to whom comes a Penalty of ignominy, and on whom descends a Penalty that abides."	Who it is unto whom cometh a doom that will abase him, and on whom there falleth everlasting doom.	Who it is to whom there shall come a punishment which will disgrace him and to whom will be due a lasting punishment.
39 041	Verily We have revealed the Book to thee in Truth, for (instructing) mankind. He, then, that receives guidance benefits his own soul: but he that strays injures his own soul. Nor art thou set over them to dispose of their affairs.	Lo! We have revealed unto thee (Muhammad) the Scripture for mankind with truth. Then whosoever goeth right it is for his soul, and whosoever strayeth, strayeth only to its hurt. And thou art not a warder over them.	Surely We have revealed to you the Book with the truth for the sake of men; so whoever follows the right way, it is for his own soul and whoever errs, he errs only to its detriment; and you are not a custodian over them.

39 042	It is Allah that takes the souls (of men) at death; and those that die not (He takes) during their sleep: those on whom He has passed the decree of death, He keeps back (from returning to life), but the rest He sends (to their bodies) for a term appointed verily in this are Signs for those who reflect.	Allah receiveth (men's) souls at the time of their death, and that (soul) which dieth not (yet) in its sleep. He keepeth that (soul) for which He hath ordained death and dismisseth the rest till an appointed term. Lo! herein verily are portents for people who take thought.	Allah takes the souls at the time of their death, and those that die not during their sleep; then He withholds those on whom He has passed the decree of death and sends the others back till an appointed term; most surely there are signs in this for a people who reflect.
39 043	What! Do they take for intercessors others besides Allah? Say. Even if they have no power whatever and no intelligence?	Or choose they intercessors other than Allah? Say. What! Even though they have power over nothing and have no intelligence?	Or have they taken intercessors besides Allah? Say: what! even though they did not ever have control over anything, nor do they understand.
39 044	Say: "To Allah belongs exclusively (the right to grant) intercession: to Him belongs the dominion of the heavens and the earth: In the End, it is to Him that ye shall be brought back."	Say: Unto Allah belongeth all intercession. His is the Sovereignty of the heavens and the earth. And afterward unto Him ye will be brought back.	Say: Allah's is the intercession altogether; His is the kingdom of the heavens and the earth, then to Him you shall be brought back.
39 045	When Allah, the One and Only, is mentioned, the hearts of those who believe not in the Hereafter are filled with disgust and horror; but when (gods) other than He are mentioned, behold, they are filled with joy!	And when Allah alone is mentioned, the hearts of those who believe not in the Hereafter are repelled, and when those (whom they worship) beside Him are mentioned, behold! they are glad.	And when Allah alone is mentioned, the hearts of those who do not believe in the hereafter shrink, and when those besides Him are mentioned, lo! they are joyful.
39 046	Say: "O Allah! Creator of the heavens and the earth! Knower of all that is hidden and open! it is Thou that wilt judge between Thy Servants in those matters about which they have differed."	Say: O Allah! Creator of the heavens and the earth! Knower of the Invisible and the Visible! Thou wilt judge between Thy slaves concerning that wherein they used to differ.	Say: O Allah! Originator of the heavens and the earth, Knower of the unseen and the seen! Thou (only) judgest between Thy servants as to that wherein they differ.
39 047	Even if the wrong-doers had all that there is on earth, and as much more, (in vain) would they offer it for ransom from the pain of the Penalty on the Day of Judgment: but something will confront them from Allah, which they could never have counted upon!	And though those who do wrong possess all that is in the earth, and therewith as much again, they verily will seek to ransom themselves therewith on the Day of Resurrection from the awful doom; and there will appear unto them, from their Lord, that wherewith they never reckoned.	And had those who are unjust all that is in the earth and the like of it with it, they would certainly offer it as ransom (to be saved) from the evil of the punishment on the day of resurrection; and what they never thought of shall become plain to them from Allah.
39 048	For the evils of their Deeds will confront them, and they will be (completely) encircled by that which they used to mock at!	And the evils that they earned will appear unto them, and that whereat they used to scoff will surround them.	And the evil (consequences) of what they wrought shall become plain to them, and the very thing they mocked at shall beset them.
39 049	Now, when trouble touches man, he cries to Us: But when We bestow a favour upon him as from Ourselves, he says, "This has been given to me because of a certain knowledge (I have)!" Nay, but this is but a trial, but most of them understand not!	Now when hurt toucheth a man he crieth unto Us, and afterward when We have granted him a boon from Us, he saith: Only by force of knowledge I obtained it. Nay, but it is a test. But most of them know not.	So when harm afflicts a man he calls upon Us; then, when We give him a favor from Us, he says: I have been given it only by means of knowledge. Nay, it is a trial, but most of them do not know.
39 050	Thus did the (generations) before them say! But all that they did was of no profit to them.	Those before them said it, yet (all) that they had earned availed them not;	Those before them did say it indeed, but what they earned availed them not.

39 051	Nay, the evil results of their Deeds overtook them. And the wrong-doers of this (generation)- the evil results of their Deeds will soon overtake them (too), and they will never be able to frustrate (Our Plan)!	But the evils that they earned smote them; and such of these as do wrong, the evils that they earn will smite them; they cannot escape.	So there befell them the evil (consequences) of what they earned; and (as for) those who are unjust from among these, there shall befall them the evil (consequences) of what they earn, and they shall not escape.
39 052	Know they not that Allah enlarges the provision or restricts it, for any He pleases? Verily, in this are Signs for those who believe!	Know they not that Allah enlargeth providence for whom He will, and straiteneth it (for whom He will). Lo! herein verily are portents for people who believe.	Do they not know that Allah makes ample the means of subsistence to whom He pleases, and He straitens; most surely there are signs in this for a people who believe.
39 053	Say: "O my Servants who have transgressed against their souls! Despair not of the Mercy of Allah: for Allah forgives all sins: for He is Oft-Forgiving, Most Merciful."	Say: O My slaves who have been prodigal to their own hurt! Despair not of the mercy of Allah, Who forgiveth all sins. Lo! He is the Forgiving, the Merciful.	Say: O my servants! who have acted extravagantly against their own souls, do not despair of the mercy of Allah; surely Allah forgives the faults altogether; surely He is the Forgiving the Merciful.
39 054	"Turn ye to our Lord (in repentance) and bow to His (Will), before the Penalty comes on you: after that ye shall not be helped."	Turn unto your Lord repentant, and surrender unto Him, before there come unto you the doom, when ye cannot be helped.	And return to your Lord time after time and submit to Him before there comes to you the punishment, then you shall not be helped.
39 055	"And follow the best of (the courses) revealed to you from your Lord, before the Penalty comes on you - of a sudden while ye perceive not!"-	And follow the better (guidance) of that which is revealed unto you from your Lord, before the doom cometh on you suddenly when ye know not,	And follow the best that has been revealed to you from your Lord before there comes to you the punishment all of a sudden while you do not even perceive;
39 056	"Lest the soul should (then) say: 'Ah! Woe is me!- In that I neglected (my duty) towards Allah, and was but among those who mocked!'"-	Lest any soul should say: Alas, my grief that I was unmindful of Allah, and I was indeed among the scoffers!	Lest a soul should say: O woe to me! for what I fell short of my duty to Allah, and most surely I was of those who laughed to scorn;
39 057	"Or (lest) it should say: 'If only Allah had guided me, I should certainly have been among the righteous!'"-	Or should say: If Allah had but guided me I should have been among the dutiful!	Or it should say: Had Allah guided me, I would certainly have been of those who guard (against evil);
39 058	"Or (lest) it should say when it (actually) sees the penalty: 'If only I had another chance, I should certainly be among those who do good!'"	Or should say, when it seeth the doom: Oh, that I had but a second chance that I might be among the righteous!	Or it should say when it sees the punishment: Were there only a returning for me, I should be of the doers of good.
39 059	"(The reply will be:) 'Nay, but there came to thee my Signs, and thou didst reject them: thou wast Haughty, and became one of those who reject faith!'"	(But now the answer will be): Nay, for My revelations came unto thee, but thou didst deny them and wast scornful and wast among the disbelievers.	Aye! My communications came to you, but you rejected them, and you were proud and you were one of the unbelievers.
39 060	On the Day of Judgment wilt thou see those who told lies against Allah;- their faces will be turned black; is there not in Hell an abode for the Haughty?	And on the Day of Resurrection thou (Muhammad) seest those who lied concerning Allah with their faces blackened. Is not the home of the scorners in hell?	And on the day of resurrection you shall see those who lied against Allah; their faces shall be blackened. Is there not in hell an abode for the proud?
39 061	But Allah will deliver the righteous to their place of salvation: no evil shall touch them, nor shall they grieve.	And Allah delivereth those who ward off (evil) because of their deserts. Evil toucheth them not, nor do they grieve.	And Allah shall deliver those who guard (against evil) with their achievement; evil shall not touch them, nor shall they grieve.
39 062	Allah is the Creator of all things, and He is the Guardian and Disposer of all affairs.	Allah is Creator of all things, and He is Guardian over all things.	Allah is the Creator of every thing and He has charge over every thing.

39 063	To Him belong the keys of the heavens and the earth: and those who reject the Signs of Allah,- it is they who will be in loss.	His are the keys of the heavens and the earth, and they who disbelieve the revelations of Allah - such are they who are the losers.	His are the treasures of the heavens and the earth; and (as for) those who disbelieve in the communications of Allah, these it is that are the losers.
39 064	Say: "Is it some one other than Allah that ye order me to worship, O ye ignorant ones?"	Say (O Muhammad, to the disbelievers): Do ye bid me serve other than Allah? O ye fools!	Say: What! Do you then bid me serve others than Allah, O ignorant men?
39 065	But it has already been revealed to thee,- as it was to those before thee,- "If thou wert to join (gods with Allah), truly fruitless will be thy work (in life), and thou wilt surely be in the ranks of those who lose (all spiritual good)".	And verily it hath been revealed unto thee as unto those before thee (saying). If thou ascribe a partner to Allah thy work will fail and thou indeed wilt be among the losers.	And certainly, it has been revealed to you and to those before you: Surely if you associate (with Allah), your work would certainly come to naught and you would certainly be of the losers.
39 066	Nay, but worship Allah, and be of those who give thanks.	Nay, but Allah must thou serve, and be among the thankful!	Nay! but serve Allah alone and be of the thankful.
39 067	No just estimate have they made of Allah, such as is due to Him: On the Day of Judgment the whole of the earth will be but His handful, and the heavens will be rolled up in His right hand: Glory to Him! High is He above the Partners they attribute to Him!	And they esteem not Allah as He hath the right to be esteemed, when the whole earth is His handful on the Day of Resurrection, and the heavens are rolled in His right hand. Glorified is He and High Exalted from all that they ascribe as partner (unto Him).	And they have not honored Allah with the honor that is due to Him; and the whole earth shall be in His grip on the day of resurrection and the heavens rolled up in His right hand; glory be to Him, and may He be exalted above what they associate (with Him).
39 068	The Trumpet will (just) be sounded, when all that are in the heavens and on earth will swoon, except such as it will please Allah (to exempt). Then will a second one be sounded, when, behold, they will be standing and looking on!	And the trumpet is blown, and all who are in the heavens and all who are in the earth swoon away, save him whom Allah willeth. Then it is blown a second time, and behold them standing waiting!	And the trumpet shall be blown, so all those that are in the heavens and all those that are in the earth shall swoon, except such as Allah please; then it shall be blown again, then lo! they shall stand up awaiting.
39 069	And the Earth will shine with the Glory of its Lord: the Record (of Deeds) will be placed (open); the prophets and the witnesses will be brought forward and a just decision pronounced between them; and they will not be wronged (in the least).	And the earth shineth with the light of her Lord, and the Book is set up, and the prophets and the witnesses are brought, and it is judged between them with truth, and they are not wronged.	And the earth shall beam with the light of its Lord, and the Book shall be laid down, and the prophets and the witnesses shall be brought up, and judgment shall be given between them with justice, and they shall not be dealt with unjustly.
39 070	And to every soul will be paid in full (the fruit) of its Deeds; and (Allah) knoweth best all that they do.	And each soul is paid in full for what it did. And He is Best Aware of what they do.	And every soul shall be paid back fully what it has done, and He knows best what they do.
39 071	The Unbelievers will be led to Hell in crowd: until, when they arrive, there, its gates will be opened. And its keepers will say, "Did not messengers come to you from among yourselves, rehearsing to you the Signs of your Lord, and warning you of the Meeting of This Day of yours?" The answer will be: "True: but the Decree of Punishment has been proved true against the Unbelievers!"	And those who disbelieve are driven unto hell in troops till, when they reach it and the gates thereof are opened, and the warders thereof say unto them: Came there not unto you messengers of your own, reciting unto you the revelations of your Lord and warning you of the meeting of this your Day? they say: Yea, verily. But the word of doom of disbelievers is fulfilled.	And those who disbelieve shall be driven to hell in companies; until, when they come to it, its doors shall be opened, and the keepers of it shall say to them: Did not there come to you messengers from among you reciting to you the communications of your Lord and warning you of the meeting of this day of yours? They shall say: Yea! But the sentence of punishment was due against the unbelievers.

39 072	(To them) will be said: "Enter ye the gates of Hell, to dwell therein: and evil is (this) Abode of the Arrogant!"	It is said (unto them): Enter ye the gates of hell to dwell therein. Thus hapless is the journey's end of the scorners.		It shall be said: Enter the gates of hell to abide therein; so evil is the abode of the proud.
39 073	And those who feared their Lord will be led to the Garden in crowds: until behold, they arrive there; its gates will be opened; and its keepers will say: "Peace be upon you! well have ye done! enter ye here, to dwell therein."	And those who keep their duty to their Lord are driven unto the Garden in troops till, when they reach it, and the gates thereof are opened, and the warders thereof say unto them: Peace be unto you! Ye are good, so enter ye (the Garden of delight), to dwell therein;		And those who are careful of (their duty to) their Lord shall be conveyed to the garden in companies; until when they come to it, and its doors shall be opened, and the keepers of it shall say to them: Peace be on you, you shall be happy; therefore enter it to abide.
39 074	They will say: "Praise be to Allah, Who has truly fulfilled His Promise to us, and has given us (this) land in heritage: We can dwell in the Garden as we will: how excellent a reward for those who work (righteousness)!"	They say: Praise be to Allah, Who hath fulfilled His promise unto us and hath made us inherit the land, sojourning in the Garden where we will! So bounteous is the wage of workers.		And they shall say: (All) praise is due to Allah, Who has made good to us His promise, and He has made us inherit the land; we may abide in the garden where we please; so goodly is the reward of the workers.
39 075	And thou wilt see the angels surrounding the Throne (Divine) on all sides, singing Glory and Praise to their Lord. The Decision between them (at Judgment) will be in (perfect) justice, and the cry (on all sides) will be, "Praise be to Allah, the Lord of the Worlds!"	And thou (O Muhammad) seest the angels thronging round the Throne, hymning the praises of their Lord. And they are judged aright. And it is said: Praise be to Allah, the Lord of the Worlds!		And you shall see the angels going round about the throne glorifying the praise of their Lord; and judgment shall be given between them with justice, and it shall be said: All praise is due to Allah, the Lord of the worlds.

Chapter 40:

AL-GHAFIR (THE FORGIVER (GOD))

Total Verses: 85 Revealed At: MAKKA

In the name of Allah, the Most Beneficent, the Most Merciful.

40 001	Ha Mim.	Ha. Mim.	Ha Mim.
40 002	The revelation of this Book is from Allah, Exalted in Power, Full of Knowledge,-	The revelation of the Scripture is from Allah, the Mighty, the Knower,	The revelation of the Book is from Allah, the Mighty, the Knowing,
40 003	Who forgiveth sin, accepteth repentance, is strict in punishment, and hath a long reach (in all things). there is no god but He: to Him is the final goal.	The Forgiver of sin, the Accepter of repentance, the Stern in punishment, the Bountiful. There is no God save Him. Unto Him is the journeying.	The Forgiver of the faults and the Acceptor of repentance, Severe to punish, Lord of bounty; there is no god but He; to Him is the eventual coming.
40 004	None can dispute about the Signs of Allah but the Unbelievers. Let not, then, their strutting about through the land deceive thee!	None argue concerning the revelations of Allah save those who disbelieve, so let not their turn of fortune in the land deceive thee (O Muhammad).	None dispute concerning the communications of Allah but those who disbelieve, therefore let not their going to and fro in the cities deceive you.

40 005	But (there were people) before them, who denied (the Signs),- the People of Noah, and the Confederates (of Evil) after them; and every People plotted against their prophet, to seize him, and disputed by means of vanities, therewith to condemn the Truth; but it was I that seized them! and how (terrible) was My Requital!	The folk of Noah and the factions after them denied (their messengers) before these, and every nation purposed to seize their messenger and argued falsely, (thinking) thereby to refute the Truth. Then I seized them, and how (awful) was My punishment.	The people of Nuh and the parties after them rejected (prophets) before them, and every nation purposed against their messenger to destroy him, and they disputed by means of the falsehood that they might thereby render null the truth, therefore I destroyed them; how was then My retribution!
40 006	Thus was the Decree of thy Lord proved true against the Unbelievers; that truly they are Companions of the Fire!	Thus was the word of thy Lord concerning those who disbelieve fulfilled: That they are owners of the Fire.	And thus did the word of your Lord prove true against those who disbelieved that they are the inmates of the fire.
40 007	Those who sustain the Throne (of Allah) and those around it sing Glory and Praise to their Lord; believe in Him; and implore Forgiveness for those who believe: "Our Lord! Thy Reach is over all things, in Mercy and Knowledge. Forgive, then, those who turn in Repentance, and follow Thy Path; and preserve them from the Penalty of the Blazing Fire!"	Those who bear the Throne, and all who are round about it, hymn the praises of their Lord and believe in Him and ask forgiveness for those who believe (saying): Our Lord! Thou comprehendest all things in mercy and knowledge, therefor forgive those who repent and follow Thy way. Ward off from them the punishment of hell.	Those who bear the power and those around Him celebrate the praise of their Lord and believe in Him and ask protection for those who believe: Our Lord! Thou embracest all things in mercy and knowledge, therefore grant protection to those who turn (to Thee) and follow Thy way, and save them from the punishment of the hell:
40 008	"And grant, our Lord! that they enter the Gardens of Eternity, which Thou hast promised to them, and to the righteous among their fathers, their wives, and their posterity! For Thou art (He), the Exalted in Might, Full of Wisdom."	Our Lord! And make them enter the Gardens of Eden which thou hast promised them, with such of their fathers and their wives and their descendants as do right. Lo! Thou, only Thou, art the Mighty, the Wise.	Our Lord! and make them enter the gardens of perpetuity which Thou hast promised to them and those who do good of their fathers and their wives and their offspring, surely Thou are the Mighty, the Wise.
40 009	"And preserve them from (all) ills; and any whom Thou dost preserve from ills that Day,- on them wilt Thou have bestowed Mercy indeed: and that will be truly (for them) the highest Achievement".	And ward off from them ill-deeds; and he from whom Thou wardest off ill-deeds that day, him verily hast Thou taken into mercy. That is the supreme triumph.	And keep them from evil deeds, and whom Thou keepest from evil deeds this day, indeed Thou hast mercy on him, and that is the mighty achievement.
40 010	The Unbelievers will be addressed: "Greater was the aversion of Allah to you than (is) your aversion to yourselves, seeing that ye were called to the Faith and ye used to refuse."	Lo! (on that day) those who disbelieve are informed by proclamation: Verily Allah's abhorrence is more terrible than your abhorrence one of another, when ye were called unto the faith but did refuse.	Surely those who disbelieve shall be cried out to: Certainly Allah's hatred (of you) when you were called upon to the faith and you rejected, is much greater than your hatred of yourselves.
40 011	They will say: "Our Lord! twice hast Thou made us without life, and twice hast Thou given us Life! Now have we recognised our sins: Is there any way out (of this)?"	They say: Our Lord! Twice hast Thou made us die, and twice hast Thou made us live. Now we confess our sins. Is there any way to go out?	They shall say: Our Lord! twice didst Thou make us subject to death, and twice hast Thou given us life, so we do confess our faults; is there then a way to get out?
40 012	(The answer will be:) "This is because, when Allah was invoked as the Only (object of worship), ye did reject Faith, but when partners were joined to Him, ye believed! the Command is with Allah, Most High, Most Great!"	(It is said unto them): This is (your plight) because, when Allah only was invoked, ye disbelieved, but when some partner was ascribed to Him ye were believing. But the command belongeth only to Allah, the Sublime, the Majestic.	That is because when Allah alone was called upon, you disbelieved, and when associates were given to Him, you believed; so judgment belongs to Allah, the High, the Great.

40 013	He it is Who showeth you his Signs, and sendeth down sustenance for you from the sky: but only those receive admonition who turn (to Allah).	He it is Who showeth you His portents, and sendeth down for you provision from the sky. None payeth heed save him who turneth (unto Him) repentant.	He it is Who shows you His signs and sends down for you sustenance from heaven, and none minds but he who turns (to Him) again and again.
40 014	Call ye, then, upon Allah with sincere devotion to Him, even though the Unbelievers may detest it.	Therefor (O believers) pray unto Allah, making religion pure for Him (only), however much the disbelievers be averse -	Therefore call upon Allah, being sincere to Him in obedience, though the unbelievers are averse:
40 015	Raised high above ranks (or degrees), (He is) the Lord of the Throne (of Authority): by His Command doth He send the Spirit (of inspiration) to any of His servants he pleases, that it may warn (men) of the Day of Mutual Meeting,-	The Exalter of Ranks, the Lord of the Throne. He causeth the Spirit of His command upon whom He will of His slaves, that He may warn of the Day of Meeting,	Possessor of the highest rank, Lord of power: He makes the inspiration to light by His command upon whom He pleases of His servants, that he may warn (men) of the day of meeting.
40 016	The Day whereon they will (all) come forth: not a single thing concerning them is hidden from Allah. Whose will be the dominion that Day? That of Allah, the One the Irresistible!	The day when they come forth, nothing of them being hidden from Allah. Whose is the Sovereignty this day? It is Allah's, the One, the Almighty.	(Of) the day when they shall come forth, nothing concerning them remains hidden to Allah. To whom belongs the kingdom this day? To Allah, the One, the Subduer (of all).
40 017	That Day will every soul be requited for what it earned; no injustice will there be that Day, for Allah is Swift in taking account.	This day is each soul requited that which it hath earned; no wrong (is done) this day. Lo! Allah is swift at reckoning.	This day every soul shall be rewarded for what it has earned; no injustice (shall be done) this day; surely Allah is quick in reckoning.
40 018	Warn them of the Day that is (ever) drawing near, when the hearts will (come) right up to the throats to choke (them); No intimate friend nor intercessor will the wrong-doers have, who could be listened to.	Warn them (O Muhammad) of the Day of the approaching (doom), when the hearts will be choking the throats, (when) there will be no friend for the wrong-doers, nor any intercessor who will be heard.	And warn them of the day that draws near, when hearts shall rise up to the throats, grieving inwardly; the unjust shall not have any compassionate friend nor any intercessor who should be obeyed.
40 019	(Allah) knows of (the tricks) that deceive with the eyes, and all that the hearts (of men) conceal.	He knoweth the traitor of the eyes, and that which the bosoms hide.	He knows the stealthy looks and that which the breasts conceal.
40 020	And Allah will judge with (justice and) Truth: but those whom (men) invoke besides Him, will not (be in a position) to judge at all. Verily it is Allah (alone) Who hears and sees (all things).	Allah judgeth with truth, while those to whom they cry instead of Him judge not at all. Lo! Allah, He is the Hearer, the Seer.	And Allah judges with the truth; and those whom they call upon besides Him cannot judge aught; surely Allah is the Hearing, the Seeing.
40 021	Do they not travel through the earth and see what was the End of those before them? They were even superior to them in strength, and in the traces (they have left) in the land: but Allah did call them to account for their sins, and none had they to defend them against Allah.	Have they not travelled in the land to see the nature of the consequence for those who disbelieved before them? They were mightier than these in power and (in the) traces (which they left behind them) in the earth. Yet Allah seized them for their sins, and they had no protector from Allah.	Have they not travelled in the earth and seen how was the end of those who were before them? Mightier than these were they in strength-- and in fortifications in the land, but Allah destroyed them for their sins; and there was not for them any defender against Allah.
40 022	That was because there came to them their messengers with Clear (Signs), but they rejected them: So Allah called them to account: for He is Full of Strength, Strict in Punishment.	That was because their messengers kept bringing them clear proofs (of Allah's Sovereignty) but they disbelieved; so Allah seized them. Lo! He is Strong, severe in punishment.	That was because there came to them their messengers with clear arguments, but they rejected (them), therefore Allah destroyed them; surely He is Strong, Severe in retribution.

40 023	Of old We sent Moses, with Our Signs and an authority manifest,	And verily We sent Moses with Our revelations and a clear warrant	And certainly We sent Musa with Our communications and clear authority,
40 024	To Pharaoh, Haman, and Qarun; but they called (him) "a sorcerer telling lies!"...	Unto Pharaoh and Haman and Korah, but they said: A lying sorcerer!	To Firon and Haman and Qaroun, but they said: A lying magician.
40 025	Now, when he came to them in Truth, from Us, they said, "Slay the sons of those who believe with him, and keep alive their females," but the plots of Unbelievers (end) in nothing but errors (and delusions)!...	And when he brought them the Truth from Our presence, they said: Slay the sons of those who believe with him, and spare their women. But the plot of disbelievers is in naught but error.	So when he brought to them the truth from Us, they said: Slay the sons of those who believe with him and keep their women alive; and the struggle of the unbelievers will only come to a state of perdition.
40 026	Said Pharaoh: "Leave me to slay Moses; and let him call on his Lord! What I fear is lest he should change your religion, or lest he should cause mischief to appear in the land!"	And Pharaoh said: Suffer me to kill Moses, and let him cry unto his Lord. Lo! I fear that he will alter your religion or that he will cause confusion in the land.	And Firon said: Let me alone that I may slay Musa and let him call upon his Lord; surely I fear that he will change your religion or that he will make mischief to appear in the land.
40 027	Moses said: "I have indeed called upon my Lord and your Lord (for protection) from every arrogant one who believes not in the Day of Account!"	Moses said: Lo! I seek refuge in my Lord and your Lord from every scorner who believeth not in a Day of Reckoning.	And Musa said: Surely I take refuge with my Lord and-- your Lord from every proud one who does not believe in the day of reckoning.
40 028	A believer, a man from among the people of Pharaoh, who had concealed his faith, said: "Will ye slay a man because he says, 'My Lord is Allah'?- when he has indeed come to you with Clear (Signs) from your Lord? and if he be a liar, on him is (the sin of) his lie: but, if he is telling the Truth, then will fall on you something of the (calamity) of which he warns you: Truly Allah guides not one who transgresses and lies!"	And a believing man of Pharaoh's family, who hid his faith, said: Would ye kill a man because he saith: My Lord is Allah, and hath brought you clear proofs from your Lord? If he is lying, then his lie is upon him; and if he is truthful, then some of that wherewith he threateneth you will strike you. Lo! Allah guideth not one who is a prodigal, a liar.	And a believing man of Firon's people who hid his faith said: What! will you slay a man because he says: My Lord is Allah, and indeed he has brought to you clear arguments from your Lord? And if he be a liar, on him will be his lie, and if he be truthful, there will befall you some of that which he threatens you (with); surely Allah does not guide him who is extravagant, a liar:
40 029	"O my People! Yours is the dominion this day: Ye have the upper hand in the land: but who will help us from the Punishment of Allah, should it befall us?" Pharaoh said: "I but point out to you that which I see (myself); Nor do I guide you but to the Path of Right!"	O my people! Yours is the kingdom to-day, ye being uppermost in the land. But who would save us from the wrath of Allah should it reach us? Pharaoh said: I do but show you what I think, and I do but guide you to wise policy.	O my people! yours is the kingdom this day, being masters in the land, but who will help us against the punishment of Allah if it come to us? Firon said: I do not show you aught but that which I see (myself), and I do not make you follow any but the right way.
40 030	Then said the man who believed: "O my people! Truly I do fear for you something like the Day (of disaster) of the Confederates (in sin)!"-	And he who believed said: O my people! Lo! I fear for you a fate like that of the factions (of old);	And he who believed said: O my people! surely I fear for you the like of what befell the parties:
40 031	"Something like the fate of the People of Noah, the 'Ad, and the Thamud, and those who came after them: but Allah never wishes injustice to his Servants."	A plight like that of Noah's folk, and A'ad and Thamud, and those after them, and Allah willeth no injustice for (His) slaves.	The like of what befell the people of Nuh and Ad and Samood and those after them, and Allah does not desire injustice for (His) servants;
40 032	"And O my people! I fear for you a Day when there will be Mutual calling (and wailing),"-	And, O my people! Lo! I fear for you a Day of Summoning,	And, O my people! I fear for you the day of calling out,

40 033	"A Day when ye shall turn your backs and flee: No defender shall ye have from Allah: Any whom Allah leaves to stray, there is none to guide..."	A day when ye will turn to flee, having no preserver from Allah: and he whom Allah sendeth astray, for him there is no guide.	The day on which you will turn back retreating; there shall be no savior for you from Allah, and whomsoever Allah causes to err, there is no guide for him:
40 034	"And to you there came Joseph in times gone by, with Clear Signs, but ye ceased not to doubt of the (Mission) for which he had come: At length, when he died, ye said: 'No messenger will Allah send after him.' thus doth Allah leave to stray such as transgress and live in doubt,"-	And verily Joseph brought you of old clear proofs, yet ye ceased not to be in doubt concerning what he brought you till, when he died, ye said: Allah will not send any messenger after him. Thus Allah deceiveth him who is a prodigal, a doubter.	And certainly Yusuf came to you before with clear arguments, but you ever remained in doubt as to what he brought; until when he died, you said: Allah will never raise a messenger after him. Thus does Allah cause him to err who is extravagant, a doubter,
40 035	"(Such) as dispute about the Signs of Allah, without any authority that hath reached them, grievous and odious (is such conduct) in the sight of Allah and of the Believers. Thus doth Allah, seal up every heart - of arrogant and obstinate Transgressors."	Those who wrangle concerning the revelations of Allah without any warrant that hath come unto them, it is greatly hateful in the sight of Allah and in the sight of those who believe. Thus doth Allah print on every arrogant, disdainful heart.	Those who dispute concerning the communications of Allah without any authority that He has given them; greatly hated is it by Allah and by those who believe. Thus does Allah set a seal over the heart of every proud, haughty one.
40 036	Pharaoh said: "O Haman! Build me a lofty palace, that I may attain the ways and means-"	And Pharaoh said: O Haman! Build for me a tower that haply I may reach the roads,	And Firon said: O Haman! build for me a tower that I may attain the means of access,
40 037	"The ways and means of (reaching) the heavens, and that I may mount up to the god of Moses: But as far as I am concerned, I think (Moses) is a liar!" Thus was made alluring, in Pharaoh's eyes, the evil of his deeds, and he was hindered from the Path; and the plot of Pharaoh led to nothing but perdition (for him).	The roads of the heavens, and may look upon the god of Moses, though verily I think him a liar. Thus was the evil that he did made fairseeming unto Pharaoh, and he was debarred from the (right) way. The plot of Pharaoh ended but in ruin.	The means of access to the heavens, then reach the god of Musa, and I surely think him to be a liar. And thus the evil of his deed was made fairseeming to Firon, and he was turned away from the way; and the struggle of Firon was not (to end) in aught but destruction.
40 038	The man who believed said further: "O my people! Follow me: I will lead you to the Path of Right."	And he who believed said: O my people! Follow me. I will show you the way of right conduct.	And he who believed said: O my people! follow me, I will guide you to the right course;
40 039	"O my people! This life of the present is nothing but (temporary) convenience: It is the Hereafter that is the Home that will last."	O my people! Lo! this life of the world is but a passing comfort, and lo! the Hereafter, that is the enduring home.	O my people! this life of the world is only a (passing) enjoyment, and surely the hereafter is the abode to settle;
40 040	"He that works evil will not be requited but by the like thereof: and he that works a righteous deed - whether man or woman - and is a Believer- such will enter the Garden (of Bliss): Therein will they have abundance without measure."	Whoso doeth an ill-deed, he will be repaid the like thereof, while whoso doeth right, whether male or female, and is a believer, (all) such will enter the Garden, where they will be nourished without stint.	Whoever does an evil, he shall not be recompensed (with aught) but the like of it, and whoever does good, whether male or female, and he is a believer, these shall enter the garden, in which they shall be given sustenance without measure.
40 041	"And O my people! How (strange) it is for me to call you to Salvation while ye call me to the Fire!"	And, O my people! What aileth me that I call you unto deliverance when ye call me unto the Fire?	And, O my people! how is it that I call you to salvation and you call me to the fire?
40 042	"Ye do call upon me to blaspheme against Allah, and to join with Him partners of whom I have no knowledge; and I call you to the Exalted in Power, Who forgives again and again!"	Ye call me to disbelieve in Allah and ascribe unto Him as partners that whereof I have no knowledge, while I call you unto the Mighty, the Forgiver.	You call on me that I should disbelieve in Allah and associate with Him that of which I have no knowledge, and I call you to the Mighty, the most Forgiving;

40 043	"Without doubt ye do call me to one who is not fit to be called to, whether in this world, or in the Hereafter; our return will be to Allah; and the Transgressors will be Companions of the Fire!"	Assuredly that whereunto ye call me hath no claim in the world or in the Hereafter, and our return will be unto Allah, and the prodigals will be owners of the Fire.	No doubt that what you call me to has no title to be called to in this world, nor in the hereafter, and that our turning back is to Allah, and that the extravagant are the inmates of the fire;
40 044	"Soon will ye remember what I say to you (now), My (own) affair I commit to Allah: for Allah (ever) watches over His Servants."	And ye will remember what I say unto you. I confide my cause unto Allah. Lo! Allah is Seer of (His) slaves.	So you shall remember what I say to you, and I entrust my affair to Allah, Surely Allah sees the servants.
40 045	Then Allah saved him from (every) ill that they plotted (against him), but the burnt of the Penalty encompassed on all sides the People of Pharaoh.	So Allah warded off from him the evils which they plotted, while a dreadful doom encompassed Pharaoh's folk,	So Allah protected him from the evil (consequences) of what they planned, and the most evil punishment overtook Firon's people:
40 046	In front of the Fire will they be brought, morning and evening: And (the sentence will be) on the Day that Judgment will be established: Cast ye the People of Pharaoh into the severest Penalty!	The Fire; they are exposed to it morning and evening; and on the day when the Hour upriseth (it is said): Cause Pharaoh's folk to enter the most awful doom.	The fire; they shall be brought before it (every) morning and evening and on the day when the hour shall come to pass: Make Firon's people enter the severest chastisement.
40 047	Behold, they will dispute with each other in the Fire! The weak ones (who followed) will say to those who had been arrogant, "We but followed you: Can ye then take (on yourselves) from us some share of the Fire?"	And when they wrangle in the Fire, the weak say unto those who were proud: Lo! we were a following unto you; will ye therefor rid us of a portion of the Fire?	And when they shall contend one with another in the fire, then the weak shall say to those who were proud: Surely we were your followers; will you then avert from us a portion of the fire?
40 048	Those who had been arrogant will say: "We are all in this (Fire)! Truly, Allah has judged between (his) Servants!"	Those who were proud say: Lo! we are all (together) herein. Lo! Allah hath judged between (His) slaves.	Those who were proud shall say: Surely we are all in it: surely Allah has judged between the servants.
40 049	Those in the Fire will say to the Keepers of Hell: "Pray to your Lord to lighten us the Penalty for a day (at least)!"	And those in the Fire say unto the guards of hell: Entreat your Lord that He relieve us of a day of the torment.	And those who are in the fire shall say to the keepers of hell: Call upon your Lord that He may lighten to us one day of the punishment.
40 050	They will say: "Did there not come to you your messengers with Clear Signs?" They will say, "Yes". They will reply, "Then pray (as ye like)! But the prayer of those without Faith is nothing but (futile wandering) in (mazes of) error!"	They say: Came not your messengers unto you with clear proofs? They say: Yea, verily. They say: Then do ye pray, although the prayer of disbelievers is in vain.	They shall say: Did not your messengers come to you with clear arguments? They shall say: Yea. They shall say: Then call. And the call of the unbelievers is only in error.
40 051	We will, without doubt, help our messengers and those who believe, (both) in this world's life and on the Day when the Witnesses will stand forth,-	Lo! We verily do help Our messengers, and those who believe, in the life of the world and on the day when the witnesses arise,	Most surely We help Our messengers, and those who believe, in this world's life and on the day when the witnesses shall stand up,
40 052	The Day when no profit will it be to Wrong-doers to present their excuses, but they will (only) have the Curse and the Home of Misery.	The day when their excuse availeth not the evil-doers, and theirs is the curse, and theirs the ill abode.	The day on which their excuse shall not benefit the unjust, and for them is curse and for them is the evil abode.
40 053	We did aforetime give Moses the (Book of) Guidance, and We gave the book in inheritance to the Children of Israel,-	And We verily gave Moses the guidance, and We caused the Children of Israel to inherit the Scripture,	And certainly We gave Musa the guidance, and We made the children of Israel inherit the Book,
40 054	A Guide and a Message to men of Understanding.	A guide and a reminder for men of understanding.	A guidance and a reminder to the men of understanding.

40 055	Patiently, then, persevere: for the Promise of Allah is true: and ask forgiveness for thy fault, and celebrate the Praises of thy Lord in the evening and in the morning.	Then have patience (O Muhammad). Lo! the promise of Allah is true. And ask forgiveness of thy sin, and hymn the praise of thy Lord at fall of night and in the early hours.	Therefore be patient; surely the promise of Allah is true; and ask protection for your fault and sing the praise of your Lord in the evening and the morning.
40 056	Those who dispute about the signs of Allah without any authority bestowed on them,- there is nothing in their breasts but (the quest of) greatness, which they shall never attain to: seek refuge, then, in Allah: It is He Who hears and sees (all things).	Lo! those who wrangle concerning the revelations of Allah without a warrant having come unto them, there is naught else in their breasts save pride which they will never attain. So take thou refuge in Allah. Lo! He, only He, is the Hearer, the Seer.	Surely (as for) those who dispute about the communications of Allah without any authority that has come to them, there is naught in their breasts but (a desire) to become great which they shall never attain to; Therefore seek refuge in Allah, surely He is the Hearing, the Seeing.
40 057	Assuredly the creation of the heavens and the earth is a greater (matter) than the creation of men: Yet most men understand not.	Assuredly the creation of the heavens and the earth is greater than the creation of mankind; but most of mankind know not.	Certainly the creation of the heavens and the earth is greater than the creation of the men, but most people do not know.
40 058	Not equal are the blind and those who (clearly) see: Nor are (equal) those who believe and work deeds of righteousness, and those who do evil. Little do ye learn by admonition!	And the blind man and the seer are not equal, neither are those who believe and do good works (equal with) the evil-doer. Little do ye reflect!	And the blind and the seeing are not alike, nor those who believe and do good and the evil-doer; little is it that you are mindful.
40 059	The Hour will certainly come: Therein is no doubt: Yet most men believe not.	Lo! the Hour is surely coming, there is no doubt thereof; yet most of mankind believe not.	Most surely the hour is coming, there is no doubt therein, but most people do not believe.
40 060	And your Lord says: "Call on Me; I will answer your (Prayer): but those who are too arrogant to serve Me will surely find themselves in Hell - in humiliation!"	And your Lord hath said: Pray unto Me and I will hear your prayer. Lo! those who scorn My service, they will enter hell, disgraced.	And your Lord says: Call upon Me, I will answer you; surely those who are too proud for My service shall soon enter hell abased.
40 061	It is Allah Who has made the Night for you, that ye may rest therein, and the Day as that which helps (you) to see. Verily Allah is full of Grace and Bounty to men: yet most men give no thanks.	Allah it is Who hath appointed for you night that ye may rest therein, and day for seeing. Lo! Allah is a Lord of bounty for mankind, yet most of mankind give not thanks.	Allah is He Who made for you the night that you may rest therein and the day to see; most surely Allah is Gracious to men, but most men do not give thanks.
40 062	Such is Allah, your Lord, the Creator of all things, there is no god but He: Then how ye are deluded away from the Truth!	Such is Allah, your Lord, the Creator of all things, There is no God save Him. How then are ye perverted?	That is Allah, your Lord, the Creator of everything; there is no God but He; whence are you then turned away?
40 063	Thus are deluded those who are wont to reject the Signs of Allah.	Thus are they perverted who deny the revelations of Allah.	Thus were turned away those who denied the communications of Allah.
40 064	It is Allah Who has made for you the earth as a resting place, and the sky as a canopy, and has given you shape- and made your shapes beautiful,- and has provided for you Sustenance, of things pure and good;- such is Allah your Lord. So Glory to Allah, the Lord of the Worlds!	Allah it is Who appointed for you the earth for a dwelling-place and the sky for a canopy, and fashioned you and perfected your shapes, and hath provided you with good things. Such is Allah, your Lord. Then blessed be Allah, the Lord of the Worlds!	Allah is He Who made the earth a resting-place for you and the heaven a canopy, and He formed you, then made goodly your forms, and He provided you with goodly things; that is Allah, your Lord; blessed then is Allah, the Lord of the worlds.

40 065	He is the Living (One): There is no god but He: Call upon Him, giving Him sincere devotion. Praise be to Allah, Lord of the Worlds!	He is the Living One. There is no God save Him. So pray unto Him, making religion pure for Him (only). Praise be to Allah, the Lord of the Worlds!	He is the Living, there is no god but He, therefore call on Him, being sincere to Him in obedience; (all) praise is due to Allah, the Lord of the worlds.
40 066	Say: "I have been forbidden to invoke those whom ye invoke besides Allah,- seeing that the Clear Signs have come to me from my Lord; and I have been commanded to bow (in Islam) to the Lord of the Worlds."	Say (O Muhammad): I am forbidden to worship those unto whom ye cry beside Allah since there have come unto me clear proofs from my Lord, and I am commanded to surrender to the Lord of the Worlds.	Say: I am forbidden to serve those whom you call upon besides Allah when clear arguments have come to me from my Lord, and I am commanded that I should submit to the Lord of the worlds.
40 067	It is He Who has created you from dust then from a sperm-drop, then from a leech-like clot; then does he get you out (into the light) as a child: then lets you (grow and) reach your age of full strength; then lets you become old,- though of you there are some who die before;- and lets you reach a Term appointed; in order that ye may learn wisdom.	He it is Who created you from dust, then from a drop (of seed) then from a clot, then bringeth you forth as a child, then (ordaineth) that ye attain full strength and afterward that ye become old men - though some among you die before - and that ye reach an appointed term, that haply ye may understand.	He it is Who created you from dust, then from a small life-germ, then from a clot, then He brings you forth as a child, then that you may attain your maturity, then that you may be old-- and of you there are some who are caused to die before-- and that you may reach an appointed term, and that you may understand.
40 068	It is He Who gives Life and Death; and when He decides upon an affair, He says to it, "Be", and it is.	He it is Who quickeneth and giveth death. When He ordaineth a thing, He saith unto it only: Be! and it is.	He it is Who gives life and brings death, so when He decrees an affair, He only says to it: Be, and it is.
40 069	Seest thou not those that dispute concerning the Signs of Allah? How are they turned away (from Reality)?-	Hast thou not seen those who wrangle concerning the revelations of Allah, how they are turned away? -	Have you not seen those who dispute with respect to the communications of Allah: how are they turned away?
40 070	Those who reject the Book and the (revelations) with which We sent our messengers: but soon shall they know,-	Those who deny the Scripture and that wherewith We send Our messengers. But they will come to know,	Those who reject the Book and that with which We have sent Our Messenger; but they shall soon come to know,
40 071	When the yokes (shall be) round their necks, and the chains; they shall be dragged along-	When carcans are about their necks and chains. They are dragged	When the fetters and the chains shall be on their necks; they shall be dragged
40 072	In the boiling fetid fluid: then in the Fire shall they be burned;	Through boiling waters; then they are thrust into the Fire.	Into boiling water, then in the fire shall they be burned;
40 073	Then shall it be said to them: "Where are the (deities) to which ye gave part-worship-"	Then it is said unto them: Where are (all) that ye used to make partners (in the Sovereignty)	Then shall it be said to them: Where is that which you used to set up
40 074	"In derogation of Allah?" They will reply: "They have left us in the lurch: Nay, we invoked not, of old, anything (that had real existence)." Thus does Allah leave the Unbelievers to stray.	Beside Allah? They say: They have failed us; but we used not to pray to anything before. Thus doth Allah send astray the disbelievers (in His guidance).	Besides Allah? They shall say: They are gone away from us, nay, we used not to call upon anything before. Thus does Allah confound the unbelievers.
40 075	"That was because ye were wont to rejoice on the earth in things other than the Truth, and that ye were wont to be insolent."	(And it is said unto them): This is because ye exulted in the earth without right, and because ye were petulant.	That is because you exulted in the land unjustly and because you behaved insolently.
40 076	"Enter ye the gates of Hell, to dwell therein: and evil is (this) abode of the arrogant!"	Enter ye the gates of hell, to dwell therein. Evil is the habitation of the scornful.	Enter the gates of hell to abide therein, evil then is the abode of the proud.

40 077	So persevere in patience; for the Promise of Allah is true: and whether We show thee (in this life) some part of what We promise them,- or We take thy soul (to Our Mercy) (before that),-(in any case) it is to Us that they shall (all) return.	Then have patience (O Muhammad). Lo! the promise of Allah is true. And whether we let thee see a part of that which We promise them, or (whether) We cause thee to die, still unto Us they will be brought back.	So be patient, surely the promise of Allah is true. So should We make you see part of what We threaten them with, or should We cause you to die, to Us shall they be returned.
40 078	We did aforetime send messengers before thee: of them there are some whose story We have related to thee, and some whose story We have not related to thee. It was not (possible) for any messenger to bring a sign except by the leave of Allah: but when the Command of Allah issued, the matter was decided in truth and justice, and there perished, there and then those who stood on Falsehoods.	Verily We sent messengers before thee, among them those of whom We have told thee, and some of whom We have not told thee; and it was not given to any messenger that he should bring a portent save by Allah's leave, but when Allah's commandment cometh (the cause) is judged aright, and the followers of vanity will then be lost.	And certainly We sent messengers before you: there are some of them that We have mentioned to you and there are others whom We have not mentioned to you, and it was not meet for a messenger that he should bring a sign except with Allah's permission, but when the command of Allah came, judgment was given with truth, and those who treated (it) as a lie were lost.
40 079	It is Allah Who made cattle for you, that ye may use some for riding and some for food;	Allah it is Who hath appointed for you cattle, that ye may ride on some of them, and eat of some -	Allah is He Who made the cattle for you that you may ride on some of them, and some of them you eat.
40 080	And there are (other) advantages in them for you (besides); that ye may through them attain to any need (there may be) in your hearts; and on them and on ships ye are carried.	(Many) benefits ye have from them - and that ye may satisfy by their means a need that is in your breasts, and may be borne upon them as upon the ship.	And there are advantages for you in them, and that you may attain thereon a want which is in your breasts, and upon them and upon the ships you are borne.
40 081	And He shows you (always) His Signs: then which of the Signs of Allah will ye deny?	And He showeth you His tokens. Which, then, of the tokens of Allah do ye deny?	And He shows you His signs: which then of Allah's signs will you deny?
40 082	Do they not travel through the earth and see what was the End of those before them? They were more numerous than these and superior in strength and in the traces (they have left) in the land: Yet all that they accomplished was of no profit to them.	Have they not travelled in the land to see the nature of the consequence for those before them? They were more numerous than these, and mightier in power and (in the) traces (which they left behind them) in the earth. But all that they used to earn availed them not.	Have they not then journeyed in the land and seen how was the end of those before them? They were more (in numbers) than these and greater in strength and in fortifications in the land, but what they earned did not avail them.
40 083	For when their messengers came to them with Clear Signs, they exulted in such knowledge (and skill) as they had; but that very (Wrath) at which they were wont to scoff hemmed them in.	And when their messengers brought them clear proofs (of Allah's Sovereignty) they exulted in the knowledge they (themselves) possessed. And that which they were wont to mock befell them.	Then when their messengers came to them with clear arguments, they exulted in what they had with them of knowledge, and there beset them that which they used to mock.
40 084	But when they saw Our Punishment, they said: "We believe in Allah,- the one Allah - and we reject the partners we used to join with Him."	Then, when they saw Our doom, they said: We believe in Allah only and reject (all) that we used to associate (with Him).	But when they saw Our punishment, they said: We believe in Allah alone and we deny what we used to associate with Him.
40 085	But their professing the Faith when they (actually) saw Our Punishment was not going to profit them. (Such has been) Allah's Way of dealing with His Servants (from the most ancient times). And even thus did the Rejecters of Allah perish (utterly)!	But their faith could not avail them when they saw Our doom. This is Allah's law which hath ever taken course for His bondmen. And then the disbelievers will be ruined.	But their belief was not going to profit them when they had seen Our punishment; (this is) Allah's law, which has indeed obtained in the matter of His servants, and there the unbelievers are lost.

Chapter 41:

FUSSILAT (EXPLAINED IN DETAIL)

Total Verses: 54 Revealed At: MAKKA

In the name of Allah, the Most Beneficent, the Most Merciful.

41 001	Ha Mim:	Ha. Mim.	Ha Mim!
41 002	A Revelation from (Allah), Most Gracious, Most Merciful;-	A revelation from the Beneficent, the Merciful,	A revelation from the Beneficent, the Merciful Allah:
41 003	A Book, whereof the verses are explained in detail;- a Qur'an in Arabic, for people who understand;-	A Scripture whereof the verses are expounded, a Lecture in Arabic for people who have knowledge,	A Book of which the verses are made plain, an Arabic Quran for a people who know:
41 004	Giving good news and admonition: yet most of them turn away, and so they hear not.	Good tidings and a warning. But most of them turn away so that they hear not.	A herald of good news and a warner, but most of them turn aside so they hear not.
41 005	They say: "Our hearts are under veils, (concealed) from that to which thou dost invite us, and in our ears in a deafness, and between us and thee is a screen: so do thou (what thou wilt); for us, we shall do (what we will!)"	And they say: Our hearts are protected from that unto which thou (O Muhammad) callest us, and in our ears there is a deafness, and between us and thee there is a veil. Act, then. Lo! we also shall be acting.	And they say: Our hearts are under coverings from that to which you call us, and there is a heaviness in our ears, and a veil hangs between us and you, so work, we too are working.
41 006	Say thou: "I am but a man like you: It is revealed to me by Inspiration, that your Allah is one Allah: so stand true to Him, and ask for His Forgiveness." And woe to those who join gods with Allah,-	Say (unto them O Muhammad): I am only a mortal like you. It is inspired in me that your Allah is One Allah, therefor take the straight path unto Him and seek forgiveness of Him. And woe unto the idolaters,	Say: I am only a mortal like you; it is revealed to me that your Allah is one Allah, therefore follow the right way to Him and ask His forgiveness; and woe to the polytheists;
41 007	Those who practise not regular Charity, and who even deny the Hereafter.	Who give not the poor-due, and who are disbelievers in the Hereafter.	(To) those who do not give poor-rate and they are unbelievers in the hereafter.
41 008	For those who believe and work deeds of righteousness is a reward that will never fail.	Lo! as for those who believe and do good works, for them is a reward enduring.	(As for) those who believe and do good, they shall surely have a reward never to be cut off.
41 009	Say: Is it that ye deny Him Who created the earth in two Days? And do ye join equals with Him? He is the Lord of (all) the Worlds.	Say (O Muhammad, unto the idolaters): Disbelieve ye verily in Him Who created the earth in two Days, and ascribe ye unto Him rivals? He (and none else) is the Lord of the Worlds.	Say: What! do you indeed disbelieve in Him Who created the earth in two periods, and do you set up equals with Him? That is the Lord of the Worlds.
41 010	He set on the (earth), mountains standing firm, high above it, and bestowed blessings on the earth, and measure therein all things to give them nourishment in due proportion, in four Days, in accordance with (the needs of) those who seek (sustenance).	He placed therein firm hills rising above it, and blessed it and measured therein its sustenance in four Days, alike for (all) who ask;	And He made in it mountains above its surface, and He blessed therein and made therein its foods, in four periods: alike for the seekers.

41 011	Moreover He comprehended in His design the sky, and it had been (as) smoke: He said to it and to the earth: "Come ye together, willingly or unwillingly." They said: "We do come (together), in willing obedience."	Then turned He to the heaven when it was smoke, and said unto it and unto the earth: Come both of you, willingly or loth. They said: We come, obedient.	Then He directed Himself to the heaven and it is a vapor, so He said to it and to the earth: Come both, willingly or unwillingly. They both said: We come willingly.
41 012	So He completed them as seven firmaments in two Days, and He assigned to each heaven its duty and command. And We adorned the lower heaven with lights, and (provided it) with guard. Such is the Decree of (Him) the Exalted in Might, Full of Knowledge.	Then He ordained them seven heavens in two Days and inspired in each heaven its mandate; and We decked the nether heaven with lamps, and rendered it inviolable. That is the measuring of the Mighty, the Knower.	So He ordained them seven heavens in two periods, and revealed in every heaven its affair; and We adorned the lower heaven with brilliant stars and (made it) to guard; that is the decree of the Mighty, the Knowing.
41 013	But if they turn away, say thou: "I have warned you of a stunning Punishment (as of thunder and lightning) like that which (overtook) the 'Ad and the Thamud!"	But if they turn away, then say: I warn you of a thunderbolt like the thunderbolt (which fell of old upon the tribes) of A'ad and Thamud;	But if they turn aside, then say: I have warned you of a scourge like the scourge of Ad and Samood.
41 014	Behold, the messengers came to them, from before them and behind them, (preaching): "Serve none but Allah." They said, "If our Lord had so pleased, He would certainly have sent down angels (to preach). Now we reject your mission (altogether)."	When their messengers came unto them from before them and behind them, saying: Worship none but Allah! they said: If our Lord had willed, He surely would have sent down angels (unto us), so lo! we are disbelievers in that wherewith ye have been sent.	When their messengers came to them from before them and from behind them, saying, Serve nothing but Allah, they said: If our Lord had pleased He would certainly have sent down angels, so we are surely unbelievers in that with which you are sent.
41 015	Now the 'Ad behaved arrogantly through the land, against (all) truth and reason, and said: "Who is superior to us in strength?" What! did they not see that Allah, Who created them, was superior to them in strength? But they continued to reject Our Signs!	As for A'ad, they were arrogant in the land without right, and they said: Who is mightier than us in power? Could they not see that Allah Who created them, He was mightier than them in power? And they denied Our revelations.	Then as to Ad, they were unjustly proud in the land, and they said: Who is mightier in strength than we? Did they not see that Allah Who created them was mightier than they in strength, and they denied Our communications?
41 016	So We sent against them a furious Wind through days of disaster, that We might give them a taste of a Penalty of humiliation in this life; but the Penalty of a Hereafter will be more humiliating still: and they will find no help.	Therefor We let loose on them a raging wind in evil days, that We might make them taste the torment of disgrace in the life of the world. And verily the doom of the Hereafter will be more shameful, and they will not be helped.	So We sent on them a furious wind in unlucky days, that We may make them taste the chastisement of abasement in this world's life; and certainly the chastisement of the hereafter is much more abasing, and they shall not be helped.
41 017	As to the Thamud, We gave them Guidance, but they preferred blindness (of heart) to Guidance: so the stunning Punishment of humiliation seized them, because of what they had earned.	And as for Thamud, We gave them guidance, but they preferred blindness to the guidance, so the bolt of the doom of humiliation overtook them because of what they used to earn.	And as to Samood, We showed them the right way, but they chose error above guidance, so there overtook them the scourge of an abasing chastisement for what they earned.
41 018	But We delivered those who believed and practised righteousness.	And We delivered those who believed and used to keep their duty to Allah.	And We delivered those who believed and guarded (against evil).
41 019	On the Day that the enemies of Allah will be gathered together to the Fire, they will be marched in ranks.	And (make mention of) the day when the enemies of Allah are gathered unto the Fire, they are driven on	And on the day that the enemies of Allah shall be brought together to the fire, then they shall be formed into groups.

41 020	At length, when they reach the (Fire), their hearing, their sight, and their skins will bear witness against them, as to (all) their deeds.	Till, when they reach it, their ears and their eyes and their skins testify against them as to what they used to do.	Until when they come to it, their ears and their eyes and their skins shall bear witness against them as to what they did.
41 021	They will say to their skins: "Why bear ye witness against us?" They will say: "Allah hath given us speech,- (He) Who giveth speech to everything: He created you for the first time, and unto Him were ye to return."	And they say unto their skins: Why testify ye against us? They say: Allah hath given us speech Who giveth speech to all things, and Who created you at the first, and unto Whom ye are returned.	And they shall say to their skins: Why have you borne witness against us? They shall say: Allah Who makes everything speak has made us speak, and He created you at first, and to Him you shall be brought back.
41 022	"Ye did not seek to hide yourselves, lest your hearing, your sight, and your skins should bear witness against you! But ye did think that Allah knew not many of the things that ye used to do!"	Ye did not hide yourselves lest your ears and your eyes and your skins should testify against you, but ye deemed that Allah knew not much of what ye did.	And you did not veil yourselves lest your ears and your eyes and your skins should bear witness against you, but you thought that Allah did not know most of what you did.
41 023	"But this thought of yours which ye did entertain concerning your Lord, hath brought you to destruction, and (now) have ye become of those utterly lost!"	That, your thought which ye did think about your Lord, hath ruined you; and ye find yourselves (this day) among the lost.	And that was your (evil) thought which you entertained about your Lord that has tumbled you down into perdition, so are you become of the lost ones.
41 024	If, then, they have patience, the Fire will be a home for them! and if they beg to be received into favour, into favour will they not (then) be received.	And though they are resigned, yet the Fire is still their home; and if they ask for favour, yet they are not of those unto whom favour can be shown.	Then if they will endure, still the fire is their abode, and if they ask for goodwill, then are they not of those who shall be granted goodwill.
41 025	And We have destined for them intimate companions (of like nature), who made alluring to them what was before them and behind them; and the sentence among the previous generations of jinns and men, who have passed away, is proved against them; for they are utterly lost.	And We assigned them comrades (in the world), who made their present and their past fairseeming unto them. And the Word concerning nations of the jinn and humankind who passed away before them hath effect for them. Lo! they were ever losers.	And We have appointed for them comrades so they have made fairseeming to them what is before them and what is behind them, and the word proved true against them-- among the nations of the jinn and the men that have passed away before them-- that they shall surely be losers.
41 026	The Unbelievers say: "Listen not to this Qur'an, but talk at random in the midst of its (reading), that ye may gain the upper hand!"	Those who disbelieve say: Heed not this Qur'an, and drown the hearing of it; haply ye may conquer.	And those who disbelieve say: Do not listen to this Quran and make noise therein, perhaps you may overcome.
41 027	But We will certainly give the Unbelievers a taste of a severe Penalty, and We will requite them for the worst of their deeds.	But verily We shall cause those who disbelieve to taste an awful doom, and verily We shall requite them the worst of what they used to do.	Therefore We will most certainly make those who disbelieve taste a severe punishment, and We will most certainly reward them for the evil deeds they used to do.
41 028	Such is the requital of the enemies of Allah,- the Fire: therein will be for them the Eternal Home: a (fit) requital, for that they were wont to reject Our Signs.	That is the reward of Allah's enemies: the Fire. Therein is their immortal home, payment forasmuch as they denied Our revelations.	That is the reward of the enemies of Allah-- the fire; for them therein shall be the house of long abiding; a reward for their denying Our communications.
41 029	And the Unbelievers will say: "Our Lord! Show us those, among jinns and men, who misled us: We shall crush them beneath our feet, so that they become the vilest (before all)."	And those who disbelieve will say: Our Lord! Show us those who beguiled us of the jinn and humankind. We will place them underneath our feet that they may be among the nethermost.	And those who disbelieve will say: Our Lord! show us those who led us astray from among the jinn and the men that we may trample them under our feet so that they may be of the lowest.

41 030	In the case of those who say, "Our Lord is Allah", and, further, stand straight and steadfast, the angels descend on them (from time to time): "Fear ye not!" (they suggest), "Nor grieve! but receive the Glad Tidings of the Garden (of Bliss), the which ye were promised!"	Lo! those who say: Our Lord is Allah, and afterward are upright, the angels descend upon them, saying: Fear not nor grieve, but hear good tidings of the paradise which ye are promised.	(As for) those who say: Our Lord is Allah, then continue in the right way, the angels descend upon them, saying: Fear not, nor be grieved, and receive good news of the garden which you were promised.
41 031	"We are your protectors in this life and in the Hereafter: therein shall ye have all that your souls shall desire; therein shall ye have all that ye ask for!"-	We are your protecting friends in the life of the world and in the Hereafter. There ye will have (all) that your souls desire, and there ye will have (all) for which ye pray.	We are your guardians in this world's life and in the hereafter, and you shall have therein what your souls desire and you shall have therein what you ask for:
41 032	"A hospitable gift from one Oft-Forgiving, Most Merciful!"	A gift of welcome from One Forgiving, Merciful.	A provision from the Forgiving, the Merciful.
41 033	Who is better in speech than one who calls (men) to Allah, works righteousness, and says, "I am of those who bow in Islam"?	And who is better in speech than him who prayeth unto his Lord and doeth right, and saith: Lo! I am of those who are muslims (surrender unto Him).	And who speaks better than he who calls to Allah while he himself does good, and says: I am surely of those who submit?
41 034	Nor can goodness and Evil be equal. Repel (Evil) with what is better: Then will he between whom and thee was hatred become as it were thy friend and intimate!	The good deed and the evil deed are not alike. Repel the evil deed with one which is better, then lo! he, between whom and thee there was enmity (will become) as though he was a bosom friend.	And not alike are the good and the evil. Repel (evil) with what is best, when lo! he between whom and you was enmity would be as if he were a warm friend.
41 035	And no one will be granted such goodness except those who exercise patience and self-restraint,- none but persons of the greatest good fortune.	But none is granted it save those who are steadfast, and none is granted it save the owner of great happiness.	And none are made to receive it but those who are patient, and none are made to receive it but those who have a mighty good fortune.
41 036	And if (at any time) an incitement to discord is made to thee by the Evil One, seek refuge in Allah. He is the One Who hears and knows all things.	And if a whisper from the devil reach thee (O Muhammad) then seek refuge in Allah. Lo! He is the Hearer, the Knower.	And if an interference of the Shaitan should cause you mischief, seek refuge in Allah; surely He is the Hearing, the Knowing.
41 037	Among His Signs are the Night and the Day, and the Sun and the Moon. Do not prostrate to the sun and the moon, but prostrate to Allah, Who created them, if it is Him ye wish to serve.	And of His portents are the night and the day and the sun and the moon. Do not prostrate to the sun or the moon; but prostrate to Allah Who created them, if it is in truth Him Whom ye worship.	And among His signs are the night and the day and the sun and the moon; do not prostrate to the sun nor to the moon; and prostrate to Allah Who created them, if Him it is that you serve.
41 038	But if they (Unbelievers) are arrogant, (no matter): for in the presence of thy Lord are those who celebrate His praises by night and by day. And they never flag (nor feel themselves above it).	But if they are too proud - still those who are with thy Lord glorify Him night and day, and tire not.	But if they are proud, yet those with your Lord glorify Him during the night and the day, and they are not tired.
41 039	And among His Signs in this: thou seest the earth barren and desolate; but when We send down rain to it, it is stirred to life and yields increase. Truly, He Who gives life to the (dead) earth can surely give life to (men) who are dead. For He has power over all things.	And of His portents (is this): that thou seest the earth lowly, but when We send down water thereon it thrilleth and groweth. Lo! He Who quickeneth it is verily the Quickener of the Dead. Lo! He is Able to do all things.	And among His signs is this, that you see the earth still, but when We send down on it the water, it stirs and swells: most surely He Who gives it life is the Giver of life to the dead; surely He has power over all things.

41 040	Those who pervert the Truth in Our Signs are not hidden from Us. Which is better?- he that is cast into the Fire, or he that comes safe through, on the Day of Judgment? Do what ye will: verily He seeth (clearly) all that ye do.	Lo! those who distort Our revelations are not hid from Us. Is he who is hurled into the Fire better, or he who cometh secure on the Day of Resurrection? Do what ye will. Lo! He is Seer of what ye do.	Surely they who deviate from the right way concerning Our communications are not hidden from Us. What! is he then who is cast into the fire better, or he who comes safe on the day of resurrection? Do what you like, surely He sees what you do.
41 041	Those who reject the Message when it comes to them (are not hidden from Us). And indeed it is a Book of exalted power.	Lo! those who disbelieve in the Reminder when it cometh unto them (are guilty), for lo! it is an unassailable Scripture.	Surely those who disbelieve in the reminder when it comes to them, and most surely it is a Mighty Book:
41 042	No falsehood can approach it from before or behind it: It is sent down by One Full of Wisdom, Worthy of all Praise.	Falsehood cannot come at it from before it or from behind it. (It is) a revelation from the Wise, the Owner of Praise.	Falsehood shall not come to it from before it nor from behind it; a revelation from the Wise, the Praised One.
41 043	Nothing is said to thee that was not said to the messengers before thee: that thy lord has at his Command (all) forgiveness as well as a most Grievous Penalty.	Naught is said unto thee (Muhammad) save what was said unto the messengers before thee. Lo! thy Lord is owner of forgiveness, and owner (also) of dire punishment.	Naught is said to you but what was said indeed to the messengers before you; surely your Lord is the Lord of forgiveness and the Lord of painful retribution.
41 044	Had We sent this as a Qur'an (in the language) other than Arabic, they would have said: "Why are not its verses explained in detail? What! (a Book) not in Arabic and (a Messenger) an Arab?" Say: "It is a Guide and a Healing to those who believe; and for those who believe not, there is a deafness in their ears, and it is blindness in their (eyes): They are (as it were) being called from a place far distant!"	And if We had appointed it a Lecture in a foreign tongue they would assuredly have said: If only its verses were expounded (so that we might understand)? What! A foreign tongue and an Arab? - Say unto them (O Muhammad): For those who believe it is a guidance and a healing; and as for those who disbelieve, there is a deafness in their ears, and it is blindness for them. Such are called to from afar.	And if We had made it a Quran in a foreign tongue, they would certainly have said: Why have not its communications been made clear? What! a foreign (tongue) and an Arabian! Say: It is to those who believe a guidance and a healing; and (as for) those who do not believe, there is a heaviness in their ears and it is obscure to them; these shall be called to from a far-off place.
41 045	We certainly gave Moses the Book aforetime: but disputes arose therein. Had it not been for a Word that went forth before from thy Lord, (their differences) would have been settled between them: but they remained in suspicious disquieting doubt thereon.	And We verily gave Moses the Scripture, but there hath been dispute concerning it; and but for a Word that had already gone forth from thy Lord, it would ere now have been judged between them; but lo! they are in hopeless doubt concerning it.	And certainly We gave the Book to Musa, but it has been differed about, and had not a word already gone forth from your Lord, judgment would certainly have been given between them; and most surely they are in a disquieting doubt about it.
41 046	Whoever works righteousness benefits his own soul; whoever works evil, it is against his own soul: nor is thy Lord ever unjust (in the least) to His Servants.	Whoso doeth right it is for his soul, and whoso doeth wrong it is against it. And thy Lord is not at all a tyrant to His slaves.	Whoever does good, it is for his own soul, and whoever does evil, it is against it; and your Lord is not in the least unjust to the servants.
41 047	To Him is referred the Knowledge of the Hour (of Judgment: He knows all): No date-fruit comes out of its sheath, nor does a female conceive (within her womb) nor bring forth (Young) but by His knowledge. The Day that (Allah) will propound to them the (question), Where are the partners (ye attributed) to Me? They will say, We do assure thee not one of us can bear witness!	Unto Him is referred (all) knowledge of the Hour. And no fruits burst forth from their sheaths, and no female carrieth or bringeth forth but with His knowledge. And on the day when He calleth unto them: Where are now My partners? they will say: We confess unto Thee, not one of us is a witness (for them).	To Him is referred the knowledge of the hour, and there come not forth any of the fruits from their coverings, nor does a female bear, nor does she give birth, but with His knowledge; and on the day when He shall call out to them, Where are (those whom you called) My associates? They shall say: We declare to Thee, none of us is a witness.

41 048	The (deities) they used to invoke aforetime will leave them in the lurch, and they will perceive that they have no way of escape.	And those to whom they used to cry of old have failed them, and they perceive they have no place of refuge.	And away from them shall go what they called upon before, and they shall know for certain that there is no escape for them.
41 049	Man does not weary of asking for good (things), but if ill touches him, he gives up all hope (and) is lost in despair.	Man tireth not of praying for good, and if ill toucheth him, then he is disheartened, desperate.	Man is never tired of praying for good, and if evil touch him, then he is despairing, hopeless.
41 050	When we give him a taste of some Mercy from Ourselves, after some adversity has touched him, he is sure to say, "This is due to my (merit): I think not that the Hour (of Judgment) will (ever) be established; but if I am brought back to my Lord, I have (much) good (stored) in His sight!" But We will show the Unbelievers the truth of all that they did, and We shall give them the taste of a severe Penalty.	And verily, if We cause him to taste mercy after some hurt that hath touched him, he will say: This is my own; and I deem not that the Hour will ever rise, and if I am brought back to my Lord, I surely shall be better off with Him - But We verily shall tell those who disbelieve (all) that they did, and We verily shall make them taste hard punishment.	And if We make him taste mercy from Us after distress that has touched him, he would most certainly say: This is of me, and I do not think the hour will come to pass, and if I am sent back to my Lord, I shall have with Him sure good; but We will most certainly inform those who disbelieved of what they did, and We will most certainly make them taste of hard chastisement.
41 051	When We bestow favours on man, he turns away, and gets himself remote on his side (instead of coming to Us); and when evil seizes him, (he comes) full of prolonged prayer!	When We show favour unto man, he withdraweth and turneth aside, but when ill toucheth him then he aboundeth in prayer.	And when We show favor to man, he turns aside and withdraws himself; and when evil touches him, he makes lengthy supplications.
41 052	Say: "See ye if the (Revelation) is (really) from Allah, and yet do ye reject it? Who is more astray than one who is in a schism far (from any purpose)?"	Bethink you: If it is from Allah and ye reject it - Who is further astray than one who is at open feud (with Allah)?	Say: Tell me if it is from Allah; then you disbelieve in it, who is in greater error than he who is in a prolonged opposition?
41 053	Soon will We show them our Signs in the (furthest) regions (of the earth), and in their own souls, until it becomes manifest to them that this is the Truth. Is it not enough that thy Lord doth witness all things?	We shall show them Our portents on the horizons and within themselves until it will be manifest unto them that it is the Truth. Doth not thy Lord suffice, since He is Witness over all things?	We will soon show them Our signs in the Universe and in their own souls, until it will become quite clear to them that it is the truth. Is it not sufficient as regards your Lord that He is a witness over all things?
41 054	Ah indeed! Are they in doubt concerning the Meeting with their Lord? Ah indeed! It is He that doth encompass all things!	How! Are they still in doubt about the meeting with their Lord? Lo! Is not He surrounding all things?	Now surely they are in doubt as to the meeting of their Lord; now surely He encompasses all things.

Chapter 42:

ASH-SHURA (COUNCIL, CONSULTATION)

Total Verses: 53 Revealed At: MAKKA

In the name of Allah, the Most Beneficent, the Most Merciful.

42 001	Ha-Mim.	Ha. Mim.	Ha Mim.
42 002	Ain. Sin. Qaf.	A'in. Sin. Qaf.	Ain Sin Qaf.
42 003	Thus doth (He) send inspiration to thee as (He did) to those before thee,- Allah, Exalted in Power, Full of Wisdom.	Thus Allah the Mighty, the Knower inspireth thee (Muhammad) as (He inspired) those before thee.	Thus does Allah, the Mighty, the Wise, reveal to you, and (thus He revealed) to those before you.
42 004	To Him belongs all that is in the heavens and on earth: and He is Most High, Most Great.	Unto Him belongeth all that is in the heavens and all that is in the earth, and He is the Sublime, the Tremendous.	His is what is in the heavens and what is in the earth, and He is the High, the Great.
42 005	The heavens are almost rent asunder from above them (by Him Glory): and the angels celebrate the Praises of their Lord, and pray for forgiveness for (all) beings on earth: Behold! Verily Allah is He, the Oft-Forgiving, Most Merciful.	Almost might the heavens above be rent asunder while the angels hymn the praise of their Lord and ask forgiveness for those on the earth. Lo! Allah, He is the Forgiver, the Merciful.	The heavens may almost rend asunder from above them and the angels sing the praise of their Lord and ask forgiveness for those on earth; now surely Allah is the Forgiving, the Merciful.
42 006	And those who take as protectors others besides Him,- Allah doth watch over them; and thou art not the disposer of their affairs.	And as for those who choose protecting friends beside Him, Allah is Warden over them, and thou art in no wise a guardian over them.	And (as for) those who take guardians besides Him, Allah watches over them, and you have not charge over them.
42 007	Thus have We sent by inspiration to thee an Arabic Qur'an: that thou mayest warn the Mother of Cities and all around her,- and warn (them) of the Day of Assembly, of which there is no doubt: (when) some will be in the Garden, and some in the Blazing Fire.	And thus We have inspired in thee a Lecture in Arabic, that thou mayst warn the mother-town and those around it, and mayst warn of a day of assembling whereof there is no doubt. A host will be in the Garden, and a host of them in the Flame.	And thus have We revealed to you an Arabic Quran, that you may warn the mother city and those around it, and that you may give warning of the day of gathering together wherein is no doubt; a party shall be in the garden and (another) party in the burning fire.
42 008	If Allah had so willed, He could have made them a single people; but He admits whom He will to His Mercy; and the wrongdoers will have no protector nor helper.	Had Allah willed, He could have made them one community, but Allah bringeth whom He will into His mercy. And the wrong-doers have no friend nor helper.	And if Allah had pleased He would surely have made them a single community, but He makes whom He pleases enter into His mercy, and the unjust it is that shall have no guardian or helper.
42 009	What! Have they taken (for worship) protectors besides Him? But it is Allah,- He is the Protector, and it is He Who gives life to the dead: It is He Who has power over all things,	Or have they chosen protecting friends besides Him? But Allah, He (alone) is the Protecting Friend. He quickeneth the dead, and He is Able to do all things.	Or have they taken guardians besides Him? But Allah is the Guardian, and He gives life to the dead, and He has power over all things.

42 010	Whatever it be wherein ye differ, the decision thereof is with Allah: such is Allah my Lord: In Him I trust, and to Him I turn.	And in whatsoever ye differ, the verdict therein belongeth to Allah. Such is my Lord, in Whom I put my trust, and unto Whom I turn.	And in whatever thing you disagree, the judgment thereof is (in) Allah's (hand); that is Allah, my Lord, on Him do I rely and to Him do I turn time after time.
42 011	(He is) the Creator of the heavens and the earth: He has made for you pairs from among yourselves, and pairs among cattle: by this means does He multiply you: there is nothing whatever like unto Him, and He is the One that hears and sees (all things).	The Creator of the heavens and the earth. He hath made for you pairs of yourselves, and of the cattle also pairs, whereby He multiplieth you. Naught is as His likeness; and He is the Hearer, the Seer.	The Originator of the heavens and the earth; He made mates for you from among yourselves, and mates of the cattle too, multiplying you thereby; nothing like a likeness of Him; and He is the Hearing, the Seeing.
42 012	To Him belong the keys of the heavens and the earth: He enlarges and restricts. The Sustenance to whom He will: for He knows full well all things.	His are the keys of the heavens and the earth. He enlargeth providence for whom He will and straiteneth (it for whom He will). Lo! He is Knower of all things.	His are the treasures of the heavens and the earth; He makes ample and straitens the means of subsistence for whom He pleases; surely He is Cognizant of all things.
42 013	The same religion has He established for you as that which He enjoined on Noah - the which We have sent by inspiration to thee - and that which We enjoined on Abraham, Moses, and Jesus: Namely, that ye should remain steadfast in religion, and make no divisions therein: to those who worship other things than Allah, hard is the (way) to which thou callest them. Allah chooses to Himself those whom He pleases, and guides to Himself those who turn (to Him).	He hath ordained for you that religion which He commended unto Noah, and that which We inspire in thee (Muhammad), and that which We commended unto Abraham and Moses and Jesus, saying: Establish the religion, and be not divided therein. Dreadful for the idolaters is that unto which thou callest them. Allah chooseth for Himself whom He will, and guideth unto Himself him who turneth (toward Him).	He has made plain to you of the religion what He enjoined upon Nuh and that which We have revealed to you and that which We enjoined upon Ibrahim and Musa and Isa that keep to obedience and be not divided therein; hard to the unbelievers is that which you call them to; Allah chooses for Himself whom He pleases, and guides to Himself him who turns (to Him), frequently.
42 014	And they became divided only after Knowledge reached them,- through selfish envy as between themselves. Had it not been for a Word that went forth before from thy Lord, (tending) to a Term appointed, the matter would have been settled between them: But truly those who have inherited the Book after them are in suspicious (disquieting) doubt concerning it.	And they were not divided until after the knowledge came unto them, through rivalry among themselves; and had it not been for a Word that had already gone forth from thy Lord for an appointed term, it surely had been judged between them. And those who were made to inherit the Scripture after them are verily in hopeless doubt concerning it.	And they did not become divided until after knowledge had come to them out of envy among themselves; and had not a word gone forth from your Lord till an appointed term, certainly judgment would have been given between them; and those who were made to inherit the Book after them are most surely in disquieting doubt concerning it.
42 015	Now then, for that (reason), call (them to the Faith), and stand steadfast as thou art commanded, nor follow thou their vain desires; but say: "I believe in the Book which Allah has sent down; and I am commanded to judge justly between you. Allah is our Lord and your Lord: for us (is the responsibility for) our deeds, and for you for your deeds. There is no contention between us and you. Allah will bring us together, and to Him is (our) Final Goal."	Unto this, then, summon (O Muhammad). And be thou upright as thou art commanded, and follow not their lusts, but say: I believe in whatever scripture Allah hath sent down, and I am commanded to be just among you. Allah is our Lord and your Lord. Unto us our works and unto you your works; no argument between us and you. Allah will bring us together, and unto Him is the journeying.	To this then go on inviting, and go on steadfastly on the right way as you are commanded, and do not follow their low desires, and say: I believe in what Allah has revealed of the Book, and I am commanded to do justice between you: Allah is our Lord and your Lord; we shall have our deeds and you shall have your deeds; no plea need there be (now) between us and you: Allah will gather us together, and to Him is the return.

42 016	But those who dispute concerning Allah after He has been accepted,- futile is their dispute in the Sight of their Lord: on them will be a Penalty terrible.	And those who argue concerning Allah after He hath been acknowledged, their argument hath no weight with their Lord, and wrath is upon them and theirs will be an awful doom.	And (as for) those who dispute about Allah after that obedience has been rendered to Him, their plea is null with their Lord, and upon them is wrath, and for them is severe punishment.
42 017	It is Allah Who has sent down the Book in Truth, and the Balance (by which to weigh conduct). And what will make thee realise that perhaps the Hour is close at hand?	Allah it is Who hath revealed the Scripture with truth, and the Balance. How canst thou know? It may be that the Hour is nigh.	Allah it is Who revealed the Book with truth, and the balance, and what shall make you know that haply the hour be nigh?
42 018	Only those wish to hasten it who believe not in it: those who believe hold it in awe, and know that it is the Truth. Behold, verily those that dispute concerning the Hour are far astray.	Those who believe not therein seek to hasten it, while those who believe are fearful of it and know that it is the Truth. Are not they who dispute, in doubt concerning the Hour, far astray?	Those who do not believe in it would hasten it on, and those who believe are in fear from it, and they know that it is the truth. Now most surely those who dispute obstinately concerning the hour are in a great error.
42 019	Gracious is Allah to His servants: He gives Sustenance to whom He pleases: and He has power and can carry out His Will.	Allah is gracious unto His slaves. He provideth for whom He will. And He is the Strong, the Mighty.	Allah is Benignant to His servants; He gives sustenance to whom He pleases, and He is the Strong, the Mighty.
42 020	To any that desires the tilth of the Hereafter, We give increase in his tilth, and to any that desires the tilth of this world, We grant somewhat thereof, but he has no share or lot in the Hereafter.	Whoso desireth the harvest of the Hereafter, We give him increase in its harvest. And whoso desireth the harvest of the world, We give him thereof, and he hath no portion in the Hereafter.	Whoever desires the gain of the hereafter, We will give him more of that again; and whoever desires-- the gain of this world, We give him of it, and in the hereafter he has no portion.
42 021	What! have they partners (in godhead), who have established for them some religion without the permission of Allah? Had it not been for the Decree of Judgment, the matter would have been decided between them (at once). But verily the wrongdoers will have a grievous Penalty.	Or have they partners (of Allah) who have made lawful for them in religion that which Allah allowed not? And but for a decisive word (gone forth already), it would have been judged between them. Lo! for wrong-doers is a painful doom.	Or have they associates who have prescribed for them any religion that Allah does not sanction? And were it not for the word of judgment, decision would have certainly been given between them; and surely the unjust shall have a painful punishment.
42 022	Thou wilt see the Wrong-doers in fear on account of what they have earned, and (the burden of) that must (necessarily) fall on them. But those who believe and work righteous deeds will be in the luxuriant meads of the Gardens: they shall have, before their Lord, all that they wish for. That will indeed be the magnificent Bounty (of Allah).	Thou seest the wrong-doers fearful of that which they have earned, and it will surely befall them, while those who believe and do good works (will be) in flowering meadows of the Gardens, having what they wish from their Lord. This is the great preferment.	You will see the unjust fearing on account of what they have earned, and it must befall them; and those who believe and do good shall be in the meadows of the gardens; they shall have what they please with their Lord: that is the great grace.
42 023	That is (the Bounty) whereof Allah gives Glad Tidings to His Servants who believe and do righteous deeds. Say: "No reward do I ask of you for this except the love of those near of kin." And if any one earns any good, We shall give him an increase of good in respect thereof: for Allah is Oft-Forgiving, Most Ready to appreciate (service).	This it is which Allah announceth unto His bondmen who believe and do good works. Say (O Muhammad, unto mankind): I ask of you no fee therefor, save loving kindness among kinsfolk. And whoso scoreth a good deed We add unto its good for him. Lo! Allah is Forgiving, Responsive.	That is of which Allah gives the good news to His servants, (to) those who believe and do good deeds. Say: I do not ask of you any reward for it but love for my near relatives; and whoever earns good, We give him more of good therein; surely Allah is Forgiving, Grateful.

42 024	What! Do they say, "He has forged a falsehood against Allah"? But if Allah willed, He could seal up thy heart. And Allah blots out Vanity, and proves the Truth by His Words. For He knows well the secrets of all hearts.	Or say they: He hath invented a lie concerning Allah? If Allah willed, He could have sealed thy heart (against them). And Allah will wipe out the lie and will vindicate the truth by His words. Lo! He is Aware of what is hidden in the breasts (of men).	Or do they say: He has forged a lie against Allah? But if Allah pleased, He would seal your heart; and Allah will blot out the falsehood and confirm the truth with His words; surely He is Cognizant of what is in the breasts.
42 025	He is the One that accepts repentance from His Servants and forgives sins: and He knows all that ye do.	And He it is Who accepteth repentance from His bondmen, and pardoneth the evil deeds, and knoweth what ye do,	And He it is Who accepts repentance from His servants and pardons the evil deeds and He knows what you do;
42 026	And He listens to those who believe and do deeds of righteousness, and gives them increase of His Bounty: but for the Unbelievers their is a terrible Penalty.	And accepteth those who do good works, and giveth increase unto them of His bounty. And as for disbelievers, theirs will be an awful doom.	And He answers those who believe and do good deeds, and gives them more out of His grace; and (as for) the unbelievers, they shall have a severe punishment.
42 027	If Allah were to enlarge the provision for His Servants, they would indeed transgress beyond all bounds through the earth; but he sends (it) down in due measure as He pleases. For He is with His Servants Well acquainted, Watchful.	And if Allah were to enlarge the provision for His slaves they would surely rebel in the earth, but He sendeth down by measure as He willeth. Lo! He is Informed, a Seer of His bondmen.	And if Allah should amplify the provision for His servants they would certainly revolt in the earth; but He sends it down according to a measure as He pleases; surely He is Aware of, Seeing, His servants.
42 028	He is the One that sends down rain (even) after (men) have given up all hope, and scatters His Mercy (far and wide). And He is the Protector, Worthy of all Praise.	And He it is Who sendeth down the saving rain after they have despaired, and spreadeth out His mercy. He is the Protecting Friend, the Praiseworthy.	And He it is Who sends down the rain after they have despaired, and He unfolds His mercy; and He is the Guardian, the Praised One.
42 029	And among His Signs is the creation of the heavens and the earth, and the living creatures that He has scattered through them: and He has power to gather them together when He wills.	And of His portents is the creation of the heaven and the earth, and of whatever beasts He hath dispersed therein. And He is Able to gather them when He will.	And one of His signs is the creation of the heavens and the earth and what He has spread forth in both of them of living beings; and when He pleases He is all-powerful to gather them together.
42 030	Whatever misfortune happens to you, is because on the things your hands have wrought, and for many (of them) He grants forgiveness.	Whatever of misfortune striketh you, it is what your right hands have earned. And He forgiveth much.	And whatever affliction befalls you, it is on account of what your hands have wrought, and (yet) He pardons most (of your faults).
42 031	Nor can ye frustrate (aught), (fleeing) through the earth; nor have ye, besides Allah, any one to protect or to help.	Ye cannot escape in the earth, for beside Allah ye have no protecting friend nor any helper.	And you cannot escape in the earth, and you shall not have a guardian or a helper besides Allah.
42 032	And among His Signs are the ships, smooth-running through the ocean, (tall) as mountains.	And of His portents are the ships, like banners on the sea;	And among His signs are the ships in the sea like mountains.
42 033	If it be His Will He can still the Wind: then would they become motionless on the back of the (ocean). Verily in this are Signs for everyone who patiently perseveres and is grateful.	If He will He calmeth the wind so that they keep still upon its surface - Lo! herein verily are signs for every steadfast grateful (heart)-	If He pleases, He causes the wind to become still so that they lie motionless on its back; most surely there are signs in this for every patient, grateful one,
42 034	Or He can cause them to perish because of the (evil) which (the men) have earned; but much doth He forgive.	Or He causeth them to perish on account of that which they have earned - And He forgiveth much -	Or He may make them founder for what they have earned, and (even then) pardon most;

42 035	But let those know, who dispute about Our Signs, that there is for them no way of escape.	And that those who argue concerning Our revelations may know they have no refuge.	And (that) those who dispute about Our communications may know; there is no place of refuge for them.
42 036	Whatever ye are given (here) is (but) a convenience of this life: but that which is with Allah is better and more lasting: (it is) for those who believe and put their trust in their Lord:	Now whatever ye have been given is but a passing comfort for the life of the world, and that which Allah hath is better and more lasting for those who believe and put their trust in their Lord,	So whatever thing you are given, that is only a provision of this world's life, and what is with Allah is better and more lasting for those who believe and rely on their Lord.
42 037	Those who avoid the greater crimes and shameful deeds, and, when they are angry even then forgive;	And those who shun the worst of sins and indecencies and, when they are wroth, forgive,	And those who shun the great sins and indecencies, and whenever they are angry they forgive.
42 038	Those who hearken to their Lord, and establish regular Prayer; who (conduct) their affairs by mutual Consultation; who spend out of what We bestow on them for Sustenance;	And those who answer the call of their Lord and establish worship, and whose affairs are a matter of counsel, and who spend of what We have bestowed on them,	And those who respond to their Lord and keep up prayer, and their rule is to take counsel among themselves, and who spend out of what We have given them.
42 039	And those who, when an oppressive wrong is inflicted on them, (are not cowed but) help and defend themselves.	And those who, when great wrong is done to them, defend themselves,	And those who, when great wrong afflicts them, defend themselves.
42 040	The recompense for an injury is an injury equal thereto (in degree): but if a person forgives and makes reconciliation, his reward is due from Allah: for (Allah) loveth not those who do wrong.	The guerdon of an ill-deed is an ill the like thereof. But whosoever pardoneth and amendeth, his wage is the affair of Allah. Lo! He loveth not wrong-doers.	And the recompense of evil is punishment like it, but whoever forgives and amends, he shall have his reward from Allah; surely He does not love the unjust.
42 041	But indeed if any do help and defend themselves after a wrong (done) to them, against such there is no cause of blame.	And whoso defendeth himself after he hath suffered wrong - for such, there is no way (of blame) against them.	And whoever defends himself after his being oppressed, these it is against whom there is no way (to blame).
42 042	The blame is only against those who oppress men and wrong-doing and insolently transgress beyond bounds through the land, defying right and justice: for such there will be a penalty grievous.	The way (of blame) is only against those who oppress mankind, and wrongfully rebel in the earth. For such there is a painful doom.	The way (to blame) is only against those who oppress men and revolt in the earth unjustly; these shall have a painful punishment.
42 043	But indeed if any show patience and forgive, that would truly be an exercise of courageous will and resolution in the conduct of affairs.	And verily whoso is patient and forgiveth - lo! that, verily, is (of) the steadfast heart of things.	And whoever is patient and forgiving, these most surely are actions due to courage.
42 044	For any whom Allah leaves astray, there is no protector thereafter. And thou wilt see the Wrong-doers, when in sight of the Penalty, Say: Is there any way (to effect) a return?	He whom Allah sendeth astray, for him there is no protecting friend after Him. And thou (Muhammad) wilt see the evil-doers when they see the doom, (how) they say: Is there any way of return?	And whomsoever Allah makes err, he has no guardian after Him; and you shall see the unjust, when they see the punishment, saying: Is there any way to return?

42 045	And thou wilt see them brought forward to the (Penalty), in a humble frame of mind because of (their) disgrace, (and) looking with a stealthy glance. And the Believers will say: "Those are indeed in loss, who have given to perdition their own selves and those belonging to them on the Day of Judgment. Behold! Truly the Wrong-doers are in a lasting Penalty!"		And thou wilt see them exposed to (the Fire), made humble by disgrace, and looking with veiled eyes. And those who believe will say: Lo! the (eternal) losers are they who lose themselves and their housefolk on the Day of Resurrection. Lo! are not the wrong-doers in perpetual torment?	And you shall see them brought before it humbling themselves because of the abasements, looking with a faint glance. And those who believe shall say: Surely the losers are they who have lost themselves and their followers on the resurrection day. Now surely the iniquitous shall remain in lasting chastisement.
42 046	And no protectors have they to help them, other than Allah. And for any whom Allah leaves to stray, there is no way (to the Goal).		And they will have no protecting friends to help them instead of Allah. He whom Allah sendeth astray, for him there is no road.	And they shall have no friends to help them besides Allah; and--whomsoever Allah makes err, he shall have no way.
42 047	Hearken ye to your Lord, before there come a Day which there will be no putting back, because of (the Ordainment of) Allah! that Day there will be for you no place of refuge nor will there be for you any room for denial (of your sins)!		Answer the call of your Lord before there cometh unto you from Allah a Day which there is no averting. Ye have no refuge on that Day, nor have ye any (power of) refusal.	Hearken to your Lord before there comes the day from Allah for which there shall be no averting; you shall have no refuge on that day, nor shall it be yours to make a denial.
42 048	If then they run away, We have not sent thee as a guard over them. Thy duty is but to convey (the Message). And truly, when We give man a taste of a Mercy from Ourselves, he doth exult thereat, but when some ill happens to him, on account of the deeds which his hands have sent forth, truly then is man ungrateful!		But if they are averse, We have not sent thee as a warder over them. Thine is only to convey (the message). And lo! when We cause man to taste of mercy from Us he exulteth therefor. And if some evil striketh them because of that which their own hands have sent before, then lo! man is an ingrate.	But if they turn aside, We have not sent you as a watcher over them; on you is only to deliver (the message); and surely when We make man taste mercy from Us, he rejoices thereat; and if an evil afflicts them on account of what their hands have already done, then-surely man is ungrateful.
42 049	To Allah belongs the dominion of the heavens and the earth. He creates what He wills (and plans). He bestows (children) male or female according to His Will (and Plan),		Unto Allah belongeth the Sovereignty of the heavens and the earth. He createth what He will. He bestoweth female (offspring) upon whom He will, and bestoweth male (offspring) upon whom He will;	Allah's is the kingdom of the heavens and the earth; He creates what He pleases; He grants to whom He pleases daughters and grants to whom He pleases sons.
42 050	Or He bestows both males and females, and He leaves barren whom He will: for He is full of Knowledge and Power.		Or He mingleth them, males and females, and He maketh barren whom He will. Lo! He is Knower, Powerful.	Or He makes them of both sorts, male and female; and He makes whom He pleases barren; surely He is the Knowing, the Powerful.
42 051	It is not fitting for a man that Allah should speak to him except by inspiration, or from behind a veil, or by the sending of a messenger to reveal, with Allah's permission, what Allah wills: for He is Most High, Most Wise.		And it was not (vouchsafed) to any mortal that Allah should speak to him unless (it be) by revelation or from behind a veil, or (that) He sendeth a messenger to reveal what He will by His leave. Lo! He is Exalted, Wise.	And it is not for any mortal that Allah should speak to them, they could not bear to hear and they did not see.
42 052	And thus have We, by Our Command, sent inspiration to thee: thou knewest not (before) what was Revelation, and what was Faith; but We have made the (Qur'an) a Light, wherewith We guide such of Our servants as We will; and verily thou dost guide (men) to the Straight Way,-		And thus have We inspired in thee (Muhammad) a Spirit of Our command. Thou knewest not what the Scripture was, nor what the Faith. But We have made it a light whereby We guide whom We will of Our bondmen. And lo! thou verily dost guide unto a right path,	And thus did We reveal to you an inspired book by Our command. You did not know what the Book was, nor (what) the faith (was), but We made it a light, guiding thereby whom We please of Our servants; and most surely you show the way to the right path:

42 053	The Way of Allah, to Whom belongs whatever is in the heavens and whatever is on earth. Behold (how) all affairs tend towards Allah!	The path of Allah, unto Whom belongeth whatsoever is in the heavens and whatsoever is in the earth. Do not all things reach Allah at last?	The path of Allah, Whose is whatsoever is in the heavens and whatsoever is in the earth; now surely to Allah do all affairs eventually come.

Chapter 43:

AZ-ZUKHRUF (ORNAMENTS OF GOLD, LUXURY)

Total Verses: 89 Revealed At: MAKKA

In the name of Allah, the Most Beneficent, the Most Merciful.

43 001	Ha-Mim.	Ha. Mim.	Ha Mim.
43 002	By the Book that makes things clear,-	By the Scripture which maketh plain,	I swear by the Book that makes things clear:
43 003	We have made it a Qur'an in Arabic, that ye may be able to understand (and learn wisdom).	Lo! We have appointed it a Lecture, in Arabic that haply ye may understand.	Surely We have made it an Arabic Quran that you may understand.
43 004	And verily, it is in the Mother of the Book, in Our Presence, high (in dignity), full of wisdom.	And Lo! in the Source of Decrees, which We possess, it is indeed sublime, decisive.	And surely it is in the original of the Book with Us, truly elevated, full of wisdom.
43 005	Shall We then take away the Message from you and repel (you), for that ye are a people transgressing beyond bounds?	Shall We utterly ignore you because ye are a wanton folk?	What! shall We then turn away the reminder from you altogether because you are an extravagant people?
43 006	But how many were the prophets We sent amongst the peoples of old?	How many a prophet did We send among the men of old!	And how many a prophet have We sent among the ancients.
43 007	And never came there a prophet to them but they mocked him.	And never came there unto them a prophet but they used to mock him.	And there came not to them a prophet but they mocked at him.
43 008	So We destroyed (them)- stronger in power than these;- and (thus) has passed on the Parable of the peoples of old.	Then We destroyed men mightier than these in prowess; and the example of the men of old hath gone (before them).	Then We destroyed those who were stronger than these in prowess, and the case of the ancients has gone before,
43 009	If thou wert to question them, 'Who created the heavens and the earth?' They would be sure to reply, 'they were created by (Him), the Exalted in Power, Full of Knowledge';-	And if thou (Muhammad) ask them: Who created the heavens and the earth, they will surely answer: The Mighty, the Knower created them;	And if you should ask them, Who created the heavens and the earth? they would most certainly say: The Mighty, the Knowing One, has created them;
43 010	(Yea, the same that) has made for you the earth (like a carpet) spread out, and has made for you roads (and channels) therein, in order that ye may find guidance (on the way);	Who made the earth a resting-place for you, and placed roads for you therein, that haply ye may find your way;	He Who made the earth a resting-place for you, and made in it ways for you that you may go aright;
43 011	That sends down (from time to time) rain from the sky in due measure;- and We raise to life therewith a land that is dead; even so will ye be raised (from the dead);-	And Who sendeth down water from the sky in (due) measure, and We revive a dead land therewith. Even so will ye be brought forth;	And He Who sends down water from the cloud according to a measure, then We raise to life thereby a dead country, even thus shall you be brought forth;

43 012	That has created pairs in all things, and has made for you ships and cattle on which ye ride,	He Who created all the pairs, and appointed for you ships and cattle whereupon ye ride.	And He Who created pairs of all things, and made for you of the ships and the cattle what you ride on,
43 013	In order that ye may sit firm and square on their backs, and when so seated, ye may celebrate the (kind) favour of your Lord, and say, Glory to Him Who has subjected these to our (use), for we could never have accomplished this (by ourselves),"	That ye may mount upon their backs, and may remember your Lord's favour when ye mount thereon, and may say: Glorified be He Who hath subdued these unto us, and we were not capable (of subduing them);	That you may firmly sit on their backs, then remember the favor of your Lord when you are firmly seated thereon, and say: Glory be to Him Who made this subservient to us and we were not able to do it,
43 014	"And to our Lord, surely, must we turn back!"	And lo! unto our Lord we surely are returning.	And surely to our Lord we must return.
43 015	Yet they attribute to some of His servants a share with Him (in his godhead)! truly is man a blasphemous ingrate avowed!	And they allot to Him a portion of His bondmen! Lo! man is verily a mere ingrate.	And they assign to Him a part of His servants; man, to be sure, is clearly ungrateful.
43 016	What! has He taken daughters out of what He himself creates, and granted to you sons for choice?	Or chooseth He daughters of all that He hath created, and honoureth He you with sons?	What! has He taken daughters to Himself of what He Himself creates and chosen you to have sons?
43 017	When news is brought to one of them of (the birth of) what he sets up as a likeness to (Allah) Most Gracious, his face darkens, and he is filled with inward grief!	And if one of them hath tidings of that which he likeneth to the Beneficent One, his countenance becometh black and he is full of inward rage.	And when one of them is given news of that of which he sets up as a likeness for the Beneficent Allah, his face becomes black and he is full of rage.
43 018	Is then one brought up among trinkets, and unable to give a clear account in a dispute (to be associated with Allah)?	(Liken they then to Allah) that which is bred up in outward show, and in dispute cannot make itself plain?	What! that which is made in ornaments and which in contention is unable to make plain speech!
43 019	And they make into females angels who themselves serve Allah. Did they witness their creation? Their evidence will be recorded, and they will be called to account!	And they make the angels, who are the slaves of the Beneficent, females. Did they witness their creation? Their testimony will be recorded and they will be questioned.	And they make the angels-- them who are the servants of the Beneficent Allah-- female (divinities). What! did they witness their creation? Their evidence shall be written down and they shall be questioned.
43 020	("Ah!") they say, "If it had been the will of (Allah) Most Gracious, we should not have worshipped such (deities)!" Of that they have no knowledge! they do nothing but lie!	And they say: If the Beneficent One had (so) willed, we should not have worshipped them. They have no knowledge whatsoever of that. They do but guess.	And they say: If the Beneficent Allah had pleased, we should never have worshipped them. They have no knowledge of this; they only lie.
43 021	What! have We given them a Book before this, to which they are holding fast?	Or have We given them any scripture before (this Qur'an) so that they are holding fast thereto?	Or have We given them a book before it so that they hold fast to it?
43 022	Nay! they say: "We found our fathers following a certain religion, and we do guide ourselves by their footsteps."	Nay, for they say only: Lo! we found our fathers following a religion, and we are guided by their footprints.	Nay! they say: We found our fathers on a course, and surely we are guided by their footsteps.
43 023	Just in the same way, whenever We sent a Warner before thee to any people, the wealthy ones among them said: "We found our fathers following a certain religion, and we will certainly follow in their footsteps."	And even so We sent not a warner before thee (Muhammad) into any township but its luxurious ones said: Lo! we found our fathers following a religion, and we are following their footprints.	And thus, We did not send before you any warner in a town, but those who led easy lives in it said: Surely we found our fathers on a course, and surely we are followers of their footsteps.

43 024	He said: "What! Even if I brought you better guidance than that which ye found your fathers following?" They said: "For us, we deny that ye (prophets) are sent (on a mission at all)."	(And the warner) said: What! Even though I bring you better guidance than that ye found your fathers following? They answered: Lo! in what ye bring we are disbelievers.	(The warner) said: What! even if I bring to you a better guide than that on which you found your fathers? They said: Surely we are unbelievers in that with which you are sent.
43 025	So We exacted retribution from them: now see what was the end of those who rejected (Truth)!	So We requited them. Then see the nature of the consequence for the rejecters!	So We inflicted retribution on them, then see how was the end of the rejecters.
43 026	Behold! Abraham said to his father and his people: "I do indeed clear myself of what ye worship:"	And when Abraham said unto his father and his folk. Lo! I am innocent of what ye worship	And when Ibrahim said to his father and his people: Surely I am clear of what you worship,
43 027	"(I worship) only Him Who made me, and He will certainly guide me."	Save Him Who did create me, for He will surely guide me.	Save Him Who created me, for surely He will guide me.
43 028	And he left it as a Word to endure among those who came after him, that they may turn back (to Allah).	And he made it a word enduring among his seed, that haply they might return.	And he made it a word to continue in his posterity that they may return.
43 029	Yea, I have given the good things of this life to these (men) and their fathers, until the Truth has come to them, and a messenger making things clear.	Nay, but I let these and their fathers enjoy life (only) till there should come unto them the Truth and a messenger making plain.	Nay! I gave them and their fathers to enjoy until there came to them the truth and a Messenger making manifest (the truth).
43 030	But when the Truth came to them, they said: "This is sorcery, and we do reject it."	And now that the Truth hath come unto them they say: This is mere magic, and lo! we are disbelievers therein.	And when there came to them the truth they said: This is magic, and surely we are disbelievers in it.
43 031	Also, they say: "Why is not this Qur'an sent down to some leading man in either of the two (chief) cities?"	And they say: If only this Qur'an had been revealed to some great man of the two towns?	And they say: Why was not this Quran revealed to a man of importance in the two towns?
43 032	Is it they who would portion out the Mercy of thy Lord? It is We Who portion out between them their livelihood in the life of this world: and We raise some of them above others in ranks, so that some may command work from others. But the Mercy of thy Lord is better than the (wealth) which they amass.	Is it they who apportion thy Lord's mercy? We have apportioned among them their livelihood in the life of the world, and raised some of them above others in rank that some of them may take labour from others; and the mercy of thy Lord is better than (the wealth) that they amass.	Will they distribute the mercy of your Lord? We distribute among them their livelihood in the life of this world, and We have exalted some of them above others in degrees, that some of them may take others in subjection; and the mercy of your Lord is better than what they amass.
43 033	And were it not that (all) men might become of one (evil) way of life, We would provide, for everyone that blasphemes against (Allah) Most Gracious, silver roofs for their houses and (silver) stair-ways on which to go up,	And were it not that mankind would have become one community, We might well have appointed, for those who disbelieve in the Beneficent, roofs of silver for their houses and stairs (of silver) whereby to mount,	And were it not that all people had been a single nation, We would certainly have assigned to those who disbelieve in the Beneficent Allah (to make) of silver the roofs of their houses and the stairs by which they ascend.
43 034	And (silver) doors to their houses, and thrones (of silver) on which they could recline,	And for their houses doors (of silver) and couches of silver whereon to recline,	And the doors of their houses and the couches on which they recline,
43 035	And also adornments of gold. But all this were nothing but conveniences of the present life: The Hereafter, in the sight of thy Lord is for the Righteous.	And ornaments of gold. Yet all that would have been but a provision of the life of the world. And the Hereafter with your Lord would have been for those who keep from evil.	And (other) embellishments of gold; and all this is naught but provision of this world's life, and the hereafter is with your Lord only for those who guard (against evil).

43 036	If anyone withdraws himself from remembrance of (Allah) Most Gracious, We appoint for him an evil one, to be an intimate companion to him.	And he whose sight is dim to the remembrance of the Beneficent, We assign unto him a devil who becometh his comrade;		And whoever turns himself away from the remembrance of the Beneficent Allah, We appoint for him a Shaitan, so he becomes his associate.
43 037	Such (evil ones) really hinder them from the Path, but they think that they are being guided aright!	And lo! they surely turn them from the way of Allah, and yet they deem that they are rightly guided;		And most surely they turn them away from the path, and they think that they are guided aright:
43 038	At length, when (such a one) comes to Us, he says (to his evil companion): "Would that between me and thee were the distance of East and West!" Ah! evil is the companion (indeed)!	Till, when he cometh unto Us, he saith (unto his comrade): Ah, would that between me and thee there were the distance of the two horizons - an evil comrade!		Until when he comes to Us, he says: O would that between me and you there were the distance of the East and the West; so evil is the associate!
43 039	When ye have done wrong, it will avail you nothing, that Day, that ye shall be partners in Punishment!	And it profiteth you not this day, because ye did wrong, that ye will be sharers in the doom.		And since you were unjust, it will not profit you this day that you are sharers in the chastisement.
43 040	Canst thou then make the deaf to hear, or give direction to the blind or to such as (wander) in manifest error?	Canst thou (Muhammad) make the deaf to hear, or canst thou guide the blind or him who is in error manifest?		What! can you then make the deaf to hear or guide the blind and him who is in clear error?
43 041	Even if We take thee away, We shall be sure to exact retribution from them,	And if We take thee away, We surely shall take vengeance on them,		But if We should take you away, still We shall inflict retribution on them;
43 042	Or We shall show thee that (accomplished) which We have promised them: for verily We shall prevail over them.	Or (if) We show thee that wherewith We threaten them; for lo! We have complete command of them.		Rather We will certainly show you that which We have promised them; for surely We are the possessors of full power over them.
43 043	So hold thou fast to the Revelation sent down to thee; verily thou art on a Straight Way.	So hold thou fast to that which is inspired in thee. Lo! thou art on a right path.		Therefore hold fast to that which has been revealed to you; surely you are on the right path.
43 044	The (Qur'an) is indeed the message, for thee and for thy people; and soon shall ye (all) be brought to account.	And lo! it is in truth a Reminder for thee and for thy folk; and ye will be questioned.		And most surely it is a reminder for you and your people, and you shall soon be questioned.
43 045	And question thou our messengers whom We sent before thee; did We appoint any deities other than (Allah) Most Gracious, to be worshipped?	And ask those of Our messengers whom We sent before thee: Did We ever appoint gods to be worshipped beside the Beneficent?		And ask those of Our messengers whom We sent before you: Did We ever appoint gods to be worshipped besides the Beneficent Allah?
43 046	We did send Moses aforetime, with Our Signs, to Pharaoh and his Chiefs: He said, "I am a messenger of the Lord of the Worlds."	And verily We sent Moses with Our revelations unto Pharaoh and his chiefs, and he said: I am a messenger of the Lord of the Worlds.		And certainly We sent Musa with Our communications to Firon and his chiefs, so he said: Surely I am the messenger of the Lord of the worlds.
43 047	But when he came to them with Our Signs, behold they ridiculed them.	But when he brought them Our tokens, behold! they laughed at them.		But when he came to them with Our signs, lo! they laughed at them.
43 048	We showed them Sign after Sign, each greater than its fellow, and We seized them with Punishment, in order that they might turn (to Us).	And every token that We showed them was greater than its sister (token), and We grasped them with the torment, that haply they might turn again.		And We did not show them a sign but it was greater than its like, and We overtook them with chastisement that they may turn.
43 049	And they said, "O thou sorcerer! Invoke thy Lord for us according to His covenant with thee; for we shall truly accept guidance."	And they said: O wizard! Entreat thy Lord for us by the pact that He hath made with thee. Lo! we verily will walk aright.		And they said: O magician! call on your Lord for our sake, as He has made the covenant with you; we shall surely be the followers of the right way.

43 050	But when We removed the Penalty from them, behold, they broke their word.	But when We eased them of the torment, behold! they broke their word.	But when We removed from them the chastisement, lo! they broke the pledge.
43 051	And Pharaoh proclaimed among his people, saying: "O my people! Does not the dominion of Egypt belong to me, (witness) these streams flowing underneath my (palace)? What! see ye not then?"	And Pharaoh caused a proclamation to be made among his people saying: O my people! Is not mine the sovereignty of Egypt and these rivers flowing under me? Can ye not then discern?	And Firon proclaimed amongst his people: O my people! is not the kingdom of Egypt mine? And these rivers flow beneath me; do you not then see?
43 052	"Am I not better than this (Moses), who is a contemptible wretch and can scarcely express himself clearly?"	I am surely better than this fellow, who is despicable and can hardly make (his meaning) plain!	Nay! I am better than this fellow, who is contemptible, and who can hardly speak distinctly:
43 053	"Then why are not gold bracelets bestowed on him, or (why) come (not) with him angels accompanying him in procession?"	Why, then, have armlets of gold not been set upon him, or angels sent along with him?	But why have not bracelets of gold been put upon him, or why have there not come with him angels as companions?
43 054	Thus did he make fools of his people, and they obeyed him: truly were they a people rebellious (against Allah).	Thus he persuaded his people to make light (of Moses), and they obeyed him. Lo! they were a wanton folk.	So he incited his people to levity and they obeyed him: surely they were a transgressing people.
43 055	When at length they provoked Us, We exacted retribution from them, and We drowned them all.	So, when they angered Us, We punished them and drowned them every one.	Then when they displeased Us, We inflicted a retribution on them, so We drowned them all together,
43 056	And We made them (a people) of the Past and an Example to later ages.	And We made them a thing past, and an example for those after (them).	And We made them a precedent and example to the later generations.
43 057	When (Jesus) the son of Mary is held up as an example, behold, thy people raise a clamour threat (in ridicule)!	And when the son of Mary is quoted as an example, behold! the folk laugh out,	And when a description of the son of Marium is given, lo! your people raise a clamor threat.
43 058	And they say, "Are our gods best, or he?" This they set forth to thee, only by way of disputation: yea, they are a contentious people.	And say: Are our gods better, or is he? They raise not the objection save for argument. Nay! but they are a contentious folk.	And they say: Are our gods better, or is he? They do not set it forth to you save by way of disputation; nay, they are a contentious people.
43 059	He was no more than a servant: We granted Our favour to him, and We made him an example to the Children of Israel.	He is nothing but a slave on whom We bestowed favour, and We made him a pattern for the Children of Israel.	He was naught but a servant on whom We bestowed favor, and We made him an example for the children of Israel.
43 060	And if it were Our Will, We could make angels from amongst you, succeeding each other on the earth.	And had We willed We could have set among you angels to be viceroys in the earth.	And if We please, We could make among you angels to be successors in the land.
43 061	And (Jesus) shall be a Sign (for the coming of) the Hour (of Judgment): therefore have no doubt about the (Hour), but follow ye Me: this is a Straight Way.	And lo! verily there is knowledge of the Hour. So doubt ye not concerning it, but follow Me. This is the right path.	And most surely it is a knowledge of the hour, therefore have no doubt about it and follow me: this is the right path.
43 062	Let not the Evil One hinder you: for he is to you an enemy avowed.	And let not Satan turn you aside. Lo! he is an open enemy for you.	And let not the Shaitan prevent you; surely he is your open enemy.
43 063	When Jesus came with Clear Signs, he said: "Now have I come to you with Wisdom, and in order to make clear to you some of the (points) on which ye dispute: therefore fear Allah and obey me."	When Jesus came with clear proofs (of Allah's Sovereignty), he said: I have come unto you with wisdom, and to make plain some of that concerning which ye differ. So keep your duty to Allah, and obey me.	And when Isa came with clear arguments he said: I have come to you indeed with wisdom, and that I may make clear to you part of what you differ in; so be careful of (your duty to) Allah and obey me:
43 064	"For Allah, He is my Lord and your Lord: so worship ye Him: this is a Straight Way."	Lo! Allah, He is my Lord and your Lord. So worship Him. This is a right path.	Surely Allah is my Lord and your Lord, therefore serve Him; this is the right path:

43 065	But sects from among themselves fell into disagreement: then woe to the wrong-doers, from the Penalty of a Grievous Day!	But the factions among them differed. Then woe unto those who do wrong from the doom of a painful day.	But parties from among them differed, so woe to those who were unjust because of the chastisement of a painful day.
43 066	Do they only wait for the Hour - that it should come on them all of a sudden, while they perceive not?	Await they aught save the Hour, that it shall come upon them suddenly, when they know not?	Do they wait for aught but the hour, that it should come upon them all of a sudden while they do not perceive?
43 067	Friends on that day will be foes, one to another,- except the Righteous.	Friends on that day will be foes one to another, save those who kept their duty (to Allah).	The friends shall on that day be enemies one to another, except those who guard (against evil).
43 068	My devotees! no fear shall be on you that Day, nor shall ye grieve,-	O My slaves! For you there is no fear this day, nor is it ye who grieve;	O My servants! there is no fear for you this day, nor shall you grieve.
43 069	(Being) those who have believed in Our Signs and bowed (their wills to Ours) in Islam.	(Ye) who believed Our revelations and were self-surrendered,	Those who believed in Our communications and were submissive:
43 070	Enter ye the Garden, ye and your wives, in (beauty and) rejoicing.	Enter the Garden, ye and your wives, to be made glad.	Enter the garden, you and your wives; you shall be made happy.
43 071	To them will be passed round, dishes and goblets of gold: there will be there all that the souls could desire, all that their ayes could delight in: and ye shall abide therein (for eye).	Therein are brought round for them trays of gold and goblets, and therein is all that souls desire and eyes find sweet. And ye are immortal therein.	There shall be sent round to them golden bowls and drinking-cups and therein shall be what their souls yearn after and (wherein) the eyes shall delight, and you shall abide therein.
43 072	Such will be the Garden of which ye are made heirs for your (good) deeds (in life).	This is the Garden which ye are made to inherit because of what ye used to do.	And this is the garden which you are given as an inheritance on account of what you did.
43 073	Ye shall have therein abundance of fruit, from which ye shall have satisfaction.	Therein for you is fruit in plenty whence to eat.	For you therein are many fruits of which you shall eat.
43 074	The sinners will be in the Punishment of Hell, to dwell therein (for aye):	Lo! the guilty are immortal in hell's torment.	Surely the guilty shall abide in the chastisement of hell.
43 075	Nowise will the (Punishment) be lightened for them, and in despair will they be there overwhelmed.	It is not relaxed for them, and they despair therein.	It shall not be abated from them and they shall therein be despairing.
43 076	Nowise shall We be unjust to them: but it is they who have been unjust themselves.	We wronged them not, but they it was who did the wrong.	And We are not unjust to them, but they themselves were unjust.
43 077	They will cry: "O Malik! would that thy Lord put an end to us!" He will say, "Nay, but ye shall abide!"	And they cry: O master! Let thy Lord make an end of us. He saith: Lo! here ye must remain.	And they shall call out: O Malik! let your Lord make an end of us. He shall say: Surely you shall tarry.
43 078	Verily We have brought the Truth to you: but most of you have a hatred for Truth.	We verily brought the Truth unto you, but ye were, most of you, averse to the Truth.	Certainly We have brought you the truth, but most of you are averse to the truth.
43 079	What! have they settled some plan (among themselves)? But it is We Who settle things.	Or do they determine any thing (against the Prophet)? Lo! We (also) are determining.	Or have they settled an affair? Then surely We are the settlers.
43 080	Or do they think that We hear not their secrets and their private counsels? Indeed (We do), and Our messengers are by them, to record.	Or deem they that We cannot hear their secret thoughts and private confidences? Nay, but Our envoys, present with them, do record.	Or do they think that We do not hear what they conceal and their secret discourses? Aye! and Our messengers with them write down.
43 081	Say: "If (Allah) Most Gracious had a son, I would be the first to worship."	Say (O Muhammad): If the Beneficent One hath a son, then, I shall be first among the worshippers. (But there is no son).	Say: If the Beneficent Allah has a son, I am the foremost of those who serve.

43 082	Glory to the Lord of the heavens and the earth, the Lord of the Throne (of Authority)! (He is free) from the things they attribute (to him)!	Glorified be the Lord of the heavens and the earth, the Lord of the Throne, from that which they ascribe (unto Him)!	Glory to the Lord of the heavens and the earth, the Lord of Power, from what they describe.
43 083	So leave them to babble and play (with vanities) until they meet that Day of theirs, which they have been promised.	So let them flounder (in their talk) and play until they meet the Day which they are promised.	So leave them plunging into false discourses and sporting until they meet their day which they are threatened with.
43 084	It is He Who is Allah in heaven and Allah on earth, and He is full of Wisdom and Knowledge.	And He it is Who in the heaven is Allah, and in the earth Allah. He is the Wise, the Knower.	And He it is Who is Allah in the heavens and Allah in the earth; and He is the Wise, the Knowing.
43 085	And blessed is He to Whom belongs the dominion of the heavens and the earth, and all between them: with Him is the Knowledge of the Hour (of Judgment): and to Him shall ye be brought back.	And blessed be He unto Whom belongeth the Sovereignty of the heavens and the earth and all that is between them, and with Whom is knowledge of the Hour, and unto Whom ye will be returned.	And blessed is He Whose is the kingdom of the heavens and the earth and what is between them, and with Him is the knowledge of the hour, and to Him shall you be brought back.
43 086	And those whom they invoke besides Allah have no power of intercession;- only he who bears witness to the Truth, and they know (him).	And those unto whom they cry instead of Him possess no power of intercession, saving him who beareth witness unto the Truth knowingly.	And those whom they call upon besides Him have no authority for intercession, but he who bears witness of the truth and they know (him).
43 087	If thou ask them, who created them, they will certainly say, Allah: How then are they deluded away (from the Truth)?	And if thou ask them who created them, they will surely say: Allah. How then are they turned away?	And if you should ask them who created them, they would certainly say: Allah. Whence are they then turned back?
43 088	(Allah has knowledge) of the (Prophet's) cry, "O my Lord! Truly these are people who will not believe!"	And he saith: O my Lord! Lo! these are a folk who believe not.	Consider his cry: O my Lord! surely they are a people who do not believe.
43 089	But turn away from them, and say "Peace!" But soon shall they know!	Then bear with them (O Muhammad) and say: Peace. But they will come to know.	So turn away from them and say, Peace, for they shall soon come to know.

Chapter 44:

AD-DUKHAN (SMOKE)

Total Verses: 59 Revealed At: MAKKA

In the name of Allah, the Most Beneficent, the Most Merciful.

44 001	Ha-Mim.	Ha. Mim.	Ha Mim!
44 002	By the Book that makes things clear;-	By the Scripture that maketh plain	I swear by the Book that makes manifest (the truth).
44 003	We sent it down during a Blessed Night: for We (ever) wish to warn (against Evil).	Lo! We revealed it on a blessed night - Lo! We are ever warning -	Surely We revealed it on a blessed night surely We are ever warning--
44 004	In the (Night) is made distinct every affair of wisdom,	Whereon every wise command is made clear	Therein every wise affair is made distinct,
44 005	By command, from Our Presence. For We (ever) send (revelations),	As a command from Our presence - Lo! We are ever sending -	A command from Us; surely We are the senders (of messengers),
44 006	As Mercy from thy Lord: for He hears and knows (all things);	A mercy from thy Lord. Lo! He, even He is the Hearer, the Knower,	A mercy from your Lord, surely He is the Hearing, the Knowing,

44 007	The Lord of the heavens and the earth and all between them, if ye (but) have an assured faith.	Lord of the heavens and the earth and all that is between them, if ye would be sure.	The Lord of the heavens and the earth and what is between them, if you would be sure.
44 008	There is no god but He: It is He Who gives life and gives death,- The Lord and Cherisher to you and your earliest ancestors.	There is no God save Him. He quickeneth and giveth death; your Lord and Lord of your forefathers.	There is no god but He; He gives life and causes death, your Lord and the Lord of your fathers of yore.
44 009	Yet they play about in doubt.	Nay, but they play in doubt.	Nay, they are in doubt, they sport.
44 010	Then watch thou for the Day that the sky will bring forth a kind of smoke (or mist) plainly visible,	But watch thou (O Muhammad) for the day when the sky will produce visible smoke	Therefore keep waiting for the day when the heaven shall bring an evident smoke,
44 011	Enveloping the people: this will be a Penalty Grievous.	That will envelop the people. This will be a painful torment.	That shall overtake men; this is a painful punishment.
44 012	(They will say:) "Our Lord! remove the Penalty from us, for we do really believe!"	(Then they will say): Our Lord relieve us of the torment. Lo! we are believers.	Our Lord! remove from us the punishment; surely we are believers.
44 013	How shall the message be (effectual) for them, seeing that an Messenger explaining things clearly has (already) come to them,-	How can there be remembrance for them, when a messenger making plain (the Truth) had already come unto them,	How shall they be reminded, and there came to them a Messenger making clear (the truth),
44 014	Yet they turn away from him and say: "Tutored (by others), a man possessed!"	And they had turned away from him and said: One taught (by others), a madman?	Yet they turned their backs on him and said: One taught (by others), a madman.
44 015	We shall indeed remove the Penalty for a while, (but) truly ye will revert (to your ways).	Lo! We withdraw the torment a little. Lo! ye return (to disbelief).	Surely We will remove the punishment a little, (but) you will surely return (to evil).
44 016	One day We shall seize you with a mighty onslaught: We will indeed (then) exact Retribution!	On the day when We shall seize them with the greater seizure, (then) in truth We shall punish.	On the day when We will seize (them) with the most violent seizing; surely We will inflict retribution.
44 017	We did, before them, try the people of Pharaoh: there came to them a messenger most honourable,	And verily We tried before them Pharaoh's folk, when there came unto them a noble messenger,	And certainly We tried before them the people of Firon, and there came to them a noble messenger,
44 018	Saying: "Restore to me the Servants of Allah: I am to you a messenger worthy of all trust;"	Saying: Give up to me the slaves of Allah. Lo! I am a faithful messenger unto you.	Saying: Deliver to me the servants of Allah, surely I am a faithful messenger to you,
44 019	"And be not arrogant as against Allah: for I come to you with authority manifest."	And saying: Be not proud against Allah. Lo! I bring you a clear warrant.	And that do not exalt yourselves against Allah, surely I will bring to you a clear authority:
44 020	"For me, I have sought safety with my Lord and your Lord, against your injuring me."	And lo! I have sought refuge in my Lord and your Lord lest ye stone me to death.	And surely I take refuge with my Lord and your Lord that you should stone me to death:
44 021	"If ye believe me not, at least keep yourselves away from me."	And if ye put no faith in me, then let me go.	And if you do not believe in me, then leave me alone.
44 022	(But they were aggressive:) then he cried to his Lord: "These are indeed a people given to sin."	And he cried unto his Lord, (saying): These are guilty folk.	Then he called upon his Lord: These are a guilty people.
44 023	(The reply came:) "March forth with My Servants by night: for ye are sure to be pursued."	Then (his Lord commanded): Take away My slaves by night. Lo! ye will be followed,	So go forth with My servants by night; surely you will be pursued:
44 024	"And leave the sea as a furrow (divided): for they are a host (destined) to be drowned."	And leave the sea behind at rest, for lo! they are a drowned host.	And leave the sea intervening; surely they are a host that shall be drowned.
44 025	How many were the gardens and springs they left behind,	How many were the gardens and the watersprings that they left behind,	How many of the gardens and fountains have they left!
44 026	And corn-fields and noble buildings,	And the cornlands and the goodly sites	And cornfields and noble places!

44 027	And wealth (and conveniences of life), wherein they had taken such delight!	And pleasant things wherein they took delight!	And goodly things wherein they rejoiced;
44 028	Thus (was their end)! And We made other people inherit (those things)!	Even so (it was), and We made it an inheritance for other folk;	Thus (it was), and We gave them as a heritage to another people.
44 029	And neither heaven nor earth shed a tear over them: nor were they given a respite (again).	And the heaven and the earth wept not for them, nor were they reprieved.	So the heaven and the earth did not weep for them, nor were they respited.
44 030	We did deliver aforetime the Children of Israel from humiliating Punishment,	And We delivered the Children of Israel from the shameful doom;	And certainly We delivered the children of Israel from the abasing chastisement,
44 031	Inflicted by Pharaoh, for he was arrogant (even) among inordinate transgressors.	(We delivered them) from Pharaoh. Lo! he was a tyrant of the wanton ones.	From Firon; surely he was haughty, (and) one of the extravagant.
44 032	And We chose them aforetime above the nations, knowingly,	And We chose them, purposely, above (all) creatures.	And certainly We chose them, having knowledge, above the nations.
44 033	And granted them Signs in which there was a manifest trial.	And We gave them portents wherein was a clear trial.	And We gave them of the communications wherein was clear blessing.
44 034	As to these (Quraish), they say forsooth:	Lo! these, forsooth, are saying:	Most surely these do say:
44 035	"There is nothing beyond our first death, and we shall not be raised again."	There is naught but our first death, and we shall not be raised again.	There is naught but our first death and we shall not be raised again.
44 036	"Then bring (back) our forefathers, if what ye say is true!"	Bring back our fathers, if ye speak the truth!	So bring our fathers (back), if you are truthful.
44 037	What! Are they better than the people of Tubba and those who were before them? We destroyed them because they were guilty of sin.	Are they better, or the folk of Tubb'a and those before them? We destroyed them, for surely they were guilty.	Are they better or the people of Tubba and those before them? We destroyed them, for surely they were guilty.
44 038	We created not the heavens, the earth, and all between them, merely in (idle) sport:	And We created not the heavens and the earth, and all that is between them, in play.	And We did not create the heavens and the earth and what is between them in sport.
44 039	We created them not except for just ends: but most of them do not understand.	We created them not save with truth; but most of them know not.	We did not create them both but with the truth, but most of them do not know.
44 040	Verily the Day of sorting out is the time appointed for all of them,-	Assuredly the Day of Decision is the term for all of them,	Surely the day of separation is their appointed term, of all of them
44 041	The Day when no protector can avail his client in aught, and no help can they receive,	A day when friend can in naught avail friend, nor can they be helped,	The day on which a friend shall not avail (his) friend aught, nor shall they be helped,
44 042	Except such as receive Allah's Mercy: for He is Exalted in Might, Most Merciful.	Save him on whom Allah hath mercy. Lo! He is the Mighty, the Merciful.	Save those on whom Allah shall have mercy; surely He is the Mighty the Merciful.
44 043	Verily the tree of Zaqqum	Lo! the tree of Zaqqum,	Surely the tree of the Zaqqum,
44 044	Will be the food of the Sinful,-	The food of the sinner!	Is the food of the sinful
44 045	Like molten brass; it will boil in their insides.	Like molten brass, it seetheth in their bellies	Like dregs of oil; it shall boil in (their) bellies,
44 046	Like the boiling of scalding water.	As the seething of boiling water.	Like the boiling of hot water.
44 047	(A voice will cry:) "Seize ye him and drag him into the midst of the Blazing Fire!"	(And it will be said): Take him and drag him to the midst of hell,	Seize him, then drag him down into the middle of the hell;
44 048	"Then pour over his head the Penalty of Boiling Water,"	Then pour upon his head the torment of boiling water.	Then pour above his head of the torment of the boiling water:

44 049	"Taste thou (this)! Truly wast thou mighty, full of honour!"	(Saying): Taste! Lo! thou wast forsooth the mighty, the noble!	Taste; you forsooth are the mighty, the honorable:
44 050	"Truly this is what ye used to doubt!"	Lo! this is that whereof ye used to doubt.	Surely this is what you disputed about.
44 051	As to the Righteous (they will be) in a position of Security,	Lo! those who kept their duty will be in a place secured.	Surely those who guard (against evil) are in a secure place,
44 052	Among Gardens and Springs;	Amid gardens and watersprings,	In gardens and springs;
44 053	Dressed in fine silk and in rich brocade, they will face each other;	Attired in silk and silk embroidery, facing one another.	They shall wear of fine and thick silk, (sitting) face to face;
44 054	So; and We shall join them to fair women with beautiful, big, and lustrous eyes.	Even so (it will be). And We shall wed them unto fair ones with wide, lovely eyes.	Thus (shall it be), and We will wed them with Houris pure, beautiful ones.
44 055	There can they call for every kind of fruit in peace and security;	They call therein for every fruit in safety.	They shall call therein for every fruit in security;
44 056	Nor will they there taste Death, except the first death; and He will preserve them from the Penalty of the Blazing Fire,-	They taste not death therein, save the first death. And He hath saved them from the doom of hell,	They shall not taste therein death except the first death, and He will save them from the punishment of the hell,
44 057	As a Bounty from thy Lord! that will be the supreme achievement!	A bounty from thy Lord. That is the supreme triumph.	A grace from your Lord; this is the great achievement.
44 058	Verily, We have made this (Qur'an) easy, in thy tongue, in order that they may give heed.	And We have made (this Scripture) easy in thy language only that they may heed.	So have We made it easy in your tongue that they may be mindful.
44 059	So wait thou and watch; for they (too) are waiting.	Wait then (O Muhammad). Lo! they (too) are waiting.	Therefore wait; surely they are waiting.

Chapter 45:

AL-JATHIYA (CROUCHING)

Total Verses: 37 Revealed At: MAKKA

In the name of Allah, the Most Beneficent, the Most Merciful.

45 001	Ha-Mim.	Ha. Mim.	Ha Mim.
45 002	The revelation of the Book is from Allah the Exalted in Power, Full of Wisdom.	The revelation of the Scripture is from Allah, the Mighty, the Wise.	The revelation of the Book is from Allah, the Mighty, the Wise.
45 003	Verily in the heavens and the earth, are Signs for those who believe.	Lo! in the heavens and the earth are portents for believers.	Most surely in the heavens and the earth there are signs for the believers.
45 004	And in the creation of yourselves and the fact that animals are scattered (through the earth), are Signs for those of assured Faith.	And in your creation, and all the beasts that He scattereth in the earth, are portents for a folk whose faith is sure.	And in your (own) creation and in what He spreads abroad of animals there are signs for a people that are sure;
45 005	And in the alternation of Night and Day, and the fact that Allah sends down Sustenance from the sky, and revives therewith the earth after its death, and in the change of the winds,- are Signs for those that are wise.	And the difference of night and day and the provision that Allah sendeth down from the sky and thereby quickeneth the earth after her death, and the ordering of the winds, are portents for a people who have sense.	And (in) the variation of the night and the day, and (in) what Allah sends down of sustenance from the cloud, then gives life thereby to the earth after its death, and (in) the changing of the winds, there are signs for a people who understand.

45 006	Such are the Signs of Allah, which We rehearse to thee in Truth; then in what exposition will they believe after (rejecting) Allah and His Signs?	These are the portents of Allah which We recite unto thee (Muhammad) with truth. Then in what fact, after Allah and His portents, will they believe?	These are the communications of Allah which We recite to you with truth; then in what announcement would they believe after Allah and His communications?
45 007	Woe to each sinful dealer in Falsehoods:	Woe unto each sinful liar,	Woe to every sinful liar,
45 008	He hears the Signs of Allah rehearsed to him, yet is obstinate and lofty, as if he had not heard them: then announce to him a Penalty Grievous!	Who heareth the revelations of Allah recited unto him, and then continueth in pride as though he heard them not. Give him tidings of a painful doom.	Who hears the communications of Allah recited to him, then persists proudly as though he had not heard them, so announce to him a painful punishment.
45 009	And when he learns something of Our Signs, he takes them in jest: for such there will be a humiliating Penalty.	And when he knoweth aught of Our revelations he maketh it a jest. For such there is a shameful doom.	And when he comes to know of any of Our communications, he takes it for a jest; these it is that shall have abasing chastisement.
45 010	In front of them is Hell: and of no profit to them is anything they may have earned, nor any protectors they may have taken to themselves besides Allah: for them is a tremendous Penalty.	Beyond them there is hell, and that which they have earned will naught avail them, nor those whom they have chosen for protecting friends beside Allah. Theirs will be an awful doom.	Before them is hell, and there shall not avail them aught of what they earned, nor those whom they took for guardians besides Allah, and they shall have a grievous punishment.
45 011	This is (true) Guidance and for those who reject the Signs of their Lord, is a grievous Penalty of abomination.	This is guidance. And those who disbelieve the revelations of their Lord, for them there is a painful doom of wrath.	This is guidance; and (as for) those who disbelieve in the communications of their Lord, they shall have a painful punishment on account of uncleanness.
45 012	It is Allah Who has subjected the sea to you, that ships may sail through it by His command, that ye may seek of his Bounty, and that ye may be grateful.	Allah it is Who hath made the sea of service unto you that the ships may run thereon by His command, and that ye may seek of His bounty, and that haply ye may be thankful;	Allah is He Who made subservient to you the sea that the ships may run therein by His command, and that you may seek of His grace, and that you may give thanks.
45 013	And He has subjected to you, as from Him, all that is in the heavens and on earth: Behold, in that are Signs indeed for those who reflect.	And hath made of service unto you whatsoever is in the heavens and whatsoever is in the earth; it is all from Him. Lo! herein verily are portents for a people who reflect.	And He has made subservient to you whatsoever is in the heavens and whatsoever is in the earth, all, from Himself; most surely there are signs in this for a people who reflect.
45 014	Tell those who believe, to forgive those who do not look forward to the Days of Allah: It is for Him to recompense (for good or ill) each People according to what they have earned.	Tell those who believe to forgive those who hope not for the days of Allah; in order that He may requite folk what they used to earn.	Say to those who believe (that) they forgive those who do not fear the days of Allah that He may reward a people for what they earn.
45 015	If any one does a righteous deed, it ensures to the benefit of his own soul; if he does evil, it works against (his own soul). In the end will ye (all) be brought back to your Lord.	Whoso doeth right, it is for his soul, and whoso doeth wrong, it is against it. And afterward unto your Lord ye will be brought back.	Whoever does good, it is for his own soul, and whoever does evil, it is against himself; then you shall be brought back to your-- Lord.
45 016	We did aforetime grant to the Children of Israel the Book, the Power of Command, and Prophethood; We gave them, for Sustenance, things good and pure; and We favoured them above the nations.	And verily we gave the Children of Israel the Scripture and the Command and the Prophethood, and provided them with good things and favoured them above (all) peoples;	And certainly We gave the Book and the wisdom and the prophecy to the children of Israel, and We gave them of the goodly things, and We made them excel the nations.

45	017	And We granted them Clear Signs in affairs (of Religion): it was only after knowledge had been granted to them that they fell into schisms, through insolent envy among themselves. Verily thy Lord will judge between them on the Day of Judgment as to those matters in which they set up differences.	And gave them plain commandments. And they differed not until after the knowledge came unto them, through rivalry among themselves. Lo! thy Lord will judge between them on the Day of Resurrection concerning that wherein they used to differ.	And We gave them clear arguments in the affair, but they did not differ until after knowledge had come to them out of envy among themselves; surely your Lord will judge between them on the day of resurrection concerning that wherein they differed.
45	018	Then We put thee on the (right) Way of Religion: so follow thou that (Way), and follow not the desires of those who know not.	And now have We set thee (O Muhammad) on a clear road of (Our) commandment; so follow it, and follow not the whims of those who know not.	Then We have made you follow a course in the affair, therefore follow it, and do not follow the low desires of those who do not know.
45	019	They will be of no use to thee in the sight of Allah: it is only wrong-doers (that stand as) protectors, one to another: but Allah is the Protector of the Righteous.	Lo! they can avail thee naught against Allah. And lo! as for the wrong-doers, some of them are friends of others; and Allah is the Friend of those who ward off (evil).	Surely they shall not avail you in the least against Allah; and surely the unjust are friends of each other, and Allah is the guardian of those who guard (against evil).
45	020	These are clear evidences to men and a Guidance and Mercy to those of assured Faith.	This is clear indication for mankind, and a guidance and a mercy for a folk whose faith is sure.	These are clear proofs for men, and a guidance and a mercy for a people who are sure.
45	021	What! Do those who seek after evil ways think that We shall hold them equal with those who believe and do righteous deeds,- that equal will be their life and their death? Ill is the judgment that they make.	Or do those who commit ill-deeds suppose that We shall make them as those who believe and do good works, the same in life and death? Bad is their judgment!	Nay! do those who have wrought evil deeds think that We will make them like those who believe and do good-- that their life and their death shall be equal? Evil it is that they judge.
45	022	Allah created the heavens and the earth for just ends, and in order that each soul may find the recompense of what it has earned, and none of them be wronged.	And Allah hath created the heavens and the earth with truth, and that every soul may be repaid what it hath earned. And they will not be wronged.	And Allah created the heavens and the earth with truth and that every soul may be rewarded for what it has earned and they shall not be wronged.
45	023	Then seest thou such a one as takes as his god his own vain desire? Allah has, knowing (him as such), left him astray, and sealed his hearing and his heart (and understanding), and put a cover on his sight. Who, then, will guide him after Allah (has withdrawn Guidance)? Will ye not then receive admonition?	Hast thou seen him who maketh his desire his god, and Allah sendeth him astray purposely, and sealeth up his hearing and his heart, and setteth on his sight a covering? Then who will lead him after Allah (hath condemned him)? Will ye not then heed?	Have you then considered him who takes his low desire for his god, and Allah has made him err having knowledge and has set a seal upon his ear and his heart and put a covering upon his eye. Who can then guide him after Allah? Will you not then be mindful?
45	024	And they say: "What is there but our life in this world? We shall die and we live, and nothing but time can destroy us." But of that they have no knowledge: they merely conjecture:	And they say: There is naught but our life of the world; we die and we live, and naught destroyeth us save time; when they have no knowledge whatsoever of (all) that; they do but guess.	And they say: There is nothing but our life in this world; we live and die and nothing destroys us but time, and they have no knowledge of that; they only conjecture.
45	025	And when Our Clear Signs are rehearsed to them their argument is nothing but this: They say, "Bring (back) our forefathers, if what ye say is true!"	And when Our clear revelations are recited unto them their only argument is that they say: Bring (back) our fathers then, if ye are truthful.	And when Our clear communications are recited to them, their argument is no other than that they say: Bring our fathers (back) if you are truthful.

45 026	Say: "It is Allah Who gives you life, then gives you death; then He will gather you together for the Day of Judgment about which there is no doubt": But most men do not understand.	Say (unto them, O Muhammad): Allah giveth life to you, then causeth you to die, then gathereth you unto the Day of Resurrection whereof there is no doubt. But most of mankind know not.	Say: Allah gives you life, then He makes you die, then will He gather you to the day of resurrection wherein is no doubt, but most people do not know.
45 027	To Allah belongs the dominion of the heavens and the earth, and the Day that the Hour of Judgment is established,- that Day will the dealers in Falsehood perish!	And unto Allah belongeth the Sovereignty of the heavens and the earth; and on the day when the Hour riseth, on that day those who follow falsehood will be lost.	And Allah's is the kingdom of the heavens and the earth; and on the day when the hour shall come to pass, on that day shall they perish who say false things.
45 028	And thou wilt see every sect bowing the knee: Every sect will be called to its Record: "This Day shall ye be recompensed for all that ye did!"	And thou wilt see each nation crouching, each nation summoned to its record. (And it will be said unto them): This day ye are requited what ye used to do.	And you shall see every nation kneeling down; every nation shall be called to its book: today you shall be rewarded for what you did.
45 029	"This Our Record speaks about you with truth: For We were wont to put on Record all that ye did."	This Our Book pronounceth against you with truth. Lo! We have caused (all) that ye did to be recorded.	This is Our book that speaks against you with justice; surely We wrote what you did,
45 030	Then, as to those who believed and did righteous deeds, their Lord will admit them to His Mercy that will be the achievement for all to see.	Then, as for those who believed and did good works, their Lord will bring them in unto His mercy. That is the evident triumph.	Then as to those who believed and did good, their Lord will make them enter into His mercy; that is the manifest achievement.
45 031	But as to those who rejected Allah, (to them will be said): "Were not Our Signs rehearsed to you? But ye were arrogant, and were a people given to sin!"	And as for those who disbelieved (it will be said unto them): Were not Our revelations recited unto you? But ye were scornful and became a guilty folk.	As to those who disbelieved: What! were not My communications recited to you? But you were proud and you were a guilty people.
4 032	"And when it was said that the promise of Allah was true, and that the Hour- there was no doubt about its (coming), ye used to say, 'We know not what is the hour: we only think it is an idea, and we have no firm assurance.'"	And when it was said: Lo! Allah's promise is the truth, and there is no doubt of the Hour's coming, ye said: We know not what the Hour is. We deem it naught but a conjecture, and we are by no means convinced.	And when it was said, Surely the promise of Allah is true and as for the hour, there is no doubt about it, you said: We do not know what the hour is; we do not think (that it will come to pass) save a passing thought, and we are not at all sure.
45 033	Then will appear to them the evil (fruits) of what they did, and they will be completely encircled by that which they used to mock at!	And the evils of what they did will appear unto them, and that which they used to deride will befall them.	And the evil (consequences) of what they did shall become manifest to them and that which they mocked shall encompass them.
45 034	It will also be said: "This Day We will forget you as ye forgot the meeting of this Day of yours! and your abode is the Fire, and no helpers have ye!"	And it will be said: This day We forget you, even as ye forgot the meeting of this your day; and your habitation is the Fire, and there is none to help you.	And it shall be said: Today We forsake you as you neglected the meeting of this day of yours and your abode is the fire, and there are not for you any helpers:
45 035	"This, because ye used to take the Signs of Allah in jest, and the life of the world deceived you:" (From) that Day, therefore, they shall not be taken out thence, nor shall they be received into Grace.	This, forasmuch as ye made the revelations of Allah a jest, and the life of the world beguiled you. Therefor this day they come not forth from thence, nor can they make amends.	That is because you took the communications of Allah for a jest and the life of this world deceived you. So on that day they shall not be brought forth from it, nor shall they be granted goodwill.
45 036	Then Praise be to Allah, Lord of the heavens and Lord of the earth,- Lord and Cherisher of all the Worlds!	Then praise be to Allah, Lord of the heavens and Lord of the earth, the Lord of the Worlds.	Therefore to Allah is due (all) praise, the Lord of the heavens and the Lord of the earth, the Lord of the worlds.
45 037	To Him be glory throughout the heavens and the earth: and He is Exalted in Power, Full of Wisdom!	And unto Him (alone) belongeth Majesty in the heavens and the earth, and He is the Mighty, the Wise.	And to Him belongs greatness in the heavens and the earth, and He is the Mighty, the Wise.

Chapter 46:

AL-AHQAF (THE WIND-CURVED SANDHILLS, THE DUNES)

Total Verses: 35 Revealed At: MAKKA

In the name of Allah, the Most Beneficent, the Most Merciful.

46 001	Ha-Mim.	Ha. Mim.	Ha Mim.
46 002	The Revelation of the Book is from Allah the Exalted in Power, Full of Wisdom.	The revelation of the Scripture is from Allah the Mighty, the Wise.	The revelation of the Book is from Allah, the Mighty, the Wise.
46 003	We created not the heavens and the earth and all between them but for just ends, and for a Term Appointed: But those who reject Faith turn away from that whereof they are warned.	We created not the heavens and the earth and all that is between them save with truth, and for a term appointed. But those who disbelieve turn away from that whereof they are warned.	We did not create the heavens and the earth and what is between them two save with truth and (for) an appointed term; and those who disbelieve turn aside from what they are warned of.
46 004	Say: "Do ye see what it is ye invoke besides Allah? Show me what it is they have created on earth, or have they a share in the heavens bring me a book (revealed) before this, or any remnant of knowledge (ye may have), if ye are telling the truth!"	Say (unto them, O Muhammad): Have ye thought on all that ye invoke beside Allah? Show me what they have created of the earth. Or have they any portion in the heavens? Bring me a scripture before this (Scripture), or some vestige of knowledge (in support of what ye say), if ye are truthful.	Say: Have you considered what you call upon besides Allah? Show me what they have created of the earth, or have they a share in the heavens? Bring me a book before this or traces of knowledge, if you are truthful.
46 005	And who is more astray than one who invokes besides Allah, such as will not answer him to the Day of Judgment, and who (in fact) are unconscious of their call (to them)?	And who is further astray than those who, instead of Allah, pray unto such as hear not their prayer until the Day of Resurrection, and are unconscious of their prayer,	And who is in greater error than he who calls besides Allah upon those that will not answer him till the day of resurrection and they are heedless of their call?
46 006	And when mankind are gathered together (at the Resurrection), they will be hostile to them and reject their worship (altogether)!	And when mankind are gathered (to the Judgment) will become enemies for them, and will become deniers of having been worshipped.	And when men are gathered together they shall be their enemies, and shall be deniers of their worshipping (them).
46 007	When Our Clear Signs are rehearsed to them, the Unbelievers say, of the Truth when it comes to them: "This is evident sorcery!"	And when Our clear revelations are recited unto them, those who disbelieve say of the Truth when it reacheth them: This is mere magic.	And when Our clear communications are recited to them, those who disbelieve say with regard to the truth when it comes to them: This is clear magic.
46 008	Or do they say, "He has forged it"? Say: "Had I forged it, then can ye obtain no single (blessing) for me from Allah. He knows best of that whereof ye talk (so glibly)! Enough is He for a witness between me and you! And he is Oft-Forgiving, Most Merciful."	Or say they: He hath invented it? Say (O Muhammad): If I have invented it, still ye have no power to support me against Allah. He is Best Aware of what ye say among yourselves concerning it. He sufficeth for a witness between me and you. And He is the Forgiving, the Merciful.	Nay! they say: He has forged it. Say: If I have forged it, you do not control anything for me from Allah; He knows best what you utter concerning it; He is enough as a witness between me and you, and He is the Forgiving, the Merciful.

46 009	Say: "I am no bringer of new-fangled doctrine among the messengers, nor do I know what will be done with me or with you. I follow but that which is revealed to me by inspiration; I am but a Warner open and clear."	Say: I am no new thing among the messengers (of Allah), nor know I what will be done with me or with you. I do but follow that which is inspired in me, and I am but a plain warner.	Say: I am not the first of the messengers, and I do not know what will be done with me or with you: I do not follow anything but that which is revealed to me, and I am nothing but a plain warner.
46 010	Say: "See ye? If (this teaching) be from Allah, and ye reject it, and a witness from among the Children of Israel testifies to its similarity (with earlier scripture), and has believed while ye are arrogant, (how unjust ye are!) truly, Allah guides not a people unjust."	Bethink you: If it is from Allah and ye disbelieve therein, and a witness of the Children of Israel hath already testified to the like thereof and hath believed, and ye are too proud (what plight is yours)? Lo! Allah guideth not wrong-doing folk.	Say: Have you considered if it is from Allah, and you disbelieve in it, and a witness from among the children of Israel has borne witness of one like it, so he believed, while you are big with pride; surely Allah does not guide the unjust people.
46 011	The Unbelievers say of those who believe: "If (this Message) were a good thing, (such men) would not have gone to it first, before us!" And seeing that they guide not themselves thereby, they will say, "this is an (old,) falsehood!"	And those who disbelieve say of those who believe: If it had been (any) good, they would not have been before us in attaining it. And since they will not be guided by it, they say: This is an ancient lie;	And those who disbelieve say concerning those who believe: If it had been a good, they would not have gone ahead of us therein. And as they do not seek to be rightly directed thereby, they say: It is an old lie.
46 012	And before this, was the Book of Moses as a guide and a mercy: And this Book confirms (it) in the Arabic tongue; to admonish the unjust, and as Glad Tidings to those who do right.	When before it there was the Scripture of Moses, an example and a mercy; and this is a confirming Scripture in the Arabic language, that it may warn those who do wrong and bring good tidings for the righteous.	And before it the Book of Musa was a guide and a mercy: and this is a Book verifying (it) in the Arabic language that it may warn those who are unjust and as good news for the doers of good.
46 013	Verily those who say, "Our Lord is Allah," and remain firm (on that Path),- on them shall be no fear, nor shall they grieve.	Lo! those who say: Our Lord is Allah, and thereafter walk aright, there shall no fear come upon them neither shall they grieve.	Surely those who say, Our Lord is Allah, then they continue on the right way, they shall have no fear nor shall they grieve.
46 014	Such shall be Companions of the Gardens, dwelling therein (for aye): a recompense for their (good) deeds.	Such are rightful owners of the Garden, immortal therein, as a reward for what they used to do.	These are the dwellers of the garden, abiding therein: a reward for what they did.
46 015	We have enjoined on man kindness to his parents: In pain did his mother bear him, and in pain did she give him birth. The carrying of the (child) to his weaning is (a period of) thirty months. At length, when he reaches the age of full strength and attains forty years, he says, "O my Lord! Grant me that I may be grateful for Thy favour which Thou has bestowed upon me, and upon both my parents, and that I may work righteousness such as Thou mayest approve; and be gracious to me in my issue. Truly have I turned to Thee and truly do I bow (to Thee) in Islam."	And We have commended unto man kindness toward parents. His mother beareth him with reluctance, and bringeth him forth with reluctance, and the bearing of him and the weaning of him is thirty months, till, when he attaineth full strength and reacheth forty years, he saith: My Lord! Arouse me that I may give thanks for the favour wherewith Thou hast favoured me and my parents, and that I may do right acceptable unto Thee. And be gracious unto me in the matter of my seed. Lo! I have turned unto Thee repentant, and lo! I am of those who surrender (unto Thee).	And We have enjoined on man doing of good to his parents; with trouble did his mother bear him and with trouble did she bring him forth; and the bearing of him and the weaning of him was thirty months; until when he attains his maturity and reaches forty years, he says: My Lord! grant me that I may give thanks for Thy favor which Thou hast bestowed on me and on my parents, and that I may do good which pleases Thee and do good to me in respect of my offspring; surely I turn to Thee, and surely I am of those who submit.

46 016	Such are they from whom We shall accept the best of their deeds and pass by their ill deeds: (They shall be) among the Companions of the Garden: a promise! of truth, which was made to them (in this life).	Those are they from whom We accept the best of what they do, and overlook their evil deeds. (They are) among the owners of the Garden. This is the true promise which they were promised (in the world).	These are they from whom We accept the best of what they have done and pass over their evil deeds, among the dwellers of the garden; the promise of truth which they were promised.
46 017	But (there is one) who says to his parents, "Fie on you! Do ye hold out the promise to me that I shall be raised up, even though generations have passed before me (without rising again)?" And they two seek Allah's aid, (and rebuke the son): "Woe to thee! Have faith! for the promise of Allah is true." But he says, "This is nothing but tales of the ancients!"	And whoso saith unto his parents: Fie upon you both! Do ye threaten me that I shall be brought forth (again) when generations before me have passed away? And they twain cry unto Allah for help (and say): Woe unto thee! Believe! Lo! the promise of Allah is true. But he saith: This is naught save fables of the men of old:	And he who says to his parents: Fie on you! do you threaten me that I shall be brought forth when generations have already passed away before me? And they both call for Allah's aid: Woe to you! believe, surely the promise of Allah is true. But he says: This is nothing but stories of the ancients.
46 018	Such are they against whom is proved the sentence among the previous generations of jinns and men, that have passed away; for they will be (utterly) lost.	Such are those on whom the Word concerning nations of the jinn and mankind which have passed away before them hath effect. Lo! they are the losers.	These are they against whom the word has proved true among nations of the jinn and the men that have already passed away before them; surely they are losers.
46 019	And to all are (assigned) degrees according to the deeds which they (have done), and in order that (Allah) may recompense their deeds, and no injustice be done to them.	And for all there will be ranks from what they do, that He may pay them for their deeds; and they will not be wronged.	And for all are degrees according to what they did, and that He may pay them back fully their deeds and they shall not be wronged.
46 020	And on the Day that the Unbelievers will be placed before the Fire, (It will be said to them): "Ye received your good things in the life of the world, and ye took your pleasure out of them: but today shall ye be recompensed with a Penalty of humiliation: for that ye were arrogant on earth without just cause, and that ye (ever) transgressed."	And on the day when those who disbelieve are exposed to the Fire (it will be said): Ye squandered your good things in the life of the world and sought comfort therein. Now this day ye are rewarded with the doom of ignominy because ye were disdainful in the land without a right, and because ye used to transgress.	And on the day when those who disbelieve shall be brought before the fire: You did away with your good things in your life of the world and you enjoyed them for a while, so today you shall be rewarded with the punishment of abasement because you were unjustly proud in the land and because you transgressed.
46 021	Mention (Hud) one of 'Ad's (own) brethren: Behold, he warned his people about the winding Sand-tracts: but there have been warners before him and after him: "Worship ye none other than Allah: Truly I fear for you the Penalty of a Mighty Day."	And make mention (O Muhammad) of the brother of A'ad when he warned his folk among the wind-curved sandhills - and verily warners came and went before and after him - saying: Serve none but Allah. Lo! I fear for you the doom of a tremendous Day.	And mention the brother of Ad; when he warned his people in the sandy plains,-- and indeed warners came before him and after him-- saying Serve none but Allah; surely I fear for you the punishment of a grievous day.
46 022	They said: "Hast thou come in order to turn us aside from our gods? Then bring upon us the (calamity) with which thou dost threaten us, if thou art telling the truth?"	They said: Hast come to turn us away from our gods? Then bring upon us that wherewith thou threatenest us, if thou art of the truthful.	They said: Have you come to us to turn us away from our gods; then bring us what you threaten us with, if you are of the truthful ones.
46 023	He said: "The Knowledge (of when it will come) is only with Allah: I proclaim to you the mission on which I have been sent: But I see that ye are a people in ignorance!"..	He said: The knowledge is with Allah only. I convey unto you that wherewith I have been sent, but I see you are a folk that know not.	He said: The knowledge is only with Allah, and I deliver to you the message with which I am sent, but I see you are a people who are ignorant.

46 024	Then, when they saw the (Penalty in the shape of) a cloud traversing the sky, coming to meet their valleys, they said, "This cloud will give us rain!" "Nay, it is the (Calamity) ye were asking to be hastened!- A wind wherein is a Grievous Penalty!"	Then, when they beheld it as a dense cloud coming toward their valleys, they said: Here is a cloud bringing us rain. Nay, but it is that which ye did seek to hasten, a wind wherein is painful torment,	So when they saw it as a cloud appearing in the sky advancing towards their valleys, they said: This is a cloud which will give us rain. Nay! it is what you sought to hasten on, a blast of wind in which is a painful punishment,
46 025	"Everything will it destroy by the command of its Lord!" Then by the morning they - nothing was to be seen but (the ruins of) their houses! thus do We recompense those given to sin!	Destroying all things by commandment of its Lord. And morning found them so that naught could be seen save their dwellings. Thus do We reward the guilty folk.	Destroying everything by the command of its Lord, so they became such that naught could be seen except their dwellings. Thus do We reward the guilty people.
46 026	And We had firmly established them in a (prosperity and) power which We have not given to you (ye Quraish!) and We had endowed them with (faculties of) hearing, seeing, heart and intellect: but of no profit to them were their (faculties of) hearing, sight, and heart and intellect, when they went on rejecting the Signs of Allah; and they were (completely) encircled by that which they used to mock at!	And verily We had empowered them with that wherewith We have not empowered you, and had assigned them ears and eyes and hearts; but their ears and eyes and hearts availed them naught since they denied the revelations of Allah; and what they used to mock befell them.	And certainly We had established them in what We have not established you in, and We had given-- them ears and eyes and hearts, but neither their ears, nor their eyes, nor their hearts availed them aught, since they denied the communications of Allah, and that which they mocked encompassed them.
46 027	We destroyed aforetime populations round about you; and We have shown the Signs in various ways, that they may turn (to Us).	And verily We have destroyed townships round about you, and displayed (for them) Our revelation, that haply they might return.	And certainly We destroyed the towns which are around you, and We repeat the communications that they might turn.
46 028	Why then was no help forthcoming to them from those whom they worshipped as gods, besides Allah, as a means of access (to Allah)? Nay, they left them in the lurch: but that was their falsehood and their invention.	Then why did those whom they had chosen for gods as a way of approach (unto Allah) not help them? Nay, but they did fail them utterly. And (all) that was their lie, and what they used to invent.	Why did not then those help them whom they took for gods besides Allah to draw (them) nigh (to Him)? Nay! they were lost to them; and this was their lie and what they forged.
46 029	Behold, We turned towards thee a company of jinns (quietly) listening to the Qur'an: when they stood in the presence thereof, they said, Listen in silence! When the (reading) was finished, they returned to their people, to warn (them of their sins).	And when We inclined toward thee (Muhammad) certain of the jinn, who wished to hear the Qur'an and, when they were in its presence, said: Give ear! and, when it was finished, turned back to their people, warning.	And when We turned towards you a party of the jinn who listened to the Quran; so when they came to it, they said: Be silent; then when it was finished, they turned back to their people warning (them).
46 030	They said, "O our people! We have heard a Book revealed after Moses, confirming what came before it: it guides (men) to the Truth and to a Straight Path."	They said: O our people! Lo! we have heard a Scripture which hath been revealed after Moses, confirming that which was before it, guiding unto the truth and a right road.	They said: O our people! we have listened to a Book revealed after Musa verifying that which is before it, guiding to the truth and to a right path:
46 031	"O our people, hearken to the one who invites (you) to Allah, and believe in him: He will forgive you your faults, and deliver you from a Penalty Grievous."	O our people! respond to Allah's summoner and believe in Him. He will forgive you some of your sins and guard you from a painful doom.	O our people! accept the Divine caller and believe in Him, He will forgive you of your faults and protect you from a painful punishment.

46 032	"If any does not hearken to the one who invites (us) to Allah, he cannot frustrate (Allah's Plan) on earth, and no protectors can he have besides Allah: such men (wander) in manifest error."	And whoso respondeth not to Allah's summoner he can nowise escape in the earth, and he hath no protecting friends instead of Him. Such are in error manifest.	And whoever does not accept the Divine caller, he shall not escape in the earth and he shall not have guardians besides Him, these are in manifest error.
46 033	See they not that Allah, Who created the heavens and the earth, and never wearied with their creation, is able to give life to the dead? Yea, verily He has power over all things.	Have they not seen that Allah, Who created the heavens and the earth and was not wearied by their creation, is Able to give life to the dead? Aye, He verily is Able to do all things.	Have they not considered that Allah, Who created the heavens and the earth and was not tired by their creation, is able to give life to the dead? Aye! He has surely power over all things.
46 034	And on the Day that the Unbelievers will be placed before the Fire, (they will be asked,) "Is this not the Truth?" they will say, "Yea, by our Lord!" (One will say:) "Then taste ye the Penalty, for that ye were wont to deny (Truth)!"	And on the day when those who disbelieve are exposed to the Fire (they will be asked): Is not this real? They will say: Yea, by our Lord. He will say: Then taste the doom for that ye disbelieved.	And on the day when those who disbelieve shall be brought before the fire: Is it not true? They shall say: Aye! by our Lord! He will say: Then taste the punishment, because you disbelieved.
46 035	Therefore patiently persevere, as did (all) messengers of inflexible purpose; and be in no haste about the (Unbelievers). On the Day that they see the (Punishment) promised them, (it will be) as if they had not tarried more than an hour in a single day. (Thine but) to proclaim the Message: but shall any be destroyed except those who transgress?	Then have patience (O Muhammad) even as the stout of heart among the messengers (of old) had patience, and seek not to hasten on (the doom) for them. On the day when they see that which they are promised (it will seem to them) as though they had tarried but an hour of daylight. A clear message. Shall any be destroyed save evil-living folk?	Therefore bear up patiently as did the messengers endowed with constancy bear up with patience and do not seek to hasten for them (their doom). On the day that they shall see what they are promised they shall be as if they had not tarried save an hour of the day. A sufficient exposition! Shall then any be destroyed save the transgressing people?

Chapter 47:

MUHAMMAD (MUHAMMAD)

Total Verses: 38 Revealed At: MADINA

In the name of Allah, the Most Beneficent, the Most Merciful.

47 001	Those who reject Allah and hinder (men) from the Path of Allah,- their deeds will Allah render astray (from their mark).	Those who disbelieve and turn (men) from the way of Allah, He rendereth their actions vain.	(As for) those who disbelieve and turn away from Allah's way, He shall render their works ineffective.
47 002	But those who believe and work deeds of righteousness, and believe in the (Revelation) sent down to Muhammad - for it is the Truth from their Lord,- He will remove from them their ills and improve their condition.	And those who believe and do good works and believe in that which is revealed unto Muhammad - and it is the truth from their Lord - He riddeth them of their ill-deeds and improveth their state.	And (as for) those who believe and do good, and believe in what has been revealed to Muhammad, and it is the very truth from their Lord, He will remove their evil from them and improve their condition.

47 003	This because those who reject Allah follow vanities, while those who believe follow the Truth from their Lord: Thus does Allah set forth for men their lessons by similitudes.	That is because those who disbelieve follow falsehood and because those who believe follow the truth from their Lord. Thus Allah coineth their similitudes for mankind.	That is because those who disbelieve follow falsehood, and have given them their dowries, taking (them) in marriage, not fornicating nor taking them for paramours in secret; and whoever denies faith, his work indeed is of no account, and in the hereafter he shall be one of the losers.
47 004	Therefore, when ye meet the Unbelievers (in fight), smite at their necks; At length, when ye have thoroughly subdued them, bind a bond firmly (on them): thereafter (is the time for) either generosity or ransom: Until the war lays down its burdens. Thus (are ye commanded): but if it had been Allah's Will, He could certainly have exacted retribution from them (Himself); but (He lets you fight) in order to test you, some with others. But those who are slain in the Way of Allah,- He will never let their deeds be lost.	Now when ye meet in battle those who disbelieve, then it is smiting of the necks until, when ye have routed them, then making fast of bonds; and afterward either grace or ransom till the war lay down its burdens. That (is the ordinance). And if Allah willed He could have punished them (without you) but (thus it is ordained) that He may try some of you by means of others. And those who are slain in the way of Allah, He rendereth not their actions vain.	So when you meet in battle those who disbelieve, then smite the necks until when you have overcome them, then make (them) prisoners, and afterwards either set them free as a favor or let them ransom (themselves) until the war terminates. That (shall be so); and if Allah had pleased He would certainly have exacted what is due from them, but that He may try some of you by means of others; and (as for) those who are slain in the way of Allah, He will by no means allow their deeds to perish.
47 005	Soon will He guide them and improve their condition,	He will guide them and improve their state,	He will guide them and improve their condition.
47 006	And admit them to the Garden which He has announced for them.	And bring them in unto the Garden which He hath made known to them.	And cause them to enter the garden which He has made known to them.
47 007	O ye who believe! If ye will aid (the cause of) Allah, He will aid you, and plant your feet firmly.	O ye who believe! If ye help Allah, He will help you and will make your foothold firm.	O you who believe! if you help (the cause of) Allah, He will help you and make firm your feet.
47 008	But those who reject (Allah),- for them is destruction, and (Allah) will render their deeds astray (from their mark).	And those who disbelieve, perdition is for them, and He will make their actions vain.	And (as for) those who disbelieve, for them is destruction and He has made their deeds ineffective.
47 009	That is because they hate the Revelation of Allah; so He has made their deeds fruitless.	That is because they are averse to that which Allah hath revealed, therefor maketh He their actions fruitless.	That is because they hated what Allah revealed, so He rendered their deeds null.
47 010	Do they not travel through the earth, and see what was the End of those before them (who did evil)? Allah brought utter destruction on them, and similar (fates await) those who reject Allah.	Have they not travelled in the land to see the nature of the consequence for those who were before them? Allah wiped them out. And for the disbelievers there will be the like thereof.	Have they not then journeyed in the land and seen how was the end of those before them: Allah brought down destruction upon them, and the unbelievers shall have the like of it.
47 011	That is because Allah is the Protector of those who believe, but those who reject Allah have no protector.	That is because Allah is patron of those who believe, and because the disbelievers have no patron.	That is because Allah is the Protector of those who believe, and because the unbelievers shall have no protector for them.
47 012	Verily Allah will admit those who believe and do righteous deeds, to Gardens beneath which rivers flow; while those who reject Allah will enjoy (this world) and eat as cattle eat; and the Fire will be their abode.	Lo! Allah will cause those who believe and do good works to enter Gardens underneath which rivers flow; while those who disbelieve take their comfort in this life and eat even as the cattle eat, and the Fire is their habitation.	Surely Allah will make those who believe and do good enter gardens beneath which rivers flow; and those who disbelieve enjoy themselves and eat as the beasts eat, and the fire is their abode.

47 013	And how many cities, with more power than thy city which has driven thee out, have We destroyed (for their sins)? and there was none to aid them.	And how many a township stronger than thy township (O Muhammad) which hath cast thee out, have We destroyed, and they had no helper!	And how many a town which was far more powerful than the town of yours which has driven you out: We destroyed them so there was no helper for them.
47 014	Is then one who is on a clear (Path) from his Lord, no better than one to whom the evil of his conduct seems pleasing, and such as follow their own lusts?	Is he who relieth on a clear proof from his Lord like those for whom the evil that they do is beautified while they follow their own lusts?	What! is he who has a clear argument from his Lord like him to whom the evil of his work is made fairseeming: and they follow their low desires.
47 015	(Here is) a Parable of the Garden which the righteous are promised: in it are rivers of water incorruptible; rivers of milk of which the taste never changes; rivers of wine, a joy to those who drink; and rivers of honey pure and clear. In it there are for them all kinds of fruits; and Grace from their Lord. (Can those in such Bliss) be compared to such as shall dwell for ever in the Fire, and be given, to drink, boiling water, so that it cuts up their bowels (to pieces)?	A similitude of the Garden which those who keep their duty (to Allah) are promised: Therein are rivers of water unpolluted, and rivers of milk whereof the flavour changeth not, and rivers of wine delicious to the drinkers, and rivers of clear-run honey; therein for them is every kind of fruit, with pardon from their Lord. (Are those who enjoy all this) like those who are immortal in the Fire and are given boiling water to drink so that it teareth their bowels?	A parable of the garden which those guarding (against evil) are promised: Therein are rivers of water that does not alter, and rivers of milk the taste whereof does not change, and rivers of drink delicious to those who drink, and rivers of honey clarified and for them therein are all fruits and protection from their Lord. (Are these) like those who abide in the fire and who are made to drink boiling water so it rends their bowels asunder.
47 016	And among them are men who listen to thee, but in the end, when they go out from thee, they say to those who have received Knowledge, "What is it he said just then?" Such are men whose hearts Allah has sealed, and who follow their own lusts.	Among them are some who give ear unto thee (Muhammad) till, when they go forth from thy presence they say unto those who have been given knowledge: What was that he said just now? Those are they whose hearts Allah hath sealed, and they follow their own lusts.	And there are those of them who seek to listen to you, until when they go forth from you, they say to those who have been given the knowledge: What was it that he said just now? These are they upon whose hearts Allah has set a seal and they follow their low desires.
47 017	But to those who receive Guidance, He increases the (light of) Guidance, and bestows on them their Piety and Restraint (from evil).	While as for those who walk aright, He addeth to their guidance, and giveth them their protection (against evil).	And (as for) those who follow the right direction, He increases them in guidance and gives them their guarding (against evil).
47 018	Do they then only wait for the Hour,- that it should come on them of a sudden? But already have come some tokens thereof, and when it (actually) is on them, how can they benefit then by their admonition?	Await they aught save the Hour, that it should come upon them unawares? And the beginnings thereof have already come. But how, when it hath come upon them, can they take their warning?	Do they then wait for aught but the hour that it should come to them all of a sudden? Now indeed the tokens of it have (already) come, but how shall they have their reminder when it comes on them?
47 019	Know, therefore, that there is no god but Allah, and ask forgiveness for thy fault, and for the men and women who believe: for Allah knows how ye move about and how ye dwell in your homes.	So know (O Muhammad) that there is no God save Allah, and ask forgiveness for thy sin and for believing men and believing women. Allah knoweth (both) your place of turmoil and your place of rest.	So know that there is no god but Allah, and, ask protection for your fault and for the believing men and the believing women; and Allah knows the place of your returning and the place of your abiding.

47 020	Those who believe say, "Why is not a sura sent down (for us)?" But when a sura of basic or categorical meaning is revealed, and fighting is mentioned therein, thou wilt see those in whose hearts is a disease looking at thee with a look of one in swoon at the approach of death. But more fitting for them-	And those who believe say: If only a surah were revealed! But when a decisive surah is revealed and war is mentioned therein, thou seest those in whose hearts is a disease looking at thee with the look of men fainting unto death. Therefor woe unto them!	And those who believe say: Why has not a Chapter been revealed? But when a decisive Chapter is revealed, and fighting is mentioned therein you see those in whose hearts is a disease look to you with the look of one fainting because of death. Woe to them then!
47 021	Were it to obey and say what is just, and when a matter is resolved on, it were best for them if they were true to Allah.	Obedience and a civil word. Then, when the matter is determined, if they are loyal to Allah it will be well for them.	Obedience and a gentle word (was proper), but when the affair becomes settled, then if they remain true to Allah it would certainly be better for them.
47 022	Then, is it to be expected of you, if ye were put in authority, that ye will do mischief in the land, and break your ties of kith and kin?	Would ye then, if ye were given the command, work corruption in the land and sever your ties of kinship?	But if you held command, you were sure to make mischief in the land and cut off the ties of kinship!
47 023	Such are the men whom Allah has cursed for He has made them deaf and blinded their sight.	Such are they whom Allah curseth so that He deafeneth them and maketh blind their eyes.	Those it is whom Allah has cursed so He has made them deaf and blinded their eyes.
47 024	Do they not then earnestly seek to understand the Qur'an, or are their hearts locked up by them?	Will they then not meditate on the Qur'an, or are there locks on the hearts?	Do they not then reflect on the Quran? Nay, on the hearts there are locks.
47 025	Those who turn back as apostates after Guidance was clearly shown to them,- the Evil One has instigated them and busied them up with false hopes.	Lo! those who turn back after the guidance hath been manifested unto them, Satan hath seduced them, and He giveth them the rein.	Surely (as for) those who return on their backs after that guidance has become manifest to them, the Shaitan has made it a light matter to them; and He gives them respite.
47 026	This, because they said to those who hate what Allah has revealed, We will obey you in part of (this) matter; but Allah knows their (inner) secrets.	That is because they say unto those who hate what Allah hath revealed: We will obey you in some matters; and Allah knoweth their secret talk.	That is because they say to those who hate what Allah has revealed: We will obey you in some of the affairs; and Allah knows their secrets.
47 027	But how (will it be) when the angels take their souls at death, and smite their faces and their backs?	Then how (will it be with them) when the angels gather them, smiting their faces and their backs!	But how will it be when the angels cause them to die smiting their backs.
47 028	This because they followed that which called forth the Wrath of Allah, and they hated Allah's good pleasure; so He made their deeds of no effect.	That will be because they followed that which angereth Allah, and hated that which pleaseth Him. Therefor He hath made their actions vain.	That is because they follow what is displeasing to Allah and are averse to His pleasure, therefore He has made null their deeds.
47 029	Or do those in whose hearts is a disease, think that Allah will not bring to light all their rancour?	Or do those in whose hearts is a disease deem that Allah will not bring to light their (secret) hates?	Or do those in whose hearts is a disease think that Allah will not bring forth their spite?
47 030	Had We so wiled, We could have shown them up to thee, and thou shouldst have known them by their marks: but surely thou wilt know them by the tone of their speech! And Allah knows all that ye do.	And if We would, We could show them unto thee (Muhammad) so that thou shouldst know them surely by their marks. And thou shalt know them by the burden of their talk. And Allah knoweth your deeds.	And if We please We would have made you know them so that you would certainly have recognized them by their marks and most certainly you can recognize them by the intent of (their) speech; and Allah knows your deeds.
47 031	And We shall try you until We test those among you who strive their utmost and persevere in patience; and We shall try your reported (mettle).	And verily We shall try you till We know those of you who strive hard (for the cause of Allah) and the steadfast, and till We test your record.	And most certainly We will try you until We have known those among you who exert themselves hard, and the patient, and made your case manifest.

47 032	Those who reject Allah, hinder (men) from the Path of Allah, and resist the Messenger, after Guidance has been clearly shown to them, will not injure Allah in the least, but He will make their deeds of no effect.	Lo! those who disbelieve and turn from the way of Allah and oppose the messenger after the guidance hath been manifested unto them, they hurt Allah not a jot, and He will make their actions fruitless.	Surely those who disbelieve and turn away from Allah's way and oppose the Messenger after that guidance has become clear to them cannot harm Allah in any way, and He will make null their deeds.
47 033	O ye who believe! Obey Allah, and obey the messenger, and make not vain your deeds!	O ye who believe! Obey Allah and obey the messenger, and render not your actions vain.	O you who believe! obey Allah and obey the Messenger, and do not make your deeds of no effect.
47 034	Those who reject Allah, and hinder (men) from the Path of Allah, then die rejecting Allah,- Allah will not forgive them.	Lo! those who disbelieve and turn from the way of Allah and then die disbelievers, Allah surely will not pardon them.	Surely those who disbelieve and turn away from Allah's way, then they die while they are unbelievers, Allah will by no means forgive them.
47 035	Be not weary and faint-hearted, crying for peace, when ye should be uppermost: for Allah is with you, and will never put you in loss for your (good) deeds.	So do not falter and cry out for peace when ye (will be) the uppermost, and Allah is with you, and He will not grudge (the reward of) your actions.	And be not slack so as to cry for peace and you have the upper hand, and Allah is with you, and He will not bring your deeds to naught.
47 036	The life of this world is but play and amusement: and if ye believe and guard against Evil, He will grant you your recompense, and will not ask you (to give up) your possessions.	The life of the world is but a sport and a pastime. And if ye believe and ward off (evil). He will give you your wages, and will not ask of you your wordly wealth.	The life of this world is only idle sport and play, and if you believe and guard (against evil) He will give you your rewards, and will not ask of you your possessions.
47 037	If He were to ask you for all of them, and press you, ye would covetously withhold, and He would bring out all your ill-feeling.	If He should ask it of you and importune you, ye would hoard it, and He would bring to light your (secret) hates.	If He should ask you for it and urge you, you will be niggardly, and He will bring forth your malice.
47 038	Behold, ye are those invited to spend (of your substance) in the Way of Allah: But among you are some that are niggardly. But any who are niggardly are so at the expense of their own souls. But Allah is free of all wants, and it is ye that are needy. If ye turn back (from the Path), He will substitute in your stead another people; then they would not be like you!	Lo! ye are those who are called to spend in the way of Allah, yet among you there are some who hoard. And as for him who hoardeth, he hoardeth only from his soul. And Allah is the Rich, and ye are the poor. And if ye turn away He will exchange you for some other folk, and they will not be the likes of you.	Behold! you are those who are called upon to spend in Allah's way, but among you are those who are niggardly, and whoever is niggardly is niggardly against his own soul; and Allah is Self-sufficient and you have need (of Him), and if you turn back He will bring in your place another people, then they will not be like you.

Chapter 48:

AL-FATH (VICTORY, CONQUEST)

Total Verses: 29 Revealed At: MADINA

In the name of Allah, the Most Beneficent, the Most Merciful.

48 001	Verily We have granted thee a manifest Victory:	Lo! We have given thee (O Muhammad) a signal victory,	Surely We have given to you a clear victory
48 002	That Allah may forgive thee thy faults of the past and those to follow; fulfil His favour to thee; and guide thee on the Straight Way;	That Allah may forgive thee of thy sin that which is past and that which is to come, and may perfect His favour unto thee, and may guide thee on a right path,	That Allah may forgive your community their past faults and those to follow and complete His favor to you and keep you on a right way,
48 003	And that Allah may help thee with powerful help.	And that Allah may help thee with strong help -	And that Allah might help you with a mighty help.
48 004	It is He Who sent down tranquillity into the hearts of the Believers, that they may add faith to their faith;- for to Allah belong the Forces of the heavens and the earth; and Allah is Full of Knowledge and Wisdom;-	He it is Who sent down peace of reassurance into the hearts of the believers that they might add faith unto their faith. Allah's are the hosts of the heavens and the earth, and Allah is ever Knower, Wise -	He it is Who sent down tranquillity into the hearts of the believers that they might have more of faith added to their faith-- and Allah's are the hosts of the heavens and the earth, and Allah is Knowing, Wise-
48 005	That He may admit the men and women who believe, to Gardens beneath which rivers flow, to dwell therein for aye, and remove their ills from them;- and that is, in the sight of Allah, the highest achievement (for man),-	That He may bring the believing men and the believing women into Gardens underneath which rivers flow, wherein they will abide, and may remit from them their evil deeds - That, in the sight of Allah, is the supreme triumph -	That He may cause the believing men and the believing women to enter gardens beneath which rivers flow to abide therein and remove from them their evil; and that is a grand achievement with Allah;
48 006	And that He may punish the Hypocrites, men and women, and the Polytheists, men and women, who imagine an evil opinion of Allah. On them is a round of Evil: the Wrath of Allah is on them: He has cursed them and got Hell ready for them: and evil is it for a destination.	And may punish the hypocritical men and the hypocritical women, and the idolatrous men and the idolatrous women, who think an evil thought concerning Allah. For them is the evil turn of fortune, and Allah is wroth against them and hath cursed them, and hath made ready for them hell, a hapless journey's end.	And (that) He may punish the hypocritical men and the hypocritical women, and the polytheistic men and the polytheistic women, the entertainers of evil thoughts about Allah. On them is the evil turn, and Allah is wroth with them and has cursed them and prepared hell for them, and evil is the resort.
48 007	For to Allah belong the Forces of the heavens and the earth; and Allah is Exalted in Power, Full of Wisdom.	Allah's are the hosts of the heavens and the earth, and Allah is ever Mighty, Wise.	And Allah's are the hosts of the heavens and the earth; and Allah is Mighty, Wise.
48 008	We have truly sent thee as a witness, as a bringer of Glad Tidings, and as a Warner:	Lo! We have sent thee (O Muhammad) as a witness and a bearer of good tidings and a warner,	Surely We have sent you as a witness and as a bearer of good news and as a warner,
48 009	In order that ye (O men) may believe in Allah and His Messenger, that ye may assist and honour Him, and celebrate His praise morning and evening.	That ye (mankind) may believe in Allah and His messenger, and may honour Him, and may revere Him, and may glorify Him at early dawn and at the close of day.	That you may believe in Allah and His Messenger and may aid him and revere him; and (that) you may declare His glory, morning and evening.

48 010	Verily those who plight their fealty to thee do no less than plight their fealty to Allah: the Hand of Allah is over their hands: then any one who violates his oath, does so to the harm of his own soul, and any one who fulfils what he has covenanted with Allah,- Allah will soon grant him a great Reward.	Lo! those who swear allegiance unto thee (Muhammad), swear allegiance only unto Allah. The Hand of Allah is above their hands. So whosoever breaketh his oath, breaketh it only to his soul's hurt; while whosoever keepeth his covenant with Allah, on him will He bestow immense reward.	Surely those who swear allegiance to you do but swear allegiance to Allah; the hand of Allah is above their hands. Therefore whoever breaks (his faith), he breaks it only to the injury of his own soul, and whoever fulfills what he has covenanted with Allah, He will grant him a mighty reward.
48 011	The desert Arabs who lagged behind will say to thee: "We were engaged in (looking after) our flocks and herds, and our families: do thou then ask forgiveness for us." They say with their tongues what is not in their hearts. Say: "Who then has any power at all (to intervene) on your behalf with Allah, if His Will is to give you some loss or to give you some profit? But Allah is well acquainted with all that ye do."	Those of the wandering Arabs who were left behind will tell thee: Our possessions and our households occupied us, so ask forgiveness for us! They speak with their tongues that which is not in their hearts. Say: Who can avail you aught against Allah, if He intend you hurt or intend you profit? Nay, but Allah is ever Aware of what ye do.	Those of the dwellers of the desert who were left behind will say to you: Our property and our families kept us busy, so ask forgiveness for us. They say with their tongues what is not in their hearts. Say: Then who can control anything for you from Allah if He intends to do you harm or if He intends to do you good; nay, Allah is Aware of what you do:
48 012	"Nay, ye thought that the Messenger and the Believers would never return to their families; this seemed pleasing in your hearts, and ye conceived an evil thought, for ye are a people lost (in wickedness)."	Nay, but ye deemed that the messenger and the believers would never return to their own folk, and that was made fairseeming in your hearts, and ye did think an evil thought, and ye were worthless folk.	Nay! you rather thought that the Messenger and the believers would not return to their families ever, and that was made fairseeming to your hearts and you thought an evil thought and you were a people doomed to perish.
48 013	And if any believe not in Allah and His Messenger, We have prepared, for those who reject Allah, a Blazing Fire!	And so for him who believeth not in Allah and His messenger - Lo! We have prepared a flame for disbelievers.	And whoever does not believe in Allah and His Messenger, then surely We have prepared burning fire for the unbelievers.
48 014	To Allah belongs the dominion of the heavens and the earth: He forgives whom He wills, and He punishes whom He wills: but Allah is Oft-Forgiving, Most Merciful.	And Allah's is the Sovereignty of the heavens and the earth. He forgiveth whom He will, and punisheth whom He will. And Allah is ever Forgiving, Merciful.	And Allah's is the kingdom of the heavens and the earth; He forgives whom He pleases and punishes whom He pleases, and Allah is Forgiving, Merciful.
48 015	Those who lagged behind (will say), when ye (are free to) march and take booty (in war): "Permit us to follow you." They wish to change Allah's decree: Say: "Not thus will ye follow us: Allah has already declared (this) beforehand": then they will say, "But ye are jealous of us." Nay, but little do they understand (such things).	Those who were left behind will say, when ye set forth to capture booty: Let us go with you. They fain would change the verdict of Allah. Say (unto them, O Muhammad): Ye shall not go with us. Thus hath Allah said beforehand. Then they will say: Ye are envious of us. Nay, but they understand not, save a little.	Those who are left behind will say when you set forth for the gaining of acquisitions: Allow us (that) we may follow you. They desire to change the world of Allah. Say: By no means shall you follow us; thus did Allah say before. But they will say: Nay! you are jealous of us. Nay! they do not understand but a little.
48 016	Say to the desert Arabs who lagged behind: "Ye shall be summoned (to fight) against a people given to vehement war: then shall ye fight, or they shall submit. Then if ye show obedience, Allah will grant you a goodly reward, but if ye turn back as ye did before, He will punish you with a grievous Penalty."	Say unto those of the wandering Arabs who were left behind: Ye will be called against a folk of mighty prowess, to fight them until they surrender; and if ye obey, Allah will give you a fair reward; but if ye turn away as ye did turn away before, He will punish you with a painful doom.	Say to those of the dwellers of the desert who were left behind: You shall soon be invited (to fight) against a people possessing mighty prowess; you will fight against them until they submit; then if you obey, Allah will grant you a good reward; and if you turn back as you turned back before, He will punish you with a painful punishment.

48 017	No blame is there on the blind, nor is there blame on the lame, nor on one ill (if he joins not the war): But he that obeys Allah and his Messenger,- (Allah) will admit him to Gardens beneath which rivers flow; and he who turns back, (Allah) will punish him with a grievous Penalty.	There is no blame for the blind, nor is there blame for the lame, nor is there blame for the sick (that they go not forth to war). And whoso obeyeth Allah and His messenger, He will make him enter Gardens underneath which rivers flow; and whoso turneth back, him will He punish with a painful doom.	There is no harm in the blind, nor is there any harm in the lame, nor is there any harm in the sick (if they do not go forth); and whoever obeys Allah and His Messenger, He will cause him to enter gardens beneath which rivers flow, and whoever turns back, He will punish him with a painful punishment.
48 018	Allah's Good Pleasure was on the Believers when they swore Fealty to thee under the Tree: He knew what was in their hearts, and He sent down Tranquillity to them; and He rewarded them with a speedy Victory;	Allah was well pleased with the believers when they swore allegiance unto thee beneath the tree, and He knew what was in their hearts, and He sent down peace of reassurance on them, and hath rewarded them with a near victory;	Certainly Allah was well pleased with the believers when they swore allegiance to you under the tree, and He knew what was in their hearts, so He sent down tranquillity on them and rewarded them with a near victory,
48 019	And many gains will they acquire (besides): and Allah is Exalted in Power, Full of Wisdom.	And much booty that they will capture. Allah is ever Mighty, Wise.	And many acquisitions which they will take; and Allah is Mighty, Wise.
48 020	Allah has promised you many gains that ye shall acquire, and He has given you these beforehand; and He has restrained the hands of men from you; that it may be a Sign for the Believers, and that He may guide you to a Straight Path;	Allah promiseth you much booty that ye will capture, and hath given you this in advance, and hath withheld men's hands from you, that it may be a token for the believers, and that He may guide you on a right path.	Allah promised you many acquisitions which you will take, then He hastened on this one for you and held back the hands of men from you, and that it may be a sign for the believers and that He may guide you on a right path.
48 021	And other gains (there are), which are not within your power, but which Allah has compassed: and Allah has power over all things.	And other (gain), which ye have not been able to achieve, Allah will compass it, Allah is Able to do all things.	And others which you have not yet been able to achieve Allah has surely encompassed them, and Allah has power over all things.
48 022	If the Unbelievers should fight you, they would certainly turn their backs; then would they find neither protector nor helper.	And if those who disbelieve join battle with you they will take to flight, and afterward they will find no protecting friend nor helper.	And if those who disbelieve fight with you, they would certainly turn (their) backs, then they would not find any protector or a helper.
48 023	(Such has been) the practice (approved) of Allah already in the past: no change wilt thou find in the practice (approved) of Allah.	It is the law of Allah which hath taken course aforetime. Thou wilt not find for the law of Allah aught of power to change.	Such has been the course of Allah that has indeed run before, and you shall not find a change in Allah's course.
48 024	And it is He Who has restrained their hands from you and your hands from them in the midst of Makka, after that He gave you the victory over them. And Allah sees well all that ye do.	And He it is Who hath withheld men's hands from you, and hath withheld your hands from them, in the valley of Mecca, after He had made you victors over them. Allah is Seer of what ye do.	And He it is Who held back their hands from you and your hands from them in the valley of Mecca after He had given you victory over them; and Allah is Seeing what you do.

48 025	They are the ones who denied Revelation and hindered you from the Sacred Mosque and the sacrificial animals, detained from reaching their place of sacrifice. Had there not been believing men and believing women whom ye did not know that ye were trampling down and on whose account a crime would have accrued to you without (your) knowledge, (Allah would have allowed you to force your way, but He held back your hands) that He may admit to His Mercy whom He will. If they had been apart, We should certainly have punished the Unbelievers among them with a grievous Punishment.	These it was who disbelieved and debarred you from the Inviolable Place of Worship, and debarred the offering from reaching its goal. And if it had not been for believing men and believing women, whom ye know not - lest ye should tread them under foot and thus incur guilt for them unknowingly; that Allah might bring into His mercy whom He will - If (the believers and the disbelievers) had been clearly separated We verily had punished those of them who disbelieved with painful punishment.	It is they who disbelieved and turned you away from the Sacred Mosque and (turned off) the offering withheld from arriving at its destined place; and were it not for the believing men and the believing women, whom, not having known, you might have trodden down, and thus something hateful might have afflicted you on their account without knowledge-- so that Allah may cause to enter into His mercy whomsoever He pleases; had they been widely separated one from another, We would surely have punished those who disbelieved from among them with a painful punishment.	
48 026	While the Unbelievers got up in their hearts heat and cant - the heat and cant of ignorance,- Allah sent down His Tranquillity to his Messenger and to the Believers, and made them stick close to the command of self-restraint; and well were they entitled to it and worthy of it. And Allah has full knowledge of all things.	When those who disbelieve had set up in their hearts zealotry, the zealotry of the Age of Ignorance, then Allah sent down His peace of reassurance upon His messenger and upon the believers and imposed on them the word of self-restraint, for they were worthy of it and meet for it. And Allah is Aware of all things.	When those who disbelieved harbored in their hearts (feelings of) disdain, the disdain of (the days of) ignorance, but Allah sent down His tranquillity on His Messenger and on the believers, and made them keep the word of guarding (against evil), and they were entitled to it and worthy of it; and Allah is Cognizant of all things.	
48 027	Truly did Allah fulfil the vision for His Messenger: ye shall enter the Sacred Mosque, if Allah wills, with minds secure, heads shaved, hair cut short, and without fear. For He knew what ye knew not, and He granted, besides this, a speedy victory.	Allah hath fulfilled the vision for His messenger in very truth. Ye shall indeed enter the Inviolable Place of Worship, if Allah will, secure, (having your hair) shaven and cut, not fearing. But He knoweth that which ye know not, and hath given you a near victory beforehand.	Certainly Allah had shown to His Messenger the vision with truth: you shall most certainly enter the Sacred Mosque, if Allah pleases, in security, (some) having their heads shaved and (others) having their hair cut, you shall not fear, but He knows what you do not know, so He brought about a near victory before that.	
48 028	It is He Who has sent His Messenger with Guidance and the Religion of Truth, to proclaim it over all religion: and enough is Allah for a Witness.	He it is Who hath sent His messenger with the guidance and the religion of truth, that He may cause it to prevail over all religion. And Allah sufficeth as a Witness.	He it is Who sent His Messenger with the guidance and the true religion that He may make it prevail over all the religions; and Allah is enough for a witness.	

48 029	Muhammad is the messenger of Allah; and those who are with him are strong against Unbelievers, (but) compassionate amongst each other. Thou wilt see them bow and prostrate themselves (in prayer), seeking Grace from Allah and (His) Good Pleasure. On their faces are their marks, (being) the traces of their prostration. This is their similitude in the Taurat; and their similitude in the Gospel is: like a seed which sends forth its blade, then makes it strong; it then becomes thick, and it stands on its own stem, (filling) the sowers with wonder and delight. As a result, it fills the Unbelievers with rage at them. Allah has promised those among them who believe and do righteous deeds forgiveness, and a great Reward.	Muhammad is the messenger of Allah. And those with him are hard against the disbelievers and merciful among themselves. Thou (O Muhammad) seest them bowing and falling prostrate (in worship), seeking bounty from Allah and (His) acceptance. The mark of them is on their foreheads from the traces of prostration. Such is their likeness in the Torah and their likeness in the Gospel - like as sown corn that sendeth forth its shoot and strengtheneth it and riseth firm upon its stalk, delighting the sowers - that He may enrage the disbelievers with (the sight of) them. Allah hath promised, unto such of them as believe and do good works, forgiveness and immense reward.	Muhammad is the Messenger of Allah, and those with him are firm of heart against the unbelievers, compassionate among themselves; you will see them bowing down, prostrating themselves, seeking grace from Allah and pleasure; their marks are in their faces because of the effect of prostration; that is their description in the Taurat and their description in the Injeel; like as seed-produce that puts forth its sprout, then strengthens it, so it becomes stout and stands firmly on its stem, delighting the sowers that He may enrage the unbelievers on account of them; Allah has promised those among them who believe and do good, forgiveness and a great reward.

Chapter 49:

AL-HUJRAAT (THE PRIVATE APARTMENTS, THE INNER APARTMENTS)

Total Verses: 18 Revealed At: MADINA

In the name of Allah, the Most Beneficent, the Most Merciful.

49 001	O Ye who believe! Put not yourselves forward before Allah and His Messenger; but fear Allah: for Allah is He Who hears and knows all things.	O ye who believe! Be not forward in the presence of Allah and His messenger, and keep your duty to Allah. Lo! Allah is Hearer, Knower.	O you who believe! be not forward in the presence of Allah and His Messenger, and be careful of (your duty to) Allah; surely Allah is Hearing, Knowing.
49 002	O ye who believe! Raise not your voices above the voice of the Prophet, nor speak aloud to him in talk, as ye may speak aloud to one another, lest your deeds become vain and ye perceive not.	O ye who believe! Lift not up your voices above the voice of the Prophet, nor shout when speaking to him as ye shout one to another, lest your works be rendered vain while ye perceive not.	O you who believe! do not raise your voices above the voice of the Prophet, and do not speak loud to him as you speak loud to one another, lest your deeds became null while you do not perceive.
49 003	Those that lower their voices in the presence of Allah's Messenger,- their hearts has Allah tested for piety: for them is Forgiveness and a great Reward.	Lo! they who subdue their voices in the presence of the messenger of Allah, those are they whose hearts Allah hath proven unto righteousness. Theirs will be forgiveness and immense reward.	Surely those who lower their voices before Allah's Messenger are they whose hearts Allah has proved for guarding (against evil); they shall have forgiveness and a great reward.
49 004	Those who shout out to thee from without the inner apartments - most of them lack understanding.	Lo! those who call thee from behind the private apartments, most of them have no sense.	(As for) those who call out to you from behind the private chambers, surely most of them do not understand.
49 005	If only they had patience until thou couldst come out to them, it would be best for them: but Allah is Oft-Forgiving, Most Merciful.	And if they had had patience till thou camest forth unto them, it had been better for them. And Allah is Forgiving, Merciful.	And if they wait patiently until you come out to them, it would certainly be better for them, and Allah is Forgiving, Merciful.

49 006	O ye who believe! If a wicked person comes to you with any news, ascertain the truth, lest ye harm people unwittingly, and afterwards become full of repentance for what ye have done.	O ye who believe! If an evil-liver bring you tidings, verify it, lest ye smite some folk in ignorance and afterward repent of what ye did.	O you who believe! if an evil-doer comes to you with a report, look carefully into it, lest you harm a people in ignorance, then be sorry for what you have done.
49 007	And know that among you is Allah's Messenger: were he, in many matters, to follow your (wishes), ye would certainly fall into misfortune: But Allah has endeared the Faith to you, and has made it beautiful in your hearts, and He has made hateful to you Unbelief, wickedness, and rebellion: such indeed are those who walk in righteousness;-	And know that the messenger of Allah is among you. If he were to obey you in much of the government, ye would surely be in trouble; but Allah hath endeared the faith to you and hath beautified it in your hearts, and hath made disbelief and lewdness and rebellion hateful unto you. Such are they who are the rightly guided.	And know that among you is Allah's Messenger; should he obey you in many a matter, you would surely fall into distress, but Allah has endeared the faith to you and has made it seemly in your hearts, and He has made hateful to you unbelief and transgression and disobedience; these it is that are the followers of a right way.
49 008	A Grace and Favour from Allah; and Allah is full of Knowledge and Wisdom.	(It is) a bounty and a grace from Allah; and Allah is Knower, Wise.	By grace from Allah and as a favor; and Allah is Knowing, Wise.
49 009	If two parties among the Believers fall into a quarrel, make ye peace between them: but if one of them transgresses beyond bounds against the other, then fight ye (all) against the one that transgresses until it complies with the command of Allah; but if it complies, then make peace between them with justice, and be fair: for Allah loves those who are fair (and just).	And if two parties of believers fall to fighting, then make peace between them. And if one party of them doeth wrong to the other, fight ye that which doeth wrong till it return unto the ordinance of Allah; then, if it return, make peace between them justly, and act equitably. Lo! Allah loveth the equitable.	And if two parties of the believers quarrel, make peace between them; but if one of them acts wrongfully towards the other, fight that which acts wrongfully until it returns to Allah's command; then if it returns, make peace between them with justice and act equitably; surely Allah loves those who act equitably.
49 010	The Believers are but a single Brotherhood: So make peace and reconciliation between your two (contending) brothers; and fear Allah, that ye may receive Mercy.	The believers are naught else than brothers. Therefore make peace between your brethren and observe your duty to Allah that haply ye may obtain mercy.	The believers are but brethren, therefore make peace between your brethren and be careful of (your duty to) Allah that mercy may be had on you.
49 011	O ye who believe! Let not some men among you laugh at others: It may be that the (latter) are better than the (former): Nor let some women laugh at others: It may be that the (latter) are better than the (former): Nor defame nor be sarcastic to each other, nor call each other by (offensive) nicknames: Ill-seeming is a name connoting wickedness, (to be used of one) after he has believed: And those who do not desist are (indeed) doing wrong.	O ye who believe! Let not a folk deride a folk who may be better than they (are), not let women (deride) women who may be better than they are; neither defame one another, nor insult one another by nicknames. Bad is the name of lewdness after faith. And whoso turneth not in repentance, such are evil-doers.	O you who believe! let not (one) people laugh at (another) people perchance they may be better than they, nor let women (laugh) at (other) women, perchance they may be better than they; and do not find fault with your own people nor call one another by nicknames; evil is a bad name after faith, and whoever does not turn, these it is that are the unjust.
49 012	O ye who believe! Avoid suspicion as much (as possible): for suspicion in some cases is a sin: And spy not on each other behind their backs. Would any of you like to eat the flesh of his dead brother? Nay, ye would abhor it...But fear Allah: For Allah is Oft-Returning, Most Merciful.	O ye who believe! Shun much suspicion; for lo! some suspicion is a crime. And spy not, neither backbite one another. Would one of you love to eat the flesh of his dead brother? Ye abhor that (so abhor the other)! And keep your duty (to Allah). Lo! Allah is Relenting, Merciful.	O you who believe! avoid most of suspicion, for surely suspicion in some cases is a sin, and do not spy nor let some of you backbite others. Does one of you like to eat the flesh of his dead brother? But you abhor it; and be careful of (your duty to) Allah, surely Allah is Oft-returning (to mercy), Merciful.

49 013	O mankind! We created you from a single (pair) of a male and a female, and made you into nations and tribes, that ye may know each other (not that ye may despise each other). Verily the most honoured of you in the sight of Allah is (he who is) the most righteous of you. And Allah has full knowledge and is well acquainted (with all things).	O mankind! Lo! We have created you male and female, and have made you nations and tribes that ye may know one another. Lo! the noblest of you, in the sight of Allah, is the best in conduct. Lo! Allah is Knower, Aware.	O you men! surely We have created you of a male and a female, and made you tribes and families that you may know each other; surely the most honorable of you with Allah is the one among you most careful (of his duty); surely Allah is Knowing, Aware.
49 014	The desert Arabs say, "We believe." Say, "Ye have no faith; but ye (only) say, 'We have submitted our wills to Allah,' For not yet has Faith entered your hearts. But if ye obey Allah and His Messenger, He will not belittle aught of your deeds: for Allah is Oft-Forgiving, Most Merciful."	The wandering Arabs say: We believe. Say (unto them, O Muhammad): Ye believe not, but rather say "We submit," for the faith hath not yet entered into your hearts. Yet, if ye obey Allah and His messenger, He will not withhold from you aught of (the reward of) your deeds. Lo! Allah is Forgiving, Merciful.	The dwellers of the desert say: We believe. Say: You do not believe but say, We submit; and faith has not yet entered into your hearts; and if you obey Allah and His Messenger, He will not diminish aught of your deeds; surely Allah is Forgiving, Merciful.
49 015	Only those are Believers who have believed in Allah and His Messenger, and have never since doubted, but have striven with their belongings and their persons in the Cause of Allah: Such are the sincere ones.	The (true) believers are those only who believe in Allah and His messenger and afterward doubt not, but strive with their wealth and their lives for the cause of Allah. Such are the sincere.	The believers are only those who believe in Allah and His Messenger then they doubt not and struggle hard with their wealth and their lives in the way of Allah; they are the truthful ones.
49 016	Say: "What! Will ye instruct Allah about your religion? But Allah knows all that is in the heavens and on earth: He has full knowledge of all things."	Say (unto them, O Muhammad): Would ye teach Allah your religion, when Allah knoweth all that is in the heavens and all that is in the earth, and Allah is Aware of all things?	Say: Do you apprise Allah of your religion, and Allah knows what is in the heavens and what is in the earth; and Allah is Cognizant of all things.
49 017	They impress on thee as a favour that they have embraced Islam. Say, Count not your Islam as a favour upon me: Nay, Allah has conferred a favour upon you that He has guided you to the faith, if ye be true and sincere."	They make it a favour unto thee (Muhammad) that they have surrendered (unto Him). Say: Deem not your Surrender a favour unto me; but Allah doth confer a favour on you, inasmuch as He hath led you to the Faith, if ye are earnest.	They think that they lay you under an obligation by becoming Muslims. Say: Lay me not under obligation by your Islam: rather Allah lays you under an obligation by guiding you to the faith if you are truthful.
49 018	"Verily Allah knows the secrets of the heavens and the earth: and Allah Sees well all that ye do."	Lo! Allah knoweth the Unseen of the heavens and the earth. And Allah is Seer of what ye do.	Surely Allah knows the unseen things of the heavens and the earth; and Allah sees what you do.

Chapter 50:

QAF (THE LETTER QAF)

Total Verses: 45 Revealed At: MAKKA

In the name of Allah, the Most Beneficent, the Most Merciful.

50 001	Qaf: By the Glorious Qur'an (Thou art Allah's Messenger).	Qaf. By the Glorious Qur'an,	Qaf. I swear by the glorious Quran (that Muhammad is the Messenger of Allah)
50 002	But they wonder that there has come to them a Warner from among themselves. So the Unbelievers say: "This is a wonderful thing!"	Nay, but they marvel that a warner of their own hath come unto them; and the disbelievers say: This is a strange thing:	Nay! they wonder that there has come to them a warner from among themselves, so the unbelievers say: This is a wonderful thing:
50 003	"What! When we die and become dust, (shall we live again?) That is a (sort of) return far (from our understanding)."	When we are dead and have become dust (shall we be brought back again)? That would be a far return!	What! when we are dead and have become dust? That is afar (from probable) return.
50 004	We already know how much of them the earth takes away: With Us is a record guarding (the full account).	We know that which the earth taketh of them, and with Us is a recording Book.	We know indeed what the earth diminishes of them, and with Us is a writing that preserves.
50 005	But they deny the Truth when it comes to them: so they are in a confused state.	Nay, but they have denied the truth when it came unto them, therefor they are now in troubled case.	Nay, they rejected the truth when it came to them, so they are (now) in a state of confusion.
50 006	Do they not look at the sky above them?- How We have made it and adorned it, and there are no flaws in it?	Have they not then observed the sky above them, how We have constructed it and beautified it, and how there are no rifts therein?	Do they not then look up to heaven above them how We have made it and adorned it and it has no gaps?
50 007	And the earth- We have spread it out, and set thereon mountains standing firm, and produced therein every kind of beautiful growth (in pairs)-	And the earth have We spread out, and have flung firm hills therein, and have caused of every lovely kind to grow thereon,	And the earth, We have made it plain and cast in it mountains and We have made to grow therein of all beautiful kinds,
50 008	To be observed and commemorated by every devotee turning (to Allah).	A vision and a reminder for every penitent slave.	To give sight and as a reminder to every servant who turns frequently (to Allah).
50 009	And We send down from the sky rain charted with blessing, and We produce therewith gardens and Grain for harvests;	And We send down from the sky blessed water whereby We give growth unto gardens and the grain of crops,	And We send down from the cloud water abounding in good, then We cause to grow thereby gardens and the grain that is reaped,
50 010	And tall (and stately) palm-trees, with shoots of fruit-stalks, piled one over another;-	And lofty date-palms with ranged clusters,	And the tall palm-trees having spadices closely set one above another,
50 011	As sustenance for (Allah's) Servants;- and We give (new) life therewith to land that is dead: Thus will be the Resurrection.	Provision (made) for men; and therewith We quicken a dead land. Even so will be the resurrection of the dead.	A sustenance for the servants, and We give life thereby to a dead land; thus is the rising.
50 012	Before them was denied (the Hereafter) by the People of Noah, the Companions of the Rass, the Thamud,	The folk of Noah denied (the truth) before them, and (so did) the dwellers at Ar-Rass and (the tribe of) Thamud,	(Others) before them rejected (prophets): the people of Nuh and the dwellers of Ar-Rass and Samood,

50 013	The 'Ad, Pharaoh, the brethren of Lut,	And (the tribe of) A'ad, and Pharaoh, and the brethren of Lot,		And Ad and Firon and Lut's brethren,
50 014	The Companions of the Wood, and the People of Tubba'; each one (of them) rejected the messengers, and My warning was duly fulfilled (in them).	And the dwellers in the wood, and the folk of Tubb'a: every one denied their messengers, therefor My threat took effect.		And the dwellers of the grove and the people of Tuba; all rejected the messengers, so My threat came to pass.
50 015	Were We then weary with the first creation, that they should be in confused doubt about a new Creation?	Were We then worn out by the first creation? Yet they are in doubt about a new creation.		Were We then fatigued with the first creation? Yet are they in doubt with regard to a new creation.
50 016	It was We Who created man, and We know what dark suggestions his soul makes to him: for We are nearer to him than (his) jugular vein.	We verily created man and We know what his soul whispereth to him, and We are nearer to him than his jugular vein.		And certainly We created man, and We know what his mind suggests to him, and We are nearer to him than his life-vein.
50 017	Behold, two (guardian angels) appointed to learn (his doings) learn (and noted them), one sitting on the right and one on the left.	When the two Receivers receive (him), seated on the right hand and on the left,		When the two receivers receive, sitting on the right and on the left.
50 018	Not a word does he utter but there is a sentinel by him, ready (to note it).	He uttereth no word but there is with him an observer ready.		He utters not a word but there is by him a watcher at hand.
50 019	And the stupor of death will bring Truth (before his eyes): "This was the thing which thou wast trying to escape!"	And the agony of death cometh in truth. (And it is said unto him): This is that which thou wast wont to shun.		And the stupor of death will come in truth; that is what you were trying to escape.
50 020	And the Trumpet shall be blown: that will be the Day whereof Warning (had been given).	And the trumpet is blown. This is the threatened Day.		And the trumpet shall be blown; that is the day of the threatening.
50 021	And there will come forth every soul: with each will be an (angel) to drive, and an (angel) to bear witness.	And every soul cometh, along with it a driver and a witness.		And every soul shall come, with it a driver and a witness.
50 022	(It will be said:) "Thou wast heedless of this; now have We removed thy veil, and sharp is thy sight this Day!"	(And unto the evil-doer it is said): Thou wast in heedlessness of this. Now We have removed from thee thy covering, and piercing is thy sight this day.		Certainly you were heedless of it, but now We have removed from you your veil, so your sight today is sharp.
50 023	And his Companion will say: "Here is (his Record) ready with me!"	And (unto the evil-doer) his comrade saith: This is that which I have ready (as testimony).		And his companions shall say: This is what is ready with me.
50 024	(The sentence will be:) "Throw, throw into Hell every contumacious Rejecter (of Allah)!"-	(And it is said): Do ye twain hurl to hell each rebel ingrate,		Do cast into hell every ungrateful, rebellious one,
50 025	"Who forbade what was good, transgressed all bounds, cast doubts and suspicions;"	Hinderer of good, transgressor, doubter,		Forbidder of good, exceeder of limits, doubter,
50 026	"Who set up another god beside Allah: Throw him into a severe penalty."	Who setteth up another god along with Allah. Do ye twain hurl him to the dreadful doom.		Who sets up another god with Allah, so do cast him into severe chastisement.
50 027	His Companion will say: "Our Lord! I did not make him transgress, but he was (himself) far astray."	His comrade saith: Our Lord! I did not cause him to rebel, but he was (himself) far gone in error.		His companion will say: Our Lord! I did not lead him into inordinacy but he himself was in a great error.
50 028	He will say: "Dispute not with each other in My Presence: I had already in advance sent you Warning."	He saith: Contend not in My presence, when I had already proffered unto you the warning.		He will say: Do not quarrel in My presence, and indeed I gave you the threatening beforehand:

50 029	"The Word changes not before Me, and I do not the least injustice to My Servants."	The sentence that cometh from Me cannot be changed, and I am in no wise a tyrant unto the slaves.	My word shall not be changed, nor am I in the least unjust to the servants.
50 030	One Day We will ask Hell, "Art thou filled to the full?" It will say, Are there any more (to come)?	On the day when We say unto hell: Art thou filled? and it saith: Can there be more to come?	On the day that We will say to hell: Are you filled up? And it will say: Are there any more?
50 031	And the Garden will be brought nigh to the Righteous,- no more a thing distant.	And the Garden is brought nigh for those who kept from evil, no longer distant.	And the garden shall be brought near to those who guard (against evil), not far off:
50 032	(A voice will say:) "This is what was promised for you,- for every one who turned (to Allah) in sincere repentance, who kept (His Law),"	(And it is said): This is that which ye were promised. (It is) for every penitent and heedful one,	This is what you were promised, (it is) for every one who turns frequently (to Allah), keeps (His limits);
50 033	"Who feared (Allah) Most Gracious Unseen, and brought a heart turned in devotion (to Him):"	Who feareth the Beneficent in secret and cometh with a contrite heart.	Who fears the Beneficent Allah in secret and comes with a penitent heart:
50 034	"Enter ye therein in Peace and Security; this is a Day of Eternal Life!"	Enter it in peace. This is the day of immortality.	Enter it in peace, that is the day of abiding.
50 035	There will be for them therein all that they wish, and more besides in Our Presence.	There they have all that they desire, and there is more with Us.	They have therein what they wish and with Us is more yet.
50 036	But how many generations before them did We destroy (for their sins),- stronger in power than they? Then did they wander through the land: was there any place of escape (for them)?	And how many a generation We destroyed before them, who were mightier than these in prowess so that they overran the lands! Had they any place of refuge (when the judgment came)?	And how many a generation did We destroy before them who were mightier in prowess than they, so they went about and about in the lands. Is there a place of refuge?
50 037	Verily in this is a Message for any that has a heart and understanding or who gives ear and earnestly witnesses (the truth).	Lo! therein verily is a reminder for him who hath a heart, or giveth ear with full intelligence.	Most surely there is a reminder in this for him who has a heart or he gives ear and is a witness.
50 038	We created the heavens and the earth and all between them in Six Days, nor did any sense of weariness touch Us.	And verily We created the heavens and the earth, and all that is between them, in six Days, and naught of weariness touched Us.	And certainly We created the heavens and the earth and what is between them in six periods and there touched Us not any fatigue.
50 039	Bear, then, with patience, all that they say, and celebrate the praises of thy Lord, before the rising of the sun and before (its) setting.	Therefor (O Muhammad) bear with what they say, and hymn the praise of thy Lord before the rising and before the setting of the sun;	Therefore be patient of what they say, and sing the praise of your Lord before the rising of the sun and before the setting.
50 040	And during part of the night, (also,) celebrate His praises, and (so likewise) after the postures of adoration.	And in the night-time hymn His praise, and after the (prescribed) prostrations.	And glorify Him in the night and after the prayers.
50 041	And listen for the Day when the Caller will call out from a place quiet near,-	And listen on the day when the crier crieth from a near place,	And listen on the day when the crier shall cry from a near place
50 042	The Day when they will hear a (mighty) Blast in (very) truth: that will be the Day of Resurrection.	The day when they will hear the (Awful) Cry in truth. That is the day of coming forth (from the graves).	The day when they shall hear the cry in truth; that is the day of coming forth.
50 043	Verily it is We Who give Life and Death; and to Us is the Final Goal-	Lo! We it is Who quicken and give death, and unto Us is the journeying.	Surely We give life and cause to die, and to Us is the eventual coming;
50 044	The Day when the Earth will be rent asunder, from (men) hurrying out: that will be a gathering together,- quite easy for Us.	On the day when the earth splitteth asunder from them, hastening forth (they come). That is a gathering easy for Us (to make).	The day on which the earth shall cleave asunder under them, they will make haste; that is a gathering together easy to Us.

50 045	We know best what they say; and thou art not one to overawe them by force. So admonish with the Qur'an such as fear My Warning!	We are Best Aware of what they say, and thou (O Muhammad) art in no wise a compeller over them. But warn by the Qur'an him who feareth My threat.	We know best what they say, and you are not one to compel them; therefore remind him by means of the Quran who fears My threat.

Chapter 51:

ADH-DHARIYAT (THE WINNOWING WINDS)

Total Verses: 60 Revealed At: MAKKA

In the name of Allah, the Most Beneficent, the Most Merciful.

51 001	By the (Winds) that scatter broadcast;	By those that winnow with a winnowing	I swear by the wind that scatters far and wide,
51 002	And those that lift and bear away heavy weights;	And those that bear the burden (of the rain)	Then those clouds bearing the load (of minute things in space).
51 003	And those that flow with ease and gentleness;	And those that glide with ease (upon the sea)	Then those (ships) that glide easily,
51 004	And those that distribute and apportion by Command;-	And those who distribute (blessings) by command,	Then those (angels who) distribute blessings by Our command;
51 005	Verily that which ye are promised is true;	Lo! that wherewith ye are threatened is indeed true,	What you are threatened with is most surely true,
51 006	And verily Judgment and Justice must indeed come to pass.	And lo! the judgment will indeed befall.	And the judgment must most surely come about.
51 007	By the Sky with (its) numerous Paths,	By the heaven full of paths,	I swear by the heaven full of ways.
51 008	Truly ye are in a doctrine discordant,	Lo! ye, forsooth, are of various opinion (concerning the truth).	Most surely you are at variance with each other in what you say,
51 009	Through which are deluded (away from the Truth) such as would be deluded.	He is made to turn away from it who is (himself) averse.	He is turned away from it who would be turned away.
51 010	Woe to the falsehood-mongers,-	Accursed be the conjecturers	Cursed be the liars,
51 011	Those who (flounder) heedless in a flood of confusion:	Who are careless in an abyss!	Who are in a gulf (of ignorance) neglectful;
51 012	They ask, "When will be the Day of Judgment and Justice?"	They ask: When is the Day of Judgment?	They ask: When is the Day of Judgment?
51 013	(It will be) a Day when they will be tried (and tested) over the Fire!	(It is) the day when they will be tormented at the Fire,	(It is) the day on which they shall be tried at the fire.
51 014	"Taste ye your trial! This is what ye used to ask to be hastened!"	(And it will be said unto them): Taste your torment (which ye inflicted). This is what ye sought to hasten.	Taste your persecution! this is what you would hasten on.
51 015	As to the Righteous, they will be in the midst of Gardens and Springs,	Lo! those who keep from evil will dwell amid gardens and watersprings,	Surely those who guard (against evil) shall be in gardens and fountains.
51 016	Taking joy in the things which their Lord gives them, because, before then, they lived a good life.	Taking that which their Lord giveth them; for lo! aforetime they were doers of good;	Taking what their Lord gives them; surely they were before that, the doers of good.
51 017	They were in the habit of sleeping but little by night,	They used to sleep but little of the night,	They used to sleep but little in the night.
51 018	And in the hour of early dawn, they (were found) praying for Forgiveness;	And ere the dawning of each day would seek forgiveness,	And in the morning they asked forgiveness.

51 019	And in their wealth and possessions (was remembered) the right of the (needy), him who asked, and him who (for some reason) was prevented (from asking).	And in their wealth the beggar and the outcast had due share.	And in their property was a portion due to him who begs and to him who is denied (good).
51 020	On the earth are signs for those of assured Faith,	And in the earth are portents for those whose faith is sure.	And in the earth there are signs for those who are sure,
51 021	As also in your own selves: Will ye not then see?	And (also) in yourselves. Can ye then not see?	And in your own souls (too); will you not then see?
51 022	And in heaven is your Sustenance, as (also) that which ye are promised.	And in the heaven is your providence and that which ye are promised;	And in the heaven is your sustenance and what you are threatened with.
51 023	Then, by the Lord of heaven and earth, this is the very Truth, as much as the fact that ye can speak intelligently to each other.	And by the Lord of the heavens and the earth, it is the truth, even as (it is true) that ye speak.	And by the Lord of the heavens and the earth! it is most surely the truth, just as you do speak.
51 024	Has the story reached thee, of the honoured guests of Abraham?	Hath the story of Abraham's honoured guests reached thee (O Muhammad)?	Has there come to you information about the honored guests of Ibrahim?
51 025	Behold, they entered his presence, and said: "Peace!" He said, Peace! (and thought), "These seem unusual people."	When they came in unto him and said: Peace! he answered, Peace! (and thought): Folk unknown (to me).	When they entered upon him, they said: Peace. Peace, said he, a strange people.
51 026	Then he turned quickly to his household, brought out a fatted calf,	Then he went apart unto his housefolk so that they brought a fatted calf;	Then he turned aside to his family secretly and brought a fat (roasted) calf,
51 027	And placed it before them... He said, "Will ye not eat?"	And he set it before them, saying: Will ye not eat?	So he brought it near them. He said: What! will you not eat?
51 028	(When they did not eat), He conceived a fear of them. They said, Fear not, and they gave him glad tidings of a son endowed with knowledge.	Then he conceived a fear of them. They said: Fear not! and gave him tidings of (the birth of) a wise son.	So he conceived in his mind a fear on account of them. They said: Fear not. And they gave him the good news of a boy possessing knowledge.
51 029	But his wife came forward (laughing) aloud: she smote her forehead and said: "A barren old woman!"	Then his wife came forward, making moan, and smote her face, and cried: A barren old woman!	Then his wife came up in great grief, and she struck her face and said: An old barren woman!
51 030	They said, "Even so has thy Lord spoken: and He is full of Wisdom and Knowledge."	They said: Even so saith thy Lord. Lo! He is the Wise, the Knower.	They said: Thus says your Lord: Surely He is the Wise, the Knowing.
51 031	(Abraham) said: "And what, O ye Messengers, is your errand (now)?"	(Abraham) said: And (afterward) what is your errand, O ye sent (from Allah)?	He said: What is your affair then, O messengers!
51 032	They said, "We have been sent to a people (deep) in sin;"-	They said: Lo! we are sent unto a guilty folk,	They said: Surely we are sent to a guilty people,
51 033	"To bring on, on them, (a shower of) stones of clay (brimstone),"	That we may send upon them stones of clay,	That we may send down upon them stone of clay,
51 034	"Marked as from thy Lord for those who trespass beyond bounds."	Marked by thy Lord for (the destruction of) the wanton.	Sent forth from your Lord for the extravagant.
51 035	Then We evacuated those of the Believers who were there,	Then We brought forth such believers as were there.	Then We brought forth such as were therein of the believers.
51 036	But We found not there any just (Muslim) persons except in one house:	But We found there but one house of those surrendered (to Allah).	But We did not find therein save a (single) house of those who submitted (the Muslims).
51 037	And We left there a Sign for such as fear the Grievous Penalty.	And We left behind therein a portent for those who fear a painful doom.	And We left therein a sign for those who fear the painful punishment.
51 038	And in Moses (was another Sign): Behold, We sent him to Pharaoh, with authority manifest.	And in Moses (too, there is a portent) when We sent him unto Pharaoh with clear warrant,	And in Musa: When We sent him to Firon with clear authority.

51 039	But (Pharaoh) turned back with his Chiefs, and said, "A sorcerer, or one possessed!"	But he withdrew (confiding) in his might, and said: A wizard or a madman.	But he turned away with his forces and said: A magician or a mad man.
51 040	So We took him and his forces, and threw them into the sea; and his was the blame.	So We seized him and his hosts and flung them in the sea, for he was reprobate.	So We seized him and his hosts and hurled them into the sea and he was blamable.
51 041	And in the 'Ad (people) (was another Sign): Behold, We sent against them the devastating Wind:	And in (the tribe of) A'ad (there is a portent) when we sent the fatal wind against them.	And in Ad: When We sent upon them the destructive wind.
51 042	It left nothing whatever that it came up against, but reduced it to ruin and rottenness.	It spared naught that it reached, but made it (all) as dust.	It did not leave aught on which it blew, but it made it like ashes.
51 043	And in the Thamud (was another Sign): Behold, they were told, Enjoy (your brief day) for a little while!	And in (the tribe of) Thamud (there is a portent) when it was told them: Take your ease awhile.	And in Samood: When it was said to them: Enjoy yourselves for a while.
51 044	But they insolently defied the Command of their Lord: So the stunning noise (of an earthquake) seized them, even while they were looking on.	But they rebelled against their Lord's decree, and so the thunderbolt overtook them even while they gazed;	But they revolted against the commandment of their Lord, so the rumbling overtook them while they saw.
51 045	Then they could not even stand (on their feet), nor could they help themselves.	And they were unable to rise up, nor could they help themselves.	So they were not able to rise up, nor could they defend themselves-
51 046	So were the People of Noah before them for they wickedly transgressed.	And the folk of Noah aforetime. Lo! they were licentious folk.	And the people of Nuh before, surely they were a transgressing people.
51 047	With power and skill did We construct the Firmament: for it is We Who create the vastness of pace.	We have built the heaven with might, and We it is Who make the vast extent (thereof).	And the heaven, We raised it high with power, and most surely We are the makers of things ample.
51 048	And We have spread out the (spacious) earth: How excellently We do spread out!	And the earth have We laid out, how gracious is the Spreader (thereof)!	And the earth, We have made it a wide extent; how well have We then spread (it) out.
51 049	And of every thing We have created pairs: That ye may receive instruction.	And all things We have created by pairs, that haply ye may reflect.	And of everything We have created pairs that you may be mindful.
51 050	Hasten ye then (at once) to Allah: I am from Him a Warner to you, clear and open!	Therefor flee unto Allah; lo! I am a plain warner unto you from him.	Therefore fly to Allah, surely I am a plain warner to you from Him.
51 051	And make not another an object of worship with Allah: I am from Him a Warner to you, clear and open!	And set not any other god along with Allah; lo! I am a plain warner unto you from Him.	And do not set up with Allah another god: surely I am a plain warner to you from Him.
51 052	Similarly, no messenger came to the People before them, but they said (of him) in like manner, "A sorcerer, or one possessed"!	Even so there came no messenger unto those before them but they said: A wizard or a madman!	Thus there did not come to those before them a messenger but they said: A magician or a mad man.
51 053	Is this the legacy they have transmitted, one to another? Nay, they are themselves a people transgressing beyond bounds!	Have they handed down (the saying) as an heirloom one unto another? Nay, but they are froward folk.	Have they charged each other with this? Nay! they are an inordinate people.
51 054	So turn away from them: not thine is the blame.	So withdraw from them (O Muhammad), for thou art in no wise blameworthy,	Then turn your back upon them for you are not to blame;
51 055	But teach (thy Message) for teaching benefits the Believers.	And warn, for warning profiteth believers.	And continue to remind, for surely the reminder profits the believers.
51 056	I have only created jinns and men, that they may serve Me.	I created the jinn and humankind only that they might worship Me.	And I have not created the jinn and the men except that they should serve Me.

51 057	No Sustenance do I require of them, nor do I require that they should feed Me.	I seek no livelihood from them, nor do I ask that they should feed Me.	I do not desire from them any sustenance and I do not desire that they should feed Me.
51 058	For Allah is He Who gives (all) Sustenance,- Lord of Power,- Steadfast (for ever).	Lo! Allah! He it is that giveth livelihood, the Lord of unbreakable might.	Surely Allah is the Bestower of sustenance, the Lord of Power, the Strong.
51 059	For the wrong-doers, their portion is like unto the portion of their fellows (of earlier generations): then let them not ask Me to hasten (that portion)!	And lo! for those who (now) do wrong there is an evil day like unto the evil day (which came for) their likes (of old); so let them not ask Me to hasten on (that day).	So surely those who are unjust shall have a portion like the portion of their companions, therefore let them not ask Me to hasten on.
51 060	Woe, then, to the Unbelievers, on account of that Day of theirs which they have been promised!	And woe unto those who disbelieve, from (that) their day which they are promised.	Therefore woe to those who disbelieve because of their day which they are threatened with.

Chapter 52:

AT-TUR (THE MOUNT)

Total Verses: 49 Revealed At: MAKKA

In the name of Allah, the Most Beneficent, the Most Merciful.

52 001	By the Mount (of Revelation);	By the Mount,	I swear by the Mountain,
52 002	By a Decree Inscribed	And a Scripture inscribed	And the Book written
52 003	In a Scroll unfolded;	On fine parchment unrolled,	In an outstretched fine parchment,
52 004	By the much-frequented Fane;	And the House frequented,	And the House (Kaaba) that is visited,
52 005	By the Canopy Raised High;	And the roof exalted,	And the elevated canopy
52 006	And by the Ocean filled with Swell;-	And the sea kept filled,	And the swollen sea
52 007	Verily, the Doom of thy Lord will indeed come to pass;-	Lo! the doom of thy Lord will surely come to pass;	Most surely the punishment of your Lord will come to pass;
52 008	There is none can avert it;-	There is none that can ward it off.	There shall be none to avert it;
52 009	On the Day when the firmament will be in dreadful commotion.	On the day when the heaven will heave with (awful) heaving,	On the day when the heaven shall move from side to side
52 010	And the mountains will fly hither and thither.	And the mountains move away with (awful) movement,	And the mountains shall pass away passing away (altogether).
52 011	Then woe that Day to those that treat (Truth) as Falsehood;-	Then woe that day unto the deniers	So woe on that day to those who reject (the truth),
52 012	That play (and paddle) in shallow trifles.	Who play in talk of grave matters;	Those who sport entering into vain discourses.
52 013	That Day shall they be thrust down to the Fire of Hell, irresistibly.	The day when they are thrust with a (disdainful) thrust, into the fire of Hell.	The day on which they shall be driven away to the fire of hell with violence.
52 014	"This," it will be said, "Is the Fire,- which ye were wont to deny!"	(And it is said unto them): This is the Fire which ye were wont to deny.	This is the fire which you used to give the lie to.
52 015	"Is this then a fake, or is it ye that do not see?"	Is this magic, or do ye not see?	Is it magic then or do you not see?

52 016	"Burn ye therein: the same is it to you whether ye bear it with patience, or not: Ye but receive the recompense of your (own) deeds."	Endure the heat thereof, and whether ye are patient of it or impatient of it is all one for you. Ye are only being paid for what ye used to do.	Enter into it, then bear (it) patiently, or do not bear (it) patiently, it is the same to you; you shall be requited only (for) what you did.
52 017	As to the Righteous, they will be in Gardens, and in Happiness,-	Lo! those who kept their duty dwell in gardens and delight,	Surely those who guard (against evil) shall be in gardens and bliss
52 018	Enjoying the (Bliss) which their Lord hath bestowed on them, and their Lord shall deliver them from the Penalty of the Fire.	Happy because of what their Lord hath given them, and (because) their Lord hath warded off from them the torment of hell fire.	Rejoicing because of what their Lord gave them, and their Lord saved them from the punishment of the burning fire.
52 019	(To them will be said:) "Eat and drink ye, with profit and health, because of your (good) deeds."	(And it is said unto them): Eat and drink in health (as a reward) for what ye used to do,	Eat and drink pleasantly for what you did,
52 020	They will recline (with ease) on Thrones (of dignity) arranged in ranks; and We shall join them to Companions, with beautiful big and lustrous eyes.	Reclining on ranged couches. And we wed them unto fair ones with wide, lovely eyes.	Reclining on thrones set in lines, and We will unite them to large-eyed beautiful ones.
52 021	And those who believe and whose families follow them in Faith,- to them shall We join their families: Nor shall We deprive them (of the fruit) of aught of their works: (Yet) is each individual in pledge for his deeds.	And they who believe and whose seed follow them in faith, We cause their seed to join them (there), and We deprive them of nought of their (life's) work. Every man is a pledge for that which he hath earned.	And (as for) those who believe and their offspring follow them in faith, We will unite with them their offspring and We will not diminish to them aught of their work; every man is responsible for what he shall have wrought.
52 022	And We shall bestow on them, of fruit and meat, anything they shall desire.	And We provide them with fruit and meat such as they desire.	And We will aid them with fruit and flesh such as they desire.
52 023	They shall there exchange, one with another, a (loving) cup free of frivolity, free of all taint of ill.	There they pass from hand to hand a cup wherein is neither vanity nor cause of sin.	They shall pass therein from one to another a cup wherein there shall be nothing vain nor any sin.
52 024	Round about them will serve, (devoted) to them, young male servants (handsome) as Pearls well-guarded.	And there go round, waiting on them menservants of their own, as they were hidden pearls.	And round them shall go boys of theirs as if they were hidden pearls.
52 025	They will advance to each other, engaging in mutual enquiry.	And some of them draw near unto others, questioning,	And some of them shall advance towards others questioning each other.
52 026	They will say: "Aforetime, we were not without fear for the sake of our people."	Saying: Lo! of old, when we were with our families, we were ever anxious;	Saying: Surely we feared before on account of our families:
52 027	"But Allah has been good to us, and has delivered us from the Penalty of the Scorching Wind."	But Allah hath been gracious unto us and hath preserved us from the torment of the breath of Fire.	But Allah has been gracious to us and He has saved us from the punishment of the hot wind:
52 028	"Truly, we did call unto Him from of old: truly it is He, the Beneficent, the Merciful!"	Lo! we used to pray unto Him of old. Lo! He is the Benign, the Merciful.	Surely we called upon Him before: Surely He is the Benign, the Merciful.
52 029	Therefore proclaim thou the praises (of thy Lord): for by the Grace of thy Lord, thou art no (vulgar) soothsayer, nor art thou one possessed.	Therefor warn (men, O Muhammad). By the grace of Allah thou art neither soothsayer nor madman.	Therefore continue to remind, for by the grace of your Lord, you are not a soothsayer, or a madman.
52 030	Or do they say:- "A Poet! we await for him some calamity (hatched) by Time!"	Or say they: (he is) a poet, (one) for whom we may expect the accident of time?	Or do they say: A poet, we wait for him the evil accidents of time.
52 031	Say thou: "Await ye!- I too will wait along with you!"	Say (unto them): Except (your fill)! Lo! I am with you among the expectant.	Say: Wait, for surely I too with you am of those who wait.

52 032	Is it that their faculties of understanding urge them to this, or are they but a people transgressing beyond bounds?	Do their minds command them to do this, or are they an outrageous folk?	Nay! do their understandings bid them this? Or are they an inordinate people?
52 033	Or do they say, "He fabricated the (Message)"? Nay, they have no faith!	Or say they: He hath invented it? Nay, but they will not believe!	Or do they say: He has forged it. Nay! they do not believe.
52 034	Let them then produce a recital like unto it,- If (it be) they speak the truth!	Then let them produce speech the like thereof, if they are truthful.	Then let them bring an announcement like it if they are truthful.
52 035	Were they created of nothing, or were they themselves the creators?	Or were they created out of naught? Or are they the creators?	Or were they created without there being anything, or are they the creators?
52 036	Or did they create the heavens and the earth? Nay, they have no firm belief.	Or did they create the heavens and the earth? Nay, but they are sure of nothing!	Or did they create the heavens and the earth? Nay! they have no certainty.
52 037	Or are the Treasures of thy Lord with them, or are they the managers (of affairs)?	Or do they own the treasures of thy Lord? Or have they been given charge (thereof)?	Or have they the treasures of your Lord with them? Or have they been set in absolute authority?
52 038	Or have they a ladder, by which they can (climb up to heaven and) listen (to its secrets)? Then let (such a) listener of theirs produce a manifest proof.	Or have they any stairway (unto heaven) by means of which they overhear (decrees). Then let their listener produce some warrant manifest!	Or have they the means by which they listen? Then let their listener bring a clear authority.
52 039	Or has He only daughters and ye have sons?	Or hath He daughters whereas ye have sons?	Or has He daughters while you have sons?
52 040	Or is it that thou dost ask for a reward, so that they are burdened with a load of debt?-	Or askest thou (Muhammad) a fee from them so that they are plunged in debt?	Or do you ask them for a reward, so that they are overburdened by a debt?
52 041	Or that the Unseen in it their hands, and they write it down?	Or possess they the Unseen so that they can write (it) down?	Or have they the unseen so that they write (it) down?
52 042	Or do they intend a plot (against thee)? But those who defy Allah are themselves involved in a Plot!	Or seek they to ensnare (the messenger)? But those who disbelieve, they are the ensnared!	Or do they desire a war? But those who disbelieve shall be the vanquished ones in war.
52 043	Or have they a god other than Allah? Exalted is Allah far above the things they associate with Him!	Or have they any god beside Allah? Glorified be Allah from all that they ascribe as partner (unto Him)!	Or have they a god other than Allah? Glory be to Allah from what they set up (with Him).
52 044	Were they to see a piece of the sky falling (on them), they would (only) say: "Clouds gathered in heaps!"	And if they were to see a fragment of the heaven falling, they would say: A heap of clouds.	And if they should see a portion of the heaven coming down, they would say: Piled up clouds.
52 045	So leave them alone until they encounter that Day of theirs, wherein they shall (perforce) swoon (with terror),-	Then let them be (O Muhammad), till they meet their day, in which they will be thunder-stricken,	Leave them then till they meet that day of theirs wherein they shall be made to swoon (with terror):
52 046	The Day when their plotting will avail them nothing and no help shall be given them.	A day in which their guile will naught avail them, nor will they be helped.	The day on which their struggle shall not avail them aught, nor shall they be helped.
52 047	And verily, for those who do wrong, there is another punishment besides this: But most of them understand not.	And verily, for those who do wrong, there is a punishment beyond that. But most of them know not.	And surely those who are unjust shall have a punishment besides that (in the world), but most of them do not know.
52 048	Now await in patience the command of thy Lord: for verily thou art in Our eyes: and celebrate the praises of thy Lord the while thou standest forth,	So wait patiently (O Muhammad) for thy Lord's decree, for surely thou art in Our sight; and hymn the praise of thy Lord when thou uprisest,	And wait patiently for the judgment of your Lord, for surely you are before Our eyes, and sing the praise of your Lord when you rise;

52 049	And for part of the night also praise thou Him,- and at the retreat of the stars!	And in the night-time also hymn His praise, and at the setting of the stars.	And in the night, give Him glory too, and at the setting of the stars.

Chapter 53:

AN-NAJM (THE STAR)

Total Verses: 62 Revealed At: MAKKA

In the name of Allah, the Most Beneficent, the Most Merciful.

53 001	By the Star when it goes down,-	By the Star when it setteth,	I swear by the star when it goes down.
53 002	Your Companion is neither astray nor being misled.	Your comrade erreth not, nor is deceived;	Your companion does not err, nor does he go astray;
53 003	Nor does he say (aught) of (his own) Desire.	Nor doth he speak of (his own) desire.	Nor does he speak out of desire.
53 004	It is no less than inspiration sent down to him:	It is naught save an inspiration that is inspired,	It is naught but revelation that is revealed,
53 005	He was taught by one Mighty in Power,	Which one of mighty powers hath taught him,	The Lord of Mighty Power has taught him,
53 006	Endued with Wisdom: for he appeared (in stately form);	One vigorous; and he grew clear to view	The Lord of Strength; so he attained completion,
53 007	While he was in the highest part of the horizon:	When he was on the uppermost horizon.	And he is in the highest part of the horizon.
53 008	Then he approached and came closer,	Then he drew nigh and came down	Then he drew near, then he bowed
53 009	And was at a distance of but two bow-lengths or (even) nearer;	Till he was (distant) two bows' length or even nearer,	So he was the measure of two bows or closer still.
53 010	So did (Allah) convey the inspiration to His Servant- (conveyed) what He (meant) to convey.	And He revealed unto His slave that which He revealed.	And He revealed to His servant what He revealed.
53 011	The (Prophet's) (mind and) heart in no way falsified that which he saw.	The heart lied not (in seeing) what it saw.	The heart was not untrue in (making him see) what he saw.
53 012	Will ye then dispute with him concerning what he saw?	Will ye then dispute with him concerning what he seeth?	What! do you then dispute with him as to what he saw?
53 013	For indeed he saw him at a second descent,	And verily he saw him yet another time	And certainly he saw him in another descent,
53 014	Near the Lote-tree beyond which none may pass:	By the lote-tree of the utmost boundary,	At the farthest lote-tree;
53 015	Near it is the Garden of Abode.	Nigh unto which is the Garden of Abode.	Near which is the garden, the place to be resorted to.
53 016	Behold, the Lote-tree was shrouded (in mystery unspeakable!)	When that which shroudeth did enshroud the lote-tree,	When that which covers covered the lote-tree;
53 017	(His) sight never swerved, nor did it go wrong!	The eye turned not aside nor yet was overbold.	The eye did not turn aside, nor did it exceed the limit.
53 018	For truly did he see, of the Signs of his Lord, the Greatest!	Verily he saw one of the greater revelations of his Lord.	Certainly he saw of the greatest signs of his Lord.
53 019	Have ye seen Lat. and 'Uzza,	Have ye thought upon Al-Lat and Al-'Uzza	Have you then considered the Lat and the Uzza,
53 020	And another, the third (goddess), Manat?	And Manat, the third, the other?	And Manat, the third, the last?
53 021	What! for you the male sex, and for Him, the female?	Are yours the males and His the females?	What! for you the males and for Him the females!

53 022	Behold, such would be indeed a division most unfair!	That indeed were an unfair division!	This indeed is an unjust division!
53 023	These are nothing but names which ye have devised,- ye and your fathers,- for which Allah has sent down no authority (whatever). They follow nothing but conjecture and what their own souls desire!- Even though there has already come to them Guidance from their Lord!	They are but names which ye have named, ye and your fathers, for which Allah hath revealed no warrant. They follow but a guess and that which (they) themselves desire. And now the guidance from their Lord hath come unto them.	They are naught but names which you have named, you and your fathers; Allah has not sent for them any authority. They follow naught but conjecture and the low desires which (their) souls incline to; and certainly the guidance has come to them from their Lord.
53 024	Nay, shall man have (just) anything he hankers after?	Or shall man have what he coveteth?	Or shall man have what he wishes?
53 025	But it is to Allah that the End and the Beginning (of all things) belong.	But unto Allah belongeth the after (life), and the former.	Nay! for Allah is the hereafter and the former (life).
53 026	How many-so-ever be the angels in the heavens, their intercession will avail nothing except after Allah has given leave for whom He pleases and that he is acceptable to Him.	And how many angels are in the heavens whose intercession availeth naught save after Allah giveth leave to whom He chooseth and accepteth.	And how many an angel is there in the heavens whose intercession does not avail at all except after Allah has given permission to whom He pleases and chooses.
53 027	Those who believe not in the Hereafter, name the angels with female names.	Lo! it is those who disbelieve in the Hereafter who name the angels with the names of females.	Most surely they who do not believe in the hereafter name the angels with female names.
53 028	But they have no knowledge therein. They follow nothing but conjecture; and conjecture avails nothing against Truth.	And they have no knowledge thereof. They follow but a guess, and lo! a guess can never take the place of the truth.	And they have no knowledge of it; they do not follow anything but conjecture, and surely conjecture does not avail against the truth at all.
53 029	Therefore shun those who turn away from Our Message and desire nothing but the life of this world.	Then withdraw (O Muhammad) from him who fleeth from Our remembrance and desireth but the life of the world.	Therefore turn aside from him who turns his back upon Our reminder and does not desire anything but this world's life.
53 030	That is as far as knowledge will reach them. Verily thy Lord knoweth best those who stray from His Path, and He knoweth best those who receive guidance.	Such is their sum of knowledge. Lo! thy Lord is Best Aware of him who strayeth, and He is Best Aware of him whom goeth right.	That is their goal of knowledge; surely your Lord knows best him who goes astray from His path and He knows best him who follows the right direction.
53 031	Yea, to Allah belongs all that is in the heavens and on earth: so that He rewards those who do evil, according to their deeds, and He rewards those who do good, with what is best.	And unto Allah belongeth whatsoever is in the heavens and whatsoever is in the earth, that He may reward those who do evil with that which they have done, and reward those who do good with goodness.	And Allah's is what is in the heavens and what is in the earth, that He may reward those who do evil according to what they do, and (that) He may reward those who do good with goodness.
53 032	Those who avoid great sins and shameful deeds, only (falling into) small faults,- verily thy Lord is ample in forgiveness. He knows you well when He brings you out of the earth, and when ye are hidden in your mothers' wombs. Therefore justify not yourselves: He knows best who it is that guards against evil.	Those who avoid enormities of sin and abominations, save the unwilled offences - (for them) lo! thy Lord is of vast mercy. He is Best Aware of you (from the time) when He created you from the earth, and when ye were hidden in the bellies of your mothers. Therefor ascribe not purity unto yourselves. He is Best Aware of him who wardeth off (evil).	Those who keep aloof from the great sins and the indecencies but the passing idea; surely your Lord is liberal in forgiving. He knows you best when He brings you forth from the earth and when you are embryos in the wombs of your mothers; therefore do not attribute purity to your souls; He knows him best who guards (against evil).
53 033	Seest thou one who turns back,	Didst thou (O Muhammad) observe him who turned away,	Have you then seen him who turns his back?

53 034	Gives a little, then hardens (his heart)?	And gave a little, then was grudging?	And gives a little and (then) withholds.
53 035	What! Has he knowledge of the Unseen so that he can see?	Hath he knowledge of the Unseen so that he seeth?	Has he the knowledge of the unseen so that he can see?
53 036	Nay, is he not acquainted with what is in the Books of Moses-	Or hath he not had news of what is in the books of Moses	Or, has he not been informed of what is in the scriptures of Musa?
53 037	And of Abraham who fulfilled his engagements?-	And Abraham who paid his debt:	And (of) Ibrahim who fulfilled (the commandments):
53 038	Namely, that no bearer of burdens can bear the burden of another;	That no laden one shall bear another's load,	That no bearer of burden shall bear the burden of another-
53 039	That man can have nothing but what he strives for;	And that man hath only that for which he maketh effort,	And that man shall have nothing but what he strives for-
53 040	That (the fruit of) his striving will soon come in sight:	And that his effort will be seen.	And that his striving shall soon be seen-
53 041	Then will he be rewarded with a reward complete;	And afterward he will be repaid for it with fullest payment;	Then shall he be rewarded for it with the fullest reward-
53 042	That to thy Lord is the final Goal;	And that thy Lord, He is the goal;	And that to your Lord is the goal-
53 043	That it is He Who granteth Laughter and Tears;	And that He it is who maketh laugh, and maketh weep,	And that He it is Who makes (men) laugh and makes (them) weep;
53 044	That it is He Who granteth Death and Life;	And that He it is Who giveth death and giveth life;	And that He it is Who causes death and gives life-
53 045	That He did create in pairs,- male and female,	And that He createth the two spouses, the male and the female,	And that He created pairs, the male and the female
53 046	From a seed when lodged (in its place);	From a drop (of seed) when it is poured forth;	From the small seed when it is adapted
53 047	That He hath promised a Second Creation (Raising of the Dead);	And that He hath ordained the second bringing forth;	And that on Him is the bringing forth a second time;
53 048	That it is He Who giveth wealth and satisfaction;	And that He it is Who enricheth and contenteth;	And that He it is Who enriches and gives to hold;
53 049	That He is the Lord of Sirius (the Mighty Star);	And that He it is Who is the Lord of Sirius;	And that He is the Lord of the Sirius;
53 050	And that it is He Who destroyed the (powerful) ancient 'Ad (people),	And that He destroyed the former (tribe of) A'ad,	And that He did destroy the Ad of old
53 051	And the Thamud nor gave them a lease of perpetual life.	And (the tribe of) Thamud He spared not;	And Samood, so He spared not
53 052	And before them, the people of Noah, for that they were (all) most unjust and most insolent transgressors,	And the folk of Noah aforetime, Lo! they were more unjust and more rebellious;	And the people of Nuh before; surely they were most unjust and inordinate;
53 053	And He destroyed the Overthrown Cities (of Sodom and Gomorrah).	And Al-Mu'tafikah He destroyed	And the overthrown cities did He overthrow,
53 054	So that (ruins unknown) have covered them up.	So that there covered them that which did cover.	So there covered them that which covered.
53 055	Then which of the gifts of thy Lord, (O man,) wilt thou dispute about?	Concerning which then, of the bounties of thy Lord, canst thou dispute?	Which of your Lord's benefits will you then dispute about?
53 056	This is a Warner, of the (series of) Warners of old!	This is a warner of the warners of old.	This is a warner of the warners of old.
53 057	The (Judgment) ever approaching draws nigh:	The threatened Hour is nigh.	The near event draws nigh.
53 058	No (soul) but Allah can lay it bare.	None beside Allah can disclose it.	There shall be none besides Allah to remove it.
53 059	Do ye then wonder at this recital?	Marvel ye then at this statement,	Do you then wonder at this announcement?
53 060	And will ye laugh and not weep,-	And laugh and not weep,	And will you laugh and not weep?
53 061	Wasting your time in vanities?	While ye amuse yourselves?	While you are indulging in varieties.

53 062	But fall ye down in prostration to Allah, and adore (Him)!	Rather prostrate yourselves before Allah and serve Him.	So make obeisance to Allah and serve (Him).

Chapter 54:

AL-QAMAR (THE MOON)

Total Verses: 55 Revealed At: MAKKA

In the name of Allah, the Most Beneficent, the Most Merciful.

54 001	The Hour (of Judgment) is nigh, and the moon is cleft asunder.	The hour drew nigh and the moon was rent in twain.	The hour drew nigh and the moon did rend asunder.
54 002	But if they see a Sign, they turn away, and say, "This is (but) transient magic."	And if they behold a portent they turn away and say: Prolonged illusion.	And if they see a miracle they turn aside and say: Transient magic.
54 003	They reject (the warning) and follow their (own) lusts but every matter has its appointed time.	They denied (the Truth) and followed their own lusts. Yet everything will come to a decision.	And they call (it) a lie, and follow their low desires; and every affair has its appointed term.
54 004	There have already come to them Recitals wherein there is (enough) to check (them),	And surely there hath come unto them news whereof the purport should deter,	And certainly some narratives have come to them wherein is prevention--
54 005	Mature wisdom;- but (the preaching of) Warners profits them not.	Effective wisdom; but warnings avail not.	Consummate wisdom-- but warnings do not avail;
54 006	Therefore, (O Prophet,) turn away from them. The Day that the Caller will call (them) to a terrible affair,	So withdraw from them (O Muhammad) on the day when the Summoner summoneth unto a painful thing.	So turn (your) back on them (for) the day when the inviter shall invite them to a hard task,
54 007	They will come forth,- their eyes humbled - from (their) graves, (torpid) like locusts scattered abroad,	With downcast eyes, they come forth from the graves as they were locusts spread abroad,	Their eyes cast down, going forth from their graves as if they were scattered locusts,
54 008	Hastening, with eyes transfixed, towards the Caller!- "Hard is this Day!", the Unbelievers will say.	Hastening toward the summoner; the disbelievers say: This is a hard day.	Hastening to the inviter. The unbelievers shall say: This is a hard day.
54 009	Before them the People of Noah rejected (their messenger): they rejected Our servant, and said, "Here is one possessed!", and he was driven out.	The folk of Noah denied before them, yea, they denied Our slave and said: A madman; and he was repulsed.	Before them the people of Nuh rejected, so they rejected Our servant and called (him) mad, and he was driven away.
54 010	Then he called on his Lord: "I am one overcome: do Thou then help (me)!"	So he cried unto his Lord, saying: I am vanquished, so give help.	Therefore he called upon his Lord: I am overcome, come Thou then to help.
54 011	So We opened the gates of heaven, with water pouring forth.	Then opened We the gates of heaven with pouring water	So We opened the gates of the cloud with water pouring
54 012	And We caused the earth to gush forth with springs, so the waters met (and rose) to the extent decreed.	And caused the earth to gush forth springs, so that the waters met for a predestined purpose.	And We made water to flow forth in the land in springs, so the water gathered together according to a measure already ordained.
54 013	But We bore him on an (Ark) made of broad planks and caulked with palm-fibre:	And We carried him upon a thing of planks and nails,	And We bore him on that which was made of planks and nails
54 014	She floats under our eyes (and care): a recompense to one who had been rejected (with scorn)!	That ran (upon the waters) in Our sight, as a reward for him who was rejected.	Sailing, before Our eyes, a reward for him who was denied.

54 015	And We have left this as a Sign (for all time): then is there any that will receive admonition?	And verily We left it as a token; but is there any that remembereth?	And certainly We left it as a sign, but is there anyone who
54 016	But how (terrible) was My Penalty and My Warning?	Then see how (dreadful) was My punishment after My warnings!	How (great) was then My punishment and My warning!
54 017	And We have indeed made the Qur'an easy to understand and remember: then is there any that will receive admonition?	And in truth We have made the Qur'an easy to remember; but is there any that remembereth?	And certainly We have made the Quran easy for remembrance, but is there anyone who will mind?
54 018	The 'Ad (people) (too) rejected (Truth): then how terrible was My Penalty and My Warning?	(The tribe of) A'ad rejected warnings. Then how (dreadful) was My punishment after My warnings.	Ad treated (the truth) as a lie, so how (great) was My punishment and My warning!
54 019	For We sent against them a furious wind, on a Day of violent Disaster,	Lo! We let loose on them a raging wind on a day of constant calamity,	Surely We sent on them a tornado in a day of bitter ill-luck
54 020	Plucking out men as if they were roots of palm-trees torn up (from the ground).	Sweeping men away as though they were uprooted trunks of palm-trees.	Tearing men away as if they were the trunks of palm-trees torn up.
54 021	Yea, how (terrible) was My Penalty and My Warning!	Then see how (dreadful) was My punishment after My warnings!	How (great) was then My punishment and My warning!
54 022	But We have indeed made the Qur'an easy to understand and remember: then is there any that will receive admonition?	And in truth We have made the Qur'an easy to remember; but is there any that remembereth?	And certainly We have made the Quran easy for remembrance, but is there anyone who will mind?
54 023	The Thamud (also) rejected (their) Warners.	(The tribe of) Thamud rejected warnings	Samood rejected the warning.
54 024	For they said: "What! a man! a solitary one from among ourselves! shall we follow such a one? Truly should we then be straying in mind, and mad!"	For they said; Is it a mortal man, alone among us, that we are to follow? Then indeed we should fall into error and madness.	So they said: What! a single mortal from among us! Shall we follow him? Most surely we shall in that case be in sure error and distress:
54 025	"Is it that the Message is sent to him, of all people amongst us? Nay, he is a liar, an insolent one!"	Hath the remembrance been given unto him alone among us? Nay, but he is a rash liar.	Has the reminder been made to light upon him from among us? Nay! he is an insolent liar!
54 026	Ah! they will know on the morrow, which is the liar, the insolent one!	(Unto their warner it was said): To-morrow they will know who is the rash liar.	Tomorrow shall they know who is the liar, the insolent one.
54 027	For We will send the she-camel by way of trial for them. So watch them, (O Salih), and possess thyself in patience!	Lo! We are sending the she-camel as a test for them; so watch them and have patience;	Surely We are going to send the she-camel as a trial for them; therefore watch them and have patience.
54 028	And tell them that the water is to be divided between them: Each one's right to drink being brought forward (by suitable turns).	And inform them that the water is to be shared between (her and) them. Every drinking will be witnessed.	And inform them that the water is shared between them; every share of the water shall be regulated.
54 029	But they called to their companion, and he took a sword in hand, and hamstrung (her).	But they call their comrade and he took and hamstrung (her).	But they called their companion, so he took (the sword) and slew (her).
54 030	Ah! how (terrible) was My Penalty and My Warning!	Then see how (dreadful) was My punishment after My warnings!	How (great) was then My punishment and My warning!
54 031	For We sent against them a single Mighty Blast, and they became like the dry stubble used by one who pens cattle.	Lo! We sent upon them one Shout, and they became as the dry twigs (rejected by) the builder of a cattle-fold.	Surely We sent upon them a single cry, so they were like the dry fragments of trees which the maker of an enclosure collects.
54 032	And We have indeed made the Qur'an easy to understand and remember: then is there any that will receive admonition?	And in truth We have made the Qur'an easy to remember; but is there any that remembereth?	And certainly We have made the Quran easy for remembrance, but is there anyone who will mind?
54 033	The people of Lut rejected (his) warning.	The folk of Lot rejected warnings.	The people of Lut treated the warning as a lie.

54 034	We sent against them a violent Tornado with showers of stones, (which destroyed them), except Lut's household: them We delivered by early Dawn,-	Lo! We sent a storm of stones upon them (all) save the family of Lot, whom We rescued in the last watch of the night,	Surely We sent upon them a stonestorm, except Lut's followers; We saved them a little before daybreak,
54 035	As a Grace from Us: thus do We reward those who give thanks.	As grace from Us. Thus We reward him who giveth thanks.	A favor from Us; thus do We reward him who gives thanks.
54 036	And (Lut) did warn them of Our Punishment, but they disputed about the Warning.	And he indeed had warned them of Our blow, but they did doubt the warnings.	And certainly he warned them of Our violent seizure, but they obstinately disputed the warning.
54 037	And they even sought to snatch away his guests from him, but We blinded their eyes. (They heard:) "Now taste ye My Wrath and My Warning."	They even asked of him his guests for an ill purpose. Then We blinded their eyes (and said): Taste now My punishment after My warnings!	And certainly they endeavored to turn him from his guests, but We blinded their eyes; so taste My chastisement and My warning.
54 038	Early on the morrow an abiding Punishment seized them:	And in truth the punishment decreed befell them early in the morning.	And certainly a lasting chastisement overtook them in the morning.
54 039	"So taste ye My Wrath and My Warning."	Now taste My punishment after My warnings!	So taste My chastisement and My warning.
54 040	And We have indeed made the Qur'an easy to understand and remember: then is there any that will receive admonition?	And in truth We have made the Qur'an easy to remember; but is there any that remembereth?	And certainly We have made the Quran easy for remembrance, but is there anyone who will mind?
54 041	To the People of Pharaoh, too, aforetime, came Warners (from Allah).	And warnings came in truth unto the house of Pharaoh	And certainly the warning came to Firon's people.
54 042	The (people) rejected all Our Signs; but We seized them with such Penalty (as comes) from One Exalted in Power, able to carry out His Will.	Who denied Our revelations, every one. Therefore We grasped them with the grasp of the Mighty, the Powerful.	They rejected all Our communications, so We overtook them after the manner of a Mighty, Powerful One.
54 043	Are your Unbelievers, (O Quraish), better than they? Or have ye an immunity in the Sacred Books?	Are your disbelievers better than those, or have ye some immunity in the scriptures?	Are the unbelievers of yours better than these, or is there an exemption for you in the scriptures?
54 044	Or do they say: "We acting together can defend ourselves"?	Or say they: We are a host victorious?	Or do they say: We are a host allied together to help each other?
54 045	Soon will their multitude be put to flight, and they will show their backs.	The hosts will all be routed and will turn and flee.	Soon shall the hosts be routed, and they shall turn (their) backs.
54 046	Nay, the Hour (of Judgment) is the time promised them (for their full recompense): And that Hour will be most grievous and most bitter.	Nay, but the Hour (of doom) is their appointed tryst, and the Hour will be more wretched and more bitter (than their earthly failure).	Nay, the hour is their promised time, and the hour shall be most grievous and bitter.
54 047	Truly those in sin are the ones straying in mind, and mad.	Lo! the guilty are in error and madness.	Surely the guilty are in error and distress.
54 048	The Day they will be dragged through the Fire on their faces, (they will hear:) "Taste ye the touch of Hell!"	On the day when they are dragged into the Fire upon their faces (it is said unto them): Feel the touch of hell.	On the day when they shall be dragged upon their faces into the fire; taste the touch of hell.
54 049	Verily, all things have We created in proportion and measure.	Lo! We have created every thing by measure.	Surely We have created everything according to a measure.
54 050	And Our Command is but a single (Act),- like the twinkling of an eye.	And Our commandment is but one (commandment), as the twinkling of an eye.	And Our command is but one, as the twinkling of an eye.
54 051	And (oft) in the past, have We destroyed gangs like unto you: then is there any that will receive admonition?	And verily We have destroyed your fellows; but is there any that remembereth?	And certainly We have already destroyed the likes of you, but is there anyone who will mind?

54 052	All that they do is noted in (their) Books (of Deeds):	And every thing they did is in the scriptures,		And everything they have done is in the writings.
54 053	Every matter, small and great, is on record.	And every small and great thing is recorded.		And everything small and great is written down.
54 054	As to the Righteous, they will be in the midst of Gardens and Rivers,	Lo! the righteous will dwell among gardens and rivers,		Surely those who guard (against evil) shall be in gardens and rivers,
54 055	In an Assembly of Truth, in the Presence of a Sovereign Omnipotent.	Firmly established in the favour of a Mighty King.		In the seat of honor with a most Powerful King.

Chapter 55:

AR-RAHMAN (THE BENEFICENT, THE MERCY GIVING)

Total Verses: 78 Revealed At: MAKKA

In the name of Allah, the Most Beneficent, the Most Merciful.

55 001	(Allah) Most Gracious!	The Beneficent	The Beneficent Allah,
55 002	It is He Who has taught the Qur'an.	Hath made known the Qur'an.	Taught the Quran.
55 003	He has created man:	He hath created man.	He created man,
55 004	He has taught him speech (and intelligence).	He hath taught him utterance.	Taught him the mode of expression.
55 005	The sun and the moon follow courses (exactly) computed;	The sun and the moon are made punctual.	The sun and the moon follow a reckoning.
55 006	And the herbs and the trees - both (alike) prostrate in adoration.	The stars and the trees prostrate.	And the herbs and the trees do prostrate (to Him).
55 007	And the Firmament has He raised high, and He has set up the Balance (of Justice),	And the sky He hath uplifted; and He hath set the measure,	And the heaven, He raised it high, and He made the balance
55 008	In order that ye may not transgress (due) balance.	That ye exceed not the measure,	That you may not be inordinate in respect of the measure.
55 009	So establish weight with justice and fall not short in the balance.	But observe the measure strictly, nor fall short thereof.	And keep up the balance with equity and do not make the measure deficient.
55 010	It is He Who has spread out the earth for (His) creatures:	And the earth hath He appointed for (His) creatures,	And the earth, He has set it for living creatures;
55 011	Therein is fruit and date-palms, producing spathes (enclosing dates);	Wherein are fruit and sheathed palm-trees,	Therein is fruit and palms having sheathed clusters,
55 012	Also corn, with (its) leaves and stalk for fodder, and sweet-smelling plants.	Husked grain and scented herb.	And the grain with (its) husk and fragrance.
55 013	Then which of the favours of your Lord will ye deny?	Which is it, of the favours of your Lord, that ye deny?	Which then of the bounties of your Lord will you deny?
55 014	He created man from sounding clay like unto pottery,	He created man of clay like the potter's,	He created man from dry clay like earthen vessels,
55 015	And He created jinns from fire free of smoke:	And the jinn did He create of smokeless fire.	And He created the jinn of a flame of fire.
55 016	Then which of the favours of your Lord will ye deny?	Which is it, of the favours of your Lord, that ye deny?	Which then of the bounties of your Lord will you deny?
55 017	(He is) Lord of the two Easts and Lord of the two Wests:	Lord of the two Easts, and Lord of the two Wests!	Lord of the East and Lord of the West.

55 018	Then which of the favours of your Lord will ye deny?	Which is it, of the favours of your Lord, that ye deny?	Which then of the bounties of your Lord will you deny?
55 019	He has let free the two bodies of flowing water, meeting together:	He hath loosed the two seas. They meet.	He has made the two seas to flow freely (so that) they meet together:
55 020	Between them is a Barrier which they do not transgress:	There is a barrier between them. They encroach not (one upon the other).	Between them is a barrier which they cannot pass.
55 021	Then which of the favours of your Lord will ye deny?	Which is it, of the favours of your Lord, that ye deny?	Which then of the bounties of your Lord will you deny?
55 022	Out of them come Pearls and Coral:	There cometh forth from both of them the pearl and coral-stone.	There come forth from them pearls, both large and small.
55 023	Then which of the favours of your Lord will ye deny?	Which is it, of the favours of your Lord, that ye deny?	Which then of the bounties of your Lord will you deny?
55 024	And His are the Ships sailing smoothly through the seas, lofty as mountains:	His are the ships displayed upon the sea, like banners.	And His are the ships reared aloft in the sea like mountains.
55 025	Then which of the favours of your Lord will ye deny?	Which is it, of the favours of your Lord, that ye deny?	Which then of the bounties of your Lord will you deny?
55 026	All that is on earth will perish:	Everyone that is thereon will pass away;	Everyone on it must pass away.
55 027	But will abide (for ever) the Face of thy Lord,- full of Majesty, Bounty and Honour.	There remaineth but the Countenance of thy Lord of Might and Glory.	And there will endure for ever the person of your Lord, the Lord of glory and honor.
55 028	Then which of the favours of your Lord will ye deny?	Which is it, of the favours of your Lord, that ye deny?	Which then of the bounties of your Lord will you deny?
55 029	Of Him seeks (its need) every creature in the heavens and on earth: every day in (new) Splendour doth He (shine)!	All that are in the heavens and the earth entreat Him. Every day He exerciseth (universal) power.	All those who are in the heavens and the earth ask of Him; every moment He is in a state (of glory).
55 030	Then which of the favours of your Lord will ye deny?	Which is it, of the favours of your Lord, that ye deny?	Which then of the bounties of your Lord will you deny?
55 031	Soon shall We settle your affairs, O both ye worlds!	We shall dispose of you, O ye two dependents (man and jinn).	Soon will We apply Ourselves to you, O you two armies.
55 032	Then which of the favours of your Lord will ye deny?	Which is it, of the favours of your Lord, that ye deny?	Which then of the bounties of your Lord will you deny?
55 033	O ye assembly of jinns and men! If it be ye can pass beyond the zones of the heavens and the earth, pass ye! not without authority shall ye be able to pass!	O company of jinn and men, if ye have power to penetrate (all) regions of the heavens and the earth, then penetrate (them)! Ye will never penetrate them save with (Our) sanction.	O assembly of the jinn and the men! If you are able to pass through the regions of the heavens and the earth, then pass through; you cannot pass through but with authority.
55 034	Then which of the favours of your Lord will ye deny?	Which is it, of the favours of your Lord, that ye deny?	Which then of the bounties of your Lord will you deny?
55 035	On you will be sent (O ye evil ones twain!) a flame of fire (to burn) and a smoke (to choke): no defence will ye have:	There will be sent, against you both, heat of fire and flash of brass, and ye will not escape.	The flames of fire and smoke will be sent on you two, then you will not be able to defend yourselves.
55 036	Then which of the favours of your Lord will ye deny?	Which is it, of the favours of your Lord, that ye deny?	Which then of the bounties of your Lord will you deny?
55 037	When the sky is rent asunder, and it becomes red like ointment:	And when the heaven splitteth asunder and becometh rosy like red hide-	And when the heaven is rent asunder, and then becomes red like red hide.
55 038	Then which of the favours of your Lord will ye deny?	Which is it, of the favours of your Lord, that ye deny? -	Which then of the bounties of your Lord will you deny?
55 039	On that Day no question will be asked of man or jinn as to his sin.	On that day neither man nor jinni will be questioned of his sin.	So on that day neither man nor jinni shall be asked about his sin.
55 040	Then which of the favours of your Lord will ye deny?	Which is it, of the favours of your Lord, that ye deny?	Which then of the bounties of your Lord will you deny?

55 041	(For) the sinners will be known by their marks: and they will be seized by their forelocks and their feet.	The guilty will be known by their marks, and will be taken by the forelocks and the feet.	The guilty shall be recognized by their marks, so they shall be seized by the forelocks and the feet.
55 042	Then which of the favours of your Lord will ye deny?	Which is it, of the favours of your Lord, that ye deny?	Which then of the bounties of your Lord will you deny?
55 043	This is the Hell which the Sinners deny.	This is hell which the guilty deny.	This is the hell which the guilty called a lie.
55 044	In its midst and in the midst of boiling hot water will they wander round!	They go circling round between it and fierce, boiling water.	Round about shall they go between it and hot, boiling water.
55 045	Then which of the favours of your Lord will ye deny?	Which is it, of the favours of your Lord, that ye deny?	Which then of the bounties of your Lord will you deny?
55 046	But for such as fear the time when they will stand before (the Judgment Seat of) their Lord, there will be two Gardens-	But for him who feareth the standing before his Lord there are two gardens.	And for him who fears to stand before his Lord are two gardens.
55 047	Then which of the favours of your Lord will ye deny?-	Which is it, of the favours of your Lord, that ye deny?	Which then of the bounties of your Lord will you deny?
55 048	Containing all kinds (of trees and delights);-	Of spreading branches.	Having in them various kinds.
55 049	Then which of the favours of your Lord will ye deny?-	Which is it, of the favours of your Lord, that ye deny?	Which then of the bounties of your Lord will you deny?
55 050	In them (each) will be two Springs flowing (free);	Wherein are two fountains flowing.	In both of them are two fountains flowing.
55 051	Then which of the favours of your Lord will ye deny?-	Which is it, of the favours of your Lord, that ye deny?	Which then of the bounties of your Lord will you deny?
55 052	In them will be Fruits of every kind, two and two.	Wherein is every kind of fruit in pairs.	In both of them are two pairs of every fruit.
55 053	Then which of the favours of your Lord will ye deny?	Which is it, of the favours of your Lord, that ye deny?	Which then of the bounties of your Lord will you deny?
55 054	They will recline on Carpets, whose inner linings will be of rich brocade: the Fruit of the Gardens will be near (and easy of reach).	Reclining upon couches lined with silk brocade, the fruit of both the gardens near to hand.	Reclining on beds, the inner coverings of which are of silk brocade; and the fruits of the two gardens shall be within reach.
55 055	Then which of the favours of your Lord will ye deny?	Which is it, of the favours of your Lord, that ye deny?	Which then of the bounties of your Lord will you deny?
55 056	In them will be (Maidens), chaste, restraining their glances, whom no man or jinn before them has touched;-	Therein are those of modest gaze, whom neither man nor jinn will have touched before them.	In them shall be those who restrained their eyes; before them neither man nor jinn shall have touched them.
55 057	Then which of the favours of your Lord will ye deny?-	Which is it, of the favours of your Lord, that ye deny?	Which then of the bounties of your Lord will you deny?
55 058	Like unto Rubies and coral.	(In beauty) like the jacynth and the coral-stone.	As though they were rubies and pearls.
55 059	Then which of the favours of your Lord will ye deny?	Which is it, of the favours of your Lord, that ye deny?	Which then of the bounties of your Lord will you deny?
55 060	Is there any Reward for Good - other than Good?	Is the reward of goodness aught save goodness?	Is the reward of goodness aught but goodness?
55 061	Then which of the favours of your Lord will ye deny?	Which is it, of the favours of your Lord, that ye deny?	Which then of the bounties of your Lord will you deny?
55 062	And besides these two, there are two other Gardens,-	And beside them are two other gardens,	And besides these two are two (other) gardens:
55 063	Then which of the favours of your Lord will ye deny?-	Which is it, of the favours of your Lord, that ye deny?	Which then of the bounties of your Lord will you deny?
55 064	Dark-green in colour (from plentiful watering).	Dark green with foliage.	Both inclining to blackness.
55 065	Then which of the favours of your Lord will ye deny?	Which is it, of the favours of your Lord, that ye deny?	Which then of the bounties of your Lord will you deny?

55 066	In them (each) will be two Springs pouring forth water in continuous abundance:	Wherein are two abundant springs.	In both of them are two springs gushing forth.
55 067	Then which of the favours of your Lord will ye deny?	Which is it, of the favours of your Lord, that ye deny?	Which then of the bounties of your Lord will you deny?
55 068	In them will be Fruits, and dates and pomegranates:	Wherein is fruit, the date-palm and pomegranate.	In both are fruits and palms and pomegranates.
55 069	Then which of the favours of your Lord will ye deny?	Which is it, of the favours of your Lord, that ye deny?	Which then of the bounties of your Lord will you deny?
55 070	In them will be fair (Companions), good, beautiful:-	Wherein (are found) the good and beautiful companions-	In them are goodly things, beautiful ones.
55 071	Then which of the favours of your Lord will ye deny?-	Which is it, of the favours of your Lord, that ye deny? -	Which then of the bounties of your Lord will you deny?
55 072	Companions restrained (as to their glances), in (goodly) pavilions;-	Fair ones, close-guarded in pavilions -	Pure ones confined to the pavilions.
55 073	Then which of the favours of your Lord will ye deny?-	Which is it, of the favours of your Lord, that ye deny? -	Which then of the bounties of your Lord will you deny?
55 074	Whom no man or jinn before them has touched;-	Whom neither man nor jinn will have touched before them -	Man has not touched them before them nor jinn.
55 075	Then which of the favours of your Lord will ye deny?-	Which is it, of the favours of your Lord, that ye deny?	Which then of the bounties of your Lord will you deny?
55 076	Reclining on green Cushions and rich Carpets of beauty.	Reclining on green cushions and fair carpets.	Reclining on green cushions and beautiful carpets.
55 077	Then which of the favours of your Lord will ye deny?	Which is it, of the favours of your Lord, that ye deny?	Which then of the bounties of your Lord will you deny?
55 078	Blessed be the name of thy Lord, full of Majesty, Bounty and Honour.	Blessed be the name of thy Lord, Mighty and glorious!	Blessed be the name of your Lord, the Lord of Glory and Honor!

Chapter 56:

AL-WAQIA (THE EVENT, THE INEVITABLE)

Total Verses: 96 Revealed At: MAKKA

In the name of Allah, the Most Beneficent, the Most Merciful.

56 001	When the Event inevitable cometh to pass,	When the event befalleth -	When the great event comes to pass,
56 002	Then will no (soul) entertain falsehood concerning its coming.	There is no denying that it will befall -	There is no belying its coming to pass--
56 003	(Many) will it bring low; (many) will it exalt;	Abasing (some), exalting (others);	Abasing (one party), exalting (the other),
56 004	When the earth shall be shaken to its depths,	When the earth is shaken with a shock	When the earth shall be shaken with a (severe) shaking,
56 005	And the mountains shall be crumbled to atoms,	And the hills are ground to powder	And the mountains shall be made to crumble with (an awful) crumbling,
56 006	Becoming dust scattered abroad,	So that they become a scattered dust,	So that they shall be as scattered dust.
56 007	And ye shall be sorted out into three classes.	And ye will be three kinds:	And you shall be three sorts.
56 008	Then (there will be) the Companions of the Right Hand;- What will be the Companions of the Right Hand?	(First) those on the right hand; what of those on the right hand?	Then (as to) the companions of the right hand; how happy are the companions of the right hand!

56 009	And the Companions of the Left Hand,- what will be the Companions of the Left Hand?	And (then) those on the left hand; what of those on the left hand?	And (as to) the companions of the left hand; how wretched are the companions of the left hand!
56 010	And those Foremost (in Faith) will be Foremost (in the Hereafter).	And the foremost in the race, the foremost in the race:	And the foremost are the foremost,
56 011	These will be those Nearest to Allah:	Those are they who will be brought nigh	These are they who are drawn nigh (to Allah),
56 012	In Gardens of Bliss:	In gardens of delight;	In the gardens of bliss.
56 013	A number of people from those of old,	A multitude of those of old	A numerous company from among the first,
56 014	And a few from those of later times.	And a few of those of later time.	And a few from among the latter.
56 015	(They will be) on Thrones encrusted (with gold and precious stones),	On lined couches,	On thrones decorated,
56 016	Reclining on them, facing each other.	Reclining therein face to face.	Reclining on them, facing one another.
56 017	Round about them will (serve) youths of perpetual (freshness),	There wait on them immortal youths	Round about them shall go youths never altering in age,
56 018	With goblets, (shining) beakers, and cups (filled) out of clear-flowing fountains:	With bowls and ewers and a cup from a pure spring	With goblets and ewers and a cup of pure drink;
56 019	No after-ache will they receive therefrom, nor will they suffer intoxication:	Wherefrom they get no aching of the head nor any madness,	They shall not be affected with headache thereby, nor shall they get exhausted,
56 020	And with fruits, any that they may select:	And fruit that they prefer	And fruits such as they choose,
56 021	And the flesh of fowls, any that they may desire.	And flesh of fowls that they desire.	And the flesh of fowl such as they desire.
56 022	And (there will be) Companions with beautiful, big, and lustrous eyes,-	And (there are) fair ones with wide, lovely eyes,	And pure, beautiful ones,
56 023	Like unto Pearls well-guarded.	Like unto hidden pearls,	The like of the hidden pearls:
56 024	A Reward for the deeds of their past (life).	Reward for what they used to do.	A reward for what they used to do.
56 025	Not frivolity will they hear therein, nor any taint of ill,-	There hear they no vain speaking nor recrimination	They shall not hear therein vain or sinful discourse,
5 026	Only the saying, "Peace! Peace".	(Naught) but the saying: Peace, (and again) Peace.	Except the word peace, peace.
56 027	The Companions of the Right Hand,- what will be the Companions of the Right Hand?	And those on the right hand; what of those on the right hand?	And the companions of the right hand; how happy are the companions of the right hand!
56 028	(They will be) among Lote-trees without thorns,	Among thornless lote-trees	Amid thornless lote-trees,
56 029	Among Talh trees with flowers (or fruits) piled one above another,-	And clustered plantains,	And banana-trees (with fruits), one above another.
56 030	In shade long-extended,	And spreading shade,	And extended shade,
56 031	By water flowing constantly,	And water gushing,	And water flowing constantly,
56 032	And fruit in abundance.	And fruit in plenty	And abundant fruit,
56 033	Whose season is not limited, nor (supply) forbidden,	Neither out of reach nor yet forbidden,	Neither intercepted nor forbidden,
56 034	And on Thrones (of Dignity), raised high.	And raised couches;	And exalted thrones.
56 035	We have created (their Companions) of special creation.	Lo! We have created them a (new) creation	Surely We have made them to grow into a (new) growth,

56 036	And made them virgin - pure (and undefiled), -	And made them virgins,		Then We have made them virgins,
56 037	Beloved (by nature), equal in age,-	Lovers, friends,		Loving, equals in age,
56 038	For the Companions of the Right Hand.	For those on the right hand;		For the sake of the companions of the right hand.
56 039	A (goodly) number from those of old,	A multitude of those of old		A numerous company from among the first,
56 040	And a (goodly) number from those of later times.	And a multitude of those of later time.		And a numerous company from among the last.
56 041	The Companions of the Left Hand,- what will be the Companions of the Left Hand?	And those on the left hand: What of those on the left hand?		And those of the left hand, how wretched are those of the left hand!
56 042	(They will be) in the midst of a Fierce Blast of Fire and in Boiling Water,	In scorching wind and scalding water		In hot wind and boiling water,
56 043	And in the shades of Black Smoke:	And shadow of black smoke,		And the shade of black smoke,
56 044	Nothing (will there be) to refresh, nor to please:	Neither cool nor refreshing.		Neither cool nor honorable.
56 045	For that they were wont to be indulged, before that, in wealth (and luxury),	Lo! heretofore they were effete with luxury		Surely they were before that made to live in ease and plenty.
56 046	And persisted obstinately in wickedness supreme!	And used to persist in the awful sin.		And they persisted in the great violation.
56 047	And they used to say, "What! when we die and become dust and bones, shall we then indeed be raised up again?"-	And they used to say: When we are dead and have become dust and bones, shall we then, forsooth, be raised again,		And they used to say: What! when we die and have become dust and bones, shall we then indeed be raised?
56 048	"(We) and our fathers of old?"	And also our forefathers?		Or our fathers of yore?
56 049	Say: "Yea, those of old and those of later times,"	Say (unto them, O Muhammad): Lo! those of old and those of later time		Say: The first and the last,
56 050	"All will certainly be gathered together for the meeting appointed for a Day well-known."	Will all be brought together to the tryst of an appointed day.		Shall most surely be gathered together for the appointed hour of a known day.
56 051	"Then will ye truly,- O ye that go wrong, and treat (Truth) as Falsehood!"-	Then lo! ye, the erring, the deniers,		Then shall you, O you who err and call it a lie!
56 052	"Ye will surely taste of the Tree of Zaqqum."	Ye verily will eat of a tree called Zaqqum		Most surely eat of a tree of Zaqqoom,
56 053	"Then will ye fill your insides therewith,"	And will fill your bellies therewith;		And fill (your) bellies with it;
56 054	"And drink Boiling Water on top of it:"	And thereon ye will drink of boiling water,		Then drink over it of boiling water;
56 055	"Indeed ye shall drink like diseased camels raging with thirst!"	Drinking even as the camel drinketh.		And drink as drinks the thirsty camel.
56 056	Such will be their entertainment on the Day of Requital!	This will be their welcome on the Day of Judgment.		This is their entertainment on the day of requital.
56 057	It is We Who have created you: why will ye not witness the Truth?	We created you. Will ye then admit the truth?		We have created you, why do you not then assent?
56 058	Do ye then see?- The (human Seed) that ye throw out,-	Have ye seen that which ye emit?		Have you considered the seed?
56 059	Is it ye who create it, or are We the Creators?	Do ye create it or are We the Creator?		Is it you that create it or are We the creators?
56 060	We have decreed Death to be your common lot, and We are not to be frustrated	We mete out death among you, and We are not to be outrun,		We have ordained death among you and We are not to be overcome,

56 061	From changing your Forms and creating you (again) in (forms) that ye know not.	That We may transfigure you and make you what ye know not.	In order that We may bring in your place the likes of you and make you grow into what you know not.
56 062	And ye certainly know already the first form of creation: why then do ye not celebrate His praises?	And verily ye know the first creation. Why, then, do ye not reflect?	And certainly you know the first growth, why do you not then mind?
56 063	See ye the seed that ye sow in the ground?	Have ye seen that which ye cultivate?	Have you considered what you sow?
56 064	Is it ye that cause it to grow, or are We the Cause?	Is it ye who foster it, or are We the Fosterer?	Is it you that cause it to grow, or are We the causers of growth?
56 065	Were it Our Will, We could crumble it to dry powder, and ye would be left in wonderment,	If We willed, We verily could make it chaff, then would ye cease not to exclaim:	If We pleased, We should have certainly made it broken down into pieces, then would you begin to lament:
56 066	(Saying), "We are indeed left with debts (for nothing):"	Lo! we are laden with debt!	Surely we are burdened with debt:
56 067	"Indeed are we shut out (of the fruits of our labour)"	Nay, but we are deprived!	Nay! we are deprived.
56 068	See ye the water which ye drink?	Have ye observed the water which ye drink?	Have you considered the water which you drink?
56 069	Do ye bring it down (in rain) from the cloud or do We?	Is it ye who shed it from the raincloud, or are We the Shedder?	Is it you that send it down from the clouds, or are We the senders?
56 070	Were it Our Will, We could make it salt (and unpalatable): then why do ye not give thanks?	If We willed We verily could make it bitter. Why then, give ye not thanks?	If We pleased, We would have made it salty; why do you not then give thanks?
56 071	See ye the Fire which ye kindle?	Have ye observed the fire which ye strike out;	Have you considered the fire which you strike?
56 072	Is it ye who grow the tree which feeds the fire, or do We grow it?	Was it ye who made the tree thereof to grow, or were We the grower?	Is it you that produce the trees for it, or are We the producers?
56 073	We have made it a memorial (of Our handiwork), and an article of comfort and convenience for the denizens of deserts.	We, even We, appointed it a memorial and a comfort for the dwellers in the wilderness.	We have made it a reminder and an advantage for the wayfarers of the desert.
56 074	Then celebrate with praises the name of thy Lord, the Supreme!	Therefor (O Muhammad), praise the name of thy Lord, the Tremendous.	Therefore glorify the name of your Lord, the Great.
56 075	Furthermore I call to witness the setting of the Stars,-	Nay, I swear by the places of the stars -	But nay! I swear by the falling of stars;
56 076	And that is indeed a mighty adjuration if ye but knew,-	And lo! that verily is a tremendous oath, if ye but knew -	And most surely it is a very great oath if you only knew;
56 077	That this is indeed a Qur'an Most Honourable,	That (this) is indeed a noble Qur'an	Most surely it is an honored Quran,
56 078	In Book well-guarded,	In a Book kept hidden	In a book that is protected
56 079	Which none shall touch but those who are clean:	Which none toucheth save the purified,	None shall touch it save the purified ones.
56 080	A Revelation from the Lord of the Worlds.	A revelation from the Lord of the Worlds.	A revelation by the Lord of the worlds.
56 081	Is it such a Message that ye would hold in light esteem?	Is it this Statement that ye scorn,	Do you then hold this announcement in contempt?
56 082	And have ye made it your livelihood that ye should declare it false?	And make denial thereof your livelihood?	And to give (it) the lie you make your means of subsistence.
56 083	Then why do ye not (intervene) when (the soul of the dying man) reaches the throat,-	Why, then, when (the soul) cometh up to the throat (of the dying)	Why is it not then that when it (soul) comes up to the throat,
56 084	And ye the while (sit) looking on,-	And ye are at that moment looking	And you at that time look on--

56 085	But We are nearer to him than ye, and yet see not,-	And We are nearer unto him than ye are, but ye see not-		And We are nearer to it than you, but you do not see-
56 086	Then why do ye not,- If you are exempt from (future) account,-	Why then, if ye are not in bondage (unto Us),		Then why is it not-- if you are not held under authority--
56 087	Call back the soul, if ye are true (in the claim of independence)?	Do ye not force it back, if ye are truthful?		That you send it (not) back-- if you are truthful?
56 088	Thus, then, if he be of those Nearest to Allah,	Thus if he is of those brought nigh,		Then if he is one of those drawn nigh (to Allah),
56 089	(There is for him) Rest and Satisfaction, and a Garden of Delights.	Then breath of life, and plenty, and a Garden of delight.		Then happiness and bounty and a garden of bliss.
56 090	And if he be of the Companions of the Right Hand,	And if he is of those on the right hand,		And if he is one of those on the right hand,
56 091	(For him is the salutation), "Peace be unto thee", from the Companions of the Right Hand.	Then (the greeting) "Peace be unto thee" from those on the right hand.		Then peace to you from those on the right hand.
56 092	And if he be of those who treat (Truth) as Falsehood, who go wrong,	But if he is of the rejecters, the erring,		And if he is one of the rejecters, the erring ones,
56 093	For him is Entertainment with Boiling Water.	Then the welcome will be boiling water		He shall have an entertainment of boiling water,
56 094	And burning in Hell-Fire.	And roasting at hell-fire.		And burning in hell.
56 095	Verily, this is the Very Truth and Certainly.	Lo! this is certain truth.		Most surely this is a certain truth.
56 096	So celebrate with praises the name of thy Lord, the Supreme.	Therefor (O Muhammad) praise the name of thy Lord, the Tremendous.		Therefore glorify the name of your Lord, the Great.

Chapter 57:

AL-HADID (THE IRON)

Total Verses: 29 Revealed At: MADINA

In the name of Allah, the Most Beneficent, the Most Merciful.

57 001	Whatever is in the heavens and on earth,- let it declare the Praises and Glory of Allah: for He is the Exalted in Might, the Wise.	All that is in the heavens and the earth glorifieth Allah; and He is the Mighty, the Wise.		Whatever is in the heavens and the earth declares the glory of Allah, and He is the Mighty, the Wise.
57 002	To Him belongs the dominion of the heavens and the earth: It is He Who gives Life and Death; and He has Power over all things.	His is the Sovereignty of the heavens and the earth; He quickeneth and He giveth death; and He is Able to do all things.		His is the kingdom of the heavens and the earth; He gives life and causes death; and He has power over all things.
57 003	He is the First and the Last, the Evident and the Immanent: and He has full knowledge of all things.	He is the First and the Last, and the Outward and the Inward; and He is Knower of all things.		He is the First and the Last and the Ascendant (over all) and the Knower of hidden things, and He is Cognizant of all things.

57 004	He it is Who created the heavens and the earth in Six Days, and is moreover firmly established on the Throne (of Authority). He knows what enters within the earth and what comes forth out of it, what comes down from heaven and what mounts up to it. And He is with you wheresoever ye may be. And Allah sees well all that ye do.	He it is Who created the heavens and the earth in six Days; then He mounted the Throne. He knoweth all that entereth the earth and all that emergeth therefrom and all that cometh down from the sky and all that ascendeth therein; and He is with you wheresoever ye may be. And Allah is Seer of what ye do.	He it is who created the heavens and the earth in six periods, and He is firm in power; He knows that which goes deep down into the earth and that which comes forth out of it, and that which comes down from the heaven and that which goes up into it, and He is with you wherever you are; and Allah sees what you do.
57 005	To Him belongs the dominion of the heavens and the earth: and all affairs are referred back to Allah.	His is the Sovereignty of the heavens and the earth, and unto Allah (all) things are brought back.	His is the kingdom of the heavens and the earth; and to Allah are (all) affairs returned.
57 006	He merges Night into Day, and He merges Day into Night; and He has full knowledge of the secrets of (all) hearts.	He causeth the night to pass into the day, and He causeth the day to pass into the night, and He is knower of all that is in the breasts.	He causes the night to enter in upon the day, and causes the day to enter in upon the night, and He is Cognizant of what is in the hearts.
57 007	Believe in Allah and His messenger, and spend (in charity) out of the (substance) whereof He has made you heirs. For, those of you who believe and spend (in charity),- for them is a great Reward.	Believe in Allah and His messenger, and spend of that whereof He hath made you trustees; and such of you as believe and spend (aright), theirs will be a great reward.	Believe in Allah and His Messenger, and spend out of what He has made you to be successors of; for those of you who believe and spend shall have a great reward.
57 008	What cause have ye why ye should not believe in Allah?- and the Messenger invites you to believe in your Lord, and has indeed taken your Covenant, if ye are men of Faith.	What aileth you that ye believe not in Allah, when the messenger calleth you to believe in your Lord, and He hath already made a covenant with you, if ye are believers?	And what reason have you that you should not believe in Allah? And the Messenger calls on you that you may believe in your Lord, and indeed He has made a covenant with you if you are believers.
57 009	He is the One Who sends to His Servant Manifest Signs, that He may lead you from the depths of Darkness into the Light and verily Allah is to you most Kind and Merciful.	He it is Who sendeth down clear revelations unto His slave, that He may bring you forth from darkness unto light; and lo! for you, Allah is Full of Pity, Merciful.	He it is who sends down clear communications upon His servant, that he may bring you forth from utter darkness into light; and most surely Allah is Kind, Merciful to you.
57 010	And what cause have ye why ye should not spend in the cause of Allah?- For to Allah belongs the heritage of the heavens and the earth. Not equal among you are those who spent (freely) and fought, before the Victory, (with those who did so later). Those are higher in rank than those who spent (freely) and fought afterwards. But to all has Allah promised a goodly (reward). And Allah is well acquainted with all that ye do.	And what aileth you that ye spend not in the way of Allah when unto Allah belongeth the inheritance of the heavens and the earth? Those who spent and fought before the victory are not upon a level (with the rest of you). Such are greater in rank than those who spent and fought afterwards. Unto each hath Allah promised good. And Allah is Informed of what ye do.	And what reason have you that you should not spend in Allah's way? And Allah's is the inheritance of the heavens and the earth, not alike among you are those who spent before the victory and fought (and those who did not): they are more exalted in rank than those who spent and fought afterwards; and Allah has promised good to all; and Allah is Aware of what you do.
57 011	Who is he that will Loan to Allah a beautiful loan? for (Allah) will increase it manifold to his credit, and he will have (besides) a liberal Reward.	Who is he that will lend unto Allah a goodly loan, that He may double it for him and his may be a rich reward?	Who is there that will offer to Allah a good gift so He will double it for him, and he shall have an excellent reward.

57 012	One Day shalt thou see the believing men and the believing women- how their Light runs forward before them and by their right hands: (their greeting will be): "Good News for you this Day! Gardens beneath which flow rivers! to dwell therein for aye! This is indeed the highest Achievement!"	On the day when thou (Muhammad) wilt see the believers, men and women, their light shining forth before them and on their right hands, (and wilt hear it said unto them): Glad news for you this day: Gardens underneath which rivers flow, wherein ye are immortal. That is the supreme triumph.	On that day you will see the faithful men and the faithful women-- their light running before them and on their right hand-- good news for you today: gardens beneath which rivers flow, to abide therein, that is the grand achievement.
57 013	One Day will the Hypocrites- men and women - say to the Believers: Wait for us! Let us borrow (a Light) from your Light! It will be said: Turn ye back to your rear! then seek a Light (where ye can)! So a wall will be put up betwixt them, with a gate therein. Within it will be Mercy throughout, and without it, all alongside, will be (Wrath and) Punishment!	On the day when the hypocritical men and the hypocritical women will say unto those who believe: Look on us that we may borrow from your light! it will be said: Go back and seek for light! Then there will separate them a wall wherein is a gate, the inner side whereof containeth mercy, while the outer side thereof is toward the doom.	On the day when the hypocritical men and the hypocritical women will say to those who believe: Wait for us, that we may have light from your light; it shall be said: Turn back and seek a light. Then separation would be brought about between them, with a wall having a door in it; (as for) the inside of it, there shall be mercy in it, and (as for) the outside of it, before it there shall be punishment.
57 014	(Those without) will call out, "Were we not with you?" (The others) will reply, "True! but ye led yourselves into temptation; ye looked forward (to our ruin); ye doubted (Allah's Promise); and (your false) desires deceived you; until there issued the Command of Allah. And the Deceiver deceived you in respect of Allah."	They will cry unto them (saying): Were we not with you? They will say: Yea, verily; but ye tempted one another, and hesitated, and doubted, and vain desires beguiled you till the ordinance of Allah came to pass; and the deceiver deceived you concerning Allah;	They will cry out to them: Were we not with you? They shall say: Yea! but you caused yourselves to fall into temptation, and you waited and doubted, and vain desires deceived you till the threatened punishment of Allah came, while the archdeceiver deceived you about Allah.
57 015	"This Day shall no ransom be accepted of you, nor of those who rejected Allah. Your abode is the Fire: that is the proper place to claim you: and an evil refuge it is!"	So this day no ransom can be taken from you nor from those who disbelieved. Your home is the Fire; that is your patron, and a hapless journey's end.	So today ransom shall not be accepted from you nor from those who disbelieved; your abode is the fire; it is your friend and evil is the resort.
57 016	Has not the time arrived for the Believers that their hearts in all humility should engage in the remembrance of Allah and of the Truth which has been revealed (to them), and that they should not become like those to whom was given Revelation aforetime, but long ages passed over them and their hearts grew hard? For many among them are rebellious transgressors.	Is not the time ripe for the hearts of those who believe to submit to Allah's reminder and to the truth which is revealed, that they become not as those who received the scripture of old but the term was prolonged for them and so their hearts were hardened, and many of them are evil-livers.	Has not the time yet come for those who believe that their hearts should be humble for the remembrance of Allah and what has come down of the truth? And (that) they should not be like those who were given the Book before, but the time became prolonged to them, so their hearts hardened, and most of them are transgressors.
57 017	Know ye (all) that Allah giveth life to the earth after its death! already have We shown the Signs plainly to you, that ye may learn wisdom.	Know that Allah quickeneth the earth after its death. We have made clear Our revelations for you, that haply ye may understand.	Know that Allah gives life to the earth after its death; indeed, We have made the communications clear to you that you may understand.
57 018	For those who give in Charity, men and women, and loan to Allah a Beautiful Loan, it shall be increased manifold (to their credit), and they shall have (besides) a liberal reward.	Lo! those who give alms, both men and women, and lend unto Allah a goodly loan, it will be doubled for them, and theirs will be a rich reward.	Surely (as for) the charitable men and the charitable women and (those who) set apart for Allah a goodly portion, it shall be doubled for them and they shall have a noble reward.

57 019	And those who believe in Allah and His messengers- they are the Sincere (lovers of Truth), and the witnesses (who testify), in the eyes of their Lord: They shall have their Reward and their Light. But those who reject Allah and deny Our Signs,- they are the Companions of Hell-Fire.	And those who believe in Allah and His messengers, they are the loyal, and the martyrs are with their Lord; they have their reward and their light; while as for those who disbelieve and deny Our revelations, they are owners of hell-fire.	And (as for) those who believe in Allah and His messengers, these it is that are the truthful and the faithful ones in the sight of their Lord: they shall have their reward and their light, and (as for) those who disbelieve and reject Our communications, these are the inmates of the hell.
57 020	Know ye (all), that the life of this world is but play and amusement, pomp and mutual boasting and multiplying, (in rivalry) among yourselves, riches and children. Here is a similitude: How rain and the growth which it brings forth, delight (the hearts of) the tillers; soon it withers; thou wilt see it grow yellow; then it becomes dry and crumbles away. But in the Hereafter is a Penalty severe (for the devotees of wrong). And Forgiveness from Allah and (His) Good Pleasure (for the devotees of Allah). And what is the life of this world, but goods and chattels of deception?	Know that the life of the world is only play, and idle talk, and pageantry, and boasting among you, and rivalry in respect of wealth and children; as the likeness of vegetation after rain, whereof the growth is pleasing to the husbandman, but afterward it drieth up and thou seest it turning yellow, then it becometh straw. And in the Hereafter there is grievous punishment, and (also) forgiveness from Allah and His good pleasure, whereas the life of the world is but matter of illusion.	Know that this world's life is only sport and play and gaiety and boasting among yourselves, and a vying in the multiplication of wealth and children, like the rain, whose causing the vegetation to grow, pleases the husbandmen, then it withers away so that you will see it become yellow, then it becomes dried up and broken down; and in the hereafter is a severe chastisement and (also) forgiveness from Allah and (His) pleasure; and this world's life is naught but means of deception.
57 021	Be ye foremost (in seeking) Forgiveness from your Lord, and a Garden (of Bliss), the width whereof is as the width of heaven and earth, prepared for those who believe in Allah and His messengers: that is the Grace of Allah, which He bestows on whom he pleases: and Allah is the Lord of Grace abounding.	Race one with another for forgiveness from your Lord and a Garden whereof the breadth is as the breadth of the heavens and the earth, which is in store for those who believe in Allah and His messengers. Such is the bounty of Allah, which He bestoweth upon whom He will, and Allah is of Infinite Bounty.	Hasten to forgiveness from your Lord and to a garden the extensiveness of which is as the extensiveness of the heaven and the earth; it is prepared for those who believe in Allah and His messengers; that is the grace of Allah: He gives it to whom He pleases, and Allah is the Lord of mighty grace.
57 022	No misfortune can happen on earth or in your souls but is recorded in a decree before We bring it into existence: That is truly easy for Allah:	Naught of disaster befalleth in the earth or in yourselves but it is in a Book before we bring it into being - Lo! that is easy for Allah -	No evil befalls on the earth nor in your own souls, but it is in a book before We bring it into existence; surely that is easy to Allah:
57 023	In order that ye may not despair over matters that pass you by, nor exult over favours bestowed upon you. For Allah loveth not any vainglorious boaster,-	That ye grieve not for the sake of that which hath escaped you, nor yet exult because of that which hath been given. Allah loveth not all prideful boasters,	So that you may not grieve for what has escaped you, nor be exultant at what He has given you; and Allah does not love any arrogant boaster:
57 024	Such persons as are covetous and commend covetousness to men. And if any turn back (from Allah's Way), verily Allah is Free of all Needs, Worthy of all Praise.	Who hoard and who enjoin upon the people avarice. And whosoever turneth away, still Allah is the Absolute, the Owner of Praise.	Those who are niggardly and enjoin niggardliness on men; and whoever turns back, then surely Allah is He Who is the Self-sufficient, the Praised.

57 025	We sent aforetime our messengers with Clear Signs and sent down with them the Book and the Balance (of Right and Wrong), that men may stand forth in justice; and We sent down Iron, in which is (material for) mighty war, as well as many benefits for mankind, that Allah may test who it is that will help, Unseen, Him and His messengers: For Allah is Full of Strength, Exalted in Might (and able to enforce His Will).	We verily sent Our messengers with clear proofs, and revealed with them the Scripture and the Balance, that mankind may observe right measure; and He revealed iron, wherein is mighty power and (many) uses for mankind, and that Allah may know him who helpeth Him and His messengers, though unseen. Lo! Allah is Strong, Almighty.	Certainly We sent Our messengers with clear arguments, and sent down with them the Book and the balance that men may conduct themselves with equity; and We have made the iron, wherein is great violence and advantages to men, and that Allah may know who helps Him and His messengers in the secret; surely Allah is Strong, Mighty.
57 026	And We sent Noah and Abraham, and established in their line Prophethood and Revelation: and some of them were on right guidance. But many of them became rebellious transgressors.	And We verily sent Noah and Abraham and placed the Prophethood and the Scripture among their seed, and among them there is he who goeth right, but many of them are evil-livers.	And certainly We sent Nuh and Ibrahim and We gave to their offspring the (gift of) prophecy and the Book; so there are among them those who go aright, and most of them are transgressors.
57 027	Then, in their wake, We followed them up with (others of) Our messengers: We sent after them Jesus the son of Mary, and bestowed on him the Gospel; and We ordained in the hearts of those who followed him Compassion and Mercy. But the Monasticism which they invented for themselves, We did not prescribe for them: (We commanded) only the seeking for the Good Pleasure of Allah; but that they did not foster as they should have done. Yet We bestowed, on those among them who believed, their (due) reward, but many of them are rebellious transgressors.	Then We caused Our messengers to follow in their footsteps; and We caused Jesus, son of Mary, to follow, and gave him the Gospel, and placed compassion and mercy in the hearts of those who followed him. But monasticism they invented - We ordained it not for them - only seeking Allah's pleasure, and they observed it not with right observance. So We give those of them who believe their reward, but many of them are evil-livers.	Then We made Our messengers to follow in their footsteps, and We sent Isa son of Marium afterwards, and We gave him the Injeel, and We put in the hearts of those who followed him kindness and mercy; and (as for) monkery, they innovated it-- We did not prescribe it to them-- only to seek Allah's pleasure, but they did not observe it with its due observance; so We gave to those of them who believed their reward, and most of them are transgressors.
57 028	O ye that believe! Fear Allah, and believe in His Messenger, and He will bestow on you a double portion of His Mercy: He will provide for you a Light by which ye shall walk (straight in your path), and He will forgive you (your past): for Allah is Oft-Forgiving, Most Merciful.	O ye who believe! Be mindful of your duty to Allah and put faith in His messenger. He will give you twofold of His mercy and will appoint for you a light wherein ye shall walk, and will forgive you. Allah is Forgiving, Merciful;	O you who believe! be careful of (your duty to) Allah and believe in His Messenger: He will give you two portions of His mercy, and make for you a light with which you will walk, and forgive you, and Allah is Forgiving, Merciful;
57 029	That the People of the Book may know that they have no power whatever over the Grace of Allah, that (His) Grace is (entirely) in His Hand, to bestow it on whomsoever He wills. For Allah is the Lord of Grace abounding.	That the People of the Scripture may know that they control naught of the bounty of Allah, but that the bounty is in Allah's hand to give to whom He will. And Allah is of Infinite Bounty.	So that the followers of the Book may know that they do not control aught of the grace of Allah, and that grace is in Allah's hand, He gives it to whom He pleases; and Allah is the Lord of mighty grace.

Chapter 58:

AL-MUJADILA (SHE THAT DISPUTETH, THE PLEADING WOMAN)

Total Verses: 22 Revealed At: MADINA

In the name of Allah, the Most Beneficent, the Most Merciful.

58 001	Allah has indeed heard (and accepted) the statement of the woman who pleads with thee concerning her husband and carries her complaint (in prayer) to Allah: and Allah (always) hears the arguments between both sides among you: for Allah hears and sees (all things).	Allah hath heard the saying of her that disputeth with thee (Muhammad) concerning her husband, and complaineth unto Allah. And Allah heareth your colloquy. Lo! Allah is Hearer, Knower.	Allah indeed knows the plea of her who pleads with you about her husband and complains to Allah, and Allah knows the contentions of both of you; surely Allah is Hearing, Seeing.
58 002	If any men among you divorce their wives by Zihar (calling them mothers), they cannot be their mothers: None can be their mothers except those who gave them birth. And in fact they use words (both) iniquitous and false: but truly Allah is one that blots out (sins), and forgives (again and again).	Such of you as put away your wives (by saying they are as their mothers) - They are not their mothers; none are their mothers except those who gave them birth - they indeed utter an ill word and a lie. And lo! Allah is Forgiving, Merciful.	(As for) those of you who put away their wives by likening their backs to the backs of their mothers, they are not their mothers; their mothers are no others than those who gave them birth; and most surely they utter a hateful word and a falsehood and most surely Allah is Pardoning, Forgiving.
58 003	But those who divorce their wives by Zihar, then wish to go back on the words they uttered,- (It is ordained that such a one) should free a slave before they touch each other: Thus are ye admonished to perform: and Allah is well acquainted with (all) that ye do.	Those who put away their wives (by saying they are as their mothers) and afterward would go back on that which they have said, (the penalty) in that case (is) the freeing of a slave before they touch one another. Unto this ye are exhorted; and Allah is Informed of what ye do.	And (as for) those who put away their wives by likening their backs to the backs of their mothers then would recall what they said, they should free a captive before they touch each other; to that you are admonished (to conform); and Allah is Aware of what you do.
58 004	And if any has not (the wherewithal), he should fast for two months consecutively before they touch each other. But if any is unable to do so, he should feed sixty indigent ones, this, that ye may show your faith in Allah and His Messenger. Those are limits (set by) Allah. For those who reject (Him), there is a grievous Penalty.	And he who findeth not (the wherewithal), let him fast for two successive months before they touch one another; and for him who is unable to do so (the penance is) the feeding of sixty needy ones. This, that ye may put trust in Allah and His Messenger. Such are the limits (imposed by Allah); and for disbelievers is a painful doom.	But whoever has not the means, let him fast for two months successively before they touch each other; then as for him who is not able, let him feed sixty needy ones; that is in order that you may have faith in Allah and His Messenger, and these are Allah's limits, and the unbelievers shall have a painful punishment.
58 005	Those who resist Allah and His Messenger will be humbled to dust, as were those before them: for We have already sent down Clear Signs. And the Unbelievers (will have) a humiliating Penalty,-	Lo! those who oppose Allah and His messenger will be abased even as those before them were abased; and We have sent down clear tokens, and for disbelievers is a shameful doom	Surely those who act in opposition to Allah and His Messenger shall be laid down prostrate as those before them were laid down prostrate; and indeed We have revealed clear communications, and the unbelievers shall have an abasing chastisement.

58 006	On the Day that Allah will raise them all up (again) and show them the Truth (and meaning) of their conduct. Allah has reckoned its (value), though they may have forgotten it, for Allah is Witness to all things.	On the day when Allah will raise them all together and inform them of what they did. Allah hath kept account of it while they forgot it. And Allah is Witness over all things.	On the day when Allah will raise them up all together, then inform them of what they did: Allah has recorded it while they have forgotten it; and Allah is a witness of all things.
58 007	Seest thou not that Allah doth know (all) that is in the heavens and on earth? There is not a secret consultation between three, but He makes the fourth among them, - Nor between five but He makes the sixth,- nor between fewer nor more, but He is in their midst, wheresoever they be: In the end will He tell them the truth of their conduct, on the Day of Judgment. For Allah has full knowledge of all things.	Hast thou not seen that Allah knoweth all that is in the heavens and all that is in the earth? There is no secret conference of three but He is their fourth, nor of five but He is their sixth, nor of less than that or more but He is with them wheresoever they may be; and afterward, on the Day of Resurrection, He will inform them of what they did. Lo! Allah is Knower of all things.	Do you not see that Allah knows whatever is in the heavens and whatever is in the earth? Nowhere is there a secret counsel between three persons but He is the fourth of them, nor (between) five but He is the sixth of them, nor less than that nor more but He is with them wheresoever they are; then He will inform them of what they did on the day of resurrection: surely Allah is Cognizant of all things.
58 008	Turnest thou not thy sight towards those who were forbidden secret counsels yet revert to that which they were forbidden (to do)? And they hold secret counsels among themselves for iniquity and hostility, and disobedience to the Messenger. And when they come to thee, they salute thee, not as Allah salutes thee, (but in crooked ways): And they say to themselves, "Why does not Allah punish us for our words?" Enough for them is Hell: In it will they burn, and evil is that destination!	Hast thou not observed those who were forbidden conspiracy and afterward returned to that which they had been forbidden, and (now) conspire together for crime and wrongdoing and disobedience toward the messenger? And when they come unto thee they greet thee with a greeting wherewith Allah greeteth thee not, and say within themselves: Why should Allah punish us for what we say? Hell will suffice them; they will feel the heat thereof - a hapless journey's end!	Have you not seen those who are forbidden secret counsels, then they return to what they are forbidden, and they hold secret counsels for sin and revolt and disobedience to the Messenger, and when they come to you they greet you with a greeting with which Allah does not greet you, and they say in themselves: Why does not Allah punish us for what we say? Hell is enough for them; they shall enter it, and evil is the resort.
58 009	O ye who believe! When ye hold secret counsel, do it not for iniquity and hostility, and disobedience to the Prophet; but do it for righteousness and self-restraint; and fear Allah, to Whom ye shall be brought back.	O ye who believe! When ye conspire together, conspire not together for crime and wrongdoing and disobedience toward the messenger, but conspire together for righteousness and piety, and keep your duty toward Allah, unto whom ye will be gathered.	O you who believe! when you confer together in private, do not give to each other counsel of sin and revolt and disobedience to the Messenger, and give to each other counsel of goodness and guarding (against evil); and be careful of (your duty to) Allah, to Whom you shall be gathered together.
58 010	Secret counsels are only (inspired) by the Evil One, in order that he may cause grief to the Believers; but he cannot harm them in the least, except as Allah permits; and on Allah let the Believers put their trust.	Lo! Conspiracy is only of the devil, that he may vex those who believe; but he can harm them not at all unless by Allah's leave. In Allah let believers put their trust.	Secret counsels are only (the work) of the Shaitan that he may cause to grieve those who believe, and he cannot hurt them in the least except with Allah's permission, and on Allah let the believers rely.

58 011	O ye who believe! When ye are told to make room in the assemblies, (spread out and) make room: (ample) room will Allah provide for you. And when ye are told to rise up, rise up: Allah will raise up, to (suitable) ranks (and degrees), those of you who believe and who have been granted (mystic) Knowledge: And Allah is well acquainted with all ye do.	O ye who believe! when it is said unto you: Make room! in assemblies, then make room; Allah will make way for you (hereafter). And when it is said: Come up higher! go up higher; Allah will exalt those who believe among you, and those who have knowledge, to high ranks. Allah is informed of what ye do.	O you who believe! when it is said to you, Make room in (your) assemblies, then make ample room, Allah will give you ample, and when it is said: Rise up, then rise up. Allah will exalt those of you who believe, and those who are given knowledge, in high degrees; and Allah is Aware of what you do.
58 012	O ye who believe! When ye consult the Messenger in private, spend something in charity before your private consultation. That will be best for you, and most conducive to purity (of conduct). But if ye find not (the wherewithal), Allah is Oft-Forgiving, Most Merciful.	O ye who believe! When ye hold conference with the messenger, offer an alms before your conference. That is better and purer for you. But if ye cannot find (the wherewithal) then lo! Allah is Forgiving, Merciful.	O you who believe! when you consult the Messenger, then offer something in charity before your consultation; that is better for you and purer; but if you do not find, then surely Allah is Forgiving, Merciful.
58 013	Is it that ye are afraid of spending sums in charity before your private consultation (with him)? If, then, ye do not so, and Allah forgives you, then (at least) establish regular prayer; practise regular charity; and obey Allah and His Messenger. And Allah is well acquainted with all that ye do.	Fear ye to offer alms before your conference? Then, when ye do it not and Allah hath forgiven you, establish worship and pay the poor-due and obey Allah and His messenger. And Allah is Aware of what ye do.	Do you fear that you will not (be able to) give in charity before your consultation? So when you do not do it and Allah has turned to you (mercifully), then keep up prayer and pay the poor-rate and obey Allah and His Messenger; and Allah is Aware of what you do.
58 014	Turnest thou not thy attention to those who turn (in friendship) to such as have the Wrath of Allah upon them? They are neither of you nor of them, and they swear to falsehood knowingly.	Hast thou not seen those who take for friends a folk with whom Allah is wroth? They are neither of you nor of them, and they swear a false oath knowingly.	Have you not seen those who befriend a people with whom Allah is wroth? They are neither of you nor of them, and they swear falsely while they know.
58 015	Allah has prepared for them a severe Penalty: evil indeed are their deeds.	Allah hath prepared for them a dreadful doom. Evil indeed is that which they are wont to do.	Allah has prepared for them a severe punishment; surely what they do is evil.
58 016	They have made their oaths a screen (for their misdeeds): thus they obstruct (men) from the Path of Allah: therefore shall they have a humiliating Penalty.	They make a shelter of their oaths and turn (men) from the way of Allah; so theirs will be a shameful doom.	They make their oaths to serve as a cover so they turn away from Allah's way; therefore they shall have an abasing chastisement.
58 017	Of no profit whatever to them, against Allah, will be their riches nor their sons: they will be Companions of the Fire, to dwell therein (for aye)!	Their wealth and their children will avail them naught against Allah. Such are rightful owners of the Fire; they will abide therein.	Neither their wealth nor their children shall avail them aught against Allah; they are the inmates of the fire, therein they shall abide.
58 018	One day will Allah raise them all up (for Judgment): then will they swear to Him as they swear to you: And they think that they have something (to stand upon). No, indeed! they are but liars!	On the day when Allah will raise them all together, then will they swear unto Him as they (now) swear unto you, and they will fancy that they have some standing. Lo! is it not they who are the liars?	On the day that Allah will raise them up all, then they will swear to Him as they swear to you, and they think that they have something; now surely they are the liars.
58 019	The Evil One has got the better of them: so he has made them lose the remembrance of Allah. They are the Party of the Evil One. Truly, it is the Party of the Evil One that will perish!	The devil hath engrossed them and so hath caused them to forget remembrance of Allah. They are the devil's party. Lo! is it not the devil's party who will be the losers?	The Shaitan has gained the mastery over them, so he has made them forget the remembrance of Allah; they are the Shaitan's party; now surely the Shaitan's party are the losers.

58 020	Those who resist Allah and His Messenger will be among those most humiliated.	Lo! those who oppose Allah and His messenger, they will be among the lowest.	Surely (as for) those who are in opposition to Allah and His Messenger; they shall be among the most abased.
58 021	Allah has decreed: "It is I and My messengers who must prevail": For Allah is One full of strength, able to enforce His Will.	Allah hath decreed: Lo! I verily shall conquer, I and My messengers. Lo! Allah is Strong, Almighty.	Allah has written down: I will most certainly prevail, I and My messengers; surely Allah is Strong, Mighty.
58 022	Thou wilt not find any people who believe in Allah and the Last Day, loving those who resist Allah and His Messenger, even though they were their fathers or their sons, or their brothers, or their kindred. For such He has written Faith in their hearts, and strengthened them with a spirit from Himself. And He will admit them to Gardens beneath which Rivers flow, to dwell therein (for ever). Allah will be well pleased with them, and they with Him. They are the Party of Allah. Truly it is the Party of Allah that will achieve Felicity.	Thou wilt not find folk who believe in Allah and the Last Day loving those who oppose Allah and His messenger, even though they be their fathers or their sons or their brethren or their clan. As for such, He hath written faith upon their hearts and hath strengthened them with a Spirit from Him, and He will bring them into Gardens underneath which rivers flow, wherein they will abide. Allah is well pleased with them, and they are well pleased with Him. They are Allah's party. Lo! is it not Allah's party who are the successful?	You shall not find a people who believe in Allah and the latter day befriending those who act in opposition to Allah and His Messenger, even though they were their (own) fathers, or their sons, or their brothers, or their kinsfolk; these are they into whose hearts He has impressed faith, and whom He has strengthened with an inspiration from Him: and He will cause them to enter gardens beneath which rivers flow, abiding therein; Allah is well-pleased with them and they are well-pleased with Him these are Allah's party: now surely the party of Allah are the successful ones.

Chapter 59:

AL-HASHR (EXILE, BANISHMENT)

Total Verses: 24 Revealed At: MADINA

In the name of Allah, the Most Beneficent, the Most Merciful.

59 001	Whatever is in the heavens and on earth, let it declare the Praises and Glory of Allah: for He is the Exalted in Might, the Wise.	All that is in the heavens and all that is in the earth glorifieth Allah, and He is the Mighty, the Wise.	Whatever is in the heavens and whatever is in the earth declares the glory of Allah, and He is the Mighty, the Wise.
59 002	It is He Who got out the Unbelievers among the People of the Book from their homes at the first gathering (of the forces). Little did ye think that they would get out: And they thought that their fortresses would defend them from Allah! But the (Wrath of) Allah came to them from quarters from which they little expected (it), and cast terror into their hearts, so that they destroyed their dwellings by their own hands and the hands of the Believers, take warning, then, O ye with eyes (to see)!	He it is Who hath caused those of the People of the Scripture who disbelieved to go forth from their homes unto the first exile. Ye deemed not that they would go forth, while they deemed that their strongholds would protect them from Allah. But Allah reached them from a place whereof they reckoned not, and cast terror in their hearts so that they ruined their houses with their own hands and the hands of the believers. So learn a lesson, O ye who have eyes!	He it is Who caused those who disbelieved of the followers of the Book to go forth from their homes at the first banishment you did not think that they would go forth, while they were certain that their fortresses would defend them against Allah; but Allah came to them whence they did not expect, and cast terror into their hearts; they demolished their houses with their own hands and the hands of the believers; therefore take a lesson, O you who have eyes!

59	003	And had it not been that Allah had decreed banishment for them, He would certainly have punished them in this world: And in the Hereafter they shall (certainly) have the Punishment of the Fire.	And if Allah had not decreed migration for them, He verily would have punished them in the world, and theirs in the Hereafter is the punishment of the Fire.	And had it not been that Allah had decreed for them the exile, He would certainly have punished them in this world, and in the hereafter they shall have chastisement of the fire.
59	004	That is because they resisted Allah and His Messenger: and if any one resists Allah, verily Allah is severe in Punishment.	That is because they were opposed to Allah and His messenger; and whoso is opposed to Allah, (for him) verily Allah is stern in reprisal.	That is because they acted in opposition to Allah and His Messenger, and whoever acts in opposition to Allah, then surely Allah is severe in retributing (evil).
59	005	Whether ye cut down (O ye Muslim!) The tender palm-trees, or ye left them standing on their roots, it was by leave of Allah, and in order that He might cover with shame the rebellious transgresses.	Whatsoever palm-trees ye cut down or left standing on their roots, it was by Allah's leave, in order that He might confound the evil-livers.	Whatever palm-tree you cut down or leave standing upon its roots, It is by Allah's command, and that He may abase the transgressors.
59	006	What Allah has bestowed on His Messenger (and taken away) from them - for this ye made no expedition with either cavalry or camelry: but Allah gives power to His messengers over any He pleases: and Allah has power over all things.	And that which Allah gave as spoil unto His messenger from them, ye urged not any horse or riding-camel for the sake thereof, but Allah giveth His messenger lordship over whom He will. Allah is Able to do all things.	And whatever Allah restored to His Messenger from them you did not press forward against it any horse or a riding camel but Allah gives authority to His messengers against whom He pleases, and Allah has power over all things.
59	007	What Allah has bestowed on His Messenger (and taken away) from the people of the townships,- belongs to Allah,- to His Messenger and to kindred and orphans, the needy and the wayfarer; In order that it may not (merely) make a circuit between the wealthy among you. So take what the Messenger assigns to you, and deny yourselves that which he withholds from you. And fear Allah; for Allah is strict in Punishment.	That which Allah giveth as spoil unto His messenger from the people of the townships, it is for Allah and His messenger and for the near of kin and the orphans and the needy and the wayfarer, that it become not a commodity between the rich among you. And whatsoever the messenger giveth you, take it. And whatsoever he forbiddeth, abstain (from it). And keep your duty to Allah. Lo! Allah is stern in reprisal.	Whatever Allah has restored to His Messenger from the people of the towns, it is for Allah and for the Messenger, and for the near of kin and the orphans and the needy and the wayfarer, so that it may not be a thing taken by turns among the rich of you, and whatever the Messenger gives you, accept it, and from whatever he forbids you, keep back, and be careful of (your duty to) Allah; surely Allah is severe in retributing (evil):
59	008	(Some part is due) to the indigent Muhajirs, those who were expelled from their homes and their property, while seeking Grace from Allah and (His) Good Pleasure, and aiding Allah and His Messenger: such are indeed the sincere ones:-	And (it is) for the poor fugitives who have been driven out from their homes and their belongings, who seek bounty from Allah and help Allah and His messenger. They are the loyal.	(It is) for the poor who fled their homes and their possessions, seeking grace of Allah and (His) pleasure, and assisting Allah and His Messenger: these it is that are the truthful.
59	009	But those who before them, had homes (in Medina) and had adopted the Faith,- show their affection to such as came to them for refuge, and entertain no desire in their hearts for things given to the (latter), but give them preference over themselves, even though poverty was their (own lot). And those saved from the covetousness of their own souls,- they are the ones that achieve prosperity.	Those who entered the city and the faith before them love those who flee unto them for refuge, and find in their breasts no need for that which hath been given them, but prefer (the fugitives) above themselves though poverty become their lot. And whoso is saved from his own avarice - such are they who are successful.	And those who made their abode in the city and in the faith before them love those who have fled to them, and do not find in their hearts a need of what they are given, and prefer (them) before themselves though poverty may afflict them, and whoever is preserved from the niggardliness of his soul, these it is that are the successful ones.

59 010	And those who came after them say: "Our Lord! Forgive us, and our brethren who came before us into the Faith, and leave not, in our hearts, rancour (or sense of injury) against those who have believed. Our Lord! Thou art indeed Full of Kindness, Most Merciful."	And those who came (into the faith) after them say: Our Lord! Forgive us and our brethren who were before us in the faith, and place not in our hearts any rancour toward those who believe. Our Lord! Thou art Full of Pity, Merciful.	And those who come after them say: Our Lord! forgive us and those of our brethren who had precedence of us in faith, and do not allow any spite to remain in our hearts towards those who believe, our Lord! surely Thou art Kind, Merciful.
59 011	Hast thou not observed the Hypocrites say to their misbelieving brethren among the People of the Book? - "If ye are expelled, we too will go out with you, and we will never hearken to any one in your affair; and if ye are attacked (in fight) we will help you". But Allah is witness that they are indeed liars.	Hast thou not observed those who are hypocrites, (how) they tell their brethren who disbelieve among the People of the Scripture: If ye are driven out, we surely will go out with you, and we will never obey anyone against you, and if ye are attacked we verily will help you. And Allah beareth witness that they verily are liars.	Have you not seen those who have become hypocrites? They say to those of their brethren who disbelieve from among the followers of the Book: If you are driven forth, we shall certainly go forth with you, and we will never obey any one concerning you, and if you are fought against, we will certainly help you, and Allah bears witness that they are most surely liars.
59 012	If they are expelled, never will they go out with them; and if they are attacked (in fight), they will never help them; and if they do help them, they will turn their backs; so they will receive no help.	(For) indeed if they are driven out they go not out with them, and indeed if they are attacked they help them not, and indeed if they had helped them they would have turned and fled, and then they would not have been victorious.	Certainly if these are driven forth, they will not go forth with them, and if they are fought against, they will not help them, and even if they help-them, they will certainly turn (their) backs, then they shall not be helped.
59 013	Of a truth ye are stronger (than they) because of the terror in their hearts, (sent) by Allah. This is because they are men devoid of understanding.	Ye are more awful as a fear in their bosoms than Allah. That is because they are a folk who understand not.	You are certainly greater in being feared in their hearts than Allah; that is because they are a people who do not understand.
59 014	They will not fight you (even) together, except in fortified townships, or from behind walls. Strong is their fighting (spirit) amongst themselves: thou wouldst think they were united, but their hearts are divided: that is because they are a people devoid of wisdom.	They will not fight against you in a body save in fortified villages or from behind walls. Their adversity among themselves is very great. Ye think of them as a whole whereas their hearts are divers. That is because they are a folk who have no sense.	They will not fight against you in a body save in fortified towns or from behind walls; their fighting between them is severe, you may think them as one body, and their hearts are disunited; that is because they are a people who have no sense.
59 015	Like those who lately preceded them, they have tasted the evil result of their conduct; and (in the Hereafter there is) for them a grievous Penalty;-	On the likeness of those (who suffered) a short time before them, they taste the ill effects of their own conduct, and theirs is painful punishment.	Like those before them shortly; they tasted the evil result of their affair, and they shall have a painful punishment.
59 016	(Their allies deceived them), like the Evil One, when he says to man, Deny Allah: but when (man) denies Allah, (the Evil One) says, "I am free of thee: I do fear Allah, the Lord of the Worlds!"	(And the hypocrites are) on the likeness of the devil when he telleth man to disbelieve, then, when he disbelieveth saith: Lo! I am quit of thee. Lo! I fear Allah, the Lord of the Worlds.	Like the Shaitan when he says to man: Disbelieve, but when he disbelieves, he says: I am surely clear of you; surely I fear Allah, the Lord of the worlds.
59 017	The end of both will be that they will go into the Fire, dwelling therein for ever. Such is the reward of the wrong-doers.	And the consequence for both will be that they are in the Fire, therein abiding. Such is the reward of evil-doers.	Therefore the end of both of them is that they are both in the fire to abide therein, and that is the reward of the unjust.

59 018	O ye who believe! Fear Allah, and let every soul look to what (provision) He has sent forth for the morrow. Yea, fear Allah: for Allah is well-acquainted with (all) that ye do.	O ye who believe! Observe your duty to Allah. And let every soul look to that which it sendeth on before for the morrow. And observe your duty to Allah. Lo! Allah is Informed of what ye do.	O you who believe! be careful of (your duty to) Allah, and let every soul consider what it has sent on for the morrow, and be careful of (your duty to) Allah; surely Allah is Aware of what you do.
59 019	And be ye not like those who forgot Allah; and He made them forget their own souls! Such are the rebellious transgressors!	And be not ye as those who forgot Allah, therefor He caused them to forget their souls. Such are the evil-doers.	And be not like those who forsook Allah, so He made them forsake their own souls: these it is that are the transgressors.
59 020	Not equal are the Companions of the Fire and the Companions of the Garden: it is the Companions of the Garden, that will achieve Felicity.	Not equal are the owners of the Fire and the owners of the Garden. The owners of the Garden, they are the victorious.	Not alike are the inmates of the fire and the dwellers of the garden: the dwellers of the garden are they that are the achievers.
59 021	Had We sent down this Qur'an on a mountain, verily, thou wouldst have seen it humble itself and cleave asunder for fear of Allah. Such are the similitudes which We propound to men, that they may reflect.	If We had caused this Qur'an to descend upon a mountain, thou (O Muhammad) verily hadst seen it humbled, rent asunder by the fear of Allah. Such similitudes coin We for mankind that haply they may reflect.	Had We sent down this Quran on a mountain, you would certainly have seen it falling down, splitting asunder because of the fear of Allah, and We set forth these parables to men that they may reflect.
59 022	Allah is He, than Whom there is no other god;- Who knows (all things) both secret and open; He, Most Gracious, Most Merciful.	He is Allah, than Whom there is no other God, the Knower of the Invisible and the Visible. He is the Beneficent, Merciful.	He is Allah besides Whom there is no god; the Knower of the unseen and the seen; He is the Beneficent, the Merciful.
59 023	Allah is He, than Whom there is no other god;- the Sovereign, the Holy One, the Source of Peace (and Perfection), the Guardian of Faith, the Preserver of Safety, the Exalted in Might, the Irresistible, the Supreme: Glory to Allah! (High is He) above the partners they attribute to Him.	He is Allah, than Whom there is no other God, the Sovereign Lord, the Holy One, Peace, the Keeper of Faith, the Guardian, the Majestic, the Compeller, the Superb. Glorified be Allah from all that they ascribe as partner (unto Him).	He is Allah, besides Whom there is no god; the King, the Holy, the Giver of peace, the Granter of security, Guardian over all, the Mighty, the Supreme, the Possessor of every greatness Glory be to Allah from what they set up (with Him).
59 024	He is Allah, the Creator, the Evolver, the Bestower of Forms (or Colours). To Him belong the Most Beautiful Names: whatever is in the heavens and on earth, doth declare His Praises and Glory: and He is the Exalted in Might, the Wise.	He is Allah, the Creator, the Shaper out of naught, the Fashioner. His are the most beautiful names. All that is in the heavens and the earth glorifieth Him, and He is the Mighty, the Wise.	He is Allah the Creator, the Maker, the Fashioner; His are the most excellent names; whatever is in the heavens and the earth declares His glory; and He is the Mighty, the Wise.

Chapter 60:

AL-MUMTAHINA (SHE THAT IS TO BE EXAMINED, EXAMINING HER)

Total Verses: 13 Revealed At: MADINA

In the name of Allah, the Most Beneficent, the Most Merciful.

60 001	O ye who believe! Take not my enemies and yours as friends (or protectors),- offering them (your) love, even though they have rejected the Truth that has come to you, and have (on the contrary) driven out the Prophet and yourselves (from your homes), (simply) because ye believe in Allah your Lord! If ye have come out to strive in My Way and to seek My Good Pleasure, (take them not as friends), holding secret converse of love (and friendship) with them: for I know full well all that ye conceal and all that ye reveal. And any of you that does this has strayed from the Straight Path.	O ye who believe! Choose not My enemy and your enemy for allies. Do ye give them friendship when they disbelieve in that truth which hath come unto you, driving out the messenger and you because ye believe in Allah, your Lord? If ye have come forth to strive in My way and seeking My good pleasure, (show them not friendship). Do ye show friendship unto them in secret, when I am Best Aware of what ye hide and what ye proclaim? And whosoever doeth it among you, he verily hath strayed from the right way.	O you who believe! do not take My enemy and your enemy for friends: would you offer them love while they deny what has come to you of the truth, driving out the Messenger and yourselves because you believe in Allah, your Lord? If you go forth struggling hard in My path and seeking My pleasure, would you manifest love to them? And I know what you conceal and what you manifest; and whoever of you does this, he indeed has gone astray from the straight path.
60 002	If they were to get the better of you, they would behave to you as enemies, and stretch forth their hands and their tongues against you for evil: and they desire that ye should reject the Truth.	If they have the upper hand of you, they will be your foes, and will stretch out their hands and their tongues toward you with evil (intent), and they long for you to disbelieve.	If they find you, they will be your enemies, and will stretch forth towards you their hands and their tongues with evil, and they ardently desire that you may disbelieve.
60 003	Of no profit to you will be your relatives and your children on the Day of Judgment: He will judge between you: for Allah sees well all that ye do.	Your ties of kindred and your children will avail you naught upon the Day of Resurrection. He will part you. Allah is Seer of what ye do.	Your relationship would not profit you, nor your children on the day of resurrection; He will decide between you; and Allah sees what you do.
60 004	There is for you an excellent example (to follow) in Abraham and those with him, when they said to their people: "We are clear of you and of whatever ye worship besides Allah: we have rejected you, and there has arisen, between us and you, enmity and hatred for ever,- unless ye believe in Allah and Him alone": But not when Abraham said to his father: "I will pray for forgiveness for thee, though I have no power (to get) aught on thy behalf from Allah." (They prayed): "Our Lord! in Thee do we trust, and to Thee do we turn in repentance: to Thee is (our) Final Goal."	There is a goodly pattern for you in Abraham and those with him, when they told their folk: Lo! we are guiltless of you and all that ye worship beside Allah. We have done with you. And there hath arisen between us and you hostility and hate for ever until ye believe in Allah only - save that which Abraham promised his father (when he said): I will ask forgiveness for thee, though I own nothing for thee from Allah - Our Lord! In Thee we put our trust, and unto Thee we turn repentant, and unto Thee is the journeying.	Indeed, there is for you a good example in Ibrahim and those with him when they said to their people: Surely we are clear of you and of what you serve besides Allah; we declare ourselves to be clear of you, and enmity and hatred have appeared between us and you forever until you believe in Allah alone-- but not in what Ibrahim said to his father: I would certainly ask forgiveness for you, and I do not control for you aught from Allah-- Our Lord! on Thee do we rely, and to Thee do we turn, and to Thee is the eventual coming:

60 005	"Our Lord! Make us not a (test and) trial for the Unbelievers, but forgive us, our Lord! for Thou art the Exalted in Might, the Wise."	Our Lord! Make us not a prey for those who disbelieve, and forgive us, our Lord! Lo! Thou, only Thou, are the Mighty, the Wise.	Our Lord! do not make us a trial for those who disbelieve, and forgive us, our Lord! surely Thou art the Mighty, the Wise.
60 006	There was indeed in them an excellent example for you to follow,- for those whose hope is in Allah and in the Last Day. But if any turn away, truly Allah is Free of all Wants, Worthy of all Praise.	Verily ye have in them a goodly pattern for everyone who looketh to Allah and the Last Day. And whosoever may turn away, lo! still Allah, He is the Absolute, the Owner of Praise.	Certainly there is for you in them a good example, for him who fears Allah and the last day; and whoever turns back, then surely Allah is the Self-sufficient, the Praised.
60 007	It may be that Allah will grant love (and friendship) between you and those whom ye (now) hold as enemies. For Allah has power (over all things); And Allah is Oft-Forgiving, Most Merciful.	It may be that Allah will ordain love between you and those of them with whom ye are at enmity. Allah is Mighty, and Allah is Forgiving, Merciful.	It may be that Allah will bring about friendship between you and those whom you hold to be your enemies among them; and Allah is Powerful; and Allah is Forgiving, Merciful.
60 008	Allah forbids you not, with regard to those who fight you not for (your) Faith nor drive you out of your homes, from dealing kindly and justly with them: for Allah loveth those who are just.	Allah forbiddeth you not those who warred not against you on account of religion and drove you not out from your homes, that ye should show them kindness and deal justly with them. Lo! Allah loveth the just dealers.	Allah does not forbid you respecting those who have not made war against you on account of (your) religion, and have not driven you forth from your homes, that you show them kindness and deal with them justly; surely Allah loves the doers of justice.
60 009	Allah only forbids you, with regard to those who fight you for (your) Faith, and drive you out of your homes, and support (others) in driving you out, from turning to them (for friendship and protection). It is such as turn to them (in these circumstances), that do wrong.	Allah forbiddeth you only those who warred against you on account of religion and have driven you out from your homes and helped to drive you out, that ye make friends of them. Whosoever maketh friends of them - (All) such are wrongdoers.	Allah only forbids you respecting those who made war upon you on account of (your) religion, and drove you forth from your homes and backed up (others) in your expulsion, that you make friends with them, and whoever makes friends with them, these are the unjust.
60 010	O ye who believe! When there come to you believing women refugees, examine (and test) them: Allah knows best as to their Faith: if ye ascertain that they are Believers, then send them not back to the Unbelievers. They are not lawful (wives) for the Unbelievers, nor are the (Unbelievers) lawful (husbands) for them. But pay the Unbelievers what they have spent (on their dower), and there will be no blame on you if ye marry them on payment of their dower to them. But hold not to the guardianship of unbelieving women: ask for what ye have spent on their dowers, and let the (Unbelievers) ask for what they have spent (on the dowers of women who come over to you). Such is the command of Allah: He judges (with justice) between you. And Allah is Full of Knowledge and Wisdom.	O ye who believe! When believing women come unto you as fugitives, examine them. Allah is Best Aware of their faith. Then, if ye know them for true believers, send them not back unto the disbelievers. They are not lawful for them (the disbelievers), nor are they (the disbelievers) lawful for them. And give them (the disbelievers) that which they have spent (upon them). And it is no sin for you to marry such women when ye have given them their dues. And hold not to the ties of disbelieving women; and ask for (the return of) that which ye have spent; and let them (the disbelievers) ask for that which they have spent. That is the judgment of Allah. He judgeth between you. Allah is Knower, Wise.	O you who believe! when believing women come to you flying, then examine them; Allah knows best their faith; then if you find them to be believing women, do not send them back to the unbelievers, neither are these (women) lawful for them, nor are those (men) lawful for them, and give them what they have spent; and no blame attaches to you in marrying them when you give them their dowries; and hold not to the ties of marriage of unbelieving women, and ask for what you have spent, and let them ask for what they have spent. That is Allah's judgment; He judges between you, and Allah is Knowing, Wise.

60	011	And if any of your wives deserts you to the Unbelievers, and ye have an accession (by the coming over of a woman from the other side), then pay to those whose wives have deserted the equivalent of what they had spent (on their dower). And fear Allah, in Whom ye believe.	And if any of your wives have gone from you unto the disbelievers and afterward ye have your turn (of triumph), then give unto those whose wives have gone the like of that which they have spent, and keep your duty to Allah in Whom ye are believers.	And if anything (out of the dowries) of your wives has passed away from you to the unbelievers, then your turn comes, give to those whose wives have gone away the like of what they have spent, and be careful of (your duty to) Allah in Whom you believe.
60	012	O Prophet! When believing women come to thee to take the oath of fealty to thee, that they will not associate in worship any other thing whatever with Allah, that they will not steal, that they will not commit adultery (or fornication), that they will not kill their children, that they will not utter slander, intentionally forging falsehood, and that they will not disobey thee in any just matter,- then do thou receive their fealty, and pray to Allah for the forgiveness (of their sins): for Allah is Oft-Forgiving, Most Merciful.	O Prophet! If believing women come unto thee, taking oath of allegiance unto thee that they will ascribe no thing as partner unto Allah, and will neither steal nor commit adultery nor kill their children, nor produce any lie that they have devised between their hands and feet, nor disobey thee in what is right, then accept their allegiance and ask Allah to forgive them. Lo! Allah is Forgiving, Merciful.	O Prophet! when believing women come to you giving you a pledge that they will not associate aught with Allah, and will not steal, and will not commit fornication, and will not kill their children, and will not bring a calumny which they have forged of themselves, and will not disobey you in what is good, accept their pledge, and ask forgiveness for them from Allah; surely Allah is Forgiving, Merciful.
60	013	O ye who believe! Turn not (for friendship) to people on whom is the Wrath of Allah, of the Hereafter they are already in despair, just as the Unbelievers are in despair about those (buried) in graves.	O ye who believe! Be not friendly with a folk with whom Allah is wroth, (a folk) who have despaired of the Hereafter as the disbelievers despair of those who are in the graves.	O you who believe! do not make friends with a people with whom Allah is wroth; indeed they despair of the hereafter as the unbelievers despair of those in tombs.

Chapter 61:

AS-SAFF (THE RANKS, BATTLE ARRAY)

Total Verses: 14 Revealed At: MADINA

In the name of Allah, the Most Beneficent, the Most Merciful.

61	001	Whatever is in the heavens and on earth, let it declare the Praises and Glory of Allah: for He is the Exalted in Might, the Wise.	All that is in the heavens and all that is in the earth glorifieth Allah, and He is the Mighty, the Wise.	Whatever is in the heavens and whatever is in the earth declares the glory of Allah; and He is the Mighty, the Wise.
61	002	O ye who believe! Why say ye that which ye do not?	O ye who believe! Why say ye that which ye do not?	O you who believe! why do you say that which you do not do?
61	003	Grievously odious is it in the sight of Allah that ye say that which ye do not.	It is most hateful in the sight of Allah that ye say that which ye do not.	It is most hateful to Allah that you should say that which you do not do.
61	004	Truly Allah loves those who fight in His Cause in battle array, as if they were a solid cemented structure.	Lo! Allah loveth them who battle for His cause in ranks, as if they were a solid structure.	Surely Allah loves those who fight in His way in ranks as if they were a firm and compact wall.

61 005	And remember, Moses said to his people: "O my people! why do ye vex and insult me, though ye know that I am the messenger of Allah (sent) to you?" Then when they went wrong, Allah let their hearts go wrong. For Allah guides not those who are rebellious transgressors.	And (remember) when Moses said unto his people: O my people! Why persecute ye me, when ye well know that I am Allah's messenger unto you? So when they went astray Allah sent their hearts astray. And Allah guideth not the evil-living folk.	And when Musa said to his people: O my people! why do you give me trouble? And you know indeed that I am Allah's messenger to you; but when they turned aside, Allah made their hearts turn aside, and Allah does not guide the transgressing people.
61 006	And remember, Jesus, the son of Mary, said: "O Children of Israel! I am the messenger of Allah (sent) to you, confirming the Law (which came) before me, and giving Glad Tidings of a Messenger to come after me, whose name shall be Ahmad." But when he came to them with Clear Signs, they said, "This is evident sorcery!"	And when Jesus son of Mary said: O Children of Israel! Lo! I am the messenger of Allah unto you, confirming that which was (revealed) before me in the Torah, and bringing good tidings of a messenger who cometh after me, whose name is the Praised One. Yet when he hath come unto them with clear proofs, they say: This is mere magic.	And when Isa son of Marium said: O children of Israel! surely I am the messenger of Allah to you, verifying that which is before me of the Taurat and giving the good news of a Messenger who will come after me, his name being Ahmad, but when he came to them with clear arguments they said: This is clear magic.
61 007	Who doth greater wrong than one who invents falsehood against Allah, even as he is being invited to Islam? And Allah guides not those who do wrong.	And who doeth greater wrong than he who inventeth a lie against Al-Islam? And Allah guideth not wrongdoing folk.	And who is more unjust than he who forges a lie against Allah and he is invited to Islam, and Allah does not guide the unjust people.
61 008	Their intention is to extinguish Allah's Light (by blowing) with their mouths: But Allah will complete (the revelation of) His Light, even though the Unbelievers may detest (it).	Fain would they put out the light of Allah with their mouths, but Allah will perfect His light however much the disbelievers are averse.	They desire to put out the light of Allah with their mouths but Allah will perfect His light, though the unbelievers may be averse.
61 009	It is He Who has sent His Messenger with Guidance and the Religion of Truth, that he may proclaim it over all religion, even though the Pagans may detest (it).	He it is Who hath sent His messenger with the guidance and the religion of truth, that He may make it conqueror of all religion however much idolaters may be averse.	He it is Who sent His Messenger with the guidance and the true religion, that He may make it overcome the religions, all of them, though the polytheists may be averse.
61 010	O ye who believe! Shall I lead you to a bargain that will save you from a grievous Penalty?-	O ye who believe! Shall I show you a commerce that will save you from a painful doom?	O you who believe! shall I lead you to a merchandise which may deliver you from a painful chastisement?
61 011	That ye believe in Allah and His Messenger, and that ye strive (your utmost) in the Cause of Allah, with your property and your persons: That will be best for you, if ye but knew!	Ye should believe in Allah and His messenger, and should strive for the cause of Allah with your wealth and your lives. That is better for you, if ye did but know.	You shall believe in Allah and His Messenger, and struggle hard in Allah's way with your property and your lives; that is better for you, did you but know!
61 012	He will forgive you your sins, and admit you to Gardens beneath which Rivers flow, and to beautiful mansions in Gardens of Eternity: that is indeed the Supreme Achievement.	He will forgive you your sins and bring you into Gardens underneath which rivers flow, and pleasant dwellings in Gardens of Eden. That is the supreme triumph.	He will forgive you your faults and cause you to enter into gardens, beneath which rivers flow, and goodly dwellings in gardens of perpetuity; that is the mighty achievement;
61 013	And another (favour will He bestow,) which ye do love,- help from Allah and a speedy victory. So give the Glad Tidings to the Believers.	And (He will give you) another (blessing) which ye love: help from Allah and present victory. Give good tidings (O Muhammad) to believers.	And yet another (blessing) that you love: help from Allah and a victory near at hand; and give good news to the believers.

61 014	O ye who believe! Be ye helpers of Allah: As said Jesus the son of Mary to the Disciples, "Who will be my helpers to (the work of) Allah?" Said the disciples, "We are Allah's helpers!" then a portion of the Children of Israel believed, and a portion disbelieved: But We gave power to those who believed, against their enemies, and they became the ones that prevailed.	O ye who believe! Be Allah's helpers, even as Jesus son of Mary said unto the disciples: Who are my helpers for Allah? They said: We are Allah's helpers. And a party of the Children of Israel believed, while a party disbelieved. Then We strengthened those who believed against their foe, and they became the uppermost.		O you who believe! be helpers (in the cause) of Allah, as Isa son of Marium said to (his) disciples: Who are my helpers in the cause of Allah? The disciples said: We are helpers (in the cause) of Allah. So a party of the children of Israel believed and another party disbelieved; then We aided those who believed against their enemy, and they became uppermost.

Chapter 62:

AL-JUMUA (THE CONGREGATION, FRIDAY)

Total Verses: 11 Revealed At: MADINA

In the name of Allah, the Most Beneficent, the Most Merciful.

62 001	Whatever is in the heavens and on earth, doth declare the Praises and Glory of Allah,- the Sovereign, the Holy One, the Exalted in Might, the Wise.	All that is in the heavens and all that is in the earth glorifieth Allah, the Sovereign Lord, the Holy One, the Mighty, the Wise.	Whatever is in the heavens and whatever is in the earth declares the glory of Allah, the King, the Holy, the Mighty, the Wise.
62 002	It is He Who has sent amongst the Unlettered a messenger from among themselves, to rehearse to them His Signs, to sanctify them, and to instruct them in Scripture and Wisdom,- although they had been, before, in manifest error;-	He it is Who hath sent among the unlettered ones a messenger of their own, to recite unto them His revelations and to make them grow, and to teach them the Scripture and wisdom, though heretofore they were indeed in error manifest,	He it is Who raised among the inhabitants of Mecca a Messenger from among themselves, who recites to them His communications and purifies them, and teaches them the Book and the Wisdom, although they were before certainly in clear error,
62 003	As well as (to confer all these benefits upon) others of them, who have not already joined them: And He is exalted in Might, Wise.	Along with others of them who have not yet joined them. He is the Mighty, the Wise.	And others from among them who have not yet joined them; and He is the Mighty, the Wise.
62 004	Such is the Bounty of Allah, which He bestows on whom He will: and Allah is the Lord of the highest bounty.	That is the bounty of Allah; which He giveth unto whom He will. Allah is of Infinite Bounty.	That is Allah's grace; He grants it to whom He pleases, and Allah is the Lord of mighty grace.
62 005	The similitude of those who were charged with the (obligations of the) Mosaic Law, but who subsequently failed in those (obligations), is that of a donkey which carries huge tomes (but understands them not). Evil is the similitude of people who falsify the Signs of Allah: and Allah guides not people who do wrong.	The likeness of those who are entrusted with the Law of Moses, yet apply it not, is as the likeness of the ass carrying books. Wretched is the likeness of folk who deny the revelations of Allah. And Allah guideth not wrongdoing folk.	The likeness of those who were charged with the Taurat, then they did not observe it, is as the likeness of the ass bearing books, evil is the likeness of the people who reject the communications of Allah; and Allah does not guide the unjust people.
62 006	Say: "O ye that stand on Judaism! If ye think that ye are friends to Allah, to the exclusion of (other) men, then express your desire for Death, if ye are truthful!"	Say (O Muhammad): O ye who are Jews! If ye claim that ye are favoured of Allah apart from (all) mankind, then long for death if ye are truthful.	Say: O you who are Jews, if you think that you are the favorites of Allah to the exclusion of other people, then invoke death if you are truthful.

62 007	But never will they express their desire (for Death), because of the (deeds) their hands have sent on before them! and Allah knows well those that do wrong!	But they will never long for it because of all that their own hands have sent before, and Allah is Aware of evil-doers.	And they will never invoke it because of what their hands have sent before; and Allah is Cognizant of the unjust.
62 008	Say: "The Death from which ye flee will truly overtake you: then will ye be sent back to the Knower of things secret and open: and He will tell you (the truth of) the things that ye did!"	Say (unto them, O Muhammad): Lo! the death from which ye shrink will surely meet you, and afterward ye will be returned unto the Knower of the Invisible and the Visible, and He will tell you what ye used to do.	Say: (As for) the death from which you flee, that will surely overtake you, then you shall be sent back to the Knower of the unseen and the seen, and He will inform you of that which you did.
62 009	O ye who believe! When the call is proclaimed to prayer on Friday (the Day of Assembly), hasten earnestly to the Remembrance of Allah, and leave off business (and traffic): That is best for you if ye but knew!	O ye who believe! When the call is heard for the prayer of the day of congregation, haste unto remembrance of Allah and leave your trading. That is better for you if ye did but know.	O you who believe! when the call is made for prayer on Friday, then hasten to the remembrance of Allah and leave off trading; that is better for you, if you know.
62 010	And when the Prayer is finished, then may ye disperse through the land, and seek of the Bounty of Allah: and celebrate the Praises of Allah often (and without stint): that ye may prosper.	And when the prayer is ended, then disperse in the land and seek of Allah's bounty, and remember Allah much, that ye may be successful.	But when the prayer is ended, then disperse abroad in the land and seek of Allah's grace, and remember Allah much, that you may be successful.
62 011	But when they see some bargain or some amusement, they disperse headlong to it, and leave thee standing. Say: "The (blessing) from the Presence of Allah is better than any amusement or bargain! and Allah is the Best to provide (for all needs)."	But when they spy some merchandise or pastime they break away to it and leave thee standing. Say: That which Allah hath is better than pastime and than merchandise, and Allah is the Best of providers.	And when they see merchandise or sport they break up for it, and leave you standing. Say: What is with Allah is better than sport and (better) than merchandise, and Allah is the best of Sustainers.

Chapter 63:

AL-MUNAFIQOON (THE HYPOCRITES)

Total Verses: 11 Revealed At: MADINA

In the name of Allah, the Most Beneficent, the Most Merciful.

63 001	When the Hypocrites come to thee, they say, "We bear witness that thou art indeed the Messenger of Allah." Yea, Allah knoweth that thou art indeed His Messenger, and Allah beareth witness that the Hypocrites are indeed liars.	When the hypocrites come unto thee (O Muhammad), they say: We bear witness that thou art indeed Allah's messenger. And Allah knoweth that thou art indeed His messenger, and Allah beareth witness that the hypocrites indeed are speaking falsely.	When the hypocrites come to you, they say: We bear witness that you are most surely Allah's Messenger; and Allah knows that you are most surely His Messenger, and Allah bears witness that the hypocrites are surely liars.
63 002	They have made their oaths a screen (for their misdeeds): thus they obstruct (men) from the Path of Allah: truly evil are their deeds.	They make their faith a pretext so that they may turn (men) from the way of Allah. Verily evil is that which they are wont to do,	They make their oaths a shelter, and thus turn away from Allah's way; surely evil is that which they do.

63 003	That is because they believed, then they rejected Faith: So a seal was set on their hearts: therefore they understand not.	That is because they believed, then disbelieved, therefore their hearts are sealed so that they understand not.	That is because they believe, then disbelieve, so a seal is set upon their hearts so that they do not understand.
63 004	When thou lookest at them, their exteriors please thee; and when they speak, thou listenest to their words. They are as (worthless as hollow) pieces of timber propped up, (unable to stand on their own). They think that every cry is against them. They are the enemies; so beware of them. The curse of Allah be on them! How are they deluded (away from the Truth)!	And when thou seest them their figures please thee; and if they speak thou givest ear unto their speech. (They are) as though they were blocks of wood in striped cloaks. They deem every shout to be against them. They are the enemy, so beware of them. Allah confound them! How they are perverted!	And when you see them, their persons will please you, and If they speak, you will listen to their speech; (they are) as if they were big pieces of wood clad with garments; they think every cry to be against them. They are the enemy, therefore beware of them; may Allah destroy them, whence are they turned back?
63 005	And when it is said to them, "Come, the Messenger of Allah will pray for your forgiveness", they turn aside their heads, and thou wouldst see them turning away their faces in arrogance.	And when it is said unto them: Come! The messenger of Allah will ask forgiveness for you! they avert their faces and thou seest them turning away, disdainful.	And when it is said to them: Come, the Messenger of Allah will ask forgiveness for you, they turn back their heads and you may see them turning away while they are big with pride.
63 006	It is equal to them whether thou pray for their forgiveness or not. Allah will not forgive them. Truly Allah guides not rebellious transgressors.	Whether thou ask forgiveness for them or ask not forgiveness for them is all one for them; Allah will not forgive them. Lo! Allah guideth not the evil-living folk.	It is alike to them whether you beg forgiveness for them or do not beg forgiveness for them; Allah will never forgive them; surely Allah does not guide the transgressing people.
63 007	They are the ones who say, "Spend nothing on those who are with Allah's Messenger, to the end that they may disperse (and quit Medina)." But to Allah belong the treasures of the heavens and the earth; but the Hypocrites understand not.	They it is who say: Spend not on behalf of those (who dwell) with Allah's messenger that they may disperse (and go away from you); when Allah's are the treasures of the heavens and the earth; but the hypocrites comprehend not.	They it is who say: Do not spend upon those who are with the Messenger of Allah until they break up. And Allah's are the treasures of the heavens and the earth, but the hypocrites do not understand.
63 008	They say, "If we return to Medina, surely the more honourable (element) will expel therefrom the meaner." But honour belongs to Allah and His Messenger, and to the Believers; but the Hypocrites know not.	They say: Surely, if we return to Al-Madinah the mightier will soon drive out the weaker; when might belongeth to Allah and to His messenger and to the believers; but the hypocrites know not.	They say: If we return to Medina, the mighty will surely drive out the meaner therefrom; and to Allah belongs the might and to His Messenger and to the believers, but the hypocrites do not know.
63 009	O ye who believe! Let not your riches or your children divert you from the remembrance of Allah. If any act thus, the loss is their own.	O ye who believe! Let not your wealth nor your children distract you from remembrance of Allah. Those who do so, they are the losers.	O you who believe! let not your wealth, or your children, divert you from the remembrance of Allah; and whoever does that, these are the losers.
63 010	and spend something (in charity) out of the substance which We have bestowed on you, before Death should come to any of you and he should say, "O my Lord! why didst Thou not give me respite for a little while? I should then have given (largely) in charity, and I should have been one of the doers of good".	And spend of that wherewith We have provided you before death cometh unto one of you and he saith: My Lord! If only thou wouldst reprieve me for a little while, then I would give alms and be among the righteous.	And spend out of what We have given you before death comes to one of you, so that he should say: My Lord! why didst Thou not respite me to a near term, so that I should have given alms and been of the doers of good deeds?

63 011	But to no soul will Allah grant respite when the time appointed (for it) has come; and Allah is well acquainted with (all) that ye do.	But Allah reprieveth no soul when its term cometh, and Allah is Informed of what ye do.	And Allah does not respite a soul when its appointed term has come, and Allah is Aware of what you do.

Chapter 64:

AT-TAGHABUN (MUTUAL DISILLUSION, HAGGLING)

Total Verses: 18 Revealed At: MAKKA

In the name of Allah, the Most Beneficent, the Most Merciful.

64 001	Whatever is in the heavens and on earth, doth declare the Praises and Glory of Allah: to Him belongs dominion, and to Him belongs praise: and He has power over all things.	All that is in the heavens and all that is in the earth glorifieth Allah; unto Him belongeth Sovereignty and unto Him belongeth praise, and He is Able to do all things.	Whatever is in the heavens and whatever is in the earth declares the glory of Allah; to Him belongs the kingdom, and to Him is due (all) praise, and He has power over all things.
64 002	It is He Who has created you; and of you are some that are Unbelievers, and some that are Believers: and Allah sees well all that ye do.	He it is Who created you, but one of you is a disbeliever and one of you is a believer, and Allah is Seer of what ye do.	He it is Who created you, but one of you is an unbeliever and another of you is a believer; and Allah sees what you do.
64 003	He has created the heavens and the earth in just proportions, and has given you shape, and made your shapes beautiful: and to Him is the final Goal.	He created the heavens and the earth with truth, and He shaped you and made good your shapes, and unto Him is the journeying.	He created the heavens and the earth with truth, and He formed you, then made goodly your forms, and to Him is the ultimate resort.
64 004	He knows what is in the heavens and on earth; and He knows what ye conceal and what ye reveal: yea, Allah knows well the (secrets) of (all) hearts.	He knoweth all that is in the heavens and the earth, and He knoweth what ye conceal and what ye publish. And Allah is Aware of what is in the breasts (of men).	He knows what is in the heavens and the earth, and He knows what you hide and what you manifest; and Allah is Cognizant of what is in the hearts.
64 005	Has not the story reached you, of those who rejected Faith aforetime? So they tasted the evil result of their conduct; and they had a grievous Penalty.	Hath not the story reached you of those who disbelieved of old and so did taste the ill-effects of their conduct, and theirs will be a painful doom.	Has there not come to you the story of those who disbelieved before, then tasted the evil result of their conduct, and they had a painful punishment?
64 006	That was because there came to them messengers with Clear Signs, but they said: "Shall (mere) human beings direct us?" So they rejected (the Message) and turned away. But Allah can do without (them): and Allah is free of all needs, worthy of all praise.	That was because their messengers (from Allah) kept coming unto them with clear proofs (of Allah's Sovereignty), but they said: Shall mere mortals guide us? So they disbelieved and turned away, and Allah was independent (of them). Allah is Absolute, Owner of Praise.	That is because there came to them their messengers with clear arguments, but they said: Shall mortals guide us? So they disbelieved and turned back, and Allah does not stand in need (of anything), and Allah is Self-sufficient, Praised.
64 007	The Unbelievers think that they will not be raised up (for Judgment). Say: "Yea, by my Lord, Ye shall surely be raised up: then shall ye be told (the truth) of all that ye did. And that is easy for Allah."	Those who disbelieve assert that they will not be raised again. Say (unto them, O Muhammad): Yea, verily, by my Lord! ye will be raised again and then ye will be informed of what ye did; and that is easy for Allah.	Those who disbelieve think that they shall never be raised. Say: Aye! by my Lord! you shall most certainly be raised, then you shall most certainly be informed of what you did; and that is easy to Allah.

64 008	Believe, therefore, in Allah and His Messenger, and in the Light which we have sent down. And Allah is well acquainted with all that ye do.	So believe in Allah and His messenger and the light which We have revealed. And Allah is Informed of what ye do.	Therefore believe in Allah and His Messenger and the Light which We have revealed; and Allah is Aware of what you do.
64 009	The Day that He assembles you (all) for a Day of Assembly,- that will be a Day of mutual loss and gain (among you), and those who believe in Allah and work righteousness,- He will remove from them their ills, and He will admit them to Gardens beneath which Rivers flow, to dwell therein for ever: that will be the Supreme Achievement.	The day when He shall gather you unto the Day of Assembling, that will be a day of mutual disillusion. And whoso believeth in Allah and doeth right, He will remit from him his evil deeds and will bring him unto Gardens underneath which rivers flow, therein to abide for ever. That is the supreme triumph.	On the day that He will gather you for the day of gathering, that is the day of loss and gain; and whoever believes in Allah and does good, He will remove from him his evil and cause him to enter gardens beneath which rivers flow, to abide therein forever; that is the great achievement.
64 010	But those who reject Faith and treat Our Signs as falsehoods, they will be Companions of the Fire, to dwell therein for aye: and evil is that Goal.	But those who disbelieve and deny Our revelations, such are owners of the Fire; they will abide therein - a hapless journey's end!	And (as for) those who disbelieve and reject Our communications, they are the inmates of the fire, to abide therein and evil is the resort.
64 011	No kind of calamity can occur, except by the leave of Allah: and if any one believes in Allah, (Allah) guides his heart (aright): for Allah knows all things.	No calamity befalleth save by Allah's leave. And whosoever believeth in Allah, He guideth his heart. And Allah is Knower of all things.	No affliction comes about but by Allah's permission; and whoever believes in Allah, He guides aright his heart; and Allah is Cognizant of all things.
64 012	So obey Allah, and obey His Messenger: but if ye turn back, the duty of Our Messenger is but to proclaim (the Message) clearly and openly.	Obey Allah and obey His messenger; but if ye turn away, then the duty of Our messenger is only to convey (the message) plainly.	And obey Allah and obey the Messenger, but if you turn back, then upon Our Messenger devolves only the clear delivery (of the message).
64 013	Allah! There is no god but He: and on Allah, therefore, let the Believers put their trust.	Allah! There is no God save Him. In Allah, therefore, let believers put their trust.	Allah, there is no god but He; and upon Allah, then, let the believers rely.
64 014	O ye who believe! Truly, among your wives and your children are (some that are) enemies to yourselves: so beware of them! But if ye forgive and overlook, and cover up (their faults), verily Allah is Oft-Forgiving, Most Merciful.	O ye who believe! Lo! among your wives and your children there are enemies for you, therefor beware of them. And if ye efface and overlook and forgive, then lo! Allah is Forgiving, Merciful.	O you who believe! surely from among your wives and your children there is an enemy to you; therefore beware of them; and if you pardon and forbear and forgive, then surely Allah is Forgiving, Merciful.
64 015	Your riches and your children may be but a trial: but in the Presence of Allah, is the highest, Reward.	Your wealth and your children are only a temptation, whereas Allah! with Him is an immense reward.	Your possessions and your children are only a trial, and Allah it is with Whom is a great reward.
64 016	So fear Allah as much as ye can; listen and obey and spend in charity for the benefit of your own soul and those saved from the covetousness of their own souls,- they are the ones that achieve prosperity.	So keep your duty to Allah as best ye can, and listen, and obey, and spend; that is better for your souls. And whoso is saved from his own greed, such are the successful.	Therefore be careful of (your duty to) Allah as much as you can, and hear and obey and spend, it is better for your souls; and whoever is saved from the greediness of his soul, these it is that are the successful.
64 017	If ye loan to Allah, a beautiful loan, He will double it to your (credit), and He will grant you Forgiveness: for Allah is most Ready to appreciate (service), Most Forbearing,-	If ye lend unto Allah a goodly loan, He will double it for you and will forgive you, for Allah is Responsive, Clement,	If you set apart for Allah a goodly portion, He will double it for you and forgive you; and Allah is the Multiplier (of rewards), Forbearing,
64 018	Knower of what is open, Exalted in Might, Full of Wisdom.	Knower of the Invisible and the Visible, the Mighty, the Wise.	The Knower of the unseen and the seen, the Mighty, the Wise.

Chapter 65:

AT-TALAQ (DIVORCE)

Total Verses: 12 Revealed At: MADINA

In the name of Allah, the Most Beneficent, the Most Merciful.

65 001	O Prophet! When ye do divorce women, divorce them at their prescribed periods, and count (accurately), their prescribed periods: And fear Allah your Lord: and turn them not out of their houses, nor shall they (themselves) leave, except in case they are guilty of some open lewdness, those are limits set by Allah: and any who transgresses the limits of Allah, does verily wrong his (own) soul: thou knowest not if perchance Allah will bring about thereafter some new situation.	O Prophet! When ye (men) put away women, put them away for their (legal) period and reckon the period, and keep your duty to Allah, your Lord. Expel them not from their houses nor let them go forth unless they commit open immorality. Such are the limits (imposed by) Allah; and whoso transgresseth Allah's limits, he verily wrongeth his soul. Thou knowest not: it may be that Allah will afterward bring some new thing to pass.		O Prophet! when you divorce women, divorce them for their prescribed time, and calculate the number of the days prescribed, and be careful of (your duty to) Allah, your Lord. Do not drive them out of their houses, nor should they themselves go forth, unless they commit an open indecency; and these are the limits of Allah, and whoever goes beyond the limits of Allah, he indeed does injustice to his own soul. You do not know that Allah may after that bring about reunion.
65 002	Thus when they fulfil their term appointed, either take them back on equitable terms or part with them on equitable terms; and take for witness two persons from among you, endued with justice, and establish the evidence (as) before Allah. Such is the admonition given to him who believes in Allah and the Last Day. And for those who fear Allah, He (ever) prepares a way out,	Then, when they have reached their term, take them back in kindness or part from them in kindness, and call to witness two just men among you, and keep your testimony upright for Allah. Whoso believeth in Allah and the Last Day is exhorted to act thus. And whosoever keepeth his duty to Allah, Allah will appoint a way out for him,		So when they have reached their prescribed time, then retain them with kindness or separate them with kindness, and call to witness two men of justice from among you, and give upright testimony for Allah. With that is admonished he who believes in Allah and the latter day; and whoever is careful of (his duty to) Allah, He will make for him an outlet,
65 003	And He provides for him from (sources) he never could imagine. And if any one puts his trust in Allah, sufficient is (Allah) for him. For Allah will surely accomplish his purpose: verily, for all things has Allah appointed a due proportion.	And will provide for him from (a quarter) whence he hath no expectation. And whosoever putteth his trust in Allah, He will suffice him. Lo! Allah bringeth His command to pass. Allah hath set a measure for all things.		And give him sustenance from whence he thinks not; and whoever trusts in Allah, He is sufficient for him; surely Allah attains His purpose; Allah indeed has appointed a measure for everything.
65 004	Such of your women as have passed the age of monthly courses, for them the prescribed period, if ye have any doubts, is three months, and for those who have no courses (it is the same): for those who carry (life within their wombs), their period is until they deliver their burdens: and for those who fear Allah, He will make their path easy.	And for such of your women as despair of menstruation, if ye doubt, their period (of waiting) shall be three months, along with those who have it not. And for those with child, their period shall be till they bring forth their burden. And whosoever keepeth his duty to Allah, He maketh his course easy for him.		And (as for) those of your women who have despaired of menstruation, if you have a doubt, their prescribed time shall be three months, and of those too who have not had their courses; and (as for) the pregnant women, their prescribed time is that they lay down their burden; and whoever is careful of (his duty to) Allah He will make easy for him his affair.

65 005	That is the Command of Allah, which He has sent down to you: and if any one fears Allah, He will remove his ills, from him, and will enlarge his reward.	That is the commandment of Allah which He revealeth unto you. And whoso keepeth his duty to Allah, He will remit from him his evil deeds and magnify reward for him.		That is the command of Allah which He has revealed to you, and whoever is careful of (his duty to) Allah, He will remove from him his evil and give him a big reward.
65 006	Let the women live (in 'iddat) in the same style as ye live, according to your means: Annoy them not, so as to restrict them. And if they carry (life in their wombs), then spend (your substance) on them until they deliver their burden: and if they suckle your (offspring), give them their recompense: and take mutual counsel together, according to what is just and reasonable. And if ye find yourselves in difficulties, let another woman suckle (the child) on the (father's) behalf.	Lodge them where ye dwell, according to your wealth, and harass them not so as to straiten life for them. And if they are with child, then spend for them till they bring forth their burden. Then, if they give suck for you, give them their due payment and consult together in kindness; but if ye make difficulties for one another, then let some other woman give suck for him (the father of the child).		Lodge them where you lodge according to your means, and do not injure them in order that you may straiten them; and if they are pregnant, spend on them until they lay down their burden; then if they suckle for you, give them their recompense and enjoin one another among you to do good; and if you disagree, another (woman) shall suckle for him.
65 007	Let the man of means spend according to his means: and the man whose resources are restricted, let him spend according to what Allah has given him. Allah puts no burden on any person beyond what He has given him. After a difficulty, Allah will soon grant relief.	Let him who hath abundance spend of his abundance, and he whose provision is measured, let him spend of that which Allah hath given him. Allah asketh naught of any soul save that which He hath given it. Allah will vouchsafe, after hardship, ease.		Let him who has abundance spend out of his abundance and whoever has his means of subsistence straitened to him, let him spend out of that which Allah has given him; Allah does not lay on any soul a burden except to the extent to which He has granted it; Allah brings about ease after difficulty.
65 008	How many populations that insolently opposed the command of their Lord and of His messengers, did We not then call to account,- to severe account?- and We imposed on them an exemplary Punishment.	And how many a community revolted against the ordinance of its Lord and His messengers, and We called it to a stern account and punished it with dire punishment,		And how many a town which rebelled against the commandment of its Lord and His messengers, so We called it to account severely and We chastised it (with) a stern chastisement.
65 009	Then did they taste the evil result of their conduct, and the End of their conduct was Perdition.	So that it tasted the ill-effects of its conduct, and the consequence of its conduct was loss.		So it tasted the evil result of its conduct, and the end of its affair was perdition.
65 010	Allah has prepared for them a severe Punishment (in the Hereafter). Therefore fear Allah, O ye men of understanding - who have believed!- for Allah hath indeed sent down to you a Message,-	Allah hath prepared for them stern punishment; so keep your duty to Allah, O men of understanding! O ye who believe! Now Allah hath sent down unto you a reminder,		Allah has prepared for them severe chastisement, therefore be careful of (your duty to) Allah, O men of understanding who believe! Allah has indeed revealed to you a reminder,
65 011	A Messenger, who rehearses to you the Signs of Allah containing clear explanations, that he may lead forth those who believe and do righteous deeds from the depths of Darkness into Light. And those who believe in Allah and work righteousness, He will admit to Gardens beneath which Rivers flow, to dwell therein for ever: Allah has indeed granted for them a most excellent Provision.	A messenger reciting unto you the revelations of Allah made plain, that He may bring forth those who believe and do good works from darkness unto light. And whosoever believeth in Allah and doeth right, He will bring him into Gardens underneath which rivers flow, therein to abide for ever. Allah hath made good provision for him.		A Messenger who recites to you the clear communications of Allah so that he may bring forth those who believe and do good deeds from darkness into light; and whoever believes in Allah and does good deeds, He will cause him to enter gardens beneath which rivers now, to abide therein forever, Allah has indeed given him a goodly sustenance.

65 012	Allah is He Who created seven Firmaments and of the earth a similar number. Through the midst of them (all) descends His Command: that ye may know that Allah has power over all things, and that Allah comprehends, all things in (His) Knowledge.	Allah it is who hath created seven heavens, and of the earth the like thereof. The commandment cometh down among them slowly, that ye may know that Allah is Able to do all things, and that Allah surroundeth all things in knowledge.		Allah is He Who created seven heavens, and of the earth the like of them; the decree continues to descend among them, that you may know that Allah has power over all things and that Allah indeed encompasses all things in (His) knowledge.

Chapter 66:

AT-TAHRIM (BANNING, PROHIBITION)

Total Verses: 12 Revealed At: MADINA

In the name of Allah, the Most Beneficent, the Most Merciful.

66 001	O Prophet! Why holdest thou to be forbidden that which Allah has made lawful to thee? Thou seekest to please thy consorts. But Allah is Oft-Forgiving, Most Merciful.	O Prophet! Why bannest thou that which Allah hath made lawful for thee, seeking to please thy wives? And Allah is Forgiving, Merciful.	O Prophet! why do you forbid (yourself) that which Allah has made lawful for you; you seek to please your wives; and Allah is Forgiving, Merciful.
66 002	Allah has already ordained for you, (O men), the dissolution of your oaths (in some cases): and Allah is your Protector, and He is Full of Knowledge and Wisdom.	Allah hath made lawful for you (Muslims) absolution from your oaths (of such a kind), and Allah is your Protector. He is the Knower, the Wise.	Allah indeed has sanctioned for you the expiation of your oaths and Allah is your Protector, and He is the Knowing the Wise.
66 003	When the Prophet disclosed a matter in confidence to one of his consorts, and she then divulged it (to another), and Allah made it known to him, he confirmed part thereof and repudiated a part. Then when he told her thereof, she said, "Who told thee this?" He said, "He told me Who knows and is well-acquainted (with all things)."	When the Prophet confided a fact unto one of his wives and when she afterward divulged it and Allah apprised him thereof, he made known (to her) part thereof and passed over part. And when he told it her she said: Who hath told thee? He said: The Knower, the Aware hath told me.	And when the prophet secretly communicated a piece of information to one of his wives-- but when she informed (others) of it, and Allah made him to know it, he made known part of it and avoided part; so when he informed her of it, she said: Who informed you of this? He said: The Knowing, the one Aware, informed me.
66 004	If ye two turn in repentance to Him, your hearts are indeed so inclined; But if ye back up each other against him, truly Allah is his Protector, and Gabriel, and (every) righteous one among those who believe,- and furthermore, the angels - will back (him) up.	If ye twain turn unto Allah repentant, (ye have cause to do so) for your hearts desired (the ban); and if ye aid one another against him (Muhammad) then lo! Allah, even He, is his Protecting Friend, and Gabriel and the righteous among the believers; and furthermore the angels are his helpers.	If you both turn to Allah, then indeed your hearts are already inclined (to this); and if you back up each other against him, then surely Allah it is Who is his Guardian, and Jibreel and the believers that do good, and the angels after that are the aiders.
66 005	It may be, if he divorced you (all), that Allah will give him in exchange consorts better than you,- who submit (their wills), who believe, who are devout, who turn to Allah in repentance, who worship (in humility), who travel (for Faith) and fast,- previously married or virgins.	It may happen that his Lord, if he divorce you, will give him in your stead wives better than you, submissive (to Allah), believing, pious, penitent, devout, inclined to fasting, widows and maids.	Maybe, his Lord, if he divorce you, will give him in your place wives better than you, submissive, faithful, obedient, penitent, adorers, fasters, widows and virgins.

66 006	O ye who believe! save yourselves and your families from a Fire whose fuel is Men and Stones, over which are (appointed) angels stern (and) severe, who flinch not (from executing) the Commands they receive from Allah, but do (precisely) what they are commanded.	O ye who believe! Ward off from yourselves and your families a Fire whereof the fuel is men and stones, over which are set angels strong, severe, who resist not Allah in that which He commandeth them, but do that which they are commanded.	O you who believe! save yourselves and your families from a fire whose fuel is men and stones; over it are angels stern and strong, they do not disobey Allah in what He commands them, and do as they are commanded.
66 007	(They will say), "O ye Unbelievers! Make no excuses this Day! Ye are being but requited for all that ye did!"	(Then it will be said): O ye who disbelieve! Make no excuses for yourselves this day. Ye are only being paid for what ye used to do.	O you who disbelieve! do not urge excuses today; you shall be rewarded only according to what you did.
66 008	O ye who believe! Turn to Allah with sincere repentance: In the hope that your Lord will remove from you your ills and admit you to Gardens beneath which Rivers flow,- the Day that Allah will not permit to be humiliated the Prophet and those who believe with him. Their Light will run forward before them and by their right hands, while they say, "Our Lord! Perfect our Light for us, and grant us Forgiveness: for Thou hast power over all things."	O ye who believe! Turn unto Allah in sincere repentance! It may be that your Lord will remit from you your evil deeds and bring you into Gardens underneath which rivers flow, on the day when Allah will not abase the Prophet and those who believe with him. Their light will run before them and on their right hands; they will say: Our Lord! Perfect our light for us, and forgive us! Lo! Thou art Able to do all things.	O you who believe! turn to Allah a sincere turning; maybe your Lord will remove from you your evil and cause you to enter gardens beneath which rivers flow, on the day on which Allah will not abase the Prophet and those who believe with him; their light shall run on before them and on their right hands; they shall say: Our Lord! make perfect for us our light, and grant us protection, surely Thou hast power over all things.
66 009	O Prophet! Strive hard against the Unbelievers and the Hypocrites, and be firm against them. Their abode is Hell,- an evil refuge (indeed).	O Prophet! Strive against the disbelievers and the hypocrites, and be stern with them. Hell will be their home, a hapless journey's end.	O Prophet! strive hard against the unbelievers and the hypocrites, and be hard against them; and their abode is hell; and evil is the resort.
66 010	Allah sets forth, for an example to the Unbelievers, the wife of Noah and the wife of Lut: they were (respectively) under two of our righteous servants, but they were false to their (husbands), and they profited nothing before Allah on their account, but were told: "Enter ye the Fire along with (others) that enter!"	Allah citeth an example for those who disbelieve: the wife of Noah and the wife of Lot, who were under two of Our righteous slaves yet betrayed them so that they (the husbands) availed them naught against Allah and it was said (unto them): Enter the Fire along with those who enter.	Allah sets forth an example to those who disbelieve the wife of Nuh and the wife of Lut: they were both under two of Our righteous servants, but they acted treacherously towards them so they availed them naught against Allah, and it was said: Enter both the fire with those who enter.
66 011	And Allah sets forth, as an example to those who believe the wife of Pharaoh: Behold she said: "O my Lord! Build for me, in nearness to Thee, a mansion in the Garden, and save me from Pharaoh and his doings, and save me from those that do wrong";	And Allah citeth an example for those who believe: the wife of Pharaoh when she said: My Lord! Build for me a home with thee in the Garden, and deliver me from Pharaoh and his work, and deliver me from evil-doing folk;	And Allah sets forth an example to those who believe the wife of Firon when she said: My Lord! build for me a house with Thee in the garden and deliver me from Firon and his doing, and deliver me from the unjust people:
66 012	And Mary the daughter of 'Imran, who guarded her chastity; and We breathed into (her body) of Our spirit; and she testified to the truth of the words of her Lord and of His Revelations, and was one of the devout (servants).	And Mary, daughter of 'Imran, whose body was chaste, therefor We breathed therein something of Our Spirit. And she put faith in the words of her Lord and His scriptures, and was of the obedient.	And Marium, the daughter of Imran, who guarded her chastity, so We breathed into her of Our inspiration and she accepted the truth of the words of her Lord and His books, and she was of, the obedient ones.

Chapter 67:

AL-MULK (THE SOVEREIGNTY, CONTROL)

Total Verses: 30 Revealed At: MAKKA

In the name of Allah, the Most Beneficent, the Most Merciful.

67 001	Blessed be He in Whose hands is Dominion; and He over all things hath Power;-	Blessed is He in Whose hand is the Sovereignty, and, He is Able to do all things.	Blessed is He in Whose hand is the kingdom, and He has power over all things,
67 002	He Who created Death and Life, that He may try which of you is best in deed: and He is the Exalted in Might, Oft-Forgiving;-	Who hath created life and death that He may try you which of you is best in conduct; and He is the Mighty, the Forgiving,	Who created death and life that He may try you-- which of you is best in deeds; and He is the Mighty, the Forgiving,
67 003	He Who created the seven heavens one above another: No want of proportion wilt thou see in the Creation of (Allah) Most Gracious. So turn thy vision again: seest thou any flaw?	Who hath created seven heavens in harmony. Thou (Muhammad) canst see no fault in the Beneficent One's creation; then look again: Canst thou see any rifts?	Who created the seven heavens one above another; you see no incongruity in the creation of the Beneficent Allah; then look again, can you see any disorder?
67 004	Again turn thy vision a second time: (thy) vision will come back to thee dull and discomfited, in a state worn out.	Then look again and yet again, thy sight will return unto thee weakened and made dim.	Then turn back the eye again and again; your look shall come back to you confused while it is fatigued.
67 005	And we have, (from of old), adorned the lowest heaven with Lamps, and We have made such (Lamps) (as) missiles to drive away the Evil Ones, and have prepared for them the Penalty of the Blazing Fire.	And verily We have beautified the world's heaven with lamps, and We have made them missiles for the devils, and for them We have prepared the doom of flame.	And certainly We have adorned this lower heaven with lamps and We have made these missiles for the Shaitans, and We have prepared for them the chastisement of burning.
67 006	For those who reject their Lord (and Cherisher) is the Penalty of Hell: and evil is (such), Destination.	And for those who disbelieve in their Lord there is the doom of hell, a hapless journey's end!	And for those who disbelieve in their Lord is the punishment of hell, and evil is the resort.
67 007	When they are cast therein, they will hear the (terrible) drawing in of its breath even as it blazes forth,	When they are flung therein they hear its roaring as it boileth up,	When they shall be cast therein, they shall hear a loud moaning of it as it heaves,
67 008	Almost bursting with fury: Every time a Group is cast therein, its Keepers will ask, "Did no Warner come to you?"	As it would burst with rage. Whenever a (fresh) host is flung therein the wardens thereof ask them: Came there unto you no warner?	Almost bursting for fury. Whenever a group is cast into it, its keeper shall ask them: Did there not come to you a warner?
67 009	They will say: "Yes indeed; a Warner did come to us, but we rejected him and said, 'Allah never sent down any (Message): ye are nothing but an egregious delusion!'"	They say: Yea, verily, a warner came unto us; but we denied and said: Allah hath naught revealed; ye are in naught but a great error.	They shall say: Yea! indeed there came to us a warner, but we rejected (him) and said: Allah has not revealed anything, you are only in a great error.
67 010	They will further say: "Had we but listened or used our intelligence, we should not (now) be among the Companions of the Blazing Fire!"	And they say: Had we been wont to listen or have sense, we had not been among the dwellers in the flames.	And they shall say: Had we but listened or pondered, we should not have been among the inmates of the burning fire.

67 011	They will then confess their sins: but far will be (Forgiveness) from the Companions of the Blazing Fire!	So they acknowledge their sins; but far removed (from mercy) are the dwellers in the flames.	So they shall acknowledge their sins, but far will be (forgiveness) from the inmates of the burning fire.
67 012	As for those who fear their Lord unseen, for them is Forgiveness and a great Reward.	Lo! those who fear their Lord in secret, theirs will be forgiveness and a great reward.	(As for) those who fear their Lord in secret, they shall surely have forgiveness and a great reward.
67 013	And whether ye hide your word or publish it, He certainly has (full) knowledge, of the secrets of (all) hearts.	And keep your opinion secret or proclaim it, lo! He is Knower of all that is in the breasts (of men).	And conceal your word or manifest it; surely He is Cognizant of what is in the hearts.
67 014	Should He not know,- He that created? and He is the One that understands the finest mysteries (and) is well-acquainted (with them).	Should He not know what He created? And He is the Subtile, the Aware.	Does He not know, Who created? And He is the Knower of the subtleties, the Aware.
67 015	It is He Who has made the earth manageable for you, so traverse ye through its tracts and enjoy of the Sustenance which He furnishes: but unto Him is the Resurrection.	He it is Who hath made the earth subservient unto you, so Walk in the paths thereof and eat of His providence. And unto Him will be the resurrection (of the dead).	He it is Who made the earth smooth for you, therefore go about in the spacious sides thereof, and eat of His sustenance, and to Him is the return after death.
67 016	Do ye feel secure that He Who is in heaven will not cause you to be swallowed up by the earth when it shakes (as in an earthquake)?	Have ye taken security from Him Who is in the heaven that He will not cause the earth to swallow you when lo! it is convulsed?	Are you secure of those in the heaven that He should not make the earth to swallow you up? Then lo! it shall be in a state of commotion.
67 017	Or do ye feel secure that He Who is in Heaven will not send against you a violent tornado (with showers of stones), so that ye shall know how (terrible) was My warning?	Or have ye taken security from Him Who is in the heaven that He will not let loose on you a hurricane? But ye shall know the manner of My warning.	Or are you secure of those in the heaven that He should not send down upon you a punishment? Then shall you know how was My warning.
67 018	But indeed men before them rejected (My warning): then how (terrible) was My rejection (of them)?	And verily those before them denied, then (see) the manner of My wrath (with them)!	And certainly those before them rejected (the truth), then how was My disapproval.
67 019	Do they not observe the birds above them, spreading their wings and folding them in? None can uphold them except (Allah) Most Gracious: Truly (Allah) Most Gracious: Truly it is He that watches over all things.	Have they not seen the birds above them spreading out their wings and closing them? Naught upholdeth them save the Beneficent. Lo! He is Seer of all things.	Have they not seen the birds above them expanding (their wings) and contracting (them)? What is it that withholds them save the Beneficent Allah? Surely He sees everything.
67 020	Nay, who is there that can help you, (even as) an army, besides (Allah) Most Merciful? In nothing but delusion are the Unbelievers.	Or who is he that will be an army unto you to help you instead of the Beneficent? The disbelievers are in naught but illusion.	Or who is it that will be a host for you to assist you besides the Beneficent Allah? The unbelievers are only in deception.
67 021	Or who is there that can provide you with Sustenance if He were to withhold His provision? Nay, they obstinately persist in insolent impiety and flight (from the Truth).	Or who is he that will provide for you if He should withhold His providence? Nay, but they are set in pride and frowardness.	Or who is it that will give you sustenance if He should withhold His sustenance? Nay! they persist in disdain and aversion.
67 022	Is then one who walks headlong, with his face grovelling, better guided,- or one who walks evenly on a Straight Way?	Is he who goeth groping on his face more rightly guided, or he who walketh upright on a straight road?	What! is he who goes prone upon his face better guided or he who walks upright upon a straight path?
67 023	Say: "It is He Who has created you (and made you grow), and made for you the faculties of hearing, seeing, feeling and understanding: little thanks it is ye give."	Say (unto them, O Muhammad): He it is who gave you being, and hath assigned unto you ears and eyes and hearts. Small thanks give ye!	Say: He it is Who brought you into being and made for you the ears and the eyes and the hearts: little is it that you give thanks.

67 024	Say: "It is He Who has multiplied you through the earth, and to Him shall ye be gathered together."	Say: He it is Who multiplieth you in the earth, and unto Whom ye will be gathered.	Say: He it is Who multiplied you in the earth and to Him you shall be gathered.
67 025	They ask: When will this promise be (fulfilled)? - If ye are telling the truth.	And they say: When (will) this promise (be fulfilled), if ye are truthful?	And they say: When shall this threat be (executed) if you are truthful?
67 026	Say: "As to the knowledge of the time, it is with Allah alone: I am (sent) only to warn plainly in public."	Say: The knowledge is with Allah only, and I am but a plain warner;	Say: The knowledge (thereof) is only with Allah and I am only a plain warner.
67 027	At length, when they see it close at hand, grieved will be the faces of the Unbelievers, and it will be said (to them): "This is (the promise fulfilled), which ye were calling for!"	But when they see it nigh, the faces of those who disbelieve will be awry, and it will be said (unto them): This is that for which ye used to call.	But when they shall see it nigh, the faces of those who disbelieve shall be sorry, and it shall be said; This is that which you used to call for.
67 028	Say: "See ye?- If Allah were to destroy me, and those with me, or if He bestows His Mercy on us,- yet who can deliver the Unbelievers from a grievous Penalty?"	Say (O Muhammad): Have ye thought: Whether Allah causeth me (Muhammad) and those with me to perish or hath mercy on us, still, who will protect the disbelievers from a painful doom?	Say: Have you considered if Allah should destroy me and those with me-- rather He will have mercy on us; yet who will protect the unbelievers from a painful punishment?
67 029	Say: "He is (Allah) Most Gracious: We have believed in Him, and on Him have we put our trust: So, soon will ye know which (of us) it is that is in manifest error."	Say: He is the Beneficent. In Him we believe and in Him we put our trust. And ye will soon know who it is that is in error manifest.	Say: He is the Beneficent Allah, we believe in Him and on Him do we rely, so you shall come to know who it is that is in clear error.
67 030	Say: "See ye?- If your stream be some morning lost (in the underground earth), who then can supply you with clear-flowing water?"	Say: Have ye thought: If (all) your water were to disappear into the earth, who then could bring you gushing water?	Say: Have you considered if your water should go down, who is it then that will bring you flowing water?

Chapter 68:

AL-QALAM (THE PEN)

Total Verses: 52 Revealed At: MAKKA

In the name of Allah, the Most Beneficent, the Most Merciful.

68 001	Nun. By the Pen and the (Record) which (men) write,-	Nun. By the pen and that which they write (therewith),	Noon. I swear by the pen and what the angels write,
68 002	Thou art not, by the Grace of thy Lord, mad or possessed.	Thou art not, for thy Lord's favour unto thee, a madman.	By the grace of your Lord you are not mad.
68 003	Nay, verily for thee is a Reward unfailing:	And lo! thine verily will be a reward unfailing.	And most surely you shall have a reward never to be cut off.
68 004	And thou (standest) on an exalted standard of character.	And lo! thou art of a tremendous nature.	And most surely you conform (yourself) to sublime morality.
68 005	Soon wilt thou see, and they will see,	And thou wilt see and they will see	So you shall see, and they (too) shall see,
68 006	Which of you is afflicted with madness.	Which of you is the demented.	Which of you is afflicted with madness.

68 007	Verily it is thy Lord that knoweth best, which (among men) hath strayed from His Path: and He knoweth best those who receive (true) Guidance.	Lo! thy Lord is Best Aware of him who strayeth from His way, and He is Best Aware of those who walk aright.	Surely your Lord best knows him who errs from His way, and He best knows the followers of the right course.
68 008	So hearken not to those who deny (the Truth).	Therefor obey not thou the rejecters	So do not yield to the rejecters.
68 009	Their desire is that thou shouldst be pliant: so would they be pliant.	Who would have had thee compromise, that they may compromise.	They wish that you should be pliant so they (too) would be pliant.
68 010	Heed not the type of despicable men,- ready with oaths,	Neither obey thou each feeble oath-monger,	And yield not to any mean swearer
68 011	A slanderer, going about with calumnies,	Detracter, spreader abroad of slanders,	Defamer, going about with slander
68 012	(Habitually) hindering (all) good, transgressing beyond bounds, deep in sin,	Hinderer of the good, transgressor, malefactor	Forbidder of good, outstepping the limits, sinful,
68 013	Violent (and cruel),- with all that, base-born,-	Greedy therewithal, intrusive.	Ignoble, besides all that, base-born;
68 014	Because he possesses wealth and (numerous) sons.	It is because he is possessed of wealth and children	Because he possesses wealth and sons.
68 015	When to him are rehearsed Our Signs, "Tales of the ancients", he cries!	That, when Our revelations are recited unto him, he saith: Mere fables of the men of old.	When Our communications are recited to him, he says: Stories of those of yore.
68 016	Soon shall We brand (the beast) on the snout!	We shall brand him on the nose.	We will brand him on the nose.
68 017	Verily We have tried them as We tried the People of the Garden, when they resolved to gather the fruits of the (garden) in the morning.	Lo! We have tried them as We tried the owners of the garden when they vowed that they would pluck its fruit next morning,	Surely We will try them as We tried the owners of the garden, when they swore that they would certainly cut off the produce in the morning,
68 018	But made no reservation, ("If it be Allah's Will").	And made no exception (for the Will of Allah);	And were not willing to set aside a portion (for the poor).
68 019	Then there came on the (garden) a visitation from thy Lord, (which swept away) all around, while they were asleep.	Then a visitation from thy Lord came upon it while they slept	Then there encompassed it a visitation from your Lord while they were sleeping.
68 020	So the (garden) became, by the morning, like a dark and desolate spot, (whose fruit had been gathered).	And in the morning it was as if plucked.	So it became as black, barren land.
68 021	As the morning broke, they called out, one to another,-	And they cried out one unto another in the morning,	And they called out to each other in the morning,
68 022	"Go ye to your tilth (betimes) in the morning, if ye would gather the fruits."	Saying: Run unto your field if ye would pluck (the fruit).	Saying: Go early to your tilth if you would cut (the produce).
68 023	So they departed, conversing in secret low tones, (saying)-	So they went off, saying one unto another in low tones:	So they went, while they consulted together secretly,
68 024	"Let not a single indigent person break in upon you into the (garden) this day."	No needy man shall enter it to-day against you.	Saying: No poor man shall enter it today upon you.
68 025	And they opened the morning, strong in an (unjust) resolve.	They went betimes, strong in (this) purpose.	And in the morning they went, having the power to prevent.
68 026	But when they saw the (garden), they said: "We have surely lost our way:"	But when they saw it, they said: Lo! we are in error!	But when they saw it, they said: Most surely we have gone astray
68 027	"Indeed we are shut out (of the fruits of our labour)!"	Nay, but we are desolate!	Nay! we are made to suffer privation.

68 028	Said one of them, more just (than the rest): "Did I not say to you, 'Why not glorify (Allah)?'"	The best among them said: Said I not unto you: Why glorify ye not (Allah)?	The best of them said: Did I not say to you, Why do you not glorify (Allah)?
68 029	They said: "Glory to our Lord! Verily we have been doing wrong!"	They said: Glorified be our Lord! Lo! we have been wrong-doers.	They said: Glory be to our Lord, surely we were unjust.
68 030	Then they turned, one against another, in reproach.	Then some of them drew near unto others, self-reproaching.	Then some of them advanced against others, blaming each other.
68 031	They said: "Alas for us! We have indeed transgressed!"	They said: Alas for us! In truth we were outrageous.	Said they: O woe to us! surely we were inordinate:
68 032	"It may be that our Lord will give us in exchange a better (garden) than this: for we do turn to Him (in repentance)!"	It may be that our Lord will give us better than this in place thereof. Lo! we beseech our Lord.	Maybe, our Lord will give us instead one better than it; surely to our Lord do we make our humble petition.
68 033	Such is the Punishment (in this life); but greater is the Punishment in the Hereafter,- if only they knew!	Such was the punishment. And verily the punishment of the Hereafter is greater if they did but know.	Such is the chastisement, and certainly the chastisement of the hereafter is greater, did they but know!
68 034	Verily, for the Righteous, are Gardens of Delight, in the Presence of their Lord.	Lo! for those who keep from evil are gardens of bliss with their Lord.	Surely those who guard (against evil) shall have with their Lord gardens of bliss.
68 035	Shall We then treat the People of Faith like the People of Sin?	Shall We then treat those who have surrendered as We treat the guilty?	What! shall We then make (that is, treat) those who submit as the guilty?
68 036	What is the matter with you? How judge ye?	What aileth you? How foolishly ye judge!	What has happened to you? How do you judge?
68 037	Or have ye a book through which ye learn-	Or have ye a scripture wherein ye learn	Or have you a book wherein you read,
68 038	That ye shall have, through it whatever ye choose?	That ye shall indeed have all that ye choose?	That you have surely therein what you choose?
68 039	Or have ye Covenants with Us to oath, reaching to the Day of Judgment, (providing) that ye shall have whatever ye shall demand?	Or have ye a covenant on oath from Us that reacheth to the Day of Judgment, that yours shall be all that ye ordain?	Or have you received from Us an agreement confirmed by an oath extending to the day of resurrection that you shall surely have what you demand?
68 040	Ask thou of them, which of them will stand surety for that!	Ask them (O Muhammad) which of them will vouch for that!	Ask them which of them will vouch for that,
68 041	Or have they some "Partners" (in Godhead)? Then let them produce their "partners", if they are truthful!	Or have they other gods? Then let them bring their other gods if they are truthful,	Or have they associates if they are truthful.
68 042	The Day that the shin shall be laid bare, and they shall be summoned to bow in adoration, but they shall not be able,-	On the day when it befalleth in earnest, and they are ordered to prostrate themselves but are not able,	On the day when there shall be a severe affliction, and they shall be called upon to make obeisance, but they shall not be able,
68 043	Their eyes will be cast down,- ignominy will cover them; seeing that they had been summoned aforetime to bow in adoration, while they were whole, (and had refused).	With eyes downcast, abasement stupefying them. And they had been summoned to prostrate themselves while they were yet unhurt.	Their looks cast down, abasement shall overtake them; and they were called upon to make obeisance indeed while yet they were safe.
68 044	Then leave Me alone with such as reject this Message: by degrees shall We punish them from directions they perceive not.	Leave Me (to deal) with those who give the lie to this pronouncement. We shall lead them on by steps from whence they know not.	So leave Me and him who rejects this announcement; We will overtake them by degrees, from whence they perceive not:
68 045	A (long) respite will I grant them: truly powerful is My Plan.	Yet I bear with them, for lo! My scheme is firm.	And I do bear with them, surely My plan is firm.
68 046	Or is it that thou dost ask them for a reward, so that they are burdened with a load of debt?-	Or dost thou (Muhammad) ask a fee from them so that they are heavily taxed?	Or do you ask from them a reward, so that they are burdened with debt?

68 047	Or that the Unseen is in their hands, so that they can write it down?	Or is the Unseen theirs that they can write (thereof)?	Or have they (the knowledge of) the unseen, so that they write (it) down?
68 048	So wait with patience for the Command of thy Lord, and be not like the Companion of the Fish,- when he cried out in agony.	But wait thou for thy Lord's decree, and be not like him of the fish, who cried out in despair.	So wait patiently for the judgment of your Lord, and be not like the companion of the fish, when he cried while he was in distress.
68 049	Had not Grace from his Lord reached him, he would indeed have been cast off on the naked shore, in disgrace.	Had it not been that favour from his Lord had reached him he surely had been cast into the wilderness while he was reprobate.	Were it not that favor from his Lord had overtaken him, he would certainly have been cast down upon the naked Found while he was blamed.
68 050	Thus did his Lord choose him and make him of the Company of the Righteous.	But his Lord chose him and placed him among the righteous.	Then his Lord chose him, and He made him of the good.
68 051	And the Unbelievers would almost trip thee up with their eyes when they hear the Message; and they say: "Surely he is possessed!"	And lo! those who disbelieve would fain disconcert thee with their eyes when they hear the Reminder, and they say: Lo! he is indeed mad;	And those who disbelieve would almost smite you with their eyes when they hear the reminder, and they say: Most surely he is mad.
68 052	But it is nothing less than a Message to all the worlds.	When it is naught else than a Reminder to creation.	And it is naught but a reminder to the nations.

Chapter 69:

AL-HAAQQA (THE REALITY)

Total Verses: 52 Revealed At: MAKKA

In the name of Allah, the Most Beneficent, the Most Merciful.

69 001	The Sure Reality!	The Reality!	The sure calamity!
69 002	What is the Sure Reality?	What is the Reality?	What is the sure calamity!
69 003	And what will make thee realise what the Sure Reality is?	Ah, what will convey unto thee what the reality is!	And what would make you realize what the sure calamity is!
69 004	The Thamud and the 'Ad People (branded) as false the Stunning Calamity!	(The tribes of) Thamud and A'ad disbelieved in the judgment to come.	Samood and Ad called the striking calamity a lie.
69 005	But the Thamud,- they were destroyed by a terrible Storm of thunder and lightning!	As for Thamud, they were destroyed by the lightning.	Then as to Samood, they were destroyed by an excessively severe punishment.
69 006	And the 'Ad, they were destroyed by a furious Wind, exceedingly violent;	And as for A'ad, they were destroyed by a fierce roaring wind,	And as to Ad, they were destroyed by a roaring, violent blast.
69 007	He made it rage against them seven nights and eight days in succession: so that thou couldst see the (whole) people lying prostrate in its (path), as they had been roots of hollow palm-trees tumbled down!	Which He imposed on them for seven long nights and eight long days so that thou mightest have seen men lying overthrown, as they were hollow trunks of palm-trees.	Which He made to prevail against them for seven nights and eight days unremittingly, so that you might have seen the people therein prostrate as if they were the trunks of hollow palms.
69 008	Then seest thou any of them left surviving?	Canst thou (O Muhammad) see any remnant of them?	Do you then see of them one remaining?

69 009	And Pharaoh, and those before him, and the Cities Overthrown, committed habitual Sin.	And Pharaoh and those before him, and the communities that were destroyed, brought error,	And Firon and those before him and the overthrown cities continuously committed sins.
69 010	And disobeyed (each) the messenger of their Lord; so He punished them with an abundant Penalty.	And they disobeyed the messenger of their Lord, therefor did He grip them with a tightening grip.	And they disobeyed the Messenger of their Lord, so He punished them with a vehement punishment.
69 011	We, when the water (of Noah's Flood) overflowed beyond its limits, carried you (mankind), in the floating (Ark),	Lo! when the waters rose, We carried you upon the ship	Surely We bore you up in the ship when the water rose high,
69 012	That We might make it a Message unto you, and that ears (that should hear the tale and) retain its memory should bear its (lessons) in remembrance.	That We might make it a memorial for you, and that remembering ears (that heard the story) might remember.	So that We may make it a reminder to you, and that the retaining ear might retain it.
69 013	Then, when one blast is sounded on the Trumpet,	And when the trumpet shall sound one blast	And when the trumpet is blown with a single blast,
69 014	And the earth is moved, and its mountains, and they are crushed to powder at one stroke,-	And the earth with the mountains shall be lifted up and crushed with one crash,	And the earth and the mountains are borne away and crushed with a single crushing.
69 015	On that Day shall the (Great) Event come to pass.	Then, on that day will the Event befall.	On that day shall the great event come to pass,
69 016	And the sky will be rent asunder, for it will that Day be flimsy,	And the heaven will split asunder, for that day it will be frail.	And the heaven shall cleave asunder, so that on that day it shall be frail,
69 017	And the angels will be on its sides, and eight will, that Day, bear the Throne of thy Lord above them.	And the angels will be on the sides thereof, and eight will uphold the Throne of thy Lord that day, above them.	And the angels shall be on the sides thereof; and above them eight shall bear on that day your Lord's power.
69 018	That Day shall ye be brought to Judgment: not an act of yours that ye hide will be hidden.	On that day ye will be exposed; not a secret of you will be hidden.	On that day you shall be exposed to view-- no secret of yours shall remain hidden.
69 019	Then he that will be given his Record in his right hand will say: Ah here! Read ye my Record!	Then, as for him who is given his record in his right hand, he will say: Take, read my book!	Then as for him who is given his book in his right hand, he will say: Lo! read my book:
69 020	"I did really understand that my Account would (One Day) reach me!"	Surely I knew that I should have to meet my reckoning.	Surely I knew that I shall meet my account.
69 021	And he will be in a life of Bliss,	Then he will be in blissful state	So he shall be in a life of pleasure,
69 022	In a Garden on high,	In a high garden	In a lofty garden,
69 023	The Fruits whereof (will hang in bunches) low and near.	Whereof the clusters are in easy reach.	The fruits of which are near at hand:
69 024	"Eat ye and drink ye, with full satisfaction; because of the (good) that ye sent before you, in the days that are gone!"	(And it will be said unto those therein): Eat and drink at ease for that which ye sent on before you in past days.	Eat and drink pleasantly for what you did beforehand in the days gone by.
69 025	And he that will be given his Record in his left hand, will say: Ah! Would that my Record had not been given to me!	But as for him who is given his record in his left hand, he will say: Oh, would that I had not been given my book	And as for him who is given his book in his left hand he shall say: O would that my book had never been given me:
69 026	"And that I had never realised how my account (stood)!"	And knew not what my reckoning!	And I had not known what my account was:
69 027	"Ah! Would that (Death) had made an end of me!"	Oh, would that it had been death!	O would that it had made an end (of me):
69 028	"Of no profit to me has been my wealth!"	My wealth hath not availed me,	My wealth has availed me nothing:

69 029	"My power has perished from me!"...	My power hath gone from me.	My authority is gone away from me.
69 030	(The stern command will say): "Seize ye him, and bind ye him,"	(It will be said): Take him and fetter him	Lay hold on him, then put a chain on him,
69 031	"And burn ye him in the Blazing Fire."	And then expose him to hell-fire	Then cast him into the burning fire,
69 032	"Further, make him march in a chain, whereof the length is seventy cubits!"	And then insert him in a chain whereof the length is seventy cubits.	Then thrust him into a chain the length of which is seventy cubits.
69 033	"This was he that would not believe in Allah Most High."	Lo! He used not to believe in Allah the Tremendous,	Surely he did not believe in Allah, the Great,
69 034	"And would not encourage the feeding of the indigent!"	And urged not on the feeding of the wretched.	Nor did he urge the feeding of the poor.
69 035	"So no friend hath he here this Day."	Therefor hath he no lover here this day,	Therefore he has not here today a true friend,
69 036	"Nor hath he any food except the corruption from the washing of wounds,"	Nor any food save filth	Nor any food except refuse,
69 037	"Which none do eat but those in sin."	Which none but sinners eat.	Which none but the wrongdoers eat.
69 038	So I do call to witness what ye see,	But nay! I swear by all that ye see	But nay! I swear by that which you see,
69 039	And what ye see not,	And all that ye see not	And that which you do not see.
69 040	That this is verily the word of an honoured messenger;	That it is indeed the speech of an illustrious messenger.	Most surely, it is the Word brought by an honored Messenger,
69 041	It is not the word of a poet: little it is ye believe!	It is not poet's speech - little is it that ye believe!	And it is not the word of a poet; little is it that you believe;
69 042	Nor is it the word of a soothsayer: little admonition it is ye receive.	Nor diviner's speech - little is it that ye remember!	Nor the word of a soothsayer; little is it that you mind.
69 043	(This is) a Message sent down from the Lord of the Worlds.	It is a revelation from the Lord of the Worlds.	It is a revelation from the Lord of the worlds.
69 044	And if the messenger were to invent any sayings in Our name,	And if he had invented false sayings concerning Us,	And if he had fabricated against Us some of the sayings,
69 045	We should certainly seize him by his right hand,	We assuredly had taken him by the right hand	We would certainly have seized him by the right hand,
69 046	And We should certainly then cut off the artery of his heart:	And then severed his life-artery,	Then We would certainly have cut off his aorta.
69 047	Nor could any of you withhold him (from Our wrath).	And not one of you could have held Us off from him.	And not one of you could have withheld Us from him.
69 048	But verily this is a Message for the Allah-fearing.	And lo! it is a warrant unto those who ward off (evil).	And most surely it is a reminder for those who guard (against evil).
69 049	And We certainly know that there are amongst you those that reject (it).	And lo! We know that some among you will deny (it).	And most surely We know that some of you are rejecters.
69 050	But truly (Revelation) is a cause of sorrow for the Unbelievers.	And lo! it is indeed an anguish for the disbelievers.	And most surely it is a great grief to the unbelievers.
69 051	But verily it is Truth of assured certainty.	And lo! it is absolute truth.	And most surely it is the true certainty
69 052	So glorify the name of thy Lord Most High.	So glorify the name of thy Tremendous Lord.	Therefore-glorify the name of your Lord, the Great.

Chapter 70:

AL-MAARIJ (THE ASCENDING STAIRWAYS)

Total Verses: 44 Revealed At: MAKKA

In the name of Allah, the Most Beneficent, the Most Merciful.

70 001	A questioner asked about a Penalty to befall-	A questioner questioned concerning the doom about to fall	One demanding, demanded the chastisement which must befall
70 002	The Unbelievers the which there is none to ward off,-	Upon the disbelievers, which none can repel,	The unbelievers-- there is none to avert it--
70 003	(A Penalty) from Allah, Lord of the Ways of Ascent.	From Allah, Lord of the Ascending Stairways	From Allah, the Lord of the ways of Ascent.
70 004	The angels and the spirit ascend unto him in a Day the measure whereof is (as) fifty thousand years:	(Whereby) the angels and the Spirit ascend unto Him in a Day whereof the span is fifty thousand years.	To Him ascend the angels and the Spirit in a day the measure of which is fifty thousand years.
70 005	Therefore do thou hold Patience,- a Patience of beautiful (contentment).	But be patient (O Muhammad) with a patience fair to see.	Therefore endure with a goodly patience.
70 006	They see the (Day) indeed as a far-off (event):	Lo! they behold it afar off	Surely they think it to be far off,
70 007	But We see it (quite) near.	While we behold it nigh:	And We see it nigh.
70 008	The Day that the sky will be like molten brass,	The day when the sky will become as molten copper,	On the day when the heaven shall be as molten copper
70 009	And the mountains will be like wool,	And the hills become as flakes of wool,	And the mountains shall be as tufts of wool
70 010	And no friend will ask after a friend,	And no familiar friend will ask a question of his friend	And friend shall not ask of friend
70 011	Though they will be put in sight of each other,- the sinner's desire will be: Would that he could redeem himself from the Penalty of that Day by (sacrificing) his children,	Though they will be given sight of them. The guilty man will long to be able to ransom himself from the punishment of that day at the price of his children	(Though) they shall be made to see each other. The guilty one would fain redeem himself from the chastisement of that day by (sacrificing) his children,
70 012	His wife and his brother,	And his spouse and his brother	And his wife and his brother
70 013	His kindred who sheltered him,	And his kin that harboured him	And the nearest of his kinsfolk who gave him shelter,
70 014	And all, all that is on earth,- so it could deliver him:	And all that are in the earth, if then it might deliver him.	And all those that are in the earth, (wishing) then (that) this might deliver him.
70 015	By no means! for it would be the Fire of Hell!-	But nay! for lo! it is the fire of hell	By no means! Surely it is a flaming fire
70 016	Plucking out (his being) right to the skull!-	Eager to roast;	Dragging by the head,
70 017	Inviting (all) such as turn their backs and turn away their faces (from the Right).	It calleth him who turned and fled (from truth),	It shall claim him who turned and fled (from truth),
70 018	And collect (wealth) and hide it (from use)!	And hoarded (wealth) and withheld it.	And amasses (wealth) then shuts it up.
70 019	Truly man was created very impatient;-	Lo! man was created anxious,	Surely man is created of a hasty temperament

70 020	Fretful when evil touches him;	Fretful when evil befalleth him	Being greatly grieved when evil afflicts him
70 021	And niggardly when good reaches him;-	And, when good befalleth him, grudging;	And niggardly when good befalls him
70 022	Not so those devoted to Prayer;-	Save worshippers.	Except those who pray,
70 023	Those who remain steadfast to their prayer;	Who are constant at their worship	Those who are constant at their prayer
70 024	And those in whose wealth is a recognised right.	And in whose wealth there is a right acknowledged	And those in whose wealth there is a fixed portion.
70 025	For the (needy) who asks and him who is prevented (for some reason from asking);	For the beggar and the destitute;	For him who begs and for him who is denied (good)
70 026	And those who hold to the truth of the Day of Judgment;	And those who believe in the Day of Judgment,	And those who accept the truth of the judgment day
70 027	And those who fear the displeasure of their Lord,-	And those who are fearful of their Lord's doom -	And those who are fearful of the chastisement of their Lord--
70 028	For their Lord's displeasure is the opposite of Peace and Tranquillity;-	Lo! the doom of their Lord is that before which none can feel secure-	Surely the chastisement of their Lord is (a thing) not to be felt secure of--
70 029	And those who guard their chastity,	And those who preserve their chastity	And those who guard their private parts,
70 030	Except with their wives and the (captives) whom their right hands possess,- for (then) they are not to be blamed,	Save with their wives and those whom their right hands possess, for thus they are not blameworthy;	Except in the case of their wives or those whom their right hands possess-- for these surely are not to be blamed,
70 031	But those who trespass beyond this are transgressors;-	But whoso seeketh more than that, those are they who are transgressors;	But he who seeks to go beyond this, these it is that go beyond the limits--
70 032	And those who respect their trusts and covenants;	And those who keep their pledges and their covenant,	And those who are faithful to their trusts and their covenant
70 033	And those who stand firm in their testimonies;	And those who stand by their testimony	And those who are upright in their testimonies,
70 034	And those who guard (the sacredness) of their worship;-	And those who are attentive at their worship.	And those who keep a guard on their prayer,
70 035	Such will be the honoured ones in the Gardens (of Bliss).	These will dwell in Gardens, honoured.	Those shall be in gardens, honored.
70 036	Now what is the matter with the Unbelievers that they rush madly before thee-	What aileth those who disbelieve, that they keep staring toward thee (O Muhammad), open-eyed,	But what is the matter with those who disbelieve that they hasten on around you,
70 037	From the right and from the left, in crowds?	On the right and on the left, in groups?	On the right hand and on the left, in sundry parties?
70 038	Does every man of them long to enter the Garden of Bliss?	Doth every man among them hope to enter the Garden of Delight?	Does every man of them desire that he should be made to enter the garden of bliss?
70 039	By no means! For We have created them out of the (base matter) they know!	Nay, verily. Lo! We created them from what they know.	By no means! Surely We have created them of what they know.
70 040	Now I do call to witness the Lord of all points in the East and the West that We can certainly-	But nay! I swear by the Lord of the rising-places and the setting-places (of the planets) that We verily are Able	But nay! I swear by the Lord of the Easts and the Wests that We are certainly able
70 041	Substitute for them better (men) than they; And We are not to be defeated (in Our Plan).	To replace them by (others) better than them. And we are not to be outrun.	To bring instead (others) better than them, and We shall not be overcome.

70 042	So leave them to plunge in vain talk and play about, until they encounter that Day of theirs which they have been promised!-	So let them chat and play until they meet their Day which they are promised,	Therefore leave them alone to go on with the false discourses and to sport until they come face to face with that day of theirs with which they are threatened;
70 043	The Day whereon they will issue from their sepulchres in sudden haste as if they were rushing to a goal-post (fixed for them),-	The day when they come forth from the graves in haste, as racing to a goal,	The day on which they shall come forth from their graves in haste, as if they were hastening on to a goal,
70 044	Their eyes lowered in dejection,- ignominy covering them (all over)! such is the Day the which they are promised!	With eyes aghast, abasement stupefying them: Such is the Day which they are promised.	Their eyes cast down; disgrace shall overtake them; that is the day which they were threatened with.

Chapter 71:

NOOH (NOOH)

Total Verses: 28 Revealed At: MAKKA

In the name of Allah, the Most Beneficent, the Most Merciful.

71 001	We sent Noah to his People (with the Command): "Do thou warn thy People before there comes to them a grievous Penalty."	Lo! We sent Noah unto his people (saying): Warn thy people ere the painful doom come unto them.	Surely We sent Nuh to his people, saying: Warn your people before there come upon them a painful chastisement.
71 002	He said: "O my People! I am to you a Warner, clear and open:"	He said: O my people! Lo! I am a plain warner unto you	He said: O my people! Surely I am a plain warner to you:
71 003	"That ye should worship Allah, fear Him and obey me:"	(Bidding you): Serve Allah and keep your duty unto Him and obey me,	That you should serve Allah and be careful of (your duty to) Him and obey me:
71 004	"So He may forgive you your sins and give you respite for a stated Term: for when the Term given by Allah is accomplished, it cannot be put forward: if ye only knew."	That He may forgive you somewhat of your sins and respite you to an appointed term. Lo! the term of Allah, when it cometh, cannot be delayed, if ye but knew.	He will forgive you some of your faults and grant you a delay to an appointed term; surely the term of Allah when it comes is not postponed; did you but know!
71 005	He said: "O my Lord! I have called to my People night and day:"	He said: My Lord! Lo! I have called unto my people night and day	He said: O my Lord! surely I have called my people by night and by day!
71 006	"But my call only increases (their) flight (from the Right)."	But all my calling doth but add to their repugnance;	But my call has only made them flee the more:
71 007	"And every time I have called to them, that Thou mightest forgive them, they have (only) thrust their fingers into their ears, covered themselves up with their garments, grown obstinate, and given themselves up to arrogance."	And lo! whenever I call unto them that Thou mayst pardon them they thrust their fingers in their ears and cover themselves with their garments and persist (in their refusal) and magnify themselves in pride.	And whenever I have called them that Thou mayest forgive them, they put their fingers in their ears, cover themselves with their garments, and persist and are puffed up with pride:
71 008	"So I have called to them aloud;"	And lo! I have called unto them aloud,	Then surely I called to them aloud:
71 009	"Further I have spoken to them in public and secretly in private,"	And lo! I have made public proclamation unto them, and I have appealed to them in private.	Then surely I spoke to them in public and I spoke to them in secret:
71 010	"Saying, 'Ask forgiveness from your Lord; for He is Oft-Forgiving;'"	And I have said: Seek pardon of your Lord. Lo! He was ever Forgiving.	Then I said, Ask forgiveness of your Lord, surely He is the most Forgiving:

71 011	"'He will send rain to you in abundance;'"	He will let loose the sky for you in plenteous rain,	He will send down upon you the cloud, pouring down abundance of rain:
71 012	"'Give you increase in wealth and sons; and bestow on you gardens and bestow on you rivers (of flowing water).'"	And will help you with wealth and sons, and will assign unto you Gardens and will assign unto you rivers.	And help you with wealth and sons, and make for you gardens, and make for you rivers.
71 013	"'What is the matter with you, that ye place not your hope for kindness and long-suffering in Allah,'"-	What aileth you that ye hope not toward Allah for dignity	What is the matter with you that you fear not the greatness of Allah?
71 014	"'Seeing that it is He that has created you in diverse stages?'"	When He created you by (divers) stages?	And indeed He has created you through various grades:
71 015	"'See ye not how Allah has created the seven heavens one above another,'"	See ye not how Allah hath created seven heavens in harmony,	Do you not see how Allah has created the seven heavens one above another,
71 016	"'And made the moon a light in their midst, and made the sun as a (Glorious) Lamp?'"	And hath made the moon a light therein, and made the sun a lamp?	And made the moon therein a light, and made the sun a lamp?
71 017	"'And Allah has produced you from the earth growing (gradually),'"	And Allah hath caused you to grow as a growth from the earth,	And Allah has made you grow out of the earth as a growth:
71 018	"'And in the End He will return you into the (earth), and raise you forth (again at the Resurrection)?'"	And afterward He maketh you return thereto, and He will bring you forth again, a (new) forthbringing.	Then He returns you to it, then will He bring you forth a (new) bringing forth:
71 019	"'And Allah has made the earth for you as a carpet (spread out),'"	And Allah hath made the earth a wide expanse for you	And Allah has made for you the earth a wide expanse,
71 020	"'That ye may go about therein, in spacious roads.'"	That ye may thread the valley-ways thereof.	That you may go along therein in wide paths.
71 021	Noah said: "O my Lord! They have disobeyed me, but they follow (men) whose wealth and children give them no increase but only Loss."	Noah said: My Lord! Lo! they have disobeyed me and followed one whose wealth and children increase him in naught save ruin;	Nuh said: My Lord! surely they have disobeyed me and followed him whose wealth and children have added to him nothing but loss.
71 022	"And they have devised a tremendous Plot."	And they have plotted a mighty plot,	And they have planned a very great plan.
71 023	"And they have said (to each other), 'Abandon not your gods: Abandon neither Wadd nor Suwa', neither Yaguth nor Ya'uq, nor Nasr';"-	And they have said: Forsake not your gods. Forsake not Wadd, nor Suwa', nor Yaghuth and Ya'uq and Nasr.	And they say: By no means leave your gods, nor leave Wadd, nor Suwa; nor Yaghus, and Yauq and Nasr.
71 024	"They have already misled many; and grant Thou no increase to the wrong-doers but in straying (from their mark)."	And they have led many astray, and Thou increasest the wrong-doers in naught save error.	And indeed they have led astray many, and do not increase the unjust in aught but error.
71 025	Because of their sins they were drowned (in the flood), and were made to enter the Fire (of Punishment): and they found- in lieu of Allah- none to help them.	Because of their sins they were drowned, then made to enter a Fire. And they found they had no helpers in place of Allah.	Because of their wrongs they were drowned, then made to enter fire, so they did not find any helpers besides Allah.
71 026	And Noah, said: "O my Lord! Leave not of the Unbelievers, a single one on earth!"	And Noah said: My Lord! Leave not one of the disbelievers in the land.	And Nuh said: My Lord! leave not upon the land any dweller from among the unbelievers:
71 027	"For, if Thou dost leave (any of) them, they will but mislead Thy devotees, and they will breed none but wicked ungrateful ones."	If Thou shouldst leave them, they will mislead Thy slaves and will beget none save lewd ingrates.	For surely if Thou leave them they will lead astray Thy servants, and will not beget any but immoral, ungrateful (children)

71 028	"O my Lord! Forgive me, my parents, all who enter my house in Faith, and (all) believing men and believing women: and to the wrong-doers grant Thou no increase but in perdition!"	My Lord! Forgive me and my parents and him who entereth my house believing, and believing men and believing women, and increase not the wrong-doers in aught save ruin.	My Lord! forgive me and my parents and him who enters my house believing, and the believing men and the believing women; and do not increase the unjust in aught but destruction!

Chapter 72:

AL-JINN (THE JINN)

Total Verses: 28 Revealed At: MAKKA

In the name of Allah, the Most Beneficent, the Most Merciful.

72 001	Say: It has been revealed to me that a company of jinns listened (to the Qur'an). They said, 'We have really heard a wonderful Recital!	Say (O Muhammad): It is revealed unto me that a company of the jinn gave ear, and they said: Lo! we have heard a marvellous Qur'an,	Say: It has been revealed to me that a party of the jinn listened, and they said: Surely we have heard a wonderful Quran,
72 002	It gives guidance to the Right, and we have believed therein: we shall not join (in worship) any (gods) with our Lord.	Which guideth unto righteousness, so we believe in it and we ascribe no partner unto our Lord.	Guiding to the right way, so we believe in it, and we will not set up any one with our Lord:
72 003	And Exalted is the Majesty of our Lord: He has taken neither a wife nor a son.	And (we believe) that He - exalted be the glory of our Lord! - hath taken neither wife nor son,	And that He-- exalted be the majesty of our Lord-- has not taken a consort, nor a son:
72 004	There were some foolish ones among us, who used to utter extravagant lies against Allah;	And that the foolish one among us used to speak concerning Allah an atrocious lie.	And that the foolish amongst us used to forge extravagant things against Allah:
72 005	But we do think that no man or spirit should say aught that is untrue against Allah.'	And lo! we had supposed that humankind and jinn would not speak a lie concerning Allah -	And that we thought that men and jinn did not utter a lie against Allah:
72 006	True, there were persons among mankind who took shelter with persons among the jinns, but they increased them in folly.	And indeed (O Muhammad) individuals of humankind used to invoke the protection of individuals of the jinn, so that they increased them in revolt (against Allah);	And that persons from among men used to seek refuge with persons from among jinn, so they increased them in wrongdoing:
72 007	And they (came to) think as ye thought, that Allah would not raise up any one (to Judgment).'	And indeed they supposed, even as ye suppose, that Allah would not raise anyone (from the dead) -	And that they thought as you think, that Allah would not raise anyone:
72 008	And we pried into the secrets of heaven; but we found it filled with stern guards and flaming fires.'	And (the jinn who had listened to the Qur'an said): We had sought the heaven but had found it filled with strong warders and meteors.	And that we sought to reach heaven, but we found it filled with strong guards and flaming stars.
72 009	We used, indeed, to sit there in (hidden) stations, to (steal) a hearing; but any who listen now will find a flaming fire watching him in ambush.'	And we used to sit on places (high) therein to listen. But he who listeneth now findeth a flame in wait for him;	And that we used to sit in some of the sitting-places thereof to steal a hearing, but he who would (try to) listen now would find a flame lying in wait for him:
72 010	And we understand not whether ill is intended to those on earth, or whether their Lord (really) intends to guide them to right conduct.'	And we know not whether harm is boded unto all who are in the earth, or whether their Lord intendeth guidance for them.	And that we know not whether evil is meant for those who are on earth or whether their Lord means to bring them good:

72 011	There are among us some that are righteous, and some the contrary: we follow divergent paths.'	And among us there are righteous folk and among us there are far from that. We are sects having different rules.	And that some of us are good and others of us are below that: we are sects following different ways:
72 012	But we think that we can by no means frustrate Allah throughout the earth, nor can we frustrate Him by flight.'	And we know that we cannot escape from Allah in the earth, nor can we escape by flight.	And that we know that we cannot escape Allah in the earth, nor can we escape Him by flight:
72 013	And as for us, since we have listened to the Guidance, we have accepted it: and any who believes in his Lord has no fear, either of a short (account) or of any injustice.'	And when we heard the guidance, we believed therein, and whoso believeth in his Lord, he feareth neither loss nor oppression.	And that when we heard the guidance, we believed in it; so whoever believes in his Lord, he should neither fear loss nor being overtaken (by disgrace):
72 014	Amongst us are some that submit their wills (to Allah), and some that swerve from justice. Now those who submit their wills - they have sought out (the path) of right conduct':	And there are among us some who have surrendered (to Allah) and there are among us some who are unjust. And whoso hath surrendered to Allah, such have taken the right path purposefully.	And that some of us are those who submit, and some of us are the deviators; so whoever submits, these aim at the right way:
72 015	But those who swerve,- they are (but) fuel for Hell-fire'-	And as for those who are unjust, they are firewood for hell.	And as to the deviators, they are fuel of hell:
72 016	(And Allah's Message is): "If they (the Pagans) had (only) remained on the (right) Way, We should certainly have bestowed on them Rain in abundance."	If they (the idolaters) tread the right path, We shall give them to drink of water in abundance	And that if they should keep to the (right) way, We would certainly give them to drink of abundant water,
72 017	"That We might try them by that (means). But if any turns away from the remembrance of his Lord, He will cause him to undergo a severe Penalty."	That We may test them thereby, and whoso turneth away from the remembrance of his Lord; He will thrust him into ever-growing torment.	So that We might try them with respect to it; and whoever turns aside from the reminder of his Lord, He will make him enter into an afflicting chastisement:
72 018	"And the places of worship are for Allah (alone): So invoke not any one along with Allah;"	And the places of worship are only for Allah, so pray not unto anyone along with Allah.	And that the mosques are Allah's, therefore call not upon any one with Allah:
72 019	"Yet when the Devotee of Allah stands forth to invoke Him, they just make round him a dense crowd."	And when the slave of Allah stood up in prayer to Him, they crowded on him, almost stifling.	And that when the servant of Allah stood up calling upon Him, they wellnigh crowded him (to death).
72 020	Say: "I do no more than invoke my Lord, and I join not with Him any (false god)."	Say (unto them, O Muhammad): I pray unto Allah only, and ascribe unto Him no partner.	Say: I only call upon my Lord, and I do not associate any one with Him.
72 021	Say: "It is not in my power to cause you harm, or to bring you to right conduct."	Say: Lo! I control not hurt nor benefit for you.	Say: I do not control for you evil or good.
72 022	Say: "No one can deliver me from Allah (If I were to disobey Him), nor should I find refuge except in Him,"	Say: Lo! none can protect me from Allah, nor can I find any refuge beside Him	Say: Surely no one can protect me against Allah, nor can I find besides Him any place of refuge:
72 023	"Unless I proclaim what I receive from Allah and His Messages: for any that disobey Allah and His Messenger,- for them is Hell: they shall dwell therein for ever."	(Mine is) but conveyance (of the Truth) from Allah, and His messages; and whoso disobeyeth Allah and His messenger, lo! his is fire of hell, wherein such dwell for ever.	(It is) only a delivering (of communications) from Allah and His messages; and whoever disobeys Allah and His Messenger surely he shall have the fire of hell to abide therein for a long time.

72 024	At length, when they see (with their own eyes) that which they are promised,- then will they know who it is that is weakest in (his) helper and least important in point of numbers.	Till (the day) when they shall behold that which they are promised (they may doubt); but then they will know (for certain) who is weaker in allies and less in multitude.	Until when they see what they are threatened with, then shall they know who is weaker in helpers and fewer in number.
72 025	Say: "I know not whether the (Punishment) which ye are promised is near, or whether my Lord will appoint for it a distant term."	Say (O Muhammad, unto the disbelievers): I know not whether that which ye are promised is nigh, or if my Lord hath set a distant term for it.	Say: I do not know whether that with which you are threatened be nigh or whether my Lord will appoint for it a term:
72 026	"He (alone) knows the Unseen, nor does He make any one acquainted with His Mysteries,"-	(He is) the Knower of the Unseen, and He revealeth unto none His secret,	The Knower of the unseen! so He does not reveal His secrets to any,
72 027	"Except a messenger whom He has chosen: and then He makes a band of watchers march before him and behind him,"	Save unto every messenger whom He hath chosen, and then He maketh a guard to go before him and a guard behind him	Except to him whom He chooses as a messenger; for surely He makes a guard to march before him and after him,
72 028	"That He may know that they have (truly) brought and delivered the Messages of their Lord: and He surrounds (all the mysteries) that are with them, and takes account of every single thing."	That He may know that they have indeed conveyed the messages of their Lord. He surroundeth all their doings, and He keepeth count of all things.	So that He may know that they have truly delivered the messages of their Lord, and He encompasses what is with them and He records the number of all things.

Chapter 73:

AL-MUZZAMMIL (THE ENSHROUDED ONE, BUNDLED UP)

Total Verses: 20 Revealed At: MAKKA

In the name of Allah, the Most Beneficent, the Most Merciful.

73 001	O thou folded in garments!	O thou wrapped up in thy raiment!	O you who have wrapped up in your garments!
73 002	Stand (to prayer) by night, but not all night,-	Keep vigil the night long, save a little -	Rise to pray in the night except a little,
73 003	Half of it,- or a little less,	A half thereof, or abate a little thereof	Half of it, or lessen it a little,
73 004	Or a little more; and recite the Qur'an in slow, measured rhythmic tones.	Or add (a little) thereto - and chant the Qur'an in measure,	Or add to it, and recite the Quran as it ought to be recited.
73 005	Soon shall We send down to thee a weighty Message.	For we shall charge thee with a word of weight.	Surely We will make to light upon you a weighty Word.
73 006	Truly the rising by night is most potent for governing (the soul), and most suitable for (framing) the Word (of Prayer and Praise).	Lo! the vigil of the night is (a time) when impression is more keen and speech more certain.	Surely the rising by night is the firmest way to tread and the best corrective of speech.
73 007	True, there is for thee by day prolonged occupation with ordinary duties:	Lo! thou hast by day a chain of business.	Surely you have in the day time a long occupation.
73 008	But keep in remembrance the name of thy Lord and devote thyself to Him whole-heartedly.	So remember the name of thy Lord and devote thyself with a complete devotion -	And remember the name of your Lord and devote yourself to Him with (exclusive) devotion.

73 009	(He is) Lord of the East and the West: there is no god but He: take Him therefore for (thy) Disposer of Affairs.	Lord of the East and the West; there is no God save Him; so choose thou Him alone for thy defender -	The Lord of the East and the West-- there is no god but He-- therefore take Him for a protector.
73 010	And have patience with what they say, and leave them with noble (dignity).	And bear with patience what they utter, and part from them with a fair leave-taking.	And bear patiently what they say and avoid them with a becoming avoidance.
73 011	And leave Me (alone to deal with) those in possession of the good things of life, who (yet) deny the Truth; and bear with them for a little while.	Leave Me to deal with the deniers, lords of ease and comfort (in this life); and do thou respite them awhile.	And leave Me and the rejecters, the possessors of ease and plenty, and respite them a little.
73 012	With Us are Fetters (to bind them), and a Fire (to burn them),	Lo! with Us are heavy fetters and a raging fire,	Surely with Us are heavy fetters and a flaming fire,
73 013	And a Food that chokes, and a Penalty Grievous.	And food which choketh (the partaker), and a painful doom	And food that chokes and a painful punishment,
73 014	One Day the earth and the mountains will be in violent commotion. And the mountains will be as a heap of sand poured out and flowing down.	On the day when the earth and the hills rock, and the hills become a heap of running sand.	On the day when the earth and the mountains shall quake and the mountains shall become (as) heaps of sand let loose.
73 015	We have sent to you, (O men!) a messenger, to be a witness concerning you, even as We sent a messenger to Pharaoh.	Lo! We have sent unto you a messenger as witness against you, even as We sent unto Pharaoh a messenger.	Surely We have sent to you a Messenger, a witness against you, as We sent a messenger to Firon.
73 016	But Pharaoh disobeyed the messenger; so We seized him with a heavy Punishment.	But Pharaoh rebelled against the messenger, whereupon We seized him with no gentle grip.	But Firon disobeyed the messenger, so We laid on him a violent hold.
73 017	Then how shall ye, if ye deny (Allah), guard yourselves against a Day that will make children hoary-headed?-	Then how, if ye disbelieve, will ye protect yourselves upon the day which will turn children grey,	How, then, will you guard yourselves, if you disbelieve, on the day which shall make children grey-headed?
73 018	Whereon the sky will be cleft asunder? His Promise needs must be accomplished.	The very heaven being then rent asunder. His promise is to be fulfilled.	The heaven shall rend asunder thereby; His promise is ever brought to fulfillment.
73 019	Verily this is an Admonition: therefore, whoso will, let him take a (straight) path to his Lord!	Lo! This is a Reminder. Let him who will, then, choose a way unto his Lord.	Surely this is a reminder, then let him, who will take the way to his Lord.

73 020	Thy Lord doth know that thou standest forth (to prayer) nigh two-thirds of the night, or half the night, or a third of the night, and so doth a party of those with thee. But Allah doth appoint night and day in due measure He knoweth that ye are unable to keep count thereof. So He hath turned to you (in mercy): read ye, therefore, of the Qur'an as much as may be easy for you. He knoweth that there may be (some) among you in ill-health; others travelling through the land, seeking of Allah's bounty; yet others fighting in Allah's Cause, read ye, therefore, as much of the Qur'an as may be easy (for you); and establish regular Prayer and give regular Charity; and loan to Allah a Beautiful Loan. And whatever good ye send forth for your souls ye shall find it in Allah's Presence,- yea, better and greater, in Reward and seek ye the Grace of Allah: for Allah is Oft-Forgiving, Most Merciful.	Lo! thy Lord knoweth how thou keepest vigil sometimes nearly two-thirds of the night, or (sometimes) half or a third thereof, as do a party of those with thee. Allah measureth the night and the day. He knoweth that ye count it not, and turneth unto you in mercy. Recite, then, of the Qur'an that which is easy for you. He knoweth that there are sick folk among you, while others travel in the land in search of Allah's bounty, and others (still) are fighting for the cause of Allah. So recite of it that which is easy (for you), and establish worship and pay the poor-due, and (so) lend unto Allah a goodly loan. Whatsoever good ye send before you for your souls, ye will find it with Allah, better and greater in the recompense. And seek forgiveness of Allah. Lo! Allah is Forgiving, Merciful.	Surely your Lord knows that you pass in prayer nearly two-thirds of the night, and (sometimes) half of it, and (sometimes) a third of it, and (also) a party of those with you; and Allah measures the night and the day. He knows that you are not able to do it, so He has turned to you (mercifully), therefore read what is easy of the Quran. He knows that there must be among you sick, and others who travel in the land seeking of the bounty of Allah, and others who fight in Allah's way, therefore read as much of it as is easy (to you), and keep up prayer and pay the poor-rate and offer to Allah a goodly gift, and whatever of good you send on beforehand for yourselves, you will find it with Allah; that is best and greatest in reward; and ask forgiveness of Allah; surely Allah is Forgiving, Merciful.

Chapter 74:

AL-MUDDATHTHIR (THE CLOAKED ONE, THE MAN WEARING A CLOAK)

Total Verses: 56 Revealed At: MAKKA

In the name of Allah, the Most Beneficent, the Most Merciful.

74 001	O thou wrapped up (in the mantle)!	O thou enveloped in thy cloak,	O you who are clothed!
74 002	Arise and deliver thy warning!	Arise and warn!	Arise and warn,
74 003	And thy Lord do thou magnify!	Thy Lord magnify,	And your Lord do magnify,
74 004	And thy garments keep free from stain!	Thy raiment purify,	And your garments do purify,
74 005	And all abomination shun!	Pollution shun!	And uncleanness do shun,
74 006	Nor expect, in giving, any increase (for thyself)!	And show not favour, seeking wordly gain!	And bestow not favors that you may receive again with increase,
74 007	But, for thy Lord's (Cause), be patient and constant!	For the sake of thy Lord, be patient!	And for the sake of your Lord, be patient.
74 008	Finally, when the Trumpet is sounded,	For when the trumpet shall sound,	For when the trumpet is sounded,
74 009	That will be- that Day - a Day of Distress,-	Surely that day will be a day of anguish,	That, at that time, shall be a difficult day,
74 010	Far from easy for those without Faith.	Not of ease, for disbelievers.	For the unbelievers, anything but easy.

74 011	Leave Me alone, (to deal) with the (creature) whom I created (bare and) alone!-	Leave Me (to deal) with him whom I created lonely,	Leave Me and him whom I created alone,
74 012	To whom I granted resources in abundance,	And then bestowed upon him ample means,	And give him vast riches,
74 013	And sons to be by his side!-	And sons abiding in his presence	And sons dwelling in his presence,
74 014	To whom I made (life) smooth and comfortable!	And made (life) smooth for him.	And I adjusted affairs for him adjustably;
74 015	Yet is he greedy-that I should add (yet more);-	Yet he desireth that I should give more.	And yet he desires that I should add more!
74 016	By no means! For to Our Signs he has been refractory!	Nay! For lo! he hath been stubborn to Our revelations.	By no means! surely he offers opposition to Our communications.
74 017	Soon will I visit him with a mount of calamities!	On him I shall impose a fearful doom.	I will make a distressing punishment overtake him.
74 018	For he thought and he plotted;-	For lo! he did consider; then he planned -	Surely he reflected and guessed,
74 019	And woe to him! How he plotted!-	(Self-)destroyed is he, how he planned!	But may he be cursed how he plotted;
74 020	Yea, Woe to him; How he plotted!-	Again (self-)destroyed is he, how he planned! -	Again, may he be cursed how he plotted;
74 021	Then he looked round;	Then looked he,	Then he looked,
74 022	Then he frowned and he scowled;	Then frowned he and showed displeasure.	Then he frowned and scowled,
74 023	Then he turned back and was haughty;	Then turned he away in pride	Then he turned back and was big with pride,
74 024	Then said he: "This is nothing but magic, derived from of old;"	And said: This is naught else than magic from of old;	Then he said: This is naught but enchantment, narrated (from others);
74 025	"This is nothing but the word of a mortal!"	This is naught else than speech of mortal man.	This is naught but the word of a mortal.
74 026	Soon will I cast him into Hell-Fire!	Him shall I fling unto the burning.	I will cast him into hell.
74 027	And what will explain to thee what Hell-Fire is?	- Ah, what will convey unto thee what that burning is! -	And what will make you realize what hell is?
74 028	Naught doth it permit to endure, and naught doth it leave alone!-	It leaveth naught; it spareth naught	It leaves naught nor does it spare aught.
74 029	Darkening and changing the colour of man!	It shrivelleth the man.	It scorches the mortal.
74 030	Over it are Nineteen.	Above it are nineteen.	Over it are nineteen.

74 031	And We have set none but angels as Guardians of the Fire; and We have fixed their number only as a trial for Unbelievers,- in order that the People of the Book may arrive at certainty, and the Believers may increase in Faith,- and that no doubts may be left for the People of the Book and the Believers, and that those in whose hearts is a disease and the Unbelievers may say, "What symbol doth Allah intend by this?" Thus doth Allah leave to stray whom He pleaseth, and guide whom He pleaseth: and none can know the forces of thy Lord, except He and this is no other than a warning to mankind.	We have appointed only angels to be wardens of the Fire, and their number have We made to be a stumbling-block for those who disbelieve; that those to whom the Scripture hath been given may have certainty, and that believers may increase in faith; and that those to whom the Scripture hath been given and believers may not doubt; and that those in whose hearts there is disease, and disbelievers, may say: What meaneth Allah by this similitude? Thus Allah sendeth astray whom He will, and whom He will He guideth. None knoweth the hosts of thy Lord save Him. This is naught else than a Reminder unto mortals.	And We have not made the wardens of the fire others than angels, and We have not made their number but as a trial for those who disbelieve, that those who have been given the book may be certain and those who believe may increase in faith, and those who have been given the book and the believers may not doubt, and that those in whose hearts is a disease and the unbelievers may say: What does Allah mean by this parable? Thus does Allah make err whom He pleases, and He guides whom He pleases, and none knows the hosts of your Lord but He Himself; and this is naught but a reminder to the mortals.
74 032	Nay, verily: By the Moon,	Nay, by the Moon	Nay; I swear by the moon,
74 033	And by the Night as it retreateth,	And the night when it withdraweth	And the night when it departs,
74 034	And by the Dawn as it shineth forth,-	And the dawn when it shineth forth,	And the daybreak when it shines;
74 035	This is but one of the mighty (portents),	Lo! this is one of the greatest (portents)	Surely it (hell) is one of the gravest (misfortunes),
74 036	A warning to mankind,-	As a warning unto men,	A warning to mortals,
74 037	To any of you that chooses to press forward, or to follow behind;-	Unto him of you who will advance or hang back.	To him among you who wishes to go forward or remain behind.
74 038	Every soul will be (held) in pledge for its deeds.	Every soul is a pledge for its own deeds;	Every soul is held in pledge for what it earns,
74 039	Except the Companions of the Right Hand.	Save those who will stand on the right hand.	Except the people of the right hand,
74 040	(They will be) in Gardens (of Delight): they will question each other,	In gardens they will ask one another	In gardens, they shall ask each other
74 041	And (ask) of the Sinners:	Concerning the guilty:	About the guilty:
74 042	"What led you into Hell Fire?"	What hath brought you to this burning?	What has brought you into hell?
74 043	They will say: "We were not of those who prayed;"	They will answer: We were not of those who prayed	They shall say: We were not of those who prayed;
74 044	"Nor were we of those who fed the indigent;"	Nor did we feed the wretched.	And we used not to feed the poor;
74 045	"But we used to talk vanities with vain talkers;"	We used to wade (in vain dispute) with (all) waders,	And we used to enter into vain discourse with those who entered into vain discourses.
74 046	"And we used to deny the Day of Judgment,"	And we used to deny the Day of Judgment,	And we used to call the Day of Judgment a lie;
74 047	"Until there came to us (the Hour) that is certain."	Till the Inevitable came unto us.	Till death overtook us.
74 048	Then will no intercession of (any) intercessors profit them.	The mediation of no mediators will avail them then.	So the intercession of intercessors shall not avail them.
74 049	Then what is the matter with them that they turn away from admonition?-	Why now turn they away from the Admonishment,	What is then the matter with them, that they turn away from the admonition,

74 050	As if they were affrighted asses,	As they were frightened asses	As if they were asses taking fright
74 051	Fleeing from a lion!	Fleeing from a lion?	That had fled from a lion?
74 052	Forsooth, each one of them wants to be given scrolls (of revelation) spread out!	Nay, but everyone of them desireth that he should be given open pages (from Allah).	Nay; every one of them desires that he may be given pages spread out;
74 053	By no means! But they fear not the Hereafter,	Nay, verily. They fear not the Hereafter.	Nay! but they do not fear the hereafter.
74 054	Nay, this surely is an admonition:	Nay, verily. Lo! this is an Admonishment.	Nay! it is surely an admonition.
74 055	Let any who will, keep it in remembrance!	So whosoever will may heed.	So whoever pleases may mind it.
74 056	But none will keep it in remembrance except as Allah wills: He is the Lord of Righteousness, and the Lord of Forgiveness.	And they will not heed unless Allah willeth (it). He is the fount of fear. He is the fount of Mercy.	And they will not mind unless Allah please. He is worthy to be feared and worthy to forgive.

Chapter 75:

AL-QIYAMA (THE RISING OF THE DEAD, RESURRECTION)

Total Verses: 40 Revealed At: MAKKA

In the name of Allah, the Most Beneficent, the Most Merciful.

75 001	I do call to witness the Resurrection Day;	Nay, I swear by the Day of Resurrection;	Nay! I swear by the day of resurrection.
75 002	And I do call to witness the self-reproaching spirit: (Eschew Evil).	Nay, I swear by the accusing soul (that this Scripture is true).	Nay! I swear by the self-accusing soul.
75 003	Does man think that We cannot assemble his bones?	Thinketh man that We shall not assemble his bones?	Does man think that We shall not gather his bones?
75 004	Nay, We are able to put together in perfect order the very tips of his fingers.	Yea, verily. We are Able to restore his very fingers!	Yea! We are able to make complete his very fingertips
75 005	But man wishes to do wrong (even) in the time in front of him.	But man would fain deny what is before him.	Nay! man desires to give the lie to what is before him.
75 006	He questions: "When is the Day of Resurrection?"	He asketh: When will be this Day of Resurrection?	He asks: When is the day of resurrection?
75 007	At length, when the sight is dazed,	But when sight is confounded	So when the sight becomes dazed,
75 008	And the moon is buried in darkness.	And the moon is eclipsed	And the moon becomes dark,
75 009	And the sun and moon are joined together,-	And sun and moon are united,	And the sun and the moon are brought together,
75 010	That Day will Man say: "Where is the refuge?"	On that day man will cry: Whither to flee!	Man shall say on that day: Whither to fly to?
75 011	By no means! No place of safety!	Alas! No refuge!	By no means! there shall be no place of refuge!
75 012	Before thy Lord (alone), that Day will be the place of rest.	Unto thy Lord is the recourse that day.	With your Lord alone shall on that day be the place of rest.
75 013	That Day will Man be told (all) that he put forward, and all that he put back.	On that day man is told the tale of that which he hath sent before and left behind.	Man shall on that day be informed of what he sent before and (what he) put off.
75 014	Nay, man will be evidence against himself,	Oh, but man is a telling witness against himself,	Nay! man is evidence against himself,

75 015	Even though he were to put up his excuses.	Although he tender his excuses.		Though he puts forth his excuses.
75 016	Move not thy tongue concerning the (Qur'an) to make haste therewith.	Stir not thy tongue herewith to hasten it.		Do not move your tongue with it to make haste with it,
75 017	It is for Us to collect it and to promulgate it:	Lo! upon Us (resteth) the putting together thereof and the reading thereof.		Surely on Us (devolves) the collecting of it and the reciting of it.
75 018	But when We have promulgated it, follow thou its recital (as promulgated).	And when We read it, follow thou the reading;		Therefore when We have recited it, follow its recitation.
75 019	Nay more, it is for Us to explain it (and make it clear):	Then lo! upon Us (resteth) the explanation thereof.		Again on Us (devolves) the explaining of it.
75 020	Nay, (ye men!) but ye love the fleeting life,	Nay, but ye do love the fleeting Now		Nay! But you love the present life,
75 021	And leave alone the Hereafter.	And neglect the Hereafter.		And neglect the hereafter.
75 022	Some faces, that Day, will beam (in brightness and beauty);-	That day will faces be resplendent,		(Some) faces on that day shall be bright,
75 023	Looking towards their Lord;	Looking toward their Lord;		Looking to their Lord.
75 024	And some faces, that Day, will be sad and dismal,	And that day will other faces be despondent,		And (other) faces on that day shall be gloomy,
75 025	In the thought that some back-breaking calamity was about to be inflicted on them;	Thou wilt know that some great disaster is about to fall on them.		Knowing that there will be made to befall them some great calamity.
75 026	Yea, when (the soul) reaches to the collar-bone (in its exit),	Nay, but when the life cometh up to the throat		Nay! When it comes up to the throat,
75 027	And there will be a cry, "Who is a magician (to restore him)?"	And men say: Where is the wizard (who can save him now)?		And it is said: Who will be a magician?
75 028	And he will conclude that it was (the Time) of Parting;	And he knoweth that it is the parting;		And he is sure that it is the (hour of) parting
75 029	And one leg will be joined with another:	And agony is heaped on agony;		And affliction is combined with affliction;
75 030	That Day the Drive will be (all) to thy Lord!	Unto thy Lord that day will be the driving.		To your Lord on that day shall be the driving.
75 031	So he gave nothing in charity, nor did he pray!-	For he neither trusted, nor prayed.		So he did not accept the truth, nor did he pray,
75 032	But on the contrary, he rejected Truth and turned away!	But he denied and flouted.		But called the truth a lie and turned back,
75 033	Then did he stalk to his family in full conceit!	Then went he to his folk with glee.		Then he went to his followers, walking away in haughtiness.
75 034	Woe to thee, (O men!), yea, woe!	Nearer unto thee and nearer,		Nearer to you (is destruction) and nearer,
75 035	Again, Woe to thee, (O men!), yea, woe!	Again nearer unto thee and nearer (is the doom).		Again (consider how) nearer to you and nearer.
75 036	Does man think that he will be left uncontrolled, (without purpose)?	Thinketh man that he is to be left aimless?		Does man think that he is to be left to wander without an aim?
75 037	Was he not a drop of sperm emitted (in lowly form)?	Was he not a drop of fluid which gushed forth?		Was he not a small seed in the seminal elements,
75 038	Then did he become a leech-like clot; then did (Allah) make and fashion (him) in due proportion.	Then he became a clot; then (Allah) shaped and fashioned		Then he was a clot of blood, so He created (him) then made (him) perfect.
75 039	And of him He made two sexes, male and female.	And made of him a pair, the male and female.		Then He made of him two kinds, the male and the female.
75 040	Has not He, (the same), the power to give life to the dead?	Is not He (Who doeth so) Able to bring the dead to life?		Is not He able to give life to the dead?

Chapter 76:

AL-INSAN (MAN)

Total Verses: 31 Revealed At: MAKKA

In the name of Allah, the Most Beneficent, the Most Merciful.

76 001	Has there not been over Man a long period of Time, when he was nothing - (not even) mentioned?	Hath there come upon man (ever) any period of time in which he was a thing unremembered?	There surely came over man a period of time when he was a thing not worth mentioning.
76 002	Verily We created Man from a drop of mingled sperm, in order to try him: So We gave him (the gifts), of Hearing and Sight.	Lo! We create man from a drop of thickened fluid to test him; so We make him hearing, knowing.	Surely We have created man from a small life-germ uniting (itself): We mean to try him, so We have made him hearing, seeing.
76 003	We showed him the Way: whether he be grateful or ungrateful (rests on his will).	Lo! We have shown him the way, whether he be grateful or disbelieving.	Surely We have shown him the way: he may be thankful or unthankful.
76 004	For the Rejecters we have prepared chains, yokes, and a blazing Fire.	Lo! We have prepared for disbelievers manacles and carcans and a raging fire.	Surely We have prepared for the unbelievers chains and shackles and a burning fire.
76 005	As to the Righteous, they shall drink of a Cup (of Wine) mixed with Kafur,-	Lo! the righteous shall drink of a cup whereof the mixture is of Kafur,	Surely the righteous shall drink of a cup the admixture of which is camphor,
76 006	A Fountain where the Devotees of Allah do drink, making it flow in unstinted abundance.	A spring wherefrom the slaves of Allah drink, making it gush forth abundantly,	A fountain from which the servants of Allah shall drink; they make it to flow a (goodly) flowing forth.
76 007	They perform (their) vows, and they fear a Day whose evil flies far and wide.	(Because) they perform the vow and fear a day whereof the evil is wide-spreading,	They fulfill vows and fear a day the evil of which shall be spreading far and wide.
76 008	And they feed, for the love of Allah, the indigent, the orphan, and the captive,-	And feed with food the needy wretch, the orphan and the prisoner, for love of Him,	And they give food out of love for Him to the poor and the orphan and the captive:
76 009	(Saying), "We feed you for the sake of Allah alone: no reward do we desire from you, nor thanks."	(Saying): We feed you, for the sake of Allah only. We wish for no reward nor thanks from you;	We only feed you for Allah's sake; we desire from you neither reward nor thanks:
76 010	"We only fear a Day of distressful Wrath from the side of our Lord."	Lo! we fear from our Lord a day of frowning and of fate.	Surely we fear from our Lord a stern, distressful day.
76 011	But Allah will deliver them from the evil of that Day, and will shed over them a Light of Beauty and (blissful) Joy.	Therefor Allah hath warded off from them the evil of that day, and hath made them find brightness and joy;	Therefore Allah win guard them from the evil of that day and cause them to meet with ease and happiness;
76 012	And because they were patient and constant, He will reward them with a Garden and (garments of) silk.	And hath awarded them for all that they endured, a Garden and silk attire;	And reward them, because they were patient, with garden and silk,
76 013	Reclining in the (Garden) on raised thrones, they will see there neither the sun's (excessive heat) nor (the moon's) excessive cold.	Reclining therein upon couches, they will find there neither (heat of) a sun nor bitter cold.	Reclining therein on raised couches, they shall find therein neither (the severe heat of) the sun nor intense cold.
76 014	And the shades of the (Garden) will come low over them, and the bunches (of fruit), there, will hang low in humility.	The shade thereof is close upon them and the clustered fruits thereof bow down.	And close down upon them (shall be) its shadows, and its fruits shall be made near (to them), being easy to reach.

76	015	And amongst them will be passed round vessels of silver and goblets of crystal,-	Goblets of silver are brought round for them, and beakers (as) of glass	And there shall be made to go round about them vessels of silver and goblets which are of glass,
76	016	Crystal-clear, made of silver: they will determine the measure thereof (according to their wishes).	(Bright as) glass but (made) of silver, which they (themselves) have measured to the measure (of their deeds).	(Transparent as) glass, made of silver; they have measured them according to a measure.
76	017	And they will be given to drink there of a Cup (of Wine) mixed with Zanjabil,-	There are they watered with a cup whereof the mixture is of Zanjabil,	And they shall be made to drink therein a cup the admixture of which shall be ginger,
76	018	A fountain there, called Salsabil.	(The water of) a spring therein, named Salsabil.	(Of) a fountain therein which is named Salsabil.
76	019	And round about them will (serve) youths of perpetual (freshness): If thou seest them, thou wouldst think them scattered Pearls.	There wait on them immortal youths, whom, when thou seest, thou wouldst take for scattered pearls.	And round about them shall go youths never altering in age; when you see them you will think them to be scattered pearls.
76	020	And when thou lookest, it is there thou wilt see a Bliss and a Realm Magnificent.	When thou seest, thou wilt see there bliss and high estate.	And when you see there, you shall see blessings and a great kingdom.
76	021	Upon them will be green Garments of fine silk and heavy brocade, and they will be adorned with Bracelets of silver; and their Lord will give to them to drink of a Wine Pure and Holy.	Their raiment will be fine green silk and gold embroidery. Bracelets of silver will they wear. Their Lord will slake their thirst with a pure drink.	Upon them shall be garments of fine green silk and thick silk interwoven with gold, and they shall be adorned with bracelets of silver, and their Lord shall make them drink a pure drink.
76	022	"Verily this is a Reward for you, and your Endeavour is accepted and recognised."	(And it will be said unto them): Lo! this is a reward for you. Your endeavour (upon earth) hath found acceptance.	Surely this is a reward for you, and your striving shall be recompensed.
76	023	It is We Who have sent down the Qur'an to thee by stages.	Lo! We, even We, have revealed unto thee the Qur'an, a revelation;	Surely We Ourselves have revealed the Quran to you revealing (it) in portions.
76	024	Therefore be patient with constancy to the Command of thy Lord, and hearken not to the sinner or the ingrate among them.	So submit patiently to thy Lord's command, and obey not of them any guilty one or disbeliever.	Therefore wait patiently for the command of your Lord, and obey not from among them a sinner or an ungrateful one.
76	025	And celebrate the name or thy Lord morning and evening,	Remember the name of thy Lord at morn and evening.	And glorify the name of your Lord morning and evening.
76	026	And part of the night, prostrate thyself to Him; and glorify Him a long night through.	And worship Him (a portion) of the night. And glorify Him through the livelong night.	And during part of the night adore Him, and give glory to Him (a) long (part of the) night.
76	027	As to these, they love the fleeting life, and put away behind them a Day (that will be) hard.	Lo! these love fleeting life, and put behind them (the remembrance of) a grievous day.	Surely these love the transitory and neglect a grievous day before them.
76	028	It is We Who created them, and We have made their joints strong; but, when We will, We can substitute the like of them by a complete change.	We, even We, created them, and strengthened their frame. And when We will, We can replace them, bringing others like them in their stead.	We created them and made firm their make, and when We please We will bring in their place the likes of them by a change.
76	029	This is an admonition: Whosoever will, let him take a (straight) Path to his Lord.	Lo! this is an Admonishment, that whosoever will may choose a way unto his Lord.	Surely this is a reminder, so whoever pleases takes to his Lord a way.
76	030	But ye will not, except as Allah wills; for Allah is full of Knowledge and Wisdom.	Yet ye will not, unless Allah willeth. Lo! Allah is Knower, Wise.	And you do not please except that Allah please, surely Allah is Knowing, Wise;
76	031	He will admit to His Mercy whom He will; But the wrong-doers,- for them has He prepared a grievous Penalty.	He maketh whom He will to enter His mercy, and for evil-doers hath prepared a painful doom.	He makes whom He pleases to enter into His mercy; and (as for) the unjust, He has prepared for them a painful chastisement.

Chapter 77:

AL-MURSALAT (THE EMISSARIES, WINDS SENT FORTH)

Total Verses: 50 Revealed At: MAKKA

In the name of Allah, the Most Beneficent, the Most Merciful.

77 001	By the (Winds) sent forth one after another (to man's profit);	By the emissary winds, (sent) one after another	I swear by the emissary winds, sent one after another (for men's benefit),
77 002	Which then blow violently in tempestuous Gusts,	By the raging hurricanes,	By the raging hurricanes,
77 003	And scatter (things) far and wide;	By those which cause earth's vegetation to revive;	Which scatter clouds to their destined places,
77 004	Then separate them, one from another,	By those who winnow with a winnowing,	Then separate them one from another,
77 005	Then spread abroad a Message,	By those who bring down the Reminder,	Then I swear by the angels who bring down the revelation,
77 006	Whether of Justification or of Warning;-	To excuse or to warn,	To clear or to warn.
77 007	Assuredly, what ye are promised must come to pass.	Surely that which ye are promised will befall.	Most surely what you are threatened with must come to pass.
77 008	Then when the stars become dim;	So when the stars are put out,	So when the stars are made to lose their light,
77 009	When the heaven is cleft asunder;	And when the sky is riven asunder,	And when the heaven is rent asunder,
77 010	When the mountains are scattered (to the winds) as dust;	And when the mountains are blown away,	And when the mountains are carried away as dust,
77 011	And when the messengers are (all) appointed a time (to collect);-	And when the messengers are brought unto their time appointed -	And when the messengers are gathered at their appointed time
77 012	For what Day are these (portents) deferred?	For what day is the time appointed?	To what day is the doom fixed?
77 013	For the Day of Sorting out.	For the Day of Decision.	To the day of decision.
77 014	And what will explain to thee what is the Day of Sorting out?	And what will convey unto thee what the Day of Decision is! -	And what will make you comprehend what the day of decision is?
77 015	Ah woe, that Day, to the Rejecters of Truth!	Woe unto the repudiators on that day!	Woe on that day to the rejecters.
77 016	Did We not destroy the men of old (for their evil)?	Destroyed We not the former folk,	Did We not destroy the former generations?
77 017	So shall We make later (generations) follow them.	Then caused the latter folk to follow after?	Then did We follow them up with later ones.
77 018	Thus do We deal with men of sin.	Thus deal We ever with the guilty.	Even thus shall We deal with the guilty.
77 019	Ah woe, that Day, to the Rejecters of Truth!	Woe unto the repudiators on that day!	Woe on that day to the rejecters.
77 020	Have We not created you from a fluid (held) despicable?-	Did We not create you from a base fluid	Did We not create you from contemptible water?
77 021	The which We placed in a place of rest, firmly fixed,	Which We laid up in a safe abode	Then We placed it in a secure resting-place,
77 022	For a period (of gestation), determined (according to need)?	For a known term?	Till an appointed term,

77 023	For We do determine (according to need); for We are the best to determine (things).	Thus We arranged. How excellent is Our arranging!	So We proportion it-- how well are We at proportioning (things).
77 024	Ah woe, that Day! to the Rejecters of Truth!	Woe unto the repudiators on that day!	Woe on that day to the rejecters.
77 025	Have We not made the earth (as a place) to draw together.	Have We not made the earth a receptacle	Have We not made the earth to draw together to itself,
77 026	The living and the dead,	Both for the living and the dead,	The living and the dead,
77 027	And made therein mountains standing firm, lofty (in stature); and provided for you water sweet (and wholesome)?	And placed therein high mountains and given you to drink sweet water therein?	And made therein lofty mountains, and given you to drink of sweet water?
77 028	Ah woe, that Day, to the Rejecters of Truth!	Woe unto the repudiators on that day!	Woe on that day to the rejecters.
77 029	(It will be said:) "Depart ye to that which ye used to reject as false!"	(It will be said unto them:) Depart unto that (doom) which ye used to deny;	Walk on to that which you called a lie.
77 030	"Depart ye to a Shadow (of smoke ascending) in three columns,"	Depart unto the shadow falling threefold,	Walk on to the covering having three branches,
77 031	"(Which yields) no shade of coolness, and is of no use against the fierce Blaze."	(Which yet is) no relief nor shelter from the flame.	Neither having the coolness of the shade nor availing against the flame.
77 032	"Indeed it throws about sparks (huge) as Forts,"	Lo! it throweth up sparks like the castles,	Surely it sends up sparks like palaces,
77 033	"As if there were (a string of) yellow camels (marching swiftly)."	(Or) as it might be camels of bright yellow hue.	As if they were tawny camels.
77 034	Ah woe, that Day, to the Rejecters of Truth!	Woe unto the repudiators on that day!	Woe on that day to the rejecters.
77 035	That will be a Day when they shall not be able to speak.	This is a day wherein they speak not,	This is the day on which they shall not speak,
77 036	Nor will it be open to them to put forth pleas.	Nor are they suffered to put forth excuses.	And permission shall not be given to them so that they should offer excuses.
77 037	Ah woe, that Day, to the Rejecters of Truth!	Woe unto the repudiators on that day!	Woe on that day to the rejecters.
77 038	That will be a Day of Sorting out! We shall gather you together and those before (you)!	This is the Day of Decision, We have brought you and the men of old together.	This is the day of decision: We have gathered you and those of yore.
77 039	Now, if ye have a trick (or plot), use it against Me!	If now ye have any wit, outwit Me.	So if you have a plan, plan against Me (now).
77 040	Ah woe, that Day, to the Rejecters of Truth!	Woe unto the repudiators on that day!	Woe on that day to the rejecters.
77 041	As to the Righteous, they shall be amidst (cool) shades and springs (of water).	Lo! those who kept their duty are amid shade and fountains,	Surely those who guard (against evil) shall be amid shades and fountains,
77 042	And (they shall have) fruits,- all they desire.	And fruits such as they desire.	And fruits such as they desire.
77 043	"Eat ye and drink ye to your heart's content: for that ye worked (Righteousness)."	(Unto them it is said:) Eat, drink and welcome, O ye blessed, in return for what ye did.	Eat and drink pleasantly because of what you did.
77 044	Thus do We certainly reward the Doers of Good.	Thus do We reward the good.	Surely thus do We reward the doers of good.
77 045	Ah woe, that Day, to the Rejecters of Truth!	Woe unto the repudiators on that day!	Woe on that day to the rejecters.
77 046	(O ye unjust!) Eat ye and enjoy yourselves (but) a little while, for that ye are Sinners.	Eat and take your ease (on earth) a little. Lo! ye are guilty.	Eat and enjoy yourselves for a little; surely you are guilty.

77 047	Ah woe, that Day, to the Rejecters of Truth!	Woe unto the repudiators on that day!	Woe on that day to the rejecters.
77 048	And when it is said to them, "Prostrate yourselves!" they do not so.	When it is said unto them: Bow down, they bow not down!	And where it is said to them: Bow down, they do not bow down.
77 049	Ah woe, that Day, to the Rejecters of Truth!	Woe unto the repudiators on that day!	Woe on that day to the rejecters.
77 050	Then what Message, after that, will they believe in?	In what statement, after this, will they believe?	In what announcement, then, after it, will they believe?

Chapter 78:

AN-NABA (THE TIDINGS, THE ANNOUNCEMENT)

Total Verses: 40 Revealed At: MAKKA

In the name of Allah, the Most Beneficent, the Most Merciful.

78 001	Concerning what are they disputing?	Whereof do they question one another?	Of what do they ask one another?
78 002	Concerning the Great News,	(It is) of the awful tidings,	About the great event,
78 003	About which they cannot agree.	Concerning which they are in disagreement.	About which they differ?
78 004	Verily, they shall soon (come to) know!	Nay, but they will come to know!	Nay! they shall soon come to know
78 005	Verily, verily they shall soon (come to) know!	Nay, again, but they will come to know!	Nay! Nay! they shall soon know.
78 006	Have We not made the earth as a wide expanse,	Have We not made the earth an expanse,	Have We not made the earth an even expanse?
78 007	And the mountains as pegs?	And the high hills bulwarks?	And the mountains as projections (thereon)?
78 008	And (have We not) created you in pairs,	And We have created you in pairs,	And We created you in pairs,
78 009	And made your sleep for rest,	And have appointed your sleep for repose,	And We made your sleep to be rest (to you),
78 010	And made the night as a covering,	And have appointed the night as a cloak,	And We made the night to be a covering,
78 011	And made the day as a means of subsistence?	And have appointed the day for livelihood.	And We made the day for seeking livelihood.
78 012	And (have We not) built over you the seven firmaments,	And We have built above you seven strong (heavens),	And We made above you seven strong ones,
78 013	And placed (therein) a Light of Splendour?	And have appointed a dazzling lamp,	And We made a shining lamp,
78 014	And do We not send down from the clouds water in abundance,	And have sent down from the rainy clouds abundant water,	And We send down from the clouds water pouring forth abundantly,
78 015	That We may produce therewith corn and vegetables,	Thereby to produce grain and plant,	That We may bring forth thereby corn and herbs,
78 016	And gardens of luxurious growth?	And gardens of thick foliage.	And gardens dense and luxuriant.
78 017	Verily the Day of Sorting out is a thing appointed,	Lo! the Day of Decision is a fixed time,	Surely the day of decision is (a day) appointed:
78 018	The Day that the Trumpet shall be sounded, and ye shall come forth in crowds;	A day when the trumpet is blown and ye come in multitudes,	The day on which the trumpet shall be blown so you shall come forth in hosts,

78 019	And the heavens shall be opened as if there were doors,	And the heaven is opened and becometh as gates,	And the heaven shall be opened so that it shall be all openings,
78 020	And the mountains shall vanish, as if they were a mirage.	And the hills are set in motion and become as a mirage.	And the mountains shall be moved off so that they shall remain a mere semblance.
78 021	Truly Hell is as a place of ambush,	Lo! hell lurketh in ambush,	Surely hell lies in wait,
78 022	For the transgressors a place of destination:	A home for the rebellious.	A place of resort for the inordinate,
78 023	They will dwell therein for ages.	They will abide therein for ages.	Living therein for ages.
78 024	Nothing cool shall they taste therein, nor any drink,	Therein taste they neither coolness nor (any) drink	They shall not taste therein cool nor drink
78 025	Save a boiling fluid and a fluid, dark, murky, intensely cold,	Save boiling water and a paralysing cold:	But boiling and intensely cold water,
78 026	A fitting recompense (for them).	Reward proportioned (to their evil deeds).	Requital corresponding.
78 027	For that they used not to fear any account (for their deeds),	For lo! they looked not for a reckoning;	Surely they feared not the account,
78 028	But they (impudently) treated Our Signs as false.	They called Our revelations false with strong denial.	And called Our communications a lie, giving the lie (to the truth).
78 029	And all things have We preserved on record.	Everything have We recorded in a Book.	And We have recorded everything in a book,
78 030	"So taste ye (the fruits of your deeds); for no increase shall We grant you, except in Punishment."	So taste (of that which ye have earned). No increase do We give you save of torment.	So taste! for We will not add to you aught but chastisement.
78 031	Verily for the Righteous there will be a fulfilment of (the heart's) desires;	Lo! for the duteous is achievement -	Surely for those who guard (against evil) is achievement,
78 032	Gardens enclosed, and grapevines;	Gardens enclosed and vineyards,	Gardens and vineyards,
78 033	And voluptuous women of equal age;	And voluptuous women of equal age;	And voluptuous women of equal age;
78 034	And a cup full (to the brim).	And a full cup.	And a pure cup.
78 035	No vanity shall they hear therein, nor Untruth:-	There hear they never vain discourse, nor lying -	They shall not hear therein any vain words nor lying.
78 036	Recompense from thy Lord, a gift, (amply) sufficient,	Requital from thy Lord - a gift in payment -	A reward from your Lord, a gift according to a reckoning:
78 037	(From) the Lord of the heavens and the earth, and all between, (Allah) Most Gracious: None shall have power to argue with Him.	Lord of the heavens and the earth, and (all) that is between them, the Beneficent; with Whom none can converse.	The Lord of the heavens and the earth and what is between them, the Beneficent Allah, they shall not be able to address Him.
78 038	The Day that the Spirit and the angels will stand forth in ranks, none shall speak except any who is permitted by (Allah) Most Gracious, and He will say what is right.	On the day when the angels and the Spirit stand arrayed, they speak not, saving him whom the Beneficent alloweth and who speaketh right.	The day on which the spirit and the angels shall stand in ranks; they shall not speak except he whom the Beneficent Allah permits and who speaks the right thing.
78 039	That Day will be the sure Reality: Therefore, whoso will, let him take a (straight) return to his Lord!	That is the True Day. So whoso will should seek recourse unto his Lord.	That is the sure day, so whoever desires may take refuge with his Lord.
78 040	Verily, We have warned you of a Penalty near, the Day when man will see (the deeds) which his hands have sent forth, and the Unbeliever will say, "Woe unto me! Would that I were (mere) dust!"	Lo! We warn you of a doom at hand, a day whereon a man will look on that which his own hands have sent before, and the disbeliever will cry: "Would that I were dust!"	Surely We have warned you of a chastisement near at hand: the day when man shall see what his two hands have sent before, and the unbeliever shall say: O! would that I were dust!

Chapter 79:

AN-NAZIAT (THOSE WHO DRAG FORTH, SOUL-SNATCHERS)

Total Verses: 46 Revealed At: MAKKA

In the name of Allah, the Most Beneficent, the Most Merciful.

79 001	By the (angels) who tear out (the souls of the wicked) with violence;	By those who drag forth to destruction,	I swear by the angels who violently pull out the souls of the wicked,
79 002	By those who gently draw out (the souls of the blessed);	By the meteors rushing,	And by those who gently draw out the souls of the blessed,
79 003	And by those who glide along (on errands of mercy),	By the lone stars floating,	And by those who float in space,
79 004	Then press forward as in a race,	By the angels hastening,	Then those who are foremost going ahead,
79 005	Then arrange to do (the Commands of their Lord),	And those who govern the event,	Then those who regulate the affair.
79 006	One Day everything that can be in commotion will be in violent commotion,	On the day when the first trump resoundeth.	The day on which the quaking one shall quake,
79 007	Followed by oft-repeated (commotions):	And the second followeth it,	What must happen afterwards shall follow it.
79 008	Hearts that Day will be in agitation;	On that day hearts beat painfully	Hearts on that day shall palpitate,
79 009	Cast down will be (their owners') eyes.	While eyes are downcast	Their eyes cast down.
79 010	They say (now): "What! shall we indeed be returned to (our) former state?"	(Now) they are saying: Shall we really be restored to our first state	They say: Shall we indeed be restored to (our) first state?
79 011	"What! - when we shall have become rotten bones?"	Even after we are crumbled bones?	What! when we are rotten bones?
79 012	They say: "It would, in that case, be a return with loss!"	They say: Then that would be a vain proceeding.	They said: That then would be a return occasioning loss.
79 013	But verily, it will be but a single (Compelling) Cry,	Surely it will need but one shout,	But it shall be only a single cry,
79 014	When, behold, they will be in the (full) awakening (to Judgment).	And lo! they will be awakened.	When lo! they shall be wakeful.
79 015	Has the story of Moses reached thee?	Hath there come unto thee the history of Moses?	Has not there come to you the story of Musa?
79 016	Behold, thy Lord did call to him in the sacred valley of Tuwa:-	How his Lord called him in the holy vale of Tuwa,	When his Lord called upon him in the holy valley, twice,
79 017	"Go thou to Pharaoh for he has indeed transgressed all bounds:"	(Saying:) Go thou unto Pharaoh - Lo! he hath rebelled -	Go to Firon, surely he has become inordinate.
79 018	"And say to him, 'Wouldst thou that thou shouldst be purified (from sin)'?"-	And say (unto him): Hast thou (will) to grow (in grace)?	Then say: Have you (a desire) to purify yourself:
79 019	"'And that I guide thee to thy Lord, so thou shouldst fear Him?'"	Then I will guide thee to thy Lord and thou shalt fear (Him).	And I will guide you to your Lord so that you should fear.
79 020	Then did (Moses) show him the Great Sign.	And he showed him the tremendous token.	So he showed him the mighty sign.
79 021	But (Pharaoh) rejected it and disobeyed (guidance);	But he denied and disobeyed,	But he rejected (the truth) and disobeyed.
79 022	Further, he turned his back, striving hard (against Allah).	Then turned he away in haste,	Then he went back hastily.

79 023	Then he collected (his men) and made a proclamation,	Then gathered he and summoned	Then he gathered (men) and called out.
79 024	Saying, "I am your Lord, Most High".	And proclaimed: "I (Pharaoh) am your Lord the Highest."	Then he said: I am your lord, the most high.
79 025	But Allah did punish him, (and made an) example of him, - in the Hereafter, as in this life.	So Allah seized him (and made him) an example for the after (life) and for the former.	So Allah seized him with the punishment of the hereafter and the former life.
79 026	Verily in this is an instructive warning for whosoever feareth (Allah).	Lo! herein is indeed a lesson for him who feareth.	Most surely there is in this a lesson to him who fears.
79 027	What! Are ye the more difficult to create or the heaven (above)? (Allah) hath constructed it:	Are ye the harder to create, or is the heaven that He built?	Are you the harder to create or the heaven? He made it.
79 028	On high hath He raised its canopy, and He hath given it order and perfection.	He raised the height thereof and ordered it;	He raised high its height, then put it into a right good state.
79 029	Its night doth He endow with darkness, and its splendour doth He bring out (with light).	And He made dark the night thereof, and He brought forth the morn thereof.	And He made dark its night and brought out its light.
79 030	And the earth, moreover, hath He extended (to a wide expanse);	And after that He spread the earth,	And the earth, He expanded it after that.
79 031	He draweth out therefrom its moisture and its pasture;	And produced therefrom the water thereof and the pasture thereof,	He brought forth from it its water and its pasturage.
79 032	And the mountains hath He firmly fixed;-	And He made fast the hills,	And the mountains, He made them firm,
79 033	For use and convenience to you and your cattle.	A provision for you and for your cattle.	A provision for you and for your cattle.
79 034	Therefore, when there comes the great, overwhelming (Event),-	But when the great disaster cometh,	But when the great predominating calamity comes;
79 035	The Day when man shall remember (all) that he strove for,	The day when man will call to mind his (whole) endeavour,	The day on which man shall recollect what he strove after,
79 036	And Hell-Fire shall be placed in full view for (all) to see,-	And hell will stand forth visible to him who seeth,	And the hell shall be made manifest to him who sees
79 037	Then, for such as had transgressed all bounds,	Then, as for him who rebelled	Then as for him who is inordinate,
79 038	And had preferred the life of this world,	And chose the life of the world,	And prefers the life of this world,
79 039	The Abode will be Hell-Fire;	Lo! hell will be his home.	Then surely the hell, that is the abode.
79 040	And for such as had entertained the fear of standing before their Lord's (tribunal) and had restrained (their) soul from lower desires,	But as for him who feared to stand before his Lord and restrained his soul from lust,	And as for him who fears to stand in the presence of his Lord and forbids the soul from low desires,
79 041	Their abode will be the Garden.	Lo! the Garden will be his home.	Then surely the garden-- that is the abode.
79 042	They ask thee about the Hour,- 'When will be its appointed time?	They ask thee of the Hour: when will it come to port?	They ask you about the hour, when it will come.
79 043	Wherein art thou (concerned) with the declaration thereof?	Why (ask they)? What hast thou to tell thereof?	About what! You are one to remind of it.
79 044	With thy Lord in the Limit fixed therefor.	Unto thy Lord belongeth (knowledge of) the term thereof.	To your Lord is the goal of it.
79 045	Thou art but a Warner for such as fear it.	Thou art but a warner unto him who feareth it.	You are only a warner to him who would fear it.
79 046	The Day they see it, (It will be) as if they had tarried but a single evening, or (at most till) the following morn!	On the day when they behold it, it will be as if they had but tarried for an evening or the morn thereof.	On the day that they see it, it will be as though they had not tarried but the latter part of a day or the early part of it.

Chapter 80:

ABASA (HE FROWNED)

Total Verses: 42 Revealed At: MAKKA

In the name of Allah, the Most Beneficent, the Most Merciful.

80 001	(The Prophet) frowned and turned away,	He frowned and turned away	He frowned and turned (his) back,
80 002	Because there came to him the blind man (interrupting).	Because the blind man came unto him.	Because there came to him the blind man.
80 003	But what could tell thee but that perchance he might grow (in spiritual understanding)?-	What could inform thee but that he might grow (in grace)	And what would make you know that he would purify himself,
80 004	Or that he might receive admonition, and the teaching might profit him?	Or take heed and so the reminder might avail him?	Or become reminded so that the reminder should profit him?
80 005	As to one who regards Himself as self-sufficient,	As for him who thinketh himself independent,	As for him who considers himself free from need (of you),
80 006	To him dost thou attend;	Unto him thou payest regard.	To him do you address yourself.
80 007	Though it is no blame to thee if he grow not (in spiritual understanding).	Yet it is not thy concern if he grow not (in grace).	And no blame is on you if he would not purify himself
80 008	But as to him who came to thee striving earnestly,	But as for him who cometh unto thee with earnest purpose	And as to him who comes to you striving hard,
80 009	And with fear (in his heart),	And hath fear,	And he fears,
80 010	Of him wast thou unmindful.	From him thou art distracted.	From him will you divert yourself.
80 011	By no means (should it be so)! For it is indeed a Message of instruction:	Nay, but verily it is an Admonishment,	Nay! surely it is an admonishment.
80 012	Therefore let whoso will, keep it in remembrance.	So let whosoever will pay heed to it,	So let him who pleases mind it.
80 013	(It is) in Books held (greatly) in honour,	On honoured leaves	In honored books,
80 014	Exalted (in dignity), kept pure and holy,	Exalted, purified,	Exalted, purified,
80 015	(Written) by the hands of scribes-	(Set down) by scribes	In the hands of scribes
80 016	Honourable and Pious and Just.	Noble and righteous.	Noble, virtuous.
80 017	Woe to man! What hath made him reject Allah;	Man is (self-)destroyed: how ungrateful!	Cursed be man! how ungrateful is he!
80 018	From what stuff hath He created him?	From what thing doth He create him?	Of what thing did He create him?
80 019	From a sperm-drop: He hath created him, and then mouldeth him in due proportions;	From a drop of seed. He createth him and proportioneth him,	Of a small seed; He created him, then He made him according to a measure,
80 020	Then doth He make His path smooth for him;	Then maketh the way easy for him,	Then (as for) the way-- He has made it easy (for him)
80 021	Then He causeth him to die, and putteth him in his grave;	Then causeth him to die, and burieth him;	Then He causes him to die, then assigns to him a grave,

80	022	Then, when it is His Will, He will raise him up (again).	Then, when He will, He bringeth him again to life.	Then when He pleases, He will raise him to life again.
80	023	By no means hath he fulfilled what Allah hath commanded him.	Nay, but (man) hath not done what He commanded him.	Nay; but he has not done what He bade him.
80	024	Then let man look at his food, (and how We provide it):	Let man consider his food:	Then let man look to his food,
80	025	For that We pour forth water in abundance,	How We pour water in showers	That We pour down the water, pouring (it) down in abundance,
80	026	And We split the earth in fragments,	Then split the earth in clefts	Then We cleave the earth, cleaving (it) asunder,
80	027	And produce therein corn,	And cause the grain to grow therein	Then We cause to grow therein the grain,
80	028	And Grapes and nutritious plants,	And grapes and green fodder	And grapes and clover,
80	029	And Olives and Dates,	And olive-trees and palm-trees	And the olive and the palm,
80	030	And enclosed Gardens, dense with lofty trees,	And garden-closes of thick foliage	And thick gardens,
80	031	And fruits and fodder,-	And fruits and grasses:	And fruits and herbage
80	032	For use and convenience to you and your cattle.	Provision for you and your cattle.	A provision for you and for your cattle.
80	033	At length, when there comes the Deafening Noise,-	But when the Shout cometh	But when the deafening cry comes,
80	034	That Day shall a man flee from his own brother,	On the day when a man fleeth from his brother	The day on which a man shall fly from his brother,
80	035	And from his mother and his father,	And his mother and his father	And his mother and his father,
80	036	And from his wife and his children.	And his wife and his children,	And his spouse and his son--
80	037	Each one of them, that Day, will have enough concern (of his own) to make him indifferent to the others.	Every man that day will have concern enough to make him heedless (of others).	Every man of them shall on that day have an affair which will occupy him.
80	038	Some faces that Day will be beaming,	On that day faces will be bright as dawn,	(Many) faces on that day shall be bright,
80	039	Laughing, rejoicing.	Laughing, rejoicing at good news;	Laughing, joyous.
80	040	And other faces that Day will be dust-stained,	And other faces, on that day, with dust upon them,	And (many) faces on that day, on them shall be dust,
80	041	Blackness will cover them:	Veiled in darkness,	Darkness shall cover them.
80	042	Such will be the Rejecters of Allah, the doers of iniquity.	Those are the disbelievers, the wicked.	These are they who are unbelievers, the wicked.

Chapter 81:

AT-TAKWIR (THE OVERTHROWING)

Total Verses: 29 Revealed At: MAKKA

In the name of Allah, the Most Beneficent, the Most Merciful.

81 001	When the sun (with its spacious light) is folded up;	When the sun is overthrown,	When the sun is covered,
81 002	When the stars fall, losing their lustre;	And when the stars fall,	And when the stars darken,
81 003	When the mountains vanish (like a mirage);	And when the hills are moved,	And when the mountains are made to pass away,
81 004	When the she-camels, ten months with young, are left untended;	And when the camels big with young are abandoned,	And when the camels are left untended,
81 005	When the wild beasts are herded together (in the human habitations);	And when the wild beasts are herded together,	And when the wild animals are made to go forth,
81 006	When the oceans boil over with a swell;	And when the seas rise,	And when the seas are set on fire,
81 007	When the souls are sorted out, (being joined, like with like);	And when souls are reunited,	And when souls are united,
81 008	When the female (infant), buried alive, is questioned -	And when the girl-child that was buried alive is asked	And when the female infant buried alive is asked
81 009	For what crime she was killed;	For what sin she was slain,	For what sin she was killed,
81 010	When the scrolls are laid open;	And when the pages are laid open,	And when the books are spread,
81 011	When the world on High is unveiled;	And when the sky is torn away,	And when the heaven has its covering removed,
81 012	When the Blazing Fire is kindled to fierce heat;	And when hell is lighted,	And when the hell is kindled up,
81 013	And when the Garden is brought near;-	And when the Garden is brought nigh,	And when the garden is brought nigh,
81 014	(Then) shall each soul know what it has put forward.	(Then) every soul will know what it hath made ready.	Every soul shall (then) know what it has prepared.
81 015	So verily I call to witness the planets - that recede,	Oh, but I call to witness the planets,	But nay! I swear by the stars,
81 016	Go straight, or hide;	The stars which rise and set,	That run their course (and) hide themselves,
81 017	And the Night as it dissipates;	And the close of night,	And the night when it departs,
81 018	And the Dawn as it breathes away the darkness;-	And the breath of morning	And the morning when it brightens,
81 019	Verily this is the word of a most honourable Messenger,	That this is in truth the word of an honoured messenger,	Most surely it is the Word of an honored messenger,
81 020	Endued with Power, with rank before the Lord of the Throne,	Mighty, established in the presence of the Lord of the Throne,	The processor of strength, having an honorable place with the Lord of the Dominion,
81 021	With authority there, (and) faithful to his trust.	(One) to be obeyed, and trustworthy;	One (to be) obeyed, and faithful in trust.
81 022	And (O people!) your companion is not one possessed;	And your comrade is not mad.	And your companion is not gone mad.
81 023	And without doubt he saw him in the clear horizon.	Surely he beheld Him on the clear horizon.	And of a truth he saw himself on the clear horizon.

81 024	Neither doth he withhold grudgingly a knowledge of the Unseen.	And he is not avid of the Unseen.	Nor of the unseen is he a tenacious concealer.
81 025	Nor is it the word of an evil spirit accursed.	Nor is this the utterance of a devil worthy to be stoned.	Nor is it the word of the cursed Shaitan,
81 026	When whither go ye?	Whither then go ye?	Whither then will you go?
81 027	Verily this is no less than a Message to (all) the Worlds:	This is naught else than a reminder unto creation,	It is naught but a reminder for the nations,
81 028	(With profit) to whoever among you wills to go straight:	Unto whomsoever of you willeth to walk straight.	For him among you who pleases to go straight.
81 029	But ye shall not will except as Allah wills,- the Cherisher of the Worlds.	And ye will not, unless (it be) that Allah willeth, the Lord of Creation.	And you do not please except that Allah please, the Lord of the worlds.

Chapter 82:

AL-INFITAR (THE CLEAVING, BURSTING APART)

Total Verses: 19 Revealed At: MAKKA

In the name of Allah, the Most Beneficent, the Most Merciful.

82 001	When the Sky is cleft asunder;	When the heaven is cleft asunder,	When the heaven becomes cleft asunder,
82 002	When the Stars are scattered;	When the planets are dispersed,	And when the stars become dispersed,
82 003	When the Oceans are suffered to burst forth;	When the seas are poured forth,	And when the seas are made to flow forth,
82 004	And when the Graves are turned upside down;-	And the sepulchres are overturned,	And when the graves are laid open,
82 005	(Then) shall each soul know what it hath sent forward and (what it hath) kept back.	A soul will know what it hath sent before (it) and what left behind.	Every soul shall know what it has sent before and held back.
82 006	O man! What has seduced thee from thy Lord Most Beneficent?-	O man! What hath made thee careless concerning thy Lord, the Bountiful,	O man! what has beguiled you from your Lord, the Gracious one,
82 007	Him Who created thee. Fashioned thee in due proportion, and gave thee a just bias;	Who created thee, then fashioned, then proportioned thee?	Who created you, then made you complete, then made you symmetrical?
82 008	In whatever Form He wills, does He put thee together.	Into whatsoever form He will, He casteth thee.	Into whatever form He pleased He constituted you.
82 009	Nay! but ye do reject Right and Judgment!	Nay, but ye deny the Judgment.	Nay! but you give the lie to the judgment day,
82 010	But verily over you (are appointed angels) to protect you,-	Lo! there are above you guardians,	And most surely there are keepers over you
82 011	Kind and honourable,- Writing down (your deeds):	Generous and recording,	Honorable recorders,
82 012	They know (and understand) all that ye do.	Who know (all) that ye do.	They know what you do.
82 013	As for the Righteous, they will be in bliss;	Lo! the righteous verily will be in delight.	Most surely the righteous are in bliss,
82 014	And the Wicked - they will be in the Fire,	And lo! the wicked verily will be in hell;	And most surely the wicked are in burning fire,
82 015	Which they will enter on the Day of Judgment,	They will burn therein on the Day of Judgment.	They shall enter it on the Day of Judgment.

82 016	And they will not be able to keep away therefrom.	And will not be absent thence.		And they shall by no means be absent from it.
82 017	And what will explain to thee what the Day of Judgment is?	Ah, what will convey unto thee what the Day of Judgment is!		And what will make you realize what the Day of Judgment is?
82 018	Again, what will explain to thee what the Day of Judgment is?	Again, what will convey unto thee what the Day of Judgment is!		Again, what will make you realize what the Day of Judgment Is?
82 019	(It will be) the Day when no soul shall have power (to do) aught for another: For the command, that Day, will be (wholly) with Allah.	A day on which no soul hath power at all for any (other) soul. The (absolute) command on that day is Allah's.		The day on which no soul shall control anything for (another) soul; and the command on that day shall be entirely Allah's.

Chapter 83:

AL-MUTAFFIFIN (DEFRAUDING, THE CHEATS, CHEATING)

Total Verses: 36 Revealed At: MAKKA

In the name of Allah, the Most Beneficent, the Most Merciful.

83 001	Woe to those that deal in fraud,-	Woe unto the defrauders:	Woe to the defrauders,
83 002	Those who, when they have to receive by measure from men, exact full measure,	Those who when they take the measure from mankind demand it full,	Who, when they take the measure (of their dues) from men take it fully,
83 003	But when they have to give by measure or weight to men, give less than due.	But if they measure unto them or weight for them, they cause them loss.	But when they measure out to others or weigh out for them, they are deficient.
83 004	Do they not think that they will be called to account?-	Do such (men) not consider that they will be raised again	Do not these think that they shall be raised again
83 005	On a Mighty Day,	Unto an Awful Day,	For a mighty day,
83 006	A Day when (all) mankind will stand before the Lord of the Worlds?	The day when (all) mankind stand before the Lord of the Worlds?	The day on which men shall stand before the Lord of the worlds?
83 007	Nay! Surely the record of the wicked is (preserved) in Sijjin.	Nay, but the record of the vile is in Sijjin -	Nay! most surely the record of the wicked is in the Sijjin.
83 008	And what will explain to thee what Sijjin is?	Ah! what will convey unto thee what Sijjin is! -	And what will make you know what the Sijjin is?
83 009	(There is) a Register (fully) inscribed.	A written record.	It is a written book.
83 010	Woe, that Day, to those that deny-	Woe unto the repudiators on that day!	Woe on that day to the rejecters,
83 011	Those that deny the Day of Judgment.	Those who deny the Day of Judgment	Who give the lie to the Day of Judgment.
83 012	And none can deny it but the Transgressor beyond bounds the Sinner!	Which none denieth save each criminal transgressor,	And none gives the lie to it but every exceeder of limits, sinful one
83 013	When Our Signs are rehearsed to him, he says, "Tales of the ancients!"	Who, when thou readest unto him Our revelations, saith: (Mere) fables of the men of old.	When Our communications are recited to him, he says: Stories of those of yore.
83 014	By no means! but on their hearts is the stain of the (ill) which they do!	Nay, but that which they have earned is rust upon their hearts.	Nay! rather, what they used to do has become like rust upon their hearts.
83 015	Verily, from (the Light of) their Lord, that Day, will they be veiled.	Nay, but surely on that day they will be covered from (the mercy of) their Lord.	Nay! most surely they shall on that day be debarred from their Lord.

83 016	Further, they will enter the Fire of Hell.	Then lo! they verily will burn in hell,	Then most surely they shall enter the burning fire.
83 017	Further, it will be said to them: "This is the (reality) which ye rejected as false!"	And it will be said (unto them): This is that which ye used to deny.	Then shall it be said: This is what you gave the lie to.
83 018	Nay, verily the record of the Righteous is (preserved) in 'Illiyin.	Nay, but the record of the righteous is in 'Illiyin -	Nay! Most surely the record of the righteous shall be in the Iliyin.
83 019	And what will explain to thee what 'Illiyun is?	Ah, what will convey unto thee what 'Illiyin is! -	And what will make you know what the highest Iliyin is?
83 020	(There is) a Register (fully) inscribed,	A written record,	It is a written book,
83 021	To which bear witness those Nearest (to Allah).	Attested by those who are brought near (unto their Lord).	Those who are drawn near (to Allah) shall witness it.
83 022	Truly the Righteous will be in Bliss:	Lo! the righteous verily are in delight,	Most surely the righteous shall be in bliss,
83 023	On Thrones (of Dignity) will they command a sight (of all things):	On couches, gazing,	On thrones, they shall gaze;
83 024	Thou wilt recognise in their faces the beaming brightness of Bliss.	Thou wilt know in their faces the radiance of delight.	You will recognize in their faces the brightness of bliss.
83 025	Their thirst will be slaked with Pure Wine sealed:	They are given to drink of a pure wine, sealed,	They are made to quaff of a pure drink that is sealed (to others).
83 026	The seal thereof will be Musk: And for this let those aspire, who have aspirations:	Whose seal is musk - for this let (all) those strive who strive for bliss -	The sealing of it is (with) musk; and for that let the aspirers aspire.
83 027	With it will be (given) a mixture of Tasnim:	And mixed with water of Tasnim,	And the admixture of it is a water of Tasnim,
83 028	A spring, from (the waters) whereof drink those Nearest to Allah.	A spring whence those brought near (to Allah) drink.	A fountain from which drink they who are drawn near (to Allah).
83 029	Those in sin used to laugh at those who believed,	Lo! the guilty used to laugh at those who believed,	Surely they who are guilty used to laugh at those who believe.
83 030	And whenever they passed by them, used to wink at each other (in mockery);	And wink one to another when they passed them;	And when they passed by them, they winked at one another.
83 031	And when they returned to their own people, they would return jesting;	And when they returned to their own folk, they returned jesting;	And when they returned to their own followers they returned exulting.
83 032	And whenever they saw them, they would say, "Behold! These are the people truly astray!"	And when they saw them they said: Lo! these have gone astray.	And when they saw them, they said: Most surely these are in error;
83 033	But they had not been sent as keepers over them!	Yet they were not sent as guardians over them.	And they were not sent to be keepers over them.
83 034	But on this Day the Believers will laugh at the Unbelievers:	This day it is those who believe who have the laugh of disbelievers,	So today those who believe shall laugh at the unbelievers;
83 035	On Thrones (of Dignity) they will command (a sight) (of all things).	On high couches, gazing.	On thrones, they will look.
83 036	Will not the Unbelievers have been paid back for what they did?	Are not the disbelievers paid for what they used to do?	Surely the disbelievers are rewarded as they did.

Chapter 84:

AL-INSHIQAQ (THE SUNDERING, SPLITTING OPEN)

Total Verses: 25 Revealed At: MAKKA

In the name of Allah, the Most Beneficent, the Most Merciful.

84 001	When the sky is rent asunder,	When the heaven is split asunder	When the heaven bursts asunder,
84 002	And hearkens to (the Command of) its Lord, and it must needs (do so);-	And attentive to her Lord in fear,	And obeys its Lord and it must.
84 003	And when the earth is flattened out,	And when the earth is spread out	And when the earth is stretched,
84 004	And casts forth what is within it and becomes (clean) empty,	And hath cast out all that was in her, and is empty	And casts forth what is in it and becomes empty,
84 005	And hearkens to (the Command of) its Lord,- and it must needs (do so);- (then will come Home the full reality).	And attentive to her Lord in fear!	And obeys its Lord and it must.
84 006	O thou man! Verily thou art ever toiling on towards thy Lord- painfully toiling,- but thou shalt meet Him.	Thou, verily, O man, art working toward thy Lord a work which thou wilt meet (in His presence).	O man! surely you must strive (to attain) to your Lord, a hard striving until you meet Him.
84 007	Then he who is given his Record in his right hand,	Then whoso is given his account in his right hand	Then as to him who is given his book in his right hand,
84 008	Soon will his account be taken by an easy reckoning,	He truly will receive an easy reckoning	He shall be reckoned with by an easy reckoning,
84 009	And he will turn to his people, rejoicing!	And will return unto his folk in joy.	And he shall go back to his people joyful.
84 010	But he who is given his Record behind his back,-	But whoso is given his account behind his back,	And as to him who is given his book behind his back,
84 011	Soon will he cry for perdition,	He surely will invoke destruction	He shall call for perdition,
84 012	And he will enter a Blazing Fire.	And be thrown to scorching fire.	And enter into burning fire.
84 013	Truly, did he go about among his people, rejoicing!	He verily lived joyous with his folk,	Surely he was (erstwhile) joyful among his followers.
84 014	Truly, did he think that he would not have to return (to Us)!	He verily deemed that he would never return (unto Allah).	Surely he thought that he would never return.
84 015	Nay, nay! for his Lord was (ever) watchful of him!	Nay, but lo! his Lord is ever looking on him!	Yea! surely his Lord does ever see him.
84 016	So I do call to witness the ruddy glow of Sunset;	Oh, I swear by the afterglow of sunset,	But nay! I swear by the sunset redness,
84 017	The Night and its Homing;	And by the night and all that it enshroudeth,	And the night and that which it drives on,
84 018	And the Moon in her fullness:	And by the moon when she is at the full,	And the moon when it grows full,
84 019	Ye shall surely travel from stage to stage.	That ye shall journey on from plane to plane.	That you shall most certainly enter one state after another.
84 020	What then is the matter with them, that they believe not?-	What aileth them, then, that they believe not	But what is the matter with them that they do not believe,
84 021	And when the Qur'an is read to them, they fall not prostrate,	And, when the Qur'an is recited unto them, worship not (Allah)?	And when the Quran is recited to them they do not make obeisance?

84 022	But on the contrary the Unbelievers reject (it).	Nay, but those who disbelieve will deny;	Nay! those who disbelieve give the lie to the truth.
84 023	But Allah has full knowledge of what they secrete (in their breasts)	And Allah knoweth best what they are hiding.	And Allah knows best what they hide,
84 024	So announce to them a Penalty Grievous,	So give them tidings of a painful doom,	So announce to them a painful punishment,
84 025	Except to those who believe and work righteous deeds: For them is a Reward that will never fail.	Save those who believe and do good works, for theirs is a reward unfailing.	Except those who believe and do good; for them is a reward that shall never be cut off.

Chapter 85:

AL-BUROOJ (THE MANSIONS OF THE STARS, CONSTELLATIONS)

Total Verses: 22 Revealed At: MAKKA

In the name of Allah, the Most Beneficent, the Most Merciful.

85 001	By the sky, (displaying) the Zodiacal Signs;	By the heaven, holding mansions of the stars,	I swear by the mansions of the stars,
85 002	By the promised Day (of Judgment);	And by the Promised Day.	And the promised day,
85 003	By one that witnesses, and the subject of the witness;-	And by the witness and that whereunto he beareth testimony,	And the bearer of witness and those against whom the witness is borne.
85 004	Woe to the makers of the pit (of fire),	(Self-)destroyed were the owners of the ditch	Cursed be the makers of the pit,
85 005	Fire supplied (abundantly) with fuel:	Of the fuel-fed fire,	Of the fire (kept burning) with fuel,
85 006	Behold! they sat over against the (fire),	When they sat by it,	When they sat by it,
85 007	And they witnessed (all) that they were doing against the Believers.	And were themselves the witnesses of what they did to the believers.	And they were witnesses of what they did with the believers.
85 008	And they ill-treated them for no other reason than that they believed in Allah, Exalted in Power, Worthy of all Praise!-	They had naught against them save that they believed in Allah, the Mighty, the Owner of Praise,	And they did not take vengeance on them for aught except that they believed in Allah, the Mighty, the Praised,
85 009	Him to Whom belongs the dominion of the heavens and the earth! And Allah is Witness to all things.	Him unto Whom belongeth the Sovereignty of the heavens and the earth; and Allah is of all things the Witness.	Whose is the kingdom of the heavens and the earth; and Allah is a Witness of all things.
85 010	Those who persecute (or draw into temptation) the Believers, men and women, and do not turn in repentance, will have the Penalty of Hell: They will have the Penalty of the Burning Fire.	Lo! they who persecute believing men and believing women and repent not, theirs verily will be the doom of hell, and theirs the doom of burning.	Surely (as for) those who persecute the believing men and the believing women, then do not repent, they shall have the chastisement of hell, and they shall have the chastisement of burning.
85 011	For those who believe and do righteous deeds, will be Gardens; beneath which rivers flow: That is the great Salvation, (the fulfilment of all desires),	Lo! those who believe and do good works, theirs will be Gardens underneath which rivers flow. That is the Great Success.	Surely (as for) those who believe and do good, they shall have gardens beneath which rivers flow, that is the great achievement.
85 012	Truly strong is the Grip (and Power) of thy Lord.	Lo! the punishment of thy Lord is stern.	Surely the might of your Lord is great.
85 013	It is He Who creates from the very beginning, and He can restore (life).	Lo! He it is Who produceth, then reproduceth,	Surely He it is Who originates and reproduces,

85 014	And He is the Oft-Forgiving, Full of Loving-Kindness,	And He is the Forgiving, the Loving,		And He is the Forgiving, the Loving,
85 015	Lord of the Throne of Glory,	Lord of the Throne of Glory,		Lord of the Arsh, the Glorious,
85 016	Doer (without let) of all that He intends.	Doer of what He will.		The great doer of what He will.
85 017	Has the story reached thee, of the forces-	Hath there come unto thee the story of the hosts		Has not there come to you the story of the hosts,
85 018	Of Pharaoh and the Thamud?	Of Pharaoh and (the tribe of) Thamud?		Of Firon and Samood?
85 019	And yet the Unbelievers (persist) in rejecting (the Truth)!	Nay, but those who disbelieve live in denial		Nay! those who disbelieve are in (the act of) giving the lie to the truth.
85 020	But Allah doth encompass them from behind!	And Allah, all unseen, surroundeth them.		And Allah encompasses them on every side.
85 021	Nay, this is a Glorious Qur'an,	Nay, but it is a glorious Qur'an.		Nay! it is a glorious Quran,
85 022	(Inscribed) in a Tablet Preserved!	On a guarded tablet.		In a guarded tablet.

Chapter 86:

AT-TARIQ (THE MORNING STAR, THE NIGHTCOMER)

Total Verses: 17 Revealed At: MAKKA

In the name of Allah, the Most Beneficent, the Most Merciful.

86 001	By the Sky and the Night-Visitant (therein);-	By the heaven and the Morning Star	I swear by the heaven and the comer by night;
86 002	And what will explain to thee what the Night-Visitant is?-	- Ah, what will tell thee what the Morning Star is!	And what will make you know what the comer by night is?
86 003	(It is) the Star of piercing brightness;-	- The piercing Star!	The star of piercing brightness;
86 004	There is no soul but has a protector over it.	No human soul but hath a guardian over it.	There is not a soul but over it is a keeper.
86 005	Now let man but think from what he is created!	So let man consider from what he is created.	So let man consider of what he is created:
86 006	He is created from a drop emitted-	He is created from a gushing fluid	He is created of water pouring forth,
86 007	Proceeding from between the backbone and the ribs:	That issued from between the loins and ribs.	Coming from between the back and the ribs.
86 008	Surely (Allah) is able to bring him back (to life)!	Lo! He verily is Able to return him (unto life)	Most surely He is able to return him (to life).
86 009	The Day that (all) things secret will be tested,	On the day when hidden thoughts shall be searched out.	On the day when hidden things shall be made manifest,
86 010	(Man) will have no power, and no helper.	Then will he have no might nor any helper.	He shall have neither strength nor helper.
86 011	By the Firmament which returns (in its round),	By the heaven which giveth the returning rain,	I swear by the raingiving heavens,
86 012	And by the Earth which opens out (for the gushing of springs or the sprouting of vegetation),-	And the earth which splitteth (with the growth of trees and plants)	And the earth splitting (with plants);
86 013	Behold this is the Word that distinguishes (Good from Evil):	Lo! this (Qur'an) is a conclusive word,	Most surely it is a decisive word,

86 014	It is not a thing for amusement.	It is no pleasantry.	And it is no joke.
86 015	As for them, they are but plotting a scheme,	Lo! they plot a plot (against thee, O Muhammad)	Surely they will make a scheme,
86 016	And I am planning a scheme.	And I plot a plot (against them).	And I (too) will make a scheme.
86 017	Therefore grant a delay to the unbelievers: Give respite to them gently (for awhile).	So give a respite to the disbelievers. Deal thou gently with them for a while.	So grant the unbelievers a respite: let them alone for a

Chapter 87:

AL-ALA (THE MOST HIGH, GLORY TO YOUR LORD IN THE HIGHEST)

Total Verses: 19 Revealed At: MAKKA

In the name of Allah, the Most Beneficent, the Most Merciful.

87 001	Glorify the name of thy Guardian-Lord Most High,	Praise the name of thy Lord the Most High,	Glorify the name of your Lord, the Most High,
87 002	Who hath created, and further, given order and proportion;	Who createth, then disposeth;	Who creates, then makes complete,
87 003	Who hath ordained laws. And granted guidance;	Who measureth, then guideth;	And Who makes (things) according to a measure, then guides (them to their goal),
87 004	And Who bringeth out the (green and luscious) pasture,	Who bringeth forth the pasturage,	And Who brings forth herbage,
87 005	And then doth make it (but) swarthy stubble.	Then turneth it to russet stubble.	Then makes it dried up, dust-colored.
87 006	By degrees shall We teach thee to declare (the Message), so thou shalt not forget,	We shall make thee read (O Muhammad) so that thou shalt not forget	We will make you recite so you shall not forget,
87 007	Except as Allah wills: For He knoweth what is manifest and what is hidden.	Save that which Allah willeth. Lo! He knoweth the disclosed and that which still is hidden;	Except what Allah pleases, surely He knows the manifest, and what is hidden.
87 008	And We will make it easy for thee (to follow) the simple (Path).	And We shall ease thy way unto the state of ease.	And We will make your way smooth to a state of ease.
87 009	Therefore give admonition in case the admonition profits (the hearer).	Therefor remind (men), for of use is the reminder.	Therefore do remind, surely reminding does profit.
87 010	The admonition will be received by those who fear (Allah):	He will heed who feareth,	He who fears will mind,
87 011	But it will be avoided by those most unfortunate ones,	But the most hapless will flout it,	And the most unfortunate one will avoid it,
87 012	Who will enter the Great Fire,	He who will be flung to the great Fire	Who shall enter the great fire;
87 013	In which they will then neither die nor live.	Wherein he will neither die nor live.	Then therein he shall neither live nor die.
87 014	But those will prosper who purify themselves,	He is successful who groweth,	He indeed shall be successful who purifies himself,
87 015	And glorify the name of their Guardian-Lord, and (lift their hearts) in prayer.	And remembereth the name of his Lord, so prayeth,	And magnifies the name of his Lord and prays.
87 016	Nay (behold), ye prefer the life of this world;	But ye prefer the life of the world	Nay! you prefer the life of this world,
87 017	But the Hereafter is better and more enduring.	Although the Hereafter is better and more lasting.	While the hereafter is better and more lasting.

87 018	And this is in the Books of the earliest (Revelation),-	Lo! This is in the former scrolls.	Most surely this is in the earlier scriptures,
87 019	The Books of Abraham and Moses.	The Books of Abraham and Moses.	The scriptures of Ibrahim and Musa.

Chapter 88:

AL-GHASHIYA (THE OVERWHELMING, THE PALL)

Total Verses: 26 Revealed At: MAKKA

In the name of Allah, the Most Beneficent, the Most Merciful.

88 001	Has the story reached thee of the overwhelming (Event)?	Hath there come unto thee tidings of the Overwhelming?	Has not there come to you the news of the overwhelming calamity?
88 002	Some faces, that Day, will be humiliated,	On that day (many) faces will be downcast,	(Some) faces on that day shall be downcast,
88 003	Labouring (hard), weary,-	Toiling, weary,	Laboring, toiling,
88 004	The while they enter the Blazing Fire,-	Scorched by burning fire,	Entering into burning fire,
88 005	The while they are given, to drink, of a boiling hot spring,	Drinking from a boiling spring,	Made to drink from a boiling spring.
88 006	No food will there be for them but a bitter Dhari'	No food for them save bitter thorn-fruit	They shall have no food but of thorns,
88 007	Which will neither nourish nor satisfy hunger.	Which doth not nourish nor release from hunger.	Which will neither fatten nor avail against hunger.
88 008	(Other) faces that Day will be joyful,	In that day other faces will be calm,	(Other) faces on that day shall be happy,
88 009	Pleased with their striving,-	Glad for their effort past,	Well-pleased because of their striving,
88 010	In a Garden on high,	In a high Garden	In a lofty garden,
88 011	Where they shall hear no (word) of vanity:	Where they hear no idle speech,	Wherein you shall not hear vain talk.
88 012	Therein will be a bubbling spring:	Wherein is a gushing spring,	Therein is a fountain flowing,
88 013	Therein will be Thrones (of dignity), raised on high,	Wherein are couches raised	Therein are thrones raised high,
88 014	Goblets placed (ready),	And goblets set at hand	And drinking-cups ready placed,
88 015	And cushions set in rows,	And cushions ranged	And cushions set in a row,
88 016	And rich carpets (all) spread out.	And silken carpets spread.	And carpets spread out.
88 017	Do they not look at the Camels, how they are made?-	Will they not regard the camels, how they are created?	Will they not then consider the camels, how they are created?
88 018	And at the Sky, how it is raised high?-	And the heaven, how it is raised?	And the heaven, how it is reared aloft,
88 019	And at the Mountains, how they are fixed firm?-	And the hills, how they are set up?	And the mountains, how they are firmly fixed,
88 020	And at the Earth, how it is spread out?	And the earth, how it is spread?	And the earth, how it is made a vast expanse?
88 021	Therefore do thou give admonition, for thou art one to admonish.	Remind them, for thou art but an admonisher,	Therefore do remind, for you are only a reminder.

88 022	Thou art not one to manage (men's) affairs.	Thou art not at all a warder over them.	You are not a watcher over them;
88 023	But if any turn away and reject Allah,-	But whoso is averse and disbelieveth,	But whoever turns back and disbelieves,
88 024	Allah will punish him with a mighty Punishment,	Allah will punish him with direst punishment.	Allah will chastise him with the greatest chastisement.
88 025	For to Us will be their return;	Lo! unto Us is their return	Surely to Us is their turning back,
88 026	Then it will be for Us to call them to account.	And Ours their reckoning.	Then surely upon Us is the taking of their account.

Chapter 89:

AL-FAJR (THE DAWN, DAYBREAK)

Total Verses: 30 Revealed At: MAKKA

In the name of Allah, the Most Beneficent, the Most Merciful.

89 001	By the break of Day	By the Dawn	I swear by the daybreak,
89 002	By the Nights twice five;	And ten nights,	And the ten nights,
89 003	By the even and odd (contrasted);	And the Even and the Odd,	And the even and the odd,
89 004	And by the Night when it passeth away;-	And the night when it departeth,	And the night when it departs.
89 005	Is there (not) in these an adjuration (or evidence) for those who understand?	There surely is an oath for thinking man.	Truly in that there is an oath for those who possess understanding.
89 006	Seest thou not how thy Lord dealt with the 'Ad (people),-	Dost thou not consider how thy Lord dealt with (the tribe of) A'ad,	Have you not considered how your Lord dealt with Ad,
89 007	Of the (city of) Iram, with lofty pillars,	With many-columned Iram,	(The people of) Aram, possessors of lofty buildings,
89 008	The like of which were not produced in (all) the land?	The like of which was not created in the lands;	The like of which were not created in the (other) cities;
89 009	And with the Thamud (people), who cut out (huge) rocks in the valley?-	And with (the tribe of) Thamud, who clove the rocks in the valley;	And (with) Samood, who hewed out the rocks in the valley,
89 010	And with Pharaoh, lord of stakes?	And with Pharaoh, firm of might,	And (with) Firon, the lord of hosts,
89 011	(All) these transgressed beyond bounds in the lands,	Who (all) were rebellious (to Allah) in these lands,	Who committed inordinacy in the cities,
89 012	And heaped therein mischief (on mischief).	And multiplied iniquity therein?	So they made great mischief therein?
89 013	Therefore did thy Lord pour on them a scourge of diverse chastisements:	Therefore thy Lord poured on them the disaster of His punishment.	Therefore your Lord let down upon them a portion of the chastisement.
89 014	For thy Lord is (as a Guardian) on a watch-tower.	Lo! thy Lord is ever watchful.	Most surely your Lord is watching.
89 015	Now, as for man, when his Lord trieth him, giving him honour and gifts, then saith he, (puffed up), "My Lord hath honoured me."	As for man, whenever his Lord trieth him by honouring him, and is gracious unto him, he saith: My Lord honoureth me.	And as for man, when his Lord tries him, then treats him with honor and makes him lead an easy life, he says: My Lord honors me.

89 016	But when He trieth him, restricting his subsistence for him, then saith he (in despair), "My Lord hath humiliated me!"	But whenever He trieth him by straitening his means of life, he saith: My Lord despiseth me.	But when He tries him (differently), then straitens to him his means of subsistence, he says: My Lord has disgraced me.
89 017	Nay, nay! but ye honour not the orphans!	Nay, but ye (for your part) honour not the orphan	Nay! but you do not honor the orphan,
89 018	Nor do ye encourage one another to feed the poor!-	And urge not on the feeding of the poor.	Nor do you urge one another to feed the poor,
89 019	And ye devour inheritance - all with greed,	And ye devour heritages with devouring greed.	And you eat away the heritage, devouring (everything) indiscriminately,
89 020	And ye love wealth with inordinate love!	And love wealth with abounding love.	And you love wealth with exceeding love.
89 021	Nay! When the earth is pounded to powder,	Nay, but when the earth is ground to atoms, grinding, grinding,	Nay! when the earth is made to crumble to pieces,
89 022	And thy Lord cometh, and His angels, rank upon rank,	And thy Lord shall come with angels, rank on rank,	And your Lord comes and (also) the angels in ranks,
89 023	And Hell, that Day, is brought (face to face),- on that Day will man remember, but how will that remembrance profit him?	And hell is brought near that day; on that day man will remember, but how will the remembrance (then) avail him)?	And hell is made to appear on that day. On that day shall man be mindful, and what shall being mindful (then) avail him?
89 024	He will say: "Ah! Would that I had sent forth (good deeds) for (this) my (Future) Life!"	He will say: Ah, would that I had sent before me (some provision) for my life!	He shall say: O! would that I had sent before for (this) my life!
89 025	For, that Day, His Chastisement will be such as none (else) can inflict,	None punisheth as He will punish on that day!	But on that day shall no one chastise with (anything like) His chastisement,
89 026	And His bonds will be such as none (other) can bind.	None bindeth as He then will bind.	And no one shall bind with (anything like) His binding.
89 027	(To the righteous soul will be said:) "O (thou) soul, in (complete) rest and satisfaction!"	But ah! thou soul at peace!	O soul that art at rest!
89 028	"Come back thou to thy Lord,- well pleased (thyself), and well-pleasing unto Him!"	Return unto thy Lord, content in His good pleasure!	Return to your Lord, well-pleased (with him), well-pleasing (Him),
89 029	"Enter thou, then, among My devotees!"	Enter thou among My bondmen!	So enter among My servants,
89 030	"Yea, enter thou My Heaven!"	Enter thou My Garden!	And enter into My garden.

Chapter 90:

AL-BALAD (THE CITY, THIS COUNTRYSIDE)

Total Verses: 20 Revealed At: MAKKA

In the name of Allah, the Most Beneficent, the Most Merciful.

90 001	I do call to witness this City;-	Nay, I swear by this city -	Nay! I swear by this city.
90 002	And thou art a freeman of this City;-	And thou art an indweller of this city -	And you shall be made free from obligation in this city--
90 003	And (the mystic ties of) parent and child;-	And the begetter and that which he begat,	And the begetter and whom he begot.
90 004	Verily We have created man into toil and struggle.	We verily have created man in an atmosphere:	Certainly We have created man to be in distress.

90 005	Thinketh he, that none hath power over him?	Thinketh he that none hath power over him?	Does he think that no one has power over him?
90 006	He may say (boastfully); Wealth have I squandered in abundance!	And he saith: I have destroyed vast wealth:	He shall say: I have wasted much wealth.
90 007	Thinketh he that none beholdeth him?	Thinketh he that none beholdeth him?	Does he think that no one sees him?
90 008	Have We not made for him a pair of eyes?-	Did We not assign unto him two eyes	Have We not given him two eyes,
90 009	And a tongue, and a pair of lips?-	And a tongue and two lips,	And a tongue and two lips,
90 010	And shown him the two highways?	And guide him to the parting of the mountain ways?	And pointed out to him the two conspicuous ways?
90 011	But he hath made no haste on the path that is steep.	But he hath not attempted the Ascent -	But he would not attempt the uphill road,
90 012	And what will explain to thee the path that is steep?-	Ah, what will convey unto thee what the Ascent is! -	And what will make you comprehend what the uphill road is?
90 013	(It is:) freeing the bondman;	(It is) to free a slave,	(It is) the setting free of a slave,
90 014	Or the giving of food in a day of privation	And to feed in the day of hunger.	Or the giving of food in a day of hunger
90 015	To the orphan with claims of relationship,	An orphan near of kin,	To an orphan, having relationship,
90 016	Or to the indigent (down) in the dust.	Or some poor wretch in misery,	Or to the poor man lying in the dust.
90 017	Then will he be of those who believe, and enjoin patience, (constancy, and self-restraint), and enjoin deeds of kindness and compassion.	And to be of those who believe and exhort one another to perseverance and exhort one another to pity.	Then he is of those who believe and charge one another to show patience, and charge one another to show compassion.
90 018	Such are the Companions of the Right Hand.	Their place will be on the right hand.	These are the people of the right hand.
90 019	But those who reject Our Signs, they are the (unhappy) Companions of the Left Hand.	But those who disbelieve Our revelations, their place will be on the left hand.	And (as for) those who disbelieve in our communications, they are the people of the left hand.
90 020	On them will be Fire vaulted over (all round).	Fire will be an awning over them.	On them is fire closed over.

Chapter 91:

ASH-SHAMS (THE SUN)

Total Verses: 15 Revealed At: MAKKA

In the name of Allah, the Most Beneficent, the Most Merciful.

91 001	By the Sun and his (glorious) splendour;	By the sun and his brightness,	I swear by the sun and its brilliance,
91 002	By the Moon as she follows him;	And the moon when she followeth him,	And the moon when it follows the sun,
91 003	By the Day as it shows up (the Sun's) glory;	And the day when it revealeth him,	And the day when it shows it,
91 004	By the Night as it conceals it;	And the night when it enshroudeth him,	And the night when it draws a veil over it,
91 005	By the Firmament and its (wonderful) structure;	And the heaven and Him Who built it,	And the heaven and Him Who made it,

91 006	By the Earth and its (wide) expanse:	And the earth and Him Who spread it,		And the earth and Him Who extended it,
91 007	By the Soul, and the proportion and order given to it;	And a soul and Him Who perfected it		And the soul and Him Who made it perfect,
91 008	And its enlightenment as to its wrong and its right;-	And inspired it (with conscience of) what is wrong for it and (what is) right for it.		Then He inspired it to understand what is right and wrong for it;
91 009	Truly he succeeds that purifies it,	He is indeed successful who causeth it to grow,		He will indeed be successful who purifies it,
91 010	And he fails that corrupts it!	And he is indeed a failure who stunteth it.		And he will indeed fail who corrupts it.
91 011	The Thamud (people) rejected (their prophet) through their inordinate wrong-doing,	(The tribe of) Thamud denied (the truth) in their rebellious pride,		Samood gave the lie (to the truth) in their inordinacy,
91 012	Behold, the most wicked man among them was deputed (for impiety).	When the basest of them broke forth		When the most unfortunate of them broke forth with
91 013	But the Messenger of Allah said to them: "It is a She-camel of Allah! And (bar her not from) having her drink!"	And the messenger of Allah said: It is the she-camel of Allah, so let her drink!		So Allah's messenger said to them (Leave alone) Allah's she-camel, and (give) her (to) drink.
91 014	Then they rejected him (as a false prophet), and they hamstrung her. So their Lord, on account of their crime, obliterated their traces and made them equal (in destruction, high and low)!	But they denied him, and they hamstrung her, so Allah doomed them for their sin and razed (their dwellings).		But they called him a liar and slaughtered her, therefore their Lord crushed them for their sin and levelled them (with the ground).
91 015	And for Him is no fear of its consequences.	He dreadeth not the sequel (of events).		And He fears not its consequence.

Chapter 92:

AL-LAIL (THE NIGHT)

Total Verses: 21 Revealed At: MAKKA

In the name of Allah, the Most Beneficent, the Most Merciful.

92 001	By the Night as it conceals (the light);	By the night enshrouding		I swear by the night when it draws a veil,
92 002	By the Day as it appears in glory;	And the day resplendent		And the day when it shines in brightness,
92 003	By (the mystery of) the creation of male and female;-	And Him Who hath created male and female,		And the creating of the male and the female,
92 004	Verily, (the ends) ye strive for are diverse.	Lo! your effort is dispersed (toward divers ends).		Your striving is most surely (directed to) various (ends).
92 005	So he who gives (in charity) and fears (Allah),	As for him who giveth and is dutiful (toward Allah)		Then as for him who gives away and guards (against evil),
92 006	And (in all sincerity) testifies to the best,-	And believeth in goodness;		And accepts the best,
92 007	We will indeed make smooth for him the path to Bliss.	Surely We will ease his way unto the state of ease.		We will facilitate for him the easy end.
92 008	But he who is a greedy miser and thinks himself self-sufficient,	But as for him who hoardeth and deemeth himself independent,		And as for him who is niggardly and considers himself free from need (of Allah),

92 009	And gives the lie to the best,-	And disbelieveth in goodness;	And rejects the best,
92 010	We will indeed make smooth for him the path to Misery;	Surely We will ease his way unto adversity.	We will facilitate for him the difficult end.
92 011	Nor will his wealth profit him when he falls headlong (into the Pit).	His riches will not save him when he perisheth.	And his wealth will not avail him when he perishes.
92 012	Verily We take upon Ourselves to guide,	Lo! Ours it is (to give) the guidance	Surely Ours is it to show the way,
92 013	And verily unto Us (belong) the End and the Beginning.	And lo! unto Us belong the latter portion and the former.	And most surely Ours is the hereafter and the former.
92 014	Therefore do I warn you of a Fire blazing fiercely;	Therefor have I warned you of the flaming Fire	Therefore I warn you of the fire that flames:
92 015	None shall reach it but those most unfortunate ones	Which only the most wretched must endure,	None shall enter it but the most unhappy,
92 016	Who give the lie to Truth and turn their backs.	He who denieth and turneth away.	Who gives the lie (to the truth) and turns (his) back.
92 017	But those most devoted to Allah shall be removed far from it,-	Far removed from it will be the righteous	And away from it shall be kept the one who guards most (against evil),
92 018	Those who spend their wealth for increase in self-purification,	Who giveth his wealth that he may grow (in goodness).	Who gives away his wealth, purifying himself
92 019	And have in their minds no favour from anyone for which a reward is expected in return,	And none hath with him any favour for reward,	And no one has with him any boon for which he should be rewarded,
92 020	But only the desire to seek for the Countenance of their Lord Most High;	Except as seeking (to fulfil) the purpose of his Lord Most High.	Except the seeking of the pleasure of his Lord, the Most High.
92 021	And soon will they attain (complete) satisfaction.	He verily will be content.	And he shall soon be well-pleased.

Chapter 93:

AD-DHUHA (THE MORNING HOURS, MORNING BRIGHT)

Total Verses: 11 Revealed At: MAKKA

In the name of Allah, the Most Beneficent, the Most Merciful.

93 001	By the Glorious Morning Light,	By the morning hours	I swear by the early hours of the day,
93 002	And by the Night when it is still,-	And by the night when it is stillest,	And the night when it covers with darkness.
93 003	Thy Guardian-Lord hath not forsaken thee, nor is He displeased.	Thy Lord hath not forsaken thee nor doth He hate thee,	Your Lord has not forsaken you, nor has He become displeased,
93 004	And verily the Hereafter will be better for thee than the present.	And verily the latter portion will be better for thee than the former,	And surely what comes after is better for you than that which has gone before.
93 005	And soon will thy Guardian-Lord give thee (that wherewith) thou shalt be well-pleased.	And verily thy Lord will give unto thee so that thou wilt be content.	And soon will your Lord give you so that you shall be well pleased.
93 006	Did He not find thee an orphan and give thee shelter (and care)?	Did He not find thee an orphan and protect (thee)?	Did He not find you an orphan and give you shelter?
93 007	And He found thee wandering, and He gave thee guidance.	Did He not find thee wandering and direct (thee)?	And find you lost (that is, unrecognized by men) and guide (them to you)?

93 008	And He found thee in need, and made thee independent.	Did He not find thee destitute and enrich (thee)?	And find you in want and make you to be free from want?
93 009	Therefore, treat not the orphan with harshness,	Therefor the orphan oppress not,	Therefore, as for the orphan, do not oppress (him).
93 010	Nor repulse the petitioner (unheard);	Therefor the beggar drive not away,	And as for him who asks, do not chide (him),
93 011	But the bounty of thy Lord - rehearse and proclaim!	Therefor of the bounty of thy Lord be thy discourse.	And as for the favor of your Lord, do announce (it).

Chapter 94:

AL-INSHIRAH (SOLACE, CONSOLATION, RELIEF)

Total Verses: 8 Revealed At: MAKKA

In the name of Allah, the Most Beneficent, the Most Merciful.

94 001	Have We not expanded thee thy breast?-	Have We not caused thy bosom to dilate,	Have We not expanded for you your breast,
94 002	And removed from thee thy burden	And eased thee of the burden	And taken off from you your burden,
94 003	The which did gall thy back?-	Which weighed down thy back;	Which pressed heavily upon your back,
94 004	And raised high the esteem (in which) thou (art held)?	And exalted thy fame?	And exalted for you your esteem?
94 005	So, verily, with every difficulty, there is relief:	But lo! with hardship goeth ease,	Surely with difficulty is ease.
94 006	Verily, with every difficulty there is relief.	Lo! with hardship goeth ease;	With difficulty is surely ease.
94 007	Therefore, when thou art free (from thine immediate task), still labour hard,	So when thou art relieved, still toil	So when you are free, nominate.
94 008	And to thy Lord turn (all) thy attention.	And strive to please thy Lord.	And make your Lord your exclusive object.

Chapter 95:

AT-TIN (THE FIG, THE FIGTREE)

Total Verses: 8 Revealed At: MAKKA

In the name of Allah, the Most Beneficent, the Most Merciful.

95 001	By the Fig and the Olive,	By the fig and the olive,	I swear by the fig and the olive,
95 002	And the Mount of Sinai,	By Mount Sinai,	And mount Sinai,
95 003	And this City of security,-	And by this land made safe;	And this city made secure,
95 004	We have indeed created man in the best of moulds,	Surely We created man of the best stature	Certainly We created man in the best make.
95 005	Then do We abase him (to be) the lowest of the low,-	Then we reduced him to the lowest of the low,	Then We render him the lowest of the low.

95 006	Except such as believe and do righteous deeds: For they shall have a reward unfailing.	Save those who believe and do good works, and theirs is a reward unfailing.		Except those who believe and do good, so they shall have a reward never to be cut off.
95 007	Then what can, after this, contradict thee, as to the judgment (to come)?	So who henceforth will give the lie to thee about the judgment?		Then who can give you the lie after (this) about the judgment?
95 008	Is not Allah the wisest of judges?	Is not Allah the most conclusive of all judges?		Is not Allah the best of the Judges?

Chapter 96:

AL-ALAQ (THE CLOT, READ)

Total Verses: 19 Revealed At: MAKKA

In the name of Allah, the Most Beneficent, the Most Merciful.

96 001	Proclaim! (or read!) in the name of thy Lord and Cherisher, Who created-	Read: In the name of thy Lord Who createth,	Read in the name of your Lord Who created.
96 002	Created man, out of a (mere) clot of congealed blood:	Createth man from a clot.	He created man from a clot.
96 003	Proclaim! And thy Lord is Most Bountiful,-	Read: And thy Lord is the Most Bounteous,	Read and your Lord is Most Honorable,
96 004	He Who taught (the use of) the pen,-	Who teacheth by the pen,	Who taught (to write) with the pen
96 005	Taught man that which he knew not.	Teacheth man that which he knew not.	Taught man what he knew not.
96 006	Nay, but man doth transgress all bounds,	Nay, but verily man is rebellious	Nay! man is most surely inordinate,
96 007	In that he looketh upon himself as self-sufficient.	That he thinketh himself independent!	Because he sees himself free from want.
96 008	Verily, to thy Lord is the return (of all).	Lo! unto thy Lord is the return.	Surely to your Lord is the return.
96 009	Seest thou one who forbids-	Hast thou seen him who dissuadeth	Have you seen him who forbids
96 010	A votary when he (turns) to pray?	A slave when he prayeth?	A servant when he prays?
96 011	Seest thou if he is on (the road of) Guidance?-	Hast thou seen if he relieth on the guidance (of Allah)	Have you considered if he were on the right way,
96 012	Or enjoins Righteousness?	Or enjoineth piety?	Or enjoined guarding (against evil)?
96 013	Seest thou if he denies (Truth) and turns away?	Hast thou seen if he denieth (Allah's guidance) and is froward?	Have you considered if he gives the lie to the truth and turns (his) back?
96 014	Knoweth he not that Allah doth see?	Is he then unaware that Allah seeth?	Does he not know that Allah does see?
96 015	Let him beware! If he desist not, We will drag him by the forelock,-	Nay, but if he cease not We will seize him by the forelock -	Nay! if he desist not, We would certainly smite his forehead,
96 016	A lying, sinful forelock!	The lying, sinful forelock -	A lying, sinful forehead.
96 017	Then, let him call (for help) to his council (of comrades):	Then let him call upon his henchmen!	Then let him summon his council,
96 018	We will call on the angels of punishment (to deal with him)!	We will call the guards of hell.	We too would summon the braves of the army.

96 019	Nay, heed him not: But bow down in adoration, and bring thyself the closer (to Allah)!	Nay, Obey not thou him. But prostrate thyself, and draw near (unto Allah).	Nay! obey him not, and make obeisance and draw nigh (to Allah).	

Chapter 97:

AL-QADR (POWER, FATE)

Total Verses: 5 Revealed At: MAKKA

In the name of Allah, the Most Beneficent, the Most Merciful.

97 001	We have indeed revealed this (Message) in the Night of Power:	Lo! We revealed it on the Night of Predestination.	Surely We revealed it on the grand night.
97 002	And what will explain to thee what the night of power is?	Ah, what will convey unto thee what the Night of Power is!	And what will make you comprehend what the grand night
97 003	The Night of Power is better than a thousand months.	The Night of Power is better than a thousand months.	The grand night is better than a thousand months.
97 004	Therein come down the angels and the Spirit by Allah's permission, on every errand:	The angels and the Spirit descend therein, by the permission of their Lord, with all decrees.	The angels and Gibreel descend in it by the permission of their Lord for every affair,
97 005	Peace!... This until the rise of morn!	(The night is) Peace until the rising of the dawn.	Peace! it is till the break of the morning.

Chapter 98:

AL-BAYYINA (THE CLEAR PROOF, EVIDENCE)

Total Verses: 8 Revealed At: MADINA

In the name of Allah, the Most Beneficent, the Most Merciful.

98 001	Those who reject (Truth), among the People of the Book and among the Polytheists, were not going to depart (from their ways) until there should come to them Clear Evidence,-	Those who disbelieve among the People of the Scripture and the idolaters could not have left off (erring) till the clear proof came unto them,	Those who disbelieved from among the followers of the Book and the polytheists could not have separated (from the faithful) until there had come to them the clear evidence:
98 002	A messenger from Allah, rehearsing scriptures kept pure and holy:	A messenger from Allah, reading purified pages	A messenger from Allah, reciting pure pages,
98 003	Wherein are laws (or decrees) right and straight.	Containing correct scriptures.	Wherein are all the right ordinances.
98 004	Nor did the People of the Book make schisms, until after there came to them Clear Evidence.	Nor were the People of the Scripture divided until after the clear proof came unto them.	And those who were given the Book did not become divided except after clear evidence had come to them.
98 005	And they have been commanded no more than this: To worship Allah, offering Him sincere devotion, being true (in faith); to establish regular prayer; and to practise regular charity; and that is the Religion Right and Straight.	And they are ordered naught else than to serve Allah, keeping religion pure for Him, as men by nature upright, and to establish worship and to pay the poor-due. That is true religion.	And they were not enjoined anything except that they should serve Allah, being sincere to Him in obedience, upright, and keep up prayer and pay the poor-rate, and that is the right religion.

98 006	Those who reject (Truth), among the People of the Book and among the Polytheists, will be in Hell-Fire, to dwell therein (for aye). They are the worst of creatures.	Lo! those who disbelieve, among the People of the Scripture and the idolaters, will abide in fire of hell. They are the worst of created beings.	Surely those who disbelieve from among the followers of the Book and the polytheists shall be in the fire of hell, abiding therein; they are the worst of men.
98 007	Those who have faith and do righteous deeds,- they are the best of creatures.	(And) lo! those who believe and do good works are the best of created beings.	(As for) those who believe and do good, surely they are the best of men.
98 008	Their reward is with Allah: Gardens of Eternity, beneath which rivers flow, they will dwell therein for ever; Allah well pleased with them, and they with Him: all this for such as fear their Lord and Cherisher.	Their reward is with their Lord: Gardens of Eden underneath which rivers flow, wherein they dwell for ever. Allah hath pleasure in them and they have pleasure in Him. This is (in store) for him who feareth his Lord.	Their reward with their Lord is gardens of perpetuity beneath which rivers flow, abiding therein for ever; Allah is well pleased with them and they are well pleased with Him; that is for him who fears his Lord.

Chapter 99:

AL-ZALZALA (THE EARTHQUAKE)

Total Verses: 8 Revealed At: MAKKA

In the name of Allah, the Most Beneficent, the Most Merciful.

99 001	When the earth is shaken to her (utmost) convulsion,	When Earth is shaken with her (final) earthquake	When the earth is shaken with her (violent) shaking,
99 002	And the earth throws up her burdens (from within),	And Earth yieldeth up her burdens,	And the earth brings forth her burdens,
99 003	And man cries (distressed): 'What is the matter with her?'-	And man saith: What aileth her?	And man says: What has befallen her?
99 004	On that Day will she declare her tidings:	That day she will relate her chronicles,	On that day she shall tell her news,
99 005	For that thy Lord will have given her inspiration.	Because thy Lord inspireth her.	Because your Lord had inspired her.
99 006	On that Day will men proceed in companies sorted out, to be shown the deeds that they (had done).	That day mankind will issue forth in scattered groups to be shown their deeds.	On that day men shall come forth in sundry bodies that they may be shown their works.
99 007	Then shall anyone who has done an atom's weight of good, see it!	And whoso doeth good an atom's weight will see it then,	So, he who has done an atom's weight of good shall see it
99 008	And anyone who has done an atom's weight of evil, shall see it.	And whoso doeth ill an atom's weight will see it then.	And he who has done an atom's weight of evil shall see it.

Chapter 100:

AL-ADIYAT (THE COURSER, THE CHARGERS)

Total Verses: 11 Revealed At: MAKKA

In the name of Allah, the Most Beneficent, the Most Merciful.

100 001	By the (Steeds) that run, with panting (breath),	By the snorting courses,	I swear by the runners breathing pantingly,
100 002	And strike sparks of fire,	Striking sparks of fire	Then those that produce fire striking,

100 003	And push home the charge in the morning,	And scouring to the raid at dawn,	Then those that make raids at morn,
100 004	And raise the dust in clouds the while,	Then, therewith, with their trail of dust,	Then thereby raise dust,
100 005	And penetrate forthwith into the midst (of the foe) en masse;-	Cleaving, as one, the centre (of the foe),	Then rush thereby upon an assembly:
100 006	Truly man is, to his Lord, ungrateful;	Lo! man is an ingrate unto his Lord	Most surely man is ungrateful to his Lord.
100 007	And to that (fact) he bears witness (by his deeds);	And lo! he is a witness unto that;	And most surely he is a witness of that.
100 008	And violent is he in his love of wealth.	And lo! in the love of wealth he is violent.	And most surely he is tenacious in the love of wealth.
100 009	Does he not know,- when that which is in the graves is scattered abroad,	Knoweth he not that, when the contents of the graves are poured forth	Does he not then know when what is in the graves is raised,
100 010	And that which is (locked up) in (human) breasts is made manifest-	And the secrets of the breasts are made known,	And what is in the breasts is made apparent?
100 011	That their Lord had been Well-acquainted with them, (even to) that Day?	On that day will their Lord be perfectly informed concerning them.	Most surely their Lord that day shall be fully aware of them.

Chapter 101:

AL-QARIA (THE CALAMITY, THE STUNNING BLOW, THE DISASTER)

Total Verses: 11 Revealed At: MAKKA

In the name of Allah, the Most Beneficent, the Most Merciful.

101 001	The (Day) of Noise and Clamour:	The Calamity!	The terrible calamity!
101 002	What is the (Day) of Noise and Clamour?	What is the Calamity?	What is the terrible calamity!
101 003	And what will explain to thee what the (Day) of Noise and Clamour is?	Ah, what will convey unto thee what the Calamity is!	And what will make you comprehend what the terrible calamity is?
101 004	(It is) a Day whereon men will be like moths scattered about,	A day wherein mankind will be as thickly-scattered moths	The day on which men shall be as scattered moths,
101 005	And the mountains will be like carded wool.	And the mountains will become as carded wool.	And the mountains shall be as loosened wool.
101 006	Then, he whose balance (of good deeds) will be (found) heavy,	Then, as for him whose scales are heavy (with good works),	Then as for him whose measure of good deeds is heavy,
101 007	Will be in a life of good pleasure and satisfaction.	He will live a pleasant life.	He shall live a pleasant life.
101 008	But he whose balance (of good deeds) will be (found) light,-	But as for him whose scales are light,	And as for him whose measure of good deeds is light,
101 009	Will have his home in a (bottomless) Pit.	A bereft and Hungry One will be his mother,	His abode shall be the abyss.
101 010	And what will explain to thee what this is?	Ah, what will convey unto thee what she is! -	And what will make you know what it is?
101 011	(It is) a Fire blazing fiercely!	Raging Fire.	A burning fire.

Chapter 102:

AT-TAKATHUR (RIVALRY IN WORLD INCREASE, COMPETITION)

Total Verses: 8 Revealed At: MAKKA

In the name of Allah, the Most Beneficent, the Most Merciful.

102 001	The mutual rivalry for piling up (the good things of this world) diverts you (from the more serious things),	Rivalry in worldly increase distracteth you	Abundance diverts you,
102 002	Until ye visit the graves.	Until ye come to the graves.	Until you come to the graves.
102 003	But nay, ye soon shall know (the reality).	Nay, but ye will come to know!	Nay! you shall soon know,
102 004	Again, ye soon shall know!	Nay, but ye will come to know!	Nay! Nay! you shall soon know.
102 005	Nay, were ye to know with certainty of mind, (ye would beware!)	Nay, would that ye knew (now) with a sure knowledge!	Nay! if you had known with a certain knowledge,
102 006	Ye shall certainly see Hell-Fire!	For ye will behold hell-fire.	You should most certainly have seen the hell;
102 007	Again, ye shall see it with certainty of sight!	Aye, ye will behold it with sure vision.	Then you shall most certainly see it with the eye of certainty;
102 008	Then, shall ye be questioned that Day about the joy (ye indulged in)!	Then, on that day, ye will be asked concerning pleasure.	Then on that day you shall most certainly be questioned about the boons.

Chapter 103:

AL-ASR (THE DECLINING DAY, EVENTIDE, THE EPOCH)

Total Verses: 3 Revealed At: MAKKA

In the name of Allah, the Most Beneficent, the Most Merciful.

103 001	By (the Token of) Time (through the ages),	By the declining day,	I swear by the time,
103 002	Verily Man is in loss,	Lo! man is a state of loss,	Most surely man is in loss,
103 003	Except such as have Faith, and do righteous deeds, and (join together) in the mutual teaching of Truth, and of Patience and Constancy.	Save those who believe and do good works, and exhort one another to truth and exhort one another to endurance.	Except those who believe and do good, and enjoin on each other truth, and enjoin on each other patience.

Chapter 104:

AL-HUMAZA (THE TRADUCER, THE GOSSIPMONGER)

Total Verses: 9 Revealed At: MAKKA

In the name of Allah, the Most Beneficent, the Most Merciful.

104 001	Woe to every (kind of) scandal-monger and-backbiter,	Woe unto every slandering traducer,		Woe to every slanderer, defamer,
104 002	Who pileth up wealth and layeth it by,	Who hath gathered wealth (of this world) and arranged it.		Who amasses wealth and considers it a provision (against mishap);
104 003	Thinking that his wealth would make him last for ever!	He thinketh that his wealth will render him immortal.		He thinks that his wealth will make him immortal.
104 004	By no means! He will be sure to be thrown into That which Breaks to Pieces,	Nay, but verily he will be flung to the Consuming One.		Nay! he shall most certainly be hurled into the crushing disaster,
104 005	And what will explain to thee That which Breaks to Pieces?	Ah, what will convey unto thee what the Consuming One is!		And what will make you realize what the crushing disaster is?
104 006	(It is) the Fire of (the Wrath of) Allah kindled (to a blaze),	(It is) the fire of Allah, kindled,		It is the fire kindled by Allah,
104 007	The which doth mount (right) to the Hearts:	Which leapeth up over the hearts (of men).		Which rises above the hearts.
104 008	It shall be made into a vault over them,	Lo! it is closed in on them		Surely it shall be closed over upon them,
104 009	In columns outstretched.	In outstretched columns.		In extended columns.

Chapter 105:

AL-FIL (THE ELEPHANT)

Total Verses: 5 Revealed At: MAKKA

In the name of Allah, the Most Beneficent, the Most Merciful.

105 001	Seest thou not how thy Lord dealt with the Companions of the Elephant?	Hast thou not seen how thy Lord dealt with the owners of the Elephant?		Have you not considered how your Lord dealt with the possessors of the elephant?
105 002	Did He not make their treacherous plan go astray?	Did He not bring their stratagem to naught,		Did He not cause their war to end in confusion,
105 003	And He sent against them Flights of Birds,	And send against them swarms of flying creatures,		And send down (to prey) upon them birds in flocks,
105 004	Striking them with stones of baked clay.	Which pelted them with stones of baked clay,		Casting against them stones of baked clay,
105 005	Then did He make them like an empty field of stalks and straw, (of which the corn) has been eaten up.	And made them like green crops devoured (by cattle)?		So He rendered them like straw eaten up?

Chapter 106:

QURAISH (WINTER, QURAYSH)

Total Verses: 4 Revealed At: MAKKA

In the name of Allah, the Most Beneficent, the Most Merciful.

106 001	For the covenants (of security and safeguard enjoyed) by the Quraish,	For the taming of Qureysh.		For the protection of the Qureaish--
106 002	Their covenants (covering) journeys by winter and summer,-	For their taming (We cause) the caravans to set forth in winter and summer.		Their protection during their trading caravans in the winter and the summer--
106 003	Let them adore the Lord of this House,	So let them worship the Lord of this House,		So let them serve the Lord of this House
106 004	Who provides them with food against hunger, and with security against fear (of danger).	Who hath fed them against hunger and hath made them safe from fear.		Who feeds them against hunger and gives them security against fear.

Chapter 107:

AL-MAUN (SMALL KINDNESSES, ALMSGIVING, HAVE YOU SEEN)

Total Verses: 7 Revealed At: MAKKA

In the name of Allah, the Most Beneficent, the Most Merciful.

107 001	Seest thou one who denies the Judgment (to come)?	Hast thou observed him who believeth religion?	Have you considered him who calls the judgment a lie?
107 002	Then such is the (man) who repulses the orphan (with harshness),	That is he who repelleth the orphan,	That is the one who treats the orphan with harshness,
107 003	And encourages not the feeding of the indigent.	And urgeth not the feeding of the needy.	And does not urge (others) to feed the poor.
107 004	So woe to the worshippers	Ah, woe unto worshippers	So woe to the praying ones,
107 005	Who are neglectful of their prayers,	Who are heedless of their prayer;	Who are unmindful of their prayers,
107 006	Those who (want but) to be seen (of men),	Who would be seen (at worship)	Who do (good) to be seen,
107 007	But refuse (to supply) (even) neighbourly needs.	Yet refuse small kindnesses!	And withhold the necessaries of life.

Chapter 108:

AL-KAUTHER (ABUNDANCE, PLENTY)

Total Verses: 3 Revealed At: MAKKA

In the name of Allah, the Most Beneficent, the Most Merciful.

108 001	To thee have We granted the Fount (of Abundance).	Lo! We have given thee Abundance;	Surely We have given you Kausar,
108 002	Therefore to thy Lord turn in Prayer and Sacrifice.	So pray unto thy Lord, and sacrifice.	Therefore pray to your Lord and make a sacrifice.
108 003	For he who hateth thee, he will be cut off (from Future Hope).	Lo! it is thy insulter (and not thou) who is without posterity.	Surely your enemy is the one who shall be without posterity,

Chapter 109:

AL-KAFIROON (THE DISBELIEVERS, ATHEISTS)

Total Verses: 6 Revealed At: MAKKA

In the name of Allah, the Most Beneficent, the Most Merciful.

109 001	Say: O ye that reject Faith!	Say: O disbelievers!	Say: O unbelievers!
109 002	I worship not that which ye worship,	I worship not that which ye worship;	I do not serve that which you serve,
109 003	Nor will ye worship that which I worship.	Nor worship ye that which I worship.	Nor do you serve Him Whom I serve:
109 004	And I will not worship that which ye have been wont to worship,	And I shall not worship that which ye worship.	Nor am I going to serve that which you serve,
109 005	Nor will ye worship that which I worship.	Nor will ye worship that which I worship.	Nor are you going to serve Him Whom I serve:
109 006	To you be your Way, and to me mine.	Unto you your religion, and unto me my religion.	You shall have your religion and I shall have my religion.

Chapter 110:

AN-NASR (SUCCOUR, DIVINE SUPPORT)

Total Verses: 3 Revealed At: MADINA

In the name of Allah, the Most Beneficent, the Most Merciful.

110 001	When comes the Help of Allah, and Victory,	When Allah's succour and the triumph cometh	When there comes the help of Allah and the victory,
110 002	And thou dost see the people enter Allah's Religion in crowds,	And thou seest mankind entering the religion of Allah in troops,	And you see men entering the religion of Allah in companies,

110 003	Celebrate the praises of thy Lord, and pray for His Forgiveness: For He is Oft-Returning (in Grace and Mercy).	Then hymn the praises of thy Lord, and seek forgiveness of Him. Lo! He is ever ready to show mercy.	Then celebrate the praise of your Lord, and ask His forgiveness; surely He is oft-returning (to mercy).

Chapter 111:

AL-MASADD (PALM FIBRE, THE FLAME)

Total Verses: 5 Revealed At: MAKKA

In the name of Allah, the Most Beneficent, the Most Merciful.

111 001	Perish the hands of the Father of Flame! Perish he!	The power of Abu Lahab will perish, and he will perish.	Perdition overtake both hands of Abu Lahab, and he will perish.
111 002	No profit to him from all his wealth, and all his gains!	His wealth and gains will not exempt him.	His wealth and what he earns will not avail him.
111 003	Burnt soon will he be in a Fire of Blazing Flame!	He will be plunged in flaming Fire,	He shall soon burn in fire that flames,
111 004	His wife shall carry the (crackling) wood - As fuel!-	And his wife, the wood-carrier,	And his wife, the bearer of fuel,
111 005	A twisted rope of palm-leaf fibre round her (own) neck!	Will have upon her neck a halter of palm-fibre.	Upon her neck a halter of strongly twisted rope.

Chapter 112:

AL-IKHLAS (SINCERITY)

Total Verses: 4 Revealed At: MAKKA

In the name of Allah, the Most Beneficent, the Most Merciful.

112 001	Say: He is Allah, the One and Only;	Say: He is Allah, the One!	Say: He, Allah, is One.
112 002	Allah, the Eternal, Absolute;	Allah, the eternally Besought of all!	Allah is He on Whom all depend.
112 003	He begetteth not, nor is He begotten;	He begetteth not nor was begotten.	He begets not, nor is He begotten.
112 004	And there is none like unto Him.	And there is none comparable unto Him.	And none is like Him.

Chapter 113:

AL-FALAQ (THE DAYBREAK, DAWN)

Total Verses: 5 Revealed At: MAKKA

In the name of Allah, the Most Beneficent, the Most Merciful.

113 001	Say: I seek refuge with the Lord of the Dawn,	Say: I seek refuge in the Lord of the Daybreak		Say: I seek refuge in the Lord of the dawn,
113 002	From the mischief of created things;	From the evil of that which He created;		From the evil of what He has created,
113 003	From the mischief of Darkness as it overspreads;	From the evil of the darkness when it is intense,		And from the evil of the utterly dark night when it comes,
113 004	From the mischief of those who practise secret arts;	And from the evil of malignant witchcraft,		And from the evil of those who blow on knots,
113 005	And from the mischief of the envious one as he practises envy.	And from the evil of the envier when he envieth.		And from the evil of the envious when he envies

Chapter 114:

AN-NAS (MANKIND)

Total Verses: 6 Revealed At: MAKKA

In the name of Allah, the Most Beneficent, the Most Merciful.

114 001	Say: I seek refuge with the Lord and Cherisher of Mankind,	Say: I seek refuge in the Lord of mankind,		Say: I seek refuge in the Lord of men,
114 002	The King (or Ruler) of Mankind,	The King of mankind,		The King of men,
114 003	The God (or Judge) of Mankind,-	The God of mankind,		The God of men,
114 004	From the mischief of the Whisperer (of Evil), who withdraws (after his whisper),-	From the evil of the sneaking whisperer,		From the evil of the whisperings of the slinking (Shaitan),
114 005	(The same) who whispers into the hearts of Mankind,-	Who whispereth in the hearts of mankind,		Who whispers into the hearts of men,
114 006	Among jinns and among men.	Of the jinn and of mankind.		From among the jinn and the men.

www.ingramcontent.com/pod-product-compliance
Lightning Source LLC
Chambersburg PA
CBHW081837230426
43669CB00018B/2736